AutoCAD® 2000:
A Problem-Solving Approach

Sham Tickoo

Professor
Department of Manufacturing Engineering Technologies
And Supervision
Purdue University Calumet
Hammond, Indiana

CADCIM Technologies

Schererville, Indiana, U.S.A.

D1314261

Thomson Learning™

Africa • Australia • Canada • Denmark • Japan • Mexico • New Zealand
Phillipines • Puerto Rico • Singapore • Spain • United Kingdom • United States

NOTICE TO THE READER

Publisher does not warrant or guarantee any of the products described herein or perform any independent analysis in connection with any of the product information contained herein. Publisher does not assume, and expressly disclaims, any obligation to obtain and include information other than that provided to it by the manufacturer.

The reader is expressly warned to consider and adopt all safety precautions that might be indicated by the activities herein and to avoid all potential hazards. By following the instructions contained herein, the reader willingly assumes all risks in connection with such instructions.

The publisher makes no representation or warranties of any kind, including but not limited to, the warranties of fitness for particular purpose or merchantability, nor are any such representations implied with respect to the material set forth herein, and the publisher takes no responsibility with respect to such material. The publisher shall not be liable for any special, consequential, or exemplary damages resulting, in whole or part, from the readers' use of, or reliance upon, this material. Autodesk does not guarantee the performance of the software and Autodesk assumes no responsibility or liability for the performance of the software or for errors in this manual.

Autodesk Press Staff
Executive Director: Alar Elken
Executive Editor: Sandy Clark
Developmental Editor: John Fisher
Editorial Assistant: Allyson Powell
Executive Marketing Manager: Maura Theriault
Executive Production Manager: Mary Ellen Black
Production Coordinator: Jennifer Gaines
Art and Design Coordinator: Mary Beth Vought
Marketing Coordinator: Paula Collins
Technology Project Manager: Tom Smith

Cover illustration by Brucie Rosch

For more information, contact
Autodesk Press
3 Columbia Circle, Box 15-015
Albany, New York USA 12212-15015;
or find us on the World Wide Web at http://www.autodeskpress.com

Library of Congress Cataloging-in-Publication Data
Tickoo, Sham.
　　AutoCAD 2000: a problem-solving approach / Sham Tickoo.
　　　　p.　　　　cm.
　　ISBN 0-7668-1234-0
　　1. Computer graphics. 2. AutoCAD. 3. Computer-aided design.
　　I. Title.
　　T385.T523　　1999
　　604.2'0285' 5369—dc21　　　　　　　　　　　　99-16264
　　　　　　　　　　　　　　　　　　　　　　　　CIP

Table of Contents

Chapter 3: Drawing Aids

Chapter 4: Editing Commands

Chapter 5: Controlling Drawing Display and Creating Text

Chapter 6: Basic Dimensioning

Chapter 7: Editing Dimensions

Chapter 8: Dimension Styles and Dimensioning System Variables

Chapter 9: Geometric Dimensioning and Tolerancing

Chapter 10: Editing with GRIPS

Chapter 11: Hatching

Chapter 12: Blocks

Advanced AutoCAD

Chapter 13: Defining Block Attributes

Chapter 14: External References

Chapter 15: Plotting Drawings and Draw Commands

Chapter 16: Object Grouping and Editing Commands

Chapter 17: Inquiry Commands, Data Exchange, and Object Linking and Embedding

Chapter 18: Technical Drawing with AutoCAD

Chapter 19: Isometric Drawing

Chapter 20: User Coordinate System

Chapter 21: Drawing Predefined 3D Objects, Viewing and Editing 3D Objects, and Drawing 3D Surfaces

Chapter 22: Model Space Viewports, Paper Space Viewports, Layouts and Dynamic Viewing of 3D Objects

Chapter 23: Solid Modeling

Chapter 24: Rendering

Chapter 25: Geometry Calculator

Chapter 26: Accessing External Datbases

Chapter 27: AutoCAD on Internet

Customizing AutoCAD

Chapter 28: Template Drawings

Chapter 29: Script Files and Slide Shows

Chapter 30: Creating Linetypes and Hatch Patterns

Chapter 31: Customizing the ACAD.PGP File

Chapter 36: AutoLISP

Chapter 37: Visual LISP

Chapter 38: DIESEL: A String Expression Language

Appendices

Index

Preface

AutoCAD, developed by Autodesk Inc., is the most popular PC-CAD system available in the market. Over two million people in 80 countries around the world use AutoCAD to generate various kinds of drawings. In 1998 the market share of AutoCAD grew to 78 percent, making it the worldwide standard for generating drawings. Also, AutoCAD's open architecture has allowed third-party developers to write application software that has significantly added to its popularity. For example, the author of this book has developed a software package, "SMLayout" for sheet metal products, that generates flat layout of various geometrical shapes such as transitions, intersections, cones, elbows, and tank heads. Several companies in Canada and the United States are using this software package with AutoCAD to design and manufacture various products. AutoCAD has also provided facilities that allow users to customize AutoCAD to make it more efficient and therefore increase their productivity.

This book contains a detailed explanation of AutoCAD 2000 commands and how to use them in solving drafting and design problems. The book also unravels the customizing power of AutoCAD. Every AutoCAD command and customizing technique is thoroughly explained with examples and illustrations that make it easy to understand their function and application. At the end of each topic, there are examples that illustrate the function of the command and how it can be used in the drawing. When you are done reading this book, you will be able to use AutoCAD commands to make a drawing, create text, make and insert symbols, dimension a drawing, create 3D objects and solid models, write script files, define linetypes and hatch patterns, write your own menus, define new commands, write programs in the AutoLISP and Visual LISP programming languages, customize the status line using DIESEL, and edit the Program Parameter file (ACAD.PGP).

The book also covers basic drafting and design concepts — such as orthographic projections, dimensioning principles, sectioning, auxiliary views, and assembly drawings — that provide you with the essential drafting skills you need to solve drawing problems with AutoCAD. In the process, you will discover some new applications of AutoCAD that are unique and might have a significant effect on your drawings. You will also get a better idea of why AutoCAD has become such a popular software package and an international standard in PC-CAD. Please refer to the following table for conventions used in this text.

Convention	**Example**
• Command names are capitalized and bold.	The **MOVE** command
• A key icon appears when you should respond by pressing the ENTER or RETURN key.	[Enter]
• Command sequences are indented. Responses are indicated by boldface. Directions are indicated by italics. Comments are enclosed in parentheses.	Command: **MOVE** Select object: **G** Enter group name: *Enter a group name* *(the group name is group1)*

Convention

- The command selection from the toolbars, pull-down menus, and Command: prompt are enclosed in a shaded box.

- AutoCAD 2000 features are indicated by an asterisk symbol at the end of the feature.

- Project exercises are designated by the project number and the part number of the project.

Convention

Toolbar:	Draw>Arc
Pull-down:	Draw>Arc
Command:	ARC or A

AutoCAD Design Center*

Project Exercise 1-3

e-resource

This is an educational resource that creates a truly electronic classroom. It is a CD-ROM containing tools and instructional resources that enrich your classroom and make your preparation time shorter. The elements of **e-resource** link directly to the text and tie together to provide a unified instructional system. With **e-resource** you can spend your time teaching, not preparing to teach. (ISBN: 0-7668-1237-5)

Features contained in e-resource include:

Syllabus: Lesson plans created by chapter. You have the option of using these lesson plans with your own course information.

Chapter Hints: Objectives and teaching hints that provide the basis for a lecture outline that helps you to present concepts and material.

Answers to Review Questions: These solutions enable you to grade and evaluate end-of-chapter tests.

PowerPoint® Presentation: These slides provide the basis for a lecture outline that helps you to present concepts and material. Key points and concepts can be graphically highlighted for student retention.

World Class Test Computerized Test Bank: Over 800 questions of varying levels of difficulty are provided in true/false and multiple-choice formats so you can assess student comprehension.

AVI Files: AVI files, listed by topic, allow you to view a quick video illustrating and explaining key concepts.

Drawing and Program Files: Drawing and program files used in the examples and exercises.

World Class Manager: World Class Manager allows you to automatically extract and track data from on-line tests, practice tests and tutorials created by World Class Test. You can also create reports such as individual student reports, missing assignment reports, a summary of grade distribution, class lists and more. All statistics are updated automatically as data is entered or changed.

Author's Web Sites

For Faculty: Please contact the author at **stickoo@calumet.purdue.edu** to access the Web Site that contains the following:
   1. **Power Point presentations, programs, and drawings used in this textbook.**
   2. **Syllabus, chapter objectives and hints, and questions with answers for every chapter.**

For Students:You can download drawing-exercises, tutorials, programs, and special topics by accessing authors Web Site at **http://www.calumet.purdue.edu/public/mets/tickoo/index.html**.

DEDICATION

To teachers, who make it possible to disseminate knowledge
to enlighten the young and curious minds
of our future generations

To students, who are dedicated to learning new technologies
and making the world a better place to live

Thanks

To the faculty and students of the MET department of
Purdue University Calumet for their cooperation

To Renu Muthoo, Anupama Pande, and Santosh Tickoo
of CADCIM Technologies
for their valuable help

Basic AutoCAD

Author's Web Sites

For Faculty: Please contact the author at **stickoo@calumet.purdue.edu** to access the Web Site that contains the following:

1. **Power Point presentations, programs, and drawings used in this textbook.**
2. **Syllabus, chapter objectives and hints, and questions with answers for every chapter.**

For Students:You can download drawing-exercises, tutorials, programs, and special topics by accessing authors Web Site at **http://www.calumet.purdue.edu/public/mets/tickoo/index.html**.

Chapter 1

Getting Started

Learning Objectives

**After completing this chapter, you will be able to*:*
* *Invoke AutoCAD commands from the menu, screen menu, digitizer, command line, or toolbars.*
* *Understand the functioning of dialog boxes in AutoCAD.*
* *Draw lines using the **LINE** command and its options.*
* *Understand different coordinate systems used in AutoCAD.*
* *Use the **ERASE** and **MOVE** commands.*
* *Create selection sets using Window and Crossing options.*
* *Draw circles using different options of the **CIRCLE** command.*
* *Use **REDRAW**, **ZOOM**, and **PAN** commands.*
* *Plot drawings.*
* *Save the work using different file-saving commands.*
* *Open an existing file and start a new drawing.*
* *Use the **Options** dialog box to specify the settings.*
* *Recall and edit command line.*
* *Use Learning Assistance and AutoCAD's help.*

STARTING AUTOCAD

When you turn on your computer, the operating system (Windows 95, Windows NT or Windows 98) is automatically loaded (Figure 1-1). This will display the Windows screen with various application icons. You can load AutoCAD by double-clicking on the AutoCAD 2000 icon. You can also load AutoCAD from the task bar by choosing the **Start** button at the bottom left corner of the screen (default position) to display the menu. Choose Programs to display the program folders. Now, choose the AutoCAD 2000 folder to display AutoCAD programs and then choose AutoCAD 2000 to start AutoCAD.

Figure 1-1 *Windows screen with taskbar and application icons*

STARTING A DRAWING*

When you start AutoCAD, AutoCAD displays the **Startup** dialog box on the screen (Figure 1-2). The dialog box is disabled if you clear the **Show Startup dialog** check box in the **Startup** dialog box. To turn on the display of the dialog box, Choose **Options** from the **Tools** menu. Choose the **System** tab and under the **General Options** area, select **Show Startup dialog** check box and choose **OK**. The **Startup** dialog box provides the following four options for starting a new drawing.

Open a Drawing

When you choose the **Open a Drawing** button (Figure 1-3), a list of the four most recently opened drawings is displayed for you to select from. The **Browse** button allows you to look for another file. The dialog box is disabled if **FILEDIA** system variable is set to 0.

Start from Scratch

When you choose the **Start from Scratch** button (Figure 1-4), AutoCAD starts a new drawing that contains the default AutoCAD setup for English (acad.dwt) or Metric drawings (acadiso.dwt). For example, if you select English default setting, the limits are 12x9, text height is 0.20, dimensions and linetype scale factors are 1.

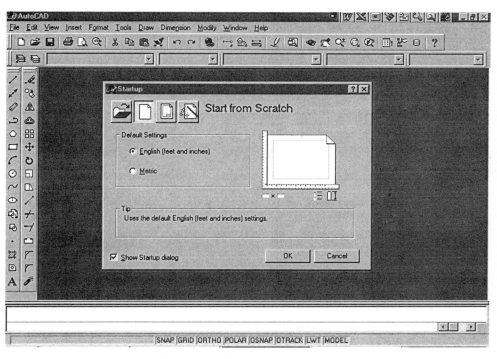

Figure 1-2 Startup dialog box

Figure 1-3 *When using Open a Drawing, AutoCAD displays a list of four most recently opened drawings.*

Figure 1-4 When using Start from Scratch, the new drawing contains the default settings.

Use a Template

When you choose the **Use a Template** button in the **Startup** dialog box, AutoCAD displays a list of templates supplied with AutoCAD (Figure 1-5). The default template file is acad.dwt or acadiso.dwt, depending on the installation. If you use the template file, the new drawing will have the same setting as the template file. You can also define your own template files that are customized to your requirements (See Chapter 28, Template Drawings). To differentiate the template files from the drawing files, the template files have **.dwt** extension whereas the drawing files have **.dwg** extension. Any drawing files can be saved as a template file. You can use the **Browse** button to select other template files. When you choose the **Browse** button, the **Select a template file** dialog box is displayed.

Figure 1-5 When using Use a Template, AutoCAD displays a list of template files.

Use a Wizard

When you choose the **Use a Wizard** button, you have the choice of using **Quick Setup** or **Advanced Setup**. In the **Quick Setup**, you specify the units, width, and length of the work area. In the **Advanced Setup** you specify units, angle, angle measure, angle direction, and area.

INVOKING COMMANDS IN AUTOCAD

This chapter assumes that the software is loaded on your system and that you are familiar with the hardware you are using. When you start AutoCAD and you are in the drawing editor, you need to invoke AutoCAD commands to perform any operation. For example, if you want to draw a line, first you have to invoke the **LINE** command, and then you define the start point and endpoint of the line. Similarly, if you want to erase objects, you must enter the **ERASE** command, and then select the objects you want to erase. AutoCAD has provided the following methods to enter or select commands:

Keyboard	Menu	Toolbar
Digitizing tablet	Screen menu	

Keyboard

You can invoke any AutoCAD command at the keyboard by typing the command name at the Command prompt, and then pressing ENTER or the SPACEBAR. Before you enter a command, make sure the Command prompt is displayed as the last line in the command prompt area. If the Command prompt is not displayed, you must cancel the existing command by pressing ESC (escape) on the keyboard. The following example shows how to invoke the **LINE** command from the keyboard:

Command: **LINE** Enter

Menu

You can also select commands from the menu. The **menu bar** that displays the menu bar titles is at the top of the screen. As you move the pointing device sideways, different menu bar titles are highlighted. You can choose the desired item by pressing the pick button of your pointing device. Once the item is selected, the corresponding menu is displayed directly under the title. You can invoke a command from the menu by pressing the pick button of your pointing device. Some of the menu items in the menu display an arrow on the right side, which indicates that the menu item has a cascading menu. You can display the cascading menu by selecting the menu item or by just moving the arrow pointer to the right of that item. You can then select any item in the cascading menu by highlighting the item or command and pressing the pick button of your pointing device, or simply by pressing the stylus (pen) down if you are using a stylus with your digitizer. For example, if you want to draw an ellipse using the Center option, choose **Draw** from the menu bar, choose **Ellipse** from the **Draw** menu, then choose **Center** from the cascading menu (Figure 1-6). In this text this command selection sequence will be referenced as Choose **Draw > Ellipse > Center.**

*Figure 1-6 Invoking the **ELLIPSE** command from the **Draw** menu.*

Toolbar

In Windows, the toolbar is an easy and convenient way to invoke a command. For example, you can invoke the **LINE** command by choosing the **Line** tool (the upper left tool, Figure 1-7) in the **Draw** toolbar. When you select a command from the toolbar, the Command prompts are displayed in the Command prompt area.

Displaying Toolbars. The toolbars can be displayed by selecting the respective check boxes in the **Toolbars** dialog box (Figure 1-8). The **Toolbars** dialog box can be invoked by selecting **Toolbars** in the **View** menu. Each toolbar contains a group of tools representing different AutoCAD commands. When you move the cursor over the tools of a toolbar, the tool-tip (name of command) is displayed below the tool on which the cursor is resting. Once you locate the desired tool, the command associated with that tool can be invoked by choosing the tool.

*Figure 1-7 Selecting the **LINE** command from the **Draw** toolbar*

*Figure 1-8 **Toolbars** dialog box*

The toolbars can be moved anywhere on the screen by placing the cursor on the title bar area and then dragging it to the desired location. You must hold the pick button down while dragging. You can also change the shape of the toolbars by placing the cursor anywhere on the border of the toolbar and then dragging it in the desired direction (Figures 1-9 and 1-10). You can also customize toolbars to meet your requirements (See Chapter 32, Pull-down, Shortcut, and Partial Menus and Customizing Toolbars).

*Figure 1-9 Reshaping the **Draw** toolbar*

*Figure 1-10 **Draw** toolbar reshaped*

Screen Menu

In AutoCAD the screen menus are not displayed by default. To display the screen menus, select the **Display screen menu** check box in the **Options** (**Display** tab) dialog box. This dialog box can be accessed by choosing **Options** from the **Tools** menu. The screen menus are then displayed on the right side of the computer screen (Figure 1-11). The screen menu can be docked on either side of

Figure 1-11 *AutoCAD screen display showing the **File** menu, **Draw** toolbar, and the screen menu*

the screen. You can choose an item from the screen menu by moving the cursor up or down along the screen menu bar until the item you want is highlighted. You can then choose it by pressing the pick button of your pointing device. The first screen menu that AutoCAD displays is the root menu. In the screen menus the commands are arranged in different groups. For example, if you want to invoke the **ELLIPSE** command, you must first choose **DRAW 1** from the root menu, and then choose **Ellipse:**. A menu item that consists of all uppercase letters without a colon at the end (**DRAW 1**) represents a group heading. If you choose this item

*Figure 1-12 Invoking the **ELLIPSE** command from the screen menu*

it will automatically load that submenu and display the submenu items in the screen menu area. If you select a command, AutoCAD will automatically invoke that command and also display its options in the screen menu area. You can always return to the root menu by selecting the menu item **AutoCAD**, which is displayed at the top of every screen menu.

Digitizing Tablet

In the digitizing tablet, the commands are selected from the template that is secured on the surface of the tablet. To use the tablet menu you need a digitizing tablet and a pointing device. You also need a tablet template that contains AutoCAD commands arranged in various groups for easy identification. To invoke a command from the digitizer, move your pointing device so that the crosshairs of the pointing device (or the tip of the stylus) are directly over the cell that contains the command you want to invoke. Now press the pick button of the pointing device, or simply press down the stylus, and AutoCAD will automatically invoke that command.

AUTOCAD DIALOG BOXES

A dialog box can consist of a dialog label, toggle buttons, radio buttons, edit boxes, slider bars, image boxes, and a box that encloses these components. These components are also referred to as TILES. Some of the components of a dialog box are shown in Figure 1-12.

Figure 1-12 Components of a dialog box

DRAWING LINES IN AUTOCAD

Toolbar:	Draw > Line
Menu:	Draw > Line
Command:	LINE or L

The most fundamental object in a drawing is the line. A line can be drawn between any two points by using AutoCAD's **LINE** command. Once you have invoked the **LINE** command, the next prompt, **Specify first point:** requires you to specify the starting point of the line. After the first point is selected, Au-

Figure 1-13 Invoking the LINE command from the Draw toolbar

toCAD will prompt you to enter the second point at the **Specify next point or [Undo]:** prompt. When you select the second point of the line, AutoCAD will again display the prompt **Specify next** point or [Undo]:. At this point you may continue to select points or terminate the **LINE** command by pressing ENTER, ESC, or the SPACEBAR. If you press the ENTER key, the shortcut menu is displayed. Select Enter in the shortcut menu to terminate the **LINE** command. You can also right-click to display the shortcut menu from where you can choose Enter or Cancel options to exit from the **LINE** command. After terminating the **LINE** command, AutoCAD will again display the Command prompt. The prompt sequence for drawing Figure 1-15 is as follows:

*Figure 1-14 Invoking the **LINE** command from the **Draw** menu*

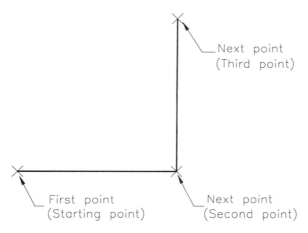

*Figure 1-15 Drawing lines using the **LINE** command*

Command: **LINE** `Enter`
Specify first point: *Move the cursor (mouse) and left-click to specify the first point.*
Specify next point or [Undo]: *Move the cursor and left-click to specify the second point.*
Specify next point or [Undo]: *Specify the third point.*
Specify next point or [Close/Undo]: `Enter`   *(Press ENTER to terminate the **LINE** command.)*

Note

*To clear the graphics area (drawing screen) to gain space to work out the exercises and the examples, type **ERASE** at the Command prompt and press ENTER. The screen crosshairs will change into a box called a pick box and AutoCAD will prompt you to select objects. You can select the object by positioning the pick box anywhere on the object and pressing the pick button of the pointing device. Once you have finished selecting the objects, press ENTER to terminate the **ERASE** command and the objects you selected will be erased. If you enter All at the **Select objects:** prompt, AutoCAD will erase all objects from the screen. (See **ERASE** command "Erasing Objects" discussed later in this chapter). You can use the **U** (undo) command to undo the last command.*

Command: **ERASE** `Enter`
Select objects: *Select objects.*   *(Select objects using the pick box.)*
Select objects: `Enter`
Command: **R** `Enter`   *(Type **R** for redraw.)*

Command: **ERASE** [Enter]
Select objects: **ALL** [Enter]
Select objects: [Enter]
Command: **U** [Enter]   *(**U** command will undo the last command.)*

The **LINE** command has the following three options:

Continue   Close   Undo

The Continue Option

After exiting from the **LINE** command, you may want to draw another line starting from the point where the previous line ended. In such cases you can use the **Continue** option. This option enables you to grab the endpoint of the previous line and to continue drawing the line from that point (Figure 1-16). The following is the prompt sequence for the **Continue** option:

Command: **LINE** [Enter]
Specify first point: *Pick first point of the line.*
Specify next point or [Undo]: *Pick second point.*
Specify next point or [Undo]: [Enter]
Command: **LINE** [Enter]   *(Or press ENTER to repeat the command.)*
Specify first point: [Enter]   *(Press ENTER or choose Continue from the screen menu to*
                                                continue the line from the last line.)
Specify next point or [Undo]: *Pick second point of the second line (Third point in Figure 1-16).*
Specify next point or [Undo]: [Enter]

You can also type the @ symbol to start the line from the **last point**. For example, if you draw a line and then immediately repeat the **LINE** command, the @ will snap to the endpoint of the last line. The Continue option will snap to the endpoint of the last line or arc, even if other points have been defined after the line was drawn.

Command: **LINE** [Enter]
Specify first point: *Pick first point of the line.*
Specify next point or [Undo]: *Pick second point.*
Specify next point or [Undo]: [Enter]
Command: **LINE or L** [Enter]   *(**L** is command alias for **LINE**)*
Specify first point: @ [Enter]   *(Continues the drawing line from the last point.)*
Specify next point or [Undo]: *Pick second point of the second line.*
Specify next point or [Undo]: [Enter]

The Close Option

The **Close** option can be used to join the current point with the initial point of the first line when two or more lines are **drawn in continuation**. For example, this option can be used when an open figure needs one more line to close it and make a polygon (a polygon is a closed figure with at least three sides, for example, a triangle or rectangle). The following is the prompt sequence for the **Close** option (Figure 1-17):

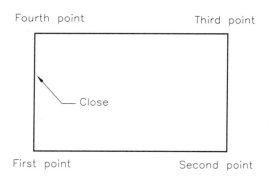

*Figure 1-16 Using the **Continue** option with the*
LINE command

*Figure 1-17 Using the **Close** option with the*
LINE command

Command: **LINE** [Enter]
Specify first point: *Pick first point.*
Specify next point or [Undo]: *Pick second point.*
Specify next point or [Undo]: *Pick third point.*
Specify next point or [Close/Undo]: *Pick fourth point.*

Specify next point or [Close/Undo]: **C** [Enter]   *(Joins the fourth point with the first point.)*

You can also choose the **Close** option from the shortcut menu, which appears when you right-click
in the drawing area.

The Undo Option

If you draw a line, and then realize that you made an error, you can remove the line using the
Undo option. If you need to remove more than one line, you can use this option multiple times
and go as far back as you want. In this option, you can type **Undo** (or just **U**) at the **Specify next
point or [Undo]:** prompt. You can also right-click to display the shortcut menu which gives you
the **Undo** option. The following example illustrates the use of the **Undo** option (Figure 1-18):

Command: **LINE** [Enter]
Specify first point: *Pick first point (Point 1 in Figure 1-18).*
Specify next point or [Undo]: *Pick second point (Point 2).*
Specify next point or [Undo]: *Pick third point.*
Specify next point or [Close/Undo]: *Pick fourth point.*
Specify next point or [Close/Undo]: **U** [Enter]   *(Removes last line from Point 3 to Point 4.)*
Specify next point or [Close/Undo]: **U** [Enter]   *(Removes next line from Point 2 to Point3.)*
Specify next point or [Close/Undo]: [Enter]

Chapter 1

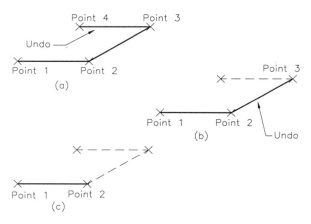

Figure 1-18 *Removing lines using the* **Undo** *option of the* **LINE**

COORDINATE SYSTEMS

To specify a point in a plane, we take two mutually perpendicular lines as references. The horizontal line is called the **X axis**, and the vertical line is called the **Y axis.** The point of intersection of these two axes is called the **origin**. The X and Y axes divide the XY plane into four parts, generally known as quadrants. The X coordinate measures the horizontal distance from the origin (how far left or right) on the X axis. The Y coordinate measures the vertical distance from the origin (how far up or down) on the Y axis. The origin has the coordinate values of X = 0, Y = 0. The origin is taken as the reference for locating any point in the XY plane. The X coordinate is positive if measured to the right of the origin and negative if measured to the left of the origin. The Y coordinate is positive if measured above the origin and negative if measured below the origin. This method of specifying points is called the **Cartesian coordinate system** (Figure 1-19). In AutoCAD, the default origin is located at the lower left corner of the graphics area of the screen. AutoCAD uses the following coordinate systems to locate a point in an XY plane:

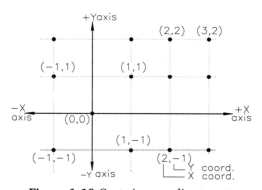

Figure 1-19 *Cartesian coordinate system*

      Absolute coordinates
      Relative coordinates
      Polar coordinates
      Direct distance entry

Absolute Coordinates

In the absolute coordinate system the points are located with respect to the origin (0,0), Figure 1-20.

For example, a point with X = 4 and Y = 3 is measured 4 units horizontally (displacement along the X axis) and 3 units vertically (displacement along the Y axis) from the origin (Figure 1-21).

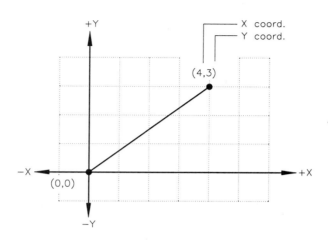

Figure 1-20 *Absolute coordinate system*

In AutoCAD, the absolute coordinates are specified by entering X and Y coordinates, separated by a comma. The following example illustrates the use of absolute coordinates (Figure 1-21):

Command: **LINE** Enter
Specify first point: **1,1** Enter
        (X = 1 and Y = 1.)
Specify next point or [Undo]: **4,1** Enter
        (X = 4 and Y = 1.)
Specify next point or [Undo]: **4,3** Enter
Specify next point or [Close /Undo]: **1,3** Enter
Specify next point or [Close/Undo]: **1,1** Enter
Specify next point or [Close/Undo]: Enter

Figure 1-21 *Drawing lines using absolute coordinates*

Example 1

For Figure 1-22, enter the absolute coordinates of the points in the given table. Then draw the figure using absolute coordinates.

Point	Coordinates	Point	Coordinates
1	3,1	5	5,2
2	3,6	6	6,3
3	4,6	7	7,3
4	4,2	8	7,1

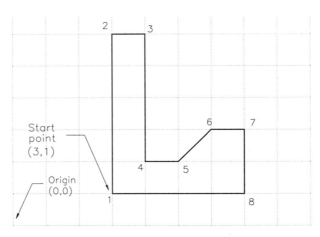

Figure 1-22 *Drawing a figure using absolute coordinates*

Once the coordinates of the points are known you can draw the figure by using AutoCAD's **LINE** command. The prompt sequence is:

Command: **LINE** [Enter]
Specify first point: **3,1** [Enter]   *(Start point.)*
Specify next point or [Undo]: **3,6** [Enter]
Specify next point or [Undo]: **4,6** [Enter]
Specify next point or [Close/Undo]: **4,2** [Enter]
Specify next point or [Close/Undo]: **5,2** [Enter]
Specify next point or [Close/Undo]: **6,3** [Enter]
Specify next point or [Close/Undo]: **7,3** [Enter]
Specify next point or [Close/Undo]: **7,1** [Enter]
Specify next point or [Close/Undo]: **3,1** [Enter]
Specify next point or [Close/Undo]: [Enter]

Exercise 1   *General*

For Figure 1-23, enter the absolute coordinates of the points in the given table, then use those coordinates to draw that same figure.

Point	Coordinates	Point	Coordinates
1	2, 1	6	2 < 225
2	2, 5	7	2 < -45 or 2 < 325
3	7, 5	8	7, 2
4	7, 4	9	7, 1
5	4, 4		

Figure 1-23 Drawing for Exercise 1

Relative Coordinates

In the relative coordinate system, the displacements along the X and Y axes (DX and DY) are measured with reference to the previous point rather than to the origin. In AutoCAD the relative coordinate system is designated by the symbol @ and it should precede any relative entry. The following prompt sequence illustrates the use of the relative coordinate system to draw a rectangle that has the lower left corner at point (1,1). The length of the rectangle is 4 units and the width is 3 units (Figure 1-24).

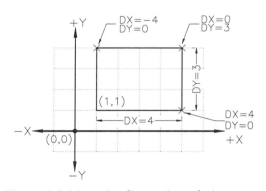

Figure 1-24 Drawing lines using relative coordinates

Command: **LINE** [Enter]
Specify first point: **1,1** [Enter]
      (Start point.)
Specify next point or [Undo]: **@4,0** [Enter]   *(Second point DX = 4, DY = 0.)*
Specify next point or [Undo]: **@0,3** [Enter]   *(Third point DX = 0, DY = 3.)*
Specify next point or [Close/Undo]: **@-4,0** [Enter]   *(Fourth point DX = -4, DY = 0.)*
Specify next point or [Close/Undo]: **@0,-3** [Enter]   *(Start point DX = 0, DY = -3.)*
Specify next point or [Close/Undo]: [Enter]

Sign Convention. As just mentioned, in the relative coordinate system the displacements along the X and Y axes are measured with respect to the previous point. Imagine a horizontal line and a vertical line passing through the previous point so that you get four quadrants. If the new point is located in the first quadrant, the displacements DX and DY are both positive. If the new point is located in the third quadrant, the displacements DX and DY are both negative. In other words up or right are positive and down or left are negative.

Example 2

Draw Figure 1-25 using relative coordinates of the points given in the table below.

Point	Coordinates	Point	Coordinates
1	3,1	8	@-1,-1
2	@4,0	9	@-1,1
3	@0,1	10	@-1,0
4	@-1,0	11	@0,-2
5	@1,1	12	@1,-1
6	@0,2	13	@-1,0
7	@-1,0	14	@0,-1

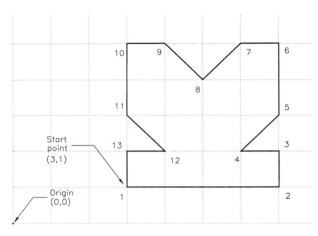

*Figure 1-25 Using relative coordinates with the **LINE** command*

Once you know the coordinates of the points, you can draw the figure by using AutoCAD's **LINE** command and entering the coordinates of the points.

Command: **LINE** ⏎
Specify first point: **3,1** ⏎   *(Start point.)*
Specify next point or [Undo]: **@4,0** ⏎
Specify next point or [Undo]: **@0,1** ⏎
Specify next point or [Close/Undo]: **@-1,0** ⏎
Specify next point or [Close/Undo]: **@1,1** ⏎
Specify next point or [Close/Undo]: **@0,2** ⏎
Specify next point or [Close/Undo]: **@-1,0** ⏎
Specify next point or [Close/Undo]: **@-1,-1** ⏎
Specify next point or [Close/Undo]: **@-1,1** ⏎
Specify next point or [Close/Undo]: **@-1,0** ⏎
Specify next point or [Close/Undo]: **@0,-2** ⏎
Specify next point or [Close/Undo]: **@1,-1** ⏎
Specify next point or [Close/Undo]: **@-1,0** ⏎

Specify next point or [Close/Undo]: **@0,-1** Enter
Specify next point or [Close/Undo]: Enter

Exercise 2 *General*

For Figure 1-26, enter the relative coordinates of the points in the given table, then use these coordinates to draw the figure.

Figure1-26 *Drawing for Exercise 2*

Point	Coordinates	Point	Coordinates
1	2, 1	12	_____
2	@ 5,0	13	_____
3	@ 0 1	14	_____
4	@ -1 0	15	_____
5	@ .5 < 270	16	_____
6	@ 1 < 180	17	_____
7	@ 1 < 90	18	_____
8	_____	19	_____
9	_____	20	_____
10	_____	21	_____
11	_____	22	_____

Polar Coordinates

In the polar coordinate system, a point can be located by defining both the distance of the point from the current point and the angle that the line between the two points makes with the positive X axis. The prompt sequence to draw a line from a point at 1,1 to a point at a distance of 5 units from the point (1,1), and at an angle of 30 degrees to the X axis, is (Figure 1-27):

Command: **LINE** Enter
Specify first point: **1,1** Enter
Specify next point or [Undo]: **@5<30** Enter

Sign Convention. In the polar coordinate system the angle is measured from the horizontal axis (3 o' clock) as the zero degree baseline. Also, the angle is positive if measured in a counterclockwise direction and negative if measured in a clockwise direction. Here we assume that the default setup of angle measurement has not been changed. For more information about changing the default setup, see "Setting Units" in Chapter 3.

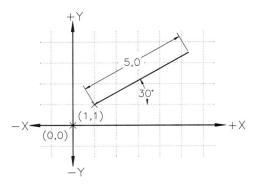

Figure 1-27 *Drawing a line using polar coordinates*

Example 3

For Figure 1-28, enter the polar coordinates of each point in the table, then generate the drawing. Use absolute coordinates for the start point (1.5, 1.75). The dimensions are shown in the drawing.

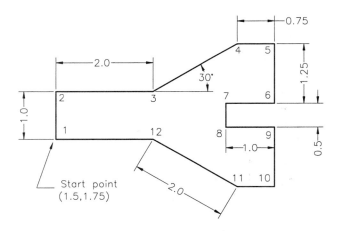

Figure 1-28 *Drawing for Example 3*

Point	Coordinates	Point	Coordinates
1	1.5,1.75	7	@1.0<180
2	@1.0<90	8	@0.5<270
3	@2.0<0	9	@1.0<0
4	@2.0<30	10	@1.25<270
5	@0.75<0	11	@0.75<180
6	@1.25<-90 (or <270)	12	@2.0<150

Once you know the coordinates of the points, you can generate the drawing by using AutoCAD's **LINE** command and entering the coordinates of the points.

Command: **LINE** [Enter]
Specify first point: **1.5,1.75** [Enter]   *(Start point.)*
Specify next point or [Undo]: **@1<90** [Enter]
Specify next point or [Undo]: **@2.0<0** [Enter]
Specify next point or [Close/Undo]: **@2<30** [Enter]
Specify next point or [Close/Undo]: **@0.75<0** [Enter]
Specify next point or [Close/Undo]: **@1.25<-90** [Enter]
Specify next point or [Close/Undo]: **@1.0<180** [Enter]
Specify next point or [Close/Undo]: **@0.5<270** [Enter]
Specify next point or [Close/Undo]: **@1.0<0** [Enter]
Specify next point or [Close/Undo]: **@1.25<270** [Enter]
Specify next point or [Close/Undo]: **@0.75<180** [Enter]
Specify next point or [Close/Undo]: **@2.0<150** [Enter]
Specify next point or [Close/Undo]: **C** [Enter]   *(Joins the last point with the first point.)*

Exercise 3   *General*

Draw the object shown in Figure 1-29 using the absolute, relative, and polar coordinate systems to locate the points. Do not draw the dimensions; they are for reference only. Assume the missing dimensions.

Figure 1-29 *Drawing for Exercise 3*

Direct Distance Entry

You can draw a line by specifying the length of the line and its direction, using the Direct Distance Entry, (Figure 1-30). The direction is determined by the position of the cursor, and the length of the line is entered from the keyboard. If Ortho is on, you can draw lines along the X or Y axis by specifying the length of line and positioning the cursor along ortho direction. You can also use it with other draw commands like **RECTANGLE**. You can also use the Direct Distance Entry with polar tracking and **SNAPANG.** For example, if **SNAPANG** is 45 degrees and ortho is off, you can draw a line at 45 or 135 degrees direction by positioning the cursor and entering the distance from the keyboard. Similarly, if the polar tracking is on, you can position the cursor at the predefined angles and then enter the length of the line from the keyboard.

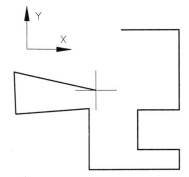

Command: **LINE**
Specify first point: *Start point.*
Specify next point or [Undo]: *Position the cursor and then enter distance.*
Specify next point or [Undo]: *Position the cursor and then enter distance.*

Figure 1-30 Using Direct Distance Entry to draw lines

Example 4

In this example you will draw the object as shown in Figure 1-31, using Direct Distance Entry. The starting point is 1,1.

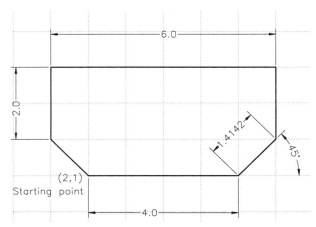

Figure 1-31 Drawing for Example 4

Before you invoke the **LINE** command, you should turn on polar tracking. This will make it easier to specify the direction of lines. To turn polar tracking on, choose the **Polar Tracking** button in the status bar. You can also turn polar tracking on or off while you are in a command. As you move the cursor, AutoCAD displays a dotted line when the position of the cursor matches one of the predefined angles for polar tracking. The following is the Command prompt sequence for drawing the object in Figure 1-31:

Command: **LINE**
Specify first point: **2,1**
Specify next point or [Close/Undo]: **4** ⏎   *(Move the cursor horizontally and enter the length of the line (4) from the keyboard.)*

Specify next point or [Close/Undo]: **1.4142** *(Position the cursor in a 45-degree direction and enter 1.4142.)*

Specify next point or [Close/Undo]: **2** *Move the cursor up vertically, then enter 2.*

Specify next point or [Close/Undo]: **6** *Move the cursor left horizontally then enter 6.*

Specify next point or [Close/Undo]: **2** *Move the cursor down vertically then enter 2.*

Specify next point or [Close/Undo]: **C**

Exercise 4 *General*

Use the direct distance entry method to draw a parallelogram. The base of the parallelogram = 4 units, side = 2.25 units, and the angle = 45 degrees. Draw the same parallelogram using absolute, relative, and polar coordinates. Note the differences and the advantage of using Direct Distance Entry.

ERASING OBJECTS

Toolbar:	Modify > Erase
Menu:	Modify > Erase
Command:	ERASE

Figure 1-32 Invoking the ERASE command from the Modify toolbar

After drawing some objects you may want to erase some of them from the screen. To erase you can use AutoCAD's **ERASE** command. This command is used exactly the same way as an eraser is used in manual drafting to remove unwanted information. When you invoke the **ERASE** command, a small box known as the pick box replaces the screen cursor. To erase an object, move the **pick box** so it touches the object. You can select the object by pressing the pick button of your pointing device (Figure 1-34). AutoCAD confirms the selection by changing the selected objects into dashed lines, and the **Select objects:** prompt returns. You can either continue selecting objects or press ENTER to terminate the object selection process and erase the selected objects. If you are entering the command from the keyboard, you can type **E** or **ERASE**. The following is the prompt sequence:

Command: **ERASE** Enter
Select objects: *Select first object.*

Figure 1-33 Invoking the ERASE command from the Modify menu

Select objects: *Select second object.*
Select objects: [Enter]

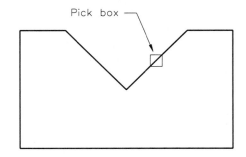

If you enter All at the **Select objects:** prompt, AutoCAD will erase all objects in the drawing, even if the objects are outside the screen display area.

> Command: **ERASE** [Enter]
> Select objects: **All**

You can also first select the objects to be erased from the drawing and then right-click on the drawing area to display the shortcut menu. From here, you can choose the **Erase** option.

Figure 1-34 Selecting objects by positioning the pick box at the top of the object and then pressing the pick button on the pointing device

CANCELING AND UNDOING A COMMAND

If you are in a command and you want to cancel or get out of that command, press the ESC (Escape) key on the keyboard.

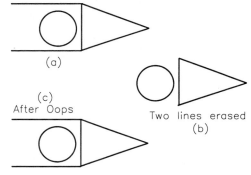

> Command: **ERASE** [Enter]
> Select objects: *Press ESC (Escape) to cancel the command.*

Similarly, sometimes you unintentionally erase some object from the screen. When you discover such an error, you can correct it by restoring the erased object by means of the **OOPS** command. The **OOPS** command restores objects that have been accidentally erased by the previous **ERASE** command, Figure 1-35. You can also use the **U** (Undo) command to undo the last command.

*Figure 1-35 Use of the **OOPS** command*

> Command: **OOPS** [Enter]   *(Restores erased objects.)*
> Command: **U** [Enter]   *(Undoes the last command.)*

CREATING SELECTION SETS

One of the ways to select objects is to select them individually, which can be time-consuming if you have a number of objects to edit. This problem can be solved by creating a selection set that enables you to select several objects at a time. The selection set options can be used with those commands that require object selection, such as **MOVE** and **ERASE**. There are many selection options for creating a selection set, like All, Last, and Add. At this point we will explore two options: **Window** and **Crossing.** The remaining options are discussed in the next chapter.

The Window Option

This option is used to select an object or group of objects by drawing a box or window around them. The objects to be selected should be completely enclosed within the window; those objects that lie partially inside the boundaries of the window are not selected. You can select the **Window** option by typing W at the **Select objects:** prompt. AutoCAD will prompt you to select the two opposite corners of the window. After selecting the first corner, you can select the other corner by moving the cursor to the desired position and specifying the particular point. As you move the cursor, a box or window is displayed that changes in size as you move the cursor. The objects selected by the **Window** option are displayed as dashed objects, i.e. highlighted (Figure 1-36). The following prompt sequence illustrates the use of the **Window** option with the **ERASE** command:

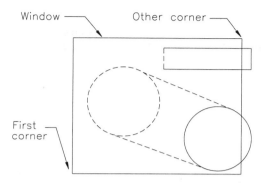

Figure 1-36 *Selecting objects using the* **Window** *option*

> Command: **ERASE** [Enter]
> Select objects: **W** [Enter]
> Specify first corner: *Select the first corner.*
> Specify opposite corner: *Select the second corner.*
> Select objects: [Enter]

You can also select the **Window** option by selecting a blank point on the screen at the **Select objects:** prompt. This is automatically taken as the first corner of the window. Dragging the cursor to the right will display a window. After getting all the objects to be selected inside this window, you can specify the other corner with your pointing device. The objects that are completely enclosed within the window will be selected and highlighted. The following is the prompt sequence for automatic window selection with the **ERASE** command:

> Command: **ERASE** [Enter]
> Select objects: *Select a blank point as the first corner of the window.*
> Specify opposite corner: *Drag the cursor to the right to select the other corner of the window.*
> Select objects: [Enter]

The Crossing Option

This option is used to select an object or group of objects by creating a box or window around them. The objects to be selected should be touching the window boundaries or completely enclosed within the window. You can invoke the **Crossing** option by entering **C** at the **Select objects:** prompt. After you choose the Crossing option, AutoCAD prompts you to select the first corner at the **Specify first corner:** prompt. Once you have selected the first corner, a box or window made of dashed lines is displayed. By moving the cursor you can change the size of the crossing box, hence putting the objects to be selected within (or touching) the box. Here you can select the other corner. The objects selected by the Crossing option are highlighted by displaying them as dashed objects (Figure 1-37). The following prompt sequence illustrates the use of the Crossing option with the **ERASE** command:

Command: **ERASE** Enter
Select objects: **C** Enter
Specify first corner: *Select the first corner of
the crossing window.*
Specify opposite corner: *Select the other
corner of the crossing window.*
Select objects: Enter

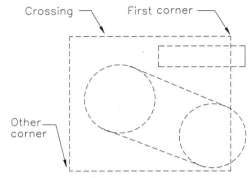

Figure 1-37 *Selecting objects using the Crossing
option*

You can also select the **Crossing** option automatically by selecting a blank point on the
screen at the **Select objects:** prompt and dragging the cursor to the left. The blank point you
selected becomes the first corner of the crossing window and AutoCAD will then prompt you
to select the other corner. As you move the cur-
sor, a box or window made of dashed lines is displayed. The objects that are touching or completely enclosed within the window will be selected. The objects selected by the Crossing option
are highlighted by being displayed as dashed objects. The prompt sequence for automatic crossing selection is:

Command: **ERASE** Enter
Select objects: *Select a blank point as the first corner of the crossing window.*
Specify opposite corner: *Drag the cursor to the left to select the other corner of the crossing window.*
Select objects: Enter

MOVE COMMAND

Toolbar:	Modify > Move
Menu:	Modify > Move
Command:	MOVE

Sometimes objects may not be located where they should be.
In such situations you can use the **MOVE** command. This
command lets you move the object (or objects) from their
present location to a new one. This shifting does not change
the size or orientation of the objects. After you enter this

Figure 1-38 *Invoking the MOVE
command from the Modify toolbar*

command, AutoCAD will prompt you to select the objects to be moved. You can select the objects
individually or use any selection techniques discussed earlier (Window, Crossing, etc.). Next, AutoCAD prompts you for the base point. This is any point on or next to the object. It is better to
select a point on the object, a corner (if the object has one), or the center of a circle. The next
prompt asks you for a second point of displacement. This is the location where you want to move
the object. The selected objects are moved from the specified base point to the second point of
displacement (Figure 1-40). The prompt sequence is as follows:

Command: **MOVE** Enter
Select objects: *Choose objects individually or use the selection set.*
Select objects: Enter

Specify base point or displacement: *Specify any point on or near the object.*
Specify second point of displacement or <use first point as displacement>: *Select the new location by specifying a point on the screen.*

Figure 1-40 *Moving an object using the **MOVE** command*

We can also move the selected objects by using the short-cut menu by clicking the right button. If null response is given at **Specify second point of displacement or <use first point as displacement>:**prompt by pressing enter, AutoCAD interprets the first point as relative value of displacement in X,Y, and Z directions respectively.

Figure 1-39 *Invoking the **MOVE** command from the **Modify** menu*

DRAWING CIRCLES

Toolbar:	Draw > Circle
Menu:	Draw > Circle
Command:	CIRCLE

To draw a circle you can use the AutoCAD **CIRCLE** command. The following is the prompt sequence for the **CIRCLE** command:

Figure 1-41 *Invoking the **CIRCLE** command from the **Draw** toolbar*

Command: **CIRCLE** [Enter]
Specify center point for circle or [3P/2P/Ttr(tan tan radius)]:

The different options of the **CIRCLE** command follow.

The Center and Radius Option
In this option you can draw a circle by defining the center and the radius of the circle, Figure 1-43.

After entering the **CIRCLE** command, AutoCAD will prompt you to enter the center of the circle, which can be selected by specifying a point on the screen or by entering the coordinates of the center point. Next, you will be prompted to enter the radius of the circle. Here you can accept the default value, enter a new value, or select a point on the circumference of the circle to specify the radius. The following is the prompt sequence for drawing a circle with a center at 3,2 and a radius of 1 unit:

Command: **CIRCLE** [Enter]
Specify center point for circle or [3P/2P/Ttr(tan tan radius): **3,2** [Enter]
Specify radius of circle or [Diameter]<current>: **1** (or @1<0, or @1,0) [Enter]

Note
You can also set the radius by assigning a value to the ***CIRCLERAD*** *system variable. The value you assign becomes the default value for radius.*

The Center and Diameter Option

In this option you can draw a circle by defining the center and diameter of the circle. After invoking the **CIRCLE** command, AutoCAD prompts you to enter the center of the circle, which can be selected by specifying a point on the screen or by entering the coordinates of

Figure 1-42 *Invoking the* ***CIRCLE*** *command from the* ***Draw*** *menu*

the center point. Next, you will be prompted to enter the radius of the circle. At this prompt enter **D**. After this you will be prompted to enter the diameter of the circle. For entering the diameter you can accept the default value, enter a new value, or drag the circle to the desired diameter and select a point. If you use a menu option to select the **CIRCLE** command with the **Diameter** option, the menu automatically enters the **Diameter** option and prompts for the diameter after you specify the center. The following is the prompt sequence for drawing a circle with the center at (2,3) and a diameter of 2 units (Figure 1-44):

Command: **CIRCLE** [Enter]
Specify center point for circle or [3P/2P/Ttr(tan tan radius): **2,3** [Enter]
Specify radius of circle or [Diameter]<current>: **D** [Enter]
Specify diameter of circle <current>: **2** [Enter]

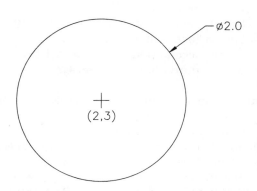

Figure 1-43 *Drawing a circle using the Center and Radius option*

Figure 1-44 *Drawing a circle using the Center and Diameter option*

The Two-Point Option

You can also draw a circle using the **Two-Point** option. In this option AutoCAD lets you draw the circle by specifying the two endpoints of the circle's diameter. For example, if you want to draw a circle that passes through the points (1,1) and (2,1), you can use the **CIRCLE** command with 2P option, as shown in the following example (Figure 1-45):

    Command: **CIRCLE** Enter

    Specify center point for circle or [3P/2P/Ttr(tan tan radius): **2P** Enter

    Specify first end point of circle's diameter: **1,1** Enter

    Second end point of circle's diameter: **2,1** Enter   *(You can also use polar or relative coordinates.)*

The Three-Point Option

For drawing a circle, you can also use the **Three-Point** option by defining three points on the circumference of the circle. The three points may be entered in any order. To draw a circle that passes through the points 3,3, 3,1 and 4,2 (Figure 1-46), the prompt sequence is:

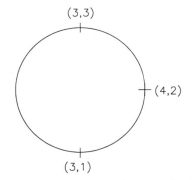

Figure 1-45 *Drawing a Circle using the Two-Point option*

Figure 1-46 *Drawing a Circle using the Three-Point option*

Command: **CIRCLE** Enter
Specify center point for circle or [3P/2P/Ttr(tan tan radius)]: 3P Enter
Specify first point on circle: **3,3** Enter
Specify second point on circle: **3,1** Enter
Specify third point on circle: **4,2** Enter

You can also use **relative coordinates** to define the points:

Command: **CIRCLE** Enter
Specify center point for circle or [3P/2P/Ttr(tan tan radius)]: **3P** Enter
Specify first point on circle: **3,3** Enter
Specify second point on circle: **@0,-2** Enter
Specify third point on circle: **@1,1** Enter

The Tangent Tangent Radius Option

A tangent is an object (line, circle, or arc) that contacts the circumference of a circle at only one point. In this option AutoCAD uses the Tangent object snap to locate two tangent points on the selected objects that are to be tangents to the circle. Then you have to specify the radius of the circle. The prompt sequence for drawing a circle using the **Ttr** option:

Command: **CIRCLE** Enter
Specify center point for circle or [3P/2P/Ttr(tan tan radius)]: **T** Enter
Specify point on object for first tangent of circle: *Select first line, circle, or arc.*
Specify point on object for second tangent of circle: *Select second line, circle, or arc.*
Specify radius of circle <current>: **0.75** Enter

In Figures 1-47 through 1-50, the dotted circles represent the circles that are drawn by using the **Ttr** option. The circle AutoCAD actually draws depends on how you select the objects that are to be tangent to the new circle. The figures show the effect of selecting different points on the objects. The dashed circles represent the circles that are drawn using the **Ttr** option. If you specify too small or large a radius, you may get unexpected results or a "Circle does not exist" prompt.

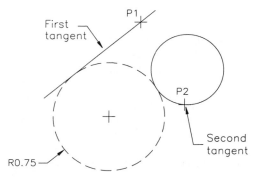

Figure 1-47 *Tangent, tangent, radius (Ttr) option*

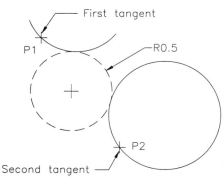

Figure1-48 *Drawing a circle using the tangent, tangent, radius (Ttr) option*

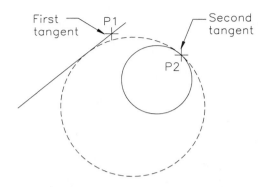

Figure 1-49 *Tangent, tangent, radius (Ttr) option*

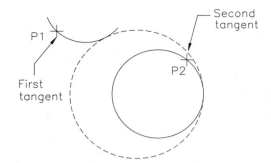

Figure 1-50 *Tangent, tangent, radius (Ttr) option*

The Tangent, Tangent, Tangent Option

You can invoke this option from the menu bar or the screen menu. This option is a modification of the Three-Point option. In this option AutoCAD uses the Tangent osnap to locate three points on three selected objects to which the circle is drawn tangent. The following is the prompt sequence for drawing a circle using the **Tan, Tan, Tan** option (Figure 1-51):

> Command: **CIRCLE** Enter
> Specify center point for circle or [3P/2P/ Ttr(tan tan radius): *Select Tan, Tan, Tan option from the **Draw** menu.*
> _ 3P Specify first point on circle: _tan to *Select the first object.*
> Specify second point on circle: _tan to *Select the second object.*
> Specify third point on circle: _tan to *Select the third object.*

Figure 1-51 *Drawing a circle using the Tan, Tan, Tan option*

| **Exercise 5** | *Mechanical* |

Generate Figure 1-52 using different options of the **LINE** and **CIRCLE** commands. Use absolute, relative, or polar coordinates for drawing the triangle. The vertices of the triangle will be used as the center of the circles. The circles can be drawn using the Center and Radius, Center and Diameter, or TTT option. (Height of triangle = 2.25 x sin 60 = 1.949.) Do not draw the dimensions; they are for reference only.

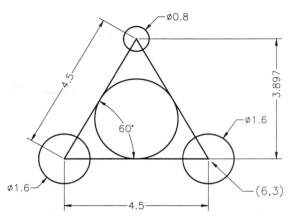

Figure 1-52 *Drawing for Exercise 5*

BASIC DISPLAY COMMANDS

Drawing in AutoCAD is much simpler than manual drafting in many ways. Sometimes while drawing, it is very difficult to see and alter minute details. In AutoCAD, you can overcome this problem by viewing only a specific portion of the drawing. This is done using the **ZOOM** command, which lets you enlarge or reduce the size of the drawing displayed on the screen. We will introduce here some of the drawing display commands, like **REDRAW**, **ZOOM**, and **PAN**. A detailed explanation of these commands and other display options appears in Chapter 5, Controlling Drawing Display and Creating Text.

REDRAW Command

 The **REDRAW** command redraws the screen, thereby removing the cross marks that appear when a point is specified on the screen. These marks, known as blip marks or **blips**, indicate the points you have selected (points specified).

Command: **REDRAW** or **R** Enter

ZOOM Command

Toolbar:	Zoom toolbar, Standard > Zoom flyout
Menu:	View > Zoom
Command:	ZOOM

The **ZOOM** command enlarges or reduces the view of the drawing on the screen, but it does not affect the actual size of the drawing. After the **ZOOM** command has been invoked, different options can be used to obtain the desired display. If you use a menu, it issues the appropriate option at the initial **ZOOM** prompt. The following is the prompt sequence of the **ZOOM** command and some of the **ZOOM** options:

Figure 1-53 *Selecting **Zoom** options from the **Standard** toolbar*

Command: **ZOOM** or **Z** Enter
Specify corner of window, enter a scale factor (nX or nXP), or [All/Center/Dynamic/Extents/Previous/Scale/Window]<Realtime>:

Realtime Zooming

You can use the **Realtime Zoom** to zoom in and zoom out interactively. To zoom in, invoke the command, then hold the pick button down and move the cursor up. If you want to zoom in further, bring the cursor down, Specify a point and move the cursor up. Similarly, to zoom out, hold the pick button down and move the cursor down. Realtime zoom is the default setting for the **ZOOM** command. Pressing ENTER after entering the **ZOOM** command automatically invokes the realtime zoom.

*Figure 1-54 Invoking the **ZOOM** command from the **View** menu*

Window Option

This is the most commonly used option of the **ZOOM** command. It lets you specify the area you want to zoom in on by letting you specify two opposite corners of a rectangular window. The center of the specified window becomes the center of the new display screen. The area inside the window is magnified in size to fill the display as completely as possible. The points can be specified by selecting them with the help of the pointing device or by entering their coordinates.

Previous Option

While working on a complex drawing, you may need to zoom in on a portion of the drawing to edit some minute details. When you have completed the editing you may want to return to the previous view. This can be done using the **Previous** option of the **ZOOM** command. AutoCAD remembers the last ten views which can be recalled by using the **Previous** option.

Panning in Realtime

You can use the **Realtime Pan** to pan the drawing interactively. To pan a drawing, invoke the command and then hold the pick button down and move the cursor in any direction. When you select the realtime pan, AutoCAD displays an image of a hand indicating that you are in PAN mode. When in realtime zoom or pan, you can right-click to display the shortcut menu, Figure 1-55. You can use the shortcut menu to select **Zoom**, **Pan**, **Exit**, or other zoom options.

*Figure 1-55 Shortcut menu when in realtime **ZOOM** and **PAN** commands*

CREATING TEXT

Menu:	Draw > Text > Single-Line Text
Command:	DTEXT or TEXT

The **DTEXT** or **TEXT** command lets you write several lines of text on a drawing. The prompt sequence is:

Command: **DTEXT** [Enter]
Current text style: "current" Text height: current
Specify start point of text or [Justify/Style]:
Specify the starting point of text.
Specify height <current>: *Enter the text height.*
Specify rotation angle <0>: [Enter]
Enter text: *Enter the text.*
Enter text: *Enter the second line of text.*
Enter text: [Enter]

You can use the BACKSPACE key to edit the text on the screen while you are writing the text. The text commands are discussed in detail in Chapter 5.

Figure 1-56 Invoking the DTEXT or TEXT command from the Draw menu

PLOTTING DRAWINGS*

Toolbar:	Standard toolbar > Plot
Menu:	File > Plot...
Command:	PLOT or PRINT

 Drawings can be plotted by using the **PLOT** command. AutoCAD will display the **Plot** dialog box (Figure 1-59) when you enter or select the **PLOT** command.

Command: **PLOT**

The values in this dialog box are the ones that were set during the configuring of AutoCAD. If the displayed values conform to your requirements, you can start plotting without making any changes. If necessary, you can make changes in the default values according to your plotting requirements.

Basic Plotting

In this section you will learn how to set up the basic plotting parameters. Later, you will learn about the advance option, that allows you to plot according to your plot drawing specifications. Basic plotting involves selecting the correct output device (plotter), specifying the area to plot, selecting paper size, specifying the plot origin, orientation, and the plot scale.

***Figure 1-57** Invoking the PLOT command from the File*

Example 5

You will plot the drawing of Example 4 (Figure 1-58) using the **Window** option to select the area to plot. Assume that AutoCAD is configured for two output devices, System Printer and HP 7475A.

Figure 1-58 Drawing for Example 5

Step 1

Invoke the **Plot** dialog box from the **Standard** toolbar, or the **File** menu (Choose **Plot**) or by entering **PLOT** at the Command prompt.

Step 2

Choose the **Plot Device** tab, Figure 1-59. Under **Plotter Configuration**, select the name of the device by choosing the drop-down arrow button in the **Name:** edit box, to display the drop-down list of the currently configured devices. Related information about the selected device is displayed below this box. For example, if you have configured AutoCAD for two output devices, System Printer and HP 7475A, AutoCAD will display these names in the **Name:** edit box drop-down list. If you want to plot the drawing on the System Printer, select System Printer (if it is not already selected).

Step 3

Now choose the **Plot Settings** tab and here, choose the **Window** button (located under **Plot** area) in the **Plot** dialog box. You can enter the first and second corners of the area you want to plot by specifying points on the screen. When you choose the **Window** button, the dialog box will temporarily disappear and the drawing will appear on the screen. Now, select the first and second corners (Points P1 and P2), specifying the plot area (the area you want to plot). Once you have defined the two corners, the **Plot** dialog box will reappear.

Figure 1-59 Plot dialog box with the Plot Device tab

Step 4

To set the size for the plot, select from the **Paper size:** edit box drop-down list under **Paper size and paper units** area (Figure 1-60), which lists all the plotting sizes that the present plotter can support. You can select any one of the sizes listed in the dialog box or specify a size (width and height) of your own through the **Plotter Manager**. (This option is discussed later in Chapter 15, Plotting Drawings and Draw Commands.) Once you select a size, you can also select the orientation by choosing either the **Landscape** or **Portrait** radio buttons under **Drawing orientation**. The sections in the **Plot** dialog box pertaining to paper size and orientation are automatically revised to reflect the new paper size and orientation. In this example you will specify Paper size A (8.5 by 11 inches).

Step 5

You can also modify values for **Plot offset**, the default values for X and Y are 0. Similarly, you can enter values for **Plot scale**. Choose the **Scale: edit** box drop-down list arrow button to display the various scale factors. From this list you can select a scale factor you want to use. For example if you select the scale factor 1/4"=1'-0", the **Custom:** edit boxes show 1 inch= 48 drawing units. If you want the drawing to be plotted so that it fits on the specified sheet of paper, select the **Scaled to Fit** option. When you select this option, AutoCAD will determine the scale factor and display the scale factor in the **Custom:** edit boxes. In this example, you will plot the drawing so that it fits on 8.5 x 11 paper. Therefore, select the Scaled to Fit option and notice the change in the **Custom:** (Inches = Drawing Units) edit boxes. Selecting the **Custom** option, allows you to enter your own values.

Figure 1-60 Plot dialog box with Plot Settings tab

Step 6

You can view the plot on the specified paper size before actually plotting it by choosing the **Preview...** buttons in the **Plot** dialog box. This way you can save time and stationery. AutoCAD provides two types of Plot Previews, partial and full. To generate partial preview of a plot, choose the **Partial Preview** button. The **Partial Plot Preview** dialog box is displayed (Figure 1-61). To display the drawing just as it would be plotted on the paper, choose the **Full Preview** button. **Full Preview** takes more time than **Partial Preview** because the drawing is regenerated. Once regeneration is complete, the preview image is displayed on the screen, Figure 1-62. In place of the cursor a realtime zoom icon is displayed. You can hold the pick button of your pointing device and then move it up to zoom into the preview image and move the cursor down to zoom out of the preview image. To exit the preview image, press the ESC or ENTER key. You can also right-click to display the shortcut menu where you can choose **Exit** to exit the preview image.

Step 7

If the plot preview is satisfactory and you want to plot the drawing, choose the **OK** button in the **Plot** dialog box. You can also choose **Plot** from the shortcut menu displayed in the previous step. AutoCAD will plot the drawing on the specified plotter.

Figure 1-61 Partial Plot Preview dialog

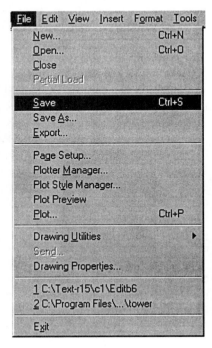

Figure 1-62 Full plot preview

SAVING YOUR WORK

Toolbar:	Standard > Save
Menu:	File >Save or Save As
Command:	SAVE > SAVEAS > QSAVE

In AutoCAD or any computer system, you must save your work before you exit from the drawing editor or turn the system off. Also, it is recommended that you save your drawings after regular time intervals. In case of a power failure, a serious editing error, or some other problem, all work saved prior to the problem will be retained. The commands that AutoCAD has provided to save the work can be entered at the Command prompt or by selecting the appropriate command from the menu bar (Choose **File**) (Figure 1-63).

AutoCAD has provided the following commands that let you save your work on the hard disk of the computer or on the floppy diskette:

SAVE   SAVEAS   QSAVE

*Figure 1-63 Different Save options in the **File** menu*

The **SAVE**, **SAVEAS**, and **QSAVE** commands allow you to save your drawing by writing it to a permanent storage device, such as a hard drive, or on a diskette in the A or B drive. When you invoke the **SAVEAS** command or the **SAVE** command (**SAVE** command can be invoked from the

Command prompt only. **SAVE** in the **File** menu and the **Standard** toolbar invoke the **QSAVE** command), the **Save Drawing As** dialog box (Figure 1-64) is displayed. In this dialog box, you are supposed to enter the file name in which the drawing will be saved. The **SAVEAS** command works in the same way as the **SAVE** command, but in addition to saving the drawing it sets the name of the current drawing to the file name you specify. The **QSAVE** command saves the current named drawing without asking you to enter a file name, thus allowing you to do a quick save. If the current drawing is unnamed, **QSAVE** acts like **SAVEAS** and will prompt you to enter the file name in the **Save Drawing As** dialog box.

The **Save Drawing As** dialog box displays the information related to the drawing files on your system. To save your work, enter the name of the drawing in the **File Name:** edit box or select a file from the list box. The drawing extension **.dwg** is not required as it is the default (AutoCAD drawing) and is displayed in the **Save as type:** list box. You can change the directory through the **Save in:** drop-down list. If you want to save the drawing on the A drive, enter **a:house**, and AutoCAD will write the information to the diskette in the A drive. After entering the name, choose the **Save** button.

Figure 1-64 Save Drawing As dialog box

Note
*If you want to save a drawing on the A or B drive, make sure the diskette you are using to save the drawings is formatted. Other features of the **Save Drawing As** dialog box are described near the end of this chapter.*

OPENING AN EXISTING FILE

Toolbar:	Standard toolbar > Open
Menu:	File > Open
Command:	OPEN

Chapter 1

To open an existing file in the drawing editor, you can use the **OPEN** command. When you invoke the **OPEN** command, AutoCAD displays the **Select File** dialog box (Figure 1-65). You can enter the name of the drawing file you want to open in the **File Name:** edit box, or you can select the name of the drawing from the **Files Name:** list box.

Command: **OPEN** [Enter]

Figure 1-65 Select File dialog box

STARTING A NEW DRAWING

Toolbar:	Standard toolbar > New
Menu:	File > New
Command:	NEW

When you run AutoCAD, and you are in the drawing editor, the drawing you create is named **Drawing 1.dwg** by default. You can save this drawing under a different name by using the **SAVE** or **SAVEAS** command. You can either specify the file name first and then begin work or do it before exiting. The **NEW** command is used to create a new drawing while you are in an editing session.

Command: **NEW** [Enter]

After you invoke the **NEW** command, AutoCAD will display the **Create New Drawing** dialog box (Figure 1-66). Choose **OK** to accept the **Start from Scratch** option (default). A new drawing having the default AutoCAD setup is started.

QUITTING A DRAWING

You can exit from the drawing editor by using the **EXIT** or **QUIT** command. If the changes you have made to the drawing have been saved, AutoCAD allows you to exit without saving them again. In case the drawing has not been saved, it allows you to save the work first through a dialog box. This box gives you an option to discard the current drawing or changes made to it. It also gives you an option to cancel the command.

Figure 1-66 Create New Drawing dialog box

Note
*The following sections describe in detail the **Save Drawing As** and **Select File** dialog boxes. If you are using AutoCAD for the first time, you can skip this portion and come back to it later.*

SAVE DRAWING AS DIALOG BOX

Save as type: List Boxes

The **Save as type:** drop-down list (Figure 1-67) is used to specify the drawing format in which you want to save the file. For example, to save the file as AutoCAD 2000 drawing file, select **AutoCAD 2000** Drawing from the drop-down list.

Figure 1-67 Save as type list box

File name Edit Box

The **File name:** edit box is used to enter the name of the file you want the drawing to be saved as. This can be done by typing the file name or selecting it from the list box. If you select the file name you want from the list box, the name you select automatically appears in the **File name:** edit box. If you have already assigned a name to the drawing, the current drawing name is taken as default. If the drawing is unnamed, the default name **Drawing1** is displayed in the **File Name:** edit box.

Save in: List Box

The current drive and path information is listed in the **Save in:** drop-down list (Figure 1-68). AutoCAD will initially save the drawing in the default directory, but if you want to save the drawing in a different directory, you have to specify the path. For example, if you want to save the present drawing under the file name **HOUSE** in C1 subdirectory, choose the arrow button in the **Save in:** list box to display the drop-down list and select C:. When you select C: all directories in C drive will be listed in the file list box. Double-click on TEXT-R15 or select TEXT-R15 and choose the **Open** button to display its directories. Again Double-click on C1 or select C1 and choose the **Open** button to display drawing names in the file list box. Select HOUSE from the list, if it is already listed there, or enter it in the **File name:** edit box and then choose the **Save** button. Your drawing (House) will be saved in the C1 folder (C:\TEXT-R15\C1\HOUSE.dwg).

Figure 1-68   Save in: list box

List and Detail Buttons

If you choose the **List** button (Figure 1-69), all files present in the current directory will be listed in the file list box. If you choose the **Detail** button, it will display detailed information about the files (size, type, date, and time of modification).

Figure 1-69 Save in: list box

Folder Button

If you choose the **Create New Folder** button, AutoCAD creates a new directory under the name **New Folder**. The new folder is displayed in the file list box. You can accept the name or change it to your requirement.

Up One Level Button

The **Up One Level** button displays the directories which are up by one level.

Options Button

The **Options** button displays the **Saveas Options** dialog box where you can save the proxy images of custom objects. It has the **DWG** and **DXF** options tabs.

Search the Web

It displays the **Browse the Web** dialog box that enables you to access and store AutoCAD files on the internet.

Look in Favorites

Sets the search path to look in the system's Favorites folder.

Add to Favorites

Creates a shortcut to the selected file or folder and adds it to the systems Favorites folder.

SELECT FILE DIALOG BOX

When you enter the **OPEN** command or choose **Open** from the **File** menu or the **Standard** toolbar, AutoCAD displays the **Select File** dialog box. This box is similar to the **Save Drawing As** dialog box (described earlier, Figure 1-69), except the **Preview box**, **Locate**, **Partial Open** and **Find File** buttons, **Select Initial View** and **Open as read-only** check boxes.

Select Initial View

A view is defined as the way you look at an object. The **Select Initial View** option allows you to specify the view you want to load initially when AutoCAD loads the drawing. This option will work if the drawing has saved views. You can save a desired view by using AutoCAD's **VIEW** command (see "**VIEW** Command," Chapter 5). If the drawing has no saved views, selecting this option will load the last view. If you select the **Select Initial View** check box and then the **OK** button, AutoCAD will display the **Select Initial View** dialog box (Figure 1-70). You can select the view name from this dialog box, and AutoCAD will load the drawing with the selected view displayed.

Figure 1-70 Select Initial View dialog box.

Open as read-only

If you want to view a drawing without altering it, you must select the **Open as read-only** check box. In other words, read only protects the drawing file from changes. AutoCAD does not prevent you from editing the drawing, but if you try to save the opened drawing to the original file name, AutoCAD warns you that the drawing file is **write protected.** However, you can save the edited drawing to a file with a different file name.

Find File

Select this button to display the **Browse/Search** dialog box (Figure 1-71). This allows you to search files in different drives and subdirectories.

Browse

The file name of the drawing that is currently selected is displayed in the **File Name:** drop-down list. The bitmap images of the drawings in the current directory are displayed in the **Preview** box. The drawing display size can be made small, medium, or large by selecting the desired option in the **Size:** list box. The **Drives:** and **Directories:** list boxes display the different drives and directories available.

Search

To activate the **Search** dialog box (Figure 1-72), choose the **Search** tab. To start the search routine, choose the **Search** button. Searching for files depends on the file type or creation date. As the search continues, the search progress is updated in the **Preview** box. After the search is completed, the bitmap images and the file names of those files that fulfill the search criteria are displayed in the list box. The total number of these files is also displayed. The **Search Pattern** allows you to

Figure 1-71 Browse/Search *dialog box*

search for files having a specific pattern of specified file type. In the list box you can select the desired file type for searching. In the **Date Filter** box you can specify a certain time and date so that only those files are searched that have been created before or after the particular time and date. The time and date can be specified in the **Time** and **Date** text boxes in the **Date Filter** box. In the **Search Location** area you can specify the drives and paths for searching. In the **Drives** list box you can specify the drive for searching. The **All Drives** list box displays all the fixed drives. In the **Path** edit box you can specify the directories to be searched. The **Edit** button opens the **Edit Path** dialog box which is used to edit a path.

Partial Open*

The **Partial Open** button displays the **Partial Open** dialog box that enables you to import geometry from a selected view or layer into a drawing.

Locate

The **Locate** button enables you to search a specified File by using the search path specified in the **Options** dialog box.

Preview

If you select a file name from the **File Name:** list box, the bitmap image of that particular file is displayed in the Preview box.

Figure 1-72 Browse/Search dialog box

AUTOMATIC TIMED SAVE

AutoCAD allows you to save your work automatically at specific intervals. To change the time intervals you can use the system variable **SAVETIME**. You can also change the time intervals from the **Options** dialog box (**General** tab), which can be invoked from the **Tools** menu. Depending on the power supply, hardware, and type of drawings, you should decide on an appropriate time and assign that time to this variable. AutoCAD saves the drawing under the file name **AUTO.SV$**. The extension of the auto-save file is **.SV$**.

> Command: **SAVETIME** Enter
> Enter new value for SAVETIME <120>: *Enter time, in minutes.*

CREATION OF BACKUP FILES

If the drawing file already exists and you use **SAVE** or **SAVEAS** commands to update the current drawing, AutoCAD creates a backup file. AutoCAD takes the previous copy of the drawing and changes it from a file type **.DWG** to **.BAK**, and the updated drawing is saved as a drawing file with the **.DWG** extension. For example, if the name of the drawing is **MYPROJ.DWG**, AutoCAD will change it to **MYPROJ.BAK** and save the current drawing as **MYPROJ.DWG.**

OPTIONS DIALOG BOX*

You can use the **Options** dialog box (Figure 1-73) to change the settings that affect the drawing environment or the AutoCAD interface. For example, you can use the **Options** dialog box to display the screen menu or specify the support directories that contain the files you need. The Current profile: name and the Current drawing: name are displayed on the top, above the tabs.

*Figure 1-73 **Options** dialog box*

The Options Dialog Box Tabs

Files
Stores the directories in which AutoCAD looks for driver, menu, support, and other files. It uses three icons: folder, paper stack, and file cabinet. The folder icon is for search path, the paper stack icon is for files, and the file cabinet icon is for a specific folder.

Display
Controls drawing and window settings like screen menu display and scroll bar. For example, if you want to display the screen menu, invoke the **Options** dialog box by selecting **Options** in the **Tools** menu. In the **Options** dialog box choose the **Display** tab and then select the **Display screen menu** check box under the **Window Elements** area. Similarly, you can change the color of the graphics window background. It also allows you to modify the Display resolution and Display performance.

Open and Save
Controls parameters related to opening and saving of files in AutoCAD like the Automatic Save feature.

Output

Controls parameters related to plotting of drawings in AutoCAD like the Default output device.

System

Contains AutoCAD system settings options like the 3D graphics display and Pointing device settings options.

User Preferences

Controls settings that depend on the way the user prefers working on AutoCAD, like the Right-click Customization.

Drafting

Controls settings like the Autosnap Settings and the Aperture Size.

Selection

Controls settings related to the methods of Object Selection like the Grips.

Profiles

Saves and restores the system settings. To set the Profile in the **Options** dialog box, choose the **Profile** tab and then choose the **Add to list** button. The **Add Profile** dialog box appears. Enter the Profile name and description. Then choose the **Apply & Close** button. Next, make the new profile current and then specify the settings. The settings are saved in the new profile and can be restored anytime by making the profile current.

Example 6

In the following example you will use the **Options** dialog box to create a profile that contains the specified settings.

1. To invoke the **Options** dialog box choose **Options** from the **Tools** menu. You can also right-click in the Command window to display a shortcut menu and choose **Options**. Typing **OPTIONS** in the Command line also displays the **Options** dialog box.

2. In the **Options** dialog box choose the **Profiles** tab.

3. Choose the **Add to list:** button to display the **Add Profile** dialog box. Enter the name of the new profile (**Myprofile1**) and description of the new profile and then choose the **Apply and Close** button to exit.

4. Make sure **Myprofile1** profile is selected and then choose the **Set Current** button to make **Myprofile1** current. Choose the **Display** tab and then select the **Display screen menu** check box.

5. Now, choose the **Color** button. The **AutoCAD color options** dialog box is displayed. Change the color of the graphics window background to white. Choose the **Apply & Close** button to return to the **Options** dialog box.

Chapter 1

6. Choose the **Output** tab and then select the **Add or Configure Plotters** button to add another printer. When you choose this button, the **Plotters** dialog box is displayed on the screen. Double-click on the **Add-A-Plotter Wizard** icon, which guides you through the process of selecting and adding a plotter. When you choose the **Finish** button in the **Add-A-Plotter Wizard**, an icon for the newly configured plotter appears in the **Plotters** dialog box. Close this box. From the Use default device edit box drop-down list, select a printer.

7. Choose the **Drafting** tab and change the AutoSnap Marker Size to the maximum. Choose the **Apply** button and then the **OK** button to exit. Notice the changes in screen color and AutoSnapMarker size. Press ENTER to invoke the **Options** dialog box again or choose **Options** from the **Tools** menu.

9. Choose the **Profile** tab and then select the default profile (<<Unnamed Profile>>). Choose the **Set Current** button to load the default settings. The screen settings will change as specified in the Default profile.

10. Select the **Myprofile1** profile and then choose the **Set Current** button to change the settings assigned to **Myprofile1** profile.

COMMAND LINE RECALL AND EDITING

You can recall a command by using the up and down arrow key in the History Window. As you press the arrow key, previously entered commands and the Command prompt entries are displayed at the Command prompt. Once the desired command is displayed at the Command prompt, you can execute the command by pressing the ENTER key. You can also edit the command or the values displayed in the History Window.

The commands and command prompt entries that are displayed in the History Window can be selected, copied, and pasted in the command line. To copy and paste, select the lines and then right-click in the History Window (Command prompt area) to display the shortcut menu (Figure 1-74). In the shortcut menu select copy and then paste the selected lines in the command line. After the lines are pasted, you can edit them.

Figure 1-74 The shortcut menu, displayed on right-clicking on the command prompt area

AUTOCAD'S HELP

You can get the on-line help and documentation on the working of AutoCAD 2000 commands from the **Help** menu (Figure 1-75).

AutoCAD Help Topics

Toolbar:	Standard > Help
Menu:	Help > AutoCAD Help Topics
Command:	HELP

Invoking **HELP** displays the **Help Topics: AutoCAD Help** dialog box (Figure 1-76). You can use this dialog box to ac-

Figure 1-75 Help menu

cess help on different topics and commands. It has four tabs: **Contents**, **Index**, **Find**, and **Using AutoCAD Help**, which display the corresponding help topics. If you are in the middle of a command and require help regarding it, choosing the **Help** button, displays information about that particular command.

Contents

This tab displays the help topics that are organized by categories pertaining to different sections of AutoCAD. To select a category, double-click on the corresponding book icon or select the book icon and then choose the **Open** button. The topics associated with that category are displayed in a window. Select a topic and then double-click or choose the **Open** button; AutoCAD displays information about the selected topic or command. In this display, if you select the items that are underlined and green in color, a step-by-step tutorial on that topic is displayed. If you select the bulleted items, AutoCAD displays information about the selected item.

Index

This tab displays the complete index (search keywords) in an alphabetical order. To display information about an item or command, type the item (word) or command name in the edit box, (Figure 1-76). With each letter entered the listing keeps on changing in the list area, displaying the possible topics. When you enter the word and if AutoCAD finds that word, it is automatically highlighted in the list area. Choose the **Display** button to display information about it.

Figure 1-76 Help Topics: AutoCAD Help dialog box (Index tab)

Find

This tab creates a word list based on all the keywords present in the online help files. You can use the Options button to refine this list. When you type a word you are looking for, a list of matching words appears in a window below to narrow down your search. The display window below this one further narrows down your search by giving you an option of selecting a topic it is associated with.

What's New

This option gives you an interactive list of all the new features in AutoCAD 2000. You can choose this option from the **Help** menu that displays the **What's New** screen with a list of new features. When you choose the button next to a topic, a brief description of the feature improvement is displayed. Choose a feature to display a list of subtopics. You can choose a particular topic (written and underlined in green) by positioning your cursor on it (cursor changes into a pointing hand icon), and then pressing the pick button of the pointing device. An explanation of the selected topic is displayed. You can go back to the main menu by choosing the **Back** button or you can exit the **What's New** by selecting the **Exit** option from the **File** menu in **What's New**.

Learning Assistance

This is a multimedia learning option that provides you an online environment where you can learn the AutoCAD software application interactively. You can choose this option from the **Help** menu. Choosing this option displays an **Insert Disc** dialog box. On inserting the disc and after specifying the path for it, choose **OK** to display the **AutoCAD Learning Assistance-Microsoft Intenet Explorer** screen, (Figure 1-77). This screen is divided into two areas, the one on the left displays the various topics to select from. When you choose a heading, the related items under that particular topic are displayed on the right-hand side. When you choose an item, AutoCAD displays the related explanation. At the top of this screen is the **Play Animation** button. Choose this button to give you an animated working of the selected command or feature. The animation is also supported by voice (audio) which explains the working interactively with the animation. You can exit the animation by selecting **Back** from the **Go** menu. You can exit from the Learning Assistance by choosing **Exit** from the **File** menu or by selecting the **Close (X)** button.

Support Assistance

This help option displays the Autodesk Support Assistance screen having five main headings: **Search for solution, Download, What's hot, More Resources** and **Phone Support**. Choosing any one of these topics displays further sub topics to choose from with their brief explanations. You can choose any of these to look for their respective descriptions and related topics. To go to search or Up one level, you choose the **Search** or **Up one level** buttons, provided at the end of the screen. This option gives you all the Technical Support information in a question and answer format. It also provides information about other help resources.

Autodesk on the Web

This utility connects you to the various AutoCAD/ Autodesk web pages and sites through the Microsoft Internet Explorer.

AutoCAD 2000 Web Site

This option connects you to the AutoCAD 2000 web site.

Figure 1-77 Learning Assistance

About AutoCAD

This option gives you information about the Release, Serial Number, and Licensed To and also the legal description about AutoCAD.

ADDITIONAL HELP RESOURCES

1. You can get help for a command while working by pressing the F1 key. The **Help** dialog box containing information about the command is displayed. You can exit the dialog box and continue with the command.

2. You can get help about a certain dialog box by choosing the **Help** button in that dialog box.

3. Some of the dialog boxes have a **question mark** (**?**) button at the top-right corner just adjacent to the **close** button. When you choose this button the ? gets attached to the cursor. You can then drop it on any item in the dialog box to display information about that particular item.

4. Autodesk has provided several resources that you can use to get assistance with your AutoCAD questions. You can also use these resources to get information on Autodesk products, product updates, and other services provided by Autodesk. The following is a list of some of the resources:

    a. Autodesk Web Site **http://www.autodesk.com**
    b. AutoCAD 2000 Web Site: **http://www.autodesk.com/autocad**

   c.   Autodesk Fax Information System: **(415) 446-1919**

   d.   AutoCAD Technical Assistance Website **autodesk.com/support**.

   e.   AutoCAD Discussion Groups Website **autodesk.com/support/discsgrp/acad.htm**.

5.   You can also get help by contacting the author, Sham Tickoo, at **stickoo@calumet.purdue.edu**.

6.   You can download AutoCAD drawings, programs, and special topics by accessing authors Web Site at **http://www.calumet.purdue.edu/public/mets/tickoo/index.html**.

Self-Evaluation Test

Answer the following questions and then compare your answers to the correct answers given at the end of this chapter.

1.   If you exit the **LINE** command after drawing a line and then select **LINE** command again, the _____ option can be used to draw a line from the endpoint of the last line.

2.   The _____coordinates of a point are located with reference to the previous point.

3.   To draw a line from point (2,2) to another point at a distance of 3 units and an angle of 60 degrees, you will have the prompt sequence:

   Command: _____
   Specify first point: _____
   Specify next point or [Undo]: _____

4.   When using the **Window** option in the **ERASE** command, the objects to be erased must _____lie within the window.

5.   The prompt sequence for drawing a circle with its center at (4,5) and a diameter of 3 units is:
   Command: _____
   Specify center point or [3P/2P/Ttr(tan tan radius)]<Center point>:_____
   Specify radius of circle or [Diameter]<current>: _____
   Specify diameter of circle <current>: _____

6.   The _____option of the **CIRCLE** command can be used to draw a circle, if you want the circle to be tangent to two previously drawn objects.

7.   You can erase a previously drawn line using the _____option of the **LINE** command.

8. The _____ system variable can be used to change the time interval for automatic save.

9. When you select the **ERASE** command, a small box known as the _____ replaces the screen cursor.

10. The _____ command is used to plot a drawing.

11. By choosing the _____ button in the **Plot** dialog box, you can specify the section of the drawing to be plotted with the help of a _____.

Review Questions

1. The prompt sequence for the **LINE** command is:

   Command: _____

   _____

   _____

2. The _____ option can be used to draw the last side of a polygon.

3. In the two mutually intersecting lines for the X and Y coordinates, the X coordinate value is calculated along the _____ line, and the Y coordinate value is calculated along the _____ line.

4. In the _____ coordinate system, the points are located with respect to origin 0,0.

5. In the relative coordinate system, if you want a displacement of 6 units along the Y axis and 0 displacement along the X axis, you should enter _____ at the **Specify next point or [Undo]:** prompt.

6. In the polar coordinate system, you need to specify the _____ of the point from the _____ point and the _____ it makes with the positive X axis.

7. The **ERASE** command can be selected from the _____ screen menu or by entering _____ at the Command prompt.

8. When AutoCAD puts you in the drawing editor, the _____ command is used to create a new drawing.

9. The **NEW** command can be invoked from the _____ menu or by entering _____ at the Command prompt.

10. The prompt sequence for drawing a circle with (2,2), (4,5), and (7,1) as three points on its circumference is:

    Command: _____
    Specify center point for circle or [3P/2P/Ttr(tan tan radius)]: _____
    Specify first point on circle: _____
    Specify second point on circle: _____
    Specify third point on circle: _____

11. To open or load an existing file into the drawing editor, you can use the _____ command.

12. A file name for a new drawing can also be specified from the command line if the _____ system variable is set to 0.

13. When you enter the **SAVEAS** command, AutoCAD displays the standard file dialog box entitled _____ .

14. What is the difference between the **Window** option and the **Crossing** option?

15. Explain the function of various boxes in the **Select File** dialog box.

16. Explain briefly the function of the **Create New Drawing** dialog box.

17. How will you create a new file with the name **DRAW** using the command line and not through the dialog box?

18. Explain the differences between the **SAVE**, **SAVEAS**, and **QSAVE** commands.

19. Explain the functions of various components of the **Save Drawing As** dialog box.

20. You can view the plot on the specified paper size before actually plotting it by choosing the _____ button in the **Plot** dialog box.

Exercises

Exercise 6   *Mechanical*

Use the following relative and absolute coordinate values in the **LINE** command to draw the object.

Point	Coordinates	Point	Coordinates
1	3.0, 3.0	5	@3.0,5.0
2	@3,0	6	@3,0
3	@-1.5,3.0	7	@-1.5,-3
4	@-1.5,-3.0	8	@-1.5,3

Exercise 7   *Mechanical*

For Figure 1-78, enter the relative coordinates of the points in the given table, then use these coordinates to draw the figure.

Figure 1-78 *Drawing for Exercise 7*

1	3.0, 1.0	9	
2	@ 2∠0	10	
3	@ 1∠60	11	
4	@ 1.5∠0	12	
5	@ 1∠120	13	
6	@ 1∠60	14	
7	@ 1∠135	15	
8	@ 2∠180	16	

Exercise 8

For Figure 1-79, enter the polar coordinates of the points in the given table. Then use those coordinates to draw the figure. Do not draw the dimensions.

Figure 1-79 Drawing for Exercise 8

Point	Coordinates	Point	Coordinates
1	1.0, 1.0	6	@ 2<-45°
2	@ 6.186∠90	7	@ 2< 225°
3	@ 2< -60	8	@ 3< 200°
4	@ 2< 10	9	@ 2< 170°
5	@ 3< -20		

Exercise 9

Generate the drawing in Figure 1-80, using the absolute, relative, or polar coordinate system. Draw according to the dimensions shown in the figure, but do not draw the dimensions.

Figure 1-80 Drawing for Exercise 9

Exercise 10 *Mechanical*

Draw Figure 1-81, using the **LINE** command and the **Ttr** option of the **CIRCLE** command.

Figure 1-81 Drawing for Exercise 10

Exercise 11 *Architectural*

Create the drawing in Figure 1-82, using the pointing device to select points. The drawing you generate should resemble the one in the figure.

Figure 1-82 Drawing for Exercise 11

Problem-Solving Exercise 1   *Mechanical*

Draw the object shown in Figure 1-83, using the **LINE** and **CIRCLE** commands. In this exercise only the diameters of the circles are given. In order to draw the lines and small circles (R0.6), you need to find the coordinate points for the lines and the center points of the circles. For example, if the center of concentric circles is at 5,3.5, then the X coordinate of the lower left corner of the rectangle is 5.0 - 2.4=2.6.

Figure 1-83 *Drawing for Problem-Solving Exercise 1*

Problem-Solving Exercise 2   *Mechanical*

Draw Figure 1-84, using various options of the **CIRCLE** and **LINE** commands. In this exercise you have to find the coordinate points for drawing the lines and circles. Also, you need to determine the best and easiest method to draw the 1.7 diameter circles along the outermost circle.

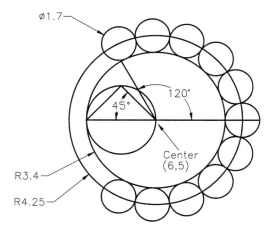

Figure 1-84 *Drawing for Problem-Solving Exercise 2*

Project Exercise 1-1   *Mechanical*

Generate the drawing in Figure 1-85, using the absolute, relative, or polar coordinate system. Draw according to the dimensions shown in the figure, but do not draw the dimensions. Save the drawing as BENCH1-2. (See Chapters 2, 6, 7, 19, and 23 for other drawings of Project Exercise 1)

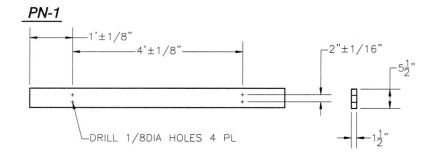

Figure 1-85 *Drawing for Project Exercise 1-1*

Answers to Self-evaluation Test

1 - Continue, **2** - Relative, **3** - **LINE** / 2,2 / @3<60, **4** - completely, **5** - **CIRCLE** / 4,5 / D / 3, **6** - Tangent tangent radius, **7** - Undo, **8** - **SAVETIME**, **9** - pick box, **10** - **PLOT**, **11**- window, window

Chapter 2

Draw Commands

Learning Objectives

After completing this chapter, you will be able to:
- *Draw arcs using different options.*
- *Draw rectangles, ellipses, and elliptical arcs.*
- *Draw polygons like hexagons and pentagons.*
- *Draw traces, polylines, and doughnuts.*
- *Draw points and change point style and point size.*

DRAWING ARCS

Toolbar:	Draw > Arc
Menu:	Draw > Arc
Command:	ARC or A

*Figure 2-1 Invoking the **ARC** command from the **Draw** toolbar*

*Figure 2-2 Invoking the **ARC** command from the **Draw** menu*

An arc is defined as a part of a circle; it can be drawn using the **ARC** command. An arc can be drawn in **11** distinct ways using the options listed under the **ARC** command. The default method for drawing an arc is the **3 Points** option. Other options can be invoked by entering the appropriate letter to select an option. If you have set the **DRAGMODE** variable to Auto, the last parameter to be specified in any arc generation is automatically dragged into the relevant location.

The 3 Points Option

When you enter ARC at the Command: prompt, you automatically get into the **3 Points** option. The 3 points option requires the start point, the second point, and the endpoint of the arc (Figure 2-3 and Figure 2-4). The arc can be drawn in a clockwise or counterclockwise direction by dragging the arc with the cursor. The following is the prompt sequence to draw an arc with a start point at (2,2), second point at (3,3), and an endpoint at (3,4). (You can also specify the points by moving the cursor and then specifying points on the screen.)

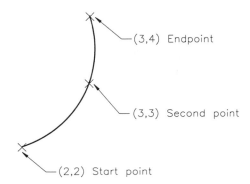

Figure 2-3 Drawing an arc using the 3 points option

Command: **ARC** [Enter]
Specify startpoint of arc or [CEnter]: **2,2** [Enter]
Specify second point of arc or [CEnter/ENd]: **3,3** [Enter]
Specify end point of arc: **3,4** [Enter]

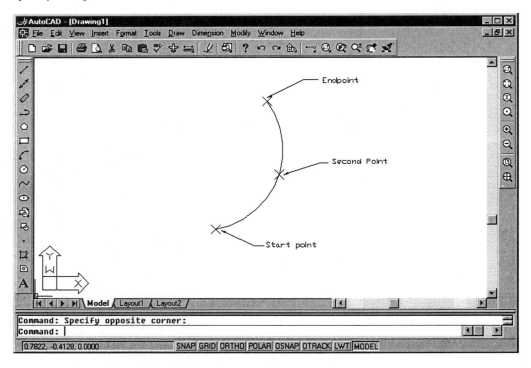

Figure 2-4 Drawing an arc using the 3 points option

Exercise 1   *General*

Draw several arcs using the 3 Points option. The points can be selected by entering coordinates or by specifying points on the screen. Also, try to create a circle by drawing two separate arcs and by drawing a single arc. Notice the limitations of the **ARC** command.

The Start, Center, End Option

This option is slightly different from the 3 points option. In this option, instead of entering the second point, you enter the center of the arc. Choose this option when you know the start point, endpoint, and center point of the arc. The arc is drawn in a counterclockwise direction from the start point to the endpoint around the specified center. The endpoint specified need not be on the arc and is used only to calculate the angle at which the arc ends. The radius of the arc is determined by the distance between the center point and the start point. The prompt sequence for drawing an arc with a start point of (3,2), center point of (2,2), and endpoint of (2,3.5) (Figure 2-5) is as follows:

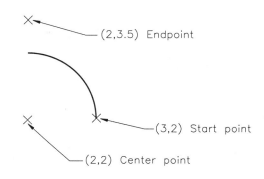

Figure 2-5 *Drawing an arc using the Start, Center, End option*

> Command: **ARC** [Enter]
> Specify start point of arc or [CEnter]: **3,2** [Enter]
> Specify second point of arc or [CEnter/ENd]: **CE** [Enter]
> Specify center point of arc: **2,2** [Enter]
> Specify end point of the arc or [Angle/ chord Length]: **2,3.5** [Enter]

The Start, Center, Angle Option

This option is the best choice if you know the **included angle** of the arc. The included angle is the angle formed by the start point and the endpoint of the arc with the specified center. This option draws an arc in a counterclockwise direction with the specified center and start point spanning the indicated angle (Figure 2-6). If the specified angle is negative, the arc is drawn in a clockwise direction (Figure 2-7).

The prompt sequence for drawing an arc with center at (2,2), a start point of (3,2), and an included angle of 60 degrees (Figure 2-6) is:

> Command: **ARC** [Enter]
> Specify start point of arc or [CEnter]: **3,2** [Enter]
> Specify second point of arc or [CEnter/ENd]: **CE** [Enter]
> Specify center point of arc: **2,2** [Enter]
> Specify end point of the arc or [Angle/ chord Length]: **A** [Enter]
> Specify included angle: **60** [Enter]

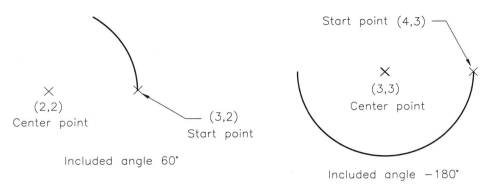

Figure 2-6 *Drawing an arc using the Start, Center, Angle option*

Figure 2-7 *Drawing an arc using a negative angle in the Start, Center, Angle option*

You can draw arcs with negative angle values in the Start, Center, Included Angle (St,C,Ang) option by entering "-" (negative sign) followed by the angle values of your requirement at the **Specify included angle:** prompt (Figure 2-7). This is illustrated by the following prompt sequence:

Command: **ARC** [Enter]
Specify start point of arc or [CEnter]: **4,3** [Enter]
Specify second point of arc or [CEnter/ENd]: **CE** [Enter]
Specify center point of arc: **3,3** [Enter]
Specify end point of the arc or [Angle/ chord Length]: **A** [Enter]
Specify included angle: **-180** [Enter]

Exercise 2   *Mechanical*

a.   Draw an arc using the **St,C,Ang** option. The start point is (6,3), the centerpoint is (3,3), and the angle is 240 degrees.

b.   Make the drawing shown in Figure 2-8. The distance between the dotted lines is 1.0 units. Create the radii by using the arc command options as indicated in the drawing.

Figure 2-8 *Drawing for Exercise 2(b)*

The Start, Center, Length Option

In this option you are required to specify the start point, center point, and length of chord. A **chord** is defined as the straight line connecting the start point and the endpoint of an arc. The chord length needs to be specified so that AutoCAD can calculate the ending angle. Identical start, center, and chord length specifications can be used to define four different arcs. AutoCAD settles this problem by always drawing this type of arc counterclockwise from the start point. Therefore, a positive chord length gives the smallest possible arc with that length. This is known as the minor arc. The minor arc is less than 180 degrees. A negative value for chord length results in the largest possible arc, also known as the major arc. The chord length can be determined by using the standard chord length tables or using the mathematical relation ($L = 2*Sqrt\ [h(2r-h)]$). For example, an arc of radius 1 unit, with an included angle of 30 degrees, has a chord length of 0.51764 units. The prompt sequence for drawing an arc that has a start point of (3,1), center of (2,2) and the chord length of (2) (Figure 2-9) is:

> Command: **ARC** [Enter]
> Specify start point of arc or [CEnter]: **3,1** [Enter]
> Specify second point of arc or [CEnter/ENd]: **CE** [Enter]
> Specify center point of arc: **2,2** [Enter]
> Specify end point of the arc or [Angle/ chord Length]: **L** [Enter]
> Length of chord: **2** [Enter]

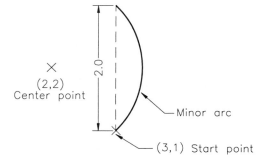

Figure 2-9 *Drawing an arc using the Start, Center, Length option*

Figure 2-10 *Drawing an arc using a negative chord length value in the Start, Center, Length option*

You can draw the major arc by defining the length of the chord as negative (Figure 2-10). In this case the arc with a start point of (3,1), a center point of (2,2), and a negative chord length of (-2) is drawn with the following prompt sequence:

> Command: **ARC** [Enter]
> Specify start point of arc or [CEnter]: **3,3** [Enter]
> Specify second point of arc or [CEnter/ENd]: **CE** [Enter]
> Specify center point of arc: **2,2** [Enter]
> Specify end point of the arc or [Angle/ chord Length]: **L** [Enter]
> Length of chord: **-2** [Enter]

Exercise 3   *General*

Draw a minor arc with the center point at (3,4), start point at (4,2), and chord length of 4 units.

The Start, End, Angle Option

With this option you can draw an arc by specifying the start point of the arc, the endpoint, and the included angle. A positive included angle value draws an arc in a counterclockwise direction from the start point to the endpoint, spanning the included angle; a negative included angle value draws the arc in a clockwise direction. The prompt sequence for drawing an arc with a start point of (3,2), endpoint of (2,4), and included angle of 120 degrees (Figure 2-11) is:

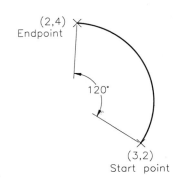

Figure 2-11 Drawing an arc using the Start, End, Angle option

Command: **ARC** Enter
Specify start point of arc or [CEnter]: **3,2** Enter
Specify second point of arc or [CEnter/ENd]: **EN** Enter
Specify end point of arc: **2,4** Enter
Specify center point of arc or [Angle/Direction/Radius]: **A** Enter
Specify included angle: **120** Enter

The Start, End, Direction Option

In this option you can draw an arc by specifying the start point, endpoint, and starting direction of the arc, in degrees. In other words, the arc starts in the direction you specify (the start of the arc is established tangent to the direction you specify). This option can be used to draw a major or minor arc, in a clockwise or counterclockwise direction. The size and position of the arc are determined by the distance between the start point and endpoint and the direction specified. To illustrate the positive direction option (Figure 2-12), the prompt sequence for an arc having a start point of (4,3), endpoint of (3,5), and direction of 90 degrees is:

Command: **ARC** Enter
Specify start point of arc or [CEnter]: **4,3** Enter
Specify second point of arc or [CEnter/ENd]: **EN** Enter
Specify end point of arc: **3,5** Enter
Specify center point of arc or [Angle/Direction/Radius]: **D** Enter
Specify tangent direction for the start of arc: **90** Enter

To illustrate the option using a negative direction degree specification (Figure 2-13), the prompt sequence for an arc having a start point of (4,3), endpoint of (3,4), and direction of -90 degrees is:

Command: **ARC** Enter
Specify start point of arc or [CEnter]: **4,3** Enter
Specify second point of arc or [CEnter/ENd]: **EN** Enter
Specify end point of arc: **3,4** Enter

Specify center point of arc or [Angle/Direction/Radius]: **D** [Enter]
Specify tangent direction for the start of arc: **- 90** [Enter]

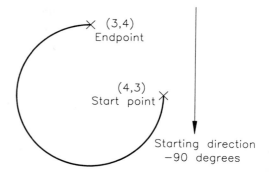

Figure 2-12 *Drawing an arc using the Start, End, Direction option*

Figure 2-13 *Drawing an arc using a negative direction in the Start, End, Direction option*

Exercise 4

Mechanical

a. Specify the directions and the coordinates of two arcs in such a way that they form a circular figure.

b. Make the drawing shown in Figure 2-14. Create the radii by using the arc command options indicated in the drawing. (Use the @ symbol to snap to the previous point. Example: Center/ <Start point>:@)

Figure 2-14 *Drawing for Exercise 4(b)*

The Start, End, Radius Option

This option is used when you know the start point, endpoint, and radius of the arc. The same values for the three variables (start point, endpoint, and radius) can result in four different arcs. AutoCAD resolves this by always drawing this type of arc in a counterclockwise direction from the start point. Hence, a positive radius value results in a **minor arc** (smallest arc between the start point and the endpoint) Figure 2-15(b), while a negative radius value results in a **major arc** (the largest arc between two endpoints) Figure 2-15(a). The prompt sequence to draw a major arc having a start point of (3,3), endpoint of (2,5), and radius of -2 ,Figure 2-15(a), is:

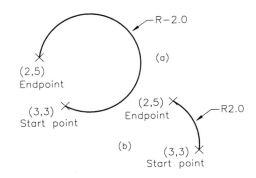

Figure 2-15 *Drawing an arc using the Start, End, Radius option*

Command: **ARC** Enter
Specify start point of arc or [CEnter]: **3,3** Enter
Specify second point of arc or [CEnter/ENd]: **EN** Enter
Specify end point of arc: **2,5** Enter
Specify center point of arc or [Angle/Direction/Radius]: **R** Enter
Radius: **-2** Enter

The prompt sequence to draw a minor arc having its start point at (3,3), endpoint at (2,5), and radius as 2 (Figure 2-15b) is:

Command: **ARC** Enter
Specify start point of arc or [CEnter]: **3,3** Enter
Specify second point of arc or [CEnter/ENd]: **EN** Enter
Specify end point of arc: **2,5** Enter
Specify center point of arc or [Angle/Direction/Radius]: **R** Enter
Radius: **2** Enter

The Center, Start, End Option

The Center, Start, End option is a modification of the Start, Center, End option. Use this option whenever it is easier to start drawing an arc by establishing the center first. Here the arc is always drawn in a counterclockwise direction from the start point to the endpoint, around the specified center. The prompt sequence for drawing an arc that has a center point at (3,3), start point at (5,3), and endpoint at (3,5) (Figure 2-16) is:

Command: **ARC** Enter
Specify start point of arc or [CEnter]: **CE** Enter
Specify center point of arc: **3,3** Enter
Specify start point of arc: **5,3** Enter
Specify end point of arc or [Angle/chord Length]: **3,5** Enter

Figure 2-16 *Drawing an arc using the Center, Start, End option*

Figure 2-17 *Drawing an arc using the Center, Start, Angle option*

The Center, Start, Angle Option

This option is a variation of the Start, Center, Angle option. Use this option whenever it is easier to draw an arc by establishing the center first. The prompt sequence for drawing an arc that has a center point at (4,5), start point at (5,4), and included angle of 120 degrees (Figure 2-17) is:

> Command: **ARC** [Enter]
> Specify start point of arc or [CEnter]: **CE** [Enter]
> Specify center point of arc: **4,5** [Enter]
> Specify start point of arc: **5,4** [Enter]
> Specify end point of arc or [Angle/chord Length]: **A** [Enter]
> Specify included angle: **120** [Enter]

The Center, Start, Length Option

The **Center, Start, Length** option is a modification of the Start, Center, Length option. This option is used whenever it is easier to draw an arc by establishing the center first. The prompt sequence for drawing an arc that has a center point at (2,2), start point at (4,3), and length of chord of 3 (Figure 2-18) is:

> Command: **ARC** [Enter]
> Specify start point of arc or [CEnter]: **CE** [Enter]
> Specify center point of arc: **2,2** [Enter]
> Specify start point of arc: **4,3** [Enter]
> Specify end point of arc or [Angle/chord Length]: **L** [Enter]
> Specify length of chord: **3** [Enter]

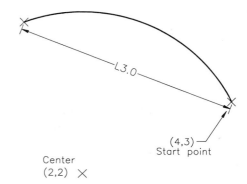

Figure 2-18 *Drawing an arc using the Center, Start, Length option*

Continue Option

With this option you can continue drawing an arc from a previously drawn arc or line. This option resembles the **Start, End, Direction** option in that if you do not specify a start point but just press ENTER, or you select the **Continue** option (draw menu), then the start point and direction of the arc will be taken from the **endpoint and ending direction** of the previous line or arc drawn on the current screen. When this option is used to draw arcs, each successive arc is tangent to the previous one. Most often this option is used to draw arcs tangent to a previously drawn line.

The prompt sequence to draw an arc tangent to an earlier drawn line using the Continue option (Figure 2-19) is:

Command: **LINE** [Enter]
Specify first point: **2,2** [Enter]
Specify next point or [Undo]: **4,3** [Enter]
Specify next point or [Undo]: [Enter]
Command: **ARC** [Enter]
Specify start point of arc or [CEnter]: *Select the* **Continue** *option or press* ENTER.
Specify endpoint of arc : **4,5** [Enter]

The prompt sequence to draw an arc continued from a previously drawn arc (Figure 2-20) is:

Command: **ARC** [Enter]
Specify start point of arc or [CEnter]: **2,2** [Enter]
Specify second point of arc or [CEnter/ENd]: **EN** [Enter]
Specify endpoint of arc : **3,4** [Enter]
Specify center point of arc or [Angle/Direction/Radius]: **R** [Enter]
Specify radius of arc: **2** [Enter]
Command: **ARC** [Enter]
Specify start point of arc or [CEnter]: [Enter]
Endpoint: **5,4** [Enter]

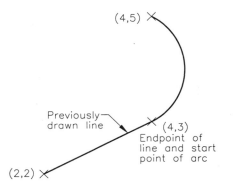

Figure 2-19 *Drawing an arc using the Continue option*

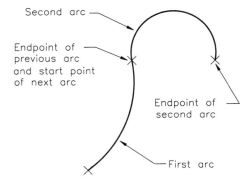

Figure 2-20 *Drawing an arc using the Continue option*

Continue (LineCont:) Option

This option is available only in the **Arc:** screen menu. With this option you can continue drawing a line from the endpoint of a previously drawn arc. When you select this option, the start point and direction of the line will be taken from the **endpoint and ending direction** of the previous arc. In other words, the line will be tangent to the arc drawn on the current screen. The prompt sequence to draw a line tangent to an earlier drawn arc using the LineCont: option (Figure 2-21) is:

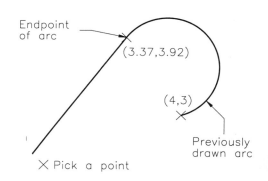

Figure 2-21 *Drawing an arc using the LineCont: option*

Command: **ARC** [Enter]
Specify start point of arc or [CEnter]: **4,3** [Enter]
Specify second point of arc or [CEnter/ENd]: **EN** [Enter]
Specify end point of arc : **3.37,3.92** [Enter]
Specify center point of arc or [Angle/Direction/Radius]: *Specify the center point.*
Command: **ARC** [Enter]
Specify start point of arc or [CEnter]: Select *the LineCont option from ARC screen menu.*
Length of line: **1.5**

You can also use the **LINE** command to draw a line that is tangent to an arc.

Command: **LINE** [Enter]
Specify first point: [Enter]
Length of line: *Enter a value.*

Exercise 5   *Graphics*

a. Use the **Center, Start, Angle** and the **Continue** options to draw the figures shown in Figure 2-22.

b. Make the drawing shown in Figure 2-23. The distance between the dotted lines is 1.0 units. Create the radii as indictated in the drawing by using the **ARC** command options.

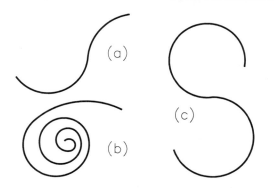

Figure 2-22 *Drawing for Exercise 5(a)*

Figure 2-23 Drawing for Exercise 5(b)

DRAWING RECTANGLES

Toolbar:	Draw > Rectangle
Menu:	Draw > Rectangle
Command:	RECTANG

Figure 2-24 Invoking the **RECTANG** command from the **Draw** toolbar

Figure 2-25 Invoking the **RECTANG** command from the **Draw** menu

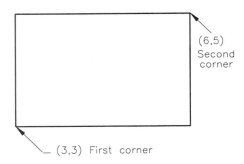

Figure 2-26 Drawing a rectangle using the **RECTANG** command

A rectangle can be drawn using the **RECTANGLE** command. After invoking the **RECTANGLE** command, you are prompted to specify the first corner of the rectangle at the **Specify first corner**

point: prompt. Here you can enter the coordinates of the first corner or specify the desired point with the pointing device. The first corner can be any one of the four corners. Then you are prompted to enter the coordinates or specify the other corner at the **Specify other corner point**: prompt. This corner is taken as the corner diagonally opposite the first corner. The prompt sequence for drawing a rectangle with (3,3) as its lower left corner coordinate and (6,5) as its upper right corner (Figure 2-26) is:

> Command: **RECTANG or RECTANGLE** [Enter]
> Specify first corner point or [Chamfer/Elevation/Fillet/Thickness/Width]: **3,3** [Enter] *(Lower left corner location.)*
> Specify other corner point: **6,5** [Enter]   *(Upper right corner location.)*

You can also specify the first corner and drag the cursor to specify the other corner. The **RECTANG** command has the following options:

Chamfer

The **Chamfer** option creates a chamfer by specifying the chamfer distances (Figure 2-27).

> Command: **RECTANG or RECTANGLE** [Enter]
> Specify first corner point or [Chamfer/Elevation/Fillet/Thickness/Width]: **C** [Enter]
> Specify first chamfer distance for rectangles <0.0000>: *Enter a value.*
> Specify second chamfer distance for rectangles <0.0000>: *Enter a value.*
> Specify first corner point or [Chamfer/Elevation/Fillet/Thickness/Width]: *Select a point as lower left corner location.*
> Specify other corner point : *Select a point as upper right corner location.*

Figure 2-27 Drawing a rectangle with chamfer   *Figure 2-28 Drawing a rectangle with fillet*

Fillet

The **Fillet** option allows you to create a filleted rectangle by specifying the fillet radius (Figure 2-28).

> Specify first corner point or [Chamfer/Elevation/Fillet/Thickness/Width]: **F** [Enter]
> Specify fillet radius for rectangles <0.0000>: *Enter a value.*

Now, if you draw a rectangle it will be filleted provided the length and width of the rectangle is equal to or greater than twice the value of the specified fillet. Otherwise, AutoCAD will draw a rectangle without fillet.

Width

The **Width** option allows you to control the line width of the rectangle by specifying the width (Figure 2-29).

> Specify first corner point or [Chamfer/Elevation/Fillet/Thickness/Width]: **W** [Enter]
> Specify lines width for rectangles <0.0000>: *Enter a value.*

Figure 2-29 Drawing a rectangle with specified width

Figure 2-30 Drawing rectangles with thickness and elevation specified

Thickness

The **Thickness** option allows you to draw a rectangle that is extruded in the Z direction by the specified value of thickness. For example, if you draw a rectangle with thickness of 2 units, you will get a rectangular box whose height is 2 units (Figure 2-30).

> Specify first corner point or [Chamfer/Elevation/Fillet/Thickness/Width]: **T** [Enter]
> Specify thickness for rectangles <0.0000>: *Enter a value.*

Elevation

The **Elevation** option allows you to draw a rectangle at a specified distance from the XY plane along the Z axis. For example, if the elevation is 2 units, the rectangle will be drawn two units above the XY plane. If the thickness of the rectangle is 1 unit, you will get a rectangular box of 1 unit height located 2 units above the XY plane (Figure 2-30).

> Chamfer/Elevation/Fillet/Thickness/Width/<First corner>: **E** [Enter]
> Specify elevation for rectangles <0.0000>: *Enter a value.*

To view the objects in 3D space, change the viewpoint (Select View, 3D Viewpoint > SE Isometric).

Note

The value you enter for Fillet, Width, Elevation, and Thickness becomes the current value for the subsequent rectangle command. Therefore, you must reset the values if they are different from the current values. The thickness of rectangle is always controlled by its thickness settings.

The rectangle generated on the screen is treated as a single object. Hence, the individual sides can be edited only after the rectangle has been exploded using the **EXPLODE** *command.*

Exercise 6 *General*

Draw a rectangle 4 units long, 3 units high, and with its first corner at (1,1). Inside the first rectangle draw another rectangle whose sides are 0.5 units.

DRAWING ELLIPSES

Toolbar:	Draw > Ellipse
Menu:	Draw > Ellipse
Command:	ELLIPSE

— Ellipse

Figure 2-31 Invoking the **ELLIPSE** *command from the* **Draw** *toolbar*

(a) PELLIPSE=1
(POLYLINE based ellipse)
(Release 12 ellipse)

(b)

(c) PELLIPSE=0 (Default)
(NURBS−based ellipse)

(d)

Figure 2-32 Drawing polyline and NURBS-based

 If a circle is observed from an angle, the shape seen is called an **Ellipse**. An ellipse can be created using various options listed within the **ELLIPSE** command. If the **PELLIPSE** is set to 0 (default), AutoCAD creates a true ellipse, also known as NURBS-based (Non-Uniform Rational Bezier Spline) ellipse. The true ellipse has a center and quadrant points. If you select it, the grips will be displayed at the center and the quadrant points of the ellipse. If you move one of the grips located on the perimeter of the ellipse, the major or minor axis will change, which changes the size of the ellipse, as shown in Figure 2-32(d).

Note
Up to Release 12, ellipses were based on polylines. They were made of multiple polyarcs as a result, it was difficult to edit an ellipse. For example, if you select an ellipse, the grips will be displayed at the endpoints of each polyarc. If you move a vertex point, you get the shape shown in Figure 2-32(b). Also, you cannot snap to the center or the quadrant points of a polyline-based ellipse. In AutoCAD 2000, you can still draw the polyline-based ellipse by setting the value of **PELLIPSE** *system variable to 1.*

Figure 2-33 Invoking the **ELLIPSE** *command from the* **Draw** *menu*

Once you invoke the **ELLIPSE** command, AutoCAD will acknowledge with the prompt **Specify axis endpoint of ellipse or [Arc/Center]:** or **Specify axis endpoint of ellipse or [Arc/Center/ Isocircle]:**(if isometric snap is on). The response to this prompt depends on the option you want to choose. The different options are explained next.

Drawing an Ellipse Using the Axis and Eccentricity Option

In this option you draw an ellipse by specifying one of its axes and its eccentricity. To use this option, acknowledge the **Specify axis endpoint of ellipse or [Arc/Center]:** prompt by specifying a point, either by specifying a point using a pointing device or by entering its coordinates. This is the first endpoint of one axis of the ellipse. AutoCAD will then respond with the prompt **Specify other endpoint of axis:**. Here, specify the other endpoint of the axis. The angle at which the ellipse is drawn depends on the angle made by these two axis endpoints. Your response to the next prompt determines whether the axis is the **major axis** or the **minor axis.**

The next prompt is **Specify distance to other axis or [Rotation]:**. If you specify a distance, it is presumed as half the length of the second axis. You can also specify a point. The distance from this point to the midpoint of the first axis is again taken as half the length of this axis. The ellipse will pass through the selected point only if it is perpendicular to the midpoint of the first axis. To visually analyze the distance between the selected point and the midpoint of the first axis, AutoCAD appends an elastic line to the crosshairs, with one end fixed at the midpoint of the first axis. You can also drag the point, dynamically specifying half of the other axis distance. This helps you to visualize the ellipse. The prompt sequence for drawing an ellipse with one axis endpoint is located at (3,3), the other at (6,3), and the distance of the other axis being 1 (Figure 2-34) is:

> Command: **ELLIPSE** [Enter]
> Specify axis endpoint of ellipse or [Arc/Center]: **3,3** [Enter]
> Specify other endpoint of axis : **6,3** [Enter]
> Specify distance to other axis or [Rotation]: **1** [Enter]   *(You can also enter @1<90 or @1<0)*

Another example for drawing an ellipse (Figure 2-35) using the **Axis and Eccentricity** option is illustrated by the following prompt sequence:

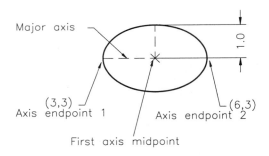

Figure 2-34 Drawing an ellipse using the Axis and Eccentricity option

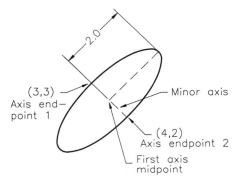

Figure 2-35 Drawing an ellipse using the Axis and Eccentricity option

Command: **ELLIPSE** Enter
Specify axis endpoint of ellipse or [Arc/Center]: **3,3** Enter
Specify other endpoint of axis : **4,2** Enter
Specify distance to other axis or [Rotation]: **2** Enter

If you enter Rotation or R at the **Specify distance to other axis or [Rotation]:** prompt, the first axis specified is automatically taken as the major axis of the ellipse. The next prompt is **Specify rotation around major axis:**. The major axis is taken as the diameter line of the circle, and the rotation takes place around this diameter line into the third dimension. The ellipse is formed when AutoCAD projects this rotated circle into the drawing plane. You can enter the rotation angle value in the range of 0 to 89.4 degrees only, because an angle value greater than 89.4 degrees changes the circle into a line. Instead of entering a definite angle value at the Rotation around major axis: prompt, you can specify a point relative to the midpoint of the major axis. This point can be dragged to specify the ellipse dynamically. The following is the prompt sequence for a rotation of 0 degrees around the major axis, as shown in Figure 2-36(a).

Command: **ELLIPSE** Enter
Specify axis endpoint of ellipse or [Arc/Center]: *Select point (P1)* Enter
Specify other endpoint of axis : *Select another point (P2)* Enter
Specify distance to other axis or [Rotation]: **R** Enter
Specify rotation around major axis: **0** Enter

The Figure 2-36 also shows rotations of 45 degrees, 60 degrees, and 89.4 degrees.

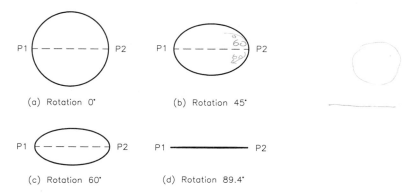

(a) Rotation 0°   (b) Rotation 45°

(c) Rotation 60°   (d) Rotation 89.4°

Figure 2-36 *Rotation about the major axis*

Note
*The Isocircle option is not available if the Isometric suboption in the Style option of the **SNAP** command is set to Off. In this section the SNAP mode Isometric option is not being used.*

The Arc option is not available if you have set the PELLIPSE system variable to 1.

Exercise 7   *General*

Draw an ellipse whose major axis is 4 units and whose rotation around this axis is 60 degrees. Draw another ellipse, whose rotation around the major axis is 15 degrees.

Drawing Ellipse Using the Center and Two Axes Option

In this option you can construct an ellipse by specifying the center point, the endpoint of one axis, and the length of the other axis. The only difference between this method and the ellipse by axis and eccentricity method is that instead of specifying the second endpoint of the first axis, the center of the ellipse is specified. The center of an ellipse is defined as the point of intersection of the major and minor axes. In this option the first axis need not be the major axis. For example, to draw an ellipse with center at (4,4), axis endpoint at (6,4), and length of the other axis as 2 units (Figure 2-37), the command sequence is:

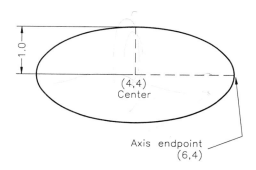

Figure 2-37 *Drawing an ellipse using the Center option*

    Command: **ELLIPSE** ⏎
    Specify axis endpoint of ellipse or [Arc/Center]: **C** ⏎
    Specify center of ellipse: **4,4** ⏎
    Specify end point of axis: **6,4** ⏎
    Specify distance to other axis or [Rotation]: **1** ⏎

Instead of entering the distance, you can enter Rotation or R at the **Specify distance to other axis [Rotation]:** prompt. This takes the first axis specified as the major axis. The next prompt, **Specify rotation around major axis:**, prompts you to enter the rotation angle value. The rotation takes place around the major axis, which is taken as the diameter line of the circle. The rotation angle values should range from 0 to 89.4 degrees.

Drawing Elliptical Arcs

You can use the Arc option of the **ELLIPSE** command to draw an elliptical arc. When you enter the **ELLIPSE** command and select the Arc option, AutoCAD will prompt you to enter information about the geometry of the ellipse and the arc limits. You can define the arc limits by using the following options:

1. Start and End angle of the arc
2. Start and Included angle of the arc
3. Specifying Start and End parameters

The angles are measured from the first point and in a counterclockwise direction if AutoCAD's default setup has not been changed. The following example illustrates the use of these three options.

Example 1

Draw the following elliptical arcs as shown in Figure 2-38:
a.   Start angle = -45, end angle = 135
b.   Start angle = -45, included angle = 225
c.   Start parameter = @1,0, end parameter = @1<225

Specifying Start and End Angle of the Arc [Figure 2-38(a)]

Command: **ELLIPSE**
Specify axis endpoint of ellipse or [Arc/Center]: **A** [Enter]
Specify axis endpoint of elliptical arc or [Center]: *Select the first endpoint.*
Specify other endpoint of axis : *Select the second point.*
Specify distance to other axis or [Rotation]: *Select a point or enter a distance.*
Specify start angle or [Parameter]: **-45** [Enter]
Specify end angle or [Parameter/Included angle]: **135** [Enter] *(Angle where arc ends.)*

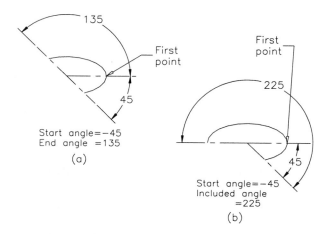

Figure 2-38 *Drawing elliptical arcs*

Specifying Start and Included Angle of the Arc [Figure 2-38(b)]

Command: **ELLIPSE**
Specify axis endpoint of ellipse or [Arc/Center]: **A** [Enter]
Specify axis endpoint of elliptical arc or [Center]: *Select the first endpoint.*
Specify other endpoint of axis : *Select the second point.*
Specify distance to other axis or [Rotation]: *Select a point or enter a distance.*
Specify start angle or [Parameter]: **-45** [Enter]
Specify end angle or [Parameter/Included angle]: **I** [Enter]
Specify included angle for arc<current>: **225** [Enter] *(Included angle.)*

Specifying Start and End Parameters (Figure 2-39)

Command: **ELLIPSE**
Specify axis endpoint of ellipse or [Arc/Center]: **A** [Enter]
Specify axis endpoint of elliptical arc or [Center]:*Select the first endpoint*
Specify other endpoint of axis : *Select the second endpoint.*
Specify distance to other axis or [Rotation]: *Select a point or enter a distance.*
Specify start angle or [Parameter]: **P**
Specify start parameter or [Angle]: **@1,0**

Specify end parameter or angle[Angle/Included angle]: **@1<225**

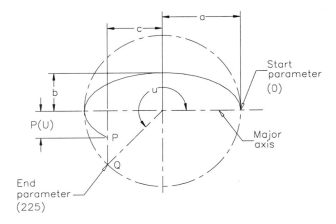

Figure 2-39 *Drawing an elliptical arc by specifying the start and end parameters*

Calculating Parameters for an Elliptical Arc

The start and end parameters of an elliptical arc are determined by specifying a point on the circle whose diameter is equal to the major diameter of the ellipse as shown in Figure 2-39. In this drawing, the major axis of the ellipse is 2.0 and the minor axis is 1.0. The diameter of the circle is 2.0. To determine the start and end parameters of the elliptical arc, you must specify the points on the circle. In the example, the start parameter is @1,0 and the end parameter is @1<225. Once you specify the points on the circle, AutoCAD will project these points on the major axis and determine the endpoint of the elliptical arc. In the Figure 2-39, Q is the end parameter of the elliptical arc. AutoCAD projects point Q on the major axis and locates intersection point P, which is the endpoint of the elliptical arc. The coordinates of point P can be calculated by using the following equations:

The equation of an ellipse with center as origin is
$$x^2/a^2 + y^2/b^2 = 1$$
In parametric form $x = a * cos(u)$
$y = b * sin(u)$
For the example $a = 1$
$b = 0.5$
Therefore $x = 1 * cos(225) = -0.707$
$y = 0.5 * sin(225) = -0.353$
The coordinates of point P are (-0.707, -0.353) with respect to the center of the ellipse.
Note: $v = atan(b/a*tan(u)) = $ end angle
$v = atan(0.5/1*tan(225)) = 206.56o$
Also $e = 1-b^2/a^2)^.5 = $ eccentricity
$e = 1-.5^2/1^2)^.5 = .866$
$r = x^2 + y^2)^.5$
$r = .707^2 + .353^2)^.5 = 0.790$

or using the polar equation r = b/(1 - e^2 * cos(v)^2)^.5
$\qquad\qquad\qquad$ r = .5/(1 - .866^2 * cos(206.56)^2)^.5
$\qquad\qquad\qquad$ r = 0.790

Exercise 8
Mechanical

a.   Construct an ellipse with center at (2,3), axis endpoint at (4,6), and the other axis endpoint a distance of 0.75 units from the midpoint of the first axis.

b.   Make the drawing as shown in Figure 2-40. The distance between the dotted lines is 1.0 units. Create the elliptical arcs using **ELLIPSE** command options.

***Figure 2-40** Drawing for Exercise 8(b)*

DRAWING REGULAR POLYGONS

Toolbar:	Draw > Polygon
Menu:	Draw > Polygon
Command:	POLYGON

***Figure 2-41** Invoking the **POLYGON** command from the **Draw** toolbar*

A **regular polygon** is a closed geometric figure with equal sides and equal angles. The number of sides varies from **3** to **1024**. For example, a triangle is a three-sided polygon and a pentagon is a five-sided polygon. In AutoCAD, the **POLYGON** command is used to draw regular two-dimensional polygons. The characteristics of a polygon drawn in AutoCAD are those of a closed polyline having 0 width. You can change the width of the polyline forming the polygon. The prompt sequence is:

$\qquad$ Command: **POLYGON** Enter
$\qquad$ Enter number of sides <4>:

Once you invoke the **POLYGON** command, it prompts you to enter the number of sides. The number of sides determines the type of polygon (for example, 6 sides defines a hexagon). The default value for the number of sides is **4**. You can change the number of sides to your requirement (in the range of 3 to 1024) and then the new value becomes the default. You can also set a different default value for the number of sides by using the **POLYSIDES** system variable. For example, if you want the default for the number of sides to be **3**, the prompt sequence is:

Command: **POLYSIDES** `Enter`
Enter new value for POLYSIDES <4>: **3** `Enter`

The Center of Polygon Option

The default option prompts you to select a point that is taken as the center point of the polygon. The next prompt is **Enter an option[Inscribed in circle/Circumscribed about circle]<I>:**. A polygon is said to be **inscribed** when it is drawn inside an imaginary circle and its vertices (corners) touch the circle (Figure 2-43). Likewise, a polygon is **circumscribed** when it is drawn outside the imaginary circle and the sides of the polygon are tangent to the circle (midpoint of each side of the polygon will lie on the circle) (Figure 2-44). If you want to have an inscribed polygon, enter **I** at the prompt. The next prompt issued is **Specify radius of circle:**. Here you are required to specify the radius of the circle on which all the vertices of the polygon will lie. Once you specify the radius, a polygon will be generated. If you want to select the circumscribed option, enter **C** at the

Figure 2-42 Invoking the **POLYGON** command from the **Draw** menu

prompt **Enter an option[Inscribed in circle/Circumscribed about circle]<I>:**. After this enter the radius of the circle. The inscribed or circumscribed circle is not drawn on the screen. The radius of the circle can be dynamically dragged instead of a numerical value entered. The prompt sequence for drawing an inscribed octagon with center at (4,4), and a radius of 1.5 units (Figure 2-43) is:

Command: **POLYGON** `Enter`
Enter number of sides<4>: **8** `Enter`
Specify center of polygon or [Edge]: **4,4** `Enter`
Enter an option[Inscribed in circle/Circumscribed about circle]<I>: **I** `Enter`
Specify radius of circle: **1.5** `Enter`

The prompt sequence for drawing a circumscribed pentagon (polygon with five sides) with center at (9,4) and a radius of 1.5 units (Figure 2-44) is:

Command: **POLYGON** `Enter`
Enter number of sides<4>: **5** `Enter`
Specify center of polygon or [Edge]: **9,4** `Enter`
Enter an option[Inscribed in circle/Circumscribed about circle]<I>: **C** `Enter`

Specify radius of circle: **1.5** Enter

Inscribed octagon

Circumscribed pentagon

Figure 2-43 *Drawing an inscribed polygon using the Center of Polygon option*

Figure 2-44 *Drawing a circumscribed polygon using the Center of Polygon option*

Note

If you select a point to specify the radius of an inscribed polygon, one of the vertices is positioned on the selected point. In the case of circumscribed polygons, the midpoint of an edge is placed on the point you have specified. In this manner you can specify the size and rotation of the polygon.

In the case of numerical specification of the radius, the bottom edge of the polygon is rotated by the prevalent snap rotation angle.

Exercise 9   *General*

Draw a circumscribed polygon of eight sides. The polygon should be drawn by the Center of Polygon method.

The Edge Option

The other method for drawing a polygon is to select the **Edge** option. This can be done by entering EDGE or E at the **Specify center of polygon or [Edge]:** prompt. The next two prompts issued are **Specify first endpoint of edge:** and **Specify second endpoint of edge:**. Here you need to specify the two endpoints of an edge of the polygon. The polygon is drawn in a counterclockwise direction, with the two points entered defining its first edge. To draw a hexagon (six-sided polygon) using the Edge option, with the first endpoint of the edge at (2,4) and the second endpoint of the edge at (2,2.5) (Figure 2-45), the following will be the prompt sequence:

Command: **POLYGON** Enter

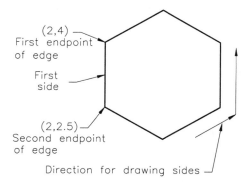

Figure 2-45 *Drawing a polygon (hexagon) using the Edge option*

Enter number of sides<4>: **6** [Enter]
Specify center of polygon or [Edge]: **E** [Enter]
Specify first endpoint of edge: **2,4** [Enter]
Specify second endpoint of edge: **2,2.5** [Enter]

Exercise 10   *Graphics*

Draw a polygon with 10 sides using the **Edge** option and an elliptical arc as shown in Figure 2-46. Let the first endpoint of the edge be at (7,1) and the second endpoint be at (8,2).

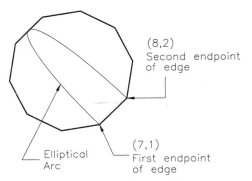

Figure 2-46 Polygon and elliptical arc for Exercise 10

DRAWING TRACES

Command:	TRACE

TRACES are lines that have a thickness (specified as its width). Traces are solid-filled if the FILLMODE is on. If the FILLMODE is off, only the trace outline is drawn. The fill option can be accessed through the **FILL** command or the **FILLMODE** system variable.

The specifications of a trace are entered just like those of a line. The difference between the **LINE** command and the **TRACE** command is that in the latter the width of the trace is entered before entering the rest of the specifications. To specify the width of the trace, you can enter the distance or select two points. AutoCAD automatically measures the distance between those two points and assumes it as the width of the trace. All of the trace segments drawn by a single **TRACE** command will have the same width. The default value for the width of the trace is the width of the previous trace drawn. This value is stored in the **TRACEWID** system variable hence you can change the default setting for the width of the trace through the **TRACEWID** variable. The endpoints of the trace lie on the center of the trace width. The start and end of traces are always cut square and are made of TRACE segments. The drawing of each segment is suspended until you specify the next segment or you end the trace by pressing ENTER. This is because trace ends are shaped to fit the start of the next segment. For example, to draw a solid-filled trace (Figure 2-47) with a width of 0.25 units, starting from (1,3), to point (3,3), to point (2,1), the prompt sequence is:

Command: **FILLMODE** [Enter]
Enter new value for FILLMODE <1>: [Enter]
Command: **TRACE** [Enter]
Specify trace width <0.0500>: **0.25** [Enter]
Specify start point: **1,3** [Enter]

Specify next point: **3,3** [Enter]
Specify next point: **2,1** [Enter]
Specify next point: [Enter]

The prompt sequence to draw a nonsolid trace (Figure 2-48) with a width of 0.25 units, starting from point (3,3), to point (5,3), to point (5,1), is:

Command: **FILLMODE** [Enter]
Enter new value for FILLMODE <1>:**0** [Enter]
Command: **TRACE** [Enter]
Specify trace width <0.0500>: **0.25** [Enter]
Specify start point: **3,3** [Enter]
Specify next point: **5,3** [Enter]
Specify next point: **5,1** [Enter]
Specify next point: [Enter]

Figure 2-47 Drawing a solid trace using the TRACE command

Figure 2-48 Drawing a nonsolid trace using the TRACE command

Note
You should always set the FILLMODE off if there are many traces to be drawn because regeneration takes less time for nonsolid traces. You can turn the FILLMODE on when the drawing has taken final shape, then use the REGEN command to fill the traces in the drawing.

The hatch pattern visibility is also controlled by FILLMODE. When FILLMODE is off, the hatch pattern will not be visible on the screen.

Exercise 11
General

Using the **TRACE** command, draw "Au" on the screen (both as a solid-filled trace and nonsolid trace) as shown in Figure 2-49. Assume the width of the trace = 0.20 units.

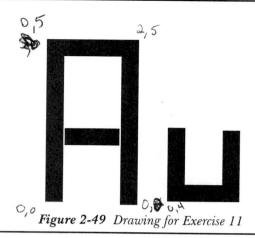

Figure 2-49 Drawing for Exercise 11

DRAWING POLYLINES

Toolbar:	Draw > Polyline
Menu:	Draw > Polyline
Command:	PLINE (or PL)

Figure 2-50 Invoking the **Polyline**
command from the **Draw** toolbar

A **polyline** is a line that can have different characteristics. The term POLYLINE can be broken into two parts: POLY and LINE. POLY means "many". This signifies that a polyline can have many features. Some of the features of polylines are:

1. Polylines, like traces, are thick lines having a desired width.
2. Polylines are very flexible and can be used to draw any shape, such as a filled circle or a doughnut.
3. Polylines can be used to draw objects in any linetype (for example, hidden linetype).
4. Advanced editing commands can be used to edit polylines (for example, **PEDIT** command).

Figure 2-51 Invoking the **Polyline**
command from the **Draw** menu

5. A single polyline object can be formed by joining polylines and polyarcs of different thickness.
6. It is easy to determine the area or perimeter of a polyline feature. Also, it is easy to offset when drawing walls.

The command to draw a polyline is **PLINE or PL**. The **PLINE** command functions fundamentally like the **LINE** command, except that additional options are provided and all the segments of the polyline form a single object. After invoking the **PLINE** command, the next prompt is:

> Specify start point: *Specify the starting point or enter its coordinates.*
> Current line width is nn.n.

Current line width is nn.n is displayed automatically, which indicates that the polyline drawn will have nn.n width. If you want the polyline to have a different width, invoke the Width option at the next prompt and then set the polyline width. The next prompt is:

> Specify next point or [Arc/Close/Halfwidth/Length/Undo/Width]: Specify *next point or enter an option.*

The options that can be invoked at this prompt, depending on your requirement, are:

Next Point of Line

This option is maintained as the default and is used to specify the next point of the current polyline segment. If additional polyline segments are added to the first polyline, AutoCAD automatically makes the endpoint of the first polyline segment the start point of the next polyline segment. The prompt sequence is:

> Command: **PLINE or PL** Enter
> Specify start point: *Specify the starting point of the polyline.*
> Current line width is 0.0000.
> Specify next point or [Arc/Close/Halfwidth/Length/Undo/Width]: *Specify the endpoint of the first polyline segment.*
> Specify next point or [Arc/Close/Halfwidth/Length/Undo/Width]: *Specify the endpoint of the second polyline segment, or press ENTER to exit the command.*

Width

You can change the current polyline width by entering W (width option) at the last prompt. Then you are prompted for the starting width and the ending width of the polyline.

> Specify next point or [Arc/Close/Halfwidth/Length/Undo/Width]: **W** Enter
> Specify starting width <current>: *Specify the starting width.*
> Specify ending width <starting width>: *Specify the ending width.*

The starting width value is taken as the default value for the ending width. Hence, to have a uniform polyline you need to give a null response (press ENTER) at the **Specify ending width <starting width>:** prompt. Just as in the case of traces, the start point and endpoint of the polyline are located at the center of the line width. To draw a uniform polyline (Figure 2-52) with a width of 0.25 units, a start point at (4,5), an endpoint at (5,5), and the next endpoint at (3,3), the following will be the prompt sequence:

> Command: **PLINE** Enter

Specify start point: **4,5** [Enter]
Current line-width is 0.0000
Specify next point or [Arc/Close/Halfwidth/Length/Undo/Width]: **W** [Enter]
Specify starting width <current>: **0.25** [Enter]
Specify ending width <0.25>: [Enter]
Specify next point or [Arc/Close/Halfwidth/Length/Undo/Width]: **5,5** [Enter]
Specify next point or [Arc/Close/Halfwidth/Length/Undo/Width]: **3,3** [Enter]
Specify next point or [Arc/Close/Halfwidth/Length/Undo/Width]: [Enter]

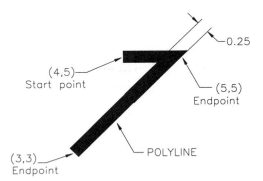

Figure 2-52 *Drawing a uniform polyline using the **PLINE** command*

Figure 2-53 *Drawing a tapered polyline using the **PLINE** command*

You can get a tapered polyline by entering two different values at the starting width and the ending width prompts. To draw a tapered polyline (Figure 2-53) with a starting width of 0.5 units and an ending width of 0.15 units, a start point at (2,4), and an endpoint at (5,4), the prompt sequence is:

Command: **PLINE** [Enter]
Specify start point: **2,4** [Enter]
Current line-width is 0.0000
Specify next point or [Arc/Close/Halfwidth/Length/Undo/Width]: **W** [Enter]
Specify starting width <0.0000>: **0.50** [Enter]
Specify ending width <0.50>: **0.15** [Enter]
Specify next point or [Arc/Close/Halfwidth/Length/Undo/Width]: **5,4** [Enter]
Specify next point or [Arc/Close/Halfwidth/Length/Undo/Width]: [Enter]

Close

This option closes the polyline by drawing a polyline segment from the most recent endpoint to the initial start point, and on doing so exits from the **PLINE** command. This option can be invoked by entering **Close** or **C** at the following prompt:

Specify next point or [Arc/Close/Halfwidth/Length/Undo/Width]: **C** [Enter]

The width of the closing segment can be changed by using the Width/Halfwidth option before invoking the Close option.

Halfwidth

With this option you can specify the starting and ending halfwidth of a polyline. This halfwidth distance is equal to half of the actual width of the polyline. This option can be invoked by entering Halfwidth or H at the following prompt:

> Specify next point or [Arc/Close/Halfwidth/Length/Undo/Width]: **H** [Enter]
> Specify starting half-width <0.0000>: **0.12** [Enter] *(Specify desired starting halfwidth.)*
> Specify ending half-width <0.1200>: **0.05** [Enter] *(Specify desired ending halfwidth.)*

Length

This option prompts you to enter the length of a new polyline segment. The new polyline segment will be the length you have entered. It will be drawn at the same angle as the last polyline segment or tangent to the previous polyarc segment. This option can be invoked by entering Length or L at the following prompt:

> Specify next point or [Arc/Close/Halfwidth/Length/Undo/Width]: **L** [Enter]
> Specify length of line: *Specify the desired length of the Pline.*

Undo

This option erases the most recently drawn polyline segment. This option can be invoked by entering Undo or U at the following prompt:

> Specify next point or [Arc/Close/Halfwidth/Length/Undo/Width]: **UNDO** or **U** [Enter]

You can use this option repeatedly until you reach the start point of the first polyline segment. Further use of **Undo** option evokes this message:

> All segments already undone.

Arc

This option is used to switch from drawing polylines to drawing polyarcs, and provides you the options associated with drawing polyarcs. The Arc option can be invoked by entering Arc or A at the following prompt:

> Specify next point or [Arc/Close/Halfwidth/Length/Undo/Width]: **A** [Enter]

The next prompt is:

> Specify end point of arc or [Angle/CEnter/CLose/Direction/Halfwidth/Line/Radius/Second pt/Undo/Width]: Enter *an option.*

By default the arc segment is drawn tangent to the previous segment of the polyline. The direction of the previous line, arc, or polyline segment is default for polyarc. The preceding prompt contains options associated with the PLINE Arc. The detailed explanation of each of these options follows:

Angle. This option prompts you to enter the included angle for the arc. If you enter a positive angle, the arc is drawn in a counterclockwise direction from the start point to the endpoint. If the angle specified is negative, the arc is drawn in a clockwise direction. The prompt issued for this option is:

Specify included angle: *Specify the included angle.*

The next prompt is:

Specify endpoint of arc or [Center/Radius]:

Center refers to the center of the arc segment, Radius refers to the radius of the arc, and Endpoint draws the arc.

CEnter. This option prompts you to specify the center of the arc to be drawn. As mentioned before, usually the arc segment is drawn so that it is tangent to the previous polyline segment; in such cases AutoCAD determines the center of the arc automatically. Hence, the **CEnter** option provides the freedom to choose the center of the arc segment. The CEnter option can be invoked by entering **CE** at the **Specify end point of arc or [Angle/CEnter/CLose/Direction/Halfwidth/ Line/Radius/Second pt/Undo/Width]:** prompt. Once you specify the center point, AutoCAD issues the following prompt:

Specify endpoint of arc or [Angle/Length]:

Angle refers to the included angle, Length refers to the length of the chord, and Endpoint refers to the endpoint of the arc.

CLose. This option closes the polyline by drawing a polyarc segment from the previous endpoint to the initial start point, and on doing so exits from the **PLINE** command. The **CLose** option can be invoked by entering **CL**.

Direction. Usually the arc drawn with the **PLINE** command is tangent to the previous polyline segment. In other words, the starting direction of the arc is the ending direction of the previous segment. The Direction option allows you to specify the tangent direction of your choice for the arc segment to be drawn. The next prompt is:

Specify tangent direction for the start point of arc: Specify *the direction.*

You can also specify the direction by specifying a point. AutoCAD takes it as a direction from the starting point. Once the direction is specified, AutoCAD prompts:

Specify endpoint of arc: *Specify the endpoint of arc.*

Halfwidth. This option is the same as for the Line option and prompts you to specify the starting and ending halfwidth of the arc segment.

Line. This option takes you back to the **Line mode**. You can draw polylines only in Line mode.

Radius. This option prompts you to specify the **radius** of the arc segment. The prompt sequence is:

> Specify radius of arc: *Specify the radius of the arc segment.*
> Specify endpoint of arc or [Angle]:

If you specify a point, the arc segment is drawn. If you enter an angle, you will have to specify the angle and the direction of the chord at the **Specify included angle:** and **Specify direction of chord for arc<current>:** prompts, respectively.

Figure 2-54 Drawing a Polyarc

Second pt. This option selects the second point of an arc in the three-point arc option. The prompt sequence is:

> Specify second point of arc: *Specify the second point on the arc.*
> Specify endpoint of arc: *Specify the third point on the arc.*

Undo. This option reverses the changes made in the previously drawn segment.

Width. This option prompts you to enter the width of the arc segment. To draw a tapered arc segment you can enter different values at the starting width and ending width prompts. The prompt sequence is identical to that for the polyline. Also, a specified point on a polyline refers to the mid-point on its width.

Endpoint of arc. This option is maintained as the default and prompts you to specify the endpoint of the current arc segment. The following is the prompt sequence for drawing an arc with start point at (3,3), endpoint at (3,5), starting width of 0.50 units, and ending width of 0.15 units (Figure 2-54):

> Command: **PLINE** [Enter]
> Specify start point: **3,3** [Enter]
> Current line-width is 0.0000
> Specify nextpoint or [Arc/Close/Halfwidth/Length/Undo/Width]: **A** [Enter]
> Specify endpoint of arc or [Angle/CEnter/CLose/Direction/Halfwidth/Line/Radius/Second pt/Undo/Width]: **W** [Enter]
> Specify starting width <current>: **0.50** [Enter]
> Specify ending width <0.50>: **0.15** [Enter]
> Specify endpoint of arc or [Angle/CEnter/CLose/Direction/Halfwidth/Line/Radius/Second pt/Undo/Width]: **3,5** [Enter]
> Specify endpoint of arc or [Angle/CEnter/CLose/Direction/Halfwidth/Line/Radius/Second pt/Undo/Width]: [Enter]

Note

*The **FILL** or **FILLMODE** applies to polylines and hatch patterns and the change is effective on regeneration. If **FILL** is on or if **FILLMODE** is 1, the polylines are drawn filled and the hatch* *patterns are visible. Also **PLINEGEN** controls the linetype pattern between the vertex points of a 2D polyline. A value of 0 centers the linetype for each polyline segment and 1 makes them continuous.*

Optimized Polylines

The optimized polylines also known as **lightweight polylines** are created when you use the **PLINE** command (an AutoCAD feature since Release 14). The optimized polylines are similar to regular 2D polylines in functionality, but the data base format of an optimized polylines is different from a 2D polyline. In case of an optimized polyline the vertices are not stored as separate entities, but as a single object with an array of information. This feature results in reduced object and file size.

If you use the **PEDIT** command on a optimized polyline and use spline fit or curve fit options, the polyline automatically becomes a regular 2D polyline. Also, when you load a Release 13 or earlier drawing, AutoCAD automatically converts the polylines into optimized polylines. Commands like **POLYGON**, **DONUT**, **SKETCH**, **ELLIPSE**, **PEDIT**, **BOUNDARY**, **RECTANG** create optimized polylines. To see the difference between these two polylines; draw a polyline consisting of several segments and then use the **LIST** command to list the information about the object. Now, use the **PEDIT** command to change this polyline into a splined polyline and then use the **LIST** command again. Notice the difference in the database associated with these polylines.

CONVERT Command

You can use the **CONVERT** command to manually change a 2D polyline to an optimized (light-weight) polyline. You can also use this command to change a Release 13 associative hatch pattern to AutoCAD 2000 hatch object, except the solid-fill hatches.

>   Command: **CONVERT** `Enter`
>   Enter type of objects to optimize [Hatch/Polylines/All]: *Enter an option.*
>   Enter object selection preference[Select/All]<All>:

Exercise 12   *General*

Draw the objects shown in Figure 2-55 and Figure 2-56. Approximate the width of different polylines.

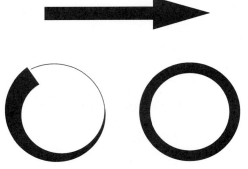

Figure 2-55 *Drawing for Exercise 12*

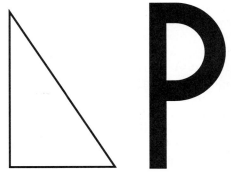

Figure 2-56 *Drawing for Exercise 12*

DRAWING DOUGHNUTS

Menu:	Draw > Donut
Command:	DONUT (or DOUGHNUT)

In AutoCAD the **DONUT** or **DOUGHNUT** command is issued to draw an object that looks like a filled circle ring called a doughnut. Actually, AutoCAD's doughnuts are made of two semicircular polyarcs having a certain width. Hence the **DONUT** command allows you to draw a thick circle. The doughnuts can have any inside and outside diameters. If the FILLMODE is off, the doughnuts look like circles (if the inside diameter is zero) or concentric circles (if the inside diameter is not zero). You can also select a point for the center of the doughnut anywhere on the screen with the help of a pointing device. The prompt sequence for drawing doughnuts is:

Command: **DONUT** or **DOUGHNUT** [Enter]
Specify inside diameter of donut <current>: *Specify the inner diameter of the donut.*
Specify outside diameter of donut <current>: *Specify the outer diameter of the donut.*
Specify center of donut or <exit>: *Specify the center of the donut.*
Specify center of donut or <exit>: *Specify the center of the donut to draw more donuts of previous specifications or give a null response to exit.*

Figure 2-57 *Invoking the **DONUT** command from the **Draw** menu*

The defaults for the inside and outside diameters are the respective diameters of the most recent doughnut drawn. The values for the inside and outside diameters are saved in the **DONUTID** and **DONUTOD** system variables. You can specify a new diameter of your choice by entering a numeric value or by specifying two points to indicate the diameter. A solid-filled circle is drawn by specifying the inside diameter as zero (FILLMODE is on). Once the diameter specification is completed, the doughnuts are formed at the crosshairs and can be placed anywhere on the screen. The location at which you want the doughnuts to be drawn has to be specified at the **Specify center of donut or <exit>:** prompt. You can enter the coordinates of the point at that prompt or specify the point by dragging the center point. Once you have specified the center of the doughnut, AutoCAD repeats the **Specify center of donut or <exit>:** prompt. As you go on specifying the locations for the center point, doughnuts with the specified diameters at specified locations are drawn. To end the **DONUT** command, give a null response to this prompt by pressing ENTER. Since doughnuts are circular polylines, the doughnut can be edited with the **PEDIT** command or any other editing command that can be used to edit polylines.

Example 2

If you want to draw an unfilled doughnut with an inside diameter of 0.75 units, an outside diameter of 2.0 units, and centered at (2,2) (Figure 2-58), the following is the prompt sequence:

Command: **FILLMODE** Enter
New value for FILLMODE <1>: **0** Enter
Command: **DONUT** Enter
Specify inside diameter of donut<0.5000>: **0.75** Enter
Specify outside diameter of donut <1.000>: **2** Enter
Specify center of donut or <exit>: **2,2** Enter
Specify center of donut or <exit>: Enter

FILLMODE 0

Figure 2-58 *Drawing an unfilled doughnut using the* ***DONUT*** *command*

FILLMODE 1

Figure 2-59 *Drawing a filled doughnut using the* ***DONUT*** *command*

The following is the prompt sequence for drawing a filled doughnut with an inside diameter of 0.5 units, outside diameter of 2.0 units, centered at a specified point (Figure 2-59).

Command: **FILLMODE** Enter
Enter new value for FILLMODE <1>: **1** Enter
Command: **DONUT** Enter
Specify inside diameter of donut<0.5000>: **0.50** Enter
Specify outside diameter of donut <1.000>: **2** Enter
Specify center of donut or <exit>: *Specify a point*
Specify center of donut or <exit>: Enter

To draw a solid-filled doughnut with an outside diameter of 2.0 units (Figure 2-60), the following is the prompt sequence:

Command: **DONUT** Enter
Specify inside diameter of donut <0.5000>: **0** Enter
Specify outside diameter of donut <1.000>: **2** Enter
Specify center of donut or <exit>: *Specify a point.*
Specify center of donut or <exit>: Enter

Doughnut with
inside diameter zero

Figure 2-60 *Solid-filled doughnut*

DRAWING POINTS

Toolbar:	Draw > Point
Menu:	Draw > Point
Command:	POINT

Figure 2-61 Invoking the POINT command from the Draw toolbar

The **point** is the basic drawing object. Points are invaluable in building a drawing file. To draw a point anywhere on the screen, AutoCAD provides the **POINT** command.

Command: **POINT** Enter
Current pointmodes: PDMODE=n PDSIZE=n.nn
Specify a point: *Specify the location where you want to plot the point.*

When a point is drawn, a mark appears on the screen. This mark, known as a **blip**, is the construction marker for the point. The blip mark is cleared once the screen

Figure 2-62 Invoking the POINT command from the Draw menu

is redrawn with the **REDRAW** command and a point of the specified point type is left on the screen. If you invoke the **POINT** by entering POINT at the Command prompt, you can draw only one point in a single point command. On the other hand, if you invoke the **POINT** command from the toolbar or the menu, you can draw as many points as you desire in a single command with **Multiple Point** option. In this case you can exit from the **POINT** command by pressing **ESC.**

Changing the Point Type

Menu:	Format > Point Style...
Command:	PDMODE

The type of point drawn is controlled by the **PDMODE** (Point Display MODE) system variable. The point type can be set either from the **Point Style** dialog box or by entering **PDMODE** at the Command prompt. There are twenty combinations of point types. The **Point Style** dialog box can be accessed from the format menu (Select Format > Point Style...). You can choose a point style in this dialog box by clicking your pointing device on the point style of your choice. A box is formed around that particular point style to acknowledge the selection made. Next, choose the OK button. Now all the points will be drawn in the selected style until you change it to a new style.

You can also invoke **PDMODE** by entering PDMODE at the Command prompt and changing its value to that of the required point type.

Command: **PDMODE** [Enter]
Enter new value for PDMODE <current>: *Enter the new value.*
Command: **POINT** [Enter]
Specify a point: *Select a point.*

*Figure 2-63 Selecting **Point Style**
from the **Format** menu*

The PDMODE values for different point types are:

*Figure 2-64 **Point Style** dialog-box*

1. A value of 0 is the default for the PDMODE variable
    and generates a dot at the specified point.
2. A value of 1 for the PDMODE variable generates nothing at the specified point.
3. A value of 2 for the PDMODE variable generates plus mark (+) through the specified point.
4. A value of 3 for the PDMODE variable generates cross mark (X) through the specified point.
5. A value of 4 for the PDMODE variable generates a vertical line in the upward direction from
    the specified point.
6. When you add **32** to the **PDMODE** values of 0 to 4, a circle is generated around the
    symbol obtained from the original **PDMODE** value. For example, to draw a point having a
    cross mark and a circle around it, the value of the **PDMODE** variable will be **3 + 32 = 35.**
    Similarly, you can generate a square around the symbol with the **PDMODE** of value 0 to 4 by
    adding **64** to the original **PDMODE** value. For example, to draw a point having a plus
    mark and a square around it, the value of the **PDMODE** variable will be **2 + 64 = 66**. You can
    also generate a square and a circle around the symbol with the **PDMODE** of value 0 to
    4 by adding **96** to the original **PDMODE** value. For example, to draw a point having a dot
    mark and a circle and a square around it, the value of the **PDMODE** variable will be **0 + 96 =
    96**.

When the value of the **PDMODE** is changed or a new point type is selected from the dialog box,
all of the previously drawn points retain their styles until the drawing is regenerated. After REGEN,
all of the points on the drawing are drawn in the shape designated by the current value of the

PDMODE variable. The **REGEN** command does the calculations for all the objects on the screen and draws them according to the new values obtained upon calculation.

Pdmode value	Point style	Pdmode value	Point style
0		64+0=64	□
1		64+1=65	□
2	+	64+2=66	⊞
3	×	64+3=67	⊠
4	ı	64+4=68	⊡
32+0=32	○	96+0=96	⬭
32+1=33	○	96+1=97	⬭
32+2=34	⊕	96+2=98	⊕
32+3=35	⊗	96+3=99	⊠
32+4=36	⊙	96+4=100	⬭

Figure 2-65 Different point types

Exercise 13   *General*

Check what types of points are drawn for each value of the PDMODE variable. Use the **REGEN** command to regenerate the drawing, and notice the change in the previously drawn points.

Changing the Point Size

Command: PDSIZE

The system variable **PDSIZE** (Point Display SIZE) governs the size of the point (except for the **PDMODE** values of 0 and 1). The size of a point can be set from the **Point Style** dialog box (Figure 2-64) by entering the desired point size in the **Point Size** edit box. The point size can also be set by entering PDSIZE at the Command prompt and then changing its value to a new one(Figure 2-66). A value of 0 for the **PDSIZE** variable generates the point at 5 percent of the graphics area height.

A positive value for **PDSIZE** defines an absolute size for the point. This can also be specified by selecting the **Set Size in Absolute Units** radio button in the Point Style dialog box. If PDSIZE is negative or if the **Set Size Relative to Screen** radio button is selected in the dialog box, the size is taken as a percentage of the viewport size, and as such the appearance (size) of the point is not altered by the use of the **ZOOM** command (the **ZOOM** command should perform regeneration). For example, a setting of 5 makes the point 5 units high; a setting of -5 makes the point 5 percent of the current drawing area. The prompt sequence for changing the size of the point is:

Figure 2-66 Changing point size using the PDSIZE variable

Command: **PDSIZE** [Enter]
Enter new value for PDSIZE <0.000>: **1** [Enter]
Command: **POINT** [Enter]
Specify a point: *Select a point.*

PDMODE and **PDSIZE** values can also be changed through the **SETVAR** command.

Exercise 14   *General*

a.   Try various combinations of the **PDMODE** and **PDSIZE** variables.

b.   Check the difference between the points generated from negative values of **PDSIZE** and points generated from positive values of **PDSIZE**. Use the **ZOOM** command to zoom in, if needed.

Self- Evaluation Test

Answer the following questions and then compare your answers to the correct answers given at the end of this chapter.

1.   Different options for drawing arcs can be invoked by entering the **ARC** command and then selecting an appropriate letter. (T/F)

2.   A negative value for chord length in the St,C,Len option results in the largest possible arc, also known as the major arc. (T/F)

3.   If you do not specify a start point but just press ENTER or select the Continue option, the start point and direction of the arc will be taken from the endpoint and ending direction of the previous line or arc drawn on the current screen. (T/F)

4.   If you select a point to specify the radius of a circumscribed polygon, one of the vertices is positioned on the selected point. In the case of inscribed polygons, the midpoint of an edge is placed on the point you have specified. (T/F)

5.   When the value of **PDMODE** is changed, all the previously drawn points also change to the type designated by the **PDMODE** variable when the drawing is regenerated. (T/F)

6.   Fill in the command, entries, and operations required to draw an arc with start point at (3,3), center at (2,3), and an included angle of 80 degrees.
Command: _____
Specify start of arc or [CEnter]: _____
Specify second point of arc or [CEnter/ENd]: _____

Specify center point of arc: _____
Specify endpoint of arc or [Angle/chord Length]: _____
Specify included angle: _____

7. Fill in the command, entries, and operations required to draw an ellipse with first and second axis endpoints are at (4,5) and (7,5), respectively, and the distance of the other axis 1 unit.
    Command: _____
    Specify axis endpoint of ellipse[Arc/Center]: _____
    Specify other endpoint of axis : _____
    Specify distance to other axis or [Rotation]: _____

8. Fill in the command, entries, and operations needed to erase the most recently drawn object in a figure comprising many objects.
    Command: _____
    Select objects: _____
    1 found
    Select objects: _____

9. The system variable _____ governs the size of the point.

10. The maximum number of sides a polygon can have in AutoCAD is _____

11. The Fill option can be accessed through the _____ command or the _____ system variable.

12. The values for the inside and outside diameters of a doughnut are saved in the _____ and _____ system variables.

13. Summarize the various ways of drawing an ellipse. _____
    _____ .

14. What is the function of the **FILLMODE** system variable? _____
    _____ .

15. Define inscribed and circumscribed polygons. _____
    _____ .

Chapter 2

Review Questions

1. The default method of drawing an arc is the three-point option. (T/F)

2. An arc can be drawn only in a counterclockwise direction. (T/F)

3. In the **St,C,Ang** option, if the specified angle is negative, the arc is drawn in a counterclockwise direction. (T/F)

4. In the **St,C,Len** option, the arc is drawn in a counterclockwise fashion from the start point. (T/F)·

5. In the **St,C,Len** option, positive chord length gives the largest possible arc (known as the major arc) with that length. (T/F)

6. A unit radius arc with an included angle of 45 degrees has a chord length of 0.765 units. (T/F)

7. In the **St,E,Rad** option, a positive radius value results in a major arc, and a negative radius value results in a minor arc. (T/F)

8. In the **St,E,Dir** option, the start of the arc is established tangent to the specified direction. (T/F)

9. Using the **RECTANG** command, the rectangle generated on the screen is treated as a combination of different objects; hence individual sides can be edited immediately. (T/F)

10. The **ELLIPSE** command draws an ellipse as a composition of small arc segments forming a polyline. (T/F)

11. The characteristics of a polygon drawn in AutoCAD are those of a closed polyline having zero width and no tangent specification. (T/F)

12. If the **FILL** mode is off, only the trace outlines are drawn. (T/F)

13. Regeneration or redrawing takes the same amount of time for both non-solid-filled traces and solid-filled traces. (T/F)

14. Polylines can be used with any type of line. (T/F)

15. Doughnuts in AutoCAD are circular polylines. (T/F)

16. After regeneration, all the points on the drawing are drawn in the shape designated by the current value of the **PDMODE** variable. (T/F)

17. The system variable PDSIZE controls the size of the point except for the **PDMODE** values of 0 and 1. (T/F)

18. Though a selection set is being formed using the **Last** option, only one object is selected, even if you use the Last option a number of times. (T/F)

19. Fill in the command, entries, and operations required to draw an arc tangent to the end point of a previously drawn arc.
Command: _____
Specify start point of arc or [CEnter]: _____
Specify second point of arc [CEnter/End]: _____

20. Fill in the command, entries, and operations required to draw an ellipse whose first and second axis endpoints are at (2,3) and (5,3) respectively, with a rotation of 45 degrees _____ around the major axis.
Command: _____
Specify axis endpoint of ellipse or [Arc/Center]: _____
Specify other endpoint of axis: _____
Specify distance to other axis or [Rotation]: _____
Specify rotation around major axis: _____

21. Give the command, entries, and operations required to draw an ellipse by the Center and Two Axes method. The center of the ellipse is located at (5,6), the axis endpoint at (6,6), and the width of the other axis is 2 units.
Command: _____
Specify axis endpoint of ellipse or [Arc/Center]: _____
Specify center of ellipse: _____
Specify endpoint of axis: _____
Specify distance to other axis or [Rotation]: _____

22. Fill in the command, entries, and operations needed to draw a pentagon with the Edge option, where the first and second endpoints of the edge are at (4,2) and (3,3), respectively.
Command: _____
Enter number of sides <4>: _____
Specify center of polygon or [Edge]>: _____
First endpoint of edge: _____
Second endpoint of edge: _____

23. Traces are solid-filled if _____ is on.

24. To save time, you can turn on the **FILL** mode when the drawing has taken the final shape and then use the _____ command to fill the traces in the drawing.

25. The _____ option of the **PLINE** command closes the polyline by drawing a polyline segment from the most recent endpoint to the initial start point.

26. The _____ option of the **PLINE** command is used to switch from drawing polylines to drawing polyarcs, and provides you the options associated with the drawing of polyarcs.

27. The type of point drawn is controlled by the _____ system variable.

28. You can have _____ combinations of point types.

29. A value of zero for the **PDSIZE** variable generates the point at _____ percent of the graphics area height.

30. A positive value for **PDSIZE** defines _____ size for the point.

31. Explain the difference between an optimized polyline and a 2D polyline. _____
_____ .

32. What is the function of **CONVERT** command? _____
_____ .

33. You cannot draw a filleted rectangle using the **RECTANG** command. (T/F)

EXERCISES

Exercise 15   *Mechanical*

Make the drawing shown in Figure 2-67. The distance between the dotted lines is 1.0 units. Create the radii by using appropriate **ARC** command options.

Figure 2-67 *Drawing for Exercise 15*

Exercise 16

Make the drawing shown in Figure 2-68. The distance between the dotted lines is 1.0 units. Create the radii using appropriate **ARC** command options.

Figure 2-68 Drawing for Exercise 16

Exercise 17

Make the drawing shown in Figure 2-69. The distance between the dotted lines is 0.5 units. Create the ellipses using the **ELLIPSE** command.

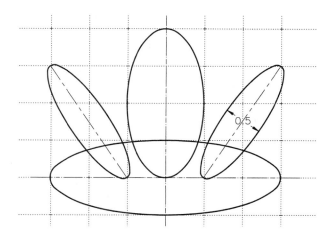

Figure 2-69 Drawing for Exercise 17

Exercise 18   *Mechanical*

Use the appropriate options of the **CIRCLE**, **LINE**, and **ARC** commands to generate the drawing in Figure 2-70. The dimensions are as shown in the figure. Use the **POINT** command to draw the center points of the circles.

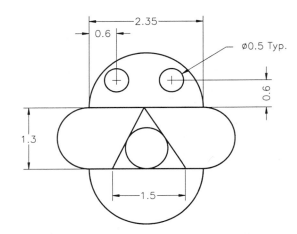

Figure 2-70 *Drawing for Exercise 18*

Exercise 19   *Mechanical*

Make the drawing shown in Figure 2-71. You must use only the **LINE**, **CIRCLE** and **ARC** command options. Use the **POINT** command to draw the center points of the circles and arcs.

Figure 2-71 *Drawing for Exercise 19*

Exercise 20

Draw the following Figure 2-72, using the **RECTANGLE** command.

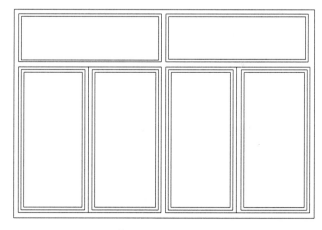

Figure 2-72 Drawing for Exercise 20

Exercise 21

Draw the following figure 2-73 using the **LINE**, **CIRCLE**, **PLINE** and **ARC** commands.

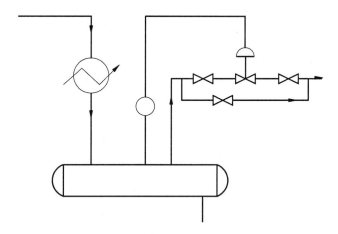

Figure 2-73 Drawing for Exercise 21

Chapter 2

Problem Solving Exercise 1   *Mechanical*

Draw Figure 2-74 using only the **LINE**, **CIRCLE**, and **ARC** commands or their options.

Figure 2-74 Drawing for Problem Solving Exercise 1

Problem Solving Exercise 2   *Mechanical*

Draw Figure 2-75 using the **POLYGON** and **CIRCLE** commands. The drawing must be created according to the given dimensions. Use the **POINT** command to draw the center lines going through the circles.

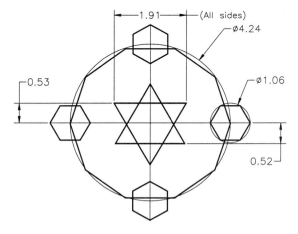

Figure 2-75 Drawing for Problem Solving Exercise 2

Project Exercise 1-2

Generate the drawing in Figure 2-76 according to the dimensions shown in the figure, but do not draw the dimensions. Save the drawing as BENCH3-4. (See Chapters 1, 6, 7, 19, and 23 for other drawings of Project Exercise 1).

Figure 2-76 *Drawing for Project Exercise 1-2*

Chapter 2

Chapter 3

Drawing Aids

Learning Objectives

After completing this chapter, you will be able to:
- *Set up units using the **Drawing Units** dialog box and the **UNITS** command.*
- *Set up and determine limits for a given drawing.*
- *Determine limits for engineering, architectural, and metric drawings.*
- *Set up layers and assign colors and linetypes to them.*
- *Set up Grid, Snap, and Ortho modes based on the drawing requirements.*
- *Use Object Snaps and understand their applications.*
- *Combine Object Snap modes and set up running object snap modes.*
- *Use Autotracking, current, and global linetype scaling.*
- *Determine **LTSCALE** factor for plotting.*

In this chapter you will learn about the drawing setup. This involves several factors that can affect the quality and accuracy of your drawing. This chapter contains a detailed description of how to set up units, limits, and layers. You will also learn about some of the drawing aids, like Grid, Snap, and Ortho. These aids will help you to draw accurately and quickly.

SETTING UNITS
Using the Drawing Units Dialog Box*

Menu:	Format > Units
Command:	UNITS

The **UNITS** command is used to select a format for the units of distance and angle measurement. You can use the **Drawing**

Figure 3-1 *Invoking the UNITS command from the Format menu*

Units dialog box to set the units. In the **Drawing Units** dialog box (Figure 3-2), you can select a desired format of units or angles from the drop-down list displayed on choosing the down arrow button to the right of the **Type:** edit box. You can also specify the precision of units and angles from the **Precision:** drop-down list. (Figure 3-3).

Figure 3-2 Drawing Units dialog box

Figure 3-3 Specifying Precision from the Drawing Units dialog box

Specifying Units. You can use the **Drawing Units** dialog box to specify the units you want in the drawing. You can select one of the following five formats:

1. Architectural
2. Decimal
3. Engineering
4. Fractional
5. Scientific

If you select the Scientific, Decimal, or Fractional format, you can enter the distances or coordinates in any of these three formats, but not in engineering or architectural units. In the following example, the units variously are set as decimal, scientific, fractional, and decimal and fractional to enter the coordinates of different points:

Command: **LINE** [Enter]
Specify from point: **1.75,0.75** [Enter]   (*Decimal.*)
Specify next point or [Undo]: **1.75E+01, 3.5E+00** [Enter]   (*Scientific.*)
Specify next point or [Undo]: **10-3/8,8-3/4** [Enter]   (*Fractional.*)
Specify next point or [Close/Undo]: **0.5,17/4** [Enter]   (*Decimal and fractional.*)

If you choose the Engineering or Architectural format, you can enter the distances or coordinates in any of the five formats. In the following example, the units are set as architectural; hence, different formats are used to enter the coordinates of points:

> Command: **LINE** [Enter]
> Specify first point: **1-3/4,3/4** [Enter]   (*Fractional.*)
> Specify next point or [Undo]: **1'1-3/4",3-1/4** [Enter]   (*Architectural.*)
> Specify next point or [Undo]: **0'10.375,0'8.75** [Enter]   (*Engineering.*)
> Specify next point or [Close/Undo]: **0.5,4-1/4"** [Enter]   (*Decimal and engineering.*)

Note

The inch symbol (") is optional. For example, 1'1-3/4" is the same as 1'1-3/4, and 3/4" is the same as 3/4.

You cannot use the feet (') or inch (") symbols if you have selected Scientific, Decimal, or Fractional unit formats.

Specifying Angle. You can select one of the following five angle measuring systems:

> 1. Decimal Degrees
> 2. Deg/min/sec
> 3. Grads
> 4. Radians
> 5. Surveyor's Units

If you select any of the first four measuring systems, you can enter the angle in the Decimal, Degrees/minutes/seconds, Grads, or Radians system, but you cannot enter the angle in Surveyor's units. However, if you select Surveyor's units, you can enter the angles in any of the five systems. If you enter an angle value without any indication of measuring system, it is taken in the current system. To enter the value in another system, use the appropriate suffixes and symbols, such as r (Radians), d (Degrees), g (Grads), or the others shown in the following examples. In the following example, the system of angle measure is Surveyor's units and different systems of angle measure are used to define the angle of the line:

> Command: **LINE** [Enter]
> Specify first point: **3,3** [Enter]
> Specify next point or [Undo]: **@3<45.5** [Enter]   (*Decimal degrees.*)
> Specify next point or [Undo]: **@3<90d30'45"** [Enter]   (*Degrees/min/sec.*)
> Specify next point or [Close/Undo]: **@3<75'0g** [Enter]   (*Grads.*)
> Specify next point or [Close/Undo]: **@3<N45d30'E** [Enter]   (*Surveyor's units.*)

In **Surveyor's units** you must specify the bearing angle that the line makes with the north-south direction (Figure 3-4). For example, if you want to define an angle of 60 degrees with north, in the Surveyor's units the angle will be specified as N60dE. Similarly, you can specify angles like S50dE, S50dW, N75dW, as shown in Figure 3-5. You cannot specify an angle that exceeds 90 degrees (N120E). The angles can also be specified in **radians** or **grads** for example, 180 de-

Figure 3-4 *Specifying angles in Surveyor's units*

Chapter 3

grees is equal to **PI** (3.14159) radians. You can convert degrees into radians or radians into degrees using the following equations:

$$\text{radians} = \text{degrees} \times 3.14159/180$$
$$\text{degrees} = \text{radians} \times 180/3.14159$$

Grads are generally used in land surveys. There are 400 grads or 360 degrees in a circle. A 90-degree angle is equal to 100 grads.

In AutoCAD, by default the angles are positive if measured in the counterclockwise direction (Figure 3-5) and the angles are measured with positive X axis (East, Figure 3-6). The angles are negative if measured clockwise. If you want the angles measured as positive in the clockwise direction, select the **Clockwise** check box. Then the positive angles will be measured in the clockwise direction and the negative angles in the counterclockwise direction.

Figure 3-5 *N,S,E,W directions*

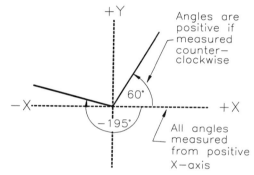

Figure 3-6 *Measuring angles counterclockwise from the positive X axis (default)*

Choosing the **Direction...** button in the **Drawing Units** dialog box, displays the **Direction Control** dialog box which gives you an option of selecting the setting for direction of the Base Angle (see Figure 3-7). If you select the **Other** option, you can set your own direction for the Base Angle by either entering a value in the **Angle:** edit box or choosing the **Pick an Angle** button to specify the angle on the screen.

Choosing the down arrow button in the **When inserting blocks in this drawing, scale them to:** edit box, for **DesignCenter blocks,** you are allowed to choose from a list of units. The default value is **Unitless.**

The Sample Output shows an example of the current format of the units and angles.

Figure 3-7 *Selecting Direction from the **Units Control** dialog box*

Using the -UNITS Command

You can also set up units by entering **-UNITS** at the Command prompt. The prompt sequence is:

Command: **-UNITS** [Enter]

The AutoCAD Text Window is displayed, which shows the following five report formats with the examples:

Report formats:	(Examples)
1. Scientific	1.55E+01
2. Decimal	15.50
3. Engineering	1'-3.50"
4. Architectural	1'-3 1/2"
5. Fractional	15 1/2

With the exception of the Engineering and Architectural formats, these formats can be used with any basic units of measurement. For example, Decimal mode is perfect for metric units as well as decimal English units.

Enter choice, 1 to 5 <default>:

AutoCAD is now waiting for you to select a format of your choice. After the selection is made, AutoCAD will prompt you to select the precision required, depending on the selected format. For selection 1, 2, or 3, the next prompt says:

Enter number of digits to right of decimal point (0 to 8) <default>:

If the default value is acceptable to you, press ENTER; otherwise, enter your choice. For example, the number 2.1250 has four digits to the right of the decimal point; therefore, you will enter 4 at this prompt. For choices 4 and 5 the prompt says:

Enter denominator of smallest fraction to display
(1, 2, 4, 8, 16, 32, 64, 128, or 256) <default>:

You can now enter your choice or choose default by pressing ENTER. For example, if you want the distances or coordinates measured up to 1/64 (2-1/64), enter 64. After you enter the format and precision for distances and coordinates, the **-UNITS** command proceeds to angles and allows you to select any one of the five listed systems of angle measurement.

Systems of angle measure:	(Examples)
1. Decimal degrees	45.0000
2. Degrees/minutes/seconds	45d0'0"
3. Grads	50.0000g
4. Radians	0.7854r
5. Surveyor's units	N 45d0'0" E

Enter choice, 1 to 5 <default>:

Chapter 3

Enter number of fractional places for display of angles (0 to 8) <default>:

After you select the system of angle measure and precision to display angles, you must select a direction for angle measurement. The prompt says:

Direction for angle 0:
    East   3 o'clock   = 0
    North   12 o'clock   = 90
    West   9 o'clock   = 180
    South   6 o'clock   = 270
Enter direction for angle <0> <current>:

You can now select any starting direction to measure angles. In the default mode, angle measurement always starts with 0 degrees corresponding to East (Figure 3-6). You can enter a new direction or press ENTER to select 0 degrees. The next prompt says:

Measure angles clockwise? [Yes/No] <current>:

If you want angles measured clockwise, enter Y. If you enter N, then a positive angle is measured in a counterclockwise direction and a negative angle is measured clockwise. This is the last prompt for setting the units, and it is followed by the Command prompt.

Example 1   *General*

In this example we will set the units for a drawing according to the following specifications and then draw Figure 3-8:

1. Set **UNITS** to fractional, with the denominator of the smallest fraction equal to 32.
2. Set the angular measurement to Surveyor's units, with the number of fractional places for display of angles equal to zero.
3. Set the direction to 90 degrees (north) and the direction of measurement of angles to clockwise (angles measured positive in clockwise direction) (Figure 3-8).

Using the Drawing Units dialog box

1. Invoke the **Drawing Units** dialog box by entering UNITS/ DDUNITS at the Command prompt or by choosing **Units** from the **Format** menu.

    Command: **UNITS** or DDUNITS [Enter]

2. Select **Fractional units** from the **Type :** edit box drop-down list in the **Length** area. From the **Precision** drop-down list, in the **Length** area, select 0 1/32 if it is not already selected.

3. In the **Angle** area of the dialog box, select **Surveyor's Units** from the **Type:** edit box drop-down list. From the **Precision** drop-down list, in the **Angle** area, select **N 0d E** if it is not already selected. Also, select the **Clockwise** check box to set clockwise angle measurement as positive.

4. Choose the **Direction** button to display the **Direction Control** dialog box.

5. Select the **North** radio button. Choose the **OK** button to exit the **Direction Control** dialog box.

6. Choose the **OK** button to exit the **Drawing Units** dialog box.

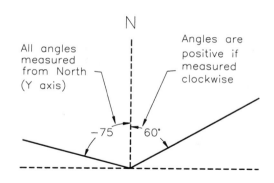

Figure 3-9 Angles measured from north (Y axis)

7. With the units set, draw Figure 3-8 using polar coordinates. Here the units are fractional and the **angles are measured from north** (90-degree axis). Also, the angles are measured as positive in a clockwise direction and **negative** in a counterclockwise direction.

Command: **LINE** [Enter]
Specify first point: **2,2** [Enter]
Specify next point or [Undo]: **@2.0<0** [Enter]
Specify next point or [Undo]: **@2.0<60** [Enter]
Specify next point or [Close/Undo]: **@1<180** [Enter]
Specify next point or [Close/Undo]: **@1<90** [Enter]
Specify next point or [Close/Undo]: **@1<180** [Enter]
Specify next point or [Close/Undo]: **@2.0<60** [Enter]
Specify next point or [Close/Undo]: **@0.5<90** [Enter]
Specify next point or [Close/Undo]: **@2.0<180** [Enter]
Specify next point or [Close/Undo]: **C** [Enter]

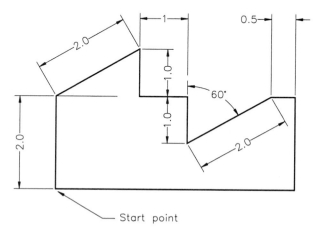

Figure 3-8 Drawing for Example 1

Using the command line

1. Invoke the **UNITS** command and select the appropriate options as shown below:

Command: **-UNITS** [Enter]

Report formats: (Examples)
1. Scientific   1.55E+01
2. Decimal   15.50
3. Engineering   1'-3.50"
4. Architectural   1'-3 1/2"
5. Fractional   15 1/2

With the exception of Engineering and Architectural formats, these formats can be used
with any basic units of measurement. For example, Decimal mode is perfect for metric units
as well as decimal English units.

Enter choice, 1 to 5 <default>: **5** [Enter]

Enter denominator of smallest fraction to display
(1,2,4,8,16,32, 64, 128, or 256) <default>: **32** [Enter]

Systems of angle measure: (Examples)
1. Decimal degrees   45.0000
2. Degrees/minutes/seconds   45d0'0"
3. Grads   50.0000g
4. Radians   0.7854r
5. Surveyor's units   N 45d0'0" E

Enter choice, 1 to 5 <default>: **5** [Enter]
Enter number of fractional places for display of angles (0 to 8) <default>: **0** [Enter]

Direction for angle E
     East   3 o'clock   = E
     North   12 o'clock   = N
     West   9 o'clock   = W
     South   6 o'clock   = S
Enter direction for angle <0> <cur-
rent>: **N** [Enter]

Measure angles clockwise? [Yes/No]
     <current>: **Y** [Enter]

Forcing Default Angles

When you define the direction by specifying the
angle, the output of the angle depends on the
following (Figure 3-10):

     Angular units
     Angle direction
     Angle base

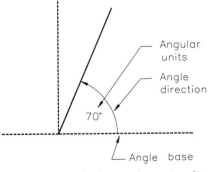

*Figure 3-10 Default angular units, direction, and
base*

For example, if you are using the AutoCAD default setting, <70 represents an angle of 70 decimal degrees from the positive X axis, measured counterclockwise. The decimal degrees represent angular units, X axis represents the angle base, and counterclockwise represents the angle direction. If you have changed the default settings for measuring angles, it might be confusing to enter the angles. AutoCAD lets you bypass the current settings by entering << or <<< before the angle. If you enter << before the angle, AutoCAD will bypass the current angle settings and use the angle as decimal degrees from the default angle base and default angle direction (angles are referenced from the positive X axis and are positive if measured counterclockwise). If you enter <<< in front of the angle, AutoCAD will use current angular units, but it will bypass the current settings for angle base and angle direction and use the default angle setting (angles are referenced from the positive X axis and are positive if measured counterclockwise).

Assume, for example, that you have changed the current settings and made the system of angle measure radians with two places of precision: angle base north (the Y axis), and the direction clockwise. Now, if you enter <1.04 or <1.04r, all the current settings will be taken into consideration and you will get an angle of 1.04 radians, measured in a clockwise direction from the positive Y axis, Figure 3-11(a). If you enter <<60, AutoCAD will bypass the current settings and reference the angle in degrees from the positive X axis, measuring 60 degrees in a counterclockwise direction, Figure 3-11(b). If you enter <<<1.04r, AutoCAD will use the current angular units, but will bypass the current angle base and angle direction. Hence, the angle will be referenced from the positive X axis, measuring 1.04 radians in a counterclockwise direction, Figure 3-11(c).

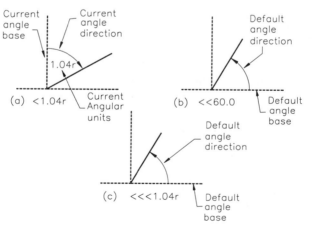

Figure 3-11 *Forcing default angles*

The effect of using the open angle brackets is summarized in the following table.

Angle prefix	Angular units	Angle direction	Angle base	Example
<	current	current	current	<1.04r
<<	degrees	counterclockwise	default	<<60.0
<<<	current	counterclockwise	default	<<<1.04r

You can also override the current angle units by entering the appropriate suffix, like 60d for degrees.

LIMITS COMMAND

Menu:	Format > Drawing Limits
Command:	LIMITS

When you start AutoCAD, the default limits are 12.00,9.00. You can use the **LIMITS** command to set up new limits. The following is the prompt sequence of the **LIMITS** command for setting the limits of 24,18:

Command: **LIMITS** Enter
Specify lower left corner or [ON/OFF]<current>: **0,0** Enter
Specify upper right corner <current>: **24,18** Enter

Figure 3-12 Choosing **Drawing Limits** *from the* **Format** *menu*

At the preceding two prompts you are required to specify the lower left corner and the upper right corner of the sheet. Normally you choose (0,0) as the lower left corner, but you can enter any other point. If the sheet size is 24 x 18, enter 24,18 as the coordinates of the upper right corner.

Setting Limits

In AutoCAD the drawings must be drawn full scale and, therefore, limits are needed to size up a drawing area. The limits of the drawing area are usually determined by the following factors:

1. The actual size of the drawing.
2. The space needed for putting down the dimensions, notes, bill of materials, and other necessary details.
3. The space between different views so that the drawing does not look cluttered.
4. The space for the border and a title block, if any.

To get a good idea of how to set up limits, it is always better to draw a rough sketch of the drawing to help calculate the area needed. For example, if an object has a front view size of 5 x 5, a side view size of 3 x 5, and a top view size of 5 x 3, the limits should be set so they can accommodate the drawing and everything associated with it. In Figure 3-13, the space between the front and side views is 4 units and between the front and top views is 3 units. Also, the space between the border and the drawing is 5 units on the left, 5 units on the right, 3 units at the bottom, and 2 units at the top. (The space between the views and between the border line and the drawing depends on the drawing.)

After you know the sizes of different views and have determined the space required between views, between the border and the drawing, and between the borderline and the edges of the paper, you can calculate the space you need as follows:

Space along (X axis) = 1 + 5 + 5 + 4 + 3 + 5 + 1 = 24
Space along (Y axis) = 1 + 3 + 5 + 3 + 3 + 2 + 1 = 18

Thus, the space or the work area you need for the drawing is 24 x18. Once you have determined the space you need, select the sheet size that can accomodate your drawing. In the above case, you will select D size (34 x 22) sheet. Therefore the actual drawing limits are 34,22.

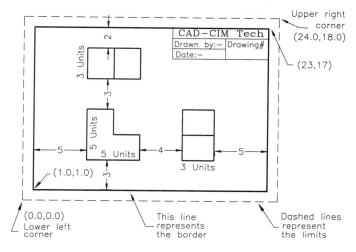

Figure 3-13 Setting limits in a drawing

Standard Sheet Sizes

When you make a drawing, you might want to plot the drawing to get a hard copy. Several standard sheet sizes are available to plot your drawing. Although in AutoCAD you can select any work area, it is recommended that you select the work area based on the sheet size you will be using to plot the drawing. The sheet size is the deciding factor for determining the limits (work area), text size (**TEXTSIZE**), dimensioning scale factor (**DIMSCALE**), linetype scale factor (**LTSCALE**) and other drawing-related parameters. The following tables list standard sheet sizes and the corresponding drawing limits for different scale factors:

Standard U.S. Size

Letter size	Sheet size	Limits (1:1)	Limits (1:4)	Limits (1/4"=1')
A	8.5 x 11	8.5,11	34,44	34',44'
B	11 x 17	11,17	44,68	44',68'
C	17 x 22	17,22	68,88	68',88'
D	22 x 34	22,34	88,136	88',136'
E	34 x 44	34,44	136,176	136'x176'

International Size

Letter size	Sheet size	Limits (1:1)	Limits (1:20)
A4	210 x 297	210,297	4200,5940

A3	297 x 420	297,420	5940,8400
A2	420 x 594	420,597	8400,11940
A1	595 x 841	595,841	11940,16820
A0	841 x 1189	841,1189	16820,23780

Limits for Architectural Drawings

Most architectural drawings are drawn at a scale of 1/4" = 1', 1/8" = 1', or 1/16" = 1'. You must set the limits accordingly. The following example illustrates how to calculate the limits in architectural drawings:

Given
Sheet size = 24 x 18
Scale is 1/4" = 1'

Calculate limits
Scale is 1/4" = 1'
    or 1/4" = 12"
      or 1" = 48"
X limit = 24 x 48
      = 1152" or 1152 Units
      = 96'
Y limit = 18 x 48
      = 864" or 864 Units
      = 72'

Thus, the scale factor is 48 and the limits are 1152",864", or 96',72'.

Example 2   *Architectural*

In this example you will calculate limits and determine an appropriate drawing scale factor for Figure 3-14. The drawing is to be plotted on a 12" x 9" sheet.

The scale factor can be calculated as follows:

Given or known
Overall length of the drawing = 31'
Length of the sheet = 12"
Approximate space between the drawing and the edges of the paper = 2"

Calculate scale factor
To calculate the scale factor, you have to try different scales until you find one that satisfies the given conditions. After some experience you will find this fairly easy to do. For this example, assume a scale factor of 1/4" = 1'.

Scale factor 1/4" = 1'
    or   1" = 4'

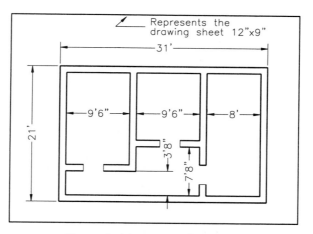

Figure 3-14 Drawing for Example 2

Thus, a line 31' long will be = 31'/4' = 7.75" on paper. Similarly, a line 21' long = 21'/4' = 5.25".

Approximate space between the drawing and the edges of paper = 2"
Therefore, total length of the sheet = 7.75 + 2 + 2 = 11.75"
Similarly, total width of the sheet = 5.25 + 2 + 2 = 9.25"

Because you selected the scale 1/4" = 1', the drawing will definitely fit on the given sheet of paper (12" x 9"). Therefore, the scale for this drawing is 1/4" = 1'.

Calculate limits
Scale factor = 1" = 48" or 1" = 4'
The length of the sheet is 12"
Therefore, X limit = 12 x 4' = 48'
Also, Y limit = 9 x 4' = 36'

Limits for Metric Drawings

When the drawing units are metric, you must use **standard metric size sheets** or calculate the limits in millimeters (mm). For example, if the sheet size you decide to use is 24 x 18, the limits after conversion to the metric system will be 609.6,457.2 (multiply length and width by 25.4). You can round these numbers to the nearest whole numbers 610,457. Note that metric drawings do not require any special setup, except for the limits. Metric drawings are like any other drawings that use decimal units. As with architectural drawings, you can draw metric drawings to a scale. For example, if the scale is 1:20 you must calculate the limits accordingly. The following example illustrates how to calculate the limits for metric drawings.

Given
Sheet size = 24" x 18"
Scale = 1 : 20

Chapter 3

Calculate limits
Scale is 1 : 20
Therefore, scale factor = 20
X limit = 24 x 25.4 x 20 = 12192 units
Y limits = 18 x 25.4 x 20 = 9144 units

Thus, the limits are 12192 and 9144.

Exercise 1   *Mechanical*

Set the units of the drawing according to the following specifications and then make the drawing shown in Figure 3-15 (Leave a space of 3 to 5 units around the drawing for dimensioning and title block). The space between the dotted lines is 1 unit.

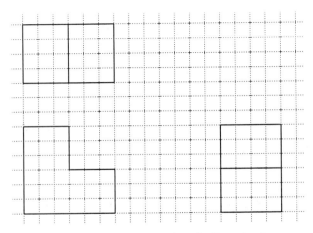

Figure 3-15 *Drawing for Exercise 1*

1. Set **UNITS** to decimal units, with two digits to the right of the decimal point.
2. Set the angular measurement to decimal degrees, with the number of fractional places for display of angles equal to 1.
3. Set the direction to 0 degrees (east) and the direction of measurement of angles to counter-clockwise (angles measured positive in counterclockwise direction).

LAYERS

The concept of layers can be best explained by using the concept of overlays in manual drafting. In manual drafting, different details of the drawing can be drawn on different sheets of paper, or overlays. Each overlay is perfectly aligned with the others, and when all of them are placed on top of each other you can reproduce the entire drawing. As shown in Figure 3-16, the object lines have been drawn in the first overlay and the dimensions in the second overlay. You can place these overlays on top of each other and get a combined look at the drawing.

In AutoCAD, instead of using overlays you use layers. Each layer is assigned a name. You can also assign a color and linetype to these layers. For example, in Figure 3-17 the object lines have been

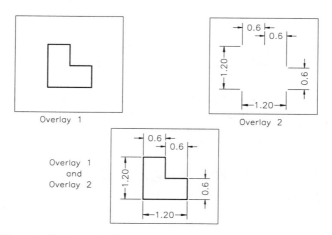

Figure 3-16 *Drawing lines and dimensions in different overlays*

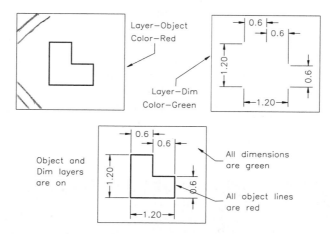

Figure 3-17 *Drawing lines and dimensions in different layers*

drawn in the OBJECT layer and the dimensions have been drawn in the DIM layer. The object lines will be red because the red color has been assigned to the OBJECT layer. Similarly, the dimension lines will be green because the DIM layer has been assigned the green color. You can display all of the layers or you can display the layers individually or in any combination.

Advantages of Layers

1. Each layer can be assigned a different color. Assigning a particular color to a group of objects is very important for plotting. For example, if all object lines are red, at the time of plotting you can assign the red color to a slot (pen) that has the desired tip width (e.g., medium). Similarly, if the dimensions are green, you can assign the green color to another slot (pen) that has a thin tip. By assigning different colors to different layers you can control the width of the lines when the drawing is plotted. You can also make a layer plottable or nonplottable.

2. The layers are useful for some editing operations. For example, if you want to erase all dimensions in a drawing, you can freeze all layers except the dimension layer and then erase all dimensions by using the **Crossing** option to select objects.
3. You can turn a layer off or freeze a layer that you do not want to be displayed or plotted.
4. You can lock a layer, which will prevent the user from accidently editing the objects in that layer.
5. The colors also help you to distinguish different groups of objects. For example, in architectural drafting, the plans for foundation, floors, plumbing, electrical, and heating systems may all be made in different layers. In electronics drafting and in PCB (printed circuit board), the design of each level of a multilevel circuit board can be drawn on separate layer.

LAYER PROPERTIES MANAGER DIALOG BOX*

Toolbar:	Object Properties > Layers
Menu:	Format > Layer...
Command:	LAYER or DDLMODES

Figure 3-18 Invoking the LAYER command from the Format menu

You can use the **Layer Properties Manager** dialog box (Figure 3-19) to perform the functions associated with the **LAYER** command. For example, you can create new layers, assign colors, assign linetypes, or perform any operation that is shown in the dialog box. Using this dialog box for layers is efficient and provides a convenient way to use various options. You can also perform some layer functions like freeze, thaw, lock, unlock, etc., directly from the **Object properties** toolbar (Figure 3-20). If you have already created some layers, they will be listed with their current status in the dialog box as shown in Figure 3-19.

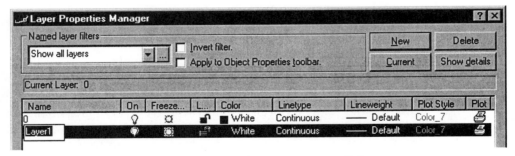

Figure 3-19 Layer Properties Manager dialog

Creating New Layers

If you want to create new layers, choose the **New** button. A new layer with name Layer1 and having the properties of the selected (highlighted) layer is created and listed in the dialog box just below the highlighted layer. You can change or edit the name by selecting it and then entering a new name. If no layer is selected, the new layer is placed at the end of the layers list and has the properties of the default layer 0. If more than one layer is selected, the new layer is placed below

Figure 3-20 Object Properties toolbar

the last highlighted layer and has its properties. Also, right-clicking anywhere in the Layers list area of the **Layer Properties Manager** dialog box, displays a shortcut menu that gives you an option to create a new layer. You can right-click a layer whose properties you want to use in the new layer and then select New Layer from the shortcut menu.

Layer Names
1. A layer name can be up to 256 characters long, including letters (a - z), numbers (0 - 9), special characters ($ _ -) and spaces. Any combination of lower and upper-case letters can be used while naming a layer.
2. The layers should be named to help the user identify the contents of the layer. For example, if the layer name is HATCH, a user can easily recognize the layer and its contents. On the other hand, if the layer name is X261, it is hard to identify the contents of the layer.
3. Layer names should be short, but should also convey the meaning.

Note

If you exchange drawings with or provide drawings to consultants or others, it is very important that you standardize and coordinate layer names and other layer settings.

Assigning a Linetype, Color, Lineweight* or Plot Style* to a Layer

To assign a new linetype to a layer, select the current linetype displayed with a particular layer. When you select the linetype, AutoCAD will display the **Select Linetype** dialog box (Figure 3-22), which displays the linetypes that are defined and loaded on your system. Select the new linetype and then choose the **OK** button. The linetype you selected is assigned to the layer you selected initially. The layers are, by default, assigned continuous linetype and white color.

If the linetypes have not been loaded on your system, choose the **Load** button in the **Select Linetype** dialog box. This displays the **Load or Reload Linetypes** dialog box (Figure 3-22), which displays all linetypes in the **ACAD.LIN** file. In this dialog box you can select individual linetypes or a number of linetypes by holding the SHIFT or CTRL key on the keyboard and then selecting the linetypes. If you right-click, AutoCAD displays the shortcut menu that you can use to select all linetypes. Then by choosing the **OK** button, the selected linetypes are loaded. You can also use the **LINETYPE** command to display the **Linetype Manager** dialog box which is similar to the **Layer Properties Manager** dialog box and allows you to load, delete linetypes, set filters or show details of linetypes. The **Linetype Manager** dialog box (Figure 3-23) can also be loaded through the

Chapter 3

Figure 3-21 Select Linetype dialog box

Figure 3-22 Load or Reload Linetypes dialog

Format menu by choosing **Linetype**. To use the command line to load the linetypes, the prompts are as follows:

Command: **-LINETYPE** Enter
Current line type: "ByLayer"
Enter an option [?/Create/Load/Set]: **L** Enter
Enter linetype(s) to load: Enter *name(s) of linetypes to load*.

The **Select Linetype File** dialog box appears that enables you to load the required linetypes from the specific files you need.

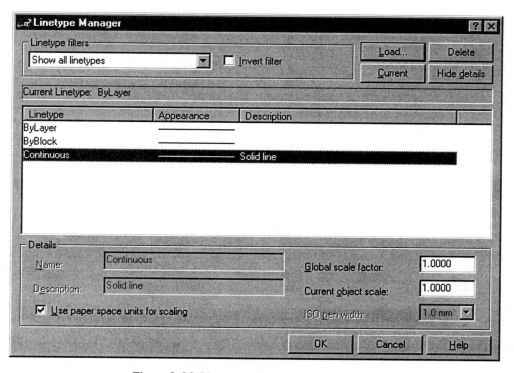

Figure 3-23 Linetype Manager dialog box.

To assign a color, select the color icon in a particular layer; AutoCAD will display a **Select Color** dialog box. Select a desired color and then choose the **OK** button. The color you selected will be assigned to the selected layer. The number of colors is determined by your graphics card and monitor. Most color systems support eight or more colors. If your system allows it, you may choose a color number between 0 and 255 (256 colors). The following are the first seven standard colors:

Color number	Color name	Color number	Color name
1	Red	5	Blue
2	Yellow	6	Magenta
3	Green	7	White
4	Cyan		

Note

Using nonstandard colors may cause compatibility problems if the drawings are used on other systems with different colors. On a light background, the color "white" appears black. Certain colors are hard to see on light backgrounds and others are hard to see on dark backgrounds, so you may have to use different colors than those specified in some examples and exercises.

To assign a Lineweight to a layer, select the layer and then click on the Lineweight associated with it; the **Lineweight** dialog box appears. Select a Lineweight from the **Lineweights:** list. Choose **OK**

Chapter 3

to return to the **Layer Properties Manager** dialog box.

Plot Style is a group of property settings like color, linetype, lineweight that can be assigned to a layer. The default Plot Style is **Normal** in which the color, linetype, and lineweight are BYLAYER. To assign a Plot Style to a layer, select the layer and then click on its plot style; the **Select Plot Style** dialog box appears where you can select a specific Plot Style from the **Plot Styles:** list of available Plot Styles. Plot Styles have to be created before you can use them. Choose **OK** to return to the **Layer Properties Manager** dialog box.

Making a Layer Current

To make a layer current, select the name of desired layer and then choose the **Current** button in the dialog box. AutoCAD will display the name of the selected layer next to **Current Layer:**. Choose **OK** to exit the dialog box. You can also make a layer current by double-clicking on it in the layer list box of the **Layer Properties Manager** dialog box. Right-clicking a layer in the Layer list box displays a shortcut menu which gives you an option to make the selected layer current. Only one layer can be made current and it is the layer where new objects will be drawn. You can also make a layer current by selecting it from the **Layer Control** drop-down list of the **Object Properties** toolbar. Choosing the **Make Object's Layer Current** button from the **Object Properties** toolbar prompts you to select the object whose layer you wish to make current and the layer associated with that object will be made current.

Controlling Display of Layers

You can control the display of the layers by selecting the **Turn a layer On or Off, Freeze or thaw in ALL viewports, Lock or Unlock a layer, Make a layer plottable or nonplottable** toggle icons in the list box of any particular layer.

Turn a layer On or Off. With the **Turn a layer On or Off** toggle icon you can turn the layers on or off. The layers that are turned on are displayed and can be plotted. The layers that are turned off are not displayed and cannot be plotted. If you turn the current layer off, AutoCAD will display a warning box informing you that the current drawing layer has been turned off.

Freeze or thaw in ALL viewports. While working on a drawing, if you do not want to see certain layers you can also use the **Freeze or thaw in ALL viewports** toggle icon to freeze the layers. The Thaw option negates the effect of the Freeze option, and the frozen layers are restored to normal. For example, while editing a drawing you may not want the dimensions displayed on the screen. To avoid this, you can freeze the DIM layer. The frozen layers are invisible and cannot be plotted. The difference between the **Off** option and the **Freeze** option is that the frozen layers are not calculated by the computer while regenerating the drawing. This saves time. The current layer cannot be frozen.

Active or New VP Freeze. When the tilemode is turned off (see Chapter 22, Drawing Predefined 3D Objects, Viewing and Editing 3D Objects, and 3D Surfaces), you can freeze or thaw the selected layers in the active floating viewport by selecting the **Active VP Freeze** icon for the selected layers. The frozen layers will still be visible in other viewports. If you want to freeze some layers in the new floating viewports, then select the **New VP Freeze** toggle icon for the selected layers. AutoCAD will freeze the layers in subsequently created new viewports without affecting the viewports that already exist. (Paper space is discussed in Chapter 22.) Also, check the **VPLAYER** command for selectively freezing the layers in viewports. The widths of the column headings in the **Layer Properties Manager** dialog box can be decreased or increased, by positioning the cursor between the column headings and then holding down the pick button of your pointing device and dragging the cursor to the right or the left.

LOck or Unlock a layer. While working on a drawing, if you do not want to accidentally edit some objects on a particular layer but still need to have them visible, you can use the **LOck/Unlock** toggle icon to lock the layers. When a layer is locked you can still use the objects in the locked layer for Object Snaps and inquiry commands like **LIST**. You can also make the locked layer the current layer and draw objects on it. The locked layers are plotted. The **Unlock** option negates the **LOck** option and allows you to edit objects on the layers previously locked.

Make a layer plottable or nonplottable*. If you do not wish to plot a particular layer, for example, construction lines, you can use the make a layer plottable or non-plottable toggle icon to make the layer nonplottable. The construction lines will not be plotted.

Deleting Layers

You can delete a layer by selecting the layer and then choosing the **Delete** button. To delete a layer it is necessary that the layer should not contain any objects. You cannot delete the Layers 0 and defpoints, a current layer and a Xref dependent layer.

You can also control the display of layers by first selecting a layer and then choosing the **Show details** button in **Layer Properties Manager** dialog box. This displays the layer details box that displays the properties associated with the selected layer. Using this box, you can change the name, color, linetype, lineweight, and other properties of the selected layer. Note that you cannot change the name of 0 layer. Once you have chosen the **Show details** button, the **Hide details** button is available.

Selective Display of Layers

If you have a limited number of layers it is easy to scan through them. However, if you have many layers it is sometimes difficult to search through the layers. To solve this problem you can use the drop-down list in the **Named layer filters area** of the **Layer Properties Manager** dialog box to display the layers selectively. If you want to display only those layers that are **XRef dependent**, you can select this option in the drop-down list. You can also define filter specification by choosing the [...] button to display the **Named Layers Filters** subdialog box (Figure 3-24). When loaded, initially this dialog box contains the default specifications. If you want to list only those layers that are red in color, enter red in the **Color:** edit box, then give this filter a name in the **Filter name:** edit box and then choose the **Add** button. This filter gets added to the list of Named Layer Filters. Now, when you select this named filter from the drop-down list in the Named layer filters area, AutoCAD will display the layers that are red in color in the **Layer Properties Manager** dialog box. If you select **All** in the Show drop-down list, all layers will be displayed. If you again want to display only those layers that are red in color, select the name of the specific filter from the drop-down list. As the specifications are already set in the **Named Layer Filters** dialog box, all the layers that are red in color are displayed.

In the **Layer Properties Manager** dialog box, selecting the Invert filter check box, inverts the filter that you have selected. For example, if you have selected the Show all layers, none of the

Figure3-24 Set Layer Filters dialog box

layers will be displayed. If you wish to apply the current layer filter to the Layer Control list in the **Object Properties** toolbar, select the **Apply to Object Properties toolbar** check box. When you do so, the tooltip indicates that the specified filter has been applied and only the filtered layers are displayed in the Layer Control drop-down list. When you right-click in the layers list box, AutoCAD displays a shortcut menu on the screen that you can use to select all layers, clear all layers, create new layer, or selectively display layers.

 Note
*You can also access the Layer options from the **Object Properties** toolbar (Figure 3-20) by selecting the appropriate icons.*

A frozen layer cannot be made current, but a layer that is turned off can be made current. However, neither can be plotted.

Setting Layers from the Command Line

You can also set layers from the command line by entering **-LAYER** at the Command prompt. The following is the prompt sequence:

Command: **-LAYER** [Enter]
Enter an option
[?/Make/Set/New/ON/OFF/Color/Ltype/Lweight/Plot/Freeze/Thaw/LOck/Unlock:

You can perform any function on the layer by entering the appropriate option at this prompt. For example, if you want to create two new layers, DIM and CEN, the prompt sequence is:

Command: **-LAYER** [Enter]
Enter an option
[?/Make/Set/New/ON/OFF/Color/Ltype/Lweight/Plot/Freeze/Thaw/LOck/Unlock: **N** [Enter]
Enter name list for new layer(s): **DIM, CEN** [Enter]

You can use the **Make** option of the **LAYER** command to simultaneously create a layer (unless it already exists) and set it current. If your current layer is VIEW and you want to create a new layer, OBJECT, and also make it the current, the prompt sequence is:

Command: **-LAYER** [Enter]
Enter an option
[?/Make/Set/New/ON/OFF/Color/Ltype/Lweight/Plot/Freeze/Thaw/LOck/Unlock: **M** [Enter]
Enter name for new layer (becomes the current layer) <VIEW>: **OBJECT** [Enter]

Example 3   *General*

Set up four layers with the following linetypes and colors. Then make the drawing (without dimensions) as shown in Figure 3-25.

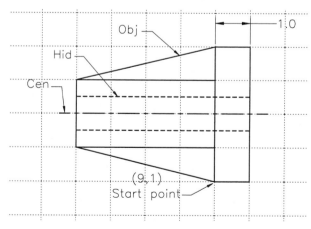

Figure 3-25 Drawing for Example 3

Layer name	Color	Linetype
Obj	Red	Continuous
Hid	Yellow	Hidden

Chapter 3

Cen	Green	Center
Dim	Blue	Continuous

In this example, assume that the limits and units are already set. Before drawing the lines, you need to create layers and assign colors and linetypes to these layers. Also, depending on the objects that you want to draw, you need to set that layer as current. In this exercise you will create the layers using the **Layer Properties Manager** dialog box and the **LAYER** command.

Using the dialog box

1. Choose the **Layers** button in the **Object Properties** toolbar to display the **Layer Properties Manager** dialog box. The default layer 0 with default properties is displayed in the list box.

2. Choose the **New** button. AutoCAD automatically creates a new layer (Layer1) having the default properties and displays it in the list box. Change its name by entering OBJ in place of Layer1.

3. Now choose the color icon to display the **Select Color** dialog box. Select color Red and then choose **OK**. Red color is assigned to layer **Obj**.

Using the command prompt

4. Now, use the **-LAYER** command to create the layer **Hid** and then assign to it the hidden linetype and yellow color.

   Command: **-LAYER** [Enter]
   Enter an option
   [?/Make/Set/New/ON/OFF/Color/Ltype/Lweight/Plot/Freeze/Thaw/LOck/Unlock]: **N** [Enter]
   Enter name list for new layer(s) name: **Hid** [Enter]
   Enter an option
   [?/Make/Set/New/ON/OFF/Color/Ltype/Lweight/Plot/Freeze/Thaw/LOck/Unlock]: **C** [Enter]
   Enter color name or number (1-255): **Yellow** or **Y** [Enter]
   Enter name list of layer(s) for color 2 (yellow) <0>: **Hid** [Enter]
   Enter an option
   [?/Make/Set/New/ON/OFF/Color/Ltype/Lweight/Plot/Freeze/Thaw/LOck/Unlock]: **L** [Enter]
   Enter loaded linetype name or [?] <CONTINUOUS>: **Hidden** [Enter]
   Enter name list for of layer(s) for linetype "HIDDEN" <0>: **Hid** [Enter]
   Enter an option
   [?/Make/Set/New/ON/OFF/Color/Ltype/Lweight/Plot/Freeze/Thaw/LOck/Unlock]: [Enter]

5. You can create the other two layers (CEN and DIM) using either the dialog box or the command prompt.

6. Enter **LAYER** at the Command prompt to invoke the **Layer Properties Manager** dialog box. Select **Obj** layer and then choose the **Current** button to make the **Obj** layer current. Choose the **OK** button to exit the dialog box.

7. Using the **LINE** command, draw the object lines in layer **Obj**.

Command: **LINE** [Enter]
Specify first point: **9,1** [Enter]
Specify next point or [Undo]: **9,9** [Enter]
Specify next point or [Undo]: **11,9** [Enter]
Specify next point or [Close/Undo]: **11,1** [Enter]
Specify next point or [Close/Undo]: **9,1** [Enter]
Specify next point or [Close/Undo]: **1,3** [Enter]
Specify next point or [Close/Undo]: **1,7** [Enter]
Specify next point or [Close/Undo]: **9,9** [Enter]
Specify next point or [Close/Undo]: [Enter]

Command: **LINE** [Enter]
Specify first point: **1,3** [Enter]
Specify next point or [Undo]: **9,3** [Enter]
Specify next point or [Undo]: [Enter]

Command: **LINE** [Enter]
Specify first point: **1,7** [Enter]
Specify next point or [Undo]: **9,7** [Enter]
Specify next point or [Undo]: [Enter]

8. Now, make the **Hid** layer current using the Command prompt and then draw the hidden lines of the drawing in the Hid layer.

Command: **-LAYER** [Enter]
Enter an option
[?/Make/Set/New/ON/OFF/Color/Ltype/Lweight/Plot/Freeze/Thaw/LOck/Unlock]: **S** [Enter]
Enter layer name to make current <OBJ>: **Hid** [Enter]
Enter an option
[?/Make/Set/New/ON/OFF/Color/Ltype/Lweight/Plot/Freeze/Thaw/LOck/Unlock]: [Enter]

Command: **LINE** [Enter]
Specify first point: **1,4** [Enter]
Specify next point or [Undo]: **11,4** [Enter]
Specify next point or [Undo]: [Enter]

Command: **LINE** [Enter]
Specify first point: **1,6** [Enter]
Specify next point or [Undo]: **11,6** [Enter]
Specify next point or [Undo]: [Enter]

9. Enter **LAYER** at the Command prompt or select **Layer** in **Format** menu to invoke the **Layer Properties Manager** dialog box. Select Cen layer and then choose the **Current** button to make the Cen layer current. Choose the **OK** button to exit the dialog box.

Command: **LINE** [Enter]
Specify first point: **0,5** [Enter]

Specify next point or [Undo]: **12,5** `Enter`
Specify next point or [Undo]: `Enter`

Exercise 2   *Mechanical*

Set up layers with the following linetypes and colors. Then make the drawing (without dimensions) as shown in Figure 3-26. The distance between the dotted lines is 1 unit.

Figure 3-26 Drawing for Exercise 2

Layer name	Color	Linetype
Object	Red	Continuous
Hidden	Yellow	Hidden
Center	Green	Center
Dimension	Blue	Continuous

DRAFTING SETTINGS DIALOG BOX*

Menu:	Tools > Drafting Settings...
Command:	DSETTINGS

You can use the **Drafting Settings** dialog box to set drawing modes such as Grid, Snap, Solid fill, Object Snap and Polar and Object Snap tracking. You can also right click on **Snap**, **Otrack**, **Grid**, **Polar** or **Otrack** buttons on the Status bar to display a shortcut menu and select **Settings...** to display the **Drafting Settings** dialog box. This dialog box operates under three main tabs: **Snap and Grid, Object Snap** and **Polar Tracking**. In the **Drafting Settings** dialog box (Figure 3-28), the Grid and Snap can be turned on or off by selecting their **Snap On** or **Grid On** check boxes. You can set the grid or snap spacing by entering either the same or different values in their respective **Snap / Grid X Spacing** and **Snap/Grid Y Spacing** edit boxes. When you exit the grid or snap X spacing edit boxes, the correspond-

*Figure 3-27 Selecting **Drafting Setting** from the **Tools** menu*

Figure 3-28 Drafting Settings dialog box

ing Y Spacing value is automatically set to match the X spacing value. Therefore, if you want different X and Y spacing values, you need to set the X spacing first, then set the Y spacing.

Setting Grid

The grid lines are lines of dots on the screen at predefined spacing (Figure 3-29). These dotted

Figure 3-29 Grid lines

lines act as a graph that can be used as reference lines in a drawing. You can change the distance between the grid dots as per your requirement. The grid pattern appears within the drawing limits, which helps to define the working area. The grid also gives you a sense of the size of the drawing objects.

Grid On (F7): Turning the Grid On or Off. You can turn the grid on/off and change the grid spacing in the **Drafting Settings** dialog box (Figure 3-28). You can also turn grid on or off by choosing the **Grid** button in the status bar (Figure 3-39). When a grid is turned on after having been off, the grid is set to the previous grid spacing. The function key F7 acts as a toggle key for turning the grid on or off.

Grid X Spacing and Grid Y Spacing. The Grid X Spacing and Grid Y Spacing edit boxes are used to define a desired grid spacing along the X and Y axis. For example, to set the grid spacing to 0.5 units, enter 0.5 in the X Spacing and Y Spacing edit boxes (Figure 3-30). You can also enter different values for horizontal and vertical grid spacing (Figure 3-31).

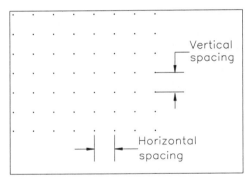

Figure 3-30 Controlling grid spacing

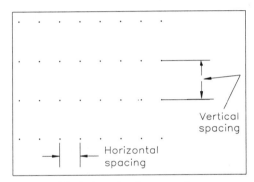

Figure 3-31 Using the Aspect option to create unequal grid spacing

You can also use the **GRID** command to set the grid. The following is the prompt sequence for the **GRID** command:

Command: **GRID** [Enter]
Specify grid spacing (X) or [ON/OFF/Snap/Aspect/Type] <0>: **0.5** [Enter]

The Aspect option is used to assign a different value to the horizontal and vertical grid spacing. The rid and the snap grid (discussed in the next section) are independent of each other. However, you can automatically display the grid lines at the same resolution as that of the Snap grid by using the **Snap** option. When you use this option, AutoCAD will automatically change the grid spacing to zero and display the grid lines at the same resolution as set for Snap.

Note
*In the **GRID** command, to specify the grid spacing as a multiple of the Snap spacing, enter X after the value (2X). In the **Drafting Settings** dialog box if the grid spacing is specified as zero, it automatically adjusts to equal the Snap resolution.*

Setting Snap

The snap is used to set increments for cursor movement. While moving the cursor it is sometimes difficult to position a point accurately. The **SNAP** command allows you to set up an invisible grid (Figure 3-32) that allows the cursor to move in fixed increments from one snap point to another. The snap points are the points where the invisible snap lines intersect. The snap spacing is independent of the grid spacing, so the two can have equal or different values. You generally set snap to an increment of the grid setting, for example, Snap=2 and Grid=10.

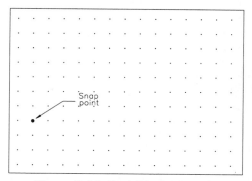

Figure 3-32 Invisible Snap grid

On: Turning the Snap On or Off. You can turn the snap on/off and set the snap spacing from the **Drafting Settings** dialog box (Figure 3-28). As in the case of GRID, the Snap On/Off selection turns the invisible snap grid on or off and moves the cursor by increments. If the SNAP is off, the cursor will not move by increments. It will move freely as you move the pointing device. When you turn the snap off, AutoCAD remembers the value of the snap, and this value is restored when you turn the snap back on. You can also turn snap on or off by choosing the **Snap** button in the status bar (Figure 3-39) or using the function key F9 as a toggle key for turning snap on or off.

Snap Angle. The **Angle:** edit box is used to rotate the snap grid through an angle (Figure 3-33). Normally, the snap grid has horizontal and vertical lines, but sometimes you need the snap grid at an angle. For example, when you are drawing an auxiliary view (a drawing view that is at an angle to other views of the drawing), it is more useful to have the snap grid at an angle. If the rotation angle is positive, the grid rotates in a counterclockwise direction; if the rotation angle is negative, it rotates in a clockwise direction.

Figure 3-33 Snap grid rotated 30 degrees

X Base and Y Base. The X Base and Y Base edit boxes can be used to define the snap and grid origin point in the current viewport relative to current UCS. The value is stored in the **SNAPBASE** system variable.

You can also use the **SNAP** command to set the snap. The following is the Command prompt sequence for the **SNAP** command:

Command: **SNAP** [Enter]
Specify snap spacing or [ON/OFF/Aspect/Rotate/Style/Type] <current>: **A** [Enter]
Specify horizontal spacing <current>: **0.5** [Enter]
Specify vertical spacing <current>: **1** [Enter]

Command: **SNAP** ⏎
Specify snap spacing or [ON/OFF/Aspect/Rotate/Style/Type] <current>: **R** ⏎
Specify base point <0,0>: **2,2** ⏎ (New base point.)
Specify rotation angle <0>: **30** ⏎

Note
It is generally preferable to rotate the UCS rather than rotating the snap grid. See Chapter 20.

Isometric Snap/Grid

You can choose the **Isometric snap** radio button to set the snap grid to isometric mode. The default is off (standard). The isometric mode is used to make isometric drawings. In isometric drawings, the isometric axes are at angles of 30, 90, and 150 degrees. The Isometric Snap/Grid enables you to display the grid lines along these axes (Figure 3-34). You can also use the **Style** option of the **SNAP** command to set the snap and grid to isometric mode.

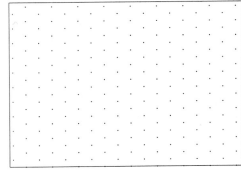

Figure 3-34 Isometric snap grid

Command: **SNAP** ⏎
Specify snap spacing or [ON/OFF/Aspect/
Rotate/Style/Type] <current>: **S** ⏎
Enter snap grid style [Standard/Isometric] <current>: **I** ⏎
Specify vertical spacing <current>: **1.5** ⏎

Once you set the isometric snap, AutoCAD automatically changes the cursor to align with the isometric axis. You can adjust the cursor orientation when you are working on the left, top, or right plane of the drawing by using the F5 key or holding down the CTRL key and then pressing the E key to cycle the cursor through different isometric planes (left, right, top).

Polar Spacing controls polar settings. The **Polar distance:** edit box, allows you to give a value to the Polar Snap. If this value is zero, it assumes the same value as the snap X spacing.

Snap Type and Style. There are two types of Snap Types, **Polar** snap and **Grid** snap. **Grid** snap snaps along the grid and is either of **Rectangular** style or **Isometric** style. **Polar** snap snaps along Polar alignment angles. These angles can be set in the **Polar Tracking** tab of the **Drafting Settings** dialog box. If you select the **Polar Snap** radio button in the **Snap Type and Style** area of the **Snap and Grid** tab of the **Drafting Settings** dialog box and if Polar or Object tracking is on, the cursor will snap along the set Polar tracking angles, relative to the last point selected or aquired. The snap type is also controlled by the **SNAPTYPE** system variable.

| **Example 4** | *General* |

Draw the auxiliary view of the object whose front view is shown in Figure 3-35. The thickness of the plate is 4 units; the length of the incline's face is 12 units. The following are the three different ways to draw the auxiliary view.

Figure 3-35 *Front view of the plate for Example 4*   **Figure 3-36** *Auxiliary view using rotated snap grid*

Rotating the Snap Grid

Command: **SNAP** `Enter`
Specify snap spacing or [ON/OFF/Aspect/Rotate/Style/Type] <current>: **R** `Enter`
Specify base point <current>: *Select point P0.*   *(Use Object snap.)*
Specify rotation angle <current>: **30** `Enter`
Command: **LINE** `Enter`
Specify first point: *Select point (P1).*
Specify next point or [Undo]: *Move the cursor 4 units right and select point (P2).*
Specify next point or [Undo]: *Move the cursor 10 units up and select point (P3).*
Specify next point or [Close/Undo]: *Move the cursor 4 units left and select point (P4).*
Specify next point or [Close/Undo]: **C** `Enter`

Using Polar Coordinates

Command: **LINE** `Enter`
Specify first point: *Select the starting point P1.*
Specify next point or [Undo]: **@4<30** `Enter`
Specify next point or [Undo]: **@10<120** `Enter`
Specify next point or [Close/Undo]: **@4<210** `Enter`
Specify next point or [Close/Undo]: **C** `Enter`

Note that the angle measurements do not change even though you have rotated the snap. The angle is still measured with reference to the positive X axis.

Rotating UCS Icon

When you rotate the UCS by 30 degrees, the X axis and Y axis also rotate through the same angle and the **UCSICON** will automatically align with the rotated snap grid (See Figure 3-36). (See the **UCS** command for a detailed explanation.)

Command: **UCS** `Enter`
Current UCS name:*WORLD*
Enter an option [New/Move/orthoGraphic/Prev/Restore/Save/Del/Apply/?/
World]<World>:**N** `Enter`

Specify origin of new UCS or [ZAxis/3Point/OBject/Face/View/X/Y/Z]<0,0,0>:**Z**
Specify rotation angle about Z axis <0>: **30** [Enter]

Command: **LINE** [Enter]
Specify first point: *Select the starting point P1.*
Specify next point or [Undo]: **@4<0** [Enter]
Specify next point or [Undo]: **@10<90** [Enter]
Specify next point or [Close/Undo]: **@4<180** [Enter]
Specify next point or [Close/Undo]: **C** [Enter]

Note that the angle measurements have changed to match the alignment of the rotated UCS.

Setting Ortho Mode

You can turn the Ortho mode on or off by choosing the **Ortho** button in the status bar (Figure 3-39). The **ORTHO** mode allows you to draw lines at right angles only. Whenever you are using the pointing device to specify the next point, the movement of the rubber-band line connected to the cursor is either horizontal (parallel to the X axis) or vertical (parallel to the Y axis). If you want to draw a line in the Ortho mode, specify the starting point at the **Specify first point:** prompt. To specify the second point, move the cursor with the pointing device and specify a desired point. The line drawn will be either vertical or horizontal, depending on the direction in which you moved the cursor (Figure 3-37 and Figure 3-38). You can also use the **ORTHO** command to turn the Ortho mode on or off. You can also use the function key F8 to turn the Ortho mode on or off.

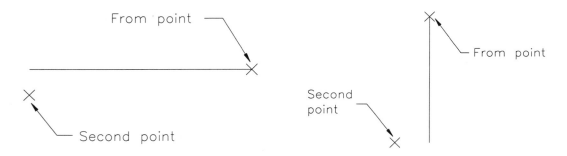

Figure 3-37 *Drawing a horizontal line using the Ortho mode*

Figure 3-38 *Drawing a vertical line using the Ortho mode*

Command: **ORTHO** [Enter]
Enter mode [ON/OFF] <current>: Enter *On or Off.*

STATUS LINE

When you are in AutoCAD, displayed is a status line at the bottom of the graphics screen (Figure 3-39). This line contains some useful information and tools that will make it easy to change the status of some AutoCAD functions. To change the status, you must choose the buttons. For example, if you want to display grid lines on the screen, choose the **GRID** button. Similarly, if you

Figure 3-39 Default Status line display

want to switch to paper space, choose **MODEL**. The status line contains the following information:

Coordinate Display. You can also use the function key F6 as a toggle key to turn the display of coordinates on or off. The **Coordinates** information displayed in the status line can be static or dynamic. The **COORDS** system variable controls the type of display of the coordinates. If the value of the **COORDS** variable is set to 0, the coordinate display is static, i.e., the coordinate values displayed in the status line change only when you specify a point . However, if the value of the **COORDS** variable is set to 1 or 2, coordinate display is dynamic (default setting), AutoCAD constantly displays the absolute coordinates of the graphics cursor with respect to the UCS origin. AutoCAD can also display the polar coordinates (length<angle) if you are in an AutoCAD command and the **COORDS** system variable is set to 2.

SNAP. If **Snap Mode** is on, the **SNAP** button is displayed as pressed in the status line; otherwise, it is not. You can also use the function key F9 as a toggle key to turn Snap off or on.

GRID. If **Grid Display** is on, grid lines are displayed on the screen. The function key F7 can also be used to turn on or off the grid display.

ORTHO. If **Ortho Mode** is on, the **ORTHO** button is displayed as pressed in the status line. You can use the F8 key to turn on or off the **Ortho Mode**.

POLAR*. Choosing the **POLAR** button in the Status line turns on the **Polar Tracking**. You can also use the function key F10. Turning the Polar Tracking on, automatically turns off the Ortho mode.

OSNAP. If **Object Snap** is on, the **OSNAP** button is displayed as pressed in the status line. You can also use the F3 key to turn the Object Snap on or off. When Object Snap is on, you can use the running object snaps. If OSNAP is off, the running Object Snaps are temporarily disabled. The status of OSNAP (Off or On) does not prevent you from using regular object snaps.

OTRACK. Choosing the **OTRACK** button, turns on **Object Snap Tracking**.

LWT. Choosing this button in the Staus line, allows you to **Show/Hide Lineweight**. If the **LWT** button is not pressed, the display of Lineweight is turned off.

MODEL and PAPER Space. AutoCAD displays MODEL in the status line when you are working in the model space. If you are working in the paper space, AutoCAD will display PAPER in place of MODEL.

OBJECT SNAPS

Toolbar:	Object Snap or
	Standard > Object Snap flyout

Object snaps are one of the most useful features of AutoCAD. They improve your performance and the accuracy of your drawing and make drafting much simpler than it normally would be. Object Snaps can also be invoked from the short-cut menu (Figure 3-40), which can be accessed by holding down the SHIFT key on the keyboard and then pressing the ENTER button on your pointing device. You can also invoke the different Object Snaps from the **Standard** toolbar by choosing the **Object Snap** button and holding the Pick button of your pointing device to display the flyout having the object snap buttons. The term OBJECT SNAP refers to the cursor's ability to snap exactly to a geometric point on an object. The advantage of using object snaps is that you do not have to specify an exact point. For example, if you want to place a point at the midpoint of a line, you may not be able to specify the exact point. Using the MIDpoint Object snap, all you do is move the cursor somewhere on the object. You will notice a marker (in the form of a geometric shape) is automatically displayed at the middle point (snap point). You can click to place a point at the position of the **marker**. You

Figure 3-40 *Selecting Object snap modes from the shortcut menu*

can also have a target box attached to the cursor when any object snap is invoked. The object snaps recognize only the objects that are visible on the screen, which include the objects on locked layers. The objects on layers that are turned off or frozen are not visible, so they cannot be used for object

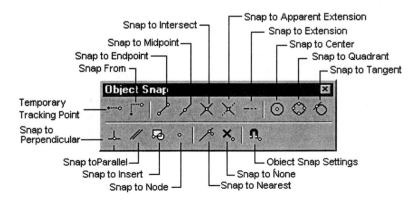

Figure 3-41 Object Snap *toolbar*

snaps. The following are the Object Snap modes available in AutoCAD:

NEArest	CENter	QUIck	TANgent
ENDpoint	QUAdrant	NONe	PERpendicular
MIDpoint	INTersection	INSertion	NODe
From	APParent Intersection	EXTension	PARallel

You can also invoke an Object snap by entering an abbreviation in the command line.

AutoSnap

Menu:	Tools > Options...
Command:	OPTIONS

The AutoSnap feature enables you to lock to geometric points of the objects. As you move the target box over the object, AutoCAD displays the geometric marker corresponding to the shapes shown in the **Object Snap** tab of the **Drafting Settings** dialog box. You can change the AutoSnap settings in the **Options** dialog box, under the **Drafting** tab. The **Options...** dialog box can be invoked from the **Tools** menu (**Tools > Options...**), or by entering **OPTIONS** at the Command prompt. When you choose the **Drafting** tab in the **Options** dialog box, the AutoSnap options are displayed (Figure 3-42). You can select the **Marker** check box to activate the marker. You can also

*Figure 3-42 **Drafting** tab of **Options** dialog box*

activate the Magnet and AutoSnap Tooltip by selecting their respective check boxes. The **AutoSnapTooltip** displays a flag that describes the name of the object snap that AutoCAD has detected. The **Magnet** automatically moves and locks to the closest snap point. Similarly, if you select the **Display AutoSnap Aperture box**, the target box is added to the screen crosshairs when you invoke an object snap. You can change the size of the marker by moving the **Marker Size** slider bar. You can also change the color of the markers through the **AutoSnap Marker Color:** list box. The size of the Aperture box can be changed by moving the Aperture size slider bar in the **Options** (**Drafting tab**) dialog box. The size of the aperture is measured in PIXELS, short for picture elements. Picture elements are dots that make up the screen picture. The aperture size can also be changed using the **APERTURE** command. In AutoCAD the default value for the aperture size is 10 pixels. The display of the Marker and the AutoSnapTooltip is controlled by the AUTOSNAP system variable. The default value of this variable is 7 and is saved with the drawing. The following are the bit values for AUTOSNAP:

Bit Values	Function
0	Turns off the Marker, AutoSnap Tooltip, and Magnet
1	Turns on the Marker
2	Turns on the AutoSnapTooltip
4.	Turns on the Magnet

NEArest

The **NEArest** Object Snap mode selects a point on an object (line, arc, circle, ellipse) that is visually closest to the graphics cursor (crosshairs). To use this mode, enter the command, then choose the NEArest object snap. Move the crosshairs near the intended point on the object so as to display the marker at the desired point and then select the object. AutoCAD will grab a point on the line where the marker was displayed. The following is the prompt sequence for drawing a line from a point on a line (Figure 3-43):

Command: **LINE** [Enter]
Specify first point: **NEA** [Enter]   *(NEArest object snap.)*
to *Select a point near an existing object.*
Specify next point or [Undo]: *Select endpoint of the line.*

ENDpoint

The **ENDpoint** Object Snap mode snaps to the closest endpoint of a line or an arc. To use this Object Snap mode, select or enter the ENDpoint, move the cursor (crosshairs) anywhere close to the endpoint of the object. The marker will be displayed at the endpoint, and then click to specify that point. AutoCAD will grab the endpoint of the object. If there are several objects near the cursor crosshairs, AutoCAD will grab the endpoint of the object that is closest to the crosshairs. The following is the prompt sequence for drawing a line from the endpoint of a line (Figure 3-44):

Command: **LINE** [Enter]
Specify first point: **END** [Enter]   *(ENDpoint object snap.)*
of *Move the target box and select the line.*
Specify next point or [Undo]: *Select the endpoint of the line.*

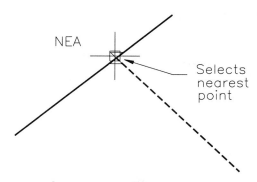

Figure 3-43 NEArest Object Snap mode

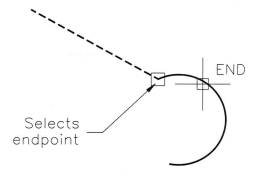

Figure 3-44 ENDpoint Object Snap mode

MIDpoint

The **MIDpoint** Object Snap mode snaps to the midpoint of a line or an arc. To use this object snap mode, select or enter MIDpoint and select the object anywhere. AutoCAD will grab the midpoint of the object. The following is the prompt sequence for drawing a line to the midpoint of a line (Figure 3-45):

Command: **LINE** [Enter]
Specify first point: *Select the starting point of the line.*
Specify next point or [Undo]: **MID** [Enter]   *(MIDpoint object snap.)*
of *Move the cursor and select the original line.*

TANgent

The **TANgent** object snap allows you to draw a tangent to or from an existing ellipse, circle, or arc. To use this object snap, the cursor should be placed on the circumference of the circle or arc to select it. The following is the prompt sequence for drawing a line tangent to a circle (Figure 3-46):

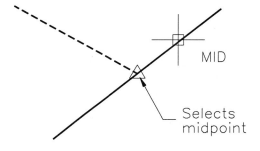

Figure 3-45 MIDpoint object snap mode

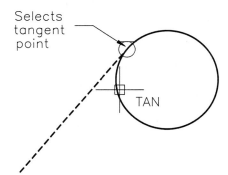

Figure 3-46 TANgent object snap mode

Command: **LINE** Enter
Specify first point: *Select the starting point of the line.*
Specify next point or [Undo]: **TAN** Enter   *(TANgent object snap).*
to *Move the cursor and select the circle.*

The Figure 3-47, shows the use of NEArest, ENDpoint, MIDpoint, and TANgent object snaps.

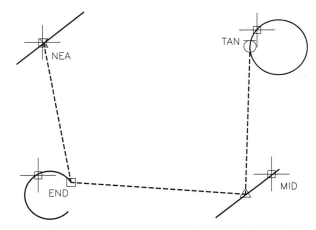

*Figure 3-47 Using NEArest, ENDpoint, MIDpoint, and TANgent
object snaps*

CENter

 The CENter Object Snap mode allows
you to snap to the center point of a ellipse, circle, or an arc. After selecting
this option, you must point to the visible part of the circumference of a circle or arc.
The following is the prompt sequence for drawing a line from the center of a circle
(Figure 3-48):

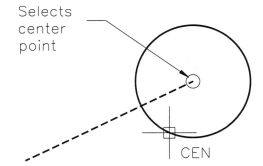

Command: **LINE** Enter
Specify first point: **CEN** Enter   *(CENter
object snap.)*

Figure 3-48 CENter object snap mode

of *Move the cursor and select the circle.*
Specify next point or [Undo]: *Select the endpoint of the line.*

INTersection

 The INTersection Object Snap mode is used if you need to snap to a point where two or
more lines, circles, ellipses or arcs intersect. To use this object snap, move the cursor close
to the desired intersection so that the intersection is within the target box, and then specify
that point. The following is the prompt sequence for drawing a line from an intersection

(Figure 3-49):

> Command: **LINE** [Enter]
> Specify first point: **INT** [Enter]   *(INTersection object snap.)*
> of *Position the cursor near the intersection and select it.*
> Specify next point or [Undo]: *Select the endpoint of the line.*

If you select only one object with INTersection object snap, AutoCAD prompts **and** for selection of another object.

QUAdrant

The **QUAdrant** Object Snap mode is used when you need to snap to a quadrant point of an ellipse, arc, or circle. A circle has four quadrants, and each quadrant subtends an angle of 90 degrees. The quadrant points are located at 0-, 90-, 180-, 270-degree positions. If the circle is inserted as a block (see Chapter 12), that is rotated, the quadrant points are also rotated by the same amount. To use this object snap, position the cursor on the circle or arc closest to the desired quadrant. The prompt sequence for drawing a line from the third quadrant of a circle (Figures 3-50,3-51,3-52) is:

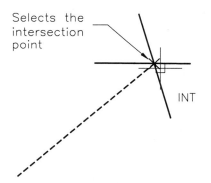

Figure 3-49 *INTersection Object Snap mode*

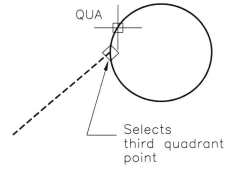

Figure 3-50 *QUAdrant Object Snap mode*

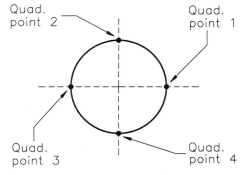

Figure 3-51 *QUAdrant Object Snap mode*

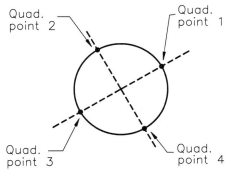

Figure 3-52 *Four quadrants of a circle*

Command: **LINE** ⏎
Specify first point: **QUA** ⏎   *(QUAdrant object snap.)*
of *Move the cursor close to the third quadrant of the circle and select it.*
Specify next point or [Undo]: *Select the endpoint of the line.*

PERpendicular

The **PERpendicular** Object Snap mode is used to draw a line perpendicular to or from another line, or normal to or from an arc or circle, or to an ellipse. When you use this mode and select an object, AutoCAD calculates the point on the selected object so that the previously selected point is perpendicular to the line. The object can be selected by positioning the cursor anywhere on the line. The following is the prompt sequence for drawing a line that is perpendicular to a given line (Figure 3-53):

Command: **LINE**   ⏎
Specify first point: *Select the starting point of the line.*
Specify next point or [Undo]: **PER** ⏎   *(PERpendicular object snap.)*
to   *Select the line on which you want to draw perpendicular.*

When you select the line first, the rubber-band feature of the line is disabled. The line will appear only after the second point is selected. The prompt sequence for drawing a line perpendicular from a given line (Figure 3-54) is:

Command: **LINE** ⏎
Specify first point: **PER** ⏎   *(PERpendicular object snap.)*
to   *Select the line on which you want to draw perpendicular.*
Specify next point or [Undo]: *Select the endpoint of the line.*

The Figure 3-55, shows the use of the CENter, INTersection, and PERpendicular Object Snaps.

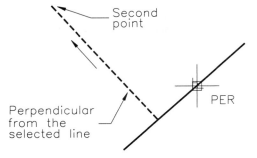

Figure 3-53 *Selecting the start point, then the perpendicular snap.*

Figure 3-54 *Selecting the perpendicular snap first*

Figure 3-55 *Using CENter, Intersection, and PERpendicular Object Snap modes*

Exercise 3 *Graphics*

In Figure 3-56, P1 and P2 are the center points of the top and bottom arcs. The space between the dotted lines is 1 unit.

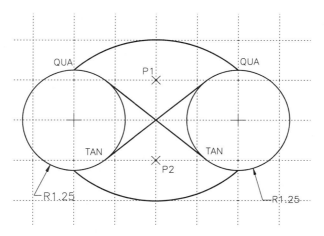

Figure 3-56 *Drawing for Exercise 3*

QUIck

If you are using an object snap when several objects cross the cursor, AutoCAD normally searches all objects for the specified Object Snap mode and selects the closest point. Depending on your hardware setup, this will cause a delay in searching for the specified point. The **QUIck** option stops searching as soon as AutoCAD finds the first object that has a point on the object qualifying for the specified object snap. With QUick mode, the point depends on the order in which the selected objects are found. You can use the QUIck option with any object snap mode. Only when the intersection snap is on, Quick is ignored and a full search for the specified point is carried out. The following is the prompt sequence for using the QUIck and MIDpoint Object Snap modes:

Command: **LINE** Enter
Specify first point: *Select the starting point of the line.*
Specify next point or [Undo]: **QUI, MID** Enter   *(QUIck and MIDpoint object snaps.)*
of *Select the line.*

NODe

The **NODe** object snap can be used to snap to a point object drawn, using the **POINT** command or placed while using the **DIVIDE** or **MEASURE** commands. In Figure 3-57, three points have been drawn using the AutoCAD **POINT** command. You can snap to these points by using NODe Snap mode, as shown on the following example, Figure 3-58:

Command: **LINE** Enter
Specify first point: **NOD** Enter   *(NODe object snap.)*
of *Select point P1.*
Specify next point or [Undo]: **NOD** Enter
of *Select point P2.*
Specify next point or [Undo]: NOD Enter
of *Select point P3.*

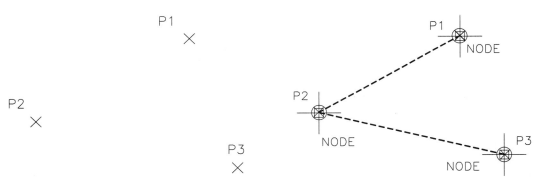

Figure 3-57 Point objects   **Figure3-58** *Using NODe object snap*

INSertion

The **INSertion** Object Snap mode is used to snap to the insertion point of a text, shape, block, attribute, or attribute definition. In Figure 3-59, the text **WELCOME** is left-justified and the text **AutoCAD** is center-justified. The point with respect to which the text is justified is the insertion point of that text string. If you want to snap to these insertion points or the insertion point of a block, you must use the INSertion Object Snap mode as shown in the following prompt sequence:

Command: **LINE** [Enter]
Specify first point: **INS** [Enter]   *(INSert object snap.)*
of *Select WELCOME text.*
Specify next point or [Undo]: **INS** [Enter]
of *Select the block.*
Specify next point or [Undo]: **INS** [Enter]
of *Select AutoCAD text.*

Figure 3-59 INSertion Object Snap mode

NONe

The **NONe** Object Snap mode turns off any running object snap (see the section "Running Object Snap Mode" that follows.) for one point. The following example illustrates the use of this Object Snap mode:

Command: **-OSNAP** [Enter]
Enter list of object snap modes: **MID, CEN**

This sets the object snaps to Mid and Cen. You can disable those using the None object snap.

Command: **LINE** [Enter]
Specify first point: *Specify a point.*
Specify next point or [Undo]: **NONe** [Enter]   *(Turns off the running object snap and allows you to select any point.)*

Once you have selected a point it continues the command with the specified object snaps.

APParent Intersection

The **APParent Intersection** Object Snap mode is similar to the INTersection Snap Mode, except that this mode selects projected or visual intersections of lines, arcs, circles, or ellipses (see Figure 3-60 and Figure 3-61). The projected intersections are those intersections that are not present on the screen, but are imaginary ones that can be formed if line, or arcs are extended. Sometimes two objects appear to intersect one another in the current view, but in 3D space the two objects do not actually intersect. The APParent Intersection snap mode also selects such visual intersections. The prompt sequence is:

Command: **LINE** [Enter]
From point: **APP**   *(APParent Intersection object snap.)*
of *Select first object.*
and *Select second object.*
To point: *Select the endpoint of the line.*

Chapter 3

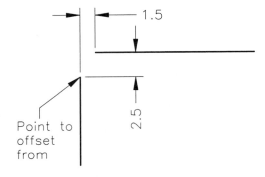

Figure 3-60 *Using the APParent Intersection snap mode*

Figure 3-61 *Using the APParent Intersection snap mode*

From

The **From** object snap can be used to locate a point relative to a given point (Figure 3-62). For example, if you want to locate a point that is 2.5 units up and 1.5 units right from the endpoint of a given line, you can use the From object snap as follows:

Command: **LINE**
Specify first point: **From**   *(or select Snap From from the **Object Snap** toolbar.)*
_from Base point: **End**   *(or select Snap to Endpoint from the **Object Snap** toolbar and specify the endpoint of the given line.).*
of <Offset>: **@1.5,2.5**

Figure 3-62 *Using the From object snap to locate a point*

Note
The From object snap cannot be used as running object snap.

PARallel*

When you need to draw a line parallel to an object on the screen, you can use the **PARallel** object snap (see Figure 3-63). For example, when you are in the middle of the line command, and you have to draw a line parallel to the one already on screen, you can use the **PARallel** object snap as follows:

Command: **LINE**   *(or choose **Line** from the **Draw** toolbar)*
Specify first point: *(Select a point on the screen.)*
Specify next point or [Undo]: PAR   *(or choose **Snap to Parallel** from the **Object Snap** toolbar)*
to   *(Specify object to which parallel is to be drawn)*

Briefly pause on the line you want to use; a mark appears on it to indicate that it has been selected. Now on moving the cursor, close to an angle parallel to the object; a parallel line symbol appears on the selected object. Select the next point. This line which has been drawn is parallel to the selected object.

EXTension*

EXTension gives you an option to locate a point on the extension path of a line or an arc (Figure 3-64). This object snap can be used to extend a line or an arc. It can also be used with INTersection or APParent Intersection to determine the point of extended intersection. To use extension, choose **Line** from the **Draw** toolbar and then choose **Snap to Extension** from the **Object Snap** toolbar. Briefly pause at the end of the line or arc you want to use. A small plus sign (+) appears at the end of the line or arc, indicating that it has been selected. Moving the cursor along the extension path, displays a temporary extension path and the tooltip displays relative polar coordinates from the end of the line. Select a point or enter a distance to begin a line and then select another point to finish the line.

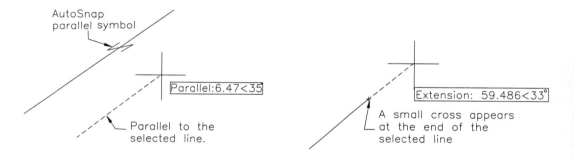

Figure 3-63 Using the Parallel object snap to draw a line parallel to a selected line

Figure 3-64 Using the Extension object snap mode

Combining Object Snap Modes

You can also combine the snaps by separating the snap modes with a comma. AutoCAD will search for the specified modes and grab the point on the object that is closest to the point where the object is selected. The prompt sequence for using the MIDpoint and ENDpoint object snaps is:

Command: **LINE** [Enter]
Specify first point: **MID, END** [Enter]   *(MIDpoint or ENDpoint object snap.)*
to   *Select the object.*

In this example, we have defined two object snap modes, MIDpoint and ENDpoint. The point that it will grab depends on where you select the line. If you select the line at a point that is closer to the midpoint of the line, AutoCAD will snap to the midpoint (Figure 3-65). If you select the line closer to the endpoint of the line, the line will snap to the endpoint of the line (Figure 3-66).

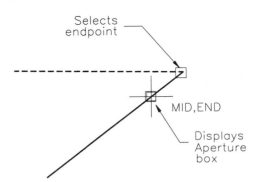

Figure 3-65 *Using MIDpoint, ENDpoint snaps (Selecting midpoint)*

Figure 3-66 *Using MIDpoint, ENDpoint snaps (Selecting endpoint)*

Cycling Through Snaps and Keyboard Entry Priority

AutoCAD displays the geometric marker corresponding to the shapes shown in the **Object snap settings** tab of **Drafting Settings** dialog box. You can use the TAB key to cycle through the snaps. For example, if you have a circle with an intersecting rectangle as shown in Figure 3-67 and you want to snap to one of the geometric points on the circle, you can use the TAB key to cycle through the geometric points. The geometric points for circle are center point, quadrant points, and in this example, the intersection points of the rectangle and circle. To snap to one of these points, the first thing you need to do is to set the snaps (center, quadrant, and intersection object snaps) in the **Drafting Settings** dialog box. After entering a command, when you drag the cursor over the objects, AutoSnap displays a marker and a SnapTip. You can cycle through the snap points available for an object by pressing the TAB key. For example, if you press the TAB key while the aperture box is on the circle, AutoSnap will display the center, quadrant, and intersection points. By selecting a point you can snap to one of these points.

The **OSNAPCOORD** system variable determines the priority between the keyboard entry and object snap. You can also set this variable through the **User Preferences** tab of the **Options** dialog box. For example, if intersection object snap is on and OSNAPCOORD is set to 1 and you enter the coordinates of the endpoint of a line very close to the intersection point (Figure 3-68), the line

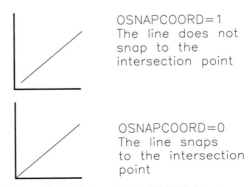

Figure 3-67 *Using TAB key to cycle through the snap*

Figure 3-68 *Using OSNAPCOORD system variable to set keyboard entry priority*

will not snap to the intersection point. If **OSNAPCOORD** is set to 0, the line will snap to the intersection point because running object snap has the priority.

Note
In the discussions of object snaps, "line" generally includes xlines, rays, and polyline segments, and "arc" generally includes polyarc segments.

Exercise 4   *General*

Make the drawing in Figure 3-69. The space between the dotted lines is 1 unit.

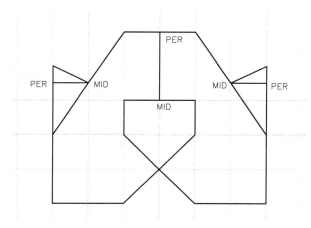

Figure 3-69 *Drawing for Exercise 4*

RUNNING OBJECT SNAP MODE

Toolbar:	Standard > Object Snap flyout, Object Snap > Object Snap Settings
Menu:	Tools > Drafting Settings...
Command:	OSNAP or DDOSNAP or DSETTINGS

In the previous sections you have learned how to use the object snaps to snap to different points of an object. One of the drawbacks of these object snaps is that you have to select them every time you use them, even if it is the same snap mode. This problem can be solved by using **running object snaps**. The Running Osnap can be invoked from the **Drafting Settings** dialog box. To invoke the **Drafting Settings** dialog box, choose **Drafting Settings...** from the **Tools** menu. You can also choose the **Object Snap Settings** button from the **Object Snap** toolbar or from the **Object snap** flyout in the **Standard** toolbar. Right-clicking on the **Osnap** button in the Status bar, displays a shortcut menu from which you can choose a setting to display the **Drafting Settings** dialog box. In the **Drafting Settings** dialog box, choose the **Object Snap** tab and set the running Object Snap modes by selecting the check boxes next to the snap modes. For example, if you want to set ENDpoint as the running object Snap mode, select the **ENDpoint** check box and then the **OK** button in the dialog box. You can also set it through the Command prompt:

Command: **-OSNAP** [Enter]
Current Osnap modes:
Enter list of object snap modes: **END** [Enter]

Once you set the running object snap mode, you are automatically in that mode and the marker is displayed when you move the crosshairs over the snap points. If you had selected a combination of modes, AutoCAD selects the mode that is closest to the screen crosshairs. The running object snap mode can be turned on or off, without losing the object snap settings, by choosing the **OSNAP** button in the Status bar located at the bottom of the screen. You can also accomplish this by pressing the function key F3 or CTRL+F keys. If no running osnaps are set, the **Drafting Settings** dialog box is displayed on choosing the **OSNAP** button in the Status bar (Figure 3-71).

Note
When you use a temporary object snap and fail to specify a suitable point, AutoCAD issues an Invalid point prompt and reissues the pending command's prompt. However, with a running object snap mode, if you fail to specify a suitable point, AutoCAD accepts the point specified without snapping to an object.

*Figure 3-70 Selecting **Drafting Settings** from the **Tools** menu.*

*Figure 3-71 **Drafting Settings** dialog box*

Overriding the Running Snap

When you select the running object snaps, all other object snap modes are ignored unless you select another object snap mode. Once you select a different osnap mode, the running OSNAP mode is temporarily overruled. After the operation has been performed, the running OSNAP mode goes into effect again. If you want to discontinue the current running object snap modes totally, choose the **Clear all** button in the **Drafting Settings** dialog box. If you want to temporarily disable the running object snap, choose the **Osnap** button in the status bar (Figure 3-39).

If you are overriding the running OSNAP modes for a point selection and no point is found to satisfy the override object snap mode, AutoCAD displays a message to this effect. For example, if you specify an override object snap mode of CENter and no circle, ellipse, or arc is found at that location, AutoCAD will display the message "No center found for specified point. Point or option keyword required."

FUNCTION AND CONTROL KEYS

You can also us the function and control keys to change the status of coordinate display, Snap, Ortho, Osnap, tablet, screen, isometric planes, running Object Snap, Grid, Polar and Object tracking. The following is a list of function and control keys.

F1	Help	F7	Grid On/Off **(Ctrl+G)**
F2	Graphics Screen/Text Window	F8	Ortho On/Off **(Ctrl+L)**
F3	Running Osnap On/Off **(Ctrl+F)**	F9	Snap On/Off **(Ctrl+B)**
F4	Tablet mode On/Off **(Ctrl+T)**	F10	Polar tracking On/Off
F5	Isoplane top/right/left **(Ctrl+E)**	F11	Object Snap tracking
F6	Coordinate display On/Off **(Ctrl+D)**		

USING AUTOTRACKING*

When using AutoTracking, the cursor moves along temporary paths to locate key points in a drawing. It can be used to locate points with respect to other points or objects in the drawing. There are two types of AutoTracking options: **Polar** and **Object Snap Tracking**. Polar Tracking can be selected by choosing the **POLAR** button in the Status bar, by using the function key F10 or by selecting the **Polar Tracking On** check box in the **Polar Tracking** tab of the **Drafting Settings** dialog box (Figure 3-72). Polar Tracking constrains the movement of the cursor along a path that is based on the Polar Angle Settings.For example, if the **Increment Angle:** edit box value is set to 5 degrees in the **Polar Angle Settings** area of the **Polar Tracking** tab of the **Drafting Settings** dialog box, the cursor will move along alignment paths that are multiples of 5 degrees and a tooltip will display a distance and angle. Selecting the **Additional angles** check box and choosing the **New** button allows you to add a new increment angle value in the **Increment Angle:** drop-down list. Polar Tracking is on only when the Ortho mode is off. Similarly, Object Snap Tracking tracks the movement of the cursor along alignment paths based on Object Snap points which are selected in the **Object Snap** tab of the **Drafting Settings** dialog box. Selecting the **Object Snap Tracking On** check box in the **Object Snap** tab of the **Drafting Settings** dialog box, choosing the **OTRACK** button in the status bar or using the function key F11 sets the Object Snap tracking on.

The direction of the path is determined by the motion of the cursor or the point you select on an object. For example, if you want to draw a circle whose center is located in line with the center of

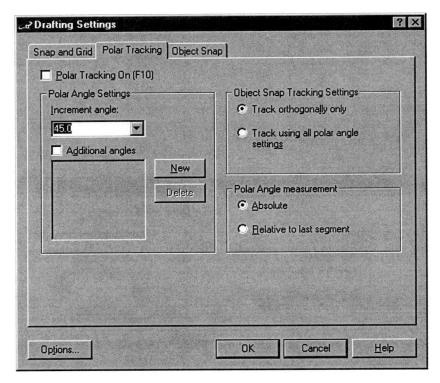

*Figure 3-72 **Polar Tracking** tab of the **Drafting Settings** dialog box*

two existing circles, you can use Autotracking as follows:

Command: **CIRCLE**
Specify center point for Circle or [3P/2P/Ttr (tan, tan, radius)]: TK   *(or choose the OTRACK button in the Status bar, after setting the running center object snap)*
First tracking point: CEN   *(or Pause the cursor briefly at the center of the first circle to attain the point and then move it along the horizontal alignment path.)*
Next point (Press ENTER to end tracking) :Cen   *(or Place the cursor briefly at the center of the second circle and then move it along the vertical alignment path.)*
Next point (Press ENTER to end tracking):Enter   *(Select the intersection of the two alignment paths)*
Specify radius of Circle or [Diameter] <current>: Enter radius or specify a point.

Similarly, you can use Autotracking in combination with the midpoint object snap to locate the center of the rectangle and then draw a circle (Figure 3-73 and Figure 3-74).

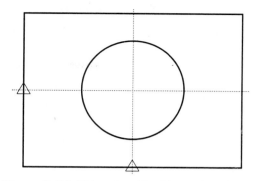

Figure 3-73 *Using AutoTracking to locate a point (Center of circle)*

Figure 3-74 *Using AutoTracking to locate a point (MIDpoint of rectangle)*

GLOBAL AND CURRENT LINETYPE SCALING

The LTSCALE system variable controls the global scale factor of the lines in a drawing. For example, if LTSCALE is set to 2, all lines in the drawing will be affected by a factor of 2. Like LTSCALE, the **CELTSCALE** system variable controls the linetype scaling. The difference is that CELTSCALE determines the current linetype scaling. For example, if you set CELTSCALE to 0.5, all lines drawn after setting the new value for CELTSCALE will have the linetype scaling factor of 0.5. The value is retained in the CELTSCALE system variable. Line (a) in Figure 3-75 is drawn with a CELTSCALE factor of 1; line (b) is drawn with a CELTSCALE factor of 0.5. The length of the dash is reduced by a factor of 0.5 when

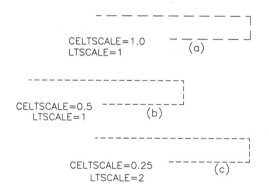

Figure 3-75 *Using **CELTSCALE** to control current linetype scaling*

CELTSCALE is 0.5. The net scale factor is equal to the product of CELTSCALE and LTSCALE. Figure 3-75(c) shows a line that is drawn with LTSCALE of 2 and CELTSCALE of 0.25. The net scale factor = LTSCALE x CELTSCALE = 2 x 0.25 = 0.5. You can also change the global and current scale factors by choosing the **Linetype** tab of **Layer and Linetype Properties** dialog box (Figure 3-76). If you choose the **Detail>>** button, the properties associated with the selected linetype are displayed. You can change the values according to your drawing requirements.

Chapter 3

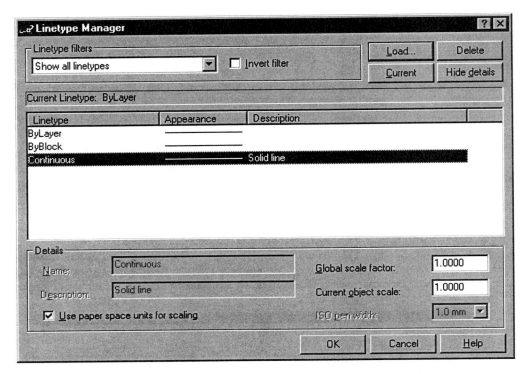

*Figure 3-76 The **Linetype** tab of **Linetype Manager** dialog box*

LTSCALE FACTOR FOR PLOTTING

The **LTSCALE** factor for plotting depends on the size of the sheet you are using to plot the drawing. For example, if the limits are 48 by 36, the drawing scale is 1:1, and you want to plot the drawing on a 48" by 36" size sheet, then the **LTSCALE** factor is 1. If you check the specification of the Hidden linetype in the **ACAD.LIN** file, the length of each dash is 0.25. Hence, when you plot a drawing with 1:1 scale, the length of each dash in a hidden line is 0.25.

However, if the drawing scale is 1/8" = 1' and you want to plot the drawing on 48" by 36" paper, the **LTSCALE** factor must 8 x 12 = 96. The length of each dash in the hidden line will increase by a factor of 96, because the **LTSCALE** factor is 96. Therefore, the length of each dash will be (0.25 x 96 = 24) units. At the time of plotting, the scale factor for plotting must be 1:96 to plot the 384' by 288' drawing on 48" by 36" paper. Each dash of the hidden line that was 24" long on the drawing will be 24/96 = 0.25" long when plotted. Similarly, if the desired text size on the paper is 1/8", the text height in the drawing must be 1/8 x 96 = 12".

Ltscale Factor for PLOTTING = Drawing Scale

Sometimes your plotter may not be able to plot a 48" by 36" drawing, or you might like to decrease the size of the plot so that the drawing fits within a specified area. To get the correct dash lengths for hidden, center, or other lines, you must adjust the **LTSCALE** factor. For example, if you want to plot the previously mentioned drawing in a 45" by 34" area, the correction factor is:

Correctionfactor $= 48/45$

                     $= 1.0666$

New LTSCALE factor $=$ **LTSCALE** factor x Correction factor

                          $= 96$ x 1.0666

                          $= 102.4$

New Ltscale Factor for PLOTTING = Drawing Scale x Correction Factor

Note

If you change the LTSCALE factor, all lines in the drawing are affected by the new ratio.

Changing Linetyype Scale Using the PROPERTIES Command*

You can also change the current linetype scale by using the **PROPERTIES** command.

Toolbar:	Object Properties > Properties
Menu:	Modify > Properties
Command:	PROPERTIES

When you choose this command, AutoCAD will display the **Properties** dialog box, Figure 3-77. All properties of the selected objects are displayed in the **Object Properties** window. To change the current linetype scale, select the objects and then invoke the **PROPERTIES** command to display the **Object Properties** window (Figure 3-78). In this dialog box, select the **Categorized** tab and locate the Linetype scale edit box. Enter the new linetype scale and then close the dialog box. The linetype scale of the selected objects is changed to the new value you entered.

*Figure 3-77 Selecting Properties from the **Object Properties** toolbar*

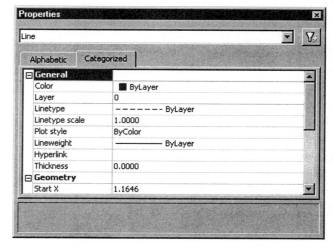

*Figure 3-78 **Properties** dialog box (**Categorized** tab)*

Self Evaluation Test

Answer the following questions and then compare your answers to the correct answers given at the end of this chapter.

1. In the default mode, the measurement of angles always starts with 90 degrees corresponding to north. (T/F)

2. The layers that are turned on are displayed on the screen and cannot be plotted. (T/F)

3. The TANgent Object Snap mode allows you to draw a tangent to or from an existing line. (T/F)

4. You can combine object snaps by separating the snap modes with a comma. (T/F)

5. The INSertion object snap mode is used to snap to the insertion point of a block only. (T/F)

6. In Surveyor's units you are required to specify the bearing angle the line makes with the _____ .

7. The layers are, by default, assigned _____ linetype and white color.

8. You can display the grid lines at the same resolution as that of the Snap by using the _____ .

9. The _____ object snap can be used to snap to a point object.

10. You can also load and display the **Layer Properties Manager** dialog box by entering _____ at the Command prompt.

Review Questions

1. You can use the decimal units mode for metric units as well as decimal English units. (T/F)

2. You cannot use the feet (') or inch (") symbols if you have selected the Scientific, Decimal, or Fractional unit format. (T/F)

3. If you select Decimal, Degrees/minutes/seconds, Grads, or Radians, you can enter an angle in any of the five measuring systems. (T/F)

4. Assigning a color to a group of objects is very important for plotting. (T/F)

5. You can lock a layer, which will prevent the user from accidentally editing the objects in that layer. (T/F)

6. The Set option of the **-LAYER** command allows you to create a new layer and simultaneously make it the current layer. (T/F)

7. When a layer is locked, you cannot use the objects in the locked layer for Osnaps. (T/F)

8. When the tilemode is turned off, you can freeze the selected layers in the current model space viewport or in the paper space environment by selecting **Active VP Freeze**. (T/F)

9. To specify the grid spacing as a multiple of the snap spacing in the **GRID** command, enter X after the value (2X). (T/F)

10. If the grid spacing is specified as 1, it automatically adjusts to the snap resolution. (T/F)

11. When you are drawing an auxiliary view (a drawing view that is at an angle to other views of the drawing), it is useful to have the UCS snap grid at an angle. (T/F)

12. The **CENter** Object Snap mode allows you to snap to the center point of a circle or an arc. (T/F)

13. To use the **QUAdrant** object snap, position the target box anywhere on the circle or arc. (T/F)

14. In AutoCAD the default is: Angles measured in the _____ direction are positive.

15. If you enter _____ before the angle, AutoCAD will bypass the current angle settings and use the angle as decimal degrees from the default angle base and default angle direction.

16. If you enter _____ in front of the angle, AutoCAD will use current angular units, but it will bypass the current settings of angle base and angle direction and use the default angle, base, and direction settings.

17. You can also load the **Drawing Units** dialog box by entering _____ at the AutoCAD, Command prompt.

18. A layer name can be up to _____ characters long, including letters, numbers, and special characters.

19. The difference between the **Off** option and the **Freeze** option is that the frozen layers are not _____ by the computer while regenerating the drawing.

20. You can use the _____ option of the **Layer Properties Manager** dialog box to selectively display the layers.

21. You can use the **Style** option to set the snap grid to a standard or _____ .

22. The _____ object snap option stops searching as soon as AutoCAD finds a point on the object qualifying for the specified object snap.

23. The size of the aperture is measured in _____ , short for picture elements.

Exercises

Exercise 5   *Architecture*

Set the units for a drawing according to the following specifications:

1. Set the **UNITS** to architectural, with the denominator of the smallest fraction equal to 16.
2. Set the angular measurement to degrees/minutes/seconds, with the number of fractional places for display of angles equal to 2.
3. Set the direction to 0 degrees (east) and the direction of measurement of angles to counterclockwise (angles measured positive in a counterclockwise direction).

Based on Figure 3-79, determine and set the limits of the drawing. Also, set an appropriate value for Grid and Snap. The scale for this drawing is 1/4" = 1'. Leave enough space around the drawing for dimensioning and title block. (HINT: Scale factor = 48; sheet size required is 12 x 9; therefore, the limits are 12 x 48, 9 x 48 = 576, 432. Use athe **ZOOM** command and then select the **All** option to display the new limits.)

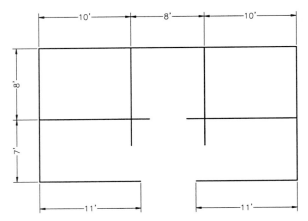

Figure 3-79 Drawing for Exercise 5

Exercise 6   *Mechanical*

Set up four layers with the following linetypes and colors. Then make the drawing (without dimensions) as shown in Figure 3-80.

Figure 3-80 *Drawing for Exercise 6*

Layer name	Color	Linetype
Object	Red	Continuous
Hidden	Yellow	Hidden
Center	Green	Center

Exercise 7

General

Set up a drawing with the following layers, linetypes, and colors. Then make the drawing as shown in Figure 3-81. The distance between the dotted lines is 1 unit.

Layer name	Color	Linetype
Object	Red	Continuous
Hidden	Yellow	Hidden

Figure 3-81 *Drawing for Exercise 7*

Exercise 8   *Mechanical*

Set up a drawing with the following layers, linetypes, and colors. Then make the drawing (without dimensions) as shown in Figure 3-82.

Layer name	Color	Linetype
Object	Red	Continuous
Center	Green	Center

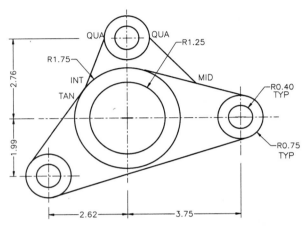

Figure 3-82 Drawing for Exercise 8

Problem-Solving Exercise 1   *Mechanical*

Make the drawing shown in Figure 3-83. To create the arcs you need to calculate their start points and end-points. Also, you need to figure out the start point for the lines (lines inside the arcs) so that the lines can be drawn with the existing dimensions.

Figure 3-83 Drawing for Problem- Solving Exercise 1

Problem-Solving Exercise 2 *Mechanical*

Based on Figure 3-84, determine and set the limits and units of the drawing. Also, set an appropriate value for Grid and Snap. The scale for this drawing is 1:10. Leave enough space around the drawing for dimensioning and the title block. (HINT: Scale factor = 10; sheet size required is 600 x 450; therefore, the limits are 600 x 10, 450 x 10 = 6000, 4500. Also, change the LTSCALE to 500 so that the hidden lines are displayed as hidden lines on screen and use the **ZOOM** command with **All** option to display the new limits.)

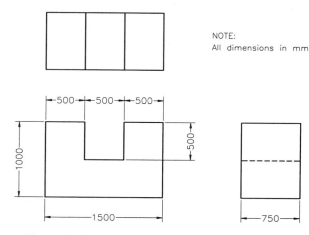

NOTE:
All dimensions in mm

Figure 3-84 *Drawing for Problem-Solving Exercise 2*

Answers to Self-Evaluation Test
1 - F, 2 - F, 3 - F, 4 - T, 5 - F, 6 - north-south direction, 7 - continuous, 8 - Snap option, 9 - NODe, 10 - **DDLMODES**

Chapter 3

Chapter 4

Editing Commands

Learning Objectives

After completing this chapter, you will be able to:
- *Create selection sets using various object selection options.*
- *Make copies of existing objects using the **COPY** command.*
- *Copying objects with base point using the **COPYBASE** command.*
- *Use the **OFFSET** and **BREAK** commands.*
- *Fillet and chamfer objects using the **FILLET** and **CHAMFER** commands.*
- *Cut and extend objects using the **TRIM** and **EXTEND** commands.*
- *Stretch objects using the **STRETCH** command.*
- *Create polar and rectangular arrays using the **ARRAY** command.*
- *Use the **ROTATE** and **MIRROR** commands.*
- *Scale objects using the **SCALE** command.*
- *Lengthen objects like line, arc, spline using **LENGTHEN** command.*
- *Use the **MEASURE** and **DIVIDE** commands.*
- *Use the **PROPERTIES** command to change object properties.*
- *Use the **QSELECT** command for quick selection of objects.*

CREATING A SELECTION SET

In Chapter 1, we discussed two options of the selection set (Window, Crossing). In this chapter you will learn additional selection set options you can use to select objects. The following options are explained here.

Last	CPolygon	Add	Undo	Previous
Fence	BOX	SIngle	ALL	Group
AUto	WPolygon	Remove	Multiple	

Note
The quickest and easiest way to enter most selection options is by typing their required (shown in uppercase) one or more character abbreviations.

Last

Last is the most convenient option if you want to select the most recently drawn object that is visible on the screen. Although a selection set is being formed using the **Last** option, only one object is selected even if you use the Last option a number of times. You can use the Last selection option with any command that requires selection of objects (e.g., **COPY, MOVE, ERASE**). After entering the particular command at the Command prompt, enter LAST or L at the **Select objects:** prompt. The most recently drawn object on the screen will be selected and highlighted.

Exercise 1   *General*

Using the **LINE** command, draw Figure 4-1(a). Then use the **ERASE** command with the **Last** option to erase the three most recently drawn lines to obtain Figure 4-1(d).

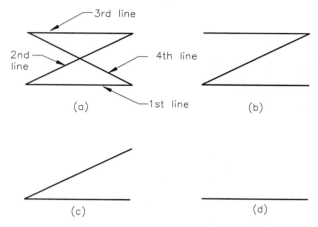

Figure 4-1 *Erasing objects using the **Last** selection option*

Previous

The Previous selection option automatically selects the objects in the most recently created selection set. To invoke this option you can enter **PREVIOUS** or **P** at the **Select objects:** prompt. AutoCAD 2000 saves the previous selection set and lets you select it again by using the Previous option. In other words, with the help of the Previous option you can edit the previous set without reselecting its objects individually. Another advantage of the Previous selection option is that you need not remember the objects if more than one editing operation has to be carried out on the same set of objects. For example, if you want to copy a number of objects and then move them, you can use the **Previous** option to select the same group of objects with the **MOVE** command. The prompt sequence will be as follows:

Command: **COPY** [Enter]
Select objects: *Select the objects.*
Select objects: [Enter]
Specify base point or displacement, or [Multiple]: *Specify the base point.*
Specify second point of displacement or <use first point as displacement>: *Specify the point for displacement.*

Command: **MOVE** [Enter]
Select objects: **P** [Enter]
found

The **Previous** option does not work with some editing commands, like **STRETCH**. A previous selection set is cleared by the various deletion operations and the commands associated with them, like **UNDO**. You cannot select the objects in model space and then use same selection set in paper space, or vice versa, because AutoCAD notes the space (paper space or model space) in which the individual selection set is obtained.

WPolygon

This option is similar to the **Window** option, except that in this option you can define a window that consists of an irregular polygon. You can specify the selection area by specifying points around the object you want to select (Figure 4-2). In other words, the objects to be selected should be completely enclosed within the polygon. The polygon is formed as you specify the points and can take any shape except one in which it intersects itself. The last segment of the polygon is automatically drawn to close the polygon. The polygon can be created by specifying the coordinates of the points or by specifying the points with the help of a pointing device. With the **Undo** option, the

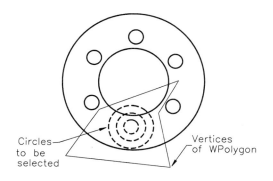

*Figure 4-2 Selecting objects using the **WPolygon** option*

most recently specified WPolygon point can be undone. To use the **WPolygon** option with object selection commands (like **ERASE, MOVE, COPY**), first enter the particular command at the Command prompt, and then enter WP at the **Select objects:** prompt. The prompt sequence for the **WPolygon** option is:

Select objects: **WP** [Enter]
First polygon point: *Specify the first point.*
Specify endpoint of line or [Undo]: *Specify the second point.*
Specify endpoint of line or [Undo]: *Specify the third point.*
Specify endpoint of line or [Undo]: *Specify the fourth point.*
Specify endpoint of line or [Undo]: [Enter] *(Press ENTER after specifying the last point of polygon.)*

Exercise 2
General

Draw a number of objects on the screen, and then erase some of them using the WPolygon to select the objects you want to erase.

CPolygon

This method of selection is similar to the WPolygon method except that **CPolygon** also selects those objects that are not completely enclosed within the polygon, but are touching the polygon boundaries. In other words, if a portion of an object is lying inside the polygon, the particular object is also selected in addition to those objects that are completely enclosed within the polygon (Figure 4-3). CPolygon is formed as you specify the points. The points can be specified at the Command line or by specifying points with a pointing device. Just as in the **WPolygon** option, the crossing polygon can take any shape except the one in which it intersects itself. Also, the last segment is drawn automatically, so the CPolygon is closed at all times. The prompt sequence for **CPolygon** option is:

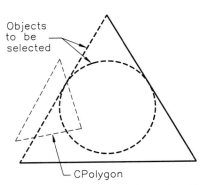

Figure 4-3 Selecting objects using the CPolygon option

Select objects: **CP** [Enter]
First polygon point: *Specify the first point.*
Specify endpoint of line or [Undo]: *Specify the second point.*
Specify endpoint of line or [Undo]: *Specify the third point.*
Specify endpoint of line or [Undo]: [Enter] *(When finished specifying the last point of the polygon.)*

Remove

The **Remove** option is used to remove an object from the selection set (but not from the drawing). After selecting many objects from a drawing by any selection method, there may be need for removing some of the objects from the selection set. You can remove the objects by selecting the objects using the pointing device with the SHIFT key depressed, when system variable **PICKADD** is set to 1(default). The following prompt sequence illustrates the use of removing objects by using the SHIFT key depressed in the **ERASE** command (Figure 4-4):

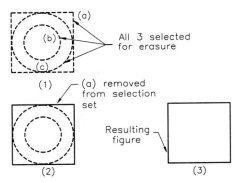

Figure 4-4 Using the Remove option

Command: **ERASE** [Enter]
Select objects: *Select objects (a), (b), and (c).*

Now if do not want to erase object (a), you can do the same by depressing the SHIFT key and selecting object (a) with the pointing device. AutoCAD will display the following message:

Select objects: 1 found, 1 removed, 2 total

Add

The **Add** option can be used to add objects to the selection set. When you begin creating a selectionset, you are in **Add** mode. After you create a selection set by any selection method, you can add more objects by simply selecting them by the pointing device, when system variable **PICKADD** is set to 1(default). When system variable **PICKADD** is set to 0, to add objects to the selection set, you need to select objects by pointing device with SHIFT key depressed.

ALL

The **ALL** selection option is used to select all the objects on the drawing screen. Objects that are in the "OFF" layers are not selected with the **ALL** option. You can use this selection option with **ERASE** or **MOVE** or any other command that requires object selection. After invoking the command, the ALL option can be entered at the **Select objects:** prompt. Once you enter this option, all the objects drawn on the screen will be highlighted (dashed). For example, if there are four objects on the screen and you want to erase all of them, the prompt sequence is:

    Command: ERASE Enter
    Select objects: ALL Enter
    4 found
    Select objects: Enter

You can use this option in combination with other selection options. To illustrate this, consider there are five objects on the drawing screen and you want to erase three of them. After invoking the **ERASE** command you can enter **ALL** at the **Select objects:** prompt, then press the SHIFT key andselect the two particular objects to remove from the selection set. Hence, the remaining three objects are erased.

Fence

In the **Fence** option, a selection set is created by drawing an open polyline fence through the objects to be selected. Any object touched by the fence polyline is selected (Figure 4-5). This mode of selection is like the **CPolygon** option, except that the last line of the selection polygon is not closed and objects that do not touch are not selected. The selection fence can be created by entering the coordinates at the Command line or by specifying the points with the pointing device. More flexibility for selection is provided, because the fence can intersect itself. The Undo option can be used to undo the most

*Figure 4-5 Erasing objects using the **Fence** option*

recently selected fence point. Like the other selection options, this option is also used with commands that need object selection. The prompt sequence is:

    Select objects: F Enter
    First fence point: *Specify the first point.*
    Specify endpoint of line or [Undo]: *Specify the second point.*
    Specify endpoint of line or [Undo]: *Specify the third point.*
    Specify endpoint of line or [Undo]: *Specify the fourth point.*
    Specify endpoint of line or [Undo]: Enter *(Press ENTER.)*

Group

The **Group** option enables you to select a group of objects by their group name. You can create a group and assign a name to it with the help of the **GROUP** command (see Chapter 16). Once a

Chapter 4

group has been created, you can select the group using the **Group** option for editing purposes. This makes the object selection process easier and faster, for a set of objects is selected by entering just the group name. The prompt sequence is:

Command: **MOVE** [Enter]
Select objects: **G** [Enter]
Enter group name: *Enter the name of the predefined group you want to select.*
4 found
Select objects: [Enter]

Exercise 3   *General*

Draw six circles and select all of them to erase using the **ERASE** command with the **ALL** option. Now change the selection set contents by removing alternate circles from the selection set by holding the SHIFT key down and selecting objects so that alternate circles are erased.

BOX

When system variable **PICKAUTO** is set to 1 (default), the **BOX** selection option is used to select objects inside a rectangle. After you enter BOX at the **Select objects:** prompt, you are required to specify the two corners of a rectangle at the **First corner:** and the **Other corner:** prompts. If you specify the first corner on the right and the second corner on the left, the BOX is equivalent to the Crossing selection option; hence, it also selects those objects that are touching the rectangle boundaries in addition to those that are completely enclosed within the rectangle. If you specify the first corner on the left and the second corner on the right, this option is equivalent to the Window option and selects only those objects that are completely enclosed within the rectangle. The prompt sequence is:

Select objects: **BOX** [Enter]
Specify first corner: *Specify a point.*
Specify Opposite corner: *Specify opposite corner point of the box.*

AUto

The **AUto** option is used to establish automatic selection. You can select a single object, by selecting that object, as well as select a number of objects, by creating a window or a crossing. If you select a single object, it is selected; if you specify a point in the blank area you are automatically in the BOX selection option and the point you have specified becomes the first corner of the box. Auto and Add are default selections.

Multiple

When you enter **M** (Multiple) at the **Select objects:** prompt, you can select multiple objects at a single **Select objects:** prompt without the objects being highlighted. Once you give a null response to the **Select objects:** prompt, all the selected objects are highlighted together. Multiple commands can also be used effectively to select two intersecting objects if the intersection point is selected twice.

Undo

This option removes the most recently selected object from the selection set.

SIngle

When you enter SI (SIngle) at the **Select objects:** prompt, the selection takes place in the SIngle selection mode. The **Select objects:** prompt repeats until you make the selection. Once you select an object or a number of objects using a Window or Crossing option, the Select objects: prompt is not repeated and AutoCAD proceeds with the command for which the selection is made.

    Command: **ERASE** [Enter]
    Select objects: **SI** [Enter]
    Select objects: *Select the object for erasing. The selected object is erased.*

You can also create a selection set with the help of **SELECT** command. The prompt sequence is:

    Command: **SELECT** [Enter]
    Select objects: *Use any selection method.*

EDITING COMMANDS

To use AutoCAD effectively, you need to know the editing commands and how to use them. In this section you will learn about the editing commands. These commands can be invoked from the toolbar, or menu, or can be entered at the Command: prompt. We are going to discuss the following editing commands (**MOVE, ERASE** and **OOPS** commands were discussed in Chapter 1):

MOVE	**SCALE**	**EXTEND**	**MIRROR**
COPY	**FILLET**	**STRETCH**	**BREAK**
OFFSET	**CHAMFER**	**LENGTHEN**	**MEASURE**
ROTATE	**TRIM**	**ARRAY**	**DIVIDE**

COPY COMMAND

Toolbar:	Modify > Copy Object
Menu:	Modify > Copy
Command:	COPY or CP

Figure 4-6 Invoking the COPY command from the Modify toolbar

The **COPY** command is used to copy an existing object. This command is similar to the **MOVE** command, in the sense that it makes copies of the selected objects and places them at specified locations, but the originals are left intact. In this command also, you need to select the objects and then specify the base point. Then you are required to specify the second point, where you want the objects to be copied, (see Figure 4-7). The prompt sequence is:

    Command: **COPY** or **CP** [Enter]
    Select objects: *Select the objects to copy.*
    Select objects: [Enter]
    Specify base point or displacement, or [Multiple]: *Specify the base point.*

Chapter 4

Specify second point or displacement, or <use first point as displacement>: *Specify a new position on the screen using pointing device or entering coordinates.*

Multiple Copies

This option of the **COPY** command is used to make multiple copies of the same object (Figure 4-8). To use this option, select the **Multiple** option or enter **M** at the **Specify base point or displacement, or [Multiple]:** prompt. Next, AutoCAD prompts you to enter the second point. When you select a point, a copy is placed at that point, and the prompt is automatically repeated until you press ENTER to terminate the **COPY** command. The prompt sequence for the **COPY** command with the **Multiple** option is:

Specify base point or displacement, or [Multiple]: **M** [Enter]
Specify base point: *Specify the base point.*
Specify second point of displacement or <use first point as displacement>: *Specify a point for placement.*
Specify second point of displacement or <use first point as displacement>: *Specify another point for placement.*
Specify second point of displacement or <use first point as displacement>: *Specify another point for placement.*
Specify second point of displacement or <use first point as displacement>: [Enter]

*Figure 4-7 Using the **COPY** command*

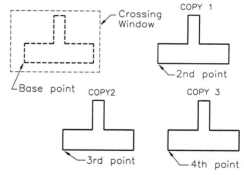

*Figure 4-8 Making multiple copies using the **COPY** command*

COPYBASE COMMAND*

Menu:	Edit > Copy with Basepoint
Command:	COPYBASE

The command **COPYBASE** is used to specify the basepoint of objects to be copied. This is a new feature in AutoCAD 2000 that can be very useful while pasting an object very precisely in the same diagram or into another diagram. The **COPYBASE** command can also be invoked from the short-cut menu by right-clicking in the drawing area and choosing **Copy with Base Point**. The command sequence is as follows:

Command: **COPYBASE** [Enter]
Specify base point: *Specify the base point of the object.*

Select objects: *Select the object to be copied.*

After copying objects with the **COPYBASE** command , you can **paste** the objects at the desired place with greater accuracy.

PASTEBLOCK COMMAND*

Menu:	Edit > Paste as Block
Command:	PASTEBLOCK

PASTEBLOCK command pastes a copied block into a new drawing. You can also invoke **PASTEBLOCK** command from the short-cut menu by right clicking in the drawing area and choosing **Paste as Block**.

PASTEORIG COMMAND*

Menu:	Edit > Paste to Original Coordinates
Command:	PASTEORIG

Figure 4-9 Invoking the Copy with Base Point from the shortcut menu

PASTEORIG command pastes a copied object into a new drawing using the coordinates from the original drawing. You can also invoke **PASTEORIG** command from the short-cut menu by right clicking in the drawing area and choosing **Paste to Original Coordinates**. **PASTEORIG** is available only when the Clipboard contains AutoCAD data from a drawing other than the current drawing.

Exercise 4   *General*

a. Draw a circle and use the **COPY** command to make a single copy of the circle or any other figure you have drawn.
b. Make four copies of the figure drawn in (a) using the Multiple (**M**) option.
c. Draw a rectangle and make a single copy of the rectangle using the **COPYBASE** command and **Paste** commands.

OFFSET COMMAND

Toolbar:	Modify > Offset
Menu:	Modify > Offset
Command:	OFFSET

If you want to draw parallel lines, polylines, concentric circles, arcs, curves, etc., you can use the **OFFSET** command (Figure 4-10). This command creates another object that is similar to the selected one. When offsetting an object you can specify the offset distance and the side to offset, or you can specify a point through which you want to offset the selected object. Depending on the side to offset, you can create smaller or larger circles, ellipses, and arcs. If the offset side is toward the inner side of the perimeter, the arc, ellipse, or circle will be smaller than the original. The prompt sequence is:

Chapter 4

Command: **OFFSET** [Enter]
Specify offset distance or [Through] <current>:

At this last prompt you can enter either the **Offset distance** or the **Through** option (Figure 4-11). The offset distance can be specified by entering a value or by specifying two points with the pointing device. AutoCAD will measure the distance between these two points and use it as the offset distance. The prompt sequence for the **Offset distance** option is:

Offset distance or [Through] <current>: *Specify two points or enter a value.*
Select object to offset or <exit>: *Select the object to offset.*
Specify point on side to offset? *Specify the side for offsetting.*
Select object to offset or <exit>: *Select another object or press ENTER to complete the command.*

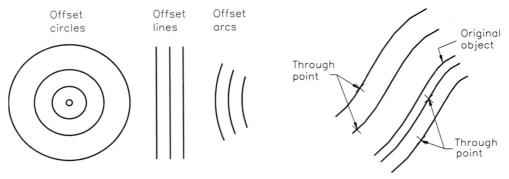

Figure 4-10 *Using the* **OFFSET** *command*

Figure 4-11 *Using the* **Through** *option in the* **OFFSET** *command*

In the case of the **Through** option, you do not have to specify a distance; you simply specify an offset point after selecting. The offset object is created at the specified point. The prompt sequence is:

Specify offset distance or [Through] <current>: **T** [Enter]
Select object to offset or <exit>: *Select the object.*
Specify through point: *Specify the offset point.*

The offset distance is stored in the **OFFSETDIST** system variable. A negative value indicates OFFSET is set to the Through option. You can offset lines, arcs, 2D polylines, xlines, circles, ellipses, elliptical arcs rays, and planar splines. If you try to offset objects other than these, the message **Cannot offset that object** is displayed.

Exercise 5   *Graphics*

1. Draw five concentric circles using the **OFFSET** command.
2. Use the **OFFSET** edit command to draw Figure 4-12(a) and 4-12(b).

Figure 4-12 *Drawing for Exercise 5*

ROTATE COMMAND

Toolbar:	Modify > Rotate
Menu:	Modify > Rotate
Command:	ROTATE

Sometimes when making drawings you may need to rotate an object or a group of objects. You can accomplish this by using the **ROTATE** command. When you invoke this command, AutoCAD will prompt you to select the objects and the base point about which the selected objects will be rotated. You should be careful when selecting the base point as it is easy to get confused if the base point is not located on a known object. After you specify the base point you are required to enter a rotation angle. Positive angles produce a counterclockwise rotation; negative angles produce a clockwise rotation (Figure 4-13). The **ROTATE** command can also invoked from the shortcut menu by selecting the object and clicking the right button in the drawing area and choosing **Rotate**. The prompt sequence is:

Command: **ROTATE** Enter
Current positive angle in UCS: ANGDIR=*current* ANGBASE=*current*
Select objects: *Select the objects for rotation.*
Select objects: Enter
Specify base point: *Specify a base point on or near the object.*
Specify rotation angle or [Reference]: *Enter a positive or negative rotation angle, or specify a point.*

If you need to rotate objects with respect to a known angle, you can do this in two different ways using the **Reference** option. The first way is by specifying the known angle as the reference angle, followed by the proposed angle to which the objects will be rotated (Figure 4-14). Here the object is first rotated clockwise from the X axis, to the reference angle. Then the object is rotated to the new angle from this reference position in a counterclockwise direction. The prompt sequence is:

Command: **ROTATE** Enter
Current positive angle in UCS: ANGDIR=*current* ANGBASE=*current*
Select objects: *Select the objects for rotation.*

Chapter 4

Select objects: [Enter]
Specify base point: *Specify the base point.*
Specify rotation angle or [Reference]: **R** [Enter]
Specify the reference angle <0>: **10** [Enter]
Specify the new angle: **90** [Enter]

Figure 4-13 Rotation of objects with different rotation angles

*Figure 4-14 Rotation using the **Reference** Angle option*

The other method is to specify two points to indicate a reference line on the object; then specify a new angle to rotate the object with respect to this line (Figure 4-15). The direction of rotation depends on the point you choose first on the reference line. The prompt sequence is:

Command: **ROTATE** [Enter]
Current positive angle in UCS:
ANGDIR=*current* ANGBASE=*current*
Select objects: *Select the object for rotation.*
Select objects: [Enter]
Specify base point: *Specify the base point.*
Specify rotation angle or [Reference]: **R** [Enter]
Specify the reference angle <0>: *Specify the first point on the reference line.*
Specify second point: *Specify the second point on the reference line.*
Specify new angle: **45** [Enter]

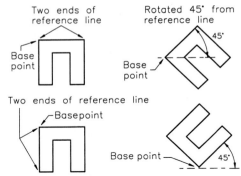

*Figure 4-15 Rotation using the **Reference** Line option*

SCALE COMMAND

Toolbar:	Modify > Scale
Menu:	Modify > Scale.
Command:	SCALE

Many times you will need to change the size of objects in a drawing. You can do this with the **SCALE** command. This command enlarges or shrinks the selected object in the same ratio for the X and Y dimensions about a base point. Application of the identical scale factor to the X and Y dimensions ensures that the shape of the objects being scaled do not change.

This is a useful and timesaving editing command because instead of redrawing objects to the required size, you can scale the objects with a single **SCALE** command. Another advantage of this command is that if you have already put the dimensions on the drawing, they will also change according to the new scale. You can also invoke the **SCALE** command from the shortcut menu by right-clicking in the drawing area and choosing **Scale**. The prompt sequence is:

> Command: **SCALE** [Enter]
> Select objects: *Select objects to be scaled.*
> Select objects: [Enter]
> Specify base point: *Specify the base point, preferably a known point.*
> Specify scale factor or [Reference]: **0.75** [Enter]

When a drawing is rescaled, a scale factor is used to change the size of selected objects around a chosen base point (Figure 4-16). The chosen base point remains fixed, whereas everything around it may increase or reduce in size according to the scale factor.

Scale factor=0.75

Original object   Scaled object

*Figure 4-16 Using the Scale factor option in the **SCALE** command*

To reduce the size of an object, the scale factor should be less than 1 and to increase the size of an object, the scale factor should be greater than 1. You can enter a scale factor or select two points to specify a distance as a factor. When you select two points to specify a distance as factor, the first point should be on the referenced object.

Sometimes it is time-consuming to calculate the relative scale factor. In such cases you can scale the object by specifying a desired size in relation to the existing size (a known dimension). In other words you can use a **reference length**. To do this, type **R** at the **Specify scale factor or [Reference]:** prompt. Then, you either specify two points to specify the length or enter a length. At the next prompt, enter the length relative to the reference length. For example, if a line is **2.5** units long and you want the length of the line to be **1.00** units, then instead of calculating the relative scale factor, you use the **Reference** option (Figure 4-17). This is illustrated as follows:

> Command: **SCALE** [Enter]
> Select objects: **Select the object**.
> Select objects: [Enter]
> Specify base point: *Specify the base point.*
> Specify scale factor or [Reference]: **R** [Enter]

Chapter 4

Specify reference length <1>: **2.5** [Enter]
Specify new length: **1.0** [Enter]

If you have not used the required drawing units for a drawing, you can use the **Reference** option of the **SCALE** command to correct the error. Select the entire drawing with the help of the All selection option. Specify the **Reference option**, then select the endpoints of the object whose desired length you know. Specify the new length, and all objects in the drawing will be rescaled automatically to the desired size.

Figure 4-17 Using the *Reference* option in the *SCALE* command

FILLET COMMAND

Toolbar:	Modify > Fillet
Menu:	Modify > Fillet
Command:	FILLET

The **FILLET** command is used to create smooth round arcs to connect two objects. In mechanical drafting, inside rounded corners are known as FILLETS and outside ones are known as ROUNDS, but in AutoCAD all rounded corners are referred to as fillets. The **FILLET** command helps you form round corners between any two lines by asking you to identify the two lines. This can be done by selecting them with the cursor. A fillet can be drawn between two intersecting parallel lines as well as nonintersecting and nonparallel lines, arcs, polylines, xlines, rays, splines, circles, and true ellipses. The radius of the arc to create the fillet has to be specified. The prompt sequence is:

Command: **FILLET** [Enter]
Current Settings: Mode= TRIM, Radius= 0.5000
Select first object or [Polyline/Radius/Trim]:

Select First Object Option

This is the default method to fillet two objects. As the name implies, it prompts for the first object required for filleting. The prompt sequence is:

Command: **FILLET** [Enter]
Current Settings: Mode= TRIM, Radius= 0.5000
Select first object or [Polyline/Radius/Trim]: *Specify first object.*
Select second object: *Select second object.*

You can select lines with the Window, Crossing, or Last option, but to avoid unexpected results it is safer to select by picking objects individually. Also, selection by picking objects is necessary in the case of arcs and circles that have the possibility of more than one fillet. They are filleted closest to the select points (Figures 4-18 and 4-19).

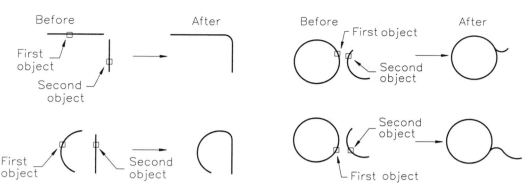

Figure 4-18 *Using the* **FILLET** *command*

Figure 4-19 *Using the* **FILLET** *command on circles and arcs*

You also can fillet a 3D solid (see Chapter 23 for details). Here you have to select different edges to fillet, but the edges should be selected individually. The prompt sequence is:

Command: **FILLET** [Enter]
Current Settings: Mode= TRIM, Radius= 0.5000
Select first object or [Polyline/Radius/Trim]: *Select an edge of the solid.*
Enter fillet radius <current>: *Specify a radius.*
Select an edge or [Chain/Radius]:

Select edge. You can go on selecting individual edges. Press ENTER to come out of this option.

Chain. Here you can select a single edge or chain. If you select Chain, all the tangential edges to the selected single edge are chosen automatically. The prompt sequence is:

Select an edge or [Chain/Radius]: **C** [Enter]
Select an edge chain or [Edge/Radius]: *Select edge chain, or enter* **E** *to shift to single edge mode, or* **R** *to specify a radius.*

The **FILLET** command can also be used to cap the ends of two parallel lines (Figure 4-20). The cap is a semicircle whose radius is equal to half the distance between the two parallel lines. The cap distance is calculated automatically when you select the two parallel lines for filleting.

Command: **FILLET**
Current Settings: Mode= TRIM, Radius= 0.5000
Select first object or [Polyline/Radius/Trim]: *Select the first parallel line.*
Select second object: *Select the second parallel line.*

Radius Option

The fillet you create depends on the radius distance you specify. The default radius is 0.5000. You can enter a distance or two points. The new radius you enter becomes the default and remains in effect until changed. Fillet with zero radius creates sharp corners and is used to clean up lines at corners (in case they overlap or have a gap). The prompt sequence is:

Chapter 4

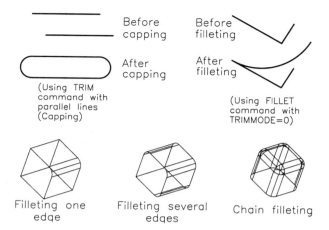

Figure 4-20 *Capping parallel lines with the **FILLET** command, filleting without cutting the geometry, filleting polylines, and solid models.*

Select first object or [Polyline/Radius/Trim]: **R** `Enter`
Specify fillet radius <current>: *Enter a fillet radius or press ENTER to accept current value.*

 Note
FILLETRAD system variable controls and stores the current fillet radius.

Trim Option

If this option is set to Trim, the selected objects are either trimmed or extended to the fillet arc endpoints. If set to NoTrim they are left intact. The prompt sequence is:

Select first object or [Polyline/Radius/Trim]: **T** `Enter`
Specify trimmode option [Trim/No trim] <current>: *Enter **T** to trim the edges, **N** to leave them intact.*

Setting TRIMMODE. TRIMMODE is a system variable that eliminates any size restriction on the **FILLET** command. By setting **TRIMMODE** to 0, you can create a fillet of any size without actually cutting the existing geometry. Also, there is no restriction on the fillet radius; the fillet radius can be larger than one or both objects that are being filleted. The value of the **TRIMMODE** system variable can also be set by entering **TRIMMODE** at the Command prompt:

Command: **TRIMMODE**
Enter new value for TRIMMODE <1>: **0**

 Note
TRIMMODE = 0   *Fillet or chamfer without cutting the existing geometry.*
TRIMMODE = 1   *Extend or trim the geometry.*
*When you enter the **FILLET** command, AutoCAD displays the current **TRIMMODE** and the current fillet radius.*

Polyline Option

Using this option you can fillet a single polyline (Figure 4-21). If the polyline is selected with the Window, Crossing, or Last option, the most recent vertex is filleted. If you select the P option, AutoCAD prompts you to select a polyline, and then all its vertices are filleted. If the selected polyline is not closed, then the beginning corner is not filleted. The prompt sequence is:

Command: **FILLET** `Enter`
Current Settings: Mode= *current*,
Radius= *current*
Select first object or [Polyline/Radius/Trim]: **P** `Enter`
Select 2D polyline: *Select the polyline.*

Figure 4-21 Using the FILLET command on polylines

Filleting Objects with Different UCS

The fillet command will also fillet objects that are not in the current UCS plane. To create a fillet for such objects, AutoCAD will automatically change the UCS transparently so that it can generate a fillet between the selected objects.

Note

*The **FILLET** command can fillet between a polyline and other objects, or between two adjacent segments of a single polyline, but it cannot fillet between two separate polylines. You can select the segments to fillet, or enter C or W and use Crossing or Window selection. If you select more than two segments with a Crossing or Window selection, the two segments found nearest the polyline's first endpoint will be filleted.*

CHAMFER COMMAND

Toolbar:	Modify >
Chamfer	
Menu:	Modify > Chamfer

In drafting, the **CHAMFER** is defined as the taper provided on a surface. Sometimes the chamfer is used to avoid a sharp corner. In AutoCAD a chamfer is any angled corner of a drawing. A beveled line connects two separate objects to create a chamfer. The size of a chamfer depends on its distance from the corner. If a chamfer is equidistant from the corner in both directions, it is a 45-degree chamfer. A chamfer can be drawn between two lines that may or may not intersect. This command also works on a single polyline. The prompt sequence is:

Command: **CHAMFER** `Enter`
(TRIM mode) Current chamfer Dist1 = 0.5000, Dist2 = 0.5000
Select first line or [Polyline/Distances/Angle/Trim/Method]:

The next prompts displayed are dependent on the option you choose at this last prompt.

Select First Line Option

In this option you need to select two nonparallel objects so that they are joined with a beveled line. The prompt sequence is:

Command: **CHAMFER** [Enter]
(TRIM mode) Current chamfer Dist1 = 0.5000, Dist2 = 0.5000
Select first line or [Polyline/Distance/Angle/Trim/Method]: *Specify the first line.*
Select second line: *Select the second line.*

You can also chamfer a 3D solid using this command (see Chapter 23 for details). Here AutoCAD prompts you to specify the base surface, which can be either of the two edges that are adjacent to the selected edge. The prompt sequence for a 3D solid is:

Base surface selection...
Enter surface selection option [Next/OK(current)] <OK>:

At the **Enter surface selection option[Next/OK(current)] <OK>:** prompt, enter OK if the selected surface itself is the base surface. If you enter N, AutoCAD selects one of the surfaces adjacent to the selected edge as the base surface. The next prompts are:

Specify base surface distance <current>: *Enter distance.*
Specify other surface distance <current>: *Enter distance.*
Select an edge or [Loop]:

The default is the **Select an edge** option where you can select a single edge to chamfer. If you enter **L**, you are in the **Loop** option and you need to select a loop edge at the **Select an edge or [Loop]:** prompt. This chamfers all the edges on the loop surface. See Figure 4-22.

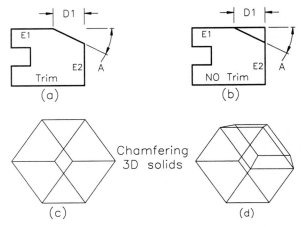

Figure 4-22 *Using the **CHAMFER** command to create a chamfer*

Distances Option

Under this option you can enter the chamfer distance. To do this, type **D** at the **Select first line or [Polyline/Distance/Angle/Trim/Method]:** prompt. Next, enter the first and the second chamfer distances. The default value for the chamfer distance is 0.5. The new chamfer distances remain in effect until you change them. Instead of entering the distance values, you can specify two points to indicate each distance, (Figure 4-23). The prompt sequence is:

Select first line or [Polyline/Distance/Angle/Trim/Method]: **D** [Enter]
Specify first chamfer distance <current>: *Enter a distance or specify two points.*
Specify second chamfer distance <current>: *Enter a distance or specify two points.*

The first and second chamfer distances are stored in the **CHAMFERA** and **CHAMFERB** system variables.

Figure 4-23 Different types of chamfers

 Note
*If Dist 1 and Dist 2 are set to zero, the **CHAMFER** command will extend or trim the selected lines so that they end at the same point.*

Polyline Option

You can use the **CHAMFER** command to chamfer all corners of a closed or open polyline (Figure 4-24). To do this, select the **Polyline** option after entering the command. Next, select the polyline. In case of a closed polyline, all the corners of the polyline are chamfered to the set distance values. Sometimes the polyline may appear closed. But if the **Close** option was not used to create it, it may not be. In this case, the beginning corner is not chamfered. The prompt sequence is:

Command: **CHAMFER** [Enter]
(TRIM mode) Current chamfer Dist1 = 0.5000, Dist2 = 0.5000
Select first line or [Polyline/Distance/Angle/Trim/Method]: **P** [Enter]
Select 2D polyline: *Select the polyline.*

Figure 4-24 *Using the* **CHAMFER** *command to create a chamfer between two lines or polyline segments*

Angle Option

The **Angle** option is used to set the chamfer distance by specifying an angle and a distance. The prompt sequence is:

Select first line or [Polyline/Distance/Angle/Trim/Method]: **A** Enter
Specify chamfer length on the first line <current>: *Specify a length.*
Specify chamfer angle from the first line <current>: *Specify an angle.*

Trim Option

Depending on this option, the selected objects are either trimmed extended to the endpoints of the chamfer line or left intact. The prompt sequence is:

Select first line or [Polyline/Distance/Angle/Trim/Method]: **T** Enter
Enter Trim mode option [Trim/No Trim] <current>:

Method Option

By using this option you can choose between the Distance option and the Angle option using the current distance or angle settings. The prompt sequence is:

Select first line or [Polyline/Distance/Angle/Trim/Method]: **M** Enter
Enter trim method [Distance/Angle] <current>: *Enter* **D** *for Distance option,* **A** *for Angle option.*

Note

If you set the **TRIMMODE** *system variable to 1 (Default value), the objects will be trimmed or extended after they are chamfered and filleted. If* **TRIMMODE** *is set to zero, the objects are left untrimmed.*

Setting the CHAMFER System Variables

The chamfer modes, distances, length, and angle can also be set by using the following system variables:

CHAMMODE = 0 Distance/Distance (default)
CHAMMODE = 1 Length/Angle
CHAMFERA Sets first chamfer distance on the first selected line (default = 0.5000)
CHAMFERB Sets second chamfer distance on the second selected line (default = 0.5000)
CHAMFERC Sets the chamfer length (default = 1.0000)
CHAMFERD Sets the chamfer angle from the first line (default = 0)

TRIM COMMAND

Toolbar:	Modify > Trim
Menu:	Modify > Trim
Command:	TRIM

You may need to trim existing objects of a drawing. Breaking individual objects takes time if you are working on a complex drawing with many objects. The **TRIM** command trims objects that extend beyond a required point of intersection. With this command you must select the cutting edges or boundaries first. There can be more than one cutting edge and you can use any selection method to select them. After the cutting edge or edges are selected, you must select each object to be trimmed. If you want to break a single object into two by deleting a portion, you can select two cutting edges on the same object and then select the object to trim between those two cutting edges. An object can be both a cutting edge and an object to trim. You can trim lines, circles, arcs, polylines, splines, ellipses, xlines, and rays. The prompt sequence is:

Command: **TRIM** [Enter]
Current settings:Projection=UCS Edge = None
Select cutting edges...
Select objects: *Select the cutting edges*.
Select objects: [Enter]
Select object to trim or [Project/Edge/Undo]:

Select Object to Trim Option

Here you have to specify the objects you want to trim. This prompt is repeated until you press ENTER. This way you can select several objects with a single **TRIM** command (Figure 4-26). The prompt sequence is:

Figure 4-25 Invoking the TRIM command from the Modify menu

Command: **TRIM** [Enter]
Current settings: Projection= UCS Edge= None
Select cutting edges...
Select objects: *Select the first cutting edge.*
Select objects: *Select the second cutting edge.*
Select objects: [Enter]
Select object to trim or [Project/Edge/Undo]: *Select the first object to trim.*
Select object to trim or [Project/Edge/Undo]: *Select the second object to trim.*
Select object to trim or [Project/Edge/Undo]: [Enter]

Edge Option

This option is used whenever you want to trim those objects that do not intersect the cutting edges, but would intersect if the cutting edges were extended and intersected the selected objects in 3D space, (Figure 4-27). The prompt sequence is:

Command: **TRIM** [Enter]
Current settings: Projection= UCS Edge= None
Select cutting edges...
Select objects: *Select the cutting edge.*
Select objects: [Enter]
Select object to trim or [Project/Edge/Undo]: **E** [Enter]
Enter an implied edge extension mode [Extend/No extend] <current>: **E** [Enter]
Select object to trim or [Project/Edge/Undo]: *Select the object to trim.*

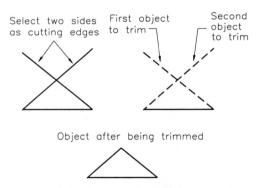

*Figure 4-26 Using the **TRIM** command*

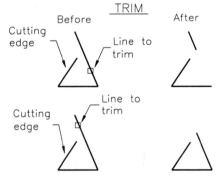

*Figure 4-27 Trimming an object using the **Edge** option (Extend)*

Project Option

In this option you can use Project mode while trimming objects. The prompt sequence is:

Select object to trim or [Project/Edge/Undo]: **P** [Enter]
Enter an projection option [None/Ucs/View] <current>:

The **None** option is used whenever the objects to trim intersect the cutting edges in 3D space. If you want to trim those objects that do not intersect the cutting edges in 3D space, but do visually appear to intersect in a particular UCS or the current view, use the **UCS** or View options. The UCS option projects the objects to the XY plane of the current UCS, while the **View** option projects the objects to the current view direction (trims to their apparent visual intersections).

Undo Option

If you want to remove the previous change created by the **TRIM** command, enter **U** at the **Select object to trim or [Project/Edge/Undo]:** prompt.

Exercise 6 *Mechanical*

Draw the top illustration in Figure 4-28. Then use the **FILLET**, **CHAMFER**, and **TRIM** commands to obtain the figure shown in the bottom of Figure 4-28. (Set the SNAP = 0.05; assume the missing dimensions.)

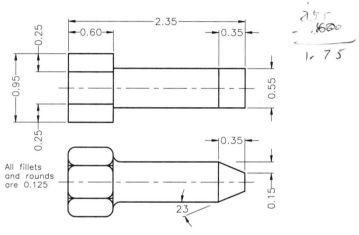

Figure 4-28 Drawing for Exercise 6

EXTEND COMMAND

Toolbar:	Modify > Extend
Menu:	Modify > Extend.
Command:	EXTEND

This command may be considered the opposite of the **TRIM** command. In the **TRIM** command you trim objects; in the **EXTEND** command you can lengthen or extend lines, polylines, rays, and arcs to meet other objects. This command does not extend closed polylines. The command format is similar to that of the **TRIM** command. You are required to select the boundary edges first. The boundary edges are those objects that the selected lines or arcs extend to meet. These edges can be lines, polylines, circles, arcs, ellipses, xlines, rays, splines, text, or even viewports. If a polyline is selected as the boundary edge, the line extends to the polyline's center. The following is the prompt sequence:

Command: **EXTEND** [Enter]
Current settings: Projection= UCS Edge= None

Select boundary edges ...
Select objects: *Select the boundary edges.*
Select objects: [Enter]
Select object to extend or [Project/Edge/Undo]:

Project Option

In this option you can use the projection mode while trimming objects. The prompt sequence is:

Command: **EXTEND** [Enter]
Current settings: Projection= UCS Edge= None
Select boundary edges ...
Select objects: *Select the boundary edges.*
Select objects: [Enter]
Select object to extend or [Project/Edge/Undo]: **P** [Enter]
Enter a projection option [None/UCS/View] <current>:

The **None** option is used whenever the objects to be extended intersect with the boundary edge in 3D space. If you want to extend those objects that do not intersect the boundary edge in 3D space, use the **UCS** or **View** options. The UCS option projects the objects to the XY plane of the current UCS, while the View option projects the objects to the current view.

Select Object to Extend Option

Here you have to specify the object you want to extend to the particular boundary (Figure 4-29). This prompt is repeated until you press ENTER. This way you can select a number of objects in a single **EXTEND** command.

Edge Option

You can use this option whenever you want to extend objects that do not actually intersect the boundary edge, but would intersect its edge if the boundary edge were extended (Figure 4-30). If you enter **E** at the prompt, the selected object is extended to the implied boundary edge. If you enter **N** at the prompt, only those objects that would actually intersect the real boundary edge are extended (the default). The prompt sequence is:

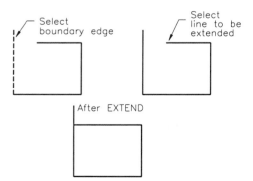

Figure 4-29 *Using the **EXTEND** command*

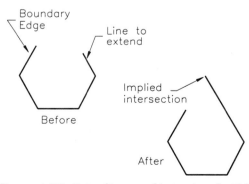

Figure 4-30 *Extending an object using the **Edge** option*

Command: **EXTEND** `Enter`
Current settings: Projection= UCS Edge= None
Select boundary edges ...
Select objects: *Select the boundary edge.*
Select objects: `Enter`
Select object to extend or [Project/Edge/Undo]: **E** `Enter`
Enter an implied extension mode [Extend/No extend] <current>: **E** `Enter`
Select object to extend or [Project/Edge/Undo]: *Select the line to extend.*

Undo Option

If you want to remove the previous change created by the **EXTEND** command, enter **U** at the **Select object to extend or [Project/Edge/Undo]:** prompt.

Trimming and Extending with Text, Region, or Spline

The **TRIM** and **EXTEND** commands can be used with text, regions, or splines as edges (Figure 4-31). This makes the **TRIM** and **EXTEND** commands two of the most useful editing commands in AutoCAD. The **TRIM** and **EXTEND** commands can also be used with arcs, elliptical arcs, splines, ellipses, 3D Pline, rays, and lines. See Figure 4-32.

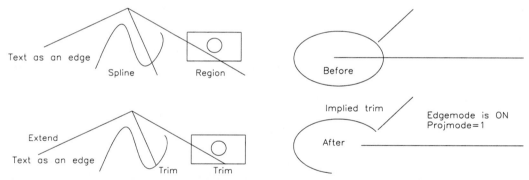

*Figure 4-31 Using the **TRIM** and **EXTEND** commands with text, spline, and region*

*Figure 4-32 Using the **Edge** option to do an implied trim*

The system variables **PROJMODE** and **EDGEMODE** determine how the **TRIM** and **EXTEND** commands are executed. The following is the list of the values that can be assigned to these variables:

Value	PROJMODE	EDGEMODE
0	True 3D mode	Use regular edge without extension (default)
1	Project to current UCS XY plane (default)	Extend the edge to natural boundary
2	Project to current view plane	

STRETCH COMMAND

Toolbar:	Modify > Stretch
Menu:	Modify > Stretch
Command:	STRETCH

This command can be used to stretch objects, altering selected portions of the objects. With this command you can lengthen objects, shorten them, and alter their shapes, (see Figure 4-33). You must use a Crossing, or CPolygon selection to specify the objects to stretch. The prompt sequence is:

Command: **STRETCH** [Enter]
Select objects to stretch by crossing-window or crossing-polygon ...
Select objects: *Select the objects using crossing window or polygon.*
Select objects: [Enter]

After selecting the objects, you have to specify the point of displacement. You should select only that portion of the object that needs stretching.

Specify base point or displacement: *Specify the base point.*
Specify second point of displacement: *Specify the displacement point.*

You normally use a Crossing or CPolygon selection with **STRETCH** because if you use a Window, those objects that cross the window are not selected, and the objects selected because they are fully within the window are moved, not stretched. The object selection and stretch specification process of **STRETCH** is a little unusual. You are really specifying two things: first, you are selecting objects. Second, you are specifying the portions of those selected objects to be stretched. You can use a Crossing or CPolygon selection to simultaneously specify both, or you can select objects by any method, and then use any window or crossing specification to specify what parts of those objects to stretch. Objects or portions of selected objects which are completely within the window or crossing specification are moved. If selected objects cross the window or crossing specification, their defining points within the window or crossing specification are moved, their defining points outside the window or crossing specification remain fixed, and the parts crossing the window or crossing specification are stretched. Only the last window or crossing specification made determines what is stretched or moved. Figure 4-33 illustrates using a crossing selection to simultaneously select the two angled lines and specify that their right ends will be stretched. Alternatively, you could select the lines by any method and then use a Window selection (which would not actually select anything) to specify that their right ends will be stretched.

*Figure 4-33 Using the **STRETCH** command*

LENGTHEN COMMAND

Toolbar:	Modify > Lengthen
Menu:	Modify > Lengthen
Command:	LENGTHEN

 Like the **TRIM** and **EXTEND** commands, the **LENGTHEN** command can be used to extend or shorten lines, polylines, elliptical arcs, and arcs. The **LENGTHEN** command has several options that allow you to change the length of objects by dynamically dragging the object endpoint, entering the delta value, entering the percentage value, or entering the total length of the object. The **LENGTHEN** command also allows the repeated selection of objects for editing. The **LENGTHEN** command has no effect on closed objects, like circles. The prompt sequence is:

Command: **LENGTHEN**
Select an object or [DElta/Percent/Total/DYnamic]:

<Select object>

This is the default option, which returns the current length or the angle of the selected object. If the object is a line, AutoCAD returns only the length. However, if the selected object is an arc, AutoCAD returns the length and the angle.

DElta

The **DElta** option is used to increase or decrease the length or angle of an object by defining the delta distance or delta angle. The delta value can be entered by entering a numerical value or by specifying two points. A positive value will increase (Extend) the length of the selected object and a negative value will decrease the length (Trim). The following is the command prompt sequence for decreasing the angle of an arc by 30 degrees (Figure 4-34):

Chapter 4

Command: **LENGTHEN** [Enter]
Select an object or [DElta/Percent/Total/DYnamic]: **DE** [Enter]
Enter delta length or [Angle] <current>: **A** [Enter]
Enter delta angle <current>: **-30** [Enter]
Select object to change or [Undo]: *Select object.*
Select object to change or [Undo]: [Enter]

Percent

The **Percent** option is used to extend or trim an object by defining the change as a percentage of the original length of the angle. For example, a positive number of 150 will increase the length by 50 percent and a positive number of 75 will decrease the length by 25 percent of the original value. (Negative values are not allowed).

Total

The **Total** option is used to extend or trim an object by defining the new total length or angle. For example, if you enter a total length of 1.25, AutoCAD will automatically increase or decrease the length of the object so that the new length of the object is 1.25. The value can be entered by entering a numerical value or by specifying two points. The object is shortened or lengthened with respect to the endpoint that is closest to the selection point. The selection point is determined by where the object was selected. The prompt sequence in Total option is:

Specify total length or [Angle] <current>: *Specify the length or enter* **A** *for angle.*

If you enter a positive value in the above prompt then the length of the selected objects is changed accordingly. You can change the angle of an arc by entering A and giving the new value.

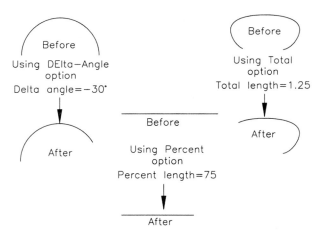

*Figure 4-34 Using the **LENGTHEN** command with DElta, Percent, and Total options*

DYnamic

The **DYnamic** option allows you to dynamically change the length or angle of an object by specifying one of the endpoints and dragging it to a new location. The other end of the object stays fixed and is not affected by dragging. The angle of lines, radius of arcs, and shape of elliptical arcs are unaffected.

ARRAY COMMAND

Toolbar:	Modify >
Array	
Menu:	Modify > Array

In some drawings you may need to specify an object multiple times in a rectangular or circular arrangement. For example, suppose you have to draw six chairs around a table. This job can be accomplished by drawing each chair separately or by using the **COPY** command to make multiple copies of the chair. You could also draw one chair and then, with the help of the **ARRAY** command, create the other five. This method is more efficient and less time-consuming. The **ARRAY** command allows you to make multiple copies of selected objects in a **rectangular** or **polar** fashion. Each resulting element of the array can be controlled separately. The prompt sequence is:

> Command: **ARRAY** [Enter]
> Select objects: *Select objects to copy.*
> Select objects: [Enter]
> Enter type of array [Rectangular/Polar] <last>:

The option that is used in the previous **ARRAY** command is set as current and the "<>" is placed around it. The function and results obtained by using the **ARRAY** command vary, depending on which type of array you want to generate: rectangular or polar.

Rectangular Array

A rectangular array is formed by making copies of the selected object along the X and Y axes (along rows and columns). The command allows you to choose the number of rows and columns. The row and column counts must be whole numbers. The default value for each of these numbers is 1. The prompt sequence is:

> Enter type of array [Rectangular/Polar] <last>: **R** [Enter]
> Enter the number of rows (---) <1>: **3** [Enter]
> Enter the number of columns (|||) <1>: **3** [Enter]

The direction is shown in the parentheses: (—) for horizontal and (|||) for vertical. Next, you are prompted to enter the distances between the rows and the columns. You can simply enter the distance between the rows and the distance between the columns (Figure 4-35):

> Enter the distance between rows or specify unit cell (---): **0.5** [Enter]
> Specify distance between columns(|||): **0.75** [Enter]

Another way to designate the unit cell or distance is by selecting two opposite corners of the rectangle to specify the row and the column spacing. In both cases the height of the original object is included in the distance between rows and the width is included in the distance between columns (Figure 4-36).

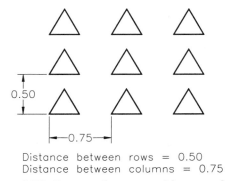

Distance between rows = 0.50
Distance between columns = 0.75

Figure 4-35 *Rectangular array with row and column distance*

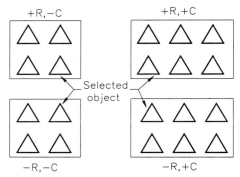

Figure 4-36 *Rectangular array selecting unit cell distance*

If both the distances between rows and columns are positive, the array is generated above and to the right of the cornerstone element. If the row distance is negative, rows are added downward. Similarly, a negative column distance causes columns to be added to the left, (see Figure 4-37). The prompt sequence for **-R, -C** is as follows:

Enter the number of rows (---): **2** [Enter]
Enter the number of columns (|||): **2** [Enter]
Enter the distance between rows or specify unit cell (---): **-0.40** [Enter]
Specify distance between columns (|||): **-0.40** [Enter]

Figure 4-37 *Specification of the direction of arrays*

As with any command, the process can be terminated before completion by pressing ESC.

Rotated Rectangular Array

Normally, in the default UCS, the **Snap rotation angle** is 0 degrees and AutoCAD builds the array along a baseline defined by this angle. Because of this, rectangular arrays are normally orthogonal. You can change this and create a rotated array by first changing the UCS or Snap rotation angle. If you then create an array, it is constructed along a baseline defined by the current Snap rotation angle of the current UCS. In the following example the array is constructed with the Snap rotation angle at **30 degrees**, (Figure 4-38). The prompt sequence is:

Command: **SNAP** [Enter]
Specify snap spacing or [ON/OFF/Aspect/Rotate/Style] <0.5000>: **R** [Enter]
Specify base point <0.0000,0.0000>: *Specify base point.*

Rotation angle <0>: **30** [Enter]

Command: **ARRAY** [Enter]
Select objects: *Select object to be arrayed.*
Select objects: [Enter]
Enter type of array [Rectangular or Polar array]<R>: **R** [Enter]
Enter the number of rows (---): **3** [Enter]
Enter the number of columns (|||): **3** [Enter]
Enter the distance between rows or specify unit cell (---): **0.50** [Enter]
Specify distance between columns (|||): **0.75** [Enter]

Figure 4-38 Rotated rectangular array

Polar Array

A polar array is an arrangement of objects around a point in a circular pattern. You can use the **Polar** option of the **ARRAY** command to draw this kind of array (Figure 4-39). The prompt sequence is:

Command: **ARRAY** [Enter]
Select objects: *Select object to be arrayed.*
Select objects: [Enter]
Enter type of array [Rectangular or Polar array]<R>: **P** [Enter]

The next prompt is:

Specify center point of array:

Here you enter the point around which you want the array to be constructed. In the next three prompts, AutoCAD asks you to enter three parameters:

The number of items in the array.
The angle to fill.
The angle between the items in the array.

You have the option of specifying any two of the three parameters. For the first prompt, **Specify the number of items:**, enter the total number of items in the array, including the original item. If you give a null response to this written prompt, you will have to specify the angle to fill as well as the angle between the items. The next prompt sequence is **Specify the angle to fill (+=CCW,-=CW)<360>:**. The letters in the parentheses stand for the counterclockwise and clockwise directions. As is clear from the prompt, a positive angle generates an

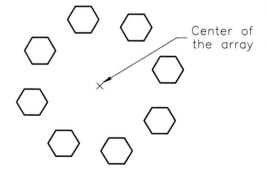

*Figure 4-39 Using the **Polar** option to create a circular array*

array in a counterclockwise direction, and a negative angle generates it in a clockwise direction. The array is completely defined if you specify the number of items and the angle to fill. If you supply only one of the two parameters, AutoCAD prompts you for the angle between the items in the array at the prompt **Angle between items:**. You should specify the direction of the array at this prompt. If you have not previously specified the number of items, AutoCAD will calculate them automatically. To construct the array, AutoCAD calculates the distance from the array's center point to a point of reference on the last object selected. The reference point applied depends on the object. For example:

Object	Reference point
Point	Insertion point
Circle, Arc	Center point
Block, Shape	Insertion base point
Text	Starting point
Line, Trace, Cone	Endpoint

If you select a group of objects, the entire selection is considered an array item. The copied object is placed at the calculated distance from the array's center point. The next prompt is:

Rotate arrayed objects [Yes/No] <Y>:

If you respond to this prompt with **N**, the objects are not rotated as they are copied. This means that the replicated objects remain in the same orientation as the original object. You can have the objects rotated as they are copied around a pivot point by entering **Y** at this prompt. Here, the same face of each object points toward the pivot point. The prompt sequence for objects not rotated (Figure 4-40) is:

Enter type of array [Rectangular or Polar array]<R>: **P** [Enter]
Specify center point of array: *Specify the center point.*
Enter the number of items in the array: **6** [Enter]
Specify the angle to fill (+ =ccw, -=cw)<360>: [Enter]
Rotate arrayed objects [Yes/No] <Y>: **N** [Enter]

To rotate the objects (Figure 4-41), enter Y or simply press the ENTER key at the last prompt.

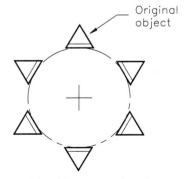

Figure 4-40 Objects not rotated as they are   *Figure 4-41 Objects rotated as they are arrayed*

MIRROR COMMAND

Toolbar:	Modify > Mirror
Menu:	Modify > Mirror
Command:	MIRROR

The **MIRROR** command creates a mirror copy of the selected objects; the objects can be mirrored at any angle. This command is helpful in drawing symmetrical figures. When you invoke this command, AutoCAD will prompt you to select the objects and then the mirror line.

After you select the objects to be mirrored, AutoCAD prompts you to enter the beginning point and endpoint of a mirror line (the imaginary line about which objects are reflected). You can specify the endpoints of the mirror line by specifying the points or by entering their coordinates. The mirror line can be specified at any angle. After the first endpoint has been selected, AutoCAD displays the selected objects as they would appear in a mirror. Next, you need to specify the second endpoint of the mirror line. Once this is accomplished, AutoCAD prompts you to specify whether you want to retain the original figure (Figure 4-42) or delete it and just keep the mirror image of the figure (Figure 4-43). The prompt sequence is:

Command: **MIRROR** [Enter]
Select objects: *Select the objects to be mirrored.*
Select objects: [Enter]
Specify first point of mirror line: *Specify the first endpoint.*
Specify second point of mirror line: *Specify the second endpoint.*
Delete source objects ? [Yes/No] <N>: *Enter Y for deletion, N for retaining the previous objects.*

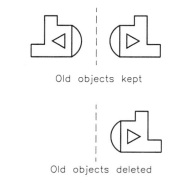

Figure 4-42 *Reflecting an object using the* ***MIRROR*** *command*

Figure 4-43 *Retaining and deleting old objects using the* ***MIRROR*** *command*

Text Mirroring

By default, the **MIRROR** command reverses all the objects, including texts and dimensions. But you may not want the text reversed (written backward). In such a situation, you should use the system variable **MIRRTEXT**. The **MIRRTEXT** variable has the following two values (Figure 4-44):

1 = Text is reversed in relation to the original object. This is the default value.

0 = Inhibits the text from being reversed with respect to the original object.

Hence, if you want the existing object to be mirrored, but at the same time you want the text to be readable and not reversed, set the **MIRRTEXT** variable to 0, then use the **MIRROR** command.

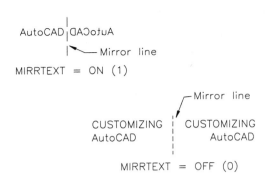

Figure 4-44 *Using the* **MIRRTEXT** *variable to mirror the text*

Command: **MIRRTEXT** [Enter]
Enter new value for MIRRTEXT <1>: **0** [Enter]
Command: **MIRROR** [Enter]
Select objects: *Select the objects.*
Select objects: [Enter]
Specify first point of mirror line: *Specify the first point of the mirror line.*
Specify second point of mirror line: *Specify the second point.*
Delete source objects?[Yes/No] <N>: *Enter* **Y** *to delete,* **N** *to retain the original objects.*

BREAK COMMAND

Toolbar:	Modify > Break
Menu:	Modify > Break
Command:	BREAK

The **BREAK** command cuts existing objects into two or erases portions of the objects. This command can be used to remove a part of the selected objects or to break objects like lines, arcs, circles, ellipses, xlines, rays, splines, and polylines. After entering this command, AutoCAD prompts you to select the object to be broken, and then the break points. The four different options for using the **BREAK** command are discussed next.

1 Point Option

Using this option, you can break the object into two parts. Here, the selection point is taken as the break point, and the object is broken there. The prompt sequence is:

Command: **BREAK** [Enter]
Select object: *Select the object to be broken.*
Enter second break point or [First point]: @ [Enter]

1 Point Select Option

Using this option, you can break the object into two parts, but you are allowed to specify a different breakpoint. The selection point does not affect the break point. The prompt sequence is:

Command: **BREAK** [Enter]
Select object: *Select the object to be broken.*

Enter second break point or [First point]: **F** `Enter`
Specify first break point: *Specify a new break point.*
Specify second break point: @ `Enter`

2 Points Option

Here you are allowed to break an object between two selected points. The point at which you select the object becomes your first break point and then you are prompted to enter the second break point. The prompt sequence is:

Command: **BREAK** `Enter`
Select object: *Select the object to be broken.*
Enter second break point or [First point]: *Specify the second break point.*

The object is broken between those two points and the in-between portion of the object is removed (Figure 4-45).

2 Points Select Option

This option is similar to the 2 Points option; the only difference is that instead of making the selection point as the first break point, you are allowed to specify a new first point. The prompt sequence is:

Command: **BREAK** `Enter`
Select object: *Select the object to be broken.*
Enter second break point or [First point]: **F** `Enter`
Specify first break point: *Specify a new break point.*
Specify second break point: *Specify second point.*

If you need to work on arcs or circles, make sure that you work in a counterclockwise direction, or you may end up cutting the wrong part. In this case the second point should be selected in a counterclockwise direction with respect to the first one (Figure 4-46). You can use the 2 Points and 2 Points Select options to break an object into two without removing a portion in between. This can be achieved by specifying the same point on the object as the first and the second break points. If

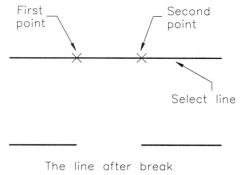

Figure 4-45 *Using the* **BREAK** *command on a line*

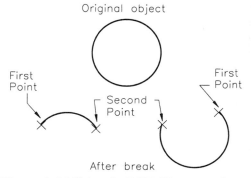

Figure 4-46 *Using the* **BREAK** *command on arcs and circles*

you specify the first break point on the line and the second break point beyond the end of the line, one complete end starting from the first break point will be removed. The extrusion direction of the selected object need not be parallel to the Z axis of the UCS.

Exercise 7 *General*

Break a line at five different points and then erase the alternate segments. Next, draw a circle and break it into four equal parts.

MEASURE COMMAND

Pull-down:	Draw > Point > Measure
Command:	MEASURE

While drawing, you may need to segment an object at fixed distances without actually dividing it. You can use the **MEASURE** command to do so. This command places point (nodes) on the given object at a specified distance. The shape of these points is determined by the **PDMODE** system variable and the size is determined by the **PDSIZE** variable. The **MEASURE** command starts measuring the object from the endpoint closest to where the object is selected. When a circle is to be measured, an angle from the center is formed that is equal to the Snap rotation angle. This angle becomes the starting point of measurement, and the markers are placed at equal intervals in a counterclockwise direction.

This command goes on placing markers at equal intervals of the specified distance without considering whether the last segment is the same distance or not. Instead of entering a value, you can also select two points that will be taken as the distance. In the following example a line and a circle is measured at .80 unit distance

*Figure 4-47 Invoking the **MEASURE** command from the **Draw** menu*

(Figure 4-48). The Snap rotation angle is zero degrees. The **PDMODE** variable is set to 3 so that X marks are placed as markers. The prompt sequence is:

Command: **MEASURE** Enter
Select object to measure: *Select the object to be measured.*
Specify length of segment or [Block]: **.80** Enter

You can also place blocks as markers (Figure 4-49), but the block must already be defined within the drawing. You can align these blocks with the object to be measured. The prompt sequence is:

Command: **MEASURE** Enter
Select object to measure: *Select the object to be measured.*

Specify length of segment or [Block]: **B** Enter
Enter name of block to insert: *Enter the name of the block.*
Align block with object? [Yes/No] <Y>: *Enter* Y *to align,* N *to not align.*
Specify length of segment: *Enter distance.*

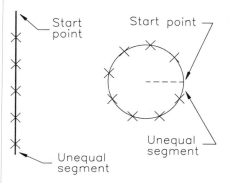

Figure 4-48 *Using the MEASURE command*

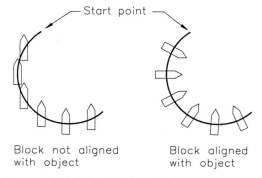

Figure 4-49 *Using blocks with the MEASURE command*

DIVIDE COMMAND

Menu:	Draw >Point > Divide
Command:	DIVIDE

The **DIVIDE** command is used to divide an object into a number of segments of equal length without actually breaking it. This command is similar to the **MEASURE** command except that here you do not have to specify the distance. The **DIVIDE** command calculates the full length of the object and places markers at equal intervals. This makes the last interval equal to the rest of the intervals. If you want a line to be divided, first enter the **DIVIDE** command and select the object to be divided. After this you enter the number of divisions or segments. The number of divisions entered can range from 2 to 32,767. The prompt sequence for dividing a line and circle into five equal parts is (Figure 4-50):

Command: **DIVIDE** Enter
Select object to divide: *Select the object you want to divide.*
Enter number of segments or [Block]: **5** Enter

You can also place blocks as markers, but the block must be defined within the drawing. You can align these blocks with the object to be measured. The prompt sequence is (Figure 4-51):

Command: **DIVIDE** Enter
Select object to divide: *Select the object to be measured.*
Enter number of segments or [Block]: **B** Enter
Enter name of block to insert: *Enter the name of the block.*
Align block with object? [Yes/No] <Y>: *Enter* Y *to align, N to not align.*
Enter number of segments: *Enter the number of segments.*

Chapter 4

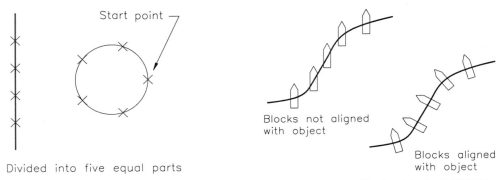

Figure 4-50 Using the **DIVIDE** command

Figure 4-51 Using blocks with the **DIVIDE** command

Note
*The size and shape of points placed by the **DIVIDE** and **MEASURE** commands are controlled by the **PDSIZE** and **PDMODE** system variables.*

Exercise 8   *General*

a.   Use the **MEASURE** command to divide a circle into parts with a of length 0.75" and divide a line into 10 equal segments (set **PDMODE** variable to 3).

b.   Draw the Figure 4-52. Use the **DIVIDE** command to divide the circle and use the NODE object snap to select the points.

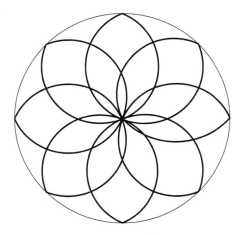

Figure 4-52 Drawing for Exercise 8

MATCHING PROPERTIES

Toolbar:	Standard > Match Properties
Menu:	Modify > Match Properties
Command:	MATCHPROP or PAINTER

The **MATCHPROP** or **PAINTER** command can be used to change some properties like color, layer, linetype, and linetype scale of the selected objects to the source object. When you invoke this command, AutoCAD will prompt you to select the source object and then the destination objects. The properties of the destination objects will be changed to that of the source object.

> Command: **MATCHPROP** or **PAINTER**
> Select Source Object: *Select the source object.*
> Current active settings: Color Layer ltype Ltscale Lineweight Thickness Plotstyle Text Dim Hatch
> Select Destination Object(s) or [Settings]: *Select the objects whose properties you want to change.*

When you select the Setting option, AutoCAD displays the **Properties settings** dialog box (Figure 4-54). The properties displayed in this dialog box are those of the source object. You can use this dialog box to change the properties that are copied from source to destination objects. The following table lists the properties associated with different types of objects:

Match Properties

*Figure 4-53 Invoking **Match Properties** from the **Standard** toolbar*

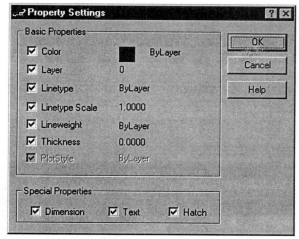

*Figure 4-54 **Properties Settings** dialog box*

Object	Color & layer	Linetype & Linetype Scale	Lineweight	Thickness	Text	Dimension	Hatch	Plot style
3dface	x	x	x					x
Arc	x	x	x	x				x
AttDef	x			x	x			x
Body	x	x						x
Circle	x	x	x	x				x
Dimension	x	x				x		x
Ellipse	x	x	x					x
Hatch	x		x			+	x	
Image	x	x						x
Insert	x	x	x					x
Leader	x	x	x			x		x
Line	x	x	x	x			x	
Mtext	x				x			x
OLE object								
Point	x		x	x			x	

Object								
2D polyline	x	x		x		x		x
3D polyline	x	x		x				x
3D mesh	x	x		x				x
Pface mesh	x	x		x				x
Ray	x	x		x				x
Region	x	x		x		x		x
2D solid	x	x		x				x
ACIS solid	x	x		x				x
Spline	x	x		x				x
Text	x	x	x		x			x
Tolerance	x	x		x		x		x
Trace	x	x		x		x		x
Viewport	x		x				x	
Xline	x	x		x				x
Xref	x	x		x				x
Zombie	x	x		x				x

PROPERTIES COMMAND*

Toolbar:	Standard > Properties
Menu:	Modify, Tools > Properties
Command:	PROPERTIES

 You can also modify an object by using the **PROPERTIES** command. When you invoke this command, AutoCAD will display **Objects Properties Window** on the screen (Figure 4-56). Similarly, if you select text, the Objects Properties Window is displayed. For example, if you select a object in the drawing area, the properties of that object will be displayed in the Object Properties Window. The contents of the Objects Properties Window changes according to the objects selected.

The **Object Properties** Window can also be invoked from shortcut menu by right-clicking in the drawing area and choosing **Properties** from the menu.

The **Object Properties Window** shows the common properties of the multiple objects if more than one object is selected. To

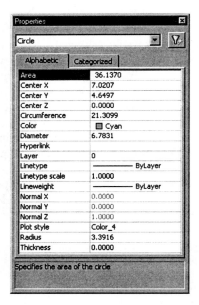

Figure 4-56 Using **Properties** command to edit (Objects Properties Window)

Figure 4-55 Selecting Properties from the **Object Properties** toolbar

change properties of the selected objects, you can click in the cell next to the name of the property and change the values manually or you can choose from the available options in the drop-down list if one is available. You can cycle through the options by double-clicking in the property cell.

QSELECT COMMAND*

Menu:	Tools > Quick Select
Command:	QSELECT

Figure 4-57 Quick Select dialog box

Quick Select is a new feature of AutoCAD 2000. This creates a new selection set which will either include or exclude all objects that matches specified object type and property criteria. The **QSELECT** command can be applied to the entire drawing or existing selection set. If a drawing is partially opened, QSELECT does not consider the objects that are not loaded. **QSELECT** command can be invoked by choosing the **Quick Select** button in the **Object Properties** Window. In the shortcut menu, the **QSELECT** command can be invoked by selecting **Quick Select**. The prompt sequence is as follows:

Command: **QSELECT** Enter

AutoCAD 2000 displays the **Quick Select** dialog box (Figure 4-57).

The **Quick Select** dialog box specifies the object filtering criteria and creates a selection set from that criteria.

Apply To. Apply to specifies whether to apply the filtering criteria to the entire drawing or to the current selection set. If there is some existing current selection set, Current Selection is the default value. Otherwise entire drawing is the default value.

Object Type. This specifies the type of object to be filtered. It lists all the available object types and if some objects are selected, it lists all selected object types. Multiple is the default setting.

Properties. It specifies the properties to be filtered.

Operator. It specifies the range of the filter for the chosen property:

Chapter 4

- Equals   =
- Does not Equal   < >
- Greater than   >
- Less than   <

Value. It specifies the property value of the filter. If values are known, then it becomes a list of the available values from which you can select a value. Otherwise you can enter a value.

How to Apply. It gives you choice of inclusion or exclusion from the new selection set. You can choose Include in new selection set for creating a new selection set only composed of those objects that conform to the filtering criteria. The other option creates a new selection set of objects that does not conform to the filtering criteria.

Append to Current Selection Set. This creates a cumulative selection set by using multiple uses of the Quick Select. It specifies whether **QSELECT** replaces or is appended to the current selection set.

Quick Select supports custom objects (objects that are created by some other applications) and their properties. If custom objects has other properties than AutoCAD 2000, then the source application of the object should be running in order for the properties to be available by the **QSELECT**.

Self-Evaluation Test

Answer the following questions and then compare your answers to the correct answers given at the end of this chapter.

1. When you shift a group of objects using the **MOVE** command, the size and orientation of these objects is changed. (T/F)

2. The **COPY** command makes copies of the selected object, leaving the original object intact. (T/F)

3. Depending on the side to offset, you can create smaller or larger circles, ellipses, and arcs with the **OFFSET** command. (T/F)

4. With the **BREAK** command, when you select an object, the selection point becomes the first break point. (T/F)

5. A fillet cannot be created between two parallel and nonintersecting lines. (T/F)

6. The _____ command prunes objects that extend beyond a required point of intersection.

7. The offset distance is stored in the _____ system variable.

8. Instead of specifying the scale factor, you can use the **Reference** option to scale an object. (T/F)

9. If the **MIRRTEXT** system variable is set to a value of 1, the mirrored text is not reversed with respect to the original object. (T/F)

10. A Rectangular array can be rotated. (T/F)

11. There are two types of arrays: _____ and _____.

12. The _____ option of the _____ command is used to draw an array in which the objects of the array are placed in a circular pattern around a point.

Review Questions

1. In the case of the **Through** option of the **OFFSET** command, you do not have to specify a distance; you simply have to specify an offset point. (T/F)

2. With the **BREAK** command, you cannot break an object in two without removing a portion in between. (T/F)

3. With the **FILLET** command, the extrusion direction of the selected object must be parallel to the Z axis of the UCS. (T/F)

4. With the **FILLET** command, there can be more than one fillet for arcs and circles. (T/F)

5. The _____ command helps you form round corners between any two lines by asking you to identify the two lines.

6. The _____ command does not work on closed lines or polylines.

7. If an entire selected object is within a window or crossing specification, the _____ command works like the **MOVE** command.

8. The _____ option of the **EXTEND** command is used to extend objects to the implied boundary.

9. With the **FILLET** command, using the **Polyline** option, if the selected polyline is not closed, the _____ corner is not filleted.

10. When the chamfer distance is zero, the chamfer created is in the form of a _____.

11. Compare the commands **EXTEND** and **STRETCH**. _____

_____

12. Describe the commands **FILLET** and **CHAMFER**. _____
_____

13. Explain how you can move an object from one position to another._____
_____

14. AutoCAD saves the previous selection set and lets you select it again by using the _____ selection option.

15. The **R (Remove)** option is used to shift from Add mode to _____ .

16. The _____ command restores objects that have been erased by the previous **ERASE** command.

17. Objects on frozen or locked layers are selected by the **All** selection option. (T/F)

18. The **Remove** selection option removes the selected object from the drawing. (T/F)

19. When you use the **SIngle** selection option with the **ERASE** command, you can select either a single object or multiple objects. (T/F)

20. The _____ selection option is used to select objects by touching the objects to be selected with the selection line.

21. The _____ variable is used to set the default for the number of sides in a polygon.

22. In the case of numerical specification of a radius, the bottom edge of the polygon is rotated by the prevalent _____ angle in the current UCS.

23. The _____ selection option is used if you want to select the most recently drawn object on the screen.

24. The _____ selection option enables you to select all the objects on the drawing screen.

25. With the **ARRAY** command, if you specify _____ column distance, the columns are added to the left.

26. You can use the _____ option of the _____ command to rotate an object that has been rotated previously with respect to a known angle.

27. What is the purpose of the **ARRAY** command? _____
_____.

28. Explain the difference between a polar array and a rectangular array. _____
_____.

29. Before creating a rectangular array, what values should you know _____
_____.

30. Define a unit cell._____
_____.

31. Suppose an object is 2 inches wide and you want a rectangular array with 1-inch spacing between objects. What should the column distance be? _____
_____.

32. Explain how you can create a rotated rectangular array. _____
_____.

33. In a polar array, suppose you enter a value for "Number of items" prompt. From the following options, select the one you are not required to give:
    A. Angle to fill.
    B. Angle between items.
    C. Center point.
    D. Rotate objects as they are copied.

Exercises

Exercise 9

Mechanical

Draw the object shown in Figure 4-58 and save the drawing. Assume the missing dimensions.

Figure 4-58 Drawing for Exercise 9

Chapter 4

Exercise 10   *Mechanical*

Make the drawing shown in Figure 4-59 and save the drawing. You can use the **ARRAY** command to make copies of the bolt hole details.

Figure 4-59 *Drawing for Exercise 10*

Exercise 11   *Mechanical*

Make the drawing shown in Figure 4-60 and save the drawing.

Figure 4-60 *Drawing for Exercise 11*

Exercise 12

Mechanical

Make the drawing shown in Figure 4-61 and save the drawing. Assume the missing dimensions.

Figure 4-61 Drawing for Exercise 12

Problem-Solving Exercise 1

Mechanical

Draw Figure 4-62 using draw and edit commands. Use the **MIRROR** command to mirror the shape 9 units across the Y axis so that the distance between two center points is 9 units. Mirror the shape across the X axis and then reduce the mirrored shape by 75 percent. Join the two ends to complete the shape of the open end spanner. Save the file. Assume the missing dimensions

Figure 4-62 Partial drawing for Problem-Solving Exercise 1

Chapter 4

Problem-Solving Exercise 2 *Architecture*

Draw the floor plan as shown in Figure 4-63 using AutoCAD commands that you have learned in Chapters 1 through 4. Assume the missing dimensions or measure the relative dimensions from the given drawing (the drawing is not to scale).

Figure4-63 *Drawing for Problem-Solving Exercise 2*

Chapter 5

Controlling Drawing Display and Creating Text

Learning Objectives

After completing this chapter, you will be able to:

- *Use the* **REDRAW** *and* **REGEN** *commands.*
- *Use the* **ZOOM** *command and its options.*
- *Understand the* **PAN** *and* **VIEW** *commands.*
- *Use AutoCAD text commands such as* **TEXT** *and* **DTEXT**.
- *Edit text using the* **DDEDIT** *command.*
- *Draw special characters in AutoCAD.*
- *Create paragraph text using the* **MTEXT** *command.*
- *Edit text using the* **DDEDIT** *and* **PROPERTIES** *commands.*
- *Substitute fonts and specify alternate default fonts.*
- *Create text styles using the* **STYLE** *command.*
- *Determine text height and check spelling.*
- *Format paragraph text.*

BASIC DISPLAY OPTIONS

Drawing in AutoCAD is much simpler than manual drafting in many ways. Sometimes while drawing, it is very difficult to see and alter minute details. In AutoCAD, you can overcome this problem by viewing only a specific portion of the drawing. For example, if you want to display a part of the drawing on a larger area, you can use the **ZOOM** command, which lets you enlarge or reduce the size of the drawing displayed on the screen. Similarly, you can use **REGEN** command to regenerate the drawing and **REDRAW** to refresh the screen. In this chapter you will learn some of the drawing display commands, like **REDRAW**, **REGEN**, **PAN**, **ZOOM**, and **VIEW**. These commands can also be used in the transparent mode. Transparent commands are commands that can be used while another command is in progress. Once you have completed the process involved with a transparent command, AutoCAD automatically returns you to the command with which you were working before you invoked the transparent command.

REDRAW COMMAND

Toolbar:	Standard toolbar > Redrawall
Menu:	View > Redraw
Command:	REDRAW (or R)

This command redraws the screen, thereby removing the small cross marks that appear when a point is specified on the screen. These marks, known as blip marks or **blips**, indicate the points you have selected (points picked). The blip mark is not treated as an element of the drawing. In AutoCAD, several commands redraw the screen automatically (for example, when a grid is turned off), but it is sometimes useful to redraw the screen explicitly. Redrawing is used to remove blips and fill empty spaces left on the screen after objects have been deleted from the drawing. It also redraws the objects that do not display on the screen as a result of editing some other object. In AutoCAD, the **REDRAW** command can also be used in the transparent mode. Use of the **REDRAW** command does not involve a prompt sequence; instead, the redrawing process takes place without any prompting for information. You can also invoke this command from the tablet menu if you have the tablet facility. The prompt sequence is:

Figure 5-1 Invoking the REDRAW command from the View menu

Command: **REDRAW or (R)** [Enter]

If the command is to be entered while you are working inside another command, type an apostrophe in front of the command. The apostrophe appended to a command indicates that the command is to be used as a transparent command (Command: **'REDRAW** [Enter]).

As with any other command, pressing ESC stops the command from taking effect and takes you back to the Command prompt. The **REDRAW** command affects only the current viewport. If you have more than one viewport you can use the **REDRAWALL** command to redraw all the viewports.

While working on complex drawings it may be better to set the blipmode off instead of using **REDRAW** command to clear blips. This can be done by using the **BLIPMODE** command. The prompt sequence is:

Command: **BLIPMODE** [Enter]
Enter mode [ON/OFF]<ON>: **OFF** [Enter]

REGEN COMMAND

Menu:	View > Regen
Command:	REGEN

The **REGEN command** makes AutoCAD regenerate the entire drawing to update it. The need for regeneration usually occurs when you change certain aspects of the drawing. All the objects in the drawing are recalculated and the current viewport is redrawn. This is a longer process than **REDRAW** and is seldom needed. One of the advantages of this command is that the drawing is refined by smoothing out circles and arcs. To use this command, enter **REGEN** at the Command prompt:

Command: **REGEN** [Enter]

AutoCAD displays the message **Regenerating model** while it regenerates the drawing. The **REGEN** command affects only the current viewport. If you have more than one viewport, you can use the **REGENALL** command to regenerate all the viewports. The **REGEN** command can be aborted by pressing ESC. This saves time if you are going to use another command that causes automatic regeneration.

Note
*Under certain conditions, the **ZOOM** and **PAN** commands automatically regenerate the drawing. Some other commands also perform regenerations under certain conditions.*

ZOOM COMMAND

Toolbar:	Zoom toolbar or Standard > Zoom flyout
Menu:	View > Zoom
Command:	ZOOM

Creating drawings on the screen would not be of much use if you could not magnify the drawing view to work on minute details. Getting close to or away from the drawing is the function of the **ZOOM** command. In other words, this command enlarges or reduces the view of the drawing on the screen, but it does not affect the actual size of the objects. In this way the **ZOOM** command functions like the zoom lens on a camera. When you magnify the apparent size of a section of the drawing, you see that area in greater detail. On the other hand, if you reduce the apparent size of the drawing, you see a larger area.

The ability to zoom in, or magnify, has been helpful in creating the miniscule circuits used in the electronics and computer industries. This is one of the most frequently used commands. Also, this command can be used transparently, which means that it can be used while working in other commands. The **ZOOM** command can be invoked from the shortcut menu by right-clicking in the drawing area and choosing **Zoom** from the menu (Figure 5-3). This command has several options and can be used in a number of ways. After the **ZOOM** command has been entered, different options are listed:

Chapter 5

Figure 5-2 Selecting *Zoom* options from the *Zoom* toolbar

Figure 5-3 Invoking the **ZOOM** command from the **shortcut** menu, when in **LINE** Command

Command: **ZOOM** [Enter]
Specify corner of window, enter a scale factor (nX or nXP) , or
[All/Center/Dynamic/Extents/Previous/Scale/Window] <real time>:

Realtime Zooming

You can use the **Realtime Zoom** to zoom in and zoom out interactively. To zoom in, invoke the command, then hold the pick button down and move the cursor up. If you want to zoom in further, bring the cursor down. Specify a point and move the cursor up. Similarly, to zoom out, hold the pick button down and move the cursor down. If you move the cursor vertically up from the midpoint of the screen to the top of the window, the drawing is magnified by 100% (Zoom in 2x magnification). Similarly, if you move the cursor vertically down from the midpoint of the screen to the bottom of the window, the drawing display is reduced 100% (Zoom out 0.5x magnification). Realtime zoom is the default setting for the **ZOOM** command. Pressing Enter after entering the **ZOOM** command automatically invokes the realtime zoom.

When you use the realtime zoom, AutoCAD displays a plus sign (+) and a minus sign (-). When you reach the zoom out limit, AutoCAD does not display the minus sign (-) with the cursor. Similarly, when you reach the zoom in limit, AutoCAD does not display the plus sign (+) with the cursor. To exit the realtime zoom, press Enter, Esc, or select Exit from the cursor menu.

All Option

This option of the **ZOOM** command displays the drawing limits (Figure 5-4) or extents, whichever is greater. Even if the objects are not within the limits, they are still included in the display. Hence, with the help of the **All** option, you can view the entire drawing in the current viewport (Figure 5-5).

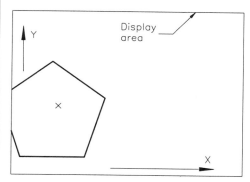

Figure 5-4 *Drawing showing limits*

Figure 5-5 *The Zoom All option*

Center Option

This option lets you define a new display window by specifying its center point (Figures 5-6 and 5-7). Here, you are required to enter the **center** and the **height** of the subsequent screen display. If you press ENTER instead of entering a new center point, the center of the view will remain unchanged. Instead of entering a height, you can enter the **magnification factor** by typing a number. If you press ENTER at the height prompt, or if the height you enter is the same as the current height, magnification does not take place. For example, if the current height is 2.7645 and you press ENTER at the **magnification or height <2.7645>:** prompt, magnification will not take place. The smaller the value, the greater the enlargement of the image. You can also enter a number followed by **X**. This indicates the change in magnification, not as an absolute value, but as a value relative to the current screen. The following is the prompt sequence:

Command : **ZOOM** [Enter]
Specify corner of window, enter a scale factor (nX or nXP), or
[All/Center/Dynamic/Extents/Previous/Scale/Window] <realtime>: C [Enter]
Specify center point : *Specify a center point.*
Enter magnification or height <current>: 5X [Enter]

Figure 5-6 *Drawing before using the* **ZOOM Center** *option*

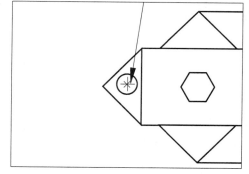

Figure 5-7 *Drawing after using the* **ZOOM Center** *option*

In Figure 5-7, the current magnification height is 5, which magnified the display 5 times. If you enter a value of 2, the size (height and width) of the display area changes to 2 x 2, that will change the size of the object in graphics window. In Figure 5-8, since the diameter of the circle is 2 units, it will fit in the 2 x 2 window. The prompt sequence is:

Command: **ZOOM** [Enter]
Specify corner of window,enter a scale factor (nX or nXP), or
[All/Center/Dynamic/Extents/Previous/Scale/Window]<realtime>:**C** [Enter]
Center point: *Select the center of the circle.*
Magnification or Height <5.0>:**2** [Enter]

Extents Option

As the name indicates , this option lets you zoom to the extents of the drawing. The extents of the drawing comprise the area that has the drawings in it . The rest of the empty area is neglected . With this option, all the objects in the drawing are magnified to the largest possible display (Figure 5-9).

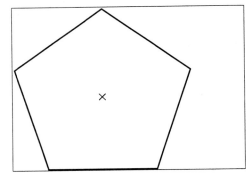

*Figure 5-8 Drawing after using the **ZOOM** Center option*

*Figure 5-9 The **ZOOM Extents** option*

Dynamic Option

This option displays the portion of the drawing that you have already specified. The prompt sequence for using this option of the **ZOOM** command is:

Command: **ZOOM** [Enter]
Specify corner of window,enter a scale factor (nX or nXP), or
[All/Center/Dynamic/Extents/Previous/Scale/Window]<realtime>: **D** [Enter]

You can then specify the area you want to be displayed by manipulating a view box representing your viewport. This option lets you enlarge or shrink the view box and move it around. When you have the view box in the proper position and size, the current viewport is cleared by AutoCAD and a special view selection screen is displayed. This special screen comprises information regarding the current view as well as available views. In a color display, the different viewing windows are very easy to distinguish because of their different colors, but in a monochrome monitor, they can be distinguished by their shape.

Blue Dashed Box Representing Drawing Extents. Drawing extents are represented by a dashed blue box (Figure 5-10), which constitutes the larger of the drawing limits or the actual area occupied by the drawing.

Green Dashed Box Representing the Current View. A green dotted box is formed to represent the area that the current viewport comprises when the **Dynamic** option of the **ZOOM** command is invoked (Figure 5-11).

Figure 5-10 Box representing drawing extents

Figure 5-11 Representation of the current view

Panning View Box (X in the center). A view box initially of the same size as the current view box (the green or magenta box) is displayed with an X in the center (Figure 5-12). You can move this box with the help of your pointing device. This box, known as the **panning view box**, helps you to find the center point of the zoomed display you want. When you have found the center, you press the pick button to make the zooming view box appear.

Zooming View Box (arrow on the right side). After you press the pick button in the center of the panning view box, the X in the center of the view box is replaced by an arrow pointing to the right edge of the box. This **zooming view box** (Figure 5-13) indicates the ZOOM mode. You can now increase or decrease the area of this box according to the area you want to zoom into. To shrink the box, move the pointer to the left; to increase it, move the pointer to the right. The top, right, and bottom sides of the zooming view box move as you move the pointer, but the left side remains fixed, with the zoom base point at the midpoint of the left side. When you have the

Figure 5-12 The panning view box

Figure 5-13 The zooming view box

zooming view box in the desired size for your zoom display, press ENTER to complete the command and zoom into the desired area of the drawing. Before pressing ENTER, if you want to change the position of the zooming view box, click the pick button of your pointing device to make the panning view box reappear. After repositioning, press ENTER.

Previous Option

While working on a complex drawing, you may need to zoom in on a portion of the drawing to edit some minute details. Once the editing is over you may want to return to the previous view. This can be done using the **Previous** option of the **ZOOM** command. Without this option it would be very tedious to zoom back to previous views. AutoCAD saves the view specification of the current viewport whenever it is being altered by any of the ZOOM options or by the PAN, VIEW Restore, **DVIEW** or **PLAN** commands (which are discussed later). Up to 10 views are saved for each viewport. The prompt sequence for this option is:

Command: **ZOOM** (Enter)
Specify corner of window, enter a scale factor (nX or nXP), or
[All/Center/Dynamic/Extents/Previous/Scale/Window]<realtime>: **P** (Enter)

Successive **ZOOM,** P commands can restore upto 10 previous views. **VIEW** here refers to the area of the drawing defined by its display extents. If you erase some objects and then issue a **ZOOM** Previous command, the previous view is restored, but the erased objects are not.

Window Option

This is the most commonly used option of the **ZOOM** command. It lets you specify the area you want to zoom in on, by letting you specify two opposite corners of a rectangular window. The center of the specified window becomes the center of the new display screen. The area inside the window is magnified or reduced in size to fill the display as completely as possible. The points can be specified either by selecting them with the help of the pointing device or by entering their coordinates. The prompt sequence is:

Command: **ZOOM** (Enter)
Specify corner of window, enter a scale factor (nX or nXP), or
[All/Center/Dynamic/Extents/Previous/Scale/Window]<realtime>: *Specify a point.*
Specify opposite corner: *Specify another point.*

Whenever the **ZOOM** command is invoked, the window method is one of two default options. This is illustrated by the prompt sequence above, where you can specify the two corner points of the window without invoking any option of the **ZOOM** command. The **Window** option can also be used by entering **W**. In this case the prompt sequence is:

Command: **ZOOM** (Enter)
Specify corner of window, enter a scale factor (nX or nXP), or
[All/Center/Dynamic/Extents/Previous/Scale/Window]<realtime>: **W** (Enter)
Specify first corner: *Specify a point.*
Specify opposite corner: *Specify another point.*

Scale Option

The Scale option is used in the following ways.

Scale: Relative to Full View. This option of the **ZOOM** command lets you magnify or reduce the size of a drawing according to a scale factor, (Figure 5-14). A scale factor equal to 1 displays an area equal in size to the area defined by the established limits. This may not display the entire drawing if the previous view was not centered on the limits or if you have drawn outside the limits. To get a magnification relative to the full view, you can enter any other number. For example, you can type 4 if you want the displayed image to be enlarged four times. If you want to decrease the magnification relative to the full view, you need to enter a number that is less than 1. In Figure 5-15, the image size decreased because the scale factor is less than 1. In other words, the image size is half of the full view because the scale factor is 0.5. The prompt sequence is:

Command: **ZOOM** [Enter]
Specify corner of window, enter a scale factor (nX or nXP), or
[All/Center/Dynamic/Extents/Previous/Scale/Window]<realtime>: **S** [Enter]
Enter a scale factor (nX or nXP) : **0.5** [Enter]

Figure 5-14 *Drawing before* **ZOOM** *Scale option*

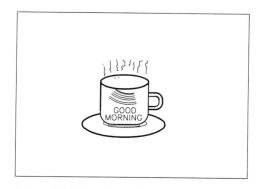

Figure 5-15 *Drawing after* **ZOOM** *Scale option*

Scale: Relative to Current View. The second way to scale is with respect to the current view (Figure 5-16). In this case, instead of entering only a number, enter a number followed by an **X**. The scale is calculated with reference to the current view. For example, if you enter **0.25X**, each object in the drawing will be displayed at one fourth (1/4) of its current size. The following example increases the display magnification by a factor of 2 relative to its current value (Figure 5-17):

Command: **ZOOM** [Enter]
Specify corner of window, enter a scale factor (nX or nXP), or
[All/Center/Dynamic/Extents/Previous/Scale/Window]<realtime>: **2X** [Enter]

Scale: Relative to Paper Space Units. The third method of scaling is with respect to paper space. You can use paper space in a variety of ways and for various reasons. For example, you can array and plot various views of your model in paper space. To scale each view relative to paper space units, you can use the **ZOOM XP** option. Each view can have an individual scale. The

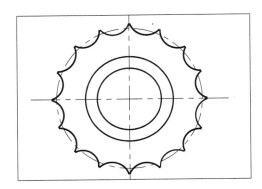

Figure 5-16 *Drawing before* **ZOOM** *Scale(X)* *option*

Figure 5-17 *Drawing after* **ZOOM** *Scale (X) option*

drawing view can be at any scale of your choice in a model space viewport. For example, to display a model space at one fourth (1/4) the size of the paper space units, the prompt sequence is:

Command: **ZOOM** [Enter]
Specify corner of window, enter a scale factor (nX or nXP), or
[All/Center/Dynamic/Extents/Previous/Scale/Window]<realtime>: **1/4XP** [Enter]

Note
For a better understanding of this topic, refer to "Model Space and Paper Space" in Chapter 22.

Zoom In and Out

You can also zoom into the drawing using the **In** option, which doubles the image size.

Similarly, you can use the **Out** option to decrease the size of the image by half. To invoke these options from the command line, enter **ZOOM 2X** for the **In** option or **ZOOM .5X** for the **Out** option at the Command prompt.

Exercise 1   *Mechanical*

Draw Figure 5-18 according to the given dimensions. Use the **ZOOM** command to get a bigger view of the drawing. Do not dimension the drawing.

Figure 5-18 Drawing for Exercise 1

PAN REALTIME COMMAND

Toolbar:	Standard toolbar > Pan
Menu:	View > Pan
Command:	PAN

You may want to view or draw on a particular area outside the current viewport. You can do this using the **PAN** command. If done manually, this would be like holding one corner of the drawing and dragging it across the screen. The **PAN** command allows you to bring into view portions of the drawing that are outside the current viewport. This is done without changing the magnification of the drawing. The effect of this command can also be illustrated by imagining that you are looking at a big drawing through a window known as the **display window** that allows you to slide the drawing right, left, up, and down to bring the part you want to view inside this window. You can invoke **PAN** command from the shortcut menu also.

Figure 5-19 Invoking the PAN command from the View menu

Panning in Realtime

You can use the **Realtime PAN** to pan the drawing interactively. To pan a drawing, invoke the command and then hold the pick button down and move the cursor in any direction. When you select the realtime pan, AutoCAD displays an image of a hand indicating that you are in PAN mode.

Realtime pan is the default setting for the **PAN** command. Pressing ENTER after entering the **PAN** command automatically invokes the realtime pan. To exit the realtime pan, press ENTER, ESC, or choose **Exit** from the shortcut menu.

Chapter 5

There are different menu items and buttons predefined for the **PAN** command, which can be used to pan the drawing in a particular direction. These items can be invoked from the menu.

Point. In this option you are required to specify the displacement. To do this you need to specify in what direction to move the drawing and by what distance. You can give the displacement either by entering the coordinates of the points or by specifying the coordinates by using a pointing device. The coordinates can be entered in two ways. One way is to specify a single coordinate pair. In this case, AutoCAD takes it as a relative displacement of the drawing with respect to the screen. For example, in the following case the **PAN** command would shift the displayed portion of the drawing 2 units to the right and 2 units up.

> Command: *Specify the Point item from the **View** menu.*
> Specify base point or displacement: **2,2** [Enter]
> Specify second point: [Enter]

In the second case, you can specify two coordinate pairs. AutoCAD computes the displacement from the first point to the second. Here, displacement is calculated between point (3,3) and point (5,5).

> Command: *Specify the Point item from the View menu*
> Specify base point or displacement: **3,3** [Enter]   *(Or specify a point)*
> Specify second point: **5,5** [Enter]   *(Or specify a point)*

Left. Moves the drawing so that some of the left portion of the screen is brought into view.

Right. Moves the drawing so that some of the right portion of the screen is brought into view.

Up. Moves the drawing toward the bottom so that some of the top portion of the screen is brought into view.

Down. Moves the drawing toward the top so that some of the bottom portion of the screen is brought into view.

CREATING VIEWS

While working on a drawing, you may frequently be working with the **ZOOM** and **PAN** commands, and you may need to work on a particular drawing view (some portion of the drawing) more often than others. Instead of wasting time by recalling your zooms and pans and selecting up the same area from the screen over and over again, you can store the view under a name and restore the view using the name you have given it. The **View dialog box** (Figure 5-21) is used to save the current view under a name so that you can restore (display) it later. It does not save any drawing object data, only the view parameters needed to redisplay that portion of the drawing.

View Dialog Box

Toolbar:	Viewpoint > Named Views
	Standard > Named Views
Menu:	View > Named Views
Command:	DDVIEW or View

*Figure 5-20 Invoking Named Views from the **View** toolbar*

You can save and restore the views from the **View** dialog box (Figure 5-21). This dialog box is very useful when you are saving and restoring many view names. With this dialog box you can name the current view or restore some other view. The list box shows all the existing named views. The following are the different options in the **View** dialog box:

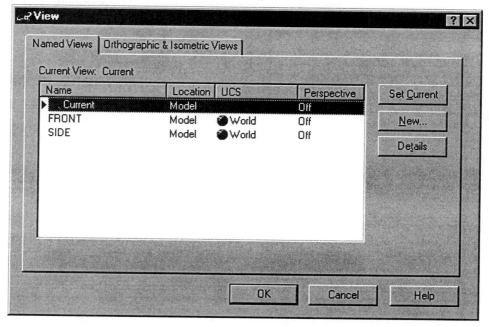

Figure 5-21 View Dialog box

Current Views List Box

The Views list box displays a list of the named views in the drawing. The list appears with the names of all saved views and the space in which each was defined (as discussed in Chapter 21).

New

The new button allows you to create a new view and save it by giving it a name. When you choose the New button, the **New View** dialog box (Figure 5-22) is displayed. Enter a name for the view in the **View** edit box. If you want to save the current view, then activate the **Current display** radio button. If you want to save a rectangular portion of the current drawing as a view (without first zooming in on that area), then choose the **Define window** radio button to activate it. You can specify two points on the screen to describe the window by choosing the **define view window** button or you can enter the X and Y coordinates in the **Specify first corner** and **Specify other corner** in the command lines. After specifying the view, choose the **Save View** button to save the named view.

Figure 5-22 New View Dialog box

Set Current

The **Set Current** button allows you to replace the current viewport by the view you specify. AutoCAD uses the center point and magnification of each saved view and executes a **ZOOM Center** with this information when a view is restored.

Note
*Refer to Chapter 22. Also, if **TILEMODE** is on, you cannot restore a Paper space view.*

Details

You can also see the description of the general parameters of a view by selecting the particular view and then choosing the **Details** button.

Using the Command prompt

You can also use the **-VIEW** command to work with views at the Command: prompt.

Command: **-VIEW** [Enter]
Enter an option [?/Orthographic/Delete/Restore/Save/UCS/Window]:

You can use the different options to save, restore, delete, or list the views. If you try to restore a Model space while working in Paper space, AutoCAD automatically switches to Model space, and vice versa. In this case AutoCAD will prompt you further as follows:

Enter view name to restore: Select *viewport for restoring*

You can select the viewport you want by selecting its border. That particular viewport must be on and active. The restored viewport also becomes the current one. You can use the Window option to define the view; the prompt sequence is:

Command: **-VIEW** ⏎
Enter an option [?/Orthographic/Delete/Restore/Save/UCS/Window]: **W** ⏎
Enter view name to save: *Enter the name.*
Specify first corner: *Specify a point.*
Specify other corner: *Specify another point.*

AERIAL VIEW

Menu: View > Aerial View
Command: DSVIEWER

As a navigational tool, AutoCAD provides you with the option of opening another drawing display window along with the graphics screen window you are working on. This window, called the **Aerial View** window, can be used to view the entire drawing and select those portions you want to quickly zoom or pan. The AutoCAD graphics screen window resets itself to display the portion of the drawing you have selected for Zoom or Pan in the Aerial View window. You can keep the Aerial View window open as you work on the graphics screen, or minimize it so that it stays on the screen as an button which can be restored when required (Figure 5-23). As with all windows, you can resize or move it. The Aerial View window can also be invoked when you are in the midst of any command other than the **DVIEW** command.

Figure 5-23 AutoCAD graphics screen with the Aerial View window

The Aerial View window has two menus, View and Options. It also has a toolbar containing zoom in, zoom out, and zoom global options. The following is a description of the available options in the Aerial View:

Toolbar Buttons

The Aerial View window has three buttons: **Zoom In**, **Zoom Out**, and **Zoom Global** (Figure 5-24).

Zoom In. This option leads to the magnification by a factor of **2** which is centered on the current view box.

Zoom Out. This option leads to the reduction by **half** centered on the current view box.

Zoom Global. The Global option displays the complete drawing in the Aerial Viewport.

Menus

The menus available in the menu title bar are **View** and **Options**. They are described as follows:

Figure 5-24 Aerial View window

View. The **View** menu contains **Zoom In**, **Zoom Out**, and **Global options**. The **Zoom Out** and **Zoom In** options magnify or reduce the display, and the **Global option** acts like Zoom Extents in the Aerial View window.

Options. The **Options** menu has the following three options:

Auto Viewport. When you are working with viewports, you may need to change the view in the Aerial View window to display the current viewport view. You can achieve this by selecting the Auto Viewport option from the **Options** menu. If you are working in multiple viewports and you zoom or pan in the Aerial Viewport window, only the view in the current viewport is affected.

Dynamic Update. When you make any changes in the current drawing, the View box is updated simultaneously in the Aerial View window if you have selected the Dynamic Update option. If Dynamic Update is unselected, the drawing is not updated simultaneously. The drawing in the Aerial View window is updated only when you move the cursor in the Aerial View window or invoke any of the menus or the toolbar buttons.

Realtime Zoom. This option if on, updates the drawing area when you are zooming in Aerial view in realtime.

CREATING TEXT

In manual drafting, lettering is accomplished by hand using a lettering device, pen, or pencil. This is a very time-consuming and tedious job. Computer-aided drafting has made this process extremely simple. Engineering drawings invoke certain standards to be followed in connection with the placement of a text in a drawing. In this section, you will learn how text can be added in a drawing by using **TEXT**, **DTEXT**, and **MTEXT** commands. The following is a list of some of the functions associated with **TEXT**, **DTEXT**, and **MTEXT** commands that are described in this section:

1. Using the **TEXT**, **DTEXT** and **MTEXT** commands to create text.
2. Changing text styles using the **STYLE** command.
3. Drawing special symbols using the proper control characteristics.
4. Editing single line and paragraph text.

TEXT AND DTEXT COMMAND

Menu:	Draw > Text > Single Line Text
Command:	TEXT or DTEXT

The **TEXT** and **DTEXT** commands lets you write text on a drawing. These commands allow you to delete what has been typed by using the BACKSPACE key. They also let you enter multiple lines in one command. The **TEXT** and **DTEXT** commands display a line after you enter the start point, height, and the rotation angle. This line identifies the start point and the size of the text height entered. The characters appear on the screen as you enter them. When you press Enter after typing a line, the cursor automatically places itself at the start of the next line and repeats the prompt **Enter text:**. You can end the command by giving null response (pressing the ENTER key) to the **Enter text:** prompt. This command can be canceled by pressing ESC. If you do this, the entire text entered during this particular command sequence is erased.

The screen crosshairs can be moved irrespective of the cursor line for the text. If you specify a point, this command will complete the current line of the text and move the cursor line to the point you selected. This cursor line can be moved and placed anywhere on the screen; hence, multiple lines of text can be entered at any desired locations on the screen with a single **TEXT** command. By pressing BACKSPACE you can delete one character to the left of the current position of the cursor box. Even if you have entered several lines of the text, you can use Backspace and go on deleting until you reach the start point of the first line entered. Upon deletion of an entire line, **DTEXT** displays a ***Deleted*** message in the command prompt area.

This command can be used with most of the text alignment modes, although it is most useful in the case of left-justified texts. In the case of aligned texts, this command assigns a height appropriate for the width of the first line to every line of the text. Irrespective of the **Justify** option chosen, the text is first left-aligned at the selected point. After the **DTEXT** command ends, the text is momentarily erased from the screen and regenerated with the requested alignment. For example, if you use the **Middle** option, the text will first appear on the screen as left-justified, starting at the point you designated as the middle point. After you end the command and press Enter, it is regenerated with the proper alignment. The sequence of prompts in the **DTEXT** command is the same as for the **TEXT** command and both perform the same function.

Command: **TEXT** or **DTEXT** `Enter`
Specify start point of text or [Justify/Style]: *Specify the start point.*
Specify height <0.25>:**0.15** `Enter`
Specify rotation angle of text <0>: `Enter`
Enter text: *Enter first line of the text.*
Enter text: *Enter second line of the text.*
Enter text: `Enter` *Press ENTER to terminate the text command.*

Chapter 5

Start Point Option

This is the default and the most commonly used option in the **DTEXT** command. By specifying a start point, the text is left-justified along its baseline starting from the location of the starting point. Specifying a start point does let you **left-justify** your text; however, before AutoCAD draws the text, it needs some more parameters. AutoCAD must know the text height, the rotation angle for the baseline, and the text string to be drawn. It prompts you for all this information. The prompt sequence is:

     Specify height <default>:
     Specify rotation angle of text <default>
     Enter text:

The **Specify height:** prompt determines the distance by which the text extends above the baseline, measured by the capital letters. This distance is specified in drawing units. You can specify the text height by specifying two points or entering a value. In the case of a null response, the default height, i.e., the height used for the previous text drawn in the same style, will be used.

Next comes the **Specify rotation angle of text:** prompt. It determines the angle at which the text line will be drawn. The default value of the rotation angle is **0 degrees** (3 o'clock, or east), and in this case the text is drawn horizontally from the specified start point. The rotation angle is measured in a counterclockwise direction. The last angle specified becomes the current rotation angle, and if you give a null response the last angle specified will be used as default. You can also specify the rotation angle by specifying a point. The text is drawn upside down if a point is specified at a location to the left of the start point.

As a response to the **Enter text:** prompt, enter the text string. Spaces are allowed between words. After entering the text, press ENTER. The following example illustrates these prompts:

     Command: **DTEXT** [Enter]
     Specify start point of text or [Justify/Style]: **1,1** [Enter]
     Specify height <0.25>:**0.15** [Enter]
     Specify rotation angle of text <0>: [Enter]
     Enter text: *Enter the text string.*

Justify Option

AutoCAD offers different options to align the text. **Alignment** refers to the layout of the text. The main text alignment modes are **left, center,** and **right**. You can align a text using a combination of modes; e.g., top/middle/baseline/bottom and left/center/right (Figure 5-25). **Top** refers to the line along which lie the top points of the capital letters ; **Baseline** refers to the line along which lie their bases. Letters with descenders (such as p, g, y) dip below the baseline to the bottom.

When the **Justify** option is invoked, the user can place text in one of the 14 various alignment types by selecting the desired alignment option. The orientation of the text style determines the command interaction for Text Justify. (Text styles and fonts are discussed later in this chapter). For now, assume that the text style orientation is horizontal. The prompt sequence using this option of the **DTEXT** command is:

Text justifications
for text alignment

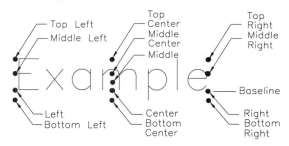

Figure 5-25 *Text alignment positions*

Command: **DTEXT** `Enter`
Specify start point of text or [Justify/style]: **J** `Enter`
Enter an option [Align/Fit/Center/Middle/Right/TL/TC/TR/ML/MC/MR/BL/BC/ BR]: *Select any of these options.*

If the text style is vertically oriented (refer to the "**STYLE** Command" section later in this chapter), the prompt sequence is as follows:

Command: **DTEXT** `Enter`
Specify start point of text or [Justify/Style]: **J** `Enter`
Enter an option [Align/Center/Middle/Right]:

If you know what justification you want, you can enter it directly at the **Specify start point of text or [Justify/Style]:** prompt instead of first entering J to display the justification prompt. If you need to specify a style as well as a justification, you must specify the style first. The available text justification options with alignment, the corresponding abbreviations, and the text style orientations (horizontal or vertical) are as follows:

Alignment	**Abbreviation**	**Orientation**
Align	A	Horizontal/Vertical
Fit	F	Horizontal
Center	C	Horizontal/Vertical
Middle	M	Horizontal/Vertical
Right	R	Horizontal/Vertical
Top/left	TL or Tleft	Horizontal
Top/center	TC or Tcenter	Horizontal
Top/right	TR or Tright	Horizontal
Middle/left	ML or Mleft	Horizontal
Middle/center	MC or Mcenter	Horizontal
Middle/right	MR or Mright	Horizontal
Bottom/left	BL or Bleft	Horizontal

| Bottom/center | BC or Bcenter | Horizontal |
| Bottom/right | BR or Bright | Horizontal |

Align Option. This option is invoked under the Justify option. Here, enter A at the **Enter an option[Align/Fit/Center/Middle/Right/TL/TC/TR/ML/MC/MR/BL/BC/BR]:** prompt. In this option the text string is written between two points (Figure 5-26). You must specify the two points that act as the endpoints of the baseline. The two points may be specified horizontally or at an angle. AutoCAD adjusts the text width (compresses or expands) so that it fits between the two points. The text height is also changed, depending on the distance between points and number of letters.

Command: **DTEXT** [Enter]
Specify start point of text or [Justify/Style]: **J** [Enter]
Enter an option [Align/Fit/Center/Middle/Right/TL/TC/TR/ML/MC/MR/BL/BC/BR]: **A** [Enter]
Specify first endpoint of text baseline: *Specify a point.*
Specify second endpoint of text baseline: *Specify a point.*
Enter text: *Enter the text string.*

Fit Option. This option is very similar to the previous one. The only difference is that in this case you select the text height, and it does not vary according to the distance between the two points. AutoCAD adjusts the letter width to fit the text between the two given points, but the height remains constant (Figure 5-26). The Fit option is not accessible for vertically oriented text styles. If you try the Fit option on the vertical text style, you will notice that the text string does not appear in the prompt. The prompt sequence is:

Command: **DTEXT** [Enter]
Specify start point of text or[Justify/Style]: **J** [Enter]
Enter an option [Align/Fit/Center/Middle/Right/TL/TC/TR/ML/MC/MR/BL/BC/BR]: **F** [Enter]
Specify first endpoint of text baseline: *Specify a point.*
Specify second endpoint of text baseline: *Specify a point.*
Specify height<current>: *Enter the height.*
Enter text: *Enter the text.*

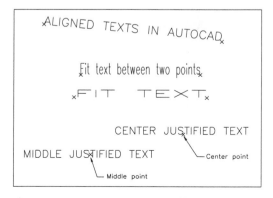

*Figure 5-26 Writing the text using **Align**, **Fit**, **Center**, and **Middle** options*

Note

*You do not need to select the **Justify** option (J) for selecting the text justification. You can enter the text justification by directly entering justification when AutoCAD prompts "Specify start point of text or [Justify/Style]:"*

Center Option. You can use this option to select the midpoint of the baseline for the text. This option can be invoked by entering **Justify** and then **Center** or **C**. After you select or specify the center point, you must enter the letter height and the rotation angle (Figure 5-26). The prompt sequence is:

Command: **DTEXT** [Enter]
Specify start point of text or [Justify/Style]: C [Enter]
Specify center point of text: *Specify a point.*
Specify height<current>: **0.15** [Enter]
Specify rotation angle of text<0>: [Enter]
Enter text: **CENTER JUSTIFIED TEXT** [Enter]

Middle Option. Using this option you can center text not only horizontally, as with the previous option, but also vertically. In other words, you can specify the middle point of the text string (Figure 5-26). You can alter the text height and the angle of rotation to your requirement. The prompt sequence is:

Command: **DTEXT** [Enter]
Specify start point of text or[Justify/Style]: **M** [Enter]
Specify middle point of text : *Specify a point.*
Specify height<current>: **0.15** [Enter]
Specify rotation angle of text<0>: [Enter]
Enter text: **MIDDLE JUSTIFIED TEXT** [Enter]

Right Option. This option is similar to the default left-justified Start point option. The only difference is that the text string is aligned with the lower right corner (the endpoint you specify); i.e., the text is **right-justified** (Figure 5-27). The prompt sequence is :

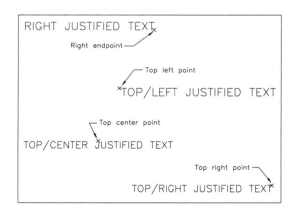

Figure 5-27 Writing text using the Right, Top-Left, Top-Center, and Top-Right options

Command: **DTEXT** [Enter]
Specify start point of text or [Justify/Style]: R [Enter]
Specify right endpoint of text baseline : *Specify a point.*
Specify height<current>: **0.15** [Enter]
Specify rotation angle of text<0>: [Enter]
Enter text: **RIGHT JUSTIFIED TEXT** [Enter]

TL Option. The full form of this abbreviation has already been written. In this option the text string is justified from the **top left** (Figure 5-27). The command prompt sequence is:

Command: **DTEXT** [Enter]
Specify start point of text or[Justify/Style]: **TL** [Enter]
Specify top-left point of text : *Specify a point.*
Specify height<current>: **0.15** [Enter]
Specify rotation angle of text <0>: [Enter]
Enter text: **TOP/LEFT JUSTIFIED TEXT** [Enter]

Note
The rest of the text alignment options are similar to those just discussed, and you can try them on your own. The prompt sequence is almost the same as those given for the previous examples.

Style Option

With this option you can specify another existing text style. Different text styles can have different text fonts, heights, obliquing angles, and other features. This option can be invoked by entering **TEXT** and then S at the next prompt. The prompt sequence is:

Command: **DTEXT** [Enter]
Specify start point of text or [Justify/Style]: **S** [Enter]
Enter style name or [?] <current>:

If you want to work in the previous text style, just press ENTER at the last prompt. If you want to activate another text style, enter the name of the style at the last prompt. You can also choose from a list of available text styles, which can be displayed by entering ?. After you enter ?, the next prompt is:

Enter text style(s) to list <*>:

Press ENTER to display the available text style names and the details of the current styles and commands in the **AutoCAD Text Window**. The prompt sequence in the AutoCAD Text Window is as follows :

Specify start point of text or [Justify/Style]: S [Enter]
Enter style name or [?] <current>: *Enter a style name and press F2 to return to the screen.*

Note
*With the help of the **Style** option of the **TEXT** command, you can select a text style from an existing list. If you want to create a new style, make use of the **STYLE** command, which is explained later in this chapter.*

DRAWING SPECIAL CHARACTERS

In almost all drafting applications, you need to draw **special characters** (symbols) in the normal text and in the dimension text. For example, you may want to draw the degree symbol (ø) or the diameter symbol (f), or you may want to underscore or overscore some text. This can be achieved with the appropriate sequence of control characters (control code). For each symbol, the control sequence starts with a percent sign written twice (%%). The character immediately following the double percent sign depicts the symbol. The control sequences for some of the symbols are:

Control sequence	Special character
%%c	Diameter symbol (f)
%%d	Degree symbol (ø)
%%p	Plus/minus tolerance symbol (ñ)
%%o	Toggle for overscore mode on/off
%%u	Toggle for underscore mode on/off
%%%	Single percent sign (%)

For example, if you want to draw **25⁰ Celsius**, you need to enter 25%%dCelsius. If you enter **43.0%%c**, you get **43.0ø** on the drawing screen. To underscore (underline) text, use the **%%u** control sequence followed by the text to be underscored. For example, to underscore the text: **UNDERSCORED TEXT IN AUTOCAD**, enter **%%uUNDERSCORED TEXT IN AUTOCAD** at the prompt asking for text to be entered. To underscore and overscore a text string, include **%%u%%o** at the text string.

Note

*The special characters %%O and %%U act as toggles. For example, if you enter "**This %%Utoggles%%U the underscore**", the word **toggles** will be underscored (toggles).*

None of these codes will be translated in the **DTEXT** command until this command is complete. For example, to draw the degree symbol, you can enter **%%d**. As you are entering these symbols, they will appear as %%d on the screen. After you have completed the command and pressed ENTER, the code %%d will be replaced by the degree symbol (ø).

You may be wondering why a percent sign should have a control sequence when a percent sign can easily be entered at the keyboard by pressing the percent (%) key. The reason is that sometimes a percent symbol is immediately followed (without a space) by a control sequence. In this case, the **%%%** control sequence is needed to draw a single percent symbol. To make the concept clear, assume you want to draw **67%±3.5.** Try drawing this text string by entering **67%%%p3.5.** The result will be **67%p3.5,** which is wrong. Now enter **67%%%%p3.5** and notice the result on the screen. Here you obtain the correct text string on the screen, i.e., **67%±3.5.** If there were a space between the 67% and ±3.5, you could enter 67% %%p3.5 and the result would be **67% ±3.5.** Figure 5-28 illustrates some special characters.

In addition to the control sequences shown earlier, you can use the %%nnn control sequence to draw special characters. The nnn can take a value in the range of 1 to 126. For example, to draw the & symbol, enter the text string **%%038**.

Exercise 2   *General*

Draw the text on the screen as shown in Figure 5-30. Use the text justification options shown in the drawing. The text height is 0.25 units.

Figure 5-28 *Special characters*

Figure 5-29 *Drawing for Exercise 2*

CREATING PARAGRAPH TEXT (MTEXT COMMAND)

Toolbar:	Draw > Multiline Text
Menu:	Draw > Text > Multiline Text
Command:	MTEXT

You can use the **MTEXT** command to write a paragraph text whose width can be specified by defining two corners of the text boundary or by entering a width, using coordinate entry. The text created by the **MTEXT** command is a single object regardless of the number of lines it contains. After specifying the width, you have to enter the text in the **Multiline Text Editor** dialog box (Figure 5-31).The following is the prompt sequence:

Figure 5-30 *Invoking* **Multiline Text** *from the* **Draw** *toolbar*

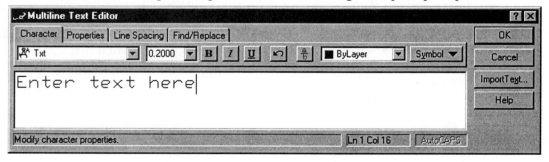

Figure 5-31 Multiline Text Editor *dialog box (Character tab)*

Command: **MTEXT** [Enter]
Current text style: STANDARD. Text height: 0.2000
Specify first corner: *Select a point to specify first corner.*

Specify opposite corner or [Height/Justify/Line spacing/Rotation/Style/Width]: *Select an option or select a point to specify other corner.*

After selecting the first corner, or you can drag the pointing device so that a box that shows the location and size of the paragraph text is formed. An arrow is displayed within the boundary, which indicates the direction of the text flow. When you define the text boundary, it does not mean that the text paragraph will fit within the defined boundary. AutoCAD only uses the width of the defined boundary as the width of the text paragraph. The height of the text boundary has no effect on the text paragraph. Once you have defined the boundary of the paragraph text, AutoCAD will display the **Multiline Text Editor** dialog box (Figure 5-31).

In addition to a Text Box , the **Multiline Text Editor** dialog box has four tabs: **Character**, **Properties**, **Line Spacing**, and **Find/Replace**. The following is the description of these tabs and the options available in each tab.

Text Box

The Text Box area displays the text you enter. The width of the active text area is determined by the specified width of paragraph text. The initial height of the text box is approximately equal to three lines of text. You can increase the size of the dialog box by dragging the edges of the box. You can also use the scroll bar to move up or down to display the text.

Character Tab

From the **Character** tab (default) you can use the following options that you can apply to the text.

Font. If you choose the font drop-down arrow, AutoCAD will display a list of different fonts available (Figure 5-32). You can select any font to apply to the text.

Font Height. You can enter the new value of the text height in the Text Height edit box to change the text height of the entire paragraph text. Once you specify the height, AutoCAD retains that value unless you change it. The **MTEXT** height does not affect the size (**TEXTSIZE** system variable) specified for **TEXT** or **DTEXT** commands.

Bold, Italic, Underline. You can use the appropriate tool icons to make the selected text boldface, italics, or create underlined text. Boldface and italics are not supported by SHX fonts.

Text Color. You can choose the color for the text from the Text color list box. You can also choose the color from the **Select Color** dialog box which is displayed by selecting **Other** in the list box.

Stacking Text. To stack the text you must use the special characters / and ^. The character / stacks the text above a line and the character ^ stacks the text without a line. After you enter the text with the special character and select the text, the stacking button is highlighted. The stacked text is displayed equal to 70 percent of the actual height. If you enter two numbers separated by / or ^, AutoCAD displays the **AutoStack Properties** dialog box (Figure 5-33). You can use this dialog box to control the stacking properties.

Chapter 5

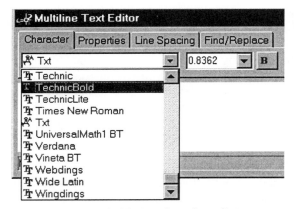

Figure 5-32 Font drop-down list

Figure 5-33 AutoStack Properties dialog box

Symbol. You can select the special characters from the Symbol menu that you can insert in the text. You can select Others to display Character Map of other special characters. To insert these characters, select the characters you want to copy and then choose the **Select** button. Once you are done selecting the special characters, choose the **Copy** button and then close the dialog box. In the text box of the Multiline Text Editor, position the cursor where you want to insert the special characters and right-click to display the shortcut menu. Select **Paste** to insert the selected special characters in the MultiLine Text Editor.

Properties Tab

From the **Properties** tab (Figure 5-34) you can use the following options that can be applied to the text.

Figure 5-34 Multiline Text Editor dialog box (Properties tab)

Style. You can select the drop-down arrow to display the predefined styles and select a new text style. The text style that you want to use must be predefined.

Justification. You can choose the drop-down arrow to display the predefined text justifications and then choose a new justification from the list box. The justification is used to control the justification of the text paragraph. For example, if the text justification is bottom-right (BR), the text paragraph will spill to the left and above the insertion point, regardless of how you define the width of the paragraph. Figure 5-35 shows different text justifications for **MTEXT**.

You can also choose the justification options from the command line.

Command: **-MTEXT**
Current text style: STANDARD. Text height: 0.2000
Specify first corner: *Select a point to specify first corner.*
Specify opposite corner or [Height/Justify/Line spacing/Rotation/Style/Width]: **J**

Enter justification [TL/TC/TR/ML/MC/MR/BL/BC/BR]<current>: *Select an option.*

Figure 5-35 *Text justifications for* **MTEXT**. *P1 is the text insertion point.*

Width. You can enter a new width for the paragraph text or select the width from the previously defined values. The (no wrap) option is the same as entering a width of 0.

Rotation. You can choose a rotation for the text from the drop-down list box. The angles are in 15 degree increments. The rotation angle specifies the rotation of the text. For example, if the rotation angle is 15 degrees, the text will rotate 15 degrees counterclockwise.

Line Spacing Tab

From the **Line Spacing** tab (Figure 5-36) you can use the following options that you can apply to change the text.

Figure 5-36 Multiline Text Editor *dialog box(Line Spacing tab)*

Line Spacing. This has two options. **Atleast** is the default setting in AutoCAD where spacing is based upon the height of the largest character in the line, while the **Exactly** option forces the line spacing for all the lines to be uniform, Figure 5-37. This can be used effectively for making the tables.

Single[1.0x]. This option determines the vertical distance between the two lines in multiline text, Figure 5-38. Single gap is the default setting. Single line spacing is equal to 1.66 times the height of the text. The available options include Single (1x), 1.5 lines (1.5x), and Double (2x). You can

Chapter 5

also enter an absolute value for line spacing in the range of 0.0833 (0.25x) to 1.333 (4x) by entering a value in the edit box.

Figure 5-37 Specifying linespacing in multiline text

Find/Replace Tab

From the **Find/Replace** tab (Figure 5-38) you can use the following options that you can apply to the text.

Figure 5-38 Multiline Text Editor dialog box (Find/Replace tab)

Find. In this edit box, you can define the text string to be searched.

Replace With. If you want some text to be replaced, enter new text for replacement in this edit box.

Replace button. Select this icon to replace the highlighted text with the text in the **Replace With** edit box.

Match Case. Activate this check box if you want to find the text, only if all characters in text object are identical to the text in the Find box.

Whole Word. Activate this check box if you want to match the text in the Find box, only if it is a single word.

Import Text

When you choose this option, AutoCAD displays the **Open** dialog box. In this dialog box you can select any text file you want to import in the **Multiline Text Editor** dialog box. The imported text is displayed in the text area. Note that only ASCII or RTF files are interpreted properly.

Example 1

In this example you will use the **Multiline Text Editor** dialog box to write the following text on the screen.

For long, complex entries, create multiline text using the MTEXT option. The angle is 10 degrees. Diameter =1/2" and Length=32 1/2".

The font of the text is **Swis721 BT,** text height is 0.20, color Red, and written at an angle of 10 degrees with Middle-Left justification. Make the word "multiline" bold, underline the text "multiline text", and make the word "angle" italic. The line spacing type and line spacing between the lines are AtLeast and 1.5x respectively. Use the symbol for degrees and replace the word "option" with "command".

1. The first step is to enter the **MTEXT** command at the command prompt. You can also invoke this command from the **Draw** menu or the **Draw** toolbar. After invoking the command, specify two corners on the screen to define the paragraph text boundary. The prompt sequence is :

    Command: **MTEXT** ⏎
    Current text style: STANDARD. Text height: 0.1000
    Specify first corner: *Select a point to specify first corner.*
    Specify opposite corner or [Height/Justify/Rotation/ Style/ Width]: *Select a point to specify other corner.*
    The **Multiline Text Editor** dialog box is displayed with the Character tab activated (default).

2. Choose the arrow in the **Font** list box to display the drop-down list. Select **Swis721 BT** true type font from the list.

3. Enter 0.20 in the **Font height** edit box.

4. Choose the **Color** icon to display the list box and select Red from the list.

5. Now enter the text in the Text Editor (Figure 5-39) and to put the degrees symbol, choose the Symbol to display the menu and select **Degrees.** When you type 1/2 and then press the SPACEBAR, AutoCAD displays the **AutoStack Properties** dialog box. Select **Convert it to a diagonal fraction**, if it is not already selected, and then choose **OK**.

Figure 5-39 Multiline Text Editor dialog box (Character tab)

6. Double-click on the word "multiline" to select it and then choose the **Underline** button.

7. Similarly, highlight the word "text" to select it and then again select the **Underline** button to underline it.

8. Now highlight on the word "multiline" (or pick and drag to select the text) and then choose the **Bold** button to make it boldface.

Chapter 5

9. Highlight on the word "angle" (or pick and drag to select the text) and then choose the **Italic** button, Figure 5-39.

10. Select the **Properties** tab to display its options.

11. From the **Justification** drop-down list choose **ML**, and from the **Rotation** drop-down list choose **10**.

12. Select the **Line Spacing** tab to change the line spacing.

13. In the **line spacing type** drop-down list choose the **AtLeast** option and in the **spacing** drop-down list choose the **1.5Lines(1.5x)** option.

14. Now select the **Find/Replace** tab (Figure 5-40) to display its different options.

15. In the **Find** edit box, enter o**ption** and in the **Replace** edit box, enter **command**.

16. Choose the **Find** button. AutoCAD finds the word "option", Figure 5-40. Choose the **Replace** button to replace **option** by **command**.

Figure 5-39 Multiline Text Editor dialog box (Find/Replace tab)

17. Choose the **OK** button to exit the dialog box and the text is displayed in the selected width on the screen, Figure 5-41.

Figure 5-41 Multiline text for Example 1

EDITING TEXT

The contents of **MTEXT**, **TEXT**, and **DTEXT** object can be edited by using the **DDEDIT** and **PROPERTIES** commands. You can also use the AutoCAD editing commands, like **MOVE**, **ERASE**, **ROTATE**, **COPY**, **MIRROR**, and **GRIPS** with any text object.

Editing Text Using DDEDIT Command

Toolbar:	Modify II > Edit Text
Pull-down:	Modify > Text
Command:	DDEDIT

 You can use the **DDEDIT** command to edit the text. If you select **TEXT** or **DTEXT** object, AutoCAD displays the **Edit Text** dialog box (Figure 5-42), where the selected text is displayed in the **Text:** edit box. You can make the changes and then choose the **OK** button. If you select the paragraph text, AutoCAD displays the text in the **Multiline Text Editor** dialog box. You can make the changes using the different options in the dialog box. The text in the dialog box can be selected by double-clicking on the word to select a word, by holding down the pick button of the pointing device and then dragging the cursor, or by triple-clicking on the text to select the entire line or paragraph.

Command: **DDEDIT** [Enter]
Select an annotation object or [Undo]: Select *a text object*

*Figure 5-42 Using the **Edit Text** dialog box to edit text*

Editing Text Using Properties Command

When you enter the **PROPERTIES** command and select the text, AutoCAD displays the **Object Properties** dialog box (Figure 5-43). You can also invoke the **PROPERTIES** command by choosing **Properties** button in the **Standard** toolbar. You need to select the text which you want to edit. To select the text, choose **Quick Select** in the **Object Properties** dialog box. In the **Quick Select** dialog box, choose **Select objects** and then select the text. Choose **OK** to return to **Object Properties** dialog box. Move the slider bar down till you see Text and Contents. If the text is a **TEXT** or **DTEXT** object, you can make the changes in the **Contents** edit box If you are editing multiline text, you must choose the **Full editor** button in the **Content** edit box, AutoCAD automatically switches to the **Multiline Text Editor** dialog box, where you can make changes to the paragraph text.

Note
*The **PROPERTIES** command has replaced the **DDMODIFY** command. If you invoke the **DDMODIFY** command, AutoCAD displays the **Object Properties** dialog box. You can also edit multiline text by using the **MTPROP** command. After entering the command you are required to select the Mtext for editing. Once you select the Mtext, the **Multiline Text Editor** dialog box is displayed. This command cannot be used to edit the text created by **TEXT** or **DTEXT** commands.*

Chapter 5

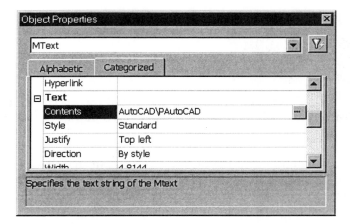

Figure 5-43 Properties dialog box

Using Shortcut Menu

You can edit the text by using the **Shortcut** menu. Select the text object and right-click in the drawing area, AutoCAD displays the **Shortcut** menu, Figure 5-44. From the **Shortcut** menu select **Text Edit** or **Mtext Edit**, depending on if the selected text is a paragraph text created by **MTEXT** command or text created by **TEXT** or **DTEXT** commands. If you select **Mtext Edit** from the **Shortcut** menu, **Multiline Text Editor** dialog box is displayed. If you select Text Edit, **Edit Text** dialog box is displayed.

SUBSTITUTING FONTS

AutoCAD provides the facility to designate the fonts that you want to substitute for other fonts used in the drawing. The information about font mapping is specified in the font mapping file (ACAD.FMP). The font mapping has the following advantages :

Figure 5-44 Shortcut menu when paragraph text is selected

1.   You can specify a font to be used when AutoCAD cannot find a font used in the drawing.

2.   You can enforce the use of a particular font in your drawings. If you load a drawing that uses different fonts, you can use the font mapping to substitute the desired font for the fonts used in the drawing.

3.   You can use .shx fonts when creating or editing a drawing. When you are done and ready to plot the drawing, you can substitute other fonts for .shx fonts.

The Font mapping file is an ASCII file with FMP extension containing one font mapping per line. The format on the line is:

Base name of the font file;Name of the substitute font with extension (ttf, shx, etc.)

For example, if you want to substitute the ROMANC font for SWISS.TTF; the entry is:

SWISS;ROMANC.SHX

You can enter this line in the ACAD.FMP file or create a new file. You may use the **FONTMAP** system variable or use the **Options** dialog box to specify the new font map file. To specify a font mapping table in the **Options** dialog box, choose **Options** from the **Tools** menu to display the **Options** dialog box. Choose the **File** tab and click on the **plus** sign next to Text Editor, Dictionary, and Font File Names. Now, click on the plus sign next to Font Mapping File to display the path and the name of the font mapping file. Double click on the file to display the **Select a File** dialog box. Select the new font mapping file and exit the **Options** dialog box. At the Command prompt enter **REGEN** to convert the existing text font to the font as specified in the new font mapping file.

Command: **FONTMAP** ⏎
Enter new value for FONTMAP, or . for none <"Acad.fmp">: *Enter the name of the font mapping file.*

The following file is a partial listing of ACAD.FMP file with the new font mapping line added (swiss;romanc.shx).

swiss;romanc.shx
cibt;CITYB___.TTF
cobt;COUNB___.TTF
eur;EURR____.TTF
euro;EURRO__.TTF
par;PANROMAN.TTF
rom;ROMANTIC.TTF
romb;ROMAB___.TTF
romi;ROMAI__.TTF
sas;SANSS__.TTF
sasb;SANSSB__.TTF
sasbo;SANSSBO_.TTF
saso;SANSSO__.TTF
suf;SUPEF___.TTF

Note
The text styles that were created using the PostScript fonts are substituted with an equivalent True Type font and plotted using the substituted font.

Specifying an Alternate Default Font

When you open a drawing file that specifies a font file that is not on your system or is not specified in the font mapping file, AutoCAD, by default, substitutes the simplex.shx font file. You can specify a different font file in the **Options** dialog box or by changing the **FONTALT** system variable.

Chapter 5

Command: **FONTALT** [Enter]
New value for FONTALT, or . for none <"simplex.shx">: *Enter the font file name.*

STYLE COMMAND

Pull-down:	Format > Text Style
Command:	STYLE or DDSTYLE

You can change the current text styles in the **TEXT** or **DTEXT** commands using the **Style** option, but to create new text styles and modify the existing style you need the **STYLE** command. When you enter **STYLE** or **DDSTYLE** at the Command prompt, or select **Text Style** in the **Format** menu, the **Text Style** dialog box (Figure 5-45) is displayed.

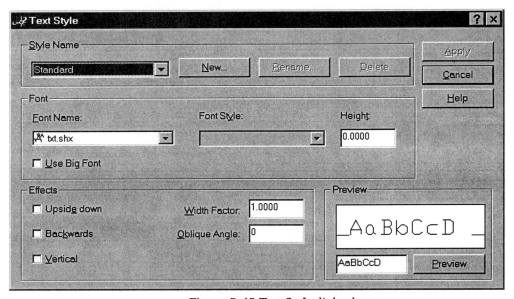

Figure 5-45 Text Style dialog box

In the Style Name edit box the default style (STANDARD) will be displayed. For creating a new style, choose the **New** button to display the **New Text Style** dialog box (Figure 5-46) and enter the name of the style you want to create. A new style having the entered name and the properties present in the **Text Style** dialog box will be created. To modify this style, select the style name from the list box and then change the different settings by entering new values in the appropriate

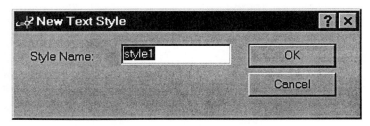

Figure 5-46 New Text Style dialog box

boxes. You can change the font by selecting a new font from the Font drop-down list. Similarly, you can change the text height, width, and oblique angle. If you specify the height of the text in the dialog box, AutoCAD will not prompt you to enter the text height when you use the **TEXT** or **DTEXT** commands. The text will be created using the height specified in the text style. If you want AutoCAD to prompt you for the text height, specify 0 text height in the dialog box. For **Width factor,** 1 is the default. If you want the letters expanded, give a width factor greater than 1; for compressed letters, give a width factor less than 1. Similarly, for the **Oblique angle,** 0 is the default. If you want the slant of the letters toward the right, the value should be greater than 0; to slant the letters toward the left, the value should be less than 0. You can also force the text to be written upside down (Figure 5-47), backwards and vertically by checking their respective check boxes. As you make the changes, you can see their effect in the **Preview** box. After making the desired changes, choose the **Apply** button and the **Close** button to exit the dialog box. You can also use the **-STYLE** command to define a new test style from the command line.

Figure 5-48 *Specifying different features to text style files*

DETERMINING TEXT HEIGHT

The actual text height is equal to the product of the **scale factor** and the **plotted text height**. Hence, scale factors are important numbers for plotting the text at the correct height. This factor is a reciprocal of the drawing plot scale. For example, if you plot a drawing at a scale of 1/4 = 1, you calculate the scale factor for text height as follows:

1/4" = 1" (i.e., the scale factor is 4)

The scale factor for an architectural drawing that is to be plotted at a scale of 1/4" = 1'0" is calculated as:

1/4" = 1'0", or 1/4" = 12", or 1 = 48

Therefore, in this case, the scale factor is 48.

For a civil engineering drawing with a scale 1"= 50', the scale factor is as follows:

1" = 50', or 1" = 50 * 12", or 1 = 600

Therefore, the scale factor is 600.

Next, calculate the height of the AutoCAD text. If it is a full-scale drawing (1=1) and the text is to be plotted at 1/8" (0.125), it should be drawn at that height. However, in a civil engineering drawing a text drawn 1/8" high will look like a dot. This is because the scale for a civil engineering drawing is 1"= 50', which means that the drawing you are working on is 600 times larger. To draw a normal text height, multiply the text height by 600. Now the height will be:

0.125" x 600 = 75

Similarly, in an architectural drawing, which has a scale factor of 48, a text that is to be 1/8" high on paper must be drawn 6 units high, as shown in the following calculation:

0.125 x 48 = 6.0

It is very important to evaluate scale factors and text heights before you begin a drawing. It would be even better to include the text height in your prototype drawing by assigning the value to the **TEXTSIZE** system variable.

CHECKING SPELLING

Toolbar:	Standard toolbar > Spelling
Menu:	Tools > Spelling
Command:	SPELL

 You can check the spelling of text (text generated by the **TEXT**, **DTEXT**, or **MTEXT** commands) by using the **SPELL** command. The prompt sequence is:

Command: **SPELL**
Select object: *Select the text for spell check or enter ALL to select all text objects.*

If no misspelled words are found in the selected text, then AutoCAD displays a message. If the spelling is not correct for any word in the selected text, AutoCAD displays the **Check Spelling** dialog box (Figure 5-48). The misspelled word is displayed under **Current word**, and correctly spelled alternate words are listed in the **Suggestions**: box. The dialog box also displays the misspelled word with the surrounding text in the **Context** box. You may select a word from the list, ignore the correction, and continue with the spell check, or accept the change. To add the listed word in the custom dictionary, choose the **Add** button. The dictionary can be changed from the **Check Spelling** dialog box or by specifying the name in the **DCTMAIN** or **DCTCUST** system variables. Dictionary must be specified for spell check.

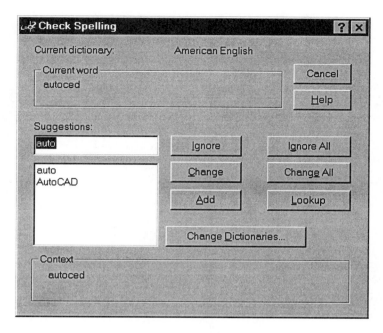

Figure 5-48 Check Spelling dialog box

Note

*You can also rename and use the Word'97 dictionary. Choose the **Change Dictionaries** button to display the **Change Dictionaries** dialog box and enter the new dictionary name with the .cus extension.*

FORMATTING PARAGRAPH TEXT

The text can be formatted by entering formatting codes in the text. To enter a paragraph text, you can use the **MTEXT** command at the command line. With the formatting codes you can underline or overline a text string, create stacked text, or insert nonbreaking space between two words. You can also use the formatting codes to change the color, font, text height, obliquing angle, or width of the text. (Figure 5-50) lists the formatting codes for paragraph text.

To obtain the paragraph text shown in Figure 5-49, use the following formatting codes in the **MTEXT** command using the command line. The prompt sequence is:

> Command: **-MTEXT**
> Specify first corner: *Select a point to specify first corner.*
> Specify opposite corner or [Height/Justify/Rotation/Style/Width]: *Select a point to specify opposite corner.*
> MText: {\H0.15{\FROMANC;{\LNOTE}}}
> MText: {\FROMANC;Hardness} **unless**

Note
_____

Hardess **unless**

otherwise specified

60RC ±3

Figure 5-49 Using True Type font with TEXTQLTY set to 100

\O...\o	Turns overline on and off	Turns \Ooverline\o on and off	Turns overline on and off
\L...\l	Turns underline on and off	Turns \Lunderline\l on and off	Turns underline on and off
\~	Inserts a nonbreaking space	Keeps the\~words together	
\\	Inserts a backslash	Inserts \\ a backslash	Keeps the words together
\{...\}	Inserts an opening and closing brace	This is \{bracketed\} word	Inserts \ a backslash The {bracketed} word
\Cvalue;	Changes to the specified color	Change \C1; the color	Change the color
\File name;	Changes to the specified font file	Chnage \Fromanc; this word	Change this word
\Hvalue;	Changes to the specified text height	Change \H0.15; this word	Change this word
\S...^...	Stacks the subsequent text at the \ or ^ symbol	2.005\S+0.001^-0.001	+0.001 2.005-0.001
\Tvalue;	Adjusts the space between characters from .75 to 4 times	\T2;TRACKING	T R A C K I N G
\Qangle;	Changes obliquing angle	\Q15;OBLIQUE TEXT	OBLIQUE TEXT
\Wvalue;	Changes width factor to produce wide text	\W2;WIDE LETTERS	WIDE LETTERS
\P	Ends paragraph	First paragraph\PSecond paragraph	First paragraph Second paragraph

Figure 5-50 *Formatting codes for paragraph text*

MText: **otherwise specified**
Mtext: **{\FROMANC;60RC}\S+3.0^-2.0**
MText:

Note
Use the curly braces if you want to apply the format codes only to the text within the braces. The curly braces can be nested up to eight levels deep.

TEXT QUALITY AND TEXT FILL

AutoCAD supports **TrueType fonts**. You can use your own TrueType fonts by adding them to the Fonts directory. You can also keep your fonts in a separate directory, in which case you must specify the location of your fonts directory in the AutoCAD search path.

The resolution and text fill of the TrueType font text is controlled by the **TEXTFILL** and **TEXTQLTY** system variables. If **TEXTFILL** is set to 1, the text will be filled. If the value is set to 0, the text will not be filled. On the screen the text will appear filled, but when it is plotted the text will not be filled. The **TEXTQLTY** variable controls the quality of the TrueType font text. The value of this variable can range from 0 to 100. The default value is 50, which gives a resolution of 300 dpi (dots per inch). If the value is set to 100, the text will be drawn at 600 dpi. The higher the resolution, the more time it takes to regenerate or plot the drawing.

FINDING AND REPLACING TEXT

Toolbar:	Standard Toolbar > Find and Replace
Pull-down:	Edit > Find
Command:	FIND

 You can use the **FIND** command to find and replace the text. The text could be a line text created by **TEXT** and **DTEXT** commands, paragraph text created by **MTEXT** command, dimension annotation text, block attribute value, hyperlinks, or hyperlink description. When you invoke this command, AutoCAD displays the **Find and Replace** dialog box, Figure 5-51. You can use this dialog box to perform the following functions:

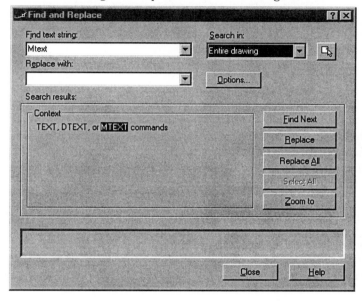

Figure 5-51 Find and Replace dialog box

Find Text

To find the text, enter the text you want to find in the **Find text string** edit box. You can do the search in entire drawing or confine the search to selected text. To select text, choose the **Select Objects** button: AutoCAD temporarily switches to drawing window. Once you are done selecting text, the **Find and Replace** dialog box reappears. In the **Search in** drop-down list you can specify if you want to search the entire drawing or current selection. If you choose the Options button, AutoCAD displays the **Find and Replace Options** dialog box, Figure 5-52. In this dialog box you can specify whether to find the whole word and whether to match the case of the specified text. To find the text, choose the **Find** button. AutoCAD displays the found text with the surrounding text in the Context area. To find the next occurrence of the text choose the **Find Next** button.

Replacing Text

If you want to replace the specified text with new text, enter the new text in the **Replace with** edit box. Now, if you choose the **Replace** button, only the found text will be replaced. If you choose the **Replace All** button, all occurrences of the specified text will be replaced with the new text.

Chapter 5

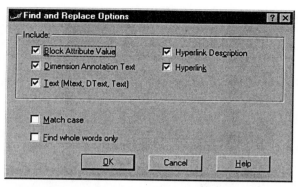

Figure 5-53 Find and Replace Options dialog box

Self-Evaluation Test

Answer the following questions and then compare your answers to the answers given at the end of this chapter.

1. Transparent commands cannot be used while another command is in progress. (T/F)

2. The virtual screen contains the last regeneration of the graphics database. (T/F)

3. An absolute magnification value is specified by a value followed by X. (T/F)

4. The **DTEXT** command does not allow you to enter multiple lines of text with a single **DTEXT** command. (T/F)

5. The **DTEXT** command does not allow you to delete typed text with the BACKSPACE key. (T/F)

6. Regeneration does not involve redrawing action. (T/F)

7. The **TEXT** command does not allow you to enter multiple lines of text with a single **TEXT** command. (T/F)

8. Give the prompt sequence to create a view of the current view under name **VIEW1**.
   Command: _____
   Enter an option [?/Orthographic/Delete/Restore/Save/Window]: _____
   Enter view name to save: _____

9. The scale factor for scaling the text is a reciprocal of the _____.

10. The four main text alignment modes are_____, _____, _____, and _____.

11. To scale a view relative to paper space units, the **ZOOM** _____ option is used.

12. While using the **ZOOM Previous** option, you can go back up to _____ views for a viewport.

13. You can use _____ to write a paragraph text whose width can be specified by defining _____ of the text boundary or by entering the _____ of the paragraph.

14 The **Justify** option is used to control the _____ of paragraph text.

15. AutoCAD supports TrueType fonts. (T/F)

Review Questions

1. Blip marks are a part of the drawing. (T/F)

2. The **REDRAW** command can be used as a transparent command. (T/F)

3. After completion of a transparent command, AutoCAD returns you to the Command prompt. (T/F)

4. If the **BLIPMODE** variable is set to On, blip marks do not appear on the screen. (T/F)

5. Drawn objects are recalculated after a **REGEN** command. (T/F)

6. Drawn objects are recalculated after a **REDRAW** command. (T/F)

7. With the **ZOOM** command, the actual size of the object changes. (T/F)

8. You can use the **ZOOM** command an indefinite number of times on a drawing. (T/F)

9. A relative magnification value is specified by a value followed by X. (T/F)

10 The **DTEXT** command allows you to see the text on the screen as you type it. (T/F)

11. The **TEXT** command does not allow you to see the text on the screen as you type it. (T/F)

12. In **DTEXT** command, the screen crosshairs can be moved to specify a new location of the cursor box for the text. (T/F)

Chapter 5

13. Give the prompt sequence to zoom in on the center of a drawing with a magnification of 2.
    Command: _____
    Specify corner of window, enter a scale factor (nX or nXP), or
    [All/ Center/ Dynamic/ Extents/ Previous/ Scale / Window] <Realtime>: _____
    Specify center point: _____
    Enter magnification or height<current>: _____

14. By specifying the start point you need, your text is _____-justified along its _____.

15. The _____ of a text determines how far above the baseline the capital letters can extend.

16. The _____ determines the orientation of the text baseline with respect to the start point.

17. You can view the entire drawing (even if it is beyond limits) with the help of the
    _____ option.

18. In the **ZOOM** Window option, the area inside the window is _____ to completely
    _____ the current viewport.

19. Explain the difference between the **REDRAW** and **REGEN** commands._____
    _____

20. What are blips and what commands make them disappear from the screen?_____
    _____

21. Name the command that allows you to change the display of blips. _____
    _____

22. Explain the difference between the **Extents** and the **All** options of the **ZOOM** command._____
    _____

23. When during the drawing process should you use the **ZOOM** command? _____
    _____

24. Name the view boxes that are displayed during the **ZOOM** Dynamic command, and explain
    the significance of each one. _____

25. What is the **PAN** command and how does it work? _____

26. Give the letter you must enter at the prompt after entering the **Justify** option for the **TEXT**
    command for:
    a. Top/left justified text
    b. Right justified text

27. What command do you use to see the text on the screen as it is typed?

28. Calculate the AutoCAD text height for a text to be plotted 1/8" using a half scale; i.e., 1" = 2"

scale.

29. Find the AutoCAD text height for a text to be plotted 1/8" high using a scale of 1/16" = 1'-0".

30. What is the function of the **REGENALL** and **REDRAWALL** commands? _____

_____

31. The text created by the **MTEXT** command is a single object regardless of the number of lines it contains. (T/F)

32. The text boundary of paragraph text is also plotted when you plot the drawing. (T/F).

33. The contents of an **MTEXT** object (paragraph text) can be edited by using the _____ and the _____ commands.

34. When using **MTEXT** command, the special characters _____ and _____ are used to stack the text.

Exercises

Exercise 3   *General*

Draw the text on the screen as shown in Figure 5-53(a). Use the text justification that will produce the text as shown in the drawing . Assume a value for text height. Use the text related commands to change the text as shown in Figure 5-53(b).

Figure 5-53(a) Drawing for Exercise 3

Figure 5-53(b) Drawing for Exercise 3 (After changing the text)

Chapter 5

Exercise 4   *General*

Draw the text on the screen shown in Figure 5-54. You must first define text style files with the attributes as shown in the drawing. The text height is 0.25 units. Do not dimension the drawing.

Figure 5-54 *Drawing for Exercise 4*

Exercise 5   *Graphics*

Draw Figure 5-55 using the **MIRROR** command to duplicate the features that are symmetrical. Also, Use display commands to facilitate the drawing process . Do not dimension the drawing.

Figure 5-55 *Drawing for Exercise 5*

Exercise 6

Draw Figure 5-56 making use of the draw, edit, and display commands.

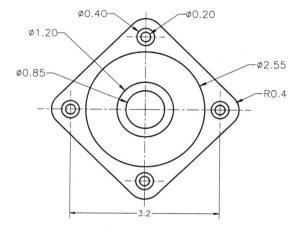

Figure 5-56 Drawing for Exercise 6

Exercise 7

Draw Figure 5-57 using the commands studied in this chapter to the maximum advantage. Do not dimension the drawing.

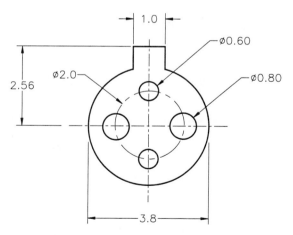

Figure 5-57 Drawing for Exercise 7

Exercise 8   *Architecture*

Make the drawing shown in Figure 5-58 . Assume the distance between the dotted lines.

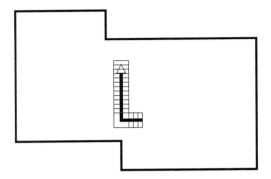

Figure 5-58 Drawing for Exercise 8

Exercise 9   *Architecture*

Make the drawing shown in Figure 5-59. Assume the distance between the dotted lines.

Figure5-59 Drawing for Exercise 9

Answers to Self-evaluation Test
1 - F, **2** - T, **3** - F , **4** - F, **5** - F, **6** - F , **7** - T , **8** - **VIEW**/Save/VIEW1, **9** - drawing scale,**10** - Align/Center/
Middle/Right, **11** - XP, **12** - 10, **13** - **MTEXT,** two corners, width, 14 - justification , **15** - T

Chapter 6

Basic Dimensioning

Learning Objectives

After completing this chapter, you will be able to:
- *Understand the need for dimensioning in drawings.*
- *Understand the fundamental dimensioning terms.*
- *Understand associative dimensioning.*
- *Select dimensioning commands in AutoCAD.*
- *Use the **QDIM** command for quick dimensioning.*
- *Create linear, aligned, rotated, baseline, and continue dimensions.*
- *Create angular, radial, diameter, and ordinate dimensions.*
- *Create center marks and centerlines.*
- *Use the **QLEADER** command to attach annotation to an object.*
- *Use the **LEADER** command.*

NEED FOR DIMENSIONING

To make designs more informative and practical, the drawing must convey more than just the graphic picture of the product. To manufacture an object, the drawing must contain size descriptions such as the length, width, height, angle, radius, diameter, and location of features. All of this information is added to the drawing with the help of **dimensioning**. Some drawings also require information about tolerances with the size of features. All of this information conveyed through dimensioning is vital and often just as important as the drawing itself. With the advances in computer-aided design/drafting and computer-aided manufacturing, it has become mandatory to draw the part to actual size so that the dimensions reflect the actual size of the features. At times it may not be necessary to draw the object the same size as the actual object would be when manufactured, but it is absolutely essential that the dimensions be accurate. Incorrect dimensions will lead to manufacturing errors.

By dimensioning, you are not only giving the size of a part, you are also giving a series of instructions to a machinist, an engineer, or an architect. The way the part is positioned in a machine, the sequence of machining operations, and the location of different features of the part depend on how you dimension the part. For example, the number of decimal places in a dimension (2.000) determines the type of machine that will be used to do that machining operation. The machining cost of such an operation is significantly higher than for a dimension that has only one digit after the decimal (2.0). Similarly, whether a part is to be forged or cast, the radii of the edges and the tolerance you provide to these dimensions determine the cost of the product, the number of defective parts, and the number of parts you get from a single die.

DIMENSIONING IN AUTOCAD

The objects that can be dimensioned in AutoCAD range from straight lines to arcs. The dimensioning commands provided by AutoCAD can be classified into four categories:

Dimension Drawing Commands
Dimension Style Commands
Dimension Editing Commands
Dimension Utility Commands

While dimensioning an object, AutoCAD automatically calculates the length of the object or the distance between two specified points. Also, settings like a gap between the dimension text and the dimension line, the space between two consecutive dimension lines, arrow size, and text size are maintained and used when the dimensions are being generated for a particular drawing. The generation of arrows, lines (dimension lines, extension lines), and other objects that form a dimension are automatically performed by AutoCAD to save the user's time. This also results in uniform drawings. However, you can override the default measurements computed by AutoCAD and change the settings of various standard values. The modification of dimensioning standards can be achieved through the dimension variables.

The dimensioning functions offered by AutoCAD provide you with extreme flexibility in dimensioning by letting you dimension various objects in a variety of ways. This is of great help because different industries, like architectural, mechanical, civil, or electrical, have different standards for the placement of dimensions.

FUNDAMENTAL DIMENSIONING TERMS

Before studying AutoCAD's dimensioning commands, it is important to know and understand various dimensioning terms that are common to linear, angular, radius, diameter, and ordinate dimensioning. Figure 6-1 shows some dimensioning objects.

Dimension Line

The **dimension line** indicates which distance or angle is being measured. Usually this line has arrows at both ends, and the dimension text is placed along the dimension line. By default the dimension line is drawn between the extension lines (Figure 6-2). If the dimension line does not fit inside, two short lines with arrows pointing inward are drawn outside the extension lines. The dimension line for angular dimensions (which are used to dimension angles) is an arc. You can control the positioning and various other features of the dimension lines by setting the dimensioning system variables. (The dimensioning system variables are discussed in Chapter 8.)

Figure 6-1 AutoCAD's dimensioning terms

Dimension Text

Dimension text is a text string that reflects the actual measurement (dimension value) between the selected points as calculated by AutoCAD. You can accept the value that AutoCAD returns or enter your own value. In case you use the default text, AutoCAD can be supplied with instructions to append the tolerances to it. Also, you can attach prefixes or suffixes of your choice to the dimension text.

Arrowheads

An **arrowhead** is a symbol used at the end of a dimension line (where dimension lines meet the extension lines). Arrowheads are also called **terminators** because they signify the end of the dimension line. Since the drafting standards differ from company to company, AutoCAD allows you to draw arrows, tick marks, closed arrows, open arrows, dots, right angle arrows, or user-defined blocks (Figure 6-2). The user-defined blocks at the two ends of the dimension line can be customized to your requirements. The size of the arrows, tick marks, user blocks, etc., can be regulated by using the dimension variables.

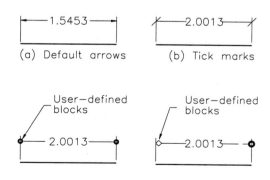

Figure 6-2 Using arrows, tick marks, and user-defined blocks

Chapter 6

Extension Lines

Extension lines are drawn from the object measured to the dimension line (Figure 6-3). These lines are also called **witness lines.** Extension lines are used in linear and angular dimensioning. Generally, extension lines are drawn perpendicular to the dimension line. However, you can make extension lines incline at an angle by using the **DIMEDIT** command (Oblique option) or by selecting **Dimension Edit** from the **Dimension** toolbar. AutoCAD also allows you to suppress either one or both extension lines in a dimension (Figure 6-4). Other aspects of the extension line can be controlled by using the dimension variables (these variables are discussed in Chapter 8).

Figure 6-3 Extension lines

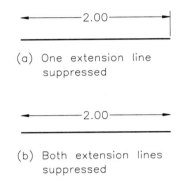

Figure 6-4 Extension line suppression

Leader

A **leader** is a line that stretches from the dimension text to the object being dimensioned. Sometimes the text for dimensioning and other annotations does not adjust properly near the object. In such cases, you can use a leader and place the text at the end of the leader line. For example, the circle shown in Figure 6-5 has a keyway slot that is too small to be dimensioned. In this situation, a leader can be drawn from the text to the keyway feature. Also, a leader can be used to attach annotations such as part numbers, notes, and instructions to an object.

Figure 6-5 Leader used to attach annotation

Center Mark and Centerlines

The **center mark** is a cross mark that identifies the center point of a circle or an arc. Centerlines are mutually perpendicular lines passing through the center of the circle/arc and intersecting the circumference of the circle/arc. A center mark or the centerlines are automatically drawn when you dimension a circle or arc (see Figure 6-6). The length of the center mark and the extension of the centerline beyond the circumference of the circle is determined by the value assigned to the **DIMCEN** dimension variable or the value assigned to Center Mark for Circle in the **Dimension Style Manager** dialog box.

Alternate units

With the help of **alternate units** you can generate dimensions for two systems of measurement at the same time (Figure 6-7). For example, if the dimensions are in inches, you can use the alternate units dimensioning facility to append metric dimensions to the dimensions (controlling the alternate units through the dimension variables are discussed in Chapter 8).

Figure 6-6 *Center mark and centerlines*

Figure 6-7 *Using alternate units dimensioning*

Tolerances

Tolerance is the amount by which the actual dimension can vary (Figure 6-8). AutoCAD can attach the plus/minus tolerances to the dimension text (actual measurement computed by AutoCAD). This is also known as **deviation tolerance**. The plus and minus tolerance that you specify can be the same or different. You can use the dimension variables to control the tolerance feature (these variables are discussed in Chapter 8).

Limits

Instead of appending the tolerances to the dimension text, you can apply the tolerances to the measurement itself (Figure 6-9). Once you define the tolerances, AutoCAD will automatically calculate the upper and lower **limits** of the dimension. These values are then displayed as a dimension text.

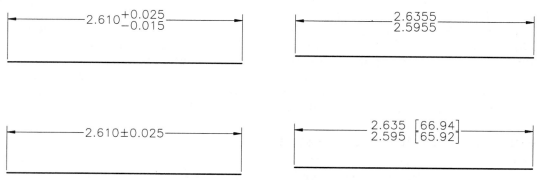

Figure 6-8 *Using tolerances with dimensions*

Figure 6-9 *Using limits dimensioning*

For example, if the actual dimension as computed by AutoCAD is 2.610 units and the tolerance values are +0.025 and -0.015, the upper and lower limits are 2.635 and 2.595. After calculating the limits, AutoCAD will display them as dimension text, as shown in Figure 6-9. The dimension variables that control the limits are discussed in Chapter 8.

ASSOCIATIVE DIMENSIONS

Associative dimensioning is a method of dimensioning in which the dimension is associated with the object that is dimensioned. In other words, the dimension is influenced by the changes in the size of the object. AutoCAD dimensions are not truly associative, but are related to the objects being dimensioned by definition points on the DEFPOINTS layer. To cause the dimension to be associatively modified, these definition points must be adjusted along with the object being changed. If, for example, you use the **SCALE** command to change an object's size and select the object, any associative dimensions will not be modified. If you select the object and its defpoints (using the Crossing selection method), then the dimension will be modified. In associative dimensioning, the items constituting a dimension (like dimension lines, arrows, extension lines, and dimension text) are drawn as a single object. If the associative dimension is disabled, the dimension lines, arrows, extension lines, and the dimension text are drawn as separate objects. In that case, you can edit the dimension lines, extension lines, text, and arrowheads as individual objects. You can also use the **EXPLODE** command to split an associative dimension into individual items (just as in the case when an associative dimension is disabled).

The dimensioning variable **DIMASO** controls associativity of dimensions. Its default setting is on. When **DIMASO** is set on and you dimension and edit the object (e.g., trimming or stretching), the dimensions associated with that object also change (Figure 6-10). Also, the appearance of associative dimensions can be preserved when they are edited by commands such as **STRETCH** and **TEDIT**. For example, a vertical associative dimension is retained as a vertical dimension even after an editing operation. The associative dimension is always generated with the same dimension variable settings as defined in the dimension style. Another advantage of associative dimensioning is that you can edit dimension objects as single objects with various commands. The dimensioning commands that are affected by associative dimensioning are the **Linear, Aligned, Rotated, Radius, Diameter**, and **Angular** commands. The **Center** and **Leader** commands are not affected by associative dimensioning. The associative dimension is always generated with the same dimension variable settings as defined in the creation of the dimension style. The present linetype and the text style are used for the drawing of text.

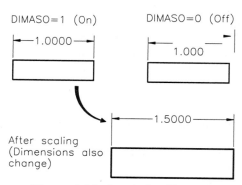

Figure 6-10 Associative dimensioning

Updating Associative Dimensions

As mentioned for this automatic revision of the associative dimension objects, the **definition points of the dimension object must be contained in the selection set** formed for the editing. Therefore, becoming familiar with the definition points of different types of dimensions will make it easier to edit the dimensions.

DEFINITION POINTS

Definition points are the points drawn at the positions used to generate an associative dimension object. The definition points are used by the associative dimensions to control their updating and rescaling. AutoCAD draws these points on a special layer called **DEFPOINTS.** These points are not plotted by the plotter because AutoCAD does not plot any object on the **DEFPOINTS** layer. If you explode an associative dimension (which is as good as turning **DIMASO** off), the definition points are converted to point objects on the **DEFPOINTS** layer. In Figure 6-11, the small circles indicate the definition points for different objects.

Figure 6-11 *Definition points of linear, angular, and ordinate dimensions*

The definition points for linear associative dimensions are the points used to specify the extension lines and the point of intersection of the first extension line and the dimension line. The definition points for the angular dimension are the endpoints of the lines used to specify the dimension and the point used to specify the dimension line arc. For example, for three-point angular dimension, the definition points are the extension line endpoints, the angle vertex, and the point used to specify the dimension line arc.

The definition points for the radius dimension are the center point of the circle or arc, and the point where the arrow touches the object. The definition points for the diameter dimension are the points where the arrows touch the circle. The definition points for the ordinate dimension are the UCS origin, the feature location, and the leader endpoint.

 Note

In addition to the definition points just mentioned, the middle point of the dimension text serves as a definition point for all types of dimensions.

SELECTING DIMENSIONING COMMANDS
Using the Toolbar and the Dimension Menu

You can select the dimension commands from the **Dimension** toolbar by choosing the desired dimension button (Figure 6-12), or from the **Dimension** menu (Figure 6-13). The **Dimension** toolbar can also be displayed by right-clicking on any toolbar and choosing **Dimensions** from the shortcut menu.

Figure 6-12 Selecting dimension commands from the **Dimension** toolbar

Using the Command Line

Using Dimensioning Commands. You can use the dimensioning commands at the Command prompt without using the **DIM** Command. For example, if you want to draw the linear dimension, the **DIMLINEAR** command can be entered directly at the Command prompt.

> Command: **DIMLINEAR**
> Specify first extension line origin or <select object>: *Select a point or press ENTER.*
> Specify second extension line origin: *Select second point.*
> Specify dimension line location or [Mtext/Text/Angle/Horizontal/Vertical/Rotated]: *Select a point to locate the position of the dimension.*
> Command: *(After you have finished dimensioning, AutoCAD returns to the Command prompt.)*

DIM and DIM1 Commands. Since dimensioning has several options, it also has its own command mode. The **DIM** command keeps you in the dimension mode, and the **Dim:** prompt is repeated after each dimensioning command until you exit the dimension mode to return to the normal AutoCAD Command prompt. To exit the dimension mode, enter EXIT (or just

Figure 6-13 Selecting dimensions from the **Dimension** menu

E) at the **Dim:** prompt. You can also exit by pressing ESC, or by pressing the third button of the digitizer puck. The previous command will be repeated if you press the SPACEBAR or ENTER at the **Dim:** prompt. In the dimension mode, it is not possible to execute the normal set of AutoCAD commands, except function keys, object snap overrides, control key combinations, transparent commands, dialog boxes, and menus.

Command: **DIM**
Dim: **Hor**
Specify first extension line origin or <select object>: *Select a point or press ENTER.*
Specify second extension line origin: *Select the second point.*
Specify dimension line location or [MText/Text/Angle]: *Select a point to locate the position of the dimension.*
Enter dimension text <default>: *Press ENTER to accept the default dimension.*
Dim: *(After you have finished dimensioning, AutoCAD returns to the **Dim:** prompt.)*

The **DIM1** command is similar to the **DIM** command. The only difference is that **DIM1** lets you execute a single dimension command and then automatically takes you back to the normal Command prompt.

Command: **DIM1**
Dim: **Hor**
Specify first extension line origin or <select object>: *Select a point or press ENTER.*
Specify second extension line origin: *Select the second point.*
Specify dimension line location or [MText/Text/Angle]: *Select a point to locate the position of the dimension.*
Enter dimension text <default>: *Press ENTER to accept the default dimension.*
Command: *(After you are done dimensioning, AutoCAD returns Command prompt.)*

AutoCAD has provided the following six fundamental dimensioning types (Figure 6-14):

Quick dimensioning   **Linear dimensioning**   **Diameter dimensioning**
Radius dimensioning   **Angular dimensioning**   **Ordinate dimensioning**Note

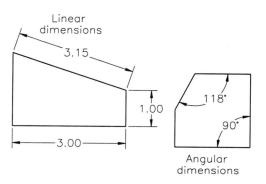

Figure 6-14(a) *Linear and angular dimensions*

Figure 6-14(b) *Radius, diameter, and ordinate dimensions*

Note

*The **DIMDEC** variable sets the number of decimal places for the value of primary dimension and the **DIMADEC** variable for angular dimensions. For example, if **DIMDEC** is set to 3, AutoCAD will display the decimal dimension up to three decimal places (2.037).*

QUICK DIMENSIONING*
Using the QDIM command

Toolbar:	Dimension > Quick Dimension
Menu:	Dimension > QDIM
Command:	QDIM

 The **QDIM** command allows you to dimension a number of objects at the same time. It also allows you to quickly edit dimension arrangements already existing in the drawing and also create new dimension arrangements. It is especially useful when creating a series of baseline or continuous dimensions. It also allows you to dimension multiple arcs and circles at the same time. When you are using the **QDIM** command, you can relocate the datum base point for baseline and ordinate dimensions. The command prompts for **QDIM** are:

Command: **QDIM**
Select geometry to dimension: *Select the objects to be dimensioned and press ENTER.*
Specify dimension line position , or [Continuous/Staggered/Baseline/Ordinate/Radius/
Diameter/datum point/Edit] <continuous>: *Press ENTER to accept default dimension arrange-
ment and specify dimension line location or enter new dimension arrangement or Edit existing
dimension arrangement.*

For example, you can dimension all circles in the drawing (Figure 6-15) by using Quick Dimensioning as follows:

Figure 6-15 *Using the **QDIM** command to quickly dimension
multiple circles*

Command: **QDIM**
Select geometry to dimension: *Select the circles and press ENTER.*
Specify dimension line position , or [Continuous/Staggered/Baseline/Ordinate/Radius/
Diameter/datum point/Edit] <continuous>: *Press R for radius dimensioning and select a point*
where you want to position the radial dimension

LINEAR DIMENSIONING

Toolbar:	Dimension > Linear Dimension
Menu:	Dimension > Linear.
Command:	DIMLIN or DIMLINEAR

Linear dimensioning applies to those dimensioning commands that measure the distance between two points. The points can be any two points in the space, the endpoints of an arc or line, or any set of points that can be identified. To achieve accuracy, selecting points must be done with the help of object snaps or by selecting an object to dimension. Linear dimensions include **Horizontal** and **Vertical** dimensioning. When you select a dimensioning command, AutoCAD will prompt you to enter information about the dimension. The dimension is not drawn until you respond to all of the dimensioning prompts.

Command: **DIMLIN**
Specify first extension line origin or <select object>: `Enter`
Select object to dimension: *Select the object.*
Specify dimension line location or
[Mtext/Text/Angle/Horizontal/Vertical/Rotated]: *Select a point to locate the position of the dimension.*

Instead of selecting the object, you can also select the two endpoints of the line that you want to dimension (Figure 6-16). Usually the points on the object are selected by using the **object snaps** (endpoints, intersection, center, etc.). The prompt sequence is as follows:

Command: **DIMLIN**
Specify first extension line origin or <select object>: *Select a point.*
Specify second extension line origin:
Select second point.
Specify dimension line location or
[Mtext/Text/Angle/Horizontal/Vertical/
Rotated]: *Select a point to locate the position*
of the dimension.

When using the **DIMLINEAR** command, you can obtain the horizontal or vertical dimension by simply defining the appropriate dimension location point. If you select a point above or below the dimension, AutoCAD creates a horizontal dimension. If you select a point that is on the left or right of the dimension, AutoCAD creates a vertical dimension through that point.

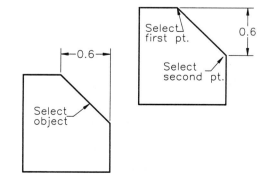

Figure 6-16 *Drawing horizontal and vertical dimension*

DIMLINEAR Options

Mtext Option. The **Mtext** option allows you to override the default dimension text and also change the font, height, etc., using the **Multiline Text Editor** dialog box. When you enter **M** at the **Specify dimension line location or [Mtext/Text/Angle/Horizontal/Vertical/Rotated]:** prompt, the **Multiline Text Editor** dialog box is displayed. By default, it includes the < > code to represent the measured associative dimension text. You can change the text by entering a new text and deleting < > code. You can also use the different options of the dialog box (explained in Chapter 5) and then choose **OK**. However, if you override the default dimensions, the dimensional associativity of the **dimension text** is lost and AutoCAD will not recalculate the dimension when the object is scaled.

Command: **DIMLIN**
Specify first extension line origin or <select object>: *Specify a point.*
Specify second extension line origin: *Specify second point.*
Specify dimension line location or
[Mtext/Text/Angle/Horizontal/Vertical/Rotated]: **M** *(Enter dimension text in **Mutiline Text Editor** dialog box; choose **OK**.)*
Specify dimension line location or
[Mtext/Text/Angle/Horizontal/Vertical/Rotated]: *Specify a point to locate the position of the dimension.*

Text Option. This option also allows you to override the default dimension. See Figure 6-17.

Command: **DIMLIN**
Specify first extension line origin or <select object>: *Select a point.*
Specify second extension line origin: *Select second point.*
Specify dimension line location or
[Mtext/Text/Angle/Horizontal/Vertical/Rotated]: **T**
Enter dimension text <Current>: *Enter new text.*
Specify dimension line location or
[Mtext/Text/Angle/Horizontal/Vertical/Rotated]: *Select a point to locate the position of the dimension.*

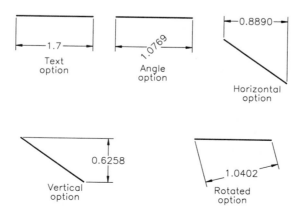

Figure 6-17 Text, Angle, Horizontal, Vertical, and Rotated options

Angle Option. This option lets you change the angle of the dimension text.

Horizontal Option. This option lets you create a horizontal dimension regardless of where you specify the dimension location.

Vertical Option. This option lets you create a vertical dimension regardless of where you specify the dimension location.

Rotated Option. This option lets you create a dimension that is rotated at a specified angle.

Note
If you override the default dimensions, the dimensional associativity of the dimension text is lost and AutoCAD will not recalculate the dimension when the object is scaled.

Example 1

In this example, you will use the **DIMLINEAR** command to dimension a line by selecting the object and by specifying the first and second extension line origins (Figure 6-18). The following is the command prompt sequence:

Selecting the Object

1. Enter the **DIMLIN** command at the Command prompt. You can also select it from the **Dimension** menu or the toolbar.

    Command: **DIMLIN**

2. At the next prompt, press ENTER to select the line. The endpoints of the line are taken as the origins for the extension line.

    Specify first extension line origin or <select object>: ⌨Enter
    Select object to dimension: *Select the line.*

3. At the next prompt, specify the location for the dimension line. This information is used by AutoCAD to set the location to place the dimension line. With the **Mtext** option, you can override the default dimension text.

    Specify dimension line location or
    [Mtext/Text/Angle/Horizontal/Vertical/
    Rotated]: **M**

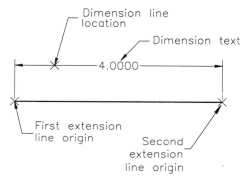

Figure 6-18 Horizontal dimension

4. When you select the Mtext option, the **Multiline Text Editor** dialog box (Figure 6-19) is displayed. Enter the dimension text in the dialog box and choose the **OK** button to exit.

Figure 6-19 Multiline Text Editor dialog box

Specify dimension line location or
[Mtext/Text/Angle/Horizontal/Vertical/Rotated]: *Specify a point.*

Specifying Extension Line Origins

1. In case you want to specify the two endpoints (extension line origin) on the line, the Command prompt sequence is as follows:

    Command: **DIMLIN**
    Specify first extension line origin or <select object>: *Select the first endpoint of the line using the Endpoint object snap.*
    Specify second extension line origin: *Select the second endpoint of the line using the Endpoint object snap.*
    Specify dimension line location or
    [Mtext/Text/Angle/Horizontal/Vertical/Rotated]: *Specify the location for the dimension line.*

ALIGNED DIMENSIONING

Toolbar:	Dimension > Aligned Dimension
Menu:	Dimension, Aligned
Command:	DIMALIGNED

You may want to dimension an object that is inclined at an angle, not parallel to the X axis or Y axis. In such a situation you can use **aligned dimensioning**. With the help of aligned dimensioning, you can measure the true distance between the two points. In horizontal or vertical dimensioning, you can only measure the distance from the first extension line origin to the second extension line origin along the horizontal or vertical axis, respectively. The working of the **ALIGNED** dimension command is similar to that of the other linear dimensioning commands. The dimension created with the **ALIGNED** command is **parallel to the object being dimensioned.**

Command: **DIMALIGNED**
or
Command: **DIM**
Dim: **ALIGNED**

Figure 6-20 illustrates aligned dimensioning. The prompt sequence for aligned dimensioning is the same as that for linear dimensions. The only difference is that you have to select the Aligned dimension option. The following is the prompt sequence for the Aligned dimensioning command:

> Command: **DIM**
> Dim: **ALIGNED**
> Specify first extension line origin or <select object>: *Select the first extension line origin.*
> Specify second extension line origin: *Select the second extension line origin.*
> Specify dimension line location or [MText/Text/Angle]: *Specify the dimension line location.*
> Enter Dimension text <measured>: *Enter new text to override the distance computed by AutoCAD or press ENTER to retain the default dimension text.*

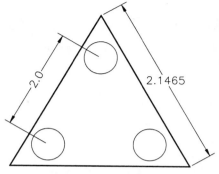

Figure 6-20 Aligned dimensioning

You can also respond to the **First extension line origin or <select object>:** prompt by pressing ENTER. AutoCAD will prompt you to select the object to dimension. Once you select the object, AutoCAD will automatically align the dimension with the selected object.

Note

*If you invoke this command from the **Dimension** menu, enter **T** at the **Specify dimension line location or [MText/Text/Angle]:** prompt.*

Exercise 1 *Mechanical*

Draw Figure 6-21, and then use the **DIMLINEAR** and **DIMALIGNED** commands to dimension the part. The distance between the dotted lines is 0.5 units. The dimensions should be upto 2 decimal places. To get dimensions up to 2 decimal places, enter DIMDEC at the Command prompt

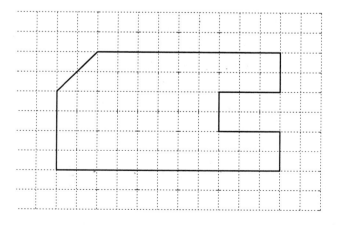

*Figure 6-21 Using the **DIMLINEAR** and **DIMALIGNED** commands to dimension the part*

and then enter 2. (For more information about dimension variable, see Chapter 8)

ROTATED DIMENSIONING

Rotated dimensioning is used when you want to place the dimension line at an angle (if you do not want to align the dimension line with the extension line origins selected) (Figure 6-22). The **ROTATED** dimension option will prompt you to specify the dimension line angle. You can invoke this command by using **DIMLINEAR** (Rotate option) or by entering **ROTATED** at the **Dim:** command prompt. The prompt sequence is:

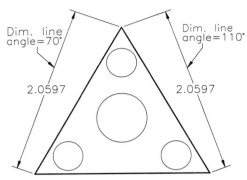

Figure 6-22 Rotated dimensioning

Dim: **ROTATED**
Specify angle of dimension line <0>: **110**
Specify first extension line origin or <select object>: *Select the lower right corner of the triangle.*
Specify second extension line origin: *Select the top corner.*
Specify dimension line location or [MText/Text/Angle]: *Select the location for the dimension line.*
Enter dimension text <2.0597>: Enter

Note
You can draw horizontal and vertical dimensioning by specifying the rotation angle of 0 degrees for horizontal dimensioning and 90 degrees for vertical dimensioning.

BASELINE DIMENSIONING

Toolbar:	Dimension > Baseline Dimension
Menu:	Dimension > Baseline
Command:	DIMBASE or DIMBASELINE

Sometimes in manufacturing you may want to locate different points and features of a part with reference to a fixed point (base point or reference point). This can be accomplished by using **BASELINE dimensioning** (Figure 6-23). With this command you can continue a linear dimension from the first extension line origin of the first dimension. The new dimension line is automatically offset by a fixed amount to avoid drawing a dimension line and dimension text on top of the previous dimension. **There must already be a linear, ordinate, or angular associative dimension to use the Baseline or Continue dimensions.** The prompt sequence for Baseline di-

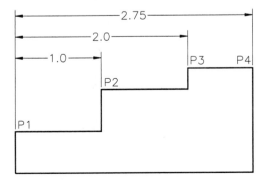

Figure 6-23 Baseline dimensioning

mension is:

>Command: **DIMLIN**
>Specify first extension line origin or <select object>: *Select left corner (P1). (Use Endpoint object snap.)*
>Specify second extension line origin: *Select the origin of the second extension line (P2).*
>Specify dimension line location or
>[Mtext/Text/Angle/Horizontal/Vertical/Rotated]: *Select the location of the first dimension line.*
>Dimension text = 1.0000

>Command: **DIMBASE**
>Specify a second extension line origin or [Undo/Select]<Select>: *Select the origin of the next extension line (P3).*
>Dimension text = 2.0000
>Specify a second extension line origin or [Undo/Select]<Select>:

When you use the **DIMBASELINE** command, you cannot change the default dimension text. The **DIM** mode commands allows you to override the default dimension text.

>Command: **DIM**
>Dim: **HOR**
>Specify first extension line origin or <select object>: *Select left corner (P1). (Use Endpoint object snap.)*
>Specify second extension line origin: *Select the origin of the second extension line (P2).*
>Specify dimension line location or [MText/Text/Angle]: **T**
>Enter dimension text <1.0000>: **1.0**
>Specify dimension line location or [MText/Text/Angle]: *Select the dimension line location.*
>Dim: **BASELINE (or BAS)**
>Specify a second extension line origin or [Select]<Select>: *Select the origin of the next extension line (P3).*
>Enter dimension text <2.0000>: **2.0**
>Dim: **BAS**
>Specify a second extension line origin or [Select]<Select>: *Select the origin of next extension line (P4).*
>Enter dimension text <3.000>: **2.75**

The next dimension line is automatically spaced and drawn by AutoCAD.

CONTINUE DIMENSIONING

Toolbar:	Dimension > Continue Dimension
Menu:	Dimension > Continue
Command:	DIMCONT or DIMCONTINUE

With this command you can continue a linear dimension from the second extension line of the previous dimension. This is also called as **chained** or **incremental dimensioning**. The **DIM** command should be used if you want to change the text (Figure 6-24).

Command: **DIM**
Dim: **HOR**
Specify first extension line origin or <select object>: *Select left corner (P1). (Use Endpoint object snap.)*
Specify second extension line origin: *Select the origin of the second extension line (P2).*
Specify dimension line location or [MText/Text/Angle]: **T**
Enter dimension text <1.0000>: **1.0**
Specify dimension line location or [MText/Text/Angle]: *Select the dimension line location.*
Dim: **CONTINUE**
Specify a second extension line origin or [Select]<Select>: *Select the origin of the next extension line (P3).*
Enter dimension text <1.0000>: Enter
Dim: **CONTINUE**
Specify a second extension line origin or [Select]<Select>: *Select the origin of next extension line (P4).*
Enter dimension text <0.7200>: **0.7500**

The default base (first extension line) for the dimensions created with the **CONTINUE** command is the previous dimension's second extension line. You can override the default by pressing ENTER at the **Specify a second extension line origin or [Select]<Select>:** prompt, and then specifying the other dimension. The extension line origin nearest to the selection point is used as the origin for the first extension line.

Figure 6-24 Continue dimensioning

Note
*When you use the **DIMCONT** command, AutoCAD does not let you change the default dimension text. Use the **DIM** command if you want to override the default dimension text.*

*There must already be a linear, angular, or ordinate dimension for the **CONTINUE** or **BASELINE** dimension commands.*

Exercise 2   *General*

Make the drawing in Figure 6-25. Then use the **BASELINE** command to dimension the top half and **CONTINUE** to dimension the bottom half. The distance between the dotted lines is 0.5 units.

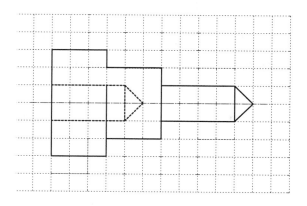

Figure 6-25 *Drawing for Exercise 2*

ANGULAR DIMENSIONING

Toolbar:	Dimension > Angular Dimension
Menu:	Dimension > Angular
Command:	DIMANGULAR or DIMANG

Angular dimensioning is used when you want to dimension an angle. This command generates a dimension arc (dimension line in the shape of an arc with arrowheads at both ends) to indicate the angle between two nonparallel lines. This command can also be used to dimension the vertex and two other points, a circle with another point, or the angle of an arc. For every set of points there exists one acute angle and one obtuse angle (inner and outer angles). If you specify the dimension arc location between the two points, you will get the acute angle; if you specify it outside the two points, you will get the obtuse angle. Figure 6-26 shows the four ways to dimension two nonparallel lines.

Command: **DIMANG**
Select arc, circle, line, or <specify vertex>:

Dimensioning the Angle Between Two Nonparallel Lines

The angle between two nonparallel lines or two straight line segments of a polyline can be dimensioned with the **DIMANGULAR** dimensioning command. The vertex of the angle is taken as the point of intersection of the two lines. The location of the extension lines and dimension arc is determined by how you specify the dimension arc location.

The following example illustrates the dimensioning of two nonparallel lines using the **DIMANGULAR** command:

Command: **DIMANG**
Select arc, circle, line, or <specify vertex>: *Select the first line.*
Select second line: *Select the second line.*

Specify dimension arc line location or [Mtext/Text/Angle]: **M** *(Enter the new value in the Multiline Text Editor dialog box.)*
Specify dimension arc line location or [Mtext/Text/Angle]: *Specify the dimension arc location.*

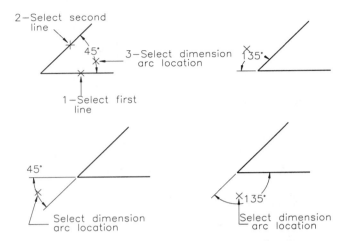

***Figure 6-26** Angular dimensioning between two nonparallel lines*

Dimensioning the Angle of an Arc

Angular dimensioning can also be used to dimension the angle of an arc. In this case, the center point of the arc is taken as the vertex and the two endpoints of the arc are used as the extension line origin points for the extension lines (Figure 6-27). The following example illustrates the dimensioning of an arc using the **DIMANGULAR** command. The prompt sequence is as follows:

Command: **DIMANG**
Select arc, circle, line, or <specify vertex>: *Select the arc.*
Specify dimension arc line location or [Mtext/Text/Angle]: **T**
Enter dimension text <current value>: *Press ENTER or specify a new value.*
Specify dimension arc line location or [Mtext/Text/Angle]: *Specify a location for the arc line.*

Angular Dimensioning of Circles

The angular feature associated with the circle can be dimensioned by selecting a circle object at the **Select arc, circle, line, or <specify vertex>:** prompt. The center of the selected circle is used as the vertex of the angle. The first point selected (when the circle is selected for angular dimensioning) is used as the origin of the first extension line. In a similar manner, the second point selected is taken as the origin of the second extension line (Figure 6-28). The following is the prompt sequence for dimensioning a circle:

Command: **DIMANG**
Select arc, circle, line, or <specify vertex>: *Select the circle at the point where you want the first extension line.*
Specify second angle endpoint: *Select the second point on or away from the circle.*

Specify dimension arc line location or [Mtext/Text/Angle]: **M** *(Enter the new value in the*
Multiline Text Editor *dialog box.)*
Specify dimension arc line location or [Mtext/Text/Angle]: *Select the location for the dimension*
line.

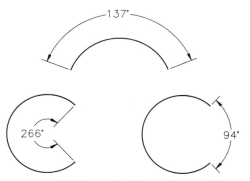

Figure 6-27 *Angular dimensioning of arcs*   ***Figure 6-28*** *Angular dimensioning of circles*

Angular Dimensioning Based on Three Points

If you press Return at the **Select arc, circle, line, or <specify vertex>:** prompt, AutoCAD allows
you to select three points to create an angular dimension. The first point is the vertex point, and
the other two points are the first and second angle endpoints of the angle (Figure 6-29). The
coordinate specifications of the first and the second angle endpoints must not be identical. However, the angle vertex coordinates and one of the angle endpoint coordinates can be identical. The
following example illustrates angular dimensioning by defining three points:

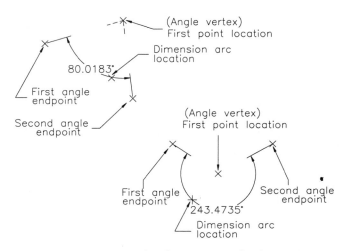

Figure 6-29 *Angular dimensioning for three points*

Command: **DIMANGULAR**
Select arc, circle, line, or <specify vertex>: *Press ENTER.*
Specify angle vertex: *Specify the first point, vertex.*

Specify first angle endpoint: *Specify the second point.*
Specify second angle endpoint: *Specify the third point.*
Specify dimension arc line location or [Mtext/Text/Angle]: *Select the location for the dimension line.*

Note

*If you use the **DIMANGULAR** command, you cannot specify the text location. With the **DIMANGULAR** command, AutoCAD positions the dimensioning text automatically. If you want to position the dimension text yourself, use the **DIM, ANGULAR** command.*

Exercise 3   *Mechanical*

Make the drawing in Figure 6-30. Then use the **DIMANGULAR** command to dimension all angles of the part. The distance between the dotted lines is 0.5 units.

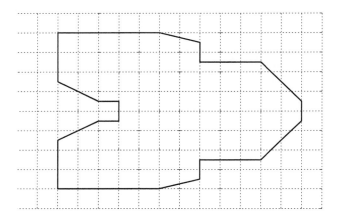

Figure 6-30 *Drawing for Exercise 3*

DIAMETER DIMENSIONING

Toolbar:	Dimension > Diameter Dimension
Pull-down:	Dimension > Diameter
Command:	DIMDIAMETER or DIMDIA

Diameter dimensioning is used to dimension a circle; you can also use it to dimension an arc. Here, the measurement is done between two diametrically opposite points on the circumference of the circle or arc (Figure 6-31). The dimension text generated by AutoCAD commences with the ø symbol, to indicate a diameter dimension. The following is the prompt sequence for dimensioning a circle:

Command: **DIMDIA**
Select arc or circle: *Select an arc or circle by selecting a point anywhere on its circumference.*
Dimension text= Current
Specify dimension line location or [Mtext/Text/Angle]: *Specify a point to position the dimension.*

If you want to override the default value of the dimension text, use the Mtext or Text option.

Command: **DIMDIA**
Select arc or circle: *Select an arc or circle.*
Dimension text= Current
Specify dimension line location or [Mtext/Text/Angle]: **T**
Enter dimension text <current>: **%%C2.5**
Specify dimension line location or [Mtext/Text/Angle]: *Move the cursor and specify a point.*

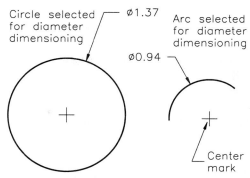

Figure 6-31 Diameter dimensioning

The control sequence %%C is used to obtain the diameter symbol Ø. It is followed by the dimension text you want to appear in the diameter dimension.

Note
The control sequence %%d can be used to generate the degree symbol "o" (45°).

RADIUS DIMENSIONING

Toolbar:	Dimension > Radius Dimension
Menu:	Dimension, Radius
Command:	DIMRADIUS or DIMRAD

 Radius dimensioning is used to dimension a circle or an arc (Figure 6-32). Radius and diameter dimensioning are similar; the only difference is that instead of the diameter line, a radius line is drawn (half of the diameter line) which is measured from the center to any point on the circumference. The dimension text generated by AutoCAD is preceded by the letter **R** to indicate a radius dimension. If you want to use the default dimension text (dimension text generated automatically by AutoCAD), simply specify a point to position the dimension at the **Specify dimension line location or [Mtext/Text/Angle]:** prompt. You can also enter a new value or specify a prefix or suffix, or suppress the entire text by entering a blank space following the **Enter dimension text <current>:** prompt. A center mark for the circle/arc is drawn automatically, provided the center mark value controlled by the **DIMCEN** variable is not 0.

Figure 6-32 Radius dimensioning

Command: **DIMRAD**
Select arc or circle: *Select the object you want to dimension.*
Dimension text= Current

Specify dimension line location or [Mtext/Text/Angle]: *Move the cursor and select a point.*

If you want to override the default value of the dimension text, use the Text option, as follows:

Command: **DIMRAD**
Select arc or circle: *Select an arc or circle.*
Dimension text= current
Specify dimension line location or [Mtext/Text/Angle]: **T**
Enter dimension text <current>: **R0.25**
Specify dimension line location or [Mtext/Text/Angle]: *Move the cursor and select a point.*

GENERATING CENTER MARKS AND CENTERLINES

Toolbar:	Dimension > Center Mark
Pull-down:	Dimension, Center Mark
Command:	DIMCENTER

 When circles or arcs are dimensioned with the **DIMRADIUS or DIMDIAMETER** command, a small mark known as a center mark may be drawn at the center of the circle/arc (Figure 6-33). Sometimes you may want to mark the center of a circle or an arc without using these dimensioning commands. This can be achieved by entering **DIMCENTER** at the Command prompt or **CENTER** (or **CEN**) at the **Dim:** prompt. You can control the size of the center mark by changing the size in the **Dimension Style Manager** dialog box or by using the **DIMCEN** variable. When the value of **DIMCEN** is negative, the centerlines are drawn (Figure 6-34).

Command: **DIMCENTER**
Select arc or circle: *Select arc or circle.*

Figure 6-33 *Using the **DIMCEN** variable to control the size of the center mark*

Figure 6-34 *Using a negative value for **DIMCEN***

 Note
*The center marks created by **DIMCENTER** or **DIM, CENTER** are lines, not associative dimensioning objects, and they have an explicit linetype.*

Exercise 4   *Mechanical*

Make the drawing in Figure 6-35. Then use the **DIMRADIUS** and **DIMDIAMETER** commands to dimension the part. Use the **DIMCENTER** command to draw the centerlines through the circles. The distance between the dotted lines is 0.5 units.

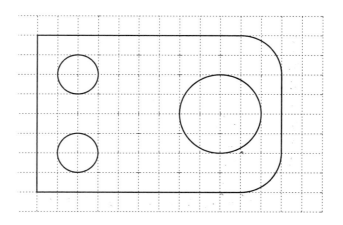

Figure 6-35 Using the *DIMRADIUS* and *DIMDIAMETER* commands to dimension a part

ORDINATE DIMENSIONING

Toolbar:	Dimension > Ordinate
Menu:	Dimension > Ordinate
Command:	DIMORDINATE or DIMORD

 Ordinate dimensioning is also known as **arrowless** dimensioning because no arrowheads are drawn in this type of dimensioning. Ordinate dimensioning is also called datum dimensioning because all dimensions are related to a common base point. The current UCS (user coordinate system) origin becomes the reference or the base point for ordinate dimensioning. With ordinate dimensioning you can determine the X or Y displacement of a selected point from the current UCS origin. To locate the UCS, you can use the **UCS** command.

In ordinate dimensioning, AutoCAD automatically places the dimension text (X or Y coordinate value) and the leader line along the X or Y axis (Figure 6-36). Since the ordinate dimensioning pertains to either the X coordinate or the Y coordinate, you should keep ORTHO on. When ORTHO is off, the leader line is automatically given a bend when you select the second leader line point that is offset from the first point. This allows you to generate offsets and avoid overlapping text on closely spaced dimensions. In ordinate dimensioning, only one extension line (leader line) is drawn.

The leader line for an X coordinate value will be drawn perpendicular to the X axis, and the leader line for a Y coordinate value will be drawn perpendicular to the Y axis. Since you cannot override this, the leader line drawn perpendicular to the X axis will have the dimension text aligned with the leader line. The dimension text is the X datum of the selected point. The leader line drawn perpendicular to the Y axis will have the dimension text, which is the Y datum of the selected point, aligned with the leader line. Any other alignment specification for the dimension text is nullified. Hence, changes in Text Alignment in the **Dimension Style Manager** dialog box (**DIMTIH** and **DIMTOH** variables) have no effect on the alignment of dimension text. You can specify the coordinate value you want to dimension at the **Specify leader endpoint or [Xdatum/ Ydatum/MText/Text/Angle]:** prompt.

Figure 6-36 Ordinate dimensioning

If you select or enter a point, AutoCAD checks the difference between the feature location and the leader endpoint. If the difference between the X coordinates is greater, the dimension measures the Y coordinate; otherwise, the X coordinate is measured. In this manner AutoCAD determines whether it is an X or Y type of ordinate dimension. However, if you enter Y instead of specifying a point, AutoCAD will dimension the Y coordinate of the selected feature. Similarly, if you enter X, AutoCAD will dimension the X coordinate of the selected point. The following is the prompt sequence for ordinate dimensioning:

Command: **DIMORD**
Specify feature location: *Select a point on an object.*
Specify leader endpoint or [Xdatum/Ydatum/Mtext/Text/Angle]: *Enter the endpoint of the leader.*

You can override the text using the **Mtext** or the **Text** options.

Command: **DIMORDINATE**
Specify feature location: *Select a point on an object.*
Specify leader endpoint or [Xdatum/Ydatum/Mtext/Text/Angle]:* **M** (*Enter the new value in the* **Multiline Text Editor** *dialog box.*)
Specify leader endpoint or [Xdatum/Ydatum/Mtext/Text/Angle]: *Specify the endpoint of the leader line.*

Exercise 5   *Mechanical*

Make the drawing in Figure 6-37. Then use the **DIMORDINATE** command to dimension the part. The distance between the dotted lines is 0.5 units.

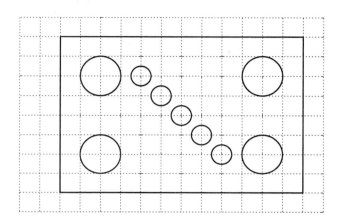

*Figure 6-37 Using the **DIMORDINATE** command to dimension the part*

DRAWING LEADERS

The leader line is used to attach annotations to an object or when the user wants to show a dimension without using another dimensioning command. Sometimes leaders for the circles or arcs are so complicated that you need to construct a leader of your own rather than using the leader generated by radius or diameter dimensioning (**DIMDIA** or **DIMRAD** command). A leader drawn by using the **LEADER** or **QLEADER** command creates the arrow and the leader lines as a single object. The text is created as a separate object. These commands can create multiline annotations and offers several options like using Mtext or copying existing annotations.

QLEADER Command

Toolbar:	Dimension > Quick Leader
Menu:	Dimension > Leader
Command:	QLEADER

The **QLEADER** command creates a leader and annotation. Choosing **Leader** from the **Dimension** menu and choosing the **Quick Leader** button from the **Dimension** toolbar, executes the **QLEADER** command. You can customize the leader and annotation by selecting the Settings option at the **Specify first leader point, or [Settings]<Settings>:** prompt. The following is the Command prompt sequence for the **QLEADER** command:

Command: **QLEADER**
Specify first leader point, or [Settings]<Settings>:*Specify the start point of the leader.*
Specify next point: Specify *end point of the leader.*

Specify next point: Specify *next point.*
Specify text width <current>: *Enter text width of multiline text.*
Enter first line of annotation text <MText>: Press *ENTER; AutoCAD displays the **Multiline Text Editor** dialog box. Enter text in the dialog box and then choose **OK** to exit.*

Press ENTER at the **Specify first leader point or [Settings]<Settings>:** prompt; the **Leader Settings** dialog box is displayed (Figure 6-38). The **Leader settings** dialog box gives you a number of options for the leader line and the text attached to it. It has the following tabs:

Annotation Tab

Gives you various options to control annotation features like Annotation Type, Mtext Options, and, Annotation Reuse.

Mtext. When selected, AutoCAD uses the **Multiline Text Editor** to create annotation. Three Mtext options are available.

Prompt for width. Selecting this check box, allows you to specify the width of the mtext annotation.

Always left justify. Left justifies the mtext annotation in all situations. Selecting this check box makes the Prompt for width option unavailable.

Frame Text. Selecting this check box draws a box around the mtext annotation.

Figure 6-38 Leader Settings dialog box, Annotation tab

Copy an Object. The copy option allows you to copy an existing annotation object (like mtext, single line text, tolerance, or block) and attach it at the end of the leader. For example, if you have a text string in the drawing that you want to place at the end of the leader, you can use the Copy option to place it at the end of the leader.

Tolerance. When you select the Tolerance option, AutoCAD displays the **Geometric Tolerance** dialog box on the screen. Specify the tolerance in the dialog box and choose OK to exit. AutoCAD will place the specified Geometric Tolerance with feature control frame at the end of the leader (Figure 6-39).

Block. The block option allows you to insert a predefined block at the end of the leader. When you select this option, AutoCAD will prompt you to enter the block name, and insertion point.

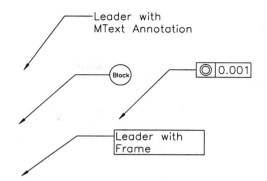

*Figure 6-39 Using the **QLEADER** command to draw a leader with MText, Block, Tolerance, and MText with Frame annotations*

None. Creates a leader without placing any annotation at the end of the leader.

Annotation Reuse. This option allows you to reuse the annotation.

> **None**. When selected, AutoCAD does not reuse the leader annotation.

> **Reuse Next**. This option allows you to reuse the annotation that you are going to create next for all subsequent leaders.

> **Reuse Current**. This option allows you to reuse the current annotation for all subsequent leaders.

Leader Line & Arrow Tab

Leader Line. Gives the options for the **leader line type** like straight or spline (Figure 6-40). The spline option draws a spline through the specified leader point and the Straight option creates straight lines.

Number of Points. With this option you can specify the number of points you can specify in a leader. For example, if it is 3, AutoCAD will prompt you for annotation after you specify two leader points. First point is the leader start point.

Arrowheads. Allows you to define a leader arrowhead from the **Arrowhead** drop-down list. The arrowhead available here are the same as the one available for dimensioning. You can also use the user defined arrows by selecting **User Arrow** from the drop-down list.

Angle Constraint. This option allows you to set the angle of the first and the second leader segments. For example, you can set the first segment to 45 degrees and the second to horizontal to get a leader line at 45 degrees with horizontal extension.

Attachment Tab

The **Attachment** tab (Figure 6-41) is available, only if you have selected **MText** in the **Annotation** tab. This tab allows you various options for attaching the Multi-line Text to the leader. It has two columns, Text on left side and Text on right side. Each column has different justifications. If you draw a leader from right to left, AutoCAD uses the settings under Text on left side. Similarly, if you draw a leader from left to right, AutoCAD uses the settings as specified under Text on right side.

Figure 6-40 Leader Settings dialog box, Leader Line & Arrow tab

Figure 6-41 Leader settings dialog box, Attachment tab

Exercise 6

Make the drawing in Figure 6-42. Then use the **LEADER** command to dimension the part as shown. The distance between the dotted lines is 0.5 units.

*Figure 6-42 Using the **LEADER** command to dimension the part*

Using the LEADER Command

The **LEADER** command draws a line that extends from the object being dimensioned to the dimension text (Figure 6-43). The following is the prompt sequence of the **LEADER** command:

*Figure 6-43 Using the **LEADER** command to draw leaders*

> Command: **LEADER**
> Specify leader start point: *Specify the starting point of the leader.*
> Specify next point: *Specify the endpoint of the leader.*
> Specify next point or [Annotation/Format/Undo]<Annotation>: *Press ENTER.*
> Enter first line of annotation text or <options>: *Enter annotation text (for example, Drill and Ream).*
> Enter the next line of annotation text: *Enter annotation text (for example, 0.75 Dia Hole).*
> Enter the next line of annotation text: Press *ENTER when done entering text.*

Annotation Options

You can also use the **Copy, Tolerance, Block,** or **Mtext** options for annotations. The following is the description of the **Copy** option.

Copy. The **Copy** option allows you to copy an existing annotation object and attach it at the end of the leader. For example, if you have a text string in the drawing that you want to place at the end of the leader, you can use the **Copy** option to place it at the end of the leader. The following is the prompt sequence for copying an existing annotation:

Command: **LEADER**
Specify leader start point: *Specify the starting point of the leader.*
Specify next point: *Specify the endpoint of the leader.*
Specify next point or [Annotation/Format/Undo]<Annotation>: *Press ENTER.*
Enter first line of annotation text or <options>: *Press ENTER.*
Enter an annotation option [Tolerance/Copy/Block/None/MText]<Mtext>: **C**
Select an object to copy: *Select an existing annotation object.*

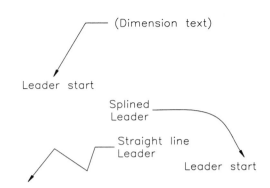

*Figure 6-44 Using the **LEADER** command to draw splined and straight leaders*

Other options like **Tolerance**, **Block**, **None**, and **MText** are similar to **QLEADER** options, discussed earlier under **Annotation Tab** heading.

Format Options

If you select the **Format** option, you can control the shape of the leader and Arrow (Figure 6-43). The available options like **Spline**, **Straight**, **Arrow**, and **None** are similar to **QLEADER** options, discussed earlier under **Leader Line & Arrow Tab** heading.

Using Leader with the DIM Command

You can also draw a leader by using the **Leader** option of the **DIM** command. The **DIM, LEADER** command creates the arrow, leader lines, and the text as separate objects. This command has the feature of defaulting to the most recently measured dimension. Once you invoke the **DIM, LEADER** command and specify the first point, the prompt sequence is similar to that of the **LINE** command. The start point of the leader should be specified at the point closest to the object being dimensioned. After drawing the leader, enter a new dimension text or keep the default one.

Command: **DIM**
Dim: **Leader** (or **L**)
Leader start: *Specify the starting point of the leader.*
To point: *Specify the endpoint of the leader.*
To point: *Specify the next point.*
To point: *Press ENTER.*
Dimension text <current>: *Enter dimension text.*

The value between the angle brackets is the current value that is the measurement of the most recently dimensioned object. If you want to retain the default text, press ENTER at the **Dimension text <current>:** prompt. You can enter text of your choice, specify a prefix/suffix, or suppress the text. The text can be suppressed by pressing the SPACEBAR, and then pressing ENTER at the **Dimension text <current>:** prompt. An arrow is drawn at the start point of the leader segment if the length of the segment is greater than two arrow lengths. If the length of the line segment is less than or equal to two arrow lengths, only a line is drawn.

Self-Evaluation Test

Answer the following questions, and then compare your answers to the answers given at the end of this chapter.

1.　With the **DIM1** command, more than one dimensioning operation can be performed at a time. (T/F)

2.　You can exit the dimension mode by entering E at the **Dim:** prompt. (T/F)

3.　Only arrow marks can be generated at the two ends of the dimension line. (T/F)

4.　You can specify dimension text of your own or accept the measured value computed by AutoCAD. (T/F)

5.　Appending suffixes to dimension text is not possible. (T/F)

6.　Appending prefixes to dimension text is not possible. (T/F)

7.　The size of the dimension arrows can be regulated. (T/F)

8.　With alternate units dimensioning, the dimension text generated is for a single system of measurement. (T/F)

9.　When using tolerances in dimensioning, if the tolerance values are equal, the tolerances are drawn one over the other. (T/F)

10.　Limits are appended to the dimension text. (T/F)

Review Questions

1.　Fill in the command and entries required to dimension an inclined line length of 3.95 units. You must change the dimension text from 3.9500 to 4.0. The dimension line must be aligned with the line being dimensioned.

　　Command: _____
　　Specify first extension line origin or <select object>: _____

Specify second extension line origin: _____
Specify dimension line location or [Mtext/Text/Angle]: _____
Enter dimension text <3.9500>: _____
Specify dimension line location or [Mtext/Text/Angle]: _____

2. Fill in the relevant information to dimension an arc. The dimension text should be R0.750. The radius of the arc is 0.75 units. After completing the dimensioning, return to the Command mode.
Command: _____
Select arc or circle: _____
Dimension text = current
Specify dimension line location or [Mtext/Text/Angle]: _____

3. Fill in the relevant information to dimension the diameter of a circle. The radius of the circle is 2.0 units. The dimension text should have a Ø symbol.
Command: _____
Select arc or circle: _____
Specify dimension line location or [Mtext/Text/Angle]: _____

4. Fill in the blanks with the command and entries required to dimension the angle by defining three points.
Command: _____
Select arc, circle, line, or <specify vertex>: _____
Specify angle vertex: _____
Specify first angle endpoint: _____
Specify second angle endpoint: _____
Specify dimension arc line location or [Mtext/Text/Angle]: _____

5. Give the command and entries required to dimension the angle of an arc.
Command: _____
Select arc, circle, line, or <specify vertex>: _____
Specify dimension arc line location or [Mtext/Text/Angle]: _____

6. Fill in the command and other entries required to draw the center mark for an existing circle/arc.
Command: _____
Select arc or circle: _____

7. Why is dimensioning needed?

8. Specify three ways to return to the Command prompt from the **Dim:** prompt (dimensioning mode).

9. What are the differences between the **DIM** and **DIM1** commands?

10. Explain briefly the five fundamental dimensioning types provided by AutoCAD. List the different dimensioning options available in each of them.

11. Explain briefly dimension line, dimension text, and dimension arrows.

12. Describe extension lines and leaders.

13. Explain the term associative dimensioning.

14. Which dimensioning type generates the coordinate value of X or Y of a location in a drawing?

15. In associative dimensioning, the dimensioning objects are drawn as individual items. (T/F)

16. In aligned dimensioning, the dimension text, by default, is aligned with the object being dimensioned. (T/F)

17. Only inner angles (acute angles) can be dimensioned with angular dimensioning. (T/F)

18. In addition to the most recently drawn dimension (the default base dimension), you can use any other linear dimension as the base dimension. (T/F)

19. In continued dimensions, the base for successive continued dimensions is the base dimension's first extension line. (T/F)

20. Horizontal dimensions measure displacement along the Y axis. (T/F)

21. Vertical dimensions measure displacement along the X axis. (T/F)

22. In rotated dimensioning, the dimension line is always aligned with the object being dimensioned. (T/F)

23. The rotated dimension can be specified to get the effect of horizontal or vertical dimension. (T/F)

24. The center point of arc/circle is taken as the vertex angle in the angular dimensioning of the arc/circle. (T/F)

25. The **DIMORDINATE** command is used to dimension the X coordinate of an object only. (T/F)

Exercises

Exercise 7   *Mechanical*

Draw the object shown in Figure 6-45, and then dimension it. Save the figure drawn in the DIMEXR7 drawing file.

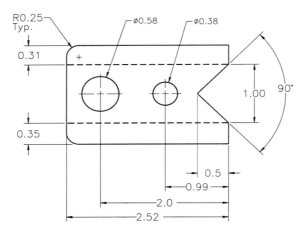

Figure 6-45 *Drawing for Exercise 7*

Exercise 8   *Mechanical*

Draw and dimension the object shown in Figure 6-46. The UCS origin is the lower left corner of the object. Save the drawing as DIMEXR8.

Figure 6-46 *Drawing for Exercise 8*

Exercise 9   *Mechanical*

Draw the object shown in Figure 6-47, then dimension it. Save the drawing as DIMEXR9.

Figure 6-47 *Drawing for Exercise 9*

Exercise 10   *Mechanical*

Draw the object shown in Figure 6-48, then dimension it. Save the drawing as DIMEXR10.

Figure 6-48 *Drawing for Exercise 10*

Exercise 11 *Mecahnical*

Draw and dimension the object shown in Figure 6-49 and save it as DIMEXR11. You can use the **ARRAY** command to facilitate drawing the figure.

Figure 6-49 *Drawing for Exercise 11*

Exercise 12 *Mechanical*

Draw and dimension Figure 6-50 and save it as DIMEXR12.

Figure 6-50 *Drawing for Exercise 12*

Exercise 13

Mechanical

Draw and dimension Figure 6-51 and save it as DIMEXR13

Figure 6-51 *Drawing for Exercise 13*

Exercise 14

Mechanical

Draw Figure 6-52 and dimension it. Save the drawing as DIMEXR14.

Figure 6-52 *Drawing for Exercise 14*

Exercise 15

Draw Figure 6-53 and dimension it. After you have drawn one of the doughnuts, use the **ARRAY** command to obtain other doughnuts. Save the drawing as DIMEXR15.

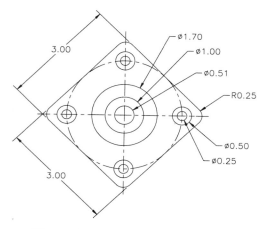

Figure 6-53 *Drawing for Exercise 15*

Exercise 16

Draw Figure 6-54 and dimension it as shown in the drawing. Use the **BASELINE** dimension command to dimension the drawing.

Figure 6-54 *Drawing for Exercise 16*

Problem-Solving Exercise 1

Draw Figure 6-55 and dimension it exactly as shown in the drawing. The **FILLET** command should be used where needed. Save the drawing as DIMPSE1.

Figure 6-55 Drawing for Problem Solving Exercise 1

Problem-Solving Exercise 2

Draw Figure 6-56 and then dimension it exactly as shown in the drawing. Save the drawing as DIMPSE2.

Figure 6-56 Drawing for Problem solving Exercise 2

Project Exercise 1-3   *Mechanical*

Generate the drawing in Figure 6-57 according to the dimensions shown in the figure. Save the drawing as BENCH5-6. (See Chapters 1, 2, 7, 19, and 23 for other drawings of Project Exercise 1.)

Figure 6-57 Drawing for Project Exercise 1-3

Answers to Self-Evaluation Test
1 - F, **2** - T, **3** - F, **4** - T, **5** - F, **6** - F, **7** - T, **8** - F, **9** - F, **10** - F

Chapter 7

Editing Dimensions

Learning Objectives

After completing this chapter, you will be able to:
- *Edit dimensions.*
- *Stretch, extend, and trim dimensions.*
- *Use the* **DIMEDIT** *and* **DIMTEDIT** *command options to edit dimensions.*
- *Update dimensions using the* **DIM**, *Update and* **DIMSTYLE**, *Apply commands.*
- *Use the* **PROPERTIES** *command to edit dimensions.*
- *Dimension in model space and paper space.*

EDITING DIMENSIONS

For editing dimensions, AutoCAD has provided some special editing commands that work with dimensions. These editing commands can be used to define new dimension text, return to home text, create oblique dimensions, and rotate and update the dimension text. You can also use the **TRIM**, **STRETCH**, and **EXTEND** commands to edit the dimensions. But unless you include the dimensioned objects in the edit selection set, objects do not change automatically. The properties of the dimensioned objects can also be changed using the **Object Properties Window** or **Dimension Style Manager**.

Stretching Dimensions

To stretch a dimension object, appropriate definition points must be included in the selection crossing box of the **STRETCH** command. Because the middle point of the dimension text is a definition point for all types of dimensions, you can use the **STRETCH** command to move the dimension text to any location you want. You can also choose **STRETCH** command from the **MODIFY** menu or **MODIFY** toolbar. If you stretch the dimension text but do not want the dimension line broken, the gap in the dimension line gets filled automatically. The dimension type remains the same after stretching. When editing, the definition points of the dimension being edited must be included in the selection crossing box. The aligned dimension adjusts itself so that it is aligned with the object being dimensioned; the dimension is automatically calculated as well. The vertical dimension maintains itself as a vertical dimension and measures the vertical distance between the base and the top of the triangle even though the line it dimensions may no longer be a vertical line. The following example illustrates the use of the **STRETCH** command in stretching a dimension.

Example 1

In this example you will stretch the objects and the dimension to a new location. The drawing in Figure 7-1(a) should already be drawn on the screen.

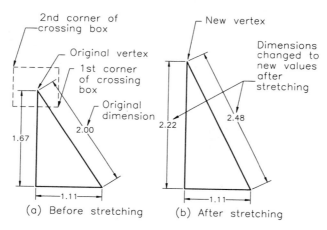

Figure 7-1 *Using the **STRETCH** command to stretch the dimensions*

1. At the AutoCAD Command prompt, enter the **STRETCH** command. At the next prompt, use the crossing option to select the objects and dimensions you want to stretch.

   Command: **STRETCH**
   Select objects to stretch by crossing-window or crossing-polygon...
   Select objects: **C**
   Specify first corner: *Select the first corner of the crossing box.*
   Specify opposite corner: *Select the second corner of the crossing box.*
   Select objects: ⏎

2. Next, AutoCAD will prompt you to enter the base point and the second point of displacement. When you enter this information, the objects and the dimensions will be stretched as shown in Figure 7-1(b).

   Specify base point or displacement: *Specify the base point.*
   Specify second point of displacement: *Specify the point where you want to stretch the objects.*

Exercise 1
Mechanical

The two dimensions in Figure 7-2(a) are too close. Fix the drawing by stretching the dimension as shown in Figure 7-2(b).

1. Stretch the outer dimension to the right so that there is some distance between the two dimensions.
2. Stretch the dimension text of the outer dimension so that the dimension text is staggered (lower than the first dimension).

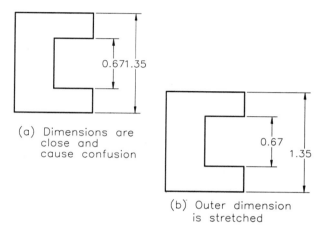

Figure 7-2 *Drawing for Exercise 1, stretching dimensions*

Trimming and Extending Dimensions

Trimming and extending operations can be carried out with all types of linear dimensions (horizontal, vertical, aligned, rotated) and the ordinate dimension. AutoCAD trims or extends a linear dimension between the extension line definition points and the object used as a boundary or trimming edge. To extend or trim an ordinate dimension, AutoCAD moves the feature location (location of the dimensioned coordinate) to the boundary edge. To retain the original ordinate value, the boundary edge to which the feature location point is moved is orthogonal to the measured ordinate. In both cases, the imaginary line drawn between the two extension line definition points is trimmed or extended by AutoCAD, and the dimension is adjusted automatically (Figure 7-3). The prompt sequence for extending the dimension is:

Command: **EXTEND**
Current Settings: Projection=UCS Edge=Extend
Select boundary edges...
Select objects: *Select the upper tip of the polygon.*
Select objects: *Press ENTER.*
Select object to extend or [Project/Edge/Undo]: *Select the dimension.*

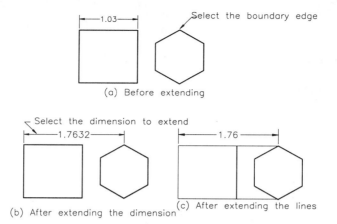

Figure 7-3 *Using the* **EXTEND** *command to extend dimensions*

Exercise 2   *General*

Use the **TRIM** command to trim the dimension at the top of Figure 7-4(a) so it looks like Figure 7-4(b).

1. Make the drawing and dimension it as shown in Figure 7-4(a). Assume the dimensions where necessary.
2. Stretch the dimension as shown in Figure 7-4(b). You can also trim the dimension by setting the **EDGEMODE** system variable to 1, and then using the **TRIM** command. In this case, you do not need to draw a line to trim.

Figure 7-4 *Drawing for Exercise 2*

EDITING DIMENSIONS (DIMEDIT Command)

The dimension text can be edited by using the **DIMEDIT** command. This command has four

Toolbar:	Dimension > Dimension Edit
Menu:	Dimension > Oblique (option)
Command:	DIMEDIT

options: New, Rotate, Home, and Oblique. The
prompt sequence for the **DIMEDIT** command is:

*Figure 7-5 Invoking **DIMEDIT** from the toolbar*

Command: **DIMEDIT**
Enter type of dimension editing (Home/New/Rotate/Oblique) <Home>: *Enter an option.*

New

You can use the **New** option to replace the existing dimension Mtext with a new text string.

Command: **DIMEDIT**
Enter type of dimension editing (Home/New/Rotate/Oblique) <Home>: **N**

The **Multiline Text Editor** dialog box is displayed (Figure 7-6). Enter the text in the Text Editor
and then choose the **OK** button. The following prompt is displayed in the command line:

Figure 7-6 Multiline Text Editor dialog box

Select objects: *Select the dimensions.*
Select objects: *Press ENTER.*

In case a null response is given at the **Enter
dimension text <current>:** prompt, the actual
dimension text is taken as the text. The <>
prefix or suffix facility can also be used when
you enter the new text string. In this case, the
prefix/suffix is appended before or after the dimension measurement that is placed instead
of the <> characters. For example, if you enter Ref-Dim before <> and mm after <> (Ref-
Dim<>mm), AutoCAD will attach Ref-Dim as
prefix and mm as suffix (Ref-Dim1.1257mm)
(see Figure 7-7).

*Figure 7-7 Using the **DIMEDIT** command to edit
dimensions*

Chapter 7

If information about the dimension style is available on the selected dimension, it is used to redraw the dimension, or the prevailing variable settings are used for the redrawing process.

You can also use the **DIM**, **NEWTEXT** commands to replace an existing text with simple text.

> Command: **DIM**
> Dim: **NEWTEXT**

The **Multiline Text Editor** dialog box is displayed where you can enter new text and then choose the **OK** button. The following prompt is displayed in the command line:

> Select objects: *Select the dimensions.*
> Select objects: *Press ENTER.*

Rotate

Using the **Rotate** option, you can position the dimension text at an angle you specify. The angle can be specified by entering its value at the **Specify angle for dimension text:** prompt or by specifying two points at the required angle. You will notice that the text rotates around its middle point. When the dimension text alignment is set to orient text horizontally, the dimension text is aligned with the dimension line. With this command, you can change the orientation (angle) of the dimension text of any number of associative dimensions. As an alternate method for rotating the text, use the **TROTATE** command at the **Dim:** prompt.

> Command: **DIMEDIT**
> Enter type of dimension editing (Home/New/Rotate/Oblique) <Home>: **R**
> Specify angle for dimension text: *Enter text angle.*
> Select objects: *Select the dimensions.*
> Select objects: *Press ENTER.*

> Dim: **TROTATE**
> Specify angle for dimension text: *Enter text angle.*
> Select objects: *Select the dimensions.*
> Select objects: *Press ENTER.*

The angle of rotation can be entered at the **Specify angle for dimension text:** prompt, or it can be specified by selecting two points. An angle value of zero places the text in its default orientation. If the text alignment is set to orient text horizontally, the dimension text is aligned with the dimension line.

Home

The Home option restores the text of an associative dimension to its original (home/default) location if the position of the text has been changed using the **STRETCH** or **DIMEDIT** command. For an alternate method use **HOMETEXT** at the **Dim:** prompt.

> Command: **DIMEDIT**
> Enter type of dimension editing (Home/New/Rotate/Oblique) <Home>: **H**
> Select objects: *Select the dimension.*

Select objects: *Press ENTER.*
Dim: **HOMETEXT**
Select objects: *Select the dimension object.*
Select objects: *Press ENTER.*

Oblique

In the linear dimensions, extension lines are drawn perpendicular to the dimension line. The **Oblique** option bends the linear associative dimensions. It draws extension lines at an oblique angle (Figure 7-8). This option is particularly important when creating isometric dimensions and can be used to resolve conflicting situations due to the overlapping of extension lines with other objects. Making an existing dimension oblique by specifying an angle oblique to it does not affect the generation of new linear dimensions. The oblique angle is maintained even after performing most editing operations. (See Chapter 19 for details about how to use this option.) The alternate method is using **OBLIQUE** at the **Dim**: prompt.

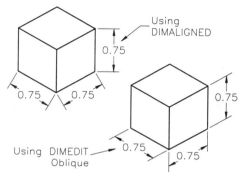

*Figure 7-8 Using **DIMEDIT-Oblique** option to edit dimensions*

Command: **DIMEDIT**
Enter type of dimension editing (Home/New/Rotate/Oblique) <Home>: **O**
Select objects: *Select the dimension.*
Select objects: *Press ENTER.*
Enter obliquing angle (press ENTER for none): *Enter an angle.*

Dim: **OBLIQUE**
Select objects: *Select the dimensions.*
Select objects: *Press ENTER.*
Enter obliquing angle (press ENTER for none): *Enter an angle.*

EDITING DIMENSION TEXT (DIMTEDIT Command)

Toolbar:	Dimension > Dimension Text Edit
Menu:	Dimension > Align Text...
Command:	DIMTEDIT

The dimension text can also be edited by using the **DIMTEDIT** command. This command is used to edit the placement and orientation of a single existing associative dimension. The practical application of this command can be, for example, in cases where dimension text of two or more dimensions are too close together, resulting in confusion. In such cases, the **DIMTEDIT** command is invoked to move the dimension text to some other location so that there is no confusion. This command has five options: **Left**, **Right**, **Center**, **Home**, and **Angle**.

Command: **DIMTEDIT**
Select dimension: *Select a dimension.*
Specify new location for dimension text or [Left/Right/Center/Home/Angle]: *Enter an option.*

As an alternate method, enter **TEDIT** at the **Dim:** prompt.

Command: **DIM**
Dim: **TEDIT**
Select dimension: *Select a dimension.*
Specify new location for dimension text or [Left/Right/Center/Home/Angle]: *Enter an option.*

*Figure 7-9 Invoking **Align Text** from the **Dimension** menu*

If the **DIMSHO** variable is on, you will notice that as you move the cursor, the dimension text of the selected associative dimension is dragged with the cursor. In this manner, you can see where to place the dimension text while you are dynamically dragging the text. Another advantage of having **DIMSHO** on is that the dimension updates dynamically as you drag it. The initial value of **DIMSHO** is on. If **DIMSHO** is off, the dimension text and the extension lines are not dragged with the cursor; hence, it is difficult to see the position of the text as you move the cursor. The splits in the dimension line are calculated while keeping track of the new location of the dimension text. **DIMSHO** is not stored in dimension style. Another method of moving text (automatically) is by using any of the **Left, Right, Center, Home,** or **Angle** options provided in the **Specify new location for dimension text or [Left/Right/Center/Home/Angle]:** prompt. The effects of these options are described next (Figure 7-10).

Left

With this option, you can left-justify the dimension text along the dimension line. The vertical placement setting determines the position of the dimension text. The horizontally aligned text is moved to the left and the vertically aligned text is moved down. This option can be used only with the linear, diameter, and radius dimensions.

Right

With this option, you can right-justify the dimension text along the dimension line. As in the case of the Left option, the vertical placement setting determines the position of the dimension text. The horizontally aligned text is moved to the right, and the vertically aligned text is moved up. This option can be used only with the linear, diameter, and radius dimensions.

Center*

With this option you can center-justify the dimension text for linear, and aligned dimensions. The vertical setting controls the vertical position of the dimension text.

Home

This option works similarly to the **HOMETEXT** command. With the use of the **Home** option, the dimension text of an associative dimension is restored (moved) to its original (home/default) location if the position of the text has been changed.

Angle

With the Angle option, you can position the dimension text at the angle you specify. This option works similarly to the **TROTATE** command. The angle can be specified by entering its value at the **Specify angle for dimension text**: prompt or by specifying two points at the required angle. You will notice that the text rotates around its middle point. If the dimension text alignment is set to Orient Text Horizontally, the dimension text is aligned with the dimension line. If information about the dimension style is available on the selected dimension, AutoCAD uses it to redraw the dimension, or the prevailing dimension variable settings are used for the redrawing process. Entering 0 degree angle changes the text to its default orientation.

*Figure 7-10 Using the **DIMTEDIT** command to edit dimension*

UPDATING DIMENSIONS

| Toolbar: | Dimension > Dimension Update |
| Dim: | UPDATE |

 The **Update** option of the **DIM** command regenerates (updates) prevailing associative dimension objects (like arrows, text height) using current settings for the dimension variables, dimension style, text style, and units.

Command: **DIM**
Dim: **UPDATE**
Select objects: *Select the dimension objects.*

The dimensions can also be updated by using the **Apply** option of the **-DIMSTYLE** command. (For details, see Chapter 8.)

Command: **-DIMSTYLE**
Current dimension style: Standard
Enter a dimension style option
[Save/Restore/STatus/Variables/Apply/?] <Restore>: **A**
Select objects: *Select the dimension objects.*

EDITING DIMENSIONS WITH GRIPS

You can also edit dimensions by using GRIP editing modes. GRIP editing is the easiest and quickest way to edit dimensions. You can perform the following operations with GRIPS (see Chapter 10 for details):

1. Position the text anywhere **along** the dimension line. You cannot move the text and position it above or below the dimension line.
2. Stretch a dimension to change the spacing between the dimension line and the object line.
3. Stretch the dimension along the length. When you stretch a dimension, the dimension text automatically changes.
4. Move, rotate, copy, or mirror the dimensions.
5. Relocate a dimension origin.
6. Change properties like color, layer, linetype, and linetype scale.
7. Load Web browser (if any *Universal Resource Locator* is associated with the object)

EDITING DIMENSIONS USING THE PROPERTIES COMMAND*

Toolbar:	Object Properties > Properties
Menu:	Modify > Properties
Command:	PROPERTIES

Figure 7-11 *Selecting Properties from the **Object Properties** toolbar*

You can also modify a dimension or leader created with the **LEADER** command by using the **PROPERTIES** command. When you choose this command, AutoCAD will display the **Object Properties Window**. All the properties of the selected objects are displayed in the **Object Properties Window** (see Figure 7-11).

OBJECT PROPERTIES WINDOW (DIMENSION)

You can use the **Object Properties Window** (Figure 7-12) to change the properties of a dimension, change the dimension text style, or change geometry, format, and annotation-related features of the selected dimension. The changes takes place dynamically in the drawing. The **Object Properties Window** is classified **Alphabetic** as well as **Category** under the respective tabs. The different categories for modification of dimensions are as follows:

General. In the general category, the various parameters displayed are **Color, Layer, Linetype, Linetype scale, Plot style, Lineweight** and **Hyperlink** with their current values. For example, if you want to change the color of the selected object, then select Color property and choose the required color from the drop-down list. Similarly, Layer, Plot style, Linetype and Lineweight can be changed from the respective drop-down lists. The Linetype scale can be changed manually at the corresponding cell.

Misc. This category displays the dimension style by name (for **DIMSTYLE** system variable use **SETVAR**). You can change the dimension style from the drop-down list for the selected dimension object.

Figure 7-12 Object Properties Window (Dimension)

Primary Units. In the primary units category, the various parameters displayed are **Decimal separator, Dim prefix, Dim suffix, Dim roundoff, Dim scale linear, Dim units, Suppress leading zeroes, Suppress trailing zeroes, Suppress zero feet, Suppress zero inches** and **Precision.** Among the above properties, Dim units, Suppress leading zeroes, Suppress trailing zeroes, Suppress zero feet, Suppress zero inches and Precision properties can be changed with the corresponding drop-down lists and the other parameters can be changed manually.

Alternate Units. In the alternate unit category, there are various parameters for the alternate units. They can be changed only if the **Alt enabled** parameter is **on.** The parameters like **Alt format, Alt precision, Alt suppress leading zeroes,** and **Alt suppress trailing zeroes, Alt suppress zero feet, Alt suppress zero inches** can be changed from the respective drop-down lists and others can be changed manually.

Fit. In the fit category, the various parameters are **Dim line forced, Dim line inside, Dim scale overall, Fit, Text inside,** and **Text movement.** All the parameters can be changed by the drop-down list except Dim scale overall (which can be changed manually).

Lines and arrows. The various parameters of the lines and arrows in the dimension objects like arrowhead size, type, arrow lineweight, etc.,can be changed in this category.

Text. The different parameters that controls the text in the dimension object like text color, text height, vertical position text offset, etc., can be changed in this category.

Tolerances. The parameters of this category can be changed only if Tolerances display parameter has some mode of tolerance selected. The various parameters are available corresponding to the mode of tolerance selected.

Tolerances and Text. This category displays the **Tolerance text height** which shows the scale factor of tolerance text as set by **DIMTXT (DIMTFAC** system variable) and can be changed manually.

OBJECT PROPERTIES WINDOW (LEADER)*

The **Object Properties Window** for **Leader** can be invoked by selecting a Leader and then choosing **Properties** from the **Modify** menu. You can also invoke the **Object Properties Window** (Figure 7-13) from the shortcut menu by right-clicking in the drawing area and choosing **Properties**. The various properties under Object Properties Window (Leader) are described as follows:

General. The parameters in the general category are the same as those discussed in the previous section (**Object Properties Window** for dimensions).

Geometry. This category displays the coordinates of the Leader. The various parameters under this category are **Vertex**, **Vertex X**, **Vertex Y**, and **Vertex Z**. You can choose any vertex of the leader and change its coordinates.

Misc. This category displays the **Dim Style** and **Type** of the Leader. You can change the style name and the type of the Leader by using these properties.

Figure 7-13 Object Properties Window (Leader)

Fit. This category displays the **Dim scale overall** property that specifies the overall scale factor applied to size, distances, or the offsets of the Leader.

Lines and Arrows. Lines and Arrows displays the different specifications of the arrowheads and line types for the Leader.

Text. Text category displays the **Text offset** to the dimension line and the vertical position (**Text pos vert**) of the dimension text and can be changed accordingly.

Example 2

Use the **PROPERTIES** command to modify the dimensions in Figure 7-14 so that it matches Figure 7-15.

Figure 7-14 *Drawing for Example 2*

Figure 7-15 *Drawing after editing the dimensions*

Chapter 7

1. Enter the **PROPERTIES** command at the Command prompt, or select it from the **Modify** menu or the toolbar.

   Command: **PROPERTIES**

   AutoCAD displays the **Object Properties Window**.
   Select the dimension 2.2500.
2. To change the number of decimal places, choose the **Precision** drop-down list from the **Primary Units** category and choose (0.00). The number of decimal places will change dynamically in the drawing.
3. To change the text style, choose the **Text style** drop-down list under **Text** category and then choose the **ROMANC** text style. The changes will take place dynamically.
4. To edit the leader, select the leader and enter the **PROPERTIES** command. AutoCAD will display the **Object Properties Window (Leader)**. Choose **Arrow size** under the **Lines and Arrows** category. Change the arrowhead size to (0.09).
5. In the **Misc** category, from the **Type** drop-down list, choose the **Spline with arrow** option. The changes will take place dynamically in the drawing.
6. To edit the radius text, choose **Text override** parameter under Text category and in the adjacent cell enter **\P{Drill and Ream} \P{0.25 Dia Hole} \P{(Through)}**. Reduce the height of the text by changing the value in **Text height** parameter to (0.06).
7. In the **Lines and arrows** category, choose the **Closed** type of arrowhead from the **Arrow** drop-down list.

Now exit the **Object Properties Window**.

MODEL SPACE AND PAPER SPACE DIMENSIONING

Figure 7-16 *Selecting paper space scaling in the* **Modify Dimension Style** *dialog box*

Dimensioning objects can be drawn in model space or paper space. If the drawings are in model space, associative dimensions should also be created in model space. If the drawings are in model space and the associative dimensions are in paper space, the dimensions will not change when you perform such editing operations as stretching, trimming, and extending, or such display operations as zoom and pan in the model space viewport. The definition points of a dimension are located in the space where the drawing is drawn. You can check for **Paper Space Scaling** under **Scale for dimension features** in the **Fit** tab of **Modify**, **New**, or **Override** dialog boxes in the **Dimension Style Manager** dialog box, depends on whether you want to modify the present style or you want to create a new style (see Figure 7-16). Choose **OK/OK** to exit from both the dialog boxes. AutoCAD calculates a scale factor that is compatible with the model space and the paper space viewports. Choose **Update** from the **Dimension** menu and select the dimension objects for updating.

The drawing shown (Figure 7-17) uses paper space scaling. The main drawing and detail drawings are located in different floating viewports (paper space). The zoom scale factors for these viewports are different: 0.75XP, 1.0XP, and 1.5XP, respectively. When you use paper scaling, AutoCAD automatically calculates the scale factor for dimensioning so that the dimensions are uniform in all the floating viewports (model space viewports).

Figure 7-17 *Dimensioning in paper model space viewports using paper space scaling or setting* **DIMSCALE** *to 0*

Self Evaluation Test

Answer the following questions, and then compare your answers to the correct answers given at the end of this chapter.

1. Explain the use and working of the **STRETCH** command._____

2. Explain the use and working of the **TRIM** command on dimensions. _____

3. In associative dimensioning, the items constituting a dimension (such as dimension lines, arrows, leaders, extension lines, and dimension text) are drawn as a **single object.** (T/F)

4. If associative dimensioning is disabled, the dimension lines, arrows, leaders, extension lines, and dimension text are drawn as **independent** objects. (T/F)

5. The **DIMASO** dimensioning variable governs the creation of associative dimensioning. (T/F)

6. In associative dimensioning, you cannot edit the dimension objects as a single object with various commands. (T/F)

7. The **horizontal, vertical, aligned,** and **rotated** dimensions cannot be associative dimensions. (T/F)

8. Only the **CENTER** and **LEADER** commands are affected by associative dimensioning. (T/F)

9. The **EXPLODE** command can be used to break an associative dimension into individual items. (T/F)

Review Questions

1. To stretch a dimension object, appropriate definition points must be included in the _____ of the **STRETCH** command.

2. Trimming and extending operations can be carried out with all types of linear (horizontal, vertical, aligned, rotated) dimensions and with the ordinate dimension. (T/F)

3. To extend or trim an ordinate dimension, AutoCAD moves the feature location (location of the dimensioned coordinate) to the boundary edge. (T/F)

4. With the _____ or _____ commands you can edit the dimension text of associative dimensions.

5. The _____ or _____ command is particularly important for creating isometric dimensions and is applicable in resolving conflicting situations due to overlapping of extension lines with other objects.

6. The _____ command is used to edit the placement and orientation of a single existing associative dimension.

7. The _____ or _____ command restores the text of an associative dimension to its original (home/default) location if the position of the text has been changed by the **STRETCH**, **TEDIT**, or **TROTATE** command.

8. The _____ command regenerates (updates) prevailing associative dimension objects (like arrows, text height) using the current settings for the dimension variables, dimension style, text style, and units.

9. If the drawings are in model space, you should create associative dimensions in _____ .

10. The _____ variable can be automatically adjusted to the zoom scale factor of the model space viewport.

11. Explain the function of the **EXPLODE** command in dimensioning. _____
_____ .

12. Explain the term **definition points**. _____
_____ .

13. Explain when to use the **EXTEND** command and how it works with dimensions. _____
_____ .

14. Explain the use and working of the **PROPERTIES** command for editing dimensions. _____
_____ .

Exercises

Exercise 3   *Mechanical*

1. Make the drawing as shown in Figure 7-18. Assume the dimensions where necessary.
2. Dimension the drawing as shown in Figure 7-18.
3. Edit the dimensions as shown in Figure 7-19, using the **STRETCH**, **EXTEND**, and **TRIM** commands.

Figure 7-18 *Drawing for Exercise 3, before editing dimensions*

Figure 7-19 *Drawing for Exercise 3, after editing dimensions*

Exercise 4   *Mechanical*

1. Make the drawing as shown in Figure 7-20 (a). Assume the dimensions where necessary.
2. Dimension the drawing and edit them as shown in Figure 7-20(b).

Figure 7-20 *Drawing for Exercise 4, showing dimensions (a) before and (b) after editing dimensions*

Chapter 7

Exercise 5   *Architecture*

1. Make the drawing as shown in Figure 7-21. Assume the dimensions where necessary.
2. Dimension, and then edit the dimension as shown.

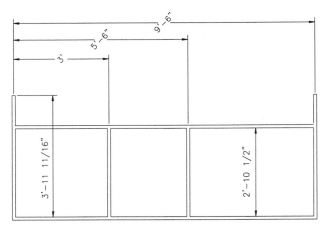

Figure 7-21 Drawing for Exercise 5, editing dimensions

Project Exercise 1-4   *Mechanical*

Generate the drawing in Figure 7-22 according to the dimensions shown in the figure. Save the drawing as BENCH7-8. (See Chapters 1, 2, 6, 19, and 23 for other drawings of Project Exercise 1.)

Figure 7-22 Drawing for Project Exercise 1-4

Project Exercise 1-5   *Mechanical*

Generate the assembly drawing with part numbers and the bill of materials as shown in Figure 7-23. Save the drawing as BENCHASM. (See Chapters 1, 2, 6, 19, and 23 for other drawings of Project Exercise 1.)

Figure 7-23 *Drawing for Project Exercise 1-5*

Answers to Self-Evaluation Test

1 - The **STRETCH** command can be used to stretch the associative dimension. For stretching a dimension object, appropriate definition points must be included in the selection crossing box of the **STRETCH** command. **2** - The trimming operations can be carried out with all types of linear (horizontal, vertical, aligned, rotated) dimensions and the ordinate dimension. AutoCAD trims a linear dimension between the extension line definition points and the object used as trimming edge. For extending or trimming an ordinate dimension, AutoCAD moves the feature location (location of the dimensioned coordinate) to the boundary edge. **3** - T, **4** - T, **5** - T, **6** - F, **7** - F, **8** - F, **9** - T

Chapter 8

Dimension Styles and Dimensioning System Variables

Learning Objectives

After completing this chapter, you will be able to:
- *Use styles and variables to control dimensions.*
- *Create dimensioning styles using dialog boxes and the command line.*
- *Set dimension variables using the different tabs of the **New**, **Modify**, and **Override Dimension Style** dialog boxes and the command line.*
- *Set other dimension variables that are not in dialog boxes.*
- *Understand dimension style families and how to apply them in dimensioning.*
- *Use dimension style overrides.*
- *Compare and list dimension styles.*
- *Import externally referenced dimension styles.*

USING STYLES AND VARIABLES TO CONTROL DIMENSIONS

In AutoCAD, the appearance of dimensions on the drawing screen and the manner in which they are saved in the drawing database are controlled by a set of dimension variables. The dimensioning commands use these variables as arguments. The variables that control the appearance of the dimensions can be managed with dimension styles. You can use the **Dimension Style Manager** dialog box to control dimension styles and dimension variables through a set of dialog boxes. You can also do this by entering relevant dimensioning variable names at the **Command:** or **Dim:** prompt.

CREATING AND RESTORING DIMENSION STYLES
Using the Dialog Box

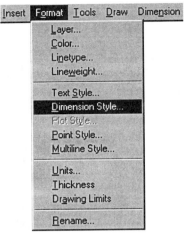

Toolbar:	Dimension > Dimension Style
Menu:	Dimension > Style...
	or Format > Dimension style
Command:	DDIM or DIMSTYLE

*Figure 8-1 Choosing **Dimension Style** from the **Dimension** toolbar*

*Figure 8-2 Choosing **Dimension Style** from the **Format** menu*

Dimension style controls the appearance and positioning of dimensions. If the default dimensioning style (STANDARD) does not meet your requirements, you can select another dimensioning style or create one that does. The default dimension style file name is **STANDARD**. Dimension styles can be created by using the **Dimension Style Manager** dialog box [Figure 8-3(a)] which appears on choosing **Style** from the **Dimension** menu or choosing **Dimension Style** from the **Format** menu. You can also invoke the **Dimension Style Manager** dialog box by choosing the

*Figure 8-3(a) **Dimension Style Manager** dialog box*

Dimension Style button in the Dimension toolbar.

In the **Dimension Style Manager** dialog box, choose the **New...** button to display the **Create New Dimension Style** dialog box [Figure 8-3(b)]. Enter the dimension style name in the **New Style Name:** text box and then select a style you want to base your style on from the **Start With:** drop-down list. The **Use for:** drop-down list, allows you to select the dimension type to which you want to apply the new dimension style. For example if you wish to use the new style for only the diameter dimension, you can select **Diameter dimension** from the **Use for:**

Figure 8-3(b) Create New Dimension Style dialog box

drop-down list. Choose the **Continue** button to display the **New Dimension Style** dialog box (Figure 8-4) where you can define the new style.

In the **Dimension Style Manager** dialog box, the current dimension style name is shown in front of **Current dimstyle:** and is also shown highlighted in the **Styles:** list box. A brief description of the current style (it's differences from the default settings) is also displayed in the **Description** box. The **Dimension Style Manager** dialog box also has a **Preview of:** window which displays a preview of the current dimension style. A style can be made current (restored) by selecting the name of the dimension style you want to make current from the list of defined dimension styles and choosing the **Set Current** button or by double-clicking on the style name you want to make current in the list box. The drop-down list in the **Dimension** toolbar also displays the dimension styles. Selecting a Dimension style from this list also sets it current.The list of dimension styles displayed in the **Styles:** list box is dependent on the option selected from the **List:** drop down list. If you select the **Styles in use** option, only the dimension styles in use will be listed in the **Style:** list box. If you right-click a style in the **Style:** list box, a shortcut menu is displayed which gives you the options to **Set current**, **Rename** or **Delete** a dimension style. Selecting the **Don't list styles in Xrefs** check box does not list the names of Xref styles in the **Styles:** list box. Choosing the **Modify** button displays the **Modify Dimension Style:** dialog box where you can modify an existing style. Choosing the **Override** button, displays the **Override Current Style:** dialog box where you can define overrides to an existing style (discussed later in this chapter). Both these dialog boxes along with the **New Dimension Style:** dialog box have identical properties. Choosing the **Compare** button displays the **Compare Dimension Styles** dialog box (also discussed later in this chapter) which allows you to compare two existing styles.

Using the Command Line

You can also create dimension styles from the command line by entering **-DIMSTYLE** at the Command prompt or by entering **SAVE** at the **Dim:** prompt:

> Command: **-DIMSTYLE**
> Current dimension style: *Displays the current style name.*
> Enter a dimension style option
> [Save/Restore/STatus/Variables/Apply/?] <Restore>: **SAVE**
> Enter name for new dimension style or [?]: *Enter the name of the dimension style.*

Command: **DIM**
Dim: **SAVE**
Enter name for new dimension style or [?]: *Enter the name of the dimension style.*

You can also restore the dimensions from the command line by entering **-DIMSTYLE** at the Command prompt or by entering **RESTORE** at the **Dim**: prompt.

Command: **-DIMSTYLE**
Current dimension style: *Displays the current style name.*
Enter a dimension Style option
[Save/Restore/STatus/Variables/Apply/?] <Restore>: **RESTORE**
Current dimension style: *Displays the current dimension style.*
Enter a dimension style name, [?] or <select dimension>: *Enter the dimension style name.*

Command: **DIM**
DIM: **RESTORE**
Current dimension style: *AutoCAD displays the current style name.*
Enter dimension style name, [?] or <select dimension>: *Enter the dimension style name.*

You can also select a dimension style by specifying a dimension on a drawing. This can be accomplished by pressing ENTER (null response) at the prompt **Enter a dimension style name, [?] or < select dimension>:**. This way, you can select the dimension style without knowing the name of the dimension style. With the help of dimension styles, you can easily create and save groups of settings for as many types of dimensions as you require. Styles can be created to support almost any standards, including ANSI, DIN, and architectural.

NEW DIMENSION STYLE: DIALOG BOX*

The **New Dimension Style** dialog box (Figure 8-4) can be used to specify the dimensioning attributes (variables) that affect the various properties of the dimensions. It has the following tabs.

Lines and Arrows Tab

The **Lines and Arrows** tab (Figure 8-4) can be used to specify the dimensioning attributes (variables) that affect the format of the dimension lines and arrows; that is, the appearance and behavior of the dimension lines, extension lines, arrowheads, and center marks. If the settings of the dimension variables have not been altered in the current editing session, the settings displayed in the dialog box are the default settings.

Dimension Line

Color. Dimension arrowheads have the same color as the dimension line because arrows constitute a part of the dimension line. You can establish a color for the dimension line and the dimension arrows. The color number or the special color label is stored in the **DIMCLRD** variable. The default color label for the dimension line is BYBLOCK. You can specify the color of the dimension line by selecting from the **Color:** drop-down list. You can also choose **Other...** from the **Color:** drop-down list to display the **Select Color** dialog box where you can choose a specific color.

Lineweight. You can specify Lineweight for the dimension line by selecting from the **Lineweight:**

Figure 8-4 Lines and Arrows tab of the New Dimension Style: dialog box

drop-down list. This value is stored in the **DIMLWD** variable. The default value is BYBLOCK.

Extend beyond ticks. The **Extend beyond ticks:** (Oblique tick extension) edit box is used to specify the distance by which the dimension line will extend beyond the extension line. The **Extend beyond ticks:** edit box can be used only when you have selected the oblique, Architectural tick or any such arrowhead type in the **1st:, 2nd:** drop-down lists in the **Arrowheads** area. The extension value entered in the **Extend beyond ticks:** edit box gets stored in the **DIMDLE** variable. By default, this edit box is disabled because the oblique arrowhead type is not selected.

Baseline Spacing. The **Baseline Spacing:** (Baseline Increment) edit box is used to control the dimension line increment (gap between successive dimension lines) for the continuation of a linear dimension drawn with the **BASELINE** command (Figure 8-5). You can specify the dimension line increment to your requirement by entering the desired value in the **Baseline Spacing:** edit box. Also, when you are creating continued dimensions with the **DIMContinue** command, the contents of a **Baseline Spacing:** edit box specify the offset distance for the successive dimension lines, if needed to avoid drawing over the previous dimension line. The default value displayed in the **Baseline Spacing:** edit box is 0.38 units. The spacing (baseline increment) value is stored in the **DIMDLI** variable.

Suppress. The **Suppress:** check boxes control the drawing of the first and second dimension

Figure 8-5 DIMDLI, *baseline increment*

lines. By default, both dimension lines will be drawn. You can suppress one or both dimension lines by selecting their corresponding check boxes. The values of these check boxes are stored in the **DIMSD1** and **DIMSD2** variables.

Note

*The first and second dimension lines are determined by how you select the extension line origins. If the first extension line origin is on the right, the first dimension line is also on the right. The initial value of **DIMSD1** and **DIMSD2** is off.*

Extension Line

Color. In the **Color:** edit box, you can examine or modify the current extension line color (Figure 8-6). The default extension line color is BYBLOCK. You can change the color by assigning a new color to the extension lines. For example, if you want the extension line color to be red, select red from the **Color:** drop-down list or select the **Other...** option from the drop-down list. On selecting this option, the **Select Color:** dialog box is displayed where you can choose the desired color. The color number or the color label is saved in the **DIMCLRE** variable.

*Figure 8-6 Changing extension line color, **DIMCLRE***

Lineweight. In this box you can examine or modify the current extension line lineweight. The default value is BYBLOCK. You can change the lineweight value by selecting a new value from the **Lineweight:** drop-down list. The value for lineweight is stored in the **DIMLWE** variable.

Extend beyond dim lines. It is the distance the extension line should extend past the dimension line. You can change the extension line offset by entering the desired distance value in the **Extend beyond dim lines:** edit box (Figure 8-7). The value of this edit box is stored in the **DIMEXE** variable. The default value for extension distance is 0.1800 units.

Offset from origin. This edit box displays the distance value the extension lines are offset from the extension line origins you specify. You may need to override this setting for specific dimensions when dimensioning curves and angled lines. You may have noticed that a small space exists between the origin points you specify and the start of the extension line (Figure 8-8). This space is due to the specified offset. You can specify an offset distance of your choice by entering it in this box. AutoCAD stores this value in the **DIMEXO** variable;. The default value for this distance is 0.0625.

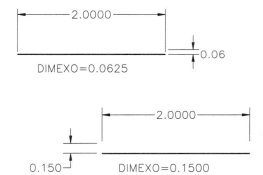

*Figure 8-7 Extension above line, **DIMEXE***

*Figure 8-8 Origin offset, **DIMEXO***

Suppress. The **Suppress:** check boxes control the display of the extension lines. By default, both extension lines will be drawn. You can suppress one or both extension lines by selecting the corresponding check boxes (Figure 8-9). The values of these check boxes are stored in the **DIMSE1** and **DIMSE2** variables (Figure 8-10).

 Note
*The first and second extension lines are determined by how you select the extension line origins. If the first extension line origin is on the right, the first extension line is also on the right. The initial value of **DIMSE1** and **DIMSE2** is off.*

*Figure 8-9 **Extension Lines** area of the **New Dimension Style** dialog box*

Figure 8-10 *Visibility of extension lines **DIMSE1** and **DIMSE2***

Arrowheads

1st: and 2nd: drop-down lists. When you create a dimension, AutoCAD draws the terminator symbols at the two ends of the dimension line. These terminator symbols, generally referred to as **arrowhead types**, represent the beginning and end of a dimension (see Figure 8-11). AutoCAD has provided nineteen standard termination symbols you can apply at each end of the dimension line. In addition to these, you can create your own arrows or terminator symbols. By default, the same arrowhead type is applied at both ends of the dimension line. If you select the first arrowhead, it is automatically applied to the second by default (see Figure 8-12). However, if you want to specify a different arrowhead at the second dimension line endpoint, you must select the desired arrowhead type or **User arrow** from the **2nd:** drop-down list.

*Figure 8-11 Arrowheads area of the **Lines &
Arrows** tab of the **New Dimension Style**
dialog box*

*Figure 8-12 Arrowheads **1st:** drop-down*

The first endpoint of the dimension line is the intersection point of the first extension line and the dimension line. The first extension line is determined by the first extension line origin. However, in angular dimensioning the second endpoint is located in a counterclockwise direction from the first point, regardless of how the points were selected when creating the angular dimension. The specified arrowhead types are selected from the **1st:** and **2nd:** drop-down lists. The first arrowhead type is saved in the **DIMBLK1** system variable, and the second arrowhead type is saved in the **DIMBLK2** system variable. As mentioned earlier, by default, arrows are drawn at the two endpoints of the dimension line. If you specify a different block from the arrowhead, the name of the block is stored in the **DIMBLK** system variable (see Chapter 12 for information on creating blocks).

User Arrow. If you want to specify that, instead of the standard arrows, a user-defined block be drawn at the ends of the dimension line, select the **User Arrow...** from the **1st:** or **2nd:** arrowheads drop-down list to display the **Select Custom Arrow Block** dialog box. Select the name of the predefined block name from the **Select from Drawing Blocks:** drop-down list and then choose the **OK** button. The size of the block is determined by the value stored in the **Arrow size:** edit box. The name of the block you select is stored in the **DIMBLK1** or **DIMBLK2** variable.

Arrow size. Arrowheads and terminator symbols are drawn according to the size specified in the **Arrow size**: edit box. The default value is 0.18 units. This value is stored in the **DIMASZ** system variable. By default, **DIMTSZ** is set to 0 and **DIMASZ** to 0.18. See Figures 8-13 and 8-14.

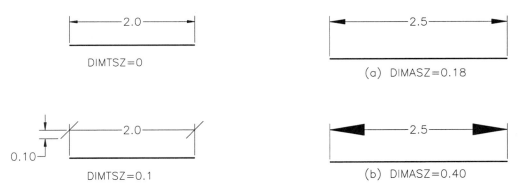

Figure 8-13 *Tick marks are drawn if* **DIMTSZ** *is not 0*

Figure 8-14 *Controlling arrow size,* **DIMASZ**

Leader. The **Leader:** drop-down list displays arrowhead types for the Leader arrow. Here also you can either select an option from the drop-down list or choose **User Arrow** which allows you to define and use a user-defined arrowhead type.

Creating Custom Arrowheads

As mentioned earlier, you can replace the default arrowheads at the end of the dimension lines with a user arrow (user-defined block). Figure 8-15, shows a block comprising a custom arrow. You can use this arrow to define a block and then use it as a user arrow. When you create a dimension, the custom arrow will automatically appear at the endpoint of the dimension line, replacing the standard arrow.

Considerations for Creating an Arrowhead Block

1. When you create a block for an arrowhead, the arrowhead block must be created in a 1 x 1 box. AutoCAD automatically scales the block's X and Y scale factors to arrowhead size x overall scale. The **DIMASZ** variable controls the length of the arrowhead. For example, if **DIMASZ** is set to 0.25, the length of the arrow will be 0.25 units. Also, if the length of the arrow is not 1

unit, it will leave a gap between the dimension line and the arrowhead block.

2. The arrowhead must be drawn as it would appear on the right-hand side of the dimension line.

3. The insertion point of the arrowhead block must be the point that will coincide with the extension line.

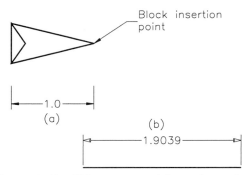

To create an arrowhead block, use the **BLOCK** command. The **Block Definition** dialog box is displayed on the screen. Enter a name for the block in the **Name:** edit box, say **MYARROW**. Choose the **Pick point** button to select the insertion base point on the screen. Once you have

Figure 8-15 *Using arrows, tick marks, and user-defined blocks*

selected the insertion base point on screen, you are returned back to the **Block Definition** dialog box. Now, choose the **Select objects** button to select objects on the screen. Select the arrow and press ENTER. In the **Block Definition** dialog box, choose **OK**. Now, when you select the **User Arrow** option from the Arrowheads drop-down lists, the **Select from Drawing Blocks:** drop-down list displays the drawing block name you just created. You can select **MYARROW** from the drop-down list and when you create a dimension, the user-defined arrow is displayed at the end of the dimension line. The following is the prompt sequence for creating a block using the command line:

> Command: **-BLOCK**
> Enter block name or [?]: *Give a name; e.g., MYARROW.*
> Specify insertion base point: *Select the endpoint as shown in the figure.*
> Select objects: *Select the arrow.*
> Select objects: *Press ENTER.*

Center Marks for Circles

This area deals with options that control the appearance of Center Marks and Centerlines in Radius and Diameter dimensioning. When using the **DIMDIAMETER** and **DIMRADIUS** commands, Center Marks are drawn only if dimensions are placed outside the circle.

Type. The **Type:** drop-down list allows you to select the type of Center Mark you wish to use, such as **None**, **Mark**, or **Line**.

Mark. This is the default option and the size of the Center mark is stored as a positive value in the **DIMCEN** variable (Figure 8-16).

Line. If you want to draw centerlines for a circle or an arc, select **Line** from the **Type:** drop-down list. The value in the **Size:** edit box determines the size of the centerlines, as shown in Figure 8-17. The value you enter in the **Size:** edit box is stored as a negative value in the **DIMCEN** variable. In the case of radius and diameter dimensioning, centerlines are drawn only when the dimension line is located outside the circle or arc. The default setting is a positive value, resulting in the generation of dimensions without centerlines.

None. If you select **None**, the center marks are not drawn and AutoCAD automatically disables the **Size:** edit box.

If you use the **DIMCEN** command, a positive value will create a center mark, and a negative value will create a centerline. If the value is 0, AutoCAD does not create center marks or centerlines.

*Figure 8-16 Center mark size, **DIMCEN***

*Figure 8-17 Mark with center lines, (negative **DIMCEN**)*

Size. The **Size:** edit box in the **Center Marks for Circles** area of the **New, Modify, Override Dimension Style** dialog box displays the current size of the center marks (Figure 8-18). The center marks are created by using the Center, Diameter, and Radius dimensioning commands. The center marks are also created if you use the

*Figure 8-18 The Center Marks for Circles area of the **New Dimension Style** dialog*

DIMCENTER command. In the case of radius and diameter dimensioning, the center mark is drawn only if the dimension line is located outside the circle or arc. You can specify the size of the center mark by entering the required value in the **Size:** edit box. If you do not want a center mark, enter 0 in the edit box or, better, select **None** in the **Type:** drop-down list. This value is stored in the **DIMCEN** variable. The default value of **DIMCEN** variable is 0.09.

 Note
*Unlike specifying a negative value for the **DIMCEN** variable, you cannot enter a negative value in the **Size:** edit box. Selecting **Line** from the **Type:** drop-down list, automatically treats the value in the **Size:** edit box as the size for the centerlines and sets **DIMCEN** to the negative of the value shown.*

Exercise 1   *Mechanical*

Draw Figure 8-19. Then set the values in the **Lines and Arrows** tab of the **New Dimension Style** dialog box to dimension the drawing as shown in this figure. (Baseline Spacing = 0.25, Extension beyond dimension line = 0.10, Offset from Origin = 0.05, Arrowhead size = 0.09.) Assume the missing dimensions.

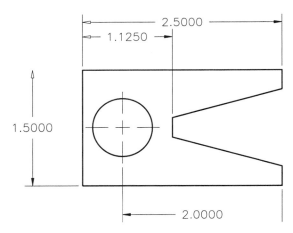

Figure 8-19 *Drawing for Exercise 1*

CONTROLLING DIMENSION TEXT FORMAT
Text Tab

You can control the dimension format through the **Text** tab of the **New Dimension Style** dialog box (Figure 8-20). In the **Text** tab, you can control the placement, appearance, horizontal and vertical alignment of dimension text. For example, you can force AutoCAD to align the dimension text along the dimension line. You can also force the dimension text to be displayed at the top of the dimension line. You can save the settings in a dimension style file for future use. The **New Dimension Style** dialog box has a Preview window that updates dynamically to display the text placement as the settings are changed. Individual items of the **Text** tab and the related dimension variables are described next.

*Figure 8-20 The **Text** tab of the **New Dimension Style** dialog box*

Text Appearance

The **Text Appearance** area of the **New Dimension Style** dialog box lets you specify the text style, text height, text format and color of the dimension text. These options are described next (Figure 8-21).

*Figure 8-21 Text Appearance area of the **Text** tab*

Text Style. The **Text Style:** drop-down list, displays the names of the predefined text styles. From this list you can select the style name that you want to use for dimensioning. You must define the text style before you can use it in dimensioning (see "**STYLE** command" in Chapter 5). Choosing the [...] button, displays the **Text Style** dialog box that allows you to create a new or modify an existing Text Style. The value of this setting is stored in the **DIMTXSTY** system variable. The change in dimension text style does not affect the text style you are using to draw other text in the drawing.

Text Color. A color can be assigned to the dimension text by selecting it from the **Text Color:** drop-down list. The color number or special color label is held in the **DIMCLRT** variable. The default color label is BYBLOCK. If you choose the **Other...** option from the **Text Color:** drop-down list, the **Select Color** dialog box is displayed where you can choose a specific color.

Text Height. You can customize the height of the dimension text (Figure 8-22) by entering the required text height in the **Text height:** edit box. You can change the dimension text height only when the current text style does not have a fixed height. In other words, the text height specified in the **STYLE** command should be zero because a predefined text height (specified in the **STYLE** command) overrides any other setting for the dimension text height. The value in the **Text height:** edit box is stored in the **DIMTXT** variable. The default text height is 0.1800 units.

*Figure 8-22 Dimension text height, **DIMTXT***

Fraction height scale. The **Fraction height scale:** edit box allows you to set the scale of the fractional units in relation to the Dimension text height. This value is stored in the **DIMTFAC** variable.

Draw frame around text. Selecting the **Draw frame around text** check box, draws a frame around the dimension text. This value is stored as a negative value in the **DIMGAP** system variable.

Text Placement

This area of the **Text** tab gives you options controlling the text placement. These options are dealt with below.

Vertical. The **Vertical:** drop-down list displays the options that control the vertical placement of the dimension text. The current setting is highlighted. Controlling the vertical placement of the dimension text is possible only when the dimension text is drawn in its normal (default) location. This setting is stored in the **DIMTAD** system variable. The vertical text placement options are described next (Figure 8-23).

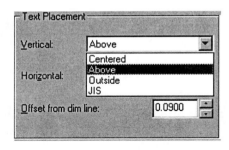

Figure 8-23 Controlling vertical placement

Centered. If this option is selected, the dimension text gets centered on the dimension line in such a way that the dimension line is split to allow for placement of the text. Selecting this option turns **DIMTAD** off. In this setting, **DIMTAD = 0** (Figure 8-24). If the **1st** or **2nd Extension Line** option is selected in the **Horizontal:** drop-down list, this centered setting will center the text on the extension line, not on the dimension line.

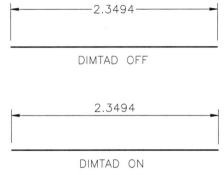

*Figure 8-24 Using Vertical placement to place text, Centered and Above a dimension line, **DIMTAD***

Above. If this option is selected, the dimension text is placed above the dimension line, except when the dimension line is not horizontal and the dimension text inside the extension lines is horizontal (**DIMTIH = 1**). The distance of the dimension text from the dimension line is controlled by the **DIMGAP** value. This results in an unbroken solid dimension line being drawn under the dimension text. In this setting, **DIMTAD=1**.

Outside. This option places the dimension text on the side of the dimension line. In this setting, **DIMTAD**=2.

JIS. This option lets you place the dimension text to conform to **JIS** (Japanese Industrial Standards) representation. In this setting, **DIMTAD=3**.

Note
The Horizontal and Vertical Placement options selected are reflected in the dimensions shown in the Preview window.

Horizontal. Horizontal Placement controls the Horizontal justification of the dimension text. To display the available options, choose the down arrow button to display the **Horizontal** drop-down list (Figure 8-25). The selected setting is stored in the **DIMJUST** system variable. The default option is **Centered**. The following is the list of the available options with **DIMJUST** values (Figure 8-26).

Option	Description	DIMJUST
Centered	Places text between extension lines	0
1st Extension Line	Places text next to first extension line	1
2nd Extension Line	Places text next to second extension line	2
Over 1st Extension	Places text aligned with and above the first extension line	3
Over 2nd Extension	Places text aligned with and above the second extension line	4

Figure 8-25 Horizontal Placement options of the Text tab of the New Dimension Style dialog box

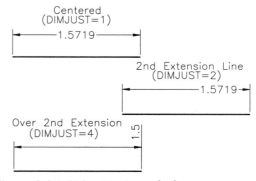

Figure 8-26 Using Horizontal Placement options to position text

Offset from dim line. The **Offset from dim line:** edit box is used to specify the distance between the dimension line and the dimension text (Figure 8-27). You can enter the text gap you need in this edit box. The Text Gap value is also used as the measure of minimum length for the segments of the dimension line and in basic tolerance. The default value specified in this box is 0.09 units. The value of this setting is stored in the **DIMGAP** system variable.

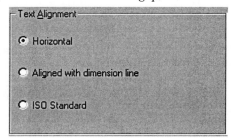

*Figure 8-27 Dimension text gap, **DIMGAP***

Text Alignment

You can use the **Text Alignment** area options (Figure 8-28) to specify the alignment of the dimension text with the dimension line. These options can be used to control the alignment of the dimension text for linear, radius, and diameter dimensions and the values are stored in the **DIMTIH** and **DIMTOH** system variables. By default, the Horizontal option is selected and both the inside and outside dimension text is drawn horizontally.

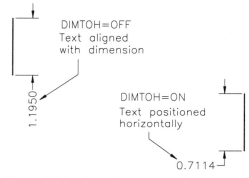

*Figure 8-28 Text Alignment area of the **Text** tab of the **New Dimension Style** dialog box*

Horizontal. By default, the dimension text is drawn horizontally with respect to the UCS (user coordinate system). Therefore, the **Horizontal** radio button is selected. The alignment of the dimension line does not affect text alignment. Selecting this option turns both the **DIMTIH** and **DIMTOH** system variables **on** (Figure 8-29 and Figure 8-30). The text is drawn horizontally even if the dimension line is at an angle.

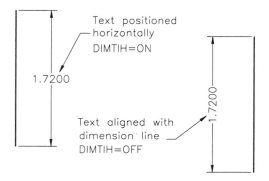

*Figure 8-29 Dimension text inside extension lines horizontal, **DIMTIH***

*Figure 8-30 Dimension text outside extension lines horizontal, **DIMTOH***

Aligned with dimension line. Selecting this radio button aligns the text with the dimension line and both the system variables **DIMTIH** and **DIMTOH** are off.

ISO Standard. By default, the dimension text is drawn horizontally with respect to the UCS (user coordinate system). Therefore, the **Horizontal** radio button is selected. The alignment of the dimension line does not affect the text alignment. If you select the **ISO Standard** radio button, the dimension text is aligned with the dimension line only when the dimension text is inside the extension lines (Figure 8-30). Selecting this option turns the system variable **DIMTOH** on, that is, the dimension text outside the extension line is horizontal regardless of the angle of the dimension line.

Exercise 2   *Mechanical*

Draw Figure 8-31. Then set the values in the **Lines and Arrows** and **Text** tab of the **New Dimension Style** dialog box to dimension the drawing as shown in the figure. (Baseline Spacing = 0.25, Extension beyond dimension lines = 0.10, Offset from Origin = 0.05, Arrow size = 0.09.) Assume the missing dimensions and set **DIMTXT** = 0.09.

Figure 8-31 Drawing for Exercise 2

FITTING DIMENSION TEXT AND ARROWHEADS
Fit Tab

The **Fit** tab of the **New Dimension Style** dialog box gives you options that control the placement of dimension lines, arrowheads, leaderlines, text and the overall dimension scale (Figure 8-32).

Fit Options

In the **Fit Options** area of the **Fit** tab, AutoCAD displays the available options for fitting the arrows and dimension text between the extension lines. The value of the **Fit Options** is stored in the **DIMATFIT**, **DIMTMOVE**, **DIMTIX**, and **DIMSOXD** system variables. The **Fit** options are described next. Selecting any of these radio buttons, sets priorities for moving the text and arrowheads outside the extension lines, if space between the extension lines is not enough to fit both of them.

Either the text or the arrows whichever fits best. This is the default option. In this option, AutoCAD places the dimension where it fits best between the extension lines. In this setting, **DIMTMOVE=0, DIMATFIT=3**.

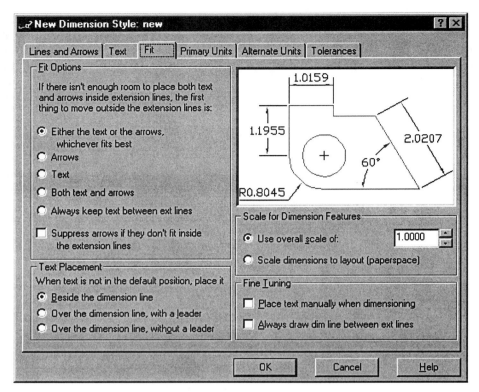

*Figure 8-32 Fit tab of the **New Dimension Style** dialog box*

Arrows. When you select this option, AutoCAD places the text and arrowheads inside the extension lines if there is enough space to fit both. If space is not available for both arrows and text, the text is placed inside the extension lines and the arrows are placed outside the extension lines. If there is not enough space for text, both text and arrowheads are placed outside the extension lines. In this setting, **DIMTMOVE=0, DIMATFIT=1** (Figure 8-33).

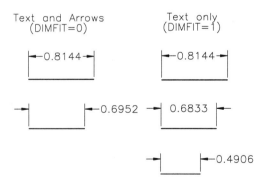

Figure 8-33 Both Text and Arrows whichever fits best and Arrows options

Text. When you select this option, AutoCAD places the text and arrowheads inside the extension lines if there is enough space to fit both. If there is enough space to fit the arrows, the arrows will be placed inside the extension lines and the dimension text moves outside the extension lines. If there is not enough space for either text or arrowheads, both are placed outside the extension lines. In this setting, **DIMTMOVE=0, DIMATFIT=2**.

Both Text and Arrows. If you select this option, AutoCAD will place the arrows and dimension text between the extension lines if there is enough space available to fit both. Otherwise, both text and arrowheads are placed outside the extension lines. In this setting, **DIMTMOVE=0**, **DIMATFIT=0** (Figure 8-33).

Always keep text between extension lines. This option always keeps the text between extension lines even in cases where AutoCAD would not do so. Selecting this radio button does not affect radius and diameter dimensions. The value is stored in the **DIMTIX** variable and the default value is **off**.

Suppress arrows if they don't fit inside the extension lines. If you select this check box, it suppresses the display of arrowheads and dimension line outside the extension line if there is insufficient space between the extension lines. The value is stored in the **DIMSOXD** variable and the default value is **off**.

Text Placement Options

The **Text Placement** area of the **Fit** tab of the **New Dimension Style** dialog box gives you options regarding positioning of dimension text when it is moved from the default position. The value is stored in the **DIMTMOVE** variable. The options are discussed as follows:

Beside the dimension line. This option places the dimension text beside the dimension line and the value for the **DIMTMOVE** variable is 0.

Over the dimension line, with a leader. Selecting this option places the dimension text away from the dimension line and a leader line is created, which connects the text to the dimension line. But, if the dimension line is too close to the text, a leader is not drawn. The Horizontal placement decides whether the text is placed to the right or left of the leader. In this setting, **DIMTMOVE=1**.

Over the dimension line, without a leader. In this option, AutoCAD does not create a leader line if there is insufficient space to fit the dimension text between the extension lines. The dimension text can be moved freely, independent of the dimension line. In this setting, **DIMTMOVE=2**.

Scale for Dimension features

Sets the value for overall Dimension scale or scaling to paper space (Figure 8-34).

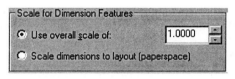

Use Overall Scale Of. The current general scaling factor that pertains to all of the size-related dimension variables, like text size, center mark size, and arrowhead size, is displayed in the **Use overall scale of:** edit box.
You can alter the scaling factor to your requirement by entering the scaling factor of your choice in the **Use overall scale of:** edit box. Altering the contents of this box alters the value of the **DIMSCALE** variable, since the current scaling factor is stored in it. The overall scale (**DIMSCALE**) is not applied to the measured lengths, coordinates, angles, or tolerance. The default value for this variable is 1.0 [Figure 8-35(a)]; and, in this case, the dimensioning variables assume their preset values and the drawing is plotted at full scale. The scale factor is the reciprocal of the drawing size so the drawing is to be plotted at half size. The overall scale factor (**DIMSCALE**) will be the reciprocal of 1/2, which is 2 [Figure 8-35(b)].

Figure 8-34 Scale for Dimension Features area of the Fit tab

Chapter 8

Note

*If you are in the middle of the dimension-
ing process and you change the
DIMSCALE value and save the changed
setting in a dimension style file, the dimen
sions with that style will be updated.*

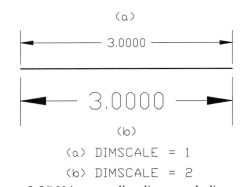

Figure 8-35 Using overall scaling to scale dimensions,
DIMSCALE

Scale dimensions to layout (paper Space).
If you select the **Scale dimensions to layout
(Paper Space)** radio button, the scale factor between the current model space viewport and
floating viewport (paper space) is computed automatically. Also, by selecting this radio button,
you disable the **Use overall scale of:** edit box
(it is disabled in the dialog box) and
DIMSCALE is set to 0. When **DIMSCALE** is assigned a value of 0, AutoCAD calculates an acceptable default value based on the scaling between the current model space viewport and paper
space. If you are in paper space (**TILEMODE=0**), or are not using the **Scale dimensions to layout
(paper Space)** feature, AutoCAD sets **DIMSCALE** to 1; otherwise, AutoCAD calculates a scale
factor that makes it possible to plot text sizes, arrow sizes, and other scaled distances at the values
in which they have been previously set. (For further details, see "Model Space and Paper Space
Dimensioning" in Chapter 7.)

Fine Tuning Options

The Fine Tuning area of the **Fit** tab of the **New Dimension Style** dialog box, provides additional
options governing placement of dimension text. The options are as follows:

Place text manually when dimensioning. When you dimension, AutoCAD places the dimension text in the middle of the dimension line (if there is enough space). If you select the **Place text
manually when dimensioning** check box, you can position the dimension text anywhere along
the dimension line (Figure 8-36). You will also notice that when you select this check box, the
Horizontal Justification is ignored. This setting is saved in the **DIMUPT** system variable. The
default value of this variable is **off**. If you set the **DIMUPT** variable on, AutoCAD will place the

dimension text at the point you have specified as the dimension line location. This enables you to position the dimension text anywhere along the dimension line.

**Always draw dimension line between ex-
tension lines**. If the dimension text and the
dimension lines are outside the extension
lines and you want the dimension lines to be
placed between the extension lines, select the
**Always draw dimension lines between ex-
tension lines** check box. When you select this
option in the radius and diameter dimensions
(when default text placement is horizontal),

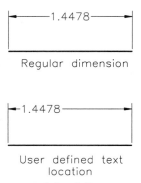

Figure 8-36 User-defined dimension text position

the dimension line and arrows are drawn inside the circle or arc, and the text and leader are drawn outside (see Figure 8-37). When you select the **Always draw dimension line between extension lines** check box, the **DIMTOFL** variable is set to on by AutoCAD. The default setting is off, resulting in generation of the dimension line outside the extension lines when the dimension text is located outside the extension lines.

Figure 8-37 Always draw dimension line between extension line option

FORMATTING PRIMARY DIMENSIONS UNITS
Primary Units Tab

You can use the **Primary Units** tab of the **New Dimension Style** dialog box to control the dimension text format and precision values (Figure 8-38). You can use this tab to control Units, Dimension Precision, and Zero Suppression for dimension measurements. AutoCAD lets you attach a user-defined prefix or suffix to the dimension text. For example, you can define the diameter symbol as a prefix by entering %%C in the **Prefix:** edit box; AutoCAD will automatically attach the diameter symbol in front of the dimension text. Similarly, you can define a unit type, such as **mm**, as a suffix; AutoCAD will then attach **mm** at the end of every dimension text. This tab also enables you to define zero suppression, precision, and dimension text format.

Linear Dimensions

The **Linear Dimensions** area of the **Primary Units** tab of the **New Dimension Style** dialog box consists of options like the Unit format, Prefix, and Suffix, and so on, which are described next.

Unit Format. When you choose the down arrow button, AutoCAD displays a drop-down list of Unit formats, such as Decimal, Scientific, Architectural to select from (Figure 8-39). You can select one of the listed units from the **Unit format:** drop-down list to use when dimensioning. Notice that by selecting a dimension unit format, the drawing units (which you might have selected by using the **DDUNITS** or **UNITS** command)

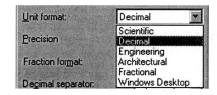

Figure 8-39 Unit Format: drop-down list

Figure 8-37 Primary Units tab of the New Dimension Style dialog box

are not affected. The unit setting for linear dimensions is stored in the **DIMUNIT** system variable.

Precision. You can also control unit precision by using the **Precision:** drop-down list. The setting for precision (number of decimal places) is saved in **DIMDEC**.

Fraction Format. Sets the format for fractions in the dimension text. You can select a format from the **Fraction format:** drop-down list. The options are Diagonal, Horizontal, and not stacked. The value is stored in the **DIMFRAC** variable.

Decimal Separator. The **Decimal separator:** drop-down list gives you options which you can select to set as decimal separators. For example, Period [.], Comma [,] or Space [ ]. If you have selected Windows desktop units in the **Unit Format:** drop-down list, AutoCAD uses the Decimal symbol settings. The value is stored in the **DIMDSEP** variable.

Round off. The **Round off:** edit box sets the value for rounding off dimension values (see Figure 8-40). For example, if the **Round off:** edit box has a value of .05, a value of .06 will round off to .10. The number of decimal places of the round off value you enter in the edit box should be less than or equal to the value in the **Precision:** edit box. The value is stored in the **DIMRND** variable and the default value in the **Round Off:** edit box

Figure 8-39 Round off area

is 0. Also see Figure 8-41.

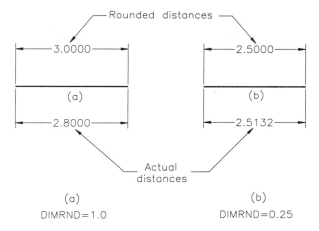

Figure 8-41 *Rounding dimension measurements,* **DIMRND**

Prefix. You can append a prefix to the dimension measurement by entering the desired prefix in the **Prefix:** edit box. The dimension text is converted into the **Prefix<dimension measurement>** format [Figure 8-42(a)]. For example, if you enter the text "Ht" in the Prefix: edit box, "Ht" will be placed in front of the dimension text. The prefix string is saved in the **DIMPOST** system variable.

 Note
*Once you specify a prefix, default prefixes such as **R** in radius dimensioning and Ø in diameter dimensioning are cancelled.*

Suffix. Just like appending a prefix, you can append a suffix to the dimension measurement by entering the desired suffix in the **Suffix:** edit box in the **Linear Dimensions** area of the **Primary Units** tab of the **New Dimension Style** dialog box [Figure 8-42 (b)]. For example, if you enter the text cm in the **Suffix:** edit box, the dimension text will have <dimension measurement>cm format. AutoCAD stores the suffix string in the **DIMPOST** variable.

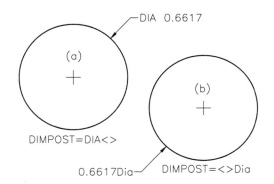

Figure 8-42 *Using text prefix (a) and text suffix (b) in dimensioning,* **DIMPOST**

The **DIMPOST** variable is used to define a prefix or suffix to the dimension text. **DIMPOST** takes a string value as its argument. For example, if you want to have a suffix for centimeters, set **DIMPOST** to cm. To establish a prefix to a dimension text, type the prefix text string and then "<>".

When you define a prefix with the **DIMPOST** variable, this prefix nullifies any default prefixes like R in radius dimensions. For angular dimensions, the <> mechanism is used. To define a prefix or suffix or to prefix the dimension text in **DIMPOST**, the < > mechanism is used. In this way, AutoCAD treats the **DIMPOST** values like text entered at the **Enter dimension text:** prompt. For example, if you want to have the prefix **Radius** and the suffix **cm** with the default text, you can set the **DIMPOST** value in the following manner:

Command: **DIMPOST**
Enter new value for DIMPOST, or . for none <" ">: **Radius < > cm**

If you want to add the user-defined text above or below the dimension line, use the separator symbol **\X**. The text that precedes the \X is aligned with the dimension line and positioned above the line. The text that follows the \X is positioned below the dimension line and aligned with the line. If you want to add more lines, use the symbol **\P**. (For a detailed description of these symbols, see the **MTEXT** Command in Chapter 5.) The following example illustrates the use of these symbols:

Command: **DIMPOST**
Enter new value for DIMPOST, or . for none <" ">: **Radius < >\X[In centimeters]**

DIMPOST value	You enter	Value	Type	Dimension text
Default (nil)	*null response*	*1*	*Linear*	*3.00*
Len < >	*null response*	*1*	*Linear*	*Len 3.00*
Default (nil)	*null response*	*3*	*Radial*	*R3.00*
< > R	*null response*	*3*	*Radial*	*3.00 R*
< > R	*< >Radius in cm*	*3*	*Radial*	*3.00 Radius in cm*
nil	*Radius < >*	*3*	*Radial*	*Radius 3.00*
mm	*null response*	*1*	*Linear*	*3.00mm*

You can also use control codes and special characters to enter special prefix and suffix symbols (See **TEXT** Command in Chapter 5).

Measurement scale. This area allows you options to set linear scale factors as follows:

Scale factor. You can specify a global scale factor for linear dimension measurements by entering the desired scale factor in the **Scale factor:** edit box. All the linear distances measured by dimensions, which includes radii, diameters, and coordinates, are multiplied by the existing value in the **Scale factor:** edit box. For example, if the value of the **Scale factor:** edit box is set to 2, two unit segments will be dimensioned as 4 units (2 x 2). The angular dimensions are not affected. In this manner, the value of the linear scaling factor affects the contents of the default (original) dimension text (Figure 8-43). Default value for linear scaling is 1. With the default value, the dimension text generated is the actual measurement of the object being dimensioned. The linear scaling value is saved in the **DIMLFAC** variable.

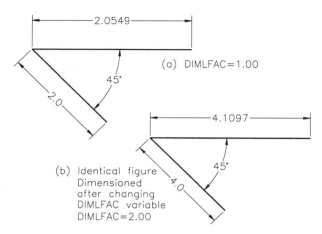

Figure 8-43 Changing the dimension length scaling factor, **DIMLFAC**

 Note
The linear scaling value is not exercised on rounding a value or on plus or minus tolerance values. Therefore, changing the linear scaling factor will not affect the tolerance values.

Apply to layout dimensions only. When you select the **Apply to layout dimensions only** check box you apply the measurement scale factor value only to dimensions in the layout. The value is stored as a negative value in the **DIMLFAC** variable. If you change the **DIMLFAC** from the **Dim:** prompt, AutoCAD displays the viewport option to calculate the **DIMLFAC**. First, the **TILEMODE** should be set to 0 (paper space), and then invoke the **MVIEW** command to get the Viewport option.

> Command: **DIM**
> Dim: **DIMLFAC**
> Enter new value for dimension variable, or Viewport <current>: **V**
> Select viewport to set scale: *Select the desired viewport.*

The **DIMLFAC** variable is automatically adjusted to the zoom scale factor of the model space viewport and assigned a negative value. In model space, AutoCAD ignores the negative value of **DIMLFAC** and assigns it a value of 1.

 Note
*Selecting the Viewport option can be accessed only from paper space (**TILEMODE** = 0).*

Zero Suppression. When Engineering or Architectural units are being used, the **Leading** and **Trailing** check boxes are disabled. If you want to suppress the feet portion of a feet-and-inches dimension when the distance is less than 1 foot (when there is a 0 in the feet portion of the text), select the **0 Feet** check box. For example, if you select the **0 Feet** check box, the dimension text 0'-8 3/4" becomes 8 3/4". By default, the 0 Feet and 0 Inches value is suppressed. If you want to suppress the inches part of a feet-and-inches dimension when the distance in the feet portion is an integer value and the inches portion is zero, select the **0 Inches** check box. For example, if you select the **0 Inches** check box, the dimension text 3'-0" becomes 3'.

If you want to suppress the leading zeros in all of the distances measured in decimals, select the **Leading** check box. For example, by selecting this box, 0.0750 becomes .0750. If you want to suppress the trailing zeros in all the distances measured in decimals, select the **Trailing** check box. For example, by selecting this box, 0.0750 becomes 0.075. AutoCAD stores zero suppression as an integer value in the **DIMZIN** variable in the following manner:

If you select the **0 Feet** check box, an integer value 3 is stored in **DIMZIN** by AutoCAD. If you select the **0 Inches** check box, an integer value 2 is stored in **DIMZIN**. If you select the **Leading** check box, an integer value 4 is stored in **DIMZIN** by AutoCAD. If you select the **Trailing** check box, an integer value 8 is stored in **DIMZIN**. A combination of not selecting the **0 Feet** and **0 Inches** check boxes results in display of the 0 feet as well as the 0 inches of a measurement. For this combination, the value stored in **DIMZIN** is 1. Selecting both the **Trailing** and **Leading** check boxes has a **DIMZIN** value of 12.

Remember that, by default, **the 0 Feet** and **0 Inches** check boxes are selected. This is displayed by a mark in these two check boxes. The following table shows the result of selecting each of the **DIMZIN** values.

DIMZIN Value	Meaning
0 (default)	Suppress zero feet and zero inches
1	Include zero feet and exactly zero inches
2	Include zero feet, suppress zero inches
3	Include zero inches, suppress zero feet

The following table illustrates the preceding results with examples.

DIMZIN Value	Examples			
0	2'-0 2/3"	8"	2'	4/5"
1	2'-0 2/3"	0'-8"	2'-0"	0'-0 4/5"
2	2'-0 2/3"	0'-8"	2'	0'-0.4/5"
3	2'-0 2/3"	8"	2'-0"	4/5"

If the dimension has feet and a fractional inch part, the number of inches is included even if it is 0. This is independent of the **DIMZIN** setting. For example, a dimension such as 1'-2/3" never exists. It will be in the form 1'-0 2/3".

The integer values 0-3 of the **DIMZIN** variable control the feet-and-inch dimension only. If you set **DIMZIN** to 4 (0 + 4 = 4), the leading zeroes will be omitted in all decimal dimensions; for example, 0.2600 becomes .2600. If you set **DIMZIN** to 8 (4 + 4 = 8), the trailing zeroes are omitted; for example, 4.9600 becomes 4.96. If you set **DIMZIN** to 12 (4 + 8 = 12), the leading and the trailing zeroes are omitted; for example, 0.2300 becomes .23. The same thing applies to zero suppression for tolerance values (**Tolerance** tab). The setting of Zero Suppression for tolerance is stored in the **DIMTZIN** system variable.

Angular Dimensions

This area gives you options to control the units format, precision, and zero suppression for Angular units.

Units Format. The **Units format:** drop-down list displays a list of unit formats for you to select from. The value governing the unit setting for angular dimensions is stored in **DIMAUNIT**.

Precision. You can select the number of decimal place display from the **Precision:** drop-down list. The value is stored in the **DIMADEC** variable.

Zero Suppression. Similar to linear dimensioning, you can suppress the **leading**, **trailing**, neither or both by selecting the respective check boxes in the Angular dimensions area of the **Primary units** tab. The value is stored in the **DIMAZIN** variable.

FORMATTING ALTERNATE UNITS
Alternate Units Tab

By default, the **Alternate Units** tab of the **New Dimension Style** dialog box is disabled and the value of the **DIMALT** variable is turned off. If you want to perform alternate units dimensioning, select the **Display Alternate Units** check box. By doing so, AutoCAD activates the various edit boxes (Figure 8-44). This tab sets the format, precision, angles, placement, scale, and so on, for the alternate units in use. In this tab you can specify the values which will be applied to alternate dimensions.

Alternate Units

This area is identical to the Linear Units area of the **Primary Units** tab and gives options to set the format for all dimension types except Angular.

Unit format. You can select a unit format to apply to the alternate dimensions from the **Unit format:** drop-down list. It has the following options which include Scientific, Decimal, Engineering, Architectural stacked, Fractional stacked, Architectural, Fractional, and Windows desktop. The value is stored in the **DIMALTU** variable. The relative size of fractions is governed by the **DIMTFAC** variable.

Precision. You can select the precision value from the **Precision:** drop-down list. The value is stored in the **DIMALTD** variable.

Multiplier for Alternate units. To generate a value in the alternate system of measurement, you need a factor with which all the linear dimensions will be multiplied. The value for this factor can be entered in the **Multiplier for alt units:** edit box located in the Alternate units area of the **Alternate Units** tab of the **New Dimension Style** dialog box. The default value of 25.4 is for dimensioning in inches with alternate units in millimeters. This scaling value (contents of the **Multiplier for alt units:** edit box) gets stored in the **DIMALTF** variable.

Round distances to. In this edit box you can enter a value to which you want all your measurements (made in alternate units) rounded off to. This value is stored in the **DIMALTRND** system

Figure 8-44 Alternate Units tab of the New Dimension Style dialog box

variable. For example if you enter a value of .25 in the **Round distances to:** edit box, all the alternate units get rounded off to the nearest .25 unit.

Prefix and Suffix. The **Prefix:** and **Suffix:** edit boxes are similar to the edit boxes in the Linear units area of the **Primary units** tab. You can enter the text or symbols that you want to precede or follow the alternate dimension text. The value is stored in the **DIMAPOST** variable. You can also use control codes and special characters to display special symbols.

Zero Suppression

This area allows you to suppress the leading or trailing zeros in decimal unit dimensions by selecting either, both, or none of the **Trailing** and **Leading** check boxes. Similarly, selecting the **0 Feet** check box, suppresses the zeros in the feet area of the dimension, when the dimension value is less than a foot. Selecting the **0 inches** check box suppresses the zeros in the inches area of the dimension. For example, 1'-0" becomes 1'. The **DIMALTZ** variable controls the suppression of zeros for alternate unit dimension values. The values that are between 0–3 affect feet-and-inch dimensions only.

Placement

This area gives options that control the positioning of the Alternate units. The value is stored in the **DIMAPOST** variable.

After Primary Value. Selecting the **After primary value** radio button, places the alternate units dimension text after the primary units. This is the default option.

Below Primary Value. Selecting the **Below pri-mary value** radio button, places the alternate units dimension text below the primary units.

Figure 8-45 illustrates the result of entering information in the **Alternate Units** tab. The decimal places get saved in the **DIMALTD** variable, the scaling value (contents of the **Multiplier for alt units:** edit box) in the **DIMALTF** variable, and the suffix string (contents of the **Suffix:** edit box) in the **DIMAPOST** variable. Similarly, the units format for alternate units in **DIMALTU**, and suppression of zeros for alternate units decimal values in **DIMALTZ**.

Figure 8-45 Dimensioning with alternate units

Tolerances Tab

The **Tolerances** tab (Figure 8-46) allows you to set values for options that control the format and display of tolerance dimension text including the alternate unit tolerance dimension text.

*Figure 8-45 **Tolerances** tab of the **New Dimension Style** dialog box*

Tolerance Format

The **Tolerance format** area of the **Tolerances** tab (Figure 8-46) lets you specify the tolerance method, tolerance value, position of tolerance text, precision and the height of the tolerance text. For example, if you do not want a dimension to deviate more than plus 0.01 and minus 0.02, you can specify this by selecting **Deviation** from the **Method:** drop-down list and then specifying the plus and minus deviation in the **Upper Value:** and the **Lower Value:** edit boxes. When you dimension, AutoCAD will automatically append the tolerance to the dimension. The **DIMTP** variable sets the maximum (or upper) tolerance limit for the dimension text and **DIMTM** variable sets the minimum (or lower) tolerance limit for dimension text. Different settings and their effects on relevant dimension variables are explained in the following sections:

Method. The **Method:** drop-down list lets you select the tolerance method. The tolerance methods supported by AutoCAD are **Symmetrical**, **Deviation**, **Limits**, and **Basic**. These tolerance methods are described next.

None. Selecting the **None** option sets the **DIMTOL** variable to 0 and does not add tolerance values to the dimension text, that is, the **Tolerances** tab is disabled.

Symmetrical. If you select **Symmetrical**, the **Lower Value:** edit box is disabled and the value specified in the **Upper Value:** edit box is applied to both plus and minus tolerance. For example, if the value specified in the **Upper Value:** edit box is 0.05, the tolerance appended to the dimension text is ± 0.05. The value of **DIMTOL** is set to 1 and the value of **DIMLIM** is set to 0.

Deviation. If you select the **Deviation** tolerance method, the values in the **Upper Value:** and **Lower Value:** edit boxes will be displayed as plus and minus dimension tolerances. If you enter values for the plus and minus tolerances, AutoCAD appends a plus sign (+) to the positive values of the tolerance and a negative sign (-) to the negative values of the tolerance. For example, if the upper value of the tolerance is 0.005 and the lower value of the tolerance is 0.002, the resulting dimension text generated will have a positive tolerance of 0.005 and a negative tolerance of 0.002 (Figure 8-47).

Even if one of the tolerance values is 0, a sign is appended to it (Figure 8-48). On specifying the deviation tolerance, AutoCAD sets the **DIMTOL** variable value to 1 and the **DIMLIM** variable value to 0. The values in the **Upper Value:** and **Lower Value:** edit boxes are saved in the **DIMTP** and **DIMTM** system variables, respectively.

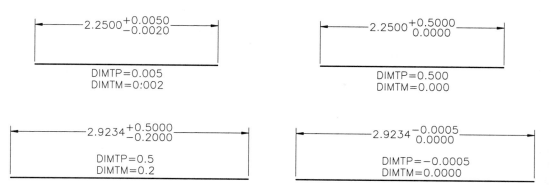

Figure 8-46 Dimensioning with deviation tolerance

Figure 8-47 Dimensioning with deviation tolerance (when one tolerance value equals 0)

Limits. If you select the **Limits** tolerance method from the **Method:** drop-down list, AutoCAD adds the upper value (contents of the **Upper Value:** edit box) to the dimension text (actual measurement) and subtracts the lower value (contents of the **Lower Value:** edit box) from the dimension text. The resulting values are drawn with the dimension text (Figure 8-49). Selecting the **Limits** tolerance method results in setting the **DIMLIM** variable value to 1 and the **DIMTOL** variable value to 0. The numeral values in the **Upper Value:** and **Lower Value:** edit boxes are saved in the **DIMTP** and **DIMTM** system variables, respectively.

Basic. A basic dimension text is dimension text with a box drawn around it (Figure 8-50). The basic dimension is also called a reference dimension. Reference dimensions are used primarily in geometric dimensioning and tolerances. The basic dimension can be realized by selecting the basic tolerance method. The distance provided around the dimension text (distance between dimension text and the rectangular box) is stored as a negative value in the **DIMGAP** variable. The negative value signifies basic dimension. The default setting is off, resulting in the generation of dimensions without the box around the dimension text.

Figure 8-49 Dimensiong with limits tolerance

Figure 8-50 Basic dimension (**DIMGAP** assigned a negative value)

Precision. The **Precision:** drop-down list lets you select the number of decimal places for the tolerance dimension text. The value is stored in **DIMTDEC** variable.

Upper Value and Lower Value. In the **Upper value:** edit box, the positive upper or maximum value is entered. If the method of tolerances is symmetrical, the same value is used as the lower value also. The value is stored in **DIMTP** variable. In the **Lower:** edit box the lower or minimum value is entered. The value is stored in **DIMTM**.

Vertical Position. It lets you justify the dimension tolerance text for deviation and symmetrical methods only. Three alignments are possible: with the **Bottom**, **Middle**, or **Top** of the main dimension text. If you select the Limits tolerance method, the **Vertical position:** drop-down list is automatically disabled. The settings are saved in the **DIMTOLJ** system variable (Bottom=0, Middle=1, and Top=2).

Scaling for Height. The **Scaling for height:** edit box lets you specify the height of the dimension tolerance text relative to the dimension text height (see Figure 8-51). The default value is 1; the height of the tolerance text is the same as the dimension text height. If you want the tolerance text to be 75 percent of the dimension height text, enter 0.75 in the **Scaling for height:** edit box. The ratio of the tolerance height to the dimension text height is calculated by AutoCAD and then stored in the **DIMTFAC** variable. **DIMTFAC = Tolerance Height/Text Height.**

Figure 8-51 *Tolerance height, DIMTFAC*

Zero Suppression. This area controls the zero suppression in the dimension tolerance text depending on which of the check boxes are selected. Selecting the **Leading** check box suppresses the leading zeros in all decimal dimension text. For example, 0.2000 becomes .2000. Trailing zeros are of significance to the tolerance. Selecting the **Trailing** check box suppresses the trailing zeros in all decimal dimensions. For example, 0.5000 becomes 0.5. Similarly, selecting both the boxes suppresses both the trailing and leading zeros and selecting none, suppresses none. If you select **0 Feet** check box, the zeros in the feet portion of the tolerance dimension text are suppressed if the dimension value is less than a foot. Similarly, selecting the **0 Inches** check box, suppresses the zeros in the inches portion of the dimension text. The value is stored in the **DIMTZIN** variable.

Alternate Unit Tolerance

Defines the precision and zero suppression settings for Alternate unit tolerance values.

Precision. From the **Precision** drop-down list you can select the precision value for alternate unit tolerance dimensions. It sets the number of decimal places to be displayed in the dimension text. The value is stored in the **DIMALTTD** variable.

Zero Suppression. Selecting the respective check boxes controls the suppression of the **Leading** and **Trailing** zeros in decimal values and the suppression of zeros in the Feet and Inches portions for dimensions in the feet and inches format. The value is stored in the **DIMALTTZ** variable.

Exercise 3   *Mechanical*

Draw Figure 8-52. Then set the values in the various tabs of the **New Dimension Style** dialog box to dimension it as shown. (Baseline Spacing = 0.25, Extension beyond dim lines = 0.10, Offset from origin = 0.05, Arrowhead size = 0.09, Text height = 0.09). Assume the missing dimensions.

Figure 8-52 Drawing for Exercise 3

OTHER DIMENSIONING VARIABLES
Positioning Dimension Text (DIMTVP)

You can position the dimension text with respect to the dimension line by using the **DIMTVP** system variable (Figure 8-53). In certain cases, **DIMTVP** is used with **DIMTAD** to control the vertical position of the dimension text. **DIMTVP** value applies only when the **DIMTAD** is off. To

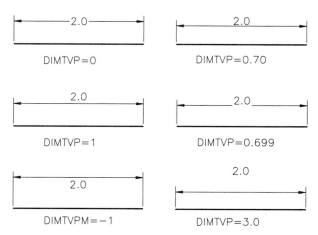

Figure 8-53 DIMTVP, dimension text vertical position

select the vertical position of the dimension text to meet your requirement (over or under the dimension line), you must first calculate the numerical value by which you want to offset the text from the dimension line. The vertical placing of the text is done by offsetting the dimension text. The magnitude of the offset of dimension text is a product of text height and **DIMTVP** value. If the value of **DIMTVP** is 1, **DIMTVP** acts as **DIMTAD**. For example, if you want to position the text 0.25 units from the dimension line, the value of **DIMTVP** is calculated as follows:

DIMTVP=Relative Position value/Text Height value
DIMTVP=0.25/ 0.09=2.7778

The value 2.7778 is stored in the dimension variable **DIMTVP**. If the absolute value is less than 0.70, the dimension line is broken to accommodate the dimension text. Relative positioning is not effective on angular dimensions.

Horizontal Placement of Text (DIMTIX and DIMSOXD)

DIMTIX System Variable. With the help of the **DIMTIX** (dimension text inside extension lines) variable, the dimension text can be placed between the extension lines even if it would normally be placed outside the lines (Figure 8-54). This can be achieved when **DIMTIX** is on (1). If DIMTIX is off (the default setting), the placement of the dimension text depends on the type of dimension. For example, if the dimensions are linear or angular, the text will be placed inside the extension lines by AutoCAD, if there is enough space available. For the radius and diameter dimensions, the text is placed outside the object being dimensioned.

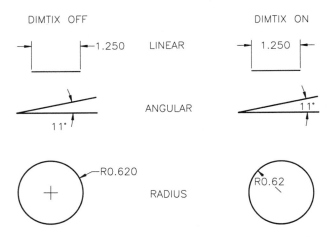

Figure 8-54 DIMTIX, dimension text inside extension lines

DIMSOXD System Variable. If you want to place the dimension text inside the extension lines, you will have to turn the **DIMTIX** variable on. If you want to suppress the dimension lines and the arrowheads, you will have to turn the **DIMDSOXD** (dimension suppress outside extension dimension lines) variable on. **DIMSOXD** suppresses the drawing of dimension lines and the arrowheads when they are placed outside the extension lines. If **DIMTIX** is on and **DIMSOXD** is off, and there is not enough space inside the extension lines to draw the dimension lines, the lines will be drawn outside the extension lines. In such a situation, if both **DIMTIX** and **DIMSOXD** are on, the dimension line will be totally suppressed. **DIMSOXD** works only when **DIMTIX** is on. The default value for **DIMSOXD** and **DIMTIX** is off (Figure 8-55).

Figure 8-55 DIMSOXD and DIMTIX suppress outside extension lines and dimension text inside extension lines

Redisplay of Dimension (DIMSHO)

The associative dimension computes and redisplays dynamically as the dimension is dragged while you are editing it. This feature is controlled by the **DIMSHO** system variable. By default, it is on, which means that the dimension will be redisplayed as it is dragged. Although it is a good feature, dynamic dragging sometimes can be very slow. In that case you can turn it off by setting **DIMSHO** to off. When you dimension a circle or an arc, the **DIMSHO** settings are ignored. The value of **DIMSHO** is not saved with the dimension style.

DIMENSION STYLE FAMILIES

The dimension style feature of AutoCAD lets the user define a dimension style with values that are common to all dimensions. For example, the arrow size, dimension text height, or color of the dimension line are generally the same in all types of dimensioning, such as linear, radial, diameter, and angular. These dimensioning types belong to the same family because they have some characteristics in common. In AutoCAD, this is called a **dimension style family,** and the values assigned to the family are called **dimension style family values.**

After you have defined the dimension style family values, you can specify variations on it for other types of dimensions, such as radial and diameter. For example, if you want to limit the number of decimal places to two in radial dimensioning, you can specify that value for radial dimensioning. The other values will stay the same as the family values to which this dimension type belongs. When you use the radial dimension, AutoCAD automatically uses the style that was defined for radial dimensioning; otherwise, it creates a radial dimension with the values as defined for the family. After you have created a dimension style family, any changes in the parent style are applied to family members if the particular property is the same. Special suffix codes are appended to the dimension style family name that correspond to different dimension types. For example, if the dimension style family name is MYSTYLE and you define a diameter type of dimension, AutoCAD will append $4 at the end of the dimension style family name. The name of the diameter type of dimension will be MYSTYLE$4. The following are the suffix codes for different types of dimensioning:

Suffix Code	Dimension Type	Suffix Code	Dimension Type
0	Linear	2	Angular
3	Radius	4	Diameter
6	Ordinate	7	Leader

Example 1

The following example illustrates the concepts of dimension style families.
1. Specify the values for the dimension style family.
2. Specify the values for linear dimension.
3. Specify the values for diameter and radius dimension.
4. After creating the dimension style, use it to dimension the given drawing.

Figure 8-56 Dimensioning using dimension style families

Step 1

Invoke the **Dimension Style Manager** dialog box by entering the **DDIM** or **DIMSTYLE** command at the AutoCAD Command prompt. You can also invoke it from the **Dimension** toolbar, or the **Dimension** or **Format** menus. If you have not defined any dimension style, AutoCAD will display STANDARD in the **Styles:** list box. Select the STANDARD style from the **Styles:** list box.

Step 2

Choose the **New...** button, to display the **New Dimension Style** dialog box. In this dialog box, enter MYSTYLE in the **New Style Name:** edit box. Select STANDARD from the **Start With:** drop-down list. Also select **All dimensions** from the **Use for:** drop-down list. Now, choose the **Continue** button to display the **New Dimension Style: MYSTYLE** dialog box. In this dialog box, choose the **Lines and Arrows** tab and enter the following values:

Baseline Spacing: 0.15   Extension beyond dim line: 0.07   Offset from origin: 0.03
Arrow size: 0.09   Center Mark for circle, Size: 0.05

In the **Text** tab, change the following values:

Text Height: 0.09   Offset from dimension line: 0.03

After entering the values, choose the **OK** button to return to the **Dimension Style Manager** dialog box. This dimension style contains the values that are common to all dimension types.

Step 3
Now, choose the **New...** button again in the **Dimension Style Manager** dialog box to display the **Create New Dimension Style:** dialog box. AutoCAD displays **Copy of MYSTYLE** in the **New Style name:** edit box. Select MYSTYLE from the **Start with:** drop down list if it is not already selected. From the **Use for:** drop-down list select **Linear dimensions**. Choose the **Continue** button to display the **New Dimension Style** dialog box and set the following values:

1. Select the **Aligned with dimension line** radio button in the Text alignment area.
2. In the Text placement area, from the **Vertical:** drop-down list, select the **Above** option.

In the **Primary units** tab, change the following:

1. **Unit format:** to Decimal units.
2. Dimension precision to two decimal places.

Step 4
Choose the **OK** button to return to the **Dimension Style Manager** dialog box. Here choose the **New** button again to display the **New Dimension Style** dialog box. Select MYSTYLE from the **Start with:** drop-down list. Also select **Diameter dimension** type from the **Use for:** drop-down list. Choose the **Continue** button to display the **New dimension Style** dialog box once again. Choose the **Primary units** tab and set the **Precision:** to two decimal places. In the **Lines and Arrows** tab, select **Line** from the Center mark for circle **Type:** drop-down list. Choose the **OK** button to return to the **Dimension Style Manager** dialog box.

In this dialog box, choose the **New** button to display the **New Dimension Style** dialog box once again. Select MYSTYLE from the **Start with:** drop-down list and **Radius dimensions** from the **Use for:** drop-down list. Choose the **Continue** button to display the **New Dimension Style** dialog box. Choose the **Primary Units** tab and set the precision to two decimal places and enter **Rad** in the **Prefix:** edit box. In the **Fit** tab, select the **Text** radio button in the **Fit Options** area. Choose the **OK** button to return to the **Dimension Style Manager** dialog box. Here, select MYSTYLE from the **Styles:** list box and choose the **Set current** button. Choose the **Close** button to exit the dialog box.

Step 5
Use the linear and baseline (**DIMLIN** and **DIMBASE**) commands to draw the linear dimensions as shown in Figure 8-55. Notice that when you enter any linear dimensioning command, AutoCAD automatically uses the values that were defined for the linear type of dimensioning.

Chapter 8

Step 6

Use the diameter dimensioning (**DIMDIA**) command to dimension the circles as shown in Figure 8-56. Again notice that the dimensions are drawn according to the values specified for the diameter type of dimensioning.

Step 7

Now, similarly use the radius dimensioning (**DIMRADIUS**) command and dimension the arc as shown in Figure 8-56.

USING DIMENSION STYLE OVERRIDES

Most of the dimension characteristics are common in a production drawing. The values that are common to different dimensioning types can be defined in the dimension style family. However, at times you might have different dimensions. For example, you may need two types of linear dimensioning: one with tolerance and one without. One way to draw these dimensions is to create two dimensioning styles. You can also use the dimension variable overrides to override the existing values. For example, you can define a dimension style (MYSTYLE) that draws dimensions without tolerance. Now, to draw a dimension with tolerance or update an existing dimension, you can override the previously defined value. You can override the values through the **Dimension Style Manager** dialog box or by setting the variable values at the Command prompt. The following example illustrates how to use the dimension style overrides.

Example 2

In this example, you will update the overall dimension (3.00) so that the tolerance is displayed with the dimension. You will also add two linear dimensions, as shown in Figure 8-57.

Figure 8-57 Overriding the dimension style values

Using Dimension Styles/ Overrides

Step 1

Invoke the **Dimension Style Manager** dialog box. Select MYSTYLE from the **Styles:** list box and choose the **Override** button to display the **Override Current Style** dialog box. The options in this dialog box are identical to the **New Dimension Style** dialog box discussed earlier in the chapter. Choose the **Tolerance** tab and specify the tolerance, symmetrical with upper value 0.02 and precision of two decimal places. Choose the **OK** button to exit the dialog box (this does not save the style). Notice that the **<style overrides>** is displayed under MYSTYLE, indicating that the style overrides the MYSTYLE dimension style.

This **<style overrides>** is displayed till you save it under a new name or under the Style it is displayed under or till you delete it. The Style overrides can be modified and compared also by choosing the **Modify** and **Compare** buttons respectively. Selecting the **style overrides** and right-clicking, displays a shortcut menu. Choosing the **Save to current Style** option from the shortcut menu saves the overrides to the current style. Choosing the **Rename** option, allows you to rename the style override and save it as a new style.

Step 2

Use the **-DIMSTYLE** command to apply the change to the existing dimensions.

> Command: **-DIMSTYLE**
> Current dimension style: MYSTYLE
> Current dimension overrides:
> DIMTOL   On
> Enter a dimension style option
> [Save/Restore/STatus/Variables/Apply/?] <Restore>: **A**
> Select objects: *Select the dimension that you want to update.*

After you select the dimension, AutoCAD will update the dimension and the tolerance will be appended to the selected dimension. If you create a new dimension, the tolerance value will be displayed automatically with the dimension, unless you make MYSTYLE (dimension style) current.

Using the PROPERTIES Command*
Step 1

You can also use the **PROPERTIES** command to modify a dimension. Select the dimension you want to modify and enter **PROPERTIES** at the Command prompt. You can also choose **Properties** from the **Modify** menu.

Step 2

AutoCAD will display the **Object Properties Window**. In this window, select Tolerances and specify the tolerance for linear dimensions, Symmetrical with Upper Value 0.02 and Precision of two decimal places. Choose the **X** button to exit the **Object Properties Window**. The dimension will be updated to new specifications (See Chapter 7, Editing Dimensions, for details). If you want to save the modified settings to a new style, select the modified dimension and right-click to display a shortcut menu. Choose the **Dim Style > Save as New style** option. Enter a name in the **Style Name:** edit box of the **Save As New Dimension Style** dialog box.

Using the DIMOVERRIDE Command

You can also use the **DIMOVERRIDE** command to override a dimension value. If you want to

Chapter 8

have tolerance displayed with the dimension, make sure the tolerances are specified. You can also choose **Override** from the **Dimension** menu.

Command: **DIMOVERRIDE**
Enter dimension variable name to override or [Clear overrides]: **DIMTOL**
Enter new value for dimension variable <Off> New value: **ON**
Enter dimension variable name to override: **DIMTP**
Enter new value for dimension variable <0.0000> New value: **0.02**
Enter dimension variable name to override: **DIMTM** [Enter]
Enter new value for dimension variable <0.0000> New value: **0.02**
Enter dimension variable name to override: [Enter]
Select objects: *Select the object that you want to update.*

You can also update a dimension by entering **Update** at the **Dim:** prompt or choosing the **Dimension Update** button from the **Dimension** toolbar. For details, see Chapter 7, Editing Dimensions.

COMPARING AND LISTING DIMENSION STYLES

Choosing the **Compare** button in the **Dimension style Manager** dialog box displays the **Compare dimension Styles** dialog box where you can compare the settings two dimensions styles or list all the settings of one of them (Figure 8-58).

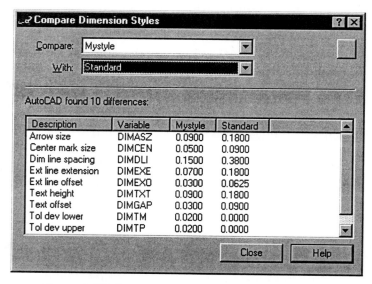

Figure 8-58 Compare Dimension styles dialog box

The **Compare:** and the **With:** drop-down lists display the dimension styles in the current drawing and selecting dimension styles from the respective lists compare the two styles. In the **With:** drop-down list, if we select **None** or the same style as selected from the **Compare:** drop-down list, all the properties of the selected style are displayed. The Comparison results are displayed under three headings: **Description** of the Dimension Style property, the **System Variable** controlling a particular settings, and the **values of the variable** which differ in the two styles in comparison. The print to clipboard button prints the comparison results to the Windows clipboard from where they can be pasted to other Windows applications.

The Save, Restore, and Apply options of the **-DIMSTYLE** command were discussed earlier in this chapter (see the section "Creating and Restoring Dimension Styles"). You can also use this command to ascertain the status of a dimension style or compare a dimension style with the current style.

Comparing Dimension Styles

You can compare the current dimension style with another style by using the Restore option and appending the tilde (~) symbol in front of the dimension style name.

> Command: **-DIMSTYLE**
> Current dimension style:
> Enter a dimension style option
> [Save/Restore/STatus/Variables/Apply/?] <Restore>: **R**
> Enter dimension style name, [?] or <select dimension>: **~Standard**

AutoCAD will display a listing of dimension variable names and their values for the standard dimension style and the current dimension style. Only those variables that have different values in the current and the named styles are listed.

> *Differences between STANDARD and current settings:*
>
> | *STANDARD* | | *Current Setting* |
> |---|---|---|
> | *DIMSOXD* | *Off* | *On* |
> | *DIMTAD* | *0* | *1* |
> | *DIMTIX* | *Off* | *On* |
> | *DIMTOL* | *Off* | *On* |
> | *DIMTP* | *0.0000* | *0.5000* |
> | *DIMTVP* | *0.0000* | *2.0000* |

Listing Dimension Styles

The **STatus** option of the **-DIMSTYLE** command displays the settings of the current dimensioning status. You can use the question mark (**?**) to display the named dimension styles in the current drawing.

> Command: **-DIMSTYLE**
> Current dimension style:
> Enter a dimension style option
> [Save/Restore/STatus/Variables/Apply/?] <Restore>: **?**
> Enter dimension style(s) to list<*>: *Press ENTER.*

If you select the **Variables** option, AutoCAD will display the dimension status of the named dimension style or the dimension style that is associated with the selected dimension.

> Command: **-DIMSTYLE**
> Current dimension style:

Enter a dimension style option
[Save/Restore/STatus/Variables/Apply/?] <Restore>: **V**
Enter dimension style name, [?] or <select dimension>: **MYSTYLE**

You can also use the **STATUS** command from the **Dim:** mode to list the dimension styles ina drawing.

USING EXTERNALLY REFERENCED DIMENSION STYLES

The externally referenced dimensions cannot be used directly in the current drawing. When you Xref a drawing, the drawing name is appended to the style name and the two are separated by the vertical bar (|) symbol. It uses the same syntax as other externally dependent symbols. For example, if the drawing (FLOOR) has a dimension style called DECIMAL and you Xref this drawing in the current drawing, AutoCAD will rename the dimension style to FLOOR|DECIMAL. You cannot make this dimension style current, nor can you modify or override it. However, you can use it as a template to create a new style. To accomplish this, invoke the **Dimension Style Manager** dialog box. If the **Don't list styles in Xrefs** check box is selected, the styles in the Xref are not displayed. Clear this check box to display the Xref dimension styles and choose the **New...** button. In the **New Style Name:** edit box of the **New Dimension Style** dialog box, enter the name of the dimension style. AutoCAD will create a new dimension style with the same values as those of the externally referenced dimension style (FLOOR|DECIMAL).

Self-Evaluation Test

Answer the following questions, and then compare your answers to the correct answers given at the end of this chapter.

1. What is the function of dimension styles (**DIMSTYLE** command)? _____

    _____

2. How can you create a dimension style of your requirement? _____

    _____

3. Fill in the command and entries required to scale the dimensioning variables that reflect sizes, distances, or offsets (such as arrow size, text size) by a value of 2.0.

    Command: _____
    DIM: _____
    Enter new value for dimension variable <current>: _____

4. The default dimension style file name is _____.

5. Dimension arrows have the same color as the _____ because arrows constitute a part of _____.

6. The size of the arrow block is determined by the value stored in the Arrow size: edit box. (T/F)

7. The center marks are created by using the _____ , _____ , and **Radius** dimensioning commands.

8. When you select Arrows option, AutoCAD places the text and arrowheads _____ .

9. If you want to add the user-defined text above or below the dimension line, use the separator symbol _____ .

10. A basic dimension text is dimension text with a _____ drawn around it.

11. A predefined text height (specified in the **STYLE** command) _____ any other setting for the dimension text height.

12. The **Text** tab of the **New Dimension Style** dialog box lets you specify the text style, text height, text gap, and _____ of the dimension text.

13. The **Suppress**: check boxes control the drawing of the _____ and _____ dimension lines.

14. The overall scale (**DIMSCALE**) is not applied to the measured lengths, coordinates, _____ , or _____ .

15. You can restore an existing dimension style as the current style with the **RESTORE** Command. (T/F)

Review Questions

1. You can use the _____ dialog box to control dimension styles and dimension variables.

2. You can also create dimension styles from the command line by entering _____ at the Command prompt.

3. The _____ tab of the **New Dimension Style** dialog box can be used to specify the dimensioning attributes (variables) that affect the geometry of the dimensions.

4. The first and second dimension lines are determined by _____ extension line origins.

5. The **Suppress**: check boxes control the display of the _____ .

6. Extension is the distance the _____ should extend past the dimension line.

7. AutoCAD has provided _____ standard termination symbols you can apply at each end of the dimension line.

8. The size of the _____ is determined by the value stored in the **Arrow size:** edit box.

9. You cannot replace the default arrowheads at the end of the dimension lines. (T/F)

10. When **DIMSCALE** is assigned a value of _____, AutoCAD calculates an acceptable default value based on the scaling between the current model space viewport and paper space.

11. If you use the **DIMCEN** command, a positive value will create a center mark, and a negative value will create a _____.

12. You can control the dimension format through the _____.

13. If you select the _____ check box, you can position the dimension text anywhere along the dimension line.

14. When you select the **Arrows** option, AutoCAD places the text and arrowheads _____ the extension lines if there is enough space to fit both.

15. The linear scaling value is not exercised on tolerance values. (T/F)

16. You can append a prefix to the dimension measurement by entering the desired prefix in the **Prefix:** edit box of the _____ dialog box.

17. If you want to add the user-defined text above or below the dimension line, use the separator symbol _____.

18. If you want to add more lines, use the symbol _____.

19. If you select the **Limits** tolerance method from the **Method:** drop-down list, AutoCAD _____ the upper value to the dimension and _____ the lower value from the dimension text.

20. The **Text** tab of the _____ dialog box lets you specify the text style, text height, text gap, and _____ of the dimension text.

21. After you have defined the dimension style family values, you can specify variations on it for other types of dimensions, such as _____, and _____.

22. The values that are common to different dimensioning types can be defined in the dimension _____.

23. Use the _____ command to apply the change to the existing dimensions.

24. You can also use the _____ command to modify a dimension.

25. You can also use the _____ command to override a dimension value.

26. You can compare the current dimension style with another style by using the Restore option and appending the _____ symbol in front of the dimension style name.

27. What is the dimension style family, and how does it help in dimensioning? _____
_____

28. What are the different ways to access the **Dimension Style Manager** dialog box? _____
_____

29. Explain various methods that can be used to change the value of a dimension variable. _
_____

30. How can you use the dimension style that has been defined in the Xref drawing? Explain.
_____

31. Explain dimension overrides. _____
_____

32. What are the different ways to override an existing dimension? _____
_____

33. How can you compare a named dimension style with the current style? _____
_____

34. Explain the use of the **DIMOVERRIDE** command and how it works. _____
_____

35. How can you compare the settings of the dimension variables of the current dimension style with those of another dimension style? _____
_____

36. Which dimensioning command is used to display the list of all dimension variables and their current settings? _____
_____

37. In oblique dimensioning, the extension lines are always drawn perpendicular to the dimension line. (T/F)

38. A group of dimension variables with some setting is termed a dimension style. (T/F)

39. Dimension style cannot have a name. (T/F)

40. The dimension style used to create a particular dimension can be revoked later by selecting that dimension. (T/F)

41. When the **DIMTVP** variable has a negative value, the dimension text is placed below the dimension line. (T/F)

42. The named dimension style associated with the dimension being updated with the **OVERRIDE** command is not updated. (T/F)

Exercises

Exercise 4 - 9   *Mechanical*

Make the drawings as shown in Figure 8-59 through Figure 8-64. You must create dimension style files and specify values for different dimension types, such as linear, radial, diameter, and ordinate. Assume the missing dimensions.

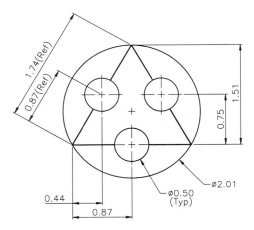

Figure 8-59 *Drawing for Exercise 4*

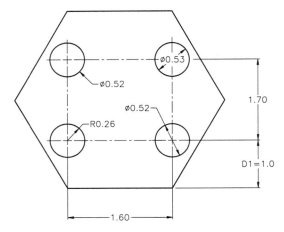

Figure 8-60 *Drawing for Exercise 5*

Figure 8-61 *Drawing for Exercise 6*

HOLE	X	Y	Z
RAD.	0.125	0.15	0.20

Figure 8-62 *Drawing for Exercise 7*

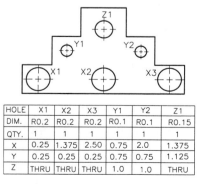

HOLE	X1	X2	X3	Y1	Y2	Z1
DIM.	R0.2	R0.2	R0.2	R0.1	R0.1	R0.15
QTY.	1	1	1	1	1	1
X	0.25	1.375	2.50	0.75	2.0	1.375
Y	0.25	0.25	0.25	0.75	0.75	1.125
Z	THRU	THRU	THRU	1.0	1.0	THRU

Figure 8-63 *Drawing for Exercise 8*

SPANNER NO.	A	B	C	D
S1	0.85	0.65	0.50	0.38
S2	1	0.75	0.59	0.44
S3	1.15	0.88	0.67	0.52
S4	1.25	0.95	0.74	0.56

Figure 8-64   *Drawing for Exercise 9*

Exercise 10   *Mechanical*

Make the drawing as shown in Figure 8-65. You must create dimension style files and specify values for different dimension types. Assume the missing dimensions.

Figure 8-65   *Drawing for Exercise 10*

Problem-Solving Exercise 1

Draw and dimension the floor plan as shown in Figure 8-66. Assume the missing dimensions or measure the relative dimensions from the given drawing (The drawing is not to scale).

Figure 8-66 *Drawing for Exercise 10*

Answers to Self-Evaluation Test

1 - Invokes **Dimension Style Manager** dialog box 2 - By using the **Dimension Style Manager** dialog box or by assigning values to dimensioning variables, 3 - **DIM/ DIMSCALE/** 2, 4 - Standard, 5 - dimension line/ dimension line, 6 - T, 7 - Center/ Diameter, 8 - inside, 9 - \X, 10 - box, 11 - Overrides, 12 - color, 13 - first/ second, 14 - angles/ tolerance, 15 - T

Chapter 9

Geometric Dimensioning and Tolerancing

Learning Objectives

After completing this chapter, you will be able to:
- *Use geometric tolerance components to specify tolerances.*
- *Use feature control frames and geometric characteristics symbols.*
- *Use tolerance values and the material condition modifier.*
- *Use complex feature control frames.*
- *Combine geometric characteristics and create composite position tolerancing.*
- *Use projected tolerance zones.*
- *Use feature control frames with leaders.*

IMPORTANCE OF GEOMETRIC DIMENSIONING AND TOLERANCING

One of the most important parts of the design process is giving the dimensions and tolerances, since every part is manufactured from the dimensions given in the drawing. Therefore, every designer must understand and have a thorough knowledge of the standard practices used in industry to make sure that the information given on the drawing is correct and can be understood by other people. Tolerancing is equally important, especially in the assembled parts. Tolerances and fits determine how the parts will fit. Incorrect tolerances could result in a product that is not usable.

In addition to dimensioning and tolerancing, the function and the relationship that exists between the mating parts is important if the part is to perform the way it was designed. This aspect of the design process is addressed by **geometric dimensioning and tolerancing**, generally known as **GDT**. Geometric dimensioning and tolerancing is a means to design and manufacture parts with respect to actual function and the relationship that exists between different features of the same part or the features of the mating parts. Therefore, a good design is not achieved by just giving dimensions and tolerances. The designer has to go beyond dimensioning and think of the intended function of the part and how the features of the part are going to affect its function. For example, in Figure 9-1, which shows a part with the required dimensions and tolerances, there is no mention of the relationship between the pin and the plate. Is the pin perpendicular to the plate? If it is, to what degree should it be perpendicular? Also, it does not mention on which surface the perpendicularity of the pin is to be measured. A design like this is open to individual interpretation based on intuition and experience. This is where geometric dimensioning and tolerancing play an important part in the product design process.

Figure 9-2 has been dimensioned using geometric dimensioning and tolerancing. The feature symbols define the datum (reference plane) and the permissible deviation in the perpendicularity of the pin with respect to the bottom surface. From a drawing like this, the chances of making a mistake are minimized. Before discussing the application of AutoCAD commands in geometric dimensioning and tolerancing, you need to understand the following feature symbols and tolerancing components.

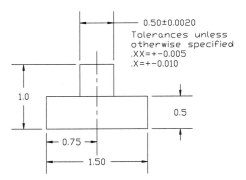

Figure 9-1 *Using traditional dimensioning and tolerancing technique*

Figure 9-2 *Using geometric dimensioning and tolerancing*

GEOMETRIC CHARACTERISTICS AND SYMBOLS

Figure 9-3 shows the geometric characteristics and symbols used in geometric dimensioning and tolerancing. These symbols are the building blocks of geometric dimensioning and tolerancing.

KIND OF FEATURE	TYPE OF FEATURE	CHARACTERISTICS	
RELATED	LOCATION	Position	⊕
		Concentricity or coaxiality	◎
		Symmetry	⊜
	ORIENTATION	Parallelism	∥
		Perpendicularity	⊥
		Angularity	∠
INDIVIDUAL	FORM	Cylindricity	⌭
		Flatness	▱
		Circularity or roundness	○
		Straightness	─
INDIVIDUAL or RELATED	PROFILE	Profile of a surface	⌓
		Profile of a line	⌒
RELATED	RUNOUT	Circular runout	↗
		Total runout	⌰

Figure 9-3 Geometric characteristics and symbols used in geometric dimensioning and tolerancing

GEOMETRIC TOLERANCING

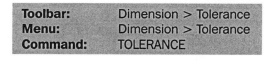

Toolbar:	Dimension > Tolerance
Menu:	Dimension > Tolerance
Command:	TOLERANCE

Figure 9-4 Choosing **Tolerance** from the **Dimension** toolbar

Geometric Tolerancing displays the deviations of profile, orientation, form, location and runout of a feature.In AutoCAD, geometrical tolerancing is displayed by feature control frames. The frames contain all the information about tolerances for a single dimension.To display feature control frames with the various tolerancing parameters, the specifications are entered in the **Geometric Tolerancing** dialog box (Figure 9-6). This dialog box can be invoked by entering the **TOLERANCE** command at the AutoCAD Command prompt.The dialog box can also be invoked by choosing **Tolerance** from the **Dimension** menu or toolbar.

Figure 9-5 Choosing **Tolerance** from the **Dimension** menu

Figure 9-6 Geometric Tolerance *dialog box*

The following list presents the geometric tolerancing components; Figure 9-7 shows their placement in the tolerance frame:

Feature control frame   **Geometric characteristics symbol**
Tolerance value   **Tolerance zone descriptor**
Material condition modifier   **Datum reference**

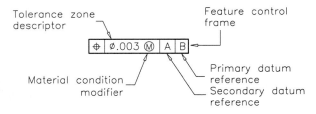

Figure 9-7 *Components of geometric tolerance*

Feature Control Frame

The **feature control frame** is a rectangular box that contains the geometric characteristics symbols and tolerance definition. The box is automatically drawn to standard specifications; you do not need to specify its size. You can copy, move, erase, rotate, and scale feature control frame. You can also snap to them using various Object snap modes. You can edit feature control frames using the **DDEDIT** command or you can also edit them using **GRIPS**. System variable **DIMCLRD** controls the color of the feature control frame. System variable **DIMGAP** controls the gap between the feature control frame and the text.

Geometric Characteristics Symbol

The geometric characteristics symbols indicate the characteristics of a feature, for example, straightness, flatness, and perpendicularity, etc. You can access the **Symbol** dialog box (Figure 9-8). by selecting the **Sym** edit box in the **Geometric Tolerance** dialog box, which is displayed when you enter the **TOLERANCE** command or choose it from the **Dimension** toolbar or menu. The different symbols can be selected from the **Symbol** dialog box.

Figure 9-8 Symbol dialog box

Tolerance Value and Tolerance Zone Descriptor

The tolerance value specifies the tolerance on the feature as indicated by the tolerance zone descriptor. For example, a value of .003 indicates that the feature must be within a 0.003 tolerance zone. Similarly, ϕ.003 indicates that this feature must be located at true position within 0.003 diameter. The tolerance value can be entered in the **Value** edit box of the **Geometric Tolerance** dialog box. The tolerance zone descriptor can be invoked by selecting the box labeled **Dia**, located to the left of the **tolerance** edit box. The **Geometric Tolerance** dialog box can be invoked by the **TOLERANCE** command or by choosing **TOLERANCE** from the **Dimension** menu or toolbar. System variable **DIMCLRT** controls the color of the tolerance text, variable **DIMTXT** controls the tolerance text size, and variable **DIMTXSTY** controls the style of the tolerance text. Using the **Projected Tolerance Zone**, inserts a projected tolerance zone symbol, which is an encircled P, after the projected tolerance zone value.

Material Condition Modifier

The **material condition modifier** specifies the material condition when the tolerance value takes effect. For example, ϕ.003(M) indicates that this feature must be located at true position within 0.003 diameter at maximum material condition (MMC). The material condition modifier symbol can be selected from the **Material Condition** dialog box (Figure 9-9). This dialog box can be invoked by selecting the **MC** button located just after **Tolerance Value** edit box in the **Geometric Tolerance** dialog box.

Figure 9-9 Material condition dialog

Datum

The datum is the origin, surface, or feature from which the measurements are made. The datum is also used to establish the geometric characteristics of a feature. The datum feature symbol consists of a reference character enclosed in a feature control frame. You can create the datum feature symbol by entering characters (like -A-) in the **Datum Identifier** edit box in the **Geometric Tolerance** dialog box and then selecting a point where you want to establish that datum.

You can also combine datum references with geometric characteristics. AutoCAD automatically positions the datum references on the right end of the feature control frame.

Chapter 9

Example 1

In the following example, you will create a feature control frame to require a perpendicularity specification (see Figure 9-10).

Step 1. Use the **TOLERANCE** command to display the **Geometric Tolerance** dialog box. Select the **Sym** edit box to display the **Symbol** dialog box. Choose the **perpendicularity** symbol in the dialog box and then choose the **OK** button.

Step 2. The perpendicularity symbol will be displayed in the **Sym** edit box in the first row of the **Geometric Tolerance** dialog box. Select the **Dia** edit box, located just before the Tolerance Value edit box, in the **Tolerance 1**

Figure 9-10 Drawing for Example 1

area on the first row. A diameter symbol will appear, to denote a cylindrical tolerance zone.

Step 3. Select the **Tolerance Value** edit box in the **Tolerance 1** area in the first row and enter **0.005**.

Step 4. Select the **Datum** edit box in the **Datum 1** area in the first row and enter **A**.

Step 5. Choose the **OK** button to accept the changes made in the **Geometric Tolerance** dialog box. The **Enter tolerance location:** prompt is displayed in the Command line area and the **Feature Control Frame** is attached to the cursor at its middle left point. Select a point to insert the frame.

Step 6. To place the datum symbol, use the **TOLERANCE** command to display the **Geometric Tolerance** dialog box. Select the **Datum Identifier** edit box, and enter **-A-**.

Step 7. Choose the **OK** button to accept the changes to the **Geometric Tolerance** dialog box, and then select a point to insert the frame.

COMPLEX FEATURE CONTROL FRAMES
Combining Geometric Characteristics

Sometimes it is not possible to specify all geometric characteristics in one frame. For example, Figure 9-11 shows the drawing of a plate with a hole in the center.

In this part, it is determined that surface C must be perpendicular to surfaces A and B within 0.002 and 0.004, respectively. Therefore, we need two frames to specify the geometric characteristics of surface C. The first frame specifies the allowable deviation in perpendicularity of surface C with respect to surface A. The second frame specifies the allowable deviation in perpendicularity of surface C with respect to surface B. In addition to these two frames, we need a third frame that identifies datum surface C.

Figure 9-11 Combining feature control frames

All the three feature control frames can be defined in one instance of the **TOLERANCE** command.

1. Enter the **TOLERANCE** command to invoke the **Geometric Tolerance** dialog box (see Figure 9-12). Select **Sym** edit box to display **Symbol** dialog box. Choose the **perpendicular** symbol, and then choose the **OK** button. AutoCAD will display the selected symbol in the first row **Sym** edit box.
2. Enter **.002** in the first row **Tolerance Value** edit box, and enter **A** in the first row of **Datum 1** edit box.
3. Select the second row **Sym** edit box to display the **Symbol** dialog box. Choose the **perpendicular** symbol, and then choose the **OK** button. AutoCAD will display the selected symbol in the second row **Sym** edit box in the **Geometric Tolerance** dialog box.
4. Enter **.004** in the second row **Tolerance Value** edit box, and enter **B** in the second row **Datum 1** edit box.

Figure 9-12 Geometric Tolerance dialog box

Chapter 9

5. In the **Datum Identifier** edit box enter **-C-**, and then choose the **OK** button to exit the dialog box.

6. In the graphics screen, select the position to place the frame.

Composite Position Tolerancing

Sometimes the accuracy required within a pattern is more important than the location of the pattern with respect to the datum surfaces. To specify such a condition, composite position tolerancing may be used. For example, Figure 9-13 shows four holes (pattern) of diameter 0.15. The design allows a maximum tolerance of 0.025 with respect to datums A, B, and C at the maximum material condition (holes are smallest). The designer wants to maintain a closer positional tolerance (0.010 at MMC) between the holes within the pattern. To specify this requirement, the designer must insert the second frame. This is generally known as composite position tolerancing. AutoCAD provides the facility to create the two composite position tolerance frames by means of the **Geometric Tolerance** dialog box. The composite tolerance frames can be created as follows:

Figure 9-13 *Using composite position tolerancing*

1. Enter the **TOLERANCE** command to invoke the **Geometric Tolerance** dialog box. Select the **Sym** edit box to display the **Symbol** dialog box. Choose the position symbol, and then Choose the **OK** button to display the symbol in the **Sym** edit box.

2. In the first row of the **Geometric Tolerance** dialog box, enter the geometric characteristics and the datum references required for the first position tolerance frame.

3. In the second row of the **Geometric Tolerance** dialog box, enter the geometric characteristics and the datum references required for the second position tolerance frame.

4. When you have finished entering the values, choose the **OK** button in the **Geometric Tolerance** dialog box, and then select the point where you want to insert the frames. AutoCAD will create the two frames and automatically align them with common position symbol, as shown in Figure 9-13.

Projected Tolerance Zone

Figure 9-14 shows two parts joined with a bolt. The lower part is threaded, and the top part has a drilled hole. When these two parts are joined, the bolt that is threaded in the lower part will have the orientation error that exists in the threaded hole. In other words, the error in the threaded hole will extend beyond the part thickness, which might cause interference, and the parts may not assemble. To avoid this problem, projected tolerance is used. The projected tolerance establishes a tolerance zone that extends above the surface. In Figure 9-14, the position tolerance for the threaded hole is 0.010, which extends 0.25 above the surface (datum A). By using the projected tolerance, you can ensure that the bolt is within the tolerance zone up to the specified distance.

Figure 9-14 *Using composite position tolerancing*

You can use the AutoCAD GDT feature to create feature control frames for the projected tolerance zone as follows:

1. Enter the **TOLERANCE** command to invoke the **Geometric Tolerance** dialog box. Choose the position symbol from the **Symbol** dialog box by selecting the **Sym** edit box, and then choose the **OK** button to exit from this dialog box.
2. In the first row of the **Geometric Tolerance** dialog box, enter the geometric characteristics and the datum references required for the first position tolerance frame (see Figure 9-15).
3. In the **Height** edit box, enter the height of the tolerance zone (0.25 for the given drawing) and select the edit box to the right of Projected Tolerance Zone. The projected tolerance zone symbol will be displayed in the box.
4. Once you are done entering the values, choose the **OK** button in the **Geometric Tolerance** dialog box, and then select the point where you want to insert the frames. AutoCAD will create the two frames and automatically align them, as shown in Figure 9-15.

Chapter 9

Figure 9-15 Geometric Tolerance dialog box

USING FEATURE CONTROL FRAMES WITH THE LEADER COMMAND

The **LEADER** command has the Tolerance option, which allows you to create the feature control frame and attach it to the end of the leader extension line. The following is the prompt sequence for using the **LEADER** command with the Tolerance option:

Command: **LEADER**
Specify leader start point: *Select a point where you want the arrow (P1).*
Specify next point: *Select a point (P2).*
Specify next point or [Annotation/Format/Undo]<Annotation>: *Select a point (P3).*
Specify next point or [Annotation/Format/Undo]<Annotation>: *Press ENTER.*
Enter first line of annotation text or <options>: *Press ENTER.*
Enter an annotation option [Tolerance/Copy/Block/None/Mtext]<Mtext>: **T**

When you select the Tolerance (**T**) option, AutoCAD will display the **Geometric Tolerance** dialog box. Select the **Sym** edit box and then from the **Symbol** dialog box choose the desired symbol, to return to the **Geometric Tolerance** dialog box. Enter the required values, and choose the **OK** button to exit the dialog box. The feature control frame with the defined geometric characteristics will be inserted at the end of the extension line, as shown in Figure 9-16.

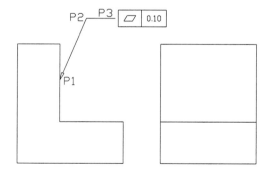

Figure 9-16 Using feature control frame with the leader

Note
*When you choose **Leader** from the Dimension menu, press ENTER to choose the **Settings** option to display the **Leader Settings** dialog box. You can select the **Tolerance** radio*

*button in the **Annotation** Type area to set the leader for Tolerance symbol. The default option is Mtext.*

Example 2

In the following example, you will create a leader with a combination feature control frame to control runout and cylindricity (Figure 9-17).

Step 1. Use the **LEADER** command to draw the leader.

Command: **LEADER**
Specify leader start point: *Select a point where you want the arrow.*
Specify next point: *Select the point for the first bend of the leader.*
Specify next point or [Annotation/Format/Undo]<Annotation>: *Select the endpoint.*
Specify next point or [Annotation/Format/Undo]<Annotation>: *Press ENTER.*
Enter first line of annotation text or <options>: *Press ENTER.*
Enter an annotation option [Tolerance/Copy/Block/None/Mtext]<Mtext>: **T**

Step 2. The **Geometric Tolerance** dialog box is displayed. Select the **Sym** edit box and from the **Symbol** dialog box, choose the **runout** symbol in the dialog box, and then return to the **Geometric Tolerance** dialog box.

Step 3. The **runout** symbol will be displayed in the **Sym** edit box on the first row of the **Geometric Tolerance** dialog box. Select the Value edit box in the Tolerance 1 area on the first row, and enter **0.15**.

Step 4. Select the **Datum** edit box in the Datum 1 area on the first row, and enter **C**.

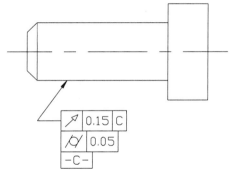

Figure 9-17 Drawing for Example 2

Step 5. Select the **Sym** edit box on the second row of the **Geometric Tolerance** dialog box to display the **Symbol** dialog box. Choose the **cylindricity** symbol in the dialog box to return to the **Geometric Tolerance** dialog box.

Step 6. The **cylindricity** symbol will be displayed in the **Sym** edit box on the second row of the **Geometric Tolerance** dialog box. Select the **Tolerance Value** edit box in the Tolerance 1 area on the second row, and enter **0.05**.

Step 7. Select the **Datum** Identifier edit box, and enter **-C-**.

Step 8. Choose the **OK** button to accept the changes to the **Geometric Tolerance** dialog box, and the control frames will be drawn at the end of the leader.

Self Evaluation Test

Answer the following questions, and then compare your answers to the correct answers given at the end of the chapter.

1. What is the advantage of showing tolerances and fits in a drawing?_____
    _____.

2. Geometric dimensioning and tolerancing is generally known as _____.

3. List the components of geometric tolerance._____
    _____.

4. Give three examples of geometric characteristics that indicate the characteristics of a feature.
    _____.

5. Give an example of a material condition modifier that specifies the material condition when
    the tolerance value takes effect. _____
    _____.

6. What is the projected tolerance zone? Explain._____
    _____.

7. The **LEADER** command has the **Tolerance** option, which allows you to create the feature
    control frame and attach it to the end of the leader extension line. (T/F)

8. Name two characteristics of the location feature._____.

9. Explain maximum material condition. _____
    _____.

Review Questions

1. One of the most important parts of the design process is to give the dimensions and tolerances.
    Why? _____.

2. Geometric dimensioning and tolerancing is a means to design and manufacture parts with
    respect to actual function and the relationship that exists between different features. (T/F)

3. _____ symbols are the building blocks of geometric dimensioning and   tolerancing.

4. The feature control frame is a circular shape that contains geometric characteristics symbols
    and tolerance definition. (T/F)

5. Give an example of tolerance value that specifies the tolerance on the feature as indicated by the tolerance zone descriptor.

6. The datum is the _____, _____, or feature from which the measurements are made.

7. Sometimes the accuracy required within a pattern is more important than the location of the pattern with respect to the datum surfaces. To specify such a condition, composite position tolerancing may be used. (T/F)

8. You cannot use the AutoCAD GDT feature to create feature control frames for the projected tolerance zone. (T/F)

9. Draw a picture of a feature control frame and explain its features.

10. Name three characteristics of the form feature._____.

Exercises

Exercise 1   *Mechanical*

Draw Figure 9-18. Then use the **TOLERANCE** and **LEADER** commands to draw the geometric tolerances as shown.

Figure 9-18 *Drawing for Exercise 1*

Project Exercise 2-1   *Mechanical*

Generate the drawing in Figure 9-19 according to the dimensions shown in the figure. Save the drawing as TOOLORGA. (See Chapters 14 and 23 for other drawings of Project Exercise 2.)

Figure 9-19 *Drawing for Project Exercise 2-1*

Project Exercise 2-2   *Mechanical*

Generate the drawing in Figure 9-20 according to the dimensions shown in the figure. Save the drawing as TOOLORGB. (See Chapters 14 and 23 for other drawings of Project Exercise 2.)

Figure 9-20 Drawing for Project Exercise 2-2

Answers to Self-Evaluation Test.

1 - Tolerances and fits determine how the parts will fit. Incorrect tolerances could result in a product that is not functional. **2** - GDT, **3** - Feature control frame, geometric characteristics symbol, tolerance value, tolerance zone descriptor, material condition modifier, datums. **4** - Straightness, flatness, perpendicularity. **5** - Example: f.003(M) indicates that this feature must be located at true position within 0.003 diameter at maximum material condition (MMC). **6** - The projected tolerance establishes a tolerance zone that extends above the surface. **7** - T, **8** - Position, concentricity, symmetry. **9** - When the part has maximum material; for example, if the part has a hole, the material will be maximum when the hole diameter is minimum.

Chapter 10

Editing with GRIPS

Learning Objectives

After completing this chapter, you will be able to:
• *Adjust grip settings.*
• *Select objects with grips.*
• *Stretch, move, rotate, scale, and mirror objects with grips.*
• *Use grips system variables.*

EDITING WITH GRIPS

Grips provide a convenient and quick means of editing objects. With grips you can stretch, move, rotate, scale, mirror objects, change properties, and load the Web browser. Grips are small squares that are displayed on an object at its definition points when the object is selected. The number of grips depends on the selected object. For example, a line has three grip points, a polyline has two, and an arc has three. Similarly, a circle has five grip points and a dimension (vertical) has five. When you select the **Enable grips** and the **Noun/Verb Selection** check boxes in the **Selection** tab of the **Options** dialog box, a small square (aperture box) at the intersection of the crosshairs is displayed (Figure 10-1).

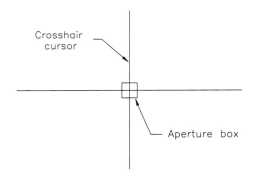

Figure 10-1 *Aperture box at the intersection of crosshair cursor*

Note
AutoCAD also displays a small square (aperture box) at the intersection of crosshairs when the ***PICKFIRST*** *(Noun/Verb Selection) system variable is set to 1 (On).*

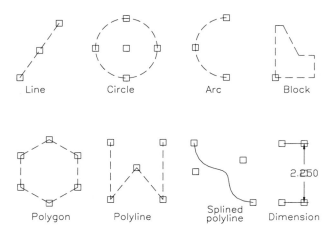

Figure 10-2 *Grip location of various objects*

ADJUSTING GRIP SETTINGS

Menu:	Tools > Options...
Command:	OPTIONS

Grip settings can be adjusted through the **Selection** tab of the **Options** dialog box (Figure 10-4).

Command: **OPTIONS**

The **Selection** tab of the **Options** dialog box has the following areas:

1. Grips
2. Grip Size

Grips

The Grips area has two check boxes: **Enable Grips** and **Enable Grips Within Blocks**. The grips can be enabled by selecting the **Enable Grips** check box. They can also be enabled by setting the **GRIPS** system variable to 1.

Command: **GRIPS**
Enter new value for GRIPS <0>: 1

The second check box, **Enable Grips Within Blocks**, enables the grips within a block. If you select this box, AutoCAD will display grips for every object in the block. If you disable the display of grips within a block, the block will have only one

Figure 10-3 *Invoking the **Options** dialog box from the **Tools** menu*

Figure 10-4 Selection tab of the Options dialog box

grip at its insertion point. You can also enable the grips within a block by setting the system variable **GRIPBLOCK** to 1 (On). If **GRIPBLOCK** is set to 0 (Off), AutoCAD will display only one grip for a block at its insertion point (Figure 10-5).

Note

*If the block has a large number of objects, and if **GRIPBLOCK** is set to 1 (On), AutoCAD will display grips for every object in the block. Therefore, it is recommended that you set the system variable **GRIPBLOCK** to 0 or clear the **Enable Grips Within Blocks** check box in the Selection tab of the **Options** dialog box.*

Grip Colors

The **Grips** area of the **Selection** tab of the **Options** dialog box has two drop-down lists, **Unselected grip color:** and **Selected grip color:**. These two drop-down lists give you options of colors to select from, for unselected and selected

*Figure 10-5 Block insertion with **GRIPBLOCK** set to 1 and to 0*

grips respectively. When you select the **More** option in either of these drop-down lists, AutoCAD displays the standard **Select Color** dialog box from which you can select a desired color. By default, the unselected grips have blue color (frame of the box) and the selected grips have red color (filled red square). The color of the unselected grips can also be changed by using the **GRIPCOLOR** system variable. Similarly, the color of the selected grips can also be changed by using the **GRIPHOT** system variable.

Grip Types. Grips can be classified into three types: hot grips, warm grips, and cold grips. When you select an object, the grips are displayed at the definition points of the object, and the object is highlighted by displaying it as a dashed line. These grips are called warm grips (blue). Now, if you select a grip on this object, the grip becomes a hot grip (filled red square). Once the grip is hot, the object can be edited. To cancel the grip, press ESC. If you press ESC once more, the hot grip changes to cold grip. When the grip is cold, the object is not highlighted, as shown in Figure 10-6. You can also snap to a cold grip.

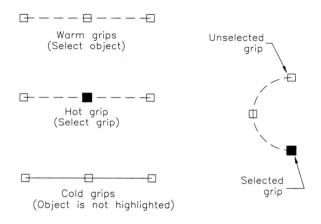

Figure 10-6 Hot, warm, cold, selected, and unselected grips

Grip Size

The **Grip Size** area of the **Selection** tab of the **Options** dialog box consists of a slider bar and a rectangular box that displays the size of the grip. To adjust the size of the grip, move the slider box left or right. The size of the grip can also be adjusted by using the system variable **GRIPSIZE**. **GRIPSIZE** is defined in pixels, and its value can range from 1 to 255 pixels.

STRETCHING OBJECTS WITH GRIPS
(Stretch Mode)

If you select an object, AutoCAD displays grips (warm grips) at the definition points of the object. When you select a grip for editing, you are automatically in the **Stretch** mode. The Stretch mode has a function similar to the **STRETCH** command. When you select a grip, it acts as a base point and is called a base grip. You can also select several grips by holding the SHIFT key down and then select the warm grips. Now, release the SHIFT key and select one of the hot grips to stretch them simultaneously. The geometry between the selected base grips is not altered. You can also make copies of the selected objects or define a new base point. When selecting grips on text objects, blocks, midpoints of lines, centers of circles and ellipses and point objects in the stretch mode, the selected objects are moved to a new location. The following example illustrates the use of the Stretch mode.

1. Use the **PLINE** command to draw a W-shaped figure as shown in Figure 10-7(a).

2. Select the object that you want to stretch [Figure 10-7(a)]. When you select the object, grips will be displayed at the endpoints of each object. A polyline has two grip points. If you use the **LINE** command to draw the object, AutoCAD will display three grips for each object.

3. Hold the SHIFT key down, and select the grips that you want to stretch [Figure 10-7(b)]. The selected grips will become hot grips, and the color of the grip will change from blue to red.

Note
By holding down the SHIFT key, you can select several grips. If you do not hold down the SHIFT key, only one grip can be selected.

4. Choose one of the selected (hot grip) grips, and specify a point to which you want to stretch the line [Figure 10-7(c)]. When you select a grip, the following prompt is displayed in the Command prompt area:

    STRETCH
    Specify stretch point or [Base point/Copy/Undo/eXit]:

    The Stretch mode has several options: **Base point**, **Copy**, **Undo**, and **eXit**. You can use the Base point option to define the base point and the Copy option to make copies.

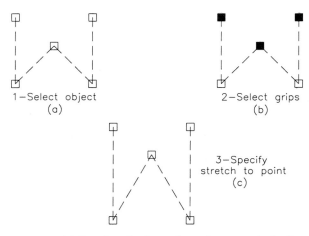

Figure 10-7 Using the Stretch mode to stretch the lines

5. Select the grip where the two lines intersect, as shown in Figure 10-9(a). Select the Copy option from the shortcut menu (Figure 10-8) by right-clicking your pointing device, or enter C for copy

at the command line, then select the points as shown in Figure 10-9(b). Each time you select a point, AutoCAD will make a copy.

If you press the SHIFT key when specifying the point to which the object is to be stretched, without selecting the copy option, then also AutoCAD allows you to make multiple copies of the selected object. Also if you press the SHIFT key again when specifying the next point, the cursor snaps to a point whose location is based on the distance between the first two points, that is the distance between the selected object and the location of the copy of the selected object.

Figure 10-8 *Selecting different Grip options from the shortcut menu*

6. Make a copy of the drawing as shown in Figure 10-9(c). Select the object, and then select the grip where the two lines intersect. When AutoCAD displays the ****STRETCH**** prompt, select the **Base Point** option from the cursor menu or enter B at the Command: prompt. Select the bottom left grip as the base point, and then give the displacement point as shown in Figure 10-9(d).

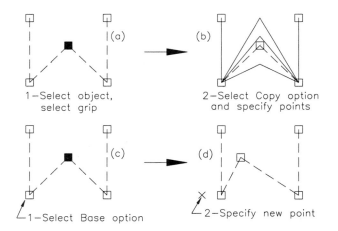

Figure 10-9 *Using the Stretch mode's* **Copy** *and* **Base point** *options*

7. To exit the grip mode, right-click to display the shortcut menu and then select **eXit**. You can also enter X at the Command: prompt or press ESC to exit.

Note

*You can select an option (**Copy** or **Base Point**) from the shortcut menu that can be invoked by right-clicking your pointing device after selecting a grip. The different modes can also be selected from the shortcut menu. You can also cycle through all the different modes by selecting a grip and pressing the ENTER key or the SPACEBAR. You can also enter keyboard shorcuts like **ST** for **STRETCH**.*

MOVING OBJECTS WITH GRIPS
(Move Mode)

The Move mode lets you move the selected objects to a new location. When you move objects, the size of the objects and their angle do not change. You can also use this mode to make copies of the selected objects or to redefine the base point. The following example illustrates the use of Move mode.

1. Use the **LINE** command to draw the shape as shown in Figure 10-10(a). When you select the objects, grips will be displayed at the definition points and the object will be highlighted.

Figure 10-10 *Using the* **Move** *mode to move and make copies of the selected objects*

2. Select the grip located at the lower left corner, and then select **Move** from the shortcut menu. You can also invoke the Move mode by entering **MOVE** or **MO** at the keyboard or giving a null response by pressing the SPACEBAR or ENTER key. AutoCAD will display the following prompt in the Command: prompt area:

   MOVE
   Specify move point or [Base point/Copy/Undo/eXit]:

3. Hold down the SHIFT key, and then enter the first displacement point. The distance between the first and the second object defines the snap offset for subsequent copies. While holding down the SHIFT key, move the screen crosshair to the next snap point and select the point. AutoCAD will make a copy of the object at that location. If you release the SHIFT key, you can specify any point where you want to place a copy of the object. You can also enter coordinates to specify the displacement.

Chapter 10

ROTATING OBJECTS WITH GRIPS
(Rotate Mode)

The **Rotate** mode allows you to rotate objects around the base point without changing their size. The options of Rotate mode can be used to redefine the base point, specify a reference angle, or make multiple copies that are rotated about the specified base point. You can access the Rotate mode by selecting the grip and then selecting **Rotate** from the shortcut menu, or by entering **ROTATE** or **RO** at the keyboard or giving a null response twice by pressing the SPACEBAR or the ENTER key. The following example illustrates the use of Rotate mode.

1. Use the **LINE** command to draw the shape as shown in Figure 10-11(a). When you select the objects, grips will be displayed at the definition points and the shape will be highlighted.

2. Select the grip located at the lower left corner and then invoke the Rotate mode. AutoCAD will display the following prompt:

    ROTATE
    Specify rotation angle or [Base point/Copy/Undo/Reference/eXit]:

3. At this prompt, enter the rotation angle. AutoCAD will rotate the selected objects by the specified angle [Figure 10-11(b)].

4. Make a copy of the original drawing as shown in Figure 10-11(c). Select the objects, and then select the grip located at the lower left corner of the object. Invoke the Rotate mode and then select the **Copy** option from the shortcut menu or enter C (Copy) at the prompt. Enter the rotation angle. AutoCAD will rotate a copy of the object through the specified angle [Figure 10-11(d)].

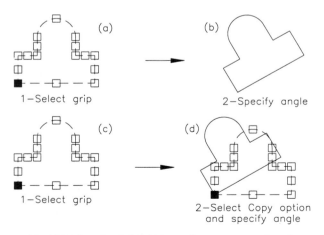

Figure 10-11 Using the **ROTATE** mode to rotate and make copies of the selected objects

5. Make another copy of the object as shown in Figure 10-12(a). Select the object, and then select

the grip at point (P0). Access the Rotate mode and copy option as described earlier. Select **Reference** option from the shortcut menu or enter R (Reference) at the following prompt:

**ROTATE (multiple) **
Specify rotation angle or [Base point/Copy/Undo/Reference/eXit]: R
Specify reference angle <0>: Select the grip at (P1).
Specify second point: Select the grip at (P2).
Specify new angle or [Base point/Copy/Undo/Reference/eXit]: 45

In response to the **Specify reference angle <0>:** prompt, select the grips at points (P1) and (P2) to define the reference angle. When you enter the new angle, AutoCAD will rotate and insert a copy at the specified angle [Figure 10-12(c)]. For example, if the new angle is 45 degrees, the selected objects will be rotated about the base point (P0) so that the line P1P2 makes a 45-degree angle with respect to the positive X axis.

Figure 10-12 *Using the* **ROTATE** *mode to rotate by giving a reference angle*

SCALING OBJECTS WITH GRIPS
(Scale Mode)

The **Scale** mode allows you to scale objects with respect to the base point without changing their orientation. The options of Scale mode can be used to redefine the base point, specify a reference length, or make multiple copies that are scaled with respect to the specified base point. You can access the Scale mode by selecting the grip and then selecting Scale from the shortcut menu, or entering **SCALE** or **SC** on the keyboard, or giving a null response three times by pressing the SPACEBAR or the ENTER key. The following example illustrates use of the Scale mode.

1. Use the **PLINE** command to draw the shape as shown in Figure 10-13(a). When you select the objects, grips will be displayed at the definition points, and the object will be highlighted.

2. Select the grip located at the lower left corner as the base grip, then invoke the **SCALE** mode.

AutoCAD will display the following prompt in the Command prompt area:

SCALE
Specify scale factor or [Base point/Copy/Undo/Reference/eXit]:

3. At this prompt enter the scale factor or move the cursor and select a point to specify a new size. AutoCAD will scale the selected objects by the specified scale factor [Figure 10-13(b)]. If the scale factor is less than 1 (<1), the objects will be scaled down by the specified factor. If the scale factor is greater than 1, the objects will be scaled up.

4. Make a copy of the original drawing as shown in Figure 10-13(c). Select the objects, and then select the grip located at the lower left corner of the object. Invoke the Scale mode. At the following prompt, enter C (Copy), and then enter B for base point:

    **SCALE (multiple) **
    Specify scale factor or [Base point/Copy/Undo/Reference/eXit]: B

5. At the **Specify base point prompt:**, select the point (P0) as the new base point, and then enter R at the following prompt.

    **SCALE (multiple) **
    Specify scale factor or [Base point/Copy/Undo/Reference/eXit]: R
    Specify reference length <1.000>: Select grips at (P1) and (P2).

After specifying the reference length at the **Specify new length or [Base point/Copy/Reference/ eXit]:** prompt, enter the actual length of the line. AutoCAD will scale the objects so that the length of the bottom edge is equal to the specified value [Figure 10-13(c)].

Figure 10-13 *Using the SCALE mode to scale and make copies of selected objects*

MIRRORING OBJECTS WITH GRIPS
(Mirror Mode)

The **Mirror** mode allows you to mirror the objects across the mirror axis without changing the size of the objects. The mirror axis is defined by specifying two points. The first point is the base point, and the second point is the point that you select when AutoCAD prompts for the second point. The options of the Mirror mode can be used to redefine the base point and make a mirror copy of the objects. You can access the Mirror mode by selecting a grip and then choosing Mirror from the shortcut menu, or by entering **MIRROR** or **MI** at the keyboard, or giving a null response four times by pressing the SPACEBAR or the ENTER key four times. The following is the example for the Mirror mode.

1. Use the **PLINE** command to draw the shape as shown in Figure 10-14(a). When you select the object, grips will be displayed at the definition points and the object will be highlighted.

2. Select the grip located at the lower right corner (P1), and then invoke the Mirror mode. The following prompt is displayed:

    MIRROR
    Specify second point or [Base point/Copy/Undo/eXit]:

3. At this prompt, enter the second point (P2). AutoCAD will mirror the selected objects with line P1P2 as the mirror axis, Figure 10-14(b).

4. Make a copy of the original figure as shown in Figure 10-14(c). Select the object, and then select the grip located at the lower right corner (P1) of the object. Invoke the Mirror mode and then select the Copy option to make mirror image while retaining the original object. Alternatively, you can also hold down the SHIFT key and make several mirror copies by specifying the second point.

Figure 10-14 *Using the Mirror mode to create a mirror image of selected objects*

5. Select point (P2) in response to the prompt **Specify second point or [Base point/Copy/Undo/ eXit]:**. AutoCAD will create a mirror image, and the original object will be retained.

Note

*You can use some editing commands, such as **ERASE**, **MOVE**, **ROTATE**, **SCALE**, **MIRROR**, and **COPY**, on an object with warm grips (Selected object), provided the system variable **PICKFIRST** is set to 1 (On).*

You cannot select an object once you select a grip (when the grip is hot).

If you want to remove an object from the selection set displaying grips, press the SHIFT key and then select the particular object. This object, which is removed from the selection set, will now not be highlighted although the grips are still displayed (Cold grips).

CHANGING PROPERTIES USING GRIPS

You can also use the grips to change the properties of a single or multiple object. To change the properties of an object, select the object to display the grips and then right-click to display the shortcut menu. In the shortcut menu, select the **Properties** option to display the **Object Properties window**. If you select a circle, AutoCAD will display Circle in the Selection drop-down list in the **Object Properties window**. Similarly, if you select text, Text is displayed in the drop-down list. If you select several objects, AutoCAD will display all the objects in the selection drop-down list of the **Object Properties window**. You can use this window to change the properties (color, layer, linetype, linetypes scale, lineweight, plot style and thickness etc.) of the gripped objects. (The **Object Properties window** has been discussed in detail in Chapter 4.) Similarly, you can use grips to edit hatch objects.

LOADING HYPERLINKS

You can also use the grips to open a file associated with the hyperlink. For example, the hyperlink could start a word processor, or activate the Web browser and load a Web page that is embedded in the selected object. If you want to launch the Web browser that provides hyperlinks to other Web pages, select the URL embedded object and then right-click to display the shortcut menu. In the shortcut menu, select the **Hyperlink** option and AutoCAD will automatically load the Web browser. When you move the cursor over or near the object that contains a hyperlink, AutoCAD displays the hyperlink information with the cursor.

EDITING GRIPPED OBJECTS

You can also edit the properties of the gripped objects by using the **Object Properties** toolbar (Figure 10-15). The gripped objects are created when you select objects without invoking a command. The gripped objects are highlighted and will display grips (rectangular boxes) at their grip points. For example, if you want to change the color of the gripped objects, select the Color drop-down list in the **Object Properties** toolbar and then select a color. The color of the gripped objects will change to the selected color. Similarly, if you want to change the layer, lineweight or linetype of the gripped objects, select the linetype, lineweight or layer from the corresponding drop-down lists. If the gripped objects have been drawn in different layers or have different colors, linetypes or lineweights, the Layer Control, Color Control, Linetype Control, Lineweight Control boxes will appear blank. You can also change the Plot Style of the selected objects.

Figure 10-15 Using the **Object Properties** *toolbar to change properties of the gripped objects*

GRIP SYSTEM VARIABLES

System variable	Default	Setting	Function
GRIPS	1	1=On, 0=Off	Enables or disables Grip mode
GRIPBLOCK	0	1=On, 0=Off	Controls the display of grips in a block
GRIPCOLOR	5	1-255	Specifies the color of unselected grips
GRIPHOT	1	1-255	Specifies the color of selected grips
GRIPSIZE	3	1-255	Specifies the size of the grip box in pixels

Self-Evaluation Test

Answer the following questions, and then compare your answers to the correct answers given at the end of this chapter.

1. What editing functions can you perform with grips? _____
   _____

2. A grip is a small square that is displayed on an object at its _____ points.

3. The number of grips depends on the selected object. (T/F)

4. A line has _____ grip points and a polyline has _____ .

5. The grip settings can be adjusted with the **GRIPS** command. (T/F)

6. The **Options** dialog box is activated by entering _____ at the Command: prompt.

7. You can enable grips within a block by setting the system variable _____ to 1 (On).

Chapter 10

8. The color of the unselected grips can also be changed by using the _____ system variable.

9. You can access the Mirror mode by selecting a grip and then entering _____ or _____ from the keyboard or giving a null response four times by pressing the SPACEBAR four times.

Review Questions

1. If you select a grip of an object, the grip becomes a cold grip. (T/F)

2. To cancel the grip, press the SHIFT and C keys. (T/F)

3. The **GRIPSIZE** is defined in pixels, and its value can range from _____ to _____ pixels.

4. The size of the grip can also be adjusted by using the system variable _____.

5. When you select a grip for editing, you are automatically in the _____ mode.

6. The _____ mode lets you move the selected objects to a new location.

7. What happens if you hold down the SHIFT key and then enter the first displacement point?
   _____

8. The Rotate mode allows you to rotate objects around the base point without changing their size. (T/F)

9. The _____ mode allows you to scale the objects with respect to the base point without changing their orientation.

10. The Mirror mode allows you to mirror the objects across the _____ without changing the size of the objects.

11. The **Go to URL** option allows you to _____ .

12. The **Properties** option allows you to _____ .

Exercises

Exercise 1   *Mechanical*

1. Use the **PLINE** or **LINE** command to make the drawing as shown in Figure 10-16(a).
2. Dimension the drawing, and place the dimensions as shown in Figure 10-16(a).
3. Use the grips to correct the dimensions and place them as shown in Figure 10-16(b).

(a)

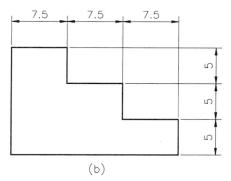

(b)

Figure 10-16(a) *Drawing for Exercise 1*   ***Figure 10-16(b)*** *Drawing for Exercise 1*

Exercise 2   *Graphics*

1. Use the **PLINE** command to draw the shape as shown in Figure 10-17(a).
2. Use grips (Stretch mode) to get the shape as shown in Figure 10-17(b).
3. Use the Rotate and Stretch modes to get the copies as shown in Figure 10-17(c)

Figure 10-17 *Drawing for Exercise 2*

Exercise 3 — *Graphics*

1. Use the **PLINE** or **LINE** command to make the drawing as shown in Figures 10-18(a) and 10-19(a).
2. Use grips to get the shapes as shown in Figures 10-18(b) and 10-19(b). (Do not use any AutoCAD command except GRIPS. Points (P1), (P2), and (P3) are midpoints. Also, X=5 units)

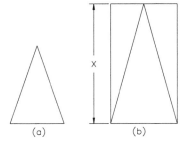

Figure10-18 *Drawing for Exercise 4*   **Figure 10-19** *Drawing for Exercise 5*

Exercise 4 — *Mechanical*

1. Make the drawing as shown in Figure 10-20(a). Assume the dimensions where necessary.
2. Dimension the drawing as shown in Figure 10-20(a).
3. Edit the dimensions as shown in Figure 10-20(b), using GRIPS.

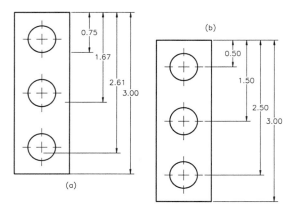

Figure 10-20 *Drawing for Exercise 6, showing dimensions*

Answers to Self-evaluation Test.
1 - With GRIPS you can stretch, move, rotate, scale, and mirror objects, **2** - definition, **3** - T,
4 - three, two, **5** - F, (**Options** dialog box), **6** - OPTIONS, **7** - GRIPBLOCK, **8** - GRIPCOLOR,
9 - MIRROR, MI.

Chapter 11

Hatching

Learning Objectives

After completing this chapter, you will be able to:
- *Use the **BHATCH** command to hatch an area.*
- *Use boundary hatch options and predefined, as well as user-defined, hatch patterns.*
- *Specify pattern properties.*
- *Preview and apply hatching.*
- *Use advanced hatching options.*
- *Edit associative hatch and hatch boundary.*
- *Hatch inserted blocks.*
- *Align hatch lines in adjacent hatch areas.*
- *Hatch by using the **HATCH** command at the Command prompt.*

HATCHING

In many drawings (such as sections of solids or sections of objects), the area must be filled with some pattern. Different filling patterns make it possible to distinguish between different parts or components of an object. Also, the material the object is made of can be indicated by the filling pattern. Filling the objects with a pattern is known as hatching (Figure 11-1). This hatching process can be accomplished by using the **BHATCH** or **HATCH** command.

Before using the **BHATCH** and **HATCH** commands, you need to understand some terms that are used when hatching. The following subsection describes some of the terms.

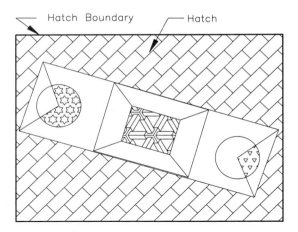

Figure 11-1 *Illustration of hatching*

Hatch Patterns

AutoCAD 2000 supports a variety of hatch patterns (Figure 11-2). Every hatch pattern is comprised of one or more hatch lines. These lines are placed at specified angles and spacing. You can change the angle and the spacing between the hatch lines. These lines may be broken into dots and dashes, or may be continuous, as required. The hatch pattern is trimmed or repeated, as required, to fill exactly the specified area. The lines comprising the hatch are drawn in the current drawing plane. The basic mechanism behind hatching is that the line objects of the pattern you have specified are generated and incorporated in the desired area in the drawing. Although a hatch can contain many lines, AutoCAD normally groups them together into an internally generated object and treats them as such for all practical purposes. For example, if you want to perform an editing operation, such as erasing the hatch, all you need to do is select any point on the hatch. The object created for the hatch lines gets deleted automatically when all references to it are

Figure 11-2 *Some hatch patterns*

deleted (only after the drawing is saved and reopened). If you want to break a pattern into individual lines to edit an individual line, you can use AutoCAD's **EXPLODE** command.

Hatch Boundary

Hatching can be used on parts of a drawing enclosed by a boundary. This boundary may be lines, circles, arcs, plines, 3D faces, or other objects, and at least part of each bounding object must be displayed within the active viewport. The **BHATCH** command automatically defines the boundary, whereas in the case of the **HATCH** command you have to define the boundary by selecting the objects that form the boundary of the hatch area.

THE BHATCH COMMAND

Toolbar:	Draw > Hatch
Menu:	Draw > Hatch...
Command:	BHATCH

*Figure 11-3 Choosing **Hatch** from the **Draw** toolbar*

The **BHATCH** (boundary hatch) command allows you to hatch a region enclosed within a boundary (closed area) by selecting a point inside the boundary or by selecting the objects to be hatched. This command automatically designates a boundary and ignores any other objects (whole or partial) that may not be a part of this boundary. One of the advantages of this command is that you do not have to select each object comprising the boundary of the area you want to hatch as in the case of the **HATCH** command (discussed later). This is because this command defines a boundary by creating a polyline from all the objects comprising the boundary. By default, this polyline gets deleted; however, if you want to retain it, you can specify that. This command also allows you to preview the hatch before actually applying it.

*Figure 11-4 Invoking the **BHATCH** command from the **Draw** menu*

When you invoke the **BHATCH** command, the **Boundary Hatch** dialog box is displayed through which you can perform the hatching operation (Figure 11-5).

Command: **BHATCH** [Enter]

Figure 11-5 Boundary Hatch dialog box

Example 1

In this example, you will hatch a circle using the default hatch settings. Later in the chapter you will learn how to change the settings to get a desired hatch pattern.

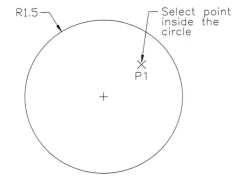

*Figure 11-6 Using the **BHATCH** command to hatch an object*

1. Invoke the **Boundary Hatch** dialog box (Figure 11-5) by entering **BHATCH** at the Command prompt.
2. Choose the **Pick Points** button from the **Boundary Hatch** dialog box (in the Boundary area). The dialog box temporarily closes.
3. Select a point inside the circle (P1) (Figure 11-6). After choosing an internal point, you can preview the hatching by choosing the **Preview** button. You can right-click to get the shortcut menu. From the shortcut menu also, you can preview the hatching by choosing **Preview**. You can also change the Island detection modes and undo selection from the shortcut menu.
4. Press ENTER to complete the point specification, and the dialog box reopens.
5. Choose the **OK** button to apply the hatch to the selected object.

BOUNDARY HATCH OPTIONS

The **Boundary Hatch** dialog box has several options that let you control various aspects of hatching, such as pattern type, scale, angle, boundary parameters, and associativity. The following is a description of these options. The options have been grouped by the tab name in which they are found in the **Boundary Hatch** dialog box. The **Boundary Hatch** dialog box has two tabs. The description of the tabs are as follows:

Quick Tab

The **Quick** Tab (Boundary **Hatch** dialog box) defines the appearance of the hatching patterns that can be applied (Figure 11-5). For quick hatching of a drawing object this dialog box can be used easily.

Type. This displays the type of the pattern that can be used for hatching drawing objects. This area lets you choose the type of hatch pattern you want. You can choose a predefined hatch pattern that comes with AutoCAD. The default hatch pattern is the predefined pattern named ANSI31. You can also choose the custom or a user-defined hatch pattern by selecting the pattern type from the drop-down list.

Pattern. The Pattern button and the drop-down list display all available predefined hatch patterns. The selected pattern is stored in the **HPNAME** system variable. ANSI31 is the default pattern in the **HPNAME** system variable. The pattern option is available only if the selected pattern is predefined. See Figures 11-7(a) and 11-7(b).

Figure 11-7(a) *Selecting pattern type from the **Boundary Hatch** dialog box*

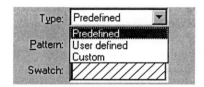

Figure 11-7(b) *Available hatch options*

When you choose the pattern [...] button, the **Hatch Pattern Palette** dialog box (Figure 11-8) is displayed that shows the images and names of the available hatch patterns. There are four tabs in the dialog box.

ANSI. This tab displays all the ANSI defined hatch patterns shipped with AutoCAD. ANSI31 pattern is default.

ISO. This tab displays all the ISO defined hatch patterns shipped with AutoCAD.

Other Predefined. This displays all the predefined hatch patterns other than ANSI or ISO patterns.

Custom. This displays all custom patterns described in any custom PAT files that is added in the search path of AutoCAD 2000.

Figure 11-8 Hatch Pattern Palette dialog box

Swatch. This box displays the preview of the selected pattern.

Custom Pattern. This drop-down list displays all the available custom hatch patterns, if any. The six most recent custom hatch patterns used appears in the list. The selected pattern is stored in **HPNAME** system variable. If you choose the Pattern [**...**] button, the **Hatch Pattern Palette** dialog box (**Custom** tab) appears. This tab displays all the available custom patterns, if any. See Figures 11-9 and 11-10.

*Figure 11-9 Selecting pattern properties (Angle and Scale) from the **Boundary Hatch** dialog box*

Figure 11-10 Pattern list box

Angle. This Pattern Properties option lets you rotate the hatch pattern with respect to the X axis of the current UCS. You can enter the angle of rotation value of your choice in the edit box next to the Angle: option. This value is stored in the **HPANG** system variable. The angle of hatch lines of a hatch pattern is governed by the values specified in the hatch definition. For example, in the ANSI31 hatch pattern definition, the specified angle of hatch lines is 45 degrees. If you select an angle of 0, the angle of hatch lines will be 45. If you enter an angle of 45 degrees, the angle of the hatch lines will be 90 degrees.

Scale. This Pattern Properties option lets you expand or contract the pattern, that is, scale the hatch pattern. You can enter the scale factor of your choice in the edit box next to the **Scale:** option. This value is stored in the **HPSCALE** system variable. Entering a value of 1 does not mean that the distance between the hatch lines is 1 unit. The distance between the hatch lines and other parameters of a hatch pattern is governed by the values specified in the hatch definition. For example, in the ANSI31 hatch pattern definition, the specified distance between the hatch lines is 0.125. If you select a scale factor of 1, the distance between the lines will be 0.125. If you enter a scale factor of 0.5, the distance between the hatch lines will be 0.5 x 0.125 = 0.0625.

Relative to Paper Space. If this check box is ticked on then AutoCAD 2000 will automatically scale the hatched pattern to the paper space units. This option can be used to display the hatch pattern at a scale that is appropriate to your layout. This option is available only in a layout.

Spacing. This displays the spacing between the lines in a predefined hatch pattern. The spacing is stored in the **HPSPACE** system variable. The default value of spacing is 1.0000.

ISO Pen Width . The ISO Pen Width option is only valid for ISO hatch patterns and linetypes. When you select any ISO pattern from the Pattern drop-down list, this option is enabled. The pen width can be selected by choosing the desired value from the ISO Pen Width drop-down list (Figure 11-11). The value selected specifies the ISO-related pattern scaling.

Figure 11-11 Selecting ISO Pen Width

User-defined Hatch Pattern

If you want to define a simple pattern, you can select the **User-Defined** pattern type in the Pattern **Type** drop-down list. You will notice that the **Angle:** and **Spacing:** edit boxes, and the **Double** check box are enabled in the dialog box. See Fgure 11-12.

Angle. You can specify an angle by entering a value in the **Angle:** edit box. This value is considered with respect to the X axis of the current UCS. This value is stored in the **HPANG** system variable.

Spacing. This edit box lets you specify the space between the hatch lines. The entered spacing value is stored in the **HPSPACE** system variable.

Double. This option makes AutoCAD draw a second set of lines at right angles to the original lines. If the Double box is selected, AutoCAD sets the **HPDOUBLE** system variable to 1.

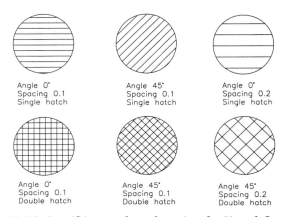

Angle 0°
Spacing 0.1
Single hatch

Angle 45°
Spacing 0.1
Single hatch

Angle 0°
Spacing 0.2
Single hatch

Angle 0°
Spacing 0.1
Double hatch

Angle 45°
Spacing 0.1
Double hatch

Angle 45°
Spacing 0.2
Double hatch

Figure 11-12 *Specifying angle and spacing for User-defined hatch*

Custom Hatch Pattern

You can select the **Custom** pattern type in the Pattern **Type** drop-down list. You will notice that the **Custom Pattern**, **Scale** and **Angle** are enabled in the dialog box.

Custom Pattern. In AutoCAD, hatch patterns are normally stored in the file named **ACAD.PAT**. You can select a hatch pattern from an individual file by selecting the Custom Pattern type, then entering the name of the stored hatch pattern in the **Custom pattern:** edit box. The Custom pattern type can be selected from the Pattern **Type** drop-down list . You can do this if you know the name of the hatch pattern. For example, you can enter BRASS or STEEL as a hatch pattern. The name is held in the **HPNAME** system variable. If AutoCAD does not locate the entered pattern in the **ACAD.PAT** file, it searches for it in a file with the same name as the pattern.

Exercise 1	*Mechanical*

In this exercise, you will hatch the given drawing using the hatch pattern named Steel. Set the hatch scale and the angle to match the drawing shown in Figure 11-13.

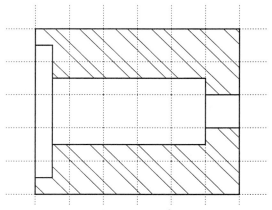

Figure 11-13 *Drawing for Exercise 1*

Selecting Hatch Boundary

The boundary selection options available in the **Boundary Hatch** dialog box allow you to define the hatch boundary by selecting a point inside the area or by selecting the objects. The other options are for removing islands, viewing the selection, and setting advanced options.

 Pick Points. This option makes AutoCAD automatically construct a boundary. When you select a point inside an object, the object and every other object inside it is selected as the boundary. To select this option, choose the **Pick Points** button in the **Boundary Hatch** dialog box. The following prompts appear:

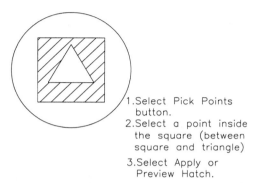

1. Select Pick Points button.
2. Select a point inside the square (between square and triangle)
3. Select Apply or Preview Hatch.

Select internal point: *Select a point inside the object to hatch.*
Selecting everything ...
Selecting everything visible...
Analyzing the selected data...
Analyzing internal islands...
Select internal point: *Select a point or press ENTER to end selection.*

Figure 11-14 Defining multiple hatch boundaries by selecting a point

In case you want to hatch an object and leave another object contained in it alone, select a point inside the object you want to hatch. By default, in the **BHATCH** command, selecting a point creates multiple boundaries, as all the objects inside the selected object are also selected. In Figure 11-14, the **Pick Points** button has been used to hatch the square but not the triangle simply by selecting the point inside the square but outside the triangle (using the default settings of the dialog box).

Boundary Definition Error. This dialog box (Figure 11-15) is displayed if AutoCAD finds that the selected point is not inside the boundary or that the boundary is not closed.

Figure 11-15 Boundary Definition Error dialog box

 Select Objects. This option in the **Boundary Hatch** dialog box lets you select objects that form the boundary for hatching. When you select this option, AutoCAD will prompt you to select objects. You can select the objects individually or use other object selection methods. In Figure 11-16, the Select Objects button is used to select the triangle. This uses the triangle as the hatch boundary, and everything inside it (text) will also be hatched. So, at the next Select objects: prompt, select the text so that it is also selected and hence, not hatched.

 Remove Islands. This option is used to remove any islands from the hatching area. For example, if you have a rectangle and circles as shown in Figure 11-17 and you use the Pick Points option to select a point inside the rectangle, AutoCAD will select both the circle and the rectangle. To remove the circle (island), you can use the Remove Islands option. When you select this option, AutoCAD will prompt you to select the islands to remove.

1. Select objects button.
2. Select the triangle for hatching.
3. Select the text.
4. Choose "Preview Hatch" or "Apply" option.

(a) Hatching without removing the islands

(b) Using the Remove Islands option to remove the islands

Figure 11-16 *Using the Select Objects option to specify the hatching boundary*

Figure 11-17 *Using the Remove Islands option to remove islands from the hatch area*

 View Selections. This option lets you view the selected boundaries and closes the dialog box temporarily. This option is unavailable when you have not selected any points or boundaries.

Inherit Properties. This option hatches the specified boundaries using the hatch properties of one object. If you select the associative hatch object whose properties you want the hatch to inherit, you can right-click in the drawing area to use the shortcut menu to toggle between the Select Objects and Pick Internal Point options to specify boundaries. When you choose the **Inherit Properties** button, the following command sequence appears:

Select associative hatch object: *Select a hatch pattern.*
Inherited Properties: Name <current>, Scale <current>, Angle <current>
Select Internal point: *Select a point inside the object to be hatched.*

When you press ENTER, the **Boundary Hatch** dialog box reappears with the name of the copied hatch pattern in the **Pattern**: edit box. The inherited hatch pattern is also displayed in the **Swatch** box. The selected pattern now becomes the current hatch pattern. If you then want to adjust the properties, such as angle or scale, you can do so.

Composition

Composition controls whether the hatch is associative or nonassociative with the hatch boundary. By default, the hatch associativity is on. One of the major advantages with the associative hatch feature is that you can edit the hatch pattern or edit the geometry that is hatched. After editing, AutoCAD will automatically regenerate the hatch and the hatch geometry to reflect the changes. The hatch pattern can be edited by using the **HATCHEDIT** command, and the hatch geometry can be edited by using grips or some AutoCAD editing commands.

Preview

You can use this option after you have selected the area to be hatched to see the hatching before it is actually applied. When you choose the **Preview** button, the dialog box is cleared and the object selected for hatching is temporarily filled with the specified hatch pattern. Previewing can also be done by right-clicking in the drawing area to get the shortcut menu; choose **Preview**. Pressing ENTER redisplays the **Boundary Hatch** dialog box so that the hatching operation can be completed and modifications made, if required. This option is available only after you have selected the area to be hatched.

OK

By choosing the **OK** button, you can apply hatching in the area specified by the hatch boundary. This option works whether or not you have previewed your hatch. This button is disabled if the hatch boundary is not defined.

Exercise 2 *Mechanical*

In this exercise, you will hatch the front view section of the drawing in Figure 11-18 using the hatch pattern for brass. Two views, top and front, are shown. In the top view, the cutting plane line indicates how the section is cut and the front view shows the full section view of the object. The section lines must be drawn only where the material is actually cut.

Figure 11-18 Drawing for Exercise 2

Advanced Tab (Boundary Hatch Dialog Box)

Defining a boundary by specifying an internal point is quite simple in the case of small and less complicated drawings. It may take more time in the case of large, complicated drawings because AutoCAD examines everything that is visible in the current viewport. Thus, the larger and more complicated the drawing, the more time it takes to locate the boundary edges. In such cases, you can improve the hatching speed by setting parameters in the **Advanced** Tab (Boundary **Hatch** dialog box), Figure 11-19.

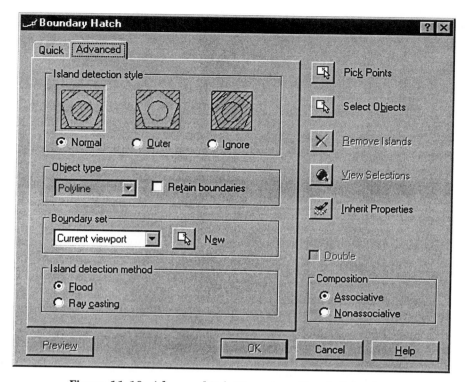

Figure 11-19 Advanced Tab (Boundary Hatch dialog box)

Island Detection Style

The island detection style can be specified by choosing style from Island detection style area (Figure 11-20). The styles are displayed with the effects in the image box. There are three styles from which you can choose: Normal, Outer, and Ignore. These styles are discussed next (Figure 11-21).

Figure 11-20 Island detection styles

Normal. This style hatches inward starting at the outermost boundary. If it encounters an internal boundary, it turns off the hatching. An internal boundary causes the hatching to turn off until another boundary is encountered. In this manner, alternate areas of the selected object are hatched, starting with the outermost area. Thus, areas separated from the outside of the hatched area by an odd number of boundaries are hatched, while those separated by an even number of boundaries are not. AutoCAD 2000 stores Normal style code by adding **, N** to the pattern name under the **HPNAME** system variable.

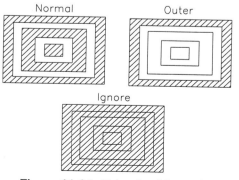

Figure 11-21 Using hatching styles

Outer. This particular option also lets you hatch inward from an outermost boundary, but the hatching is turned off if an internal boundary is encountered. Unlike the previous case, it does not turn the hatching on again. The hatching process in this case starts from both ends of each hatch line; only the outermost level of the structure is hatched, hence the name **Outer**. AutoCAD stores Outer style code by adding **, O** to the pattern name under the **HPNAME** system variable.

Ignore. In this option, all areas bounded by the outermost boundary are hatched, ignoring any hatch boundaries that are within the outer boundary. AutoCAD stores Ignore style code by adding **,I** to the pattern name under the **HPNAME** system variable.

The Normal, Outer, and Ignore options are available in the shortcut menu when you select an internal point in the drawing object and right-click in the drawing area.

Object Type

Object type specifies whether to keep the boundaries as objects or not, and AutoCAD applies object types to those objects.

Retain Boundaries. It can be used to retain the defined boundary. If the hatching was successful and you want to leave the boundary as a polyline or region to use it again, you can select the **Retain Boundaries** check box.

Object Type. The Object Type option controls the type of object AutoCAD will create when you define a boundary. It has two options: Polyline and Region. Regions are two-dimensional areas which can be created from closed shapes or loops. You can choose the desired option from the drop-down list. Object type option is available only when Retain Boundaries is selected.

Boundary Set

You can specify the boundary set by using the **Advanced** Tab (**Boundary Hatch** dialog box). The boundary set comprises the objects that the **BHATCH** command uses when constructing the boundary. The default boundary set comprises everything that is visible in the current viewport. A boundary can be produced faster by specifying a boundary set because, in this case, AutoCAD does not have to examine everything on screen.

New. This option is used to create a new boundary set. All the dialog boxes are cleared from the screen to allow selection of objects to be included in the new boundary set. While constructing the boundary set, AutoCAD uses only those objects that you select and that are hatchable. If a boundary set already exists, it is eliminated for the new one. If you do not select any hatchable objects, no new boundary set is created; AutoCAD retains the current set if there is one. Once you have formed a boundary set, you will notice that the **Existing Set** option gets added in the drop-down list. When you invoke the **BHATCH** command and you have not formed a boundary set, there is only one option, **Current Viewport** available in the drop-down list. The **Advanced** Tab (**Boundary Hatch** dialog box) reappears after you have selected the **New** button and selected objects to create a selection set. The benefit of creating a selection set is that when you select a point or select the objects to define the hatch boundary, AutoCAD will search only for the objects that are in the selection set. By confining the search to the objects in the selection set, the hatching process is faster. If you select an object that is not a part of the selection set, AutoCAD ignores objects that does not exist in the boundary set defined by using Pick Points. When a boundary set is formed, it becomes the default for hatching until you exit the **BHATCH** command or select the **Current Viewport** option from the drop-down list.

 Note
The selection of hatch style carries meaning only if the objects to be hatched are nested (that is, one or more selected boundaries is within another boundary).

Island Detection Method

Island Detection Method specifies whether to include objects within the outermost boundary as boundary objects. These internal objects are known as **islands**.

Flood. This option includes islands as boundary objects.

Ray Casting. This option runs a line from the point specified to the nearest object and then traces the boundary in a counterclockwise direction, thus excluding islands as boundary objects.

RAY CASTING OPTIONS

You can use the **ray casting** technique to define a hatch boundary. The ray casting options are available only through the **-BHATCH** command. In ray casting, AutoCAD casts an imaginary ray in all directions or a particular specified direction and locates the object that is nearest to the point you have selected. After locating the object, it takes a left turn to trace the boundary. If the first ray is intercepted by an internal area or internal text, it results in a boundary definition error. To avoid boundary definition errors, or to force the ray casting in a particular direction, you can use the Ray Casting options. These options control the direction in which AutoCAD casts the ray to form a hatch boundary. The available options are **Nearest, +X, -X, +Y**, and **-Y** . The prompt sequence for the Ray Casting options is:

Command: **-BHATCH**
Current hatch Pattern: ANSI31
Specify internal point or [Properties/Select/Remove islands/Advanced]: **A**
Enter an option [Boundary set/Retain boundary/Island detection/Style/Associativity]: **I**
Do you want island detection? [Yes/No] <Y>: **N**
Enter type of ray casting [Nearest/+X/-X/+Y/-Y/Angle] <Nearest>: *Specify an option.*

Nearest. The Nearest option is selected by default. When this option is used, AutoCAD sends an imaginary line to the nearest hatchable object, then takes a turn to the left and continues the tracing process in an effort to form a boundary around the internal point. To make this process work properly, the point you select inside the boundary should be closer to the boundary than any other object that is visible on the screen. This may be difficult when the space between two boundaries is very narrow. In such cases, it is better to use one of the other four options. Figure 11-22 shows you some of the conditions in which these options can be used.

+X, -X, +Y, and -Y options. These options can be explained better by studying Figure 11-22. Figure 11-22(a) shows that the points that can be selected are those that are nearest to the right-hand edge of the circumference of the circle because the ray casting takes place in the direction of the positive X.

Figure 11-22(b) shows that the points that can be used for selection are those that are nearest to the left-hand edge of the circle because the ray casting takes place in the negative X direction.

In Figure 11-22(c), the ray casting takes place in the positive Y direction, so the points that can be used for selection are the ones closest to the upper edge of the circle.

In Figure 11-22(d), the ray casting takes place in the negative Y direction, so the internal points that can be selected are the ones closest to the lower edge of the circle.

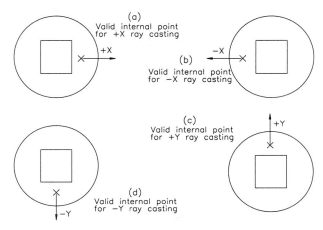

Figure 11-22 *Valid points for casting a ray in different directions to select the circle as boundary*

The effect of hatching for these ray casting options is shown Figures 11-23(a) and (b).

Figure 11-23(a) *Effect of hatching for ray casting*

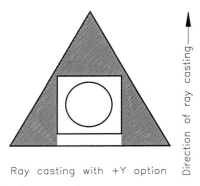

Figure 11-23(b) *Effect of hatching for ray casting*

HATCHING AROUND TEXT, TRACES, ATTRIBUTES, SHAPES, AND SOLIDS

The hatch lines do not pass through the text, attributes, or shapes present in an object being hatched because AutoCAD places an imaginary box around these objects that does not allow the hatch lines to pass through it. You must select the text/attribute/shape along with the object in which it is placed when defining the hatch boundary. If multiple line text is to be written, use the **MTEXT** command. Figure 11-24 shows you the selection of boundaries for hatching using the window selection method.

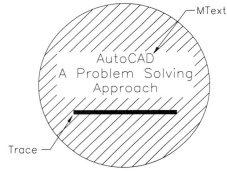

Figure 11-24 *Hatching around text and trace*

EDITING ASSOCIATIVE HATCH PATTERNS
Using the HATCHEDIT Command

Toolbar:	Modify II > Edit Hatch
Menu:	Modify > Hatch...
Command:	HATCHEDIT

Figure 11-25 *Choosing **Edit Hatch** from the **Modify II** toolbar*

The **HATCHEDIT** command can be used to edit the hatch pattern. When you enter this command and select the hatch for editing, the **Hatch Edit** dialog box (Figure 11-26) is displayed on the screen. The **Hatch Edit** dialog box can also be invoked from the shortcut menu after selecting a hatched object, right-clicking in the drawing area, and choosing **Hatch Edit**. The command sequence is as follows:

Command: **HATCHEDIT**
Select associative hatch objects: *Select a hatch object.*

AutoCAD will display **Hatch Edit** dialog box, where the hatch pattern can be changed or modified accordingly.

Figure 11-26 Using the **Hatch Edit** dialog box to edit the hatch pattern

You can redefine the hatch pattern by entering the new hatch pattern name in the **Pattern**: edit box. You can also change the scale or angle by entering the new value in the **Scale**: or **Angle**: edit box. You can also define the hatch style by choosing the Advanced Tab and then selecting Normal, Outer, or Ignore styles. If you want to copy the properties from an existing hatch pattern, choose the **Inherit Properties** button, and then select the hatch. In Figure 11-27, the object is hatched using the ANSI31 hatch pattern. Using the **HATCHEDIT** command, you can select the hatch and then edit it using the dialog box to get the hatch as shown in Figure 11-28. You can also edit an existing hatch through the command line by entering **-HATCHEDIT** at the Command prompt.

Command: **-HATCHEDIT**
Select associative hatch object: *Select the hatch pattern.*
Enter hatch option [Disassociate/Style/Properties] <Properties>: *Press ENTER*
Enter a pattern name or [?/Solid/User defined] <ANSI31>: *Enter the pattern name.*
Specify a scale for the pattern <1.0000>: *Enter scale.*
Specify an angle for the pattern <0>: *Enter angle.*

Figure 11-27 ANSI31 hatch pattern

*Figure 11-28 Using the **HATCHEDIT** command to edit the hatch pattern*

Using PROGRAMPERTIES Command*

Toolbar:	Standard > Properties
Menu:	Modify, Tools > Properties
Command:	PROPERTIES

You can also use the **PROPERTIES** command to edit the hatch pattern. When you select a hatch pattern for editing, AutoCAD displays the **Object Properties Window (Hatch)**. The categories in the **Object Properties Window** (Hatch) (Figure 11-29) are as follows:

General. You can change the hatch pattern properties like Color, Layer, Linetype, Linetype scale, Lineweight, and so on, by selecting the General category and changing the respective properties from the available drop-down list. The drop-down arrow is displayed when you select an item.

Pattern. In this category you can change the Pattern Type, Pattern name, Angle, Scale, Spacing, ISO pen width and double properties. When you choose [...] button in Type property, AutoCAD 2000 displays the **Hatch Pattern Type** dialog box (Figure 11-30). When you choose the [...] button in the Pattern name property, AutoCAD displays the **Hatch Pattern Palette** dialog box with the default pattern ANSI31 selected. The other properties can be changed manually.

Misc. In this category, Elevation, Associative, and Island detection style properties of hatching can be changed. Elevation can be changed manually while

Figure 11-29 Object Properties Window (Hatch)

Figure 11-30 Hatch Pattern Type dialog box

the Associative and Island detection styles can be changed from the available drop-down list.

EDITING HATCH BOUNDARY
Using Grips

One of the ways you can edit the hatch boundary is by using grips. You can select the hatch pattern or the hatch boundaries. If you select the hatch pattern, the hatch highlights and a grip is displayed. However, if you select an object that defines the hatch boundary, the object grips are displayed at the defining points of the selected object. Once you change the boundary definition, AutoCAD will reevaluate the hatch boundary and then hatch the area. When you edit the hatch boundary, make sure that there are no open spaces in the hatch boundary. AutoCAD will not create a hatch if the outer boundary is not closed. Figure 11-31 shows the hatch after moving the circle and text, and

Figure 11-31 Using Object Grips to edit the hatch boundary

shortening the bottom edge of the hatch boundary. The objects were edited by using grips. If you select the hatch pattern, AutoCAD will display the hatch object grip at the centroid of the hatch*. You can select the grip to make it hot and then edit the hatch object.

If the **Retain Boundaries** option was off when the hatch was created, all objects selected or found by the selection or point selection processes during the hatch creation are associated with the hatch as boundary objects. Editing any of them may affect the hatch. If, however, the Retain Boundaries option was on when the hatch was created, only the retained polyline boundary created by **BHATCH** is associated with the hatch as its boundary object. Editing it will affect the hatch, and editing the objects selected or found by selection or point selection processes during the hatch created will have no effect on the hatch. You can, of course, select and simultaneously edit the objects selected or found by the selection or point selection processes, as well as the retained polyline boundary created by the **BHATCH** command.

Using AutoCAD Editing Commands

When you use the editing commands, such as **MOVE**, **COPY**, **SCALE**, **STRETCH**, and **MIRROR**, associativity is maintained, provided all objects that define the boundary are selected for editing. If any object is missing, the associativity will be lost and AutoCAD will display the message **Hatch boundary associativity removed**. When you rotate or scale an associative hatch, the new rotation angle and the scale factor are saved with the hatch object data. This data is then used to update the hatch. If you explode an associative hatch pattern, the associativity between the hatch pattern and the defining boundary is removed. Also, when the hatch object is exploded, each line in the hatch pattern becomes a separate object.

HATCHING BLOCKS AND XREF DRAWINGS

The hatching procedure in AutoCAD works on inserted blocks and xref drawings (see Figure 11-32).

The internal structure of a block is treated by the **HATCH** and **BHATCH** commands as if the block were composed of independent objects. If you are using the **BHATCH** command, you can use the Pick Points button to generate the desired hatch in a block. If you want to hatch a block using the **BHATCH** command, the objects inside the blocks should be parallel to the current UCS. If the block is comprised of objects such as arcs, circles, or pline arc segments, they **need not be** uniformly scaled for hatching.

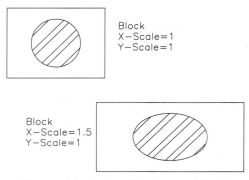

Figure 11-32 Hatching inserted blocks

When you xref a drawing, you can hatch any part of the drawing that is visible. If you use the **XCLIP** command to clip the xref drawing, the hatch pattern is not clipped. When you detach the xref drawing, the hatch pattern and its boundaries are not detached.

You can also create a hatch pattern from the Command prompt line by preceding the **BHATCH** command with a dash (-). The following is the command prompt sequence for the **-BHATCH** command:

> Command: **-BHATCH**
> Specify internal point or [Properties/Select/Remove islands/Advanced]: **P**
> Enter a pattern name or [?/Solid/User defined] <ANSI31>: *Enter the pattern name.*
> Specify a scale for the pattern <1.0000>: *Enter scale.*
> Specify an angle for the pattern <0>: *Enter angle.*
> Specify internal point or [Properties/Select/Remove islands/Advanced]: *Select internal point.*

PATTERN ALIGNMENT DURING HATCHING
(SNAPBASE Variable)

Pattern alignment is an important feature of hatching, since on many occasions you need to hatch adjacent areas with similar or sometimes identical hatch patterns while keeping the adjacent hatch patterns properly aligned. Proper alignment of hatch patterns is taken care of automatically by generating all lines of every hatch pattern from the same reference point. The reference point is normally at the origin point (0,0). Figure 11-33 shows two adjacent hatch areas. If you hatch these areas, the hatch lines may not be aligned, as shown in Figure 11-33(a). To align them, you can use the **SNAPBASE** variable so that the hatch lines are aligned, as shown in Figure 11-33(b). The reference point for hatching can be changed using the system

Figure 11-33 Aligning hatch patterns using the SNAPBASE variable

variable **SNAPBASE**. The command prompt sequence is:

Command: **SNAPBASE**
Enter new value for SNAPBASE <0.0000, 0.0000>: *Enter the new reference point.*

Note
You should set the base point back to (0,0) when you are done hatching the object.

Exercise 3   *Mechanical*

In this exercise, you will hatch the given drawing using the hatch pattern ANSI31. Use the **SNAPBASE** variable to align the hatch lines shown in the drawing (Figure 11-34).

Figure 11-34 Drawing for Exercise 3

THE BOUNDARY COMMAND

Menu:	Draw > Boundary
Command:	BOUNDARY

The **BOUNDARY** command is used to create a polyline or a region by defining a hatch boundary. When this command is entered, AutoCAD displays the **Boundary Creation** dialog box, shown in Figure 11-35.

Command: **BOUNDARY**

The options shown in the **Boundary Creation** dialog box are identical to the options in the **Advanced** Tab (**Boundary Hatch** dialog box) discussed earlier, except for the **Pick Points** option. The Pick Points option in the **Boundary Creation** dialog box is used to create a boundary by selecting a point inside the objects.

When you select the **Pick Points** option, the dialog box is cleared from the screen and the following prompt is displayed:

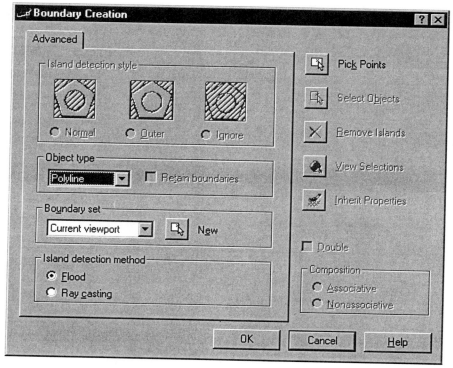

Figure 11-35 Boundary Creation dialog box

Select internal point:

Once you select an internal point, a polyline or a region is formed around the boundary (Figure 11-36). To end this process, press ENTER at the **Select internal point:** prompt. The polyline or region is determined by the **Object Type** you have specified in the Boundary Creation dialog box. If you want to edit the boundary, you can select the boundary by using the last object selection option.

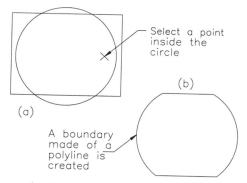

*Figure 11-36 Using **BOUNDARY** command to create a hatch boundary*

Exercise 4

Mechanical

First see Figure 11-37. Then make the drawing shown in Figure 11-38 using the **BOUNDARY** command to create a hatch boundary. Copy the boundary from the drawing shown in Figure 11-37, and then hatch.

Figure 11-37 Drawing for Exercise 4

Figure 11-38 Final drawing for Exercise 4

Chapter 11

OTHER FEATURES OF HATCHING

1. In AutoCAD the hatch patterns are separate objects. The objects store the information about the hatch pattern boundary with reference to the geometry that defines the pattern for each hatch object.

2. When you save a drawing, the hatch patterns are stored with the drawing. Therefore, the hatch patterns can be updated even if the hatch pattern file that contains the definitions of hatch patterns is not available.

3. If the system variable **FILLMODE** is 0 (Off), the hatch patterns are not displayed. After changing the value, you must use the **REGEN** command to regenerate the drawing to see the changes.

4. You can edit the boundary of a hatch pattern even when the hatch pattern is not visible (**FILLMODE**=0).

5. The hatch patterns created with earlier releases are automatically converted to AutoCAD 2000 hatch objects when the hatch pattern is edited.

6. When you save an AutoCAD 2000 drawing in Release 13 format, the hatch objects are automatically converted to Release 13 hatch blocks.

7. You can use the **CONVERT** command to change the pre-Release 14 hatch patterns to AutoCAD 2000 objects. You can also use this command to change the pre-Release 14 polylines to AutoCAD 2000 optimized format to save memory and disk space.

HATCHING BY USING THE HATCH COMMAND

Hatches can also be created with the **HATCH** command. However, such hatches are not associated with the boundary. Also, all selected objects must meet endpoint to endpoint to form a continuous series for a closed boundary because the **HATCH** command does not create its own boundary. You can invoke this command by entering **HATCH** at the AutoCAD Command prompt. When you enter the **HATCH** command, it does not display a dialog box as in the case of the **BHATCH** command. The prompt sequence is:

Command: **HATCH**
Enter a pattern name or [?/Solid/User defined] <ANSI31>: *Enter a pattern name.*

If you know the name of the pattern, enter it. You can also use the following options in response to this prompt:

? Option

If you enter **?** As the response to the **Enter a pattern name or [?/Solid/User defined] <ANSI31>:** prompt, the following prompt is displayed:

Enter pattern(s) to list <*>:

If you give a null response to this last prompt, the names and descriptions of all defined hatch patterns are displayed in the AutoCAD Text window. If you are not sure about the name of the pattern you want to use, you can select this option before entering a name. You can also list a particular pattern by specifying it at the prompt.

Solid Option

This option is used to fill the selected boundary with solid. If you enter **S** as the response to the **Enter a pattern name or [?/Solid/User defined] <ANSI31>:** prompt, the following prompt is displayed:

Select objects to define hatch boundary or <direct hatch>
Select objects: *Select a boundary for filling or press ENTER for direct hatch.*

If you select a boundary, the object is highlighted; by pressing ENTER at the next Select objects: prompt, you can complete the command and the selected area will be solid-filled.

If you press ENTER at the initial **Select objects:** prompt, you will be allowed to create a boundary for filling. The prompt sequence for the direct hatch option is:

Select objects to define hatch boundary or <direct hatch>
Select objects: *Press ENTER for direct hatch.*
Retain polyline boundary [Yes/No] <N>: *Enter **Y** to retain the polyline, **N** to lose it.*
Specify start point: *Select first point of the boundary.*
Specify next point or [Arc/ Close/ Length/ Undo]: *Select the next point of the boundary.*
Specify next point or [Arc/ Close/ Length/ Undo]: *Select the next point of the boundary.*
Specify next point or [Arc/ Close/ Length/ Undo]: **C** (*Enter **C** to close the boundary.*)
Specify start point for new boundary or <apply hatch>: *Press ENTER to complete the command.*

The created boundary will be solid-filled.

User-defined Option

This option is used for creating a user-defined array or double-hatched grid of straight lines. To invoke this option, enter **U** at the **Enter a pattern name or [?/Solid/User defined] <ANSI31>:** prompt. After you enter **U**, the following prompts are displayed:

> Specify angle for crosshatch lines <0>:
> Specify spacing between the lines <1.0000>:
> Double hatch area? [Yes/No] <N>

At the **Specify angle for crosshatch lines <0>:** prompt, you need to specify the angle at which you want the hatch to be drawn. This angle is measured with respect to the X axis of the current UCS. You can also specify the angle by selecting two points on the screen. This value is stored in the **HPANG** system variable.

At the second prompt, **Specify spacing between the lines <1.0000>:,** you can specify the space between the hatch lines. The default value for spacing is 1.0000. The specified spacing value is stored in the **HPSPACE** system variable.

At the third prompt, **Double hatch area? [Yes/No] <N>:,** you can specify whether you want double hatching. The default is no (**N**), and in this case, double hatching is disabled. You can enter **Y** (YES) if you want double hatching, and in this case, AutoCAD draws a second set of lines at right angles to the original lines. If the Double hatch is active, AutoCAD sets the **HPDOUBLE** system variable to 1.

Hatching by Specifying the Pattern Name

When you enter the **HATCH** command, you can also specify the hatch name of the hatch pattern at the pattern prompt. With the hatch name you can also specify the hatch style. The format is as follows:

> Command: **HATCH**
> Enter a pattern name or [?/Solid/User defined] <ANSI31>: **Stars, I** *(Enter a pattern name and style.)*
> Specify a scale for the pattern <1.0000>:
> Specify an angle for the pattern <0>:

By specifying **Stars, I** you are specifying the hatch pattern as Stars and the hatch style as Ignore. There are three hatch styles: **Normal**, **Outer**, and **Ignore**. They have been discussed earlier in this chapter in the "**Advanced** Tab (**Boundary Hatch** dialog box)" subsection.

All the stored hatch patterns are assigned an initial scale (size) and a rotation of 0 degrees with respect to the positive X axis. You can expand or contract according to your needs. You can scale the pattern by specifying a scale factor. You can also rotate the pattern with respect to the positive direction of the current UCS by entering a desired angle in response to the Angle prompt. You can even specify the angle manually by selecting or entering two points. For example, Figure 11-39 illustrates the hatch pattern ANSI31 with different scales and angles. The scale and angle are shown with the figures. Once you are finished specifying the pattern, AutoCAD prompts you to select objects for hatching or to create a direct hatch option (discussed earlier).

Select objects to define hatch boundary or <direct hatch>
Select objects: *Select a boundary for hatching or press ENTER for direct hatch.*

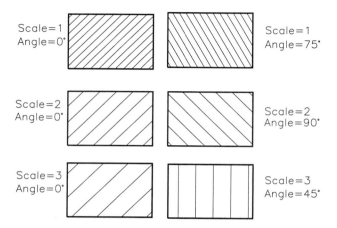

Figure 11-39 *Using different values for scale and angle*

Defining the boundaries in the **HATCH** command is a bit tedious compared with defining them with the **BHATCH** command. In the **BHATCH** command, the boundaries are automatically defined, whereas with the **HATCH** command you need to define the boundaries by selecting the objects. The objects that form the boundary must intersect at their endpoints, and the objects you select must completely define the boundary. You can use any object selection method to select the objects that define the boundary of the area to be hatched and the objects that you want to exclude from hatching. For example, in the first illustration in Figure 11-40, no hatching takes place because only two lines lie completely within the window and the boundary is not closed. In such a case, AutoCAD displays the following message:

Unable to hatch the boundary

Figure 11-40 *Selecting objects using the* **HATCH** *command*

In the second illustration, the boundary is selected by selecting objects. In this illustration, the lines LQ and MR extend beyond the hatch boundary, which makes the hatching outside the intended hatch area. You must break the top and bottom line at points Q and R so that lines LQ, QR, RM, and ML define the hatch boundary. Now, if you select the objects, AutoCAD will hatch the area bound by the four selected objects, as shown in the third illustration.

Self-Evaluation Test

Answer the following questions, and then compare your answers to the correct answers given at the end of this chapter.

1. The material the object is made of can be indicated by the hatch pattern. (T/F)

2. The _____ command automatically defines the boundary, whereas in the case of the _____ command you have to define the boundary by selecting the objects that form the boundary of the hatch area.

3. The **Boundary Hatch** dialog box can be invoked by entering _____ at the Command prompt.

4. You can define a simple pattern by selecting the **User-defined** pattern type in the **Pattern Type** list box. (T/F)

5. One of the ways to specify a hatch pattern from the group of stored hatch patterns is by selecting the down arrow in the **Pattern:** edit box. (T/F)

6. If AutoCAD does not locate the entered pattern in the _____ file, it searches for it in a file with the same name as the pattern.

7. The _____ option lets you rotate the hatch pattern with respect to the X axis of the current UCS.

8. The _____ option in the **Boundary Hatch** dialog box lets you select objects that form the boundary for hatching.

9. You can use the _____ option after you have selected the area to be hatched to see the hatching before it is actually applied.

10. By selecting the _____ button you can apply hatching in the area specified by the hatch boundary.

11. When a boundary set is formed, it does not become the default for hatching. (T/F)

12. The selection of **Normal** hatch style carries meaning only if the objects to be hatched are _____.

13. In Nearest ray casting, AutoCAD casts an imaginary ray in all directions and locates the object

that is _____ to the point that you have selected.

14. You can edit the hatch boundary by using grips. (T/F)

15. Different filling patterns make it possible to distinguish between different parts or components of an object. (T/F)

Review Questions

1. The hatching process can be accomplished by using the _____ or _____ command.

2. The hatch boundary may be comprised of Line, Circle, Arc, Plines, 3D face, or other objects, and each must be at least partially displayed within the active viewport. (T/F)

3. ・・・**BHATCH** command does not allow you to hatch a region enclosed within a boundary (closed area) by selecting a point inside the boundary. (T/F)

4. One of the advantages of the _____ command is that you don't have to select each object comprising the boundary of the area you want to hatch, as in the case of the _____ command.

5. You can cycle through the predefined hatch patterns by selecting the image box. (T/F)

6. If the **Double** hatch box is selected, AutoCAD sets the _____ system variable to 1.

7. The **Iso Pen Width** option is valid only for _____ .

8. One way to select a predefined hatch pattern is to select the **Custom** pattern type and then enter the name of the stored hatch pattern in the **Custom Pattern:** edit box. (T/F)

9. If AutoCAD does not locate the entered pattern in the ACAD.PAT file, it does not load any hatch pattern file. (T/F)

10. The _____ option lets you scale the hatch pattern.

11. A **Boundary Definition Error** dialog box is displayed if AutoCAD finds that the selected point is inside the boundary or that the boundary is not closed. (T/F)

12. The _____ option is used to remove the islands from the hatching area.

13. The _____ option lets you view the selected boundary.

14. If you want to have the same hatching pattern, style, and properties as that of an existing hatch on the screen, select the _____ button.

15. The **Associative** button controls the _____ of hatch with the hatch boundary.

16. You can improve the speed of hatching by setting parameters in the **Advanced Options** dialog box. (T/F)

17. The **Object Type** option in the **Advanced Options** dialog box controls the type of object AutoCAD will create when you define a boundary. It has two options: _____ and _____.

18. The hatching style cannot be specified by selecting a style from the **Style** list box. (T/F)

19. There are three hatching styles from which you can choose: _____, _____, and _____.

20. If you select the **Ignore** style, all areas bounded by the outermost boundary are hatched, ignoring any hatch boundaries that are within the outer boundary. (T/F)

21. Ray casting is enabled only when Island detection is turned on. (T/F)

22. You can use ray casting options to control the way AutoCAD casts the ray to form a hatch boundary. The available options are _____, _____, _____, _____, and _____.

23. The **HATCHEDIT** command can be used to edit the hatch pattern. (T/F)

24. You can also edit the hatch pattern from the Command prompt line by preceding the **BHATCH** command with a dash (-). (T/F)

25. When you use editing commands such as **MOVE, COPY, SCALE, STRETCH,** and **MIRROR,** associativity is lost. (T/F)

26. If you explode an associative hatch pattern, the associativity between the hatch pattern and the defining boundary is not affected. (T/F)

27. The hatching procedure in AutoCAD does not work on inserted blocks. (T/F)

28. If the block comprises objects such as arcs, circles or pline arc segments, it must be exploded before hatching. (T/F)

29. To align the hatches in adjacent hatch areas, you can use the _____ variable.

30. The specified hatch spacing value is stored in the _____ system variable.

Exercises

Exercise 5   *Mechanical*

Hatch the drawings in Figures 11-41 and 11-42 using the hatch pattern to match.

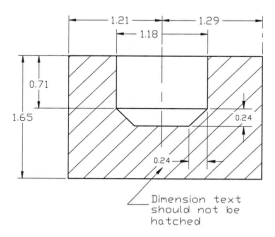

Figure 11-41 *Drawing for Exercise 5*

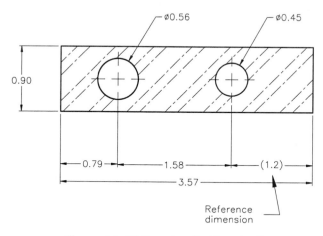

Figure 11-42 *Drawing for Exercise 5*

Exercise 6 *General*

Hatch the drawing in Figure 11-43 using the hatch pattern ANSI31. Use the **SNAPBASE** variable to align the hatch lines as shown in the drawing.

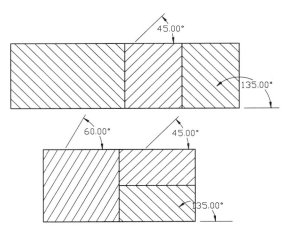

Figure 11-43 Drawign for Exercise 6

Exercise 7 *Mechanical*

Figure 11-44 shows the top and front views of an object. It also shows the cutting plane line. Based on the cutting plane line, hatch the front views in section. Use the hatch pattern of your choice.

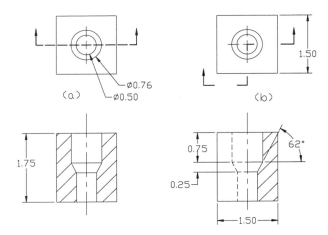

Figure 11-44 Drawign for Exercise 7

Exercise 8   *Mechanial*

Figure 11-45 shows the top and front views of an object. Hatch the front view in full section. Use the hatch pattern of your choice.

Figure 11-45 Drawing for Exercise 8

Exercise 9   *Mechanial*

Figure 11-46 shows the front and side views of an object. Hatch the side view in half-section. Use the hatch pattern of your choice.

Figure 11-46 Drawign for Exercise 9

Problem-Solving Exercise 1   *Mechanical*

Figure 11-47 shows the front and side views of an object. Hatch the aligned section view. Use the hatch pattern of your choice.

Figure 11-47 *Drawing for Problem-Solving Exercise 1*

Problem-Solving Exercise 2   *Mechanical*

Figure 11-48 shows the front view, side view, and the detail "A" of an object. Hatch the side view and draw the detail drawing as shown.

Figure 11-48 *Drawing for Problem-Solving Exercise 2*

Answers to Self-Evaluation Test
1 - T, **2** - **BHATCH, HATCH, 3** - **BHATCH, 4** - T, **5** - T, **6** - ACAD.PAT, **7** - Angle, **8** - Select Objects, **9** - Preview, **10** - Apply, **11** - F, **12** - Nested, **13** - Nearest, **14** - T, **15** - T

Chapter 12

Blocks

After completing this chapter, you will be able to*:*
* *Create blocks with the **BLOCK** command.*
* *Insert blocks with the **INSERT** and **MINSERT** commands.*
* *Perform editing operations on blocks.*
* *Create drawing files using the **WBLOCK** command.*
* *Split a block into individual objects using the **EXPLODE** and **XPLODE** commands.*
* *Define the insertion basepoint for a drawing.*
* *Rename blocks and delete unused blocks.*

THE CONCEPT OF BLOCKS

The ability to store parts of a drawing, or the entire drawing, so that they need not be redrawn when needed again in the same drawing or another drawing is extremely beneficial to the user. These parts of a drawing, entire drawings, or symbols (also known as blocks) can be placed (inserted) in a drawing at the location of your choice, in the desired orientation, with the desired scale factor. The block is given a name (block name) and the block is referenced (inserted) by its name. All the objects within a block are treated as a single object. You can **MOVE, ERASE,** or **LIST** the block as a single object; that is, you can select the entire block simply by selecting a point on it. As far as the edit and inquiry commands are concerned, the internal structure of a block is immaterial, since a block is treated as a primitive object, like a polygon. If a block definition is changed, all references to the block in the drawing are updated to incorporate the changes made to the block.

A block can be created using the **BLOCK** command. You can also create a drawing file using the **WBLOCK** command. The main difference between the two is that a wblock can be inserted in any other drawing, but a block can be inserted only in the drawing file in which it was created.

Another feature of AutoCAD is that instead of inserting a symbol as a block (which results in adding the content of the referenced drawing to the drawing in which it is inserted), you can reference drawings (Xref). This means that the contents of the referenced drawing are not added to the current drawing file, although they become part of that drawing on the screen. This is explained in detail in Chapter 14, External References.

Advantages of Using Blocks

Blocks offer many advantages; here are some of them.

1. Drawings often have some repetitive feature. Instead of drawing the same feature again and again, you can create a block of that feature and insert it wherever required. This style of working helps you to reduce drawing time and better organize your work.
2. Another advantage of using blocks is that they can be drawn and stored for future use. You can thus create a custom library of objects required for different applications. For example, if your drawings are concerned with gears, you could create blocks of gears and then integrate these blocks with custom menus (see the customizing section). In this manner, you could create an application environment of your own in AutoCAD.
3. The size of a drawing file increases as you add objects to it. AutoCAD keeps track of information about the size and position of each object in the drawing; for example, the points, scale factors, radii; and so on. If you combine several objects into a single object by forming a block out of them with the **BLOCK** command, there will be a single scale factor, rotation angle, position, and so on, for all objects in the block, thereby saving storage space. Each object repeated in multiple block insertions needs to be defined only once in the block definition. Ten insertions of a gear made of 43 lines and 41 arcs require only 94 objects (10 + 43 + 41), while ten individually drawn gears require 840 objects [10 x (43+41)].
4. If the specification for an object changes, the drawing needs to be modified. This is a very tedious task if you need to detect each location where the change is to be made and edit it individually. But if this object has been defined as a block, you can redefine it, and everywhere the object appears it is revised automatically (Figure 12-1).

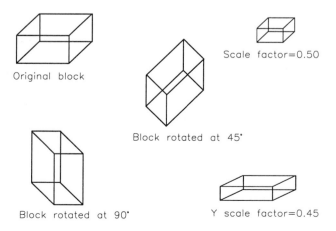

Figure 12-1 Block with different specifications

5. Attributes (textual information) can be included in blocks. Different attribute values can be specified in each insertion of a block.

6. You can create symbols and then store them as blocks with the **BLOCK** command. Later on, with the **INSERT** command, you can insert the blocks in the drawing in which they were defined. There is no limit to the number of times you can insert a block in a drawing.

7. You can store symbols as drawing files using the **WBLOCK** command and later insert those symbols into any other drawing using the **INSERT** command.

8. Blocks can have varying X, Y, and Z scales and rotation angles from one insertion to another.

FORMATION OF BLOCKS
Drawing Objects for Blocks

The first step in creating blocks is to draw the object(s) to be converted into a block. You can consider any symbol, shape, or view that may be used more than once for conversion into a block (Figure 12-2). Even a drawing that is to be used more than once can be inserted as a block. If you do not have the object to be converted into a block, use the relevant AutoCAD commands to draw it.

Figure 12-2 Symbols created to store in a library

Checking Layers

You should be particularly careful about the layers on which the objects to be converted into a block are drawn. The objects must be drawn on layer 0 if you want the block to inherit the linetype and color of the layer on which it is inserted. If you want the block to retain the linetype and color of the layer on which it was drawn, draw the objects defining the block on that layer. For example, if you want the block to have the linetype and color of layer OBJ, draw the objects comprising the block on layer OBJ. Now, even if you insert the block on any layer, the linetype and color of the block will be those of layer OBJ. If the objects in a block are drawn with the color, linetype, and lineweight as BYBLOCK, this block when inserted assumes the properties of the current layer. To change the layer associated with an object, use the **Object Properties Window**, **LAyer** option of the **CHPROP** command or any other relevant command.

CONVERTING OBJECTS INTO A BLOCK
BLOCK Command

Toolbar:	Draw > Make Block
Menu:	Draw > Block > Make...
Command:	BLOCK, BMAKE

Figure 12-3 Make Block button in the Draw toolbar

When you invoke the **BMAKE** or **BLOCK** command, the **Block Definition** dialog box (Figure 12-5) is displayed. You can use the **Block Definition** dialog box to save any object as a block.

Command: **BMAKE** or **BLOCK** [Enter]

In the **Block Definition** dialog box, you can enter the name of the block you want to create or redefine, in the **Name:** edit box. The block name can have upto 255 characters. The name can contain letters, digits, blank spaces as well as special characters like the $ (dollar sign), - (hyphen), and _ (underscore) if they are not being used for any other

Figure 12-4 Invoking the BLOCK command from the Draw menu

purpose by AutoCAD. The block name is controlled by the **EXTNAME** system variable and the default value is 1. If the **EXTNAME** is set to 0, the block name can be only 31 characters long.

If a block already exists with the block name that you have specified in the **Name:** edit box, an AutoCAD dialog box, warning that the block name already exists, is displayed at the time of choosing the **OK** button in the **Block Definition** dialog box. In this dialog box, you can either redefine the existing block by choosing the **Yes** button or you can exit it by choosing the **No** button.

After you have specified a block name, you are required to specify the insertion base point. This point is used as a reference point to insert the block. Usually, either the center of the block or the lower left corner of the block is defined as the insertion base point. Later on, when you insert the block, you will notice that the block appears at the insertion point, and you can insert the block with reference to this point. The point you specify as the insertion base point is taken as the origin point of the block's coordinate system. You can specify the insertion point by choosing the **Pick Base Point** button in the **Base Point** area of the dialog box. The dialog box is temporarily removed, and you can select a base point on the screen. You can also enter the coordinates in the **X:**, **Y:**, and **Z:** edit boxes instead of selecting a point on screen.

Figure 12-5 Block Definition dialog box

After specifying the Insertion Base point, you are required to select the objects that will constitute the block. Until the objects are not selected, AutoCAD displays a warning: **No objects selected**, at the bottom of the **Objects** area. Choose the **Select Objects** button. The dialog box is temporarily removed from the screen. You can select the objects on the screen using any selection method. After completing the selection process, right-click or press the ENTER key to return to the dialog box.

The **Object** area of the **Block Definition** dialog box also has a **Quick Select** button. If you choose this button, the **Quick Select** dialog box is displayed which allows you to define a selection set based on properties of objects. **Quick select** is used in cases where the drawings are very large and complicated. In this area, selecting the **Retain** radio button, retains the selected objects that form the block as individual objects and does not convert them into a block after the block has been defined. Selecting the **Convert to Block** radio button (default option), converts the selected objects into a block after you have defined the block and selecting the **Delete** radio button, deletes the selected objects from the drawing after the block has been defined. After objects have been selected, the bottom of the **Object** area displays the number of objects selected in the drawing to form the particular block.

The **Preview Icon** area, gives you the following options: Selecting the **Do not include an icon** radio button, does not create a preview icon and the **Preview Image box** is not displayed in this area of the dialog box. Selecting the **Create icons from block geometry** radio button creates a **Preview icon** which is saved with the block definition in the drawing. Whenever you select a block name in the **Name:** drop-down list of the **Block Definition** dialog box or the **AutoCAD Design**

Center, a Preview image is displayed. Similarly, in the **Description:** text box, if you have entered a description of the block, it is stored with the block definition and displayed on selecting the block name in the **Name:** drop-down list of the **Block Definition** dialog box or the **AutoCAD DesignCenter**. Adding a preview image and description text in the block definition, makes it easier to identify a block.

The **Insert Units:** drop-down list displays the units the inserted block in the drawing will be scaled to on insertion. The default value is Unitless.

The **Name:** drop-down list displays all the blocks defined in that drawing. This drop-down list contains the list of all the block names created in the drawing. This way you can verify whether the block you have defined has been saved. Choose the **OK** button to complete defining the block.

-BLOCK Command

You can use the **-BLOCK** command to create blocks from the command line. The following prompt sequence saves a symbol as a block named SYMBOLX.

Command: **-BLOCK** ⏎
Enter block name or [?]: SYMBOLX ⏎
Specify insertion base point: *Select a point.*
Select objects: *Select all the objects comprising the block.*
Select objects: *Press ENTER when selection is complete.*

AutoCAD acknowledges the creation of the block by removing the objects defining the block from the screen. However, you can get the objects back at the same position by entering **OOPS**.

You can use the **?** option to list all the blocks created in the drawing. The prompt sequence is:

Command: **-BLOCK** ⏎
Enter block name or [?]: ? ⏎
Enter block(s) to list <*>: ⏎

Information similar to the following is displayed in the AutoCAD Text Window:

Defined blocks
"BLK1"
"BLK2"
"SYMBOLX"

User	*External*	*Dependent*	*Unnamed*
Blocks	*References*	*Blocks*	*Blocks*
n	*n*	*n*	*n*

Here **n** denotes a numeric value.

Defined blocks. The names of all the blocks defined in the drawing.

User blocks. The number of blocks created by the user.

External references. The number of external references. These are the drawings that are referenced with the **XREF** command.

Dependent blocks. The number of externally dependent blocks. These are the blocks that are present in a referenced drawing.

Unnamed blocks. The number of unnamed blocks in the drawing. These are objects, such as associative dimensions and hatch patterns.

Exercise 1 *General*

Draw a unit radius circle, and use the **BLOCK** command to create a block. Name the block CIRCLE. Select the center as the insertion point. Use the **?** option of the **-BLOCK** command to see if the block CIRCLE was saved. Figure 12-6 shows the steps involved in creating a block.

*Figure 12-6 Using the **BLOCK** command*

INSERTING BLOCKS

Insertion of a predefined block is possible with the **INSERT** or **DDINSERT** command. With these commands, insertion is carried out using the **Insert** dialog box. In the case of the **-INSERT** command, you can insert a block by entering this command at the command line. You should determine the layer on which you want to insert the block, the location where you want to insert it, its size, and the angle by which you want the block to be rotated. If the layer on which you want to insert the block is not current, you can use the **Current** button in the **Layer Properties Manager** dialog box to make it current.

INSERT COMMAND

Toolbar:	Insert > Insert Block
	Draw > Insert
Menu:	Insert > Block...
Command:	INSERT

Figure 12-7 Invoking the INSERT command from the Insert toolbar

Figure 12-8 Invoking the INSERT command from the Insert menu

When you invoke the **INSERT** command, the **Insert** dialog box (Figure 12-9) is displayed on the screen. You can specify the different parameters of the block to be inserted in the **Insert** dialog box.

Figure 12-9 Insert dialog box

Name: Edit Box

This edit box is used to specify the name of the block to be inserted. Enter the name of the block to be inserted. You can also select the Block name from the **Name:** drop-down list. The **Browse...** button is used to insert external files. Choosing this button displays the **Select Drawing File** dialog box from where you can select a file to be inserted as a block. In the **Insert** dialog box, whichever block name you select from the **Name:** drop-down list, is displayed in the **Name:** edit box. For example, to insert a block named BLK1, select this name from the **Name:** drop-down list or enter it in the **Name:** edit box. **Path:** displays the path of the block or file to be inserted.

If you want to insert a drawing file as a block, choose the **Browse** button in the **Insert** dialog box. When you choose the **Browse** button, the **Select Drawing File** dialog box (Figure 12-10) is displayed. You can select the drawing file from the listed drawing files existing in the current directory. You can change the directory by selecting the desired directory in the **Look in:** drop-down list. Once you select the drawing file in this dialog box and choose the **Open** button, the drawing file name is displayed in the **Name:** drop-down list of the **Insert** dialog box. If you want to change the block name, just change the name in the **Name:** edit box. In this manner, the drawing can be inserted with a different block name. Changing the original drawing does not affect the inserted drawing.

Figure 12-10 Select Drawing File dialog box

Insertion Point

When a block is inserted, the coordinate system of the block is aligned parallel to the current UCS. In this area, you can specify the X, Y, and Z coordinate locations of the block insertion point. If you select the **Specify On-screen** check box, you can specify the insertion point on the screen. By default, the **Specify On-screen** check box is selected; hence, you can specify the insertion point with a pointing device.

Scale

In this area, you can specify the X, Y, and Z scale factors of the block to be inserted. By selecting the **Specify On-screen** check box, you can specify the scale of the block at which it has to be inserted, on the screen. If the **Uniform scale** check box is selected, the X scale factor value is assumed by the Y and Z scale factors. All the dimensions in the block are multiplied by the X, Y, and Z scale factors you specify. By specifying negative scale factors for X and Y, you can obtain a mirror image of the block. These scale factors allow you to stretch or compress a block along the X and Y axes, respectively, according to your needs. You can also insert 3D objects into a drawing by specifying the third scale factor (since 3D objects have three dimensions): the Z scale factor. Figure 12-11 shows variations of the X and Y scale factors for the block, CIRCLE, during insertion.

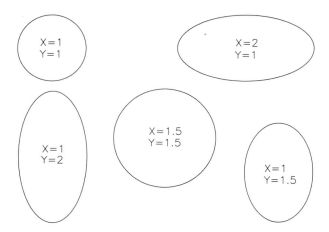

Figure 12-11 Block inserted with different scale factors

Rotation

You can enter the angle of rotation for the block to be inserted in the **Angle:** edit box. The insertion point is taken as the location about which rotation takes place. Selecting the **Specify On-screen** check box allows you to specify the angle of rotation on the screen.

Explode Check Box

By selecting this check box, the inserted block is inserted as a collection of individual objects. The function of the **Explode** check box is identical to that of the **EXPLODE** command. Once a block is exploded, the X, Y, and Z scale factors are identical. Hence, you are provided access to only one scale factor edit box (X scale factor). This scale factor is assigned to the Y and Z scale factors. You must enter a positive scale factor value.

After entering the relevant information in the dialog box, choose the **OK** button. Once you do so, the **Insert** dialog box is removed from the screen and if you have selected the **Specify On-Screen** check boxes, you can specify the insertion point, scale, and angle of rotation with a pointing device or at the command line. The following prompts appear in the command line:

Specify insertion point:
Enter X scale factor or specify opposite corner <1>:
Enter Y scale factor <Use X scale factor>:
Specify rotation angle <0>:

You can also specify these features in the **Insert** dialog box. When you clear the **Specify On-screen** check box, it activates the **Insertion Point**, **Scale**, and **Rotation** areas in the dialog box. Now you can enter these parameters in the respective edit boxes.

-INSERT COMMAND

Command: -INSERT

As mentioned before, predefined blocks can also be inserted in a drawing with the **-INSERT** command. The following is the prompt sequence for the **-INSERT** command:

Command: **-INSERT** [Enter]
Enter block name or [?] <Current>: *Enter the name of the block to be inserted.*

To display the list of blocks in the drawing, enter ? at the **Enter block name or [?]:** prompt. The next prompt issued is:

Enter block(s) to list <*>: [Enter]

If you press ENTER at this prompt, AutoCAD displays the list of blocks available in the current drawing. If you want to insert a drawing file as a block, enter the file name at the **Enter block name or [?]:** prompt. To create a block with a different name from the drawing file, enter **blockname= file name** at the **Enter block name or[?]:** prompt. If you enter ~ (tilde character) at the **Enter block name or [?]:** prompt, the **Select Drawing File** dialog box is displayed on the screen. If you enter an * (asterisk) before entering the block name, the block is automatically exploded upon insertion.

The next prompt asks you to specify the insertion point. The insertion point can be selected accurately by selecting or by using Osnaps. You can also enter the coordinate values of the insertion point. If you make changes to a block and want to update the block in the existing drawing, enter **blockname=** at the **Specify insertion point:** prompt. AutoCAD will display the prompt:

Block "current" already exists. Redefine it? [Yes/No] <No>: *Enter y to redefine it.*

The command prompt for specifying the insertion point is as follows:

Specify insertion point or [Scale/X/Y/Z/Rotate/PScale/PX/PY/PZ/PRotate]: *Select the point where you want the insertion base point for the block.*

The next two prompts ask you to specify X and Y scale factors.

Enter X scale factor, specify opposite corner or [Corner/XYZ]: *Select a point, enter a number, or press ENTER.*
Enter Y scale factor <Use X scale factor>: *Select a point, enter a number, or press ENTER.*

You can use the **XYZ** option to insert the 3D object. For this option, an additional prompt for specifying the Z scale factor is provided.

At the next prompt, you can specify the angle of rotation for the block to be inserted.

Specify rotation angle <0>: *Select a point or enter an angle.*

You can enter the numeral value of the rotation angle at the **Specify rotation angle <0>:** prompt. You can also select a point to specify the angle. In this case, AutoCAD measures the angle of an imaginary line made by joining the insertion point and the point you have selected. The block is rotated by this angle.

Inserting the Mirror Image of a Block

Scaling of the block being inserted takes place by multiplying the X and Y dimensions of the block by the X and Y scale factors (specified in the **Enter X scale factor, specify opposite corner or [Corner/XYZ]:** and **Enter Y scale factor <Use X scale factor>:** prompts, respectively). If a negative value is specified for the X or Y scale factors, you can get a mirror image of a block. For instance, a scale factor of -1 for X and -1 for Y will mirror the block in the opposite quadrant of the coordinate system. There will be no change in the block size since the magnitude of the scale factor for X and Y variables is 1. For example, we have a block named RECTANGLE. The effect of negative scale factor on the block can be marked by a change in position of insertion point marked by a (X) (Figure 12-12) for the following prompt sequence:

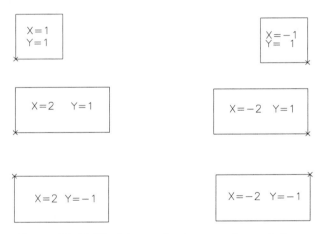

Figure 12-12 Block inserted using negative scale factors

Command: **-INSERT** [Enter]
Enter block name or [?]: RECTANGLE [Enter]
Specify insertion point or [Scale/X/Y/Z/Rotate/PScale/PX/PY/PZ/PRotate]: *Select a point.*
Enter X scale factor, specify opposite corner or [Corner/XYZ] <1>: -1 [Enter]
Enter Y scale factor [Use X scale factor]: -1 [Enter]
Specify rotation angle <0>: [Enter]

Using the Corner Option

With the **Corner** option, you can specify both X and Y scale factors at the same time. When you invoke this option, and **DRAGMODE** is turned off, you are prompted to specify the other corner (the first corner of the box is the insertion point). You can also enter a coordinate value instead of moving the cursor. The length and breadth of the box are taken as the X and Y scale factors for the block. For example, if the X and Y dimensions (length and width) of the box are the same as that of the block, the block will be drawn without any change. Points selected should be above and to the right of the insertion block. Mirror images will be produced if points selected are below or to the left of the insertion point. The prompt sequence is:

Command:**-INSERT** `Enter`
Enter block name or [?]: SQUARE `Enter`
Specify insertion point or [Scale/X/Y/Z/Rotate/PScale/PX/PY/PZ/PRotate]: *Select a point.*
Enter X scale factor, specify opposite corner or [Corner/XYZ]: C `Enter`
Specify opposite corner: *Select a point as the corner.*

The **Corner** option also allows you to use a dynamic scaling technique when **DRAGMODE** is turned on (default). You can also move the cursor at the **Enter X scale factor...** prompt to change the block size dynamically and, when the size meets your requirements, select a point.

Note
*You should try to avoid using the **Corner** option if you want to have identical X and Y scale factors because it is difficult to select a point whose X distance = Y distance, unless the **SNAP** mode is on. If you use the **Corner** option, it is better to specify the X and Y scale factors explicitly or select the corner by entering coordinates.*

Example 1

Using the dialog box, insert a block SQUARE into a drawing. The block insertion point is (1,2). The X scale factor is 2 units, the Y scale factor is 2 units, and the angle of rotation is 35 degrees. It is assumed that the block SQUARE is already defined in the current drawing.

Command: **INSERT** `Enter`

The **Insert** dialog box is displayed on the screen. In the **Name:** edit box, enter SQUARE or select the Block SQUARE from the **Name:** drop-down list. Clear the **Specify On-screen** check box. Now, under the **Insertion point** area, enter 1 in the **X:** edit box and 2 in the **Y:** edit box. Under the **Scale** area, enter 2 in the **X:** edit box and 2 in the **Y:** edit box. Under **Rotation**, enter 35 in the **Angle:** edit box. Choose the **OK** button to insert the block on the screen.

Exercise 2
General

a. Insert the block CIRCLE created in Exercise 1. Use different X and Y scale factors to get different shapes after inserting this block.
b. Insert the block CIRCLE created in Exercise 1. Use the **Corner** option to specify the scale factor.

PRESETTING THE ROTATION, ANGLE, AND SCALE FACTORS

The scale factor and the rotation of a block can be preset before specifying the block's position of insertion. This option is ideal if you want to see the scale and/or angle of the block while the block is being dragged before actually being inserted into the drawing. Once you preset any or both scale factors and angles of rotation, the effect of these values is reflected in the image of the block. For the options with P as a prefix, the preset values can be negated, if desired, when inserting the block. To realize the presetting function, enter one of the following options at the **Specify insertion point:** prompt.

Scale	**Xscale**	**Yscale**	**Zscale**	**Rotate**
PScale	**PXscale**	**PYscale**	**PZscale**	**PRotate**

Scale

If you enter Scale at the **Specify Insertion point:** prompt, you are asked to enter the scale factor. After entering the scale factor, the block assumes the specified scale factor, and AutoCAD lets you drag the block until you locate the insertion point on the screen. The X, Y, and Z axes are uniformly scaled by the specified scale factor. Once the insertion point is specified, you are not prompted for the scale factors, so you cannot change the scale factor, and the block is drawn with the previously specified (preview) scale factor. When you use the **Scale** option the prompt sequence is:

Command: **-INSERT** [Enter]
Enter block name or [?]<current>: *Enter the block name.*
Specify insertion point or [Scale/X/Y/Z/Rotate/PScale/PX/PY/PZ/PRotate]: **SCALE** [Enter]
Specify scale factor for XYZ axes: *Enter a value to preset general scale factor.*
Specify insertion point: *Select the insertion point.*
Specify rotation angle <0>: *Specify angle of rotation.*

X

With **X** as the response to the **Specify insertion point:** prompt, you can specify the X scale factor before specifying the insertion point. This option works similarly to the **Scale** option. The prompt sequence when you use the **X** option is:

Command: **-INSERT** [Enter]
Enter block name or [?]: *Enter the block name.*
Specify insertion point or [Scale/X/Y/Z/Rotate/PScale/PX/PY/PZ/PRotate]: X [Enter]
Specify X scale factor: *Enter a value to preset X scale factor.*
Specify insertion point: *Select the insertion point.*
Specify rotation angle <0>: *Specify angle of rotation.*

Y

With **Y** as the response to the **Specify insertion point:** prompt, you can specify the Y scale factor before specifying the insertion point. This option works similarly to the **Scale** option.

Z

If you enter **Z** at the **Specify insertion point:** prompt, you are asked to specify the Z scale factor before specifying the insertion point.

Rotate

If you enter **Rotate** at the **Specify insertion point:** prompt, you are asked to specify the rotation angle. You can specify the angle by specifying two points. Dragging is resumed only when you specify the angle, and the block assumes the specified rotation angle. Once the insertion point is specified, you cannot change the rotation angle, and the block is drawn with the previously specified rotation angle. The prompt sequence for this option is:

Command: **-INSERT** [Enter]
Enter block name or [?]: *Enter the block name.*
Specify insertion point or [Scale/X/Y/Z/Rotate/PScale/PX/PY/PZ/PRotate]: ROTATE [Enter]
Specify rotation angle: *Enter a value to preview the rotation angle.*
Specify insertion point: *Select the insertion point.*
Enter X scale factor, specify opposite corner, or [Corner/XYZ] <1>: *Specify the X scale factor.*
Enter Y scale factor <Use X scale factor>: *Specify the Y scale factor.*

PScale

The **PScale** option is similar to the **Scale** option. The difference is that in the case of the **PScale** option, the scale factor specified reflects only in the display of the block while it is dragged to a desired position. After you have specified the insertion point for the block, you are again prompted for a scale factor. If you do not enter the scale factor, the block is drawn exactly as it was when created. The prompt sequence for this option is:

Command: **-INSERT** [Enter]
Enter block name or [?]: *Enter the block name.*
Specify insertion point or [Scale/X/Y/Z/Rotate/PScale/PX/PY/PZ/PRotate]: PSCALE [Enter]
Specify preview scale factor for XYZ axes: *Enter a value to preview the general scale factor.*
Specify insertion point: *Specify the insertion point for the block.*
Enter X scale factor, specify opposite corner, or [Corner/XYZ] <1>: *Specify the X scale factor.*
Enter Y scale factor <Use X scale factor>: *Specify the Y scale factor.*
Specify rotation angle <0>: *Specify angle of rotation.*

PX

This option is similar to the **PScale** option. The only difference is that the X scale factor specified is reflected only in the display of the block while it is dragged to a desired position. After you have specified the insertion point for the block, you are again prompted for the X scale factor and the Y scale factor. If you do not enter the scale factor, the block is drawn exactly as it was when created.

Command: **-INSERT** [Enter]
Enter block name or [?]: *Enter the block name.*
Specify insertion point or [Scale/X/Y/Z/Rotate/PScale/PX/PY/PZ/PRotate]: PX [Enter]
Specify preview X scale factor: *Enter a value to preview the X scale factor.*
Specify insertion point: *Specify the insertion point for the block.*
Enter X scale factor, specify opposite corner, or [Corner/XYZ] <1>: *Specify the X scale factor.*
Enter Y scale factor <Use X scale factor>: *Specify the Y scale factor.*
Specify rotation angle <0>: *Specify angle of rotation.*

PY

This option is similar to the **PX** option. The difference is that in the **PY** option, you can preview the Y scale factor.

Chapter 12

PZ

This option is similar to the **PX** option. The difference is that in the **PZ** option, you can preview the Z scale factor.

PRotate

The **PRotate** option is similar to the **Rotate** option. The difference is that the rotation angle specified reflects only in the display of the block while it is dragged to a desired position. After you have specified the insertion point for the block, you are again prompted for an angle of rotation. If you do not enter the rotation angle, the block is drawn exactly as it was when created (with the same angle of rotation as specified on the creation of the block). The prompt sequence is:

Command: **-INSERT** [Enter]
Enter block name or [?] <current>: *Enter the block name.*
Specify insertion point or [Scale/X/Y/Z/Rotate/PScale/PX/PY/PZPRotate]: PROTATE [Enter]
Specify preview rotation angle: *Specify the preview value for rotation.*
Specify insertion point: Specify the insertion point for the block.
Enter X scale factor, specify opposite corner, or [Corner/XYZ]: Specify the X scale factor.
Enter Y scale factor < Use X scale factor>: *Specify the Y scale factor.*
Specify rotation angle <0>: *Specify angle of rotation.*

Exercise 3   *General*

a. Construct a triangle and form a block of it. Name the block TRIANGLE. Now, preset the Y scale factor so that on insertion, the Y scale factor of the inserted block is 2.
b. Insert the block TRIANGLE with preset rotation of 45 degrees. After defining the insertion point, enter an X and a Y scale factor of 2.

USING AUTOCAD DESIGNCENTER TO INSERT BLOCKS*

You can use the **AutoCAD DesignCenter** to copy or insert blocks from existing drawings to current drawings. On the **Standard** toolbar, choose the **AutoCAD DesignCenter** button to display the **AutoCAD Design Center** window. In this window, choose the **Tree View Toggle** and the **Desktop** buttons to display the **tree pane** on the left side. Expand **My Computer** to display the C:/Program/ACAD2000/Sample/Designcenter folder. Click on this folder to display its contents. Select a drawing file you wish to use to insert blocks from and click on the plus sign adjacent to the drawing. Select **Blocks** by clicking on it; a list of blocks in the drawing are displayed. Select the block you wish to insert and drag and drop the block into the current drawing. Now, you can move it to the desired location. You can also right-click on the block name to display a shortcut menu. Select the **Insert Block...** option from the shortcut menu. The **Insert** dialog box is displayed. Specify the **Insertion point, scale, rotation angle** in the respective edit boxes. If you select the **Specify On-Screen** check boxes you are allowed to specify these parameters on the screen.

LAYERS, COLORS, LINETYPES, AND LINEWEIGHTS* FOR BLOCKS

A block possesses the properties of the layer on which it is drawn. The block may comprise objects drawn on several different layers, with different colors, linetypes and lineweights. All this information is preserved in the block. At the time of insertion, each object in the block is drawn on its original layer with the original linetype, lineweight, and color, irrespective of the current drawing layer, object color, object linetype and object lineweights. You may want all instances of a block to have identical layer, linetype properties, lineweight, and color. This can be achieved by allocating all the properties explicitly to the objects forming the block. On the other hand, if you want the linetype and color of each instance of a block to be set according to the linetype and color of the layer on which it is inserted, draw all the objects forming the block on layer 0 and set the color, lineweight and linetype to BYLAYER. Objects with a BYLAYER color, linetype and lineweight can have their colors, linetypes, and lineweights changed after insertion by changing the layer settings. If you want the linetype, lineweight, and color of each instance of a block to be set according to the current explicit linetype, lineweight and color at the time of insertion, set the color, lineweight, and linetype of its objects to BYBLOCK. You can use the **PROPERTIES**, **CHPROP** or **CHANGE** command to change some of the characteristics associated with a block (such as layer). For a further description, refer to the **CHPROP** command or the **Properties** option of the **CHANGE** command [Chapter 16,Changing Properties and Points of an Object (**CHANGE** Command)].

 Note

The block is inserted on the layer that is current, but the objects comprising the block are drawn on the layers on which they were drawn when the block was being defined.

For example, assume block B1 includes a square and a triangle that were originally drawn on layer X and layer Y, respectively. Let the color assigned to layer X be red and to layer Y be green. Also, let the linetype assigned to layer X be continuous and for layer Y be hidden. Now, if we insert B1 on layer L1 with color yellow and linetype dot, block B1 will be on layer L1, but the square will be drawn on layer X with color red and linetype continuous, and the triangle will be drawn on layer Y with color green and linetype hidden.

The **BYLAYER** option instructs AutoCAD to give objects within the block the color and linetype of the layers on which they were created. There are three exceptions:

1. If objects are drawn on a special layer (layer 0), they are inserted on the current layer. These objects assume the characteristics of the current layer (the layer on which the block is inserted) at the time of insertion, and can be modified after insertion by changing that layer's settings.

2. Objects created with the special color BYBLOCK are generated with the color that is current at the time of insertion of the block. This color may be explicit or BYLAYER. You are thus allowed to construct blocks that assume the current object color.

3. Objects created with the special linetype BYBLOCK are generated with the linetype that is prevalent at the time the block is inserted. Blocks are thus constructed with the current object linetype, which may be BYLAYER or explicit.

 Note

If a block is inserted on a frozen layer, the block is not shown on the screen.

If you are providing drawing files to others for their use, using only BYLAYER settings provide the greatest compatibility with varying office standards for layer/ color/ linetype, and so on, because they can more easily be changed after insertion.

NESTING OF BLOCKS

The concept of having one block within another block is known as the **nesting of blocks**. For example, you can insert several blocks and then select them with the **BLOCK** command to create another block. Similarly, if you use the **INSERT** command to insert a drawing that contains several blocks into the current drawing, it creates a block containing nested blocks in the current drawing. There is no limit to the degree of nesting. The only limitation in nesting of blocks is that blocks that reference themselves cannot be inserted. The nested blocks must have different block names. Nesting of blocks affects layers, colors, and linetypes. The general rule is:

If an inner block has objects on layer 0, or objects with linetype or color BYBLOCK, these objects may be said to behave like fluids. They "float up" through the nested block structure until they find an outer block with fixed color, layer, or linetype. These objects then assume the characteristics of the fixed layer. If a fixed layer is not found in the outer blocks, then the objects with color or linetype BYBLOCK are formed; that is, they assume the color white and the linetype CONTINUOUS.

To make the concept of nested blocks clear, consider the following example:

Example 2

1. Draw a rectangle on layer 0, and form a block of it named X.
2. Change the current layer to OBJ, and set its color to red and linetype to hidden.
3. Draw a circle on OBJ layer.
4. Insert the block X in the OBJ layer.
5. Combine the circle with the block X (rectangle) to form a block Y.
6. Now, insert block Y in any layer (say, layer CEN) with color green and linetype continuous.

You will notice that block Y is generated in color red and linetype hidden. Normally, block X, which is nested in block Y and created on layer 0, should have been generated in the color (green) and linetype (continuous) of the layer CEN. The reason for this is that the object (rectangle) on layer 0 floated up through the nested block structure and assumed the color and linetype of the first outer block (Y) with a fixed color (red), layer (OBJ), and linetype (hidden). If both the blocks (X and Y) were on layer 0, the objects in block Y would assume color and linetype of the layer on which the block was inserted.

Exercise 4   *General*

1. Change the color of layer 0 to red.
2. Draw a circle and form a block of it, B1, with color BYBLOCK. It appears white because color is set to BYBLOCK.
3. Set the color to BYLAYER and draw a rectangle. The color of the rectangle is red.
4. Insert block B1. Notice that the block B1 (circle) assumes red color.
5. Create another block B2 consisting of Block B1 (circle) and rectangle.
6. Create a layer L1 with green color and hidden linetype. Insert block B2 in layer L1.
7. Explode block B2. Notice the change.
8. Explode block B1, circle. You will notice that the circle changes to white because it was drawn with color set to BYBLOCK.

Exercise 5   *General*

Part A
1. Draw a unit square on layer 0 and make it a block named B1.
2. Make a circle with radius 0.5 and change it into block B2 (Figure 12-13).
3. Insert block B1 into a drawing with an X scale factor of 3 and a Y scale factor of 4.
4. Now, insert the block B2 in the drawing and position it at the top of B1.
5. Make a block of the entire drawing and name it PLATE.
6. Insert the block Plate in the current layer.
7. Create a new layer with different colors and linetypes and insert blocks B1, B2, and Plate.

Keep in mind the layers on which the individual blocks and the inserted block were made.

Part B
Try nesting the blocks drawn on different layers and with different linetypes.

Part C
Change the layers and colors of the different blocks you have drawn so far.

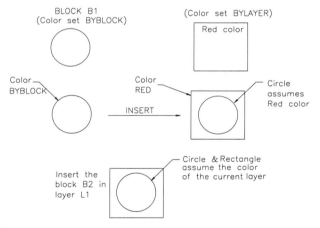

Figure 12-13 Blocks versus layers and colors

INSERTING MULTIPLE BLOCKS (MINSERT COMMAND)

Command: MINSERT

The **MINSERT** (multiple insert) command is used for multiple insertion of a block. This command comprises features of the **INSERT** and **ARRAY** commands. **MINSERT** is similar to the **-INSERT** command because it is used to insert blocks at the command level. The difference between these two commands is that the **MINSERT** command inserts more than one copy of the block in a rectangular fashion, similar to the command **ARRAY** and blocks inserted by **MINSERT** cannot be exploded. Preceding the block name with an asterisk does not explode it on insertion. With the **MINSERT** command, only one block reference is created. But, in addition to the standard features of a block definition (insert point, X/Y scaling, and rotation angle, among others), this block has repeated row and column counts. In this manner, using this command saves time and disk space. The prompt sequence is very similar to that of the **-INSERT** and **ARRAY** commands, for example, if you want to create an array with a block named BENCH with the following specifications: number of rows = 4, number of columns = 3, unit cell distance between rows = 0.50, unit cell distance between columns = 2.0:

The prompt sequence for creating this arrangement of benches in an auditorium (Figure 12-14) is:

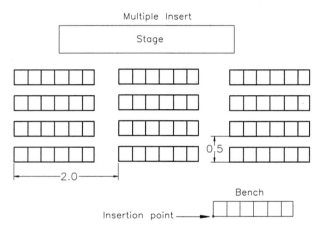

Figure 12-14 *Arrangement of benches in an auditorium*

Command: **MINSERT** [Enter]
Enter block name or [?] <current>: BENCH [Enter]
Specify insertion point or [Scale/X/Y/Z/Rotate/PScale/PX/PY/PZ/PRotate]: *Specify the insertion point.*
Enter X scale factor, specify opposite corner or [Corner/XYZ] <1>: [Enter]
Enter Y scale factor <Use X scale factor>: [Enter]
Specify rotation angle <0>: [Enter]
Enter number of rows (---)<1>: 4 [Enter]
Enter number of columns (|||) <1>: 3 [Enter]
Enter distance between rows or specify unit cell (—): 0.50 [Enter]
Specify distance between columns (|||): 2.0 [Enter]

The responses to these prompts will be clear after you use the **-INSERT** and **ARRAY** commands. The prompts pertaining to the number of rows and the number of columns require a positive nonzero integer. For the number of rows exceeding 1, you are prompted to specify the distance between the rows; if the number of columns exceeds 1, you need to specify the distance between columns. The distance between rows and columns can be a positive or a negative value. While inserting a block, if you specify block rotation, each copy of the inserted block is rotated. If you specify the rotation angle in the **MINSERT** command, the whole **MINSERT** block (array) is rotated by the specified rotation angle. If both the block and the **MINSERT** block (array) are rotated, the block does not seem rotated in the **MINSERT** pattern. This is the same as inserting an array with the rotation angle equal to 0 degrees. If you want to rotate individual blocks within the array, you should first generate a rotated block and then **MINSERT** it. The ? option of the **Enter block name or [?]:** prompt lists the names of the blocks.

When you specify the insertion point, AutoCAD prompts you for the scale factors. The options are X scale factor, Corner, and XYZ. The X scale factor is the default option and pressing ENTER at the **Enter X scale factor, specify opposite corner or [Corner/XYZ] <1>:** prompt prompts you to enter the Y scale factor. By default, Y scale factor uses the X scale factor. Using the **Corner** option, sets the scale factor by using the insertion point as the starting point and the opposite corner can be specified on screen. The command prompts on using the **Corner** option are as follows:

> Command: **MINSERT**
> Enter block name or [?]<current>:
> Specify insertion point or [Scale/X/Y/Z/Rotate/PX/PY/PZ/PRotate]: Specify *the insertion point.*
> Enter X scale factor, specify opposite corner or [Corner/XYZ] <1>: c
> Specify opposite corner: *Specify a point as the opposite corner.*
> Specify rotation angle <0>:
> Enter number of rows (---)<1>:
> Enter number of columns (|||) <1>:
> Enter distance between rows or specify unit cell(---): *Specify the distance between rows.*
> Specify distance between columns: *Specify distance between columns.*

The **XYZ** option sets the X, Y, and Z scale factors. It prompts for the X, Y, Z scale factors separately, as follows:

> Command: **MINSERT**
> Enter block name or [?] <current>: *Enter block name to insert as an array.*
> Specify insertion point or [Scale/X/Y/Z/Rotate/PScale/PX/PY/PZ/PRotate]: *Specify insertion point.*
> Enter X scale factor, specify opposite corner or [Corner/XYZ] <1>: xyz
> Specify X scale factor or [Corner] <1>: *Enter a value, press ENTER to accept the default value or type c to use the corner option.*
> Enter Y scale factor <Use X scale factor>: *Enter a value or press ENTER.*
> Specify Z scale factor <Use Z scale factor>: *Enter a value or press ENTER.*
> Specify rotation angle <0>: *Enter a value or accept default by pressing ENTER.*
> Enter number of rows (---) <1>: *Enter a positive integer.*
> Enter number of columns (|||) <1>: *Enter a positive integer.*
> Enter distance between rows or specify unit cell: *Specify a unit cell by selecting two points on screen that form a box whose width and height represent the distance between columns and rows.*

Presetting the scale factors and angle of rotation

Similar to the **-INSERT** command, when you use the **MINSERT** command, the scale factors and the angle of the block which is to be inserted can be preset and previewed prior to insertion. While using options which have P as a prefix, the preset values can be negated when finally inserting the block. The options available at the **Specify insertion point ..:** prompt are discussed next.

Scale. Sets the scale factor for the X, Y and Z axes.

Chapter 12

X. Sets the X scale factor.

Y. Sets the Y scale factor.

Z. Sets the Z scale factor.

Rotate. Sets the angle for the rotation of the array as well as the individual inserts.

PScale. Presets the preview scale for the X, Y, and Z axes before they are inserted into the specified position.

PX. Presets the preview scale factor for the X axis.

PY. Presets the preview scale factor for the Y axis.

PZ. Presets the preview scale factor for the Z axis.

PRotate. Presets the rotation angle for previewing before the object is inserted into position.

Note

*In the array of blocks generated with the use of the **MINSERT** command, you cannot alter the number of rows or columns or the spacing between them. The whole **MINSERT** pattern is considered one object that cannot be exploded.*

Exercise 6   *General*

1. Create a triangle with each side equal to 3 units.
2. Generate a block of the triangle.
3. Use the **MINSERT** command to insert the block to create a 3 by 3 array. The distance between the rows is 1 unit, and the distance between columns is 2 units.
4. Again, use the **MINSERT** command to insert the block to create a 3 by 3 array. The distance between the rows is 2 units and between the columns is 3 units, and the array is rotated 15 degrees.

CREATING DRAWING FILES (WBLOCK COMMAND)

Command: WBLOCK

The blocks or symbols created by the **BLOCK** command can be used only in the drawing in which they were created. This is a shortcoming because you may need to use a particular block in different drawings. The **WBLOCK** command is used to export symbols by writing them to new drawing files that can then be inserted in any drawing. With the **WBLOCK** command, you can create a drawing file (.DWG extension) of specified blocks or selected objects in the current drawing. All the used named objects (linetypes, layers, styles, system variables) of the current drawing are taken by the new drawing created with the **WBLOCK** command. This block can then be inserted in any drawing.

When the **WBLOCK** command is invoked, the **Write Block** dialog box is displayed (Figure 12-15).

This dialog box converts blocks into drawing files and also saves objects as drawing files. It has two main areas: the **Source** area and the **Destination** area.

Figure 12-15 Write Block dialog

The **Source** area allows you to select objects and blocks, specify insertion base points and convert them into drawing files. In this area of the dialog box, depending on the selection made by you, different default settings are displayed. If nothing is selected, the **Objects** radio button is shown as selected and in the **Destination** area, the **File Name:** edit box displays **new block.dwg** as the new file name. The **Block:** drop-down list is also not available. If a single block is selected, the **Block** radio button is shown as selected and the name of the selected block is displayed in the **Block:** edit box. **Base point** and **Objects** areas are not available. In the **Destination** area, **File Name:** edit box displays the name of the selected block. The **Block:** drop-down list displays all the block names in the current drawing. Selecting the **Entire drawing** radio button, selects the current drawing as a block and saves it as a file. Using this option, makes the **Base point** and **Objects** areas unavailable and is equivalent to entering **-WBLOCK/*** at the command line.

The **Base point** area allows you to specify the base point of a block which it uses as an insertion point. You can either enter values in the **X:**, **Y:**, and **Z:** edit boxes or choose the **Pick insertion point** button to select it on the screen. The default value is 0,0,0. The **Objects** area allows you to select objects to save as a file. You can use the **Select objects** button to select objects or use the **Quick select** button to set parameters in the **Quick Select** dialog box to select objects in the current drawing. If the **Retain** radio button is selected in the **Objects** area, the selected objects in the current drawing are kept as such after they have been saved as a new file. If the **Convert to block** radio button is selected, the selected objects in the current drawing are converted into a block with the same name as the new file after being saved as a new file. Selecting the **Delete** radio button deletes the selected objects from the current drawing after they have been saved as a file. The number of objects selected is displayed at the bottom of the **Objects** area.

The **Destination** area sets the File name, location and units of the new file in which the selected objects are saved. In the **File name:** edit box you can specify the file name of the block or the selected objects. From the **Location:** drop-down list you can select a path for the new file. You can also choose the [**...**] button to display the **Browse for folder** window, where you can specify a path for where the new file will be saved. From the **Insert Units:** drop-down list, you can select the units the new file will use when inserted as a block. The settings for units are stored in the **INSUNITS** system variable and the default option Unitless has a value of 0. On specifying the required information in the dialog box, choose **OK**. The objects or the block are saved as a new file in the path specified by you. A **WBLOCK Preview** window with the new file contents is displayed.

USING THE -WBLOCK COMMAND

When the **-WBLOCK** command is invoked, AutoCAD displays the **Create Drawing File** dialog box (Figure 12-16), except when the system variable **FILEDIA** is set to 0. This dialog box displays a list of all the drawing files in the current directory. Enter the name of the output drawing file in the **File name:** edit box and then choose the **Save** button. If the file name you specify is identical to some other file in the same directory path, AutoCAD displays a message whether you want to replace the existing drawing with the new drawing. Right-clicking on a file name in the list box, displays a shortcut menu that allows you to Select, open, print, delete, rename, move, cut, copy, and list properties of the particular drawing file.

After choosing the **Save** button, the dialog box is cleared from the screen, and AutoCAD issues the following prompt asking you for the name of an existing block that you want to convert into a permanent symbol:

Enter name of existing block or
[=(block=output file)/*(whole drawing)] <define new drawing>: *Enter the name of a predefined block.*

The drawing file with the name specified in the dialog box is created from the predefined block.

The = Sign

If you want to assign the same name to the output drawing file as that of the existing block, enter an = (equal) sign as a response to the **Enter name of existing block...:** prompt and enter same file name in the **File name:** edit box of the **Create Drawing File** dialog box.

If a block by the name you have already assigned to the output file does not exist in the current drawing, AutoCAD gives an appropriate message that no block by that name exists in the current drawing, and the **Enter name of existing block or ....:** prompt is repeated.

Figure 12-16 Create Drawing File dialog box

Creating a New WBlock

If you have not yet created a block, but want to create an output drawing file of the objects in the current drawing, enter the **-WBLOCK** command and press ENTER instead of specifying a block name at the **Enter name of existing block...:** prompt, you are then required to select an insertion point and select the objects to be incorporated in the drawing file. The prompt sequence in this case is:

    Command: **-WBLOCK** Enter

Enter a file name in the **File name:** edit box of the **Create Drawing File** dialog box.

    Enter name of existing block or
    [=(block=output file)/*(whole drawing)] <define new drawing>: Enter
    Specify insertion base point: *Select the insertion point.*
    Select objects: *Select the objects to be incorporated in the drawing file.*
    Select objects: *Press ENTER when finished selecting.*

Storing an Entire Drawing as a WBlock

You can also store an entire drawing as a WBlock. In other words, the current file is copied into a new one specified in the **File name:** edit box. To do so, respond to the prompt **Enter name of existing block ...:** with an asterisk (*). The prompt sequence is:

    Command: **-WBLOCK** Enter

Enter a file name in the **File name:** edit box of the **Create Drawing File** dialog box.

Enter name of existing block or
[=(block=output file)/*(whole drawing)] <define new drawing>:* [Enter]

Here, the entire drawing is saved in the file in the directory you have specified. The effect is identical to the **SAVE** command. The lone difference is that if you use the * response in the **-WBLOCK** command, all unused named objects are automatically purged. In this manner, the size of a drawing containing a number of unused blocks is reduced by a considerable amount. When the **FILEDIA** is set to 0, entering **-WBLOCK** at the command prompt, does not display the **Create Drawing File** dialog box and displays prompts on the command line as follows:

Command:**-WBLOCK**
Enter name of output file: *Enter a name for the output file.*
Enter name of existing block or
[=(block=output file)/*(whole drawing)] <define new drawing>: *Enter a name of an existing block, enter=, enter* or press ENTER.*

The existing block whose name you have entered will be saved as a drawing file. If you enter =, the existing block and the output file have the same name. Entering * at the **Enter name of existing block or...:** prompt, saves the entire drawing to a new output file. Pressing ENTER allows you to define a new drawing. Once the file is defined, the selected objects are deleted from the drawing. They can be restored by using the **OOPS** command.

This sequence is similar to that of the **-BLOCK** command. The drawing is saved in the current drawing symbol table and written to the disk as a drawing file.

Export Data Dialog Box
You can also use the **Export Data** dialog box (Figure 12-17) to create drawing files. The **Export Data** dialog box can be invoked from the **File** menu (**File > Export...**), or by entering **EXPORT** at the Command prompt.

In this dialog box, you can specify information about the drawing file to be created. Select the Block (*.dwg) format from the **Save as type:** drop-down list, enter the name of the drawing file in the **File name:** edit box, and then choose the **Save** button. The dialog box is cleared from the screen and AutoCAD issues the following prompt:

Enter name of existing block or
[=(block=output file)/*(whole drawing)] <define new drawing>: *Enter the name of a predefined block.*

The drawing file with the name specified in the dialog box is created from the predefined block.

Figure 12-17 Export Data dialog box

DEFINING THE INSERTION BASE POINT (BASE COMMAND)

Menu:	Draw > Block > Base
Command:	BASE

The **BASE** command lets you set the insertion base point for a drawing just as you set the base insertion point in the prompt sequence of the **-BLOCK** command. This base point is defined so that when you insert the drawing into some other drawing, the specified base point is placed on the insertion point. By default, the base point is at the origin (0,0,0). The prompt sequence is:

Command: **BASE** ⏎
Enter base point <current>: *Specify the base point or press ENTER.*

Exercise 7   *General*

a. Create a drawing file named CHAIR using the **WBLOCK** command. Get a listing of your .DWG files and make sure that CHAIR.DWG is listed. Quit the drawing editor.
b. Begin a new drawing and insert the drawing file into the drawing. Save the drawing.

EDITING BLOCKS
Breaking Up a Block

A block may be comprised of different basic objects, such as lines, arcs, polylines, and circles. All these objects are grouped together in the block and are treated as a single object. To edit any particular object of a block, the block needs to be "exploded," or split into independent parts. This is especially useful when an entire view or drawing has been inserted and a small detail needs to be corrected. This can be done in the following ways.

Entering * as the Prefix of Block Name. As we discussed, individual objects within a block cannot be edited unless the block is broken up (exploded). To insert a block as a collection of individual objects, you need to enter an asterisk before its name. The prompt sequence for exploding the block BLOCKPLAN while inserting is:

Command: **INSERT** [Enter]
Enter block name or [?] <current>: ***BLOCKPLAN**
Specify insertion point or [Scale/X/Y/Z/Rotate/PScale/PX/PY/PZ/PRotate]: *Select the insertion point.*
Scale factor <1>: [Enter]
Specify rotation angle <0>: [Enter]

The inserted object will no longer be treated as a block. The figure consists of various objects that can be edited separately.

Using the EXPLODE Command

Toolbar:	Modify > Explode
Menu:	Modify > Explode
Command:	EXPLODE

As we mentioned before, the other method to break a block into individual objects is by using the **EXPLODE** command (Figure 12-18). The prompt sequence is:

Command: **EXPLODE** [Enter]
Select objects: *Select the block to be exploded.*

*Figure 12-18 Using the **EXPLODE** command*

The **EXPLODE** command explodes a block into its component objects regardless of the scale factors. It also does not have control over the properties like, layer, linetype, lineweight, and color of the component objects. When a block is exploded, there may be no visible change in the drawing. The drawing is identical except that the color and linetype may have changed because of floating layers, colors, or linetypes. The exploded block is now a group of objects that can be edited individually. To check whether the breaking of the block has taken place, select any object that was formerly a part of the block; only that particular object should be highlighted. After a block is exploded, the block definition continues to be in the block symbol table. After exploding a block you can modify it and then redefine it by using the **BLOCK** or **BMAKE** commands. The **Block Definition** dialog box is displayed where you can choose the name of the block you wish to redefine from the **Name:** drop-down list and then, use the dialog box options and redefine it. You can also use the **-BLOCK** or the **INSERT** commands to redefine a block. Once you redefine a block, it automatically gets updated in the current drawing and for future use. Blocks inserted with **MINSERT** and External references cannot be exploded.

Using the XPLODE command*

Command: XPLODE

With the **XPLODE** command, you can explode a block or blocks into component objects and simultaneously control their properties like Layer, linetype, color, and lineweight. The scale factor of the object to be exploded should be equal and absolute, that is 1,-1,1. The command prompts are as follows:

Command: **XPLODE** [Enter]
Select objects: Use *any object selection method and select objects and then press ENTER.*

On pressing ENTER, AutoCAD reports the total number of objects selected and also the number of objects that cannot be exploded. It also further prompts for an option that decides whether changes in the properties of the component objects will be made individually or globally. The prompt is:

Enter an option [Individually/Globally] <Globally>: *Enter i, g or press ENTER to accept the default option.*

If you enter **i** at the **Enter an option [Individually/Globally] <Globally>:** prompt, AutoCAD will modify each object individually, one at a time. The command prompt is:

Enter an option [All/Color/LAyer/LType/Inherit from parent block/Explode] <Explode>: *Select an option.*

The options available are discussed below:

All. Sets all the properties like color, layer, linetype, and lineweight of selected objects after exploding them. AutoCAD prompts you to enter new color, linetype, lineweight, and layer name for the exploded component objects.

Color. Sets the color of the exploded objects. The prompt is:

Enter new color for exploded objects [Red/Yellow/Cyan/Blue/Magenta/White/BYLayer/BYBlock]<BYLAYER>: *Enter a color, option or press ENTER.*

On entering BYLAYER, the component objects take on the color of the exploded object's layer and on entering BYBLOCK, they take on the color of the exploded object.

Layer. Sets the layer of the exploded objects. The default option is inheriting the current layer. The command prompt is as follows:

Enter new layer name for exploded objects <current>: *Enter an existing layer name or press ENTER*

LType. Sets the linetype of the components of the exploded object. The command prompt is:

Enter new linetype name for exploded objects <BYLAYER>: *Enter a linetype name or press* ENTER.

Inherit from Parent Block. Sets the properties of the component objects to that of the exploded parent object, provided the component objects are drawn on layer 0 and the color, lineweight, and linetype are BYBLOCK.

Explode. Explodes the selected object exactly as in the **EXPLODE** command.

Selecting the **Globally** option, applies changes to all the selected objects at the same time and the options are similar to the ones discussed in the **Individually** option.

RENAMING BLOCKS

Menu:	Format > Rename
Command:	RENAME

Blocks can be renamed with the **RENAME** command. AutoCAD displays the **Rename** dialog box (Figure 12-19) which allows you to modify the name of an existing block.

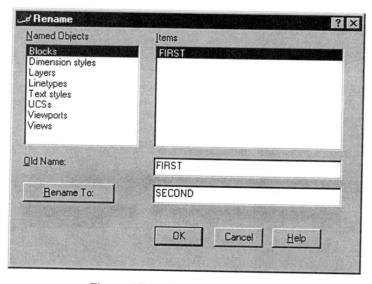

Figure 12-19 Rename dialog box

The **Named Objects** list box displays the categories of object types that can be renamed, such as: blocks, layers, dimension styles, linetypes, plot and text styles, UCSs, views, and tiled viewports. You can rename all of these except layer 0 and continuous linetype. On selecting **Blocks** from the **Named Objects** list, the **Items** list box displays all the block names in the current drawing. When you select a block name you wish to rename from the **Items** list, the block name is displayed in the **Old Name:** edit box. You can enter a block name you wish to modify in the **Old Name:** edit box or select it from the **Items** list box. Enter the new name to be assigned to the block in the **Rename To:** edit box. Choosing the **Rename To:** button, applies the change in name to the old name. Choose **OK** to exit the dialog box.

If you enter **-RENAME** at the Command prompt, command prompts are displayed at the Command line. You can rename a block using the command line. For example, if you want to rename a block named FIRST to SECOND, the prompt sequence is:

Command: **RENAME**
Enter object type to rename
[Block/Dimstyle/LAyer/LType/Style/Ucs/VIew/VPort]: B
Enter old block name: FIRST
Enter new block name: SECOND

DELETING UNUSED BLOCKS

Menu:	File > Drawing Utilities > Purge
Command:	PURGE

Unused blocks can be deleted with the **PURGE** command. For example, if you want to delete an unused block named SECOND, the prompt sequence is:

Command: **PURGE**
Enter type of unused objects to purge
[Blocks/Dimstyles/LAyers/LTypes/Plotstyles/SHapes/STyles/Mlinestyles/ All]: B
Enter names to purge <*>: SECOND
Verify each name to be purged? <Y> *Press ENTER.*
Purge block SECOND? <N>: Y

If there are no objects to remove, AutoCAD displays a message that there are no unreferenced objects to purge.

Self-Evaluation Test

Answer the following questions, and then compare your answers with the correct answers given at the end of this chapter.

1. Individual objects forming a block can be erased. (T/F)

2. A block can be mirrored by providing a scale factor of -1 for X and -1 for Y. (T/F)

3. Blocks created by the **BLOCK** command can be used in any drawing. (T/F)

4. An existing block cannot be redefined. (T/F)

5. At the time of insertion, each object that makes up a block is drawn on the current layer with the current linetype and color. (T/F)

6. If a block that is inserted is on a frozen layer, the block is generated only if portions of the block lie on nonfrozen (thawed) layers. (T/F)

7. The **WBLOCK** command lets you create a drawing file (.DWG extension) of a block defined in the current drawing. (T/F)

8. The **RENAME** command can be used to change the name of a drawing file. (T/F)

9. The _____ command is used to place a previously created block in a drawing.

10. You can delete unreferenced blocks with the _____ command.

Review Questions

1. Only blocks can be scaled. (T/F)

2. Blocks can be scaled or rotated upon insertion. (T/F)

3. Drawing files created by the **WBLOCK** command can be used in any drawing. (T/F)

4. An entire drawing can be converted into a block. (T/F)

5. Invoking the **INSERT** command causes generation of the **Insert** dialog box. (T/F)

6. The objects in a block possess the properties of the layer on which they are drawn, such as color and linetype. (T/F)

7. If the objects forming a block were drawn on layer 0 with color and linetype BYLAYER, then at the time of the insertion, each object that makes up a block is drawn on the current layer with the current linetype and color. (T/F)

8. Objects created with the special color BYBLOCK are generated with the color that is current at the time the block was inserted. (T/F)

9. Objects created with the special linetype BYBLOCK are generated with the linetype that is current at the time the block was inserted. (T/F)

10. The color, linetype, and layer on which a block is drawn can be changed with the Properties option of the **CHANGE** command. (T/F)

11. Suppose objects in Block1 have color BYBLOCK. If you incorporate Block1 into Block2 and insert with the current color set to green, Block1 also assumes the green color. (T/F)

12. Suppose objects in Block1 have color BYLAYER. If you incorporate Block1 into Block2 and insert it with the current color set to red, Block1 will assume the color of Block2, not the current color of the object's layer(s). (T/F)

13. You can create a rectangular array of a block with a single **MINSERT** command. (T/F)

14. In the array generated with the **MINSERT** command, there is no way to change the number of rows or columns or the spacing between them after insertion. The whole **MINSERT** pattern is considered one object that cannot be exploded. (T/F)

15. The **WBLOCK** command allows you to convert an existing block into a drawing file. (T/F)

16. If a block was inserted with nonuniform scales (unequal X and Y), it can be exploded. (T/F)

17. After exploding an object, the object remains identical except that the color and linetype may change because of floating layers, colors, or linetypes. (T/F)

18. **WBLOCK**-asterisk method has the same effect as the **PURGE** command. The only difference is that with the **PURGE** command, deletion takes place automatically. (T/F)

19. The **RENAME** command can be used to change the name of a block. (T/F)

20. The _____ command is used to save any object as a block.

21. The _____ command is used to place a previously created block in a drawing.

22. The Xscale factor of a block can be preset before specifying its position of insertion by entering _____ at the **Specify insertion point ...:** prompt.

23. Each X, Y, and Z scale factor of a block can be preset to a uniform value before specifying its position of insertion by entering _____ at the **Specify insertion point...:** prompt.

24. The _____ option lets you redefine the preset Y scale factor even after you have specified the insertion point for the block.

25. The concept of blocks within blocks is known as the _____.

26. The _____ command is used for multiple insertion of a specified block.

Exercises

Exercise 8   *Mechanical*

Draw part (a) of Figure 12-20 and define it as a block named A. Then, using the block insert command, insert the block in the plate as shown.

Figure 12-20 *Drawing for Exercise 8*

Exercise 9   *Piping*

Draw the diagrams in Figure 12-21 using blocks.
a. Create a block for the valve Figure 12-21(a).
b. Use a thick polyline for the flow lines.

Figure 12-21 *Drawing for Exercise 9*

Exercise 10

Mechanical

Draw part (a) of Figure 12-22 and define it as a block named B. Then, using the relevant insertion method, generate the pattern as shown. Note that the pattern is rotated at 30 degrees.

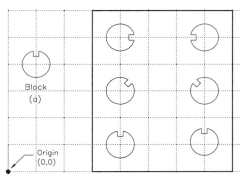

Figure 12-22 Drawing for Exercise 10

Exercise 11

Electronics

Draw the circuit diagram as shown in Figure 12-23 using blocks. Create the blocks first, and then insert the blocks to complete the circuit diagram.

Figure 12-23 Drawing for Exercise 11

Answers to Self-Evaluation Test
1 - F, **2** - T, **3** - F, **4** - F, **5** - F, **6** - F, **7** - T, **8** - F, **9** - **INSERT**, **10** - **PURGE**

Advanced AutoCAD

Author's Web Sites

For Faculty: Please contact the author at **stickoo@calumet.purdue.edu** to access the Web Site that contains the following:

1. **Power Point presentations, programs, and drawings used in this textbook.**
2. **Syllabus, chapter objectives and hints, and questions with answers for every chapter.**

For Students:You can download drawing-exercises, tutorials, programs, and special topics by accessing authors Web Site at **http://www.calumet.purdue.edu/public/mets/tickoo/index.html**.

Chapter 13

Defining Block Attributes

Learning Objectives

After completing this chapter, you will be able to:
* *Understand what attributes are and how to define attributes with a block.*
* *Edit attribute tag names.*
* *Insert blocks with attributes and assign values to attributes.*
* *Extract attribute values from the inserted blocks.*
* *Control attribute visibility.*
* *Perform global and individual editing of attributes.*
* *Insert a text file in a drawing to create bill of material.*

ATTRIBUTES

AutoCAD has provided a facility that allows the user to attach information to blocks. This information can then be retrieved and processed by other programs for various purposes. For example, you can use this information to create a bill of material, find the total number of computers in a building, or determine the location of each block in a drawing. Attributes can also be used to create blocks (such as title blocks) with prompted or preformatted text, to control text placement. The information associated with a block is known as **attribute value** or simply **attribute**. AutoCAD references the attributes with a block through tag names.

Before you can assign attributes to a block, you must create an attribute definition by using the **ATTDEF** command. The attribute definition describes the characteristics of the attribute. You can define several attribute definitions (tags) and include them in the block definition. Each time you insert the block, AutoCAD will prompt you to enter the value of the attribute. The attribute value automatically replaces the attribute tag name. The information (attribute values) assigned to a block can be extracted and written to a file by using AutoCAD's **ATTEXT** command. This file can then be inserted in the drawing as a table or processed by other programs to analyze the data. The attribute values can be edited by using the **ATTEDIT** command. The display of attributes can be controlled with **ATTDISP** command.

DEFINING ATTRIBUTES
ATTDEF Command

Menu:	Draw > Block > Define Attributes
Command:	ATTDEF

When you invoke the **ATTDEF** command, the **Attribute Definition** dialog box (Figure 13-1) is displayed. The block attributes can be defined through this dialog box. When you create an attribute definition, you must define the mode, attributes, insertion point, and text information for each attribute. All this information can be entered in the dialog box. Following is a description of each area of the **Attribute Definition** dialog box.

Figure 13-1 Attribute Definition dialog box

Mode. The **Mode** area of the Attribute Definition dialog box (Figure 13-2) has four options: Invisible, Constant, Verify, and Preset. These options determine the display and edit features of the block attributes. For example, if an attribute is invisible, the attribute is not displayed on the screen. Similarly, if an attribute is constant, its value is predefined and cannot be changed. These options are described below:

Figure 13-2 Mode area of the ***Attribute Definition*** dialog box

Invisible. This option lets you create an attribute that is not visible on the screen. This mode is useful when you do not want the attribute values to be displayed on the screen to avoid cluttering the drawing. Also, if the attributes are invisible, it takes less time to regenerate the drawing. If you want to make the invisible attribute visible, use the **ATTDISP** command discussed later in this chapter [section "Controlling Attribute Visibility (**ATTDISP** COMMAND)"].

Constant. This option lets you create an attribute that has a fixed value and cannot be changed after block insertion. When you select this mode, the Prompt: edit box and the Verify and Preset check boxes are disabled.

Verify. This option allows you to verify the attribute value you have entered when inserting a block, by asking you twice for the data. If the value is incorrect, you can correct it by entering the new value.

Preset. This option allows you to create an attribute that is automatically set to default value. The prompt is not displayed and an attribute value is not requested when you insert a block with attributes using this option to define a block attribute. Unlike a constant attribute, the preset attribute value can later be edited.

Attribute. The **Attribute** area (Figure 13-3) of the **Attribute Definition** dialog box has three edit boxes: Tag, Prompt, and Value. To enter a value, you must first select the corresponding edit box and then enter the value. You can enter up to 256 characters in these edit boxes.

Figure 13-3 *Attribute* *area of the* **Attribute** **Definition** *dialog box*

Tag. This is like a label that is used to identify an attribute. For example, the tag name COM-PUTER can be used to identify an item. The tag names can be uppercase, lowercase, or both. Any lowercase letters are automatically converted into uppercase. The tag name cannot be null. Also, the tag name must not contain any blank spaces. You should select a tag name that reflects the contents of the item being tagged. For example, the tag name COMP or COM-PUTER is an appropriate name for labeling computers.

Prompt. The text that you enter in the **Prompt:** edit box is used as a prompt when you insert a block that contains the defined attribute. If you have selected the Constant option in the Mode area, the **Prompt:** edit box is disabled because no prompt is required if the attribute is constant. If you do enter nothing in the **Prompt:** edit box, the entry made in the **Tag:** edit box is used as the prompt.

Value. The entry in the **Value:** edit box defines the default value of the specified attribute; that is, if you do not enter a value, it is used as the value for the attribute. The entry of a value is optional.

Insertion Point. The **Insertion Point** area of the **Attribute Definition** dialog box (Figure 13-4) lets you define the insertion point of block attribute text. You can define the insertion point by entering the values in the **X:**, **Y:**, and **Z:** edit boxes or by selecting **Pick Point <** button. If you select this button, the dialog box clears, and you can enter the X, Y, and Z values of the insertion point at the command line or specify the point by selecting a point on the screen. When you are done specifying the insertion point, the **Attribute Definition** dialog box reappears.

Just under the Insertion Point area of the dialog box is a check box labeled Align below previous attribute. You can use this box to place the subsequent attribute text just below the previously defined attribute automatically. This check box is disabled if no attribute has been defined. When you select this check box, the Insertion Point area and the Text Options areas are disabled because AutoCAD assumes previously defined values for text such as text height, text style,

*Figure 13-4 Insertion Point area of the **Attribute Definition** dialog box*

text justification, and text rotation. Also, the text is automatically placed on the following line. After insertion, the attribute text is responsive to the setting of the **MIRRTEXT** system variable.

Text Options. The **Text Options** area of the **Attribute Definition** dialog box (Figure 13-5) lets you define the justification, text style, height, and rotation of the attribute text. To set the text justification, select justification type in the **Justification:** drop-down list. Similarly, you can use the **Text Style:** drop-down list to define the text style. You can specify the text height and text rotation in the **Height <** and **Rotation <** edit boxes. You can also define the text height by selecting the **Height <** button. If you select this button, AutoCAD temporarily exits the dialog box and lets you enter the value

*Figure 13-5 **Text Options** area of **Attribute Definition** dialog box*

from the command line. Similarly, you can define the text rotation by selecting the **Rotation <** button and then entering the rotation angle at the command line.

 Note
The text style must be defined before it can be used to specify the text style.

*If you select a style that has the height predefined, AutoCAD automatically disables the **Height <** edit box.*

*If you have selected the Align option for the text justification, the **Height <** and **Rotation <** edit box are disabled.*

*If you have selected the **Fit** option for the text justification, the **Rotation <** edit box is disabled.*

After you complete the settings in the **Attribute Definition** dialog box and choose **OK**, the attribute tag text is inserted in the drawing at the specified insertion point.

Using Command Line

You can define block attributes through the command line by entering the **-ATTDEF** command.

Command: **-ATTDEF**
Current attribute modes: Invisible=N Constant=N Verify=N Preset=N

Enter an option to change [Invisible/Constant/Verify/Preset] <done>:
Enter attribute tag name:

The default value of all attribute modes is **N** (No). To reverse the default mode, enter **I, C, V,** or **P.** For example, if you enter **I,** AutoCAD will change the Invisible mode from **N** to **Y** (Yes). This will make the attribute visible. After setting the modes, press ENTER to go to the next prompts where you can enter the attribute tag, attribute prompt, and the attribute values.

Enter attribute tag name:
Enter attribute prompt:
Enter default attribute value:

The entry at this prompt defines the default value of the specified attribute; that is, if you do not enter a value, it is used as the value for the attribute. The entry of a value is optional. If you have selected the Constant mode, AutoCAD displays the following prompt:

Enter attribute tag name:
Enter attribute value:

Next, AutoCAD displays the following text prompts:

Current text style: "Standard" Text height: *current*
Specify start point of text or [Justify/Style]:
Specify height <*current*>:
Specify rotation angle of text <*current*>:

After you respond to these prompts, the attribute tag text will be placed at the specified location. If you press ENTER at **Specify start point of text or [Justify/Style]:,** AutoCAD will automatically place the subsequent attribute text just below the previously defined attribute, and it assumes previously defined text values such as text height, text style, text justification, and text rotation. Also, the text is automatically placed on the following line.

Example 1

In this example, you will define the following attributes for a computer and then create a block using the **BLOCK** command. The name of the block is COMP.

Mode	Tag name	Prompt	Default value
Constant	ITEM		Computer
Preset, Verify	MAKE	Enter make:	CAD-CIM
Verify	PROCESSOR	Enter processor type:	Unknown
Verify	HD	Enter Hard-Drive size:	100MB
Invisible,Verify	RAM	Enter RAM:	4MB

1. Draw the computer as shown in Figure 13-6. Assume the dimensions, or measure the dimensions of the computer you are using for AutoCAD.

Chapter 13

2. Invoke the **ATTDEF** command. The **Attribute Definition** dialog box is displayed (Figure 13-7).

3. Define the first attribute as shown in the preceding table. Select Constant in the Mode area because the mode of the first attribute is constant. In the Tag: edit box, enter the tag name, **ITEM**. Similarly, enter Computer in the **Value:** edit box. The **Prompt:** edit box is disabled because the variable is constant.

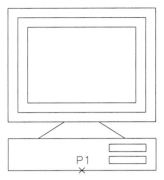

Figure 13-6 Drawing for Example 1

4. In the Insertion Point area, choose the **Pick Point <** button to define the text insertion point. Select a point below the drawing of the computer.

5. In the Text Options area, select the justification, style, height, and rotation of the text.

6. Choose the **OK** button when you are done entering information in the **Attribute Definition** dialog box.

*Figure 13-7 Enter information in the **Attribute Definition** dialog box*

7. Enter **ATTDEF** at the Command prompt to invoke the **Attribute Definition** dialog box. Enter the Mode and Attribute information for the second attribute shown in the table at the beginning of Example 1. You need not define the Insertion Point and Text Options. Check the

Align below previous attribute box that is located just below the Insertion Point area. When you check this box, the Insertion Point and Text Justification areas are disabled. AutoCAD places the attribute text just below the previous attribute text.

8. Define the remaining attributes (Figure 13-8).

9. Use the **BLOCK** command to create a block. The name of the block is COMP, and the insertion point of the block is P1, midpoint of the base. When you select the objects for the block, make sure you also select the attributes. The order of attribute selection controls the order of prompts.

ITEM
MAKE
PROCESSOR
HD
RAM

Figure 13-8 Define attributes below the computer drawing

EDITING ATTRIBUTE TAGS
Using the DDEDIT Command

Toolbar:	Modify II > Edit Text
Menu:	Modify > Text
Command:	DDEDIT

Edit Text —

Figure 13-9 Edit Text button in the ModifyII toolbar

The **DDEDIT** command lets you edit text and attribute definitions. After invoking this command, AutoCAD will prompt to **select an annotation object or [Undo]:**. If you select an attribute definition created by attribute definition, the **Edit Attribute Definition** dialog box is displayed and lists the tag name, prompt, and default value of the attribute, (Figure 13-10).

*Figure 13-10 Edit **Attribute Definition** dialog box*

You can select the edit boxes and enter the changes. Once you are done making the required changes, choose the **OK** button in the dialog box. After you exit the dialog box, AutoCAD will prompt you to select text or attribute object (Attribute tag). If you are done editing, press ENTER to return to the command line.

Command: **DDEDIT**

Select an annotation object or [Undo]: *Select the attribute tag.*

Using the CHANGE Command

You can also use the **CHANGE** command to edit text or attribute objects. The following is the Command prompt sequence for the **CHANGE** command:

Command: **CHANGE**
Select objects: *Select attribute objects.*
Select objects: [Enter]
Specify change point or [Properties]: [Enter]
Specify new text insertion point <no change>: [Enter]
Enter new text style <current>: [Enter]
Specify new height <current>: [Enter]
Specify new rotation angle <0>: [Enter]
Enter new tag <current>: *Enter new tag name or* [Enter]
Enter new prompt <current>: *Enter new prompt or* [Enter]
Enter new default value <current>: *Enter new default or* [Enter]

INSERTING BLOCKS WITH ATTRIBUTES
Using the Dialog Box

The value of the attributes can be specified during block insertion, either at the command line or in the **Edit Attributes** dialog box. The **Edit Attributes** dialog box is invoked by setting the system variable **ATTDIA** to **1** and then using the **INSERT** command to invoke **Insert** dialog box (discussed earlier in Chapter 12). The default value for **ATTDIA** is **0** which disables the dialog box. The command sequence for **INSERT** command is as follows:

Command: **ATTDIA** [Enter]
Enter new value for ATTDIA <0>: **1**

Command: **-INSERT** [Enter]
Enter block name or [?] <current>: *Enter block name that has attributes in it.*
Specify insertion point or [Scale/X/Y/Z/Rotate/PScale/PX/PY/PZ/PRotate]: *Specify a point.*
Enter X scale factor, specify opposite corner, or [Corner/XYZ] <1>: *Enter X scale factor.*
Enter Y scale factor <use X scale factor>: *Enter Y scale factor.*
Specify rotation angle <0>: *Enter rotation angle.*

After you respond to these prompts, AutoCAD will display the **Edit Attributes** dialog box (Figure 13-11). This displays the prompts and their default values that have been entered at the time of attribute definition. If there are more attributes, they can be accessed by using the **Next** or **Previous** buttons. You can enter the attribute values in the edit box located next to the attribute prompt. The block name is displayed at the top of the dialog box. After entering the new attribute values, choose **OK** button; AutoCAD will place these attribute values at the specified location.

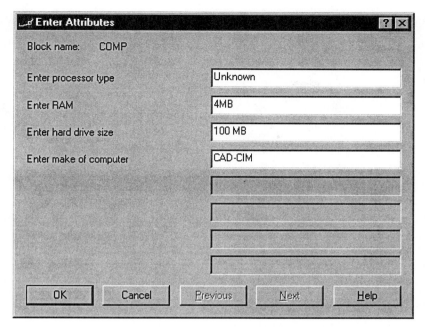

Figure 13-11 *Enter attribute values in the **Enter Attributes** dialog box*

Note

*If you use the dialog box to define the attribute values, the Verify mode is ignored because the **Enter Attributes** dialog box allows the user to examine and edit the attribute values.*

Using the Command Line

You can also define attributes from the command line by setting the system variable **ATTDIA** to **0** (default value). When you use the **-INSERT** command with **ATTDIA** set to **0**, AutoCAD does not display the **Enter Attributes** dialog box. Instead, AutoCAD will prompt you to enter the attribute values for various attributes that have been defined in the block. To define the attributes from the command line, enter the **-INSERT** command at the Command: prompt. After you define the insertion point, scale, and rotation, AutoCAD will display the following prompt:

Enter attribute values

It will be followed by the prompts that have been defined with the block using the ATTDEF command. For example:

Enter processor type <Unknown>:
Enter RAM <4MB>:
Enter Hard-Drive size <100MB>:

Example 2

In this example, you will use the **-INSERT** command to insert the block (COMP) that was defined in Example 1. The following is the list of the attribute values for computers.

ITEM	MAKE	PROCESSOR	HD	RAM
Computer	Gateway	486-60	150MB	16MB
Computer	Zenith	486-30	100MB	32MB
Computer	IBM	386-30	80MB	8MB
Computer	Del	586-60	450MB	64MB
Computer	CAD-CIM	Pentium-90	100 Min	32MB
Computer	CAD-CIM	Unknown	600MB	Standard

1. Make the floor plan drawing as shown in Figure 13-12 (assume the dimensions).

Figure 13-12 *Floor plan drawing for Example 2*

2. Set the system variable **ATTDIA** to 1. Use the **-INSERT** command to insert the blocks, and define the attribute values in the **Enter Attributes** dialog box (Figure 13-13).

   Command: **-INSERT**
   Enter block name or [?] <current>: **COMP**
   Specify insertion point or [Scale/X/Y/Z/Rotate/PScale/PX/PY/PZ/PRotate]: *Specify a point.*
   Enter X scale factor, specify opposite corner, or [Corner/XYZ] <1>: [Enter]
   Enter Y scale factor <use X scale factor>: [Enter]
   Specify rotation angle <0>: [Enter]

3. Repeat the **-INSERT** command to insert other blocks, and define their attribute values as shown in Figure 13-14

4. Save the drawing for further use.

Figure 13-13 *Enter attribute values in the **Enter Attributes** dialog box*

Figure 13-14 *The floor plan after inserting blocks and defining their attributes*

EXTRACTING ATTRIBUTES
Using the Dialog Box (ATTEXT)

Command: ATTEXT

To use the **Attribute Extraction** dialog box (Figure 13-15) for extracting the attributes, enter **ATTEXT** at the Command prompt. The information about the file format, template file, and output file must be entered in the dialog box to extract the defined attribute. Also, you must select the blocks whose attribute values you want to extract.

Figure 13-15 Attribute Extraction dialog box

File Format. This area of the dialog box lets you select the file format of the extracted data. You can select Comma Delimited File, Space Delimited File, or DXF Format Extract File (DXX). The format selection is determined by the application that you plan to use to process the data.

    Comma Delimited File (CDF). In CDF format, each character field is enclosed in single quotes, and the records are separated by a delimiter (comma by default). CDF file is a text file with the extension **.TXT.**

    Space Delimited File (SDF). In SDF format, the records are of fixed width as specified in the template file. The records are not separated by a comma, and the character fields are not enclosed in single quotes. The SDF file is a text file with the extension **.TXT.**

    DXF Format Extract File (DXX). If you select the Drawing Interchange File format, the template file name and the Template File edit box in the **Attribute Extraction** dialog box are automatically disabled. DXF™ -format extraction do not requires any template. The file created by this option contains only block references, attribute values, and end-of-sequence objects. The extension of these files is **.DXX**.

Select Objects<. This button closes the dialog box so that you can use the pointing device to select blocks with attributes. When the **Attribute Extraction** dialog box reopens, Number Found displays the number of objects you have selected.

Template File. The **template file** allows you to specify the attribute values you want to extract and the information you want to retrieve about the block. It also lets you format the display of the extracted data. The file can be created by using any text editor, such as Notepad, Windows Write, or WordPad. You can also use a word processor or a database program to write the file. The template file must be saved as an **ASCII** file and the extension of the file must be **.TXT**. The following are the fields that you can specify in a template file (the comments given on the right are for explanation only; they must not be entered with the field description):

BL:LEVEL	Nwww000	(Block nesting level)
BL:NAME	Cwww000	(Block name)
BL:X	Nwwwddd	(X coordinate of block insertion point)
BL:Y	Nwwwddd	(Y coordinate of block insertion point)
BL:Z	Nwwwddd	(Z coordinate of block insertion point)
BL:NUMBER	Nwww000	(Block counter)
BL:HANDLE	Cwww000	(Block's handle)
BL:LAYER	Cwww000	(Block insertion layer name)
BL:ORIENT	Nwwwddd	(Block rotation angle)
BL:XSCALE	Nwwwddd	(X scale factor of block)
BL:YSCALE	Nwwwddd	(Y scale factor of block)
BL:ZSCALE	Nwwwddd	(Z scale factor of block)
BL:XEXTRUDE	Nwwwddd	(X component of block's extrusion direction)
BL:YEXTRUDE	Nwwwddd	(Y component of block's extrusion direction)
BL:ZEXTRUDE	Nwwwddd	(Z component of block's extrusion direction)
Attribute tag		(The tag name of the block attribute)

The extract file may contain several fields. For example, the first field might be the item name and the second field might be the price of the item. Each line in the template file specifies one field in the extract file. Any line in a template file consists of the name of the field, the width of the field in characters, and its numerical precision (if applicable). For example:

ITEM	N015002	
BL:NAME	C015000	
	Where	**BL:NAME** ------ Field name
		Blankspaces --- Blank spaces (must not include the tab character)
		C ------------------ Designates a character field
		N ------------------ Designates a numerical field
		015 --------------- Width of field in characters
		002 --------------- Numerical precision

BL:NAME
or **ITEM**   Indicates the field names; can be of any length.

C   Designates a character field; that is, the field contains characters or it starts with characters. If the file contains numbers or starts with numbers, then C will be replaced by N. For example, **N015002**.

015   Designates a field that is 15 characters long.

002   Designates the numerical precision. In this example, the numerical precision is 2, two places following the decimal. The decimal point and the two digits following decimal are **included in the field width**. In the next example, (000), the numerical precision, is not applicable because the field does not have any numerical value (the field contains letters only).

After creating a template file, in AutoCAD 2000, if you select the **Template File...** button, the **Select Template File** dialog box (Figure 13-16) is displayed, where you can browse and select the required template file.

Figure 13-16 Select Template File dialog box

Note
You can put any number of spaces between the field name and the character C or N (ITEM N015002). However, you must not use the tab characters. Any alignment in the fields must be done by inserting spaces after the field name.

In the template file, a field name must not appear more than once. The template file name and the output file name must be different.

The template file must contain at least one field with an attribute tag name because the tag names determine which attribute values are to be extracted and from which blocks. If several blocks have different block names but the same attribute tag, AutoCAD will extract attribute values from all selected blocks. For example, if there are two blocks in the drawing with the attribute tag PRICE, then when you extract the attribute values, AutoCAD will extract the value from both blocks (if both blocks were selected). To extract the value of an attribute, the tag name must match the field name specified in the template file. AutoCAD automatically converts the tag names and the field names to uppercase letters before making a comparison.

Output File. This button specifies the name of the output file. Enter the file name in the box, or choose the **Output File...** button to search for existing template files from **Output File** dialog box (Figure 13-17). AutoCAD appends the **.TXT** file extension for CDF or SDF files and the **.DXF** file extension for DXF files.

Figure 13-17 Output File dialog box

Example 3

In this example, you will write a template file for extracting the attribute values as defined in Example 2. These attribute values must be written to a file **COMPLST1.TXT** and the values arranged as shown in the following table:

Field width in characters

< 10 >	< 12 >	< 10 >	< 12 >	< 10 >	< 10 >
COMP	Computer	Gateway	486-60	150MB	**16MB**
COMP	Computer	Zenith	486-30	100MB	**32MB**
COMP	Computer	IBM	386-30	80MB	**8MB**
COMP	Computer	Del	586-60	450MB	**64MB**
COMP	Computer	**CAD-CIM**	Pentium-90	100 Min	**32MB**
COMP	Computer	**CAD-CIM**	**Unknown**	600MB	Standard

1. Load the drawing you saved in Example 2.

2. Use the Windows Notepad to write the following template file. You can use any text editor or word processor to write the file. After writing the file, save it as an ASCII file under the file name **TEMP1.TXT**. Exit the Notepad and access AutoCAD.

BL:NAME	C010000	(Block name, 10 spaces)
Item	C012000	(Item, 12 spaces)

Make	C010000	(Computer make, 10 spaces)
Processor	C012000	(Processor type, 12 spaces)
HD	C010000	(Hard drive size, 10 spaces)
RAM	C010000	(RAM size, 10 spaces)

3. Use the **ATTEXT** command to invoke the **Attribute Extraction** dialog box (Figure 13-18), and select the Space Delimited File (SDF) radio button.

*Figure 13-18 Enter information in the **Attribute Extraction** dialog box*

4. Choose the **Select Objects <** button to select the objects (blocks) present on the screen. You can select the objects by using the Window or Crossing option. After selection is complete, right-click your pointing device to display the dialog box again.

5. In the Template File... edit box, enter the name of the template file, **TEMP1.TXT.**

6. In the Output File... edit box, enter the name of the output file, **COMPLST1.TXT.**

7. Choose the **OK** button in the **Attribute Extraction** dialog box.

8. Use the Notepad again to list the output file, **COMPLST1.TXT.** The output file will be similar to the file shown at the beginning of Example 3.

Using the Command Line (-ATTEXT)

You can also extract the attributes from the command line by entering the **-ATTEXT** command at the Command prompt. When you enter this command, AutoCAD will first prompt you to enter the type of output file. You could select CDF, SDF, DXF, or Objects. If you select the Objects option, AutoCAD will prompt you to select the objects whose attributes you want to extract. After you select the objects, AutoCAD will return the prompt, this time without the Objects option. The following is the command prompt sequence for this command.

Command: **-ATTEXT**
Enter extraction type or enable object selection [Cdf/Sdf/Dxf/Objects] <C>: **O**
Select objects: *Select objects.*
Select objects: ⌷Enter⌷
Enter attribute extraction type [Cdf/Sdf/Dxf] <C>: **C** or **S**

If you enter **C** or **S** (CDF or SDF), AutoCAD 2000 will display the **Select Template File** dialog box. You can browse for the required template file. (Template files were discussed earlier in this chapter in the subsection "Template File.")

After you select the template file name, AutoCAD 2000 will display the **Create extract file** dialog box (Figure 13-19). The extract file is the output file where you want to write the attribute values.

***Figure 13-19 Create extract file** dialog box*

If you do not enter a file name, AutoCAD assumes that the name of the extract file is the same as the drawing file name with the file extension **.TXT** or **.DXF**, depending on the attribute extract format. If you enter the file name and have selected the CDF or SDF file extraction format, the file extension must be **.TXT**; if you have selected the .DXF format, the file extension must be **.DXF**. After you enter the file name, AutoCAD will extract the attribute values from the blocks and write the data to the output file.

CONTROLLING ATTRIBUTE VISIBILITY (ATTDISP COMMAND)

Menu:	View > Display > Attribute Display
Command:	ATTDISP

The **ATTDISP** command allows you to change the visibility of all attribute values. Normally, the attributes are visible unless they are defined invisible by using the Invisible mode. The invisible attributes are not displayed, but they are a part of the block definition. The prompt sequence is:

Command: **ATTDISP**
Enter attribute visibility setting [Normal/ON/OFF] <current>:

If you enter ON and press ENTER, all attribute values will be displayed, including the attributes that are defined with the Invisible mode.

If you select OFF, all attribute values will become invisible. Similarly, if you enter N (Normal), AutoCAD will display the attribute values the way they are defined; that is, the attributes that were defined invisible will stay invisible and the attributes that were defined visible will become visible. In Example 2, the RAM attribute was defined with the Invisible mode; therefore, the RAM values are not displayed with the block. If you want to make the RAM attribute values visible (Figure 13-20), enter the **ATTDISP** command and then turn it ON.

Figure 13-20 *Using the **ATTDISP** command to make the RAM attribute values visible*

EDITING ATTRIBUTES (ATTEDIT COMMAND)
Single Block

Toolbar:	Modify II > Edit Attribute
Menu:	Modify > Attribute > Single...(Option)
Command:	ATTEDIT

Figure 13-21 Modify II toolbar

The **ATTEDIT** command allows you to edit the block attribute values through the **Edit Attributes** dialog box. When you enter this command, AutoCAD prompts you to select the block whose values you want to edit. After selecting the block, the **Edit Attribute** dialog box is displayed. The dialog box shows the prompts and the attribute values of the selected block. If an attribute has been defined with Constant mode, it is not displayed in the dialog box because a constant attribute value cannot be edited. To make any changes, choose the edit box and enter the new value. After you choose the **OK** button, the attribute values are updated in the selected block.

    Command: **ATTEDIT**
    Select block reference: *Select a block with attributes.*

If the selected block has no attributes, AutoCAD will display the alert message **That block has no editable attributes**. Similarly, if the selected object is not a block, AutoCAD again displays the alert message **That object is not a block.**.

 Note
*You cannot use the **ATTEDIT** command to do global editing of attribute values.*

*You cannot use the **ATTEDIT** command to modify position, height, or style of the attribute value.*

Example 4

In this example you will use the **ATTEDIT** command to change the attribute of the first computer (16MB to 16 Meg), which is located in Room-1.

1. Load the drawing that was created in Example 2. The drawing has six blocks with attributes. The name of the block is COMP, and it has six defined attributes, one of them invisible. Zoom in so that the first computer is displayed on the screen (Figure 13-22).

Figure 13-22 Zoomed view of the first computer

2. At the AutoCAD Command: prompt, enter the **ATTEDIT** command. AutoCAD will prompt you to select a block. Select the block, first computer located in Room-1.

    Command: **ATTEDIT**
    Select block reference: *Select a block.*

AutoCAD will display the **Edit Attributes** dialog box (Figure 13-23), which shows the attribute prompts and the attribute values.

3. Edit the values, and choose the **OK** button in the dialog box. When you exit the dialog box, the attribute values are updated.

Chapter 13

Figure 13-23 *Editing attribute values using the **Edit Attributes** dialog box*

Global Editing of Attributes

Menu:	Modify > Attribute > Global
Command:	-ATTEDIT

The **-ATTEDIT** command allows you to edit the attribute values independently of the blocks that contain the attribute reference. For example, if there are two blocks, COMPUTER and TABLE, with the attribute value PRICE, you can globally edit this value (PRICE) independently of the block that references these values. You can also edit the attribute values one at a time. For example, you can edit the attribute value (PRICE) of the block TABLE without affecting the value of the other block, COMPUTER. When you enter the **-ATTEDIT** command, AutoCAD displays the following prompt:

> Command: **-ATTEDIT**
> Edit attributes one at a time? [Yes/No] <Y>: **N**
> **Performing global editing of attribute values**

If you enter **N** at this prompt, it means that you want to do the global editing of the attributes. However, you can restrict the editing of attributes by block names, tag names, attribute values, and visibility of attributes on the screen.

Editing Visible Attributes Only

After you select global editing, AutoCAD will display the following prompt:

> Edit only attributes visible on screen? [Yes/No] <Y>: **Y**

If you enter **Y** at this prompt, AutoCAD will edit only those attributes that are visible and displayed on the screen. The attributes might have been defined with the Visible mode, but if they are not displayed on the screen they are not visible for editing. For example, if you zoom in, some of the attributes may not be displayed on the screen. Since the attributes are not displayed on the screen, they are invisible and cannot be selected for editing.

Editing All Attribute

If you enter **N** at the earlier-mentioned prompt, AutoCAD flips from graphics to text screen and displays the following message on the screen:

> **Drawing must be regenerated afterwards.**

Now, AutoCAD will edit all attributes even if they are not visible or displayed on the screen. Also, changes that you make in the attribute values are not reflected immediately. Instead, the attribute values are updated and the drawing regenerated after you are done with the command.

Editing Specific Blocks

Although you have selected global editing, you can confine the editing of attributes to specific blocks by entering the block name at the prompt. For example:

> Enter block name specification <*>: **COMP**

When you enter the name of the block, AutoCAD will edit the attributes that have the given block (COMP) reference. You can also use the wild-card characters to specify the block names. If you want to edit attributes in all blocks that have attributes defined, press ENTER

Editing Attributes with Specific Attribute Tag Names

Like blocks, you can confine attribute editing to those attribute values that have the specified tag name. For example, if you want to edit the attribute values that have the tag name MAKE, enter the tag name at the following AutoCAD prompt:

> Enter attribute tag specification <*>: **MAKE**

When you specify the tag name, AutoCAD will not edit attributes that have a different tag name, even if the values being edited are the same. You can also use the wild-card characters to specify the tag names. If you want to edit attributes with any tag name, press ENTER.

Editing Attributes with a Specific Attribute Value

Like blocks and attribute tag names, you can confine attribute editing to a specified attribute value. For example, if you want to edit the attribute values that have the value 100MB, enter the value at the following AutoCAD prompt:

> Enter attribute value specification <*>: **100MB**

When you specify the attribute value, AutoCAD will not edit attributes that have a different value, even if the tag name and block specification are the same. You can also use the wild-card characters to specify the attribute value. If you want to edit attributes with any value, press ENTER.

Sometimes the value of an attribute is null, and these values are not visible. If you want to select the null values for editing, make sure you have not restricted the global editing to visible attributes. To edit the null attributes, enter \ at the following prompt:

Enter attribute value specification <*>: \

After you enter this information, AutoCAD will prompt you to select the attributes. You can select the attributes by selecting individual attributes or by using one of the object selection options (Window, Crossing, etc).

Select Attributes: *Select the attribute values parallel to the current UCS only.*

After you select the attributes, AutoCAD will prompt you to enter the string you want to change and the new string. AutoCAD will retrieve the attribute information, edit it, and then update the attribute values.

Enter string to change:
Enter new string:

The following is the complete command prompt sequence of the **-ATTEDIT** command. It is assumed that the editing is global and for visible attributes only.

Command: **-ATTEDIT**
Edit attributes one at a time? [Yes/No] <Y>: **N**
Performing global editing of attribute values.
Edit only attributes visible on screen? [Yes/No] <Y>: **N**
Drawing must be regenerated afterwards.
Enter block name specification <*>:
Enter attribute tag specification <*>:
Enter attribute value specification <*>:
Enter string to change:
Enter new string:

Note
AutoCAD regenerates the drawing at the end of the command automatically unless system variable **REGENAUTO** *is off, which controls automatic regeneration of the drawing.*

Example 5

In this example, you will use the drawing from Example 2 to edit the attribute values that are highlighted in the following table. The tag names are given at the top of the table (ITEM, MAKE, PROCESSOR, HD, RAM). The RAM values are invisible in the drawing.

	ITEM	MAKE	PROCESSOR	HD	RAM
COMP	Computer	Gateway	486-60	150MB	**16MB**
COMP	Computer	Zenith	486-30	100MB	**32MB**
COMP	Computer	IBM	386-30	80MB	**8MB**

COMP	Computer	Del	586-60	450MB	**64MB**
COMP	Computer	**CAD-CIM**	Pentium-90	100 Min	**32MB**
COMP	Computer	**CAD-CIM**	**Unknown**	600MB	Standard

Make the following changes in the **highlighted** attribute values (Figure 13-24).

1. Change Unknown to Pentium.
2. Change CAD-CIM to Compaq.
3. Change MB to Meg for all attribute values that have the tag name RAM. (No changes should be made to the values that have the tag name HD.)

The following is the prompt sequence to change the attribute value **Unknown to Pentium**.

1. Enter the **-ATTEDIT** command at the Command prompt. At the next prompt, enter **N** (No).

   Command: **-ATTEDIT**
   Edit attributes one at a time? [Yes/No] <Y>: **N**
   Performing global editing of attribute values.

2. We want to edit only those attributes that are visible on the screen, so press ENTER at the following prompt:

   Edit only attributes visible on screen? [Yes/No] <Y>: *Press ENTER.*

3. As shown in the table, the attributes belong to a single block, COMP. In a drawing, there could be more blocks. To confine the attribute editing to the COMP block only, enter the name of the block (COMP) at the next prompt.

   Enter block name specification <*>: **COMP**

4. At the next two prompts, enter the attribute tag name and the attribute value specification. When you enter these two values, only those attributes that have the specified tag name and attribute value will be edited.

   Enter attribute tag specification<*>: **Processor**
   Enter attribute value specification<*>: **Unknown**

5. Next, AutoCAD will prompt you to select attributes. Use the Crossing option to select all blocks. AutoCAD will search for the attributes that satisfy the given criteria (attributes belong to the block COMP, the attributes have the tag name Processor, and the attribute value is Unknown). Once AutoCAD locates such attributes, they will be highlighted.

   Select Attributes:

6. At the next two prompts, enter the string you want to change, and then enter the new string.

   Enter string to change: **Unknown**

Enter new string: **Pentium**

7. The following is the command prompt sequence to change the make of the computers from **CAD-CIM** to **Compaq**.

Command: **-ATTEDIT**
Edit attributes one at a time? [Yes/No] <Y>: **N**
Performing global editing of attribute values.
Edit only attributes visible on screen? [Yes/No] <Y>: *Press ENTER.*
Drawing must be regenerated afterwards.
Enter block name specification <*>: **COMP**
Enter attribute tag specification <*>: **MAKE**
Enter attribute value specification <*>:
Select Attributes:
Enter string to change: **CAD-CIM**
Enter new string: **Compaq**

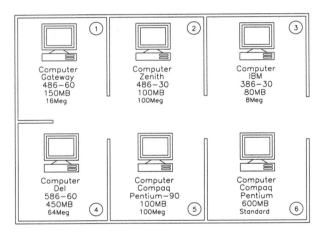

Figure 13-24 *Using* ***-ATTEDIT*** *to change the attribute values*

8. The following is the command prompt sequence to change **MB** to **Meg**.

Command: **-ATTEDIT**
Edit attributes one at a time? [Yes/No] <Y>: **N**
Performing global editing of attribute values.

At the next prompt, you must enter **N** because the attributes you want to edit (tag name, RAM) are not visible on the screen.

Edit only attributes visible on screen? [Yes/No] <Y>: **N**
Drawing must be regenerated afterwards.
Enter block name specification <*>: **COMP**

At the next prompt, about the tag specification, you must specify the tag name because the text string MB also appears in the hard drive size (tag name, HD). If you do not enter the tag name, AutoCAD will change all MB attribute values to Meg.

Enter attribute tag specification <*>: **RAM**
Enter attribute value specification <*>:
Select Attributes:
Enter string to change: **MB**
Enter new string: **Meg**

9. Use the **ATTDISP** command to display the invisible attributes on the screen.

Command: **ATTDISP**
Enter attribute visibility setting [Normal/ON/OFF] <ON>: **ON**

Individual Editing of Attributes

The **-ATTEDIT** command can also be used to edit the attribute values individually. When you enter this command, AutoCAD will prompt **Edit attributes one at a time? [Yes/No] <Y>:**. At this prompt, press ENTER to accept the default or enter **Y.** The next three prompts are about block specification, attribute tag specification, and attribute value specification, which were discussed in the previous section, in this Chapter. These options let you limit the attributes for editing. For example, if you specify a block name, AutoCAD will limit the editing to those attributes that belong to the specified block. Similarly, if you also specify the tag name, AutoCAD will limit the editing to the attributes in the specified block and with the specified tag name.

Command: **-ATTEDIT**
Edit attributes one at a time? [Yes/No] <Y>: ⌷Enter⌷
Enter block name specification<*>: ⌷Enter⌷
Enter attribute tag specification<*>: ⌷Enter⌷
Enter attribute value specification<*>: ⌷Enter⌷
Select Attributes:

At the **Select Attributes:** prompt, select the objects by choosing the objects or by using an object selection option such as Window, Crossing, WPolygon, CPolygon, or Box. By using these options you can further limit the attribute values selected for editing. After you select the objects, AutoCAD will mark the first attribute it can find with an **X.** The next prompt is:

Enter an option [Value/Position/Height/Angle/Style/Layer/Color/Next] <N>:

Value. The Value option lets you change the value of an attribute. To change the value, enter **V** at this prompt. AutoCAD will display the following prompt:

Enter type of value modification [Change/Replace] <R>:

The Change option allows you to change a few characters in the attribute value. To select the Change option, enter Change or **C** at the prompt. AutoCAD will display the next prompt:

Chapter 13

Enter string to change:
Enter new string:

At the **Enter string to change**: prompt, enter the characters you want to change and press ENTER. At the next prompt, **Enter new string:**, enter the new string.

 Note
*You can use ? and * in the string value. When these characters are used in string values, AutoCAD does not interpret them as wild-card characters.*

To use the Replace option, enter **R** or press ENTER at the **Enter type of value modification [Change/Replace] <R>:** prompt. AutoCAD will display the following prompt:

Enter new Attribute value:

At this prompt, enter the new attribute value. AutoCAD will replace the string bearing the **X** mark with the new string. If the new attribute is null, the attribute will be assigned a null value.

Position, Height, Angle. You can change the position, height, or angle of an attribute value by entering, respectively, **P**, **H**, or **A** at the following prompt:

Enter an option [Value/Position/Height/Angle/Style/Layer/Color/Next] <N>:

The Position option lets you define the new position of the attribute value. AutoCAD will prompt you to enter the new starting point, center point, or endpoint of the string. If the string is aligned, AutoCAD will prompt for two points. You can also define the new height or angle of the text string by entering, respectively, **H** or **A** at the prompt.

Layer and Color. The Layer and Color options allow you to change the layer and color of the attribute. For a color change, you can enter the new color by entering a color number (1 through 255), a color name (red, green, etc.), BYLAYER, or BYBLOCK.

Example 6

In this example, you will use the drawing in Example 2 to edit the attributes individually (Figure 13-25). Make the following changes in the attribute values.

a. Change the attribute value 100 Min to 100MB.
b. Change the height of all attributes with the tag name RAM to 0.075 units.

1. Load the drawing that you had saved in Example 2.

2. At the AutoCAD Command prompt, enter the **-ATTEDIT** command. The following is the command prompt sequence to change the value of 100 Min to 100MB.

Command: **-ATTEDIT**
Edit attributes one at a time? [Yes/No] <Y>: [Enter]

Enter block name specification <*>: **COMP**
Enter attribute tag specification <*>: `Enter`
Enter attribute value specification <*>: `Enter`
Select Attributes: *Select the attribute.*
Enter an option [Value/Position/Height/Angle/Style/Layer/Color/Next] <N>: **V**
Enter type of value modification [Change/Replace] <R>: **C**
Enter string to change: \ **Min**
Enter new string: **100MB**

When AutoCAD prompts **Enter string to change:**, enter the characters you want to change. In this example, the characters **Min** are preceded by a space. If you enter a space, AutoCAD displays the next prompt, **Enter new string:**. If you need a leading blank space, the character string must start with a backslash (\), followed by the desired number of blank spaces.

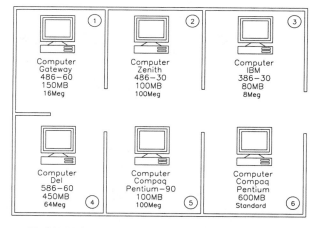

Figure 13-25 *Using* ***-ATTEDIT*** *to change the attribute values individually*

3. To change the height of the attribute text, enter the **-ATTEDIT** command as just shown. When AutoCAD displays the following prompt, enter **H** for height.

Enter an option [Value/Position/Height/Angle/Style/Layer/Color/Next] <N>: **H**
Specify new height <current>: **0.075**

After you enter the new height and press ENTER, AutoCAD will change the height of the text string that has the **X** mark. AutoCAD will then repeat the last prompt. Use the **Next** option to move the **X** mark to the next attribute. To change the height of other attribute values, repeat these steps.

Chapter 13

INSERTING TEXT FILES IN THE DRAWING
Using MTEXT Command

Toolbar:	Draw > Multiline Text
Menu:	Draw > Text > Multiline Text
Command:	MTEXT

You can insert a text file by selecting the Import Text option in the **Multiline Text Editor** dialog box. You can invoke this dialog box by using the **MTEXT** command.

    Command: **MTEXT**

Next, AutoCAD prompts you to enter the insertion point and other corner of the paragraph text box. After you enter these points, the **Multiline Text Editor** dialog box appears on screen. To insert the text file **COMPLST1.TXT** (created in Example 3), choose the Import Text button. AutoCAD displays the **Open** dialog box (Figure 13-26).

Figure 13-26 Open dialog box

In this dialog box, you can select the text file COMPLST1 and then choose the **Open** button. The imported text is displayed in the text area of the **Multiline Text Editor** dialog box (Figure 13-27). Note that only ASCII files are properly interpreted.

Now choose the **OK** button to get the imported text in the selected area on the screen (Figure 13-28). You can also use the **Multiline Text Editor** dialog box to change the text style, height, direction, width, rotation, line spacing, and attachment.

Figure 13-27 Multiline Text Editor dialog box displaying the imported text

```
COMP      Computer    CAD-CIM    Pentium-90      100  Min
COMP      Computer    CAD-CIM    Unknown         600MB
COMP      Computer    Del        586-60          450MB
COMP      Computer    Zenith     486-30          100MB
COMP      Computer    Gateway    486-60          150MB
COMP      Computer    IBM        386-30          80MB
```

Figure 13-28 Imported text file on the screen

Self-Evaluation Test

Answer the following questions, and then compare your answers to the correct answers given at the end of this chapter.

1. The **Verify** option allows you to verify the attribute value you have entered when inserting a block. (T/F)

2. Unlike a constant attribute, the **Preset** attribute cannot be edited. (T/F)

3. For tag names, any lowercase letters are automatically converted to uppercase. (T/F)

4. The entry in the **Value:** edit box of the Attribute Definition dialog box defines the _____ of the specified attribute.

5. If you have selected the **Align** option for the text justification, the Height < and Rotation < edit boxes are _____.

6. You can use the _____ command to edit text or attribute definitions.

7. The default value of the **ATTDIA** variable is _____, which disables the dialog box.

Chapter 13

8. In the Space Delimited File, the records are of fixed width as specified in the _____ File.

9. In the _____ File, the records are not separated by a comma and the character fields are not enclosed in single quotes.

10. You must not use the _____ character in template files. Any alignment in the fields must be done by inserting spaces after the field name.

11. You cannot use the **ATTEDIT** command to modify the position, height, or style of the attribute value. (T/F)

12. The _____ command allows you to edit the attribute values independently of the blocks that contain the attribute reference.

13. The **-ATTEDIT** command can also be used to edit the attribute values individually. (T/F)

14. You can use ? and * in the string value. When these characters are used in string values, AutoCAD does not interpret them as wild-card characters. (T/F)

15. You can insert the text file in the drawing by entering the _____ command at the AutoCAD Command prompt.

Review Questions

1. Give two major uses of defining block attributes. _____ .

2. The information associated with a block is known as _____ or _____ .

3. You can define the block attributes by entering _____ at the Command prompt.

4. The most convenient way to define the block attributes is by using the **Attribute Definition** dialog box, which can be invoked by entering _____ .

5. What are the options in the **Mode** area of the **Attribute Definition** dialog box? _____
   _____ .

6. The **Constant** option lets you create an attribute that has a fixed value and cannot be changed later. (T/F)

7. What is the function of the **Preset** option? _____ .

8. The attribute value is requested when you use the **Preset** option to define a block attribute. (T/F)

9. Name the three edit boxes in the **Attribute area** of the **Attribute Definition** dialog box.
   _____ .

10. The **tag** is like a label that is used to identify an attribute. (T/F)

11. The tag names can only be uppercase. (T/F)

12. The tag name cannot be null. (T/F)

13. The tag name can contain a blank space. (T/F)

14. If you select the Constant option in the Mode area of the **Attribute Definition** dialog box, the **Prompt:** edit box is _____ because no prompt is required if the attribute is _____.

15. If you do not enter anything in the **Prompt:** edit box, the entry made in the **Tag:** edit box is used as the prompt. (T/F)

16. What option, button, or check box should you select in the **Attribute Definition** dialog box to automatically place the subsequent attribute text just below the previously defined attribute? _____ .

17. The text style must be defined before it can be used to specify the text style. (T/F)

18. If you select a style that has the height predefined, AutoCAD automatically disables the Height < edit box in the Attribute Definition dialog box. (T/F)

19. If you have selected the Fit option for the text justification, the _____ edit box is disabled.

20. What is the difference between the **ATTDEF** and the **-ATTDEF** commands? _____
_____ .

21. The _____ command lets you edit both text and attribute definitions.

22. The value of the block attributes can be specified in the **Edit Attribute Definition** dialog box. (T/F)

23. The **Edit Attribute Definition** dialog box is invoked by using the _____ or _____ command with the system variable _____ set to 1.

24. If you use the **Enter Attributes** dialog box to define the attribute values, the Verify mode is _____ because the **Enter Attributes** dialog box allows the user to examine and edit the attribute values.

25. You can also define attributes from the command line by setting the system variable _____ to 0.

26. To use the **Attribute Extraction** dialog box for extracting the attributes, enter _____ at the Command prompt.

Chapter 13

27. You can select the Comma Delimited File, Space Delimited File, or Drawing Interchange File. The format selection is determined by the text editor you use. (T/F)

28. In the Comma Delimited File, each character field is enclosed in _____ and each record is separated by a _____.

Exercises

Exercise 1   *Electronics*

In this exercise, you will define the following attributes for a resistor and then create a block using the **BLOCK** command. The name of the block is RESIS.

Mode	Tag name	Prompt	Default value
Verify	RNAME	Enter name	RX
Verify	RVALUE	Enter resistance	XX
Verify, Invisible	RPRICE	Enter price	00

1. Draw the resistor as shown in Figure 13-29.
2. Enter **ATTDEF** at the AutoCAD Command prompt to invoke the **Attribute Definition** dialog box.
3. Define the attributes as shown in the preceding table, and position the attribute text as shown in Figure 13-29.
4. Use the **BLOCK** command to create a block. The name of the block is RESIS, and the insertion point of the block is at the left end of the resistor. When you select the objects for the block, make sure you also select the attributes.

Figure 13-29 *Drawing of a resistor for Exercise 1*

Exercise 2   *Electronics*

In this exercise, you will use the **INSERT** command to insert the block that was defined in Exercise 1 (RESIS). The following is the list of the attribute values for the resistances in the electric circuit.

RNAME	RVALUE	RPRICE
R1	35	0.32
R2	27	0.25
R3	52	0.40
R4	8	0.21
RX	10	0.21

1. Draw the electric circuit diagram as shown in Figure 13-30 (assume the dimensions).

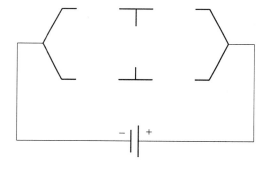

Figure 13-30 *Drawing of the electric circuit diagram without resistors for Exercise 2*

Figure 13-31 *Drawing of the electric circuit diagram with resistors for Exercise 2*

2. Set the system variable **ATTDIA** to 1. Use the **INSERT** command to insert the blocks, and define the attribute values in the **Enter Attributes** dialog box.
3. Repeat the **INSERT** command to insert other blocks, and define their attribute values as given in the table. Save the drawing as **ATTEXR2.DWG** (Figure 13-31).

Exercise 3   *Electronics*

In this exercise, you will write a template file for extracting the attribute values as defined in Exercise 2. These attribute values must be written to a file **RESISLST.TXT** and arranged as shown in the following table.

Field width in characters			
< 10 >	< 10 >	< 10 >	< 10 >
RESIS	R1	35	0.32
RESIS	R2	27	0.25
RESIS	R3	52	0.40
RESIS	R4	8	0.21
RESIS	RX	10	0.21

1. Load the drawing **ATTEXR2** that you saved in Exercise 2.
2. Use the Windows Notepad to write the template file. After writing the file, save it as an ASCII file under the file name **TEMP2.TXT.**
3. In the AutoCAD screen, use the **ATTEXT** command to invoke the **Attribute Extraction** dialog box, and select the Space Delimited File (SDF) radio button.
4. Select the objects (blocks). You can also select the objects by using the Window or Crossing option.
5. In the Template File edit box, enter the name of the template file, **TEMP2.TXT.**
6. In the Output File edit box, enter the name of the output file, **RESISLST.TXT.**
7. Choose the **OK** button in the **Attribute Extraction** dialog box.
8. Use the Windows Notepad to list the output file, **RESISLST.TXT.** The output file should be similar to the file shown in the beginning of Exercise 3.

Exercise 4   *Electronics*

In this exercise, you will use the **ATTEDIT** or **-ATTEDIT** command to change the attributes of the resistances that are highlighted in the following table. You will also extract the attribute values and insert the text file in the drawing.

1. Load the drawing **ATTEXR2** that was created in Exercise 2. The drawing has five resistances with attributes. The name of the block is RESIS, and it has three defined attributes, one of them invisible.
2. Use the AutoCAD **ATTEDIT** or **-ATTEDIT** command to edit the values that are **highlighted** in the following table.

RESIS	R1	40	0.32
RESIS	R2	29	0.25
RESIS	R3	52	0.45
RESIS	R4	8	0.25
RESIS	R5	10	0.21

3. Extract the attribute values, and write the values to a text file.
4. Use the **MTEXT** command to insert the text file in the drawing.

Exercise 5   *Electronics*

Use the information given in Exercise 3 to extract the attribute values, and write the data to the output file. The data in the output file should be Comma Delimited CDF. Use the **ATTEXT** and **-ATTEXT** commands to extract the attribute values.

Exercise 6

Electronics

In this exercise, you will draw the circuit diagram as shown in Figure 13-32, define the attributes, and then extract the attributes to create a bill of materials.

Figure 13-32 *Drawing of the circuit diagram for Exercise 6*

Answers to Self-Evaluation Test

1 - T, **2** - F, **3** - T, **4** - default value, **5** - disabled, **6** - **CHANGE**, **7** - 0, **8** - template, **9** - Space Delimited, **10** - tab, **11** - T, **12** - **ATTEDIT**, **13** - T, **14** - T, **15** - **MTEXT**

Chapter 14

External References

Learning Objectives

After completing this chapter, you will be able to:
- *Understand external references and their applications.*
- *Understand dependent symbols.*
- *Use the **XREF** command and its options.*
- *Use the **Attach, Unload, Reload, Detach**, and **Bind** options.*
- *Change the path of a drawing.*
- *Use the **XBIND** command to add dependent symbols.*
- *Use the **XCLIP** command to clip xref drawings.*
- *Understand demand loading.*
- *Use **XCLIPFRAME** and **XLOADCTL** system variables, and **XATTACH** command.*
- *Use the **REFEDIT** command for In-place editing.*

EXTERNAL REFERENCES

The external reference feature lets you reference an external drawing without making that drawing a permanent part of the existing drawing. For example, assume that we have an assembly drawing ASSEM1 that consists of two parts, SHAFT and BEARING. The SHAFT and BEARING are separate drawings created by two CAD operators or provided by two different vendors. We want to create an assembly drawing from these two parts. One way to create an assembly drawing is to insert these two drawings as blocks by using the **INSERT** command. Now assume that the design of BEARING has changed due to customer or product requirements. To update the assembly drawing we have to make sure that we insert the BEARING drawing after the changes have been made. If we forget to update the assembly drawing, then the assembly drawing will not reflect the changes made in the piece part drawing. In a production environment, this could have serious consequences.

You can solve this problem by using the **external reference** facility, which lets you link the piece part drawings with the assembly drawing. If the xref drawings (piece part) get updated, the changes are automatically reflected in the assembly drawing. This way, the assembly drawing stays updated no matter when the changes were made in the piece part drawings. There is no limit to the number of drawings that you can reference. You can also have **nested references**. For example, the piece part drawing BEARING could be referenced in the SHAFT drawing, then the SHAFT drawing could be referenced in the assembly drawing ASSEM1. When you open or plot the assembly drawing, AutoCAD automatically loads the referenced drawing SHAFT and the nested drawing BEARING.

If you use the **INSERT** command to insert the piece parts, the piece parts become a permanent part of the drawing and, therefore, the drawing has a certain size. However, if you use the external reference feature to link the drawings, the piece part drawings are not saved with the assembly drawing. AutoCAD only saves the reference information with the assembly drawing; therefore, the size of the drawing is minimized. Like blocks, the xref drawings can be scaled, rotated, or positioned at any desired location, but they cannot be exploded. You can also use only a part of the Xref by making clipped boundary of Xrefs.

DEPENDENT SYMBOLS

If you use the **INSERT** command to insert a drawing, the information about the named objects is lost if the names are duplicated. If they are unique, it is imported. The **named objects** are entries such as blocks, layers, text styles, and layers. For example, if the assembly drawing has a layer HIDDEN with green color and HIDDEN linetype, and the piece part BEARING has a layer HIDDEN with blue color and HIDDEN2 linetype, then when you insert the BEARING drawing in the assembly drawing, the values set in the assembly drawing will override the values of the inserted drawing (Figure 14-1). Therefore, in the assembly drawing, the layer HIDDEN will retain green color and HIDDEN linetype, ignoring the layer settings of the inserted drawing. Only those layers that have the same names are affected. Remaining layers that have different layer names are added to the current drawing.

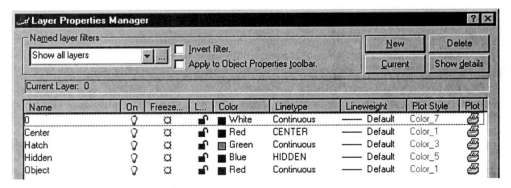

Figure 14-1 *Layer settings of the current drawing override the layers of the inserted drawing*

In the xref drawings, the information about named objects is not lost because AutoCAD will create additional named objects such as the specified layer settings as shown in Figure 14-2. For xref drawings, these named objects become dependent symbols (features such as layers, linetypes, object color, text style, and so on).

The layer HIDDEN of the xref drawing (BEARING) is appended with the name of the xref drawing BEARING, and the two are separated by the vertical bar symbol (|). Also these layers appear faded. The layer name HIDDEN changes to BEARING|HIDDEN. Similarly, CENTER is renamed BEARING|CENTER and OBJECT is renamed BEARING|OBJECT (Figure 14-2). The information added to the current drawing is not permanent. It is added only when the xref drawing is loaded. If you detach the xref drawing, the dependent symbols are automatically erased from the current drawing.

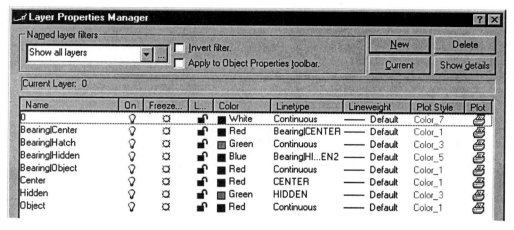

Figure 14-2 Xref creates additional layers

When you Xref a drawing, AutoCAD does not let you reference the symbols directly. For example, you cannot make the dependent layer, BEARING|HIDDEN, current. Therefore, you cannot add any objects to that layer. However, you can change the color, linetype, lineweight, or visibility (on/off, freeze/thaw) of the layer in the current drawing. If the system variable **VISRETAIN** is set to 0 (default), the settings are retained for the current drawing session. When you save and exit the drawing, the changes are discarded and the layer settings return to their default status. If the **VISRETAIN** variable is set to 1, layer settings such as color, linetype, on/off, and freeze/thaw are retained; the settings are saved with the drawing and are used when you open the drawing the next time. Whenever, you open a drawing or plot it, AutoCAD reloads each Xref in the drawing and as a result, the latest updated version of the drawing is loaded automatically.

XREF COMMAND
Managing Xrefs in a Drawing*

Toolbar:	Insert > External Reference
	Reference > External Reference
Menu:	Insert > Xref Manager
Command:	XREF

Figure 14-3 Insert toolbar

 When you invoke the **XREF** command, AutoCAD displays the **Xref Manager** dialog box (Figure 14-4). The **Xref Manager** dialog box displays the status of each Xref in the current drawing and the relation between the various Xrefs. It allows you attach a new xref, detach, unload, load an

Chapter 14

existing one, change an attachment to an overlay, or an overlay to an attachment. It also allows you to edit an xref's path and bind the xref definition to the drawing. You can also select an Xref in the current drawing and then right-click the drawing area, a shortcut menu is displayed. Choosing the **Xref Manager** option from the shortcut menu, displays the **Xref Manager** dialog box. The Upper-left corner of the dialog box has two buttons: **List View** and **Tree View**. Choosing the **List View** button displays the Xrefs in the drawing in an alphabetical list, this is the default view. It has the following headings: **Reference name**, **Status** (whether the xref is loaded, unloaded, unreferenced, not found or unresolved), **Size**, **Type** (attachment or overlay), **Date**(last saved on), and **Saved Path**. Choosing any of these headings sorts and lists the Xrefs in the current drawing according to that particular title. For example, choosing **Reference Name**, sorts and lists the xrefs as per name. You can also rename a xref in this dialog box. Choosing the **Tree View** button, displays the xrefs in the drawing in a hierarchical tree view. It displays information on nested xrefs and their relationship with one another.

Figure 14-4 Xref Manager dialog box

Attaching an Xref Drawing (Attach option)

The **Attach** button of the **Xref Manager** dialog box is used to attach an xref drawing to the current drawing. This option can be invoked by choosing the **Attach** button in the **Xref Manager** dialog box. The following examples illustrate the process of attaching an xref to the current drawing. In this example, it is assumed that there are two drawings, SHAFT and BEARING. SHAFT is the current drawing that is loaded on the screen (Figure 14-5); the BEARING drawing is saved on the disk. We want to xref the BEARING drawing in the SHAFT drawing.

1. The first step is to make sure that the SHAFT drawing is on the screen (draw the shaft drawing with assumed dimensions). (One of the drawings does not need to be on the screen. You could attach both drawings, BEARING and SHAFT, to an existing drawing, even if it is a blank drawing.)

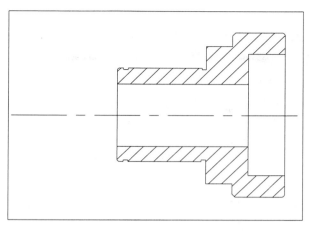

Figure 14-5 Current drawing, SHAFT

2. Invoke the **XREF** command to display the **Xref Manager** dialog box. In this dialog box, choose the **Attach** button. If you choose **External Reference** from the **Insert** menu, the **Select Reference File** dialog box (Figure 14-6) is displayed. Select the drawing that you want to attach (BEARING), and then choose the **Open** button; the **External reference** dialog box is displayed on the screen (Figure 14-7).

Figure 14-6 Select Reference File dialog box

In the **External Reference** dialog box (Figure 14-7), you can select the name of the file to attach from the **Name:** drop-down list. The selected file name is displayed in the **Name:** text box and the **Path:** of the file is also displayed below the **Name:** text box. Under the **Reference Type** area, select the **Attachment** radio button if it is not already selected (default option). You can either specify the **insertion point**, **scale**, and **rotation angle** in the respective **X:**, **Y:**, **Z:** and **Angle:** edit boxes or select the **Specify On-screen** check boxes to use the pointing device to specify them on the screen. Choose the **OK** button in the **External Reference** dialog box and then specify the Insertion, Scale and Angle parameters on the screen. After attaching the

BEARING drawing, save the current drawing with the file name SHAFT (Figure 14-8).

*Figure 14-7 **External Reference** dialog box*

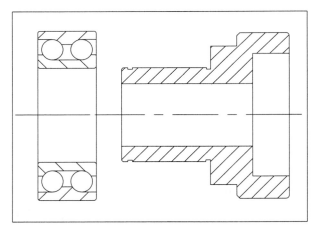

Figure 14-8 Attaching xref drawing, BEARING

You can also use the **-XREF** command to attach a drawing from the command line. If the **FILEDIA** system variable is set to 0, AutoCAD will not display the **Select Reference File** dialog box. Entering the ~ (tilde) symbol at the **Enter name of file to attach:** prompt displays the **Select Reference File** dialog box. If the file name has more than 31 characters, or has spaces or invalid characters, AutoCAD will prompt you to enter a name different from the drawing name at the **Enter name of file to attach:** prompt. Enter NEW NAME=OLD NAME at the **Enter name of file to attach:** prompt. After specifying the name of the file to attach, press ENTER. AutoCAD will now prompt you to specify the insertion point, scale factor, and the rotation angle. The command prompts are as follows:

Command: **-XREF**
Enter an option [?/Bind/Detach/Path/Unload/Reload/Overlay/Attach] <Attach>: Enter
Enter name of file to attach: BEARING   (*If **FILEDIA** = 0.*)
Specify insertion point or
[Scale/X/Y/Z/Rotate/PScale/PX/PY/PZ/PRotate]: *Select a point.*

3. Load the drawing BEARING, and make the changes shown in Figure 14-9 (draw polylines on the sides). Now, save the drawing with the file name BEARING.

Figure 14-9 Modifying the xref drawing, BEARING

4. Load the drawing SHAFT on the screen. You will notice (Figure 14-10) that the xref drawing BEARING is automatically updated. This is the most useful feature of the **XREF** command. You could also have inserted the BEARING drawing as a block, but if you had updated the BEARING drawing, the drawing in which it was inserted would not have been updated automatically.

When you attach an xref drawing, AutoCAD remembers the name of the attached drawing. If you xref the drawing again, AutoCAD displays a message to that effect as shown:

Xref "BEARING" has already been defined.
Using existing definition.
Specify insertion point or
[Scale/X/Y/Z/Rotate/PScale/PX/PY/PZ/PRotate]: *Indicate where to place another copy of the xref.*

Note
*If the xref drawing you want to attach is currently being edited, AutoCAD will attach the drawing that has been saved earlier through the **SAVE**, **WBLOCK**, or **QUIT** command.*

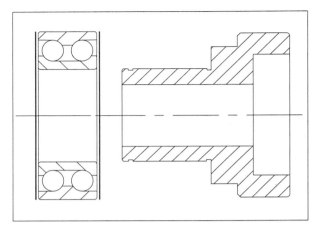

Figure 14-10 *After loading the drawing SHAFT, BEARING is automatically updated*

Points to Remember About Xref

1. When you enter the name of the xref drawing, AutoCAD checks for block names and xref names. If a block exists with the same name as the name of the xref drawing in the current drawing, the **XREF** command is terminated and an error message is displayed.
2. If you are using **-XREF** command with **FILEDIA** set to 0, you can enter ~ (tilde) at the **Enter name of file to attach:** prompt. The tilde sign displays the **Select Reference File** dialog box. Entering **?** at the **Enter an option [?/Bind/Detach/Path/Unload/Reload/Overlay/Attach] <Attach>:** prompt, displays a list of xref names, path, and type present in the current drawing.
3. When you xref a drawing, the objects that are in the model space are attached. Any objects that are in the paper space are not attached to the current drawing.
4. The layer 0, DEFPOINTS, and the linetype CONTINUOUS are treated differently. The current drawing layers 0, DEFPOINTS, and the linetype CONTINUOUS will override the layers and linetypes of the xref drawing. For example, if the layer 0 of the current drawing is white and the layer 0 of the xref drawing is red, the white color will override the red.
5. The xref drawings can be nested. For example, if the BEARING drawing contains the reference INRACE and you xref the BEARING drawing to the current drawing, the INRACE drawing is automatically attached to the current drawing. If you detach the BEARING drawing, the INRACE drawing gets detached automatically.
6. When you attach an xref drawing using the **-XREF** command with **FILEDIA** set to 0, you can assign the xref drawing a different name. For example, if the name of the xref drawing is BEARING and you want to assign it the name OBEARING, the prompt sequence is as follows:

Command: **-XREF**
Enter an option [?/Bind/Detach/Path/Unload/Reload/Overlay/Attach] <Attach>: ⏎
Enter name of file to attach: OBEARING= BEARING
Specify insertion point or
[Scale/X/Y/Z/Rotate/PScale/PX/PY/PZ/PRotate]: *Select a point.*

7. When you xref a drawing, AutoCAD stores the name and path of the drawing. If the name of the xref drawing or the path where the drawing was originally stored has changed or you cannot find it in the path specified in the **Options** dialog box, AutoCAD cannot load the drawing, plot it, or use the **Reload** option of the **XREF** command.

Detaching an Xref Drawing (Detach Option)

The **Detach** option can be used to detach the xref drawings. If there are any nested Xref drawings defined with the xref drawings, they are also detached. Once a drawing is detached, it is erased from the screen. To detach the xref drawings, select the file names in the **Xref Manager** dialog box and then choose the **Detach** button. You can also use the **-XREF** command to detach the xref drawings.

> Command: **-XREF**
> Enter an option [?/Bind/Detach/Path/Unload/Reload/Overlay/Attach] <Attach>: D
> Enter Xref name(s) to detach: *Enter names of xref drawings.*

When AutoCAD prompts for xref to detach, you can enter the name of one xref drawing or the name of several drawings separated by commas. You can also enter * (asterisk), in which case all referenced drawings, including the nested drawings, will be detached.

Updating an Xref Drawing (Reload Option)

When you load a drawing, AutoCAD automatically loads the referenced drawings. The **Reload** option of the **XREF** command lets you update the xref drawings and nested xref drawings any time. You do not need to exit the drawing editor and then reload the drawing. To reload the xref drawings, invoke the **XREF** command and select the drawings in the **Xref Manager** dialog box, then choose the **Reload** button. AutoCAD will scan for the referenced drawings and the nested xref drawings.

The **Reload** option is generally used when the xref drawings are currently being edited and you want to load the updated drawings. The xref drawings are updated based on what is saved on the disk. Therefore, before reloading an xref drawing, you should make sure that the xref drawings that are being edited have been saved. If AutoCAD encounters an error while loading the referenced drawings, the **XREF** command is terminated, and the entire reload operation is cancelled. You can also reload the xref drawings by using **-XREF** command. When you enter the **-XREF** command, AutoCAD will prompt you to enter the name of the xref drawing. You could enter the name of one xref drawing or the name of several drawings separated by commas. If you enter * (asterisk), AutoCAD will reload all xref and nested xref drawings.

> Command: **-XREF**
> Enter an option [?/Bind/Detach/Path/Unload/Reload/Overlay/Attach] <Attach>: R
> Enter Xref name(s) to reload: *Enter names of xref drawings.*

Unloading an Xref Drawing (Unload Option)

The **Unload** option allows you to unload the definition of xref drawings. However, AutoCAD retains the pointer to the xref drawings. When you unload the xref drawings, the drawings are not displayed on the screen. You can reload the xref drawings by using the **Reload** option. It is recom-

Chapter 14

mended that you unload the referenced drawings if they are not being used. Also, after unloading the xref drawings, the drawings load much faster and need less memory.

Adding an Xref Drawing (Bind Option)

The **Bind** option lets you convert the xref drawings to blocks in the current drawing. The bound drawings, including the nested xref drawings (that are no longer xrefs), become a permanent part of the current drawing. The bound drawing cannot be detached or reloaded. To bind the xref drawings, select the file names in the **Xref Manager** dialog box, and then choose the **Bind** button to display the **Bind Xrefs** dialog box (Figure 14-11). AutoCAD provides two methods to bind the xref drawing.

Bind. When you use the **Bind** option, AutoCAD binds the selected xref definition to the current drawing. For example, if you xref the drawing Bearing that has a layer named Object, a new layer Bearing|Object is created in the current drawing. When you bind this drawing, the xref dependent layer Bearing|Object will become a locally defined layer Bearing0Object (Figure 14-12). If the Bearing0Object layer already exits, AutoCAD will automatically increment the number, and the layer name becomes Bearing1Object.

Figure 14-11 Bind Xrefs dialog box

Insert. When you use the **Insert** option, AutoCAD inserts the xref drawing. For example, if you xref the drawing Bearing that has a layer named Object, a new layer Bearing|Object is created in the current drawing. If you use the **Insert** option to bind the xref drawing, the layer name Bearing|Object is renamed as Object (Figure 14-12). If the object layer already exists, then the values set in the current drawing override the values of the inserted drawing.

Figure 14-12 Layer Properties Manager dialog box

You can use this option when you want to send a copy of your drawing to a customer for review. Since all the xref drawings are a part of the existing drawing, you do not need to include the xref drawings or the path information. You can also use this option to safeguard the master drawing from accidental editing of the piece parts. You can also use the **-XREF** command to bind the xref drawings.

> Command: **-XREF**
> Enter an option [?/Bind/Detach/Path/Unload/Reload/Overlay/Attach] <Attach>: B
> Enter Xref name(s) to bind: *Enter names of xref drawings.*

Editing an XREF's Path (Path Option)

You can edit the path where the xref drawing is located by editing the path found in **Xref Found At** edit box in the **Xref Manager** dialog box. You can also use the **Browse** button to display the **Select New path** dialog box where you can locate the drawing to be used as xref. Choosing the **Open** button in this dialog box, returns you to the **Xref manager** dialog box. The drawing path and name selected is displayed in the **Xref found at** and **Name:** edit boxes respectively. To save the path, use the **Save Path** button. For example, if the drawing was originally in the C:\CAD\Proj1 subdirectory and the drawing has been moved to A:\Parts directory, the path must be edited so that

AutoCAD can load the xref drawings. When you enter the path name, AutoCAD will try to locate the file in the specified directory. If the referenced drawing is not found in the specified path, AutoCAD will automatically search the directories specified in the **Options** dialog box. If AutoCAD cannot locate the specified file, it will display an error message, prompt you to enter a new path, and display the new file name in the drawing as marker text. When using the **Browse** button in the **Xref Manager** dialog box to locate the drawing or editing the path in the **Xref found at** edit box and choosing the **Save path** button, the drawing is loaded and replaces the marker text in the drawing. You can also use the **-XREF** command to change the path.

> Command: **-XREF**
> Enter an option [?/Bind/Detach/Path/Unload/Reload/Overlay/Attach] <Attach>: P
> Edit Xref name(s) to edit path: BEARING
> Old path: C:\CAD\Proj1\Bearing
> Enter new path:

When AutoCAD prompts **Edit xref name(s) to edit path:**, you can enter the name of one xref drawing or the names of several drawings separated by commas. You can also enter * (asterisk), in which case AutoCAD will prompt you for the path name of each xref drawing. The path name stays unchanged if you press ENTER when AutoCAD prompts for a new path name.

THE OVERLAY OPTION

One of the problems with the **XREF Attach** option is that you cannot have circular reference. For example, assume you are designing the plant layout of a manufacturing unit. One person is working on the floor plan (see Figure 14-13), and the second person is working on the furniture layout in the offices. The names of the drawings are FLOORPLN and OFFICES, respectively. The person working on the office layout uses the **XREF Attach** option to insert the FLOORPLN drawing so that he or she has the latest floor plan drawing. The person who is working on the floor plan wants to XREF the OFFICES drawing. Now, if the **XREF Attach** option is used to reference the drawing, AutoCAD displays an error message because by inserting the OFFICES drawing a circular reference is created (Figure 14-14). To overcome this problem, the **Overlay** option can be used to overlay the OFFICES drawing. This is a very useful option because the **Overlay** option lets different operators avoid circular reference and share the drawing data without affecting the drawing. This option can be invoked by selecting the **Overlay** radio button in the **External Reference** dialog box or by entering O at the **Enter an option [?/Bind/Detach/Path/Unload/ Reload/Overlay/Attach] <Attach>:** prompt. Selecting the **Overlay** option, displays the **Enter Name of file to Overlay** dialog box, if the **FILEDIA** system variable is 1. Otherwise, the command prompt is:

Figure 14-13 Drawing files hierarchy

> Enter name of file to overlay: Enter *the name of the file*

Figure 14-14 AutoCAD Alert message box

When a drawing that has a nested overlay is overlaid, the nested overlay is not visible in the current drawing.

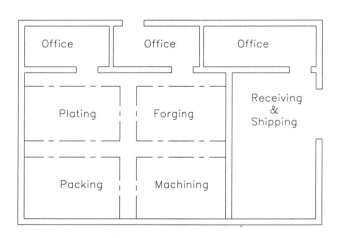

Figure 14-15 Sample plant layout drawing

Example 1

In this example you will use the **Attach** and **Overlay** options to attach and reference the drawings. Two drawings, PLAN and PLANFORG, are given. The PLAN drawing (Figure 14-15) consists of the floor plan layout, and the PLANFORG drawing (Figure 14-16) has the details of the forging section only. The CAD operator who is working on the PLANFORG drawing wants to xref the PLAN drawing for reference. Also, the CAD operator working on the PLAN drawing should be able to xref the PLANFORG drawing to complete the project. The following steps illustrate how to accomplish the defined task without creating a circular reference.

Figure 14-15 PLAN drawing

Figure 14-16 PLANFORG drawing

How circular reference is caused:

1. Load the drawing PLANFORG, and invoke the **XREF** command and choose the **Attach** option to attach the PLAN drawing. Now the drawing consists of PLANFORG and PLAN. Save the drawing.

2. Open the drawing file PLAN, and invoke the **XREF** command and attach the PLAN drawing. AutoCAD will prevent you from attaching the drawing because it causes circular reference.

   One possible solution is for the operator working on the PLANFORG drawing to detach the PLAN drawing. This way, the PLANFORG drawing does not contain any reference to the PLAN drawing and would not cause any circular reference. The other solution is to use the **-XREF** command's **Overlay** option, as follows.

How to prevent circular reference:

3. Open the drawing PLANFORG (Figure 14-17), and use the **Overlay** option of the **-XREF** command (or Select the **Overlay** radio button in the **External reference** dialog box) to overlay the PLAN drawing. The PLAN drawing is overlaid on the PLANFORG drawing (Figure 14-18).

4. Open the drawing file PLAN (Figure 14-19), and use the **Attach** option of the **XREF** command to attach the PLANFORG drawing. You will notice that only the PLANFORG drawing is attached (Figure 14-20). The drawing that was overlaid in the PLANFORG drawing (PLAN) does not appear in the current drawing. This way, the CAD operator working on the PLANFORG drawing can overlay the PLAN drawing, and the CAD operator working on the PLAN drawing can attach the PLANFORG drawing, without causing a circular reference.

Chapter 14

Figure 14-17 PLANFORG drawing

Figure 14-18 PLANFORG drawing after overlaying the PLAN drawing

Figure 14-19 PLAN drawing

Figure 14-20 PLAN drawing after attaching the PLANFORG drawing

XATTACH COMMAND

Toolbar:	Reference > External Reference Attach
Menu:	Insert > External Reference
Command:	XATTACH

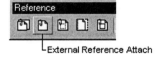

Figure 14-21 Reference toolbar

If you want to attach a drawing without invoking the **Xref Manager** dialog box, you can use the **XATTACH** command. When you invoke this command, AutoCAD displays the **Select Reference file** dialog box. This command makes it easier to attach a drawing, since most of the xref operations involve simply attaching a drawing file. After you have selected the drawing file to attach, the **External Reference** dialog box is displayed. Select the **Attachment** radio button under the **Reference Type** area. Specify the insertion point, scale, and rotation angle on screen or in the respective edit boxes.

Note

*When you attach or reference a drawing that has a drawing order created by using the **DRAWORDER** command, the drawing order is not maintained in the xref. To correct the drawing order, first open the* *xref drawing and specify the drawing order in it. Now, using the **WBLOCK** command convert it into a drawing file. Use the **XATTACH** command to now attach the newly created drawing file to the current drawing. This way the drawing order will be maintained. AutoCAD maintains a log file for xref drawings if the **XREFCTL** system variable is on. This file lists information about the date and time of loading and other operations being carried out.*

Using AutoCAD DesignCenter to Attach a Drawing As Xref*

Choose the **AutoCAD DesignCenter** button in the **Standard** toolbar to display the AutoCAD **DesignCenter** window (Figure 14-22). In the **AutoCAD DesignCenter** toolbar, choose the **Tree toggle** button to display the **tree pane**. Expand the **Tree view** and double-click the folder whose

contents you want to view. From the list of drawings diplayed in the palette, right-click the drawing you wish to attach as an xref. A shortcut menu is displayed. Choose the **Attach as Xref** option, the **External reference** dialog box is displayed. The **Name:** edit box displays the name of the selected file to be inserted as an xref and **Path:** displays the path of the file. Select the **Attachment** radio button in the **Reference type** area, if not already selected. Specify the **Insertion point**, **Scale**, and **Rotation** in the respective edit boxes or select the **Specify On-screen** check boxes to specify this information on the screen. Choose **OK** to exit the dialog box.

Figure 14-22 AutoCAD Design Center window

ADDING DEPENDENT SYMBOLS TO A DRAWING (XBIND COMMAND)

Toolbar:	Reference > External Reference Bind
Menu:	Modify > Object > External Reference > Bind
Command:	XBIND

External Reference Bind

Figure 14-23 Reference toolbar

You can use the **XBIND** command to add the selected dependent symbols of the xref drawing to the current drawing. The following example describes how to use the **XBIND** command:

1. Load the drawing BEARING that was created earlier when discussing the **Attach** option of the **XREF** command. Make sure the drawing has the following layer setup; otherwise, create the following layers.

Layer Name	Color	Linetype
0	White	Continuous
Object	Red	Continuous
Hidden	Blue	Hidden2

Center	White	Center2
Hatch	Green	Continuous

2. Draw a circle and use the **BLOCK** command to create a block. The name of the block is SIDE. Save the drawing as BEARING.

3. Start a new drawing with the following layer setup.

Layer Name	**Color**	**Linetype**
0	White	Continuous
Object	Red	Continuous
Hidden	Green	Hidden

4. Use the **XATTACH** command and attach the BEARING drawing to the current drawing. When you xref the drawing, the layers will be added to the current drawing, as discussed earlier in this chapter.

5. Invoke the **XBIND** command, and the **Xbind** dialog box (Figure 14-24) is displayed on the screen. If you want to bind the blocks defined in the xref drawing BEARING, double-click on BEARING and then double-click on the Block icon. AutoCAD lists the blocks defined in the xref drawing (Bearing). Select the block BEARING|SIDE and then select the **Add** button; the block name will be added to the **Definitions to Bind** list box. AutoCAD will bind the block with the current drawing, and the name of the block will change to BEARING0SIDE. If you want to insert the block, you must enter the new block name (BEARING0SIDE). You can also rename the block to another name that is easier to use. If the block contains reference to another xref drawing, AutoCAD binds that xref drawing and all its dependent symbols to the current drawing. Once you **XBIND** the dependent symbols, AutoCAD does not delete them. For example, the block BEARING|SIDE will not be deleted when you detach the xref drawing or end the drawing session.

Figure 14-24 Xbind dialog box

You can also use the **-XBIND** command to bind the selected dependent symbols of the xref drawing, using the command line.

> Command: **-XBIND**
> Enter symbol type to bind [Block/Dimstyle/LAyer/LType/Style]: B
> Enter dependent Block name(s): BEARING|SIDE
> 1 Block(s) bound.

6. Similarly, you can bind the dependent symbols, BEARING|STANDARD (text style), BEARING|HIDDEN, and BEARING|OBJECT layers of the xref drawing. You can also use the **-XBIND** command as follows:

> Command: **-XBIND**
> Enter symbol type to bind [Block/Dimstyle/LAyer/LType/Style]: B
> Enter dependent Layer name(s): BEARING|HIDDEN, BEARING|OBJECT
> 2 Layer(s) bound.

The layer names will change to BEARING0HIDDEN and BEARING0OBJECT. If the layer name BEARING0HIDDEN was already there, the layer will be named BEARING1HIDDEN. These two layers become a permanent part of the current drawing. If the xref drawing is detached or the current drawing is saved, the layers are not discarded. The other way of adding the dependent symbols to the current drawing is by using the **Bind** option of the **XREF** command. The bind option makes the xref drawing and the dependent symbols a permanent part of the drawing.

CLIPPING EXTERNAL REFERENCES (XCLIP COMMAND)

Toolbar:	Reference > External Reference Clip
Command:	XCLIP

Figure 14-25 Reference *toolbar*

You can clip an xref object or block by invoking the **XCLIP** command. You can also select an xref and then right-click in the drawing area to display a shortcut menu. From the shortcut menu, choose **Xref Clip**. When you invoke the command, AutoCAD will prompt you to select the objects to clip. Select the xref objects, and then define the clip boundary. The **XCLIP** command also defines a front and back clipping frame for 3D objects. The clipping boundary is specified in the same plane as the object (see Figure 14-26). The following is the prompt sequence:

> Command: **XCLIP**
> Select objects: *Select the xref drawing*.
> Enter clipping options [ON/OFF/ Clipdepth/Delete/generate Polyline/New
> · · · · · · · · · · · · · · · *Press ENTER to specify the clip boundary.*

Figure 14-26 Using **XCLIP** command to clip the xref drawings

[Select polyline/Polygonal/Rectangular] <Rectangular>: *Press ENTER to select the **Rectangular** option, and then specify two corners of the rectangular boundary.*

ON/OFF. The **ON/OFF** option allows you to turn the clipping boundary on or off. When the clipping boundary is off, you can see the complete xref drawing and when it is on, the drawing that is within the clipping polygon is displayed.

Delete. The **Delete** option deletes the predefined clipping boundary. The **ERASE** command cannot be used to delete the clipping boundary.

Generate Polyline. This option displays a polyline coinciding with the boundary of the clipped xref drawing. The polyline boundary can be edited with no effect on the clipped drawing. For example, if you stretch the boundary, it does not affect the xref drawing. The edited boundary can be used later to specify a new clipping boundary.

Clipdepth. This option allows you to define the front and back clipping planes. The objects between the front and back planes will be displayed (Figures 14-27 and 14-28). Using the **Clipdepth** option prompts you to specify a front clip point and a back clip point. Specifying these points, creates a clipping frame passing through and perpendicular to the clipping boundary. The **Distance** option for specifying the front or back clip points, creates a clipping plane at the specified distance from the clipping boundary and the **Remove** option, removes both the front and back clipping planes.

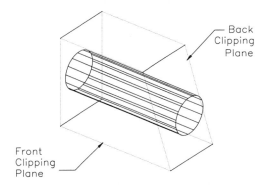

Figure 14-27 3D xref object before clipping   *Figure 14-28 3D xref object after clipping*

The clipping boundary can be specified by using the **Rectangular**, **Polygonal**, or **Select polyline** options. The **Rectangular** option generates a rectangular boundary and **polygonal** allows you to specify a boundary of any shape. You can also draw the boundary using **PLINE** or **POLYGON** commands and then use the **Select polyline** option to select this polyline as the clipping boundary. If a boundary already exists, AutoCAD prompts:

Delete old boundary? [Yes/No] <Yes>:

Displaying Clipping Frame (XCLIPFRAME)

You can use the **XCLIPFRAME** system variable to turn the clipping boundary on or off. This system variable can be set from the **Modify** menu (**Modify > Object > External Reference > Frame**), or by choosing the **External Reference Clip Frame** button from the **Reference** toolbar, or by entering **XCLIPFRAME** at the Command prompt. When the value is 0 (default) the clipping boundary is not displayed (not visible). When it is 1, the clipping boundary is displayed (visible).

Figure 14-29 Reference toolbar

DEMAND LOADING

The demand loading feature loads only that part of the referenced drawing that is required in the existing drawing. For example, if you have attached a drawing and then clipped it, only a part of the drawing (clipped portion) is displayed on the screen. The demand loading provides a mechanism by which only the clipped portion of the referenced drawing will be loaded. This makes the xref operation more efficient, especially when the drawing is reopened. This feature works with the following system variables: **XLOADPATH**, **XLOADCTL**, and **INDEXCTL**. The **XLOADPATH** system variable creates a temporary path to store demand loaded Xrefs.

XLOADCTL System Variable

The system variable **XLOADCTL** determines how the referenced drawing file is loaded. The following are the three possible settings of **XLOADCTL** system variable:

Setting	Features
0	1. Turns off demand loading.
	2. Loads entire xref drawing file.
	3. The File is locked on the server and other users cannot edit the xref drawing.
1	1. Turns on demand loading.
	2. The referenced file is kept open.
	3. Makes the referenced file read only for other users.
2	1. Turns on demand loading with copy option.
	2. A copy of referenced drawing is opened.
	3. Other users can access and edit the original referenced drawing file.

You can set the value of **XLOADCTL** at the command line or in the **External Reference** area of the **Open and Save** tab of the **Options** dialog box (Figure 14-30).

Command: **XLOADCTL**
Enter new value for XLOADCTL <1>: *Enter new value.*

Chapter 14

*Figure 14-30 Setting **XLOADCTL**, using the **Options** dialog box*

Spatial and Layer Indexes

As mentioned previously, the demand loading improves performance when the drawing contains referenced files. To make it work effectively and to take full advantage of demand loading, the **INDEXCTL** system variable must be set to 3; for example, you must store a drawing with Layer and Spatial indexes. The **INDEXCTL** variable controls the creation of layer index and spatial index. The layer index maintains a list of objects in different layers and the spatial index contains lists of objects based on their location in 3D space. The following are the settings of the **INDEXCTL** system variable:

Setting	Features
0	No index created.
1	Layer index created.
2	Spatial index created.
3	Layer and spatial index created.

EDITING REFERENCES IN PLACE*
(REFEDIT COMMAND*)

Menu:	Modify > In-place xref and Block edit > Edit Reference
Command:	REFEDIT

Often you have to make minor changes in the xref drawing and you want to save yourself the trouble of going back and forth between drawings. In such a situation you can use **In-Place Reference editing** to select the xref, modify it, and then save it after modifications. The **XEDIT** system variable controls whether the current drawing can be edited In-place when being referenced by another drawing or not. The following steps explain the referencing editing process:

1. To edit In-place, from the **Modify** menu choose **In-place Xref and Block edit > Edit Reference**. Select the xref you wish to edit; the **Reference Edit** dialog box is displayed.

2. In the **Reference name:** list box of the **Reference Edit** dialog box, the selected reference and its nested references are listed. Select the specific xref you wish to edit from the list. You can cycle between the xrefs by using the **Next** button. A **Preview** window displays an image of the selected reference.

3. Select both the **Enable unique layer and symbol names** and the **Display attribute definition for editing** check boxes. Choose **OK** to return to the current drawing. At the **Select objects:** prompt, select the objects you want to modify and press ENTER. The **Refedit** toolbar (Figure 14-31) is displayed and the objects that have not been selected for modifications become faded. The fading is controlled by the **XFADECTL** system variable or by using the **Reference fading intensity** slider bar in the **Display** tab of the **Options** dialog box. You can add or remove objects to the working set by choosing the respective buttons in the **Refedit** toolbar or by using the **REFSET** command. All the standard AutoCAD commands can be used to modify the selected objects in the xref.

Figure 14-31 The Refedit toolbar

4. When you choose the **Save back changes to the reference** button in the **Refedit** toolbar or use the **REFSAVE** command, the modifications made are saved in the drawing used as reference as well as the current drawing. Choosing the **Discard changes to reference** button in the **Refedit** toolbar does not save the changes made. After you have saved the changes to the xref, AutoCAD displays a message: **All reference edits will be saved**; choose **OK** to return to the drawing area. The current drawing is redisplayed and the fading is turned off.

Self-Evaluation Test

Answer the following questions, and then compare your answers to the correct answers given at the end of this chapter.

1. If the assembly drawing has been created by inserting a drawing, the drawing will be updated automatically if a change is made in the drawing that was inserted. (T/F)

2. The external reference facility helps you to keep the drawing updated no matter when the changes were made in the piece part drawings. (T/F)

3. AutoCAD saves only the reference information with the assembly drawing, and therefore, the size of the drawing is minimized. (T/F)

4. The _____ are entries such as blocks, layers, text styles, and layers.

5. What are dependent symbols? _____
   _____

6. Can you add objects to a dependent layer? (Y/N)

Chapter 14

7. If the **VISRETAIN** variable is set to _____, layer settings such as color, linetype, on/off, and freeze/thaw are retained. The settings are saved with the drawing and are used when you xref the drawing the next time.

8. If a block exists with the same name as the name of the xref drawing, the **XREF** command is terminated and an error message is displayed on the screen. (T/F)

9. When you enter ~ (tilde) in response to the **Enter name of file to attach:** prompt, AutoCAD displays the **Select reference file** dialog box, even if the **FILEDIA** system variable is turned off. (T/F)

10. If you insert a drawing using the **INSERT** command, the information about the named objects is not lost. (T/F)

Review Questions

1. The external reference feature lets you reference an external drawing without making that drawing a permanent part of the existing drawing. (T/F)

2. If the assembly drawing has been created by inserting a drawing, what needs to be done to update the drawing if a change has been made in the drawing that was inserted? Explain.
   _____
   _____

3. The external reference facility lets you link the piece part drawings with the assembly drawing. (T/F)

4. If the xref drawings get updated, the changes are not automatically reflected in the assembly drawing when you open the assembly drawing. (T/F)

5. There is a limit to the number of drawings you can reference. (T/F)

6. It is not possible to have nested references. (T/F)

7. If you use an external reference feature to link the drawings, the piece parts are saved with the assembly drawing. (T/F)

8. Like blocks, the xref drawings can be scaled, rotated, or positioned at any desired location. (T/F)

9. What are the named objects? Explain. _____
   _____
   _____

10. What happens to the information related to named objects when you insert a drawing?
   _____

11. In the _____ drawings the information regarding dependent symbols is not lost.

12. For xref drawings, the _____ are features such as layers, linetypes, object color, and text style.

13. The information added to the current drawing is not permanent. It is added only when the xref drawing is loaded. (T/F)

14. If you detach the xref drawing, the dependent symbols are not automatically erased from the current drawing. (T/F)

15. When you xref a drawing, AutoCAD does not let you reference the symbols directly. For example, you cannot make the dependent layer BEARING|HIDDEN current. (T/F)

16. You can change the color, linetype, or visibility (on/off, freeze/thaw) of the dependent layer. (T/F)

17. If the system variable _____ is set to 0 (default), the settings are retained for the current drawing session. When you save the drawing, the changes are discarded, and the layer settings return to their default status.

18. The _____ option of the **XREF** command can be used to attach an xref drawing to the current drawing.

19. When you attach an xref drawing, AutoCAD remembers the name of the attached drawing. At the time you attach the xref drawing, the previous xref drawing name becomes the default name. (T/F)

20. If the xref drawing you want to attach is currently being edited, AutoCAD will not attach the drawing. (T/F)

21. What is demand loading? Explain. _____
    _____
    _____

22. What is the function of the **XLOADCTL** system variable? Explain. _____
    _____
    _____

23. What is the function of the **XCLIPFRAME** system variable? Explain. _____
    _____
    _____

Chapter 14

Exercises

Exercise 1   *Mechanical*

In this exercise, you will start a new drawing and xref the drawings Part-1 and Part-2. You will also edit one of the piece parts to correct the size and use the **XBIND** command to bind some of the dependent symbols to the current drawing. Following are detailed instructions for completing this exercise.

1. Start a new drawing, Part-1, and set up the following layers.

Layer Name	Color	Linetype
0	White	Continuous
Object	Red	Continuous
Hidden	Blue	Hidden2
Center	White	Center2
Dim-Part1	Green	Continuous

2. Draw Part-1 with dimensions as shown in Figure 14-32. Save the drawing as Part-1.
3. Start a new drawing, Part-2, and set up the following layers.

Layer Name	Color	Linetype
0	White	Continuous
Object	Red	Continuous
Hidden	Blue	Hidden
Center	White	Center
Dim-Part2	Green	Continuous
Hatch	Magenta	Continuous

***Figure 14-32** Part-1, Drawing for Exercise 1*

4. Draw Part-2 with dimensions as shown in the Figure 14-33. Save the drawing as Part-2.

Figure 14-33 Part-2, Drawing for Exercise 1

5.   Start a new drawing, ASSEM1, and set up the following layers.

Layer Name	Color	Linetype
0	White	Continuous
Object	Blue	Continuous
Hidden	Yellow	Hidden

6.   Xref the two drawings Part-1 and Part-2 so that the centers of the two drilled holes coincide. Notice the overlap as shown in Figure 14-34. Save the assembly drawing as ASSEM1.

7.   Open the drawing Part-1 and correct the mistake so that there is no overlap. You can do it by editing the line (1.175 dimension) so that the dimension is 1.160.

8.   Open the assembly drawing ASSEM1 and notice the change in the overlap. The assembly drawing gets updated automatically.

Figure 14-34 Assembly drawing after attaching Part-1 and Part-2

9.   Study the layers and notice how AutoCAD renames the layers and linetypes assigned to each layer. Check to see if you can make the layers belonging to Part-1 or Part-2 current.

10. Use the **XBIND** command to bind the OBJECT and HIDDEN layers that belong to drawing Part-1. Check again to see if you can make one of these layers current.

11. Use the **Detach** option to detach the xref drawing Part-1. Study the layer again, and notice that the layers that were edited with the **XBIND** command have not been erased. Other layers

Chapter 14

belonging to Part-1 are erased.

12. Use the **Bind** option of the **XREF** command to bind the xref drawing Part-2 with the assembly drawing ASSEM1. Open the xref drawing Part-1 and add a border or make any changes in the drawing. Now, open the assembly drawing ASSEM1 and check to see if the drawing is updated.

Project Exercise 2-3 *Mechanical*

Generate the drawing in Figure 14-35 according to the dimensions shown in the figure. Save the drawing as TOOLORGC. (See Chapters 9 and 23 for other parts of Project Exercise 2)

Figure 14-35 Drawing for Project Exercise 2-3

Project Exercise 2-4

Mechanical

Where possible, use the **XREF** command, to generate the assembly drawing as shown in Figure 14-36. Also, give the bill of materials and the part numbers as shown. (See Chapters 9 and 23 for other parts of Project Exercise 2)

Part	Qty.	Description				
1	1	Lower Shelf	.75 x	7.25 x	48.00	
2	1	Upper Shelf	.75 x	3.75 x	48.00	
3	1	Lower Rail	.75 x	8.75 x	48.00	
4	1	Left Side Support	.75 x	2.75 x	32.50	
5	1	Right Side Support	.75 x	2.75 x	32.50	
6	1	Right Stile	.75 x	2.75 x	22.75	
7	1	Upper Rail	.75 x	2.75 x	48.00	
8	1	Left Stile	.75 x	2.75 x	22.75	
9	1	Tempered Pegboard	.25 x	24.00 x	48.00	
10	4	3 1/2 – No. 8 FH Wood Screw – Steel				
11	20	2 1/4 – No. 8 FH Wood Screw – Steel				
12	16	3/4 – No. 6 RH Wood Screw – Steel				

Enter university/college name

Name:	Tool Organizer
	Assembly Drawing

Figure 14-36 Drawing for Project Exercise 2-4

Answers to Self-Evaluation Test
1 - F, **2** - T, **3** - T, **4** - named objects, **5** - For xref drawings, the dependent symbols are features such as layers, linetypes, object color, and text style, **6** - N, **7** - 1, **8** - T, **9** - T, **10** - F

Chapter 15

Plotting Drawings and Draw Commands

Learning Objectives

After completing this chapter, you will be able to:
- *Set plotter specifications and plot drawings.*
- *Use Plot Styles.*
- *Define multiline style and specify properties of multilines using the **MLSTYLE** command.*
- *Draw different types of multilines using the **MLINE** command.*
- *Edit multilines using the **MLEDIT** command.*
- *Draw construction lines using the **XLINE** and **RAY** commands.*
- *Draw **NURBS** splines using the **SPLINE** command.*
- *Edit **NURBS** splines using the **SPLINEDIT** command.*
- *Use AutoCAD's **SKETCH** facility.*
- *Digitize drawings.*

PLOTTING DRAWINGS IN AUTOCAD

When you are done with a drawing, you can store it on the computer storage device, such as the hard drive or diskettes. However, to get a hard copy of the drawing you should plot the drawing on a sheet of paper using a plotter or printer. With the help of pen plotters you can obtain a high-resolution drawing.

PLOT Command

Toolbar:	Standard > Plot
Menu:	File > Plot
Command:	PLOT

The **PLOT** command is used to plot a drawing. After invoking the **PLOT** command, the **Plot** dialog box (Figure 15-1) is displayed. You can also invoke the **Plot** dialog box from the shortcut menu by right-clicking in the **Model** tab or **layout** tab and choosing **Plot**.

Command: **PLOT**

*Figure 15-1 **Plot** dialog box*

Some values in this dialog box were set when AutoCAD was first configured. You can examine these values; if they conform to your requirements, you can start plotting directly. If you want to alter the plot specifications, you can do so through the options provided in the **Plot** dialog box. The available plot options are described next.

Layout Name Area

This area displays the current layout name or displays "Selected layouts" if multiple tabs are selected. For example, if the **Model** tab is currently selected and you choose the **PLOT** command, the Layout Name shows "Model."

*Figure 15-2 Layout name area of **Plot** dialog box*

Save Changes to Layout. This check box saves the changes made in the **Plot** dialog box in the layout (Figure 15-2). This option is not available when multiple layouts are selected.

Page Setup Name Area*

The Page setup name drop-down list displays all the saved and named page setups. You can choose the base for the current page setup on a named page setup or you can add a new named page setup by choosing the **Add...** button.

Add. You can add a new page setup for the current layout by choosing the **Add...** button. When you choose this button, AutoCAD 2000 displays the **User Defined Page Setups** dialog box (Figure 15-3). You can create, delete, rename or import page setups. All the settings applied to the current layout are saved in the user defined page setup file. The description of the **User Defined Page Setups** dialog box is as follows:

Figure 15-3 User Defined Page Setups dialog box

New Page Setup Name. You can save the Name of the new user-defined page setup in this box. Then the current page setup can be based upon the named page setup.

Page Setups. This box lists all the named and saved user-defined page setups. You can select a named page setup from the list to apply to the current layout.

Rename. You can select any user-defined page setup from the list and rename the page setup.

Delete. You can select a user-defined page setup from the list and delete it by choosing the **Delete** button.

Import. You can import a user-defined page setup from another drawing and apply it to a layout in the current drawing. If you choose the **Import** button, AutoCAD displays standard file selection dialog box, where you can browse through the files for the page setup selection.

Plot Device Tab (Plot Dialog Box)

In this tab, information about the current configured plotter, plot style table, the layout or layouts to be plotted and information about plotting to a file is displayed. The tab contains the following parameters:

Plotter configuration area. This area displays the name of the plotter currently selected in the Name edit box with its location and description.

>   **Properties**. If you want to check the information about the configured printer or plotter, choose the **Properties...** button. When you select this button, the **Plotter Configuration Editor** (discussed later in the "Editing Plotter Configuration" subsection of this chapter) is displayed.

>   **Hints**. If you choose the **Hints...** button, AutoCAD displays information about the specific plotting device.

Plot Style Table (Pen Assignments) area. This area in the **Plot** dialog box sets the plot style table, edits the current plot style table, or creates a new plot style table.

>   **Name**. **Name** drop-down list displays the plot style table assigned to the current Model tab or layout tab and also lists the available plot style tables. If you select more than one layout tab with different plot style tables assigned to them, the list displays "**Varies**."

>   **Edit**. If you choose the **Edit...** button, AutoCAD displays the **Plot Style Table Editor** (discussed later in the "Using Plot Styles" subsection of this chapter), where you can edit the selected plot style table. There are three tabs: **General**, **Table View**, and **Form View** in the **Plot Style Table Editor**.

>   **New**. If you choose the **New...** button, AutoCAD displays the **Add-a-Plot Style Table wizard**, which can be used to create a new plot style table.

What to Plot area. This area in the **Plot** dialog box defines what you want to plot whether you select the **Model** tab, a **layout** tab, or multiple layout tabs. You can also plot a multiple number of copies of the plots.

>   **Current Tab**. If this radio button is selected, AutoCAD plots the current **Model** or **layout** tab. If you select multiple tabs, the tab that shows its viewing area is plotted.

>   **Selected Tabs**. If you select this radio button, AutoCAD plots the multiple Model or layout tabs that were selected previously by holding down CTRL during the selection of tabs. If you select only one tab, this option is unavailable.

>   **All Layout Tabs**. This option in the **Plot** dialog box plots all layout tabs, independent of your selection of layout tabs.

Number of Copies. This box shows the number of copies that will be plotted. If multiple layouts and copies are selected, any layouts that are set for plotting to a file or AutoSpool produces a single plot. You can plot the desired number of plots by changing the value in this box.

Plot to File area. This is used for plotting a drawing to a file instead of plotter. AutoCAD plots output to a file rather than to the plotter.

Plot to File. If you select this check box, AutoCAD plots the drawing to a file.

File Name. You can specify the file name of the plot. The default plot file name is the drawing name with the tab name, separated by a hyphen, with a .plt file extension.

Location. This box displays the location of the directory where the plot file will be stored. The default location of the plot file is the directory where the drawing file resides.

[...]. If you choose this button, AutoCAD displays a standard **Browse for Folder** dialog box, where you can choose a location of the directory to store a plot file.

Browse the Web. By choosing this button, you can browse the web and send the plot file to other locations via e-mail.

Plot Settings Tab (Plot Dialog Box)

The **Plot Settings** tab in the **Plot** dialog box controls the paper size, orientation, scale of plotting, plot offset, and other plotting options. The description of this tab is as follows:

Paper Size and Paper Units area. The **Paper Size and Paper Units** area displays available standard paper sizes for the selected plotting device. Actual paper size is indicated by the width (in X-axis direction) and the height (in Y-axis direction). The paper size selected is saved with a layout and overrides the PC3 file settings created by **Add-A-Plotter-Wizard** (discussed in the "Plotter Manager command" subsection of this chapter). If there is no plotter selected, AutoCAD displays the full standard paper size list and is available for selection. If a raster image is plotted, such as a **BMP** or **TIFF** file, the size of the plot is specified in terms of pixels, not in inches or millimeters.

Plot Device. The name of the currently selected plot device is displayed here.

Paper Size. All the available paper sizes are displayed in the drop-down list. You can select any size from the list to make it current.

Printable Area. The actual dimension of the area on the paper that is used for plotting based on the current paper size selected.

Inches or MM. The radio button specifies the units to be used for plotting.

Drawing Orientation area. This area specifies the orientation of the drawing on the paper for the plotters that support landscape or portrait orientation. You can change the drawing orientation by selecting **Portrait**, **Landscape**, or **Plot Upside-Down** radio button. The paper icon shows the media orientation of the selected paper and the letter icon shows the orientation of the drawing on the page.

Plot Area. In this area you can specify the portion of the drawing to be plotted. You can also control the way the plotting will be carried out. The various options in this area are described next.

Layout. If you select this radio button, AutoCAD plots everything within the margins of the specified paper size and the origin is calculated from 0,0 in the layout. This option is available only when a layout is selected.

Limits. If you select the **Limits** radio button, the whole area defined by the drawing limits is plotted. The exception is when the current view is not the top view. In this case, the Limits option works exactly as the Extents option by scaling all the objects in the drawing to fit into the plotting area.

Extents. If you select this option, the section of drawing that currently holds objects is plotted. In this way, this option resembles the ZOOM Extents option. If you add objects to the drawing, they are also included in the plot because the extents of the drawing may also be altered. If you reduce the drawing extents by erasing, moving, or scaling objects, you must use the ZOOM Extents or ZOOM All option. Only after this does the Extents option understand the extents of the drawing to be plotted. If you are in model space, the plot is created in relation to the model space extents; if you are in paper space, the plot is created in relation to the paper space extents. If you invoke the Extents option when the perspective view is on and the position of the camera is not outside the drawing extents, the following message is displayed: PLOT Extents incalculable, using display. In this case, the plot is created as it would be with the Display option. This option is disabled if the current drawing does not have extents.

Display. If you select this radio button while you are in model space, the whole current viewport is plotted. If you are in paper space, the whole current view is plotted.

View. Selecting the View radio button enables you to plot a view that was created with the **VIEW** command. The view must be defined in the current drawing. If no view has been created, the **View** radio button and the drop-down are disabled. These two options can be activated by creating a view in the current drawing. To select a view for plotting, select a named view you want to plot from the drop-down list (Figure 15-4) and then choose **OK**. In this case, the specifications of the plot depend on the specifications of the named view.

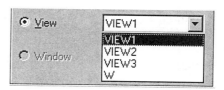

Figure 15-4 *Selecting a named view for plotting*

Window. With this option, you can specify the section of the drawing to be plotted. The section of the drawing to be plotted is defined by a lower left corner and an upper right corner of the section. A window can be defined by choosing the **Window <** button. The following command sequence is displayed:

Specify window for printing
Specify first corner: *Specify a point.*
Specify other corner: *Specify a point.*

When you are defining the window, the dialog box disappears temporarily and when the selection is completed, the box reappears.

Plot Scale area. This area controls the drawing scale of the plot area. The default scale setting is **1:1** when you are plotting a layout. But if you are plotting in a Model tab, the default setting is **Scaled to Fit**. When you are selecting a standard scale from the drop-down list, the scale is displayed in the **Custom** edit box. You can change the scale factor manually in the Custom edit box. You can also scale lineweights in proportion to the plot scale. The settings are controlled by the **LWSCALE** system variable. Lineweights generally specifies the linewidth of the printable objects and are plotted with the original linewidth size regardless of the plot scale.

Plot Offset area. This area of the **Plot Settings** tab (**Plot** dialog box) specifies an offset of the plotting area from the lower-left corner of the paper. In the layout tab, the lower-left corner of a specified plot area is positioned at the lower-left margin of the paper. If you select the Center the plot check box, AutoCAD automatically centers the plot on the paper by calculating the X and Y offset values. You can also specify an offset from the origin by entering a positive or negative value in the **X** and **Y** edit boxes. The plotter unit values are either in inches or millimeters on the paper.

Plot Options area. This area specifies the various options like lineweights, plot styles, and the current plot style table. You can select whether the lineweights are to be plotted.

    Plot with Lineweights. If you select this check box, AutoCAD plots the drawing with the lineweights. Plotting with lineweights will plot the drawing with the specified line widths.

    Plot with Plot Styles. By selecting **Plot with Plot Style, AutoCAD** plots using the plot styles applied to objects in the drawing and defined in the plot style table. The different property characteristics associated with the different style definitions are stored in the plot style tables and can be easily attached to the geometry. This setting replaces pen mapping in earlier versions of AutoCAD.

    Plot Paperspace Last. By selecting **Plot Paperspace Last**, you get an option of plotting model space geometry first. Usually paper space geometry is plotted before model space geometry. This option is available only when multiple layout is selected.

    Hide Objects. When **Hide Objects** is selected, AutoCAD plots layouts with hidden lines removed for objects in the layout environment (paper space). But in model space, hidden line removal of objects in viewports is controlled by the Viewports Hide property in the **Object Property Manager**. The hidden lines will be displayed in the plot preview, but not in the layout.

Plot Preview

You can view the plot on the specified paper size before actually plotting it by selecting the **Full Preview...** or **Partial Preview...** buttons in the Plot dialog box. AutoCAD provides two types of Plot

Chapter 15

Previews: partial and full.

Full Preview. When you choos the **Full Preview...** button AutoCAD displays the drawing on the screen just as it would be plotted on the paper. **Full preview** takes more time than the Partial preview because regeneration of the drawing takes place. Once regeneration is performed, the dialog boxes on the screen are removed temporarily, and an outline of the paper size is shown. The **Plot Preview** (Figure 15-5) with the **Zoom Realtime** icon is displayed. This Realtime icon can be used to zoom in and out interactively by holding the pick button down and then moving the pointing device. You can right-click to display the shortcut menu and then select **Exit** to exit the preview. You can also use the other options from the shortcut menu.

Partial. To generate a **Partial Preview** of a plot, choose the **Partial Preview...** button in the **Plot** dialog box. The **Partial Plot Preview** dialog box (Figure 15-6) is displayed. The paper size is graphically represented by the white paper icon. The paper size is also given numerically. The dashed rectangle shows the printable area. The dimensions of the printable area is also shown numerically. The blue rectangle is the section in the paper that is used by the image. This area is also known as the **effective area**. The size of the effective area is also given numerically. If the paper boundary and the effective area boundary overlap (are the same), this is graphically represented by a red triangle. If you define the origin of the plot so that the effective area is not accommodated in the graphic area of the dialog box, AutoCAD displays a warning. Hence, with the help of a partial preview, you can accurately see how the plot will fit on the paper. If there is something wrong with the specifications of the plot, AutoCAD provides a warning message so that corrections can be made before actual plotting takes place.

Figure 15-5   *Full Plot Preview with short-cut menu*

Figure 15-6 Partial Plot Preview dialog box

After you have finished with all the settings and other parameters, if you choose the **OK** button, AutoCAD starts plotting the drawing in the file or plotters as specified. AutoCAD displays the **Plot Progress** dialog box (Figure 15-7), where you can view the actual progress in plotting.

Figure 15-7 Plot progress dialog box

PLOTTERMANAGER Command*

Menu:	File > Plotter Manager
Command:	PLOTTERMANAGER

This is a new feature of AutoCAD 2000. If you enter **PLOTTERMANAGER** at the Command prompt, AutoCAD will display **Plotter Manager** (Figure 15-8). You can also invoke Plotter Manager by choosing **Plotter Manager** from the **File** menu. The **Plotter Manager** is basically a Windows Explorer window. Plotter Manager displays all the configured Plotters with a option of **Add-A-Plotter-Wizard**.

Figure 15-8 Plotter Manager

Add-A-Plotter-Wizard. If you double-click your pointing device on **Add-A-Plotter-Wizard** in **Plotter Manager**, AutoCAD guides you to configure a nonsystem plotter for plotting your drawing files. AutoCAD 2000 stores all the information of a configured plotter in configured plot (PC3) files. The **PC3** file are stored in **AutoCAD2000\Plotters** folder by default. The steps for configuring a new plotter using **Add-A-Plotter-Wizard** is as follows:

1. Open the **Plotter Manager** by choosing from the **File** menu.
2. In the Plotter Manager, double-click the **Add-A-Plotter-Wizard**.
3. In the **Add-A-Plotter-Wizard**, carefully read the Introduction page, and then choose the **Next** button to advance to the **Add Plotter - Begin** page.
4. On the **Add Plotter - Begin** page, choose the **My Computer** radio button (selected by default). Choose the **Next** button.
5. On the **Add Plotter - Plotter Model** page, select a manufacturer and model of your nonsystem plotter from the list and choose the **Next** button. If your plotter is not present in the list of available plotters, and you have a driver disk for your plotter, choose the **Have Disk** button to locate the **HIF** file from the driver disk, and install the driver supplied with your plotter.

6. If you want to import configuring information from a **PCP** or a **PC2** file created with a previous version of AutoCAD, you can choose the **Import File...** button in the **Import PCP or PC2** screen (Optional) and select the file.

7. On the **Add Plotter - Ports** page, select the port from the list to use when plotting. Choose **Next**.

8. On the **Add Plotter - Plotter Name** page, you can specify the name of the currently configured plotter or the default name will be entered automatically. Choose **Next**.

9. When you reach the **Add Plotter - Finish** page, you can choose the **Finish** button to exit the **Add-A-Plotter-Wizard**.

A **PC3** file for the newly configured plotter will be displayed in the **Plotters** window and you can use the plotter for plotting in the list of devices.

Editing Plotter Configuration*

You can also change the default settings for the plotter by choosing the **Edit Plotter Configuration...** button on the **Add Plotter - Finish** page. AutoCAD 2000 will display the **Plotter Configuration Editor** (Figure 15-9). The other methods of invoking the **Plotter Configuration Editor** are as follows:

From Windows Explorer, select the **PC3** file for editing (by default, **PC3** files are stored in the **ACAD2000\Plotters** folder) and double-click the file or right-click the file and choose **Open** from the shortcut menu. You can also invoke the **Plotter Configuration Editor** by choosing **Page Setup** from the **File** menu and then choose the **Properties...** button. Or, choose **Plot** from the **File** menu and then choose the **Properties...** button.

The **Plotter Configuration Editor** has three tabs. The description of the three tabs are as follows:

General tab. This tab contains basic information about the configured plotter or the PC3 file. You can make changes in the **Description** area. The rest of the information in the tab is read only. This tab contains information of the configured plotter file name, plotter driver type, HDI driver file version number, name of the system printer (if any), and the location and name of the PMP file (if any calibration file is attached to the PC3 file).

Ports tab. The Ports tab contains information about the communication between the plotting device and your computer. You can choose between a serial (local), parallel (local), or network port. The default settings for parallel ports is **LPT1** and **COM1** for serial ports. You can also change the port name if your device is connected to a different port.

Device and Document Settings tab. The **Device and Document Settings** tab contains plotting options. Additional options are available on the **Device and Document Settings** tab depending on your configured plotting device. For example, if you configure a non-system plotter you have the option to modify the pen characteristics. You can select any plotter properties from the tree displayed in the tab and change the values as required. You can also import information and save the settings as a new PC3 file.

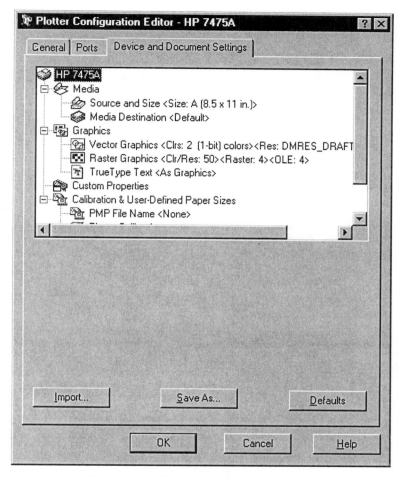

Figure 15-9 Plotter Configuration Editor

PAGESETUP Command*

Toolbar:	Layouts > Page Setup
Menu:	File > Page Setup
Command:	PAGESETUP

This is a new feature in AutoCAD 2000. The **PAGESETUP** command can be used for specifying the layout page, plotting device, paper size, and settings for all the new layouts. The **PAGESETUP** command can also be invoked from the shortcut menu by right clicking in the **Model** or **Layout** tab and choosing **Page Setup**. The command sequence for the **PAGESETUP** command is as follows:

Command: **PAGESETUP**

AutoCAD displays the **Page Setup** dialog box (Figure 15-10).

Chapter 15

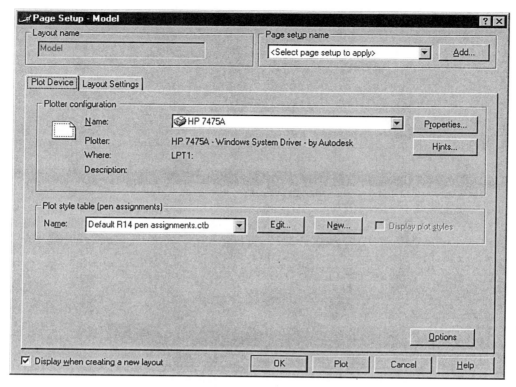

Figure 15-10 Page Setup dialog box

The **Page Setup** dialog box specifies the page layout and current plotting device settings, and is displayed every time you choose a layout tab in a drawing session. The layout settings are stored with the layout. The current Layout name is displayed in the **Layout Name** box, and in the **Page Setup Name** area, a list of all the named and saved page setups are displayed. You can choose to base the current page setup on a named page setup or you can add a new named page setup by choosing the **Add...** button, AutoCAD displays the **User Defined Page Setups** dialog box (discussed earlier in this chapter in "**PLOT** Command"). The **Page Setup** dialog box has two tabs; the **Plot Device** tab and the **Layout Settings** tab.

Plot Device tab. This tab specifies the current plotting device for plotting the layout. This tab is similar to the **Plot Device** tab of the **Plot** dialog box except for the **What to Plot** and **Plot to file** areas. The additional feature in this tab is the **Options** button. If you choose the **Options** button, AutoCAD displays the **Options** dialog box with **Output** tab selected (The **Options** dialog box is described in Chapter 3). You can make necessary changes in this dialog box.

Layout Settings tab. This tab specifies the layout settings of the drawing such as paper size, drawing orientation, plot area, plot scale, plot offset, and other plotting options. This tab is similar to the **Plot Settings** tab of the **Plot** dialog box (discussed earlier in the chapter).

The settings specified in the **Page Setup** dialog box are stored with the layout. You can also Plot the current layout from the **Page Setup** dialog box by choosing the **Plot** button after specifying all the necessary parameters in the dialog box. You can control whether the plotting should include lineweights and whether the lineweights are in proportion to the plot scale.

PSETUPIN Command*

Command:	PSETUPIN

This is a new feature added in AutoCAD 2000. You can import a User-defined Page setup into a new drawing layout by using this command. The **PSETUPIN** command facilitates importing a saved and named page setup from one drawing into a new drawing. The settings of the named page setup can be applied to layouts in the new drawing. If you enter **PSETUPIN** at the Command prompt, a standard file selection dialog box is displayed, where you can locate a drawing (.dwg) file whose pagesetups have to be imported. After you select a drawing file, AutoCAD displays the **Import User Defined Page Setups** dialog box (Figure 15-11).

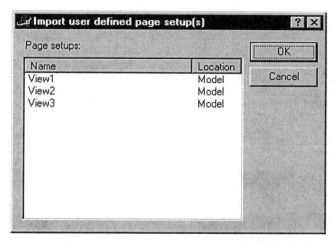

Figure 15-11 Import User Defined Page Setup(s) dialog box

To import a User-defined Page setup file using the AutoCAD command line, the prompt sequence is as follows:

Command: **-PSETUPIN**

If the system variable **FILEDIA** is set to 1, AutoCAD displays a standard file selection dialog box, but if **FILEDIA** is set to 0, AutoCAD displays the following prompt sequence:

Enter file name: *Specify the file name to be imported*
Enter user defined page setup to import or [?]: *Specify the named page setup or* **?** *for listing of available setups.*

PCINWIZARD Command*

Menu:	Tools > Wizards > Import R14 Plot Settings
Command:	PCINWIZARD

If you want to import a **PCP** or **PC2** configuration file, or plot settings created by previous releases of AutoCAD into the **Model** tab or current layout for the drawing, you can use **PCINWIZARD** command to display the **Import PCP or PC2 Plot Settings Wizard**. All the information from a **PCP** or **PC2** file regarding plot area, rotation, plot offset, plot optimization, plot to file, paper size, plot scale, and pen mapping can be imported. After you specify the name of the file for importing, you can modify the plot settings for the current layout.

USING PLOT STYLES*

Plot Styles is a new object property feature of AutoCAD 2000. This feature can change the complete look of a plotted drawing. You can use this feature to override a drawing object's color, linetype, and lineweight. You can change the end, join and fill styles of the drawing, and also change the output effects like dithering, gray scales, pen assignments, and screening. Basically, you can use **Plot Styles** effectively to plot the same drawing in various ways.

Every object and layer in the drawing has a plot style property. The plot style characteristics are defined in the plot style tables attached to the Model tab, layouts, and viewports within the layouts. You can attach and detach different plot style tables to get different looks for your plots. Basically, there are two plot style modes: Color-Dependent and Named plot style. **Color-dependent** plot styles (**.CTB** files) are based on object color and there are **255** color-dependent plot styles. **Named** plot (**.STB** files) styles are independent of object color and you can assign any plot style to any object regardless of that object's color. Every drawing in AutoCAD 2000 is in either of the modes.

STYLESMANAGER Command*

Menu:	File > Plot Style Manager
Command:	STYLESMANAGER

The **STYLESMANAGER** command is a new feature of AutoCAD 2000. If you enter **STYLESMANAGER** at the Command prompt, AutoCAD displays the **Plot Styles Manager** window (Figure 15-12).

Add-A-Plot Style Table Wizard. If you want to add a new Plot Style Table to your drawing, you can double-click on **Add-A-Plot Style Table Wizard** in the **Plot Styles Manager** window. AutoCAD will display the wizard. Following are the steps for creating a new plot style table using the wizard:

1. Read the **Introduction** page and choose the **Next** button.
2. In the **Begin** page, select the **Start from scratch**

Figure 15-12 Plot Styles Manager window

radio button and choose **Next**.
3. In the **Pick Plot Style Table** page, select **Named Plot Style Table** or **Color-Dependent Plot Style Table** according to the requirement and choose **Next**.
4. In the **File name** page, enter a file name for the new plot style table and choose **Next**.
5. A new Plot Style Table will be created with default settings. Choose **Finish** and the new Plot Style Table will be added to the **Plot Styles Manager**, which can be used for plotting.

Plot Style Table Editor. If you want to change the setting of the new Plot Style Table created by **Add-A-Plot Style Table Wizard**, choose **Plot Style Table Editor...** button in the **Finish** page and AutoCAD will display the **Plot Style Table Editor** (Figure 15-13). To edit a previously created Plot Style table, double-click the file in the **Plot Styles Manager** window and the **Plot Style Table Editor** is displayed.

Figure 15-13 Plot Style Table Editor dialog box

The **Plot Style Table Editor** has three tabs: **General**, **Table View**, and **Form View**. You can edit all the properties of an existing plot style table using the different tabs. The description of the tabs are as follows:

General tab. This tab provides the information about the file name, location of the file, version, and scale factor. All the information except the description are read only.

Table View tab. This tab displays all the plot styles available with their properties in tabular form. You can edit the existing styles or add new styles by choosing the **Add Styles** button. A new column with default style name **Style1** will be added in the table. You can change the style name and the properties in the table.

Form View tab. This tab displays all the properties in a form. All the available plot styles are displayed in the **Plot Styles** list box. You can select any style and edit its properties in the **Properties** area. If you want to add a new style, choose **Add Styles** button and AutoCAD will display the **Add Plot Style** window (Figure 15-14) with default name **Style 1**. When you choose the **OK** button, the new style will be added in the **Plot Styles** list box and you can select it for editing. If you want to delete a style, select the style and choose the **Delete Style** button.

Figure 15-14 Add Plot Style window

After editing, choose the **Save & Close** button to save and return to **Plot Styles Manager**.

PLOTSTYLE Command*

Command: PLOTSTYLE

The **PLOTSTYLE** command can be used to set the current plot style for new objects. When you enter **PLOTSTYLE** at the Command prompt, if there is no object selected then AutoCAD displays the **Current Plot Style** dialog box (Figure 15-15). But if any object selection is there in the drawing AutoCAD, displays **Select Plot Style** dialog box (Figure 15-16). The parameters in the **Current Plot Style** dialog box are as follows:

Current Plot Style. This displays the name of the current plot style.

Plot Style List. Lists all the available plot styles that can be assigned to an object, including the default plot style, **NORMAL**.

Active Plot Style Table. This dropdown list displays the name of the plot style table attached to the current layout or viewport.

Editor. If you choose the **Editor...** button, AutoCAD displays the **Plot Style Table Editor**.

Attached To. This displays to whichever tab, Model tab or a layout, the plot style table is attached

The **Select Plot Style** dialog box also displays the name of the Original and New plot styles to be assigned to the selected object.

Figure 15-15 Current Plot Style dialog box

Figure 15-16 Select Plot Style dialog box

You can also select Plotstyle using the command line. The command prompt sequence is as follows:

Command: **-PLOTSTYLE**
Current plot style is "*current style*"
Enter an option [?/Current] :

At the last prompt, enter the name of a style or type **?** and AutoCAD will display a list of all the available styles in the **AutoCAD Text Window**.

Exercise 1   *General*

Make the drawing given in Figure 15-17, and plot it according to the following specifications. It is assumed that the plotter supports six pens.

1. The object lines must be plotted with Pen-1.
2. The dimension lines and centerlines must be plotted with Pen-2.
3. The border and title block must be plotted with Pen-6.

Chapter 15

Figure 15-17 *Drawing for Exercise 1*

BATCH PLOTTING

Batch plotting is used to plot several drawings with or without their associated configuration files (PC3 files). Batch plot is not an AutoCAD command and cannot be run within AutoCAD. It is a Visual Basic batch plotting utility that can be executed at the system prompt. In Windows 95, 98 or NT operating systems, you can choose **Run**, and then select the **Batchplt.exe** from AutoCAD's **Support\Batchplt** directory (Figure 15-18) or select the Batch Plot Utility for ACAD2000 folder (Figure 15-19).

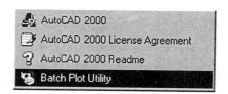

Figure 15-18 *Invoking AutoCAD* **Batch Plot Utility** *from the* **RUN** *dialog box*

Figure 15-19 *Invoking AutoCAD* **Batch Plot Utility** *from* **ACAD2000** *folder*

Batch plot allows you to create a list of files that you want to plot. You can also assign a PC3 file to the drawing name. You can save the list in a batch plot list (**BP3**) file. Batch plot allows you to change the layout for plotting, change plotting parameters, or change a plotting device. When you choose **Batch Plot Utility** by the above mentioned methods, the **AutoCAD Batch Plot Utility** window is displayed (Figure 15-20).

When you invoke the **AutoCAD Batch Plot Utility** window, the following parameters are displayed for a drawing file:

Drawing File. The file name of the drawing to be plotted is displayed here.

Figure 15-20 AutoCAD Batch Plot Utility window

Path. The full path for the drawing file is displayed.

Layout. The name of the layout of the drawing file that you want to plot is displayed here.

Page Setup. The name of the page setup for plotting this drawing is displayed with the **Default** setup selected.

Plot Device. The name of the **PC3** file for plotting the drawing is displayed with **Default** device selected.

File Menu (Batch Plot Utility Window)
The following options are available in the **File** menu of the **Batch Plot Utility** window.

Add Drawing. Displays the **Add Drawing File** dialog box that you can use to select the drawing files that you want to add to the batch plot file list.

Remove. You can use this option to remove the selected drawings from the batch plot list.

New List. You can use this option to open a new batch plot list window. If you have some unsaved changes in the current list, AutoCAD will prompt you to save the list.

Open List. Displays the Open Batch Plot List dialog box that you can use to select and load a saved Batch Plot List (BP3) file. The new file replaces the current file listing.

Append List. Appends the files saved in the Batch Plot List (BP3) file to the current file list.

Save List. Saves the existing Batch Plot List and PC3 information in the BP3 file.

Plot. Plots the drawing files listed in the Drawing File list box according to the settings as defined in the corresponding PC3 file. The AutoCAD window comes to the front and the drawing currently plotted will be displayed. If the drawing is plotted successfully, a check mark will appear next to the drawing name and if it is not plotted properly, an X mark will appear next to the drawing name.

Plot Test. AutoCAD will load but does not plot each drawing in the batch. You can check for missing xrefs, fonts, or shapes. You can use the **Plot Test** option to correct any problems that will effect the drawings during plotting.

Logging. If you select **Logging**, **Batch Plot Utility** displays the **Logging** dialog box. You can create plot journal logging and error logging. **Plot journal logging** creates a log about when and who plotted each drawing while **Error logging** shows whether any errors were encountered during plotting.

Exit. **Exit** closes the **AutoCAD Batch Plot Utility** dialog box. The existing list of files and the corresponding plot configurations will be lost if they have not been saved.

Options Menu (Batch Plot Utility Window)

The following options are available in the **Options Menu** of the **Batch Plot Utility** dialog box.

Layouts. This options displays the **Layouts** dialog box (for single or multiple drawing) depending upon the number of drawings selected. You can use these dialog boxes to change the layouts to plot. The default Layout is the "**Current Tab**" in which tab the drawing was saved last.

Page Setups. This option displays the **Page Setups** dialog box that lists all the available setups. You can also import new setups from other drawings by choosing the [...] button. You can make any setup current by selecting the setup from the list and choosing the **OK** button.

Plot Devices. This option lists all the available Plotting devices in the **Plot Devices** dialog box. You can specify each drawing a plot device while plotting.

Plot Settings. This option displays the **Plot Setting** tab of the **Plot Settings** dialog box where you can specify the area to plot, scaling, and other information related to plotting to a file.

Layers. This option displays the **Layers** tab of the **Plot Settings** dialog box where you can specify which layers to plot.

PC3 Files

PC3 files are the plot configuration files that contain the information about the plotter and all of its settings, as well as the paper or other output media. PC3 files are completely drawing- independent and can be shared among AutoCAD users. This makes it possible to use batch plotting to plot the drawings on different plotters and printers.

CREATING MULTILINES

The AutoCAD **Multiline** feature allows you to draw composite lines that consist of multiple parallel lines. Multilines consists of between 1 and 16 parallel lines, called **elements**. You can draw these lines with the **MLINE** command. Before drawing multilines, you need to set the multiline style. This can be accomplished using the **MLSTYLE** command. Also, editing of the multilines is made possible by the **MLEDIT** command.

DEFINING MULTILINE STYLE (MLSTYLE COMMAND)

Menu:	Format > Multiline Style...
Command:	MLSTYLE

The **MLSTYLE** command allows you to set the style of multilines. You can specify the number of elements in the multiline and the properties of each element. The style also controls the end caps, the end lines, and the color of multilines and fill. When you enter this command, AutoCAD displays the **Multiline Styles** dialog box (Figure 15-21). With this dialog box, you can set the spacing between the parallel lines, linetype pattern, colors, solid fill, and capping arrangements. By default, the multiline style (STANDARD) has two lines that are offset at 0.5 and -0.5.

Multiline Style Area

The Multiline Style area of the Multiline Styles dialog box has the following options.

Current. This edit box displays and sets the current multiline style. If several styles have been defined, the name of the current style is displayed in the **Current:** edit box. You can use the arrow button to display the drop-down list that has all the predefined styles. You can choose any style to make it current. The list of multiline styles can include the multiline styles that have been defined in an externally referenced drawing (xref drawing).

Figure 15-21 Multiline Styles dialog box

Name. This edit box lets you enter the name of the multiline style you are defining. The **STANDARD** style is the default style. You can also use it to rename a style.

Description. This edit box allows you to enter the description of the multiline style. The description can be up to 255 characters long, including spaces.

Load.... This button allows you to load a multiline style from an external multiline library file (acad.mln). When you choose this button, AutoCAD displays the **Load Multiline Styles** dialog box. With this dialog box, you can select the style you want to make current. You can also use this dialog box to load a predefined multiline file (.MLN file) by choosing the **File...** button and then selecting the file you want to load. Once the file is loaded, you can select a style that is defined in the .MLN file.

Save.... This button lets you save or copy the current multiline style to an external file (.MLN file). When you select this button, AutoCAD displays the **Save Multiline Style** dialog box listing the names of the predefined multiline style (.MLN) files. From the file listing, select, or enter the name of, the file where you want to save the current multiline style.

Add. This button allows you to add the multiline style name (the style name displayed in the Name: edit box) to the current multiline file (.MLN file).

Rename. This button allows you to rename the current multiline style. It will rename the multiline style that is displayed in the **Current:** edit box with the name displayed in the **Name:** edit box. You cannot rename the Standard multiline style.

Line Display Panel. The **Multiline Styles** dialog box also displays the multiline configuration in the display panel. The panel will display the color, linetype, and relative spacing of the lines.

Element Properties

If you choose the **Element Properties...** button in the **Multiline Styles** dialog box, AutoCAD will display the **Element Properties** dialog box (Figure 15-22). Before making any changes in this dialog box, you should enter a new multiline name in the **Name:** edit box of the **Multiline Styles** dialog box, and then make it current by selecting the Add button. The buttons in the **Element Properties** dialog box are activated only when the current style is not **STANDARD**. This dialog box gives you the following options for setting the properties of the individual lines (elements) that constitute the multiline.

Figure 15-22 Element Properties dialog box

Elements. This box displays the offset, color, and linetype of each line that constitutes the current multiline style. The lines are always listed in descending order based on the offset distance. For example, a line with a 0.5 offset will be listed first and a line with a 0.25 offset will be listed next.

Add. This button lets you add new lines to the current line style. The maximum number of lines you can add is **16**. When you choose the **Add** button, AutoCAD inserts a line with the offset distance of **0.00**. After the line is added, you can change its offset distance, color, or linetype by choosing the **Offset** edit box or the **Color...** or **Linetype...** button.

Delete. This button allows you to delete the line highlighted in the **Elements**: list box.

Offset. This edit box allows you to change the offset distance of the selected line in the **Elements:**

list box. The offset distance is defined with respect to the origin (0,0). The offset distance can be a positive or a negative value, which enables you to center the lines.

Color.... This button allows you to assign a color to the selected line. When you choose this button, AutoCAD displays the **Select Color** dialog box. You can select a color from the dialog box or enter a color number or name in the edit box located to the right of the color swatch box in the **Element Properties** dialog box.

Linetype.... This button allows you to assign a linetype to the selected line. When you choose this button, AutoCAD displays the **Select Linetype** dialog box. After selecting the linetype, choose the **OK** button to exit the dialog box.

Multiline Properties

If you choose the **Multiline Properties...** button from the **Multiline Styles** dialog box, AutoCAD will display the **Multiline Properties** dialog box (Figure 15-23). You can use this dialog box to define multiline properties such as display joints, end caps, and background fill. The buttons in this dialog box are activated only when the current style is not STANDARD. The dialog box provides the following options.

Figure 15-23 Multiline Properties dialog box

Display Joints. If you select the **Display joints** check box, AutoCAD will display a **miter** line (joint) across all elements of the multiline at the point where the two multilines meet. If you draw only one multiline segment, no miter line is drawn (because there is no intersection point).

Line. This option draws a line cap at the start and end of each multiline. It has two check boxes that control the start and end caps (Figure 15-24).

Outer Arc. This option draws an arc (semicircle) between the endpoints of the outermost lines.

Inner Arc. This option controls the inner arcs at the start and end of a multiline. The arc is drawn between the even-numbered inner lines. For example, if there are two inner lines, an arc will be drawn at the ends of these lines. However, if there are three inner lines, the middle line is not capped with an arc.

Angle. This option controls the cap angle at the start and end of a multiline. This angle can be from 10 degrees to 170 degrees.

Fill. This option toggles the fill on and off. If the fill is on, you can select the color of the fill by selecting the color button. When you select this button, AutoCAD displays the standard color dialog box. You can also set the color by entering the color name or color number in the edit box located to the right of the color swatch box.

Figure 15-24 Drawing multilines with different end cap specifications

DRAWING MULTILINES (MLINE COMMAND)

Toolbar:	Draw > Mulitline
Menu:	Draw > Multiline
Command:	MLINE

Figure 15-25 Selecting **Multiline** from the **Draw** toolbar

The **MLINE** command can be used to draw multilines. The following is the command prompt sequence for the **MLINE** command:

Command: **MLINE**
Current settings: Justification = Top, Scale = 1.00, Style = STANDARD
Specify start point or [Justification/Scale/STyle]: *Select a point.*
Specify next point: *Select the second point.*
Specify next point or [Undo]: *Select next point or enter* **U** *for undo.*
Specify next point or [Close/Undo]: *Select next point, enter* **U,** *or enter* **C** *for close.*

When you enter the **MLINE** command, it always displays the status of the multiline justification, scale, and style name. The command provides the following options.

Justification Option

The justification determines how a multiline is drawn between the specified points. Three justifications are available for the **MLINE** command: Top, Zero, and Bottom (Figure 15-26).

Top. This justification produces a multiline in which the top line coincides with the selected points. Since the line offsets in a multiline are arranged in descending order, the line with the largest positive offset will coincide with the selected points.

Zero. This option will produce a multiline in which the zero offset position of the multiline coincides with selected points. Multilines will be centered if positive and negative offsets are equal.

Bottom. This option will produce a multiline in which the bottom line (the line with the least offset distance) coincides with the selected point when the line is drawn from left to right.

Figure 15-26 Drawing multilines with different justifications

Scale Option

The **Scale** option allows you to change the scale of the multiline. For example, if the scale factor is 0.5, the distance between the lines (offset distance) will be reduced to half. Therefore, the width of the multiline will be half of what was defined in the multiline style. A negative scale factor will reverse the order of the offset lines. Multilines are drawn so that the line with the maximum offset distance is at the top and the line with the least offset distance is at the bottom. If you enter a scale factor of -0.5, the order in which the lines are drawn will be reversed, and the offset distances will be reduced by half. (The line with the least offset will be drawn at the top.) Here it is assumed that the lines are drawn from left to right. If the lines are drawn from right to left, the offsets are reversed. Also, if the scale factor is 0, AutoCAD forces the multiline into a single line. The line still possesses the properties of a multiline. The scale does not affect the linetype scale (**LTSCALE**).

STyle Option

The **STyle** option allows you to change the current multiline style. The style must be defined before using the STyle option to change the style.

EDITING MULTILINES (USING GRIPS)

Multilines can be edited using grips (Figure 15-27). When you select a multiline, the grips appear at the endpoints based on the justification used when drawing multilines. For example, if the multilines are top-justified, the grips will be displayed at the endpoint of the first (top) line segment. Similarly, for zero- and bottom-justified multilines, the grips are displayed on the centerline and bottom line, respectively.

Chapter 15

Note
*Multilines do not support certain editing commands, such as **BREAK**, **CHAMFER**, **FILLET**, **TRIM**, and **EXTEND**. However, commands such as **COPY**, **MOVE**, **MIRROR**, **STRETCH**, and **EXPLODE**, and certain object snap modes can be used with multilines. You must use the **MLEDIT** command to edit multilines. The **MLEDIT** command has several options that make it easier to edit these lines.*

Figure 15-27 Using grips to edit multilines

EDITING MULTILINES (USING THE MLEDIT COMMAND)

Toolbar:	Modify II > Edit Multiline
Menu:	Modify > Multiline
Command:	MLEDIT

*Figure 15-28 Invoking the **Edit Multiline** from the **Modify II** toolbar*

When you enter the **MLEDIT** command, AutoCAD displays the **Multiline Edit Tools** dialog box (Figure 15-29). This dialog box contains five basic editing tools. To edit a multiline, first select the editing operation you want to perform by double-clicking on the image tile or by selecting the image tile; then choose the **OK** button. Once you have selected the editing option, AutoCAD will prompt you to select the object or the points, depending on the option you have selected. If you press ENTER after you are done editing, the dialog box will return, and you can continue editing. The following is the list of options for editing multilines:

    Cross Intersection
        Closed Cross
        Open Cross
        Merged Cross
    Tee Intersection
        Closed Tee
        Open Tee
        Merged Tee
    Corner Joint
    Adding and Deleting Vertices
        Add Vertex
        Delete Vertex
    Cutting and Welding Multilines
        Cut Single
        Cut All
        Weld All

*Figure 15-29 **Multiline Edit Tools** dialog box*

Cross Intersection

With the **MLEDIT** command options, you can create three types of cross intersections: closed, open, and merged. You must be careful how you select the objects because the order in which you select them determines the edited shape of a multiline (Figure 15-30). The multilines can belong to the same multiline or to two completely different multilines. The following is the prompt sequence for creating the cross intersection:

Command: **MLEDIT**

The **Multiline Edit Tools** dialog box is displayed. Select the **Closed Cross** image tile and then choose the **OK** button. The dialog box is removed from the screen, and the following prompts appear in the command line.

Select first mline: *Select the first multiline.*
Select second mline: *Select the second multiline.*
Select first mline or [Undo]:

If you select **Undo**, AutoCAD undoes the operation and prompts you to select the first multiline. However, if you select another multiline, AutoCAD will prompt you to select the second multiline. If you press ENTER twice, the **Multiline Edit Tools** dialog box is returned.

Tee Intersection

With the **MLEDIT** command options, you can create three types of tee-shaped intersections: closed, open, and merged. As with the cross intersection, you must be careful how you select the objects because the order in which you select them determines the edited shape of a multiline (Figure 15-31). The prompt sequence for the tee intersection is the same as for the cross intersection.

Command: **MLEDIT**

The **Multiline Edit Tools** dialog box is displayed. Select the **Closed Tee** image tile and then choose the **OK** button. The dialog box is removed from the screen, and the following prompts appear in the command line.

*Figure 15-30 Using **MLEDIT** to edit multilines (Cross Intersection)*

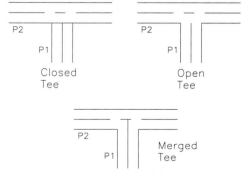

*Figure 15-31 Using **MLEDIT** to edit multilines (Tee Intersection)*

Select first mline: *Select the first multiline.*
Select second mline: *Select the intersecting multiline.*
Select first mline or [Undo]: *Select another multiline, enter Undo, or press ENTER.*

Corner Joint

The **Corner Joint** option creates a corner joint between the two selected multilines. The multilines must be two separate objects (multilines) (Figure 15-32). When you specify the two multilines, AutoCAD trims or extends the first multiline to intersect with the second one. The following is the command prompt sequence for creating a corner joint:

Command: **MLEDIT**

The **Multiline Edit Tools** dialog box is displayed. Select the Corner Joint image tile and then choose the **OK** button. The dialog box is removed from the screen, and the following prompts appear in the command line.

*Figure 15-32 Using **MLEDIT** to edit multilines (Corner Joint)*

Select first mline: *Select the multiline to trim or extend.*
Select second mline: *Select the intersecting multiline.*
Select first mline or [Undo]: *Select another multiline, enter Undo, or press ENTER.*

Adding and Deleting Vertices

You can use the **MLEDIT** command to add or delete the vertices of a multiline (Figure 15-33). When you select a multiline for adding a vertex, AutoCAD inserts a vertex point at the point where the object was selected. If you want to move the vertex, use grips. Similarly, you can use the **MLEDIT** command to delete the vertices by selecting the object whose vertex point you want to delete. AutoCAD removes the vertex that is in the positive direction of the selected multiline segment.

Command: **MLEDIT**

The **Multiline Edit Tools** dialog box is displayed. Select the **Add Vertex** image tile and then choose the **OK** button. The dialog box is removed from the screen, and the following prompts appear in the command line.

Select mline: *Select the multiline for adding vertex.*
Select mline or [Undo]: *Select another multiline, enter Undo, or press ENTER.*

Cutting and Welding Multilines

You can use the **MLEDIT** command to cut or weld the lines. When you cut a multiline, it does not create two separate multilines. They are still a part of the same object (multiline). Also, the points selected for cutting the multiline do not have to be on the same element of the multiline

(Figure 15-34).

Command: **MLEDIT**

The **Multiline Edit Tools** dialog box is displayed. Select the **Cut Single** image tile and then choose the **OK** button. The dialog box is removed from the screen, and the following prompts appear in the command line.

Select mline: *Select the multiline. (The point where you select the multiline specifies the first cut point.)*
Select second point: *Select the second cut point.*
Select mline or [Undo]: *Select another multiline, enter Undo, or press ENTER.*

The **Weld** option welds the multilines that have been cut by using the **MLEDIT** command options (Figure 15-34). You cannot weld or join separate multilines.

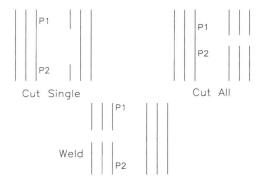

Figure 15-33 *Using **MLEDIT** to edit multilines (adding and deleting vertices)*

Figure 15-34 *Using **MLEDIT** to edit multilines (cutting and welding multilines)*

Command: **MLEDIT**

The **Multiline Edit Tools** dialog box is displayed. Select the **Weld All** image tile and then choose the **OK** button. The dialog box is removed from the screen, and the following prompts appear in the command line.

Select mline: *Select the multiline.*
Select second point: *Select the second multiline.*
Select mline or [Undo]: *Select another multiline, enter Undo, or press ENTER.*

-MLEDIT COMMAND

You can also edit the multilines using the command line and not the **Multiline Edit Tools** dialog box. To accomplish this, enter **-MLEDIT** at the Command prompt.

Command: **-MLEDIT**
Enter mline editing option [CC/OC/MC/CT/OT/MT/CJ/AV/DV/CS/CA/WA]:

After you select an option, AutoCAD will prompt you to select the multilines or specify the points. The prompt sequence will depend on the option you select, as discussed earlier in "Editing Multilines" (using the **MLEDIT** command). The following are the command line options:

AV	Add Vertex	**OT**	Open Tee
DV	Delete Vertex	**MT**	Merged Tee
CC	Closed Cross	**CJ**	Corner Joint
OC	Open Cross	**CS**	Cut Single
MC	Merged Cross	**CA**	Cut All
CT	Closed Tee	**WA**	Weld All

SYSTEM VARIABLES FOR MLINE

CMLJUST   Stores the justification of the current multiline (0-Top, 1-Middle, 2-Bottom)
CMLSCALE   Stores the scale of the current multiline (Default scale = 1.0000)
CMLSTYLE   Stores the name of the current multiline style (Default style = STANDARD)

Example 1

In the following example, you will create a multiline style that represents a wood-frame wall system. The wall system consists of 1/2" wallboard, 3 1/2" 2 x 4" wood stud, and 1/2" wallboard.

Step 1. Use the **MLSTYLE** command to display the **Multiline Styles** dialog box. The current style, STANDARD, will be edited to create the new multiline style.

Step 2. Select the **Name:** edit box and replace the word **STANDARD** with **2x4 Wood**.

Step 3. Select the **Description:** edit box and enter **Wallboard Wood Framed 2x4 Partition**.

Step 4. Choose the **Add** button to add the new style to the current multilines.

Step 5. Choose the **Element Properties...** button to display the **Element Properties** dialog box. The element properties of the STANDARD multiline style remain.

Step 6. Select the **0.5** line definition in the **Elements** display box. Select the **Offset** edit box and replace **0.500** with **1.75**. This redefines the first line as being 1.75" above the centerline of the wall.

Step 7. Select the **-0.5** line definition in the **Elements** display box. Select the **Offset** edit box and replace **0.500** with **-1.75**. This redefines the second line as being 1.75" below the centerline of the wall.

Step 8. Choose the **Add** button to add a new line to the current line style.

Step 9. The new **0.0** line definition in the **Elements** display box is already highlighted. Select the Offset edit box and replace **0.000** with **2.25**.

Step 10. Select the **Color** edit box and replace **BYLAYER** with **YELLOW**.

Step 11. Repeat steps 7 through 9, this time using the value -2.25 in step 8 to add another line to the current line style.

Step 12. Choose the **OK** button to accept the changes to the **Element Properties** and return to the **Multiline Styles** dialog box. The new multiline style will be displayed.

Step 13. Choose the **Save...** button to save the current multiline style to an external file for use in later drawing sessions. From the file listing, select the file (or enter the name of the file) where you want to save the current multiline style.

Step 14. Choose the **OK** button to return to the drawing editor. To test the new multiline style, use the **MLINE** command and draw a series of lines(Figure 15-35) .

Figure 15-35 *Creating a multiline style for a wood-frame wall system*

DRAWING CONSTRUCTION LINES (XLINE AND RAY COMMANDS)

Toolbar:	Draw > Construction Line
Menu:	Draw > Construction Line
Command:	XLINE

Figure 15-36 **Construction Line** *from the* **Draw** *toolbar*

The **XLINE** and **RAY** commands can be used to draw construction or projection lines. An **xline** is a 3D line that extends to infinity on both ends. Since the line is infinite in length, it does not have any endpoints. A **ray** is a 3D line that extends to infinity on only one end. The other end of the ray has a finite endpoint. The xlines and rays have zero extents. This means that the extents of the drawing will not change if you use the commands that change the drawing extents, such as the **ZOOM** command with the All option. Most of the object snap modes work with both xlines and rays, with some limitations: You cannot use the Endpoint object snap with the xline because by definition an xline does not have any endpoints. However, for rays you can use the Endpoint snap on one end only. Also, xlines and rays take the properties of the layer in which they are drawn. The linetype will be continuous even if the linetype assigned to the layer is not continuous (Figure 15-37). The **RAY**

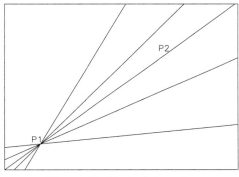

Figure 15-37 *Drawing xlines*

Chapter 15

command can be invoked from the **Draw** menu (Select Draw > Ray), or by entering **RAY** at the Command prompt.

XLINE Options

Point. If you select the default option, AutoCAD will prompt you to select two points, the **Specify a point:** and the **Specify through point:**. After you select the first point, AutoCAD will dynamically rotate the xline with the cursor. When you select the second point, an xline will be created that passes through the first and second points.

> Command: **XLINE**
> Specify a point or [Hor/Ver/Ang/Bisect/Offset]: *Specify a point.*
> Specify through point: *Specify the second point.*

Horizontal. This option will create horizontal xlines of infinite length that pass through the selected points. The xlines will be parallel to the X axis of the current UCS (Figure 15-38).

Vertical. This option will create vertical xlines of infinite length that pass through the selected points. The xlines will be parallel to the Y axis of the current UCS (Figure 15-38).

Angular. This option will create xlines of infinite length that pass through the selected point at a specified angle (Figure 15-39). The angle can be specified by entering a value at the keyboard. You can also use the reference option by selecting a line object and then specifying an angle relative to the selected line. The following is the prompt sequence for the **Angular** option:

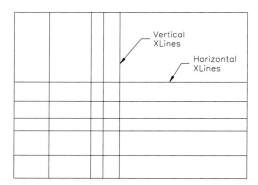

Figure 15-38 *Using the Horizontal and Vertical options to draw xlines*

Figure 15-39 *Using the Angular option to draw xlines*

> Command: **XLINE**
> Specify a point or [Hor/Ver/Ang/Bisect/Offset]: **Ang**
> Enter angle of xline (0) or [Reference]: **R**
> Select a line object: *Select a line.*
> Enter angle of xline <0>: *Enter angle (The angle will be measured counterclockwise with respect to the selected line.)*
> Specify through point: *Specify the second point.*

Bisect. This option will create an xline that passes through the angle vertex and bisects the angle. Specify the angle by selecting two points. The xline created using this option will lie in the plane defined by the selected points. You can use the object snaps to select the points on the existing objects. The following is the prompt sequence for this option (Figure 15-40):

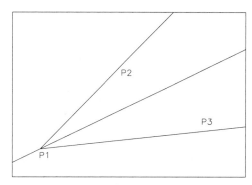

Command: **XLINE**
Specify a point or [Hor/Ver/Ang/Bisect/
Offset]: **B**
Specify angle vertex point: *Enter a point (P1).*
Specify angle start point: *Enter a point (P2).*
Specify angle end point: *Enter a point (P3).*   *(You can use object snaps to select points).*
Specify angle end point: *Press ENTER.*

Figure 15-40 Using the Bisect option to draw xlines

Offset. The **Offset** option creates xlines that are parallel to the selected line/xline at the specified offset distance. You can specify the offset distance by entering a numerical value or by selecting two points on the screen. If you select the Through option, the offset line will pass through the selected point. (This option works like the **OFFSET** editing command.)

RAY Command

A ray is a 3D line similar to the xline construction line with the difference being that it extends to infinity only in one direction. It starts from a point you specify and extends to infinity through the specified point. To exit the **RAY** command, press ESC or ENTER. The prompt sequence is:

Command: **RAY**
Specify start point: *Select the starting point for the ray.*
Specify through point: *Specify the second point.*

CREATING NURBS

Toolbar:	Draw > Spline
Menu:	Draw > Spline
Command:	SPLINE

NURBS can be created using the **SPLINE** command. NURBS is an acronym for **NonUniform Rational Bezier-Spline**. The spline created with the **SPLINE** command is different from the spline created using the **PLINE** command. The nonuniform aspect of the spline enables the spline to have sharp corners because the spacing between the spline elements that constitute a spline can be irregular. Rational means that irregular geometry, such as arcs, circles, and ellipses, can be combined with free-form curves. The Bezier-spline (B-spline) is the core that enables accurate fitting of curves to

*Figure 15-41 Invoking **SPLINE** from the **Draw** toolbar*

input data with Bezier's curve-fitting interface. The following is the command prompt sequence for creating the spline shown in Figure 15-42:

Command: **SPLINE**
Specify first point or [Object]: *Select point (P1).*
Specify next point: *Select the second point (P2).*
Specify next point or [Close/Fit tolerance] <start tangent>: *Select point (P3).*
Specify next point or [Close/Fit tolerance] <start tangent>: *Select point (P4).*
Specify next point or [Close/Fit tolerance] <start tangent>: *Select point (P5).*
Specify next point or [Close/Fit tolerance] <start tangent>: *Select point (P6).*
Specify next point or [Close/Fit tolerance] <start tangent>: *Press ENTER*
Specify start tangent: *Press ENTER for default.*
Specify end tangent: *Select point (P7).*

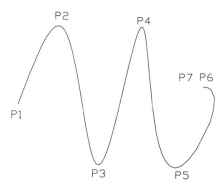

Figure 15-42 Using the **SPLINE** command to draw splines

SPLINE Command Options

Object. This option allows you to change a 2D or 3D splined polyline into a NURBS. The original splined polyline is deleted if the system variable **DELOBJ** is set to 1. To change a polyline into a splined polyline, use the **PEDIT** command.

Command: **SPLINE**
Specify first point or [Object]: **O**
Select objects to convert to splines ...
Select objects: *Select 2D or 3D splined polyline.*

Close. This option allows you to close the NURBS. When you use this option, AutoCAD will automatically join the endpoint with the start point of the spline, and you will be prompted to define the start tangent only.

Fit Tolerance. This option allows you to control the fit of the spline between specified points. If you enter a smaller value, the spline will pass through the defined points as closely as possible (Figure 15-43). If the fit tolerance value is 0, the spline passes through the fit points.

Command: **SPLINE**
Specify first point or [Object]: *Select point1.*

Specify next point: *Select second point.*

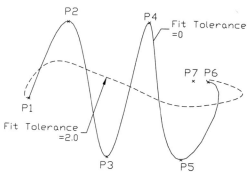

Figure 15-43 Creating a spline with a Fit Tolerance of 2

Specify next point or [Close/Fit tolerance] <start tangent>: **F**
Specify fit tolerance<current>: *Enter a value.*
Specify next point or [Close/Fit tolerance] <start tangent>: *Select third point.*

Start and End Tangents. This allows you to control the tangency of the spline at the start point and endpoint of the spline. If you press ENTER at these prompts, AutoCAD will use the default value. By default, the tangency is determined by the slope of the spline at the specified point.

EDITING SPLINES (SPLINEDIT COMMAND)

Toolbar:	Modify II > Edit Spline
Menu:	Modify > Spline
Command:	SPLINEDIT

*Figure 15-44 Selecting the **Edit Spline** button from the **Modify II** toolbar*

NURBS can be edited using the **SPLINEDIT** command. With this command, you can fit data in the selected spline, close or open the spline, move vertex points, and refine or reverse a spline. You can also invoke **SPLINEDIT** command from the shortcut menu by selecting a spline and right-clicking in the drawing area and choosing **Spline Edit**. The following is the prompt sequence of **SPLINEDIT** command:

Command: **SPLINEDIT**
Select spline:
Enter an option [Fit data/Close/Move vertex/Refine/rEverse/Undo]:

SPLINEDIT Command Options

Fit Data. When you draw a spline, the spline is fit to the specified points (data points). The Fit Data option allows you to edit these points (fit data points) (Figure 15-45). For example, if you want to redefine the start and end tangents of a spline, select the Fit Data option; then select the Tangents option, as follows:

Command: **SPLINEDIT**
Select spline:
Enter an option [Fit data/Close/Move vertex/Refine/rEverse/Undo]: **F**
Enter a fit data option
[Add/Close/Delete/Move/Purge/Tangents/toLerance/eXit] <eXit>: **T**
Specify start tangent or [System default]: *Select a point (P0).*
Specify end tangent or [System default]: *Select a point (P7).*

Close. This option allows you to close or open a spline. When you select the Close option, AutoCAD lets you open, move the vertex, or refine or reverse the spline. The following is the command prompt sequence for closing a polyline (Figure 15-46):

Enter an option [Fit data/Close/Move vertex/Refine/rEverse/Undo]: **C**
Enter an option [Open/Move vertex/Refine/rEverse/Undo/eXit] <eXit>: **X**

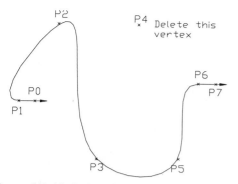

Figure 15-45 *Using the **SPLINEDIT** command to fit data points*

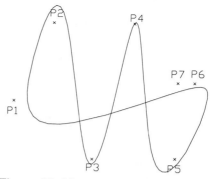

Figure 15-46 *Using the **SPLINEDIT** command to close a spline*

Move Vertex. When you draw a spline, it is associated with the Bezier control frame. The Move Vertex option allows you to move the vertices of the control frame. To display the frame with the spline, set the value of **SPLFRAME** system variable to 1. The following is the command prompt sequence for moving one of the vertex points (Figure 15-47):

Enter an option [Fit data/Close/Move vertex/Refine/rEverse/Undo]: **M**
Specify new location or [Next/Previous/Select point/eXit] <N>: **S**
Specify control point <exit>: *Select a point (P1).*
Specify new location or [Next/Previous/Select point/eXit] <N>: *Enter new location (P0).*
Specify new location or [Next/Previous/Select point/eXit] <N>: **X**

Refine. This option allows you to refine a spline by adding more control points in the spline, elevating the order, or adding weight to vertex points. For example, if you want to add more control points to a spline, the command prompt sequence is as follows (Figure 15-48):

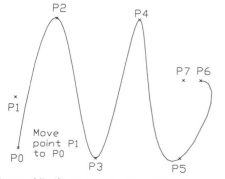

Figure 15-47 *Using the **SPLINEDIT** command to move a vertex point*

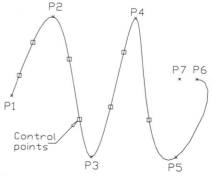

Figure 15-48 *Using the **SPLINEDIT** command to refine a spline*

Enter an option [Fit data/Close/Move vertex/Refine/rEverse/Undo]: **R**
Enter a refine option [Add control point/Elevate order/Weight/eXit] <eXit>: **A**

Specify a point on the spline <exit>: *Select a point.*
Specify a point on the spline <exit>: *Press ENTER.*
Enter a refine option [Add control point/Elevate order/Weight/eXit] <eXit>: **X**

Reverse. This option allows you to reverse the spline direction.

Undo. This option will undo the previous option.

Exit. This option exits the command line.

Exercise 2   *General*

Draw the illustration shown at the top of Figure 15-49. Then use the **SPLINE**, **SPLINEDIT**, and **GRIPS** commands to obtain the illustration shown at the bottom. (Assume the missing dimensions.)

Figure 15-49 Drawing for Exercise 2

SKETCHING IN AUTOCAD (SKETCH COMMAND)

Command: SKETCH

Sometimes you will need to draw objects that cannot be drawn with the **LINE** or other commands. For example, if you want to draw the map of a country, topographic maps, freehand designs, or signatures, you can use the AutoCAD **SKETCH** command. The **SKETCH** command lets you perform freehand sketching. To sketch, you need to have a pointing device such as a light pen, mouse, or digitizer. Since you want the freehand sketch to be as smooth as possible, you should switch SNAP and ORTHO to Off.

Command: **SKETCH**

After invoking this command, AutoCAD prompts for the length of the sketch line segment that constitutes the basic building block for sketches. This is also known as the **record increment**. The type of the sketch line segment is dependent upon the **SKPOLY** system variable. When **SKPOLY** is ON (1), it generates polyline segments. When **SKPOLY** is OFF (0), it generates line segments. You can specify the length of the sketch line segment at the following prompt:

Record increment <current>:

The default size for a single sketch segment is 0.1000 units. If you want to increase the smoothness (accuracy) of the sketch and have more flexibility in drawing sketches, reduce the record increment value (Figure 15-50). The trade-off is the computer storage area; for example, as the individual segment length decreases, the storage area required increases. After specifying the record increment, AutoCAD prompts:

Figure 15-50 Sketch with different record increments

Sketch. Pen eXit Quit Record Erase Connect.

These options are explained next.

SKETCH Command Options

Pen. With this option, you can start and stop sketching. When you enter **P** at the "**Sketch. Pen eXit Quit Record Erase Connect.**" prompt, AutoCAD responds with **<Pen down>**. Now you can start sketching by moving the cursor. If you press **P** again, AutoCAD displays **<Pen up>**, and sketching is discontinued.

. (Period). This option is used to draw a straight line between the endpoint of the most recently sketched line and a specified point. First move the cursor to the desired location and then enter [**.**]; AutoCAD automatically draws a line between that point and the endpoint of the most recently sketched line.

Connect. While sketching, many times you will need to "pen up" to access the menu or to stall sketching. After accessing the menu, or when you are ready to start sketching again, you can start sketching from the last point on the sketch with the **Connect** option. If you erase a section of the sketch, the Connect option allows you to resume sketching from the last point of the remaining sketch. To invoke this option, enter **C**.

Sketch. Pen eXit Quit Record Erase Connect . **C**
Connect: *Move to the endpoint of the line*.

Place the cursor on the last point on the sketch. Once the cursor touches the sketch line within a distance of one record increment from the endpoint of the sketch line, AutoCAD performs a "**pen down**", and you can start sketching again. If there is no sketch line on the screen and you invoke this option, the following message is displayed:

No last point known.

If you invoke the Connect option when the pen is down, you will get the following message:

Connect command meaningless when pen down.

Record. This option converts all temporary sketch lines into permanent lines.

Erase. You may make an error while sketching. The Erase option lets you erase the sketch from the endpoint to a desired point on the sketch. You can use this option when the pen is down or when the pen is up. If the pen is down, AutoCAD automatically performs a pen up.

Sketch. Pen eXit Quit Record Erase Connect . **E**
Erase: Select end of delete.<Pen up>

Place the cursor at the point up to the end of the sketch line you want to erase. If you do not want to perform the erasure, enter **E** or some other command. The following message is displayed:

Erase aborted

If you want to go forward with the erase operation after specifying the section to be erased, enter **P** or press the pick button of the pointer.

eXit. With the **eXit** option, you can record all the temporary sketch lines and return to the Command prompt. Instead of selecting the eXit option, you can press ENTER or the SPACEBAR (both have the same effect as the eXit option). AutoCAD displays a message stating the number of lines recorded.

Quit. You can use this option to exit the **SKETCH** command without recording any temporary lines sketched since the last recording of temporary lines.

DIGITIZING DRAWINGS

In digitizing, the information in the drawing is transferred to a CAD system by locating the points on the drawing that is placed on the top surface of the digitizing tablet. Sometimes it is easier to digitize an existing drawing than to create the drawing again on a CAD system. The digitizing of drawings is an important application in industry. The advantages of a drawing based on a CAD system have prompted companies to digitize drawings.

If you want to digitize a drawing, you should have a digitizer as large as the size of the largest drawing to be digitized so that you do not have to realign the drawing sheet. But situations often arise in which the digitizer is not as large as the drawing to be digitized. In such cases, after digitizing a part of the drawing (as large as the digitizer can accommodate), digitize the other parts until the entire drawing is digitized. Digitizing can be carried out in the Tablet mode. In the Tablet mode, AutoCAD uses the digitizing tablet as a digitizer, not as a screen pointing device. In this mode, the coordinate system of the paper drawings can be mapped directly into AutoCAD. The Tablet mode can be turned on or off with the **TABLET** command or by pressing function key F4.

> Command: **TABLET**
> Enter an option [ON/OFF/CAL/CFG]: **ON**   (or **OFF**)

TABLET COMMAND

Menu:	Tools > Tablet
Command:	TABLET

The first step in digitizing a drawing is to configure the tablet so that the maximum possible area on the tablet can be used. You can do this with the **TABLET** command.

> Command: **TABLET**

At the next prompt, enter CFG (Configuration option) to configure the tablet.

> Enter an option [ON/OFF/CAL/CFG]: **CFG**

After this, you are prompted to specify the number of tablet menus you want. When digitizing drawings, the whole tablet area is used for digitizing the drawing; hence, there are no tablet menus.

> Enter the number of tablet menus desired (0-4)<>: **0**

At the next prompt, enter **Y** so that reconfiguration of the tablet is possible:

> Do you want to respecify the Fixed Screen pointing area? [Yes/No] <N>: **Y**
> Digitize lower left corner of Fixed Screen pointing area: *Specify the lower left corner of the pointing area.*
> Digitize upper right corner of Fixed Screen pointing area: *Specify the upper right corner of the pointing area.*
> Do you want to specify the Floating Screen pointing area? [Yes/No]<N>: **N**

The next step in digitizing a drawing is to calibrate the tablet. For this, position the drawing to be digitized to the tablet with the help of adhesive tape. Calibration is possible in model space and paper space.

Command: **TABLET**
Enter an option [ON/OFF/CAL/CFG]: **CAL**

After you select or enter **CAL**, the Tablet mode is turned on and the screen crosshairs cursor disappears. The process of calibration involves digitizing two or more points on the drawing and then entering their coordinate values. The points to be selected can be anywhere on the drawing. Once you have specified the position of the points and the coordinate values of these positions, AutoCAD automatically calibrates the digitizing area.

Digitize point #1: *Select the first point.*
Enter coordinates for point #1: *Enter the coordinates of the first point selected.*
Digitize point #2: *Select the second point.*
Enter coordinates for point #2: *Enter the coordinates of the second point selected.*
Digitize point #3 (or RETURN to end): *Select the third point.*
Enter coordinates for point #3: *Enter the coordinates of the second point selected.*
Digitize point #4 (or RETURN to end): *Press ENTER to end.*

AutoCAD will display the Text Window displaying the transformation information (Figure 15-51).

Figure 15-51 *Tranformation Table*

Enter transformation type [Orthogonal/Affine/Projective/Repeat table] <Repeat>: **A**

You can enter any number of points. The more points you enter, the more accurate is the digitizing. If you have entered only two points, AutoCAD will automatically compute orthogonal transformation. If you have entered three or more points, AutoCAD will compute orthogonal, affine, and projective transformations and determine which best fits the configuration of the selected points. After configuring and calibrating the tablet, the crosshairs cursor is redisplayed on the screen. Now, you can use AutoCAD commands to digitize the drawing. For more information about tablets, refer to Chapter 33, Tablet Menus.

Floating Screen Pointing Area

You can configure the tablet for two pointing areas: the fixed pointing area and the floating pointing area. Before you configure the tablet, the entire tablet surface is the fixed screen pointing area.

Chapter 15

At this point the digitizer tablet performs like a pointing device. You can use the CFG option of the **TABLET** command to specify the new fixed screen pointing area. When you enter this command, AutoCAD will prompt you to specify the two points: lower left corner and upper right corner of the new screen pointing area. Now, if you move the digitizer puck within the fixed pointing area, the cursor moves on entire screen because there is one-to-one correspondence between the fixed pointing area on the digitizer and the screen. You can also define a floating screen pointing area that is the same as the screen pointing area or you can specify a different area. The following is the prompt sequence to specify a floating screen pointing area:

Command: **TABLET**
Enter an option [ON/OFF/CAL/CFG]: **CFG**
Enter the number of tablet menus desired (0-4)<>: 0

Do you want to respecify the Fixed Screen pointing area?[Yes/No]<N>: **N**
Do you want to specify the Floating Screen pointing area? [Yes/No]<N>: **Y**
Do you want the Floating Screen area to be the same size as the Fixed Screen pointing area? [Yes/No] <Y>: **N**
Digitize lower left corner of the Floating Screen pointing area: *Specify the lower left corner of the pointing area.*
Digitize upper right corner of the Floating Screen pointing area: *Specify the upper right corner of the pointing area.*

Next, AutoCAD will prompt you to specify the toggle key. By default, you can use the function key **F12** to toggle between the floating and fixed screen pointing area or you can define a button of the digitizer puck as the toggle key. You can still use the function key **F4** to turn the Tablet mode on or off to digitize a drawing.

Self-Evaluation

Answer the following questions, and then compare your answers to the correct answers given at the end of this chapter.

1. The settings for the plot parameters are saved in the _____.

2. If you want to store the plot in a file and not have it printed directly on a plotter, select the _____ check box in the **Plot** dialog box.

3. The scale for the plot can be specified in the _____ edit boxes in the **Plot** dialog box.

4. In partial preview, the _____ is graphically represented by the white rectangle. The blue rectangle is the section in the paper that is used by the _____ .

5. The **Zero** option will produce a multiline so that the zero offset position of the multiline coincides with the selected points. (T/F)

6. Multilines cannot be edited using grips. (T/F)

7. You can also edit the multilines without using the **Multiline Edit Tools** dialog box. To accomplish this, enter _____ at the Command prompt.

8. The _____ the record increment value, the greater the storage space occupied by the sketch.

9. Quitting the **SKETCH** command after recording the temporary sketch lines can be accomplished with the _____ option.

10. The size of a plot can be specified by selecting any paper size from the _____ drop-down list in the **Plot** dialog box.

11. Different objects in the same drawing can be plotted in different colors, with different linetypes and line widths. (T/F)

12. Full preview takes _____ time than Partial preview.

13. _____ can be used to edit multilines. This command edits only multilines.

14. If you select the _____ radio button in the **Plot** dialog box, the section of drawing that currently holds objects is plotted.

Review Questions

Plot

1. The _____ command is used to plot a drawing.

2. By selecting the View radio button in the **Plot** dialog box, you can plot a _____ view that was created with the _____ command in the current drawing.

3. If you do not want the hidden lines of the objects created in paper space to be plotted, select the _____ of Plot Settings tab in the **Plot** dialog box.

4. A plot can be rotated at an angle of _____ , _____ , _____ , or _____ degrees.

5. Rotation of a plot is performed in a _____ .

6. You can view the plot on the specified paper size before actually plotting it by selecting the _____ in the **Plot** dialog box.

7. In a Partial preview, if the _____ boundary and the _____ boundary overlap, this is graphically represented by a red and blue dashed line.

8. By selecting the _____ button in the **Plot** dialog box, the drawing is displayed on the screen just as it would be plotted on the paper.

Chapter 15

Mline and Mledit

9. You can draw multilines by using the _____ command.

10. The _____ command allows you to set the style of multilines.

11. The Description edit box allows you to enter the description of the _____ .

12. The **Save...** button lets you save or copy the current multiline style to an external file (.mln file). (T/F)

13. The justification does not determine how a multiline is drawn between the specified points. (T/F)

14. The _____ option allows you to change the scale of a multiline.

15. The style must be _____ before using the STyle option to change the style.

16. Using the _____ command options, you can create three types of cross intersections: closed, open, and merged.

Line, Ray, and Spline

17. The **XLINE** and **RAY** commands can be used to draw _____ or _____ lines.

18. An xline is a 3D line that extends to _____ on both ends.

19. NURBS can be created using the _____ command. NURBS is an acronym for _____ .

20. NURBS splines can be edited using the _____ command.

Sketch Command and Digitizing

21. The _____ command can be used to draw a freehand drawing in AutoCAD.

22. Sketching can be performed when the pen is _____

23. The _____ option of the **SKETCH** command is used to generate a straight line from the endpoint of the previous sketch line to the specified point.

24. Exiting the **SKETCH** command without recording temporary sketch lines can be accomplished with the _____ option.

25. The Tablet mode can be turned on and off with the help of the _____ command.

26. The process of calibration involves digitizing _____ two points on the drawing and then entering their _____ values.

27. The digitizing process can be used to convert a drawing on paper to a CAD system. (T/F)

Exercises

Exercise 3   *General*

Make the drawing given in Figure 15-52, and plot it according to the following specifications. It is assumed that the plotter supports six pens.

1. The drawing is to be plotted on 10 x 8 inch paper.
2. The border lines (polylines) must be 0.01 inches wide when plotted.
3. Change the **DIMSCALE** and text size so that the dimension text height and text height are each 0.125 inches when the drawing is plotted.
4. The object lines must be plotted with Pen-1.
5. The dimension lines and centerlines must be plotted with Pen-2.
6. The border and title block must be plotted with Pen-3.

Figure 15-52 Drawing for Exercise 3

Answers to Self-Evaluation Test

1 - PC3, **2** - **Plot to File**, **3** - Plotted Inches = Drawing Units, **4** - paper, image, **5** - T, **6** - F, **7** - **-MLEDIT**, **8** - lower, **9** - **eXit**, **10** - Paper Size, **11** - T, **12** - more, **13** - **MLEDIT**, **14** - **Extents**

Chapter 15

Chapter 16

Object Grouping and Editing Commands

Learning Objectives

After completing this chapter, you will be able to:
- *Use the **GROUP** command to group objects.*
- *Select and cycle through defined groups.*
- *Change properties and points of objects using the **CHANGE** command.*
- *Perform editing operations on polylines using the **PEDIT** command.*
- *Explode compound objects using the **EXPLODE** command.*
- *Undo previous commands using the **UNDO** command.*
- *Rename named objects using the **RENAME** command.*
- *Remove unused named objects using the **PURGE** command.*
- *Change the display order of objects using **DRAWORDER** command.*
- *Use the **AutoCAD DesignCenter** window to manage content*

OBJECT GROUPING (GROUP COMMAND)

Command:	GROUP

You can use the **Object Grouping** dialog box (Figure 16-1) to group AutoCAD objects and assign a name to the group. Once you have created groups, you can select the objects by group name. The individual characteristics of an object are not affected by forming groups. Groups are simply a mechanism that enables you to form groups and edit objects by groups. It makes the object selection process easier and faster. Objects can be members of several groups.

Although an object belongs to a group, you can still select an object as if it did not belong to any group. Groups can be selected by entering the group name or by selecting an object that belongs to the group. You can also highlight the objects in a group or sequentially highlight the groups to which an object belongs. The **Object Grouping** dialog box can be displayed by invoking the **GROUP** command. You can also use the command line form of the **GROUP** command by entering **-GROUP**.

Command: **-GROUP**
Enter a group option
[?/Order/Add/Remove/Explode/REName/Selectable/Create] <Create>:

The **Object Grouping** dialog box (Figure 16-1) provides the following options.

Figure 16-1 Object Grouping dialog box

Group Name

The **Group Name** list in the **Object Grouping** dialog box displays the names of the existing groups. The list box also displays whether a group is **selectable** or not. A **selectable** group is one, in which all members are selected on selecting a single member.

Group Identification

This area of the **Object Grouping** dialog box displays the name and description of a selected group. You can also enter the name and description of a new group that is created.

Group Name. The **Group Name:** edit box displays the name of the existing or selected group. You can also use the **Group Name:** edit box to enter the name of the new group. You can enter any name, but it is recommended that you use a name that reflects the type of objects in the group. For example, the group name WALLS can include all lines that form walls. Group names can be up to 255 characters long and can include letters, numbers and special characters ($, _, and -) which are not being used by AutoCAD for other purposes. Group names can also have spaces.

Description. The **Description:** edit box displays the description of the existing or the selected group. It can be used to enter the description of the group. The description text can be up to 64 characters long, including spaces.

Find Name <. The **Find Name <** button is used to find the group name or names associated with an object. When you select this button, the dialog box is temporarily removed; AutoCAD will prompt you to select the object. Once you select the object, the **Group Member List** dialog box (Figure 16-2) will appear, displaying the group name(s) to which the selected object belongs.

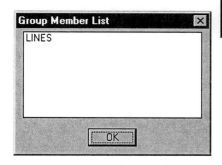

Figure 16-2 Group Member List dialog box

Highlight <. The **Highlight <** button is used to highlight the objects that are in the selected group name. You can select the group name by selecting the group name in the **Group Names** list box.

Include Unnamed. The **Include Unnamed** check box is used to display the names of the unnamed groups in the **Object Grouping** dialog box. The unnamed groups are created when you copy all objects in a named object. AutoCAD automatically groups and assigns a name to the copied objects. The format of the name is A*X* (for example, *A1, *A2, *A3). If you select the **Include Unnamed** check box, the unnamed object names (*A1, *A2, *A3, ...) will be displayed in the dialog box. The unnamed groups can also be created by not assigning a name to the group (see Unnamed in the next section, Create Group).

Create Group

New <. The **New <** button is used to define a new group after you have entered the group name in the **Group Name:** edit box. Once you choose the **New <** button, the **Object Grouping** dialog box will temporarily disappear; AutoCAD will prompt you to select objects. After selecting the objects, the dialog box will reappear and a new group is created from the selected objects using the **Group name** and **Description** in the respective edit boxes. The new group name is then displayed in the **Group Name** list. The group names in the **Group Name** list box are listed alphabetically.

Selectable. The **Selectable** check box allows you to define a group as selectable. Doing so enables you to select the entire group when one object in the group is selected. The **PICKSTYLE** system variable affects the selection ability. If **PICKSTYLE** is set at 0, you can individually select members of the group.

Unnamed. When you create a group, you can assign it a name or leave it unnamed. If you select the **Unnamed** check box, AutoCAD will automatically assign a group name to the selected objects and these unnamed groups are listed in the **Group Name** list box. The format of the name is A*n* (*A1, *A2, *A3, ...), where *n* is a number which is incremented with each new unnamed group.

Change Group

All the options in this area are activated only when you highlight a group name by selecting it. This area of the **Object Grouping** dialog box modifies the properties of the existing group

Remove <. The **Remove <** button is used to remove objects from the selected group. Once you select the group name from the **Group Name** list box and then choose the **Remove <** button, the dialog box will temporarily disappear; AutoCAD will display the following prompt on the screen:

Select objects to remove from group...
Remove objects: *Select objects.*   *(Select objects that you want to remove from the selected group.)*

If you remove all objects from the group, the group name still exists, unless you use the **Explode** option to remove the group definition. If you remove objects and then add them later in the same drawing session, the objects retain their order in the group.

Add <. The **Add <** button is used to add objects to the selected group. When you select this option, AutoCAD will prompt you to select the objects you want to add to the selected group. The prompt sequence is similar to that for the **Remove <** option.

Rename. The **Rename** button is used to rename the selected group. To rename a group, first select the group name from the **Group Name** list box and then enter the new name in the **Group Name** edit box. Then, choose the **Rename** button, and AutoCAD will rename the specified group.

Re-order. The **Re-order** option lets you change the order of the objects in the selected group. The objects are numbered in the order in which you select them when selecting objects for the group. Sometimes when creating a tool path, you may want to change the order of these objects to get a continuous tool motion. You can do this using the **Re-order** option. This option is also useful in some batch operations where one object needs to be on top of another object for display reasons. When you choose the **Re-Order** button, AutoCAD displays the **Order Group** dialog box (Figure 16-3) where you can change the order of the group members.

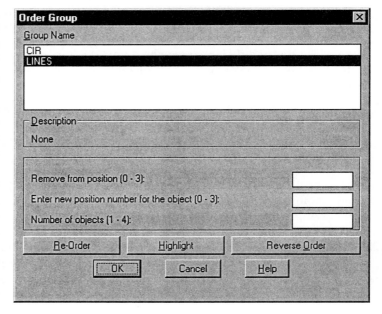

*Figure 16-3 **Order Group** dialog box*

Example 1

Figure 16-4 shows four objects that are in group G1. Determine the order of these objects and then reorder them in a clockwise direction.

1. Invoke the **Object Grouping** dialog box, and make the group (G1) current by selecting it from the **Group Name** list box.

2. Choose the **Re-Order** button from the dialog box; the **Order Group** dialog box is displayed on the screen. Select group G1, if not already selected.

Figure 16-4 Changing the order of group objects

3. Use the **Highlight <** button to highlight the current order of individual objects in the selected group. On choosing the **Highlight <** button, the **Object Grouping** dialog box is displayed. You can use the **Next** and **Previous** buttons to cycle through the group objects. Figure 16-4(a) shows the order of the objects in group G1. To create a tool path so that the tool moves in a clockwise direction, you need to reorder the objects as shown in Figure 16-4(b).

4. To get a clockwise tool path, you must switch object numbers 1 and 2. You can do this by entering the necessary information in the **Order Group** dialog box. Enter 1 in the **Remove from position:** edit box and 2 in the **Enter new position number for the object:** edit box. Enter 1 in the **Number of objects:** edit box, since there is only one object to be replaced.

5. After entering the information, choose the **Re-Order** button to define the new order of the objects. You can confirm the change by choosing the **Highlight** button again and cycling through the objects.

6. If you want to reverse the order of the objects in the group, choose the **Reverse Order** button.

Description. The **Description** button in the **Object Grouping** dialog box lets you change the description of the selected group. To change the description of a group, first select the group name from the **Group Name** list box, and then enter the new description in the **Description:** edit box. Choose the **Description** button, and AutoCAD will update the description of the specified group.

Explode. The **Explode** option deletes group definition of the selected group. The objects that were in the group become regular objects without a group reference. When an object belongs to a deleted group, it is deleted from the drawing and also from the group.

Selectable. The **Selectable** button changes the selectable status of the selected group. To change the selectable status of the group, first select the group name from the **Group Name** list box, then choose the **Selectable** button. It acts like a toggle key between the options of selectable and not selectable. If the selectable status is "Yes", you can select the entire group when one object in the group is selected. If the selectable status is "No", you cannot select the entire group by selecting one object in the group.

SELECTING GROUPS

You can select a group by name by entering G at the **Select objects:** prompt.

> Command: **MOVE**
> Select objects: G
> Enter group name: Enter group name.
> 4 found
> Select objects:

If you select any member of a selectable group at the **Select objects:** prompt, then all the group members are also selected. The **PICKSTYLE** system variable should be set to 1 or 3. Also, the group selection is turned on or off by pressing CTRL+A.

> Command: **ERASE**
> Select objects: CTRL+A   *(Press the CTRL and A keys together.)*
> <Groups on> *Select an object that belongs to a group.   (If the group has been defined as selectable, all objects belonging to that group will be selected.)*

If the group has not been defined as selectable, you cannot select all objects in the group, even if you turn the group selection on by pressing the CTRL+A keys.

Note
The combination of CTRL and A keys is used as a toggle to turn the group selection on or off.

CYCLING THROUGH GROUPS

When you use the **GROUP** command to form object groups, AutoCAD lets you sequentially highlight the groups of which the selected object is a member. For example, let us assume that an object belongs to two different groups, and you want to highlight the objects in those groups. To accomplish this, press CTRL at the **Select objects:** prompt and select the object that belongs to different groups. AutoCAD will highlight the objects in one of the groups; press the pick button of your pointing device to cycle through the groups (Figure 16-5). The prompt sequence is:

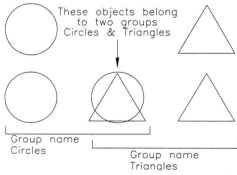

Figure 16-5 *Object selection cycling*

> Command: **ERASE**
> Select objects: *Hold down CTRL.*
> <Cycle on> *Select the object that belongs to different groups. (Press the pick button on your pointing device to cycle through the groups.)*

Select objects: [Enter]

Also, if objects are very close or directly on top of one another, such that they lie within the same selection pickbox, you can press CTRL at the **Select objects:** prompt and repeatedly click your pointing device till the object you want is highlighted. Press ENTER to select it.

CHANGING PROPERTIES AND POINTS OF AN OBJECT (CHANGE COMMAND)

Command:	CHANGE

With the help of the **CHANGE** command, you can change some of the characteristics associated with an object, such as location, color, layer, lineweight, and linetype. The **CHANGE** command has two options, **Properties** and **Change point**.

Change Point Option

You can change various features and the location of an object with the **Change point** option of the **CHANGE** command. For example, to change the endpoint of a line or a group of lines, the prompt sequence is:

> Command: **CHANGE**
> Select objects: *Select the line.*
> Select objects: [Enter]
> Select Change point or [Properties]: *Specify a point to be used as a new endpoint.*

When the **ORTHO** mode is on, using the **CHANGE** command to change the endpoint of a line or group of lines makes them parallel to either the X axis or the Y axis.

To change various features associated with the text, the prompt sequence is:

> Command: **CHANGE** [Enter]
> Select objects: *Select the text.*
> Select objects: [Enter]
> Specify new change point or [Properties]: [Enter]
> Specify new text insertion point <no change>: *Specify the new text insertion point (location of text) or press ENTER for no change.*
> Enter new text style <current>: *Enter the name of the new text style or press ENTER to accept the current style.*

The next prompt is available only for text styles that do not have a fixed height.

> Specify new text height <current>: *Specify the new text height or press ENTER to accept the current value.*
> Specify new rotation angle <current>: *Specify the new rotation angle or press ENTER to accept the current value.*
> Enter new text <current>: *Enter the new text or press ENTER to accept the current text.*

The properties of an attribute definition text can be changed just as you change the text. The prompt sequence for changing the properties of an attribute definition text is as follows:

> Command: **CHANGE**
> Select objects: *Select the attribute definition text.*
> Select objects: [Enter]
> Specify new change point or [Properties]: [Enter]
> Specify new text insertion point <no change>: *Specify the new attribute definition text insertion point (location).*
> Enter new text style <current>: *Enter the name of the new text style or press ENTER to accept the current style.*

The next prompt is available only for text styles that do not have a fixed height.

> Specify new height <current>: *Specify the new attribute definition text height.*
> Specify new rotation angle <current>: *Specify the new rotation angle.*
> Enter new tag <current>: *Enter the tag.*
> Enter new prompt <current>: *Enter the new prompt.*
> Enter new default value <current>: *Enter the new default value.*

You can also change the position of an existing block and specify a new rotation angle. The prompt sequence is as follows:

> Command: **CHANGE**
> Select objects: *Select the block.*
> Select objects: [Enter]
> Specify change point or [Properties]: [Enter]
> Specify new block insertion point <no change>: *Specify the new block insertion point.*
> Specify new block rotation angle <current>: *Specify the new rotation angle for the block.*

The radius of a circle can be changed with the **Change point** option of the **CHANGE** command by specifying the new radius in the case of the circle. To change the radius of a circle, the prompt sequence is:

> Command: **CHANGE**
> Select objects: *Select the circle.*
> Select objects: [Enter]
> Specify change point or [Properties]: *Select a point to specify the radius of the circle.*

If more than one circle is selected, after the first circle is modified, the same prompts are repeated for the next circle.

The Properties Option

The **Properties** option can be used to change the characteristics associated with an object.

Changing the Layer of an Object. If you want to change the layer on which an object exists and other characteristics associated with layers, you can use the **LAyer** option of the **Properties** option. The prompt sequence is:

> Command: **CHANGE** [Enter]
> Select objects: *Select the object whose layer you want to change.*
> Select objects: *If you have finished selection, press ENTER.*
> Specify change point or [Properties]: P [Enter]
> Enter property to change [Color/Elev/LAyer/LType/ltScale/LWeight/Thickness]: LA
> Enter new layer name <0>: *Enter a new layer name.*
> Enter property to change [Color/Elev/LAyer/LType/ltScale/LWeight/Thickness]: [Enter]

The selected object is now placed on the desired layer.

Changing the Color of an Object. You can change the color of the selected object with the **Color** option of the **CHANGE** command. If you want to change the color and linetype to match the layer, you can use the **Properties** option of the **CHANGE** command; then, change the color or linetype by entering BYLAYER as follows:

> Command: **CHANGE** [Enter]
> Select objects: *Select the block to change.*
> Select objects: *If you have finished the selection, press ENTER.*
> Specify change point or [Properties]: P [Enter]
> Enter property to change [Color/Elev/LAyer/LType/ltScale/LWeight/Thickness]: C
> Enter new color <current>: BYLAYER   *(Or enter the color name.)*
> Specify property to change [Color/Elev/LAyer/LType/ltScale/LWeight/Thickness]: [Enter]

Blocks originally created on layer 0 assume the color of the new layer; otherwise (if it was not created on layer 0), it will retain the color of the layer on which it was created.

Changing the Thickness of an Object. You can change the thickness of the selected object in the following manner:

> Command: **CHANGE** [Enter]
> Select objects: *Select the object whose thickness you want to change.*
> Select objects: [Enter]
> Specify change point or [Properties]: P [Enter]
> Enter property to change [Color/Elev/LAyer/LType/ltScale/LWeight/Thickness]: T
> Enter new thickness <current thickness>: *Specify the new thickness.*

Changing the Lineweight of an Object. You can change the lineweight of the selected object by using the **LWeight** option of the **CHANGE** command. Since the lineweight values are predefined, if you enter a value that is not predefined, a predefined value of lineweight which comes closest to the specified value is assigned to the selected object. The prompt sequence is :

> Command: **CHANGE**
> Select objects: *Select objects whose lineweight you wish to change.*
> Select objects: *If you have finished selecting objects, press ENTER.*
> Specify change point or [Properties]: P [Enter]

Enter property to change [Color/Elev/LAyer/LType/ltScale/LWeight/Thickness]: LW
Enter new lineweight <current>: *Specify new lineweight.*

You can see the effect of changing the thickness of an object in 3D view [viewpoint (1,-1,1)]. Similarly, you can change the elevation, linetype, and linetype scale of the selected objects. You can change the Z-axis elevation of a selected object provided all the points in the particular object have the same Z value.

PROPERTIES COMMAND*

Toolbar:	Standard > Properties
Menu:	Tool > Properties
Command:	PROPERTIES

Instead of using the **CHANGE** command and then the **Properties** option, you can use the **PROPERTIES** command to change the properties of an object. The **PROPERTIES** command can also be invoked by selecting an object and right-clicking to display a shortcut menu; choose **Properties** from the shortcut menu.

Command: **PROPERTIES** [Enter]

The **Object Properties Window** is displayed (Figure 16-6), from where you can change the different properties of the selected object. Select the objects whose properties you wish to change, the **Object Properties window** displays the properties of the selected object. Right-clicking in the **Object Properties** window, displays a shortcut menu where you can choose to **Allow Docking** or **Hide** the window.

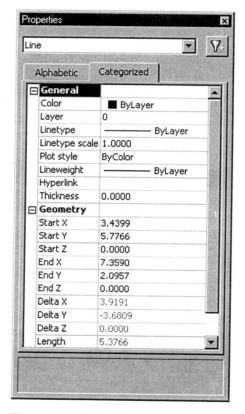

Figure 16-6 Object Properties windoow

Color

When you select **Color** from the **General** list, the color of the selected object is displayed. From the **Color** drop-down list you can select any other color you wish to assign to the selected object. Choosing the **Other...** option displays the **Select Color** dialog box (Figure 16-7). You can select the new color you want to assign to the selected object by selecting the desired color in this dialog box, and then choosing the **OK** button.

Layer

Selecting **Layer** in the **General** list of the **Object properties** window, displays the name of the layer of the object. You can select the new layer you want to assign to the selected object from the **Layer** drop-down list.

Linetype

From the **General** list in the **Object Properties** window, select **Linetype**. From the Linetype drop-

Figure 16-7 Select Color dialog box

down list, you can select the new linetype you want to assign to the selected object from the list of linetypes.

Linetype Scale

You can enter the new linetype scale factor of the selected object in the **Linetype Scale:** edit box.

Plot Style

The current Plot style is displayed in the **Plot Style** edit box under the **General** list of the **Object properties** window. You can select a different plot style for the selected object from the **Plot Style** drop-down list of Plot styles available in the current drawing.

Lineweight

Similarly, you can select a different lineweight value from the **Lineweight** drop-down list to assign to the selected object.

Hyperlink

Selecting this option under the **General** list, assigns a hyperlink to an object. The **Hyperlink** name and description assigned to the object is displayed. Choosing the [**...**] button, displays the **Insert Hyperlink** dialog box where you can enter the path of the URL or file you want to link the selected object to (Figure 16-8).

Thickness

You can enter the new 3D solid thickness of the selected object in the **Thickness:** edit box. The current value of the selected object is displayed in the **Thickness** edit box.

Figure 16-8 Insert Hyperlink dialog box

You can use the **CHPROP** command to change the properties of an object using the command line.

    Command: **CHPROP** Enter
    Select objects: *Select the object whose properties you want to change.*
    Select objects: Enter
    Enter property to change [Color/LAyer/LType/ltScale/LWeight/Plotstyle/Thickness]: *Specify the property.*

You can also use the **Object Properties** toolbar to change properties of the selected objects. This option is discussed in Chapter 10, Editing with Grips.

Exercise 1   *General*

Draw a hexagon on layer OBJ in red color. Let the linetype be hidden. Now, use the **PROPERTIES** command to change the layer to some other existing layer, the color to yellow, and the linetype to continuous. Use the **LIST** command to verify that the changes have taken place.

EXPLODE COMMAND

Toolbar:	Modify > Explode
Menu:	Modify > Explode
Command:	EXPLODE

The **EXPLODE** command is used to split compound objects such as blocks, polylines, regions, polyface meshes, polygon meshes, multilines, 3D solids, 3D meshes, bodies, or dimensions into the objects that make them up (Figure 16-10). For example, if you explode a polyline or a 3D polyline, the result will be ordinary lines or arcs (tangent specification and width are not considered). When a 3D polygon mesh is exploded, the result is 3D faces. Polyface meshes are turned into 3D faces, points, and lines. Upon exploding 3D solids, the planar surfaces of the 3D solid turn into regions, and nonplanar surfaces turn into bodies. Multilines are changed to lines. Regions turn into lines, ellipses, splines, or arcs. Two-dimensional polylines lose their width and tangent specifications; 3D polylines explode into lines. When a body is exploded, it changes into single-surface bodies, curves, or regions. When a leader is exploded, the components are lines, splines, solids, block inserts, text or Mtext, tolerance objects and so on. Mtext explodes into single line text. This command is especially useful when you have inserted an entire drawing and you need to alter a small detail.

*Figure 16-9 Choosing the **Explode** button from the **Modify** toolbar*

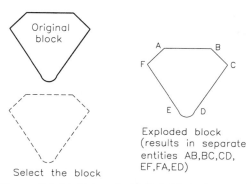

*Figure 16-10 Using the **EXPLODE** command*

Command: **EXPLODE** [Enter]
Select objects: *Select the block.*

When a block or dimension is exploded, there is no visible change in the drawing. The drawing remains the same except that the color and linetype may have changed because of floating layers, colors, or linetypes. The exploded block is turned into a group of objects that can be modified separately. To check whether the explosion of the block has taken place, select any object that was a part of the block. If the block has been exploded, only that particular object will be highlighted. With the **EXPLODE** command, only one nesting level is exploded at a time. Hence, if there is a nested block or a polyline in a block and you explode it, the inner block or the polyline will not be exploded. Attribute values are deleted when a block is exploded, and the attribute definitions are redisplayed. If a block is non-uniformly scaled, the circles in it are exploded into ellipses and the arcs are exploded into ellipses.

Note

*A block inserted using **MINSERT** and x-refs cannot be exploded.*

*While inserting a block using the **Insert** dialog box, you can insert the block as separate objects by selecting the **Explode** check box in the dialog box or using * in front of the block name when using the -**INSERT** command.*

POLYLINE EDITING (USING THE PEDIT COMMAND)

A polyline can assume various characteristics such as width, linetype, joined polyline, and closed polyline. You can edit polylines, polygons, or rectangles to attain the desired characteristics using the **PEDIT** command. In this section, we will be discussing how to edit simple 2D polylines. The following are the editing operations that can be performed on an existing polyline using the **PEDIT** command. They are discussed in detail later in this chapter.

1. A polyline of varying widths can be converted to a polyline of uniform width.
2. An open polyline can be closed and a closed one can be opened.
3. All bends and curved segments between two vertices can be removed to make a straight polyline.
4. A polyline can be split up into two.
5. Individual polylines or polyarcs connected to one another can be joined into a single polyline.
6. The appearance of a polyline can be changed by moving and adding vertices.
7. Curves of arcs and B-spline curves can be fit to all vertices in a polyline, with the specification of the tangent of each vertex being optional.
8. The linetype generation at the vertices of a polyline can be controlled.

PEDIT Command

Toolbar:	Modify II > Edit Polyline
Menu:	Modify > Polyline
Command:	PEDIT

Figure 16-11 Edit Polyline in ModifyII toolbar

You can also invoke the **PEDIT** command by selecting a polyline and right-clicking to display a shortcut menu, where you can choose **Polyline Edit**.

You can use the **PEDIT** command to edit any type of polyline. The prompt sequence is:

Command: **PEDIT** [Enter]
Select polyline: *Select the polyline to be edited using any selection method*.

If the selected line is an arc or a line (not a polyline), AutoCAD issues the following prompt:

Object selected is not a polyline.
Do you want to turn it into one? <Y>

If you want to turn the line or arc into a polyline, respond by entering a Y and pressing ENTER or by just pressing ENTER (null response). Otherwise, you can enter N and exit to the Command prompt. The subsequent prompts and editing options depend on which type of polyline has been selected. In the case of a simple 2D polyline, the next prompt displayed is:

Enter an option [Close/Join/Width/Edit vertex/Fit/Spline/Decurve/Ltype gen/Undo]: *Enter an option or press ENTER to end command*.

C (Close) Option. This option is used to close an open polyline. **Close** creates the segment that connects the last segment of the polyline to the first. You will get this option only if the polyline is not closed. Figure 16-12 illustrates this option.

O (Open) Option. If the selected polyline is closed, the **Close** option is replaced by the **Open** option. Entering O, for open, removes the closing segment.

J (Join) Option. This option appends lines, polylines, or arcs whose endpoints meet a selected polyline at any of its endpoints and adds (joins) them to it (Figure 16-13). This option can be used only if a polyline is open. After this option has been selected, AutoCAD asks you to select objects. You may also select the polyline itself. Once you have chosen the objects to be joined to the original polyline, AutoCAD ex-

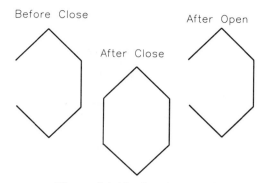

*Figure 16-12 The **Close** option*

amines them to determine whether any of them has an endpoint in common with the current polyline, and joins such an object with the original polyline. The search is then repeated using new endpoints. AutoCAD will not join if the endpoint of the object does not exactly meet the polyline. The line touching a polyline at its endpoint to form a T will not be joined. If two lines meet a polyline in a Y shape, only one of them will be selected, and this selection is unpredictable. To verify which lines have been added to the polyline, use the **LIST** command or select a part of the object. All the segments that are joined to the polyline will be highlighted. Figure 16-14 illustrates the conditions that are required to join polylines.

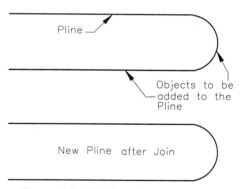

*Figure 16-13 Using the **Join** option*

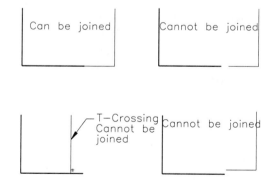

*Figure 16-14 Conditions for using the **Join** option*

Width (W) Option. The W option allows you to define a new, unvarying width for all segments of a polyline (Figure 16-15). It changes the width of a polyline with a constant or a varying width. The desired new width can be specified either by entering the width at the keyboard or by specifying the width as the distance between two specified points. Once the width has been specified, the polyline assumes it. The following prompt sequence will change the width of the given figure from 0.02 to 0.05 (Figure 16-16):

Command: **PEDIT** `Enter`
Select polyline: *Select the polyline.*
Enter an option [Close/Join/Width/Edit vertex/Fit/Spline/Decurve/Ltype gen/Undo]: W `Enter`

Specify new width for all segments: 0.05

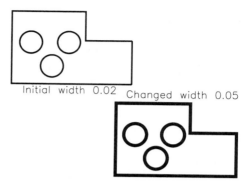

Figure 16-15 *Making the width of a polyline*
uniform

Figure 16-16 *Entering a new width for all*
segments

Note

*Circles drawn using the **CIRCLE** command cannot be changed to polylines. Polycircles can be drawn using the **Pline Arc** option (by drawing two semicircular polyarcs) or by using the **DONUT** command.*

Edit Vertex (E) Option. The **Edit vertex** option lets you select a vertex of a polyline and perform different editing operations on the vertex and the segments following it. A polyline segment has two vertices. The first one is at the start point of the polyline segment; the other one is at the endpoint of the segment. When you invoke this option, an X marker appears on the screen at the first vertex of the selected polyline. If a tangent direction has been specified for this particular vertex, an arrow is generated in that direction. After this option has been selected, the next prompt appears with a list of options for this prompt. The prompt sequence is:

Command: **PEDIT** Enter
Select polyline: *Select the polyline to be edited.*
Enter an option [Close/Join/Width/Edit vertex/Fit/Spline/Decurve/Ltype gen/Undo]: E Enter
Enter a vertex editing option
[Next/Previous/Break/Insert/Move/Regen/Straighten/Tangent/Width/eXit]<N>: *Enter an option or press ENTER to accept default.*

The options available for the **Edit vertex** option are discussed next.

Next and Previous Options. These options move the X marker to the next or the previous vertex of a polyline. The default value in the **Edit vertex** is one of these two options. The option that is selected as default is the one you chose last. In this manner, the **Next** and **Previous** options help you to move the X marker to any vertex of the polyline by selecting one of these two options, and then pressing ENTER to reach the desired vertex. These options cycle back and forth between first and last vertices, but cannot move past the first or last vertices, even if the polyline is closed (Figure 16-17).

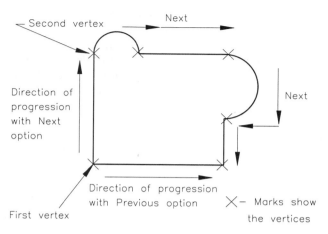

Figure 16-17 The **Next** and **Previous** options

The prompt sequence is:

Command: **PEDIT** [Enter]
Select polyline: *Select the polyline to be edited.*
Enter an option [Close/Join/Width/Edit vertex/Fit/Spline/Decurve/Ltype gen/Undo]: E [Enter]
Enter a vertex editing option
[Next/Previous/Break/Insert/Move/Regen/Straighten/Tangent/Width/eXit] <N>: *Enter N or P.*

Break Option. With the **Break** option, you
can divide a polyline into two parts (Figure
16-18). The division of the polyline can be
specified at one vertex or at two different
vertices. By specifying two different vertices, all the polyline segments and vertices
between the specified vertices are erased.
If one of the selected vertices is at the endpoint of the polyline, the **Break** option will
erase all the segments between the first vertex and the endpoint of the polyline. The
exception to this is that AutoCAD does not
erase the entire polyline if you specify the
first vertex at the start point (first vertex)

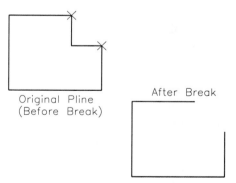

Figure 16-18 Using the **Break** option

of the polyline and the second vertex at the endpoint (last vertex) of the polyline. If both
vertices are at the endpoint of the polyline, or only one vertex is specified and its location is at
the endpoint of the polyline, no change is made to the polyline. The last two selections of
vertices are treated as invalid by AutoCAD, which acknowledges this by displaying the message ***Invalid***.

To use the **Break** option, first you need to move the marker to the first vertex where you want the split to start. Placement of the marker can be achieved with the help of the **Next** and **Previous** options. Once you have selected the first vertex to be used in the **Break** operation, invoke the **Break** option by entering B. AutoCAD takes the vertex where the marker (X) is placed as the first point of breakup. The next prompt asks you to specify the position of the next vertex for breakup. You can enter GO if you want to split the polyline at one vertex only, or use the **Next** or **Previous** option to specify the position of next vertex. The prompt sequence is:

Command: **PEDIT** [Enter]
Select polyline: *Select the polyline to be edited.*
Enter an option [Close/Join/Width/Edit vertex/Fit/Spline/Decurve/Ltype gen/Undo]: E [Enter]
Enter a vertex editing option
[Next/Previous/Break/Insert/Move/Regen/Straighten/Tangent/Width/eXit]<N>: *Enter N or P to locate the first vertex for the* ***Break*** *option.*
Enter a vertex editing option
[Next/Previous/Break/Insert/Move/Regen/Straighten/Tangent/Width/eXit]<N>: B [Enter]

Once you invoke the **Break** option, AutoCAD treats the vertex where the marker (X) is displayed as the first point for splitting the polyline. The next prompt issued is:

Enter an option [Next/Previous/Go/eXit] <N>: *Move the X marker to specify the position of next vertex for breakup.*

Enter GO if you want to split the polyline at one vertex only, or use the **Next** or **Previous** option to specify the position of the next vertex for breakup. Entering the **Go** option deletes the polyline segment between the two markers specified using the **Next** and **Previous** options. Choosing the **eXit** option, exits the **break** option.

Insert Option. The **Insert** option allows you to define a new vertex to the polyline (Figure 16-19). You can invoke this option by entering I for Insert. You should invoke it only after moving the marker (X) to the vertex that is located immediately before the new vertex. This is because the new vertex is inserted immediately after the vertex with the X mark.

Command: **PEDIT** [Enter]
Select polyline: *Select the polyline to be edited.*
Enter an option [Close/Join/Width/Edit vertex/Fit/Spline/Decurve/Ltype gen/Undo]: E [Enter]
Enter a vertex editing option
[Next/Previous/Break/Insert/Move/Regen/Straighten/Tangent/Width/eXit]<N>: *Move the marker to the vertex prior to which the new vertex is to be inserted.*
Enter a vertex editing option
[Next/Previous/Break/Insert/Move/Regen/Straighten/Tangent/Width/eXit]<N>: I [Enter]
Specify location for new vertex: *Move the cursor and select to specify the location of the new vertex.*

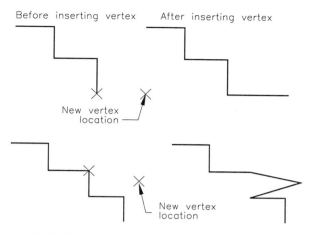

Figure 16-19 Using the **Insert** option to define new vertex points

Move Option. This option lets you move the X-marked vertex to a new position (Figure 16-20). Before invoking the **Move** option, you must move the X marker to the vertex you want to relocate by selecting the **Next** or **Previous** option. The prompt sequence is:

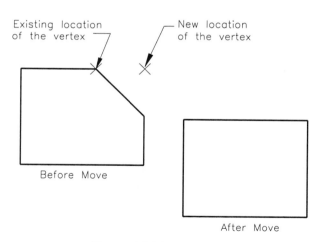

Figure 16-20 **Move** *option*

Command: **PEDIT** Enter
Select polyline: *Select the polyline to be edited.*
Enter an option [Close/Join/Width/Edit vertex/Fit/Spline/Decurve/Ltype gen/Undo]: E Enter
Enter a vertex editing option
[Next/Previous/Break/Insert/Move/Regen/Straighten/Tangent/Width/eXit]<N>: *Enter N or P to move the X marker to the vertex you want to relocate.*
Enter a vertex editing option
[Next/Previous/Break/Insert/Move/Regen/Straighten/Tangent/Width/eXit]<N>: M Enter

Specify new location for marked vertex: *Specify the new location for the selected vertex by selecting the new location or entering its coordinate values.*

Regen Option. The **Regen** option regenerates the polyline to display the effects of edits you have made. It is used most often with the **Width** option.

Straighten Option. The **Straighten** option can be used to straighten polyline segments or arcs between specified vertices (Figure 16-21). It deletes the arcs, line segments, or vertices between the two specified vertices and substitutes them with one polyline segment.

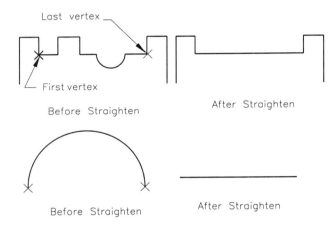

*Figure 16-21 Using the **Straighten** option to straighten polylines*

The prompt sequence is:

Command: **PEDIT** [Enter]
Select polyline: *Select the polyline to be edited.*
Enter an option [Close/Join/Width/Edit vertex/Fit/Spline/Decurve/Ltype gen/Undo]: E [Enter]
Enter a vertex editing option
[Next/Previous/Break/Insert/Move/Regen/Straighten/Tangent/Width/eXit]<N>: *Move the marker to the desired vertex with the **Next** or **Previous** option.*
Enter a vertex editing option
[Next/Previous/Break/Insert/Move/Regen/Straighten/Tangent/Width/eXit]<N>: S
Enter a vertex editing option
[Next/Previous/Break/Insert/Move/Regen/Straighten/Tangent/Width/eXit]<N>: *Move the marker to the next desired vertex.*
Enter an option [Next/Previous/Go/eXit] <N>: G [Enter]

The polyline segments between two marker locations are replaced by a single straight line segment. If you specify a single vertex, the segment following the specified vertex is straightened, if it is curved.

Tangent Option. The **Tangent** option is used to associate a tangent direction to the current vertex (marked by X). The tangent direction is used in curve fitting. This option is discussed in detail in the subsequent section on curve fitting. The prompt is:

Specify direction of vertex tangent: *Specify a point or enter an angle.*

You can specify the direction by entering an angle at the **Specify direction of vertex tangent:** prompt or by selecting a point to express the direction with respect to the current vertex.

Width Option. The **Width** option lets you change the starting and the ending widths of a polyline segment that follows the current vertex (Figure 16-22). By default, the ending width is equal to the starting width; hence, you can get a polyline segment of uniform width by accepting the default value at the **Specify ending width for next segment <starting width>:** prompt. You can specify different starting and ending widths to get a varying-width polyline. The prompt sequence is:

Enter an option [Close/Join/Width/Edit vertex/Fit/Spline/Decurve/Ltype gen/Undo]: E ⏎
Enter a vertex editing option
[Next/Previous/Break/Insert/Move/Regen/Straighten/Tangent/Width/eXit]<N>: *Move the marker to the starting vertex of the segment whose width is to be altered.*
Enter a vertex editing option
[Next/Previous/Break/Insert/Move/Regen/Straighten/Tangent/Width/eXit]<N>: W ⏎
Specify starting width for next segment <current>: *Enter the revised starting width.*
Specify ending width for next segment <starting width>: *Enter the revised ending width.*

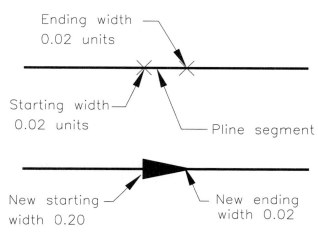

Figure 16-22 *Using the **Width** option to change the width of a polyline*

The segment with the revised widths is redrawn only after invoking the **Regen** option or when you exit the vertex mode editing.

eXit Option. This option lets you exit the Vertex mode editing and return to the main **PEDIT** prompt.

Fit Option. The **Fit** or **Fit curve** option generates a curve that passes through all the corners (vertices) of the polyline, using the tangent directions of the vertices (Figure 16-23). The curve is composed of a series of arcs passing through the corners (vertices) of the polyline. This option is used when you draw a polyline with sharp corners and need to convert it into a series of smooth curves. An example of this is a graph. In a graph, we need to show a curve by joining a series of plotted points. The process involved is called curve fitting; hence, the name of this option. These vertices of the polyline are also known as the control points. The closer together these control points are, the smoother the curve. Hence, if the **Fit** option does not give optimum results, insert more vertices into the polyline or edit the tangent directions of vertices; then, use the **Fit** option on the polyline. Before using this option you may give each vertex a tangent direction. The curve is then constructed, keeping in mind the tangent directions you have specified. The following prompt sequence illustrates the **Fit** option:

Command: **PEDIT** [Enter]
Select polyline: *Select the polyline to be edited.*
Enter an option [Close/Join/Width/Edit vertex/Fit/Spline/Decurve/Ltype gen/Undo]: F [Enter]

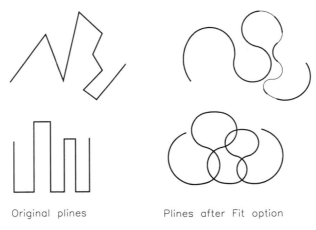

Original plines   Plines after Fit option

*Figure 16-23 The **Fit curve** option*

If the tangent directions need to be edited, use the **Edit vertex** option of the **PEDIT** command. Move the X marker to each of the vertices that need to be changed. Now, you can invoke the **tangent** option, and either enter the tangent direction in degrees or select points. The chosen direction is expressed by an arrow placed at the vertex. The prompt sequence is:

Command: **PEDIT** [Enter]
Select polyline: *Select the polyline to be edited.*
Enter an option [Close/Join/Width/Edit vertex/Fit/Spline/Decurve/Ltype gen/Undo]: E [Enter]
Enter a vertex editing option
[Next/Previous/Break/Insert/Move/Regen/Straighten/Tangent/Width/eXit]<N>: T [Enter]
Specify direction of vertex tangent: *Specify a direction in + or - degrees, or select a point in the desired direction. Press ENTER.*

Once the tangent directions are specified, use the **eXit** option to return to the previous prompt and use its **Fit curve** option.

Spline Option. The **Spline** option (Figure 16-24) also smoothens the corners of a straight segment polyline, as does the **Fit** option, but the curve passes through only the first and the last control points (vertices), except in the case of a closed polyline. The spline curve is stretched toward the other control points (vertices) but does not pass through them, as in the case of the **Fit** option. The greater the number of control points, the greater the force with which the curve is stretched toward them. The prompt sequence is as follows:

> Command: **PEDIT** ⏎
> Select polyline: *Select the polyline.*
> Enter an option [Close/Join/Width/Edit vertex/Fit/Spline/Decurve/Ltype gen/Undo]: S ⏎

The generated curve is a B-spline curve. The **frame** is the original polyline without any curves in it. If the original polyline has arc segments, these segments are straightened when the spline's frame is formed. A frame that has width produces a spline curve that tapers smoothly from the width of the first vertex to that of the last. Any other width specification between the first width specification and the last is neglected. When a spline is formed from a polyline, the frame is displayed as a polyline with zero width and continuous linetype. Also, AutoCAD saves its frame so that it may be restored to its original form. Tangent specifications on control point vertices do not affect spline construction. By default, the spline frames are not shown on screen, but you may want them displayed for reference. In such a case, system variable **SPLFRAME** needs to be manipulated. The default value for this variable is zero. If you want to see the spline frame as well, set it to 1. The prompt sequence is:

(a) Original Pline

(b) After use of Fit option

Original plines for reference

(c) After use of Spline option

*Figure 16-24 The **Spline** option*

> Command: **SPLFRAME** ⏎
> New value for SPLFRAME <0>: 1 ⏎

Now, whenever the **Spline** option is used on a polyline, the frame will also be displayed. Most editing commands such as, **MOVE, ERASE, COPY, MIRROR, ROTATE,** and **SCALE** work similarly for both the Fit curves and Spline curves. They work on both the curve and its frame, whether the frame is visible or not. The **EXTEND** command changes the frame by adding a vertex at the point the last segment intersects with the boundary. If you use any of the above mentioned commands and then use the **Decurve** option to decurve the Spline curve and later use the **Spline** option again, the same Spline curve is generated. The **BREAK, TRIM,** and **EXPLODE** commands delete the frame. The **DIVIDE, MEASURE, FILLET, CHAMFER, AREA,** and **HATCH** commands recognize only the Spline curve and do not consider the frame. The **STRETCH** command first stretches the frame and then fits the Spline curve to it. When you use the **Join** option of the **PEDIT** command, the Spline curve is decurved and the original spline information is lost. The **Next** and **Previous** options of the **Edit vertex** option of the **PEDIT** command moves the marker only to points on the frame whether visible or not. The **Break** option discards the spline curve. **Insert, Move, Straighten** and **Width** options refit the Spline curve. Object Snaps consider the Spline curve and not the frame, therefore, if you wish to snap to the frame control points, restore the original frame.

There are two types of spline curves:
Quadratic B-spline
Cubic B-spline

Both of them pass through the first and the last control points, which is characteristic of the spline curve. The cubic curves are very smooth. The cubic curve passes through the first and last control points, and the curve is closer to the other control points. The quadratic curves are not as smooth as the cubic ones, but they are smoother than the curves produced by the **Fit curve** option. The quadratic curve passes through the first and last control points, and the rest of the curve is tangent to the polyline segments between the remaining control points (Figure 16-25).

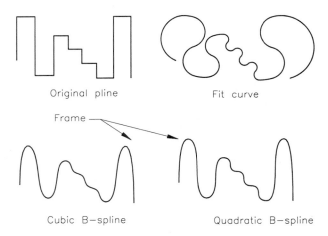

Figure 16-25 Comparison of fit curve, quad B-spline, and cubic B-spline

Generation of Different Types of Spline Curves. If you want to edit a polyline into a B-spline curve, you are first required to enter a relevant value in the **SPLINETYPE** system variable. A value of 5 produces the quadratic curve, whereas 6 produces a cubic curve. To generate a Bezier Fit Mesh, the **SURFTYPE** system variable should be set to 8.

Command: **SPLINETYPE** Enter
Enter new value for SPLINETYPE <6>: 5 Enter

Command: **SURFTYPE** Enter
New value for SURFTYPE <6>: 8 Enter

You can also get different types of splines by selecting the **Polyvars** option in the **PEDIT** screen menu. On doing so, the **Set Spline Fit Variables** dialog box (Figure 16-26) is displayed. You can select any type from the list available. The **SPLINETYPE** and **SURFTYPE** variable is automatically set to the value of the type you have chosen from the dialog box. For example, if you select the Bezier Fit Mesh type from the dialog box, the **SURFTYPE** variable is set to 8.

Figure 16-26 Set Spline Fit Variables dialog box

SPLINESEGS. The system variable **SPLINESEGS** governs the number of line segments used to construct the spline curves, so you can use this variable to control the smoothness of the curve. The default value for this variable is 8. With this value, a reasonably smooth curve that does not need much regeneration time is generated. The greater the value of this variable, the smoother the curve, the greater the regeneration time, and the more space occupied by the drawing file.

Figure 16-27 shows cubic curves with different values for the **SPLINESEGS** parameter.

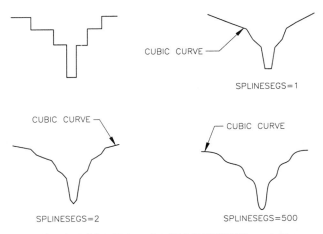

*Figure 16-28 Using the **SPLINESEGS** variable*

The prompt sequence for setting **SPLINESEGS** to a value of 500 is:

Command: **SPLINESEGS** Enter
Enter new value for SPLINESEGS <8>: 500

Decurve Option. The **Decurve** option straightens the curves generated after using the **Fit** or **Spline** option on a polyline; they return to their original shape (Figure 16-28). Polyline segments are straightened using the **Decurve** option. The vertices inserted after using the **Fit** or **Spline** option are also removed. Information entered for tangent reference is retained for use in future Fit curve operations. You can also use this command to straighten out any curve drawn with the help of the **Arc** option of the **PLINE** command. The prompt sequence is:

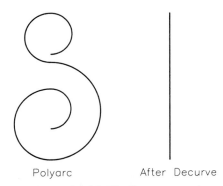

Polyarc   After Decurve

*Figure 16-28 The **Decurve** option*

Command: **PEDIT** Enter
Select polyline: *Select the polyline to be edited.*
Enter an option [Close/Join/Width/Edit vertex/Fit/Spline/Decurve/Ltype gen/Undo]: D Enter

If you use edit commands like the **BREAK** or **TRIM** commands on spline curves, the **Decurve** option cannot be used.

Ltype gen Option. You can use this option to control the linetype pattern generation for linetypes other than Continuous with respect to the vertices of the polyline (Figure 16-29). This option has two modes: ON and OFF. If turned on, this option generates the linetype in a continuous pattern with respect to the vertices of the polyline. If you turn this option off, it generates the linetype with a dash at each vertex. This option is not applicable to polylines with tapered segments. The linetype generation for new polylines can be controlled with the help of the **PLINEGEN** system variable, which acts as a toggle. The command prompt is as follows:

Enter polyline linetype generation option [ON/OFF] <Off>:

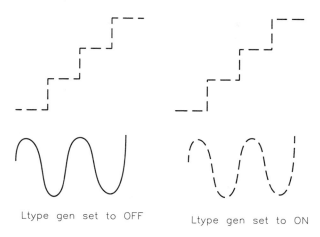

Ltype gen set to OFF   Ltype gen set to ON

*Figure 16-29 Using the **Ltype gen** option*

U (UNDO) Option. The **Undo** option negates the effect of the most recent **PEDIT** operation. You can go back as far as you need to in the current **PEDIT** session by using the **Undo** option repeatedly until you get the desired screen. If you started editing by converting an object into a polyline, and you want to change the polyline back to the object from which it was created, the **Undo** option of the **PEDIT** command will not work. In this case, you will have to exit to the Command prompt and use the **UNDO** command to undo the operation.

Exercise 2   *General*

a.   Draw a line from point (0,0) to point (6,6). Convert the line into a polyline with starting width 0.30 and ending width 0.00. Then, convert the polyline back into the original line.

b.   Draw a polyline of varying width segments and use the **Join** option to join all the segments into one polyline. Before joining the different segments, make the widths of all the segments uniform.

Exercise 3   *General*

a.   Draw a staircase-shaped polyline, then use different options of the **PEDIT** command to generate a fit curve, a quadratic B-spline, and a cubic B-spline. Then, convert the curves back into the original polyline.

b.   Draw square-wave shaped polylines, and use different options of the **Edit vertex** option to navigate around the polyline, split the polyline into two at the third vertex, insert more vertices at different locations in the original polyline, and convert the square-wave shaped polyline into a straight-line polyline.

UNDOING COMMANDS (UNDO COMMAND)

Command: UNDO

The **LINE** and **PLINE** commands have the **Undo** option, which can be used to undo (nullify) changes made within these commands. The **UNDO** command can be used to undo a previous command or to undo more than one command at one time. This command can be selected by entering **UNDO** at the Command prompt. **Undo** is also available in the **Edit** menu and the **Standard** toolbar, but this can only undo the previous command and only one command at a time. If you right-click in the drawing area a shortcut menu is displayed. Choose **Undo**. It is equivalent to **UNDO 1** or using entering **U** at the Command prompt. The **U** command can undo only one operation at a time. You can use **U** as many times as you want until AutoCAD displays the message: **Nothing to undo**. When an operation can not be undone, the message name is displayed but no action takes place. External commands like **PLOT** can not be undone. The prompt sequence for the **UNDO** command is:

> Command: **UNDO** [Enter]
> Enter the number of operations to UNDO or [Auto/Control/BEgin/End/Mark/Back]: *Enter a positive number, an option or press ENTER to undo a single operation.*

The various options of this command are discussed next.

Number (N) Option

This is the default option. This number represents the number of previous command sequences to be deleted. For example, if the number entered is 1, the previous command is undone; if the number entered is 4, the previous four commands are undone, and so on. This is identical to invoking the **U** command four times, except that only one regeneration takes place. AutoCAD lets you know which commands were undone by displaying a message after you press ENTER. The prompt sequence is:

> Command: **UNDO** [Enter]
> Enter the number of operations to UNDO or [Auto/Control/BEgin/End/Mark/Back]: 3 [Enter]
> PLINE LINE CIRCLE

Auto (A) Option

Enter A to invoke this option. The following prompt is displayed:

> Enter UNDO Auto mode [ON/OFF] <current>: *Select ON or OFF or press ENTER to accept the default.*

If Auto is On, any group of commands that was issued by one menu item is undone together. All of them are considered to be a single group and are undone as a single command. If the **Auto** option is Off, each command in the group is treated separately.

Control (C) Option

This option lets you determine how many of the options are active in the **UNDO** command. You can disable the options you do not need. With this option you can even disable the **UNDO** command. To access this option, type C. You will get the following prompt:

Enter an UNDO control option [ALL/None/One] <All>:

The options of the **Control** option are discussed next.

All (A). The **All** option activates all the features (options) of the **UNDO** command.

None (N). This option turns off **UNDO** and the **U** command. If you have used the **BEgin** and **End** options or **Mark** and **Back** options to create **UNDO** information, all of that information is undone.

Command: **UNDO**
Enter the number of operations to UNDO [Auto/Control/BEgin/End/Mark/Back]: C
Enter an UNDO control option [ALL/None/One] <All>: NONE
The prompt sequence for the **UNDO** command after issuing the **None** option is:

Command: **UNDO**
Enter an UNDO control option [All/None/One] <All>:

To enable the **UNDO** options again, you must enter the **All** or **One** (one mode) option. If you try to use the **U** command while the **UNDO** command has been disabled, AutoCAD gives you the following message:

Command: **U** [Enter]
U command disabled. Use **UNDO** command to turn it on.

One (O). This option restrains the **UNDO** command to a single operation. All **UNDO** information saved earlier during editing is scrapped.

Enter the number of operations to UNDO or [Auto/Control/BEgin/End/Mark/Back]: C
Enter an UNDO control option [All/None/One] <All>: O [Enter]

If you then enter the **UNDO** command, you will get the following prompt:

Command: **UNDO** [Enter]
Control/<1>:

In response to this last prompt, you can now either press ENTER to undo only the previous command, or go into the **Control** options by entering C. AutoCAD acknowledges undoing the previous command with messages like:

Command: **UNDO** [Enter]
Control/<1>: [Enter]
CIRCLE
Everything has been undone

BEgin (BE) and End (E) Options

A group of commands is treated as one command for the **U** and **UNDO** commands by embedding the commands between the **BEgin** and **End** options of the **UNDO** command. If you expect to remove a group of successive commands, you can use this option. Since all of the commands after the **BEgin** option and before the **End** option are treated as a single command by the **U** command, they can be undone by a single **U** command. For example, the following sequence illustrates the possibility of removal of two commands:

> Command: **UNDO** Enter
> Enter the number of operations to UNDO or [Auto/Control/BEgin/End/Mark/Back]: BE Enter
> Command: **CIRCLE** Enter
> Specify center point for Circle or [3P/2P/Ttr (tan tan radius)]: *Specify the center.*
> Specify radius of circle or [Diameter] <current>: *Specify the radius of the circle.*
> Command: **PLINE** Enter
> Specify start point or [Arc/Close/Halfwidth/Length/Undo/Width]: *Select first point.*
> Specify next point: *Select the next point.*
> Specify start point or [Arc/Close/Halfwidth/Length/Undo/Width]: *Press ENTER*
> Command: **UNDO** Enter
> Enter the number of operations to UNDO or [Auto/Control/BEgin/End/Mark/Back]: E Enter
> Command: **U** Enter

To start the next group once you are finished specifying the current group, use the **End** option to end this group. Another method is to enter the **BEgin** option to start the next group while the current group is active. This is equivalent to issuing the **End** option followed by the **BEgin** option. The group is complete only when the **End** option is invoked to match a **BEgin** option. If **U** or the **Undo** command is issued after the **BEgin** option has been invoked and before the **End** option has been issued, only one command is undone at a time until it reaches the juncture where the **BEgin** option has been entered. If you want to undo the commands issued before the **BEgin** option was invoked, you must enter the **End** option so that the group is complete. This is demonstrated in Example 2.

Example 2

Enter the following commands in the same sequence as given, and notice the changes that take place on screen.

> **CIRCLE**
> **POLYGON**
> **UNDO BEgin**
> **PLINE**
> **TRACE**
> **U**
> **DONUT**
> **UNDO End**
> **DTEXT**
> **U**
> **U**

U
U

The first **U** command will undo the **TRACE** command. If you repeat the **U** command, the **PLINE** command will be undone. Any further invoking of the **U** command will not undo any previously drawn object (**POLYGON** and **CIRCLE**, in this case), because after the **PLINE** is undone you have an **UNDO BEgin**. Only after you enter **UNDO End** can you undo the **POLYGON** and the **CIRCLE**. In the example, the second **U** command will undo the **TEXT** command, the third **U** command will undo the **DONUT** and **PLINE** commands (these are enclosed in the group), the fourth **U** command will undo the **POLYGON** command, and the fifth **U** command will undo the **CIRCLE** command. When the commands in a group are undone, the name of each command or operation is not displayed as it is undone; only the name, **GROUP**, is displayed.

Note
*You can use the **BEgin** option only when the **UNDO Control** is set to **All**.*

Mark (M) and Back Options

The **Mark** option installs a marker in the Undo file. The **Back** option lets you undo all the operations until the mark. In other words, the **Back** option returns the drawing to the point where the previous mark was inserted. For example, if you have completed a portion of your drawing and do not want anything up to this point to be deleted, you insert a marker and then proceed. Then, even if you use the **UNDO Back** option, it will work only until the marker. You can insert multiple markers, and with the help of the **Back** option you can return to the successive mark points. The following prompt sequence illustrates this:

Command: **UNDO** Enter
Enter the number of operations to UNDO or [Auto/Control/BEgin/End/Mark/Back]: M Enter

After proceeding further with your work, if you want to use the **UNDO Back** option:

Command: **UNDO** Enter
Enter the number of operations to UNDO or [Auto/Control/BEgin/End/Mark/Back]: B Enter

Once all the marks have been exhausted with the successive **Back** options, any further invoking of the **Back** option displays the message: **This will undo everything. OK? <Y>**.

If you enter Y (Yes) at this prompt, all the operations carried out since you entered the current drawing session will be undone. If you enter N (No) at this prompt, the Back option will be disregarded. You cannot undo certain commands and system variables, for example, **DIST**, **LIST**, **DELAY**, **NEW**, **OPEN**, **QUIT**, **AREA**, **HELP**, **PLOT**, **QSAVE** and **SAVE**, among many more. Actually, these commands have no effect that can be undone. Commands that change operating modes (**GRID**, **UNITS**, **SNAP**, **ORTHO**) can be undone, though the effect may not be apparent at first. This is the reason why AutoCAD displays the command names as they are undone.

REDO COMMAND

Toolbar:	Standard > Redo
Menu:	Edit > Redo
Command:	REDO

If you right-click in the drawing area, a shortcut menu is displayed. Choose **Redo** to invoke the **REDO** command. The **REDO** command brings back the objects you removed previously using the **U** and **UNDO** commands. This command undoes the **UNDO** command, but it must be entered immediately after the **UNDO** command.

Command: **REDO** Enter

The objects previously undone reappear on the screen.

RENAMING NAMED OBJECTS (RENAME COMMAND)

Menu:	Format > Rename
Command:	RENAME

You can edit the names of named objects such as blocks, dimension styles, layers, linetypes, styles, UCS, views, and viewports using the **Rename** dialog box (Figure 16-30). You can select the type of named object from the list provided in the **Named Objects** area of the dialog box. Corresponding names of all the objects of the specified type that can be renamed are displayed in the **Items** area.

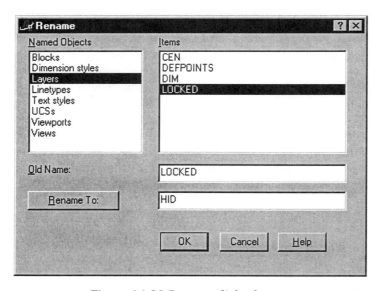

Figure 16-30 Rename dialog box

For example, if you want to rename the layer named LOCKED to HID, the process will be:

1. Select the **Layer** option from the list in the **Named Objects** area. All the layer names that can be renamed are displayed in the **Items** area.

2. Select LOCKED from the list in the Items area, such that LOCKED is displayed in the **Old Name:** edit box.
3. Enter HID in the **Rename To:** edit box, and choose the **OK** button.

Now the layer named LOCKED is renamed to HID. You can rename blocks, dimension styles, linetypes, styles, UCS, views, and viewports in the same way. You can enter **-RENAME** at the Command prompt to use the command line. The prompt sequence for changing the name of the block SQUARE to PLATE1 is:

Command: **-RENAME** [Enter]
Enter object type to rename
[Block/Dimstyle/LAyer/LType/Style/Ucs/VIew/VPort]: B [Enter]
Enter old block name: SQUARE [Enter]
Enter new block name: PLATE1 [Enter]

Note
*The **RENAME** command cannot be used to rename drawing files created using the **WBLOCK** command. You can change the name of a drawing file by using the **Rename** option of your Operating System.*

REMOVING UNUSED NAMED OBJECTS (PURGE COMMAND)

Menu:	File > Drawing Utilities > Purge
Command:	PURGE

Another editing operation used for deletion. You can delete unused named objects such as blocks, layers, dimension styles, linetypes, text styles, and shapes with the help of the **PURGE** command. When you create a new drawing or open an existing one, AutoCAD records the named objects in that drawing and notes other drawings referencing the named objects. Usually only a few of the named objects in the drawing (such as layers, linetypes, and blocks) are used. For example, when you create a new drawing, the prototype drawing settings may contain various text styles, blocks, and layers that you do not want to use. Also, you may want to delete particular unused named objects, such as unused blocks, in an existing drawing. Deleting inactive named objects is important and useful because doing so reduces the space occupied by the drawing. With the **PURGE** command, you can select the named objects you want to delete. You can use this command any time in the drawing session. The prompt sequence for the **PURGE** command is:

Command: **PURGE**
Enter type of unused object to purge
[Blocks/Dimstyles/LAyers/LTypes/Plotstyles/SHapes/STyles/Mlinestyles/All]: *Specify the object type you want to delete.*

For instance, if you want to purge a block named SQUARE from a drawing file, the prompt sequence is:

Command: **PURGE**

Enter type of unused object to purge
[Blocks/Dimstyles/LAyers/LTypes/SHapes/STyles/Mlinestyles/All]: B
Enter name(s) to purge <*>: SQUARE
Verify each name to be purged? <Y>:

The **-WBLOCK asterisk** option has the same effect as the **PURGE** command. The only difference is that in the case of the **-WBLOCK asterisk** option, unused named objects are removed automatically.

Note

*Standard objects created by AutoCAD (such as layer 0, STANDARD text style, and linetype CONTINUOUS) cannot be removed by the **PURGE** command, even if these objects are not used.*

OBJECT SELECTION MODES

Menu:	Tools > Options...
Command:	OPTIONS

When you select a number of objects, the selected objects form a **selection set**. Selection of the objects is controlled in the **Options** dialog box (Figure 16-31) which is invoked by the **OPTIONS** command. Five selection modes are provided in the **Selection** tab of this dialog box. You can select any one of these modes or a combination of various modes.

Noun/Verb Selection

By selecting the **Noun/Verb Selection** check box, you can select the objects (noun) first and then specify the operation (verb) (command) to be performed on the selection set. If this selection mode is chosen, a small pick box is displayed at the intersection of the graphic cursor (crosshairs). This mode is active by default. For example, if you want to move some objects when **Noun/Verb Selection** is enabled, first select the objects to be moved, and then invoke the **MOVE** command. The objects selected are highlighted automatically when the **MOVE** command is invoked, and AutoCAD does not issue any **Select objects:** prompt. The following commands can be used on the selected objects when the **Noun/Verb Selection** mode is active:

ALIGN	ARRAY	BLOCK	CHANGE	CHPROP
COPY	DVIEW	EXPLODE	ERASE	LIST
MIRROR	MOVE	PROPERTIES	ROTATE	SCALE
STRETCH	WBLOCK			

The following are some of the commands that are not affected by the **Noun/Verb Selection** mode. You are required to specify the objects (noun) on which an operation (command/verb) is to be performed, after specifying the command (verb):

BREAK	CHAMFER	DIVIDE	EDGESURF	EXTEND
FILLET	MEASURE	OFFSET	REVSURF	RULESURF
TABSURF	TRIM			

When the **Noun/Verb Selection** mode is active, the **PICKFIRST** system variable is set to 1 (On). In

Figure 16-31 Selection tab of the Options dialog box

other words, you can activate the **Noun/Verb Selection** mode by setting **PICKFIRST** to 1 (On).

Command: **PICKFIRST**
Enter new value for PICKFIRST <0>: 1

Use Shift to Add to Selection

The next option in the **Selection Modes** area of the **Selection** tab of the **Options** dialog box is **Use Shift to add to selection**. Selecting this option establishes additive selection mode which is the normal method of most Windows programs. In this mode, you have to hold down the SHIFT key when you want to add objects to the selection set. For example, suppose X, Y, and Z are three objects on the screen. Select object X. It is highlighted and put in the selection set. After selecting X, and while selecting object Y, if you do not hold down the SHIFT key, object Y only is highlighted and it replaces object X in the selection set. On the other hand, if you hold down the SHIFT key while selecting Y, it is added to the selection set (which contains X), and the resulting selection set contains both X and Y. Also, both X and Y are highlighted. To summarize the concept, objects are added to the selection set only when the SHIFT key is held down while objects are selected. Objects can be discarded from the selection set by reselecting these objects while the SHIFT key is held down. If you want to clear an entire selection set quickly, draw a blank selection window anywhere in a blank drawing area. You can also right-click to display a shortcut menu. Choose **Deselect All**. All selected objects in the selection set are discarded from it.

When the **Use Shift to add to selection** mode is active, the **PICKADD** system variable is set to 1 (On). In other words, you can activate the **Use Shift to add to selection** mode by setting **PICKADD** to On.

> Command: **PICKADD**
> Enter new value for PICKADD <0>: 1

Press and Drag

This selection mode is used to govern the way you can define a Selection window or Crossing window. When this option is selected, the window can be created by pressing the pick button to select one corner of the window and continuing to hold down the pick button and dragging the cursor to define the other diagonal point of the window. When you have the window you want, release the pick button. If the **Press and Drag** mode is not active, you have to select twice to specify the two diagonal corners of the window to be defined.

When the **Press and Drag** mode is active, the **PICKDRAG** system variable is set to 1 (On). In other words, you can activate the **Press and Drag** mode by setting **PICKDRAG** to On.

> Command: **PICKDRAG**
> Enter new value for PICKDRAG <0>: 1

Implied Windowing

By selecting this option, you can automatically create a Window or Crossing selection when the **Select objects:** prompt is issued. The selection window or crossing window in this case is created in the following manner:

At the **Select objects:** prompt, select a point in empty space on the screen. This becomes the first corner point of the selection window. After this, AutoCAD asks you to specify the other corner point of the selection window. If the first corner point is to the right of the second corner point, a Crossing selection is defined; if the first corner point is to the left of the second corner point, a Window selection is defined. If this option is not active, or if you need to select the first corner in a crowded area where selecting would select an object, you need to specify Window or Crossing at the **Select objects:** prompt, depending on your requirement.

When the **Implied Windowing** mode is active, the **PICKAUTO** system variable is set to 1 (On). In other words, you can activate **Implied Windowing** mode by setting **PICKAUTO** to On.

> Command: **PICKAUTO**
> Enter new value for PICKAUTO <0>: 1

Object Grouping

This turns the automatic group selection on and off. When this option is on and you select a member of a group, the whole group is selected. You can also activate this option by setting the value of the **PICKSTYLE** system variable to 1. (Groups were discussed earlier in this chapter.)

Associative Hatch

If the **Associative Hatch** check box is selected in the **Selection modes** area of the **Selection** tab of the **Options** dialog box, the boundary object is also selected when an associative hatch is selected. You can also select this option by setting the value of the **PICKSTYLE** system variable to 2.

Pickbox Size. The **Pick box** slider bar controls the size of the pickbox. The size ranges from 0 to 20. The default size is 3. You can also use the **PICKBOX** system variable.

CHANGING DISPLAY ORDER
Using DRAWORDER Command

Toolbar:	Modify II > Draworder
Menu:	Tools > Display Order
Command:	DRAWORDER

*Figure 16-32 Invoking the **DRAWORDER** command from the **Modify II** toolbar*

When you create objects, they are drawn in the order they were created. For example, if you insert a raster image and then draw a wide polyline over the image, the polyline will be displayed at the top of the raster image. At the time of plotting the raster image will be plotted first and then the polyline. You can use the **DRAWORDER** command to change the order of display and also the order of plotting.

> Command: **DRAWORDER**
> Enter object ordering option [Above object/Under object/Front/Back] <Back>: *Select an option or press ENTER.*

Above Object. With the **Above Object** option the selected object is moved above the specified object. When several objects are selected for reordering, the relative order of the selected objects is maintained. For example, in Figure 16-33 the **Above Object** option moves the objects 2, 3, and 5 above the specified object (4). When you select the **Above** or **Under object** options, the next command prompt is:

> Select reference object: *Select the object for reference.*

Original order	New order		Original order	New order
1	4		4	2
2	1		1	3
3	2		2	5
4	3		3	4
5	5		5	1
6	6		6	6

Top: Object 4 is moved to the top

Above: Objects 2,3,and 5 are moved above 4

*Figure 16-33 Using the **DRAWORDER** command to change the display order of objects*

Under Object. The **Under Object** option moves the selected object below the specified object. For example, if a wide polyline segment is overlapping an image (Figure 16-34). You can bring the image to the front (make the overlapping segment of the polyline invisible) by changing the display order of the image or polyline. Similarly, you can also change the display order two overlapping images.

Front. The **Front** option moves the selected objects to the top of the display order. For example, in Figure 16-33, the **Front** option moves the object to the top of the display order.

Figure 16-34 Effect of changing the display order

Back. The **Back** option moves the selected objects to the bottom of the display order.

When you change the display order of the objects several times, the display order might get disordered. You can use the **REGEN** command to restore the display order you set. AutoCAD cannot control the display order for nested objects in blocks and external references. The display order of the nested objects is determined by the order in which the objects were created. Similarly, the **PSOUT** command ignores the display order information and displays the objects in the same order in which they were created. By changing the display order the file size increases by 16 bytes for each object affected by the display order. This increases the file size by 1 to 5 percent.

Using the SORTENTS System Variable

The **DRAWORDER** command turns on all **Object Sorting methods** options on the **User Preferences** tab of the **Options** dialog box (Figure 16-35), which results in slower regeneration of drawings.

Figure 16-35 Object Sorting methods area in the User Preferences tab of the Options dialog box

The **SORTENTS** variable governs the display of object sort order operations using the following values:

0 - **SORTENTS** is disabled, 1 - Sorts for object selection, 2 - Sorts for object snap, 4 - Sorts for redraw, 8 - Sorts for **MSLIDE** slide creation, 16 - Sorts for **REGEN** command, 32 - Sorts for plotting, 64 - Sorts for PostScript output. More than one options can be selected by specifying the sum of the values of these options. This variable is saved in AutoCAD configuration file, not the drawing file. The initial value of **SORTENTS** is 96. This value specifies sort operations for plotting and PostScript output. When **SORTENTS** variable is set to 0, AutoCAD displays the objects in the most efficient way.

When you use the **DRAWORDER** command the values changes to 127. If you change the value of **SORTENTS** to a value other than 127, all display order information is ignored.

> Command: **SORTENTS**
> Enter new value for SORTENTS <current>:

MANAGING CONTENT*
Using the AutoCAD DesignCenter*

Toolbar:	Standard > AutoCAD DesignCenter
Menu:	Tools > AutoCAD DesignCenter
Command:	ADCENTER

When you choose the **AutoCAD DesignCenter** button in the **Standard** toolbar displays the **AutoCAD DesignCenter** window (Figure 16-36). In its default position it is docked to the left of the screen. It can be moved to any other location by clicking and dragging it with the grab bars located on the top of the window to any other position on the screen. You can also resize it by clicking the borders and dragging them to the right or left. Right-clicking on the title bar of the window displays a shortcut menu which gives options to **Allow docking**, **Hide**, **Move**, and **Resize** the **AutoCAD DesignCenter** window. The CTRL+2 key acts as toggle between hiding the window and displaying it. Also, double-clicking on the title bar of the window, docks the **AutoCAD DesignCenter** window if it is undocked and vice versa.

The **AutoCAD DesignCenter** window is used for locating and organizing drawing data, for inserting blocks, layers, external references and other customized drawing content from either your own files, local drives, network, or the internet and for viewing contents of a file. You can even access and use contents between files or from the internet.

When you choose the **Tree View Toggle** button on the **AutoCAD DesignCenter** toolbar, it displays the **Tree Pane** with a Tree view of the contents of the drives. You can also right-click in the window and choose **Tree** from the shortcut menu which is displayed. Now, the window is divided into two parts, the **Tree pane** and the **palette**. The palette displays folders, files, objects in a drawing, images, web based content and custom content. You can also resize both the tree pane and the palette by clicking and dragging the bar between them to the right or the left. In the Tree pane you can browse the contents of any folder by clicking on the plus sign (+) adjacent to it. Further expanding the contents of a file displays the following categories: **Blocks**, **Dimstyles**, **Layers**,

Figure 16-36 AutoCAD DesignCenter window in the default position

Linetypes, **Textstyles**, **Layout**, and **External References**. Clicking on any one of these categories in the **Tree pane** displays the listing under the selected category in the palette (Figure 16-37). Alternately, right-clicking a particular folder, file, or category of the file contents, displays a shortcut menu. The **Explore** option in this shortcut menu also further expands the selected folder, file, or category of contents to display the listing of contents respectively. Choosing the **Preview** button displays an image of the selected object or file in a **Preview pane** in the Palette. Choosing the **Description** button displays a brief text description of the selected item if it has one in the **Description** box.

As discussed earlier in Chapters 12 and 14, you can drag and drop any of the contents into the current drawing or add them by double-clicking on the contents. These are then reused as part of the current drawing. When you double-click on specific X-refs and Blocks, AutoCAD displays the **External Reference** dialog box and the **Insert** dialog box to help in attaching the External Reference and inserting the block, respectively. Similarly, when you right-click a specific linetype, layer, textstyle, layout or dimstyle, in the palette, a shortcut menu is displayed which gives you an option to **Add** or **Copy**. Right-clicking a block displays the options of **Insert Block** or **Copy** and right-clicking an Xref displays the options of **Attach Xref** or **Copy** in the shortcut menus.

The other options in the shortcut menu are **Add to Favorites**, **Organize Favorites**, and **Open in window**. Choosing **Add to Favorites** adds the selected file or folder to the Favorites folder, which contains the most often accessed files and folders. **Organize Favorites** allows you to reorganize the contents of the Favorites folder, and **Open in window** opens the selected drawing file as a current drawing.

Figure 16-37 The **AutoCAD DesignCenter window** *showing the Tree pane, the palette, the Preview pane and the Description box.*

Figure 16-38 The **AutoCAD DesignCenter** *toolbar*

Choosing the **Desktop** button in the **AutoCAD DesignCenter** toolbar, lists all the local and network drives. The **Open Drawings** button lists the drawings that are open, including the current drawing which is being worked on. The **History** button lists the last 20 locations accessed through the **AutoCAD DesignCenter**. The **Tree View Toggle** button displays or hides the tree pane with the tree view of the contents in a hierarchial form. This option is disabled when you choose the **History** button. Choosing the **Favorites** button displays shortcuts to files and folders that are accessed frequently by you and are stored in the **Favorites** folder. This reduces the time you take to access these files or folders from their normal location. Choosing the **Load** button displays the **Load DesignCenter Palette** dialog box (Figure 16-39) whose options are similar to the standard **Select file** dialog box. When you select a file here and choose the **Open** button, AutoCAD displays the selected file and its contents in the **AutoCad DesignCenter** window.

Choosing the **Find** button displays the **Find** dialog box (Figure 16-40). By using this dialog box, you can search for drawings that contain specific Blocks, textstyles, dimstyles, layers, layouts, external references, or linetypes, which you can select from the **Look for** drop-down list, or you can

Figure 16-39 Load DesignCenter Palette dialog box

conduct a search based on the following criteria:

1. **Date last modified on**. Choose the **Date Modified** tab in the **Find** dialog box and select the appropriate radio buttons there.
2. **Text in the block name, block and drawing description, attribute tag and value**. You can select the category to look for from the **Containing:** drop-down list in the **Advanced** tab of the **Find** dialog box. The text it contains can be entered in the **Contains text** edit box. You can also specify the **At least** or **At most** sizes in the **Size is:** edit boxes to narrow down the search.

3. **Words which are part of the File name, Title, Subject, Author's name, keyword text stored in the summary tab of the Drawing Properties**. Enter the words in the **Search for word(s)** edit box and the field can be selected from the **In the field(s)** drop-down list of the **Drawings** tab of the **Find** dialog box.

After entering the apt criteria for searching the specific file, choose the **Find Now** button. The Name, Location, File Size, Type, and Date last modified on is displayed at the bottom of the dialog box.

The **Up** button moves one level up in the tree structure from the current location. The **Views** button gives four display format options for the contents of the palette: **Large icons**, **Small icons**, **List**, and **Details**. The **List** option lists the contents in the palette while the **Details** option, gives a detailed list of the contents in the palette with the Name, File Size, and Type.

Right-clicking in the palette displays a shortcut menu with all the options provided in the AutoCAD DesignCenter in addition to **Add to Favorites**, **Organize favorites**, and **Refresh** options. The **Refresh** option refreshes the palette display if you have made any changes to it.

Figure 16-40 Find dialog box

Example 3

Use **AutoCAD DesignCenter** window to locate and view contents of the drawing KITCHENS. Also, use **AutoCAD DesignCenter** to insert a block from this drawing and also import a layer and Textstyle from the 1st floor architectural.dwg located in the Sample folder. Also import a dimstyle from Wilhome.dwg. Use these to make a drawing of a Kitchen plan (MYKITCHEN.dwg) and add text and dimensions to it as shown in Figure 16-41.

1. Open a new drawing using the **Start from Scratch** button. Make sure to select the **English (feet and inches)** radio button in the **Create New Drawing** or the **Startup** dialog box.

2. Draw a rectangle of 8" x 7".

3. Choose the **AutoCAD DesignCenter** button in the **Standard** toolbar. The **AutoCAD DesignCenter** window is displayed in its default location, docked to the left of the drawing screen.

4. In the **AutoCAD DesignCenter** toolbar, choose the **Tree View Toggle** button to display the **Tree pane** and the **Palette** (if not already displayed).

5. Now, choose the **Find** button. The **Find** dialog box is displayed. Select **Drawings** from the **Look For** drop-down list. Also select **C:** from the **In** drop-down list. Select the **Search subfolders** check box if it is not selected already. In the **Drawings** tab, type KITCHENS in the **Search**

Figure 16-41 *Drawing for Example 3*

for the word(s) edit box. Choose the **Find Now** button to commence the search. After the drawing has been located, its details and path are displayed at the bottom of the dialog box.

6. In the Tree pane, expand My Computer to display the C:\Program Files\ACAD2000\SAMPLE\DesignCenter folder. Now, click on it to display its contents in the Palette. You can also right-click to display the shortcut menu and choose **Explore** from it.

7. Right-click on KITCHEN.dwg in the palette to display the shortcut menu. Choose **Open in Window**. KITCHENS.dwg is now the current drawing. You can attach any drawing you want to use as an Xref to the current drawing by choosing the **Attach as Xref** option in the shortcut menu. After you have viewed the contents of this drawing after using the various **ZOOM** commands, close this drawing.

8. Double-click on KITCHENS.dwg in the Palette to display its contents or expand the contents by clicking on the plus sign adjacent to the File name, in the Tree pane.

9. Click on Blocks, in the Tree Pane to display the list of blocks in the drawing, in the Palette. Right-click on the block KITCHEN LAYOUT-7 x 8 ft. to display a shortcut menu. Choose **Insert Block...** to display the **Insert** dialog box. Alternately, you can double-click on the block to display the **Insert** dialog box. Select the **Specify On-Screen** check boxes and the Explode check box. Choose **OK** to exit the dialog box. Now, insert this block in the rectangle you had drawn such that the rectangle overlaps the floor area of the kitchen plan.

10. Now, double-click on 1ST FLOOR ARCHITECTURAL.DWG located in the SAMPLE folder in the same directory to display its contents in the Palette.

11. Click on Layers in the Tree Pane to display the layers in the drawing. Drag and drop or double-click the layer DIMENSIONS (COTAS) from this drawing to the current drawing. Now, you can use this layer for dimensioning in the current drawing after making it the current layer.

12. Now, click on Textstyles to display the list of Textstyles in the drawing. Select ROMAN SIM-PLEX and drag and drop it in the current drawing. You can use this textstyle for adding text to the current drawing.

13. Similarly, click on the WILHOME.DWG in the same folder. Select Dimstyles to display the Dimension styles being used in the drawing. Select ARCH and drag and drop it into the current drawing.

14. Use the imported data to add dimensions and text to the current drawing and complete it as shown in the Figure 16-41.

15. Save the current drawing as MYKITCHEN.DWG.

Self-Evaluation Test

Answer the following questions, and then compare your answers to the answers given at the end of this chapter.

1. Only the **CHANGE** command can be used to change the properties associated with a object. (T/F)

2. The **PURGE** command can be used only when you enter the drawing editor and before the drawing database has been changed by operations involving addition or deletion of objects in the drawing file. (T/F)

3. The **One** option of the **UNDO** command restrains the **U** and **UNDO** commands to a single operation. (T/F)

4. If the last (closing) segment of the polyline was drawn as a polyline and not by using the **Close** option, the effect of the **Open** option will not be visible. (T/F)

5. The **Control** option lets you determine how many of the **UNDO** options you want active. (T/F)

6. The **Width** option of the **PEDIT** command can be used to change the width of a polyline with a constant and unvarying width. (T/F)

7. You can move past the first and last vertices in a closed polyline by using either the **Next** option or the **Previous** option. (T/F)

8. The system variable _____ controls the number of line segments used to construct the spline curves.

9. If you want to edit a polyline into a B-spline curve, you have to set the system variable _____. A value equal to _____ produces the _____ curve, whereas a value equal to _____ produces a _____ curve.

10. The group names can be up to _____ characters long and can include special characters _____ .

11. The **Include Unnamed** check box is used to display the names of the unnamed objects in the **Object Grouping** dialog box. (T/F)

12. The **Selectable** check box allows you to define a group that is selectable. (T/F)

13. The **Join** option of the **PEDIT** command can be used only if a polyline is open. (T/F)

14. The **Width** option of the **PEDIT** command's main prompt can be used to change the starting and ending widths of a polyline separately to a desired value. (T/F)

Review Questions

1. You can use the _____ command to group AutoCAD objects and assign a name to the group.

2. You can also use the **GROUP** command from the command line by entering _____ at the Command prompt.

3. The _____ option in the **GROUP** command lets you change the order of the objects in the selected group.

4. A group can be selected by entering _____ at the AutoCAD **Select objects:** prompt.

5. When you use the **GROUP** command to form object groups, AutoCAD lets you sequentially highlight the groups of which the selected object is a member. (T/F)

6. The color, linetype, lineweight, and layer on which a block is drawn can be changed with the help of the **CHANGE** command. (T/F)

7. After exploding an object, the object remains identical except that the color and linetype may change because of floating layers, colors, or linetypes. (T/F)

8. The **PURGE** command has the same effect as the **WBLOCK-asterisk** method. The only difference is that with the **PURGE** command, deletion takes place automatically. (T/F)

9. The **RENAME** command can be used to change the name of a drawing file created by the **WBLOCK** command. (T/F)

10. The **RENAME** command can be used to change the name of a block. (T/F)

11. If the **Auto** option of the **UNDO** command is off, any group of commands used to insert an object is undone together. (T/F)

12. If the selected polyline is closed, the **Close** option is replaced by the **Open** option. (T/F)

13. Circles drawn using the **CIRCLE** command can be changed to polylines. (T/F)

14. When you enter the **Edit vertex** option of the **PEDIT** command, an X marker appears on the screen at the second vertex of the polyline. (T/F)

15. If a tangent direction has been specified for the vertex selected with the **Edit vertex** option, an arrow is generated in that direction. (T/F)

16. With the **Break** option of the **PEDIT** command, if there are any polyline segments or vertices between the vertices you have specified, they will be erased. (T/F)

17. The **Break** operation is valid if both the specified vertices are located at the endpoint of the polyline, or only one vertex is specified and its location is at the endpoint of the polyline. (T/F)

18. The **Move** option lets you move the X-marked vertex to a new position. (T/F)

19. The **Straighten** option of the **PEDIT** command deletes the arcs, line segments, or vertices between the desired two vertices and substitutes them with a single line segment. (T/F)

20. The **Width** option of the **Edit vertex** option of the **PEDIT** command allows you to change the starting and ending widths of an existing polyline segment. (T/F)

21. The spline curve passes through only the first and last vertices and pulls toward the other vertices but does not pass through them, unlike the **Fit** option. (T/F)

22. The fit curve passes only through the first and last vertices of the polyline. (T/F)

23. The **Decurve** option removes the vertices inserted after using the **Fit** or the **Spline** options. (T/F)

24. The **Decurve** option cannot be used to straighten out any curve drawn with the help of the **Arc** option of the **PLINE** command. (T/F)

25. Quadratic curves are extremely smooth. The quadratic curve passes through the first and last control points, and the curve is closer to the other control points. (T/F)

26. The _____ command can be used to undo any previous command or to undo several commands at once.

27. If you enter 6 at the **Enter the number of operations to undo or [Auto/Control/BEgin/End/Mark/Back]:** prompt, _____ previous commands will be undone.

28. The _____ option of the **UNDO** command disables the **UNDO** and **U** commands entirely.

29. To activate the **UNDO** options if they are disabled, you must enter either _____ or

_____ options.

30. A group of commands is caused to be treated as a single command for the **U** and **UNDO** commands by the combined work of the _____ and _____ **UNDO** options.

Exercises

Exercise 4   *Graphics*

Draw part (a) in Figure 16-42; then, using the **CHANGE** and relevant **PEDIT** options, convert it into parts (b), (c), and (d). The linetype used in part (d) is HIDDEN.

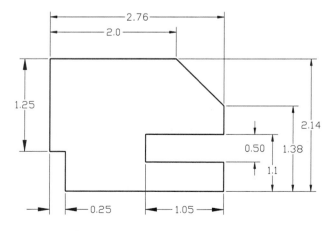

Figure 16-42 Drawing for Exercise 4

Exercise 5   *Mechanical*

Draw the object in Figure 16-43 using the **LINE** command. Change the object to a polyline with a width of 0.01.

Figure 16-43 Drawing for Exercise 5

Exercise 6 | *Graphics*

Draw part (a) in Figure 16-44; then, using the relevant **PEDIT** options, convert it into drawing (b).

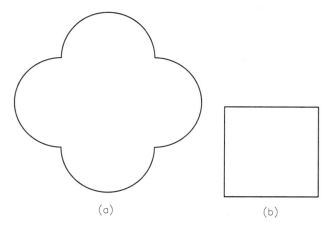

(a)

(b)

Figure 16-44 Drawing for Exercise 6

Exercise 7 | *Graphics*

Draw part (a) in Figure 16-45; then, using the relevant **PEDIT** options, convert it into drawings (b), (c), and (d). Identify the types of curves.

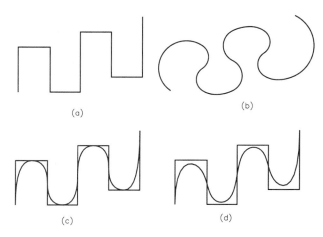

(a)

(b)

(c)

(d)

Figure 16-45 Drawing for Exercise 7

Exercise 8   *Graphics*

Draw part (a) in Figure 16-46; then, using the relevant **PEDIT** options, convert it into drawing (b).

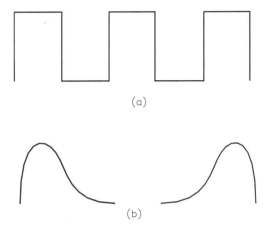

(a)

(b)

Figure 16-46 *Drawing for Exercise 8*

Exercise 9   *Graphics*

Draw part (a) in Figure 16-47; then, using the relevant **PEDIT** options, convert it into drawing (b).

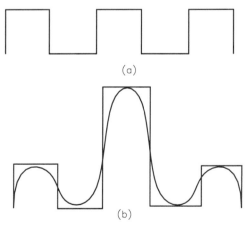

(a)

(b)

Figure 16-47 *Drawing for Exercise 9*

Answers to Self-Evaluation Test
1 - F, **2** - F, **3** - T, **4** - F, **5** - T, **6** - T, **7** - F, **8** - **SPLINESEGS**, **9** - **SPLINETYPE**, 5, quadratic, 6, cubic, **10** - 255, **11** - T, **12** - T, **13** - T, **14** - F

Chapter 17

Inquiry Commands, Data Exchange, and Object Linking and Embedding

Learning Objectives

After completing this chapter, you will be able to:
- *Make inquiries about drawings and objects.*
- *Calculate area using the **AREA** command.*
- *Calculate distances using the **DIST** command.*
- *Identify a position on the screen using the **ID** command.*
- *List information about drawings and objects using the **DBLIST** and **LIST** commands.*
- *List drawing-related information using the **STATUS** command.*
- *Import and export .dxf files using the **SAVEAS** and **OPEN** commands.*
- *Convert scanned drawings into the drawing editor using the **DXB** command.*
- *Export raster files using the **SAVEIMG** command.*
- *Understand the embedding and the linking functions of the **OLE** feature of Windows.*

MAKING INQUIRIES ABOUT A DRAWING (INQUIRY COMMANDS)

When you create a drawing or examine an existing one, you often need some information about the drawing. In manual drafting, you inquire about the drawing by performing measurements and calculations manually. Similarly, when drawing in an AutoCAD environment, you will need to make inquiries about data pertaining to your drawing. The inquiries can be about the distance from one location on the drawing to another, the area of an object like a polygon or circle, coordinates of a location on the drawing, and so on. AutoCAD keeps track of all the details pertaining to a drawing. Since inquiry commands are used to obtain information about the selected objects, these commands do not affect the drawings in any way. The following is the list of Inquiry commands:

AREA	**DIST**	**ID**	**LIST**	**DBLIST**
MASSPROP	**STATUS**	**TIME**	**DWGPROPS**	

For most of the Inquiry commands, you are prompted to select objects; once the selection is complete, AutoCAD switches from graphics mode to text mode, and all the relevant information about the selected objects is displayed. For some commands information is displayed in the AutoCAD Text Window. The display of the text screen can be tailored to your requirements with the help of a pointing device; hence, by moving the text screen to one side,

*Figure 17-1 Selecting Inquiry commands from the **Inquiry** toolbar*

you can view the drawing screen and the text screen simultaneously. If you select the **minimize** button or select the close button, you will return to the graphics screen. You can also return to the graphics screen by entering **GRAPHSCR** command at the Command prompt. Similarly, you can return to the AutoCAD Text Window by entering **TEXTSCR** at the Command prompt.

AREA COMMAND

Toolbar:	Inquiry > Area
Menu:	Tools > Inquiry > Area
Command:	AREA

Finding the area of a shape or an object manually is time-consuming. In AutoCAD, the **AREA** command is used to automatically calculate the area of an object in square units. This command saves time when calculating the area of shapes, especially when the shapes are complicated.

You can use the default option of the **AREA** command to calculate the area and perimeter or circumference of the space enclosed by the sequence of specified points. For example, to find the area of an object (one which is not formed of a single object) you have created with the help of the **LINE** command (Figure 17-2), you need to select all the vertices of that object. By selecting the points, you define the shape of the object whose area is to be found. This is the default method for determining the area of an object. The only restriction is that all the

*Figure 17-2 Using the **AREA** command*

points you specify be in a plane parallel to the XY plane of the current UCS. You can make the best possible use of object snaps such as ENDpoint, INTersect, and TANgent, or even use running Osnaps, to help you select the vertices quickly and accurately. For AutoCAD to find the area of a shape, the shapes need not have been drawn with polylines; nor do the lines need to be closed. However, curves must be approximated with short straight segments. In such cases, AutoCAD computes the area by assuming that the first point and the last point are joined. The prompt sequence in this case is:

> Command: **AREA** [Enter]
> Specify first corner point or [Object/Add/Subtract]: *Specify first point.*
> Specify next corner point or press ENTER for total: *Specify the second point.*
> Specify next corner point or press ENTER for total: *Continue selecting until all the points enclosing the area have been selected.*
> Specify next corner point or press ENTER for total: [Enter]
> Area = X, Perimeter = Y

Here, X represents the numerical value of the area and Y represents the circumference/perimeter. It is not possible to accurately determine the area of a curved object, such as an arc, with the default (Point) option. However, the approximate area under an arc can be calculated by specifying several points on the given arc. If the object whose area you want to find is not closed (formed of independent segments) and has curved lines, you should use the following steps to determine the accurate area of such an object:

1. Convert all the segments in that object into polylines using the **PEDIT** command.
2. Join all the individual polylines into a single polyline. Once you have performed these operations, the object becomes closed and you can then use the **Object** option of the **AREA** command to determine the area.

If you specify two points on the screen, the **AREA** command will display the value of the area as 0.00; the perimeter value is the distance between the two points.

Object option. You can use the **Object** option of the **AREA** command to find the area of objects such as polygons, circles, polylines, regions, solids, and splines. If the selected object is a polyline or polygon, AutoCAD displays the area and perimeter of the polyline. In case of open polylines, the area is calculated assuming that the last point is joined to the first point but the length of this segment is not added to the polyline length unlike the default option. If the selected object is a circle, ellipse, or planar closed spline curve, AutoCAD will provide information about its area and circumference. For a solid, the surface area is displayed. For a 3D polyline, all vertices must lie in a plane parallel to the XY plane of the current UCS. The extrusion direction of a 2D polyline whose area you want to determine should be parallel to the Z axis of the current UCS. In case of polylines which have a width, the area and length of the polyline is calculated using the centerline. If any of these conditions is violated, an error message is displayed on the screen. The prompt sequence is:

> Command: **AREA** [Enter]
> Specify first corner point or [Object/Add/Subtract]: O [Enter]
> Select objects : Select an object [Enter]
> Area = (X), Circumference = (Y)

The X represents the numerical value of the area, and Y represents the circumference/perimeter.

Note

*In many cases, the easiest and most accurate way to find the area of an area enclosed by multiple objects is to use the **BOUNDARY** command to create a polyline, then use the **AREA Object** option.*

Add option. Sometimes you want to add areas of different objects to determine a total area. For example, in the plan of a house, you need to add the areas of all the rooms to get the total floor area. In such cases, you can use the **Add** option. Once you invoke this option, AutoCAD activates the **Add** mode. By using the **First corner point** option at the **Specify first corner point or [Object/ Subtract]:** prompt, you can calculate the area and perimeter by selecting points on the screen. Pressing ENTER after you have selected points defining the area which is to be added, calculates the total area, since the **Add** mode is on. The command prompt is as follows:

Specify next corner point or press ENTER for total [ADD mode]:

If the polygon whose area is to be added, is not closed, the area and perimeter are calculated assuming a line is added which connects the first point to the last point to close the polygon. The length of this area is added in the perimeter. The **Object** option adds the areas and perimeters of selected objects. While using this option, if you select an open polyline, the area is calculated considering the last point is joined to the first point but the perimeter does not consider the length of this assumed segment, unlike the **First corner point** option. When you select an object, the area of the selected object is displayed on the screen. At this time the total area is equal to the area of the selected object. When you select another object, AutoCAD displays the area of the selected object as well as the combined area (total area) of the previous object and the currently selected object. In this manner you can add areas of different objects. Until the **Add** mode is active, the string ADD mode is displayed along with all subsequent object selection prompts to remind you that the **Add** mode is active. When the **AREA** command is invoked, the total area is initialized to zero.

Subtract option. The action of the **Subtract** option is the reverse of that of the **Add** option. Once you invoke this option, AutoCAD activates the **Subtract** mode. The **First corner point** and **Object** options work similar to the way they work in the ADD mode. When you select an object, the area of the selected object is displayed on the screen. At this time, the total area is equal to the area of the selected object. When you select another object, AutoCAD displays the area of the selected object as well as the area obtained by subtracting the area of the currently

*Figure 17-3 Using the **Add** and **Subtract** options*

selected object from the area of the previous object. In this manner, you can subtract areas of objects from the total area. Until the **Subtract** mode is active, the string SUBTRACT mode is displayed along with all subsequent object selection prompts, to remind you that the SUBTRACT mode is active. To exit the **AREA** command, press ENTER (null response) at the **Specify first corner point or [Object/Add/Subtract]:** prompt. The prompt sequence for these two modes for Figure 17-3 is:

Command: **AREA** [Enter]
Specify first corner point or [Object/Add/Subtract]: A [Enter]
Specify first corner point or [Object/Subtract]: O [Enter]
(ADD mode) Select objects: *Select the polyline.*
Area = 2.4438, Perimeter = 6.4999
Total area = 2.4438
(ADD mode) Select objects: [Enter]
Specify first corner point or [Object/Subtract]: S [Enter]
Specify first corner point or [Object/Add]: O [Enter]
(SUBTRACT mode) Select object: *Select the circle.*
Area = 0.0495, Circumference = 0.7890
Total area = 2.3943
(SUBTRACT mode) Select objects: *Select the second circle.*
Area = 0.0495, Circumference = 0.7890
Total area = 2.3448
(SUBTRACT mode) Select object: [Enter]
Specify first corner point or [Object/Add]: [Enter]

The **AREA** and **PERIMETER** system variables hold the area and perimeter (or circumference in the case of circles) of the previously selected polyline (or circle). Whenever you use the **AREA** command, the **AREA** variable is reset to zero.

Calculating Distance between Two Points (DIST Command)

Toolbar:	Inquiry > Distance
Menu:	Tools > Inquiry > Distance
Command:	DIST

 The **DIST** command is used to measure the distance between two selected points (Figure 17-4). The angles that the selected points make with the X axis and the XY plane are also displayed. The measurements are displayed in current units. Delta X (horizontal displacement), delta Y (vertical displacement), and delta Z are also displayed. The distance computed by the **DIST** command is saved in the **DISTANCE** variable. The prompt sequence is:

Command: **DIST** [Enter]
Specify first point: *Specify a point.*
Specify second point: *Specify a point.*

AutoCAD returns the following information:

Distance = *Calculated distance between the two points.*
Angle in XY plane = *Angle between the two points in the XY plane.*
Angle from XY plane = *Angle the specified points make with the XY plane.*
Delta X = *Change in X*, Delta Y = *Change in Y*, Delta Z = *Change in Z*.

If you enter a single number or fraction at the **Specify first point:** prompt, AutoCAD will display that number in the current unit of measurement.

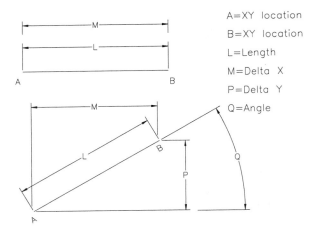

Figure 17-4 *Using the* DIST *command*

Command: **DIST**
First point: 3-3/4   *(Enter a number or a fraction.)*
Distance = 3.7500

Note
The Z coordinate is used in 3D distances. If you do not specify the Z coordinates of the two points between which you want to know the distance, AutoCAD takes the current elevation as the Z coordinate value.

Identifying a Position on the Screen (ID Command)

Toolbar:	Inquiry > Locate Point
Menu:	Tools > Inquiry > ID Point
Command:	ID

 The **ID** command identifies the position of a point you specify and tells you its coordinates.

Command: **ID** [Enter]
Specify point: *Specify the point to be identified.*
X = X coordinate   Y = Y coordinate   Z = Z coordinate

AutoCAD takes the current elevation as the Z coordinate value. If an **Osnap** mode is used to snap to a 3D object in response to the **Specify point:** prompt, the Z coordinate displayed will be that of the selected feature of the 3D object. You can also use the **ID** command to identify the location on the screen. This can be realized by entering the coordinate values you want to locate on the screen. AutoCAD identifies the point by drawing a blip mark at that location (**BLIPMODE** should be On). For example, say you want to find the position on the screen where X = 2.345, Y = 3.674, and Z = 1.0000 is located. This can be achieved with the following prompt sequence:

Command: **ID** [Enter]

> Specify point: 2.345,3.674,1.00 [Enter]
> X = 2.345   Y = 3.674   Z = 1.0000

The coordinates of the point specified in the **ID** command are saved in the **LASTPOINT** system variable. You can locate a point with respect to the **ID** point by using the relative or polar coordinate system. You can also snap to this point by typing @ when AutoCAD prompts for a point.

> Command: **ID**
> Specify point: *Select a point.*
> Command: **LINE**
> Specify first point: @   *(The line will snap to the ID point.)*

You can also use the **X/Y/Z point filters** to specify points on the screen. You can respond to the **Specify point:** prompt with any desired combination of .X, .Y, .Z, .XY, .XZ, .YZ. The 2D or 3D point is specified by specifying individual (intermediate) points and forming the desired point from the selected X, Y, and Z coordinates of the intermediate points. More simply, you can specify a 2D or 3D point by supplying separate information for the X, Y, and Z coordinates. For example, say you want to identify a point whose X, Y, and Z coordinates are marked on the screen separately. This can be achieved in the following manner:

> Command: **ID** [Enter]
> Specify point: .X [Enter]
> of   *Specify the location whose X coordinate is the X coordinate of the final desired point to be identified.*
> of (need YZ):   *Specify the location whose YZ coordinate is the YZ coordinate of the final desired point to be identified.*
> X = X coordinate   Y = Y coordinate   Z = Z coordinate

A blip mark is formed at the point of intersection of the specified X, Y, and Z coordinates. This blip mark identifies the desired point.

Listing Information about Objects (LIST Command)

Toolbar:	Inquiry > List
Menu:	Tools > Inquiry > List
Command:	LIST

The **LIST** command displays all the data pertaining to the selected objects. The prompt sequence is:

> Command: **LIST** [Enter]
> Select objects: *Select objects whose data you want to list.*
> Select objects: [Enter]

Once you select the objects to be listed, AutoCAD shifts you from the graphics screen to the AutoCAD Text Window. The information displayed (listed) varies from object to object. Information on an object's type, its coordinate position with respect to the current UCS (user coordinate system), the name of the layer on which it is drawn, and whether the object is in model space or

Chapter 17

paper space is listed for all types of objects. If the color, lineweight, and the linetype are not BYLAYER, they are also listed. Also, if the thickness of the object is greater than 0, that is also displayed. The elevation value is displayed in the form of a Z coordinate (in the case of 3D objects). If an object has an extrusion direction different from the Z axis of the current UCS, the object's extrusion direction is also provided.

More information based on the objects in the drawing is also provided. For example, for a line the following information is be displayed:

1. The coordinates of the endpoints of the line.
2. Its length (in 3D).
3. The angle made by the line with respect to the X axis of the current UCS.
4. The angle made by the line with respect to the XY plane of the current UCS.
5. Delta X, delta Y, delta Z: this is the change in each of the three coordinates from the start point to the endpoint.
6. The name of the layer in which the line was created.
7. Whether the line is drawn in Paper space or Model space.

The center point, radius, true area, and circumference of circles is displayed. For polylines, this command displays the coordinates. In addition, for a closed polyline, its true area and perimeter are also given. If the polyline is open, AutoCAD lists its length and also calculates the area by assuming a segment connecting the start point and endpoint of the polyline. In the case of wide polylines, all computation is done based on the centerlines of the wide segments. For a selected viewport, the **LIST** command displays whether the viewport is on and active, on and inactive, or off. Information is also displayed about the status of Hideplot and the scale relative to paper space. If you use the **LIST** command on a polygon mesh, the size of the mesh (in terms of M, X, N), the coordinate values of all the vertices in the mesh, and whether the mesh is closed or open in M and N directions are all displayed. As mentioned before, if all the information does not fit on a single screen, AutoCAD pauses to allow you to press ENTER to continue the listing.

Listing Information about All Objects in a Drawing (DBLIST Command)

Command:	DBLIST

The **DBLIST** command displays information pertaining to all the objects in the drawing. Once you invoke this command, information is displayed in the AutoCAD Text Window. If the information does not fit on a single screen, AutoCAD pauses to allow you to press ENTER to continue the listing. To terminate the command, press ESCAPE. To return to the graphics screen, close the AutoCAD Text Window. This command can be invoked by entering **DBLIST** at the Command prompt.

Exercise 1   *Mechanical*

Draw Figure 17-5 and save it as EX1. Using INQUIRY commands, determine the following values:

a. Area of the hexagon.
b. Perimeter of the hexagon.
c. Perimeter of the inner rectangle.
d. Circumference of each circle.
e. Area of the hexagon minus the inner rectangle.
f. Use the **DBLIST** command to get the database listing.

Figure 17-5 *Drawing for Exercise 1*

Listing Information About Solids and Regions (MASSPROP Command)

Toolbar:	Inquiry > Mass properties
Menu:	Tools > Inquiry > Mass Properties
Command:	MASSPROP

With the **MASSPROP** command, you can determine volumetric information, such as principle axes, center of gravity, and moment of inertia of 2D or 3D objects.

Command: **MASSPROP** [Enter]
Select objects: *Select an object (solid object).*

For a detailed explanation of the **MASSPROP** command, refer to Chapter 23, Solid Modelling.

CHECKING TIME-RELATED INFORMATION (TIME COMMAND)

Menu:	Tools > Inquiry > Time
Command:	TIME

The time and date maintained by your system are used by AutoCAD to provide information about several time factors related to the drawings. Hence, you should be careful about setting the current date and time in your computer. The **TIME** command can be used to display information pertaining to time related to a drawing and the drawing session. The display obtained by invoking the **TIME** command is similar to the following:

Command: **TIME**

Current time:	Monday, April 26 1999 at 11:22:35.069 AM
Times for this drawing:	
Created:	Thursday, April 15 1999 at 09:34:42.157 AM
Last updated:	Friday, April 16 1999 at 02:54:25.700 PM

Total editing time: 0 days 07:52:16.205
Elapsed timer (on)   0 days 00:43:07.304
Next automatic save in: 0 days 00:54:27:153

Enter an option [Display/ON/OFF/Reset]:

The foregoing display gives you information on the following.

Current Time
Provides today's date and the current time.

Drawing Creation Time
Provides the date and time that the current drawing was created. The creation time for a drawing is set to the system time when the **NEW**, **-WBLOCK**, or **SAVE** command is used to create that drawing file.

Last Updated Time
Provides the most recent date and time you saved the current drawing. In the beginning, it is set to the drawing creation time, and it is modified every time you use the **QUIT** or **SAVE** command to save the drawing.

Total Editing Time
This tells you the total time spent on editing the current drawing since it was created. If you terminate the editing session without saving the drawing, the time you have spent on that editing session is not added to the total time spent on editing the drawing. Also, the last update time is not revised.

Elapsed Timer
This timer operates while you are in AutoCAD. You can stop this timer by entering OFF at the **Enter an option [Display/ON/OFF/Reset]:** prompt. To activate the timer, enter ON. If you want to know how much time you have spent on the current drawing or part of the drawing in the current editing session, use the **Reset** option as soon as you start working on the drawing or part of the drawing. This resets the user-elapsed timer to zero. By default, this timer is ON. If you turn this timer OFF, the time accumulated in this timer up to the time you turned it OFF will be displayed.

Next Automatic Save In Time
This tells you when the next automatic save will be performed. The automatic save time interval can be set in the **Options** dialog box (**Open and Save** tab) or with the **SAVETIME** system variable. If the time interval has been set to zero, the **TIME** command displays the following message:

Next automatic time save in: <disabled>

If the time interval is not set to zero, and no editing has taken place since the previous save, the **TIME** command displays the following message:

Next automatic time save in: <no modification yet>

If the time interval is not set to zero, and editing has taken place since the previous save, the **TIME** command displays the following message:

Next automatic time save in: 0 days hh:mm:ss.msec

hh stands for hours
mm stands for minutes
ss stands for seconds
msec stands for milliseconds

At the end of the display of the **TIME** command, AutoCAD prompts:

Enter an option [Display/ON/OFF/Reset]:

The information displayed by the **TIME** command is static; that is, the information is not updated dynamically on the screen. If you respond to the last prompt with DISPLAY (or D), the display obtained by invoking the **TIME** command is repeated. This display contains updated time values.

With the ON response, the user-elapsed timer is started, if it was off. As mentioned earlier, when you enter the drawing editor, by default the timer is on. The OFF response is just the opposite of the ON response and stops the user-elapsed time, if it is on. With the **Reset** option, you can set the user-elapsed time to zero.

OBTAINING DRAWING STATUS INFORMATION (STATUS COMMAND)

| **Menu:** | Tools > Inquiry > Status |
| **Command:** | STATUS |

The **STATUS** command displays information about the prevalent settings of various drawing parameters, such as snap spacing, grid spacing, limits, current space, current layer, current color, and various memory parameters.

Command: **STATUS**

Once you enter this command, AutoCAD displays information similar to the following:

106 objects in Drawing.dwg

Model space limits are	X: 0.0000	Y: 0.0000(On)	
	X: 6.0000	Y: 4.4000	
Model space uses	X:0.6335	Y:-0.2459	**Over
	X:8.0497	Y: 4.9710	**Over
Display shows	X: 0.0000	Y:-0.2459	
	X: 8.0088	Y: 5.5266	

Chapter 17

Insertion base is   X: 0.0000   Y: 0.0000   Z: 0.0000
Snap resolution is   X: 0.2500   Y: 0.2500
Grid spacing is   X: 0.2500   Y: 0.2500

Current space: Model space
Current layout: Model
Current layer: OBJ
Current color: BYLAYER .... 7 (white)
Current linetype: BYLAYER .... CONTINUOUS
Current lineweight: BYLAYER
Current Plot Style: By layer
Current elevation: 0.0000   thickness: 0.0000
Fill on Grid on Ortho off Qtext off Snap off Tablet on
Object snap modes: None
Free dwg disk space: 2047.7 MBytes
Free temp disk: 2047.7 MBytes
Free physical memory: 15.0 MBytes
Free swap file space: 1987.5 MBytes

All the values (coordinates and distances) on this screen are given in the format declared in the **UNITS** command. You will also notice **Over in the **Model space uses** or **Paper space uses** line. This signifies that the drawing is not confined within the drawing limits. The amount of memory available on the disk is given in the **Free dwg disk space:** line. Information on the name of the current layer, current color, current space, current linetype, current lineweight, current Plot Style, current elevation, snap spacing (snap resolution), grid spacing, various tools that are on or off (such as Ortho, Snap, Fill, Tablet, Qtext), and which object snap modes are active is also provided by the display obtained by invoking the **STATUS** command.

Exercise 2   *General*

Use the **STATUS** command to check the disk space available on the hard drive.

Displaying Drawing Properties* (DWGPROPS Command*)

Menu:	File > Drawing Properties
Command:	DWGPROPS

On choosing **Drawing Properties** from the **File** Menu, the **Drawing Properties** dialog box is displayed (Figure 17-6). This dialog box has four tabs under which information about the drawing is displayed. The information displayed in this dialog box helps you look for the drawing more easily. The tabs are as follows:

General. This tab displays general properties about the drawing like the **Type**, **Size** and **Location**.

Summary. The **Summary** tab displays predefined properties like the Author, title, and subject.

Custom. This tab displays custom file properties including values assigned by you.

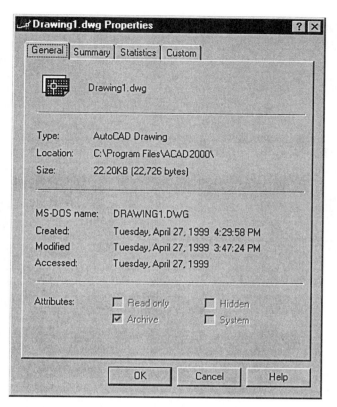

*Figure 17-6 The **Drawing Properties** dialog box*

Statistics. This tab stores and displays data such as the file size and data such as the dates when the drawing was last saved on or modified on.

DATA EXCHANGE IN AUTOCAD

Different companies have developed different software for applications such as CAD, desktop publishing, and rendering. This nonstandardization of software has led to the development of various data exchange formats that enable transfer (translation) of data from one data processing software to another. We will now discuss various data exchange formats provided in AutoCAD. AutoCAD uses the .DWG format to store drawing files. This format is not recognized by most other CAD software, such as Intergraph, CADKEY, and MicroStation. To solve this problem so that files created in AutoCAD can be transferred to other CAD software for further use, AutoCAD provides various data exchange formats, such as DXF (data interchange file) and DXB (binary drawing interchange).

DXF FILE FORMAT (DATA INTERCHANGE FILE)

The DXF file format generates a text file in ASCII code from the original drawing. This allows any computer system to manipulate (read/write) data in a DXF file. Usually, DXF format is used for CAD packages based on microcomputers. For example, packages like SmartCAM use DXF files. Some desktop publishing packages, such as Pagemaker and Ventura Publisher, also use DXF files.

Creating a Data Interchange File

The **SAVE** or the **SAVEAS** command is used to create an ASCII file with a .DXF extension from an AutoCAD drawing file. Once you invoke any of these commands, the **Save Drawing As** dialog box (Figure 17-7) is displayed. By default, the DXF file to be created assumes the name of the drawing file from which it will be created. However, you can specify a file name of your choice for the DXF file by typing the desired file name in the **File Name:** edit box. Select the extension as **DXF [*dxf]**. This can be observed in the **Save as type:** drop-down list where you can select the output file format. You can also use the **-WBLOCK** command. The **Create Drawing** dialog box is displayed, where you can enter the name of the file in the **File Name:** edit box and select **DXF [*dxf]** from the **Save as type:** drop-down list.

Figure 17-7 Save Drawing As dialog box

Choose the **Options** button to display the **Saveas Options** dialog box (Figure 17-8). In this dialog box, choose the **DXF options** tab and enter the degree of accuracy for the numeric values. The default value for the degree of accuracy is six decimal places, however, this results in less accuracy than the original drawing, which is accurate to 16 places. You can enter a value between 0 and 16 decimal places.

In this dialog box, you can also select the **Select Objects** check box, which allows you to specify objects you want to include in the DXF file. In this case, the definitions of named objects such as block definitions, text styles, and so on, are not exported. Selecting the **Save thumbnail preview image** check box, saves a preview image with the file that can be previewed in the **Preview** window of the **Select File** dialog box.

Select the **ASCII** radio button. Choose **OK** to return to the **Save Drawing As** dialog box. Choose the **Save** button here. Now an ASCII file with a .DXF extension has been created, and this file can be accessed by other CAD systems. This file contains data on the objects specified. By default, DXF files are created in ASCII format. However, you can also create binary format files by selecting the

Figure 17-8 Saveas Options dialog box

Binary radio button in the **Saveas Options** dialog box. Binary DXF files are more efficient and occupy only 75 percent of the ASCII DXF file. You can access a file in binary format more quickly than the same file in ASCII format.

Information in a DXF File

The DXF file contains data on the objects specified using the **Select objects** option in the **Save Drawing As** dialog box. You can change the data in this file to your requirement. To examine the data in this file, load the ASCII file in word processing software. A DXF file is composed of the following parts.

Header. In this part of the drawing database, all the variables in the drawing and their values are displayed.

Classes. This section deals with the internal database.

Tables. All the named objects, such as linetypes, layers, blocks, text styles, dimension styles, and views, are listed in this part.

Blocks. The objects that define blocks and their respective values are displayed in this part.

Entities. All the entities in the drawing, like Circle, and so forth, are listed in this part.

Objects. Objects in the drawing are listed in this part.

Converting DXF Files into a Drawing File (OPEN Command)

You can import a DXF file into a new AutoCAD drawing file with the **OPEN** command. From the **File** menu choose **Open**.

Command: **OPEN**

After you invoke the **OPEN** command, the **Select File** dialog box (Figure 17-9) is displayed. From the **Files of Type:** drop-down list, select **DXF [*dxf]**. In the **File Name:** edit box enter the name of the file you want to import into AutoCAD or select the file from the list. Choose the **Open** button. Once this is done, the specified DXF file is converted into a standard DWG file, regeneration is carried out, and the file is inserted into the new drawing. Now you can perform different operations on this file just as with other drawing files. You can also use the **INSERT** command to insert a DXF file into the current drawing.

Figure 17-9 Select File dialog box

Importing Scanned Files into the Drawing Editor
DXB File Format

Menu:	Insert > Drawing Exchange Binary
Command:	DXBIN

AutoCAD offers another file format for data interchange: DXB. This format is much more compressed than the binary DXF format and is used when you want to translate large amounts of data from one CAD system to another. For example, when a drawing is scanned, a DXB file is created. This file has huge amounts of data in it. The **DXBIN** command is used to create drawing files out of DXB format files.

Command: **DXBIN**

After you invoke the **DXBIN** command, the **Select DXB File** dialog box is displayed. In the **File Name:** edit box, enter the name of the file (in DXB format) you want to import into AutoCAD. Choose the **Open** button. Once this is done, the specified DXB file is converted into a standard DWG file and is inserted into the current drawing.

Note

Before importing a DXB file, you must create a new drawing file. No editing or drawing setup (limits, units, and so on) can be performed in this file. This is because if you import a DXB file into an old drawing, the settings (definitions) of layers, blocks, and so on, of the file being imported are overruled by the settings of the file into which you are importing the DXB file.

Creating and Using an ACIS file

Menu:	Tools > Export...
Command:	EXPORT, ACISOUT

Trimmed Nurbs surfaces, regions, and solids can be exported to an ACIS file with an ASCII format. Choose **Export** from the **File** menu or enter **EXPORT** at the Command prompt. The **Export Data** dialog box is displayed, enter a file name in the **File name:** edit box. From the **Save as type:** drop-down list select **ACIS [*.sat]** and then choose the **Save** button. At the **Select Objects:** prompt, select the objects you wish to save as an ACIS file and press ENTER. AutoCAD appends the file extension .sat to the file name. You can also use the **ACISOUT** command. It prompts you to select objects before the **Create ACIS File** dialog box appears on the screen.

The command **ACISIN** displays the **Select ACIS File** dialog box. Select a file to import and choose the **Open** button. This command can also be invoked by choosing **ACIS Solid** from the **Insert** menu.

Creating and Using a 3D Studio File

Menu:	Tools > Export...
Command:	EXPORT, 3DSOUT

3D geometry, views, lights and objects with surface characteristics can be saved in the 3D Studio format. In the **Export Data** dialog box, enter the file name in the **File Name:** edit box and select **3D Studio [*.3ds]** from the **Save as type:** drop-down list. Choose **Save**. At the **Select objects:** prompt, select the objects you want to save in the 3D Studio format. Press ENTER; the file extension .3ds is automatically added to the file name. You can also use the **3DSOUT** command. AutoCAD prompts you to select the objects first. When you press ENTER, the **Create 3D Studio Output File** dialog box appears. Enter the file name in the edit box and choose the **Save** button.

The **3DSIN** command displays the **3D Studio File Import** dialog box. Select the file you wish to import and choose the **Open** button. You can also invoke this command by choosing **3DStudio** from the **Insert** menu.

Creating and Using a Windows WMF File

Menu:	File > Export
Command:	EXPORT, WMFOUT

The Windows Metafile File format file contains screen vector and raster graphics format. In the **Export Data** dialog box or the **Create WMF file** dialog box, enter the file name. Select the objects you want to save in this file format. Select **Metafile [*wmf]** from the **Save as type:** drop-down list. The extension .wmf is appended to the file name.

The **WMFIN** command displays the **Import WMF** dialog box. Window metafiles are imported as blocks in AutoCAD. Select the wmf file you want to import and choose the **Open** button. Specify an insertion point, rotation angle and scale factor. Specify scaling by entering a **scale factor**, using the **corner** option to specify an imaginary box whose dimensions correspond to the scale factor or entering **xyz** to specify 3D scale factors. You can also invoke the **WMFIN** command by choosing

Chapter 17

Windows Metafile from the **Insert** menu.

Creating a BMP File

Menu:	File > Export
Command:	EXPORT, BMPOUT

This is used to create bitmap images of the objects in your drawing. In the **Export Data** dialog box, enter the name of the file, select **Bitmap [*bmp]** from the **Save as type:** drop-down list and then choose **Save**. Select the objects you wish to save as bitmap and press ENTER. Entering **BMPOUT** displays the **Create BMP File** dialog box. Enter the file name and choose **Save**. Select the objects to save as bitmap. The file extension .bmp is appended to the file name.

DATA INTERCHANGE THROUGH RASTER FILES

Until now we have discussed importing and exporting files in the DXF file format. To uphold the accuracy of the drawing, the DXF file includes almost all the information about the original drawing file. The accuracy is maintained at the expense of DXF file size and degree of complexity of these files. There are many applications in which accuracy is not very important, like desktop publishing. In such applications, you are concerned primarily with image presentation. A very simple and effective way of storing an image for import/export is in the form of **raster files**. In a raster file, information is stored in the form of a dot pattern on the screen. This bit pattern is also known as a **bit map**. For example, in a raster file a picture is stored in the form of information about the position and color of the screen pixels. AutoCAD allows you to add raster images to the vector base AutoCAD drawings, and view and plot the resulting file. We will be discussing three types of raster files: TIFF files, TGA files, and BMP files. These formats make it possible to transfer a file from AutoCAD to other software.

TIFF (tagged image file format)

TGA (targa format)

BMP (bitmap format)

Exporting the Raster Files (SAVEIMG Command)

Menu:	Tools > Display Image > Save
Command:	SAVEIMG

If there is a picture on the screen that you want to save as a raster file, use the **SAVEIMG** command. With this command, you can save a rendered image to TIFF, TGA, or BMP types of raster files. These raster files can be used by most software. Sometimes, the raster files need to be converted into some other format before they can be used by certain software. This operation is performed with a file conversion program such as Hijaak or Pizazz Plus.

Command: **SAVEIMG**

Once you invoke this command, the **Save Image** dialog box is displayed (Figures 17-10). Depending on the **Destination** option you have selected in the **Rendering Preferences** dialog box, there is a difference in the **Portion** area.

Figure 17-10 Save Image dialog box

Format. This area of the **Save Image** dialog box provides three raster formats: TGA, TIFF, and BMP. You can select any one of the formats by selecting the radio button next to the desired format. A brief description of each format follows.

> **TGA**. (default format). With this format, you can create compressed or uncompressed 32-bit RGBA Truevision v2.0 format files. These files have the extension **.tga**.

> **TIFF**. (tagged image file format). This file format has been developed by Aldus and Microsoft. With this format, you can create compressed or uncompressed 32-bit RGBA tagged image file format. These files have the extension **.tif**.

> **BMP**. (bitmap format). These files have the extension **.bmp**.

Portion. In the **Portion** area of the **Save Image** dialog box, you can specify the portion of the screen you want to save in the specified file format and the portion of the image you wish to render. In case AutoCAD is configured for rendering to a viewport (in the **Render Preferences** dialog box), the **Portion** area provides options to save either the active viewport, the drawing area, or the full screen. The **Portion** area contains an image tile that graphically represents the section of the screen to be saved. You will notice that by default the entire screen is selected for saving. If you want to save only a section of the screen, you need to specify the desired section. This can be achieved by specifying two diagonally opposite points on the image tile. Specify the lower left corner of the desired section first, then specify the upper right corner. After specifying the two corner points, AutoCAD creates a box whose lower left corner point and upper right corner point coincide with the respective points you specified. Also, the values for the X and Y Offsets and Sizes are automatically updated.

Offset. This includes **X** and **Y** edit boxes. The values you enter in these edit boxes are treated as the X and Y offsets. The start point (lower left corner) of the area to be saved as a raster file can be specified by X and Y offset values. The default value for the offset is (0,0). The values entered are taken as the pixel values. The offset values should be specified within the screen size value. When you change the offset values, the change in the start point of the image selection area is reflected by a margin formed by two intersecting lines in the image tile. The point of intersection of these two lines is the start point of the image selection area. Values of X and Y offsets greater than the screen size are not accepted by AutoCAD.

Size. With the **Offset** option, you can specify the lower left corner of the area to be selected for conversion into a raster file format. To specify the area completely, however, you need to specify the upper right corner of this area as well. This can be achieved with the **Size** option. In the case of the **Offset** option, the values entered in the **X** and **Y** edit boxes are the pixel values. The default for the **Size** option is the upper right corner of the display area. The change in location of the upper right corner of the image selection area is reflected by two intersecting lines.

Options. The display provided by choosing the **Options** button varies from one file format to another. The image compression options are displayed only for TGA and TIFF formats. For the BMP format, the image file compression is not supported, hence, the **Options** button is disabled.

 None. This is the default option. If this option is selected, compression does not take place.

 PACK. With this option, run-length encoded image compression can be realized only for TIFF files (Figure 17-11). It uses Macintosh packbits.

 RLE. This option works only for TGA format files (Figure 17-12). If you select this option, run-length encoded image compression can be realized.

Figure 17-11 TIFF Options dialog box   *Figure 17-12 TGA Options dialog box*

Reset. When you choose this button in the **Save Image** dialog box, the Offset values and the Size values are set to their default values.

Example 1

In this example, you will load a drawing or draw a figure and then use the **SAVEIMG** command to save the image.

Creating an image using the **SAVEIMG** command involves the following steps. Assume that the drawing is already loaded or drawn on the screen.

1. Invoke the **SAVEIMG** command by any one of the methods explained to display the **Save**

      Image dialog box.

2. Specify the file type in the **Format** area by selecting the radio button with the desired file type format.

3. Specify the area you want to save in the image file to be created by selecting the desired offset and size.

4. Choose the **OK** button.

5. The **Image File** dialog box is displayed. Enter the name you want to give the image file.

After this, AutoCAD starts saving the selected area to the file whose name you have specified. The saving operation is acknowledged by the following message: Writing file.

RASTER IMAGES

A raster image consists of small square-shaped dots known as pixels. In a colored image, the color is determined by the color of pixels. The raster images can be moved, copied, or clipped, and used as a cutting edge with the **TRIM** command. They can also be modified by using grips. You can also control the image contrast, transparency, and quality of the image. AutoCAD stores images in a special temporary image swap file whose default location is the Windows Temp directory. You can change the location of this file modifying it under **Temporary File Location** in the **Files** tab of the **Options** dialog box.

The images can be 8-bit gray, 8-bit color, 24-bit color, or bitonal. When image transparency is set to On, the image file formats with transparent pixels is recognized by AutoCAD and transparency is allowed. The transparent images can be in color or gray scale. AutoCAD supports the following file formats.

Image Type	File Extension	Description
BMP	.bmp, .dib, .rle	Windows and OS/2 Bitmap Format
CALS-I	.gp4, .mil, .rst	Mil-R-Raster I
FLIC	.flc, .fli	Flic Autodesk Animator Animation
GEOSPOT	.bil	GeoSPOT (BIL files must be accompanied with HDR and PAL files with connection data in the same directory.)
IG4	.ig4	Image Systems group 4
IGS	.igs	Image Systems Grayscale
JFIF or JPEG	.jpg, jpeg	Joint Photographics Expert group
PCX	.pcx	Picture PC Paintbrush Picture
PICT	.pct	Picture Macintosh Picture
PNG	.png	Portable Network Graphic
RLC	.rlc	Run-length Compressed
TARGA	.tga	True Vision Raster based Data format
TIFF/LZW	.tif	Taffed image file format

When you store images as Tiled Images, that is, in the Tagged Image File Format [TIFF], you can edit or modify any portion of the image; only the modified portion is regenerated thus saving time. Tiled images load much faster compared to nontiled images.

Chapter 17

Attaching Raster Images

Toolbar:	Reference > Image Attach
Menu:	Insert > Raster Image...
Command:	IMAGEATTACH

*Figure 17-13 Invoking the **IMAGEATTACH** command from the **Reference** toolbar*

Attaching Raster images do not make them part of the drawing. You can also drag and drop images from other files into the current drawing using the **AutoCAD DesignCenter** window. When you invoke the **IMAGEATTACH** command, AutoCAD displays the **Select Image File** dialog box (Figure 17-14). Enter the name of the image file you want to attach to the current drawing in the **File name:** edit box or select the image from the list box. The name can be up to 255 characters long and can include spaces, numbers and special characters which are not being used by AutoCAD or Windows. A preview image of the selected image is displayed in the **Preview** window of the dialog box. If you choose the **Hide Preview** button, the preview image of the selected image is not displayed in the **Preview** window. Choose the **Open** button.

Figure 17-14 Select Image File dialog box

AutoCAD displays the **Image** dialog box (Figure 17-15). The name of the selected image is displayed in the **Name:** edit box. You can select another file by using the **Browse** button. The **Name** drop-down list displays names of all the images in the current drawing. The **Path** is also displayed just below the **Name:** edit box. Select the **Specify On-Screen** check boxes to specify the **Insertion point**, **Rotation** Angle and **Scale** on screen. Alternately you can clear these check boxes and enter values in the respective edit boxes. Choosing the **Details** button gives Image information like the Horizontal and Vertical resolution values, current AutoCAD unit, and Image size in pixels and units. Choose **OK** to return to the drawing screen.

You can attach and scale an image from the Internet. In the **Select Image File** dialog box, choose the **Search the web** button. Once you have located the image file you wish to attach to the current drawing, enter the URL address in the **Look In:** edit box and the Image file name in the **File name:** edit box. Choose the **Open** button. Specify the **Insertion point**, **scale** and **Rotation** angle in the **Image** dialog box. You can also right-click the image you wish to attach to the current drawing and choose **Properties** from the shortcut menu to display the **Object Properties** window.

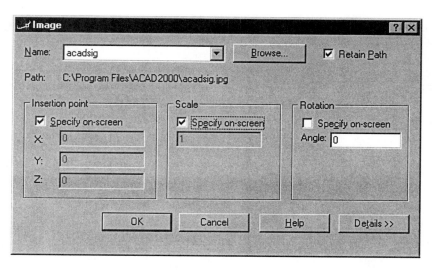

Figure 17-15 Image dialog box

From here you can select , cut and paste the URL address to the **File name:** edit box in the **Select File** dialog box.

Managing Raster Images* (Image Manager Dialog Box*)

Toolbar:	Reference > Image
	Insert > Image
Menu:	Insert > Image Manager...
Command:	IMAGE

When you invoke the **IMAGE** command, AutoCAD displays the **Image Manager** dialog box (Figure 17-17). You can also invoke the **Image Man-**

Figure 17-16 Invoking the IMAGE command from the Insert toolbar

ager dialog box by selecting an image and right-clicking to display a shortcut menu. Choose **Image > Image Manager**. You can view image information either as a list or as a tree view by choosing the respective buttons located in the upper-left corner of the **Image Manager** dialog box. The **List View** displays the names of all the images in the drawing, its loading status, size, date last modified on, and its search path. The **Tree View** displays the images in a hierarchy which shows its nesting levels within blocks and Xrefs. The **Tree View** does not display the Status, size, or any other information about the image file. You can rename an image file in this dialog box. The different options in the **Image Manager** dialog box are:

Attach. If you want to attach an image file, choose the **Attach** button; the **Select Image File** dialog box is displayed. Select the file that you want to attach to the drawing; the selected image is displayed in the **Preview** box. Choose the **Open** button. The **Image** dialog box is displayed. The name of the file and its path and extension are displayed in the **Image** dialog box. You can use the **Browse** button to select another file. Choose the **OK** button in the **Image** dialog box and specify a point where you want to insert the image. Next, AutoCAD will prompt you to enter the scale factor. You can enter the scale factor or specify a point on the screen.

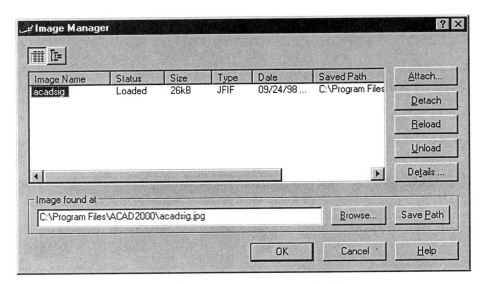

*Figure 17-17 **Image Manager** dialog box*

Detach. Detaches the selected and all associated raster images from the current drawing. Once the image is detached, no information about the image is retained in the drawing.

Reload. Reloads an image. The changes made to the image since the last insert will be loaded on the screen. You can change the status of the image file in the **Image Manager** dialog box by double-clicking on the current status. It changes from **Unload** to **Reload** and vice versa.

Unload. Unloads an image. An image is unloaded when it is not needed in the current drawing session. When you unload an image, AutoCAD retains information about the location and size of the image and the image boundary is displayed. If you reload the image, the image will appear at the same point and in the same size as the image was before unloading. Unloading the raster images enhances AutoCAD performance. Also, the unloaded images are not plotted, but unloading does not unlink the file from the drawing. If multiple images are to be loaded and the memory is insufficient, AutoCAD automatically unloads them.

Details. Displays the **Image File Details** box, which lists information about the image like file name, saved path, file creation date, file size, file type, color and color path, pixel width and height, resolution, and default size. It also displays the image in the preview box.

Image found at. This edit box displays the path of the selected image. You can edit this path and choose the **Save path** button to save the new path. If you have changed the path of an image, choose the **Browse** button to display the **Select Image File** dialog box. In this dialog box, locate the image file and then choose the **Open** button. The new path is displayed in the **Image found at** edit box. Choose the **Save Path** button to save this new path. This path is also displayed in the **Saved path** column of the dialog box.

Save Path. Saves the current path of the image.

Browse. Displays the **Select Image File** dialog box.

Using the -IMAGE Command

The options in the **Image Manager** dialog box can also be used from the command line when you use the **-IMAGE** command. The Command prompts are as follows:

Command: **-IMAGE**
Enter image option [?/Detach/Path/Reload/Unload/Attach] <Attach>: *Enter an option or press ENTER to attach an image.*

Entering ? at the above prompt gives the next prompt as follows:
Images to list<*>: *Press ENTER.*

The AutoCAD Text window lists information about the image.

EDITING RASTER IMAGE FILES
Clipping Raster Images

Toolbar:	Reference > Image Clip
Menu:	Modify > Clip > Image
Command:	IMAGECLIP

You can clip a raster image by invoking the **IMAGECLIP** command. You can select an image to clip and right-click to display a shortcut menu. Choose **Image > Clip** to invoke the **IMAGECLIP** command. When you invoke the command, AutoCAD will prompt you to select the image to clip. Select the raster image by selecting the boundary edge of the image. The image boundary must be visible to select the image. You can turn off or on the clipping boundary. To improve performance you can also make sure that on selecting an image , only the boundary is highlighted. You can turn On or Off the image highlighting that is visible when we select an image by selecting or clearing the **Highlight Raster Image Frame Only** check box in the **Display** tab of the **Options** dialog box. You can also use the **IMAGEHLT** system variable. By default, **IMAGEHLT** is set to 0, that is, only the raster image frame will be highlighted. At the **Enter image clipping option [ON/OFF/Delete/New boundary] <New Boundary>:** prompt, select the **New boundary** option and then define the clip boundary either by defining a rectangular or polygonal boundary. The clipping boundary must be specified in the same plane as the image or a plane that is parallel to it (see Figure 7-18). The following is the command prompt sequence for the **IMAGECLIP** command:

Command: **IMAGECLIP**
Select image to clip: *Select the image at the edge.*
Enter image clipping option [ON/OFF/Delete/New boundary] <New boundary>: *Press ENTER to select New boundary.*
Enter clipping type [Polygonal/Rectangular] <Rectangular>: *Type P for Polygonal and then define the polygon shape.*

ON/OF. The **ON/OFF** option allows you to turn the clipping boundary on or off. When the clipping boundary is off, you can see the complete image; when it is on, the image that is within the

Figure 17-18 Object before and after clipping

clipping polygon is displayed. In the **Object properties** window, under the **Misc** area , you can select options from the **Show Clipped** drop-down list. Selecting **Yes**, shows the clipped image and selecting **No**, displays the complete image (the clipping boundary is off).

Delete. The **Delete** option deletes the clipping boundary.

Adjusting Raster Image

Toolbar:	Reference > Image Adjust
Menu:	Modify > Object > Image > Adjust
Command:	IMAGEADJUST

The **IMAGEADJUST** command allows you to adjust the brightness, contrast, and fade of the raster image. When you choose an image and right-click, a shortcut menu is displayed. Choose **Image > Adjust** to invoke the **IMAGEADJUST** command. When you invoke this command, AutoCAD prompts you to select image(s). After selecting the image(s), AutoCAD displays the **Image Adjust** dialog box (Figure 17-19) that you can use to adjust the image. As you

*Figure 17-19 **Image Adjust** dialog box*

adjust the brightness, contrast, or fade, the image box displays the effect on the image. If you choose the **Reset** button, the values are returned to default values (Brightness= 50, Contrast= 50, and Fade= 0). You can also choose **Properties** in the shortcut menu to display the **Object Properties** window, where you can enter new values of **Brightness**, **Contrast**, and **Fade**.

Image Quality

Toolbar:	Reference > Image Quality
Menu:	Modify > Object > Image > Quality
Command:	IMAGEQUALITY

The **IMAGEQUALITY** command allows you to control the quality of the image that affects the display performance. A high quality image takes longer time to display. When you change the quality, the display changes immediately without causing a **REGEN**. The images are always plotted using high quality display. Although draft quality images appear more grainy, they are displayed more quickly. The command prompts are as follows:

Command: **IMAGEQUALITY**
Enter image quality setting [High/Draft] <High>: *Enter h or d.*

Transparency

Toolbar:	Reference > Image Transparency
Menu:	Modify > Object > Image >Transparency
Command:	TRANSPARENCY

The **TRANSPARENCY** command is used with bitonal images to turn the transparency of the image background on or off. A bitonal image is one that consists of only a foreground and a background color. When you attach a bitonal image, the image assumes the color of the current layer. Also, the bitonal image and the bitonal image boundaries are always in the same color. You can also right-click an image and choose **Properties** from the shortcut menu which is displayed. In the **Object Properties** window under the **Misc** list, select an option from the **Transparency** drop-down list. The command prompts for the **TRANSPARENCY** command are:

Command: **TRANSPARENCY**
Select image(s): *Select the image.*
Enter transparency mode [ON/OFF] <OFF>:

Image Frame

Toolbar:	Reference > Image Frame
Menu:	Modify > Object > Image > Frame
Command:	IMAGEFRAME

The **IMAGEFRAME** command is used to turn the image boundary on or off. If the image boundary is off, the image cannot be selected with the pointing device and hence, cannot be accidently moved or modified. The command prompt is as follows:

Command: **IMAGEFRAME**

Enter image frame setting [ON/OFF] <OFF>:

Other Editing Commands

You can use other editing commands like **COPY**, **MOVE**, and **STRETCH** to edit the raster image. You can also use the image as the trimming edge for trimming objects. However, you cannot trim an image. You can insert the raster image several times or make multiple copies of it. Each copy could have a different clipping boundary. You can also edit the image using grips. You can also use the **Object Properties** window to change the image layer, boundary linetype, and color, and perform other editing commands like changing the scale, rotation, width, and height by entering new values in the respective edit boxes. You can also display an image or turn off the display by selecting options from the **Show Image** drop-down list in the **Misc** field of the **Object Properties** window. If you select **Yes**, the image is displayed and if you select **No**, the display of the image is turned off. You can turn off the display of the image when you do not need it thus improving the performance.

Scaling Raster Images

The scale of the inserted image is determined by the actual size of the image and the unit of measurement (inches, feet, and so on). For example, if the image is 1" x 1.26" and you insert this image with a scale factor of 1, the size of the image on the screen will be 1 AutoCAD unit by 1.26 AutoCAD units. If the scale factor is 5, the image will be five times larger. The image that you want to insert must contain the resolution information (DPI). If the image does not contain this information, AutoCAD treats the width of the image as one unit.

POSTSCRIPT FILES

PostScript is a page description language developed by Adobe Systems. It is used mostly in DTP (desktop publishing) applications. AutoCAD allows you to work with PostScript files. You can create and export PostScript files as well as convert PostScript files into regular AutoCAD drawing files (import). PostScript images have higher resolution than raster images. The extension for these files is .EPS (Encapsulated PostScript).

PSOUT Command

Menu:	File > Export...
Command:	PSOUT, EXPORT

As just mentioned, any AutoCAD drawing file can be converted into a PostScript file. This can be accomplished with the **PSOUT** command. Once the **PSOUT** command is invoked, AutoCAD displays the **Create PostScript File** dialog box (Figure 17-20). You can also use the **EXPORT** command to display the **Export Data** dialog box. The options are similar in both the dialog boxes.

In the **File Name:** edit box, enter the name of the PostScript (EPS) file you want to create. When you use the **EXPORT** command, in the **Export Data** dialog box, select **Encapsulated PS (*.eps)** from the **Save as type:** drop-down list. Then you can choose the **Save** button to accept the default setting and create the PostScript file. You can also choose the **Options** button to change the settings through the **PostScript Out Options** dialog box (Figure 17-21) and then save the file. The **PostScript Out Options** dialog box has the following options:

Figure 17-20 Create PostScript File dialog box

Figure 17-21 PostScript Out Options dialog box

Prolog Section Name

In this edit box, you can assign a name for a prolog section to be read from the acad.psf file.

What to plot

The **What to plot** area of the dialog box has the following options:

Display. If you specify this option when you are in model space, the image in the current viewport is saved in the specified EPS file. Similarly, if you are in paper space, the current view is saved in the specified EPS file.

Extents. If you use this option, the PostScript file created will contain the section of the AutoCAD drawing that currently holds objects. In this way, this option resembles the **ZOOM Extents** option. If you add objects to the drawing, they are also included in the PostScript file to be created because the extents of the drawing are also altered. If you reduce the drawing extents by erasing, moving, or scaling objects, then you must use the **ZOOM Extents** or **ZOOM All** option. Only then does the **Extents** option of the **PSOUT** command understand the extents of the drawing to be exported. If you are in model space, the PostScript file is created in relation to the model space extents; if you are in paper space, the PostScript file is created in relation to the paper space extents. If you invoke the **PSOUT** command **Extents** option when perspective view is on and the position of camera is not out of the drawing extents, the following message is displayed:

PLOT Extents incalculable, using display

In such cases, the EPS file is created as it would be created with the **Display** option.

Limits. With this option, you can export the whole area specified by the drawing limits. If the current view is not the plan view [viewpoint (0,0,1)], the **Limits** option exports the area just as the **Extents** option would.

View. Any view created with the **VIEW** command can be exported with this option. When this radio button is activated, the **View** button is available. Choose the **View** button to display the **View Name** dialog box from where you can select the view.

Window. In this option, you need to specify the area to be exported with the help of a window. When this radio button is selected, the **Window** button is also available. Choose the **Window** button to display the **Window Selection** dialog box where you can select the **Pick** button and then specify the two corners of the window on the screen. You can also enter the coordinates of the two corners in the **Window Selection** dialog box.

Preview

The **Preview** area of the dialog box has two types of formats for preview images: **EPSI** and **TIFF**. If you want a preview image with no format, select the **None** radio button. If you select **TIFF** or **EPSI**, you are required to enter the pixel resolution of the screen preview in the **Pixels** area. You can select a preview image size of 128 x 128, 256 x 256, or 512 x 512.

Size Units

In this area, you can set the paper size units to **Inches** or **Millimeters** by selecting their corresponding radio buttons.

Scale

In this area, you can set an explicit scale by specifying how many drawing units are to be output per unit. You can select the **Fit to paper** check box so that the view to be exported is made as large as possible for the specified paper size.

Paper Size

You can select a size from the list or enter a new size in the **Width** and **Height** edit boxes to specify a paper size for the exported PostScript image.

PSIN Command

Menu:	Insert > Encapsulated PostScript
Command:	PSIN

AutoCAD allows you to import PostScript files. The **PSIN** (PostScript IN) command can be used to import a PostScript file. The PostScript file is imported into an AutoCAD drawing as a block.

Command: **PSIN**

The **Select PostScript File** dialog box (Figure 17-22) is displayed.

Figure 17-22 Select PostScript File dialog box

In this dialog box, all the EPS files in the current directory are listed. Select the file you want to import into AutoCAD, and then choose the **Open** button. The dialog box is cleared from the screen, and a rectangular box is displayed. You can move this rectangular box anywhere on the screen. The next prompts ask for the insertion point and the scale factor for the rectangular box (imported image), respectively:

Specify insertion point <0,0,0>: *Specify the location for the insertion point.*
Specify scale factor: *Specify the scale factor.*

The scale factor can also be specified by dynamically dragging the box. After you specify the scale factor, whatever is in the specified EPS file is inserted into the AutoCAD screen. From the prompts associated with **PSIN** command, it is obvious that the image is inserted into the AutoCAD drawing file as a block. By default, a box appears on the screen when you import an EPS file. This box contains the imported image, which you are unable to see until you specify the insertion point and the scale factor. If you want to see the image immediately instead of the box, set the **PSDRAG** variable to 1. By default, the value of this variable is 0; that is why, by default, you get the box. The quality of the rendering of the imported PostScript file depends on the **PSQUALITY** variable.

Command: **PSQUALITY**
New value for PSQUALITY <current>:

Different settings for **PSQUALITY** and their effects are as follows:

PSQUALITY = 0. When you insert an EPS file, the rectangular box representing the imported image is displayed. The file name of the imported EPS file is displayed in this rectangular box, and the size of this box corresponds to the size of the imported file.

PSQUALITY = A Positive Value. In this case, the imported image is displayed with the **PSQUALITY** value number of pixels per AutoCAD drawing unit. In other words, this is the resolution of the imported image. By default, the value of **PSQUALITY** is 75; hence, the imported image is displayed with 75 pixels per AutoCAD drawing unit. PostScript objects are filled.

PSQUALITY = A Negative Value. In such situations, the absolute value of the **PSQUALITY** variable controls the resolution of the imported image. The difference lies in the fact that the PostScript objects are not filled, but are displayed as outlines.

PostScript Fill Patterns (PSFILL Command)

Command: PSFILL

With the **PSFILL** command, you can fill closed 2D polylines with PostScript fill patterns. These fill patterns are declared in the acad.psf file. The declarations for a PostScript fill pattern are various parameters and arguments needed to influence the definition of a fill pattern on the screen. Some of the PostScript fill patterns are:

GRAYSCALE	LINEARGRAY	RADIALGRAY	SQUARE
WAFFLE	BRICK	ZIGZAG	STARS
AILOGO	SPECKS	RGBCOLOR	

You can also define your own fill patterns in the acad.psf file with the PostScript procedures. When you assign a fill pattern to a closed polyline, the pattern is not displayed on the screen. However, the fill pattern is recognized by the **PSOUT** command. If you import the PostScript file with a fill pattern using the **PSIN** command, the fill pattern is displayed on the screen as determined by the setting of **PSQUALITY**, **PSDRAG**, and **FILL** mode. Also, if you print such a file on a PostScript device, the fill pattern is printed. Depending on the fill pattern you specify, AutoCAD issues prompts concerning various parameters and arguments needed by the fill pattern. For example, if you want to use the STARS fill pattern, the prompt sequence is:

Command: **PSFILL**
Select polyline: *Select the polyline to be filled*.

Enter postScript fill pattern name (. = none) or [?]: STARS
Enter scale <1.0000>: *Specify the scale factor for the fill pattern.*
Enter lineWidth <1>: *Specify the line width for the fill pattern.*
Enter ForegroundGray <100>: *Press ENTER.*
Enter BackgroundGray <0>: *Press ENTER.*

To view a list of patterns, enter ? at the **Enter PostScript fill pattern name (.=none) or [?]:** prompt. If you precede the pattern name with *, the polyline outline does not appear.

Example 2

Draw a rectangle, and use the **PSFILL** command to assign the waffle pattern to the rectangle [Figure 17-23(a)]. Convert the rectangle to a PostScript file by using the **PSOUT** command, and then import the PostScript file using the **PSIN** command [Figure 17-23(b)].

1. Set **PLINEWID** to 0 and use the **RECTANG** command to draw a rectangle [Figure 17-23(a)].

2. Use the **PSFILL** command to assign the waffle pattern to the rectangle.

(a)

(b)

Figure 17-23 Assigning the waffle pattern to a polyline

Command: **PSFILL**
Select polyline: *Select the rectangle.*
Enter postScript fill pattern name (. = none) or [?] <current>: Waffle
Enter scale <1.0000>: [Enter]
Enter proportion <30>: [Enter]
Enter lineWidth <1>: [Enter]
Enter UpLeftGray <100>: [Enter]
Enter BotRightGray <0>: [Enter]
Enter TopGray <0>: [Enter]

3. Use the **PSOUT** command to convert the drawing into a PostScript file. Once the **PSOUT** command is invoked, AutoCAD displays the **Create PostScript File** dialog box. In the **File Name:** edit box, enter the name of the PostScript (EPS) file you want to create (Waffle). Then choose the **Options** button. AutoCAD displays **PostScript Out Options** dialog box.

4. In the **Preview** area of the **PostScript Out Options** dialog box, choose the **EPSI** radio button; then, choose the **128** radio button in the **Pixels** area.

5. In the **Scale** area, select the **Fit to paper** check box.

6. In the **Paper Size** area, enter 7.5 in the **Width** edit box and 10.2 in the **Height** edit box.

Chapter 17

7. Select the **Window** radio button in the **What to plot** area.

8. Choose **OK** in the **PostScript Out Options** dialog box, and then choose **Save** in the **Create PostScript File** dialog box.

9. In the command line area, the following prompts are displayed to select the window.

    Specify window for export
    Specify first corner: *Specify a point close to the lower left corner of the rectangle.*
    Specify second corner: *Specify a point close to the upper right corner of the rectangle.*

10. Set **PSQUALITY** to -75 and **PSDRAG** to 0. Use the **PSIN** command to import and insert the PostScript file.

    Command: **PSIN**　　*(Select the file Waffle from the dialog box.)*
    Specify insertion point <0,0,0>: *Specify the location for the insertion point.*
    Specify scale factor: *Specify the scale factor.*

OBJECT LINKING AND EMBEDDING

With Windows, it is possible to work with different Windows-based applications by transferring information between them. You can edit and modify the information in the original Windows application, and then update this information in other applications. This is made possible by creating links between the different applications and then updating those links, which in turn updates or modifies the information in the corresponding applications. This linking is a function of the OLE feature of Microsoft Windows. The OLE feature can also join together separate pieces of information from different applications into a single document. AutoCAD and other Windows-based applications, such as Microsoft Word, Notepad, and Windows WordPad support the Windows OLE feature.

For the OLE feature, you should have a source document where the actual object is created in the form of a drawing or a document. This document is created in an application called a **server** application. AutoCAD for Windows and Paintbrush can be used as server applications. Now this source document is to be linked to (or embedded in) the **compound** (destination) document, which is created in a different application, known as the **container** application. AutoCAD for Windows, Microsoft Word, and Windows WordPad can be used as container applications.

Clipboard

The transfer of a drawing from one Windows application to another is performed by copying the drawing or the document from the server application to the Clipboard. The drawing or document is then pasted in the container application from the Clipboard; hence, a Clipboard is used as a medium for storing the documents while transferring them from one Windows application to another. The drawing or the document on the Clipboard stays there until you copy a new drawing, which overwrites the previous one, or until you exit Windows. You can save the information present on the Clipboard with the .CLP extension.

Object Embedding

You can use the embedding function of the OLE feature when you want to ensure that there is no effect on the source document even if the destination document has been changed through the server application. Once a document is embedded, it has no connection with the source. Although editing is always done in the server application, the source document remains unchanged. Embedding can be accomplished by means of the following steps. In this example, AutoCAD for Windows is the server application and Windows WordPad is the container application.

1. Create a drawing in the server application (AutoCAD).

2. Open Windows WordPad (container application) from the Accessories group in the Program.

3. It is preferable to arrange both the container and the server windows so that both are visible (Figure 17-24).

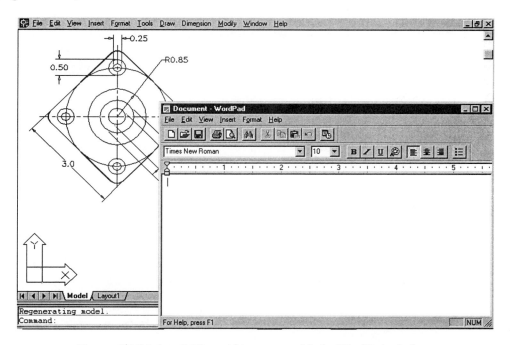

Figure 17-24 AutoCAD graphics screen with the WordPad window

4. In the AutoCAD graphics screen, use the **COPYCLIP** command. This command can be used in AutoCAD for embedding the drawings. This command can be invoked from the **Standard** toolbar by choosing the **Copy to Clipboard** button, from the **Edit** menu (Choose **Copy**), or by entering **COPYCLIP** at the command line.

Command: **COPYCLIP**

The next prompt, **Select objects:**, allows you to select the entities you want to transfer. You can either select the full drawing by entering ALL or select some of the entities by selecting them.

You can use any of the selection set options for selecting the objects. With this command the selected objects are automatically copied to the Windows Clipboard.

5. After the objects are copied to the Clipboard, make the WordPad window active. To get the drawing from the Clipboard to the WordPad application (client), select the **Paste** in the WordPad application. Choose **Paste** from the **Edit** menu in Windows WordPad (Figure 17-25). You can also use **Paste Special** from the **Edit** menu, which will display the **Paste Special** dialog box (Figure 17-26). In this dialog box, select the **Paste** radio button (default) for embedding, and then choose **OK**. The drawing is now embedded in the WordPad window.

*Figure 17-25 Pasting a drawing to the WordPad application by selecting **Paste** from the **Edit** menu*

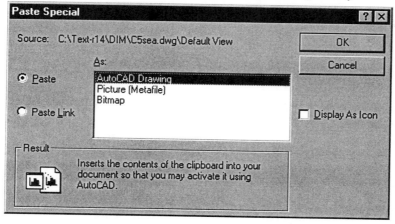

*Figure 17-26 **Paste Special** dialog box*

6.   Your drawing is now displayed in the Write window, but it may not be displayed at the proper position. You can get the drawing in the current viewport by moving the scroll button up or down in the WordPad window. You can also save your embedded drawing by choosing **Save** from the **File** menu. It displays a **Save As** dialog box where you can enter a file name. You can now exit AutoCAD.

7.   You can now edit your embedded drawing. Editing is performed in the server application, which in this case is AutoCAD for Windows. You can get the embedded drawing into the server application (AutoCAD) directly from the container application (WordPad) by double-clicking on the drawing in WordPad. The other method is by choosing **Edit Drawing Object** in the **Edit** menu. (This menu item has replaced **Object**, which was present before pasting the drawing.)

8.   Now you are in AutoCAD, with your embedded drawing displayed on the screen, but as a temporary file with a file name, such as [Drawing in Document]. Here you can edit the drawing by changing the color and linetype or by adding and deleting text, entities, and so on. In Figure 17-27 the two upper circles and their dimensions (diameter 25 and 50) have been erased, and a hexagon (diameter 50) has been drawn in its place.

9.   After you have finished modifying your drawing, choose **Update WordPad** from the **File** menu in the server (AutoCAD). This menu item has replaced the previous **Save** menu item. When you choose **Update**, AutoCAD automatically updates the drawing in Wordpad (container application). Now you can exit this temporary file in AutoCAD.

10.   This completes the embedding function so you can exit the container application. While exiting, a dialog box that asks whether or not to save changes in WordPad is displayed.

Linking Objects

The linking function of OLE is similar to the embedding function. The only difference is that here a link is created between the source document and the destination document. If you edit the source, you can simply update the link, which automatically updates the client. This allows you to place the same document in a number of applications, and if you make a change in the source document, the clients will also change by simply updating the corresponding links. Consider AutoCAD for Windows to be the server application and Windows WordPad to be the container application. Linking can be performed by means of the following.

1.   Open a drawing in the server application (AutoCAD). If you have created a new drawing, then you must save the drawing before you can link it with the container application.

2.   Open Windows WordPad (the container application) from **Accessories** in the **Program** directory.

3.   It is preferable to arrange both the container and the server windows so that both are visible.

4.   In the AutoCAD graphics screen, use the **COPYLINK** command. This command can be used in AutoCAD for linking the drawing. This command can be invoked from the **Edit** menu (Choose **Copy Link**) or by entering **COPYLINK** at the Command prompt. The prompt

Chapter 17

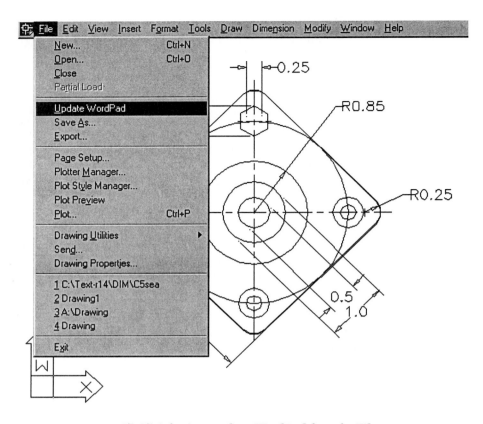

*Figure 17-27 Selecting **Update WordPad** from the **File** menu*

sequence is:

Command: **COPYLINK**

The **COPYLINK** copies the whole drawing in the current viewport directly to the Clipboard. Here you cannot select the objects for linking. If you want only a portion of the drawing to be linked, you can zoom into that view so that it is displayed in the current viewport prior to invoking the **COPYLINK** command. This command also creates a new view of the drawing having a name OLE1. Now you can exit AutoCAD.

5. Make the WordPad window active. To get the drawing from the Clipboard to the Write (container) application, choose **Paste Special** from the **Edit** menu, which will display the **Paste Special** dialog box. In this dialog box, select the **Paste Link** radio button for linking. Choose **OK**. The drawing is now linked to the WordPad window.

6. Your drawing is now displayed in the WordPad window. You can also save your linked drawing by choosing **Save** from the **File** menu. It displays a **Save As** dialog box where you can enter a file name.

7. You can now edit your linked drawing. Editing can be performed in the server application,

which in this case is AutoCAD for Windows. You can get the linked drawing in the server (AutoCAD) directly from the client (WordPad) by double-clicking on the drawing in WordPad. The other method is by choosing **Edit Linked Drawing Object** in the **Edit** menu. (This menu item has replaced **Object**, which was present before pasting the drawing.)

8. Now you are in AutoCAD, with the original drawing displayed on the screen. You can edit the drawing by changing the color and linetype or by adding and deleting text, entities, etc. Then save your drawing in AutoCAD by using the **SAVE** command. You can now exit AutoCAD.

9. You will notice that the drawing is automatically updated, and the changes made in the source drawing are present in the destination drawing also. This automatic updating is dependent on the selection of the **Automatic** radio button (default) in the **Links** dialog box (Figure 17-28). The **Links** dialog box can be invoked by choosing **Links** from the **Edit** menu. For updating manually, you can select the **Manual** radio button in the dialog box. In the manual case, after making changes in the source document and saving it, you need to invoke the **Links** dialog box and then choose the **Update Now** button; then, choose **Cancel**. This will update the drawing in the container application and display the updated drawing on the WordPad.

10. Exit the container application after saving the updated file.

Figure 17-28 Links dialog box

Linking Information into AutoCAD*

Similarly, you can also embed and link information from a server application into an AutoCAD drawing. You can also drag selected OLE objects from another application into AutoCAD, provided this application supports Microsoft Activex and the application is running and visible on the screen. Dragging and dropping is like cutting and pasting. If you press the CTRL key while you drag the object it is copied to AutoCAD. Dragging and dropping an OLE object into AutoCAD embeds it into AutoCAD.

Linking Objects into AutoCAD*

Start any server application like the Windows Wordpad and open a document in it. Select the information you wish to use in AutoCAD with your pointing device and choose **Copy** from the **Edit** menu or choose the **Copy** button in the toolbar to copy this data to the Clipboard. Open the AutoCAD drawing you wish to link this data to. Choose **Paste Special** from the **Edit** menu or use the **PASTESPEC** command. The **Paste Special** dialog box is displayed (Figure 17-29). In the **As:** list box, select the data format you wish to use. For example, for a word pad document, select **WordPad document**. Picture format uses a Metafile format. Select the **Paste Link** radio button to paste the contents of the Clipboard to the current drawing. If you select the **Paste** radio button, the data is embedded and not linked. Choose **OK** to exit the dialog box. The data is displayed in the drawing and can be positioned as needed.

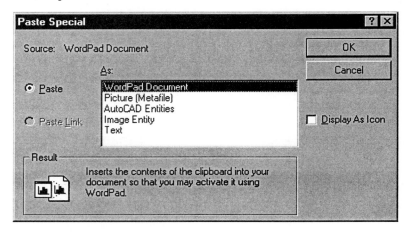

Figure 17-29 Paste Special dialog box

You can also use the **INSERTOBJ** command by entering INSERTOBJ at the Command prompt, by choosing **Ole Object...** from the **Insert** menu, or by choosing the **OLE Object** button in the **Insert** toolbar. This command links an entire file to a drawing from within AutoCAD. Using this command displays the **Insert Object** dialog box (Figure 17-30).

Select the **Create from File** radio button. Also select the **Link** check box. Choosing the **Browse** button, displays the **Browse** dialog box. Select a file you want to link from the list box or enter a name in the File name: edit box and choose the **Insert** button. The path of the file is displayed in the **File:** edit box. If you select the **Display as icon** check box, an icon is also displayed in the dialog box. Choose **OK** to exit the dialog box, the selected file is linked to the AutoCAD drawing.

AutoCAD updates the links automatically by default, whenever the server document changes, but you can use the **OLELINKS** command to display the **Links** dialog box (Figure 17-31) where you can change these settings. This dialog box can also be displayed by choosing **OLE Links...** from the **Edit** menu. In the **Links** dialog box, select the link you want to update and then choose the **Update Now** button. Then choose the **Close** button. If the server file location changes or if it is renamed, you can choose the **Change Source** button in the **Links** dialog box to display the **Change Source** dialog box. In this dialog box, locate the server file name and location and choose the **Open** button. You can also choose the **Break Link** button in the **Links** dialog box to disconnect

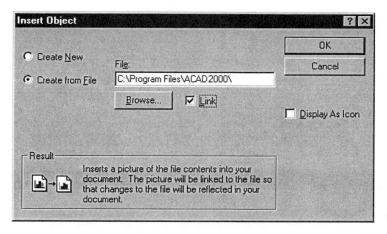

Figure 17-30 Insert Object dialog box

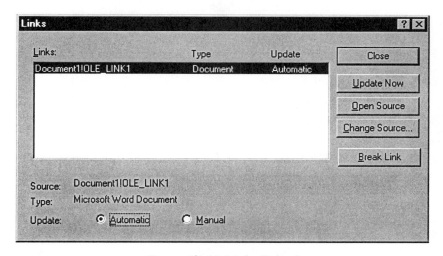

Figure 17-31 Links dialog box

the inserted information from the server application. This is done when the linking between the two is not required anymore.

Embedding Objects into AutoCAD*

Open the server application and select the data you want to embed into the AutoCAD drawing. Copy this data to the Clipboard by choosing the **Copy** button in the toolbar or choosing **Copy** from the **Edit** menu. Open the AutoCAD drawing and choose **Paste** from the AutoCAD **Edit** menu. You can also use the command **PASTECLIP**. The selected information is embedded into the AutoCAD drawing.

You can also create and embed an object into an AutoCAD drawing starting from AutoCAD itself using the **INSETOBJ** command. You can also choose **OLE Object** from the **Insert** menu or choose the **OLE Object** button from the **Insert** toolbar. The **Insert Object** dialog box is displayed

(Figure 17-32). In this dialog box, select the **Create New** radio button and select the application you wish to use from the **Object Type:** list box. Choose **OK**. The selected application opens, now, you can create the information you wish to insert in the AutoCAD drawing and save it before closing the application. The **OLE Properties** dialog box is displayed (Figure 17-33) where you can resize and rescale the inserted objects. This dialog is displayed by default. If you do not want to display this dialog box, clear the **Display dialog when pasting OLE objects** check box in the **OLE Properties** dialog box. You can also clear the **Display OLE Properties Dialog** check box in the **Systems** tab of the **Options** dialog box. You can edit information embedded in the AutoCAD drawing by opening the server application by double clicking on the inserted OLE object. You can also select the object and right-click to display a shortcut menu. Choose **Object > Edit**. After editing the data in the server application, choose **Update** from the **File** menu to reflect the modifications in the AutoCAD drawing.

Figure 17-32 Insert Object dialog box

Working with OLE Objects*

Select an OLE Object and right-click to display a shortcut menu; choose **Properties**. The **OLE Properties** dialog box is displayed (Figure 17-33). You can also select the OLE Object and use the **OLESCALE*** command. Specify a new height and a new width in the **Height:** and **Width:** edit boxes in the **Size** area or Under **Scale**, enter a value in percentage of the current values in the **Height:** and **Width:** edit boxes. Here, if you select the **Lock aspect Ratio** check box, whenever you change either the height or the width under **Scale** or **Size**, the respective width or height changes automatically to maintain the aspect ratio. If you want to change only the height or only the Width, clear this check box. Choose **OK** to apply changes.

Choosing the **Reset** button restores the selected OLE objects to their original size, that is, the size they were when inserted. If the AutoCAD drawing contains an OLE object with text with different fonts and you wish to select and modify specific text. You can select a particular font and point size from the drop-down lists under the **Text size** area and enter in the box after the = sign the value in drawing units. For example if you wish to select text in the Times Roman font, of point size 10 and modify it to size 0.5 drawing units, select Times Roman and 10 point size from the drop-down lists and in the text box after the = sign enter .5. All the text which is in Times Roman and is of

Figure 17-33 OLE Properties dialog box

point size 10 will change to 0.5 drawing units in height.

The pointing device can also be used to modify and scale an OLE Object in the AutoCAD drawing. Selecting the object displays the object frame and the move cursor. The move cursor allows you to select and drag the object to a new location. The middle handle allows you to select the frame and stretch it. It does not scale objects proportionately. The corner handle scales the object proportionately.

Select an OLE object and right-click to display the shortcut menu. Choosing **Cut** removes the object from the drawing and pastes it on the Clipboard, **Copy** places a copy of the selected object on the clipboard; and **Clear** removes the object from the drawing and does not place it on the clipboard. Choosing **Object** displays the **Convert, Open**, and **Edit** options. Choosing **Convert**, displays the **Convert** dialog box where you can convert objects from one type to another and **Edit** opens the object in the Server application where you can edit it and update it in the current drawing. **Undo** cancels the last action. **Bring to Front** and **Send to Back** options, place the OLE objects in the front of or back of the AutoCAD objects. The **Selectable** option, turns the selection of the OLE object on or off. If the **Selectable** option is on, the object frame is visible and the object is selected.

If you want to change the layer of an OLE object, select the object and right-click to display the shortcut menu, choose **Cut**. The selected object is placed on the clipboard. Change the current layer to the one you want to change the OLE object's layer to using the **Layer Properties Manager** dialog box. Now, choose **Paste** from the **Edit** menu to paste the contents of the clipboard in the AutoCAD drawing. The OLE object is pasted in the New layer, in its original size.

The **OLEHIDE** system variable controls the display of OLE objects in AutoCAD. The default value is 0, that is, all the OLE objects are visible. The different values and their effects are as follows:

0   All OLE objects are visible
1   OLE objects are visible in paper space only
2   OLE objects are visible in model space only
3   No OLE objects are visible

The **OLEHIDE** system variable affects both screen display and printing.

Self-Evaluation Test

Answer the following questions, and then compare your answers to the answers given at the end of this chapter.

1. The object whose area you want to find with the help of the **AREA** command must be a closed object. (T/F)

2. If you quit the editing session without saving the drawing, the time you spent on that editing session is added to the total time spent on editing the drawing. Also, the last update time is revised. (T/F)

3. The angle between two points can be measured with the help of the _____ command.

4. The _____ command displays all the information pertaining to the selected objects.

5. _____ time provides the most recent date and time you edited the current drawing.

6. You can set the automatic save time interval with the **Options** dialog box or with the _____ system variable.

7. You can import a DXF file into an AutoCAD drawing file with the _____ command.

8. The _____ command is used to create drawing files out of DXB format files.

9. If you import a DXB file into an old drawing, the settings of layers, blocks, and so on, of the file being imported are _____ by the settings of the file into which you are importing the DXB file.

10. A block can be imported into a drawing file only if the block definition exists in the _____ drawing file.

11. The _____ system variable holds the value of distance computed.

12. The _____ command is used to identify the coordinate values of a point on the screen.

13. If you import a PostScript file with a fill pattern using the **PSIN** command, the fill pattern is not displayed on the screen. (T/F)

14. The _____ command displays all the information pertaining to all the objects in the drawing.

15. The _____ is used as a medium for storing the documents while transferring them from one Windows application to another.

16. The _____ command can be used in AutoCAD for embedding drawings.

17. You can edit your embedded drawing in the _____ application.

18. You can get an embedded drawing into the server application directly from the container application by _____ on the drawing.

19. The _____ command can be used in AutoCAD for linking a drawing.

20. The **COPYLINK** command copies a drawing in the _____ to the Clipboard.

Review Questions

Inquiry

1. Inquiry commands are used to obtain information about the drawn figures. (T/F)

2. The default method of specifying the object whose area you want to find is by specifying all the vertices of the object. (T/F)

3. The **AREA** and **PERIMETER** system variables are reset to zero whenever you invoke the **AREA** command. (T/F)

4. To find the circumference or perimeter of an object, you can use the _____ command.

5. You can use the _____ option to add subsequently measured areas to the running total.

6. You can use the _____ option to subtract subsequently measured areas from the running total.

7. The distance between two points can be measured with the _____ command.

8. The _____ command can be used to display the data pertaining to time related to a drawing and the drawing session.

9. Drawing _____ provides the date and time the current drawing was created.

10. The drawing creation time for a drawing is set to the system time when either the _____ command, the _____ command, or the _____ command was used to create that drawing file.

Data Exchange

11. The _____ command is used to create an ASCII format file with the .DXF extension from AutoCAD drawing files.

12. With the **Binary** option of the **Save As Options** dialog box, you can also create binary format files. Binary DXF files are _____ efficient and occupy only 75 percent of the ASCII DXF file. File access for files in binary format is _____ than for the same file in ASCII format.

13. In a _____ file, information is stored in the form of a dot pattern on the screen. This bit pattern is also known as _____ .

14. If there is a picture on the screen that you want to save as a raster file, use the _____ command.

15. With the **SAVEIMG** command you can create _____ , _____ , or _____ type of raster files from the current drawing.

16. The section of screen to be saved can be specified by specifying _____ on the image tile.

17. If you are rendering to a viewport and you select the _____ option, then whatever is in the current viewport is saved to the raster file of the selected format.

18. If you are rendering to a viewport and you select the _____ option, the entire screen, including the menu area and the command line area, is saved to the raster file.

Exercises

Exercise 3   *Mechanical*

Draw Figure 17-34 without dimensions, and determine the indicated parameters using the required commands. Select the **DBLIST** command. Select **TIME**, and note the time in the drawing editor. Save the drawing.

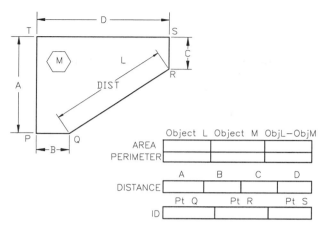

	Object L	Object M	ObjL−ObjM
AREA			
PERIMETER			

	A	B	C	D
DISTANCE				

	Pt Q	Pt R	Pt S
ID			

Figure 17-34 Drawing for Exercise 3

Exercise 4   *Graphics*

Draw two rectangles, and use the **PSFILL** command to assign stars and brick patterns to these rectangles (Figure 17-35). Convert the rectangles to the PostScript file using the **PSOUT** command, and then import the PostScript file using the **PSIN** command.

Figure 17-35 Drawing for Exercise 4

Answers to Self-Evaluation Test
1 - F, 2 - F, 3 - **DIST**, 4 - **LIST**, 5 - Last Update, 6 - **SAVETIME**, 7 - **OPEN**, 8 - **DXBIN**, 9 - overruled, 10 - importing, 11 - **DISTANCE**, 12 - **ID**, 13 - F, 14 - **DBLIST**, 15 - clipboard, 16 - **COPYCLIP**, 17 - server, 18 - double-clicking, 19 - **COPYLINK**, 20 - current viewport

Chapter 18

Technical Drawing with AutoCAD

Learning Objectives

After completing this chapter, you will be able to:
- *Understand the concepts of multiview drawings.*
- *Understand X, Y, Z axes; XY, YZ, XZ planes; and parallel planes.*
- *Draw orthographic projections and position the views.*
- *Dimension a drawing.*
- *Understand the basic dimensioning rules.*
- *Draw sectional views using different types of sections.*
- *Hatch sectioned surfaces.*
- *Understand how to use auxiliary views and how to draw them.*
- *Create assembly and detail drawings.*

MULTIVIEW DRAWINGS

When designers design a product, they visualize the shape of the product in their minds. To represent that shape on paper or to communicate the idea to other people, they must draw a picture of the product or its orthographic views. Pictorial drawings, such as isometric drawings, convey the shape of the object, but it is difficult to show all of its features and dimensions in an isometric drawing. Therefore, in industry, multiview drawings are the accepted standard for representing products. Multiview drawings are also known as **orthographic projection drawings**. To draw different views of an object, it is very important to visualize the shape of the product. The same is true when you are looking at different views of an object to determine its shape. To facilitate visualizing the shapes, you must picture the object in 3D space with reference to the X, Y, and Z axes. These reference axes can then be used to project the image into different planes. This process of visualizing objects with reference to different axes is, to some extent, natural in human beings. You might have noticed that sometimes when looking at objects that are at an angle, people tilt their heads. This is a natural reaction, an effort to position the object with respect to an imaginary reference frame (X, Y, Z axes).

UNDERSTANDING X, Y, Z AXES

To understand the X, Y, and Z axes, imagine a flat sheet of paper on the table. The horizontal edge represents the positive X axis and the other edge, the edge along the width of the sheet, represents the positive Y axis. The point where these two axes intersect is the origin. Now, if you draw a line perpendicular to the sheet passing through the origin, the line defines the positive Z axis (Figure 18-1). If you project the X, Y, and Z axes in the opposite direction beyond the origin, you will get the negative X, Y, and Z axes (Figure 18-2).

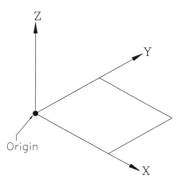

Figure 18-1 X, Y, Z axes

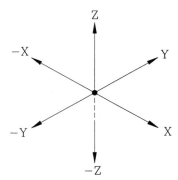

Figure 18-2 Positive and negative axes

The space between the X and Y axes is called the XY plane. Similarly, the space between the Y and Z axes is called the YZ plane, and the space between the X and Z axes is called the XZ plane (Figure 18-3). A plane that is parallel to these planes is called a parallel plane (Figure 18-4).

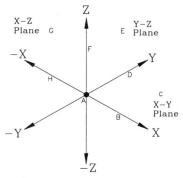

Figure 18-3 XY, YZ, and XZ planes

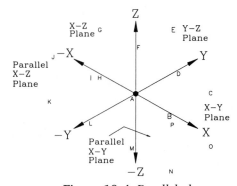

Figure 18-4 Parallel planes

ORTHOGRAPHIC PROJECTIONS

The first step in drawing an orthographic projection is to position the object along the imaginary X, Y, and Z axes. For example, if you want to draw orthographic projections of the step block shown in Figure 18-5, position the block so that the far left corner coincides with the origin, and then align the block with the X, Y, and Z axes.

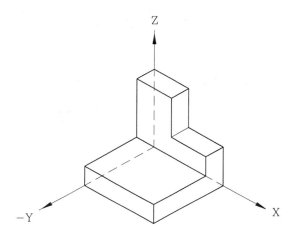

Figure 18-5 *Aligning the object with the X, Y, and Z axes*

Now you can look at the object from different directions. Looking at the object along the negative Y axis and toward the origin is called the front view. Similarly, looking at the object from the positive X direction is called the right-hand side view. To get the top view, you look at the object from the positive Z axis. See Figure 18-6.

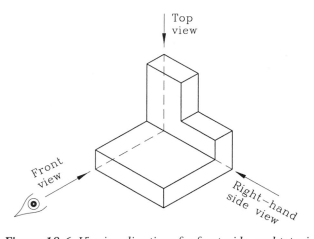

Figure 18-6 *Viewing directions for front, side, and top views*

To draw the front, side, and top views, project the points onto the parallel planes. For example, if you want to draw the front view of the step block, imagine a plane parallel to the XZ plane located at a certain distance in front of the object. Now, project the points from the object onto the parallel plane (Figure 18-7), and join the points to complete the front view.

Note

You can construct a 3D model of this object by using the layout given on the last page of this chapter. Cut the layout along the solid lines, and then fold along the hidden lines.

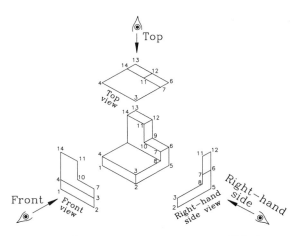

Figure18-7 *Projecting points onto parallel planes*

Repeat the same process for the side and top views. To represent these views on paper, position the views as shown Figure 18-8.

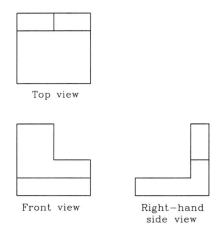

Top view

Front view   Right−hand
                    side view

Figure 18-8 *Representing views on paper*

Another way of visualizing different views is to imagine the object enclosed in a glass box (Figure 18-9).

Now, look at the object along the negative Y axis and draw the front view on the front glass panel. Repeat the process by looking along the positive X and Z axes, and draw the views on the right-hand side and the top panel of the box (Figure 18-10).

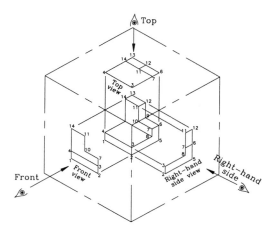

Figure 18-9 *Objects inside a glass box*

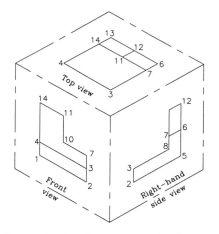

Figure 18-10 *Front, top, and side views*

To represent the front, side, and top views on paper, open the side and the top panel of the glass box (Figure 18-11). The front panel is assumed to be stationary.

After opening the panels through 90 degrees, the orthographic views will appear as shown in Figure 18-12.

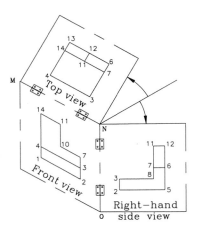

Figure 18-11 *Open the side and the top panel*

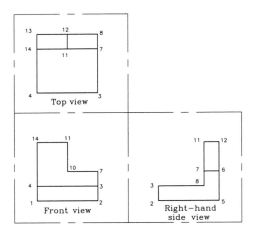

Figure 18-12 *Views after opening the box*

POSITIONING ORTHOGRAPHIC VIEWS

Orthographic views must be positioned as shown in Figure 18-13.

The right-hand side view must be positioned directly on the right side of the front view. Similarly, the top view must be directly above the front view. If the object requires additional views, they must be positioned as shown in Figure 18-14.

The different views of the step block are shown in Figure 18-15.

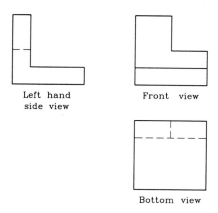

Figure 18-13 *Positioning orthographic views*

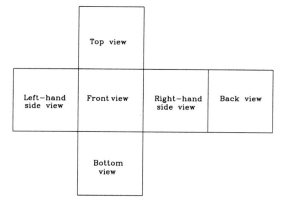

Figure 18-14 *Standard placement of orthographic views*

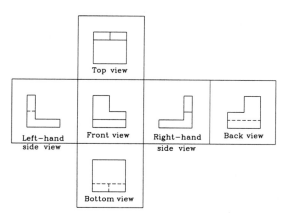

Figure 18-15 *Different views of the step block*

Chapter 18

Example 1

In this example, you will draw the required orthographic views of the object in Figure 18-16.

Figure 18-16 *Step block with hole and slot*

Drawing the orthographic views of an object involves the following steps.

Step 1. Look at the object, and determine the number of views required to show all of its features. For example, the object in Figure 18-16 will require three views only (front, side, and top).

Step 2. Based on the shape of the object, select the side you want to show as the front view. Generally the front view is the one that shows the maximum number of features or that gives a better idea about the shape of the object. Sometimes the front view is determined by how the part will be assembled in an assembly.

Step 3. Picture the object in your mind, and align it along the imaginary X, Y, Z axes (Figure 18-17).

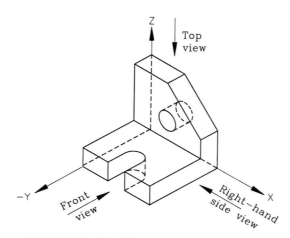

Figure 18-17 *Align the object with the imaginary X, Y, Z axes*

Step 4. Look at the object along the negative Y axis, and project the image on the imaginary XZ parallel plane, Figure 18-18.

Figure 18-18 Project the image onto the parallel planes

Step 5. Draw the front view of the object according to the given dimensions. If there are any hidden features, they must be drawn with hidden lines. The holes and slots must be shown with the centerlines.

Step 6. To draw the right-hand side view, look at the object along the positive X axis and project the image onto the imaginary YZ parallel plane.

Step 7. Draw the right-hand side view of the object according to the given dimensions. If there are any hidden features, they must be drawn with hidden lines. The holes and slots, when shown in side view, must have one centerline.

Step 8. Similarly, draw the top view to complete the drawing. Figure 18-19 shows different views of the given object.

Figure 18-19 Front, side, and top views

Chapter 18

Exercises 1 through 4   *Mechanial*

Draw the required orthographic views of the following objects in Figures 18-20 through 18-23. The distance between the dotted lines is 0.5 units.

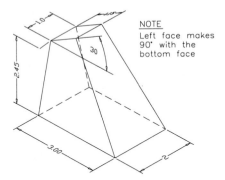

Figure 18-20 *Drawing for Exercise 1 (the object is shown as a surfaced wireframe model)*

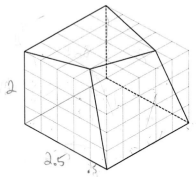

Figure 18-21 *Drawing for Exercise 2*

Figure 18-22 *Drawing for Exercise 3*

Figure 18-23 *Drawing for Exercise 4*

DIMENSIONING

Dimensioning is one of the most important things in a drawing. When you dimension, you not only give the size of a part, you give a series of instructions to a machinist, an engineer, or an architect. The way the part is positioned in a machine, the sequence of machining operations, and the location of different features of the part depend on how you dimension it. For example, the number of decimal places in a dimension (2.000) determines the type of machine that will be used to do that machining operation. The machining cost of such an operation is significantly higher than a dimension that has only one digit after the decimal (2.0). If you are using a computer numerical control (CNC) machine, locating a feature may not be a problem, but the number of pieces you can machine without changing the tool depends on the tolerance assigned to a dimension. A closer tolerance (+.0001 -.0005) will definitely increase the tooling cost and ultimately the cost of the product. Similarly, if a part is to be forged or cast, the radius of the edges and the tolerance you provide to these dimensions determine the cost of the product, the number of defective parts, and the number of parts you get from the die.

When dimensioning, you must consider the manufacturing process involved in making a part and the relationships that exist among different parts in an assembly. If you are not familiar with any operation, get help. You must not assume things when dimensioning or making a piece part drawing. The success of a product, to a large extent, depends on the way you dimension a part. Therefore, never underestimate the importance of dimensioning in a drawing.

Dimensioning Components

A dimension consists of the following components (Figure 18-24):

Extension line
Arrows or tick marks
Dimension line
Leader lines
Dimension text

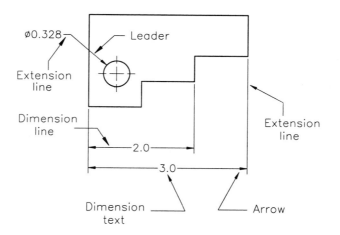

Figure 18-24 Dimensioning components

The **extension lines** are drawn to extend the points that are dimensioned. The length of the extension lines is determined by the number of dimensions and the placement of the dimension lines. These lines are generally drawn perpendicular to the surface. The **dimension lines** are drawn between the extension lines, at a specified distance from the object lines. The **dimension text** is a numerical value that represents the distance between the points. The dimension text can also consist of a variable (A, B, X, Y, Z12,...), in which case the value assigned to the variable is defined in a separate table. The dimension text can be centered around the dimension line or at the top of the dimension line. **Arrows or tick marks** are drawn at the end of the dimension line to indicate the start and end of the dimension. **Leader lines** are used when dimensioning a circle, arc, or any nonlinear element of a drawing. They are also used to attach a note to a feature or to give the part numbers in an assembly drawing.

Basic Dimensioning Rules

1. You should make the dimensions in a separate layer/layers. This makes it easy to edit or control the display of dimensions (freeze, thaw, lock, unlock). Also, the dimension layer/layers should be assigned a unique color so that at the time of plotting you can assign the desired pen to plot the dimensions. This helps to control the line width and contrast of dimensions at the time of plotting.

2. The distance of the first dimension line should at least 0.375 units (10 units for metric drawing) from the object line. In CAD drawing, this distance may be 0.75 to 1.0 units (19 to 25 units for metric drawings). Once you decide on the spacing, it should be maintained throughout the drawing.

3. The distance between the first dimension line and the second dimension line must be at least 0.25 units. In CAD drawings, this distance may be 0.25 to 0.5 units (6 to 12 units for metric drawings). If there are more dimension lines (parallel dimensions), the distances between them must be same (0.25 to 0.5 units). Once you decide on the spacing (0.25 to 0.5), the same spacing should be maintained throughout the drawing. An appropriate snap setting is useful for maintaining this spacing. If you are using baseline dimensioning, you can use AutoCAD's **DIMDLI** variable to set the spacing. You must present the dimensions so that they are not crowded, especially when there is not much space (Figure 18-25).

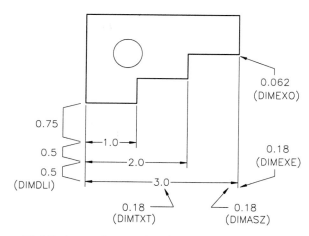

Figure 18-25 *Arrow size, text height, and spacing between dimension lines*

4. For parallel dimension lines, the dimension text can be staggered if there is not enough room between the dimension lines to place the dimension text. You can use the AutoCAD Object Grips feature or the **DIMTEDIT** command to stagger the dimension text (Figure 18-26).

Note
You can change grid, snap or UCS origin, and snap increment to make it easier to place the dimensions. You can also add the following lines to the AutoCAD menu file or toolbar buttons:

SNAP;R;\0;SNAP;0.25;GRID;0.25
SNAP;R;0,0;0;SNAP;0.25;GRID;0.5

The first line sets the snap to 0.25 units and allows the user to define the new origin of snap and grid display. The second line sets the grid to 0.5 and snap to 0.25 units. It also sets the origin for grid and snap to (0,0).

5. All dimensions should be given outside the view. However, the dimensions can be shown inside the view if they can be easily understood there and cause no confusion with other dimensions (Figure 18-27).

Figure 18-26 *Staggered dimensions*

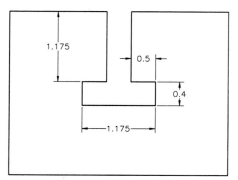

Figure 18-27 *Dimensions inside the view*

6. Dimension lines should not cross extension lines (Figure 18-28). You can accomplish this by giving the smallest dimension first and then the next largest dimension (Figure 18-29).

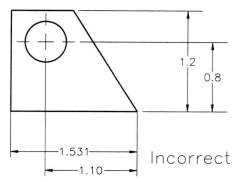

Figure 18-28 *Dimension lines should not cross extension lines*

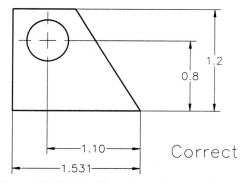

Figure 18-29 *Smallest dimension must be given first*

7. If you decide to have the dimension text aligned with the dimension line, then all dimension text in the drawing must be aligned (Figure 18-30). Similarly, if you decide to have the dimension text horizontal or above the dimension line, then to maintain uniformity in the drawing, all dimension text must be horizontal (Figure 18-31) or above the dimension line (Figure 18-32).

Chapter 18

Figure 18-30 Dimension text aligned

Figure 18-31 Dimension text horizontal

Figure 18-32 Dimension text above dimension line

8. If you have a series of continuous dimensions, they should be placed in a continuous line (Figure 18-33). Sometimes you may not be able to give the dimensions in a continuous line even after adjusting the dimension variables. In that case, give dimensions that are parallel (Figure 18-34).

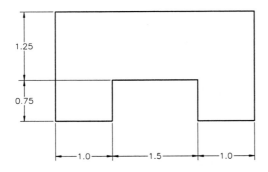

Figure 18-33 Dimensions should be continuous

Figure 18-34 Parallel dimensions

9. You should not dimension with hidden lines. The dimension must be given where the feature is visible (Figure 18-35). However, in some complicated drawings you might be justified to dimension a detail with a hidden line.

10. The dimensions must be given where the feature that you are dimensioning is obvious and shows the contour of the feature (Figure 18-36).

Figure 18-35 Do not dimension with hidden lines

Figure 18-36 Dimensions should be given where they are obvious

11. The dimensions must not be repeated; this makes it difficult to update a dimension, and sometimes the dimensions might get confusing (Figure 18-37).

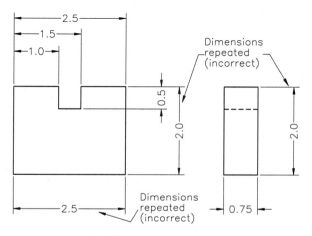

Figure 18-37 Dimension must not be repeated

12. The dimensions must be given depending on how the part will be machined and the relationship that exists between different features of the part (Figure 18-38).

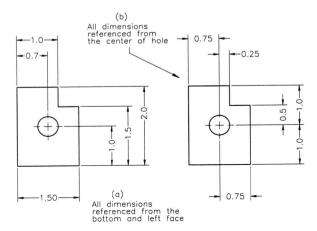

Figure 18-38 *When dimensioning, consider the machining processes involved*

13. When a dimension is not required but you want to give it for reference, it must be a reference dimension. The reference dimension must be enclosed in parentheses (Figure 18-39).

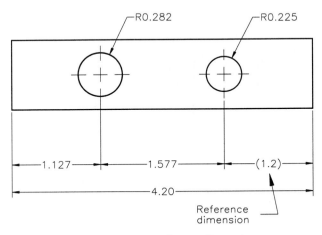

Figure 18-39 *Reference dimensions*

14. If you give continuous (incremental) dimensions for dimensioning various features of a part, the overall dimension must be omitted or given as a reference dimension (Figure 18-40). Similarly, if you give the overall dimension, one of the continuous (incremental) dimensions must be omitted or given as a reference dimension. Otherwise, there will be a conflict in tolerances. For example, the total positive tolerance on the three incremental dimensions shown in Figure 18-40 is 0.06. Therefore, the maximum size based on the incremental dimen-

sions is (1 + 0.02) + (1 + 0.02) + (1 + 0.02) = 3.06. Also, the positive tolerance on the overall 3.0 dimension is 0.02. Based on this dimension, the overall size of the part must not exceed 3.02. This causes a conflict in tolerances: with incremental dimensions, the total tolerance is 0.06, whereas with the overall dimension the total tolerance is only 0.02.

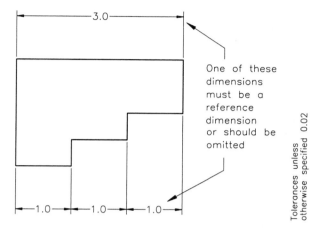

Figure 18-40 Referencing or omitting a dimension

15. If the dimension of a feature appears in a section view, you must not hatch the dimension text (Figure 18-41). You can accomplish it by selecting the dimension object when defining the hatch boundary. You can also accomplish this by drawing a rectangle around the dimension text and then hatching the area after excluding the rectangle from the hatch boundary. (You can also use the **EXPLODE** command to explode the dimension and then exclude the dimension text from hatching. This is not recommended because by exploding a dimension the associativity of the selected dimension is lost.)

Figure 18-41 Dimension text should not be hatched

16. When dimensioning a circle, the diameter should be preceded by the diameter symbol (Figure 18-42). AutoCAD automatically puts the diameter symbol in front of the diameter value. However, if you override the default diameter value, you can use %%c followed by the value of the diameter (%%c1.25) to put the diameter symbol in front of the diameter dimension.

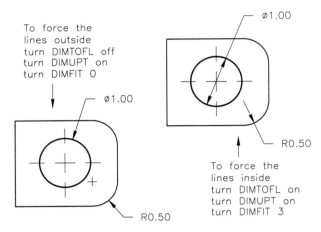

Figure 18-42 *Diameter should be preceded by the diameter symbol*

17. The circle must be dimensioned as a diameter, never as a radius. The dimension of an arc must be preceded by the abbreviation R (R1.25), and the center of the arc should be indicated by drawing a small cross. You can use the AutoCAD **DIMCEN** variable to control the size of the cross. If the value of this variable is 0, AutoCAD does not draw the cross in the center when you dimension an arc or a circle. You can also use the **DIMCENTER** command or the **CENTER** option of the **DIM** command to draw a cross at the center of the arc or circle.

18. When dimensioning an arc or a circle, the dimension line (leader) must be radial. Also, you should place the dimension text horizontally (Figure 18-43).

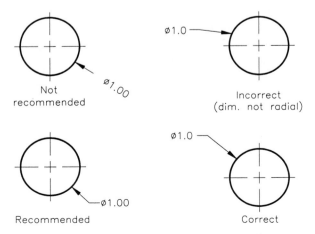

Figure 18-43 *Dimensioning a circle*

19. A chamfer can be dimensioned by specifying the chamfer angle and the distance of the chamfer from the edge. A chamfer can also be dimensioned by specifying the distances as shown in Figure 18-44.

Figure 18-44 Different ways of specifying chamfer

20. A dimension that is not to scale should be indicated by drawing a straight line under the dimension text (Figure 18-45). You can draw this line by using the **DDEDIT** command. When you invoke this command, AutoCAD will prompt you to select an annotation object. When you select the object, the **Multiline Text Editor** dialog box is displayed. Select the text (< >), and then choose the **U** (underline) button.

21. A bolt circle should be dimensioned by specifying the diameter of the bolt circle, the diameter of the holes, and the number of holes in the bolt circle (Figure 18-46).

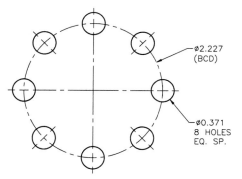

Figure 18-45 Specifying dimensions that are not to scale

Figure 18-46 Dimensioning a bolt circle

Exercises 5 through 10   *Mechanical*

Draw the required orthographic views of the following objects, and then give the dimensions (refer to Figures 18-47 through 18-52). The distance between the grid lines is 0.5 units.

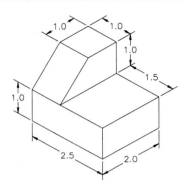

Figure 18-47 Drawing for Exercise 5

Figure 18-48 Drawing for Exercise 6

Figure 18-49 Drawing for Exercise 7

Figure 18-50 Drawing for Exercise 8

Figure 18-51 Drawing for Exercise 9

Figure 18-52 Drawing for Exercise 10(assume the missing dimensions)

SECTIONAL VIEWS

In the principal orthographic views, the hidden features are generally shown by hidden lines. In some objects, the hidden lines may not be sufficient to represent the actual shape of the hidden feature. In such situations, sectional views can be used to show the features of the object that are not visible from outside. The location of the section and the direction of sight depend on the shape of the object and the features that need to be shown. Several ways to cut a section in the object are discussed next.

Full Section

Figure 18-53 shows an object that has a drilled hole, a counterbore, and a taper. In the orthographic views, these features will be shown by hidden lines (Figure 18-54).

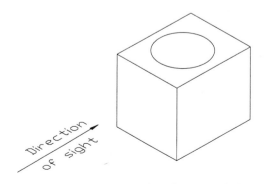

Figure 18-53 Rectangular object with hole

Figure 18-54 Front view without section

To better represent the hidden features, the object must be cut so the hidden features are visible.

In the **full section**, the object is cut along the entire length of the object. To get a better idea of a full section, imagine that the object is cut into two halves along the centerline, as shown in Figure 18-55. Now remove the left half of the object and look at the right half in the direction that is perpendicular to the sectioned surface. The view you get after cutting the section is called a **full section** view (Figure 18-56).

Figure 18-55 *One half of the object removed*

Figure 18-56 *Front view in full section*

In this section view, the features that would be hidden in a normal orthographic view are visible. Also, the part of the object where the material is actually cut is indicated by section lines. If the material is not cut, the section lines are not drawn. For example, if there is a hole, no material is cut when the part is sectioned, and so the section lines must not be drawn through that area of the section view.

Half Section

If the object is symmetrical, it is not necessary to draw a full section view. For example, in Figure 18-58 the object is symmetrical with respect to the centerline of the hole, so a full section is not required. Also, in some objects it may help to understand and visualize the shape of the hidden details better to draw the view in half section. In half section, one quarter of the object is cut, as shown in Figure 18-57. To draw the view in half section, imagine one quarter of the object removed, and then look in the direction that is perpendicular to the sectioned surface.

Figure 18-57 *One quarter of the object removed*

Figure 18-58 *Front view in half section*

You can also show the front view with a solid line in the middle, as in Figure 18-59. Sometimes the hidden lines representing the remaining part of the hidden feature are not drawn, as in Figure 18-60.

Figure 18-59 Front view in half section

Figure 18-60 Front view in half section

Broken Section

In the **broken section**, only a small portion of the object is cut to expose the features that need to be drawn in section. The broken section is designated by drawing a thick zigzag line in the section view (Figure 18-61).

Revolved Section

The **revolved section** is used to show the true shape of the object at the point where the section is cut. The revolved section is used when it is not possible to show the features clearly in

Figure 18-61 Front view with broken section

any principal view. For example, for the object in Figure 18-62, it is not possible to show the actual shape of the middle section in the front, side, or top view. Therefore, a revolved section is required to show the shape of the middle section.

The revolved section involves cutting an imaginary section through the object and then looking at the sectioned surface in a direction that is perpendicular to it. To represent the shape, the view is revolved 90 degrees and drawn in the plane of the paper, as shown Figure 18-62. Depending on the shape of the object, and for clarity, it is recommended to provide a break in the object so that the object lines do not interfere with the revolved section.

Removed Section

The **removed section** is similar to the revolved section, except that it is shown outside the object. The removed section is recommended when there is not enough space in the view to show the revolved section or if the scale of the section is different from the parent object. The removed section can be shown by drawing a line through the object at the point where the revolved section is desired and then drawing the shape of the section, as in Figure 18-63.

Figure 18-62 Front view with revolved section

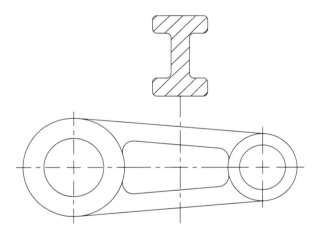

Figure 18-63 Front view with removed section

The other way of showing a removed section is to draw a cutting plane line through the object where you want to cut the section. The arrows should point in the direction in which you are looking at the sectioned surface. The section can then be drawn at a convenient place in the drawing. The removed section must be labeled as shown in Figure 18-64. If the scale has been changed, it must be mentioned with the view description.

Offset Section

The **offset section** is used when the features of the object that you want to section are not in one plane. The offset section is designated by drawing a cutting plane line that is offset through the center of the features that need to be shown in section (Figure 18-65). The arrows indicate the direction in which the section is viewed.

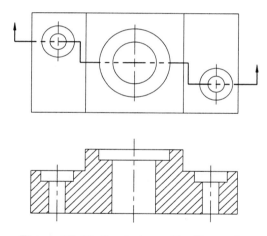

Figure 18-64 *Front view with removed section*

Figure 18-65 *Front view with offset section*

Aligned Section

In some objects, cutting a straight section might cause confusion in visualizing the shape of the section. Therefore, the aligned section is used to represent the shape along the cutting plane (Figure 18-66). Such sections are widely used in circular objects that have spokes, ribs, or holes.

Cutting Plane Lines

Cutting plane lines are thicker than object lines (Figure 18-67). You can use the **PLINE** command to draw the polylines of desired width, generally 0.005 to 0.01. However, for drawings that need to be plotted, you should assign a unique color to the cutting plane lines and then assign that color to the slot of the plotter that carries a pen of the required tip width. (For details, see Chapter 15, Plotting Drawings and Draw Commands.)

Figure 18-66 *Side view in section (aligned section)*

Figure 18-67 *Cutting plane line*

In industry, generally three types of lines are used to show the cutting plane for sectioning. The first line consists of a series of dashes 0.25 units long. The second type consists of a series of long dashes separated by two short dashes (Figure 18-68). The length of the long dash can vary from 0.75 to 1.5 units, and the short dashes are about 0.12 units long. The space between the dashes should be about 0.03 units.

Sometimes the cutting plane lines might clutter the drawing or cause confusion with other lines in the drawing. To avoid this problem, you can show the cutting plane by drawing a short line at the end of the section (Figures 18-68 and 18-69). The line should be about 0.5 units long.

Figure 18-68 Cutting plane lines

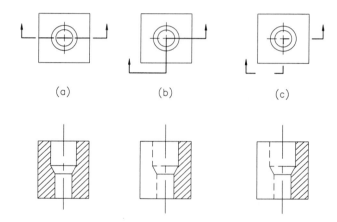

Figure 18-69 Application of cutting plane lines

Note

*In AutoCAD, you can define a new linetype that you can use to draw the cutting plane lines. See Chapter 30, Creating Linetypes and Hatching Patterns, for more information on defining linetypes. Add the following lines to the **ACAD.LIN** file, and then load the linetypes before assigning it to an object or a layer:*

*CPLANE1,___ ___ ___ ___
A,0.25,-0.03
*CPLANE2,___ ___ ___ ___
A,1.0,-0.03,0.12,-0.03,0.12,-0.03

Spacing for Hatch Lines

The spacing between the hatch (section) lines is determined by the space that is being hatched (Figure 18-70). If the hatch area is small, the spacing between the hatch lines should be smaller compared with a large hatch area.

In AutoCAD, you can control the spacing between the hatch lines by specifying the **scale factor** at the time of hatching. If the scale factor is 1, the spacing between the hatch lines is the same as defined in the hatch pattern file for that particular hatch. For example, in the following hatch pattern definition, the distance between the lines is 0.125:

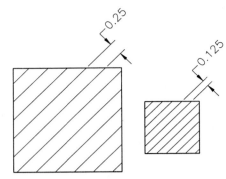

Figure 18-70 Hatch line spacing

> ***ANSI31, ANSI Iron, Brick, Stone masonry**
> **45, 0, 0, 0, .125**

When the hatch scale factor is 1, the line spacing will be 0.125; if the scale factor is 2, the spacing between the lines will be 0.125 x 2 = 0.25.

Direction of Hatch Lines

The angle for the hatch lines should be 45 degrees. However, if there are two or more hatch areas next to one another representing different parts, the hatch angle must be changed so that the hatched areas look different (Figure 18-71).

Figure 18-71 Hatch angle for adjacent parts

Also, if the hatch lines fall parallel to any edge of the hatch area, the hatch angle should be changed so that the lines are not parallel to any object line (Figure 18-72).

Points to Remember

1. Some parts, such as bolts, nuts, shafts, ball bearings, fasteners, ribs, spokes, keys, and other similar items that do not show any important feature, if sectioned, should not be shown in section.

2. Hidden details should not be shown in the section view unless the hidden lines represent an important detail or help the viewer to understand the shape of the object.

3. The section lines (hatch lines) must be thinner than the object lines. You can accomplish this by assigning a unique color to hatch lines and then assigning the color to that slot on the plotter that carries a pen with a thinner tip.

Not recommended   Recommended

Not recommended   Recommended

Figure 18-72 *Hatch angle*

4. The section lines must be drawn on a separate layer for display and editing purposes.

Exercises 11 and 12   *Mechanical*

In the following drawings (Figures 18-73 and 18-74), the views have been drawn without a section. Draw these views in section as indicated by the cutting plane lines in each object.

Figure 18-73 *Drawing for Exercise 11: draw the front view in section*

Figure 18-74 *Drawing for Exercise 12: draw the left-hand side view in section*

Exercises 13 and 14   *Mechanical*

Draw the required orthographic views for the following objects in Figures 18-75 and 18-76. Show the front view in section when the object is cut so that the cutting plane passes through the holes. Also, draw the cutting plane lines in the top view.

Figure 18-75 *Drawing for Exercise 13: draw the front view in full section*

Figure 18-76 *Drawing for Exercise 14: draw the front view with offset section*

Exercise 15   *Mechanical*

Draw the required orthographic views for the objects in Figures 18-77 and 18-78 with the front view in section. Also, draw the cutting plane lines in the top view to show the cutting plane. The material thickness is 0.25 units. (The object has been drawn as a surfaced 3D wiremesh model.)

NOTE
This is a surfaced
3D wiremesh model

Figure 18-77 *Draw the front view in half section*   **Figure 18-78** *Draw the front view in half section*

AUXILIARY VIEWS

As discussed earlier, most objects generally require three principal views (front view, side view, and top view) to show all features of the object. Round objects may require just two views. Some objects have inclined surfaces. It may not be possible to show the actual shape of the inclined surface in one of the principal views. To get the true view of the inclined surface, you must look at the surface in a direction that is perpendicular to the inclined surface. Then you can project the points onto the imaginary auxiliary plane that is parallel to the inclined surface. The view you get after projecting the points is called the **auxiliary view**, as shown in Figures 18-79 and 18-80.

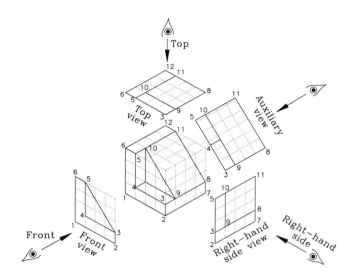

Figure 18-79 *Project points onto the auxiliary plane*

The auxiliary view in Figure 18-80 shows all features of the object as seen from the auxiliary view direction. For example, the bottom left edge is shown as a hidden line. Similarly, the lower right and upper left edges are shown as continuous lines. Although these lines are technically correct, the purpose of the auxiliary view is to show the features of the inclined surface. Therefore, in the auxiliary plane you should draw only those features that are on the inclined face, as shown in Figure 18-81. Other details that will help to understand the shape of the object may also be included in the auxiliary view. The remaining lines should be ignored because they tend to cause confusion in visualizing the shape of the object.

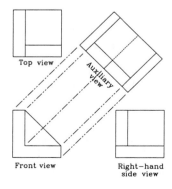

Figure 18-80 *Auxiliary, front, side, and top views*

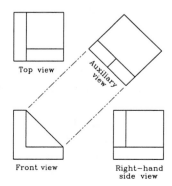

Figure 18-81 *Auxiliary, front, side, and top views*

How to Draw Auxiliary Views

The following example illustrates how to use AutoCAD to generate an auxiliary view.

Example 2

Draw the required views of the hollow triangular block with a hole in the inclined face as shown in Figure 18-82. (The block has been drawn as a solid model.)

The following steps are involved in drawing different views of this object.

Step 1. Draw the required orthographic views: the front view, side view, and the top view as shown in Figure 18-83(a). The circles on the inclined surface appear like ellipses in the front and top views. These ellipses may not be shown in the orthographic views because they tend to clutter the views [Figure 18-83(b)].

Figure 18-82 Hollow triangular block

Figure 18-83(a) Front, side, and top views

Figure 18-83(b) The ellipses may not be shown in the orthographic views

Step 2. Determine the angle of the inclined surface. In this example, the angle is 45 degrees. Use the SNAP command to rotate the snap by 45 degrees (Figure 18-84) or rotate the UCS by 45 degrees around the Z axis.

Command: **SNAP**
Specify snap spacing or [ON/OFF/Aspect/Rotate/Style/Type] <0.5000>: **R**
Specify base point <0.0000,0.0000>: *Select P1*
Specify rotation angle <0>: **45**

Using the rotate option, the snap will be rotated by 45 degrees and the grid lines will also be displayed at 45 degrees (if the **GRID** is on). Also, one of the grid lines will pass through point P1

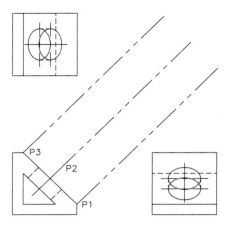

Figure 18-84 *Grid lines at 45 degrees*

because it was defined as the base point.

Step 3. Turn **ORTHO** on, and project points P1, P2, and P3 from the front view onto the auxiliary plane. Now you can complete the auxiliary view and give dimensions. The projection lines can be erased after the auxiliary view is drawn.

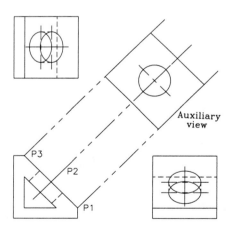

Figure 18-85 *Auxiliary, front, side, and top views*

Exercise 16   *General*

Draw the required orthographic and auxiliary views for the object in Figure 18-86. The object is drawn as a surfaced 3D wiremesh model.

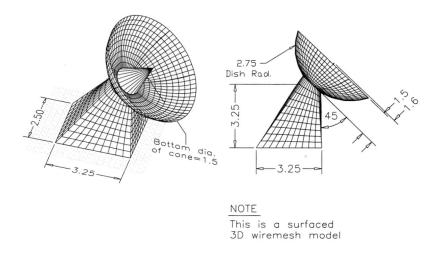

Figure 18-86 *Drawing for Exercise 16: draw the required orthographic and auxiliary views*

Exercises 17 and 18

General

Draw the required orthographic and auxiliary views for the following objects in Figures 18-87 and 18-88. The objects are drawn as 3D solid models and are shown at different angles (viewpoints are different).

Figure 18-87 *Drawing for Exercise 17: draw the required orthographic and auxiliary views*

Figure 18-88 *Drawing for Exercise 18: draw the required orthographic and auxiliary views*

DETAIL DRAWING, ASSEMBLY DRAWING, AND BILL OF MATERIALS

Detail Drawing

A detail drawing is a drawing of an individual component that is a part of the assembled product. Detail drawings are also called **piece part drawings**. Each detail drawing must be drawn and dimensioned to completely describe the size and shape of the part. It should also contain information that might be needed in manufacturing the part. The finished surfaces should be indicated by using symbols or notes and all necessary operations on the drawing. The material of which the part is made and the number of parts that are required for production of the assembled product must be given in the title block. Detail drawings should also contain part numbers. This information is used in the bill of materials and the assembly drawing. The part numbers make it easier to locate the drawing of a part. You should make a detail drawing of each part, regardless of the part's size, on a separate drawing. When required, these detail drawings can be inserted in the assembly drawing by using the **XREF** command.

Assembly Drawing

The **assembly drawing** is used to show the parts and their relative positions in an assembled product or a machine unit. The assembly drawing should be drawn so that all parts can be shown in one drawing. This is generally called the main view. The main view may be drawn in full section so that the assembly drawing shows nearly all the individual parts and their locations. Additional views should be drawn only when some of the parts cannot be seen in the main view. The hidden lines, as far as possible, should be omitted from the assembly drawing because they clutter the drawing and might cause confusion. However, a hidden line may be drawn if it helps to understand the product. Only assembly dimensions should be shown in the assembly drawing. Each part should be identified on the assembly drawing by the number used in the detail drawing and in the bill of materials. The part numbers should be given as shown in Figure 18-89. It consists of a text string for the detail number, a circle (balloon), a leader line, and an arrow or dot. The text should be made at least 0.2 inches (5 mm) high and enclosed in a 0.4 inch (10 mm) circle (balloon). The center of the circle must be located not less than 0.8 inches (20 mm) from the nearest line on the drawing. Also, the leader line should be radial with respect to the circle (balloon). The assembly drawing may also contain an exploded isometric or isometric view of the assembled unit.

Bill of Materials

A **bill of materials** is a list of parts placed on an assembly drawing just above the title block (Figure 18-89). The bill of materials contains the part number, part description, material, quantity required, and drawing numbers of the detail drawings (Figure 18-90). If the bill of materials is placed above the title block, the parts should be listed in ascending order so that the first part is at the bottom of the table (Figure 18-91). The bill of materials may also be placed at the top of the drawing. In that case, the parts must be listed in descending order with the first part at the t̪ ⌐f the table. This structure allows room for any additional items that may be added to the list.

Figure 18-89 *Assembly drawing with title block, bill of materials, and surfaced 3D wireframe model*

Figure 18-90 *Detail drawing (piece part drawing) of Part Number 2*

Figure 18-91 *Detail drawings of Part Numbers 1 and 3*

Self-Evaluation Test

Answer the following questions, and then compare your answers to the correct answers given at the end of this chapter.

1. If you draw a line perpendicular to the X and Y axes, this line defines the _____ axis.

2. The front view shows the maximum number of features or gives a better idea about the shape of the object. (T/F)

3. The number of decimal places in a dimension (for example, 2.000) determines the type of machine that will be used to do that machining operation. (T/F)

4. The dimension layer/layers should be assigned a unique color so that at the time of plotting you can assign a desired pen to plot the dimensions. (T/F)

5. All dimensions should be given inside the view. (T/F)

6. The dimensions can be shown inside the view if the dimensions can be easily understood there and cause no confusion with other object lines. (T/F)

7. The circle must be dimensioned as a(n) _____, never as a radius.

8. If you give continuous (incremental) dimensioning for dimensioning various features of a part, the overall dimension must be omitted or given as a(n) _____ dimension.

9. If the object is symmetrical, it is not necessary to draw a full section view. (T/F)

10 The removed section is similar to the _____ section, except that it is shown outside the object.

11. In AutoCAD you can control the spacing between hatch lines by specifying the _____ at the time of hatching.

12. When dimensioning, you must consider the manufacturing process involved in making a part and the relationship that exists between different parts in an assembly. (T/F)

13. The distance between the first dimension line and the second dimension line must be _____ to _____ units.

14. The reference dimension must be enclosed in _____.

15. A dimension must be given where the feature is visible. However, in some complicated drawings you might be justified to dimension a detail with a hidden line. (T/F)

Review Questions

1. Multiview drawings are also known as _____ drawings.

2. The space between the X and Y axes is called the XY plane. (T/F)

3. A plane that is parallel to the XY plane is called a parallel plane. (T/F)

4. If you look at the object along the negative Y axis and toward the origin, you will get the side view. (T/F)

5. The top view must be directly below the front view. (T/F)

6. Before drawing orthographic views, you must look at the object and determine the number of views required to show all features of the object. (T/F)

7. By dimensioning, you are not only giving the size of a part, you are giving a series of instructions to a machinist, an engineer, or an architect. (T/F)

8. What are the components of a dimension? _____
   _____

9. Why should you make the dimensions in a separate layer/layers? _____
   _____

10. The distance of the first dimension line should be _____ to _____ units from the object line.

11. You can change grid, snap or UCS origin, and snap increments to make it easier to place the dimensions. (T/F)

12. For parallel dimension lines, the dimension text can be _____ if there is not enough room between the dimension lines to place the dimension text.

13. You should not dimension with hidden lines. (T/F)

14. A dimension that is not to scale should be indicated by drawing a straight line under the dimension text. (T/F)

15. The dimensions must be given where the feature that you are dimensioning is obvious and shows the contour of the feature. (T/F)

16. When dimensioning a circle, the diameter should be preceded by the _____.

17. When dimensioning an arc or a circle, the dimension line (leader) must be _____.

18. In radial dimensioning, you should place the dimension text vertically. (T/F)

19. If the dimension of a feature appears in a section view, you must hatch the dimension text. (T/F)

20. The dimensions must not be repeated; this makes it difficult to update a dimension, and the dimensions might get confusing. (T/F)

21. A bolt circle should be dimensioned by specifying the _____ of the bolt circle, the _____ of the holes, and the _____ of the holes in the bolt circle.

22. In the _____ section, the object is cut along the entire length of the object.

23. The part of the object where the material is actually cut is indicated by drawing _____ lines.

24. The _____ section is used to show the true shape of the object at the point where the section is cut.

25. The _____ section is used when the features of the object that you want to section are not in one plane.

26. Cutting plane lines are thinner than object lines. You can use the AutoCAD PLINE command to draw the polylines of desired width. (T/F)

27. The spacing between the hatch (section) lines is determined by the space being hatched. (T/F)

28. The angle for the hatch lines should be 45 degrees. However, if there are two or more hatch areas next to one another, representing different parts, the hatch angle must be changed so that the hatched areas look different. (T/F)

29. Some parts, such as bolts, nuts, shafts, ball bearings, fasteners, ribs, spokes, keys, and other similar items that do not show any important feature, if sectioned, must be shown in section. (T/F)

30. Section lines (hatch lines) must be thicker than object lines. You can accomplish this by assigning a unique color to hatch lines and then assigning the color to that slot on the plotter carrying a pen with a thicker tip. (T/F)

31. The section lines must be drawn on a separate layer for _____ and _____ purposes.

32. In a broken section, only a _____ of the object is cut to _____ the features that need to be drawn in section.

33. The assembly drawing is used to show the _____ and their _____ in an assembled product or a machine unit.

34. In an assembly drawing, additional views should be drawn only when some of the parts cannot be seen in the main view. (T/F)

Chapter 18

35. Why shouldn't hidden lines be shown in an assembly drawing? _____

_____

Exercises

Exercises 19 through 24   *Mechanical*

Draw the required orthographic views of the following objects (the isometric view of each object is given in Figures 18-92 through 18-97). The dimensions can be determined by counting the number of grid lines. The distance between the isometric grid lines is assumed to be 0.5 units. Also dimension the drawings.

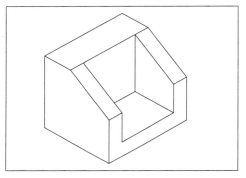

Figure 18-92 *Drawing for Exercise 19*

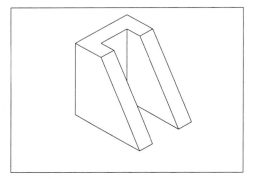

Figure 18-93 *Drawing for Exercise 20*

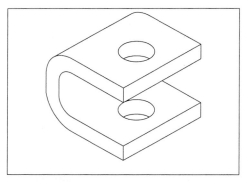

Figure 18-96 *Drawing for Exercise 23*

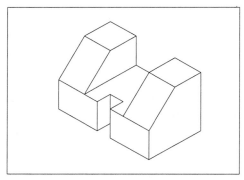

Figure 18-97 *Drawing for Exercise 24*

Figure 18-94 *Drawing for Exercise 21*   ***Figure 18-95*** *Drawing for Exercise 22*

Exercise 25   *Electronics*

Make the drawing as shown in Figure 18-98. Use layers and dimension the drawings where shown.

Figure 18-98 *Drawing for Exercise 25*

Chapter 18

Exercises 26 through 30   *Mechanial*

Make the drawings as shown in Figures 18-99 through Figure 18-103. Use layers and dimension the drawings where shown.

Figure 18-99 Drawing for Exercise 26

Figure 18-100 Drawing for Exercise 27

Figure 18-101 *Drawing for Exercise 28, exploded isometric drawing of Tool Organizer (For dimensions, see Project Exercise 2 in Chapters 9, 14, and 23)*

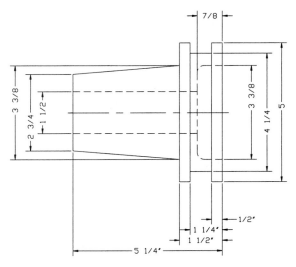

Figure 18-102 *Drawing for Exercise 29*

Figure 18-103 Drawing for Exercise 30

Answers to Self-Evaluation Test
1 - Z, **2** - T, **3** - T, **4** - T, **5** - F, **6** - T, **7** - diameter, **8** - reference, **9** - T, **10** - revolved,
11 - scale factor, **12** - T, **13** - 0.25 to 0.5, **14** - parentheses, **15** - T

Chapter 19

Isometric Drawing

ISOMETRIC DRAWINGS

Isometric drawings are generally used to help in visualizing the shape of an object. For example, if you are given the orthographic views of an object (Figure 19-1), it takes time to put the information together to visualize the shape. However, if an isometric drawing is given (Figure 19-2), it is

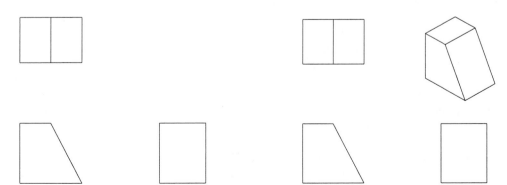

Figure 19-1 *Orthographic views of an object*

Figure 19-2 *Orthographic views with isometric drawing*

much easier to conceive the shape of the object. Thus, isometric drawings are widely used in industry to aid in understanding products and their features.

An isometric drawing should not be confused with a three-dimensional (3D) drawing. An isometric drawing is a two-dimensional (2D) drawing in a 2D plane. A 3D drawing is a true 3D model of the object. The model can be rotated and viewed from any direction. A 3D model can be a wireframe model, surface model, or solid model.

ISOMETRIC PROJECTIONS

The word isometric means "**equal measure**" because the three angles between the three principal axes of an isometric drawing are each 120 degrees (Figure 19-3). An isometric view is obtained by rotating the object 45 degrees around the imaginary vertical axis, and then tilting the object forward through a 35°16' angle. If you project the points and the edges on the frontal plane, the projected length of the edges will be approximately 81 percent (isometric length/actual length = 9/11) shorter than the actual length of the edges. However, isometric drawings are always drawn to full scale because their purpose is to help the user visualize the shape of the object. Isometric

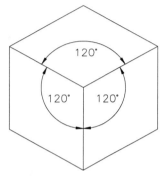

Figure 19-3 *Principal axes of an isometric drawing*

drawings are not meant to describe the actual size of the object. The actual dimensions, tolerances, and feature symbols must be shown in the orthographic views. Also, you should avoid showing any hidden lines in the isometric drawings, unless they show an important feature of the object or help in understanding the shape of the object.

ISOMETRIC AXES AND PLANES

Isometric drawings have three axes: **right horizontal axis** (P0,P1), **vertical axis** (P0,P2), and **left horizontal axis** (P0,P3). The two horizontal axes are inclined at 30 degrees to the horizontal, or X, axis (X1,X2). The vertical axis is at 90 degrees (Figure 19-4).

When you draw an isometric drawing, the horizontal object lines are drawn along or parallel to the horizontal axis. Similarly, the vertical lines are drawn along or parallel to the vertical axis. For example, if you want to make an isometric drawing of a rectangular block, the vertical edges of the block are drawn parallel to the vertical axis. The horizontal edges on the right-hand side of the block are drawn parallel to the right horizontal axis (P0,P1), and the horizontal edges on the left side of the block are drawn parallel to the left horizontal axis (P0,P3). It is important to remember that the **angles do not appear true** in isometric drawings. Therefore, the edges or surfaces that are at an angle are drawn by locating the endpoints of the edges. The lines that are parallel to the isometric axes are called **isometric lines**. The lines that are not parallel to the isometric axes are called **nonisometric lines**. Similarly, the planes can be isometric planes or nonisometric planes.

Isometric drawings have three principal planes, **isoplane right**, **isoplane top**, and **isoplane left**, as shown in Figure 19-5. The isoplane right (P0,P4,P10,P6) is the plane as defined by the vertical axis and the right horizontal axis. The isoplane top (P6,P10,P9,P7) is the plane as defined by the right and left horizontal axes. Similarly, the isoplane left (P0,P6,P7,P8) is defined by the vertical axis and the left horizontal axis.

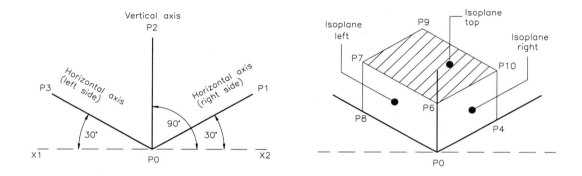

Figure 19-4 Isometric axes   *Figure 19-5 Isometric planes*

SETTING THE ISOMETRIC GRID AND SNAP

You can use the **SNAP** command to set the isometric grid and snap. The isometric grid lines are displayed at 30 degrees to the horizontal axis. Also, the distance between the grid lines is determined by the vertical spacing, which can be specified by using the **GRID** or **SNAP** command. The grid lines coincide with the three isometric axes, which makes it easier to create isometric drawings. The following command sequence illustrates the use of the **SNAP** command to set the isometric grid and snap of 0.5 units (Figure 19-6).

> Command: **SNAP**
> Specify snap spacing or [ON/OFF/Aspect/Rotate/Style/Type] <0.5000>: **S**
> Enter snap grid style [Standard/Isometric] <S>: **I**
> Specify vertical spacing <0.5000>: *Enter new snap distance.*

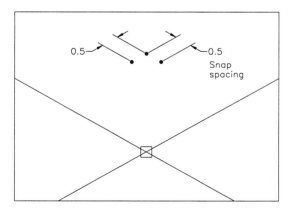

Figure 19-6 Setting isometric grid and snap

Note

*When you use the **SNAP** command to set the isometric grid, the grid lines may not be displayed. To display the grid lines, turn the grid on using the **GRID** command or press function key F7.*

You cannot set the aspect ratio for the isometric grid. Therefore, the spacing between the isometric grid lines will be the same.

You can also set the isometric grid and snap by using the **Drafting Settings** dialog box, Figure 19-7, that can be invoked by entering **DSETTINGS** at the Command prompt. You can also access this dialog box by selecting **Drafting Settings** from the **Tools** menu. You can also invoke the dialog box by right-clicking **Snap**, **Grid**, **Polar**, **Osnap**, or **Otrack** on the status bar and choosing **Settings** from the shortcut menu.

Figure 19-7 Drafting Settings dialog box

The isometric snap and grid can be turned on/off by choosing the **On** box located in the **Snap and Grid/Object Snap** tabs of the **Drafting Settings** dialog box. The **Snap and Grid** tab also contains the radio buttons to set the snap type and style. To display the grid on the screen, make sure the grid is turned on.

When you set the isometric grid, the display of the crosshairs also changes. The crosshairs are displayed at an isometric angle, and their orientation depends on the current isoplane. You can toggle among isoplane right, isoplane left, and isoplane top by pressing the CTRL and E keys simultaneously (Ctrl+E) or using the function key F5. You can also toggle among different isoplanes by using the **Drafting Settings** dialog box or by entering the **ISOPLANE** command at the Command prompt:

> Command line: **ISOPLANE**
> Enter isometric plane setting [Left/Top/Right] <Top>: **T**
> Current Isoplane: **Top**

The Ortho mode is often useful when drawing in Isometric mode. In Isometric mode, Ortho aligns with the axes of the current isoplane.

Example 1

In this example, you will create the isometric drawing in Figure 19-8.

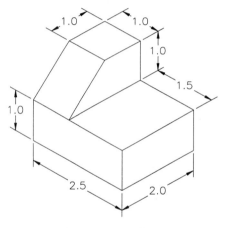

Figure 19-8 Drawing for Exercise 1

1. Use the **SNAP** command to set the isometric grid and snap. The snap value is 0.5 units.

    > Command: **SNAP**
    > Specify snap spacing or [ON/OFF/Aspect/Rotate/Style/Type] <0.5000>: **S**
    > Enter snap grid style [Standard/Isometric] <S>: **I**
    > Specify vertical spacing <0.5000>: **0.5**   (*or press ENTER.*)

2. Change the isoplane to isoplane left by pressing the **CTRL** and **E** keys. Enter the **LINE** command and draw lines between points P1, P2, P3, P4, and P1 as shown in Figure 19-9.

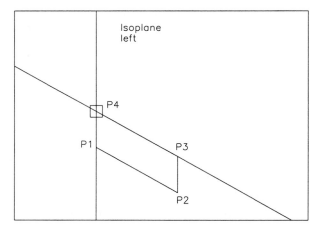

Figure 19-9 *Draw the bottom left face*

3. Change the isoplane to isoplane right by pressing the **CTRL** and **E** keys. Enter the **LINE** command and draw the lines as shown in Figure 19-10.

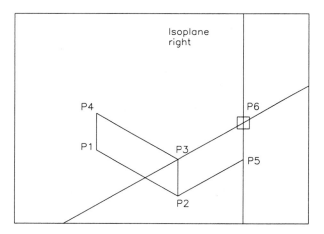

Figure 19-10 *Draw the bottom right face*

4. Change the isoplane to isoplane top by pressing the **CTRL** and **E** keys. Enter the **LINE** command and draw the lines as shown in Figure 19-11.

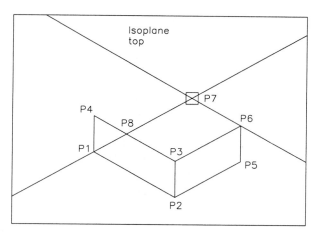

Figure 19-11 Draw the top face

5. Draw the remaining lines (Figure 19-12) according to the dimensions given in Figure 19-8.

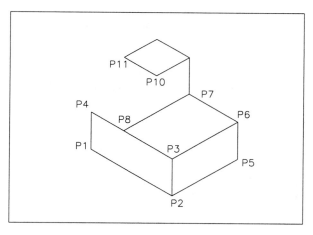

Figure 19-12 Draw the remaining lines

6. The front left end of the object is tapered at an angle. In isometric drawings, oblique surfaces (surfaces at an angle to the isometric axis) cannot be drawn like other lines. You must first locate the endpoints of the lines that define the oblique surface and then draw lines between those points. To complete the drawing of Figure 19-8, draw a line from P10 to P8 and from P11 to P4 (Figure 19-13).

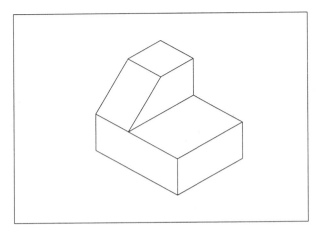

Figure 19-13 *Drawing the tapered face*

DRAWING ISOMETRIC CIRCLES

Isometric circles are drawn by using the **ELLIPSE** command and then selecting the **Isocircle** option. Before you enter the radius or diameter of the isometric circle, you must make sure you are in the required isoplane. For example, if you want to draw a circle in the right isoplane, you must toggle through the isoplanes until the required isoplane (right isoplane) is displayed. You can also set the required isoplane current before entering the **ELLIPSE** command. The crosshairs and the shape of the isometric circle will automatically change as you toggle through different isoplanes. After you enter the radius or diameter of the circle, AutoCAD will draw the isometric circle in the correct plane (Figure 19-14).

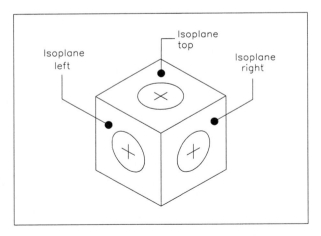

Figure 19-14 *Drawing isometric circles*

Command: **ELLIPSE**
Specify axis endpoint of ellipse or [Arc/Center/Isocircle]: **I**

Specify center of isocircle: *Select a point.*
Specify radius of isocircle or [Diameter]: *Enter circle radius.*

 Note
*You must have the isometric snap on for the **ELLIPSE** command to display the Isocircle option with the **ELLIPSE** command. If the isometric snap is not on, you cannot draw an isometric circle.*

DIMENSIONING ISOMETRIC OBJECTS

Isometric dimensioning involves two steps: (1) dimensioning the drawing using the standard dimensioning commands; (2) editing the dimensions to change them to oblique dimensions. The following example illustrates the process involved in dimensioning an isometric drawing.

Example 2

In this example, you will dimension the isometric drawing you created in Example 1.

1. Dimension the drawing as shown in Figure 19-15. You can use the aligned or vertical dimensioning command to give the dimensions. When you select the points, you must use the Intersection or Endpoint object snap to grab the endpoints of the object you are dimensioning. AutoCAD automatically leaves a gap between the object line and the extension line as specified by the **DIMGAP** variable.

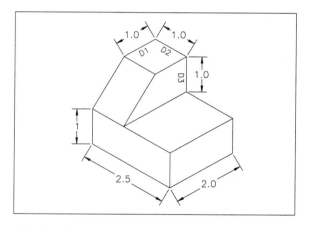

Figure 19-15 *Dimensioning an isometric drawing, before obliquing*

2. The next step is to edit the dimensions. First, enter the **DIM** command, and then enter **OBLIQUE** at the **Dim:** prompt or use the Oblique option of the **DIMEDIT** command. After you select the dimension you want to edit, AutoCAD will prompt you to enter the oblique angle. The oblique angle is determined by the angle the extension line of the isometric dimension makes with the positive X axis.

Command: **DIM**
Dim: **OBLIQUE**

Select object: Select the dimension (D1).
Enter oblique angle (Press ENTER for none): **30**

For example, the extension line of the dimension labeled D1 makes a 150-degree angle with the positive X axis [Figure 19-16(a)]; therefore, the oblique angle is 150 degrees. Similarly, the extension lines of the dimension labeled D2 makes a 30-degree angle with the positive X axis [Figure 19-16(b)]; therefore, the oblique angle is 30 degrees. After you edit all dimensions, the drawing should appear as shown in Figure 19-17.

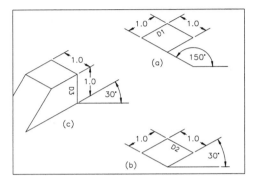

Figure 19-16 Determining the oblique angle

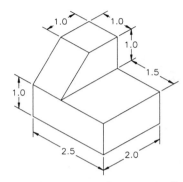

Figure 19-17 Object with isometric dimensions

ISOMETRIC TEXT

You cannot use regular text when placing text in an isometric drawing because the text in an isometric drawing is obliqued at positive or negative 30 degrees. Therefore, you must create two text styles with oblique angles of 30 degrees and negative 30 degrees. You can use the **STYLE** command and the **Text Style** dialog box to create a new text style as described here. (For more details, refer to "**STYLE** Command" in Chapter 5.)

Command: **STYLE**
Enter name of text style or [?] <Standard>: **ISOTEXT1**
Specify full font name or font filename (TTF or SHX) <txt>: **ROMANS**
Specify height of text <0.0000>: **0.075**
Specify width factor <1.0000>: *Press ENTER.*
Specify obliquing angle <0>: **30**
Display text backwards? [Yes/No] <N>: **N**
Display text upside-down? [Yes/No] <N>: **N**
Vertical? <N> **N**

Similarly, you can create another text style, **ISOTEXT2**, with a negative 30-degree oblique angle. When you place the text in an isometric drawing, you must also specify the rotation angle for the text. The text style you use and the text rotation angle depend on the placement of the text in the isometric drawing, as shown in Figure 19-18.

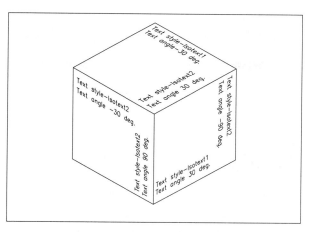

Figure 19-18 *Text style and rotation angle for isometric text*

Self-Evaluation Test

Answer the following questions, and then compare your answers with the correct answers given at the end of this chapter.

1. The word isometric means "_____" because the three angles between the three principal axes of an isometric drawing are each _____ degrees.

2. The ratio of isometric length to actual length in an isometric drawing is approximately _____.

3. The angle between the right isometric horizontal axis and the X axis is _____ degrees.

4. Isometric drawings have three principal planes: isoplane right, isoplane top, and _____.

5. What key combination or function key can you use to toggle among isoplane right, isoplane left, and isoplane top? _____.

6. You can only use the aligned dimension option to dimension an isometric drawing. (T/F)

7. Must the isometric snap be on to display the Isocircle option with the **ELLIPSE** command? (Y/N)

8. Do you need to specify the rotation angle when placing text in an isometric drawing? (Y/N)

Chapter 19

If yes, what are the possible angles? _____.

9. The lines that are not parallel to the isometric axes are called _____.

10. You should avoid showing any hidden lines in isometric drawings. (T/F)

Review Questions

1. Isometric drawings are generally used to help in _____ the shape of an object.

2. An isometric view is obtained by rotating the object _____ degrees around the imaginary vertical axis, and then tilting the object forward through a _____ angle.

3. If you project the points and the edges onto the frontal plane, the projected length of the edges will be approximately _____ percent shorter than the actual length of the edges.

4. When should hidden lines be shown in an isometric drawing? _____
   _____

5. Isometric drawings have three axes: right horizontal axis, vertical axis, and _____.

6. The angles do not appear true in isometric drawings. (T/F)

7. What are the lines called that are parallel to the isometric axis? _____.

8. What commands can you use to set the isometric grid and snap? _____.

9. Isometric grid lines are displayed at _____ degrees to the horizontal axis.

10. It is possible to set the aspect ratio for the isometric grid. (T/F)

11. You can also set the isometric grid and snap by using the **Drafting Settings** dialog box, which can be invoked by entering _____ at the Command prompt.

12. Isometric circles are drawn by using the **ELLIPSE** command and then selecting the _____ option.

13. Can you draw an isometric circle without turning the isometric snap on? (Yes/No)

14. Only aligned dimensions can be edited to change them to oblique dimensions. (T/F)

15. To place the text in an isometric drawing, you must create two text styles with oblique angles of _____ degrees and negative _____ degrees.

Exercises

Exercises 1 through 6

General

Draw the following isometric drawings (Figures 19-19 through 19-24). The dimensions can be determined by counting the number of grid lines. The distance between the isometric grid lines is assumed to be 0.5 units. Dimension the odd-numbered drawings.

Figure 19-19 *Drawing for Exercise 1*

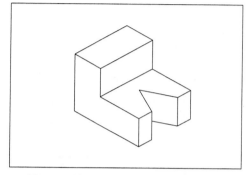

Figure 19-20 *Drawing for Exercise 2*

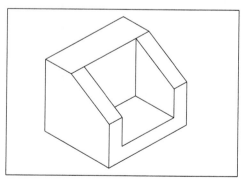

Figure 19-21 *Drawing for Exercise 3*

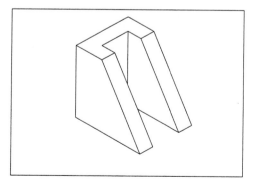

Figure 19-22 *Drawing for Exercise 4*

Figure 19-23 Drawing for Exercise 5

Figure 19-24 Drawing for Exercise 6

Project Exercise 1-7   *Mechanial*

Draw the exploded isometric drawing of the work bench as shown in Figure 19-25. (See Chapters 1, 2, 6, 7, and 23 for other drawings of Project Exercise 1.)

WORK BENCH   ISOMETRIC

Figure 19-25 Drawing for Project Exercise 1-7

Answers to Self-Evaluation Test

1 - equal measure, 120, **2** - 9/11, **3** - 30, **4** - isoplane left, **5** - CTRL and E, or F5, **6** - F, **7** - Yes, **8** - Yes, 30 degrees, -30 degrees, 90 degrees, etc., **9** - nonisometric lines, **10** - T

Chapter 20

User Coordinate System

Learning Objectives

After completing this chapter, you will be able to:
- *Use and understand the user coordinate system (UCS) and the world coordinate system (WCS).*
- *Position the UCS icon using different options of the **UCSICON** command.*
- *Use the UCS to create a 3D drawing.*
- *Use different options to redefine the UCS using the **UCS** command.*
- *Using the various tabs of the **UCS** dialog box.*

THE WORLD COORDINATE SYSTEM (WCS)

When you get into the AutoCAD drawing editor, by default, the WCS (world coordinate system) is established. In the WCS, the X, Y, and Z coordinates of any point are measured with reference to the fixed origin (0,0,0). This origin is located at the lower left corner of the screen by default. The objects you have drawn up to now use the WCS. This coordinate system is fixed and cannot be moved. The WCS is used mostly in 2D drawings. The world coordinate system and the user coordinate system (UCS), enable you to relocate and reorient the origin and X, Y, and Z axes, and were introduced in AutoCAD Release 10. Earlier releases used only the fixed origin (0,0,0).

UCSICON COMMAND

Menu:	View > Display > UCS Icon
Command:	UCSICON

The orientation of the origin of the current UCS is represented by the UCS icon (Figure 20-1). This icon is a graphic reminder of the direction of the UCS axes and the location of the origin. This icon also tells you what the viewing direction is, relative to the UCS XY plane. The default location of this symbol is a little to the right and a little above the lower left corner of the viewport. The plus (+) sign on the icon indicates that the UCS icon is placed at the origin of the current

UCS. The absence of the W on the Y axis indicates that the current coordinate system is not the WCS. If there is a box at the icon's base, it means you are viewing the UCS from above; the absence of the box indicates that you are viewing the UCS from below. Choosing **Display > UCS Icon > On**, from the **View** menu, when a check mark is displayed next to the **On** option, turns off the display of the UCS Icon. Choose the **On** option again to turn on the display of the UCS Icon. A check mark besides **On** indicates that the display of the icon is on. The **UCSICON** command also controls display of this symbol. The prompt sequence is:

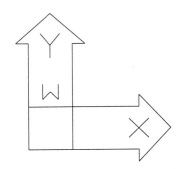

Figure 20-1 *World coordinate system (WCS) icon*

Command: **UCSICON** Enter
Enter an option [ON/OFF/All/Noorigin/ORigin] <ON>:

Also see Figure 20-2 for model space and paper space icons.

The different options of the **UCSICON** command are as follows:

ON Option. This option displays the UCS icon in the current viewport.

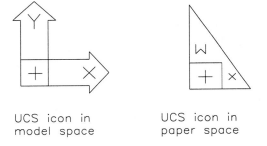

UCS icon in   UCS icon in
model space   paper space

Command: **UCSICON** Enter
Enter an option [ON/OFF/All/Noorigin/ORigin]<ON>: ON Enter

Figure 20-2 *Model space and paper space icons*

OFF Option. This option disables the UCS icon in the current viewport, causing it not to be displayed.

Enter an option [ON/OFF/All/Noorigin/ORigin]<ON>: OFF Enter

All Option. This option is used to change the UCS icons in all active viewports. Normally, changes are made only to the icon in the current viewport. For example, to turn on the UCS icons in all the viewports, the prompt sequence will be:

Enter an option [ON/OFF/All/Noorigin/ORigin]<default>: ALL
Enter an option [ON/OFF/Noorigin/ORigin] <ON>: ON

NO (Noorigin) Option. Makes AutoCAD display the icon, if enabled, at the lower left corner of the screen, whatever the position of the current UCS origin may be. This is the default setting.

Enter an option [ON/OFF/All/Noorigin/ORigin]<default>: N

OR (ORigin) Option. This option makes AutoCAD display the UCS icon (if enabled) at the origin (0,0,0) of the current coordinate system. If the current origin is off screen or it is not possible to position the icon at the origin without being clipped at the viewport edges, it is displayed at the lower left corner of the screen. Sometimes your view direction may be along the edge of the current UCS (or within one degree of the edge direction). In such cases, the UCS icon is replaced by a broken-pencil icon, to indicate that selecting locations with the pointing device is meaningless.

> Enter an option [ON/OFF/All/Noorigin/ORigin]<default>: OR

You can also choose **Display > UCS Icon > Origin** from the **View** menu to display the UCS Icon at the origin. A check mark next to Origin, indicates that the UCS Icon is displayed at the Origin of the coordinate system. The value of the current UCS origin is stored in the **UCSORG** system variable. The UCS can be different for different viewports if the **UCSVP** system variable is set to 1. When we change the UCS of the current viewport, it does not reflect in the UCSs of other active viewports if the value of **UCSVP** is set to 1; that is, the value of each UCS is stored in the specific viewport.

THE USER COORDINATE SYSTEM (UCS)

The user coordinate system (UCS) helps you to establish your own coordinate system. Changing the placement of the base point of your drawing is accomplished by changing the position/ orientation of the coordinate system. As already mentioned, the WCS is fixed, whereas the UCS can be moved and rotated to any desired position to conform to the shape of the object being drawn. Alterations in the UCS are manifested in the position and orientation of the UCS icon symbol, originally located in the lower left corner of the screen. The UCS is used mostly in 3D drawings, where you may need to specify points that vary from each other along the X, Y, and Z axes. It is also useful for relocating the origin or rotating the XY axes in 2D work, such as ordinate dimensioning, drawing auxiliary views, or controlling hatch alignment.

Figure 20-3(a) UCS toolbar

Figure 20-3(b) UCS II toolbar

Example 1

To illustrate the use of the UCS, draw a tapered rectangular block with a circle on the inclined side of it. The center of the circle is located at a given distance from the lower left corner of the tapered side. This problem can be broken into the following steps:

1. Draw the bottom side of the tapered block.
2. Draw the top side.
3. Draw the other sides.
4. Draw the circle on the inclined side of the block.

To make it easier to visualize and draw the object, the 3D object is shown in Figure 20-4. Follow the steps just given to draw an identical figure.

1. Start by drawing the bottom rectangle (Figure 20-5). Enter the **LINE** command, and select a point on the screen to draw the first line. Continue drawing lines to complete the rectangle shown in Figure 20-4. Following is the command sequence:

    Command: **LINE** ⏎
    Specify first point: 1,1 ⏎
    Specify next point or [Undo]: @2.20,0 ⏎
    Specify next point or [Undo]: @0,1.30 ⏎
    Specify next point or [Close/Undo]: @-2.20,0 ⏎
    Specify next point or [Close/Undo]: C ⏎

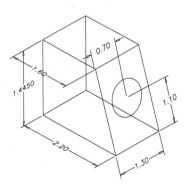

Figure 20-4 *3D object to be drawn*

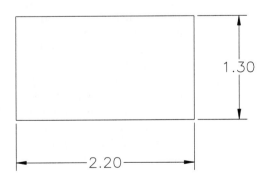

Figure 20-5 *Step 1: draw the bottom rectangle*

2. The corner of the top rectangle of the tapered block can be established with the WCS, but this could cause some confusion in locating the points since each point must be referenced with respect to the origin. With relative coordinates, you must keep track of the Z coordinate. This problem can be easily solved with the UCS by moving the origin of the coordinate system to a plane 1.4450 units above and parallel to the bottom plane. This can be accomplished by using the **UCS** command (described in detail later). Once you establish the new origin, it is much easier to draw the top side, since the drawing plane is 1.4450 units above the plane on which the bottom side was drawn (the distance between the bottom side and the top side is

1.4450 units) (Figure 20-6). The prompt sequence is:

Command: **UCS** [Enter]
Current ucs name: *WORLD*
Enter an option [New/Move/orthoGraphic/Prev/Restore/Save/Del/Apply/?/World]<World>:
N [Enter]
Specify origin of new UCS or [ZAxis/3point/OBject/Face/View/X/Y/Z] <0,0,0>: 0,0,1.445
[Enter]

After you change the UCS, the prompt sequence to draw the top side is:

Command: **LINE** [Enter]
Specify first point: 1,1
Specify next point or [Undo]: @1.6,0 [Enter]
Specify next point or [Undo]: @0,1.3 [Enter]
Specify next point or [Close/Undo]: @-1.6,0 [Enter]
Specify next point or [Close/Undo]: C [Enter]

3. Since you are looking at the object from the top side, the three edges of the top side will overlap the corresponding bottom edges; hence, you will not be able to see these three sides. Once the top and bottom are drawn, you can see the 3D shape of the object using the **VPOINT** command (discussed in detail in the next chapter) (Figure 20-7):

Command: **VPOINT** [Enter]
*** Switching to the WCS ***
Current view direction: VIEWDIR= 0.0000,0.0000,1.0000
Specify a view point or [Rotate] <display compass and tripod>: 1,-1,1 [Enter]

Figure 20-6 Step 2: draw the top rectangle   *Figure 20-7* Step 3: change Vpoint to (1,-1,1)

Join the corners of the top rectangle with the corresponding corners of the bottom rectangle (Figure 20-8). You can use the **LINE** command to draw the edges. Use the ENDpoint or INTersect snap mode to grab the corners.

4. The last step is to draw the circle on the inclined surface of the object (Figure 20-9). To do

Chapter 20

this, you need to make the inclined side (surface) the current drawing plane. This can be accomplished with the **3point** option of the **UCS** command (discussed later in this chapter). The prompt sequence is:

Command: **UCS** [Enter]
Current ucs name: *CURRENT*
Enter an option [New/Move/orthoGraphic/Prev/Restore/Save/Del/Apply/?/World] <World>: N [Enter]
Specify origin of new UCS or [ZAxis/3point/OBject/Face/View/X/Y/Z] <0,0,0>: 3 [Enter]
Specify new origin point <0,0,0>: *Specify the lower left corner (INT osnap) of the inclined side as the origin point (P1).*
Specify point on positive portion of X-axis <4.2000,1.0000,-1.4450>: *Select the endpoint of the bottom edge of the inclined surface (P2), using the INT osnap.*
Specify point on positive-Y portion of the UCS XY plane <2.2000,1.0000,-1.4450>: *Select the endpoint of the left edge of the inclined surface (P3), using the INT osnap.*

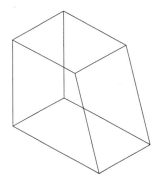

Figure 20-8 Join the corresponding corners

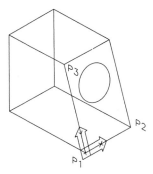

Figure 20-9 Step 4: position the UCS icon and draw a circle

Now that you have aligned the current drawing plane with the inclined surface, you can draw the circle. We know the X and Y axes displacements are between the lower corner of the inclined surface and the center of the circle. Use these X and Y displacements to specify the center of the circle, and then draw the circle. The command sequence is:

Command: **CIRCLE** [Enter]
Specify center point for circle or [3P/2P/Ttr (tan tan radius)]: 0.7,1.10 [Enter]
Specify radius of circle or [Diameter]: *Specify the desired radius.*

Using the user coordinate system, the circle can be drawn in the plane on which the inclined surface lies, and the center of the circle can easily be specified just by entering the displacements about the X and Y axes of the current UCS.

UCS COMMAND

Toolbar:	UCS > UCS
Menu:	Tools > New UCS
Command:	UCS

As already discussed, the WCS is fixed, whereas the UCS enables you to set your own coordinate system. For certain views of the drawing, it is better to have the origin of measurements at some other point on or relative to your drawing objects. This makes locating the features and dimensioning the objects easier. The origin and orientation of a coordinate system can be redefined using the **UCS** command. The prompt sequence is:

Command: **UCS** [Enter]
Current ucs name: *WORLD*
Enter an option [New/Move/orthoGraphic/Prev/Restore/Save/Del/Apply/?/World]<World>: *Select an option.*

If the **UCSFOLLOW** system variable is set to 0, any change in the UCS, does not affect the drawing view.

W (World) Option

With this option, you can set the current UCS back to the world coordinate system. To invoke this option, choose the **World UCS** button from the **UCS** toolbar or from the **UCS** flyout in the **Standard** toolbar. You can also choose **New UCS > World** from the **Tools** menu or press ENTER or enter WORLD (or W) at the following prompt:

Command: **UCS** [Enter]
Enter an option [New/Move/orthoGraphic/Prev/Restore/Save/Del/Apply/?/World]<World>: [Enter]

New Option*

The **New** option defines the origin of a new UCS by using any one of the options described below. The command prompt is :

Command: **UCS** [Enter]
Enter an option [New/Move/orthoGraphic/Prev/Restore/Save/Del/Apply/?/World]<World>: N [Enter]
Specify origin of new UCS or [ZAxis/3point/OBject/Face/View/X/Y/Z] <0,0,0>

O (Origin) Option

With this option, you can define a new UCS by changing the origin of the current UCS (Figure 20-10). The directions of the X, Y, and Z axes remain unaltered. To invoke this option, choose the **Origin UCS** button from the **UCS** toolbar or from the **UCS** flyout in the **Standard** toolbar. You can also choose **New UCS > Origin** from the **Tools** menu or enter ORIGIN (or O) at the following prompt:

Command: **UCS** [Enter]

Enter an option [New/Move/orthoGraphic/Prev/Restore/Save/Del/Apply/?/World]<World>: N [Enter]

Specify origin of new UCS or [ZAxis/3point/OBject/Face/View/X/Y/Z] <0,0,0>: *Select point (P4) using ENDpoint snap (Figure 20-10).*

At the **Specify origin of new UCS or [ZAxis/3point/OBject/Face/View/X/Y/Z] <0,0,0>:** prompt you need to specify any point relative to the current UCS. This point acts as the new origin point. For example, if you want to specify the new origin point at (2,1,0) with respect to the current UCS, enter 2,1,0 at the **Specify origin of new UCS or [ZAxis/3point/OBject/Face/View/X/Y/Z] <0,0,0>:** prompt. You can also select a point with a pointing device to specify the location of the new origin. Repeat the command and select point (P3) as new the origin.

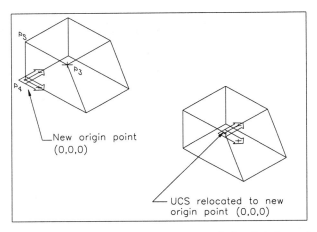

Figure 20-10 *Relocating the origin with the* **Origin** *option*

Note

If you do not provide a Z coordinate for the origin, the Z coordinate is assigned the current elevation value.

ZA (ZAxis) Option

With this option of the UCS command, you can change the coordinate system by selecting the origin point of the coordinate system and a point on the positive Z axis (Figure 20-11). After you specify a point on the Z axis, AutoCAD determines the X and Y axes of the new coordinate system accordingly. This option can be invoked by choosing the **Z Axis Vector UCS** button from the **UCS** toolbar or the **UCS** flyout in the **Standard** toolbar. You can also choose **New UCS > Z Axis Vector** from the **Tools** menu or by entering ZAXIS (or ZA) at the following prompt:

Command: **UCS** [Enter]
Current ucs name: *WORLD*
Enter an option [New/Move/orthoGraphic/Prev/Restore/Save/Del/Apply/?/World]<World>: N [Enter]
Specify origin of new UCS or [ZAxis/3point/OBject/Face/View/X/Y/Z] <0,0,0>: ZA [Enter]

Specify new origin point <0,0,0>: *Specify the origin point (P4).*
Specify point on positive portion of Z-axis <current>: *Specify a point on the positive Z axis (P6)*

If you give a null response for the **Specify point on the positive portion of Z axis <current>:** prompt, the Z axis of the new coordinate system will be parallel to (in the same direction as) the Z axis of the previous coordinate system. Null responses to the origin point and the point on the positive Z axis establish a new coordinate system in which the direction of the Z axis is identical to that of the previous coordinate system; however, the X and Y axes may be rotated around the Z axis. The positive Z axis direction is also known as the extrusion direction. In Figure 20-11, the · UCS has been relocated by specifying the origin point and a point on positive the portion of the Z axis.

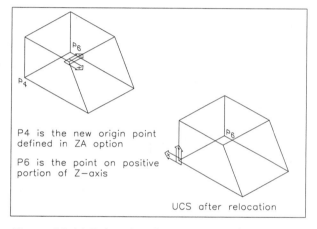

*Figure 20-11 Relocating the UCS using the **ZA** option*

3 (3point) Option

With this option, you can establish a new coordinate system by specifying the new origin point, a point on the positive X axis, and a point on the positive Y axis (Figure 20-12). The direction of the Z axis is determined by applying the right-hand rule. Align your thumb with the positive X axis and your index finger with the positive Y axis. Now bend your middle finger so it is perpendicular to the thumb and the index finger. The direction of the middle finger is the direction of the positive Z axis. The **3point** option of the **UCS** command changes the orientation of the UCS to any angled surface. This option can be invoked by selecting the **3 Point UCS** button from the **UCS** toolbar or the **UCS** flyout in the **Standard** toolbar. You can also choose **New UCS > 3Point** in the **Tools** menu or enter 3POINT (or 3) at the following prompt:

Command: **UCS** [Enter]
Current ucs name: *WORLD*
Enter an option [New/Move/orthoGraphic/Prev/Restore/Save/Del/Apply/?/World] <World>: N
Specify origin of new UCS or [ZAxis/3point/OBject/Face/View/X/Y/Z] <0,0,0>: 3

Specify new origin point <0,0,0>: *Specify the origin point.*
Specify point on positive portion of X-axis <current>: *Specify a point on the positive X axis.*
Specify point on positive-Y portion of the UCS XY plane <current>: Specify *a point on the positive Y axis.*

A null response to the **Specify new origin point <0,0,0>:** prompt will lead to a coordinate system in which the origin of the new UCS is identical to that of the previous UCS. Similarly, null responses to the Point on X or Y axis prompt will lead to a coordinate system in which the X or Y axis of the new UCS is parallel to that of the previous UCS. In Figure 20-12, the UCS has been relocated by specifying three points (the origin point, a point on the positive portion of the X axis, and a point on the positive portion of the Y axis).

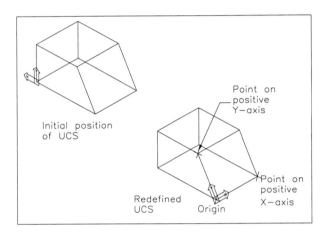

*Figure 20-12 Relocating the UCS using the **3point** option*

OB (OBject) Option

With the **OB (OBject)** option of the **UCS** command, you can establish a new coordinate system by pointing to any object in an AutoCAD drawing except a 3D polyline, 3D solid, 3D mesh, viewport object, mtext, mline, xline, ray, leader, ellipse, region, or spline. The positive Z axis of the new UCS is in the same direction as the positive Z axis of the object selected. If the X and Z axes are given, the new Y axis is determined by the right-hand rule. This option can be invoked by selecting the **Object UCS** button from the **UCS** toolbar or the **UCS** flyout in the **Standard** toolbar. You can also choose **New UCS > Object** from the **Tools** menu or enter **OBject** (or **OB**) at the following prompt:

Command: **UCS** [Enter]
Current ucs name: *WORLD*
Enter an option [New/Move/orthoGraphic/Prev/Restore/Save/Del/Apply/?/World]
<World>: N
Specify origin of new UCS or [ZAxis/3point/OBject/Face/View/X/Y/Z] <0,0,0>: OB
Select object to align UCS: *Select the circle.*

In Figure 20-13, the UCS is relocated using the **OBject** option and is aligned to the circle. The origin and the X axis of the new UCS are determined by the following rules.

Arc. When you select an arc, the center of the arc becomes the origin for the new UCS. The X axis passes through the endpoint of the arc that is closest to the point selected on the object.

Circle. The center of the circle becomes the origin for the new UCS, and the X axis passes through the point selected on the object (Figure 20-13).

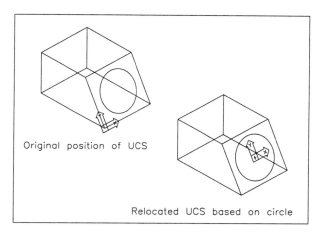

Figure 20-13 Relocating the UCS using the **OBject** option

Line. The new UCS origin is the endpoint of the line nearest the point selected on the line. The X axis is defined so that the line lies in the XY plane of the new UCS. Therefore, in the new UCS the Y coordinate of the second endpoint of the line is 0.

Trace. The origin of the new UCS is the "from" point of the Trace. The new X axis lies along the centerline of the Trace.

Dimension. The middle point of the dimension text becomes the new origin. The X axis direction is identical to the direction of the X axis of the UCS that existed when the dimension was drawn.

Point. The position of the point is the new origin.

Solid. The origin of the new UCS is the first point of the solid. The X axis of the new UCS lies along the line between the first and second points of the solid.

2D Polyline. The start point of the polyline or polyarc is treated as the new UCS origin. The X axis extends from the start point to the next vertex.

3D Face. The first point of the 3D face determines the new UCS origin. The X axis is determined from the first two points, and the positive side of the Y axis from the first and fourth points. The Z axis is determined by applying the right-hand rule.

Chapter 20

Shape/ Text/ Insert/ Attribute/ Attribute definition. The insertion point of the object becomes the new UCS origin. The new X axis is defined by the rotation of the object around its positive Z axis. Hence, the object you select will have a rotation angle of zero in the new UCS.

Note
Except for 3D faces, the XY plane of the new UCS will be parallel to the XY plane existing when the object was drawn; however, X and Y axes may be rotated.

Face (F) Option*

This option aligns the new UCS with the selected face of the solid object. You can invoke this option by choosing the **Face UCS** button from the **UCS** toolbar or the **UCS** flyout in the **Standard** toolbar. You can also choose **New UCS > Face** from the **Tools** menu or enter FACE (or F) at the following prompt:

Command: **UCS** [Enter]
Current ucs name: *WORLD*
Enter an option [New/Move/orthoGraphic/Prev/Restore/Save/Del/Apply/?/World]<World>: N
Specify origin of new UCS or [ZAxis/3point/OBject/Face/View/X/Y/Z] <0,0,0>: F
Select face of solid object: *Select within the boundary or the edge of the face to select.*
Enter an option [Next/Xflip/Yflip] <accept>:

The **Next** option, locates the new UCS on the next, adjacent face or the back face of the selected edge. **Xflip** rotates the new UCS by 180 degrees around the X axis and **Yflip** rotates it around the Y axis. Pressing ENTER at the **Enter an option [Next/Xflip/Yflip] <accept>:** accepts the location of the new UCS as specified.

V (View) Option*

The **V (View)** option of the **UCS** command lets you define a new UCS whose XY plane is perpendicular to your current viewing direction. In other words, the new XY plane is parallel to the screen. The origin of the UCS defined in this option remains unaltered. This option is used mostly to view a drawing from an oblique viewing direction. This option can be invoked by selecting the **View UCS** button from the **UCS** toolbar or the **UCS** flyout in the **Standard** toolbar. You can also choose **New UCS > View** from the **Tools** menu or enter VIEW (or V) at the following prompt:

Command: **UCS** [Enter]
Current ucs name: *WORLD*
Enter an option [New/Move/orthoGraphic/Prev/Restore/Save/Del/Apply/?/World] <World>: N
Specify origin of new UCS or [ZAxis/3point/OBject/Face/View/X/Y/Z] <0,0,0>: V [Enter]

Note
*To achieve the desired UCS, it is often easier to use the **OBject** or **View** option to establish the UCS orientation, and then use the **Origin** option to locate it, rather than using other options in a single **UCS** command.*

X/Y/Z Options*

With these options, you can rotate the current UCS around a desired axis.

> Command: **UCS** [Enter]
> Current ucs name: *WORLD*
> Enter an option [New/Move/orthoGraphic/Prev/Restore/Save/Del/Apply/?/World] <World>:
> N
> Specify origin of new UCS or [ZAxis/3point/OBject/Face/View/X/Y/Z] <0,0,0>: *Specify the axis around which you want to rotate the UCS.*
> Specify rotation angle about Z axis <90>: Specify the angle of rotation

You can specify the angle by entering the angle value at the **Specify rotation angle about Z axis <90>:** prompt or by selecting two points on the screen with the help of a pointing device. You can specify a positive or a negative angle. The new angle is taken relative to the X axis of the existing UCS. The **UCSAXISANG** system variable stores the default angle by which the UCS is rotated around the specified axis, using the **X/ Y/ Z** options of the **New** option of the **UCS** command. The right-hand rule is used to determine the positive direction of rotation around an axis. As already described, the right-hand rule states that if you visualize gripping with your right hand the axis about which you want the rotation, with your thumb pointing in the positive direction of that axis, the direction in which your fingers close indicates the positive rotation angle.

 In Figure 20-14, the UCS is relocated using the X option by specifying an angle about the X axis. The upper left part of the figure shows the UCS setting before the UCS was relocated with the X option. Enter the following prompt:

> Command: **UCS** [Enter]
> Current ucs name: *WORLD*
> Enter an option [New/Move/orthoGraphic/Prev/Restore/Save/Del/Apply/?/World] <World>:
> N
> Specify origin of new UCS or [ZAxis/3point/OBject/Face/View/X/Y/Z] <0,0,0>: X
> Specify rotation angle about Z axis <current>: 90

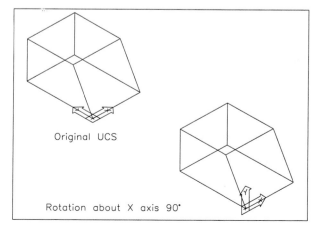

Original UCS

Rotation about X axis 90°

Figure 20-14 *Rotating the UCS about the X axis with the* ***X***

In Figure 20-15, the UCS is relocated using the **Y** option by specifying an angle about the Y axis. The upper left part of the figure shows the UCS setting before the UCS was relocated with the **Y** option. Enter the following prompt:

Command: **UCS** [Enter]
Current ucs name: *WORLD*
Enter an option [New/Move/orthoGraphic/Prev/Restore/Save/Del/Apply/?/World] <World>:
N
Specify origin of new UCS or [ZAxis/3point/OBject/Face/View/X/Y/Z] <0,0,0>: Y
Specify rotation angle about Z axis <current>: 90

Figure 20-15 *Rotating the UCS about the Y axis using the **Y** option*

 In Figure 20-16, the UCS is relocated using the **Z** option by specifying an angle about the Z axis. The upper left part of the figure shows the UCS setting before the UCS was relocated with the **Z** option. Enter the following prompt:

Command: **UCS** [Enter]
Current ucs name: *WORLD*
Enter an option [New/Move/orthoGraphic/Prev/Restore/Save/Del/Apply/?/World] <World>:
N
Specify origin of new UCS or [ZAxis/3point/OBject/Face/View/X/Y/Z] <0,0,0>: Z
Specify rotation angle about Z axis <current>: 90

Rotation about the Z axis is commonly used as an alternative to using **SNAP** command to rotate the snap and grid.

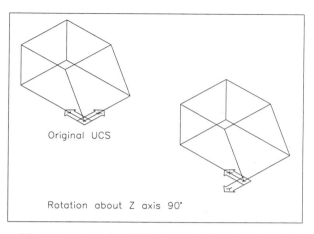

Figure 20-16 *Rotating the UCS about the Z axis using the **Z** option*

Move Option*

This option redefines the UCS by moving the UCS Origin in the positive or negative direction along the Z axis with respect to the current UCS Origin. The orientation of the XY plane remains the same. You can invoke this command by choosing the **Move UCS Origin** button in the **UCS II** toolbar. You can also choose **Move UCS** from the **Tools** menu or enter MOVE or M at the following prompt:

Command: **UCS**
Current ucs name: *WORLD*
Enter an option [New/Move/orthoGraphic/Prev/Restore/Save/Del/Apply/?/World] <World>: M
Specify new origin point or [Zdepth] <0,0,0>: *Specify a point or enter value by which the current UCS origin will move along the Z axis.*

The **New Origin point** option, moves the current UCS origin to the one specified. The **Zdepth** option specifies the distance by which the UCS origin moves along the Z axis. When we use the **Move UCS** option, in case, there are multiple viewports in the drawing, the change in the UCS is applied only to the current viewport. The **UCS Move** option is not added to the Previous list.

Orthographic Option

This option allows you to set current any one of the six Orthographic UCSs provided with AutoCAD. They are : **Top, Bottom, Front, Back, Left** and **Right**. You can specify any one of these UCSs by choosing from the **UCS II** toolbar drop-down list of predefined UCSs. The Orthographic UCSs are used normally when one is viewing and editing models. You can also select any one of the Orthographic UCSs from the List box in the **Orthographic UCSs** tab of the **UCS** dialog box and then choose the **Set current** button to apply it. You can also choose **Orthographic UCS** from the **Tools** menu or enter ORTHGRAPHIC (or G) at the command prompt as follows:

Chapter 20

Command: **UCS**
Current ucs name: *WORLD*
Enter an option [New/Move/orthoGraphic/Prev/Restore/Save/Del/Apply/?/World] <World>:
G
Enter an option [Top/Bottom/Front/BAck/Left/Right] <Top>: *Specify an option.*

The Orthographic UCSs are set with respect to the WCS. The **UCSBASE** system variable controls the UCS upon which the orthographic settings are based, the initial value is the World Coordinate System.

P (Previous) Option

The **P (Previous)** option restores the previous UCS. The last 10 user coordinate system settings are saved by AutoCAD. You can go back to the previous 10 UCS settings in the current space using the **Previous** option. If **TILEMODE** is off, the last 10 coordinate systems in paper space and in model space are saved. This option can be invoked by selecting the **Previous UCS** button from the **UCS** toolbar or the **UCS** flyout in the **Standard** toolbar. You can select the **Previous** option from the **UCS II** toolbar drop-down list or from the list box of Preset UCSs in the **Names UCSs** tab of the **UCS** dialog box. You can also enter PREVIOUS (or P) at the following prompt:

Command: **UCS** [Enter]
Enter an option [New/Move/orthoGraphic/Prev/Restore/Save/Del/Apply/?/World] <World>:
P [Enter]

R (Restore) Option

With this option of the UCS command, you can restore a previously saved named UCS. Once a saved UCS is restored, it becomes the current UCS. The viewing direction of the saved UCS is not restored. Choose **Named UCSs...** from the **Tools** menu to displays the **UCS** dialog box. The **Named UCSs** tab of this dialog box displays a list of the Named UCSs in the list box, select a UCS you want to set current and choose the **Set Current** button. You can also restore a named UCS by selecting it from the **UCS II** toolbar drop-down list. This option can also be invoked by entering RESTORE (or R) at the following prompt:

Command: **UCS** [Enter]
Current ucs name: *WORLD*
Enter an option [New/Move/orthoGraphic/Prev/Restore/Save/Del/Apply/?/World] <World>:
R [Enter]

After this, AutoCAD issues the following prompt:

Enter name of UCS to restore or [?]: *Enter the name of the UCS you want to restore.*

You can list the UCS names by entering ? at this prompt. Next AutoCAD prompts:

Enter UCS name(s) to list <*>:

You can use wild-cards, or if you want to list all the UCS names, give a null response.

S (Save) Option

With this option, you can name and save the current UCS. When you are naming the UCS, the following should be kept in mind:

1. The name can be up to 255 characters long.
2. The name can contain letters, digits, blank spaces and the special characters $ (dollar), - (hyphen), and _ (underscore).

The following is the prompt sequence:

Command: **UCS** [Enter]
Current ucs name: *WORLD*
Enter an option [New/Move/orthoGraphic/Prev/Restore/Save/Del/Apply/?/World] <World>:
S [Enter]

At the next prompt, enter a valid name for the UCS. AutoCAD saves it as a UCS.

Enter name to save current UCS or [?]:

Just as in the case of the **Restore** option, you can list the UCS names by entering ? at the prompt. Next, AutoCAD prompts:

Enter UCS name(s) to list <*>:

If you want to list all the UCS names, press ENTER.

D (Delete) Option

The **D** (**Delete**) option is used to delete the selected UCS from the list of saved coordinate systems. To invoke this option, enter DELETE (or D) at the following prompt:

Command: **UCS** [Enter]
Current ucs name: *WORLD*
Enter an option [New/Move/orthoGraphic/Prev/Restore/Save/Del/Apply/?/World]<World>:
D [Enter]
Enter UCS name(s) to delete <none>:

The UCS name you enter at this prompt is deleted. You can delete more than one UCS by separating the UCS names with commas or by using wild cards. If you delete a UCS which is current, it is renamed **UCS Unnamed**. Right-clicking a named UCS in the List box of the **Named UCSs** tab of the **UCS** dialog box, displays a shortcut menu. Choose **Delete** here to delete the selected UCS.

Apply Option*

The **Apply** Option applies the current UCS settings to a specific viewport, specified by you or to all the active viewports in a drawing session. If the **UCSVP** system variable is set to 1, each viewport saves its UCS settings. This option can be invoked by choosing the

Apply UCS button in the **UCS** toolbar or the **UCS** flyout in the **Standard** toolbar. You can also choose **New UCS > Apply** from the **Tools** menu. You can also enter APPLY (or A) at the following prompt.

Command: **UCS**
Current ucs name: *WORLD*
Enter an option [New/Move/orthoGraphic/Prev/Restore/Save/Del/Apply/?/World] <World>: A
Pick viewport to apply current UCS or [All] <current>: *Specify a viewport by clicking in it, enter A to apply the current UCS settings to all the active viewports or press ENTER.*

? Option

By invoking this option, you can list the name of the specified UCS. This option gives you the name, origin, and X, Y, and Z axes of all of the coordinate systems relative to the existing UCS. If the current UCS has no name, it is listed as WORLD or UNNAMED. The choice between these two names depends on whether the current UCS is the same as the WCS. This option can be invoked by entering ? at the following prompt:

Command: **UCS** Enter
Current ucs name: *WORLD*
Enter an option [New/Move/orthoGraphic/Prev/Restore/Save/Del/Apply/?/World] <World>: ? Enter
Enter UCS name(s) to list<*>: Enter

MANAGING UCS THROUGH DIALOG BOX (UCSMAN Command)

Toolbar:	UCS > Display UCS
Dialog	
Menu:	Tools > Named UCS...

The **UCSMAN** command displays the **UCS** dialog box (Figure 20-17). This dialog box can be used to restore to saved and orthographic UCSs, specify UCS icon and settings and name and rename UCSs. It has three tabs: **Named UCSs** tab, **Orthographic UCSs** tab and **Settings** tab.

Named UCSs Tab

The list of all the coordinate systems defined (saved) on your system is displayed in the UCS Names list of the dialog box. The first entry in this list is always the **World coordinate system**. The next entry is **Previous**, if you have defined any other coordinate systems in the current editing session. Selecting the **Previous** entry and then choosing the **OK** button repeatedly enables you to go backward through the coordinate systems defined in the current editing session. **Unnamed** is the next entry in the list if you have not named the current coordinate system. If there are a number of viewports and unnamed settings only the current viewport UCS name is displayed in the list. The current coordinate system is indicated by a small pointer icon to the right of the coordinate system name. The current UCS name is also displayed next to **Current**

Figure 20-17 UCS dialog box

UCS:. If you want to make some other coordinate system current, select that coordinate system name in the UCS Names list, and then choose the **Set Current** button. To delete a coordinate system, select that coordinate system name, and then right-click to display a shortcut menu. The options are **Set Current**, **Delete**, **Rename** and **Delete**. Choose the **Delete** button to delete the selected UCS name. To rename a coordinate system, select that coordinate system name, and then right-click to display the shortcut menu and choose **Rename**. Now, enter the desired new name. You can also double-click the name to be modified and then change the name.

 Note

*All the changes and updating of the UCS information in the drawing are carried out only after you select the **OK** button.*

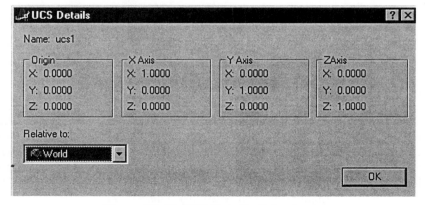

Figure 20-18 UCS Details dialog box

Chapter 20

If you want to check the current coordinate system's origin and X, Y, and Z axis values, select a UCS from the list and then choose the **Details** button. The **UCS Details** dialog box (Figure 20-18) containing that information is then displayed. You can also choose **Details** from the shortcut menu displayed on right-clicking a specific UCS name in the list box.

Setting UCS to Preset Orthographic UCSs
Using the Orthographic UCSs Tab

The **UCS** dialog box with the **Orthographic UCSs** tab is displayed also on choosing **Orthographic UCS > Preset...** from the **Tools** menu. You can select any one of the preset orthographic UCSs from the list in the **Orthographic UCSs** tab of the **UCS** dialog box (Figure 20-19). Selecting **Top** and choosing the **Set Current** button, results in creation of the UCS icon in the top view, also known as the plan view. You can also double-click the UCS name you want to set as current to make it current. You can also right-click the specific orthographic UCS name in the list and choose **Set Current** from the shortcut menu displayed. The **Current UCS:** displays the name of the current UCS name. If the current settings have not been saved and named, the **Current UCS:** name displayed is **Unnamed**.

Figure 20-19 Orthographic UCSs Tab of the UCS dialog box

The **Depth** field in the list box of this dialog box, displays the distance between the XY plane of the selected orthographic UCS setting and a parallel plane passing through the origin of the UCS base setting. The system variable **UCSBASE** stores the name of the UCS which is considered the base settings; that is, defines the origin and orientation. You can enter or modify values of **Depth** by double-clicking the Depth value of the selected UCS in the list box to display the **Orthographic UCS depth** dialog box (Figure 20-20), where you can enter new depth values. You

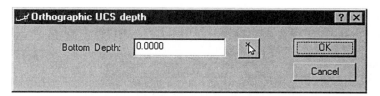

Figure 20-20 Orthographic UCS Depth dialog box

can also right-click a specific Orthographic UCS in the list box to display a shortcut menu. Choose **Depth** to display the **Orthographic UCS depth** dialog box. Enter a value in the **Front Depth:** edit box or choose the **Select new origin** button to specify a new origin or depth on the screen.

In the **Orthographic UCSs** tab of the **UCS** dialog box, you are given the choice of establishing a new UCS relative to a named UCS or to the WCS. This choice is offered from the **Relative to:** drop-down list. This list lists all the named UCSs in the current drawing. By default **World** is the base coordinate system. If you have set current any one of the preset orthographic UCSs and the you select a UCS other than World in the **Relative to:** drop-down list, the Current UCS changes to **Unnamed**. Choosing the **Details** button, displays the **UCS Details** dialog box with the origin and X, Y, Z coordinate values of the selected UCS. You can also choose **Details** from the shortcut menu that is displayed on right-clicking a UCS in the list box. The shortcut menu also has a **Reset** option. Choosing **Reset** from the shortcut menu restores the origin of the selected orthographic UCS to it's default location (0,0,0).

Figure 20-21 Settings tab of the UCS dialog box

Settings Tab

The **Settings** tab of the **UCS** dialog box (Figure 20-21), displays and modifies UCS and UCS icon settings of a specified viewport.

Chapter 20

UCS Icon Settings

Selecting the **On** check box, displays the UCS icon in the current viewport, it is similar to using the **UCSICON** command to set the display of the UCS icon to on or off. If you select the **Display at UCS origin point** check box, the UCS icon is displayed at the origin point of the coordinate system in use in the current viewport. If the origin point is not visible in the current viewport or if the check box is cleared, the UCS icon is displayed in the lower left corner of the viewport. Selecting the **Apply to all active viewports** check box, applies the current UCS icon settings to all active viewports in the current drawing.

UCS Setting

This area of the **UCS** dialog box **Settings** tab, specifies UCS settings for the current viewport. Selecting the **Save UCS with viewport** check box saves the UCS with the viewport. The value is stored in the **UCSVP** system variable. If you clear this check box, the **UCSVP** variable is set to 0 and the UCS of the viewport reflects the UCS of the current viewport. When you select the **Update view to plan** check box, the plan view is restored when the UCS in the viewport is changed. Also, when the selected UCS is restored, the plan view is restored. The value is stored in the **UCSFOLLOW** system variable.

SYSTEM VARIABLES

The coordinate value of the origin of the current UCS is held in the **UCSORG** system variable. The X and Y axis directions of the current UCS are held the in **UCSXDIR** and **UCSYDIR** system variables, respectively. The name of the current UCS is held in the **UCSNAME** variable. All these variables are read-only. If the current UCS is identical to the WCS, the **WORLDUCS** system variable is set to 1; otherwise, it holds the value 0. The current UCS icon setting can be examined and manipulated with the help of the **UCSICON** system variable. This variable holds the UCS icon setting of the current viewport. If more than one viewport is active, each one can have a different value for the **UCSICON** variable. If you are in paper space, the **UCSICON** variable will contain the setting for the UCS icon of the paper space. The **UCSFOLLOW** system variable controls the automatic display of a plan view when you switch from one UCS to another. If **UCSFOLLOW** is set to 1, a plan view is automatically displayed when you switch from one UCS to another. The **UCSAXISANG** variable stores the default angle value for the X, Y, or Z axis around which the UCS is rotated using the **X, Y, Z** options of the **New** option of the UCS command. The **UCSBASE** variable stores the name of the UCS that acts as the base; that is, defines the origin and orientation of the orthographic UCS setting. The **UCSVP** variable decides whether the UCS settings are stored with the viewport or not.

Self-Evaluation Test

Answer the following questions, and then compare your answers to the correct answers given at the end of this chapter.

1.   When you get into the AutoCAD environment (that is, the AutoCAD drawing editor), by default the _____ is established as the coordinate system.

2.   The _____ coordinate system can be moved and rotated to any desired position.

3. The _____ command controls display of the icon symbol.

4. The UCS icon is a graphic reminder only of the direction of the UCS origin. (T/F)

5. The _____ option of the **UCSICON** command enables (displays) the UCS icon in the current viewport.

6. With the _____ option of the **UCSICON** command, changes can be made to the UCS icons in all active viewports.

7. The **ORigin** option of the **UCSICON** command makes AutoCAD display the icon, if enabled, at the lower left corner of the screen, whatever the position of the current UCS origin may be. (T/F)

8. When using the **ORigin** option of the **UCSICON** command, if the current origin is off screen or it is not possible to position the icon at the origin without being clipped at the viewport edges, it is displayed at the lower left corner of the screen. (T/F)

9. The origin and orientation of a coordinate system can be redefined using the _____ command.

10. When changing the UCS with the **Origin** option of the **New** option of the **UCS** command, the directions of the **X**, **Y**, and **Z** axes can be altered. (T/F)

11. If you give a null response to the **Specify point on positive portion of Z-axis:** prompt of the **ZAxis** option of the **New** option of the **UCS** command, the Z axis of the new coordinate system will be _____ to the Z axis of the previous coordinate system.

12. With the **OBject** option of the **New** option of the UCS command, you can establish a new coordinate system by pointing to any object in an AutoCAD drawing, including a 3D polyline, 3D solid, 3D mesh, viewport object, mtext, xline, ray, leader, ellipse, region, or spline. (T/F)

13. The **View** option of the **New** option of the **UCS** command lets you define a new UCS whose XY plane is parallel to your current viewing direction. (T/F)

14. If **TILEMODE** is off, the last 10 coordinate systems in both paper space and model space are saved. (T/F)

15. Once a saved UCS is restored, it becomes the _____ UCS. The viewing direction of the saved UCS is not restored.

Review Questions

1. The user coordinate system (UCS) helps you to establish your own coordinate system. (T/F)

2. To generate the UCS icon at the new location specified in the **UCS** command, you can use the **UCSICON** command. (T/F)

3. The orientation and the origin of the current UCS are graphically represented by the _____.

4. The + sign on the icon reflects that the UCS icon is placed at the _____ of the current UCS.

5. Absence of the _____ on the Y axis indicates that the current coordinate system is not the WCS.

6. The _____ option of the **UCSICON** command disables the UCS icon in the current viewport.

7. The **NOorigin** option makes AutoCAD display the UCS icon (if enabled) at the origin (0,0,0) of the current coordinate system. (T/F)

8. Sometimes the user's view direction may be edge-on to the current UCS (or within 1 degree of edge-on). In such cases, the UCS icon is replaced by a _____ icon as an indication that the pointing locations are meaningless.

9. The **Origin** option of the **New** option of the **UCS** command lets you define a new UCS by changing the _____ of the current UCS.

10. Using the _____ option of the **New** option of the **UCS** command allows you to change the coordinate system by establishing the origin point and a point on the positive Z axis.

11. The positive X axis direction is also known as the extrusion direction. (T/F)

12. With the _____ option of the **New** option of the **UCS** command, you can establish a new coordinate system by specifying the new origin point, a point on the positive X axis, and a point on the positive Y axis.

13. If you have changed the coordinate system with the **OBject** option of the **New** option of the **UCS** command, the positive Z axis of the new UCS is in the same direction as the positive Z axis of the object selected. (T/F)

14. With the _____ option of the **New** option of the **UCS** command, you can rotate the current the UCS around the Z axis by specifying the angle value at the **Specify rotation angle about Z axis <0.0>:** prompt.

15. The _____ option restores the previous UCS.

16. With the **Restore** option of the **UCS** command, you can restore a previously saved named UCS. (T/F)

17. The name of a UCS can be only up to 21 characters long. (T/F)

18. The **D** (**Delete**) option of the **UCS** command is used to delete the selected UCS from the list of _____ coordinate systems.

19. By invoking the _____option of the **UCS** command, you can list the name of the specified UCS.

20. The _____ option of the **UCS** command gives you the name, origin, and X, Y, and Z axes of all coordinate systems relative to the existing UCS.

21. In the UCS **Orthographic UCSs** tab of the **UCS** dialog box, you are given the choice of establishing a new UCS relative to any named UCS or the _____.

22. If the current UCS is identical to the WCS, the **WORLDUCS** system variable is set to 0; otherwise, it holds the value 1. (T/F)

23. The _____system variable holds the UCS icon setting of the current viewport.

24. The _____system variable controls the automatic display of a plan view when you switch from one UCS to another.

25. If **UCSFOLLOW** is set to 0, a plan view is automatically displayed when you switch from one UCS to another. (T/F)

26. With the _____ option of the **UCS** command, you can name and save the current UCS.

27. With the _____ option of the **UCS** command, you can set the current UCS to be identical to the world coordinate system.

28. You can set the orientation of the UCS to any one of the orthographic settings in the UCS dialog box with the help of the _____ command.

29. The coordinate value of the origin of the current UCS is held in the _____ system variable.

30. The _____ dialog box lists all the coordinate systems.

Exercises

Exercises 1 through 4   *Mechanical*

Draw the given Figures 20-22 through 20-25 using the **UCS** command and its options to position the UCS icon so that you can draw the lines on different faces. The dimensions can be determined by counting the number of grid lines. The distance between the isometric grid lines can be assumed to be 0.5 or 1.0 units. The following drawings do not show the hidden edges. Your drawings should show all lines. To hide the hidden edges, you could use the **3D FACE** command (discussed later in the text).

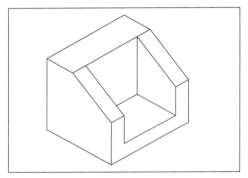

Figure 20-22 Drawing for Exercise 1

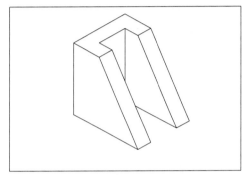

Figure 20-23 Drawing for Exercise 2

Figure 20-24 Drawing for Exercise 3

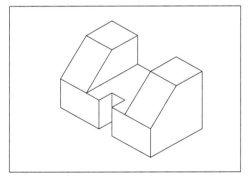

Figure 20-25 Drawing for Exercise 4

Answers to Self-Evaluation Test
1 - world coordinate system, **2** - user, **3** - **UCSICON**, **4** - F, **5** - **On**, **6** - **All**, **7** - F, **8** - T, **9** - **UCS**, **10** - F, **11** - parallel, **12** - F, **13** - F, **14** - T, **15** - current

Chapter 21

Drawing Predefined 3D Objects, Viewing and Editing 3D Objects, and Drawing 3D Surfaces

Learning Objectives

After completing this chapter, you will be able to:

- *Create predefined 3D surfaced objects: sphere, cone, dome, dish, torus, pyramid, wedge, box, and mesh.*
- *Set up viewpoints with the **VPOINT** and **PLAN** commands.*
- *Create 3D arrays using the **3DARRAY** command.*
- *Edit 3D objects using the **MIRROR3D**, **ROTATE3D**, and **ALIGN** commands.*
- *Create 3D surfaces using **RULESURF**, **REVSURF**, **TABSURF**, **EDGESURF** commands.*
- *Create 3D surfaces using the **3DMESH**, **PFACE**, and **3DFACE** commands.*

3D DRAWINGS

Until the preceding chapter, all the drawings you have seen or drawn have been two-dimensional. These drawings were generated in the XY plane. You also viewed these drawings from the Z axis, and the picture you saw in this manner is also known as the plan view. Once you start working with 3D objects, you will often need to view the drawing from different angles. For example, you may require the 3D view, the top view, or the front view of the object in space. In AutoCAD, it is possible to view an object from any position in model space. The point from which you view the drawing is known as the viewpoint. A viewpoint for the current viewport can be defined with the help of the

VPOINT command. There are three types of 3D objects that you can draw in AutoCAD: Wireframes, Surfaces and Solids. A Wireframe model is a skeletal framework of a 3D object. It has no surfaces and consists of points, lines and curves that form the edges of the object. Each of the objects forming the 3D wireframe model are to be placed individually and therefore creating these 3D objects takes the most time. You can create Wireframe objects by placing 2D objects in 3D space by entering the Z coordinate values, defining a UCS for the XY plane or using 3D polylines and splines. A surface model has both surfaces as well as edges defined. These surfaces are defined using polygonal meshes that are planar and approximate curves. They are known as meshes. You can use the **HIDE**, **SHADEMODE**, and **RENDER** commands with these objects, but they donot have the physical properties of solids.

DRAWING PREDEFINED 3D OBJECTS

In this chapter, you will first learn how to create some predefined 3D objects provided by AutoCAD. Later on, you will use these 3D objects to try out various editing operations that can be performed on them. AutoCAD supports a library of 3D objects. To draw these predefined objects, you simply specify the values of various parameters pertaining to the selected 3D object. Once you are done entering the information, the object is automatically drawn on the screen. In this manner, you can create a number of 3D objects with very little effort. You can create surface meshes (surfaced wireframes) and solid types (primitive solids, see Chapter 23) of predefined 3D shapes.

3D SURFACE MESHES

Toolbar:	Surfaces
Menu:	Draw > Surfaces > 3D Surfaces
Command:	3D

Surface mesh models define the edges and the surfaces of a 3D object. In the surface meshes category, you can create shapes like a box, cone, dome, sphere, torus, dish, wedge, pyramid, or 3D mesh. All these objects are formed as polygon meshes. Once you create surface models on the screen, you will notice that the models resemble wireframes. Only after using the **SHADEMODE**, **HIDE**, or **RENDER** command will these objects appear as surfaced objects.

Figure 21-1 Surfaces toolbar

You can also create a 3D surface object by appending AI_ as a prefix to the name of the 3D object you want to draw. For example, if you want to draw a sphere using this method, enter AI_SPHERE at the Command prompt. The AI at the start of this command is the abbreviation for the Autodesk Inc. AutoLISP command definition found in the 3D.LSP file. The specified object will be created per the specifications the user has entered. You can also choose the specific 3D object button, which you wish to draw from the **Surfaces** toolbar or you can choose **Surfaces > 3D Surfaces...** from the **Draw** menu, to display the **3D Objects** dialog box (Figure 21-2), where you can select the object you wish to draw by selecting the Preview image or from the list. Choose **OK** to exit the dialog box, the selected object will be drawn as per information you have entered about it.

Figure 21-2 3D Objects dialog box

Solids

In the solids category, you can create a box, cone, sphere, torus, wedge, or cylinder. Just as with surface models, solid models resemble wireframes when created, and only after using the **SHADEMODE**, **HIDE**, or **RENDER** command do these objects appear as solid objects. Solids have mass properties like volume, moment of inertia, and so on. The solid model can be converted into a surfaced wireframe object by exploding it (the solid sphere is an exception, since it cannot be exploded). You can create 3D solids by entering the name of the solid at the Command prompt, from the **Solids** toolbar, or from the **Draw** menu (choose **Solids**). Construction of solid primitives is discussed in Chapter 23, Solid Modelling.

Constructing a Spherical Surface Mesh

Toolbar:	Surfaces > Sphere
Menu:	Draw > Surfaces > 3D Surfaces
Command:	3D

 The spherical surface mesh (Figure 21-3) has its central axis parallel to the Z axis, and the latitudinal lines are parallel to the XY plane of the current UCS. You can also append AI_ as a prefix to SPHERE and use it as a command. The prompt sequence is as follows:

Command: **3D** [Enter]
Enter an option
[Box/Cone/DIsh/DOme/Mesh/Pyramid/Sphere/Torus/Wedge]: S [Enter]
Specify center point of sphere: *Specify the location of center point.*
Specify radius of sphere or [Diameter]: *Specify the diameter/ radius of the sphere.*
Enter number of longitudinal segments for surface of sphere <16>: *Specify the number of*

longitudinal (vertical) segments for the sphere.
Enter number of latitudinal segments for
surface of sphere <16>: *Specify the*
number of latitudinal (horizontal) segments
for the sphere.

Note
Since you cannot see a 3D object properly
from the plan view (0,0,1), side views, and
so forth, you should change the vpoint (view-
point) to a 3D viewpoint, such as (1,-1,1),
at the end of all the 3D constructions so
that you are able to view the objects three-
dimensionally.

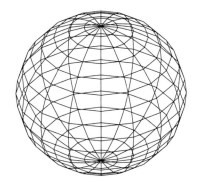

***Figure 21-3** Spherical Surface Mesh*

Constructing a 3D Box Surface Mesh

You can create a surface mesh model
of a box (Figure 21-4) by using any one
of the methods for drawing surfaced
wireframe models. The following example illustrates how to draw a box having a
length of 3 units, a width of 4 units, a height of
1.50 units, and a 0 degree rotation.

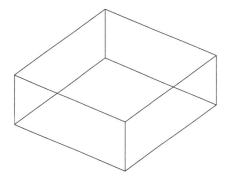

Command: **3D** [Enter]
Enter an option
[Box/Cone/DIsh/DOme/Mesh/Pyramid/
Sphere/Torus/Wedge]: B [Enter]
Specify corner point of box: *Select the*
location of the corner of the box.
Specify length of box: 3 [Enter]
Specify width of box or [Cube]: 4 [Enter]
Specify height of box: 1.50 [Enter]
Specify rotation angle of box about the Z axis or [Reference]: *Specify the rotation of the box*
about the Z axis.

***Figure 21-4** 3D Box Surface mesh*

The rotation is carried out about the first corner of the box. The base of the box is parallel to the
XY plane of the current UCS. The **Reference** option aligns the box with other objects in the
drawing or relative to the angle you specify. To draw a cube with the length of the sides equal to the
length you have specified at the **Specify length of box:** prompt, enter C at the **Specify width of**
box or [Cube]: prompt. For example, to draw a cube with the length of sides equal to 5 units and
no rotation about the Z axis, use the following prompt sequence:

Command: **3D** [Enter]
Enter an option
[Box/Cone/DIsh/DOme/Mesh/Pyramid/Sphere/Torus/Wedge]: B [Enter]
Specify corner point of box: *Select the location of the corner of the box.*

Specify length of box: 5 Enter
Specify width of box or [Cube]: C Enter
Specify rotation angle of box about the Z axis or [Reference]: 0 Enter

Constructing a Pyramid Surface Mesh

You can create a surface mesh model of a pyramid by using any one of the methods for drawing surface meshes. Choose the **Pyramid** button in the **Surfaces** toolbar. You can enter AI_PYRAMID at the Command prompt also.

Command: **AI_PYRAMID** Enter
Specify first corner point for base of pyramid: *Specify the location of the first base point.*
Specify second corner point for base of pyramid: *Specify the location of the second base point.*
Specify third corner point for base of pyramid: *Specify the location of the third base point.*

Once you have located the three base points on the screen, the next prompt issued is: **Specify fourth corner point for base of pyramid or [Tetrahedron]:**. At this prompt, you are given the choice of specifying the fourth base point of the pyramid or constructing a tetrahedron. Actually, a pyramid is any polyhedron with any polygonal base (from 3 to n base sides) and all other sides being triangles that all meet at the top. Therefore, a tetrahedron or an Egyptian-style pyramid is just a special case of pyramids, and neither can have a flattened top in true geometrical terms. A more correct description of the flattened top case would be that AutoCAD enables you to create a truncated pyramid tetrahedron with a flattened top. The **Ridge** option just plain contradicts the definition of a pyramid; it may be created with the Pyramid command, but it really is not a true pyramid.

Specify fourth corner point for base of pyramid or [Tetrahedron]: *Specify the location of the fourth base point.*

The next prompt issued is:

Specify apex point of pyramid or [Ridge/Top]:

At this prompt, you can select any one of the following options.

Pyramid with an Apex: Apex Point Option. The default option is the **Apex point** (Figure 21-5). With this option, you can specify the location of the apex of the pyramid. You must enter the X, Y, Z coordinates to specify the location of the apex or use the .X, .Y, .Z filters. If you simply select a point on the screen, the X and Y coordinates of the apex will assume the X and Y coordinates of the point selected, and the elevation, or the Z coordinate, will be the same as the Z coordinate of the base points. Hence, the apex of the pyramid will have the same elevation as the base of the pyramid. Only if you are in 3D space [for example, your viewpoint is (1,-1,1)] can you specify the apex by selecting a point on the screen.

Pyramid with a Ridge: Ridge Option. This option (Figure 21-6) can be invoked by entering R at the **Specify apex point of pyramid or [Ridge/Top]:** prompt. When you enter this option, the most recently drawn line of the base is highlighted. This indicates that the first point on the ridge will be perpendicular to the highlighted line. The next prompts displayed are:

Specify first ridge end point of pyramid: *Specify a point inside the highlighted line.*
Specify second ridge end point of pyramid: *Specify a point inside the second highlighted line.*

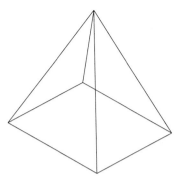

Figure 21-5 Surfaced pyramid with an apex

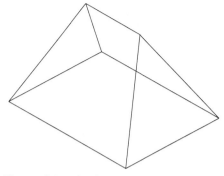

Figure 21-6 Surfaced pyramid with a ridge

Pyramid with a Top: Top Option. You can invoke this option (Figure 21-7) by entering T at
the **Specify apex point of pyramid or [Ridge/
Top]:** prompt. When you invoke this option, a
rubber-band line is attached to the first corner
of the base. The rubber-band line stretches from
the corner point to the crosshairs. This allows
you to select the first top point with respect to
the first corner, the second top point with respect to the second corner, the third top point
with respect to the third corner, and the fourth
top point with respect to the fourth corner. You
should use filters to locate the points. If you
specify the same location (coordinates) for all

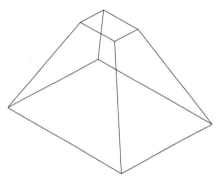

Figure 21-7 Surfaced pyramid with a top

four top points, the result is a regular pyramid with its apex at the location where all the four top
points are located.

Specify first corner point for top of pyramid: *Specify the location of the first top point.*
Specify second corner point for top of pyramid: *Specify the location of the second top point.*
Specify third corner point for top of pyramid: *Specify the location of the third top point.*
Specify fourth corner point for top of pyramid: *Specify the location of the fourth top point.*

Instead of entering the fourth base point for the pyramid, you can enter T for Tetrahedron at the
Specify fourth corner point for base of pyramid or [Tetrahedron]: prompt to draw a tetrahedron. You are going to construct two types of tetrahedrons. The first has four triangular sides and
an apex, the second has a flat top. You will first draw the tetrahedron with an apex and then a flat-
topped tetrahedron.

Tetrahedron with an Apex: Apex Option. As mentioned before, with this option you can draw a
tetrahedron that has four triangular sides and an apex (Figure 21-8). Choose the **Pyramid** button

in the **Surfaces** toolbar. The following is the prompt sequence to draw a tetrahedron with an apex:

Command: **AI_PYRAMID** [Enter]
Specify first corner point for base of pyramid: *Specify the location of the first base point.*
Specify second corner point for base of pyramid: *Specify the location of the second base point.*
Specify third corner point for base of pyramid: *Specify the location of the third base point.*
Specify fourth corner point for base of pyramid or [Tetrahedron]: T [Enter]
Specify apex point of tetrahedron or [Top]: *Specify the apex point.*

Flat-Topped Tetrahedron: Top Option. With this option, you can draw a tetrahedron that has a flat top (Figure 21-9). This option can be invoked by entering T at the **Specify apex point of tetrahedron or [Top]:** prompt. The next prompts displayed are:

Specify apex point of tetrahedron or [Top]: T [Enter]
Specify first corner point for top of tetrahedron: *Specify the location of the first top point.*
Specify first corner point for top of tetrahedron: *Specify the location of the second top point.*
Specify first corner point for top of tetrahedron: *Specify the location of the third top point.*

Figure 21-8 Tetrahedron with an apex   *Figure 21-9* Tetrahedron with a top

Note
Specify the apex point and all the top points with the .X, .Y, .Z filters, or enter the exact coordinate values.

Constructing a Cone-Shaped Surface Mesh

You can create a surface mesh model of a cone (Figure 21-10) by using any one of the methods for creating surface mesh models. If you use the **3D** command, the prompt sequence will be:

Command: **3D** [Enter]
Enter an option
[Box/Cone/DIsh/DOme/Mesh/Pyramid/Sphere/Torus/Wedge]: CONE [Enter]
You can draw a truncated cone or a pointed cone.

Pointed Cone. Three parameters are required to draw a pointed cone:

1. Center point of the base of the cone.
2. Diameter/radius of the base of the cone.
3. Height of the cone.

Choose the **Cone** button in the **Surfaces** toolbar. The prompt sequence for drawing a pointed cone is:

> Command: **AI_CONE** Enter
> Specify center point for base of cone:
> *Specify the center of base.*
> Specify radius for base of cone or [Diameter]: *Specify the radius of the base.*

Figure 21-10 Surfaced pointed cone

The next prompt asks you for the diameter/radius of the top. The default is zero (0), which results in a pointed cone.

> Specify radius for top of cone or [Diameter] <0>: *Press ENTER.*
> Specify height of cone: *Specify the height of the cone.*
> Enter number of segments for surface of cone <16>: *Specify the number of segments for the cone.*

Truncated Cone. A truncated cone is a cone whose top side (pointed side) has been truncated (Figure 21-11). To draw a truncated cone, you require four parameters:

1. Center point of the base of the cone.
2. Diameter/radius of the base of the cone.
3. Diameter/radius of the top of the cone.
4. Height of the cone.

The prompt sequence for drawing a truncated cone is:

Figure 21-11 Surfaced truncated cone

> Command: **AI_CONE** Enter
> Specify center point for base of cone: *Specify the center of base.*
> Specify radius for base of cone or [Diameter]: *Specify the radius of the base.*
> Specify radius for top of cone or [Diameter] <0>: *Specify the radius of the top.*
> Specify height of cone: *Specify the height of the cone.*
> Enter number of segments for surface of cone <16>: *Specify the number of segments for the cone.*

Note
To draw a cylinder, you draw a truncated cone with identical base and top diameters or radii.

Constructing a Surface Mesh Torus

 A torus is like a thick, hollow ring. You can create a surface mesh model of a torus (Figure 21-12) by using any one of the methods for drawing surface mesh models.

Command: **3D** [Enter]
Enter an option
[Box/Cone/DIsh/DOme/Mesh/Pyramid/Sphere/Torus/Wedge]: **T** [Enter]
Specify center point of torus: *Specify the center of the torus.*
Specify radius of torus or [Diameter]: *Specify the radius of the torus.*
Specify radius of tube or [Diameter]: *Specify the diameter of the tube.*
Enter number of segments around tube circumference <16>: *Specify the number of segments for the tube.*
Enter number of segments around torus circumference <16>: *Specify the number of segments for the torus.*

The XY plane of the current UCS is parallel to the torus. If the center point of the torus has a zero Z coordinate value (the center point of the torus lies in the present construction plane), then the XY plane bisects it.

Constructing a Surface Mesh Dome

 A dome is a hemisphere with the convex surface facing up (toward the top). You can create a surface mesh model of a dome (Figure 21-13) by using any one of the methods for drawing surface mesh models.

Command: **3D** [Enter]
Enter an option
[Box/Cone/DIsh/DOme/Mesh/Pyramid/Sphere/Torus/Wedge]: DO [Enter]
Specify center point of dome: *Specify the location of the center of the dome.*
Specify radius of dome or [Diameter]: *Specify the radius of the dome.*
Enter number of longitudinal segments for surface of dome <16>: *Specify the number of longitudinal (vertical) segments for the dome.*
Enter number of latitudinal segments for surface of dome <8>: *Specify the number of latitudinal (horizontal) segments for the dome.*

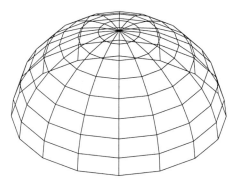

Figure 21-12 Surfaced torus   *Figure 21-13 Surfaced dome*

Constructing a Surface Mesh Dish

A dish is a hemisphere with the convex surface facing toward the bottom. Just as in the case of the dome, you can use any one of the methods described previously for drawing surface mesh models to construct a dish (Figure 21-14).

Command: **3D** [Enter]
Enter an option
[Box/Cone/DIsh/DOme/Mesh/Pyramid/Sphere/Torus/Wedge]: DI [Enter]
Specify center point of dish: *Specify the location of the center of the dish.*
Specify radius of dish or [Diameter]: *Specify the radius of the dish or enter D for the diameter.*
Enter number of longitudinal segments for surface of dish <16>: *Specify the number of longitudinal (vertical) segments for the dish.*
Enter number of latitudinal segments for surface of dish <8>: *Specify the number of latitudinal (horizontal) segments for the dish.*

Constructing a Surface Mesh Wedge

You can draw a surface mesh model of a right-angled wedge (Figure 21-15) by using any one of the methods for drawing surface mesh models. For example, you can initiate the creation of a 3D surface mesh model of a wedge by entering the **3D** command at the Command prompt and then entering WEDGE at the next prompt. You can also choose the **Wedge** button from the **Surfaces** toolbar. In the following example, you will draw a surface mesh model of a wedge using the **3D** command. Let the length of the wedge be 5 units, width 3 units, height 1 unit, and rotation 0 degrees.

Command: **3D** [Enter]
Enter an option
[Box/Cone/DIsh/DOme/Mesh/Pyramid/Sphere/Torus/Wedge]: W [Enter]
Specify corner point of wedge: *Specify the corner point of the wedge.*
Specify length of wedge: 5 [Enter]
Specify width of wedge: 3 [Enter]
Specify height of wedge: 1 [Enter]
Specify rotation angle of wedge about the Z axis: *Specify rotation around the Z axis.*

Figure 21-14 *Surfaced dish*

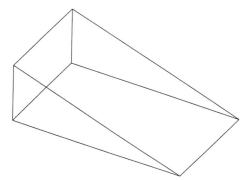

Figure 21-15 *Surfaced wedge*

The sloped side of the wedge is always opposite the first corner specified at the **Specify corner point of wedge:** prompt. The base of the wedge is always parallel to the construction plane (XY plane) of the current UCS. The height is measured parallel to the Z axis.

Note

*To draw a wedge in which the triangular sides are not parallel, use the **Ridge** option of **AI_PYRAMID** command.*

Constructing a Planar Mesh

You can create a planar model of a mesh (Figure 21-16) using any one of the methods used for drawing surface mesh objects. The type of mesh obtained is also known as planar mesh because the mesh is generated in a single plane. The prompt sequence is:

Command: **AI_MESH** [Enter]

In the next four prompts, AutoCAD asks you to specify the four corner points of the mesh.

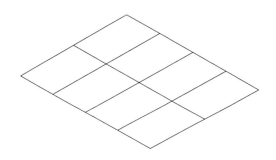

Figure 21-16 Surfaced mesh

Specify first corner point of mesh: *Specify the first corner point.*
Specify second corner point of mesh: *Specify the second corner point.*
Specify third corner point of mesh: *Specify the third corner point.*
Specify fourth corner point of mesh: *Specify the fourth corner point.*

Once you have specified the four corner points, AutoCAD prompts you to specify the number of rows (M) and the number of columns (N) of vertices. The number of vertices in both directions should be in the range 2 to 256; that is, M and N should lie in the range of 2 to 256.

Enter mesh size in the M direction: *Enter the number of rows in the mesh.*
Enter mesh size in the N direction: *Enter the number of columns in the mesh.*

VIEWING OBJECTS IN 3D SPACE

AutoCAD has provided the **VPOINT, 3DORBIT** and **DVIEW** commands to view objects in 3D space. (The **DVIEW** and **3DORBIT** commands are discussed in Chapter 22, Model space Viewports, Paper Space Viewports, and Dynamic Viewing of 3D Objects.)

VPOINT Command

Menu:	View > 3D Views > VPOINT
Command:	VPOINT

As mentioned earlier, the **VPOINT** command lets you define a viewpoint. Once you set a viewpoint, all the objects in the current viewport are regenerated and the objects are displayed as if you were viewing them from the newly defined line of sight.

Command: **VPOINT** [Enter]
Current view direction: VIEWDIR= current
Specify a view point or [Rotate] <display compass and tripod>:

At this prompt, you are supposed to enter the coordinates of the viewpoint. Regardless of the actual method or point used, the resulting view is looking towards (0,0,0) through the entire drawing, along the line of sight that the vector from that point to (0,0,0) defines or that the angle used in the **Rotate** option defines. You can enter X, Y, and Z coordinate values of the viewpoint of your choice at the **Specify a view point or [Rotate] <display compass and tripod>:** prompt. The following are some of the viewpoint settings and the sort of views obtained from each. This table will give you a fair idea of the viewing directions and viewpoints in 3D space.

Vpoint Value	View Displayed
0,0,1	Top
0,0,-1	Bottom
0,-1,0	Front
0,1,0	Rear
1,0,0	Right side
-1,0,0	Left side
1,-1,-1	Bottom, front, right side
-1,-1,-1	Bottom, front, left side
1,1,-1	Bottom, rear, right side
-1,1,-1	Bottom, rear, left side
1,-1,1	Top, front, right side
-1,-1,1	Top, front, left side
1,1,1	Top, rear, right side
-1,1,1	Top, rear, left side

Note

*The **VPOINT**, **3DORBIT**, and **DVIEW** commands cannot be used in paper space. You can use these commands in the model space.*

Using Axes Tripod and Compass to Set the Viewpoint

If you are not well-acquainted with visualizing objects in 3D space and find it difficult to imagine points in 3D space, give a null response at the **Specify a view point or [Rotate] <display compass and tripod>:** prompt instead of entering coordinates. This makes AutoCAD display a compass and an axis tripod (Figure 21-17). Now you can specify the viewpoint by moving the pointing device. You will notice that as you move the pointing device, the X, Y, Z axes tripod also moves, and so do the small crosshairs in the compass. You can now select the viewpoint with respect to the position of the X, Y, Z axes in the tripod. The

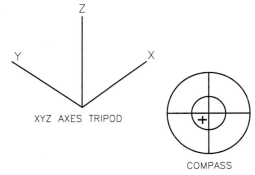

Figure 21-17 Axes tripod and compass

compass displayed is a 2D symbol of a globe. The center point of the circle is the north pole (0,0,1), and by placing the crosshairs on the north pole you can see the top view of the drawing on the screen. The inner circle in the globe depicts the equator (n,n,0). The outer circle represents the south pole (0,0,-1). By selecting crosshair locations on the screen in this manner, you can get any viewpoint (Figures 21-18 and 21-19).

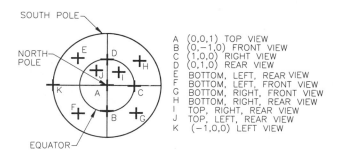

```
A  (0,0,1)  TOP  VIEW
B  (0,-1,0)  FRONT  VIEW
C  (1,0,0)  RIGHT  VIEW
D  (0,1,0)  REAR  VIEW
E  BOTTOM, LEFT, REAR VIEW
F  BOTTOM, LEFT, FRONT VIEW
G  BOTTOM, RIGHT, FRONT VIEW
H  BOTTOM, RIGHT, REAR VIEW
I  TOP, RIGHT, REAR VIEW
J  TOP, LEFT, REAR VIEW
K  (-1,0,0)  LEFT  VIEW
```

Figure 21-18 Various locations on the compass and their respective views

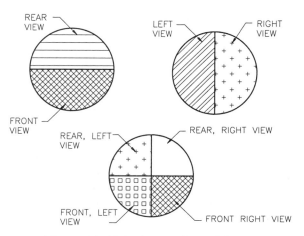

Figure 21-19 Various sections of the compass

Using the Rotate Option to Set the Viewpoint

With the **Rotate** option of the **VPOINT** command, you can set a new viewpoint by specifying values for two angles. The first angle you specify establishes the rotation (clockwise or counter-clockwise) in the XY plane from the X axis. By default, the X axis is drawn at a 0-degree angle. The second angle lets you specify the angle at which the XY plane is up (or down). On selecting the **Rotate** option, you are provided with the following prompts:

Enter angle in XY plane from X axis <current>:
Enter angle from XY plane <current>:

For example, if you specify an angle value of 0 degrees for the angle in the XY plane from the X axis, and 90 degrees for the angle from the XY plane, the resulting viewpoint will be located along the Z axis; you will get the top view of the object.

Using the Viewpoint Presets Dialog Box to Set the Viewpoint

Menu:	View > 3D Views > Viewpoint Presets
Command:	DDVPOINT

The viewpoint can also be changed from the **Viewpoint Presets** dialog box (Figure 21-20). In this dialog box, you can specify an angle from the X axis and an angle from the XY plane, thereby setting a viewpoint. Both angles can be specified by selecting the viewing angles from the image tiles or by entering the respective angle values in the edit boxes just below the image tiles. The figure on the left side of the dialog box is the plan view and the figure on the right side is called the elevation view. If you select a point inside the circle in the plan view, you can select an angle close to the desired value. If you select in between the radial lines, angles in increments of 45 degrees (starting from 0 degrees) can be specified. Similarly, in the elevation view, by selecting points on the inside of the smaller arc, you can specify an angle in increments of 15 degrees from the XY plane. The angle you specify is indicated by the white arm; the current viewing plane is indicated by the red arm. Choose the **Set to Plan View** button to display the plan as viewed from the

Figure 21-20 Viewpoint Presets dialog box

selected coordinate system. Since it is not possible to specify all angles accurately by selecting in image tiles, you can enter angle values in the **X Axis:** edit box and the **XY Plane:** edit box. You are also given the choice of specifying the viewpoint relative to the current UCS or the WCS. You can specify your choice by selecting the **Absolute to WCS** radio button or the **Relative to UCS** radio button located at the top of the dialog box.

Once you have specified both angles, choose the **OK** button to clear the dialog box and change the viewpoint according to the specifications you have provided in the **Viewpoint Presets** dialog box. Figure 21-21 shows you the pictorial effects of various viewpoints. In the following example, setting the viewpoint has been explained by entering the viewpoint coordinates at the command line as well as by specifying the viewpoint with the help of the **Viewpoint Presets** dialog box.

Figure 21-21(a) is the 3D view of the object. This view can be displayed by changing the viewpoint to (1,-1,1). You view the object from a point that makes equal angles with the X, Y, and Z axes. The **VPOINT** command can be used to change the viewpoint.

In this case, the prompt sequence is:

> Command: **VPOINT** Enter
> Current view direction: VIEWDIR=current
> Specify a view point or [Rotate] <display compass and tripod>: 1,-1,1 Enter

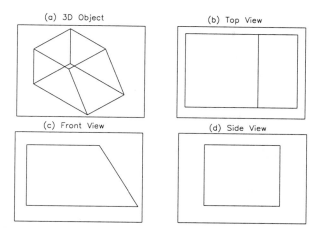

Figure 21-21 *Different views of a 3D object*

You can also change the viewpoint using the **Viewpoint Presets** dialog box. To get the 3D view, you need to rotate the viewpoint 315 degrees from the X axis and 45 degrees from the XY plane.

Figure 21-21(b) is the top view of the object. This view can be displayed by changing the viewpoint to (0,0,1). You view the object from a point along the positive Z axis (the line of sight is aligned with the positive Z axis). The **VPOINT** command can be used to change the viewpoint. In this case, the prompt sequence is:

> Command: **VPOINT** Enter
> Current view direction: VIEWDIR=current
> Specify a view point or [Rotate] <display compass and tripod>: 0,0,1 Enter

If you want to change the viewpoint using the **Viewpoint Presets** dialog box, rotate the viewpoint 0 degrees from the X axis and 90 degrees from the XY plane.

Figure 21-21(c) is the front view of the object. This view can be displayed by changing the viewpoint to (0,-1,0). We view the object from a point along the negative Y axis (the line of sight is aligned with the negative Y axis). The **VPOINT** command can be used to change the viewpoint. In this case, the prompt sequence is:

> Command: **VPOINT** Enter
> Current view direction: VIEWDIR=current
> Specify a view point or [Rotate] <display compass and tripod>: 0,-1,0 Enter

If you want to perform this operation through the **Viewpoint Presets** dialog box, rotate the viewpoint 270 degrees from the X axis and 0 degrees from the XY plane.

Figure 21-21(d) is the side view of the object. This view can be displayed by changing the viewpoint to (1,0,0). In other words, you view the object from a point along the positive X axis (the line of sight is aligned with the positive X axis). The **VPOINT** command can be used to change the viewpoint. In this case, the prompt sequence is:

> Command: **VPOINT** `Enter`
> Current view direction: VIEWDIR=current
> Specify a view point or [Rotate] <display compass and tripod>: 1,0,0, `Enter`

To accomplish this through the **Viewpoint Presets** dialog box, rotate the viewpoint 0 degrees from the X axis and 0 degrees from the XY plane.

Changing the Viewpoint Using Predefined Views

Toolbar:	View
	Standard > View flyout
Menu:	View > 3D Views
Command:	VIEW

Figure 21-22 View toolbar

You can also change the viewpoint by selecting one of the ten options: **Iso SW, Iso SE, Iso NE, Iso NW, Top, Bottom, Left, Right, Front,** and **Back.** The effects on the viewpoint are as follows:

Viewpoint Option	Corresponding Viewpoint
Top,	(0,0,1)
Bottom	(0,0,-1)
Left	(-1,0,0)
Right	(1,0,0)
Front	(0,-1,0)
Back	(0,1,0)
Iso SW	(-1,-1,1)
Iso SE	(1,-1,1)
Iso NE	(1,1,1)
Iso NW	(-1,1,1)

As discussed earlier in Chapter 5, invoking the **VIEW** command displays the **View** dialog box, where you can save and restore views in the **Named Views** tab of the dialog box. The **Orthographic and Isometric** tab (Figure 21-23) allows you to restore predefined Isometric and Orthographic views. You can select a specific orthographic and isometric view from the list box. The **Current View:** displays the name of the current view and a small icon is placed next to the view you have set current. After you have selected a specific view, choose the **Set Current** button and choose **OK** to set the selected view as current. You can also double-click the specific view or right-click it to display a shortcut menu and choose **Set Current**. When an orthographic view is set as current, the drawing is zoomed to its extents. The **Relative to:** drop-down list displays a list of all the named UCSs relative to which the orthographic views can be set current; the default is **World**. The

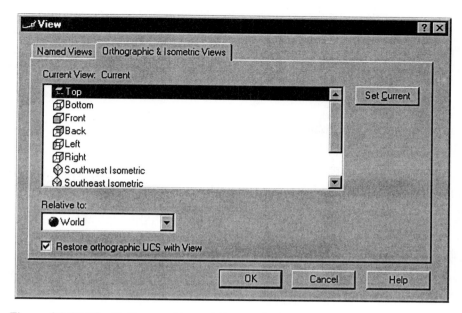

*Figure 21-23 The **Orthographic and Isometric Views** tab of the **View** dialog box*

UCSBASE variable stores the value for the name of the UCS that is selected as base for the selected view. Selecting the **Restore orthographic UCS with View** check box restores a UCS associated with the particular view when it is set current. The **UCSORTHO** variable stores the value for this option. To find out detailed information about the UCS associated with a selected named or orthographic view, choose the **Details** button in the **Named Views** tab of this dialog box.

SETTING PLAN VIEWS (PLAN COMMAND)

Menu:	View > 3D Views > Plan View
Command:	PLAN

The **PLAN** command can be used to generate the plan view of an object. The viewpoint used to obtain the plan view is always (0,0,1) relative to the current UCS, the WCS, or a previously saved UCS. In other words, a plan view is defined as the view obtained when you observe the object along the Z axis. Remember that the plan view is not necessarily the view obtained by looking at the object from the top. If you are using the WCS, the plan view is obtained by looking at the object from the top. If you want the plan view relative to the current UCS, the plan view depends totally on the direction of the Z axis. Since you can change the orientation of the X, Y, and Z axes with the UCS command, you can have a different plan view for the same object depending on the orientation of the X, Y, and Z axes.

Command: **PLAN** [Enter]
Enter an option [Current ucs/Ucs/World] <Current >:

If you have multiple viewports, the **PLAN** command generates the plan view in the current viewport only. If Perspective is on, the use of the **PLAN** command turns it off. Clipping is also turned off. The **PLAN** command cannot be used in Paper space. The prompt sequence for the **PLAN** command has the following three options.

Current UCS. This is the default option. If you invoke this option, the plan view relative to the current UCS will be generated. The display is regenerated to fit the drawing extents in the current viewport.

UCS. With the help of this option, you can generate the plan view relative to a previously defined UCS. You are prompted for the name of the UCS. You can list the names of all the saved coordinate systems by entering ? as the response to the prompt.

World. This option generates the plan view relative to the WCS. The display is regenerated to fit the drawing extents on the screen.

If the **UCSFOLLOW** system variable is set to 1, any change in the UCS changes the Plan view.

CREATING SURFACES

AutoCAD offers a wide range of commands to create 3D surfaces. The following is a description of the commands that can be used to create different types of surfaces.

RULESURF Command

Toolbar:	Surfaces > Ruled Surface
Menu:	Draw > Surfaces > Ruled Surface
Command:	RULESURF

 The **RULESURF** command can be used to generate a polygon mesh between two objects, such as lines, arcs, circles, 2D polylines, 3D polylines, splines, ellipses, or elliptical arcs (Figure 21-24). The two specified objects act as the edges of the ruled surface. The only condition for this command to work is that if one of the two objects is open (such as a line/ arc), then the other object should also be open; if one of the two objects is closed (such as a circle/ polygon), then the other object should also be closed. The exception to this rule is the point entity, which can be used as a closed object as well as an open object. Both entities cannot be points. **RULESURF** stands for ruled surface, which means that the surface between two objects is evenly divided into sections by ruled lines.

    Command: **RULESURF** [Enter]

The next two prompts ask you to select the first and second objects, respectively. The only thing you have to be careful about is that you select both entities on the same side; that is, if you selected the first entity on the left side, then the second entity must also be selected on the left side, or you will get a bowtie effect, such as a self intersecting polygon mesh.

    Current wire frame density: SURFTAB1=6
    Select first defining curve: *Select the first entity.*

Select second defining curve: *Select the second entity.*

In the case of closed curves, the location of the point you specify to select the defining curve is irrelevant because the ruled surface in such cases starts at the 0-degree quadrant location; this point depends on the current X axis and the value of the **SNAPANG** system variable. If the selected entities are closed polylines, the ruled surface starts at the last vertex and progresses backward. You can use the **ROTATE** command if you need to align the start points used. This command is frequently used to generate flat surfaces of different shapes, surfacing holes, curves on the exterior of an object, curves on the interior of an object, and so on. The mesh created by the **RULESURF** command is defined in terms of 2 x N (2 because **RULESURF** generates a polygon mesh between two objects). N stands for the mesh density. N is variable, and you can change it to your requirement. The value of N is controlled by the **SURFTAB1** system variable. N is equal to **SURFTAB1** if both defining curves are closed, or if one of them is closed and the other is a point. If both defining curves are open, N is equal to **SURFTAB1** + 1. The default setting of **SURFTAB1** is 6. You can change the value of N through **SURFTAB1** in the following manner:

Command: **SURFTAB1** [Enter]
Enter new value for SURFTAB1 <6>: *Specify the new value for N.*

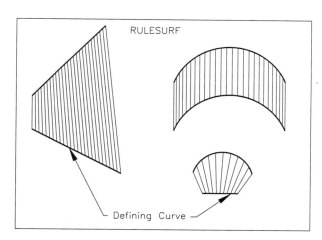

Figure 21-24 *Surface created with the **RULESURF** command*

Half of the vertices (2 x N) of the mesh are placed at equal spaces along one of the defining curves, and the rest are placed along the other defining curve.

TABSURF Command

The **TABSURF** command can be used to generate a surface extrusion (tabulated surface) from an object (Figure 21-25). There is a lot of similarity between the working of the **TABSURF** command and the **RULESURF** command. The difference lies in the fact that only one object is needed with **TABSURF**, whereas two objects are required with **RULESURF**. This object is also known as a path curve. The path curve can be a line, arc, ellipse, elliptical arc, circle, 2D polyline, or 3D polyline. The direction and the length of extrusion are governed by the length and direction of a second line or a polyline, known as the direction vector.

The endpoint of the direction vector nearest the point you select is found by AutoCAD, and the direction of the extrusion lines is set toward the opposite end of the vector line. The **SURFTAB1** variable governs the number of intervals (tabulated surfaces) along the path curve. If the path curve is a line, arc, circle, spline-fit polyline, or ellipse, the path curve is divided by the tabulation lines into intervals equal to the value of **SURFTAB1**. If the path curve is a polyline (not spline-fit), the tabulation lines are generated at the ends of the polyline segments; if there are any arc segments, each segment is divided by the tabulation lines into intervals equal to the value of **SURFTAB1**. This command can be invoked from the **Surfaces** toolbar (choose the **Tabulated Surface** button), from the **Draw** menu (choose **Surfaces > Tabulated Surface**), or by entering **TABSURF** at the **Command:** prompt.

> Command: **TABSURF** [Enter]
> Select path curve: *Select the path curve.*
> Select direction vector: *Select the direction vector.*

You can erase the direction vector once you have created the mesh.

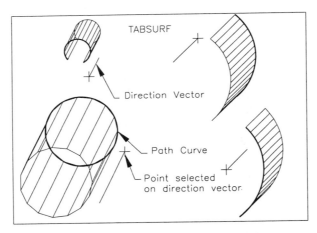

*Figure 21-25 Surface created with the **TABSURF** command*

REVSURF Command

With the **REVSURF** command, you can create a 3D mesh that trails along the path curve (profile) and rotates about the specified axis (Figure 21-26). The path curve or the profile can be an arc, line, 2D polyline, ellipse, elliptical arc, or circle. The axis of revolution can be an open 2D or 3D polyline or a line. The **SURFTAB1** and **SURFTAB2** system variables control the size (M x N) of the mesh. The value of **SURFTAB1** controls the number of faces that will be placed in the direction of rotation around the axis (M edges). **SURFTAB1** can assume a value in the range of 3 to 1,024. The value of **SURFTAB2** determines the number of equal segments that will divide the path curve (N edges). The default value for **SURFTAB1** and **SURFTAB2** is 6. If the path curve is a line, arc, circle, or spline-fit polyline, the path curve is divided by the tabulation lines into intervals equal to the value of **SURFTAB2**. If the path curve is a polyline (not spline-fit), the tabulation lines are generated at the ends of the polyline segments; if there are any arc segments, each segment is divided by the tabulation lines into intervals equal to the value of **SURFTAB2**. This command can be invoked from the **Surfaces** toolbar (select the **Revolved Surface** button), from the **Draw** menu (choose **Surfaces > Revolved Surface**), or by entering **REVSURF** at the **Command:** prompt.

Command: **REVSURF** [Enter]
Current wire frame density: SURFTAB1=6 SURFTAB2=6
Select object to revolve: *Select the line, polyline, arc or circle which defines the path curve.*
Select object that defines the axis of revolution: *Select the axis of revolution line, open 2D or 3D polyline.*

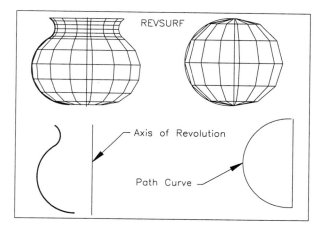

*Figure 21-26 Surface created with the **REVSURF** command*

Once you have selected the object to revolve and the axis of revolution, AutoCAD prompts you to specify the offset angle from which the surface revolution begins.

Specify start angle <0>: *Specify the start angle.*

In the next prompt, you can choose to rotate parts of the object rotated about the axis line or generate the entire 360-degree surface.

Specify included angle (+=ccw,-=cw) <360>: *Specify the included angle.*

EDGESURF Command

With the **EDGESURF** command, you can create a 3D mesh with four connected sides as the edges (boundaries), also referred to as the Coons surface path which is a bicubic surface (Figure 21-27). Basically, this mesh is a matrix of 3D faces. The number of rows and columns is governed by the **SURFTAB1** and **SURFTAB2** system variables. The four edges can be formed of lines, arcs, polyarcs, polylines, splines, elliptical arcs, or any combination of these objects. These edges must form a closed loop and have mutually shared endpoints. The only condition to create a mesh with the **EDGESURF** command is that there should be four sides (edges). The edges can be selected in any order. The M direction of the mesh depends on which edge you have specified as the first edge, and the mesh progresses from the endpoint nearest to the selected point to the other end of the edge. The N edges of the of the mesh are formed by the two edges that touch the first edge. This command can be invoked from the **Surfaces** toolbar (choose the **Edge Surface** button), from the **Draw** menu (choose **Surfaces > Edge Surface**) or by entering **EDGESURF** at the Command prompt.

Command: **EDGESURF** `Enter`
Current wireframe density: SURFTAB1=current, SURFTAB2=current
Select object 1 for surface edge 1: *Select a point on the first edge of the boundary.*
Select object 2 for surface edge 2: *Select a point on the second edge of the boundary.*
Select object 3 for surface edge 3: *Select a point on the third edge of the boundary.*
Select object 4 for surface edge 4: *Select a point on the fourth edge of the boundary.*

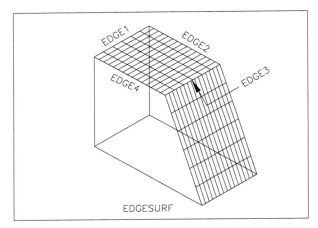

*Figure 21-27 Surface created with the **EDGESURF** command*

3DMESH COMMAND

The **3DMESH** command lets you create a free form 3D polygon mesh. The mesh is defined in terms of rows (M) and columns (N). The mesh is open in both M and N directions. You can use the **Close** option of the **PEDIT** command to close the mesh. **3DMESH** can be used to create very irregular surfaces. If the mesh points are known, **3DMESH** can be used with scripts and Autolisp routines. Wherever a row intersects a column, a vertex is formed. Hence, the total number of vertices in a mesh is the product of M and N. All the vertices of the mesh are specified by their X, Y, Z coordinate location. You can specify the vertices as 2D or 3D points. Depending on the coordinate values of the vertices, the vertices can be at any distance from each other. The definition points of the mesh are its vertices. The number of vertices in both directions should be in the range of 2 to 256. In other words, you cannot have fewer than 2 or more than 256 vertices in each direction. This command can be invoked from the **Surfaces** toolbar (choose the **3D Mesh** button), from the **Draw** menu (choose **Surfaces > 3D Mesh**) or by entering **3DMESH** at the Command prompt.

Example 1

In this example, you will create a 4 x 4 three-dimensional mesh (Figure 21-28). The prompt sequence is:

> Command: **3DMESH** ⏎
> Enter size of mesh in M direction: 6 ⏎
> Enter size of mesh in M direction: 6 ⏎
> Specify location for vertex (0,0): *Specify the coordinate location of vertex (0,0,0).*
> Specify location for vertex (0,1): *Specify the coordinate location of vertex (0,1,0).*
> Specify location for vertex (0,2): *Specify the coordinate location of vertex (0,2,0).*
> Specify location for vertex (0,3): *Specify the coordinate location of vertex (0,3,0).*
> Specify location for vertex (0,4): *Specify the coordinate location of vertex (0,4,0).*
> Specify location for vertex (0,5): *Specify the coordinate location of vertex (0,5,0).*
> Specify location for vertex (1,0): *Specify the coordinate location of vertex (1,0,0).*
> Specify location for vertex (1,1): *Specify the coordinate location of vertex (1,1,2).*
> Specify location for vertex (1,2): *Specify the coordinate location of vertex (1,2,0).*
> Specify location for vertex (1,3): *Specify the coordinate location of vertex (1,3,0).*
> Specify location for vertex (1,4): *Specify the coordinate location of vertex (1,4,0).*
> Specify location for vertex (1,5): *Specify the coordinate location of vertex (1,5,0).*

Enter the remaining vertex points to complete the mesh.

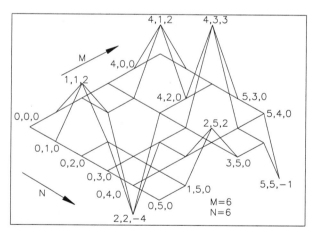

Figure 21-28 Surface created with the **3DMESH** *command*

Note

The **3DMESH** *and* **PFACE** *commands are intended primarily for use by menu items and programs to create surfaces. Using them at the command line is tedious and error-prone.*

PFACE COMMAND

Command: PFACE

The **PFACE** command is similar to the **3DFACE** command in that both allow you to create a mesh of any desired surface shape by specifying the coordinates of the vertices and assigning the vertices to the faces in the mesh. The difference between them is that when you use the **3DFACE** command, you do not select the vertices that join another face twice; with the **PFACE** command, you need to select all the vertices of a face, even if they are coincident with vertices of another face. In this way, you can avoid generating unrelated 3D faces that have coincident vertices. Also, with this command, there is no restriction on the number of faces and the number of vertices the mesh can have.

Command: **PFACE** ⏎
Specify location for vertex 1: *Specify the location of the first vertex.*
Specify location for vertex 2 or <define faces>: *Specify the location of the second vertex.*
Specify location for vertex 3 or <define faces>: *Specify the location of the third vertex.*
Specify location for vertex 4 or <define faces>: *Specify the location of the fourth vertex.*
Specify location for vertex 5 or <define faces>: *Specify the location of the fifth vertex.*
Specify location for vertex 6 or <define faces>: *Specify the location of the sixth vertex.*
Specify location for vertex 7 or <define faces>: *Specify the location of the seventh vertex.*
Specify location for vertex 8 or <define faces>: *Specify the location of the eighth vertex.*
Specify location for vertex 9 or <define faces>: ⏎

After defining the locations of all the vertices, press ENTER and you will assign vertices to the first face.

Face 1, vertex 1:
Enter a vertex number or [Color/Layer]: 1 ⏎
Face 1, vertex 2:
Enter a vertex number or [Color/Layer] <next face>: 2 ⏎
Face 1, vertex 3:
Enter a vertex number or [Color/Layer] <next face>: 3 ⏎
Face 1, vertex 4:
Enter a vertex number or [Color/Layer] <next face>: 4 ⏎

Once you have assigned the vertices to the first face, give a null response at the next prompt.

Face 1, vertex 5:
Enter a vertex number or [Color/Layer] <next face>: ⏎

You can also change the color and layer of the first face within the **PFACE** command. For example, if you want to change the color of the first face to red, the prompt sequence is:

Face 1, vertex 5:
Enter a vertex number or [Color/Layer] <next face>: COLOR ⏎
Enter a color number or standard color name <BYLAYER>: RED ⏎

Now the first face will be red.

After assigning the vertices, give a null response at the next prompt. Now, AutoCAD provides you with the prompt sequence in which you have to assign vertices to the second face:

> Face 2, vertex 1:
> Enter a vertex number or [Color/Layer]: 1 [Enter]
> Face 2, vertex 2:
> Enter a vertex number or [Color/Layer]: 4 [Enter]
> Face 2, vertex 3:
> Enter a vertex number or [Color/Layer]: 5 [Enter]
> Face 2, vertex 4:
> Enter a vertex number or [Color/Layer]: 8 [Enter]

Once you have assigned the vertices to the second face, give a null response at the next prompt:

> Face 2, vertex 5:
> Enter a vertex number or [Color/Layer]: [Enter]
> Face 3, vertex 1:
> Enter a vertex number or [Color/Layer]: [Enter]

Similarly, assign vertices to all the faces.
If you want to make an edge invisible, specify a negative number for the first vertex of the edge. The display of the invisible edges of 3D solid surfaces is governed by the **SPLFRAME** system variable. If **SPLFRAME** is set to 0, invisible edges are not displayed. If this variable is set to a number other than 0, all invisible edges are displayed. You can use the **HIDE** or **SHADEMODE** command to see the effect of the **PFACE** command (Figure 21-29).

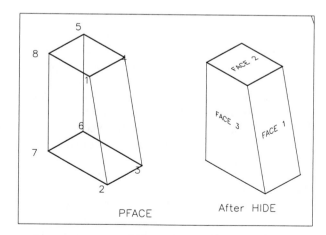

Figure 21-29 Using the *PFACE* command

3DFACE COMMAND

Toolbar:	Surfaces > 3D Face
Menu:	Draw > Surfaces > 3D Face
Command:	3DFACE

 Often, 3D models need solid surfaces for shading, hiding, and so on. Three- or four-sided surfaces are created with the help of the **3DFACE** command. The prompt sequence for the **3DFACE** command is somewhat similar to that for the **SOLID** command. The difference is that the surface created with the **SOLID** command is parallel to the current UCS, whereas with the **3DFACE** command the surface can be created anywhere in the 3D space. With this command, you can specify different Z coordinates for the different corners of a face, thereby forming a plane in 3D space.

Command: **3DFACE** [Enter]
Specify first point or [Invisible]: *Select the first point of the first face.*
Specify second point or [Invisible]: *Select the second point of the first face.*
Specify third point or [Invisible] <exit>: *Select the third point of the first face.*
Specify fourth point or [Invisible] <create three-sided face>: *Select the fourth point of the first face.*

Once you specify the first, second, third, and fourth points, AutoCAD closes the face from the fourth point to the first point (see Figure 21-30). The next prompt asks you to specify the third point. At this prompt, you can give a null response if you do not want to form any more solid surfaces. Once you give a null response, the **3DFACE** command is terminated. If you want to create more than one solid surface, the third and fourth points of the previous face will become the first and second points, respectively, of the next face. Hence, once you have the first and the second points, you need the third and fourth points to create the solid surface. AutoCAD prompts you for these two points:

Specify third point or [Invisible] <exit>: *Select the third point of the second face.*
Specify fourth point or [Invisible] <create three-sided face>: *Select the fourth point of the second face.*

If you want to create any more solid surfaces, use the procedure just described or terminate the **3DFACE** command by giving a null response. If you have a surface with only three corners (triangular) and you want to form the solid surface, select the three corners; at the **Specify third point or [Invisible] <exit>:** and **Specify fourth point or [Invisible] <create three-sided face>:** prompts, give null responses.

You may want to make some edges invisible. This can be accomplished with the **Invisible** option of the **3DFACE** command. Enter I before selecting the first point of the invisible edge. All the edges of a 3D face can be made invisible. As mentioned before, display of the invisible edges of 3D solid surfaces is governed by the **SPLFRAME** system variable. If you set **SPLFRAME** to 0, all invisible edges are not displayed; if this variable is set to a number other than 0, all invisible edges are displayed. You can control the **SPLFRAME** variable through the **ShowEdge** and **HideEdge** options (macros) listed in the screen menu. If you select the **ShowEdge** option, all the invisible edges are displayed. When **SPLFRAME** is set to 1, AutoCAD displays the following message:

Invisible edges will be SHOWN after next Regeneration

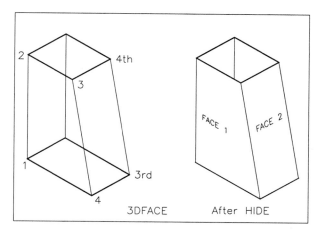

*Figure 21-30 Using the **3DFACE** command to create faces*

HideEdge can be used to hide all edges drawn with the **Invisible** option. When **SPLFRAME** is set to 0, AutoCAD displays the following message:

Invisible edges will be HIDDEN after next Regeneration

You can also control the visibility of edges through the **Object Properties** window. Select a 3D face and right-click to display a shortcut menu, choose **Properties** to display the **Object Properties** window. Under **Geometry**, choose **Visible** or **Hidden** from the **Edge** drop-down list of the specific edge whose visibility you want to modify. You can also use the **EDGE** command. This command is invoked by choosing the **Edge** button in the **Surfaces** toolbar, by choosing **Surfaces > Edge** from the **Draw** toolbar or entering **EDGE** at the Command prompt.

Command: **EDGE**
Specify edge of 3dface to toggle visibility or [Display]: *Select an edge or enter D for the Display option.*

Using the **Display** option, selects invisible edges of the 3Dfaces to redisplay them. The next prompt is:

Enter selection method for display of hidden edges [Select/ All] <All>: *Enter an option or press ENTER.*

The **All** option displays all the hidden edges of all the 3dfaces in the drawing. The **Select** option allows you to select specific hidden edges of partially visible 3dfaces and then displays them.

Setting Elevation and Thickness

You can also use Elevation and Thickness to create and view 3D objects. Elevation is based on the Z value of the XY plane on which the object is drawn. A value of 0 means the object coincides with the XY plane, a value greater than 0 means the object is above the XY plane and a negative value means it is below the plane. Thickness is the distance by which the object is extruded above or below the elevation. You can use the **THICKNESS** system variable to set the current 3D thickness. Objects with thickness can be hidden, shaded and rendered similar to meshes. The thickness of objects can be modified by using the **Object Properties** window, **CHPROP** and **CHANGE** commands. The elevation can be changed by moving the object along the Z axis. **ELEV** command also assigns elevation and extrusion thickness to new objects. The **ELEVATION** system variable stores the current elevation value.

DRAWING 3D POLYLINES (3DPOLY COMMAND)

Menu:	Draw > 3D Polyline
Command:	3DPOLY

You can draw 3D polylines using the **3DPOLY** command (Figure 21-31). The working of the **3DPOLY** and **PLINE** commands is similar. The exceptions are that a third dimension (Z) is added to the polyline, and with the **3DPOLY** you can only draw straight line segments without variable widths.

Command: **3DPOLY** [Enter]
Specify start point of polyline: *Specify a point where you want to start the 3D polyline.*
Specify endpoint of line or [Undo]: *Specify the endpoint on the screen.*
Specify endpoint of line or [Undo]: *Specify the endpoint on the screen*
Specify endpoint of line or [Close/Undo]: *Specify the endpoint on the screen or enter an option or press ENTER when finished drawing the 3D polyline.*

Figure 21-31 *Using the* **3DPOLY** *command*

The **3DPOLY** command provides the **Close** and **Undo** options.

Close Option
This option draws the connecting segment between the start point of the first polyline segment and the endpoint of the last polyline segment. Hence, you need to have at least two lines.

Undo Option
The **Undo** option reverses the effect of the previous operation. If you use the **Undo** option, the last polyline segment is erased, and a rubber-band line is fixed to the previous point while you are still in the **3DPOLY** command.

Certain editing operations cannot be performed on 3D polylines: joining, curve fitting with arc segments, and giving tangent specifications to the 3D polyline. You can use the **PEDIT** command to edit 3D polylines.

CREATING ARRAYS IN 3D SPACE (3DARRAY COMMAND)

Menu:	Modify > 3D Operation > 3D Array
Command:	3DARRAY

You can create arrays of objects in 3D space just as you can in 2D space. This can be achieved with the **3DARRAY** command. Basically, the **3DARRAY** command is similar to the **ARRAY** command. The difference, of course, is the third dimension (Z). The third dimension is nothing but a plane parallel to the XY plane along the Z axis. There are two types of 3D arrays, the **Rectangular** Array and the **Polar** Array.

3D Rectangular Array

Once you enter the **3DARRAY** command, AutoCAD displays the following message:

> Command: **3DARRAY** Enter

The next prompt asks you to select the objects you want to form the 3D array:

> Select objects: *Select the objects by using any object selection method.*

After selecting the objects, give a null response at the next **Select objects:** prompt.

The next prompt displayed is:

> Enter type of array [Rectangular/Polar] <R>:

At this prompt, specify whether you want to construct a rectangular array (R) or a polar array (P). In this example, we will construct a rectangular array.

> Enter type of array [Rectangular/Polar] <R>:

The next two prompts ask you to specify the number of rows and the number of columns you want the 3D array to have.

> Enter number of rows (—) <1>: *Specify the number of rows you want in the array.*
> Enter number of columns (|||) <1>: *Specify the number of columns you want in the array.*

The difference between the prompt sequence for the **ARRAY** command and that for the **3DARRAY** command lies in the next prompt. At this prompt, you need to specify the number of levels the array should have.

> Enter number of levels (...) <1>: *Specify the number of levels you want to have in the array.*

The next three prompts ask you to specify the distance between the rows, the distance between the columns, and the distance between the levels.

Specify the distance between rows (—):
Specify the distance between columns (| | |):
Specify the distance between levels (...):

By specifying negative values, the array will be drawn along the negative X, Y, and Z axes. If you specify positive values, the array will be drawn along the positive X, Y, and Z axes. At the end, use the **VPOINT** command to change the viewpoint to (1,-1,1) so that you can view the array from a 3D viewpoint.

Example 2

In this example, a 3D array of 3D cones will be created (Figure 21-32). The specifications of the array are:

Number of rows = 3
Number of columns = 3
Number of levels = 2
Distance between the rows = 1.00
Distance between the columns = 1.50
Distance between the levels = 5.00
Radius of the base of the cone = 0.30
Radius of the top of the cone = 0.0
Height of the cone = 0.80

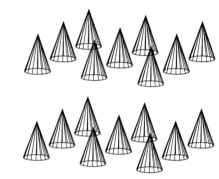

Figure 21-32 Creating a rectangular 3D array

1. First, create a 3D cone, and then generate an array. The prompt sequence for drawing a cone with the given specifications is:

    Command: **AI_CONE** [Enter]
    Specify center point for base of cone: *Specify the center point.*
    Specify radius for base of cone or [Diameter]: 0.30 [Enter]
    Specify radius for top of cone or [Diameter] <0>: [Enter]
    Specify height of cone: 0.80 [Enter]
    Enter number of segments for surface of cone <16>: *Specify the number of segments for the cone.*

2. Now that the object has been created, you can draw the 3D array. The prompt sequence is:

    Command: **3DARRAY** [Enter]
    Select objects: *Select the cone.*
    Select objects: [Enter]
    Enter the type of array [Rectangular/Polar] <R>: R [Enter]
    Enter the number of rows (---) <1>: 3 [Enter]
    Enter the number of columns (| | |) <1>: 3 [Enter]
    Enter the number of levels (...) <1>: 2 [Enter]
    Specify the distance between rows (---): 1.00 [Enter]
    Specify the distance between columns (| | |): 1.50 [Enter]

Specify the distance between levels (...): 5.00 [Enter]

3. After completion of this prompt sequence, the 3D array will be generated. If you are viewing the array from the top, use the **VPOINT** command to change the viewpoint to (1,-1,1) so that you can get a 3D view of the array.

Creating a 3D Polar Array

You can use the **3DARRAY** command to create a 3D polar array. The difference between a 2D polar array and a 3D polar array is that the 3D polar array needs an axis of rotation.

Command: **3DARRAY** [Enter]
Select objects: *Select the objects.*
Select objects: [Enter]

To specify a polar array, enter P at the next prompt:

Rectangular or Polar array (R/P): P [Enter]

The next prompt asks you to specify the number of items (selected objects) you want in the array:

Enter number of items in the array: *Specify the number of items in the array.*

AutoCAD next prompts you to enter the angle to be filled by the array. If the angle specified is positive, the array is rotated in a counterclockwise direction. If the angle specified is negative, the array is rotated in a clockwise direction.

Specify the angle to fill [+=ccw, -=cw]<360>: *Enter the angle value.*
Rotate arrayed objects ? [Yes/No] <Y>: *Specify whether to rotate objects as the array is being formed.*
Specify center point of array: *Specify the center point of the array.*
Specify second point on axis of rotation: *Select a point on the axis.*

Example 3

In this example, you will create a 3D polar array composed of 3D spheres (Figure 21-33). The specifications of the array are:

Radius of sphere = 0.50
Number of items in array = 5
Angle to fill = 360 degrees
Objects should be rotated as they are copied.

1. First, draw a sphere with the given specifications and then construct the polar array. Press the **Sphere** button in the **Surfaces**

Figure 21-33 *Creating polar 3D array*

toolbar. The prompt sequence to draw a sphere of 0.50 unit radius is:

Command: **AI_SPHERE** [Enter]
Specify center point of sphere: *Specify the center point.*
Specify radius of sphere or [Diameter]: 0.50 [Enter]
Enter number of longitudinal segments for surface of sphere <16>: *Specify the number of longitudinal (vertical) segments for the sphere.*
Enter number of latitudinal segments for surface of sphere <16>: *Specify the number of latitudinal (horizontal) segments for the sphere.*

2. Now that the sphere has been constructed, construct the polar array. The prompt sequence is:

Command: **3DARRAY** [Enter]
Select objects: *Select the sphere.*
Select objects: [Enter]
Enter the type of array [Rectangular/Polar] <R>: P [Enter]
Enter the number of items in the array: 5 [Enter]
Specify the angle to fill (+=ccw, -=cw) <360>: [Enter]
Rotate arrayed objects? [Yes/No] <Y>: [Enter]
Specify center point of array: *Specify the center point of the array.*
Specify second point on axis of rotation: *Select a point on the new Z axis.*

3. Once the polar array has been formed, change the viewpoint to (1,-1,1) so that you have a 3D view of the array.

MIRRORING 3D OBJECTS (MIRROR3D COMMAND)

Menu:	Modify > 3D Operation > Mirror
Command:	MIRROR3D

In Chapter 4, we discussed how 2D objects can be mirrored. Now, you will learn how to use the **MIRROR3D** command to mirror objects in 3D space, irrespective of the orientation of the current UCS. The prompt sequence is:

Command: **MIRROR3D** [Enter]
Select objects: *Select the objects to be mirrored.*
Select objects: *Press ENTER when done selecting.*
Specify first point of mirror plane [Object/Last/Zaxis/View/XY/YZ/ZX/3points] <3points>: *Enter an option or press ENTER.*

The different options in this prompt are discussed as follows:

3points Option

This is the default option. In this option, you specify the mirroring plane with the help of three points. The mirroring plane is the plane that passes through the three points.

Specify 1st point on mirror plane: *Specify the first point.*

Specify 2nd point on mirror plane: *Specify the second point.*
Specify 3rd point on mirror plane: *Specify the third point.*
Delete source objects? [Yes/No] <N>: *Enter Y or N to retain or delete old object.*

Object Option*

In this option, you select an object, and the mirroring plane is aligned with the plane of the selected entity.

> Command: **MIRROR3D** Enter
> Select objects: *Select the objects to be mirrored.*
> Select objects: *Press ENTER when done selecting.*
> Specify first point of mirror plane (3 points) or
> [Object/Last/Zaxis/View/XY/YZ/ZX/3points] <3points>: O
> Select a circle, arc or 2D-polyline segment: *Select the object.*
> Delete source objects? <N>: *Enter Y or N to retain or delete old object.*

Last Option

Just as in the case of the **Last** option of the **ROTATE3D** command, the **Last** option of the **MIRROR3D** command uses the last defined mirroring plane to mirror objects.

Zaxis Option

This option prompts you to specify two points. The mirroring plane is defined by a point on the plane and a point on the Z axis of that plane.

> Point on plane: *Specify a point on the plane.*
> Specify point on Z-axis (normal) of mirror plane: *Specify a point on the Z axis of the plane.*
> Delete source objects? <N>: *Enter Y or N to retain or delete old object.*

View Option

You are prompted for a point. The mirroring plane passes through the specified point and is perpendicular to the view direction.

> Specify point on view plane <0,0,0>: *Specify a point.*
> Delete source objects? <N>: *Enter Y or N to retain or delete old object.*

XY Option

You are prompted for a point. The mirroring plane is aligned with the XY plane and passes through the specified point.

> Specify point on XY plane <0,0,0>: *Specify a point.*
> Delete source objects? <N>: *Enter Y or N to retain or delete old object.*

YZ Option

You are prompted for a point. The mirroring plane is aligned with the YZ plane and passes through the specified point.

Specify point on YZ plane <0,0,0>: *Specify a point.*
Delete source objects? <N>: *Enter Y or N to retain or delete old object.*

ZX Option

You are prompted for a point. The mirroring plane is aligned with the ZX plane and passes through the specified point.

Specify point on ZX plane <0,0,0>: *Specify a point.*
Delete source objects? <N>: *Enter Y or N to retain or delete old object.*

Example 4

In the following example, Figure 21-34(a) shows the original object. You are going to perform mirroring operations on it using the XY option, ZX option, and YZ option.

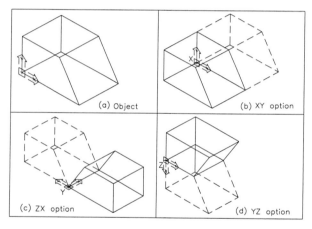

Figure 21-34 MIRROR3D options

Figure 21-34(b) shows the object that has been mirrored using the **XY** option. The original objects have been shown in hidden lines. The prompt sequence is:

Command: **MIRROR3D** Enter
Select objects: *Select the object to be mirrored as shown [Figure 21-34(a)].*
Select objects: *Press ENTER when done selecting.*
Specify first point of mirror plane (3 points) or
[Object/Last/Zaxis/View/XY/YZ/ZX/3points] <3points>: XY Enter
Specify point on XY plane <0,0,0>: *Specify X as the point on the XY plane.*
Delete source objects? <N>: Enter

Figure 21-34(c) shows the object that has been mirrored by using the **ZX** option. The original objects have been shown in hidden lines. The prompt sequence is:

Command: **MIRROR3D** Enter

Select objects: *Select the object to be mirrored.*
Select objects: *Press ENTER when done selecting.*
Specify first point of mirror plane (3 points) or
[Object/Last/Zaxis/View/XY/YZ/ZX/3points] <3points>: ZX Enter
Specify point on ZX plane <0,0,0>: *Specify Y as the point on the ZX plane.*
Delete source objects? <N>: Enter

Figure 21-34(d) shows the object that has been mirrored by using the **YZ** option. The original objects have been shown in hidden lines. The prompt sequence is:

Command: **MIRROR3D** Enter
Select objects: *Select the object to be mirrored.*
Select objects: *Press ENTER when done selecting.*
Specify first point of mirror plane (3 points) or
[Object/Last/Zaxis/View/XY/YZ/ZX/3points] <3points>: YZ Enter
Specify point on YZ plane <0,0,0>: *Specify Z as the point on YZ plane.*
Delete source objects? <N>: Enter

Example 5

Figure 21-35(a) shows the original object. In this example, you will perform mirroring operations using the **Object** option, **Zaxis** option, and **3points** option.

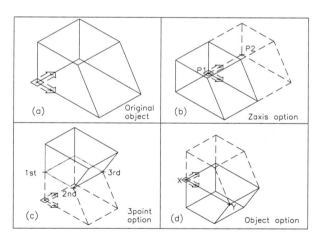

Figure 21-35 MIRROR3D options

Figure 21-35(b) shows the object that has been mirrored by using the **Zaxis** option. The original objects have been shown in hidden lines. The prompt sequence is:

Command: **MIRROR3D** Enter
Select objects: *Select the object to be mirrored [Figure 21-35(a)].*
Select objects: *Press ENTER when done selecting.*

Specify first point of mirror plane (3 points) or
[Object/Last/Zaxis/View/XY/YZ/ZX/3points] <3points>: Zaxis `Enter`
Specify point on mirror plane: *Select point P1.*
Specify point on Z-axis (normal) of mirror plane: *Select point P2.*
Delete source objects? [Yes/No] <N>: `Enter`

Figure 21-35(c) shows the object that has been mirrored using the **3points** option. The original objects have been shown in hidden lines. The prompt sequence is:

Command: **MIRROR3D** `Enter`
Select objects: *Select the object to be mirrored [Figure 21-35(a)].*
Select objects: *Press ENTER when done selecting.*
Specify first point of mirror plane (3 points) or
[Object/Last/Zaxis/View/XY/YZ/ZX/3points] <3points>: `Enter`
Specify first point on mirror plane: *Select the point at location 1.*
Specify second point on mirror plane: *Select the point at location 2.*
Specify third point on mirror plane: *Select the point at location 3.*
Delete source objects? [Yes/No] <N>: `Enter`

Figure 21-35(d) shows the object that has been mirrored by using the **Object** option. The original objects have been shown in hidden lines. Make sure the mirror line (XY) is a polyline. The prompt sequence is:

Command: **MIRROR3D** `Enter`
Select objects: *Select the object to be mirrored [Figure 21-35(a)].*
Select objects: *Press ENTER when done selecting.*
Specify first point of mirror plane (3 points) or
[Object/Last/Zaxis/View/XY/YZ/ZX/3points] <3points>: O `Enter`
Select a circle, arc, or 2D-polyline segment: *Select the line segment between points X and Y.*
Delete source objects? [Yes/No] <N>: `Enter`

ROTATING 3D OBJECTS (ROTATE3D COMMAND)

Menu:	Modify > 3D Operation > Rotate 3D
Command:	ROTATE3D

With the help of the **ROTATE3D** command, you can rotate an object in 3D space about any axis, irrespective of the orientation of the current UCS.

Command: **ROTATE3D** `Enter`
Current positive angle: ANGDIR=counterclockwise ANGBASE=0
Select objects: *Specify the objects you want to rotate.*
Select objects: `Enter`

At the next prompt, AutoCAD displays different options for selecting the axis of rotation.

Specify first point on axis or define axis by
[Object/Last/View/Xaxis/Yaxis/Zaxis/2points]:

The different options in this prompt are discussed as follows:

2points Option

This is the default option. In this option, you need to specify two points. The axis of rotation is defined by the line between the two points. The direction from the first point to the second point is positive; the direction from the second point to the first point is negative. The rotation follows the right-hand rule.

> Specify first point on axis or define axis by
> [Object/Last/View/Xaxis/Yaxis/Zaxis/2points]: [Enter]
> Specify 1st point on axis: *Specify the first point.*
> Specify 2nd point on axis: *Specify the second point.*
> Specify rotation angle or [Reference]: *Specify the angle of rotation or enter R.*

Object Option

In this case, objects like lines, polylines, circles, and arcs are used to define the axis of rotation. The axis of the circle/arc is perpendicular to its plane and passes through its center. The polyline segment (polyline or polyarc) used to specify the axis of rotation is treated as a line or arc, and then the axis of rotation is determined.

> Select a line, circle, arc or 2D-polyline segment: *Select an object.*
> Specify rotation angle or [Reference]: *Specify the angle of rotation.*

If the selected object is a line, AutoCAD aligns the axis of rotation with the line. If the selected object is a circle, AutoCAD aligns the axis of rotation with the 3D axis of the circle that passes through the center of the circle and is perpendicular to the plane of the circle. If the selected object is an arc, AutoCAD aligns the axis of rotation with the 3D axis of the arc that passes through the center of the arc. If the selected object is a pline, AutoCAD assumes a straight segment as a line and arc segment as an arc.

Last Option

If you invoke this option, the most recently used axis is selected. However, if you have not selected an axis recently, AutoCAD displays the message that no axis has been selected previously, and the axis selection prompt is again displayed.

View Option

This option allows you to specify a point in the space, and the viewing direction is aligned with this point. The axis of rotation passes through the specified point and is perpendicular to the view direction.

> Specify first point on axis or define axis by
> [Object/Last/View/Xaxis/Yaxis/Zaxis/2points]: View [Enter]
> Specify a point on the view direction axis <0,0,0>: *Specify a point.*
> Specify rotation angle or [Reference]: *Specify the angle of rotation.*

Xaxis Option

With this option, the axis of rotation is aligned with the X axis and the specified point.

Specify first point on axis or define axis by
[Object/Last/View/Xaxis/Yaxis/Zaxis/2points]: Xaxis ⏎
Specify a point on the X axis <0,0,0>: *Specify a point.*
Specify rotation angle or [Reference]: *Specify the angle of rotation.*

Yaxis Option

With this option, the axis of rotation is aligned with the Y axis and the specified point.

Specify first point on axis or define axis by
[Object/Last/View/Xaxis/Yaxis/Zaxis/2points]: Yaxis ⏎
Specify a point on the Y axis <0,0,0>: *Specify a point.*
Specify rotation angle or [Reference]: *Specify the angle of rotation.*

Zaxis Option

With this option, the axis of rotation is aligned with the Z axis and the specified point.

Specify first point on axis or define axis by
[Object/Last/View/Xaxis/Yaxis/Zaxis/2points]: Zaxis ⏎
Specify a point on Z axis <0,0,0>: *Specify a point.*
Specify rotation angle or [Reference]: *Specify the angle of rotation.*

If you use the **Reference** option to specify the angle of rotation, AutoCAD displays the prompt:

Specify the reference angle <0>: *Specify the starting angle.*
Specify the new angle: *Specify the ending angle.*

We will work out some examples of various options of the **ROTATE3D** command, which will give you a better idea of the working of **ROTATE3D** command.

Example 6

In this example, the original position of the objects to be rotated is shown in hidden lines. The new position obtained by the object upon rotation is shown in continuous lines.

In Figure 21-36(a), the object is rotated using the **Object** option of the **ROTATE3D** command. The angle of rotation is 180 degrees. The prompt sequence is:

Command: **ROTATE3D** ⏎
Current positive angle: ANGDIR=counterclockwise ANGBASE=0
Select objects: *Specify the objects you want to rotate.*
Select objects: *Press ENTER when done selecting.*
Specify first point on axis or define axis by
[Object/Last/View/Xaxis/Yaxis/Zaxis/2points]: O ⏎

Select a line, circle, arc or 2D-polyline segment: *Select the line between points (P1) and (P2).*
Specify rotation angle or [Reference]: 180 Enter

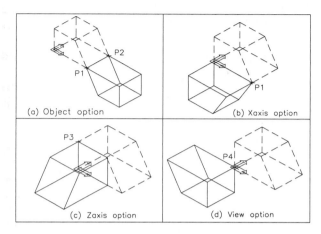

Figure 21-36 ROTATE3D Options

In Figure 21-36(b), the object is rotated using the **Xaxis** option of the **ROTATE3D** command. The angle of rotation is 180 degrees.

Command: **ROTATE3D** Enter
Select objects: *Specify the objects you want to rotate.*
Select objects: *Press ENTER when done selecting.*
Specify first point on axis or define axis by
[Object/Last/View/Xaxis/Yaxis/Zaxis/2points]: X Enter
Select a point on X axis <0,0,0>: *Select the point (P1).*
Specify rotation angle or [Reference]: 180 Enter

In Figure 21-36(c), the object is rotated using the **Zaxis** option of the **ROTATE3D** command. The angle of rotation is -90 degrees.

Command: **ROTATE3D** Enter
Select objects: *Specify the objects you want to rotate.*
Select objects: *Press ENTER when done selecting.*
Specify first point on axis or define axis by
[Object/Last/View/Xaxis/Yaxis/Zaxis/2points]: Z Enter
Select a point on Z axis <0,0,0>: *Select the point (P3).*
Specify rotation angle or [Reference]: 180 Enter

In Figure 21-36(d), the object is rotated using the **View** option of the **ROTATE3D** command. The angle of rotation is 180 degrees.

Command: **ROTATE3D** Enter
Select objects: *Specify the objects you want to rotate.*

Select objects: *Press ENTER when done selecting.*
Specify first point on axis or define axis by
[Object/Last/View/Xaxis/Yaxis/Zaxis/2points]: V [Enter]
Specify a point on the view direction axis <0,0,0>: *Select the point (P4).*
Specify rotation angle or [Reference]: 180 [Enter]

ALIGNING 3D OBJECTS (ALIGN COMMAND)

Menu:	Modify > 3D Operation > Align
Command:	ALIGN

The **ALIGN** command is used to move (translate and rotate) objects in a 3D space, irrespective of the alignment and position of the current UCS. The movement is carried out by selecting up to three points on the original object (source points) and positions where you want to move these points (destination points).

> Command: **ALIGN** [Enter]
> Select objects: *Select the objects you want to relocate.*
> Select objects: *Give a null response if selection is over.*
> Specify first source point: *Select the first point on the object to be aligned.*
> Specify first destination point: *Select the location where first point is to be relocated.*
> Specify second source point: *Select the second point on the object to be aligned.*
> Specify second destination point: *Select the location where second point is to be relocated.*
> Specify third source point or <continue>: *Select the third point on the object to be aligned.*
> Specify third destination point: *Select the location where third point is to be relocated.*

You will notice that when you select a source point, a line is drawn between the corresponding source point and the destination point. These lines are temporary and for reference only. The object can be aligned in three ways.

1. If you specify all three source points and their corresponding destination points, the movement of the object from the source position to the destination position is a combination of a translation and two rotations based on all the specified points. The first source point is moved to the first destination point. The line defined by the first and second source points is aligned with the line defined by the first and second destination points. The plane defined by the three source points is aligned with the plane defined by the three destination points.

2. If you specify only two source points and their corresponding destination points (by pressing ENTER at the **Specify third source point or <continue>:** prompt), the movement of the object from the source position to the destination position is carried out by a translation operation and a rotation operation. Using the translation operation, the first source point is moved to the first destination point. The rotation operation aligns the line passing through the two source points with the line passing through the two destination points. In this case, AutoCAD issues the following prompt:

    Scale objects based on alignment points? [Yes/No] <No>:

    Enter Y to scale the source object to the alignment points.

3. If you specify only one pair of points, the movement of the object from the source position to the destination position is carried out by a translation from the source point to the destination point. This is identical to the **MOVE** operation except that in the **MOVE** operation dynamic dragging is supported.

Example 7

Figure 21-37 shows the objects that are to be aligned and the source points and destination points. The figure also shows the resulting drawing after aligning the object.

In Figure 21-37(a), the aligning operation has been carried out by specifying a single source point (S1) and its respective destination point (D1). The prompt sequence is:

Command: **ALIGN** [Enter]
Select objects: *Select the hidden object.*
Select objects: *Give a null response if selection is over.*
Specify first source point: *Select the first source point (S1) on the object to be aligned.*
Specify first destination point: *Select the location of the first destination point (D1).*
Specify second source point: [Enter]

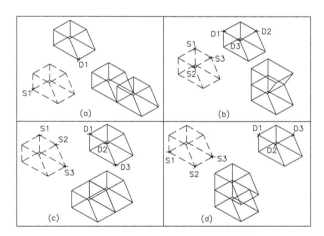

Figure 21-37 Using the ALIGN command to align objects

In the Figure 21-37(b), (c), and (d), the aligning operation has been carried out by specifying three source points (S1, S2, S3) and their respective destination points (D1, D2, D3). The prompt sequence is:

Command: **ALIGN** [Enter]
Select objects: *Select the hidden object.*
Select objects: *Give a null response if selection is completed.*
Specify first source point: *Select the first source point (S1) on the object to be aligned.*
Specify first destination point: *Select the location of the first destination point (D1).*
Specify second source point: *Select the second source point (S2) on the object to be aligned.*

Specify second source point: *Select the location of the second destination point (D2).*
Specify third source point or <continue>: *Select the location of the third source point (S3).*
Specify third destination point: *Select the location of the third destination point (D3).*

TRIM, EXTEND AND FILLET COMMANDS IN 3D

As discussed earlier in Chapter 4, you can use various options of these commands to use them in 3D space. You can also use the **PROJMODE** and **EDGEMODE** variables. The **PROJMODE** variable sets the projection mode for trimming and extending. A value of 0, implies **True 3D mode**, that is, no projection. In this case the objects must intersect in 3D space to trim or extend them. It is similar to using the **None** option of the **Project** option of the **EXTEND** and **TRIM** commands. A value of 1, projects onto the XY plane of the current UCS and is similar to using the **UCS** option of the **Project** option of the **TRIM** or **EXTEND** commands. A value of 2, projects onto the current view plane and is like using the **View** option of the **Project** option of the **TRIM** or **EXTEND** commands. The value of the **EDGEMODE** system variable controls how the cutting or trimming boundaries are decided. A value of 0, considers the selected edge with no extension. You can also use the **No Extend** option of the **Edge** option of the **TRIM** or **EXTEND** commands. A value of 1 considers an imaginary extension of the selected edge. This is similar to using the **Extend** option of the **Edge** option of the **TRIM** or **EXTEND** commands.

You can fillet coplanar objects whose extrusion directions are not parallel to the z axis of the current UCS, using the **FILLET** command. The fillet arc exists on the same plane and has the same extrusion direction as the coplanar objects. If the coplanar objects to be filleted exist in opposite directions, the fillet arc will be on the same plane but will be inclined towards the positive Z axis.

HIDE COMMAND

Toolbar:	Render > Hide
Menu:	View > Hide
Command:	HIDE

 In most 3D wireframe objects, some of the lines lie behind other lines or objects. Sometimes you may not want these hidden lines to show up on the screen, to enhance the clarity of the object. In order to do so, you can use the **HIDE** command. The prompt sequence for using the **HIDE** command is:

Command: **HIDE** [Enter]

Once you enter this command, the screen is regenerated, and all the hidden lines are suppressed in the drawing. The hidden lines are again included in the drawing when the next regeneration takes place. Circles, solids, wide polyline segments, traces, polygon and polyface meshes, 3D faces, and the extruded edges with nonzero thicknesses are treated as opaque surfaces; hence, any object behind them is suppressed once the **HIDE** command is used. Circles, traces, solids, and wide polyline segments are considered to be solid objects if they are extruded. In this case, the bottom and top faces are also considered. Objects on frozen layers or layers that have been turned off are not taken into consideration by the **HIDE** command. If you want to select specific objects to hide, use the **Hide** option of the **DVIEW** command.

CYLINDRICAL COORDINATE SYSTEM

The **cylindrical coordinate system** (Figure 21-38) is also a modification of the polar coordinate system. The location of any point is described by three things:

1. Distance from the present UCS origin.
2. Angle in the XY plane.
3. Z dimension.

This coordinate system is used mostly to locate points on a cylindrical shape. For example, a point 4 units from the UCS origin, at an angle of 25 degrees from the X axis, and having a Z dimension of 6 units would be represented in the following format:
    <Distance from the UCS origin><Angle from X axis><Z dimension>
    @4<25,6.0

SPHERICAL COORDINATE SYSTEM

The spherical coordinate system (Figure 21-39) is a modification of the polar coordinate system. The location of any point is described by three things:

1. Distance from the present UCS origin.
2. Angle in the XY plane.
3. Angle from the XY plane.

This coordinate system is somewhat similar to using longitude, latitude, and the distance from the center of earth to find the location of a point on the earth. The distance from the present UCS origin is analogous to the distance from the center of the earth. The angle in the XY plane is analogous to the longitudinal measurement. The angle from the XY plane is analogous to the latitudinal measurement. The spherical coordinate system is used mostly to locate points on a spherical surface. For example, a point 7 units from the UCS origin, at an angle of 60 degrees from the X axis, and at an angle of 50 degrees from XY plane would be represented in the following format:
    <Distance from the UCS origin><Angle from X axis><Angle from XY plane>
    @7<60<50

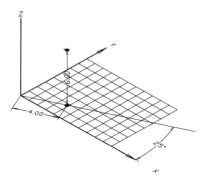

Figure 21-38 Cylindrical coordinate system

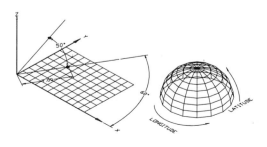

Figure 21-39 Spherical coordinate system

Self-Evaluation Test

Answer the following questions, and then compare your answers to the correct answers given at the end of this chapter.

1. To construct a 3D surfaced model, you can use the _____ command and then enter the name of the object at the next prompt.

2. The default viewpoint is _____ and the view obtained with this viewpoint is called the plan view.

3. In the **Viewpoint Presets** dialog box, you can set a viewpoint by specifying the _____ and an angle from the XY plane.

4. In a 3D array, the third dimension signifies the _____ in the array.

5. To select the _____ mirroring plane as the current mirroring plane, use the **Last** option.

6. The _____ command is used to move (translate and rotate) objects in 3D space, irrespective of the alignment and position of the current UCS.

7. With the _____ option of the **ROTATE3D** command, the axis of rotation passes through the specified point and is perpendicular to the view direction.

8. If you have multiple viewports, the **PLAN** command generates the plan view in only the _____ viewport.

9. The number of sections (surfaces) formed between the two surfaces depends on the _____ system variable.

10. With the _____ command, you can create a mesh (matrix of 3D faces) with four connected sides as the boundaries.

11. You can invoke the **Viewpoint Presets** dialog box by choosing **Viewpoint Presets** from the cascading submenu of **3D Views** in the **View** menu, or by entering _____ at the Command prompt.

12. You can invoke the **3DARRAY** command by selecting the _____ option in the **Modify > 3D Operation** menu.

13. The **MIRROR3D** command can be invoked by selecting the _____ option from the **Modify > 3D Operation** menu, or by entering the _____ command at the Command prompt.

Review Questions

3D Polygon Mesh Objects

1. To construct a 3D surfaced wireframe model of an object, you must enter _____ together with the name of the 3D object at the Command prompt.

2. You can use the _____ command to draw any desired surfaced wireframe model.

3. To construct a 3D solid model, you must enter the _____ of the object at the Command prompt.

4. If you specify any 3D object that is to be constructed through the **Surfaces** toolbar, a _____ model will be constructed.

VPOINT

5. The _____ command lets you define a viewpoint.

6. Once you set a viewpoint, _____ in the current viewport are regenerated and the objects are displayed as if you were viewing them from the direction of the newly defined viewpoint.

7. The default viewpoint is _____ and the view obtained with this viewpoint is called the plan view.

8. If you give a null response at the **Specify a view point or [Rotate] <display compass and tripod>:** prompt, AutoCAD displays a(n) _____ and _____ on the screen.

9. You can specify the viewpoint in the axis and tripod method by moving the _____ in the _____ with a pointing device.

10. As you move the small crosshairs in the compass, the _____ also moves to reflect the changes in the viewpoint.

11. You can set the viewpoint by specifying its coordinate location or by specifying the rotation in the XY plane from the X axis and the _____ .

12. In the **Viewpoint Presets** dialog box, you can set a viewpoint by specifying the _____ and an angle from the XY plane.

13. In the **Viewpoint Presets** dialog box, you can specify the viewing angles from the _____, or by entering the respective angle values in the _____ .

14. The angle you specify in the **Viewpoint Presets** dialog box is indicated by the _____, and the _____ is indicated by the red arm.

3DARRAY

15. You can create arrays of objects in 3D space with the _____ command.

16. The difference between the 2D and the 3D array is that in the 3D array, levels in the _____ also exist.

17. In a 3D array, the third dimension signifies the _____ in the array.

MIRROR3D

18. The _____ command can be used to mirror objects in 3D space, irrespective of the orientation of the current UCS.

19. With the _____ option of the **MIRROR3D** command, you specify the position of the mirroring plane with the help of three points.

20. The **Object** option of the **MIRROR3D** command lets you align the mirroring plane with the plane of the _____ .

21. To select the _____ mirror plane as the current mirroring plane, you must use the **Last** option.

22. If you want to specify the mirroring plane through the **Zaxis** option, you need to define a point on the plane and a point on the _____ of that plane.

23. In the **View** option, the mirroring plane passes through the specified point and is formed perpendicular to the _____ .

24. To align the mirroring plane with the XY plane, you must use the _____ option.

ALIGN

25. The _____ command is used to move (translate and rotate) objects in 3D space, irrespective of the alignment and position of the current UCS.

26. The movement in the **ALIGN** command is carried out by selecting _____ points on the original object and _____ points.

ROTATE3D

27. The _____ command can be used to rotate an object about any 3D axis irrespective of the orientation of the current UCS.

28. If you want to define the axis of rotation about a line between two points, you must use the _____ option of the **ROTATE3D** command.

29. In the _____ option of the **ROTATE3D** command, axes of objects like lines, polylines, circles, and arcs are used to define the axis of rotation.

30. In the _____ option of the **ROTATE3D** command, the axis of rotation passes through the specified point and is perpendicular to the view direction.

PLAN

31. The _____ command can be used to generate the plan view of an object relative to the _____ , _____ , or _____ .

32. If you have multiple viewports, the **PLAN** command generates the plan view of only the _____ viewport.

33. Perspective projection and clipping are turned _____ when you use the **PLAN** command.

HIDE

34. You can use the _____ command to suppress the display of lines that lie behind other lines or objects.

UCSFOLLOW

35. When the _____ variable is assigned a value of 1, a plan view is automatically generated if you change the UCS in a viewport.

RULESURF, TABSURF, REVSURF, EDGESURF

36. The _____ command can be used to generate a polygon mesh (ruled surface) between two _____ objects or two _____ objects.

37. The number of sections (surfaces) formed between the two surfaces depends on the _____ system variable.

38. The _____ command can be used to generate a surface extrusion (tabulated surface) from an object also known as a path curve.

39. With the _____ command, you can create a 3D mesh that trails along the path curve (profile) as it rotates around a centerline, also known as an axis.

40. In case of **REVSURF**, the value of the _____ variable determines the number of equal segments that will divide the path curve.

41. With the _____ command, you can create a mesh (matrix of 3D faces) with four connected sides as the boundaries.

3DMESH

42. The _____ command lets you create a polygon mesh in which the vertices are specified by their X, Y, Z coordinates.

3DPOLY

43. 3D polylines can be drawn using the _____ command.

44. The difference between the **3DPOLY** and **PLINE** commands is that a _____ is added to the polyline, and with the **3DPOLY** you can only draw _____ segments without variable _____ .

PFACE, 3DFACE

45. With the _____ command, you can create a mesh of any desired surface by selecting all the vertices of a face, whether or not they are coincident with the vertices of another face.

46. You can create 3D surfaces with the _____ command.

CYLINDRICAL and SPHERICAL COORDINATES

47. To find the location of a point using the cylindrical coordinate system, you need to know:
    1. _____
    2. _____
    3. _____

    Use the cylindrical coordinate system to start a line from a point that is at a distance of 3 units from the current UCS origin, making an angle of 45 degrees in the XY plane, and having the Z dimension of 4 units. Let the endpoint of the line be at an angle of 20 degrees and a distance of 2 units from the start point.

48. To find the location of a point using the spherical coordinate system, you need to know:
    1. _____
    2. _____
    3. _____

49. Use the spherical coordinate system to find the location of a point 5 units from the UCS origin, making an angle of 45 degrees in the XY plane, and at an angle of 70 degrees from the XY plane.

50. In the XZ option, the mirroring plane is aligned with the _____ plane and passes through the specified point.

Exercises

Exercises 1 through 5   *General*

1. Draw a surfaced wireframe sphere with the center at any desired position and a radius of 1 unit. Change the viewpoint to get the 3D view of the sphere.
2. Construct a torus with a torus diameter of 4 units and tube diameter of 0.50 units.
3. Draw a three-surfaced wireframe model of a pyramid. Let the first model have an apex 3 units above the base of the pyramid. Let the second model have a truncated top. The third model should have a ridge instead of an apex.
4. Draw a truncated cone. Let the bottom diameter be 1.50 units, the height be 3 units, and the top diameter be 0.25 units.
5. Construct a surfaced wireframe mesh. Let the number of rows be 4 and the number of columns be 7.

Problem Solving Exercise 1 — *Mechanical*

Construct a composite solid of the object in Figure 21-40. The model consists of four parts. The bottom part is a rectangle-to-circle transition (surface mesh). The remaining parts are solid cylinders located at different positions along the center vertical plane of the composite solid. The dimensions are as shown in the front and top views. The height of the center cylinder is 4.5. The angle is 45 degrees for the cylinder on the right side. Assume the missing dimensions.

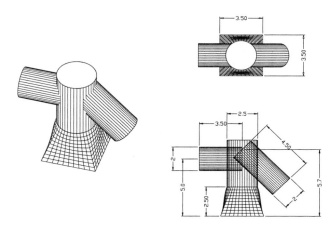

Figure 21-40 Drawing for Problem Solving Exercise 1

Chapter 22

Model Space Viewports, Paper Space Viewports, Layouts, and Dynamic Viewing of 3D Objects

Learning Objectives

After completing this chapter, you will be able to:
- *Create viewports in model space and paper space using the **VPORTS** command.*
- *Create viewports in paper space using the **-VPORTS** and **MVIEW** commands.*
- *Use paper space and model space in paper space.*
- *Shift from paper space to model space using the **MSPACE** command.*
- *Shift from model space to paper space using the **PSPACE** command.*
- *Control the visibility of viewport layers with the **VPLAYER** command.*
- *Set linetype scaling in paper space using the **PSLTSCALE** command.*
- *Dynamically view 3D objects using the **DVIEW** and **3DORBIT** commands.*

MODEL SPACE VIEWPORTS

Normally, in AutoCAD, a single viewport is displayed on the screen. AutoCAD allows you to create multiple viewports that can be used to display different views of the same object (Figure 22-1). A viewport is a rectangular part of the graphics area of the screen. Viewports can be used in different ways and for different purposes. The first reason to create viewports and divide the display screen into a number of parts is usually to create a model or layout. This is done using the **VPORTS** command. You are in the **tiled viewport** mode when you use this command. This is the default mode in AutoCAD. When you want to use the **VPORTS** command to create multiple tiled viewports, the **TILEMODE** system variable is set to 1 (default value). An arrangement of tiled viewports is a display function and cannot be plotted. The second purpose is to have different parts or different views of your drawing in different viewports. Each viewport can contain a different 2D or 3D view of your drawing, and you can use the **PAN** or **ZOOM** command to display different portions or different levels of detail of the drawing in each viewport. The Snap, Grid, and UCS icon modes can be set separately for each viewport. Using the **UCSVP** variable you can make the UCS in the viewport the same as the current UCS.

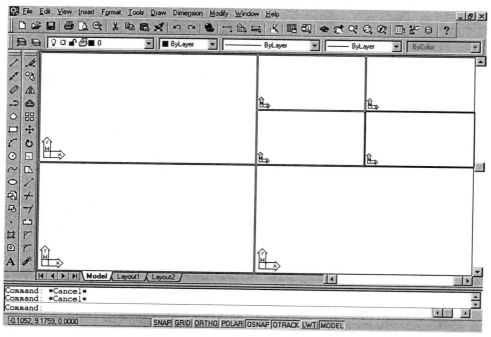

Figure 22-1 Screen display with multiple viewports

DISPLAYING VIEWPORTS AS TILED AREAS (VPORTS COMMAND)

Toolbar:	Layouts > Display Viewports Dialog
Menu:	View > Viewports > New Viewports
Command:	VPORTS

Display Viewports Dialog

*Figure 22-2 Invoking the **VPORTS** command from the **Layouts** toolbar*

As mentioned earlier, the display screen can be divided into multiple nonoverlapping tiled viewports whose number depends on the equipment and the operating system on which AutoCAD is running. Each tiled viewport contains a view of the drawing. The tiled viewports must touch at the edges without overlapping one another. While using tiled viewports, you are not allowed to edit, rearrange, or turn individual viewports on or off. These viewports are created using the **VPORTS** command when the system variable **TILEMODE** is set to 1; the **Model** tab is active. The prompt sequence is:

> Command: **TILEMODE** Enter
> Enter new value for TILEMODE <0>: 1 Enter

As required, we have set the system variable **TILEMODE** to 1. You can also set **TILEMODE** to 1 by choosing the PAPER button located in the status bar or choosing the **Model** tab. Now we will use the **VPORTS** command.

> Command: **VPORTS** Enter

The **Viewports** dialog box is displayed. You can use this dialog box to create new viewport configurations and save them. The options in the dialog box vary depending upon whether you choose the **Model** tab or the **Layout** tab. The **Viewports** dialog box has the following two tabs: **New Viewports** tab (Figure 22-3) and **Named Viewports** tab.

New Viewports Tab

You can enter a name for the viewport configuration you wish to create in the **New name:** edit box. If you do not enter a name in this edit box, the viewport configuration created by you is not saved and hence, cannot be used in layout. A list of standard viewport configurations is listed in the

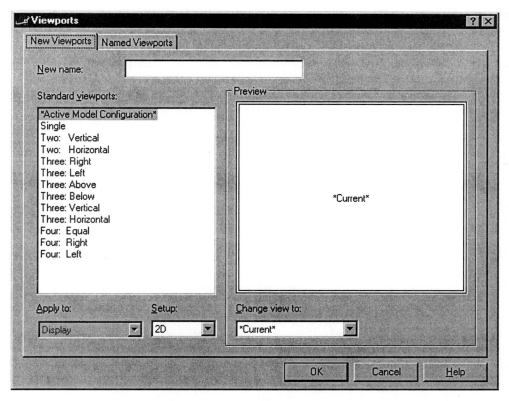

*Figure 22-3 The **New Viewports** tab of the **Viewports** dialog box*

Chapter 22

Standard viewports: list box. This list also contains the ***Active Model Configuration*** which is the current viewport configuration. From the **Standard viewports:** list, you can select any one of the listed standard viewport configurations to apply and a preview image of the selected configuration is displayed in the **Preview** window. The **Apply to:** drop-down list has two options: **Display** and **Current viewport**. Selecting the **Display** option applies the selected viewport configuration to the entire display and selecting the **Current viewport** option applies the selected viewport configuration to only the current viewport. From the **Setup:** drop-down list, you can select **2D** or **3D**. Selecting the **2D** option, creates the new viewport configuration with the current view of the drawing in all the viewports initially. Using the **3D** option, applies the standard orthogonal and isometric views to the viewports. For example if your configuration has 4 viewports, they are assigned the **Top**, **Front**, **Left** and **South East Isometric** views respectively. You can also modify these standard orthogonal and isometric views by selecting from the **Change view to:** drop-down list and replacing the existing view in the selected viewport. For example you can select the viewport which is assigned the **Top view** and then choose **Bottom view** from the **Change view to:** drop-down list to replace it. The Preview image in the **Preview** window reflects the changes you make. If you are using the **2D** option, you can select a named viewport configuration to replace the selected one. Choose **OK** to exit the dialog box and apply the created or selected configuration to the current display in the drawing. When you name and save a viewport configuration, it saves information about the number and position of viewports, the viewing direction and zoom factor and the grid, snap, coordinate system and UCS icon settings of the viewports.

Named Viewports Tab

The **Named Viewports** tab of the **Viewports** dialog box (Figure 22-4), displays the name of the current viewport next to **Current name:**. The names of all the saved viewport configurations in a drawing are displayed in the **Named viewports:** list box. You can select any one of the named viewport configurations and apply it to the current display. A preview image of the selected configuration is displayed in the **Preview** window. Choose **OK** to exit the dialog box and apply the selected viewport configuration to the current display. In the **Named viewports:** list box, you can select a name and right-click to display a shortcut menu. Choosing **Delete** deletes the selected viewport configuration and choosing **Rename**, allows you to rename the selected viewport configuration.

After we have discussed how to make a viewport current, we will describe all of the options of the **-VPORTS** command. You should know how to make a viewport current before using any of the options.

Making a Viewport Current

The viewport you are working in is called the current viewport. You can display several model space viewports on the screen, but you can work in only one of them at a time. You can switch from one viewport to another even when you are in the middle of a command. The current viewport is indicated by a border that is heavy compared with the borders of the other viewports. Also, the graphics cursor appears as a drawing cursor (screen crosshairs) only when it is within the current viewport. Outside the current viewport this cursor appears as an arrow cursor. You can enter points and select objects only from the current viewport. To make a viewport current, you can select it with the pointing device. Another way of making a viewport current is by assigning its identification number to the **CVPORT** system variable. The identification numbers of the named viewport configurations are not listed in the display. Following are the options of the **-VPORTS**

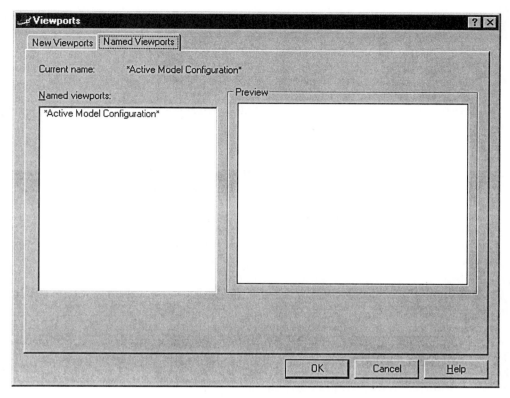

Figure 22-4 Named Viewports tab of the Viewports dialog box

command.

-VPORTS Command Options

Save option. This option is used to name and save the current viewport configuration. The prompt sequence is:

> Command: **-VPORTS** Enter
> Enter an option [Save/Restore/Delete/Join/SIngle/?/2/3/4]<3>: S Enter
> Enter name(s) for new viewport configuration or [?]: *Enter the name.*

The naming conventions are the same as those used earlier. You can use up to 31 characters and wild cards. Entering the **?** symbol causes the following prompt to be displayed:

> Enter name(s) of viewport configuration(s) to list <*>:

As a response to this prompt, you can press ENTER to get a listing of all the saved viewport configurations.

Restore option. This option restores any saved viewport configuration. You can enter the name of the viewport configuration to restore, or you can enter ? to display a list of all saved viewport configurations. The prompt sequence is:

Command: **-VPORTS** [Enter]
Enter an option [Save/Restore/Delete/Join/SIngle/?/2/3/4]<3>: R [Enter]
Enter name(s) for new viewport configuration or [?]: *Enter the name.*

You can use the ? symbol in the same way as for the **Save** option.

Delete option. You can delete a previously saved viewport configuration using this option. The prompt sequence is:

Command: **-VPORTS** [Enter]
Enter an option [Save/Restore/Delete/Join/SIngle/?/2/3/4]<3>: D [Enter]
Enter name(s) of viewport configuration(s) to delete <none>: *Enter the name.*

If you enter a wrong name, the system gives the following message: No matching viewport configurations found.

Join option. With this option, you can join two adjacent viewports into a single viewport. The view in the resulting viewport depends on which one of the two viewports you specified as the dominant viewport when they were joined. You can also select this option from the **View** menu, choose **View > Viewports > Join**.

Command: **-VPORTS** [Enter]
Enter an option [Save/Restore/Delete/Join/SIngle/?/2/3/4]<3>: J [Enter]
Select dominant viewport <current viewport>: *Select the dominant viewport.*
Select viewport to join: *Select other viewport.*

SIngle option. With this option, you can have only one viewport on the screen, and the view in this viewport depends on which one of the viewports was current when you selected the **SIngle** option. This is similar to choosing **Viewports > 1 Viewport** from the **View** menu.

? option. Invoking this option displays the identification number and screen positions of all the active viewports and the names and screen positions of the saved viewport configurations. The position of the viewports is defined by the lower left and upper right corners. The value for these corners is between (0.0,0.0) for the lower left corner of the graphics area and (1.0,1.0) for the upper right corner of the graphics area. The current viewport is the first one listed. You can also use wild-card characters to filter names. For example, entering sp* will list all configurations whose names start with sp.

2 option. This option is used to divide the current viewport into two equal parts. You can also choose **Viewports > 2 Viewports** from the **View** menu.

Enter an option [Save/Restore/Delete/Join/SIngle/?/2/3/4]<3>: 2 [Enter]
Enter a configuration option [Horizontal/Vertical] <Vertical>:

If you press ENTER at this prompt, then the current viewport is divided vertically. If you enter **Horizontal**, the current viewport is divided horizontally.

3 option. You invoke the **3 option** to divide the current viewport into three viewports in the following manner:

Enter an option [Save/Restore/Delete/Join/SIngle/?/2/3/4]<3>: 3 [Enter]

The next prompt is:

Enter a configuration option [Horizontal/Vertical/Above/Below/Left/Right] <Right>:

When you enter **Horizontal** at this prompt, the current viewport is divided horizontally into three equal parts. The **Vertical** option divides the current viewport vertically into three equal parts. The **Above**, **Below**, **Left**, and **Right** options divide the current viewport into one large and two smaller viewports. The placement of the larger viewport depends on which one of these options you specify. For example, if you select the **Above** option, the current viewport is divided horizontally into two viewports and the lower viewport is further divided vertically into two viewports. You can also invoke this option by choosing **Viewports > 3 Viewports** from the **View** menu.

4 option. Using this option, you can divide the current viewport into four equal viewports. You can also choose **Viewports > 4 Viewports** from the **View** menu.

 Note
By dividing, subdividing, and joining viewports, you can create nearly any viewport configuration you want, so long as all viewports are rectangular.

OBTAINING PLAN VIEWS AUTOMATICALLY (UCSFOLLOW SYSTEM VARIABLE)

As mentioned before, you can obtain the plan view of an object by using the **PLAN** command. If you have different viewports, you can obtain the plan view relative to the current UCS by activating a viewport, setting the UCS to your requirement, and using the default option of the **PLAN** command. This operation can be automated by using the **UCSFOLLOW** system variable. When **UCSFOLLOW** is assigned a value of 1, a plan view is automatically generated if you change the UCS. By default, this variable is assigned the value 0. All of the viewports have the **UCSFOLLOW** facility; hence, you need to specify the **UCSFOLLOW** setting separately for each viewport. The prompt sequence is:

Command: **UCSFOLLOW** [Enter]
Enter new value for UCSFOLLOW <0>: 1 [Enter]

WORKING WITH FLOATING VIEWPORTS (VPORTS COMMAND)

Invoking the **VPORTS** command in the **Layout** tab also displays the **Viewports** dialog box. This dialog box is used to create a floating viewports configuration. Floating viewports can be overlapping and can be plotted at the same time. They are used for arranging the final layout of a drawing. The **Viewports** dialog box has the same two tabs as the **Viewports** dialog box displayed in the **Model** tab, but the options vary.

New viewports tab

In this tab of the **Viewports** dialog box (Figure 22-5), the current viewport configuration name is displayed next to **Current Name:**. The **Standard viewports:** list box displays all the standard viewport configurations. Selecting a viewport configuration from this list, displays a preview image in the **Preview** window with all the default views assigned to individual viewports. In the **Viewport Spacing:** edit box, you can enter a value for the distance you want to keep between individual viewports. Selecting **2D** from the **Setup:** drop-down list, displays the current view in all the viewports of the current viewport configuration initially. Selecting the **3D** option, a set of standard orthogonal views are applied to the viewports in the configuration. You can replace a selected viewport configuration with one selected from the **Change view to:** drop-down list. In case of a **3D** setup, you can replace the default orthogonal view applied to individual viewports by selecting one from the **Change view to:** drop-down list.

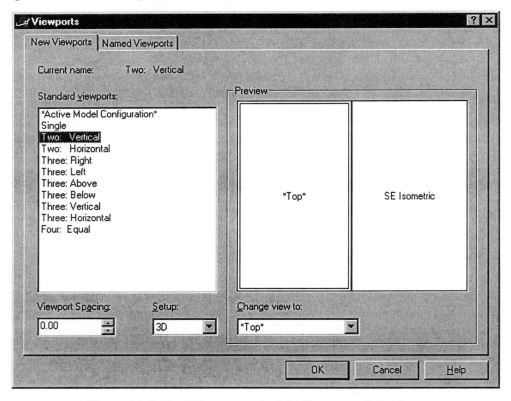

Figure 22-5 New Viewports tab of the Viewports dialog box

Named Viewports tab

The **Named Viewports** tab displays any saved and named tiled configurations for you to use in the current layout. You cannot save and name a floating viewport configuration.

-VPORTS COMMAND

In AutoCAD, you can create tiled viewports or floating viewports (untiled viewports). Tiled viewports are created by using the **VPORTS** command when the **TILEMODE** system variable is set to 1 (model space). The same command is used to create floating viewports in paper space (Figure 22-6) when you are in the layout tab. The **-VPORTS** command can be used when in the **Layout** tab to create and use floating viewports. If you invoke this command in the floating model space (TILEMODE set to 0), AutoCAD shifts you from model space to paper space, until the **-VPORT** command is active. Once the **-VPORT** command is over, AutoCAD returns you to model space. The command prompts are as follows:

Command: **-VPORTS**
Specify corner of viewport or
[ON/OFF/Fit/Hideplot/Lock/Object/Polygonal/Restore/2/3/4]<Fit>:

*Figure 22-6 Floating viewports using the **-VPORTS** command*

The purpose of creating untiled viewports in paper space by using the **-VPORT** command is that viewports are created in paper space, and these viewports can be edited as objects like circles, polygons, or text. Various settings of the first viewport created with the **-VPORT** command, such as grid, current view, and snap, are taken from the previous viewport that was current in paper space. You can also alter the size of the floating viewports and adjust them on the screen. Since viewports in paper space are just like objects, it is not possible to edit the model in paper space. For this, you need to shift from paper space to floating model space with the help of the **MSPACE** command or you can choose PAPER on the status bar.

When you enter the **-VPORT** command, AutoCAD prompts you either to select one of the options listed in the prompt line or to select the first corner point of the paper space viewport window.

-VPORT Command Options

Corner of viewport option. The **Corner of viewport** option (Figure 22-7) is the default option. With this option, you can create a single viewport. The size of the viewport is determined by the two diagonal points you specify. Once you specify the two points, a viewport is created.

Hideplot option. With the **Hideplot** option (Figure 22-8), you can choose the viewports from which you want to remove the hidden lines when you plot in paper space. If you set **Hideplot** to ON, hidden lines are not plotted. If you set **Hideplot** to OFF, hidden lines are plotted.

> Command: **-VPORT** [Enter]
> Specify corner of viewport or
> [ON/OFF/Fit/Hideplot/Lock/Object/Polygonal/Restore/2/3/4]<Fit>: H [Enter]
> Hidden line removal for plotting [ON/OFF]: ON [Enter]
> Select objects: *Select the viewports*.

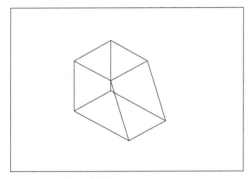

*Figure 22-7 -VPORTS command, **Corner of** viewport option*

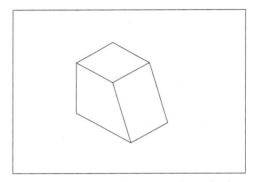

*Figure 22-8 -VPORTS command, **Hideplot** option*

Note

*When you turn **Hideplot** On, the hidden line removal takes place only at the time of plotting. It does not affect the display of the lines on screen (hidden line will be displayed). You can use the **HIDE** command to see the effect of hidden line removal.*

ON/OFF option. These options are used to turn the display in the selected viewports on or off. By default, the display inside the current viewport is on. You should turn off the viewports that are not required so that regeneration is not carried out on viewports that are turned off. Objects are not displayed in the viewports that are turned off.

Note

*The system variable **MAXACTVP** controls the number of viewports that display the objects. For example, if **MAXACTVP** is set to 16, only 16 viewports can simultaneously display the objects. The remaining viewports will not display the objects unless one or more viewports that display the objects are turned off or the **MAXACTVP** system variable is set to a higher value.*

*If you zoom or use **REGEN** in the viewport that does not display the object, AutoCAD will automati-*

cally turn off one of the other viewports to force display of the objects in the viewport.

You will not be able to work in the floating model space if all viewports are turned off; you must create a new viewport or turn on one of the viewports.

Fit option. This option generates the viewport that fits the current screen display. For example, if you want to create a single viewport, use the **Fit** option. The size of the viewport can be controlled by setting the limits or by using the **ZOOM** command to display the desired area.

2 option. You can invoke the **2** option to create two viewports in the area you specify. This option is similar to the **2** option of the **-VPORTS** command. Once you enter 2 at the **Specify corner of viewport or [ON/OFF/Fit/Hideplot/Lock/Object/Polygonal/Restore/2/3/4]<Fit>:** prompt, AutoCAD prompts you for the location and arrangement of the viewports. The prompt is:

Enter viewport arrangement [Horizontal/Vertical] <Vertical>:

At the prompt, you can choose whether the rectangular area you have specified is to be horizontally or vertically divided. The default arrangement is vertical (Figure 22-9), but you can change it to horizontal (Figure 22-10) by entering HORIZONTAL at the prompt. Once you have specified the arrangement of the viewport, the next two prompts are:

Specify first corner or [Fit]<Fit>:
Specify opposite corner:

These prompts are identical to the **Fit** and **First corner** options of the **-VPORTS** command. For example, if you enter the first corner, the next prompt asks you to specify the opposite corner of the rectangular area in which the two viewports will be created. Once these two points are defined, AutoCAD will fit the two viewports within the specified area. The **Fit** option will fit the viewports in the current screen display.

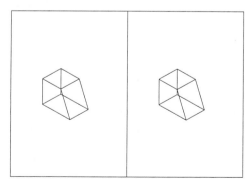

Figure 22-9 -VPORTS command, 2 option with vertical viewports

Figure 22-10 -VPORTS command, 2 option with horizontal viewports

3 option. You can invoke the **3** option to create three viewports in the area you specify. This option is similar to the **3** option of the **-VPORTS** command in the **Model** tab. Once you enter **3** at the

Specify corner of viewport or [ON/ OFF/ Fit/Hideplot/Fit/Lock/Object/Polygonal/Restore/2/3/ 4] <Fit>: prompt, AutoCAD prompts you for the location and arrangement of the viewports. The prompt is:

Enter viewport arrangement [Horizontal/Vertical/Above/Below/Left/Right] <Right>:

At the prompt, you can choose whether the rectangular area you have specified is to be divided into three viewports horizontally or vertically, and whether the third viewport is to be placed above, below, to the left of, or to the right of the other two viewports (Figures 22-11 through 22-16). The default option is **Right**, with the third viewport placed on the right side of the other two viewports. If you invoke the **Horizontal** option, the space you have specified for the viewports is divided into three equal horizontal viewports.

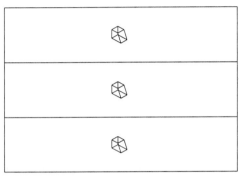

Figure 22-11 -VPORTS command, 3 option with the third viewport on right

Figure 22-12 -VPORTS command, 3 option with horizontal viewports

If you invoke the **Vertical** option, the space you have specified for the viewports is divided into three equal vertical viewports. The **Above** option places the third viewport on top of the other two viewports. The **Below** option places the third viewport under the other two viewports. If you use the **Left** option, the third viewport is placed on the left side of the other two viewports. Once you have specified the arrangement of the viewport, the next two prompts are:

Specify first corner or [Fit]<Fit>:
Specify opposite corner:

These prompts are identical to the **Fit** and **First Corner** options of the **-VPORTS** command. For example, if you specify the first corner, the next prompt asks you to specify the opposite corner of the rectangular area in which the three viewports will be created. Once these two points are defined, AutoCAD will fit the three viewports within the specified area. The **Fit** option will fit the viewports in the current screen display.

4 option. Using the 4 option, you can divide the area you have specified for the viewports into four equal viewports. If you use the **Fit** option, the graphics area on the screen is divided into four equal viewports (Figure 22-17).

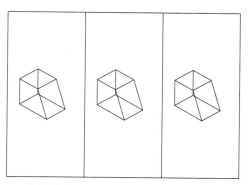

***Figure 22-13 -VPORTS** command, **3** option with the vertical viewports*

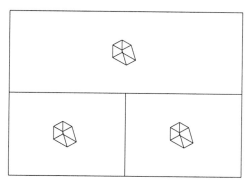

***Figure 22-14 -VPORTS** command, **3** option with one viewport above*

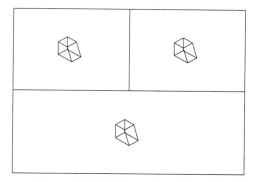

***Figure 22-15 -VPORTS** command, **3** option with one viewport below*

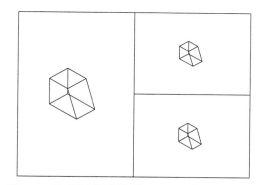

***Figure 22-16 -VPORTS** command, **3** option with one viewport on left*

Restore option. If you have used the **VPORTS** command to create and save a viewport configuration, the **Restore** option of the **-VPORTS** option can be used to obtain that configuration by specifying the name of the configuration (Figure 22-18). Once you specify the configuration name, you can specify the location and size of the viewports by using the **Fit** or **First Corner** option.

> Enter window configuration name or [?] <default>: *Specify the name of the configuration you want to restore.*
> Specify first corner or [Fit]<Fit>: Select first corner.
> Specify opposite corner: *Select second corner.*

Lock option*. You can turn the viewport locking on or off for a specific viewport. This option restricts any accidental modifications to scaling in a viewport. The command prompts are:

> Viewport View Locking [ON/OFF]: ON
> Select Objects: *Select the viewports you want to lock.*

Object option*. You can specify an object to be used as a viewport as long as the specified object

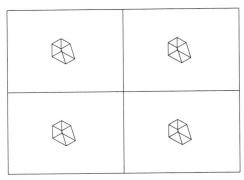

Figure 22-17 -VPORT command, 4 option

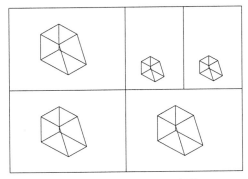

*Figure 22-18 -VPORT command, **Restore** option*

is closed and has at least three vertices. The object can be self-intersecting and can contain line as well as arc segments. This option can also be invoked by choosing the **Convert Object to Viewport** button in the **Viewports** toolbar or choosing **Viewports > Object** from the **View** menu, when you are in the **layout** tab. The command prompt is:

Select object to clip viewport: *Select the object.*

Polygonal option*. This option allows you to create an irregularly shaped viewport. This shape can include arcs also. This option can also be invoked by choosing the **Polygonal Viewport** button from the **Viewport** toolbar or by choosing **Viewports > Polygonal** from the **View** menu. The command prompts are:

Specify start point:
Specify next point or [Arc/Close/Length/Undo]: *Enter an option or specify the next point.*

Arc. The **Arc** option allows you to add an arc to the polygonal viewport. The next prompt on choosing the Arc option displays all the options available to draw an arc.

[Angle/CEnter/CLose/Direction/Line/Radius/Second point/Undo/Endpoint of arc] <End-point>: *Enter an option or press ENTER to specify the endpoint of the arc.*

Close. The **Close** option closes the boundary of the viewport, that is, it joins the first point to the last. After you have specified three points of the polygonal viewport, if you press ENTER, the viewport is closed, that is, the first point is joined to the last.

Line. This option draws a line segment of a specified length at the same angle as the previous segment. In case, the previous segment is an arc, the specified line segment will be drawn tangent to the arc. The command prompt is:

Specify length of line:

Undo. This option cancels the last line or arc segment drawn.

The Viewports Toolbar*

The **Display Viewports Dialog** button invokes the **Viewports** dialog box depending on whether you are in **Model** tab or **Layout** tab. The **Single Viewport** button creates a single viewport depending on whether you are in **Model** tab or in the **Layout** tab. The **Polygonal Viewport** button creates irregularly shaped viewports as discussed in the **Polygonal** option of the **-VPORTS** command in the **Layout** tab only. The **Convert Object to Viewport** button creates viewports of existing objects and invokes the **Object** option of the **-VPORTS** command in the **Layout** tab only. The **Clip Existing Viewport** button clips an existing viewport to an existing object or asks you to create a closed shape which it would clip the existing viewport to. This invokes the **VPCLIP** command as discussed later. The **Viewport Scale Control** drop-down list displays a list of scale factors to choose from that can be applied to a selected viewport.

Figure 22-19 Viewports toolbar

When you have selected a viewport and you right-click, a shortcut menu appears. Choosing **Viewport Clip** allows you to clip the selected viewport to an existing object or allows you to create a new viewport shape to replace it. **Display Viewport Objects** gives you the option of either displaying the objects in the selected viewport or not. **View Lock** gives you an option to either Lock or unlock the selected viewport. **Hide Plot** allows you to either turn hideplot on or off. Choosing **Properties** from the shortcut menu, displays the **Object Properties** window. The **Misc** area lists all the properties of the selected viewport. You can turn the viewport on or off by choosing **Yes** or **No** from the **On** drop-down list. You can similarly choose options to turn on or off properties like **Clipped**, **Display locking**, **Hideplot** and saving **UCS per viewport** of the selected viewport.

MVIEW COMMAND

Menu:	View > Viewports > 1 Viewports, 2 Viewports, 3 Viewports or 4 Viewports
Command:	MVIEW

The **MVIEW** command creates floating viewports and allows various options to work with them. The **TILEMODE** system variable should be set to 0. If you invoke this command in the floating Model space while you are in the **Layout** tab, AutoCAD shifts you to Paper space from Model space until the **MVIEW** command is over. Once the **MVIEW** command is over, you are returned to model space. The command prompt is:

Command: **MVIEW**
Specify corner of viewport
or[ON/OFF/Fit/Hideplot/Lock/Object/Polygonal/2/3/4]<Fit>: *Enter an option or specify the viewport on screen by specifying points by using your pointing device.*

The options displayed by the **MVIEW** command are the same as the **-VPORTS** command in the

Layout tab and have been discussed earlier in this Chapter.

VPCLIP COMMAND*

Toolbar:	Viewports > Clip Existing Viewport
Command:	VPCLIP

 The **VPCLIP** command clips the selected viewports to the specified or specified viewport boundary in the **Layout** tab. The command prompts are as follows:

Command: **VPCLIP**
Select viewport to clip:
Select clipping object or [Polygonal/Delete] <Polygonal>:

Object option. Allows you to select an object to act as a clipping boundary of the selected viewport. The objects that can be selected should be closed and include polylines, circles, ellipses, closed splines, and regions.

Polygonal option. Allows you to draw a clipping boundary by drawing line segments and arcs. The command prompts are:

Specify start point:
Specify next point or [Arc/Close/Length/Undo]:

These options of the **Polygonal** option of the **VPCLIP** command are similar to the **Polygonal** option of the **-VPORTS** command.

Delete option. Deletes the clipping boundary of a selected viewport that has been already clipped. On clipping a viewport that has been previously clipped, the original clipping boundary is deleted and gets replaced by the new boundary.

MODEL SPACE AND PAPER SPACE
Model Space (MSPACE Command)

Status bar:	PAPER
Command:	MSPACE

The **MSPACE** command is used to shift from paper space to floating model space (Figure 22-20). Before using this command, you must set **TILEMODE** to 0 (Off); you should be in the **Layout** tab. To shift from paper space to model space, at least one of the floating viewports must be on.

Command: **MSPACE** [Enter]

AutoCAD acknowledges switching into Mspace by issuing the **MSPACE** message at the command line. Also, in the status bar PAPER is changed to MODEL. You can also switch to model space by double-clicking a viewport in Paper space.

Paper Space (PSPACE Command)

Status bar:	MODEL
Command:	PSPACE

This command is used to shift from model space to paper space (Figure 22-21). Before using this command, you must set TILEMODE to 0 (Off); you should be in the Layout tab.

Command: **PSPACE** [Enter]

You can also switch to Paper space by double-clicking an area of Paper space.

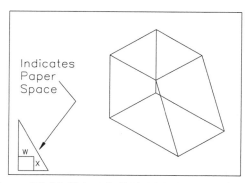

Figure 22-20 Using the *MSPACE* command to switch to model space

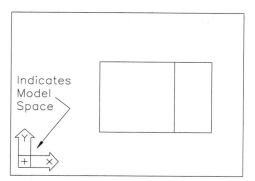

Figure 22-21 Using the *PSPACE* command to switch to paper space

MANIPULATING THE VISIBILITY OF VIEWPORT LAYERS (VPLAYER COMMAND)

Command:	VPLAYER

You can control the visibility of layers inside a floating viewport with the **VPLAYER** or **LAYER** command. The **On/Off** or **Freeze/Thaw** option of the **LAYER** command controls the visibility of layers globally, including the viewports. However, with the **VPLAYER** command you can control the visibility of layers in individual floating viewports. For example, you can use the **VPLAYER** command to freeze a layer in the selected viewport. The contents of this layer will not be displayed in the selected viewports, although in the other viewports, the contents are displayed. This command can be used from either model space or paper space. The only restriction is that **TILEMODE** be set to 0 (Off); that is, you can use this command only in the **Layout** tab.

Command: **VPLAYER** [Enter]
Enter an option [?/Freeze/Thaw/Reset/Newfrz/Vpvisdflt]:

VPLAYER Command Options

When you enter the **VPLAYER** command at the Command prompt, AutoCAD returns a prompt line that displays the available options:

Chapter 22

Command: **VPLAYER** [Enter]
Enter an option [?/Freeze/Thaw/Reset/Newfrz/Vpvisdflt]:

? option. You can use this option to obtain a listing of the frozen layers in the selected viewport. When you enter ?, AutoCAD displays the following prompt:

Select a viewport:

At this prompt, select the viewport for which you want a listing of the frozen layers. If you are in model space, AutoCAD will temporarily shift you to paper space to let you select the viewport. The complete prompt sequence of this option is:

Command: **VPLAYER** [Enter]
Enter an option [?/Freeze/Thaw/Reset/Newfrz/Vpvisdflt]: ? [Enter]
Switching to Paper space
Select a viewport: *Select a viewport.*
Layers currently frozen in viewport 1:
DIM2
DIM3
Switching to Model space
Enter an option [?/Freeze/Thaw/Reset/Newfrz/Vpvisdflt]:

Freeze option. The **Freeze** option is used to freeze a layer (or layers) in one or more viewports (Figure 22-22). When you select this option, AutoCAD displays the following prompt:

Enter layer name(s) to freeze: *Enter the layer name(s).*

In response to the prompt, specify the name of the layer you want to freeze. If you want to specify more than one layer, the layer names must be separated by commas. You can also use wild cards to specify the names of the layers you want to freeze. Once you have specified the name of the

Figure 22-22 *Using the **VPLAYER** command to freeze layers in viewports*

layer(s), AutoCAD prompts you to select the viewport(s) in which you want to freeze the specified layer(s). The prompt is:

> Enter an option [All/Select/Current]<current>: *Enter an option or press ENTER to accept default.*

The **All** option applies the changes to all viewports. **Select** allows you to specify a particular viewport to which you wish to apply changes. The **Current** option applies changes to only the current viewport.

Thaw option. With this option, you can thaw the layers that have been frozen in viewports using **VPLAYER Freeze** or the **LAYER** command. Layers that have been frozen, thawed, turned on, or turned off globally are not affected by **VPLAYER Thaw**. For example, if a layer has been frozen, the objects on the frozen layer are not regenerated on any viewport even if **VPLAYER Thaw** is used to thaw that layer in any viewport. The prompt sequence for the **VPLAYER** command with the **Thaw** option is:

> Command: **VPLAYER** [Enter]
> Enter an option [?/Freeze/Thaw/Reset/Newfrz/Vpvisdflt]: THAW [Enter]
> Enter layer name(s) to thaw: *Specify the layer(s) to be thawed.*

If you want to specify more than one layer, separate the layer names with commas. The next prompt lets you specify the viewport(s) in which you want to thaw the specified frozen layers.

> Enter an option [All/Select/Current]<Current>: *Specify the viewports.*

Reset option. With the **Reset** option, you can set the visibility of layer(s) in the specified viewports to their current default setting. The visibility defaults of a layer can be set by using the **Vpvisdflt** option of the **VPLAYER** command. The following is the prompt sequence of the **VPLAYER** command with the **Reset** option:

> Command: **VPLAYER** [Enter]
> Enter an option [?/Freeze/Thaw/Reset/Newfrz/Vpvisdflt]: RESET [Enter]
> Enter layer name(s) to reset: *Specify the names of the layer(s) you want to reset.*
> Enter an option [All/Select/Current]<current>: *Select the viewports in which you want to reset the specified layer to its default setting.*

Newfrz (New freeze) option. With this option, you can create new layers that are frozen in all viewports. This option is used mainly where you need a layer that is visible only in one viewport. This can be accomplished by creating the layer with **VPLAYER Newfrz**, and then thawing that particular layer in the viewport where you want to make the layer visible. The following is the prompt sequence of the **VPLAYER** command with the **Newfrz** option:

> Command: **VPLAYER** [Enter]
> Enter an option [?/Freeze/Thaw/Reset/Newfrz/Vpvisdflt]: NEWFRZ [Enter]
> Enter name(s) of new layers frozen in all viewports: *Specify the name of the frozen layer(s) you want to create.*

If you want to specify more than one layer, separate the layer names with commas. After you specify the name(s) of the layer(s), AutoCAD creates frozen layers in all viewports. Also, the default visibility setting of the new layer(s) is set to Frozen; hence, if you create any new viewports, the layers created with **VPLAYER Newfrz** are also frozen in the new viewports.

Vpvisdflt (Viewport visibility default) option. With this option, you can set a default for the visibility of layer(s) in the subsequent new viewports. When a new viewport is created, the frozen/thawed status of any layer depends on the **Vpvisdflt** setting for that particular layer.

> Command: **VPLAYER** [Enter]
> Enter an option [?/Freeze/Thaw/Reset/Newfrz/Vpvisdflt]: VPVISDFLT [Enter]
> Enter layer name(s) to change viewport visibility: *Specify the name(s) of the layer(s) whose default viewport visibility you want to set.*

Once you have specified the layer name(s), AutoCAD prompts:

> Enter a viewport visibility option [Frozen/Thawed]<Thawed>:

At this prompt, enter FROZEN or F if you want to set the default visibility to frozen. To set the default visibility to thawed, press ENTER or enter T for Thawed.

Controlling Viewport through the
Layer Properties Manager Dialog Box

You can use the **Layer Properties Manager** dialog box (Figure 22-23) to perform certain functions of the **VPLAYER** command, such as freezing/thawing layers in viewports.

Active VP Freeze. When the **TILEMODE** is turned off, you can freeze or thaw the selected layers in the current floating viewport by selecting the **Active viewport Freeze** toggle icon. The frozen layers will still be visible in other viewports.

New VP Freeze. If you want to freeze some layers in the new floating viewports, then select the **New VP Freeze** toggle icon. AutoCAD will freeze the layers in subsequently created new viewports without affecting the viewports that already exist (see Chapter 3, Drawing Aids, for more information).

If you start drawing on the frozen layer, objects drawn in the new viewport will not be displayed in the new viewport; however, in other viewports, the objects drawn in the new viewport will appear.

Figure 22-23 Controlling viewport display through the **Layer Properties Manager** dialog box

PAPER SPACE LINETYPE SCALING (PSLTSCALE SYSTEM VARIABLE)

By default, the linetype scaling is controlled by the **LTSCALE** system variable. Therefore, the display size of the dashes depends on the **LTSCALE** factor, on the drawing limits, or on the drawing units. If you have different viewports with different zoom (XP) factors, the size of the dashes will be different for these viewports. Figure 22-24 shows three viewports with different sizes and different zoom (XP) factors. You will notice that the dash length is different in each of these three viewports.

Generally, it is desirable to have identical line spacing in all viewports. This can be achieved with the **PSLTSCALE** system variable. By default, **PSLTSCALE** is set to 0. In this case, the size of the dashes depends on the **LTSCALE** system variable and on the zoom (XP) factor of the viewport where the objects have been drawn. If you set **PSLTSCALE** to 1 and **TILEMODE** to 0, the size of the dashes for objects in the model space are scaled to match the **LTSCALE** of objects in the paper space viewport, regardless of the zoom scale of the viewports. In other words, if **PSLTSCALE** is set to 1, even if the viewports are zoomed to different sizes, the length of the dashes will be identical

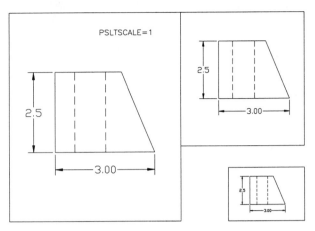

*Figure 22-24 When **PSLTSCALE** is 0 and **TILEMODE** is 0, the dash length depends on the size of the viewport*

in all viewports. Figure 22-25 shows three viewports with different limits. Notice that the dash length is identical in all three viewports.

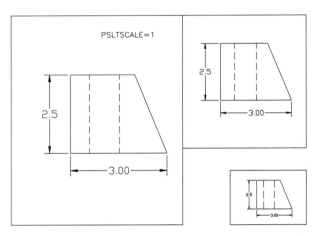

*Figure 22-25 When **PSLTSCALE** is 1 and **TILEMODE** is 0, the dash length is the same in all viewports*

CREATING AND WORKING WITH LAYOUTS (LAYOUT COMMAND*)

Toolbar:	Layouts > New Layout
Menu:	Insert > Layout > New Layout
Command:	LAYOUT

The **LAYOUT** command is used to create a new layout. It also allows you to rename, copy, save and delete existing layouts. A drawing which has been designed in the **Model** tab can be composed for plotting in the **Layout** tab. You can also add title blocks, more than one viewports and other annotations. The command prompts are:

Figure 22-26 The Layouts toolbar

> Enter layout option [Copy/Delete/New/
> Template/Rename/SAveas/Set/?]<Set>:

New option. Creates a new layout. The command prompt is :

> Enter new layout name <Layout 3>: *Specify a new name for the new layout or press ENTER to accept the default name.*

A new tab with the new layout name appears in the drawing.

Copy option. This option copies a layout. The command prompts are:

> Enter layout to copy <current>: *Enter the name of the layout you wish to copy.*
> Enter layout name for copy <default>:

If you do not enter a name for the copy of the layout, the name of the copied layout is assumed with an incremental number in brackets next to it. For example, Layout 1 is copied as Layout1(2). The name of the new layout appears as a new tab next to the copied **layout** tab.

Delete option. This option deletes an exiting layout. The most recently created layout is the default layout. The **Model** tab cannot be deleted. The command prompt is:

> Enter name of layout to delete <current>:

Template option. This option creates a new template based on an existing layout template in either .dwg or .dwt files. This option invokes the **Select File** dialog box if the **FILEDIA** system variable is 1. The layout and geometry from the specified template or drawing file is inserted into the current drawing. After the DWT or DWG file is selected, you can select one or more layouts from the **Insert** dialog box.

Choosing the **Layout from Template** button from the **Layouts** toolbar creates a layout using an existing template or drawing file. You can also choose **Layout > Layout from Template** from the **Insert** menu.

Rename option. This option allows you to rename a layout. The command prompts are:

> Enter layout to rename <current>:
> Enter new layout name:

Layout names have to be unique and can contain upto 255 characters, out of which only 32 are displayed in the tab. The characters in the name are not case sensitive.

Chapter 22

Save option. Saves a layout in the drawing template file. If the **FILEDIA** system variable is set to 1, the **Create Drawing File** dialog box appears where you can enter a file name in the **File name:** edit box. The command line prompts are:

    Enter layout to save to template <Default>:
    Enter layout template file name<current>:

Set option. Sets a layout as the current layout. The command prompt is:

    Enter layout to make current<last>:

? option. This option lists all the layouts in the current drawing.

You can choose any of the above **LAYOUT COMMAND** options from the shortcut menu which appears on right-clicking any of the **Layout** tabs.

PAGESETUP COMMAND*

Toolbar:	Layouts > Page Setup
Menu:	File > Page Setup
Command:	PAGESETUP

You can also right-click the **Model** or any of the **Layout** tabs and choose **Page Setup** from the shortcut menu which is displayed. This command allows you to specify the Layout and Plot device settings for each new layout. On invoking this command, the **Page Setup** dialog box is displayed, the details of which have been discussed in Chapter 15, Plotting Drawings and Draw Commands.

Every time you select a new **Layout** tab, the **Page Setup** dialog box is displayed automatically. These default settings are controlled in the **Layout elements** area of the **Display** tab of the **Options** dialog box.

LAYOUTWIZARD COMMAND*

Menu:	Insert > Layouts > Layout Wizard
	Tools > Wizards > Create Layout
Command:	LAYOUTWIZARD

This command displays the **Layout Wizard** which guides you step by step through the process of creating a new layout.

Example 1

In this example, you will learn how to create a drawing in the model space and then use the paper to plot the drawing.

1. Based on the drawing size, calculate the limits. Since the drawing is 50' x 48', the limits should be about 75'x60'.

2. Set the limits and layers, then draw the floor plan as shown in Figure 22-27. The overall dimensions are given in the drawing in Figure 22-28; assume other dimensions.

Figure 22-27 *Floor plan drawing for Example 1*

3. Use the **LAYOUT** command to create a new layout. You can also create a new layout by right-clicking on the **Model** or one of the **layout** tabs to display the shortcut menu. In the shortcut menu select **New layout**.

    Command: **LAYOUT**
    Enter layout option [Copy/Delete/New/Template/Rename/SAveas/Set/?]<set>:N
    Enter new layout name <Layout3>: *Specify new name or press ENTER to accept default name.*

    A new tab with the new layout name is displayed next to the last **layout** tab.

4. Next, choose the new layout (**Layout3**) tab, AutoCAD displays the **Page Setup-Layout3** dialog box. Select the **Plot Device** tab and then the select the printer or plotter that you want to use, from the Name: drop-down list. In this example, **HP Lasejet4000** is used. Choose the **Layout Settings** tab and then select the paper size that is supported by your plotting device from the Paper size: drop-down list. In this example, the paper size is 8.5 x 11. Choose the **OK** button to accept the settings and exit the dialog box. AutoCAD displays the new layout (**Layout3**) on the screen with the default viewport. Use the **ERASE** command to erase the default viewport.

5. Use the **MVIEW** command to create a viewport of 11 x 8.5 size. Once you create the viewport, the drawing will automatically appear in the viewport. Draw the border and title block according to your requirements.

6. Use the **MSPACE** command to switch to model space or double-click the viewport to switch to Model space and use the **ZOOM** command to zoom the drawing to 1/96XP. In this example, it is assumed that the scale factor is 1:96 (1/8"=1'); therefore, the zoom factor is 1/96XP.

7. Create a dimension style with the text height of 1/8" and the text above the dimension line.

Figure 22-28 Drawing plotted in paper space with 1:1 scale

Also, based on the given drawing, change other dimension settings and select the **Scale dimensions to layout (Paper Space)** radio button in the **Fit** tab of the **New Dimension Style** dialog box.

8.   Now, give the two overall dimensions as shown in the drawing. When you dimension, AutoCAD automatically adjusts the dimensions. For example, the dimension text size will increase so that when you plot the drawing the dimension text will be 1/8".

Note
For more information about dimensioning in paper space, see "Model Space and Paper Space Dimensioning" in Chapter 7.

9.   Use the **PSPACE** command or double-click on the paper area to switch to paper space and then plot the drawing at 1:1 scale (Figure 22-29).

10. Use the **MSPACE** command to switch to model space or double-click the viewport and then use the **ZOOM** command to zoom to 1/144XP. The drawing display will reduce.

11. To adjust the dimensions to the correct size, use the **UPDATE** command at the **DIM** prompt and select the dimensions to be updated. AutoCAD will automatically change the dimensions so that when the drawing is plotted, the dimension are of the right size.

12. Plot the drawing and compare the two drawings. You will notice that the dimension text height is the same in both drawings.

This way, you can use the model space to draw and dimension your drawings, and then use the paper space to draw the border, title block, and other annotations. When you are done, you can plot the drawings 1:1 size from the paper space.

Figure 22-29 Drawing plotted in paper space with 1:1 scale

DYNAMIC VIEWING OF 3D OBJECTS (DVIEW COMMAND)

Command: DVIEW

With the **DVIEW** command, you can create a parallel projection or a perspective view of objects on the screen. Basically, **DVIEW** is an improvement over the **VPOINT** command in that the **DVIEW** command allows you to visually manoeuvre around 3D objects to obtain different views. As just mentioned, the **DVIEW** command offers you a choice between parallel viewing and perspective viewing. The difference between the two is that in parallel view, parallel lines in the 3D object remain parallel, whereas in perspective view, parallel lines meet at a vanishing point. These definitions suggest that with the **VPOINT** command, only parallel viewing is possible. When the Perspective view is current, **ZOOM, PAN, 'ZOOM, 'PAN, DSVIEWER** commands and scroll bars are not available. The **DVIEW** command uses the camera and target concept to visualize an object from any desired position in 3D space. The position from which you want to view the object (the viewer's eye) is the camera, and the focus point is the target. The line formed between these two points is the line of sight, also known as the viewing direction. To get different viewing directions, you can move the camera or target or both. Once you have the required viewing direction, you can change the distance between the camera and the target by moving the camera along the line of sight. The field of view can be changed by attaching a wide-angle lens or a telephoto lens to the camera. You can pan or twist (rotate) the image. The hidden lines in the object being viewed can be suppressed. You can clip those portions of the model that you do not want to see. All these options of the **DVIEW** command demonstrate how useful this command is. The **'ZOOM, DSVIEWER, PAN** commands and Scroll bars are not available in the **DVIEW** command.

Command: **DVIEW** [Enter]
Select objects or <use DVIEWBLOCK>: *Select the objects you want to view dynamically or press ENTER to use the DVIEWBLOCK.*

Enter option
[CAmera/TArget/Distance/POints/PAn/Zoom/TWist/CLip/Hide/Off/Undo]: *Specify a point or enter an option.*

The point you specify is the start point for dragging. As you move the cursor, the viewing direction changes. The command prompt is:

Enter direction and magnitude angles: *Enter angles between 0 to 360 degrees or specify on screen.*

Direction angle determines the front of the view and the magnitude angle determines the how far the view is. The different **DVIEW** command options are discussed next.

CAmera Option

With the **CAmera** option, you can rotate the camera about the target point. To invoke the CAmera option, enter CA at the **Enter option [CAmera/TArget/Distance/POints/PAn/Zoom/TWist/CLip/ Hide/Off/Undo]:** prompt. Once you have invoked this option, the drawing is still, but you can maneuver the camera up and down (above or below the target) or you can move it left or right (clockwise or counterclockwise around the target). Remember that when you are moving the camera, the target is stationary, and that when you are moving the target, the camera is stationary. The next prompt AutoCAD displays is:

Specify camera location, or enter angle from XY plane,
or [Toggle (angle in)] <current>:

By default, this prompt asks you for the angle from the XY plane of the camera to the current UCS. This is nothing but the vertical (up or down) movement of the camera about the target. There are two ways to specify the angle.

1. You can specify the angle of rotation by moving the graphics cursor in the graphics area until you attain the desired rotation and then choosing the pick button of your pointing device. You will notice that as you move the cursor in the graphics area, the angle of rotation is continuously displayed in the status bar. Also, as you move the cursor, the object also moves dynamically. If you give a horizontal movement to the camera at the **Specify camera location, or enter angle from XY plane, or [Toggle (angle in)]** <current>: prompt, notice that the angle value displayed in the status bar does not change. This is because at the **Specify camera location, or enter angle from XY plane, or [Toggle (angle in)]** <current>: prompt, you are required to specify the vertical movement.

2. The other way to specify the angle of rotation is by entering the required angle of rotation value at the prompt. An angle of 90 degrees (default value) from the XY plane makes the camera look at the object straight down from the top side of the object, providing you with the top view (plan view). In this case, the line of sight is perpendicular to the XY plane of the current UCS. An angle of negative 90 degrees makes the camera look at the object straight up from the bottom side of the object. As you move the camera toward the top side of the object, the angle value increases. If you do not want to specify a vertical movement, press ENTER.

Once you have specified the angle from the XY plane, the next prompt displayed is:

> Specify camera location, or enter angle in XY plane from X axis,
> or [Toggle (angle from)] <current>:

This prompt asks you for the angle of the camera in the XY plane from the X axis. This is nothing but the horizontal (right or left) movement of the camera. You can enter the angle value in the range of -180 to 180 degrees. Moving the camera toward the right side of the object (counterclockwise) can be achieved by increasing the angle value; moving the camera toward the left side of the object (clockwise) can be achieved by decreasing the angle value. You can also toggle between these two prompts using the **Toggle (angle from)** or **Toggle (angle in)** option in the two prompts. The use of the **toggle** option can be illustrated as follows.

Let's say you want to enter only the angle in the XY plane from the X axis. There are two ways to do this. The first is to give a null response to the **Specify camera location, or enter angle from XY plane, or [Toggle (angle in)] <default>:** prompt. The other is by using the **Toggle (angle in)** option. Hence, to switch from the **Specify camera location, or enter angle from XY plane, or [Toggle (angle in)] <default>:** prompt to the **Specify camera location, or enter angle in XY plane from X axis, or [Toggle (angle from)] <current>:** prompt, you will have the following prompt sequence:

> Specify camera location, or enter angle from XY plane,
> or [Toggle (angle in)] <default>: T [Enter]
> Specify camera location, or enter angle in XY plane from X axis,
> or [Toggle (angle from)] <current>:

In the same manner, if you want to switch from the **Specify camera location, or enter angle in XY plane from X axis, or [Toggle (angle from)] <current>:** prompt to the **Specify camera location, or enter angle from XY plane, or [Toggle (angle in)] <default>:** prompt, the following will be the prompt sequence:

> Specify camera location, or enter angle in XY plane from X axis,
> or [Toggle (angle from)] <current>: T [Enter]
> Specify camera location, or enter angle from XY plane,
> or [Toggle (angle in)] <default>:

You have gone through the basic concept of the **CAmera** option of the **DVIEW** command. Now, you will work out some examples to apply the camera concept.

Note
*The **DVIEWBLOCK** is automatically displayed when you use **DVIEW** without selecting objects. You can define or redefine your own substitute **DVIEWBLOCK**, just like any other symbol block. Just be sure to define it to a 1x1x1 unit size so that it will be properly scaled in the **DVIEW** command.*

Example 2

In Figure 22-30, you have four sections. The house shown can be obtained by pressing ENTER at the **Select objects or <use DVIEWBLOCK>:** prompt. The drawing of the house with a window, an open door, and a chimney obtained on the screen is a block named **DVIEWBLOCK**.

Figure 22-30 CAmera option of the DVIEW command

As you use various options of the **DVIEW** command, the block is updated to reflect the changes. Once you come out of the **DVIEW** command, the entire drawing is regenerated, and the view obtained depends on the view you have selected using the various options of the **DVIEW** command. In this chapter, you will use this block to demonstrate the effect of various options of the **DVIEW** command. However, you can make a custom block of your own. The block should be of unit size. Set the lower left corner of the block as the origin point. The different views of the house block we see in Figure 22-30 can be obtained with the **CAmera** option of the **DVIEW** command. First, use the **DVIEW** command to get the image of the house on the screen.

Command: **DVIEW** `Enter`
Select objects or <use DVIEWBLOCK>: `Enter`

Now you have the image of the house on the screen. For Figure 22-30(a) (3D view), the following is the prompt sequence:

Enter option
[CAmera/TArget/Distance/POints/PAn/Zoom/TWist/CLip/Hide/Off/Undo]: CA
Specify camera location, or enter angle from XY plane,
or [Toggle (angle in)] <current>: 35.26
Specify camera location, or enter angle in XY plane from X axis,
or [Toggle (angle from)] <current>: -45
Enter option
[CAmera/TArget/Distance/POints/PAn/Zoom/TWist/CLip/Hide/Off/Undo]: *Press ENTER.*
Regenerating model.

Once you exit the **DVIEW** command, the figure of the house is removed from the screen. For Figure 22-30(b) (top view), the following is the prompt sequence:

Command: **DVIEW** `Enter`
Select objects or <use DVIEWBLOCK>: `Enter`

Enter option
[CAmera/TArget/Distance/POints/PAn/Zoom/TWist/CLip/Hide/Off/Undo]: CA
Specify camera location, or enter angle from XY plane,
or [Toggle (angle in)] <current>: 90
Specify camera location, or enter angle in XY plane from X axis,
or [Toggle (angle from)] <current>: 0
Enter option
[CAmera/TArget/Distance/POints/PAn/Zoom/TWist/CLip/Hide/Off/Undo]: *Press ENTER.*
Regenerating model.

For Figure 22-30(c) (right side view), the following is the prompt sequence:

Command: **DVIEW** [Enter]
Select objects or <use DVIEWBLOCK>: [Enter]
Enter option
[CAmera/TArget/Distance/POints/PAn/Zoom/TWist/CLip/Hide/Off/Undo]: CA
Specify camera location, or enter angle from XY plane,
or [Toggle (angle in)] <current>: 0.00
Specify camera location, or enter angle in XY plane from X axis,
or [Toggle (angle from)] <current>: 0.00
Enter option
[CAmera/TArget/Distance/POints/PAn/Zoom/TWist/CLip/Hide/Off/Undo]: *Press ENTER.*
Regenerating model.

For Figure 22-30(d) (front view), the following is the prompt sequence:

Command: **DVIEW** [Enter]
Select objects or <use DVIEWBLOCK>: [Enter]
Enter option
[CAmera/TArget/Distance/POints/PAn/Zoom/TWist/CLip/Hide/Off/Undo]: CA
Specify camera location, or enter angle from XY plane,
or [Toggle (angle in)] <current>: 0.00
Specify camera location, or enter angle in XY plane from X axis,
or [Toggle (angle from)] <current>: -90.00
Enter option
[CAmera/TArget/Distance/POints/PAn/Zoom/TWist/CLip/Hide/Off/Undo]: *Press ENTER.*
Regenerating model.

TArget Option

With the **TArget** option you can rotate the target point with respect to the camera. To invoke the **TArget** option, enter TA at the **Enter option [CAmera/ TArget/ Distance/ POints/ PAn/ Zoom/ TWist/ CLip/ Hide/ Off/ Undo]:** prompt. Once you have invoked this option, the drawing is still, but you can maneuver the target point up or down or left or right about the camera. When you move the target, the camera is stationary. The prompt sequence for the **TArget** option is:

Command: **DVIEW** [Enter]
Select objects or <use DVIEWBLOCK>: [Enter]

Enter option
[CAmera/TArget/Distance/POints/PAn/Zoom/TWist/CLip/Hide/Off/Undo]: TA [Enter]
Specify camera location, or enter angle from XY plane,
or [Toggle (angle in)] <current>: *Specify the angle about which the target will lie above or below the camera.*
Specify camera location, or enter angle in XY plane from X axis,
or [Toggle (angle from)] <current>: *Specify the angle about which the target will lie left or right of the camera.*
Enter option
[CAmera/TArget/Distance/POints/PAn/Zoom/TWist/CLip/Hide/Off/Undo]: [Enter]

The prompt sequence does not reveal the difference between the **CAmera** option and the **TArget** option. The difference lies in the actual angle of view. For example, if you specify an angle of 90 degrees in the **Specify camera location, or enter angle from XY plane, or [Toggle (angle in)] <current>:** prompt of the **CAmera** option, your viewing direction is from the top of the object toward the bottom; if you specify the same angle in the same prompt for the **TArget** option, your viewing direction is from the bottom of the object toward the top.

Example 3

The different views of the house block in Figure 22-31 can be obtained with the **TArget** option of the **DVIEW** command.

Figure 22-31 TArget option of the DVIEW command

First, use the **DVIEW** command to display the image of the house on the screen.

Command: **DVIEW** [Enter]
Select objects or <use DVIEWBLOCK>: [Enter]

For Figure 22-31(a) (3D view), the following is the prompt sequence:

Enter option
[CAmera/TArget/Distance/POints/PAn/Zoom/TWist/CLip/Hide/Off/Undo]: TA
Specify camera location, or enter angle from XY plane,
or [Toggle (angle in)] <current>: -35.26
Specify camera location, or enter angle in XY plane from X axis,
or [Toggle (angle from)] <current>: 135
Enter option
[CAmera/TArget/Distance/POints/PAn/Zoom/TWist/CLip/Hide/Off/Undo]:
Regenerating model.

For Figure 22-31(b) (top view), the following is the prompt sequence:

Command: **DVIEW** [Enter]
Select objects or <use DVIEWBLOCK>: [Enter]
Enter option
[CAmera/TArget/Distance/POints/PAn/Zoom/TWist/CLip/Hide/Off/Undo]: TA
Specify camera location, or enter angle from XY plane,
or [Toggle (angle in)] <current>: -90.00
Specify camera location, or enter angle in XY plane from X axis,
or [Toggle (angle from)] <current>:90.00
Enter option
[CAmera/TArget/Distance/POints/PAn/Zoom/TWist/CLip/Hide/Off/Undo]: *Press ENTER.*
Regenerating model

For Figure 22-31(c) (right side view), the following is the prompt sequence:

Command: **DVIEW** [Enter]
Select objects or <use DVIEWBLOCK>: [Enter]
Enter option
[CAmera/TArget/Distance/POints/PAn/Zoom/TWist/CLip/Hide/Off/Undo]: TA
Specify camera location, or enter angle from XY plane,
or [Toggle (angle in)] <current>: 0.00
Specify camera location, or enter angle in XY plane from X axis,
or [Toggle (angle from)] <current>: 180.00
Enter option
[CAmera/TArget/Distance/POints/PAn/Zoom/TWist/CLip/Hide/Off/Undo]: *Press ENTER.*
Regenerating model

For Figure 22-31(d) (front view), the following is the prompt sequence:

Command: **DVIEW** [Enter]
Select objects or <use DVIEWBLOCK>: [Enter]
Enter option
[CAmera/TArget/Distance/POints/PAn/Zoom/TWist/CLip/Hide/Off/Undo]: TA
Specify camera location, or enter angle in XY plane from X axis,
or [Toggle (angle from)]<default>: 0.00
Specify camera location, or enter angle in XY plane from X axis,

or [Toggle (angle from)]<default>: 90.00
Enter option
[CAmera/TArget/Distance/POints/PAn/Zoom/TWist/CLip/Hide/Off/Undo]: *Press ENTER.*
Regenerating model.

Distance Option

As mentioned before, the line obtained on joining the camera position and the target position is known as the line of sight. The **Distance** option can be used to move the camera toward or away from the target along the line of sight. Invoking the **Distance** option enables perspective viewing. Since we have not used the **Distance** option until now, all the previous views were in parallel projection. In perspective display, the objects nearer to the camera appear bigger than objects that are farther away from the camera position. In other words, in perspective views the parallel lines meet at a vanishing point. Another noticeable difference is that the regular coordinate system icon is replaced by the perspective icon. This icon acts as a reminder that perspective viewing is enabled. The **distance** option can be invoked by entering D at the **Enter option [CAmera/TArget/ Distance/ POints/PAn/Zoom/TWist/CLip/Hide/Off/Undo]:** prompt. Once you invoke the **Distance** option, AutoCAD prompts you to specify the new distance between the camera and the target.

Specify new camera-target distance <1.0000>: *Enter the desired distance between the camera and the target.*

On the top side of the screen, a slider bar appears. It is marked from 0x to 16x. The current distance is represented by the 1x mark. This is verified by the fact that the slider bar moves right or left with respect to the 1x mark on the slider bar. As you move the slider bar toward the right, the distance between the camera and the target increases; as you move the slider bar toward the left, the distance between the camera and the target decreases. For example, when you move the slider bar to the 16x mark, the distance between the camera and the target increases 16 times, or you can say that the camera moved away from the target on the line of sight 16 times the previous distance. The distance between the camera and the target is dynamically displayed in the status line. If you cannot display the entire object on the screen by moving the slider bar to the 16x mark, enter a larger distance at the keyboard. To revert to parallel viewing, invoke the **Off** option. If you want to magnify the drawing without turning the Perspective viewing on, you can use the **Zoom** option.

Example 4

Let Figure 22-32(a) be the default figure, in which the distance between camera and target is 4 units, which corresponds to the 1x mark on the slider bar. You can change the distance between camera and target and get different views as follows:

For Figure 22-32(b):

Command: **DVIEW** [Enter]
Select objects or <use DVIEWBLOCK>: [Enter]
Enter option
[CAmera/TArget/Distance/POints/PAn/Zoom/TWist/CLip/Hide/Off/Undo]: D [Enter]

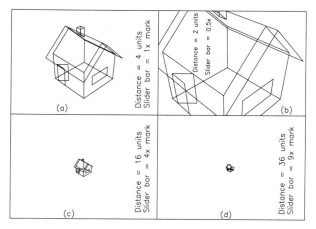

*Figure 22-32 Distance option of the **DVIEW** command*

Specify new camera-target distance <4.0000>: 2.0 [Enter]

For Figure 22-32(c):

Command: **DVIEW** [Enter]
Select objects or <use DVIEWBLOCK>: [Enter]
Enter option
[CAmera/TArget/Distance/POints/PAn/Zoom/TWist/CLip/Hide/Off/Undo]: D [Enter]
Specify new camera-target distance <4.0000>: 16.0 [Enter] *or move the pointer to the 4x mark on slider bar.*

For Figure 22-32(d):

Command: **DVIEW** [Enter]
Select objects or <use DVIEWBLOCK>: [Enter]
Enter option
[CAmera/TArget/Distance/POints/PAn/Zoom/TWist/CLip/Hide/Off/Undo]: D [Enter]
Specify new camera-target distance <4.0000>: 36.0 [Enter] *or move the pointer to the 9x mark on slider bar.*

POints Option

With the **POints** option, you can specify the camera and target positions (points) in X, Y, Z coordinates. You can specify the X, Y, Z coordinates of the point by any method used to specify points, including object snap and .X, .Y, .Z point filters. The X, Y, Z coordinate values are with respect to the current UCS. If you use the object snap to specify the points, you must type the name of the object snap. This option can be invoked by entering PO at the **Enter option [CAmera/ TArget/ Distance/POints/PAn/Zoom/TWist/CLip/Hide/Off/Undo]:** prompt.

Command: **DVIEW** [Enter]
Select objects or <use DVIEWBLOCK>: [Enter]

Chapter 22

Enter option
[CAmera/TArget/Distance/POints/PAn/Zoom/TWist/CLip/Hide/Off/Undo]: PO ⏎

The target point needs to be specified first. A rubber-band line is drawn from the current target position to the drawing crosshairs. This is the line of sight.

Specify target point <current>: *Specify the location of the target or press ENTER.*

Once you have specified the target point, you are prompted to specify the camera point. A rubber-band line is drawn between the target point and the drawing crosshairs. This helps you to place the camera relative to the target.

Enter camera point <current>: *Specify the location of the camera press ENTER.*

Establishment of the new target point and camera point should be carried in parallel projection. If you specify these two points while the perspective projection is active, the perspective projection is temporarily turned off, until you specify the camera and target points. Once this is done, the object is again displayed in perspective. If the viewing direction is changed by the new target location and camera location, the preview image is regenerated to show the change.

Example 5

In Figure 22-33, the target is located at the lower corner of the house, and the camera is located at the corner of the chimney.

In Figure 22-34, the camera is located at the lower corner of the house, and the target is located at the corner of the chimney. Both these points are marked by cross marks.

*Figure 22-33 Point option of the **DVIEW** command*

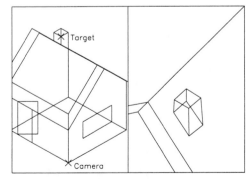

*Figure 22-34 Point option of the **DVIEW** command*

PAn Option

The **PAn** option of the **DVIEW** command resembles the **PAN** command. This option lets you shift the entire drawing with respect to the graphics display area. Just as with the **PAN** command, you have to specify the pan distance and direction by specifying two points. You must use a pointing device to specify the two points if perspective viewing is active. The prompt sequence for this option is:

Command: **DVIEW** [Enter]
Select objects or <use DVIEWBLOCK>: [Enter]
Enter option
[CAmera/TArget/Distance/POints/PAn/Zoom/TWist/CLip/Hide/Off/Undo]: PA [Enter]
Specify displacement base point: *Specify the first point.*
Specify second point: *Specify the second point.*

Zoom Option

The **Zoom** option of the **DVIEW** command resembles the **ZOOM** command. With the help of this option, you can enlarge or reduce the drawing. This option can be invoked by entering Z at the following prompt:

Enter option
[CAmera/TArget/Distance/POints/PAn/Zoom/TWist/CLip/Hide/Off/Undo]: Z [Enter]
Specify lens length <50.000mm>: *Specify the new lens length.*

Just as with the **Distance** option, in the **Zoom** option a slider bar marked from 0x to 16x is displayed on the top side of the screen. The default position on the slider bar is 1x. Two ways to zoom can now be specified. The first is when perspective is enabled. In this case, zooming is defined in terms of lens length. The 1x mark (default position) corresponds to a 50.000mm lens length. As you move the slider bar toward the right, the lens length increases; and as you move the slider bar toward the left, the lens length decreases. For example, when you move the slider bar to the 16x mark, the lens length increases 16 times, which is 16 x 50.000mm = 800.000mm. You can simulate the telephoto effect by increasing the lens length; by reducing the lens length, you can simulate the wide-angle effect. The lens length is dynamically displayed in the status bar. If perspective is not enabled, zooming is defined in terms of the zoom scale factor. In this case, the **Zoom** option resembles the **ZOOM Center** command, and the center point lies at the center of the current viewport. The 1x mark (default position) corresponds to a scale factor of 1. As you move the slider bar toward the right, the scale factor increases; as you move the slider bar toward the left, the scale factor decreases. For example, when you move the slider bar to the 16x mark, the scale factor increases 16 x 1 = 16 times. The scale factor is dynamically displayed on the status line.

Command: **DVIEW** [Enter]
Select objects or <use DVIEWBLOCK>: *Select the objects.*
Enter option
[CAmera/TArget/Distance/POints/PAn/Zoom/TWist/CLip/Hide/Off/Undo]: Z [Enter]
Specify zoom scale factor <1>: *Specify the scale factor.*

Example 6

Let's see the effect of the **Zoom** option in perspective projection. In Figure 22-35(a), the lens length is set to 25mm. This can be realized in the following manner:

Command: **DVIEW** [Enter]
Select objects or <use DVIEWBLOCK>: [Enter]

Enter option
[CAmera/TArget/Distance/POints/PAn/Zoom/TWist/CLip/Hide/Off/Undo]: Z `[Enter]`
Specify lens length <50.000mm>: 25 `[Enter]`

Similarly, for Figure 22-35(b), (c), and (d), you can set lens lengths to 50mm, 75mm, and 125mm, respectively.

*Figure 22-35 **Zoom** option of the **DVIEW** command*

TWist Option

The **TWist** option allows you to rotate (twist) the view around the line of sight. You can also say that the object on the screen is rotated around the center point of the screen because the display is always adjusted so that the target point is at the center of the screen. If you use a pointing device to specify the angle, the angle value is dynamically displayed on the status line. A rubber-band line is drawn from the center (target point) to the drawing crosshairs, and as you move the crosshairs with a pointing device, the object on the screen is rotated around the line of sight. You can also enter the angle of twist from the keyboard. The angle of twist is measured in a counterclockwise direction starting from the right side.

Command: **DVIEW** `[Enter]`
Select objects or <use DVIEWBLOCK>: `[Enter]`
Enter option
[CAmera/TArget/Distance/POints/PAn/Zoom/TWist/CLip/Hide/Off/Undo]: TW `[Enter]`
Specify view twist angle <0.00>: *Specify the angle of rotation (twist).*

Example 7

In Figure 22-36, different twist angles have been specified. For (a) the twist angle is 0, for (b) it is 338 degrees, for (c) it is 37 degrees, and for (d) it is 360 degrees.

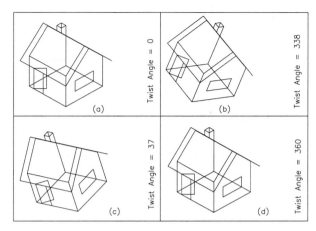

Figure 22-36 TWist option of the DVIEW command

CLip Option

The **CLip** option can be used to clip sections of the drawing (Figure 22-37). AutoCAD uses two invisible clipping planes to realize clipping. These clipping walls can be positioned anywhere on the screen and are perpendicular to the line of sight (line between target and camera). Once you position the clipping planes, AutoCAD conceals all the lines that are in front of the front clipping plane or behind the back clipping plane. The **CLip** option can be used in both parallel and perspective projections. When perspective is enabled, the front clipping plane is automatically enabled.

Note

If you have specified a positive distance, the clipping plane is placed between the target and the camera. If the distance you have specified is negative, the clipping plane is placed beyond the target.

The prompt sequence for the **CLip** option is:

Enter option
[CAmera/TArget/Distance/POints/PAn/Zoom/TWist/CLip/Hide/Off/Undo]:CL [Enter]
Enter clipping option [Back/Front/Off]<Off>: B [Enter]
Specify distance from target or [ON/OFF] <current>:

Once you have specified which clipping plane you want to set (the back clipping plane in our case), a slider bar appears on the screen. As you move the pointer toward the right side of the slider bar, the negative distance between the target and the clipping plane increases. As you move toward the left side of the slider bar, the positive distance between the target and the clipping plane increases; hence, a greater portion of the drawing is clipped. The rightmost mark on the slider bar corresponds to a distance equal to the distance between the target and the farthermost point on the object you want to clip. After specifying the distance between one of the clipping planes (back clipping plane in this prompt sequence), you need to invoke the **CLip** option again and to specify the position of the front clipping plane in terms of the distance between the front clipping plane and the target. As you move the slider bar toward the right, the negative distance between the target and the front clipping plane increases. As the negative distance increases, a greater portion of the front side of the drawing is clipped. The rightmost mark on the slider bar corresponds to a distance equal to the distance between the target and the back clipping plane.

Enter option
[CAmera/TArget/Distance/POints/PAn/Zoom/TWist/CLip/Hide/Off/Undo]:CL Enter
Enter clipping option [Back/Front/Off] <Off>: F Enter
Specify distance from target or [set to Eye(camera)/ON/OFF] <1.0000>: *Specify the distance from target.*

To illustrate the concepts behind clipping, let us display two objects (a sphere and a cone). Let the distance between the two be 10 units. Draw a line between the center of the sphere and the center of the cone. Use the **POints** option to position the target at the center of the sphere and the camera at the midpoint of the line joining the two center points. In this way, you have defined the line between the two center points as the line of sight.

Now that you have defined the target and the camera, you will see the sphere and the cone overlapping because both of them are aligned along the line of sight. You may wonder how you are able to see the cone, since it lies behind the camera position that is analogous to the eye. This is because in parallel projection, the camera is not analogous to the eye, but the line of sight is; hence, you see everything that lies in the field of vision (determined by the **Zoom** option) about the line of sight. Now, when you use the **CLip** option and the **Front** suboption to define the position of the Front clipping plane, by default the front clipping plane is positioned at the camera point. Now you cannot see the objects (cone in our case) that are behind the camera point because the default position of the front clipping plane is at the camera position; hence, any object in front of the front clipping plane is clipped. Also, if you have placed the front clipping plane behind the camera position and the perspective projection is on, the camera position is used as the front clipping plane position.

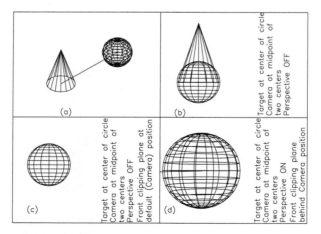

Figure 22-37 *Using the **CLip** option to clip the view*

If you change the front clipping plane position, and then at some stage you want to go back to the default front clipping plane position, you can use the **Eye** option. In perspective, without invoking the **CLip** option, the front clipping plane is placed at the camera position; hence, you are able to see only what lies in front of the camera.

Example 8

In Figure 22-38, the front clipping plane has been established at a distance of 0.50 units. The distance between the camera and the target is 3.50 units. After invoking the **CLip** option, the prompt sequence is:

Enter clipping option [Back/Front/Off]<Off>: F ⏎
Specify distance from target or [set to Eye(Camera)/On/OFF] <3.5000>: 0.50 ⏎

Figure 22-38 Front clipping with the DVIEW command

In Figure 22-39, the back clipping plane has been established at a distance of 0.50 units. The distance between the camera and the target is 3.50 units. After invoking the **CLip** option, the prompt sequence is:

Enter clipping option [Back/Front/Off]<Off>: B ⏎
Specify distance from target or [ON/OFF] <1.0000>: 0.50 ⏎

You might have noticed that if you combine the clipped shape in Figure 22-38 and the clipped shape in Figure 22-39, you get the original shape of the house. The reason is that in the first clipped figure, whatever lies between the camera and the front clipping plane is clipped, whereas in the second clipped figure, whatever lies behind the back clipping plane is clipped. Since the distances between the clipping planes and the target, and between camera and target are identical in both figures, then if you combine the clipped figures, you will get the original shape.

Hide Option

In most 3D drawings, some of the lines lie behind other lines or objects. Sometimes, you may not want these hidden lines to show up on the screen, so you can use the **Hide** option (Figure 22-40).

Figure 22-39 Back clipping with the *DVIEW* command

This option is similar to the **HIDE** command. To invoke **Hide** option, enter H at the **Enter option [CAmera/TArget/Distance/POints/PAn/Zoom/TWist/CLip/Hide/Off/Undo]:** prompt.

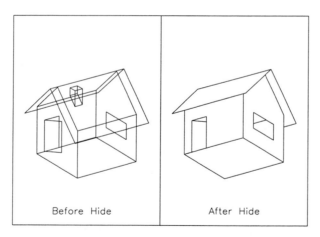

Figure 22-40 Hide option of the *DVIEW* command

Off Option

The **Off** option turns the perspective projection off. The prompt sequence is:

Enter option
[CAmera/TArget/Distance/POints/PAn/Zoom/TWist/CLip/Hide/Off/Undo]: O

When the perspective projection is turned off, you will notice that the perspective icon is replaced by the regular UCS icon.

Undo Option

The **Undo** option is similar to the **UNDO** command. The **Undo** option nullifies the result of the previous **DVIEW** operation. Just as in the case of the **UNDO** command, you can use this option a number of times to undo the results of multiple **DVIEW** operations. To invoke this option, enter U at the following prompt:

Enter option
[CAmera/TArget/Distance/POints/PAn/Zoom/TWist/CLip/Hide/Off/ Undo]: U

3DORBIT COMMAND*

Toolbar:	Standard > 3D Orbit
	3D Orbit > 3D Orbit
Menu:	View > 3D Orbit
Command:	3DORBIT

Figure 22-41 The 3D Orbit toolbar

This command activates a 3D Orbit view in the current viewport. You can click and drag your pointing device to view the 3D object from different points around it. You can select individual objects or the entire drawing to view before you invoke the **3DORBIT** command. When you invoke the **3DORBIT** command, an arcball appears, which is a circle with 4 smaller circles placed such that they divide the circle into quadrants. The UCS icon is replaced by a shaded 3D UCS icon (Figure 22-42). In the 3D orbit viewing, the target is considered stationary and the camera location is considered to be moving around it. The target is the center of the arcball. You cannot edit objects while the **3DORBIT** command is being used.

The cursor icon changes as you move the cursor in over the 3D Orbit view. The different icons indicate the different direction in which the view is being rotated. They are as follows:

Orbit mode. When you move the cursor within the arcball, the cursor looks like a sphere encircled by two lines. This icon is the **Orbit mode** cursor, and clicking and dragging the pointing device allows you to rotate the view freely as if your cursor was grabbing a sphere surrounding the objects and moving it around the target point. You can move horizontally, and vertically, as well as diagonally.

Roll mode. When you move the cursor outside the arcball, it changes to look like a sphere encircled by a circular arrow. When you click and drag, the view is rotated around an axis that extends through the center of the arcball, perpendicular to the screen.

Orbit Left-Right. When you move the cursor to the small circles placed on the left and right of the arcball, it changes into a sphere surrounded by a horizontal ellipse. When you click and drag, the view is rotated around the Y axis of the screen.

Orbit Up-down. When you move the cursor to the circles placed in the top or bottom of the arcball, it changes into a sphere surrounded by a vertical ellipse. Clicking and dragging the cursor, rotates the view around the horizontal axis or the X-axis of the screen, passing through the middle of the arcball.

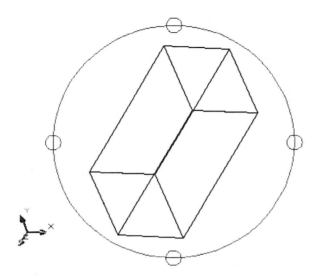

Figure 22-42 3D Orbit view, arcball with circular graphics and the 3D shaded UCS icon

You can right-click in the drawing area while the **3DORBIT** command is active to display a shortcut menu. This menu displays all the **3DORBIT** options available. To exit from the **3DORBIT** command, choose **Exit** from the shortcut menu or press ESC or ENTER. You can also shade objects while in the **3DORBIT** command by choosing **Shading Modes** from the shortcut menu and choosing any of the options available.

CAMERA COMMAND*

Toolbar:	View > Camera
Command:	CAMERA

Before you start the **3DORBIT** command for 3D viewing of the object, you can set the camera and target locations with the **CAMERA** command. The command prompts are:

Command: **CAMERA**
Current camera position: current
Current camera target: current
Specify new camera position <current>: *Enter values of the coordinates or specify point on screen.*
Specify new camera target <current>: *Enter values of the coordinates or specify point on screen.*

3DZOOM COMMAND*

Toolbar:	3D Orbit > 3D Zoom
Command:	3DZOOM

Using this command is similar to using the camera's zoom lens. It makes the object appear closer or further away but the position of the camera is not changed. When you are using perspective projection, using **3DZOOM**, exaggerates the perspective which leads to slight distortion of objects sometimes. The projection options: **Parallel** or **Perspective** can be selected from the shortcut menu displayed on right-clicking in the drawing area. Choose **Projection > Parallel** or **Perspective**. This command also starts the 3D interactive viewing. You can right-click in the drawing area to display a shortcut menu which displays all the **3D Orbit** options, the UCS icon is replaced by the shaded 3D UCS icon. **3DZOOM** can be invoked by choosing **Zoom** from the shortcut menu displayed on right-clicking in the drawing area while the **3DORBIT** command is active.

3DPAN COMMAND*

Toolbar:	3D Orbit > 3D Pan
Command:	3DPAN

This command allows you to drag the view horizontally and vertically and also starts the 3D interactive viewing. You can also invoke this command by choosing **Pan** from the shortcut menu displayed on right-clicking in the drawing area while the **3DORBIT** command is being used.

3DDISTANCE COMMAND*

Toolbar:	3D Orbit > 3D Adjust Distance
Command:	3DDISTANCE

This command is similar to taking the camera closer to or farther away from the target object i.e. it makes the object appear closer or farther away. This command also starts interactive 3D viewing. **3DDISTANCE** command unlike the **3DZOOM** command does not exaggerate perspective in a view. You can also invoke this command by right-clicking in the drawing area while the **3DORBIT** command is active to display a shortcut menu and choosing **More > Adjust Distance**. While this command is being used the cursor icon changes to a line with one arrow pointing up and one arrow pointing down. Clicking and dragging , takes the object closer or farther away from the camera i.e. changes the distance between the camera and target.

3DSWIVEL COMMAND*

Toolbar:	3D Orbit > 3D Swivel
Command:	3DSWIVEL

This command works similar to turning the camera on a tripod without changing the distance between the camera and the target. You can also invoke this command by choosing **More > Swivel Camera** from the shortcut menu displayed on right-clicking in the drawing area when the **3DORBIT** command is active. When this command is being used, the

Chapter 22

cursor icon changes to an arched arrow. This command also starts interactive 3D viewing.

VISUAL AIDS IN 3DORBIT COMMAND*

You can choose to display any of the following visual aids : **Compass**, **Grid** or **UCS Icon** in the 3D Orbit view, by choosing **Visual Aids > Compass**, **Grid** or **UCS Icon** from the shortcut menu displayed on right-clicking in the drawing area when the **3DORBIT** command is active. A check mark is displayed next to the options you have selected. Choosing **Compass**, displays a sphere drawn within the arcball with 3 lines indicating the X, Y and Z axes. Choosing **Grid** displays a grid at the current XY plane. You can specify the height by using the **ELEVATION** system variable. The **GRID** system variable controls the display options of the **Grid** before using the **3DORBIT** command. Choosing **UCS Icon** displays the UCS icon. Not selecting this option i.e. when the check mark is not placed next to the **UCS Icon** option, AutoCAD turns off the display of the UCS icon. While using any of the 3D Orbit options, interactive 3D viewing is on and a shaded 3D view UCS icon is displayed. The X axis is red, the Y axis is green and the Z axis is blue or cyan.

3DCORBIT COMMAND*

| Toolbar: | 3D Orbit > 3D Continuous Orbit |
| Command: | 3DCORBIT |

The **3DCORBIT** starts interactive 3D viewing and allows you to set the objects you select in a 3D view into continuous motion in a free form orbit. You can also invoke this command by choosing **More > Continuous Orbit** from the shortcut menu displayed on right-clicking in the drawing area while the **3DORBIT** command is active. While the **3DCORBIT** command is being used, the cursor icon changes to the **continuous orbit** cursor which is a sphere encircled by two continuous lines. Clicking in the drawing area and dragging the pointing device in any direction starts to move the object(s) in the direction you have dragged it to. When you release the pointing device button, i.e. stop clicking and dragging, the object continues to move in it's orbit in the direction you specified. The speed at which the cursor was moved determines the speed at which the objects spin. You can click and drag again to specify another direction for rotation in the continuous orbit. While using this command you can right-click in the drawing area to display the shortcut menu and add or remove **Visual Aids** from the display, choose **Projection** options, **Shading modes**, **Preset Views** or **Reset View** , without exiting the command. Choosing **Pan**, **Zoom**, **Orbit**, **Adjust Clipping Plane** ends the continuous orbit.

3DCLIP COMMAND*

| Toolbar: | 3D Orbit > 3D Adjust Clip Planes |
| Command: | 3DCLIP |

You can also invoke this command by choosing **More > Adjust Clip Planes** from the shortcut menu displayed on right-clicking in the drawing area when the 3D viewing commands are active. This command also starts interactive 3D viewing and displays the **Adjust Clipping Planes window** (Figure 22-43), where you can determine the location, turn on or off the front and back clipping planes. You can also create a slice of the object you have selected in 3D viewing.

On invoking this window, the object appears rotated at 90 degrees to the top of the current view in the window. This facilitates display of cutting planes. Setting the location of the front and back clipping planes in this window is reflected in the result in the current view. The various options of the **3DCLIP** command are displayed in the **Adjust Clipping Planes** toolbar in the window. You can also right-click in the window and choose the same options from the shortcut menu displayed.

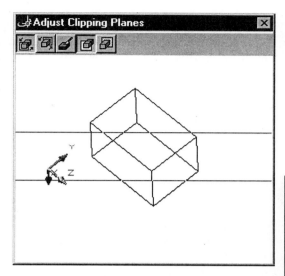

Figure 22-43 Adjust Clipping Planes window

 Adjust Front Clipping. This option is the default option and allows you to set the location of the front clipping plane. When you move the line located near the bottom of the **Adjust Clipping Planes window**, up or down, you can see the result in the current 3D Orbit view. When using this option, make sure that the **Front Clipping On** option is selected i.e. a check mark is displayed next to it in the shortcut menu or the **Front Clipping On** button is depressed in the **Adjust Clipping Planes** toolbar.

 Adjust Back Clipping. This option allows you to locate the back clipping plane. When you move the line located near the top of the **Adjust Clipping Planes window**, up or down, you can see the resulting view in the current 3D view. When using this option make sure that the **Back Clipping On** option is selected.

 Create Slice. Choosing this option, causes both the front and back clipping planes to move together. The slice is created between the two clipping planes and is displayed in the current 3D view. You can first adjust the front and the back clipping planes individually by choosing the respective options and then choose the **Create Slice** button in the toolbar to activate both the clipping planes at the same time and display the result in the current view.

 Front Clipping On. Turns On or Off the Front Clipping plane option. A check mark besides **Front Clip On** in the shortcut menu displayed on right-clicking in the **Adjust Clipping Planes window** indicates that this option is selected. You can also choose the **Front Clip On/Off** button in the **3D Orbit** toolbar also.

 Back Clipping On. Turns On or off the Back clipping plane option. A check mark next to **Back Clip On** in the shortcut menu displayed on right-clicking in the **Adjust Clipping Planes window** indicates that this option is selected. You can also choose the **Back Clip On/Off** button from the **3D Orbit** toolbar.

Choose the **Close** (**X**) button to exit the **Adjust Clipping Planes window**. When you are using the **3DORBIT** command to rotate the view of an object and if the Front and Back Clipping Planes are **On**, different portions of the object are clipped as the they cut across the clipping planes.

Preset Views*

When you are using any of the 3D Orbit commands for 3D interactive viewing, if you right-click in the drawing area a shortcut menu is displayed with all the options available. Choosing **Preset Views** allows you to choose any of the six standard orthogonal views or any one of the four standard isometric views for the selected object to be viewed. You can also select any one of the Preset views from the **View Control** drop-down list in the **3D Orbit** toolbar. Choosing **Reset View** from the shortcut menu resets the view to the view which was current when the **3DORBIT** command was started.

Self Evaluation Test

Answer the following questions, and then compare your answers to the correct answers given at the end of this chapter.

1. What are the two types of viewports in AutoCAD? _____ .

2. Tiled viewports are created by using the _____ command when the system variable a _____ is set to 1 (model space).

3. With the _____ option, you can choose the floating viewports for which you want to remove the hidden lines when you plot in paper space.

4. If you set **Hideplot** to **Off**, hidden lines are not plotted. (T/F)

5. To shift from paper space to model space, at least two viewports must be active and on. (T/F)

6. The **VPLAYER** command can be used from either model space or paper space. (T/F)

7. To use the **VPLAYER** command, the only restriction is that **TILEMODE** be set to 1 (On). (T/F)

8. The **Freeze** option of the **VPLAYER** command is used to freeze a layer (or layers) in only one viewport. (T/F)

9. Layers that have been frozen, thawed, switched on, or switched off globally are not affected by the _____ command.

10. The position from which you want to view the object (the viewer's eye) is the _____, and the focus point is the _____ .

11. The line formed between the target and the camera is known as _____ , or _____ .

12. The _____ option allows you to rotate the camera about the target point.

13. When you are moving the camera, the _____ is stationary, and when you are moving the target, the _____ is stationary.

14. If perspective is disabled, the zooming is defined in terms of the _____ .

15. The 1x mark (default position) corresponds to a scale factor of _____ .

16. When you move the slider bar to the 16x mark, the scale factor increases _____ .

17. The _____ option of the **DVIEW** command allows you to rotate (twist) the view around the line of sight.

18. The _____ option can be used to shift from perspective viewing to parallel viewing.

19. With the _____ option of the **DVIEW** command, you can specify the camera and target positions (points) in X, Y, Z coordinates.

20. The _____ option lets you shift the entire drawing with respect to the graphics display area.

21. You can edit objects while in the **3DORBIT** command. (T/F)

22. The _____ command allows you to set the objects into a continuous motion in a free form orbit.

Review Questions

VIEWPORTS
1. The _____ command can be used to create viewports and divide the display screen into a number of parts (viewports).

2. An arrangement of viewports created with the **VPORTS** command is a display function and _____ be plotted.

UCSFOLLOW
3. When the _____ variable is assigned a value of 1, a plan view is automatically generated if you change the UCS in a viewport.

MVIEW, -VPORTS
4. The **MVIEW** command is used to create _____ in paper space.

5. Before using the **-VPORTS** command, you must change the system variable _____ to 0.

6. If you invoke the **MVIEW** command in the floating model space (**TILEMODE** set to 0), AutoCAD shifts you from _____ to _____ , until the **MVIEW** command is not over.

7. It is possible to alter the size of the floating viewports and adjust them on the screen. (T/F)

8. Name five options of the **VPLAYER** command: _____, _____, _____, _____, _____ .

9. You should turn off the viewports that are not required because _____ _____ .

10. The system variable _____ controls the number of viewports that will display the objects.

11. You will not be able to work in floating model space if any viewport is turned off. (T/F)

12. What happens if you turn **Hideplot** on? _____ .

MSPACE/PSPACE

13. The _____ command is used to shift from paper space to model space.

14. Before using the **MSPACE** command, you must set _____ to 0 (Off).

15. The _____ command is used to shift from model space to paper space.

VPLAYER

16. You can control the visibility of layers inside the viewport with the _____ command.

17. With the _____ command, you can control the visibility of layers in individual viewports.

18. With the _____ option, you can set the visibility of layer(s) in the specified viewports to their current default setting.

19. The visibility defaults of subsequent new layers can be set by using the _____ option of the **VPLAYER** command.

20. With the _____ option, you can create new layers that are frozen in all viewports.

21. With the _____ option, you can set the default for the visibility of subsequent layer(s).

22. The **New VP Freeze** toggle icon governs the thawing and freezing of selected layers in _____ viewport.

DVIEW

23. With the _____ command, you can generate different views of 3D objects on the screen.

24. The **DVIEW** command offers you the choice between parallel viewing and _____viewing.

25. In _____ view, parallel lines in the 3D object remain parallel.

26. In _____ view, parallel lines meet at a vanishing point.

27. The angle from the XY plane of the camera with respect to the current UCS is used to achieve _____ movement of the camera.

28. You can use the _____ option of the **DVIEW** command to rotate the target point up or down, left or right with respect to the camera.

29. The _____ option of the **DVIEW** command can be used to move the camera toward or away from the target along the line of sight.

30. When you invoke the **Distance** option, _____ viewing is enabled.

31. In perspective display, the objects nearer to the camera appear _____ in size compared with objects that are further away from the camera position.

32. When you move the slider bar to the 16x mark, the distance between the camera and the target increases _____ .

33. If perspective is enabled, zooming is defined in terms of _____ .

34. The 1x mark (default position) corresponds to ____ lens length.

35. With the **TWist** option of the **DVIEW** command, the angle of twist is measured in a _____ direction starting from the right side.

36. The _____ option of the **DVIEW** command can be used to clip sections of the drawing.

37. The clipping planes are perpendicular to the line of sight, and AutoCAD conceals all the lines that are in _____ of the front clipping plane or _____ the back clipping plane.

38. With the front clipping plane, as you increase the negative distance, the _____ portion of the drawing is clipped.

39. With the back clipping plane, as you increase the positive distance, the _____ portion of the drawing is clipped.

40. If you change the front clipping plane position, and then at some stage you want to go back to the default front clipping plane position, you can use the _____ option.

3D ORBIT VIEWING

41. When you invoke the **3DORBIT** command, the UCS icon is replaced by a _____ .

42. The **3DCORBIT** command allows you to _____
_____ .

43. The **3DCLIP** command displays the _____
    window.

44. Choosing the _____ option, causes both the front and back clipping planes to move
    together.

45. If you are using the _____ command in the perspective projection, perspective is exag-
    gerated, sometimes leading to distortion in the shape of objects.

Exercises

Exercise 1   *General*

a.   Draw the computer as shown in Figure 22-44. Take the dimensions from the computer you are
     using. For your convenience, two images of the same computer are shown. The first one has
     the lines hidden, and the second one (Figure 22-45) shows all lines, including the lines that
     are behind the visible surfaces.

Figure 22-44 *3D view of the computer without hidden lines*

Figure 22-45 *3D view of the computer with hidden lines*

Construction of the given figure can be divided into the following steps:

1. Drawing the CPU box (central processing unit).
2. Drawing the base of the monitor.
3. Drawing the monitor.

b.   Once you have drawn the computer, create four viewports in tiled model space and obtain
     different views of the computer as shown in the screen capture (Figure 22-46). You can use the
     VPOINT command to obtain the different views.

Figure 22-46 *Four viewports in the model space*

Figure 22-47 *Using **DVIEW** options to obtain different displays of the computer*

c. Next, use the **MVIEW** command to create four viewports as shown in Figure 22-47. Center the figure of the computer in 3D view in all four of the viewports. Use the **CAmera** option of the **DVIEW** command to obtain the figure shown in the upper left viewport.

Chapter 22

Use the **Distance** option of the **DVIEW** command to obtain the figure shown in the upper right viewport.

Use the **CLip** option of the **DVIEW** command to obtain the figure shown in the lower left viewport.

Use the **TWist** option of the **DVIEW** command to obtain the figure shown in the lower right viewport.

d. What is the difference between the parallel projection and the perspective projection?

e. Use the **3DORBIT** command to view the object in 3D Orbit.

Answers to Self-Evaluation Test
1 - tiled viewports and floating viewports, **2** - **VPORTS, TILEMODE, 3** - **HIDEPLOT, 4** - F, **5** - F (One), **6** - F, **7** - F (**TILEMODE** set to 0), **8** - F (One or more), **9** - **VPLAYER, 10** - camera, target, **11** - line of sight, viewing direction, **12** - **CAmera, 13** - target, camera, **14** - zoom scale factor, **15** - 1, **16** - 16 times, **17** - **TWist, 18** - Off, **19** - **POints, 20** - **PAn, 21**- F, **22**- **3DCORBIT**

Chapter 23

Solid Modeling

Learning Objectives

After completing this chapter, you will be able to:
- *Understand solid modeling.*
- *Understand why solid modeling is used.*
- *Create solid primitives.*
- *Understand regions and how to create them.*
- *Construct composite solids.*
- *Analyze solids.*
- *Create cross sections of solids.*
- *Use **SOLIDEDIT** options to edit faces and edges of solids.*
- *Use the **SOLVIEW** and **SOLDRAW** commands to create orthographic views.*
- *Use the **SOLPROF** command to create profiles.*
- *Create shaded images.*
- *Set the shading method and diffuse reflection.*

WHAT IS SOLID MODELING?

Solid modeling is the process of building objects that have all the attributes of an actual solid object. For example, if you draw a wireframe or a surface model of a bushing, it is sufficient to define the shape and size of the object. However, in engineering, the shape and size alone are not enough to describe an object. For engineering analysis we need more information, like volume, mass, moment of inertia, and material properties (density, Young's modulus, Poissons's ratio, thermal conductivity, and so on). When you know these physical attributes of an object, it can be subjected to various tests to make sure that it performs as required by the product specifications. It eliminates the need for building expensive prototypes and makes the product development cycle shorter. Solid models also make it easy to visualize the objects because we always think of and see the objects as solids. With computers getting faster and software getting more sophisticated and affordable, solid modeling will become the core of the manufacturing process. AutoCAD solid modeling is based on the ACIS solid modeler, which is a part of the core technology.

PREDEFINED SOLID PRIMITIVES

Toolbar:	Solids
Menu:	Draw > Solids
Command:	(OBJECT NAME)

The solid primitives form the basic building blocks for a complex solid. ACIS has six predefined solid primitives you can use to construct a solid model (box, wedge, cone, cylinder, sphere, and torus). The number of lines in a solid model representation is controlled by the value assigned to the **ISO-LINES** variable. These lines are called tessellation lines. The number of lines determines the number of computations needed to generate a solid. If

Figure 23-1 Selecting Solid primitives from the Solids toolbar

the value is high, it will take significantly more time to generate a solid on the screen. Therefore, the value you assign to the **ISOLINES** variable should be realistic. When you enter commands for creating solid primitives, AutoCAD Solids will prompt you to enter information about the part geometry. The height of the primitive is always along the positive Z axis, perpendicular to the construction plane. Just like surface meshes, solids are also displayed as wireframe models unless you hide, render, or shade them. The **FACETRES** system variable controls the smoothness in the shaded and rendered objects.

Creating a Solid Box (BOX)

Toolbar:	Solids > Box
Menu:	Draw > Solids > Box
Command:	BOX

You can use the **BOX** command to create a solid rectangular box (Figure 23-2). This command has two options: **Center** and **Corner**. The **Corner** option is the default option. In this option, AutoCAD will prompt you to enter the first corner, second corner, and height of the box. The following is the prompt sequence for the **BOX** command:

Command: **BOX**
Specify corner of box or [CEnter] <0,0,0>: 1,1,0
Specify corner or [Cube/Length]: 3,2.5,0
Specify height: 2.5

Creating a Solid Cone (CONE)

Toolbar:	Solids > Cone
Menu:	Draw > Solids > Cone
Command:	CONE

The **CONE** command creates a solid cone with an elliptical or circular base (Figure 23-3). This command can be selected just as any command to create a solid primitive object. It has two options: **Elliptical** and **Center point**. The **Center point** option is the default option. The base of the cone lies on the current construction plane, and the height of the cone is along the Z axis. You can change the base plane (XY plane) by using the UCS command options. You can also define the apex point to define the cone height. The following is the command prompt sequence for the **CONE** command:

Command: **CONE**
Current frame density: ISOLINES=current
Specify center point for base of cone or [Elliptical]<0,0,0>: 5,2
Specify radius for base of cone or [Diameter]: 1.0
Specify height of cone or [Apex]: 1.5

The **Elliptical** option creates a cone with an elliptical base. The command prompt is:

Specify axis endpoint of ellipse for base of cone or [Center]: *Specify a point for the endpoint of the axis or enter C for center of base.*

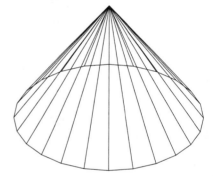

Figure 23-2 Creating a solid box using the BOX command

Figure 23-3 Creating a solid cone using the CONE command

Creating a Solid Cylinder (CYLINDER)

You can use the **CYLINDER** command to construct a solid cylinder (Figure 23-4). This command can be selected just as any command to create a solid primitive object. Like the **CONE** command, it has two options: **Elliptical** and **Center point**. The **Center point** option is the default option. The base of the cylinder lies on the current construction plane, and the height of the cylinder is along the Z axis. You can change the base plane (XY construction plane) by using the UCS command options. The following is the prompt sequence for the **CYLIN-DER** command:

Command: **CYLINDER**
Current wire frame density: ISOLINES=4
Specify center point for base of cylinder or [Elliptical] <0,0,0>: 8,2
Specify radius for base of cylinder or [Diameter]: 1.0
Specify height of cylinder or [Center of other end]: 2.5

Creating a Solid Sphere (SPHERE)

The **SPHERE** command can be used to create a solid sphere (Figure 23-5). The **SPHERE** command can be selected just as any command to create a solid primitive object. The command has only one option: **Center of sphere**. The center of the sphere automatically aligns with the Z axis of the current UCS. The following is the prompt sequence for the **SPHERE** command using the **Center point option**.

Command: **SPHERE**
Current wire frame density: ISOLINES=current
Specify center of sphere<0,0,0>: 1,5
Specify radius of sphere or [Diameter]: 1.25

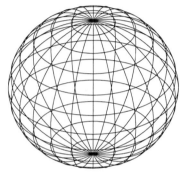

Figure 23-4 *Creating a solid cylinder using the* **CYLINDER** *command*

Figure 23-5 *Creating a solid sphere using the* **SPHERE** *command*

Creating a Solid Torus (TORUS)

You can use the **TORUS** command to create a torus (doughnut-like shape) (Figure 23-6). The **TORUS** command can be selected just as any command to create a solid primitive object. When you select this command, AutoCAD will prompt you to enter the Diameter/ or Radius of torus and the Diameter or Radius of tube. The radius of torus is the distance from the center of the torus to the centerline of the tube. This radius can have a positive or negative value. If the value is negative, the torus has a football-like shape. A torus can be self-intersecting. If both the radii of the tube and the torus are positive and the radius of the tube is greater than the radius of the torus, the resulting solid looks like a sphere with depressions at both its' ends. The torus is centered on the construction plane (the top half of the torus is above the construction plane and the other half is below the construction plane). The following is the prompt sequence for the **TORUS** command:

Command: **TORUS**
Current wire frame density: ISOLINES=current
Specify center of torus or [Diameter] <0,0,0>: 5,4
Specify radius of torus or [Diameter]: 1.75
Specify radius of tube or [Diameter]: 0.5

Creating a Solid Wedge (WEDGE)

The **WEDGE** command can be used to create a solid wedge (Figure 23-7). The **WEDGE** command can be selected just as any command to create a solid primitive object. When you enter this command, AutoCAD will prompt you to enter the first and the second corner of the wedge. These two points define the base of the wedge, which is always drawn parallel to the current construction plane. The command will also prompt you to enter the height of the wedge. The wedge will taper toward the positive X axis. The following is the prompt sequence for the **WEDGE** command:

Command: **WEDGE**
Specify first corner of wedge or [Center]<0,0,0>: 1,1,0
Specify corner or [Cube/Length]: 3,2.5,0
Specify height: 2.5

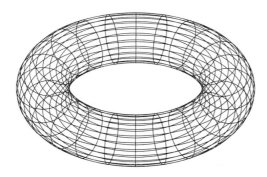

Figure 23-6 *Creating a solid torus using the* ***TORUS*** *command*

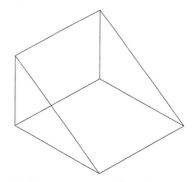

Figure 23-7 *Creating a solid wedge using the* ***WEDGE*** *command*

CONSTRUCTING A REGION

The following example explains some commands that can be used to create solids and regions.

Example 1

Use AutoCAD Solids commands to create a region, and then extrude this region to create a solid model of the object (base plate) as shown in Figure 23-8.

Creating a 2D Region Primitive

A region is a solid with zero thickness. Creating a 2D Region Primitive involves two steps: (1) create a part profile by using AutoCAD commands; (2) create a region by solidifying the part profile. A region is created by using the **REGION** command. The following steps explain the process involved in constructing a region for Example 1.

1. Use the AutoCAD drawing and editing commands to make the drawing of the base plate shown in Figure 23-9.

Figure 23-8 *Drawing for Example 1*   **Figure 23-9** *Outer profile of the base plate*

Use the **ARC** and **LINE** commands to draw the outer profile.

Command: **ARC**
Specify start point of arc or [CEnter]: CE
Specify center point of arc: 5,4
Specify start point of arc: 7,5.5
Specify endpoint of arc or [Angle/Chord length]: 7,2.5

Command: **LINE**
Specify first point: 7.0,5.5
Specify next point or [Undo]: 7.0,2.5
Specify next point or [Undo]: Enter

2. Use the **PEDIT** command to change the line into a polyline; then, use the **Join** option to join the line with the arc to create a single polyline object.

Command: **PEDIT**
Select polyline: *Select the line.*
Object selected is not a polyline
Do you want to turn it into one? <Y>: Y
Enter an option [Close/Join/Width/Edit vertex/Fit/Spline/Decurve/Ltype gen/Undo]: J
Select objects: *Select the line.*
Select objects: *Select the arc.*
Select objects: Enter
1 segment added to polyline
Enter an option [Close/Join/Width/Edit vertex/Fit/Spline/Decurve/Ltype gen/Undo]: Enter

Creating a 2D Region (REGION Command)

Toolbar:	Draw > Region
Menu:	Draw > Region
Command:	REGION

You can use the **REGION** command to create a region (Figure 23-10). AutoCAD will create a region from the selected closed polyline, line, circle, arc, ellipse, and splines and then remove the polyline from the drawing unless the **DELOBJ** system variable is set to 0.

1. Use the **REGION** command to create a region.

    Command: **REGION**
    Select objects: *Select the polyline.*
    Select objects: [Enter]
    1 loop extracted
    1 region created

2. Use the **UCS** command to move the UCS icon to the center point of the arc (5,4). (When AutoCAD prompts for the origin point, you can also use the **CENter** object snap to grab the center point of the arc.)

    Command: **UCS**
    Current UCS name: *WORLD*
    Enter an option [New/Move/orthoGraphic/Prev/Restore/Save/Del/Apply/?/World] <World>:N
    Specify new origin of new UCS or [ZAxis/3point/OBject/Face/View/X/Y/Z]<0,0,0>: 5,4

3. Draw 0.5-diameter circles located on the 4.0-diameter-bolt circle (Figure 23-11). (You can also create the circles by drawing one circle and then using the **ARRAY** command to create the remaining circles.)

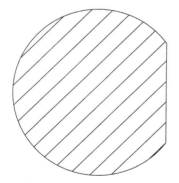

Figure 23-10 Creating a 2D Region

Figure 23-11 Creating a circular array

    Command: **CIRCLE**
    Specify center point or [3P/2P/TtR(tan tan radius)]: @2<60
    Specify radius of circle or [Diameter]: D
    Specify diameter of circle: 0.5

    Command: **ARRAY**
    Select objects: *Select 0.5 diameter circle.*
    Enter type of array [Rectangular/Polar] <R>: P

Specify center point of array: 0,0
Enter number of items in the array: 3
Specify the angle to fill (+=CCW, -=CW)<360>: 240
Rotate arrayed objects? [Yes/ No]<Y>: [Enter]

4.   Use the **REGION** command to create a region from the circles.

Subtracting Regions (SUBTRACT)

Toolbar:	Solid Editing > Subtract
Menu:	Modify > Solid Editing > Subtract
Command:	SUBTRACT

 You can use the **SUBTRACT** command to subtract regions or solids. When you use this command, AutoCAD will prompt you to select two selection sets. Once you have selected the objects, the objects of the second selection set will be subtracted from the first selection set (Figure 23-12).

Command: **SUBTRACT**
Select solids and regions to subtract
from...
Select objects: *Select the region.*
Select objects: [Enter]
Select solids and regions to subtract...
Select objects: *Select three 0.5-diameter circles.*
Select objects: [Enter]

*Figure 23-12 Subtracting regions using the **SUBTRACT** command*

The hatch lines may not get removed from the small circles until you use the **MOVE** command and move the outer profile.

Hatching a Region (Using BHATCH Command). When you create a region, the mesh lines are not visible. To hatch a region, you can use the **BHATCH** command. The hatch pattern, the hatch angle, and the hatch size can be set in the **Boundary Hatch** dialog box. You can use any hatch pattern defined in the AutoCAD ACAD.PAT file. To get hatch as shown in Figure 23-12, use the **ANSI31** hatch pattern and a scale factor of 3.5. You can also create regions with the **BOUNDARY** and **BHATCH** commands.

Creating an Extruded Solid (EXTRUDE)

Toolbar:	Solids > Extrude
Menu:	Draw > Solids > Extrude
Command:	EXTRUDE

 The next step is to add thickness to the region by using the **EXTRUDE** command (Figure 23-13). When you enter this command, AutoCAD will prompt you to select the objects for extrusion, the height of extrusion, and the extrusion taper angle. A positive angle tapers in and a negative angle tapers out. After you enter this information, AutoCAD will evaluate the boundaries and do tessellation calculations for each element in the composite region. You can also use the **ISOLINES** system variable to set the number of tessellation lines. You can extrude closed objects like polylines, polygons, rectangles, circles, ellipses, closed splines, donuts, and regions. You cannot extrude 3D objects, objects within blocks and polylines with intersecting segments.

Command: **ISOLINES**
Enter new value for ISOLINES<4>: 10

Command: **EXTRUDE**
Current wireframe density: ISOLINES=current
Select objects: *Select the region.*
Select objects: Enter
Specify height of extrusion or [Path]: 0.75   *(A positive value extrudes along the positive Z axis and a negative value extrudes along the negative Z axis.)*
Specify angle of taper for extrusion <0>: Enter

Using the path option, extrudes the object along the selected path. The extrusion path should not lie on the same plane as the object. The command prompt is:

Select extrusion path: *Select path.*

After you have completed **REGION** or **BOUNDARY** commands, the original object is deleted or retained depending on the settings of the **DELOBJ** system variable.

Next, you can use the **VPOINT** command to get a 3D view of the extruded region (Figure 23-14). Use the **ERASE** command to erase the hatch lines. Save a copy of this drawing as BASEPLT. This drawing will be used in Example 2 to construct another solid.

Command: **VPOINT**
Current view direction: VIEWDIR= current
Specify view point or [Rotate] <display compass and tripod>: 1,-1,1

Figure 23-13 Extruding a region   *Figure 23-14 3D view of the extruded region*

Chapter 23

CONSTRUCTING A COMPOSITE SOLID

A composite solid consists of two or more solid primitives. The following example explains some of the frequently used AutoCAD Solids commands that are used to create a composite solid. The example also illustrates the application of these commands.

Example 2

Use AutoCAD Solids commands to create a solid model of the object shown in Figure 23-15. The chamfer and fillet radius is 0.15. To save time, you may use the base plate drawing (BASEPLT) created in Example 1.

Figure 23-15 Drawing for Example 2

Creating a Revolved Solid (REVOLVE)

Toolbar:	Solids > Revolve
Menu:	Draw > Solids > Revolve
Command:	REVOLVE

 The **REVOLVE** command creates a solid by sweeping a closed object like a polyline or circle around an axis. The selected object can be rotated through any angle from 0 to 360 degrees. Before using the **REVOLVE** command, you must draw the profile of the surface you want to revolve. Use the **UCS** command to rotate the UCS icon by +90 degrees, and then draw the profile.

 Note
Make sure the UCS icon is at the center of the base. If it is not, use the UCS command to define the new origin.

1. Use the **UCS** command to rotate the UCS icon through 90 degrees.

   Command: **UCS**

Current UCS name: *CURRENT*
Enter an option [New/Move/orthoGraphic/Prev/Restore/Save/Del/Apply/?/World]
<World>:N
Specify new origin or [ZAxis/3point/OBject/View/X/Y/Z] <0,0,0>: X
Specify new rotation angle about X axis <0>: 90

2. Use the **PLINE** command to draw the profile of the surface (Figure 23-16).

Command: **PLINE**
Specify start point: 0,0
Current line-width is 0.0000
Specify next point or [Arc/Close/Halfwidth/Length/Undo/Width]: @0.75,0
Specify next point or [Arc/Close/Halfwidth/Length/Undo/Width]: @0,3
Specify next point or [Arc/Close/Halfwidth/Length/Undo/Width]: @0.25,0
Specify next point or [Arc/Close/Halfwidth/Length/Undo/Width]: @0,0.75
Specify next point or [Arc/Close/Halfwidth/Length/Undo/Width]: @-1,0
Specify next point or [Arc/Close/Halfwidth/Length/Undo/Width]: C

3. Use the **REVOLVE** command to revolve the profile through 360 degrees (Figure 23-17).

Command: **REVOLVE**
Current wire frame density: ISOLINES=current
Select objects: *Select the polyline.*
Select objects: [Enter]
Specify start point for axis of revolution or
define axis by [Object/X(axis)/Y(axis)]: 0,0
Specify endpoint of axis: 0,3
Specify angle of revolution <360>: [Enter]

Figure 23-16 *Creating the surface of the revolution profile*

Figure 23-17 *Creating a revolved solid*

Creating a Cylinder (CYLINDER)

The **CYLINDER** command creates a solid cylinder. The **CYLINDER** command can be selected just as any command to create a solid primitive object. When you enter this command, you will be prompted to enter the diameter and height of the cylinder. The number of lines on the cylindrical surface (tessellation lines) depends on the value of the **ISOLINES** variable. Use the following commands to draw the solid cylinder.

1. Use the **UCS** command to rotate the UCS icon -90 degrees about the X axis so that the UCS icon is parallel to the bottom face. Then, redefine the UCS origin 0.75 units up along the Z axis.

    Command: **UCS**
    Current UCS name: *CURRENT*
    Enter an option [New/Move/orthoGraphic/Prev/Restore/Save/Del/Apply/?/World]
    <World>: N
    Specify new origin or [ZAxis/3point/OBject/View/X/Y/Z] <0,0,0>: X
    Specify rotation angle about X axis <0>: -90
    Command: **UCS**
    Current UCS name: *CURRENT*
    Enter an option [New/Move/orthoGraphic/Prev/Restore/Save/Del/Apply/?/World]
    <World>: N
    Specify new origin or [ZAxis/3point/OBject/View/X/Y/Z] <0,0,0>: @0,0,0.75

2. Use the **CYLINDER** command to create a solid cylinder (Figure 23-18).

    Command: **CYLINDER**
    Current wire frame density: ISOLINES=current
    Specify center point for base of cylinder
    or [Elliptical]<0,0,0>: [Enter]
    Specify radius for base of cylinder or
    [Diameter]: 1.5
    Specify height of cylinder or [Center of
    other end]: 3.0

You have created three solids: base plate, cylinder, and inner core. The next step is to join the base plate and the cylinder using the **UNION** command. Then, you will subtract the inner core from the composite solid using the **SUBTRACT** command.

Figure 23-18 Creating a solid cylinder

Creating Composite Solids or Regions (UNION)

Toolbar:	Solid Editing > Union
Menu:	Modify > Solid Editing > Union
Command:	UNION

The **UNION** command can be used to create composite solids or regions. Several solids or regions can be combined in the same command. However, the solids cannot be combined with the regions. If the selection set contains both regions and solids, AME will automatically combine the solids and the regions separately. If the solids or the regions cannot be combined, ACIS will display the message "1 solid rejected" or "1 region rejected." (Also see the **SUBTRACT** command, discussed earlier in this chapter in the section on "Subtracting Regions.")

1. Use the **UNION** command to create a composite solid from the base plate and the cylinder.

    Command: **UNION**
    Select objects: *Select base plate.*
    Select objects: *Select cylinder.*
    Select objects: ⏎

2. Use the **SUBTRACT** command to subtract the inner core from the composite solid.

    Command: **SUBTRACT**
    Select solids and regions to subtract from...
    Select objects: *Select the composite solid.* 1 found
    Select objects: ⏎
    Select solids and regions to subtract...
    Select objects: *Select the inner core.* 1 found
    Select objects: ⏎

You will not see any change in the shape of the solid. However, if you enter the **LIST** command and select Solid, the entire solid will be highlighted, indicating that it is now a single solid with a hole through its center and a counterbore at the top. Cancel the **LIST** command or press ENTER to display the information of the selected solid on the screen. The next step is to create fillets and rounds using the **FILLET** command.

Creating Fillets and Rounds (FILLET)

Toolbar:	Modify > Fillet
Menu:	Modify > Fillet
Command:	FILLET

The **FILLET** command is used to create fillets and rounds. This command automatically unions the fillets and subtracts the rounds from the solid. The **FILLET** command does not have any special fillet or round option for Solids. The same **FILLET** command can be used for solids and other objects. Solids is intelligent enough to determine, depending on the geometry of the solid, whether to create a fillet or a round at the selected edges. If the tessellation lines are too close, use the **ISOLINES** command to change the number of lines. Next, use the **FILLET** command to create fillets and rounds on the edges, as shown in Figures 23-19 and 23-20.

    Command: **FILLET**
    Current settings: Mode = TRIM, radius = 0.000
    Select first object or [Polyline/Radius/Trim]: *Select edge A.*
    Enter fillet radius <0.000>: 0.125
    Select an edge or [Chain/Radius]: *Select edges B and C, then press ENTER.*
    3 edge(s) selected for fillet

Figure 23-19 Select edges A, B, and C

Figure 23-20 Creating fillets and rounds

Creating Chamfers (CHAMFER)

Toolbar:	Modify > Chamfer
Menu:	Modify > Chamfer
Command:	CHAMFER

The **CHAMFER** command can be used to create a chamfer, that is, to bevel the edges of a solid by a specified distance. This command automatically subtracts the chamfered volume from the solid. The **CHAMFER** command requires you to select the surface you want to chamfer; select the edge where the chamfer is needed, and indicate the chamfer distances of the base and the adjacent surfaces (Figures 23-21 and 23-22). If both the edges to be chamfered are on the same layer, the resulting chamfer assumes the same layer. In case the two edges are on different layers, the resulting chamfer assumes the current layer.

Figure 23-21 Select the base surface for creating a chamfer

Figure 23-22 Using the **CHAMFER** command to create a chamfer in solid modeling

Command: **CHAMFER**
(TRIM mode) Current chamfer Dist 1=0.5, Dist 2=0.5
Select first line or [Polyline/Distance/Angle/Trim/Method]: *Select edge E.*
Base surface selection...

Enter surface selection option [Next/OK(current)]: *Enter Next, if needed, until the cylinder edges are highlighted; then, press ENTER.*
Specify base surface chamfer distance: 0.125
Specify other surface chamfer distance <0.1250>: 0.125
Select an edge or [Loop]: *Select edge E.*
Select an edge or [Loop]: [Enter]

You might save a copy of this drawing as **SMVIEW**.

Analyzing Solids (MASSPROP)

Toolbar:	Inquiry > Mass Properties
Menu:	Tools > Inquiry > Mass Properties
Command:	MASSPROP

The **MASSPROP** command can be used to analyze a solid model. This command will automatically calculate the mass properties of the solid. The density of the solid is assumed to be 1. When you enter this command, AutoCAD will list the properties of the solid.

Command: **MASSPROP**
Select objects: *Select the solid.*

```
──────────────────── SOLIDS ────────────────────
Mass:       26.97775
Volume:     26.97775
Bounding box:      X: -2.5000 — 2.0010
                   Y: -2.5000 — 2.5000
                   Z: -0.7500 — 3.0000
Centroid:   X: -0.0623
            Y: 0.0001
            Z: 0.6068
Moments of inertia: X: 74.3905
                   Y: 71.0374
                   Z: 60.9835
Products of inertia:  XY: -0.0001
                   YZ: 0.0018
                   ZX: 0.6331
Radii of gyration:   X: 1.6606
                   Y: 1.6227
                   Z: 1.5035
Principal moments and X-Y-Z directions about centroid:
            I: 65.1039 along [0.9313 0.0001 -0.3644]
            J: 60.9993 along [-0.0004 1.0000 -0.0009]
            K: 60.2320 along [0.3644 0.0010 0.9313]
Write analysis to a file ?<N>: Y
```

If you enter Y (Yes) at this last prompt, the **Create Mass and Area Properties File** dialog box (Figure 23-23) is displayed. All the file names of the .MPR type are listed. You can enter the name of the file in the **File Name:** edit box. The file is automatically given the .MPR extension.

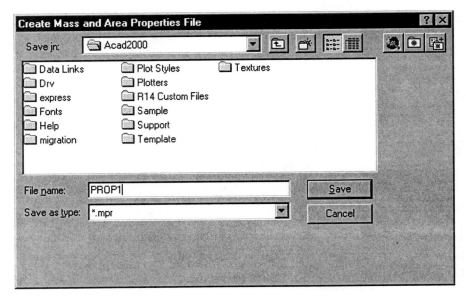

Figure 23-23 Create Mass and Area Properties File dialog box

The various terms displayed on the screen as a result of invoking the **MASSPROP** command are explained next.

For Solids. The information displayed for solids is similar to the following.

Mass. This property provides the measure of mass of a solid.

Volume. This tells you the measure of the space occupied by the solid. Since AutoCAD assigns a density of 1 to solids, the mass and volume of a solid are equal.

Bounding Box. If the solid were to be enclosed in a 3D box, the coordinates of the diagonally opposite corners would be provided by this property.

Centroid. This provides the coordinates of the center of mass for the selected solid. The density of a solid is assumed to be unvarying.

Moments of Inertia. This property provides the mass moments of inertia of a solid about the three axes. The equation used to calculate this value is:

$$mass\_moments\_of\_inertia = object\_mass * (radius\ of\ axis)2$$

The radius of axis is nothing but the radius of gyration. The values obtained are used to calculate the force required to rotate an object about the three axes.

Products of Inertia. The value obtained with this property helps to determine the force resulting in the motion of the object. The equation used to calculate this value is:

product _of_inertia YX,XZ = mass * dist centroid_to_YZ * dist centroid_to_XZ

Radii of Gyration. The equation used to calculate this value is:

gyration_radii = (moments_of_inertia/body_mass)1/2

Principal Moments and X-Y-Z Directions about Centroid. This property provides you with the highest, lowest, and middle value for the moment of inertia about an axis passing through the centroid of the object.

For Coplanar and Noncoplanar Regions. The information displayed for coplanar regions is similar to the following:

```
───────────────── REGIONS ─────────────────

    Area:        13.6480
    Perimeter:   21.2475
    Boundary box:      X: 3.3610 — 8.5063
                       Y: 4.1330 — 6.4829
    Centroid:    X: 5.9337
                 Y: 5.3127
    Moments of inertia: X: 390.8867
                        Y: 512.2000
    Product of inertia:   XY: 430.2535
    Radii of gyration:    X: 5.3516
                          Y: 6.1260
    Principal moments and X-Y directions about centroid
                I: 5.6626 along [1.0000 0.0000]
                J: 31.6536 along [0.0000 1.0000]

    Write analysis to a file ?<N>:
```

Slicing Solids (SLICE)

Toolbar:	Solids > Slice
Menu:	Draw > Solids > Slice
Command:	SLICE

 The **SLICE** command cuts a solid along the specified plane. This command cannot be used with a region. When you enter this command, AutoCAD will prompt you to select the object you want to cut and the side of the solid you want to retain (if you do not want to retain both sides). You can specify the part that you want to retain by selecting a point on that part. Use the following commands to cut the solid as shown in Figure 23-24:

1. Use the **UCS** command to rotate the UCS icon through 90 degrees about the X axis.

Command: **UCS**
Current UCS name: *CURRENT*
Enter an option [New/Move/orthoGraphic/Prev/Restore/Save/Del/Apply/?/World]
<World>: N
Specify origin of new UCS or [ZAxis/3point/OBject/View/X/Y/Z] <0,0,0>: X
Specify rotation angle about X axis<0>: 90

2. Use the **SLICE** command to cut the solid through the XY plane (Figure 23-25).

Command: **SLICE**
Select objects: *Select the solid.*
Select objects: [Enter]
Specify first point on slicing plane by [Object/Zaxis/View/XY/YZ/ZX] <3points>: XY
Specify a point on the XY-plane <0,0,0>: [Enter]
Specify point on desired side of the plane or [Keep both sides]: *Select point (F) using*
ENDpoint osnap.

Figure 23-24 *Cutting a solid through the XY plane*

Figure 23-25 *The solid after cutting*

Creating a Cross Section (SECTION)

The **SECTION** command creates the cross section of a solid through the specified plane (Figure 23-26). This command can be invoked from the **Solids** toolbar (choose the **Section** button), from the **Draw** menu (choose **Solids > Section**), or by entering **SECTION** at the Command prompt. In addition, the cross section blocks or regions are created in the current layer, not in the layer of the solid that is sectioned.

Command: **SECTION**
Select objects: *Select the solid.*
Select objects: [Enter]

Figure 23-26 *Creating the cross section of a solid*

Specify first point on Section plane by [Object/Zaxis/View/XY/YZ/ZX] <3points>: XY
Specify a point on XY plane <0,0,0>: [Enter]

First point, 3 points option

This option defines the sectioning plane by three points. After specifying the first point, AutoCAD prompts you to select the other two points on the sectioning plane.

Object option

Aligns the sectioning plane with the specific object. This object can be a circle, ellipse, circular or elliptical arc, 2D polyline segment, or spline. The command prompt is:

Select a circle, ellipse, arc, 2D spline, or 2D polyline segment:

Z Axis option

Defines the sectioning plane by one point on the sectioning plane and one on the Z axis of the plane. The command prompt is:

Specify a point on the section plane:
Specify a point on the Z-axis (normal) of the plane:

View option

Aligns the section plane with the current viewport's viewing plane. The command prompt is:

Specify a point on the current view plane<0,0,0>:

XY option

Aligns the sectioning plane with the XY plane. Specifying a point determines the location of the plane. The command prompt is:

Specify a point on the XY plane <0,0,0>:

Similarly, the **YZ** and **ZX** options align the sectioning plane with the respective planes. To see the cross section created by the **SECTION** command, use the **MOVE** command with **Last** option to move the section to another location.

OTHER SOLIDS COMMANDS
INTERSECT (Creating Composite Solids)

The **INTERSECT** command creates a composite solid or region from objects that intersect (Figure 23-27). This command can be invoked from the **Solid Editing** toolbar, from the **Modify** menu (choose **Solid Editing > Intersection**), or by entering **INTERSECT** at the Command prompt. If the objects do not intersect, they do not have any common overlapping area or volume; therefore, **INTERSECT** can be used with them, but it will delete them and prompt "Null solid created - deleted". Also, the objects could lie in any plane.

INTERFERE (Finding Interference)

The **INTERFERE** command can be used to find interference of two or more solids (Figure 23-28). It creates a composite solid from the common volume shared by the objects. If the objects do not intersect, they have no common volume; therefore, **INTERFERE** cannot be used with them. Also, the objects could lie in any plane. This command can be invoked from the **Solids** toolbar (select the **Interfere** button), from the **Draw** menu choose **Solids > Interference**, or by entering INTERFERE at the Command prompt.

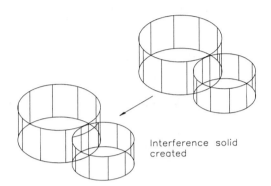

Figure 23-27 *Creating composite solids using the* **INTERSECT** *command*

Figure 23-28 *Finding Interference using the* **INTERFERE** *command*

SOLIDEDIT COMMAND*

Menu:	Modify > Solids Editing
Command:	SOLIDEDIT

With the **SOLIDEDIT** command options you can edit faces and edges of 3D solid objects. You can also invoke any of the **SOLIDEDIT** command options and suboptions from the **Solids Editing** toolbar (Figure 23-29). The command prompts are:

Figure 23-29 Solids Editing *toolbar*

Command: **SOLIDEDIT**
Solids editing automatic checking: SOLIDCHECK=1

Enter a solids editing option [Face/Edge/Body/Undo/eXit] <eXit>: *Enter an option or press ENTER to exit the command.*

Face Option

This option allows you to edit 3D solid faces. It has the following sub-options: **Extrude**, **Move**, **Rotate**, **Offset**, **Taper**, **Delete**, **Copy** and **Color**. The next prompt is:

Enter a face editing option
[Extrude/Move/Rotate/Offset/Taper/Delete/Copy/coLor/Undo/eXit]<eXit>: *Enter an option or press ENTER to exit the command.*

Extrude

This option allows you to extrude specified 3D solid object faces to a specific height or along a selected path (Figure 23-29). If you enter E at the above prompt, the next prompt is:

Select faces or [Undo/Remove]: *Select faces to extrude or enter an option.*
Select faces or [Undo/Remove/ALL]: *Select another face, an option or press ENTER.*

The **Undo** option cancels the selection of the most recent face you have selected. The **Remove** option allows you to remove a previously selected face from the selection set for extrusion. The **ALL** option selects all the faces of the specified solid. After you have selected a face for extrusion, the next prompt is:

Specify height of extrusion or [Path]: *Enter a height value or enter P.*

A positive value for the height for extrusion, extrudes the selected face outwards usually and a negative value extrudes the selected face mostly inwards. On specifying the height of extrusion, the next prompt is:

Specify angle of extrusion <0>: *Specify a value between -90 and +90 degrees or press ENTER to accept the default value of 0.*

A positive angle value tapers the selected face inwards and a negative value tapers the selected face outwards. At 0 degrees, it is tapered normal to the plane.

The Path option allows you to select a path for extrusion based on a specified line or curve. At the **Select extrusion path:** prompt, select the line, circle, arc, ellipse, elliptical arc, polyline or spline to be specified as the extrusion path. This path should not lie on the same plane as the selected face and should not have areas of high curvature.

Move

With this option you can move faces from one location to another without changing the orientation of the solid (Figure 23-30). For example, you can move holes from one place to another location. On choosing this option, the command prompts are:

Select faces or [Undo/Remove]: *Select one or more faces or enter an option.*
Select faces or [Undo/Remove/ALL]: *Select one or more faces, enter an option, or press ENTER.*

Chapter 23

Specify a base point or displacement: *Specify a base point.*
Specify a second point of displacement: *Specify a point or press ENTER.*

The face moves to the specified location.

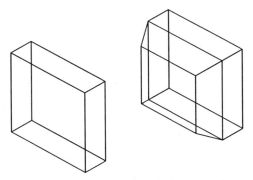

Figure 23-29 *Using the* **Extrude Faces** *option to extrude a solid face with a positive taper angle*

Figure 23-30 *Using the* **Move Faces** *option to move the hole from from the original position*

Offset

The **Offset** option allows you to offset faces uniformly through a specified distance on a 3D solid. Ofsetting takes place in the direction of the positive side of the face. For example, you can offset holes to a larger or smaller size in a 3D solid through a specified distance. A positive value increases the size of the solid and a negative value decreases the size of the solid. In Figure 23-31, the hole on the solid has been offset to a smaller size.

Rotate

This option allows you to rotate selected face(s) on a solid through a specified angle. For example, you can rotate holes around a base point through an absolute or relative angle (Figure 23-32). The direction in which the rotation takes place is determined by the current UCS and the **ANGDIR** system variable. The default value is counterclockwise with respect to the current UCS. The command prompts are:

Select faces or [Undo/Remove/ALL]: *Select face(s) or enter an option.*
Specify an axis point or [Axis by object/View/Xaxis/Yaxis/Zaxis] <2 points>: *Select a point, enter an option, or press ENTER.*

If you press ENTER to use the **2 points** option, you are prompted to select two points that will define the axis of rotation. The command prompts are:

Specify the first point on the rotation axis:
Specify the second point on the rotation axis:
Specify a rotation angle or [Reference]: *Specify the angle of rotation or enter R to use the reference option.*

The **Axis by object** option allows you to select an object to define the axis of rotation. The axis of rotation is aligned with the selected object; for example, if you select a circle, the axis of rotation is aligned along the axis that passes through the center of the circle and is normal to the plane of the circle. The selected objects could also be a line, ellipse, Arc, 2D, 3D, or LW polyline or even a spline. The command prompts are:

Select a curve to be used for the axis: *Select the object to be used to define axis of rotation.*
Specify a rotation angle or [Reference]: *Specify rotation angle or use the reference angle option.*

The **X**, **Y**, **Zaxis** options align the axis of rotation with the axis that passes through the specified point. The command prompt is:

Specify the origin of rotation <0,0,0>: *Select a point through which the axis of rotation will pass.*
Specify a rotation angle or [Reference]: *Specify rotation angle or use the reference angle option.*

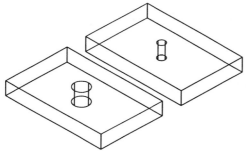

Figure 23-31 *Using the **Offset Faces** option to offset the hole on the 3D object to a smaller size*

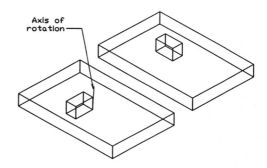

Figure 23-32 *Using the **Rotate Faces** option to rotate the hole on the 3D solid*

Taper

This option allows you to taper selected face(s) through a specified angle (Figure 23-33). The tapering takes place depending on the selection sequence of the base point and the second point along the selected face. It also depends on whether the taper angle is positive or negative. A positive value tapers the face inward and a negative value tapers the face outward. You can enter any value between -90 and +90 degrees. The default value of 0 degrees extrudes the face along the axis that is perpendicular to the selected face. If you have selected more than one face, they will all be tapered through the same angle. The command prompts are:

Select faces or [Undo/Remove/ALL]: *Select one or more faces, enter an option, or press ENTER.*
Specify the base point: *Specify a base point.*
Specify another point along the axis of tapering: *Specify a point.*
Specify the taper angle: *Specify an angle between −90 and +90 degrees.*

Delete

Removes selected face(s) from the specific 3D solid. It also removes chamfers and fillets (Figure 23-34). The command prompts are:

Select faces or [Undo/Remove/ALL]: *Select one or more faces, enter an option, or press ENTER.*

Solid validation started.
Solid validation completed.

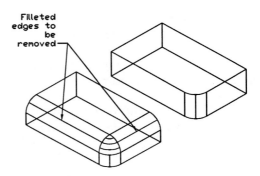

Figure 23-33 *Using the* **Taper face** *option to change the shape of the hole*

Figure 23-34 *Using the* **Delete Face** *option to remove the fillet*

Copy

The **Copy** option allows you to copy a face as a body or region (Figure 23-35). The command prompts are:

Select faces or [Undo/Remove/ALL]: *Select one or more faces, enter an option, or press ENTER.*
Specify a base point or displacement: *Specify a base point.*
Specify a second point of displacement: *Specify a point.*

Figure 23-35 *Using the* **Copy Face** *option to copy a face of the 3D solid*

Color

Changes the color of the selected face. On pressing ENTER, AutoCAD displays the Select Color dialog box for you to choose a color that you can apply to the selected face. The command prompt is :

Select faces or [Undo/Remove/ALL]: *Select one or more faces, enter an option, or press ENTER.*

Undo
This option allows you to cancel the changes made during the **SOLIDEDIT** command.

eXit
This option allows you to exit the **SOLIDEDIT** command.

Edge Option
With the **Edit** option, you can modify properties of the edge of solids. You can copy and change the color of edges. The command prompts are:

Command: **SOLIDEDIT**
Solid editing automatic checking: SOLIDCHECK=1
Enter a solids editing option [Face/Edge/Body/Undo/eXit] <eXit>: E
Enter an edge editing option [Copy/coLor/Undo/eXit] <eXit>: *Enter an option or press ENTER.*

The edge editing options are discussed in the following:

Copy
This option allows you to copy individual edges of a 3D solid (Figure 23-36). The edges are copied as lines, arcs, circles, ellipses, or splines. Entering C at the previous option, prompts as follows:

*Figure 23-36 Using the **Copy Edges** option to copy the top edge of the 3D solid*

Select edges or [Undo/Remove]: *Select an edge you wish to copy.*
Enter an edge editing option [Copy/coLor/Undo/eXit] <eXit>:*Press ENTER or enter an option.*
Solids editing automatic checking: SOLIDCHECK=1

Enter a solids editing option [Face/Edge/Body/Undo/eXit] <eXit>: *Press ENTER to exit the command or enter an option.*

Color

You can use the **coLor** option to change the color of a selected edge of a 3D solid. The command prompts are:

Select edges or [Undo/Remove]: *Select one or more edges or enter an option.*

After you select edges and press ENTER, the **Select Color** dialog box is displayed from where you can select a color to assign to the selected edges. You can also assign colors by entering their name or number. Individual edges can be assigned individual colors.

The **Undo** option cancels the modifications made during the use of the **SOLIDEDIT** command, and **eXit** option allows you to exit the command.

Body Options

These options edit the entire body of the 3D solid object. The command prompts are:

Enter a body editing option [Imprint/sePatate solids/Shell/cLean/Check/Undo/eXit] <eXit>: *Enter an option or press ENTER.*

Imprint

This option allows you to imprint an object on the 3D solid object provided the object intersects one or more faces of the solid object (Figure 23-37). The objects that can be imprinted are: arcs, circles, lines, 2D and 3D polylines, ellipses, splines, regions, bodies, and 3D solids. The command prompts are as follows:

Select a 3D solid: *Select an object.*
Select an object to imprint: *Select an object to be imprinted.*
Delete the source object <N>: *Enter y or press ENTER.*
Select an object to imprint: *Select an object or press ENTER.*

Figure 23-37 *Using the **Imprint** option to imprint part of a circle on the cube face*

seParate solids

This option allows you to disjoin 3D solids with disjointed volumes into separate 3D solids. The command prompt is:

Select a 3D solid: *Select an object.*

This option does not allow you to separate Boolean objects that form a single volume.

Shell Option

This option allows you to create a shell of a specified 3D solid. A shell is a hollow wall of a specified thickness that is created to the inside or outside perimeter of the solid (Figure 23-38). One 3D object can have only one shell. You can exclude certain faces before offsetting of faces takes place. The command prompts are:

Select a 3D solid: *Select an object.*
Remove faces or [Undo/Add]: *Select one or more faces or enter an option.*
Remove faces or [Undo/Add/ALL]: *Select a face, enter an option, or press ENTER.*
Enter the shell offset distance: *Specify a distance.*

If you have specified a positive distance, the shell that is created is to the inside perimeter of the solid and in case, it is negative, the shell is created to the outside perimeter of the 3D solid.

Clean Option

This option allows you to remove shared edges or vertices sharing the same surface or curve definition on either side of the edge or vertex. It removes all redundant edges and vertices, imprinted as well as unused geometry (Figure 23-39). It also merges faces which share the same surface. The command prompt is:

Select a 3D solid: *Select an object.*

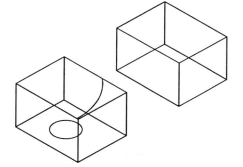

Figure 23-38 Using the **Shell** *option to create shells of a 3D cone*

Figure 23-39 Using the **Clean** *option to remove redundant and imprinted geometry*

Check Option

This option can be used to check if a solid object drawn by you is a valid 3D solid object. This option is independent of the settings of the **SOLIDCHECK** variable. The **SOLIDCHECK** variable turns on or off solid validation for the current drawing session, while using **SOLIDEDIT** options. The default value is 1; that is, solid validation is on. If the solid object is a valid 3D solid object, you can use solid editing options to modify it without AutoCAD displaying ACIS error messages. Solid editing can take place only on valid 3D solids. The command prompts are:

Select a 3D solid: *Select a solid you want to check.*
This object is a valid ACIS solid.

The **Undo** option cancels the editing modifications made and the **eXit** option allows you to exit the body editing options.

Undo Option

This option allows you to cancel or undo the editing action taken.

Exit Option

This option allows you to exit the **SOLIDEDIT** command.

Example 3

Create a 3D solid as shown in figure 23-40 and use the Solids Editing toolbar to modify it to the figure shown in 23-41.

Figure 23-40 Drawing for Example 3

Figure 23-41 Drawing after using the solid editing options

1. Choose the **Box** button in the **Solids** toolbar. Enter the following data to draw a box.

    Specify corner of box or [CEnter] <0,0,0>: 10,10
    Specify corner or [Cube/Length]: @76,76,38

2. Choose **3D Views > SE Isometric** from the **View** menu to display the model as a South East Isometric.

3. Choose **Viewports > 3 Viewports** from the **View** menu. Press ENTER at the Command prompt to accept the default settings.

4. Click on the top left viewport to make it current and choose the **Display UCS Dialog** button from the **UCS** flyout in the **Standard** toolbar. The **UCS** dialog box is displayed. Choose the **Orthographic UCSs** tab and select **Right** from the list box and choose the **Set Current** button and then choose **OK**. Similarly, set the UCS in the bottom left viewport to **Top**.

5. In the top left viewport, set Snap to 1 and choose the **Cylinder** button from the **Solids** toolbar.

Enter the following information at the command prompts:

Current wire frame density: ISOLINES=4
Specify center point for base of cylinder or [Elliptical] <0,0,0>: *Use Tracking to locate the center point for the base of the cylinder 52mm along the +Xaxis and 14mm along the +Yaxis.*
Specify radius for base of cylinder or [Diameter]: d
Specify diameter for base of cylinder: 22
Specify height of cylinder or [Center of other end]: 10

6. Similarly, draw the larger cylinder on the top face. Make the bottom left viewport current and use Object Snap tracking to locate the center of the base of the cylinder at the center of the top face of the box.

Specify radius for base of cylinder or [Diameter]: d
Specify diameter for base of cylinder: 54
Specify height of cylinder or [Center of other end]: 38

7. Zoom to the extents of the drawing in the current viewport, it resembles the drawing in Figure 23-40. Now, choose the **Union** button in the **Solids Editing** toolbar and select the three solids to unite them into a composite solid.

8. Choose the **Shell** button from the **Solids Editing** button.

Select a 3D solid: *Select the solid.*
Remove faces or [Undo/Add/ALL]: *Remove the top face of the large cylinder, the front face of the small cylinder, and the side face of the box to resemble the Figure 23-41.*
Enter the shell offset distance: -10
  Solid validation started.
  Solid validation completed.

9. Make the larger viewport in the right current and 3D Orbit and Shade modes to view the solid. Now, display it as a SE Isometric view and a 3D Wireframe model.

10. Now, in the bottom left viewport, zoom into the small cylindrical hole and choose the **Taper Faces** button from the **Solids Editing** toolbar.

Select faces or [Undo/Remove]:
Select faces or [Undo/Remove/ALL]: *Select the faces of the smaller hole.*
Specify the base point: *Specify the center of the base of the cylindrical hole.*
Specify another point along the axis of tapering:
Specify the taper angle: 10
  Solid validation started.
  Solid validation completed.

11. Now, choose the **Color Faces** button in the **Solids Editing** toolbar. Select the curved face of the hole and press ENTER. Choose the color Blue from the **Select Color** dialog box.

12. In the bottom left viewport, zoom to the top cylinder. Choose the Offset faces option and choose the larger hole. Enter the offset distance as -6. Enter L to start the Color Faces option. Choose the top face and choose the color red from the Select Color dialog box.

13. Zoom to the Extents of the drawing. Choose the Fillet button from the Modify toolbar. Set the Radius value to 3. Select all the edges to fillet and press ENTER. The model now resembles the Figure 23-41.

14. You can now review the model using 3D Orbit in any of the viewports.

SOLVIEW COMMAND

Toolbar:	Solids > Setup View
Menu:	Draw > Solids > Setup > View
Command:	SOLVIEW

 SOLVIEW is an externally defined ARX application (SOLIDS.ARX). When you invoke this command, it guides you through the process of creating orthographic or auxiliary views. The **SOLVIEW** command creates floating viewports using orthographic projections to layout sectional view and multiview drawings of solids, while you are in the layout tab.

The **SOLVIEW** command automatically creates layers for visible lines, hidden lines, and section hatching for each view. **SOLVIEW** also creates layers for dimensioning that are visible in individual viewports. You can use these layers to draw dimensions in individual viewports. The following is the naming convention for layers:

Layer name	Object type
View name-VIS	Visible lines
View name-HID	Hidden lines
View name-DIM	Dimensions
View name-HAT	Hatch patterns (for sections)

The view name is the user-defined layer name given to the view when created.

 Note
The information stored on these layers is deleted and updated when you run SOLDRAW. Therefore, do not place any permanent drawing information on these layers.

The command prompts are:

Command: **SOLVIEW**
Enter an option [Ucs/Ortho/Auxiliary/Section]: *Enter an option or press ENTER to exit the command.*

Ucs Option

This option allows you to create a profile view relative to a UCS. Although other options require existing viewports, this option can be used even if there are no existing viewports. The UCS can either be the current UCS or any other named UCS. The viewport you create will be parallel to the XY plane of the UCS. The next prompts are:

Enter an option [Named/World/?/Current] <Current>: *Enter an option or press ENTER to accept the current UCS.*

Using the **Named** option, uses a named UCS to create the profile view. The command prompts are:

Enter name of UCS to restore: *Enter the name of the UCS you want to use.*
Enter view scale <1.0>: *Enter a positive scale factor.*

This view scale value you enter is equivalent to zooming into your viewport by a factor relative to paper space. The default ratio is 1:1. The next prompts are:

Specify view center: *Specify a point and press ENTER.*

This point is based on the Model space extents. The next prompts are:

Specify the first corner of viewport: *Specify a point.*
Specify the other corner of viewport: *Specify a point.*
Enter view name: *Enter a name for the view.*

The **World** option uses the XY plane of the WCS to create a profile view. The command prompts are the same as the **Named** option.

The **?** option lists all the named UCSs. The command prompts are:

Enter UCS names to list<*>: *Enter a name or press ENTER to list all the named UCSs.*

The **Current** option uses the current XY plane of the current UCS to create the profile view. This is also the default option.

Ortho Option

The **Ortho** option creates a folded orthographic view from the existing view. AutoCAD prompts you to specify the side of the viewport from where you want to project the view. The command prompts are:

Specify side of viewport to project: *Select the edge of a viewport.*
Specify view center: *Specify a point and press ENTER.*
Specify first corner of viewport:
Specify opposite corner of viewport:
Enter view name: *Enter a name for the view.*

Auxiliary Option

This option creates an auxiliary view from an existing view. An auxiliary view is one which is projected on to a plane perpendicular to one of the orthographic views and is inclined in the adjacent view. AutoCAD prompts you to define the inclined plane used for auxiliary projection. The command prompts are:

Specify first point of inclined plane:
Specify second point of inclined plane:
Specify side to view from: *Specify a point.*
Specify view center: *Specify a point and press ENTER.*
Specify first corner of viewport:
Specify opposite corner of viewport:
Enter view name: *Enter a name for the view.*

Section Option

This option creates a sectional view of the 3D solid. The section also displays cross hatching. When you use the **SOLDRAW** command with the sectional view, a temporary copy of the solid is created and **SLICE** is used. Then **SOLDRAW** creates the visible half and discards the copy. The layer View name- HID is frozen. AutoCAD prompts you to define the cutting plane, the command prompts are:

Specify first point of cutting plane:
Specify second point of cutting plane:

Once you have defined the cutting plane, you can specify the side to view from and the view scale, relative to paper space. The command prompts are:

Specify side to view from: *Specify a point.*
Enter view scale <current>: *Enter a positive number.*
Specify view center: *Specify a point and press ENTER.*
Specify first corner of viewport:
Specify opposite corner of viewport:
Enter view name: *Enter a name for the view.*

SOLDRAW COMMAND

Toolbar:	Solids > Setup Drawing
Menu:	Draw > Solids > Setup > Drawing
Command:	SOLDRAW

The **SOLDRAW** command generates profiles and section views in the viewports that were created with the **SOLVIEW** command. It creates the visible and hidden lines that represent the silhouettes and edges of solids in a viewport, and then projects them in a plane that is perpendicular to the viewing direction. For section views, the crosshatching is automatically created using the current hatch pattern (HPNAME), hatch angle (HPANG), and hatch scale (HPSCALE). If there are any existing profiles and sections in the selected viewports, they are deleted and replaced with new ones. The command prompts are:

Select viewports to draw...
Select objects: *Select viewports to be drawn.*

Note

*You must not place any information in the view name-VIS, view name-HID, and view name-HAT layers because the information on these layers is deleted and then updated when you use the **SOLDRAW** command.*

*To redraw drawings created with the **SOLVIEW** command in AutoCAD release 12, using the **SOLDRAW** command, first convert them from AME solids to AutoCAD 3D solids using the **AMECONVERT** command.*

Example 4

In this example, you will use the **SOLVIEW** command to draw the·right-hand side and top view of a solid model object (Figure 23-42).

1. Draw a box and two cylinders. Union the box and outer cylinder, and then subtract the inner cylinder from the unioned object as shown in Figure 23-42.

2. Invoke the **SOLVIEW** command. AutoCAD automatically switches to paper space (TILEMODE= 0), creates a viewport, and issues the prompt **Enter an option [Ucs/ Ortho/ Auxiliary/ Section]:**. At this prompt, enter O for ortho.

Figure 23-42 *Solid model object for Example 4*

3. Next, AutoCAD will prompt **Specify side of viewport to project:**. At this prompt, select the right side edge of the viewport; then, select a point (view center) where you want to position the view.

4. After defining the view center, AutoCAD will prompt you to select two corners of the viewport. These two corners define the viewport for the view and clip the objects that are within the specified window.

5. Next, AutoCAD will prompt you to enter the view name that it uses to create layers. Enter RHSV for right-hand side view.

6. Repeat above steps to obtain the top view (TV) as shown in Figure 23-43. Notice that there are several lines going through the object, both in side and top views.

7. Invoke the **SOLDRAW** command. AutoCAD will prompt:

Select viewports to draw...
Select objects:

At this prompt, select the top and side viewports. The mesh lines are removed from the selected views, and the hidden lines are placed in TV-hid and RHSV-hid layers. In the Layer & Linetype Properties dialog box, change the linetype of TV-hid and RHSV-hid to hidden. The resulting view with hidden lines is shown in Figure 23-44.

Figure 23-43 *Using the **SOLVIEW** command to create views*

Figure 23-44 *Using the **SOLDRAW** command to clean the drawing*

SOLPROF COMMAND

Toolbar:	Solids > Setup Profile
Menu:	Draw > Solids > Setup > Profile
Command:	SOLPROF

 The **SOLPROF** command creates profile images of 3D solids by displaying only the edges and silhouettes of the curved surfaces of the solids in the current view. Before you can use this command, you must set the **TILEMODE** to 0 (set the **Layout** tab and create a viewport). The following example illustrates the use of the **SOLPROF** command.

Example 5

In this example, you will use the **SOLPROF** command to draw right-hand side and top profile images of a solid model object (Figure 23-42).

1. Draw a box and two cylinders. Union the box and outer cylinder, and then subtract the inner cylinder from the unioned object as shown in Figure 23-42.

2. Set the **Layout** tab. Now you are in the paper space. Use the **-VPORTS** or **MVIEW** command to create three viewports as shown in Figure 23-45.

3. Use the **MSPACE** command to switch to model space, and use the **VPOINT** command to change the view points [lower left viewport (0,-1,0), lower right viewport (1,0,0), upper left viewport (0,0,1)].

4. Make the lower left viewport active, and use the **SOLPROF** command to create the profile image. When you invoke this command, AutoCAD will issue the following prompts:

Select objects: *Select a solid model object.*
Display hidden profile lines on separate layer? [Yes/No] <Y>: *Enter Y or N.*

Entering YES will generate two blocks, one for visible lines and one for hidden lines. Entering NO considers all profile lines as visible lines and creates a block for the profile lines of the selected solid(s).

Project profile lines onto a plane? [Yes/No] <Y>: *Enter Y or N.*

Entering Y creates the profile lines with 2D objects, on to a plane normal to the viewing direction and passing through the current UCS. Entering N creates the profile lines with 3D objects.

Delete tangential edges? <Y>: Enter Y or N.

A tangential line is a transition line between two tangent faces.

5. Repeat step 4 for other viewports to create the required profiles, and then freeze the layer that contains the original solid model object. The resulting profiles are shown in Figure 23-46.

Figure 23-45 *Using the **MVIEW** and **VPOINT** commands to create viewports with different views*

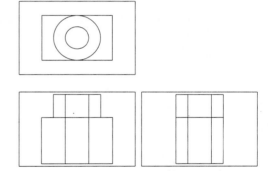

Figure 23-46 *Using the **SOLPROF** command to create profiles*

ACISIN (Importing an ACIS File)

The **ACISIN** command is used to read in a model stored as an ACIS file. After reading the file, AutoCAD creates the objects, solids, or regions from the data contained in the ACIS file. ACIS is a solid modeling file format that AutoCAD uses to store information (data) on solid objects. The file can be saved as an ASCII file with .sat extension. You can invoke the **Select ACIS File** dialog box (Figure 23-47) from the **Insert** menu by choosing **ACIS Solid**. You can also invoke this dialog box by entering **ACISIN** at the Command prompt. If you use the **IMPORT** command, the **Import File** dialog box is displayed (Figure 23-48).

Figure 23-47 Select ACIS File dialog box

Figure 23-48 Import File dialog box

ACISOUT (Exporting AutoCAD Solid Objects to an ACIS File)

The **ACISOUT** command is used to export an AutoCAD solid or a region to an ACIS solid modeling format. ACIS is a solid modeling file format that AutoCAD uses to store information (data) on solid objects. The file can be saved as an ASCII file with .sat extension. You can invoke the **Create ACIS File** dialog box (Figure 23-49) by entering **ACISOUT** at the Command prompt. AutoCAD prompts you to select objects. After selecting the object that are solids or regions, press ENTER to display the dialog box.

Figure 23-49 Create ACIS File dialog box

You can also create an ACIS file through the **File** menu (choose **Export...**). The **Export Data** dialog box is displayed (Figure 23-50). Select **ACIS (*.SAT)** from the **Save As Type:** drop-down list.

Figure 23-50 Export Data dialog box

STLOUT (Storing a Solid in Stereolithograph Format)

The **STLOUT** command can be used to write the solid model data in an ASCII or binary file format (.stl extension). The .stl file format is compatible with Stereo-Lithography Apparatus (SLA).

The SLA workstation uses this data to build the part in a series of layers; each layer defines a contour of the solid model. You can invoke the **Create STL File** dialog box (Figure 23-51) by entering **STLOUT** at the Command prompt.

Command: **STLOUT**
Select a single solid for STL output ..
Select objects: 1 found
Select objects: *Press ENTER.*
Create a binary STL file? [Yes/No] <Y>: *Enter Y or N.*

Figure 23-51 Create STL File dialog box

You can also use the **Export Data** dialog box and enter the File name in the **File name:** edit box. From the **Save As Type:** drop-down list select **Lithography(*.stl)**.

FACETRES (Adjusting Smoothness)

FACETRES is a system variable that can be used to adjust the smoothness of shaded, rendered, and hidden-line-removed objects. The default value is 0.5; the value can range from 0.01 to 10.0.

DISPSILH (Controlling Display of Silhouette)

Like **FACETRES** and **ISOLINES**, **DISPSILH** is a system variable that controls the display of silhouette curves of an object in wireframe mode. The default values is 0 (off).

AMECONVERT (Converting Existing AME Solids)

This command can be used to convert an AME solid model to an AutoCAD solid model. It can be invoked by entering **AMECONVERT** at the Command prompt. With this command, the only AME solids and regions that can be converted must have been created by AME Release 2.0 or 2.1.

All other objects are ignored. Since AutoCAD Solids uses different technology (ACIS) then does AME (PADL), you may not get an accurate conversion.

CREATING SHADED IMAGES

In a 3D object the **HIDE** command can be used to hide the hidden line in the object. By hiding the lines, you can get a better idea about the shape of the object. To get a more realistic image of the object, you can use the **SHADEMODE** command. The **SHADEMODE** command performs a hide and then creates a flat shaded picture in the current viewport. The shading uses a single light source that is assumed to be located just behind the user over the shoulder. The shaded image can be edited and the **UNDO** command cannot be used to undo shading. Use the **REGEN** or **ZOOM** command to regenerate the drawing and display the 3D wire frame of the object. This command can also be invoked by choosing **Shade** from the **View** menu. The command prompts are:

Command: **SHADEMODE**
Enter option [2D wireframe/3D wireframe/Hidden/Flat/Gouraud/fLat+edges/ gOuraud+edges]<current>: *Enter an option.*

Setting the Shading Method

You can use the **SHADEDGE** system variable to set the shading method. If **SHADEDGE** is 0, AutoCAD creates a shaded image with no edges highlighted. If **SHADEDGE** is 1, AutoCAD creates a shaded image with edges highlighted in the background color. To see the effect of these two shading methods you need 256 color display.

If **SHADEDGE** is 2, AutoCAD paints the surfaces of the object in the background color and displays the visible edges in the object's color (Figure 23-52). If **SHADEDGE** is 3 (default setting), AutoCAD paints the faces in the object's color and displays the edges in the background color (Figure 23-53).

Figure 23-52 Shading with **SHADEDGE=2**, objects white, and background white

Figure 23-53 Shading with **SHADEDGE=2**, objects red, and background white

Setting Diffuse Reflection

The system variable **SHADEDIF** is used to control the amount of light diffused that AutoCAD uses to calculate the shade for each surface. The default value of **SHADEDIF** is 70. It can range from 0 to 100.

Self-Evaluation Test

Answer the following questions, and then compare your answers to the correct answers given at the end of this chapter.

1. What is solid modeling? _____

    _____

2. ACIS can be used to create surface models and meshes. (T/F)

3. ACIS solids do not have any predefined primitives. (T/F)

4. What command can be used to check interference between solids? _____

5. The **CONE** command creates a solid cone with an elliptical or circular base. (T/F)

6. The base of the wedge is always drawn perpendicular to the current construction plane. (T/F)

7. You can create a region by solidifying the part profile. (T/F)

8. A composite solid consists of two solid primitives. (T/F)

9. The **SLICE** command cuts a solid only along the XY plane. (T/F)

10. You cannot write to a file the properties obtained by the **MASSPROP** command. (T/F)

11. You can use the _____ command to edit the faces, edges and body of existing solids.

Review Questions

1. AutoCAD Solids has _____ predefined solid primitives. Name them: _____

    _____

2. The number of tessellation lines in a solid model is controlled by the value assigned to the _____ variable.

3. You can use the _____ command to subtract solids.

4. The _____ command creates a solid by sweeping a polyline or a circle around an axis.

5. You can use the _____ to list the properties of a solid.

6. The _____ command can be used to create fillets and rounds.

7. The _____ command automatically unions the fillets and subtracts the rounds from the solid.

8. You can use the _____ command to construct a solid cylinder.

9. The _____ command lets you generate a section image of a selected object.

10. A region is created by using the _____ command.

11. To access AutoCAD **Solids** commands, you must first load the program. (T/F)

12. AutoCAD Solids is based on PADL technology. (T/F)

13. You can use the **CYLINDER** command to construct a solid cylinder. (T/F)

14. The **CYLINDER** command has only one option. (T/F)

15. A region is a solid with unit thickness. (T/F)

16. The value of the **ISOLINES** variable can be from 1 to 25. (T/F)

17. The cross section obtained by the **SECTION** command is automatically crosshatched. (T/F)

18. AME solids can be converted to AutoCAD solids. (T/F)

19. What system variable determines whether silhouette edges are drawn? _____

20. You can use the **CHAMFER** command to create a chamfer in solid objects. (T/F)

21. The _____ body editing option of the **SOLIDEDIT** command allows you to create a shell of the selected solid.

Exercises

Exercise 1 *Mechanical*

Construct a composite solid of the object shown in Figure 23-54. You may use the following instructions to create this solid:

1. Draw the outer profile of the base plate, and change the profile into a polyline.
2. Draw the circles.
3. Construct a region from the base.
4. Extrude the region.
5. Construct the solid tube.
6. Draw a rectangular solid with thickness equal to the width of the slot, and then subtract it from the tube.
7. Union the tube and the base plate.
8. Draw a solid cylinder equal to the inside diameter of the hole; then, subtract the cylinder from the object.

9. Use the **SOLVIEW** and **SOLDRAW** commands to generate the front, side, and top views.

Figure 23-54 Drawing for Exercise 1

Exercise 2   *Mechanical*

Construct a composite solid of the object shown in Figure 23-55. Use the **SOLPROF** command to generate front, side, and top profiles.

Figure 23-55 Drawing for Exercise 2

Exercise 3   *Mechanical*

Construct a composite solid of the object shown in Figure 23-56. Use the **SOLPROF** command to generate front, side, and top profiles.

Figure 23-56 *Drawing for Exercise 3*

Exercise 4   *Mechanical*

Construct a composite solid of the object shown in Figure 23-57.

Figure 23-57 *Drawing for Exercise 4*

Exercise 5   *Mechanical*

Construct a composite solid of the object shown in Figure 23-58. Use the **SOLPROF** command to generate front, side, auxiliary, and top profiles.

Figure 23-58 *Drawing for Exercise 5*

Problem-Solving Exercise 1   *Mechanical*

Construct a composite solid of the object in Exercise 15 (Chapter 18, Figure 18-77). The model consists of a bottom support, a tapered cylinder, and a set of cones at the top. The bottom support is made of four hollow cylinders joined at the ends. The wall thickness is 0.125. The tapered cylinder is also a hollow tube with 0.125 wall thickness. The lower cone located at the top slides over the tapered cylinder. The wall thickness of the cones is 0.25. Use the **SOLVIEW** and **SOLDRAW** commands to generate front and top views. Also, dimension the drawing and use the floating viewports to display different views of the object. Then, plot the drawing from the paper space on a 10.5 by 8 size sheet of paper.

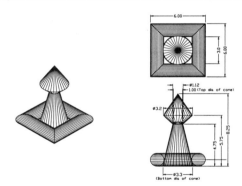

Figure 23-59 *Drawing for Problem Solving Exercise 1*

Project Exercise 2-5   *Mechanical*

Generate the solid model of the tool organizer as shown in Figure 23-60. (See Chapters 9, 14, and 23 for other drawings of Project Exercise 2.)

Figure 23-60 Drawing for Project Exercise 2-5

Project Exercise 1-6 *Mechanical*

Create a solid model of the work bench and then generate the assembly drawing with front, side and top views as shown in Figure 23-61. Use the floating viewports and the **VPOINT** command to obtain these views. (See Chapters 1, 2, 6, 7, and 19 for other drawings of Project Exercise 1)

Figure 23-61 Drawing for Project Exercise 1-6

Answers to Self-Evaluation Test

1 - The process of building objects that have all the attributes of an actual solid, **2** - F, **3** - F, **4** - **INTERFERE**, **5** - T, **6** - F (parallel), **7** - T, **8** - F (2 or more), **9** - F (any specified plane), **10** - F, **11**- **SOLIDEDIT**

Chapter 24

Rendering

Learning Objectives

After completing this chapter, you will be able to:
- *Understand rendering and why to render the objects.*
- *Configure, load, and unload AutoCAD Render.*
- *Insert and modify light sources.*
- *Select rendering type and render objects.*
- *Define and render scenes.*
- *Modify scenes.*
- *Use AutoCAD Render light sources.*
- *Attach materials to objects.*
- *Define materials and modify existing materials.*
- *Replay and print renderings.*

RENDERING

A rendered image makes it easier to visualize the shape and size of a three-dimensional (3D) object, compared to a wireframe image or a shaded image. A rendered object also makes it easier to express your design ideas to other people. For example, if you want to make a presentation of your project or a design, you do not need to build a prototype. You can use the rendered image to explain your design much more clearly because you have complete control over the shape, size, color, and surface material of the rendered image. Additionally, any required changes can be incorporated into the object, and the object can be rendered to check or demonstrate the effect of those changes. Thus, rendering is a very effective tool for communicating ideas and demonstrating the shape of an object. You can create a rendered image of a 3D object by using AutoCAD's **RENDER** command. It allows you to control the appearance of the object by defining the surface material and reflective quality of the surface and by adding lights to get the desired effects.

Determining Which Sides Are to Be Rendered in a Model

Some of the faces of a 3D model, such as the back faces and the hidden faces, need not be rendered since it would amount to an unnecessary waste of time. In the process of rendering, AutoCAD determines the front faces and the back faces of the 3D model with the use of normals on each face. A **vector** perpendicular to each face on a 3D model and whose direction is outward toward space is known as **normal**. If a face has been drawn in the clockwise direction, then the normal points inward; if a face has been drawn counterclockwise, the normal points outward. Now, depending on the location of your viewpoint, if the normal of a face points away from the viewpoint, the face is a back face. As mentioned before, rendering of such faces is not advisable (since those faces are not visible from the viewpoint) and can be avoided by invoking the Discard Back Faces option (explained later in this chapter). The faces that conceal other faces are discarded. In this manner, the time required to render objects can be decreased by discarding faces that need not be rendered.

Points to Be Remembered While Defining a Model

1. To make the rendering process as time-efficient as possible, you must use the fewest possible faces to define a plane.

2. There should be consistency in your drafting technique. Models formed of a complex mixture of faces, extruded lines, and wireframe meshes should be avoided.

3. If you are rendering circles, ellipses, or arcs, set the **VIEWRES** command to a high number. This way, the circles, arcs, or ellipses will appear smoother and the rendering of such objects will be better. But increasing the value of **VIEWRES** increases the time taken to render the objects. The smoothness of rendered curved solids depends on **FACETRES** variable.

4. If you are using the Smooth Shading option (available in the **Render** and **Rendering Preferences** dialog box, explained later), then you should specify the mesh density in such a manner that the angle described by normals of any two adjoining faces is less than 45 degrees. This is because if the angle is greater than 45 degrees, then after rendering, an edge is displayed between the faces even when the Smooth Shading option is active.

LOADING AND UNLOADING AUTOCAD RENDER

When you select any AutoCAD **RENDER** command, AutoCAD Render is loaded automatically. AutoCAD will display the following message in the command prompt area:

Command: **RENDER**
Loading Landscape Object module.
Initializing Render...
Initializing preferences... done

If you do not need AutoCAD Render, you can unload it by entering the **ARX** command at the Command prompt. AutoCAD acknowledges the unloading of Render by issuing the message "Render successfully unloaded." After unloading Render, you can reload AutoCAD Render by invoking the **RENDER** command or any other command associated with rendering (such as **SCENE** or **LIGHT**).

Command: **ARX**
Enter an option [?/Load/Unload/Commands/Options]: **U**
Enter ARX/DBX file name to unload: **ACRENDER**
ACRENDER successfully unloaded.

ELEMENTARY RENDERING

Toolbar:	Render > Render
Menu:	View > Render > Render
Command:	RENDER

Figure 24-1 Render toolbar

In this section you are going to perform an ordinary rendering. You will encounter many terms of which you will not be aware, but you need not bother about them at this stage. All the terms are explained later in this chapter. In this rendering, lights, materials, and other advanced features of rendering will not be applied. Only a default distant light is used. This will give you a feel of rendering in the simplest possible manner. Perform the following steps:

1. Using the **SPHERE** command, create four spheres on the screen as shown in Figure 24-2.
2. Invoke the **Render** dialog box (Figure 24-3).
3. In the **Render** dialog box, choose the **Render** button. AutoCAD will render all objects that are on the screen.

After some time, all the spheres are rendered and displayed on the screen (Figure 24-4). Press any key to exit the rendered image screen and return to the AutoCAD drawing screen.

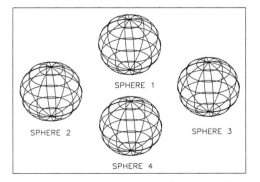

Figure 24-2 Drawing to be rendered

Figure 24-3 Render dialog box

If you want to render only some spheres (for example, SPHERE 2 and SPHERE 3), select the **Query for Selections** check box in the **Render** dialog box. When you choose the **Render** button, AutoCAD will prompt you to select the objects that you want to render. Select the objects and press ENTER; you will notice that only the selected spheres are rendered and displayed on the screen.

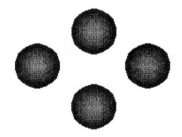

Figure 24-4 Rendering all spheres

Exercise 1   *Mechanical*

In this exercise you will render the drawing that was created in Example 2 of Chapter 23, Solid Modeling. Load and render the drawing. Figure 24-5 shows the object before rendering; Figure 24-6 shows the object after rendering.

Figure 24-5 *Drawing for Exercise 1*

Figure 24-6 *After rendering*

SELECTING DIFFERENT PROPERTIES FOR RENDERING

Toolbar:	Render > Preferences
Menu:	View > Render > Preferences
Command:	RPREF

 AutoCAD Render allows you to select various properties for the rendering. This can be achieved through the **Rendering Preferences** dialog box (Figure 24-7). The various sections of the dialog box are described next.

Figure 24-7 Rendering Preferences *dialog box*

Rendering Type

In the **Rendering Preferences** dialog box you can select the type of rendering (Render, Photo Real, Photo Raytrace) you want from the **Rendering Type** drop-down list.

Rendering Options

Various rendering options are provided in the Rendering Options area of the dialog box. These are described next.

Smooth Shade. The **Smooth Shade** allows you to smooth the rough edges. If this option is enabled, the rough-edged appearance of a multifaceted surface is smoothed. Only polygon meshes are affected by Smooth Shading. The surface normals are determined, and colors across two or more adjoining faces are blended.

Apply Materials. The Apply Materials option allows you to assign surface materials to objects. If this option is disabled, then the objects in the drawing are assigned the ***GLOBAL*** material.

Shadows. When you select this option, AutoCAD generates shadows. This option applies only to Photo Real and Photo Raytrace rendering.

Render Cache. Selecting this option results in writing rendering information to a cache file on the hard disk that can be used for subsequent renderings. This eliminates the need for AutoCAD to recalculate (tessellate) the objects for rendering. This saves time, especially when rendering solids.

More Options. If you choose the **More Options...** button, the **Render Options** dialog box (Figure 24-8) is displayed. The following is a brief description of these additional options.

Figure 24-8 Render Options dialog box

Render Quality Area. In the **Render Quality** area of this dialog box, you can choose either the Gouraud or the Phong option. These options determine the quality of shading that will be used if you have activated the Smooth Shading option.

Phong. The **Phong** option creates a high-quality rendered image. The light intensity is calculated for all the pixels, and hence, more accurate highlights are generated.

Gouraud. On the other hand, the **Gouraud** option produces a lower-quality rendered image. Light intensity at each vertex is determined, and intermediate intensities are interpolated. The advantage of the Gouraud render option is that the rendering occurs faster as compared with the Phong render option.

Face Controls Area. The **Face Controls** area governs the definition of faces of a 3D solid.

Discard Back Faces. If you select the **Discard Back Faces** option, the back faces of a 3D solid object are not taken into consideration (that is, they are made invisible), and hence, they are omitted from the calculations for the rendering. Rendering time can be reduced by enabling this option.

Back Face Normal is Negative. The **Back Face Normal** is **Negative** option can be used to define the back faces in a drawing. If this option is enabled, the faces with negative normal vectors are treated as back faces and discarded. When this option is disabled, the selection faces treated as back faces by AutoCAD are just reversed.

Rendering Procedures

The Rendering Procedure of the **Rendering Preferences** dialog box has the following options:

Query for Selections. If you select the **Query for Selections** option, AutoCAD prompts you to select objects to render.

Crop Window. When you select this option, AutoCAD will prompt you to select a window. Only the objects inside the specified window are rendered.

Skip Render Dialog. In the Rendering Procedure area, if the **Skip Render Dialog** option is invoked, the current view is rendered without displaying the Render dialog box.

Light Icon Scale. The **Icon Scale** edit box can be used to set the size of the light blocks in the drawing.

Smoothing Angle. The **Smoothing Angle** option lets you specify the angle defined by two edges. The default value for smoothing an angle is 45 degrees. Angles of less than 45 degrees are smoothed. Angles greater than 45 degrees are taken as edges.

Destination

The **Destination** area of the **Rendering Preferences** dialog box allows you to specify the destination for the rendered image output.

Viewport Option. If you select the **Viewport** option, AutoCAD renders to the current viewport.

Render Window Option. This option renders to the AutoCAD for Windows Render window.

File Option. The **File** option lets you output the rendered image to a file.

More Options. The **More Options...** button can be used to set the configuration for the output file through the **File Output Configuration** dialog box (Figure 24-9).

Chapter 24

Figure 24-9 File Output Configuration dialog box

File Type Area. In this area you can specify the output file type and rendering resolution. The file formats allowed are BMP, PCX, Postscript, TGA, and TIFF. The screen resolution can also be specified in this area. The aspect ratio of the output file can be specified in the **Aspect Ratio** edit box.

Colors Area. The colors in the output file can be specified in this area.

TGA Options Area. The **Compressed** option lets you specify compression for those file types that allow compression. The **Bottom Up** option lets you specify the scan line start point as bottom left instead of top left.

Interlace Area. Selecting the None option turns off line interlacing. The **2** to **1** and **4** to **1** options turn on interlacing.

PostScript Options Area. The **Landscape** and **Portrait** options in this area specify the orientation of the file. The **Auto** option automatically scales the image. The Custom option sets the image size in pixels. The **Image Size** edit box uses the explicit image size.

Sub Sampling

The Sub Sampling edit box controls the quality and the rendering time by reducing the number of pixels to be rendered. A **1:1** ratio (default) produces the best quality rendering. If you are just testing a rendering, you can change the value to reduce rendering time.

Background

The background option allows you to add a background to a rendering. You can use solid colors, gradient colors, or an image file as a background.

Fog/Depth Cue

You can use the Fog option to add a misty effect to a rendering. You can also assign a color to the fog.

AUTOCAD RENDER LIGHT SOURCE

Lights are vital to rendering a realistic image of an object. Without proper lighting, the rendered image may not show the features the way you expect. Colors and surface reflection can be set for the lights with RGB or HLS color systems. AutoCAD Render supports the following four light sources: ambient light, point light, distant light, and spotlight.

Ambient Light

You can visualize **ambient light** as the natural light in a room that equally illuminates all surfaces of the objects. Ambient light does not have a source and hence has no location or direction. However, you can increase or decrease the intensity of ambient light or completely turn it off. Normally, you should set the ambient light to a low value because high values give a washed-out look to the image. If you want to create a dark room or a night scene, turn off the ambient light. With ambient light alone you cannot render a realistic image. Figure 24-10 shows an object illuminated by ambient light.

Point Light

A **point light** source emits light in all directions, and the intensity of the emitted light is uniform. You can visualize an electric bulb as a point light source. In AutoCAD Render, a point source does not cast a shadow because the light is assumed to be passing **through** the object. The intensity of light radiated by a point source decreases over distance. This phenomenon is called attenuation. Figure 24-11 shows a light source that radiates light in all directions.

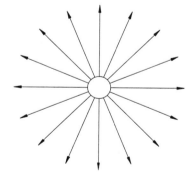

Figure 24-10 Ambient light provides constant illumination

Figure 24-11 Point light emits light in all directions

Spotlight

A **spotlight** emits light in the defined direction with a cone-shaped light beam (Figure 24-12). The direction of the light and the size of the cone can be specified. The phenomenon of **attenuation** (falloff) also applies to spotlights. This light is used mostly to highlight particular features and portions of the model. If you want to simulate a soft lighting effect, set the falloff cone angle a few degrees larger than the hot-spot cone angle.

Attenuation

Light intensity is the amount of light falling per unit area. The intensity of light is directly proportional to the degree of brightness of the object. The intensity of light decreases as the distance increases. This phenomenon, called **attenuation**, occurs only with spotlights and point light. In Figure 24-13, the light is emitted by a point source. Assume that the amount of light incident on Area-1 is I. Therefore, the intensity of light on Area-1 = I/Area. As the light travels farther from the source, it covers a larger area. The amount of light falling on Area-2 is same as on Area-1, but the area is larger. Therefore, the intensity of light for Area-2 is smaller (Intensity of light for Area-2 = I/Area). Area-1 will be brighter than Area-2 because of higher light intensity. AutoCAD Render has three options for controlling the light falloff: None, Inverse Linear, and Inverse Square.

Figure 24-12 Spotlight

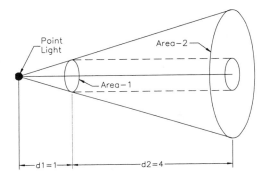

Figure 24-13 Light intensity decreases with distance

None

If you select the **None** option for light falloff, the brightness of objects is independent of distance. This means that objects that are far away from the point light source will be as bright as objects close to the light source.

Inverse Linear

In this option, the light falling on the object (brightness) is inversely proportional to the distance of the object from the light source (Brightness = 1/Distance). As distance increases, brightness decreases. For example, let us assume the intensity of the light source is **I** and the object is located at a distance of **2** units from the light source. Brightness or intensity = **I/2**. If the distance is 8 units, the intensity (light falling on the object per unit area) = **I/8**. The brightness is a linear function of the distance of the object from the light source.

Inverse Square

In this option, the light falling on the object (brightness) is inversely proportional to the square of the distance of the object from the light source (Brightness = $1/Distance^2$). For example, let us assume the intensity of the light source is **I** and the object is located at a distance of **2** units from the light source. Brightness or intensity = $I/(2)^2 = $ **I/4**. If the distance is 8 units, the intensity (light falling on the object per unit area) = $I/(8)^2 = $ **I/64**.

Distant Light

A **distant light** source emits a uniform parallel beam of light in a single direction only
(Figure 24-14). The intensity of the light beam
does not decrease with distance; it remains
constant. For example, the sun's rays can be
assumed to be a distant light source because
the light rays are parallel. When you use a distant light source in a drawing, the location of
the light source does not matter; only the direction is critical. Distant light is used mostly
to light objects or a backdrop uniformly and
for getting the effect of sunlight.

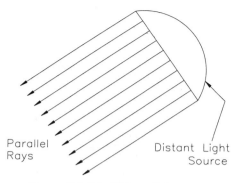

Figure 24-14 Distant light source

INSERTING AND MODIFYING LIGHTS

Toolbar:	Render > Lights
Menu:	View > Render > Lights
Command:	LIGHT

In a rendering, the lights and lighting effects are important to create a realistic representation of an object. The sides of an object that face the light must appear brighter and the
sides that are on the other side of the object must be darker. This smooth gradation of
light produces a realistic image of the object. If the light intensity is uniform over the
entire surface, the rendered object probably will not look realistic. For example, if you use the
SHADE command to shade an object, that object does not look realistic because the displayed
model lacks any gradation of light. Any number of lights can be installed in a drawing. The color,
location, and direction of all the lights can be specified individually. As mentioned before, you can
specify attenuation for point lights and spotlights. AutoCAD also allows you to change the color,
position, and intensity of any light source. The only limitation is that light types cannot be changed.
For example, you cannot change a distant light into a point light. The following sections describe
how to insert, position, and modify lights.

Inserting Distant Light

As mentioned before, the lights play an important role in producing a realistic representation of a
3D model. The gradation effect produced by the lights makes the object look realistic. In this
example, you will insert a distant light source and then render the object.

1. Use the **VPOINT** command to change the viewpoint to (1,-1,1).
    Command: **VPOINT**
    Specify a view point or [Rotate] <current>: **1,-1,1** *Press ENTER.*

2. Choose **Render** from the **View** menu.
3. Select the **Lights...** option from the cascading menu. The **Lights** dialog box is displayed
    (Figure 24-15). You can use any one of the methods just described to invoke the **Lights** dialog
    box.
4. Select the **Distant Light** option from the drop-down list, and then choose **New...** to insert a

Figure 24-15 Lights dialog box

new distant light. The **New Distant Light** dialog box is displayed [Figure 24-16(a)].

5. Enter the name of the distant light (D1) in the **New Distant Light** dialog box. Leave the intensity at its default value (1.00).

Figure 24-16(a) New Distant Light dialog box

6. Choose the **OK** button to exit this dialog box, then choose **OK** button again to exit the **Lights** dialog box.

7. Now render the image.

Modifying Distant Light

In this rendering, notice that the light falls on the object from the viewpoint direction and the right front corner is brighter than the rest of the object. We would like to modify the light source so that the light falls on the object from the right at an angle. When the light source is at an angle, the top surface also receives some light. Notice that as the oblique angle increases, the amount of light reflected by the oblique surface decreases.

1. Choose the **Lights** button from the **Render** toolbar.
2. Select the light (D1) from the **Lights** dialog box. If there is only one light, the light is automatically highlighted.
3. Choose the **Modify...** button. The **Modify Distant Light** dialog box is displayed [Figure 24-16(b)].

Figure 24-16(b) Modify Distant Light dialog box

 Note

Double-clicking on the light name is equivalent to selecting the light name and the Modify... option.

4. Choose the **Sun Angle Calculator** button to display the **Sun Angle Calculator** dialog box (Figure 24-17). Change the date and clock time, if needed.
5. Choose the **Geographic Location** button to display the **Geographic Location** dialog box (Figure 24-18). You can specify the location by choosing the name of the city in the City list box or selecting a point in the map.
6. Choose **OK** to exit the **Geographic Location** dialog box and choose **OK** again to exit the **Sun Angle Calculator** dialog box.
7. Choose **OK** to exit the **Modify Distant Lights** dialog box and choose **OK** again to exit the **Lights** dialog box.

Figure 24-17 Sun Angle Calculator dialog box

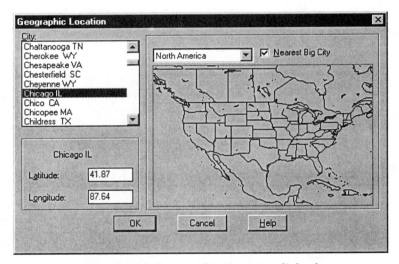

Figure 24-18 Geographic Location dialog box

8.   Render the object.

Notice that the sides (vertical faces) of the object and the horizontal surfaces have different degrees of brightness. This is because the oblique angle that the vertical surfaces make with the direction of the light rays is smaller than the oblique angle that the horizontal surfaces make. Maximum brightness occurs when the object is perpendicular to the direction of the light rays.

Inserting Point Light
In Example 1 you will insert a point light source. Then you will render the object.

Example 1

Insert a point light source and render the object of Exercise 1 with Inverse Linear and Inverse Square options.

1. Load the drawing of Exercise 1.
2. Choose the **Lights** button from the **Render** toolbar.
3. Select the Point Light option from the **Lights** dialog box.
4. Choose the **New...** button. The **New Point Light** dialog box is displayed.
5. Enter the name of the point light (P1) and set the intensity (6.0).
6. Choose the **Modify<** option from the **New Point Light** dialog box.
7. Enter the light location (-2,0,5).
8. In the **New Point Light** dialog box, select Inverse Linear, and then choose the **OK** button to exit the dialog box. Choose **OK** to exit the **Lights** dialog box.
9. Change the viewpoint to (1,-1,1), and then render the object.

Notice that the top surface of the cylindrical part and the top surface of the flange are equally bright. Next, change the falloff to Inverse Square:

10. Choose the **Lights** button from the **Render** toolbar.
11. Select the point light (P1) and then choose the **Modify...** button.
12. The **Modify Point Light** dialog box will be displayed. Select **Inverse Square**, and then choose **OK** to exit the dialog box. Choose **OK** to exit the Lights dialog box.
13. Render the object again. Now, notice that the top surface of the cylindrical part is brighter than the top surface of the flange.

DEFINING AND RENDERING A SCENE

Toolbar:	Render > Scenes
Menu:	View > Render > Scene
Command:	SCENE

The rendering depends on the view that is current and the lights that are defined in the drawing. Sometimes the current view or the lighting setup may not be enough to show all features of an object. You might need different views of the object with a certain light configuration to show different features of the object. When you change the view or define the lights for a rendering, the previous setup is lost. You can save the rendering information by defining a **scene**. For each scene, you can assign a view and the lights. When you render a particular view, AutoCAD Render uses the view information and the lights that were assigned to that scene. It ignores the lights that were not defined in the scene. Defining scenes makes it convenient to render different views with the required lighting arrangement. The following example describes the process of defining scenes and assigning views and lights to the scenes.

Example 2

In this example, you will draw a rectangular box and a sphere that is positioned at the top of the box. Next, you will insert lights, define views and scenes, and then render the scenes. You may start a new drawing or continue with the current drawing. Before defining a scene, perform the following steps in a new drawing:

1. Draw a rectangular box with length = 3, width = 3, and height = 1.5.
2. Use the **UCS** command to define the new origin at the center of the top face.
3. Draw a sphere of 1.5 radius.
4. Move the sphere so that the bottom of the sphere is resting at the top face of the box, as shown in Figure 24-19.

Next, insert the lights. In this example, you will insert a point light and a distant light. Let us first insert a distant light source.

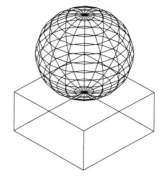

Figure 24-19 *Drawing for Example 2*

1. Select the **Render** option from the **View** menu and then select the **Lights...** option from the cascading menu. The **Lights** dialog box is displayed.
2. Select the **Distant** option, and then choose **New...** to insert a new distant light. The **New Distant Light** dialog box is displayed.
3. Enter the name of the distant light (D1) in the **Light Name:** edit box, and press ENTER. Now choose **Modify<** from the **New Distant Light** dialog box.
4. Enter the light target point (direction TO) (0,0,0) and the light location (direction FROM) (3,-3,4). Leave the intensity at 1.0.
5. Choose the **OK** button to exit the dialog box. Choose **OK** to exit the Lights dialog box.
6. Change the viewpoint to **1,-1,1,** and then render the object.

After inserting a distant light source, you need to insert a point light.

1. Choose the **Lights** button from the **Render** toolbar.
2. Select the **Point Light** option from the **Lights** dialog box and choose the **New...** button. The **New Point Light** dialog box is displayed.
3. Enter the name of the point light (P1) and set the intensity (6.0).
4. Choose the **Modify<** button from the dialog box and enter the light location (0,0,4).
5. In the **New Point Light** dialog box, select **Inverse Linear**, and then choose **OK** to exit the dialog box. Choose **OK** to exit the **Lights** dialog box.
6. Change the viewpoint to **1,-1,1,** and then render the object.

Now you will create three scenes. The first scene, SCENE1, contains distant light D1; the second scene, SCENE2, contains point light P1. The third scene, SCENE3, will contain the view VIEW1, distant light D1, and point light P1. Create the first scene by performing the following steps:

1. Choose the **Scenes** button from the **Render** toolbar.
2. Choose **New...** from the **Scenes** dialog box (Figure 24-20). The **New Scene** dialog box (Figure 24-21) will be displayed.
3. Enter the name of the scene (SCENE1) in the **Scene Name:** edit box. Select Distant Light D1 in the lights area, and then choose the **OK** button to exit the dialog box.
4. Choose the **OK** button in the **Scenes** dialog box.

Figure 24-20 Scenes dialog box

Figure 24-21 New Scene dialog box

Similarly, create the second scene, SCENE2, and assign the point light P1 to the scene. Choose the **OK** button to close the **Scenes** dialog box.

Next, create the third scene, SCENE3:

1. Use the **VPOINT** command to change the viewpoint to **1,-0.5,1** and use the **VIEW** command to save the view as **VIEW1**. Choose **OK**.
2. Invoke the **Scenes** dialog box and choose **New...** from the **Scenes** dialog box to display the **New Scene** dialog box.
3. Enter the name of the scene (SCENE3) in the **Scene Name:** edit box. Select ***ALL*** to assign Distant Light D1 and Point Light P1 to the scene. Now select VIEW1.
4. Choose the **OK** button from the **Scenes** dialog box.

You have created three scenes, and each scene has been assigned some lights. SCENE3 has been assigned a view in addition to the lights. You can render any scene, after making the scene current, as follows:

1. Invoke the **Scenes** dialog box (Figure 24-22).
2. Select on the scene name you want to render, and then choose **OK** to exit the dialog box.
3. Render the object.

*Figure 24-22 Scenes dialog box
displaying the scene names*

Modifying a Scene

You can modify a scene by changing the view and the lights that are assigned to that scene. When you render the object, AutoCAD Render will use the newly assigned view and lights to render the object.

1. Choose the **Scenes** button from the **Render** toolbar; the **Scenes** dialog box with the scene names is displayed on the screen.

2. Select the scene, SCENE3, and then choose **Modify....**
   The **Modify Scene** dialog box (Figure 24-23) is displayed.
3. Select on CURRENT, and then choose **OK** to exit the **Modify Scene** dialog box. This will assign the current view to SCENE3.
4. Choose the **OK** button to exit the **Scenes** dialog box.
5. Render the object.

Figure 24-23 Modify Scene dialog box displaying the views and lights

OBTAINING RENDERING INFORMATION

Toolbar:	Render > Statistics
Menu:	View > Render > Statistics
Command:	STATS

You can obtain information about the last rendering. When you enter the **STATS** command, AutoCAD will display the **Statistics** dialog box (Figure 24-24). Information is provided about the name of the current scene, the last rendering type used, the time taken to produce the last rendering, the number of faces processed by the last rendering, and the number of triangles processed by the last rendering. The information contained in the dialog box cannot be edited. However, the information can be saved to a file by checking the Save Statistics to

Figure 24-24 Statistics dialog box

File box and then entering the name of the file in the edit box. The file is saved as an **ASCII** file. In case a file by the specified name already exists, AutoCAD adds the present information to that file. You can use the EDIT function of any text editor to read the file.

ATTACHING MATERIALS

You can assign materials to objects, to blocks, to layers, and to an **AutoCAD color index** (ACI). Descriptions of each of them follows.

Attaching Material to an Object

Toolbar:	Render > Materials Library
Menu:	View > Render > Materials Library
Command:	MATLIB

 Any object is made up of some material; hence, to get the actual (realistic) rendered image of the object, it is necessary to assign materials to the surface of the object. AutoCAD supports different materials such as bronze, copper, brass, steel, and plastic. These materials are located in material libraries such as **RENDER.MLI**. You can assign materials to objects, to blocks, to layers, and to an AutoCAD color index (ACI). By default, only ***GLOBAL*** material is assigned to a new drawing. However, if you have an object on the screen to which you want to attach a material that is already defined in the library of materials provided by AutoCAD (**RENDER.MLI**), you need to import the desired material to the drawing and then attach it to the object. For example, if you have a sphere in the current drawing and you want to attach Aqua Glaze to it, the following steps need to be executed.

1. Invoke the **Materials Library** dialog box (Figure 24-25).
2. Once the **Materials Library** dialog box is displayed, select the material you want from the Library List box. In our case, we will select AQUA GLAZE from the list. (In case the material

Figure 24-25 Materials Library dialog box

you want to import is in a different library (other than **RENDER.MLI**), choose the **Open...** button. The **Library File** dialog box is displayed. Now you can specify the library file from which you want to select the material.) If you want to check how this material will appear after rendering, choose the **Preview** button. A rendered sphere with an Aqua Glaze material surface appears in the preview image tile in the dialog box.

3. Next, choose the **<-Import** button to import the Aqua Glaze material into the drawing. Once you do so, the entry Aqua Glaze is automatically displayed in the Materials List column. After this, you can save the materials list in a file by choosing the **Save...** button and then specifying the .mli file in the **Library File** dialog box. Next, choose the **OK** button.

Note

*When you open a new drawing, the Materials List column contains only the ***GLOBAL*** entry, which is the default material assigned to a new drawing.*

When you import a material from the library to the drawing, the material and its properties are copied to the list of materials in the drawing, and in no case is the material deleted from the library list. Unattached materials can be deleted from the Materials List by choosing the **Purge** button in the **Materials Library** dialog box.

4. Invoke the Materials dialog box (Figure 24-26). You can invoke the Materials dialog box by selecting Materials from **Render** toolbar or entering **RMAT** at the Command prompt. Notice that in the **Materials:** column, AQUA GLAZE is now listed along with ***GLOBAL***.

5. Select AQUA GLAZE from the list of materials, and then choose the **Attach <** button. AutoCAD clears the dialog box and issues the following prompt:

Select objects to attach "AQUA GLAZE" to:

Figure 24-26 Materials dialog box

6. Select the sphere. The Materials dialog box is again displayed. Choose the **OK** button. Now if you render the drawing, you will see that the Aqua Glaze material has been attached to the sphere.

Assigning Materials to the AutoCAD Color Index (ACI)

It is possible to attach materials to the AutoCAD color index (ACI). This can be realized in the following manner:

1. Invoke the **Materials** dialog box (Figure 24-26).
2. Choose the **By ACI...** button. The **Attach by AutoCAD Color Index** dialog box (Figure 24-27) is displayed.

Figure 24-27 Attach by AutoCAD Color Index dialog box

3. Select the material to be attached to an ACI from the Materials: column of the **Materials** dialog box.
4. Select the desired ACI from the **Select ACI:** list and choose the **Attach->** button.
5. Choose the **OK** button to complete the process of attaching the specified material to objects with the specified ACI.

Assigning Materials to Layers

Materials can be associated with layers. This option is useful when you want all the objects on a specified layer to have the assigned material. This can be realized in the following manner:

1. Invoke the **Materials** dialog box.
2. Choose the **By Layer...** button. The **Attach by Layer** dialog box (Figure 24-28) is displayed.
3. Select the material to be attached to all objects on a particular layer.
4. Select the desired layer and choose the **Attach->** button.
5. Choose the **OK** button.

Figure 24-28 Attach by Layer dialog box

With this, the specified material is attached to all objects on the specified layer. AutoCAD attaches a material to an object while rendering according to the following order:

1. Materials explicitly attached to objects have highest priority.
2. Next, materials attached by ACI are considered.
3. Finally, materials attached by layer are considered.
4. GLOBAL material is used if no material is attached to an object.

If you assign different materials to different objects and then combine those objects into a single block, then, upon rendering the block, the different components of the block are rendered according to the materials individually assigned to them. Now, if different components of a block have been created on different layers to which different materials have been attached, and you attach a material to the layer on which the block exists, then the block still will be rendered according to the materials attached to different layers on which the individual parts of the block were created. However, if there is some component in the block to which no material has been attached, then the material attached to the block will be attached to this component. In such a case, if no material has been attached to the block, then the component in the block to which no material has been attached will be assigned the ***GLOBAL*** material.

DETACHING MATERIALS

If you want to assign a different material to an object, it is important first to dissociate the material previously attached to it; only then can you attach another material to it. Also, sometimes it might be required that no material be attached to an object. To dissociate the material attached to an object, choose the **Detach <** button in the **Materials** dialog box. If you have attached a material by **ACI** (AutoCAD Color Index), then to detach this material, choose the **By ACI...** button in the **Materials** dialog box. The **Attach by ACI** dialog box is displayed. Choose the **Detach** button. Similarly, if you want to detach a material attached by layer, choose the **By Layer...** button in the **Materials** dialog box. The **Attach by Layer** dialog box is displayed. Choose the **Detach** button.

CHANGING THE PARAMETERS OF A MATERIAL

It is possible to change the parameters of a material, such as color and reflection properties, to meet your requirements. The **Modify Standard Material** dialog box can be effectively used for changing the parameters. The following steps need to be performed:

1. Invoke the **Materials** dialog box.
2. Select the name of the material you want to modify from the list of material names.
3. Choose the **Modify...** button. The **Modify Standard Material** dialog box appears (Figure 24-29). If you have specified the wrong material name, you can rectify this problem by entering the name of the material you want to modify in the **Material Name:** edit box.

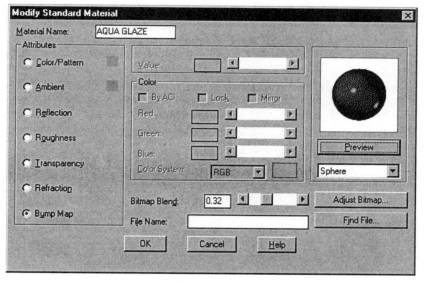

Figure 24-29 Modify Standard Material dialog box

The Modify Standard Material dialog box is comprised of the following options.

Attributes Area

The Attributes area specifies the attributes of a material. You can modify an attribute of a material by selecting it in the Attributes area and then making the alterations to it. The following attributes are listed in this area.

Color Pattern. You can change the diffuse (base) color of the material with this attribute. The intensity of the color can be changed by changing the value in the Value control with the help of the slider bar. The color can be changed by using the RGB or HLS slider bar in the Color area in this dialog box. You can also change the color with the help of the color wheel or the AutoCAD Color Index (ACI) options. The change made to the color is reflected in the color swatch next to the Color option in the Attributes area.

Ambient. By selecting this attribute, you can change the ambient color (shadow) of the material.

Changes to the intensity can be made by changing the value in the Value control box with the help of the slider bar. The color can be changed by using the RGB or HLS slider bar in the Color area in this dialog box. You can also change the color with the help of the color wheel or the AutoCAD Color Index (ACI) options. The change made to the color is reflected in the color swatch next to the Ambient option in the Attributes area.

Reflection. With this attribute, you can modify the reflective (highlight or specular) color of the material. Changes to intensity can be made by changing the value in the Value control box by using the scroll bar to increase or decrease the value. Changes to the reflective color can be made by changing the RGB or HLS slider bar in the Color area in this dialog box. You can also change the color with the help of the color wheel or the AutoCAD Color Index (ACI) options. The change made to the color is reflected in the color swatch next to the Reflection option in the Attributes area.

Roughness. With this attribute you can modify the shininess or roughness level of the material. Changes can be made by changing the value in the Value control. The size of the material's reflective highlight alters by changing the Roughness level. As you increase the level of roughness, the highlight also increases.

Transparency. With this attribute, you can change the transparency of an object. The degree of transparency can be controlled by changing the value in the **Value:** edit box.

Refraction. With this attribute, you can change how refractive a material is. The degree of refraction can be controlled by changing the value in the **Value:** edit box.

Bump Map. When you select this option, you can use the **File Name:** edit box to enter the name of a bump map that you want to assign to the object.

Note
*If you want to see the effect the changes will have on the properties of an object after rendering, choose the **Preview** button. A rendered sphere is displayed in the Preview image tile that reflects the effect of the present properties of the material.*

DEFINING NEW MATERIALS

Sometimes you may want to define a new material. To define a new material in AutoCAD, you have to perform the following steps:

1. Invoke the **Materials** dialog box.
2. Choose the **New...** button. The **New Standard Material** dialog box (Figure 24-30) appears.
3. Enter the name you want to assign to the new material in the **Material Name:** edit box. The material name cannot be more than 16 characters long, and there should be no other material by this name.
4. Just as you modified the attributes of a previously defined material in the **Modify Standard Material** dialog box, set the color and values for the Color, Ambient, Reflection, and Roughness attributes of the new material to your requirement.
5. To examine the effect of rendering with the newly defined material, choose the **Preview** button.

Figure 24-30 New Standard Material dialog box

A rendered sphere depicting the effect of rendering with the new material is displayed in the image tile.

6. After defining the attributes, choose the **OK** button. In this manner, a new material has been defined.

EXPORTING A MATERIAL FROM A DRAWING TO THE LIBRARY OF MATERIALS

Sometimes you may have a material attached to a drawing, but the material may not be present in the library of materials. One way this situation can arise is when you have transferred a drawing that has materials assigned to it from one system to another system that does not have the materials in its library of materials. It is possible to export a material from a drawing to the library of materials. The following steps need to be performed:

1. Open the drawing that has the material you want to export.
2. Invoke the **Materials** Library dialog box.
3. Select the material you want to export from the **Materials List:** column.
4. Choose the **Export->** button. You will notice that the material name is appended to the list of materials in the **Library List**: column.
5. With the **Save...** button just below the **Library List**: column, save the material in the present drawing to a library.

SAVING A RENDERING

A rendered image can be saved by rendering to a file or by rendering to the screen and then saving the image. Redisplaying a saved rendered image requires very little time compared to the time involved in rendering.

Saving a Rendering to a File

You can save a rendering directly to a file. One advantage of doing so is that you can replay the rendering in a short time. Another advantage is that when you render to the screen, the resolution of the rendering is limited by the resolution of your current display. Now if you render to a file, you can render to a higher resolution than that of your current display. Later on you can play this rendered image on a computer having a higher-resolution display. The rendered images can be saved in different formats, such as TGA, TIFF, BMP, PostScript, BMP, PCX, and IFF. To perform this operation, carry out the following steps:

1. Invoke the **Render** dialog box from the menu (Tools >Render > Render) or by entering **RENDER** at the Command prompt.
2. In the Destination area, select File in the pop-up window.
3. Choose the **More Options...** button. The **File Output Configuration** dialog box is displayed.
4. Specify the file type, rendering resolution, colors, and other options. Then choose the **OK** button. The **File Output Configuration** dialog box is cleared from the screen.
5. Choose the **Render** button in the **Render** dialog box. The **Rendering File** dialog box is displayed. Specify the name of the file to which you want to save the rendering, then choose the **OK** button.

Saving a Viewport Rendering

Menu:	View > Display Image > Save
Command:	SAVEIMG

A rendered image in the viewport can be saved with the **SAVEIMG** command. In this case, the file formats that can be used are TGA, TIFF, and BMP. To perform this operation, carry out the following steps:

1. Invoke the **Render** dialog box and choose the **Render** button to render the object.
2. Invoke the **Save Image** dialog box.
3. Specify the file format (TGA, TIFF, BMP), size, and offsets for the image, then choose the **OK** button.
4. The **Image File** dialog box is displayed.
5. Specify the name of the file to which you want to save the rendering, and then choose the **OK** button. In this way, a rendered image in the viewport can be saved in the specified file format.

Saving a Render-Window Rendered Image

A rendered image in the Render window can be saved with the **SAVE** command, which is available in the **Render** window. In this case, the file format in which the Render-window rendered image can be saved is bitmap (.BMP). To perform this operation carry out the following steps:

1. Invoke the **Render** dialog box, and select the **Render Window** option in the **Destination** area. Choose the **Render** button to render the object. In our case, we have a single sphere to be rendered. Shortly after you select the object (sphere), the **Render window** is displayed. The rendered object is displayed in this window.
2. From the **File** menu, select **Options**. The **Window Render Options** dialog box is displayed. In this dialog box, you can set the size and color depth of the rendered image. In our case, the

size is 640 x 480 and the color depth is 8 bit.

3. Next, from choose the **Save** button in **Render window** to save the rendered image. The **Save BMP** dialog box is displayed. Enter the file name in the **File Name:** edit box, and then choose the **OK** button.

The problem with bitmap images is that when you scale them up, the images become nonuniform (blocky) and cannot be printed properly. On the other hand, if you scale down these images, they lose information.

REPLAYING A RENDERED IMAGE

In the previous section, saving a rendered image was explained. In this section, we will explain how to replay the saved rendered image.

Replaying a Rendered Image to a Viewport

Menu:	Tools > Display Image > View
Command:	REPLAY

If you have saved the rendered image in a TGA, TIFF, or BMP format, you can use the **REPLAY** command to display the image on the screen. This operation can be performed in the following manner.

1. Invoke the **REPLAY** command to display the **Replay** dialog box.
2. Select the file you want to replay and choose the **OK** button.
3. Next, the **Image Specification** dialog box (Figure 24-31) is displayed. You can define the size and offsets, or take the default full screen size for displaying the rendered image.
4. After specifying the size and offsets, choose the **OK** button. The selected image is displayed on the screen per the specified size and offsets.

Figure 24-31 Image Specification dialog box

Replaying a Rendered Image to the Windows Render Window

1. Select the **Open** option in the **Render Window File** menu.
2. The **Render Open** dialog box (Figure 24-32) is displayed. Select the file you want AutoCAD to replay, and then choose the **OK** button. The selected image is displayed.

Figure 24-32 **Render Open** *dialog box*

Self-Evaluation Test

Answer the following questions, and then compare your answers to the answers given at the end of this chapter.

1. A rendered image makes it easier to visualize the shape and size of a 3D object. (T/F)

2. You can unload AutoCAD Render by invoking the **ARX** command. (T/F)

3. Falloff occurs only with a distant source of light. (T/F)

4. You cannot assign a view to a scene. (T/F)

5. You can modify a scene by changing the lights that are assigned to that scene. (T/F)

6. You can use a spotlight to create a light source that emits light in a conical fashion in the defined direction. (T/F)

7. The Phong render option produces a _____ quality image, but it is computationally _____ and takes more time to display the image.

8. Name the three methods that AutoCAD Render has provided for controlling light falloff:
   1._____ 2._____ 3._____

9. A _____ light source emits light in all directions, and the intensity of the emitted light is uniform.

10. A rendered image in the viewport can be saved with the _____ command.

11. Materials can be imported from a(n) _____ file.

12. A predefined material cannot be modified. (T/F)

13. By default, only _____ material is assigned to a new drawing.

14. Materials once attached to an object cannot be detached. (T/F)

15. In case you have saved the rendered image in a TGA, TIFF, or BMP format, you can use the _____ command to display the image.

Review Questions

1. Rendering is not an effective tool for communicating design ideas. (T/F)

2. When you select any AutoCAD Render command, AutoCAD Render is loaded automatically. (T/F)

3. You cannot render a drawing without inserting any lights or defining reflective characteristics of the surface. (T/F)

4. The Gouraud render option saves computation time, but does not generate a good quality image. (T/F)

5. You can increase or decrease the intensity of ambient light, but you cannot turn it completely off. (T/F)

6. AutoCAD Render allows you to control the appearance of an object by defining the reflective quality of the surface and by adding lights to get the desired effects. (T/F)

7. The gradation effect produced by the lights does not make any difference in the appearance of the object. (T/F)

8. By default, AutoCAD Render uses smooth shading to render the image. (T/F)

9. In the _____ option, the light falling on the object (brightness) is inversely proportional to the distance of the object from the light source (Brightness = 1/Distance).

10. _____ light does not have a source, and hence, has no location or direction.

11. The intensity of the light radiated by a point source _____ with the distance.

12. You can create a rendered image of a 3D object by using the _____ command.

13. You can load AutoCAD Render from the Command prompt by entering _____.

14. The intensity of light _____ as distance increases.

15. In the _____ option, the light falling on the object (brightness) is inversely proportional to the square of the distance of the object from the light source (Brightness = 1/Distance ^ 2).

16. A distant light source emits _____ beam of light in one direction only.

17. The intensity of a light beam from a(n) _____ light source does not change with the distance.

18. What are the names of the two rendering shading types available in AutoCAD Render?
    1._____ 2._____

19. As the oblique angle _____, the amount of light reflected by the oblique surface decreases.

20. By defining _____, it is convenient to render different views with the required lighting arrangement.

21. Materials can only be assigned explicitly to objects. (T/F)

22. When you import a material from the library of materials to a drawing, the material and its properties are copied to the list of materials in the drawing. (T/F)

23. When you import a material from the library of materials to a drawing, it gets deleted from the library of materials. (T/F)

24. New materials can be defined. (T/F)

25. A material existing in a drawing can be exported to the library of materials (.mli file). (T/F)

26. A rendered image can be saved by _____.

27. Redisplaying a saved rendered image takes _____ time as compared to the time involved in rendering.

28. You can output a _____ directly to a hard-copy device if the hard-copy device driver software is loaded and the AutoCAD renderer is configured to output to hard copy.

29. Name the light sources that AutoCAD Render supports. _____

30. Define **intensity**. _____

31. What is **attenuation**? _____

Exercises

Exercise 2

Mechanical

Make the drawing shown in Figure 24-33. This drawing will then be used for rendering. You can also load this drawing from the accompanying disk. The name of the drawing is REND. The following is the description of one of the methods of making this drawing.

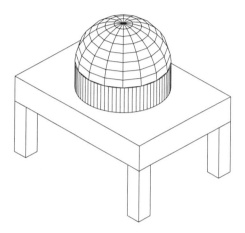

Figure 24-33 *Drawing for Exercise 2*

1. Draw a rectangle 2.75 x 2.0.
2. Use the **CHANGE** command to change the thickness to 0.25.
3. Use the **3DFACE** command to draw a 3dface at the top of the rectangular box.
4. Draw another rectangle 0.25 x 0.25.
5. Use the **CHANGE** command to change the thickness to 1.0.
6. Copy the leg of the table to four corners.
7. Define the center point of the table as the new origin.
8. Draw a circle at the top surface of the table. The center of the circle must be at the center of the table.
9. Use the **CHANGE** command to change the thickness to 0.5.
10. Draw a dome that has a diameter of 1.5. The bottom edge of the dome must coincide with the top edge of the cylinder, as shown in Figure 24-33.
11. To render the drawing, first position a distant light source at (3,-2,5) and the target at (0,0,0). Now render the drawing.
12. Position a point light source at (-1,0,5) with the falloff set to Inverse Square. Render the object again.
13. Modify the distant and the point light sources to study the effect of lighting on the rendering.

Chapter 24

Exercise 3　　　　　　　　　　　　　　*General*

Generate the 3D drawings as shown in Figures 24-34 and 24-35. Next, render the 3D view of the drawing after inserting the lights at appropriate locations so as to get a realistic 3D image of the object.

Figure 24-34 Drawing for Exercise 3

Figure 24-35 Drawing for Exercise 3

Exercise 4　　　　　　　　　　　　　　*General*

a.　Draw different objects on the screen, and assign different materials explicitly to them. Then render the drawing.

b.　Detach the materials previously assigned to the objects and assign new materials to them.

Exercise 5 *General*

Attach copper material to some layer on your system. Draw objects on this layer, and then render the drawing. Observe the results carefully.

Exercise 6 *General*

a. Define a new material named NEWMAT. Assign desired attribute values to it in the New Standard Material dialog box, and then attach this material to an object and render it to a viewport.
b. Save the rendered image in the desired size and offset. Give it any name.
c. Redisplay the saved image on the screen.

Exercise 7 *Mechanical*

Generate the 3D drawing shown in Figure 24-36. (Assume a value for the missing dimensions.). Next, render the 3D view of the drawing after inserting the lights at appropriate locations so as to get a realistic 3D image of the object.

Figure 24-36 *Drawing for Exercise 7*

Answers to Self-Evaluation Test
1 - T, **2** - T, **3** - F, **4** - F, **5** - T, **6** - T, **7** - higher/ more accurate, **8** - None, Inverse Linear, Inverse Square, **9** - point, **10** - **SAVEIMG**, **11** - .mli, **12** - F, **13** - *GLOBAL*, **14** - F, **15** - **REPLAY**

Chapter 25

Geometry Calculator

Learning Objectives

After completing this chapter, you will be able to:
- *Understand how the geometry calculator functions.*
- *Use real, integer, vector, and numeric expressions.*
- *Use snap modes in the geometry calculator.*
- *Obtain the radius of an object and locate a point on a line.*
- *Understand applications of the geometry calculator.*
- *Use AutoLISP variables and filter X, Y, and Z coordinates.*

GEOMETRY CALCULATOR

The **Geometry Calculator** is an ADS application that can be used as an online calculator. The calculator can be used to evaluate vector, real, and integer expressions. It can also access the existing geometry by using the first three characters of the standard AutoCAD object snap functions (MID, CEN, END). You can use the calculator to evaluate arithmetic and vector expressions. For example, you can use the calculator to evaluate an expression like $3.5 \wedge 12.5*[234*\log(12.5) - 3.5*\cos(30)]$. The results of a calculation can be returned as input to the current AutoCAD prompt.

Another application of the calculator is in assigning a value to an AutoLISP variable. For example, you can use an AutoLISP variable in the arithmetic expression, and then assign the value of the expression to an AutoLISP variable. You can invoke the **CAL** command by entering **CAL** or **'CAL** (for transparent use) at the AutoCAD Command prompt.

REAL, INTEGER, AND VECTOR EXPRESSIONS
Real and Integer Expressions

A **real expression** consists of real numbers and/or functions that are combined with numeric operators. Similarly, an **integer expression** consists of integer numbers and/or functions combined with numeric operators. The following is the list of numeric operators:

Operator	Operation	Example
+	Adds numbers	2 + 3
-	Subtracts numbers	15.5 - 3.754
*	Multiplies numbers	12.34 * 4
/	Divides numbers	345.5/2.125
^	Exponentiation of numbers	$25.5 ^ 2.5$
( )	Used to group expressions	$4.5 + (4.35 ^ 2)$

Example
Command: **CAL**
Initializing...>> Expression: **(4.5 + (4.35 ^ 2))**
23.4225

Vector Expression

A vector expression consists of points, vectors, numbers, and functions that are combined with the following operators:

Operator	Operation / Example
+	Adds vectors
	[a,b,c] + [x,y,z] = [a + x, b + y, c + z]
	[2,4,3] + [5,4,7] = [2 + 5, 4 + 4, 3 + 7] = [7.0 8.0 10.0]
-	Subtracts vectors
	[a,b,c] - [x,y,z] = [a - x, b - y, c - z]
	[2,4,3] - [5,4,7.5] = [2 - 5, 4 - 4, 3 - 7.5] = [-3.0 0.0 -4.5]
*	Multiplies a vector by a real number
	a * [x,y,z] = [a * x, a * y, a * z]
	3 * [2,8,3.5] = [3 * 2, 3 * 8, 3 * 3.5] = [6.0 24.0 10.5]
/	Divides a vector by a real number
	[x,y,z] / a = [x/a, y/a, z/a]
	[4,8,4.5] / 2 = [4/2, 8/2, 4.5/2] = [2.0 4.0 2.25]
&	Multiplies vectors
	[a,b,c] & [x,y,z] = [(b * z)-(c * y), (c * x)-(a * z), (a * y)-(b * x)]
	[2,4,6] & [3,5,8] = [(4 * 8)-(6 * 5), (6 * 3)-(2 * 8), (2 * 5)-(4 * 3)] = [2.0 2.0 -2.0]
( )	Used to group expressions $a + (b ^ c)$

Example
Command: **CAL**
Initializing...>> Expression: **[2,4,3] - [5,4,7.5]**
-3.0 0.0 4.5

NUMERIC FUNCTIONS

The **geometry calculator** (**CAL**) supports the following numeric functions:

Function	Description
sin(angle)	Calculates the **sine** of an angle
cos(angle)	Calculates the **cosine** of an angle
tang(angle)	Calculates the **tangent** of an angle
asin(real)	Calculates the **arcsine** of a number (The number must be between -1 and 1)
acos(real)	Calculates the **arccosine** of a number (The number must be between -1 and 1)
atan(real)	Calculates the **arctangent** of a number
ln(real)	Calculates the **natural log** of a number
log(real)	Calculates the **log, to the base 10**, of a number
exp(real)	Calculates the **natural exponent** of a number
exp 10(real)	Calculates the **exponent, to the base 10**, of a number
sqr(real)	Calculates the **square** of a number
sqrt(real)	Calculates the **square root** of a number
abs(real)	Calculates the **absolute value** of a number
round(real)	Rounds the number to the **nearest integer**
trunc(real)	Returns the **integer portion** of a number
r2d(angle)	Converts the **angle in radians** to degrees
d2r(angle)	Converts the **angle in degrees** to radians
pi	pi has a **constant value** (**3.14159**)

Example
Command: **CAL**
Initializing...>> Expression: **Sin (60)**
0.866025

USING SNAP MODES

You can use AutoCAD's snap modes with **CAL** functions to evaluate an expression. When you use snaps in an expression, AutoCAD will prompt you to select an object, and the returned value will be used in the expression. For example, if the **CAL** function is **(cen+end)/2**, the calculator will first prompt you to select an object for CENter snap mode and then select another object for ENDpoint snap mode. The corresponding coordinates of the two point values will be added and divided by **2**. The returned value is a point located midway between the center of the circle and the endpoint of the selected object. Following is the list of **CAL snap modes** and the corresponding AutoCAD snap modes:

CAL Snap Modes	AutoCAD Snap Modes
END	ENDpoint
EXT	EXTension
INS	INSert
INT	INTersection
MID	MIDpoint
CEN	CENter
NEA	NEArest
NOD	NODe
QUA	QUAdrant
PAR	PARallel
PER	PERpendicular
TAN	TANgent

Example 1

In this example, you will use the **CAL snap modes** to retrieve the point values (coordinates), and then use these values to draw a line (P3,P4). It is assumed that the circle and line (P1,P2) are already drawn (Figure 25-1).

Command: **LINE**
Specify first point: **'CAL**
>> Expression: **(cen+end)/2**
>> Select entity for CEN snap:
Select the circle.
>> Select entity for END snap:
Select one end of line (P1,P2).
Resuming **LINE** command.
Specify next point or [Undo]: **'CAL**
>> Expression: **(cen+end)/2**
>> Select entity for CEN snap:
Select the circle.
>> Select entity for END snap:
Select the other end of line (P1,P2).

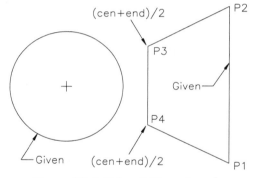

Figure 25-1 Using CAL snap modes

Now, join point (P4) with point (P1) and point (P3) with point (P2) to complete the drawing, as shown in Figure 25-1. The **'CAL** function initializes the geometry calculator transparently. The single quote in front of the cal function (') makes the cal function transparent. The expression **(cen+end)/2** will prompt you to select the objects for **CEN snap** and **END snap**. After you select these objects, the calculator will add the corresponding coordinate of these point values and then divide the sum of each coordinate by 2. The point value that this function returns is the midpoint between the center of the circle and the first endpoint of the line.

OBTAINING THE RADIUS OF AN OBJECT

You can use the **rad** function to obtain the radius of an object. The object can be a circle, an arc, or a 2D polyline arc.

Example 2

In this example, you are given a circle of certain radius (R). You will draw a second circle whose radius is 0.75 times the radius of the given circle (0.75 * R) (Figure 25-2).

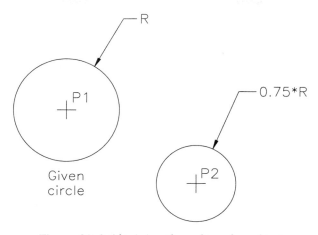

Figure 25-2 *Obtaining the radius of an object*

Command: **CIRCLE**
Specify center point for circle or [3P/2P/Ttr (tan tan radius)]: *Select a point (P2).*
Specify radius of circle or [Diameter] <current>: '**CAL**
>> Expression: **0.75*rad**
>> Select circle, arc or polyline segment for RAD function: *Select the given circle.*

Now you can enter the function name in response to the calculator prompt (**>>Expression**). In this example, the expression is **0.75*rad**. The **rad** function prompts the user to select an object, and it retrieves its radius. This radius is then multiplied by 0.75. The product of rad and 0.75 determines the radius of the new circle.

LOCATING A POINT ON A LINE

You can use the functions **pld** and **plt** to locate a point at a specified distance along a line between two points. The format of the **pld** function is **pld(p1,p2,dist)**. This function will locate a point on line (P1,P2) that is at a distance of **dist** from point (P1). For example, if the function is pld(p1,p2,0.7) and the length of the line is 1.5, the calculator will locate a point at a distance of 0.7 from point (P1) along line (P1,P2).

The format of the **plt** function is **plt(p1,p2,t)**. This function will locate a point on line (P1,P2) at a proportional distance as determined by the parameter, **t**. If **t = 0**, the point that this function will locate is at P1. Similarly, if **t = 1**, the point is located at (P2). However, if the value of **t** is greater than 0 and less than 1 (0> t <1), then the location of the point is determined by the value of **t**. For example, if the function is plt(p1,p2,0.3) and the length of the line is 1.5, the calculator will locate the point at a distance of 0.3 * 1.5 = 0.45 from point (P1).

Chapter 25

Example 3

In this example, you will use the **pld** and **plt** functions to locate the centers of the circles. Lines (P1,P2) and (P3,P4) are given (Figure 25-3).

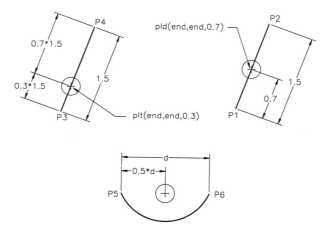

Figure 25-3 Locating a point on a line

Figure 25-3 illustrates the use of the **plt** and **pld** functions. The **plt** function, plt(**end,end,0.3**), will prompt the user to select the two endpoints of the line (P3,P4), and the function will return a point at a distance of 0.3 * 1.5 from point (P1).

> Command: **CIRCLE**
> Specify center point for circle or [3P/2P/Ttr (tan tan radius)]: '**CAL**
> >> Expression: **plt(end,end,0.3)**
> >> Select entity for END snap: *Select the first endpoint of line (P3,P4).*
> >> Select entity for END snap: *Select the second endpoint of line (P3,P4).*
> Specify radius of circle or [Diameter] <current>: *Enter radius.*

Similarly, the **pld** function, **pld(end,end,0.7)**, will prompt the user to select the two endpoints of line (P1,P2); it will return a point that is located at a distance of 0.7 units from point (P1).

> Command: **CIRCLE**
> Specify center point for circle or [3P/2P/Ttr (tan tan radius)]: '**CAL**
> >>Expression: **pld(end,end,0.7)**
> >>Select entity for END snap: *Select the first endpoint of line (P1,P2).*
> >>Select entity for END snap: *Select the second endpoint of line (P1,P2).*
> Specify radius of circle or [Diameter] <current>: *Enter radius.*

The **plt** function can also be used to locate the midpoint by selecting the two endpoints of an arc as shown in the following:

> Command: **CIRCLE**

Specify center point for circle or [3P/2P/Ttr (tan tan radius)]: **'CAL**
>>Expression: **plt(end,end,0.5)**
>>Select entity for END snap: *Select the first endpoint of arc (P5,P6).*
>>Select entity for END snap: *Select the second endpoint of arc (P5,P6).*
Specify radius of circle or [Diameter] <current>: **'CAL**
>> Expression: **0.125*dee**

OBTAINING AN ANGLE

You can use the **ang** function to obtain the angle between two lines. The function can also be used to obtain the angle that a line makes with the positive X axis. The function has the following formats (Figure 25-4):

ang(v)
ang(p1,p2)
ang(apex,p1,p2)
ang(apex,p1,p2,p)

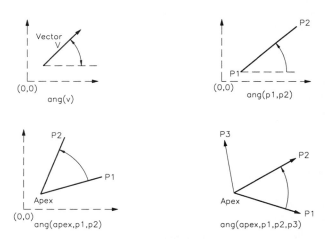

Figure 25-4 Obtaining an angle

ang(v)

The **ang(v)** function can be used to obtain the angle that a vector makes with the positive X axis. Assume a vector [2,2,0], and obtain its angle. You can use the ang(v) function to obtain the angle.

Command: **CAL**
>>Expression: **v=[2,2,0]**   *(Defines a vector v.)*
Command: **CAL**
>>Expression: **ang(v)**   *(v is a predefined vector.)*
45.0

The vector v makes a 45 degree angle with the positive X axis.

ang(p1,p2)

The **ang(p1,p2)** function can be used to obtain the angle that a line (P1,P2) makes with the positive X axis. For example, if you want to obtain the angle of a line with start point and endpoint coordinates of (1,1,0) and (4,4,0), respectively:

Command: **CAL**
\>>Expression: **p1=[1,1,0]** *(Defines a vector p1.)*
Command: **CAL**
\>>Expression: **p2=[4,4,0]** *(Defines a vector p2.)*
Command: **CAL**
\>>Expression: **ang(p1,p2)**
45.00

If the line exists, you can obtain the angle by using the following function:

Command: **CAL**
\>>Expression: **ang(end,end)**
\>>Select entity for END snap: *Select first endpoint of line (P1,P2).*
\>>Select entity for END snap: *Select second endpoint of line (P1,P2).*
31.7134   *(This is the angle that the function returns.)*

ang(apex,p1,p2)

The **ang(apex,p1,p2)** function can be used to obtain the angle that a line (apex,P1) makes with (apex,P2). For example, if you want to obtain the angle between the two given lines as shown in the third drawing of Figure 25-4, use the following commands:

Command: **CAL**
\>>Expression: **ang(end,end,end)**
\>>Select entity for END snap: *Select first endpoint (apex).*
\>>Select entity for END snap: *Select second endpoint (P1).*
\>>Select entity for END snap: *Select third endpoint (P2).*
51.41459   *(This is the angle that the function returns.)*

ang(apex,p1,p2,p)

The **ang(apex,p1,p2,p)** function can be used to obtain the angle that a line (apex,P1) makes with (apex,P2). The last point, **p**, is used to determine the orientation of the angle.

LOCATING THE INTERSECTION POINT

You can obtain the intersection point of two lines (P1,P2) and (P3,P4) by using the following function:

  ill(p1,p2,p3,p4)

(P1,P2) are two points on the first line, and (P3,P4) are two points on the second line, as shown in Figure 25-5.

Example 4

In this example, you will draw a circle whose center point is located at the intersection point of two lines (P1,P2) and (P3,P4). It is assumed that the two lines are given as shown in Figure 25-5.

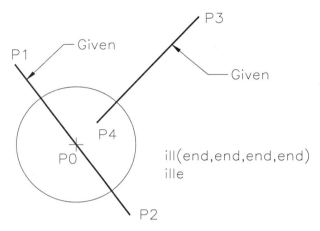

Figure 25-5 Obtaining intersection point

Use the following commands to obtain the intersection point and to draw a circle with the intersection point as the center of the circle:

Command: **CIRCLE**
Specify center point for circle or [3P/2P/Ttr (tan tan radius)]: '**CAL**
>>Expression: **ill(end,end,end,end)**
>>Select entity for END snap: *Select the first point on line (P1,P2).*
>>Select entity for END snap: *Select the second point on line (P1,P2).*
>>Select entity for END snap: *Select the first point on line (P3,P4).*
>>Select entity for END snap: *Select the second point on line (P3,P4).*
Specify radius of circle or [Diameter] <current>: *Enter radius.*

The expression ill(end,end,end,end) can be replaced by the shortcut function **ille**. When used, it will automatically prompt for four endpoints to locate the point of intersection.

APPLICATIONS OF THE GEOMETRY CALCULATOR

The following examples illustrate some additional applications of the geometry calculator.

Example 5

In this example, you will draw a circle whose center (P0) is located midway between endpoints (P4) and (P2) (Figure 25-6).

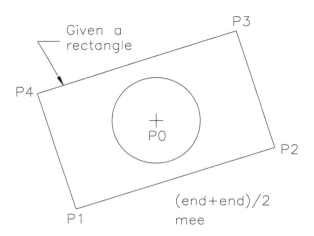

*Figure 25-6 Using the shortcut function **mee***

The center of the circle can be located by using the calculator snap modes. For example, to locate the center you can use the expression **(end+end)/2**. The other way of locating the center is by using the shortcut function **mee**, as shown here (Figure 25-6):

> Command: **CIRCLE**
> Specify center point for circle or [3P/2P/Ttr (tan tan radius)]: **'CAL**
> >>Expression: **mee**
> >>Select entity for END snap: *Select the first endpoint (P2).*
> >>Select entity for END snap: *Select the second endpoint (P4).*
> Specify radius of circle or [Diameter] <current>: *Enter the radius.*

Example 6

In this example, you will draw a circle that is tangent to a given line. The radius of the circle is 0.5 units, and the circle must pass through the selected point shown in Figure 25-7.

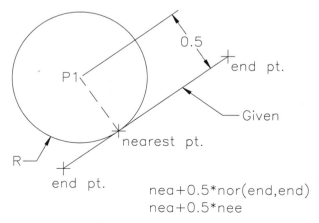

*Figure 25-7 Using the shortcut function **nee***

To draw a circle that is tangent to a line, you must first locate the center of the circle that is at a distance of 0.5 units from the selected point. This can be accomplished by using the function **nor(p1,p2)**, which returns a unit vector normal to the line (P1,P2). You can also use the shortcut function **nee**. The function will automatically prompt you to select the two endpoints of the given line. The unit vector must be multiplied by the radius (0.5) to locate the center of the circle.

> Command: **CIRCLE**
> Specify center point for circle or [3P/2P/Ttr (tan tan radius)]: **'CAL**
> >>Expression: **NEA+0.5*nee**
> >>Select entity for NEA snap: *Select a point on the given line.*
> >>Select one endpoint for NEE: *Select the first endpoint on the given line.*
> >>Select another endpoint for NEE: *Select the second endpoint on the given line.*
> Specify radius of circle or [Diameter] <current>: **0.5**

Example 7

In this example, you will draw a circle with its center on a line. The radius of the circle is 0.25 times the length of the line, and it is assumed that the line is given(Figure 25-8).

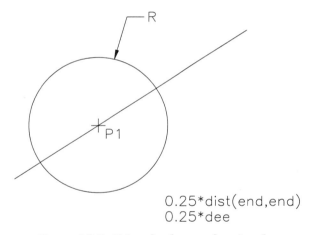

0.25*dist(end,end)
0.25*dee

*Figure 25-8 Using the shortcut function **dee***

The radius of the circle can be determined by multiplying the length of the line by 0.25. The length of the line can be obtained by using the function dist(p1,p2) or by using the shortcut function **dee**. When you use the function **dee**, the calculator will automatically prompt you to select the two endpoints of the given line. It is equivalent to using the function dist(end,end).

> Command: **CIRCLE**
> Specify center point for circle or [3P/2P/Ttr (tan tan radius)]: *Select a point on the line.*
> Specify radius of circle or [Diameter] <current>: **'CAL**
> >>Expression: **0.25*dee**
> >>Select entity for END snap: *Select the first endpoint on the given line.*
> >>Select entity for END snap: *Select the second endpoint on the given line.*

USING AUTOLISP VARIABLES

The geometry calculator allows you to use an AutoLISP variable in the arithmetic expression. You can also use the calculator to assign a value to an AutoLISP variable. The variables can be integer, real, or a 2D or 3D point. The next example illustrates the use of AutoLISP variables.

Example 8

In this example, you will draw two circles that are in the middle and are offset 0.5 units from the center. It is assumed that the other two circles are given.

To locate the center of the top circle, you must first determine the point that is midway between the centers of the two given circles. This can be accomplished by defining a variable **midpoint** where **midpoint=(cen+cen)/2**. Similarly, you can define another variable for the offset distance: **offset=[0,0.5]**. The center of the circle can be obtained by adding these two variables **(midpoint+offset)** (Figure 25-9).

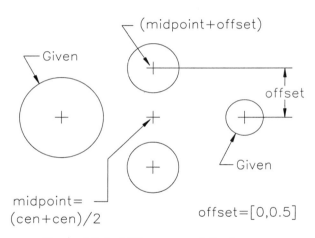

Figure 25-9 *Adding two predefined vectors*

Command: **CAL**
>>Expression: **midpoint=(cen+cen)/2**
>>Select entity for CEN snap: *Select the first circle.*
>>Select entity for CEN snap: *Select the second circle.*

Command: **CAL**
>>Expression: **offset=[0,0.5]**

Command: **CIRCLE**
Specify center point for circle or [3P/2P/Ttr (tan tan radius)]: **'CAL**
>>Expression: **(midpoint+offset)**
Specify radius of circle or [Diameter] <current>: *Enter radius.*

To locate the center point of the bottom circle, you must subtract offset from midpoint:

Command: **CIRCLE**
Specify center point for circle or [3P/2P/Ttr (tan tan radius)]: **'CAL**
\>\>Expression: **(midpoint-offset)**
Specify radius of circle or [Diameter] <current>: *Enter radius.*

The same results can be obtained by using AutoLISP expressions, as follows:

Command: **(Setq NEWPOINT "(CEN+CEN)/2+[0,0.5]")**
Command: **CIRCLE**
Specify center point for circle or [3P/2P/Ttr (tan tan radius)]: **(cal NEWPOINT)**
(Recalls the expression.)
\>\>Select entity for CEN snap: *Select the first circle.*
\>\>Select entity for CEN snap: *Select the second circle.*

FILTERING X, Y, AND Z COORDINATES

The following functions are used to retrieve the coordinates of a point.

Function	Description
xyof(p)	Retrieves the **X** and **Y** coordinates of a point (p) and returns a point; the Z coordinate is automatically set to 0.0
xzof(p)	Retrieves the **X** and **Z** coordinates of a point (p) and returns a point; the Y coordinate is automatically set to 0.0
yzof(p)	Retrieves the **Y** and **Z** coordinates of a point (p) and returns a point; the X coordinate is automatically set to 0.0
xof(p)	Retrieves the **X coordinate** of a point (p) and returns a point; the Y and Z coordinates are automatically set to 0.0
yof(p)	Retrieves the **Y coordinate** of a point (p) and returns a point; the X and Z coordinates are automatically set to 0.0
zof(p)	Retrieves the **Z coordinate** of a point (p) and returns a point; the X and Y coordinates are automatically set to 0.0
rxof(p)	Retrieves the **X coordinate** of a point (p)
ryof(p)	Retrieves the **Y coordinate** of a point (p)
rzof(p)	Retrieves the **Z coordinate** of a point (p)

Example 9

In this example, you will draw a line by using filters to extract coordinates and points. It is assumed that the two lines are as shown in Figure 25-10.

To draw a line, you need to determine the coordinates of the two endpoints of the line. The X coordinate of the first point can be obtained from point (P1), and the Y coordinate from point (P2). To obtain these coordinate points, you can use the filter function **rxof(end)** to extract the X coordinate and **ryof(end)** to extract the Y coordinate. To determine the coordinates of the endpoint of the line, you can filter the XY coordinates of point (P3) and then add the offset of 0.25 units by defining a vector [0.25,0,0].

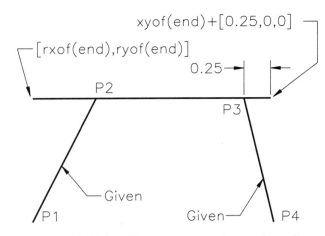

Figure 25-10 *Using filters to extract points and coordinates*

Command: **LINE**
Specify first point: 'cal
>>Expression: **[rxof(end),ryof(end)]**
>>Select entity for END snap: *Select the first endpoint (P1).*
>>Select entity for END snap: *Select the second endpoint (P2).*
Specify next point or [Undo]: **'CAL**
>>Expression: **xyof(end)+[0.25,0,0]**

CONVERTING UNITS

You can use the calculator function **cvunit** to change a given value from one system of units to another. You can also use this function to change the unit format. For example, you can change the units from feet to inches, meters to centimeters, and vice versa. The value can be a number or a point. The units available are defined in the ACAD.UNT file which is an ASCII file that you can examine. The format of the cvunit expression is:

cvunit(value, units from, units to)

Examples
Command: **CAL**
>>Expression: **cvunit(100,cm,inch)**
>>Expression: **cvunit(100,feet,meter)**
>>Expression: **cvunit(1,feet,inch)**

ADDITIONAL FUNCTIONS

The following is the list of additional calculator functions. The description given next to the function summarizes the application of the function.

Function	Description
abs(real)	Calculates the **absolute value** of a number
abs(v)	Calculates the **length of vector v**
ang(v)	Calculates the **angle** between the X axis and vector v
ang(p1,p2)	Calculates the **angle** between the X axis and line (P1,P2)
cur	Retrieves **coordinates of a point** from the location of the graphics cursor
cvunit(val,from,to)	**Converts the given value** (val) from one unit measurement system to another
dee	Measures the **distance between two endpoints**; equivalent to the function dist(end,end)
dist(p1,p2)	**Measures distance** between two specified points (P1,P2)
getvar(var_name)	Retrieves the value of the AutoCAD **system variable**
ill(p1,p2,p3,p4)	Returns the **intersection point** of lines (P1,P2) and (P3,P4)
ille	Returns the **intersection point** of lines defined by four endpoints; equivalent to the function ill(end,end,end,end)
mee	Returns the **midpoint** between two endpoints; equivalent to the function (end+end)/2
nee	Returns a **unit vector** normal to two endpoints; equivalent to the function nor(end,end)
nor	Returns a **unit vector** that is normal to a circle or an arc
nor(v)	Returns a **unit vector** in the **xy** plane that is normal to vector v
nor(p1,p2)	Returns a **unit vector** in the **xy** plane that is normal to line (P1,P2)
nor(p1,p2,p3)	Returns a **unit vector** that is normal to the specified plane defined by points (P1,P2,P3)
pld(p1,p2,dist)	**Locates a point** on the line (P1,P2) that is **dist** units from point (P1)
plt(p1,p2,t)	Locates a point on the line (P1,P2) that is **t*dist** units from point (P1) (Note: when t = 0, the point is (P1). Also, when t = 1, the point is (P2))
rad	**Retrieves the radius** of the selected object
rot(p,org,ang)	Returns a point that is rotated through angle **ang** about point **org**
u2w(p)	Locates a point with respect to WCS from the current UCS
vec(p1,p2)	**Calculates a vector** from point (P1) to point (P2)
vec(p1,p2)	**Calculates a unit vector** from point (P1) to point (P2)
vee	**Calculates a vector** from two endpoints; equivalent to the function vec(end,end)
vee1	Calculates a unit vector from two endpoints; equivalent to the function vec1(end,end)
w2u(p)	Locates a point with respect to the current UCS from WCS

Self-Evaluation Test

Answer the following questions, and then compare your answers to the correct answers given at the end of this chapter.

1. The length of a line can be obtained by using the function **dist(p1,p2)** or by using the shortcut function _____.

2. The function **xzof(p)** retrieves the _____ coordinates of a point (P) and returns a point. The Y coordinate is automatically set to (0,0).

3. What function can be used to retrieve the X coordinate of a point (P)? _____

4. The function **nor(v)** returns a _____ in the XY plane that is normal to vector v.

5. What function will calculate the absolute value of a number? _____

6. The **ang(v)** function can be used to obtain the angle that a vector makes with the _____ _____ axis.

7. What function can be used to obtain the angle that a line (P1,P2) makes with the positive X axis? _____

8. How can you obtain the intersection point of two lines (P1,P2) and (P3,P4)? _____ _____

9. What is the shortcut function for (end+end)/2? _____

10. The shortcut function **nee** is equivalent to what function? _____

Review Questions

1. What can the calculator be used for? _____

2. The calculator can also access the existing geometry by using standard AutoCAD object snap functions. (T/F)

3. The calculator cannot be used to assign a value to an AutoLISP variable. (T/F)

4. What is a real expression? _____

5. What is a vector expression, and what does it consists of? _____ _____

6. Evaluate the expression 3 * [72,18,13.5]. _____

7.   Evaluate the expression [14,8,14.5] / 2. _____

8.   Evaluate the expression [12,15.5,0.5] + [2.5,11,7]. _____

9.   Evaluate the expression [2,5,3] & [7,3,5]. _____

10. You cannot use AutoCAD snap modes with CAL functions to evaluate an expression. (T/F)

11. What function can you use to obtain the radius of an object? _____

12. Name the functions that can be used to locate a point on an object. _____

13. What is the format of the **pld** function? _____

14. What is the format of the **plt** function? _____

15. How can you obtain the angle between two given lines? _____

Exercises

Exercise 1   *General*

Make the drawing shown in Figure 25-11. Use the real operators of the geometry calculator to calculate the value of L, H, and TL.

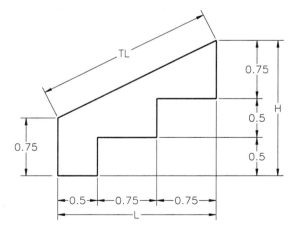

Figure 25-11 *Drawing for Exercise 1*

Exercise 2   *General*

Make the drawing shown in Figure 25-12; assume the dimensions. Draw a circle whose center is at point (P3). Use the calculator function to locate the center of the circle (P3) that is midway between

(P1) and (P2). The points (P1) and (P2) are the midpoints on the top and bottom lines, respectively.

Exercise 3   *General*

Make the drawing shown in Figure 25-13; assume the dimensions.
1. Draw a circle whose center is at point (P5). Use the calculator function to locate the center of the circle (P5) that is midway between (P3) and (P4). Points (P3) and (P4) are the midpoints on the top and bottom lines, respectively.
2. Draw a circle whose radius is 0.6 times the radius of the circle in part 1. The center of the circle (P6) is located midway between the center of that first circle (P5) and the midpoint of line (P1,P2).

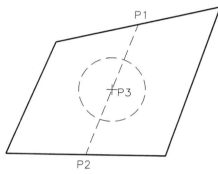

Figure 25-12 *Drawing for Exercise 2*

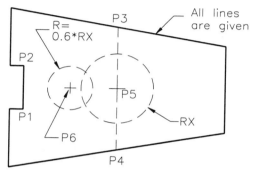

Figure 25-13 *Drawing for Exercise 3*

Problem-Solving Exercise 1   *General*

Make the drawing shown in Figure 25-14; assume the dimensions.
1. Use the calculator function to locate the point (P3). Point (P3) is midway between (P1) and (P2). The points (P1) and (P2) are the midpoints on the top and the bottom lines, respectively.
2. Use the calculator function to locate the point (P4) that is normal to the line (P1,P2) at a distance of 0.25 units.
3. Draw a circle whose center is located at (P4).

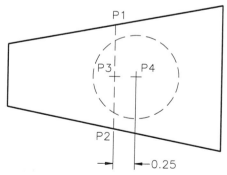

Figure 25-14 *Drawing for Problem-Solving Exercise 1*

Answers to Self-Evaluation Test

1 - dee, **2** - X and Z, **3** - rxof(p), **4** - unit vector, **5** - abs(real), **6** - positive X, **7** - ang(p1,p2), **8** - ill(p1,p2,p3,p4), **9** - mee, **10** - nor(p1,p2)

Chapter 26

Accessing External Databases

Learning Objectives

After completing this chapter, you will be able to:
* *Understand databases, and the database management system (DBMS).*
* *Understand the **AutoCAD database connectivity** feature.*
* ***Configure** external databases.*
* *Access and edit a database using **dbConnect Manager**.*
* *Create **Links** with graphical objects.*
* *Create and display **Labels** in a drawing.*
* *Understand **AutoCAD SQL Environment** (ASE) and Create queries using **Query Editor**.*
* *Form selction sets using **Link Select**.*
* *Convert ASE links into AutoCAD 2000 format.*

UNDERSTANDING DATABASES
Database

A **database** is a collection of data that is arranged in a logical order. For example, there are six computers in an office, and we want to keep a record of these computers on a sheet of paper. In a database, the columns are known as **fields, and** the individual rows are called **records** and the entries in the database tables are known as **cells** that store data for a particular variable. One of the ways of recording the computer information is to make a table with rows and columns as shown in Figure 37-1. Each column will have a heading that specifies a certain feature of the computer, such as COMP_CFG, CPU, HDRIVE, or RAM. Once the columns are labeled, the computer data can be placed in the columns for each computer. By doing this, we have created a database on a sheet of paper that contains information on our computers. The same information can be stored in a computer; this is generally known as a computerized database.

COMPUTER					
COMP_CFG	CPU	HDRIVE	RAM	GRAPHICS	INPT_DEV
1	PENTIUM350	4300MB	64MB	SUPER VGA	DIGITIZER
2	PENTIUM233	2100MB	32MB	SVGA	MOUSE
3	MACIIC	40MB	2MB	STANDARD	MOUSE
4	386SX/16	80MB	4MB	VGA	MOUSE
5	386/33	300MB	6MB	VGA	MOUSE
6	SPARC2	600MB	16MB	STANDARD	MOUSE

Figure 37-1 A table containing computer information

Most of the Database systems are extremely flexible and any modifications or additions of fields or records can be done easily. Database systems also allow you to define relationships between multiple tables, so that if the data of one table is altered, automatically the corresponding values of another table with predefined relationships will change accordingly.

Database Management System

The database management system (DBMS) is a program or a collection of programs (software) used to manage the data in the database. For example, PARADOX, dBASE, INFORMIX, and ORACLE are database management systems.

Components of a Table

A database **table** is a two-dimensional data structure (Figure 37-2) that consists of rows and columns.

COMPUTER					
COMP_CFG	CPU	HDRIVE	RAM	GRAPHICS	INPT_DEV
1	PENTIUM350	4300MB	64MB	SUPER VGA	DIGITIZER
2	PENTIUM233	2100MB	32MB	SVGA	MOUSE
3	MACIIC	40MB	2MB	STANDARD	MOUSE
4	386SX/16	80MB	4MB	VGA	MOUSE
5	386/33	300MB	6MB	VGA	MOUSE
6	SPARC2	600MB	16MB	STANDARD	MOUSE

3	MACIIC	40MB	2MB	STANDARD	MOUSE

ROWS

6	SPARC2	600MB	16MB	STANDARD	MOUSE

Figure 37-2 Rows in a table (the horizontal group of data)

Row. The horizontal group of data is called a **row**. For example, Figure 37-2 shows a table, and just below the full table are two rows of the table. Each value in a row defines an attribute of the item. For example, in Figure 37-2, the attributes assigned to COMP_CFG (1) include PENTIUM350, 4300MB, 64MB, and so on. These attributes are arranged in the first row of the table.

Column. A vertical group of data (attribute) is called a **column**. Three of the columns in Figure 37-2 are shown in Figure 37-3. HDRIVE is the column heading that represents a feature of the computer, and the HDRIVE attributes of each computer are placed vertically in this column.

COLUMNS

CPU
PENTIUM350
PENTIUM233
MACIIC
386SX/16
386/33
SPARC2

HDRIVE
4300MB
2100MB
40MB
80MB
300MB
600MB

GRAPHICS
SUPER VGA
SVGA
STANDARD
VGA
VGA
STANDARD

Figure 37-3 Columns in a table (the vertical group of data)

AUTOCAD DATABASE CONNECTIVITY

AutoCAD can be effectively used in associating data contained in an external database table with the AutoCAD graphical objects by linking. **Links** are the pointers to the database tables from which the data can be referred to. AutoCAD can also be used to attach **Labels** that will display data from the selected tables as text objects. AutoCAD database connectivity offers the following facilities:

1. A **dbConnect Manager** that can be used to associate links, labels, and queries with AutoCAD drawings.
2. An **external configuration utility** that enables AutoCAD to access the data from a database system.
3. A **Data View window** that displays the records of a database table within the AutoCAD session.
4. A **Query Editor** that can be used to construct, store, and execute SQL queries. **SQL** is an acronym for **structured query language**.
5. A **migration tool** that converts links and other displayable attributes of files created by earlier releases to AutoCAD 2000.
6. A **Link Select operation** that creates iterative selection sets based on queries and graphical objects.

DATABASE CONFIGURATION

External database can be accessed within AutoCAD only after configuring AutoCAD using Microsoft **ODBC**
(Open Database Connectivity) and **OLE DB** (Object Linking and Embedding Database) programs. AutoCAD is capable of utilizing data from other applications, regardless of the format and the platform on which the file is stored. Configuration of database involves creating a new **data source** that points to a collection of data and information about the required drivers to access it. A **data source** is an individual table or a collection of tables created and stored in an environment, catalog, or schema. Environments, catalogs, and schemas are the hierarchical database elements in most of the database management systems and they are analogous to Window-based directory structure in many ways. Schemas contain a collection of tables, while Catalogs contain subdirectories

of schemas and Environment holds subdirectories of catalogs. The external applications supported by AutoCAD 2000 are **dBASE® V** and **III**, **Oracle®8.0** and **7.3**, **Microsoft® Access®**, **PARADOX 7.0**, **Microsoft Visual FoxPro®6.0**, **SQL Server 7.0** and **6.5**. The configuration process varies slightly from one database system to other.

DBCONNECT MANAGER*

Menu:	Tools > dbConnect
Command:	DBCONNECT

This is a new feature with AutoCAD 2000 that enables you to access information from external databases more effectively than previous releases of AutoCAD. The **dbConnect Manager** is a dockable as well as resizable window and contains a set of buttons and a tree view showing all the configured and available databases. You can use **dbConnect Manager** for associating various database objects with an AutoCAD drawing. You can invoke **dbConnect Manager** (Figure 37-4) by entering **DBCONNECT** at the AutoCAD Command prompt or choosing **dbConnect** from the **Tools** menu. The **dbConnect Manager** contains two nodes in the tree view. The **Drawing nodes** displays all the open drawings and each node will display all the associated database objects with the drawing. **Data Sources node** displays all the configured data on your system.

Figure 37-4 dbconnect Manager

AutoCAD 2000 contains several Microsoft Access sample database tables and a direct driver (*jet_dbsamples.udl*). The following example shows the procedure to configure a database with your drawing using the **dbConnect Manager**.

Example 1

Configure a data source of Microsoft Access database with your diagram. Update and use the **jet_samples.udl** configuration file with new information.

Step 1. Invoke **dbConnect Manager** either by entering **DBCONNECT** at the Command prompt or choosing from the **Tools** menu. The **dbConnect** menu will be inserted between **Modify** and **Window** menus.

Step 2. From the **dbconnect** menu, choose **Data Sources > Configure** to display the **Configure a Data Source** dialog box (Figure 37-5). You can also invoke the **Configure a Data Source** dialog box by selecting **Data Sources** in **dbConnect Manager** tree view, right-clicking and choosing **Configure Data Source....**

Figure 37-5 Configure a Data Source dialog box

Step 3. From the **Data Sources:** list box in **Configure a Data Source** dialog box, select **jet_dbsamples** and choose the **OK** button. AutoCAD will display **Data Link Properties (Connection** tab) dialog box (Figure 37-6).

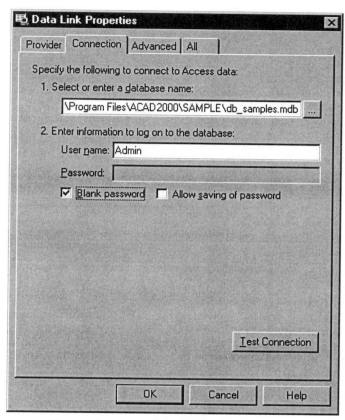

Figure 37-6 Data Link Properties dialog box

Step 4. In the **Data Link Properties (Connection** tab) dialog box, choose the [**...**] button adjacent to **Select or enter a database name:** text box. AutoCAD will display the **Select Access Database** dialog box (Figure 37-7). Select **db_samples (.mdb file)** and choose **Open** button. You can also type in the text box as **C:\Program Files\ACAD2000\SAMPLE\db_samples.mdb**, if you have selected default during the setup procedure.

Note

*If you are configuring any other driver than **Microsoft Jet** for database linking, you should consult the appropriate documentation for the configuring process.*

*The other tabs in the **Data Links Properties** dialog box are required for configuring different Database Providers supported by AutoCAD 2000.*

Figure 37-7 Select Access Database dialog box

Step 5. From the **Data Link Properties** (**Connection** tab) dialog box, choose the **Test Connection** button to ensure that the database source has been configured correctly and AutoCAD will display the **Microsoft Data Link** message box (Figure 37-8). Choose **OK** button to end the message and again choose the **OK** button to complete the configuration process.

After configuring a data source when you double click on **jet_dbsamples** in **dbConnect Manager,** all the sample tables will be displayed in the tree view and you can connect any table and link its records to your diagram.

Figure 37-8 Microsoft Data Link message box

VIEWING AND EDITING TABLE DATA FROM AUTOCAD

After you have configured a data source using the **dbConnect Manager,** you can view as well as edit its tables within the AutoCAD session. The **Data View window** can be used for viewing and editing a database table. You can open tables in **Read-only** mode to view its content. But you cannot edit its records in **Read-only** mode. Some database systems may require a valid user-name and password before connecting to AutoCAD drawing files. The records of a database table can be edited by opening in **Edit** mode. The procedures to open a table in various modes follow.

 Read-only mode: Choose **dbConnect** menu > **View Data** > **View External Table** and the table will be opened in **Read-only** mode. You can also view a table in the Read-only mode by selecting the table, right-clicking to invoke the shortcut menu, and choosing **View Table**.

 Edit mode: Choose **dbConnect** menu > **View Data** > **Edit External Table** to open the table in **Edit** mode. You can also open a table in the **Edit** mode by double-clicking on it in the tree view of the **dbConnect Manager** or choosing **Edit Table** from the shortcut menu.

Example 2

From the **jet_dbsamples** data source, select Computer table and edit each row in the table. Add a new computer and replace one by editing the table and save your changes.

Step 1. Select **Computer** table from the **jet_dbsamples** in the **dbConnect Manager** and right-click to invoke the shortcut menu. Choose **Edit Table** from the menu (Figure 37-9). You can also do the same by double clicking on the **Computer** table.

Step 2. AutoCAD will display the **Data View window** with the **Computer** table in it. In the **Data View window**, you can resize, sort, hide, or freeze the columns according to your requirement.

Step 3. To **add a new item** in the table, double-click on the first empty row. In TAG_NUM column, type **24675**. Then type:

MANUFACTURER:	**IBM**
Equipment_Description:	**PIII/450, 4500GL, NETX**
Item_Type:	**CPU**
Room:	**6035**

Figure 37-9 Choosing the **Edit Table** from the shortcut menu

Step 4. To **Edit the record** for TAG_NUM **60298**, and display the following in **Data View window** (Figure 37-10), double-click on each cell and type:

MANUFACTURER:	**CREATIVE**
Equipment_Description:	**INFRA 6000, 40XR**
Item_Type:	**CD DRIVE**
Room:	**6996**

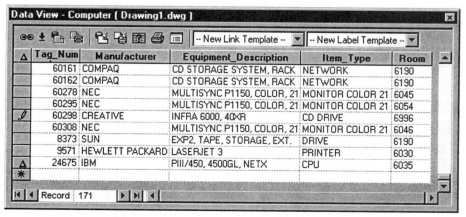

Figure 37-10 Data View window after editing

Step 5. After you have made all the changes in the database table, you have to save the changes for further use. To **save the changes** in the table, right-click on the **Data View grid header** and choose **Commit** from the shortcut menu and the changes will be saved.

 Note
After making changes, if you do not want to save the changes, from the above shortcut menu choose **Restore** *and AutoCAD will restore the orginal values.*

If you quit **Data View window** *without* **Committing**, *AutoCAD will automatically commit all the changes you have made during the editing session.*

CREATING LINKS WITH GRAPHICAL OBJECTS

The main function of the database connectivity feature of AutoCAD is to associate data from external sources with its graphical objects. You can establish the association of the database table with the drawing objects by developing a **link**, which will make reference to one or more record from the table. But you **cannot** link nongraphical objects such as layers or linetypes with the external database. Links are very closely related with graphical objects and change with the change in graphical objects.

To develop links between database tables and graphical objects, you must create a **Link Template**, which will identify the fields of the tables with which links are associated to share the template. For example, you can create a link template that uses the **Tag_number** from the **COMPUTER database table**. Link template also acts as a shortcut that points to the associated database tables. You can associate multiple links to a single graphical object using different link templates. This is useful in associating multiple database tables with a single drawing object. The following example will describe the procedure of linking using link template creation.

Example 3

Create a link template between **COMPUTER** database table from **Jet_dbsamples** and your drawing and use **Tag_Number** as the **key field** for linking.

Step 1. Open your drawing that has to be linked with the **COMPUTER** database table.

 Step 2. From the **Tools** menu, choose **dbConnect** to invoke **dbConnect Manager**. Select COMPUTER from the **jet_dbsamples** data source and right click on it to invoke the shortcut menu.

Step 3. In the shortcut menu, choose **New Link Template...** to Invoke the **New Link Template** dialog box (Figure 37-11). You can also invoke the dialog box by selecting the table in the tree view and then choosing the **New Link Template** button.

Step 4. Choose the **Continue** button to accept the default link template name **Computer Link1**. AutoCAD will display the **Link Template** dialog box (Figure 37-12). Select the check box adjacent to **Tag_Number** to accept it as the **Key field** for associating the template with the block reference in the diagram.

Figure 37-11 *New Link Template dialog box*

Step 5. Choose the **OK** button to complete the new link template; the name of the link template will be displayed under the Drawing name node of the tree view in **dbConnect Manager**.

Figure 37-12 **Link Template** *dialog box*

Step 6. To **link a record with the block reference**, double-click on the COMPUTER table to invoke the **Data View window** (Edit mode). In the table, go to Tag_Number **24675** and highlight the record (row).

 Step 7. Right-click on the row header and choose **Link!** from the shortcut menu (Figure 37-13). You can also link by choosing **Link!** button from the toolbar in **Data View window**.

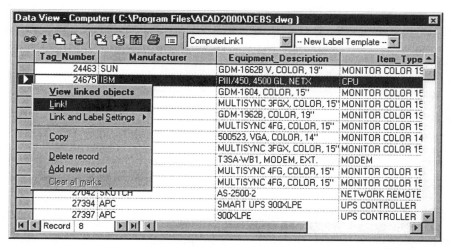

Figure 37-13 *Selecting* **Link!** *from the shortcut menu in the* **Data View** *window*

Step 8. When AutoCAD prompts you to **Select Objects:**, you can choose the block references you want to link with the record. Repeat the process to link all the records to the corresponding block references in the diagram.

 Step 9. After linking, you can **view the linked objects**, by choosing the **View Linked Objects in Drawing** button in the **Data View** dialog box, and the linked objects will get selected in the drawing area.

Additional Link Viewing Settings

You can set a number of viewing options for linked graphical objects and linked records by using the **Data View and Query Options** dialog box (Figure 37-14).

Figure 37-14 Data View and Query Options dialog box

You can set the **Automatically Pan Drawing** option so that AutoCAD will pan the drawing automatically to display objects linked with the current set of selected records in the **Data View** window. You can also set options for **Automatically zoom drawing** and the **Zoom factor**. You can also change the Record Indication settings and the indication marking color.

Editing Link Data

After linking data with the drawing objects, you may need to edit the data or update their **Key field** values. For example, you may need to reallocate the Tag-Number for the computer equipments or Room for each of the linked items. **Link Manager** can be used for changing the Key values. The next example describes the procedure of editing linked data.

Example 4

Use **Link Manager** to edit linked data from the Computer table and change the Key Value from **24352** to **24675**.

Step 1. Open the diagram that was linked with the Computer table and then from the **dbConnect** menu, choose **Links > Link Manager....** AutoCAD will prompt you to select the linked object.

Step 2. Select the linked object to invoke the **Link Manager** dialog box for the Computer table (Figure 37-15).

Step 3. Choose **Computer link1** from the **Link Template:** drop-down list.

Step 4. Select **24352** field in the **Value** column and choose the [**...**] button to invoke the **Column Values** dialog box (Figure 37-16). Select **24675** from the list and choose **OK** button.

Figure 37-15 Link Manager dialog box

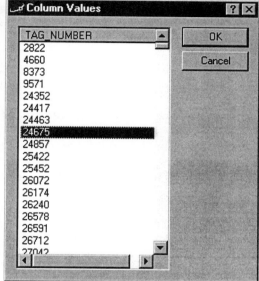

Figure 37-16 Column Values dialog box

Step 5. Again choose the **OK** button in **Link Manager** to accept the changes.

CREATING LABELS*

You can use linking as a powerful mechanism to associate drawing objects with external database tables. You can directly access associated records in the database table by selecting linked objects in the drawing. But linking has some limitations. Suppose you want to include the associated external data with the drawing objects. Since during printing, the links are only the pointers to the external database table, they will not appear in the printed drawing. In such situations, AutoCAD provides you a feature called **Labels** that can be used for visible representation of external data in drawing.

Labels are the multiline text objects that display data from the selected fields in the AutoCAD drawing. Labels are generally one of two types:

Freestanding labels. Freestanding labels exists in the AutoCAD drawing independent of the graphical objects. Their properties do not change with any change of graphical objects in the drawing.

Attached labels. Attached labels are very closely connected with the graphical objects they are associated with. If the graphical objects are moved, then the labels also move and if the objects are deleted, then the labels attached with them also get deleted.

Labels associated with the graphical objects in AutoCAD drawing are displayed with a leader. Labels are created and displayed by **Label Templates** and all the properties of label display can be controlled by using the **Label Template** dialog box. The next example will demonstrate the complete procedure of creating and displaying labels in AutoCAD drawing using label template.

Example 5

Create a new label template in the Computer database table and use the following specifications for the display of labels in the drawing:

1. The label includes **Tag_Number**, **Manufacturer** and **Item_Type** fields.
2. The fields in the label are **0.25** in height, **Times New Roman** font, **black** (**Color 18**) in color and **Middle-left** justified.
3. The label offset starts with **Middle Center** justified and leader offset is **X=1.5** and **Y=1.5**.

Step 1. Open the drawing where you want to attach a label with the drawing objects.

Step 2. Choose **Tools menu > dbConnect** to invoke **dbConnect Manager**. Select **Computer** table from **jet_dbsamples** data source.

Step 3. Right-click on the table and choose **New Label Template...** from the shortcut menu to invoke the **New Label Template** dialog box (Figure 37-17). You can also invoke the dialog box by choosing the **New Label Template** button from the **dbConnect Manager** toolbar.

Step 4. In the **New Label Template** dialog box, choose the **Continue** button to accept the default label template name **Computer Label1**. AutoCAD will display the **Label Template** dialog box.

Step 5. In the **Label Template** dialog box, choose the **Label Fields** tab and from the

Figure 37-17 New Label Template dialog box

Field: drop-down list, add **Tag_Number**, **Manufacturer**, **Item_Type** fields by using the **Add** button (Figure 37-18).

Step 6. Highlight the field names in the edit box and choose the **Character** tab. In the **Character** tab, select the **Times New Roman** font and font height to **0.25** and **Color 18** color (Figure 37-19). Also select **Middle-left** justification in the **Properties** tab.

*Figure 37-18 Label Template dialog box (**Label Fields** tab)*

*Figure 37-19 Label Template dialog box (**Character** tab)*

Step 7. Choose the **Label Offset** tab and select **Middle-center** in the **Start:** drop-down list. Set the **Leader offset:** value to **X: 1.5** and **Y: 1.5** (Figure 37-20).

*Figure 37-20 Label Template dialog box (**Label Offset** tab)*

Step 8. To display the label in the drawing, select the Computer table in the tree view of **dbConnect Manager**. Right-click on the table and choose **Edit Table...** from the shortcut menu.

Step 9. Select **Computer link1** (created in an earlier example) from the **link name** drop-down list and **Computer label1** from the **label name** drop-down list in the **Data View** window.

Step 10. Select the record (row) you want to use as a label. Then choose the **Link and Label Setting** button and select **Create Attached Label** from the menu (Figure 37-21). Then choose the

Create Attached Label button (adjacent to the **Link and Label setting** button) and select the drawing object you want to label.

Data View - Computer [C:\Program Files\ACAD2000\DEBS.dwg]   ☒

			ComputerLink1 ▼	ComputerLabel1 ▼
Create Links		**Equipment_Description**	**Item_Type**	
✔ Create Attached Labels		HL6605ATK, COLOR, 16"	MONITOR COLOR 16	
Create Freestanding Labels		HL6605ATK, COLOR, 16"	MONITOR COLOR 16	
24465 SUN		GDM-1662B V, COLOR, 19"	MONITOR COLOR 19	
24857 SUN		GDM-1604, COLOR, 15"	MONITOR COLOR 15	
25422 NEC		MULTISYNC 3FGX, COLOR, 15"	MONITOR COLOR 15	
25452 SUN		GDM-1962B, COLOR, 19"	MONITOR COLOR 19	
26072 NEC		MULTISYNC 4FG, COLOR, 15"	MONITOR COLOR 15	
26174 AST		500523, VGA, COLOR, 14"	MONITOR COLOR 14	
26240 NEC		MULTISYNC 3FGX, COLOR, 15"	MONITOR COLOR 15	
26578 TELEBIT		T3SA-WB1, MODEM, EXT.	MODEM	
26591 NEC		MULTISYNC 4FG, COLOR, 15"	MONITOR COLOR 15	
26712 NEC		MULTISYNC 4FG, COLOR, 15"	MONITOR COLOR 15	
27042 SKUTCH		AS-2500-2	NETWORK REMOTE RESE	
27394 APC		SMART UPS 900XLPE	UPS CONTROLLER	

Record 3

*Figure 37-21 Choosing the **Create Attached Label** in the **Data View** window*

AutoCAD will display the Label with given specifications in the drawing.

Note
*You can create **Freestanding Labels** in the same way by selecting **Create Freestanding Label** from the **Link and Label setting** menu in the **Data View** window.*

Updating Labels with New Database Values

There is a strong possibility that you may have to change the data values in the database table after adding a label in the AutoCAD drawing. So you should update the labels in the drawing after making any alteration in the database table the drawing is linked with. The following is the procedure for updating all label values in the AutoCAD drawing:

1. After editing the database table, open the drawing that has to be updated.

2. From the **dbConnect** menu, choose **Labels > Reload Labels...** to invoke the **Select a Database Object** dialog box (Figure 37-22).

3. In the dialog box, select the label template from the list box and choose the **OK** button for updating with the new database values.

Figure 37-22 Select a Database Object dialog box

Importing and Exporting Link and Label Templates

You may want to use the link and label templates that have been developed by some other AutoCAD users. This is very useful when developing a set of common tools to be shared by all of the team members in a project. AutoCAD is capable of importing as well as exporting all the link and label templates that are associated with a drawing. The following is the procedure to **import** a set of templates into the current drawing:

1. From the **dbConnect** menu, choose **Templates > Import Template Set** to invoke the **Import Template Set** dialog box.
2. In the dialog box, select the template set to be imported.
3. Choose **Open** to import the template set into the current drawing.

AutoCAD will display an **alert box** that can be used to provide a unique name for the template if there is a link or label template with the same name already associated with the current drawing.

The following is the procedure to **export** a set of templates from the current drawing:

1. From the **dbConnect** menu, choose **Templates > Export Template Set** to **Export Template Set** dialog box.
2. In the dialog box in the **Save In list**, select the directory where you want to save the template set.
3. Under **File Name**, specify a name for the template set, and then choose the **Save** button to save the template in the specified directory.

AUTOCAD SQL ENVIRONMENT (ASE)

SQL is an acronym for **structured query language**. It is often referred to as **sequel**. SQL is a format in computer programming that lets the user ask questions about a database according to specific rules. The **AutoCAD SQL environment** (ASE) lets you access and manipulate the data that is stored in the external database table and link data from the database to objects in a drawing.

Once you access the table, you can manipulate the data. The connection is made through a database management system (DBMS). The DBMS programs have their own methodology for working with databases. However, the ASE commands work the same way regardless of the database being used. This is made possible by the ASE drivers that come with AutoCAD software. In AutoCAD 2000, SQL has been incorporated. For example, you want to prepare a report that lists all the computer equipment that costs more then $25. **AutoCAD Query Editor** can be used to easily construct a query that returns a subset of records or linked graphical objects that follow the previously mentioned criterion.

AUTOCAD QUERY EDITOR*

The **AutoCAD Query Editor** consists of four tabs that can be used to create new queries. The tabs are arranged in order of increasing complexities. For example, if you are not familiar with **SQL** (Structured Query Language), you can start with **Quick Query** and **Range Query** initially to get familiar with query syntax.

You can start developing a query in one tab and subsequently add and refine the query conditions in the next tabs. For example, if you have created a query in the **Quick Query** tab and then decide to add an additional query using **Query Builder** tab, when you choose the **Query Builder** tab, all the values initially selected in the previous tabs are displayed in this tab and additional conditions can be added to the query. But it is not possible to go backwards through the tabs once you have created queries with one of the advanced tabs because additional functions are not available in the simpler tabs. AutoCAD will prompt a warning indicating that the query will be reset to its default values if you attempt to move backward through the query tabs.

The AutoCAD **Query Editor** has the following tabs for building queries:

Quick Query: This tab provides an environment where your simple queries can be developed based on a single database field, single operator, and a single value. For example, you can find all records from the current table where the value of the **"Item_type"** field equals **"CPU"**.

Range Query: This tab provides an environment where you a query can be developed that returns all records that fall within a given range of values. For example, you can find all records from the current table where the value of the **"Room"** field is **greater than or equal to 6050** and **less than or equal to 6150**.

Query Builder: This tab provides an environment where more complicated queries can be developed based on multiple search criteria. For example, you can find all records from the current table where the **"Item_type"** equals **"CPU"** and **"Room"** number is greater than **6050**.

SQL Query: This tab provides an environment where sophisticated queries can be developed that conform with the SQL 92 protocol. For example, you can select * from **Item type.Room. Tag_Number** where:

> **Item_type = 'CPU' ;   Room >= 6050** and **<= 6150**
> and
> **Tag_number > 26072**

The following example describes the complete procedure of creating a new query using all the tabs of the **Query Editor**.

Example 6

Create a new Query for the **Computer** database table and use all the tabs of the **Query Editor** to prepare a SQL query.

Step 1. To create a new query, from the **dbconnect** menu choose **Query > New Query...** to invoke the **New Query** dialog box (Figure 37-23). You can also invoke the dialog box by right clicking on the table (Computer) and choosing **New Query...** from the short-cut menu.

Step 2. In the **New Query** dialog box, choose the **Continue** button to accept the default query name **Computer Query1**. AutoCAD will display **Query Editor**.

Step 3. In the **Quick Query** tab of **Query Editor**, select '**Item_Type**' from the **Field:** list box, '**=Equal**' from the **Operator:** drop-down list, and type '**CPU**' in the **Value:** text

Figure 37-23 New Query dialog box

box. You can also select '**CPU**' from the **Column Values** dialog box by choosing the **Look up values** button. Choose the **Store** button to save the query (Figure 37-24).

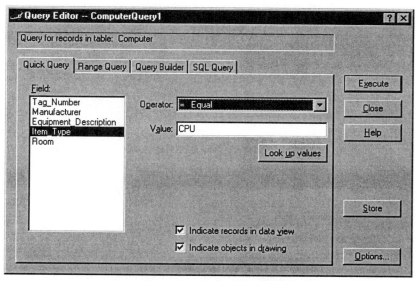

Figure 37-24 Query Editor (Quick Query tab)

Step 4. Choose the **Range Query** tab, and select **Room_Number** from the **Field:** list box. Enter **6050** in the **From:** text box and **6150** in the **Through:** text box. You can also select the values from the **Column Values** dialog box by choosing the **Look up values** button (Figure 37-25). Choose the **Store** button to save the query.

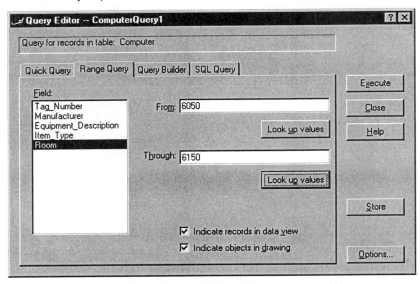

*Figure 37-25 Query Editor (**Range Query** tab)*

Step 5. Choose the **Query Builder** tab, and add **Item_Type** in **Show fields:** list box by Selecting **Item_Type** from the **Fields in table:** list box and choosing the **Add** button. In the table area, change the entries of fields, Operator, Value, logical, and Parenthetical grouping criteria as shown in Figure 37-26, by selecting each cell and selecting the values from the respective drop-down list or options lists. Choose the **Store** button to save the query.

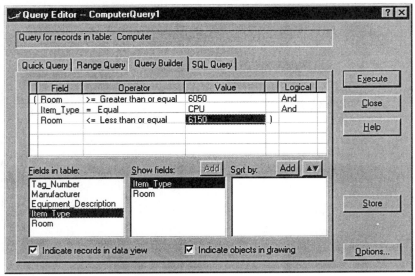

*Figure 37-26 Query Editor (**Query Builder** tab)*

Step 6. Choose the **SQL Query** tab; the query conditions specified earlier will be carried to the tab automatically. Here you can create a query using multiple tables. But select **'Computer'** from the **Table:** list box, **'Tag_Number'** from the **Fields:** list box, **'>= Greater than or equal to'** from the **Operator:** drop-down list and enter **26072** in the **Values:** edit box. You can also select from the available values by choosing the [...] button (Figure 37-27). Choose the **Store** button to save the query.

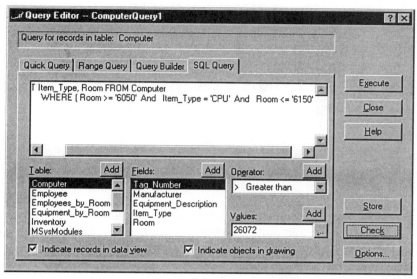

Figure 37-27 Query Editor (SQL Query tab)

Step 7. To check whether the SQL syntax is correct, choose the **Check** button and AutoCAD will display the **Information box** (Figure 37-28) to determine whether the syntax is correct.

Step 8. Choose the **Execute** button to display the **Data View** window showing a subset of records matching the specified query criteria.

Figure 37-28 Information box

Note

You can view the subset of records conforming to your criterion with any of the four tabs during the creation of queries.

Importing and Exporting SQL Queries

You may occasionally be required to use the queries made by some other user in your drawing or vice-versa. AutoCAD allows you to import or export stored queries. Sharing queries is very useful when developing common tools used by all team members on a project. Following is the procedure of **importing a set of queries** into the current drawing:

1. From the **dbConnect** menu, choose **Queries > Import Query Set** to invoke **Import Query Set** dialog box.
2. In the dialog box, select the query set to be imported.

3.   Choose the **Open** button to import the query set into the current drawing.

AutoCAD displays an alert box that you can use to provide a unique name for the query, if there is a query with the same name that is already associated with the current drawing. Following is the procedure of **exporting a set of queries** from the current drawing:

1.   From the **dbConnect** menu, choose **Queries > Export Query Set** to invoke **Export Query Set** dialog box.
2.   In the dialog box, select the directory you want to save the query set to from the **Save In** list.
3.   Under File Name box, specify a name for the query set, and then choose the **Save** button.

FORMING SELECTION SETS USING LINK SELECT*

It is possible to locate objects on the drawing on the basis of the linked nongraphic information. For example, you can locate the object that is linked to the first row of the COMPUTER table or to the first and second rows of the COMPUTER table. You can highlight specified objects or form a selection set of the selected objects. **Link Select** is an advanced feature of the **Query Editor** that can be used to construct iterative selection sets of AutoCAD graphical objects and the database records. You can start constructing a query or selecting AutoCAD graphical objects for iterative selection process. The initial selection set is referred to as **set A**. Now you can select an additional set of queries or graphical objects to further refine your selection set. The second selection set is referred to as **set B**. To refine your final selection set you must establish a relation between set A and set B. The following is the list of available relationships or set operations (Figure 37-29):

Select. This creates an initial query or graphical objects selection set. This selection set can be further refined or modified using subsequent Link Select operations.

Union. This operation adds the outcome of new selection set or query to the existing selection set. Union returns all the records that are member of set A **or** set B.

Intersect. This operation returns the intersection of the new selection set and the existing or running selection set. Intersection returns only the records that are common to both set A **and** set B.

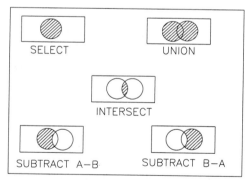

Figure 37-29 Available relationships or Set operations

Subtract A - B. This operation subtracts the result of the new selection set or query from the existing selection set.

Subtract B - A. This operation subtracts the result of the existing selection set or query from the new selection set.

After any of the Link Selection operation is executed, the result of the operation becomes the new running selection set and assigned as set A. You can extend refining your selection set by creating

a new set B and then continuing with the iterative process.
Following is the procedure to use **Link Select** for refining selection set:

1. Choose **Links > Link Select...** from the **dbConnect** menu to invoke the **Link Select** dialog
    box (Figure 37-30).

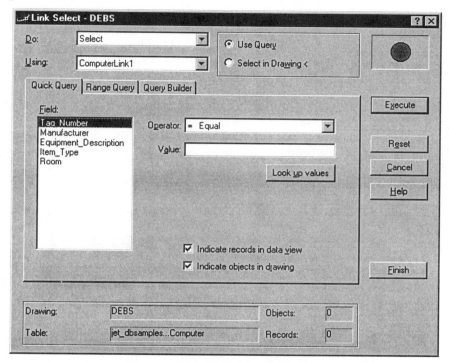

Figure 37-30 Link Select dialog box

2. Select the **Select** option from the **Do:** drop-down list for creating a new selection set. Also
    select a link template from the **Using:** drop-down list.

3. Choose either the **Use Query** or **Select in Drawing <** option for creating a new query or
    drawing object selection set.

4. Choose the **Execute** button to execute the refining operation or **Select** to add your query or
    graphical object selection set.

5. Again choose any **Link Selection** operation from the **Do:** drop-down list.

6. Repeat steps 2 through 4 for creating a set B to the **Link Select** operation and then choose the
    Finish: button to complete the operation.

 Note
*You can choose the **Use Query** option to construct a new query or **Select in Drawing <** to select a
graphical object from the drawing as a selection set.*

If you select **Indicate Records in Data View**, *then the Link Select operation result will be displayed in the* **Data View** *window and if you select* **Indicate objects in drawing**, *then AutoCAD displays a set of linked graphics objects in the drawing.*

CONVERSION OF ASE LINKS TO AUTOCAD 2000 FORMAT*

AutoCAD 2000 stores links in a different format than the previous releases. So if you want to work with your links in AutoCAD 2000, you need to convert them to the AutoCAD 2000 format. You will also have to create a AutoCAD 2000 configuration file that will point to the data source referred by the legacy links. When you open a drawing in AutoCAD 2000 where links were created by earlier releases, AutoCAD attempts to perform an automatic conversion of legacy information. But in some cases, where automatic conversion is not possible or a legacy data source might not match exactly the data source in the AutoCAD 2000 format, you can use the **Link Conversion** dialog box (Figure 37-31). During the conversion process, AutoCAD writes the data source mapping information in **asi.ini** file and applies the information for further usage of the same data source. You can use the following steps to Convert AutoCAD R13 and R14 links to the AutoCAD 2000 format:

1.   To invoke the **Link Conversion** dialog box, choose **dbConnect** menu > **Link Conversion....**

Figure 37-31 Link Conversion dialog box

2.   In **Old Link Format**, enter the following specifications:

Select R13/R14 link format to be converted.
Name of the Environment, Catalog, Schema, and Table.
Link path name of the link that has to be formatted.

3.   In the **New Link Format**, enter the following specifications:

Name of the AutoCAD 2000 data source (for example, **jet_dbsamples**).
Name of the new AutoCAD 2000 Environment, Catalog, Schema, and Table.
Name of the AutoCAD 2000 link template.

4.   Choose **Apply** and then the **OK** button to complete the conversion procedure.

5.   Open the drawing you want to convert and save it in AutoCAD 2000 format drawing.

Saving AutoCAD 2000 Links to R13/R14 Formats*

You can convert Links created in AutoCAD 2000 format as R13 or R14 formats. But you cannot save AutoCAD 2000 links in R12 format. When you select SAVE AS for saving the links with drawings, select links to R13 or R14 formats and AutoCAD will automatically convert into earlier releases format.

Review Questions

1.   The horizontal group of data is called a _____ .

2.   A vertical group of data (attribute) is called a _____ .

3.   AutoCAD can access data contained in a particular database system using _____ _____ .

4.   You can connect to external database table by using _____ manager.

5.   You can edit external database table within AutoCAD session. (T/F)

6.   You can resize, dock as well as hide **Data View** window. (T/F)

7.   Once you define a link, AutoCAD does not store that information with the drawing. (T/F)

8.   To display the associated records with the drawing objects, AutoCAD provides _____ .

9.   Labels are of two types, _____ and _____ .

10. It is possible to import as well as export Link and label templates. (T/F)

11. The SQL statements let you search through the database and retrieve the information as specified in the SQL statements. (T/F)

12. What does ASE stand for? _____

13. What is a database? _____

14. What is a database management system (DBMS)? _____
_____ .

15. A row is also referred as a _____ .

16. A column is sometimes called a _____ .

17. The _____ acts like an identification tag for locating and linking a row.

18. Only one row can be manipulated at a time. This row is called the _____ .

19. **AutoCAD Query Editor** has four tabs, namely _____, _____,
_____, and _____.

20. It is possible to go back to the previous query tab without resetting the values. (T/F)

21. You can execute query after any tab in **Query Editor**.(T/F)

22. Link select is an _____ implementation of AutoCAD **Query Editor**, which constructs selection sets of graphical objects or database records.

23. AutoCAD writes data source mapping information in the _____ file during the conver sion process of links.

24. AutoCAD 2000 links _____ be converted into AutoCAD R12 format.

Exercises

Exercise 1

General

In this exercise, you will select **Employee** table from **Jet_dbsamples** data source in **dbConnect Manager**, then edit the sixth row of the table (EMP_ID=1006, Keyser). You will also add a new row to the table, set the new row current, and then view it.

The row to be added has the following values:

EMP_ID	**1064**
LAST_NAME	**Joel**
FIRST_NAME	**Billy**
Gender	**M**
TITLE	**Marketing Executive**
Department	**Marketing**
ROOM	**6071**

Exercise 2

General

From the **Inventory** table in **Jet_dbsamples** data source, build a SQL query step-by step using all the tabs of the AutoCAD Query Editor. The conditions to be implemented are as follows:

1. Type of Item = **Furniture**   and
2. Range of Cost = **200 to 650**   and
3. Manufacturer = **Office master**

Chapter 27

AutoCAD on the Internet

Learning Objectives

The Internet has become the most important way to exchange information in the world. AutoCAD allows you to interact with the Internet in several ways. It can open and save files that are located on the Internet; it can launch a Web browser (AutoCAD 2000 includes a simple Web browser); and it can create drawing Web format (DWF) files for viewing as drawings on Web pages. After completing this chapter, you will be able to:

- *Launch a Web browser from AutoCAD.*
- *Understand the importance of the uniform resource locator (URL).*
- *Open and save drawings to and from the Internet.*
- *Place hyperlinks in a drawing.*
- *Convert drawings to DWF file format.*
- *View DWF files with a Web browser.*
- *Learn about the Whip plug-in and the DWF file format.*

INTRODUCTION

Before you can use the Internet features in AutoCAD 2000, some components of Microsoft's Internet Explorer must be present in your computer. If Internet Explorer v4.0 (or later) is already set up on your computer, then you already have these required components. If not, then the components are installed automatically when during AutoCAD 2000's setup you select: (1) the **Full Install**; or (2) the **Internet Tools** option during the **Custom** installation.

This chapter introduces you to the following Web-related commands:

BROWSER:
1   Launches a Web browser from within AutoCAD.

HYPERLINK*:
l   Attaches and removes a URL to an object or an area in the drawing.

HYPERLINKFWD*:
l   Move to the next hyperlink (an undocumented command).

HYPERLINKBACK*:
l   Moves back to the previous hyperlink (an undocumented command).

HYPERLINKSTOP*:
l   Stops the hyperlink access action (an undocumented command).

PASTEASHYPERLINK*:
l   Attaches a URL to an object in the drawing from text stored in the Windows Clipboard (an
     undocumented command).

HYPERLINKBASE*:
l   A system variable for setting the path used for relative hyperlinks in the drawing.

In addition, all of AutoCAD 2000's file-related dialog boxes are "Web enabled."

Changes From AutoCAD Release 14

If you used the Internet features in AutoCAD Release 14, then you should be aware of changes in
AutoCAD 2000.

Attached URLs from R14

In AutoCAD R14, attached URLs were not active until the drawing was converted to a DWF file; in
AutoCAD 2000, URLs are active in the drawing.

If you attached URLs to drawing in Release 14 (as well as LT 97 and LT 98), they are converted to
AutoCAD 2000-style hyperlinks the first time you save the drawing in AutoCAD 2000 DWG format.

When you use the **SAVEAS** command to save an AutoCAD 2000 drawing in R14 format, hyperlinks
are converted back to R14-style URLs. Hyperlink descriptions are stored as proxy data and not
displayed in R14/LT (this ensures that hyperlink descriptions are available again when the drawing is brought back to AutoCAD 2000 format.)

WHIP v3.1 Limitations

AutoCAD 2000 can create DWF files compatible with the WHIP v3.1 plug-in. It is recommended,
however, that you download WHIP v4.0 from the Autodesk Web site. Whip v3.1 does not display
the following AutoCAD 2000-specific features:

- Hyperlink descriptions are not saved in v3.1 DWF format.
- All objects, except polylines and traces, are displayed at minimum lineweight.
- Linetypes defined by a plot style table are displayed as continuous lines.
- Nonrectangular viewports are displayed by rectangular viewports.

Changed Internet Commands

Many of Release 14's Internet-related commands have been discontinued and replaced. The following summary describes the status of all R14 Internet commands:

BROWSER (launches Web browser from within AutoCAD): continues to work in AutoCAD 2000; the default is now Home.Html, a Web page located on your computer.

ATTACHURL (attaches a URL to an object or an area in the drawing): continues to work in AutoCAD 2000, but has been superceded by the **-HYPERLINK** command's **Insert** option.

SELECTURL (selects all objects with attached URLs): continues to work in AutoCAD 2000, but has been superceded by the **QSelect** dialog box's **Hyperlink** option.

LISTURL (lists URLs embedded in the drawing): removed from AutoCAD 2000. As a replacement, use the **Properties** dialog box's **Hyperlink** option.

DETACHURL (removes the URL from an object): continues to work in AutoCAD 2000, but has been superceded by the **-HYPERLINK** command's **Remove** option.

DWFOUT (exports the drawing and embedded URLs as a DWF file): continues to work in AutoCAD 2000, but has been superceded by the **Plot** dialog box's **ePlot** option.

DWFOUTD (exports drawing in DWF format without a dialog box): removed from AutoCAD 2000. As a replacement, use the **-PLOT** command's **ePlot** option.

INETCFG (configures AutoCAD for Internet access): removed from AutoCAD 2000; it has been replaced by the **Internet** applet of the Windows Control Panel (choose the **Connection** tab).

INSERTURL (inserts a block from the Internet into the drawing): automatically executes the **INSERT** command and displays the **Insert** dialog box. You may type a URL for the block name.

OPENURL (opens a drawing from the Internet): automatically executes the **OPEN** command and displays the **Select File** dialog box. You may type a URL for the filename.

SAVEURL (saves the drawing to the Internet): automatically executes the **SAVE** command and displays the **Save Drawing As** dialog box. You may type a URL for the filename.

You are probably already familiar with the best-known uses for the Internet: email (electronic mail) and the Web (short for "World Wide Web"). Email lets users exchange messages and data at very low cost. The Web brings together text, graphics, audio, and movies in an easy-to-use format. Other uses of the Internet include FTP (file transfer protocol) for effortless binary file transfer, Gopher (presents data in a structured, subdirectory-like format), and USENET, a collection of more than 10,000 news groups.

AutoCAD allows you to interact with the Internet in several ways. AutoCAD is able to launch a Web browser from within AutoCAD with the **BROWSER** command. Hyperlinks can be inserted in drawings with the **HYPERLINK** command, which lets you link the drawing with other documents on your computer and the Internet. With the **PLOT** command's **ePlot** option (short for "electronic plot"), AutoCAD creates DWF (short for "drawing Web format") files for viewing drawings in 2D format on Web pages. AutoCAD can open, insert, and save drawings to and from the Internet via the **OPEN**, **INSERT**, and **SAVEAS** commands.

Understanding URLs

The uniform resource locator, known as the URL, is the file naming system of the Internet. The URL system allows you to find any resource (a file) on the Internet. Example resources include a text file, a Web page, a program file, an audio or movie clip—in short, anything you might also find on your own computer. The primary difference is that these resources are located on somebody else's computer. A typical URL looks like the following examples:

ExampleURL	Meaning
http://www.autodesk.com	Autodesk Primary Web Site
news://adesknews.autodesk.com	Autodesk News Server
ftp://ftp.autodesk.com	Autodesk FTP Server
http://www.autodeskpress.com	Autodesk Press Web Site
http://users.uniserve.com/~ralphg	Editor Ralph Grabowski's Web site

Note that the **http://** prefix is not required. Most of today's Web browsers automatically add in the *routing* prefix, which saves you a few keystrokes.

URLs can access several different kinds of resources—such as Web sites, email, news groups—but always take on the same general format, as follows:

scheme://netloc

The scheme accesses the specific resource on the Internet, including these:

Scheme	Meaning
file://	File is located on your computer's hard drive or local network
ftp://	File Transfer Protocol (used for downloading files)
http://	Hyper Text Transfer Protocol (the basis of Web sites)
mailto://	Electronic mail (email)
news://	Usenet news (news groups)
telnet://	Telnet protocol
gopher://	Gopher protocol

The **://** characters indicate a network address. Autodesk recommends the following format for specifying URL-style filenames with AutoCAD:

Resource	URL Format
Web Site	**http://**servername/pathname/filename
FTP Site	**ftp://**servername/pathname/filename
Local File	**file:///**drive:/pathname/filename
or	drive:\pathname\filename
or	**file:///**drive|/pathname/filename

or	**file://**/*localPC**pathname**filename*
or	**file://**///*localPC*/*pathname*/*filename*
Network File	**file://**localhost/*drive***:**/*pathname*/*filename*
or	*localhost**drive***:***pathname**filename*
or	**file://**localhost/*drive*│/*pathname*/*filename*

The terminology can be confusing. The following definitions will help to clarify these terms.

Term	Meaning
servername	The name or location of a computer on the Internet, for example: *www.autodesk.com*
pathname	The same as a subdirectory or folder name
drive	The driver letter, such as C: or D:
localpc	A file located on your computer
localhost	The name of the network host computer

If you are not sure of the name of the network host computer, use Windows Explorer to check the Network Neighborhood for the network names of computers.

Launching A Web Browser

The **BROWSER** command lets you start a Web browser from within AutoCAD. Commonly used Web browsers include Netscape's Navigator, Microsoft's Internet Explorer, and Operasoft's Opera.

By default, the **BROWSER** command uses whatever brand of Web browser program is registered in your computer's Windows operating system. AutoCAD prompts you for the uniform resource locator (URL), such as *http://www.autodeskpress.com*. The **BROWSER** command can be used in scripts, toolbar or menu macros, and AutoLISP routines to automatically access the Internet.

Command: **BROWSER**
Browse <C:\CAD\ACAD 2000\Home.htm>: *Enter the URL.*

The default URL is an HTML file added to your computer during AutoCAD's installation. After you type the URL and press *, AutoCAD launches the Web browser and contacts the Web site. Figure 27-1 shows the popular Netscape Navigator with the Autodesk Web site at *http://www.autodesk.com*.

Changing Default Web Site

To change the default Web page that your browser starts with from within AutoCAD, change the setting in the **INETLOCATION** system variable. The variable stores the URL used by the **BROWSER** command and the **Browse the Web** dialog box. Make the change, as follows:

Command: **INETLOCATION**
Enter new value for INETLOCATION <"C:\CAD\ACAD 2000\Home.htm">: *(Type URL.)*

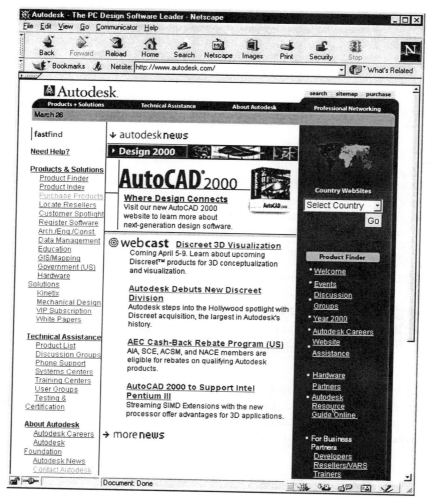

Figure 27-1 Netscape Navigator Displaying the Autodesk Web Site

Drawings on the Internet

When a drawing is stored on the Internet, you access it from within AutoCAD 2000 using the standard **OPEN**, **INSERT**, and **SAVE** commands. (In Release 14, these commands were known as **OPENURL**, **INSERTURL**, and **SAVEURL**.) Instead of specifying the file's location with the usual drive-subdirectory-file name format, such as c:\acad14\filename.dwg, use the URL format. (Recall that the URL is the universal file naming system used by the Internet to access any file located on any computer hooked up to the Internet.)

Opening Drawings from the Internet

To open a drawing from the Internet (or your firm's intranet), use the **OPEN** command (**File > Open**). Notice the three buttons at the upper right of the **Select File** dialog box (see Figure 27-2).

These are specifically for use with the Internet. From left to right, they are:

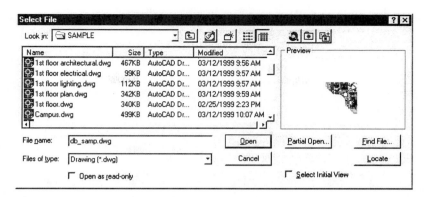

Figure 27-2 Select File dialog box

Search the Web: Displays the **Browse the Web** dialog box, a simplified Web browser.

Look in Favorites: Opens the **Favorites** folder, equivalent to "bookmarks" that store Web addresses.

Add to Favorites: Saves the current URL (hyperlink) to the **Favorites** folder.

When you click the **Search the Web** button, AutoCAD opens the **Browse the Web** dialog box (Figure 27-3). This dialog box is a simplified version of the Microsoft brand of Web browser. The purpose of this dialog box is to allow you to browse files at a Web site.

By default, the **Browse the Web** dialog box displays the contents of the URL stored in the **INETLOCATION** system variable. You can easily change this to another folder or Web site, as noted earlier.

Along the top, the dialog box has six buttons:

Back: Go back to the previous URL.

Forward: Go forward to the next URL.

Stop: Halt displaying the Web page (useful if the connection is slow or the page is very large.)

Refresh: Redisplay the current Web page.

Home: Return to the location specified by the **INETLOCATION** system variable.

Favorites: List stored URLs (hyperlinks) or bookmarks. If you have previously used Internet Explorer, you will find all your favorites listed here. Favorites are stored in the **\Windows\Favorites** folder on your computer.

The **Look in** field allows you to type the URL. Alternatively, click the down arrow to select a previous destination. If you have stored Web site addresses in the Favorites folder, then select a

Figure 27-3 Browse the Web dialog box

URL from that list.

You can either double-click a filename in the window, or type a URL in the **File name** field. The following table gives templates for typing the URL to open a drawing file:

Drawing Location	**Template URL**
Web or HTTP Site	*http://servername/pathname/filename.dwg*
	http://practicewrench.autodeskpress.com/wrench.dwg
FTP Site	*ftp://servername/pathname/filename.dwg*
	ftp://ftp.autodesk.com
Local File	*drive:\pathname\filename.dwg*
	c:\acad 2000\sample\tablet2000.dwg
Network File	*\\localhost\drive:\pathname\filename.dwg*
	\\upstairs\e:\install\sample.dwg

When you open a drawing over the Internet, it will probably take much longer than opening a file found on your computer. During the file transfer, AutoCAD displays a dialog box to report the progress (Figure 27-4). If your computer uses a 28.8Kbps modem, you should allow about five to ten minutes per megabyte of drawing file size. If your computer has access to a faster T1 connection to the Internet, you should expect a transfer speed of about one minute per megabyte.

Figure 27-4 File Download *Dialog Box*

It may be helpful to understand that the **OPEN** command does not copy the file from the Internet location directly into AutoCAD. Instead, it copies the file from the Internet to your computer's designated **Temporary** subdirectory, such as C:\Windows\Temp (and then loads the drawing from the hard drive into AutoCAD). This is known as *caching*. It helps to speed up the processing of the drawing, since the drawing file is now located on your computer's fast hard drive, instead of the relatively slow Internet.

Note that the **Locate** and **Find File** buttons (in the **Select File** dialog box) do not work for locating files on the Internet.

Example 1

The Autodesk Press Web site has an area that allows you to practice using the Internet with AutoCAD. In this example, you open a drawing file located at that Web site.

1.   Start AutoCAD.

2.   Ensure that you have a live connection to the Internet. If you normally access the Internet via a telephone (modem) connection, dial your Internet service provider now.

3.   From the menu bar, select **File > Open.** Or, choose the **Open** button on the toolbar. Notice that AutoCAD displays the **Select File** dialog box.

4.   Click the **Search the Web** button. Notice that AutoCAD displays the **Browse the Web** dialog box.

5.   In the **Look in** field, type:

     practicewrench.autodeskpress.com

     and press ENTER. After a few seconds, the **Browse the Web** dialog box displays the Web site (Figure 27-5).

Chapter 27

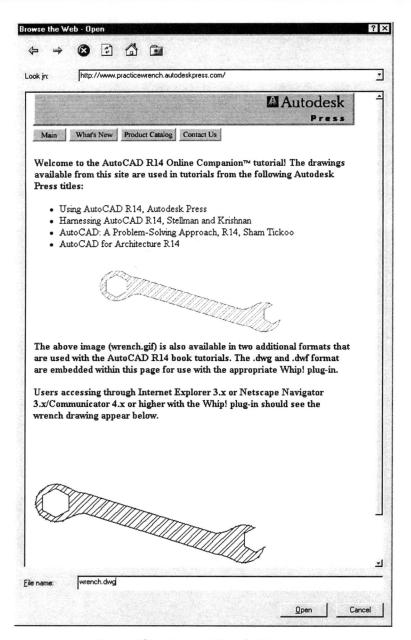

Figure 27-5 Practice Wrench Web site

6. In the Filename field, type:

wrench.dwg
and press ENTER. AutoCAD begins transferring the file. Depending on the speed of your Internet connection, this will take between a couple of seconds and a half-minute. Notice the drawing of the wrench in AutoCAD (Figure 27-6).

Figure 27-6 *Wrench drawing in AutoCAD*

Inserting a Block from the Internet

When a block (symbol) is stored on the Internet, you can access it from within AutoCAD using the **INSERT** command. When the **Insert** dialog box appears, choose the **Browse** button to display the **Select Drawing File** dialog box. This is identical to the dialog box discussed previously.

After you choose the select the file, AutoCAD downloads the file and continues with the **INSERT** command's familiar prompts.

The process is identical for accessing external reference (xref) and raster image files. Other files that AutoCAD can access over the Internet include: 3D Studio, SAT (ACIS solid modeling), DXB (drawing exchange binary), WMF (Windows metafile), and EPS (encapsulated PostScript). All of these options are found in the **Insert** menu on the menu bar.

Accessing Other Files on the Internet

Most other file-related dialog boxes allow you to access files from the Internet or intranet. This allows your firm or agency to have a central location that stores drawing standards. When you need to use a linetype or hatch pattern, for example, you access the LIN or PAT file over the Internet. More than likely, you would have the location of those files stored in the Favorites list. Some examples include:

Linetypes: From the menu bar, choose **Format** > **Linetype**. In the **Linetype Manager** dialog box, choose the **Load**, **File**, and **Look in Favorites** buttons.

Hatch Patterns: Use the Web browser to copy .PAT files from a remote location to your computer.

Multiline Styles: From the menu bar, choose **Format** > **Multiline Style**. In the **Multiline Styles** dialog box, choose the **Load**, **File**, and **Look in Favorites** buttons.

Layer Name: From the menu bar, choose **Express** > **Layers** > **Layer Manager**. In the **Layer Manager** dialog box, choose the **Import** and **Look in Favorites** buttons.

LISP and ARX Applications: From the menu bar, choose **Tools** > **Load Applications**.

Scripts: From the menu bar, choose **Tools** > **Run Scripts**.

Menus: From the menu bar, choose **Tools** > **Customize Menus**. In the **Menu Customization** dialog box, choose the **Browse** and **Look in Favorites** buttons.

Images: From the menu bar, select **Tools** > **Displays Image** > **View**.

You cannot access text files, text fonts (SHX and TTF), color settings, lineweights, dimension styles, plot styles, OLE objects, or named UCSs over the Internet.

Saving the Drawing to the Internet

When you are finished editing a drawing in AutoCAD, you can save it to a file server on the Internet with the **SAVE** command. If you inserted the drawing from the Internet (using **INSERT**) into the default Drawing.Dwg drawing, AutoCAD insists you first save the drawing to your computer's hard drive.

When a drawing of the same name already exists at that URL, AutoCAD warns you, just as it does when you use the **SAVEAS** command. Recall from the **OPEN** command that AutoCAD uses your computer system's Temporary subdirectory, hence the reference to it in the dialog box.

Using Hyperlinks with AutoCAD*

AutoCAD 2000 allows you to employ URLs in two ways: (1) directly within an AutoCAD drawing; and (2) indirectly in DWF files displayed by a Web browser. (URLs are also known as *hyperlinks*, the term we use from now on.)

Hyperlinks are created, edited, and removed with the **HYPERLINK** command (displays a dialog box) and the **-HYPERLINKS** command (for prompts at the command line). The **HYPERLINK** command (**Insert** > **Hyperlink**) prompts you to "Select objects" and then displays the **Insert Hyperlink** dialog box. (As a shortcut, you may press CTRL+K or choose the **Insert Hyperlink** button on the toolbar.)

*Figure 27-7(a) Invoking the **HYPERLINK** command from the **Standard** toolbar*

As an alternative, you may use the **–HYPERLINK** command. This command displays its prompts at the command line, and is useful for scripts and AutoLISP routines. The **–HYPERLINK** command has the following syntax:

*Figure 27-7(b) The **Insert Hyperlink** dialog box*

Command: **-HYPERLINK**
Enter an option [Remove/Insert] <Insert>: *Press ENTER.*
Enter hyperlink insert option [Area/Object] <Object>: *Press ENTER.*
Select objects: *Select an object.*
1 found Select objects: *Press ENTER.*
Enter hyperlink <current drawing>: *Enter the name of the document or Web site.*
Enter named location <none>: *Enter the name of a bookmark or AutoCAD view.*
Enter description <none>: *Enter a description of the hyperlink.*

Notice that the command also allows you to remove a hyperlink. It does not, however, allow you to edit a hyperlink. To do this, use the **Insert** option and respecify the hyperlink data.

In addition, this command allows you to create hyperlink *areas*, which is a rectangular area that can be thought of as a 2D hyperlink (the dialog box-based **HYPERLINK** command does not create hyperlink areas). When you select the **Area** option, the rectangle is placed automatically on layer URLLAYER and colored red (Figure 27-8).

In the following sections, you learn how to apply and use hyperlinks in an AutoCAD drawing and in a Web browser via the dialog box-based **HYPERLINK** command.

Figure 27-8 A rectangular hyperlink area

Hyperlinks Inside AutoCAD*

AutoCAD allows you to add a hyperlink to any object in the
drawing. An object is permitted just a single hyperlink; on the
other hand, a single hyperlink may be applied to a selection set
of objects.

You can tell an object has a hyperlink by passing the cursor
over it. The cursor displays the "linked Earth" icon, as well as a
tooltip describing the link. See Figure 27-9.

Figure 27-9 The cursor reveals a
hyperlink

If, for some reason, you do not want to see the hyperlink cursor, you can turn it off. From the **Tools**
menu, choose **Options**, then choose the **User Preferences** tab. The **Display hyperlink cursor and
shortcut menu** item toggles the display of the hyperlink cursor, as well as the **Hyperlink** tooltip
option on the shortcut menu.

Attaching Hyperlinks*

Let's see how this works with an example.

Example 2

In this example, we have the drawing of a floorplan. To this drawing, we will add hyperlinks to
another AutoCAD drawing, a Word document, and a Web site. Hyperlinks must be attached to
objects. For this reason, we will place some text in the drawing, then attach the hyperlinks to the
text.

1. Start AutoCAD 2000.

2. Open the **1st floor plan.dwg** file found in the AutoCAD 2000 **Sample** folder. (If necessary,
    choose the **Model** tab to display the drawing in model space.)

3. Invoke the **TEXT** command and place the following text in the drawing (Figure 27-10):

    Command: **TEXT**
    Current text style: "Standard" Text height: 0.20000
    Specify start point of text or [Justify/Style]: *Specify a point in the drawing.*
    Specify height <0.2000>: **2**
    Specify rotation angle of text <0>: *Press ENTER.*
    Enter text: **Site Plan**
    Enter text: **Lighting Specs**
    Enter text: **Electrical Bylaw**
    Enter text: *Press ENTER.*

4. Select the "Site Plan" text to select it.

5. Choose the **Insert Hyperlink** button on the toolbar. Notice the **Insert Hyperlinks** dialog box.

Figure 27-10 *Text placed in drawing*

6. Next to the **Link to File or URL** field, choose the **Browse** button. Notice the **Browse the Web – Select Hyperlink** dialog box (Figure 27-11).

Figure 27-11 Browse the Web – Select Hyperlink *dialog box*

7. Go to AutoCAD 2000's **Sample** folder and select the **City base map.dwg** file. Choose **Open**. AutoCAD does not open the drawing; rather, it copies the file's name to the **Insert Hyperlinks** dialog box (Figure 27-12). Notice the name of the drawing you selected in the **Link to File or URL** field.

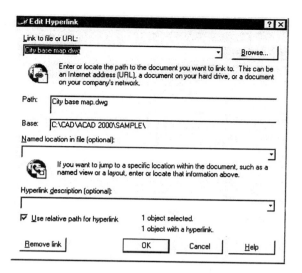

*Figure 27-12 The **Insert Hyperlinks** dialog box*

You can fill in two other fields:

Named Location in File: When the hyperlinked file is opened, it goes to the named location, called a "Bookmark." In AutoCAD, the bookmark is a named view (created with the **VIEW** command).

Hyperlink Description: You may type a description for the hyperlink, which is displayed by the tooltip. If you leave this blank, the URL is displayed by the tooltip.

8.   Choose **OK** to dismiss the dialog box. Move the cursor over the Site Plan text. Notice the display of the "linked Earth" icon; a moment later, the tooltip displays "City base map.dwg"(Figure 27-13).

Figure 27-13 The Hyperlink cursor and tooltip

9.   Repeat the **HYPERLINK** command twice more, attaching these files to the drawing text:

Text	URL
Lighting Specs	License.Rtf (found in the AutoCAD 2000 folder)
Electrical Bylaw	Home.Htm (also found in the AutoCAD 2000 folder)

You have now attached a drawing, a text document, and a Web document to objects in the drawing. Let's try out the hyperlinks.

10. Click "Site Plan" to select it. Right-click and select **Hyperlink > Open "City base map.dwg"** from the shortcut menu (Figure 27-14).

Figure 27-14 Selecting a hyperlink from the shortcut menu

Notice that AutoCAD opens "City base map.dwg". To see both drawings, select **Window > Tile Vertically** from the menu bar (Figure 27-15).

11. Select, then right-click "Lighting Specs" hyperlink. Choose **Hyperlink > Open**. Notice that Windows starts a word processor and opens the License.Rtf file.

Figure 27-15 Viewing two drawings

12. If your word processor has a **Web** toolbar, open it. Choose the **Back** button (the back arrow), as shown in Figure 27-16. Notice how that action sends you back to AutoCAD.

13. Select, then right-click "Electrical Bylaw" hyperlink. Select **Hyperlink > Open**. Notice that Windows starts your Web browser and opens the Home.Html file (Figure 27-17).

14. Back in AutoCAD, right-click any toolbar and choose **Web**. Notice that the **Web** toolbar has four buttons. From left to right, these are:

*Figure 27-18 AutoCAD's **Web** Toolbar*

Button	Command	Meaning
Go Back	**HYPERLINKBACK**	Move back to the previous hyperlink.
Go Forward	**HYPERLINKFWD**	Move to the next hyperlink.
Stop Navigation	**HYPERLINKSTOP**	Stops the hyperlink access action.
Browse the Web	**BROWSER**	Launches the Web browser.

Figure 27-16 *Viewing a Word Document*

15. Try choosing the **Go Forward** and **Go Back** buttons. Notice how these allow you to navigate between the two drawings, the RTF document, and the Web page.
    When you work with hyperlinks in AutoCAD, you may come across these limitations:

    • AutoCAD does not check that the URL you type is valid.
    • If you attach a hyperlink to a block, be aware that the hyperlink data is lost when you scale the block unevenly, stretch the block, or explode it.
    • Wide polylines and rectangular hyperlink areas are only "sensitive" on their outline.

Figure 27-17 Viewing a Web Site

Pasting As Hyperlink*

AutoCAD 2000 has a shortcut method for creating hyperlinks in the drawing. The undocumented **PASTEASHYPERLINK** command pastes any text in the Windows Clipboard as a hyperlink to any object in the drawing. Here is how it works:

1. In a word processor, select some text and copy it to the Clipboard (via CTRL+C or choose **Edit > Copy**). The text can be a URL (such as http://www.autodeskpress.com) or any other text.

2. Switch to AutoCAD and select **Edit > Paste As Hyperlink** from the menu bar. Note that this command does not work (is grayed out) if anything else is in the Clipboard, such as a picture.

3. Select one or more objects, as prompted:
    Command: _pasteashyperlink
    Select objects: *Select an object.*
    1 found Select objects: *Press ENTER.*

4. Pass the cursor over the object and note the hyperlink cursor and tooltip. The tooltip displays the same text that you copied from the document.

If the text you copy to the Clipboard is very long, AutoCAD displays only portions of it in the tooltip, using ellipses (...) to shorten the text. You cannot select text in the AutoCAD drawing to paste as a hyperlink.

You can, however, copy the hyperlink from one object to another. Select the object, right-click, and select **Hyperlink > Copy Hyperlink** from the shortcut menu. The hyperlink is copied to the Clipboard. You can now paste the hyperlink into another document, or use AutoCAD's **Edit > Paste as Hyperlink** command to attach the hyperlink to another object in the drawing.

 Note

*The **MATCHPROP** command does not work with hyperlinks.*

Highlighting Objects with URLs*

Although you can see the rectangle of area URLs, the hyperlinks themselves are invisible. For this reason, AutoCAD has the **QSELECT** command, which highlights all objects that match specifications. From the menu bar, choose **Tools > Quick Select**. AutoCAD displays the **Quick Select** dialog box (Figure 27-19).

In the fields, enter these specifications:

> Apply to: **Entire drawing**
> Object type: **Multiple**
> Properties: **Hyperlink**
> Operator: *** Wildcard Match**
> Value: *****

*Figure 27-19 The **Quick Select** dialog box*

Choose **OK** and AutoCAD highlights all objects that have a hyperlink. Depending on your computer's display system, the highlighting shows up as dashed lines or as another color.

Editing Hyperlinks*

Now that you know where the objects with hyperlinks are located, you can use the **HYPERLINK** command to edit the hyperlinks and related data. Select the hyperlinked object and invoke the **HYPERLINK** command. When the **Edit Hyperlink** dialog box appears (it looks identical to the **Insert Hyperlink** dialog box), make the changes and choose **OK**.

Removing Hyperlinks from Objects*

To remove a URL from an object, use the **HYPERLINK** command on the object. When the **Edit Hyperlink** dialog box appears, choose the **Remove Hyperlink** button.

To remove a rectangular area hyperlink, you can simply use the **ERASE** command; select the rectangle and AutoCAD erases the rectangle. (Unlike in Release 14, AutoCAD no longer purges the URLLAYER layer.)

As an alternative, you may use the **–HYPERLINK** command's **Remove** option, as follows:

> Command: **-HYPERLINK**
> Enter an option [Remove/Insert] <Insert>: R
> Select objects: ALL
> 1 found Select objects: *Press ENTER.*
> 1. *www.autodesk.com*
> 2. *www.autodeskpress.com*
> Enter number, hyperlink, or * for all: 1
> Remove, deleting the Area.
> 1 hyperlink deleted.

Hyperlinks Outside AutoCAD*

The hyperlinks you place in the drawing are also available for use outside of AutoCAD. The Web browser makes use of the hyperlink(s) when the drawing is exported in DWF format. To help make the process clearer, here are the steps that you need to go through:

Step 1

1   Open a drawing in AutoCAD.

Step 2

1   Attach hyperlinks to objects in the drawing with the **HYPERLINK** command. To attach hyperlinks to areas, use the **–HYPERLINK** command's **Area** option.

Step 3

1   Export the drawing in DWF format using the **PLOT** command's "DWF ePlot PC2" plotter configuration.

Step 4

1   Copy the DWF file to your Web site.

Step 5

1   Start your Web browser with the **BROWSER** command.

Step 6

1   View the DWF file and click on a hyperlink spot.

THE DRAWING WEB FORMAT

To display AutoCAD drawings on the Internet, Autodesk invented a new file format called drawing Web format (DWF). The DWF file has several benefits and some drawbacks over DWG files. The DWF file is compressed as much as eight times smaller than the original DWG drawing file so that it takes less time to transmit over the Internet, particularly with the relatively slow telephone modem connections. The DWF format is more secure, since the original drawing is not being displayed; another user cannot tamper with the original DWG file.

However, the DWF format has some drawbacks:

- You must go through the extra step of translating from DWG to DWF.
- DWF files cannot display rendered or shaded drawings.
- DWF is a flat 2D-file format; therefore, it does not preserve 3D data, although you can export a 3D view.
- AutoCAD itself cannot display DWF files.
- DWF files cannot be converted back to DWG format without using file translation software from a third-party vendor.
- Earlier versions of DWF did not handle paperspace objects (version 2.x and earlier), or linewidths and non-rectangular viewports (version 3.x and earlier).

To view a DWF file on the Internet, your Web browser needs a *plug-in*—a software extension that lets a Web browser handle a variety of file formats. Autodesk makes the DWF plug-in freely available from its Web site at *http://www.autodesk.com/whip*. It is a good idea to regularly check for updates to the DWF plug-in, which is updated about twice a year.

Other DWF Viewing Options

In addition to Whip with a Web browser, Autodesk provides two other options for viewing DWF files.
CADViewer Light is designed to be a DWF viewer that works on all operating systems and computer hardware because it is written in Java. As long as your Windows, Mac, or Unix computer has access to Java (included with most Web browsers), you can view DWF files.

Volo View Express is a stand-alone viewer that views and prints DWG, DWF, and DXF files. Both products can be downloaded free from the Autodesk Web site.

Viewing DWG Files

To view AutoCAD DWG and DXF files on the Internet, your Web browser needs a DWG-DXF plug-in. At the time of publication, the plug-ins were available from the following vendors:

Autodesk: *http://www.autodesk.com/whip*

SoftSource: *http://www.softsource.com/*
California Software Labs: *http://www.cswl.com*
Cimmetry systems: *http://www.cimmetry.com*

Creating a DWF File*

To create a DWF file from AutoCAD 2000, follow these steps:

1. Type the **PLOT** command or choose **Plot** from the **File** menu. Notice that AutoCAD displays the **Plot** dialog box (Figure 27-20).

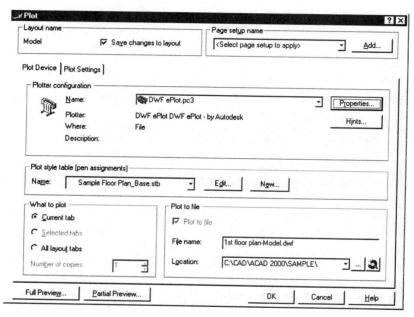

***Figure 27-20 Plot** Dialog Box*

2. In the **Name** list box (found in the **Plotter Configuration** area), select **DWF ePlot pc3**.

3. Choose the **Properties** button. Notice the **Plotter Configuration Editor** dialog box (Figure 27-21).

4. Choose **Custom Properties** in the tree view. Notice the **Custom Properties** button, which appears in the lower half of the dialog box.

5. Choose the **Custom Properties** button. Notice the **DWF Properties** dialog box (Figure 27-22).

Figure 27-21 Plotter Configuration Editor dialog box

Figure 27-22 DWF Properties Dialog Box.

Resolution

Unlike AutoCAD DWG files, which are based on real numbers, DWF files are saved using integer numbers. The **Medium** precision setting saves the drawing using 16-bit integers, which is adequate for all but the most complex drawings. **High** resolution saves the DWF file using 20-bit integers, while **Extreme** resolution saves using 32-bit integers. Figure 27-23 shows an extreme close-up of a drawing exported in DWF format. The portion at left was saved at medium resolution and shows some bumpiness in the arcs. The portion at right was saved at extreme resolution.

More significant is the difference in file size. When a DWF file was created from the "1st floor plan.dwg" file (342KB), the medium resolution DWF file was just 27KB, while the extreme resolution file became 1,100KB – some 40 times larger. That means that the medium resolution DWF file transmits over the Internet 40 times faster, a significant savings in time.

Figure 27-23 DWF output in medium resolution (at left) and extreme resolution (at right).

Format

Compression further reduces the size of the DWF file. You should always use compression, unless you know that another application cannot decompress the DWF file. Compressed binary format is seven times smaller than ASCII format (7,700KB). Again, that means the compressed DWF file transmits over the Internet seven times faster than an ASCII DWF file.

Other Options

Background Color Shown in Viewer: While white is probably the best background color, you may choose any of AutoCAD's 255 colors.

Include Layer Information: This option includes layers, which allows you to toggle layers off and on when the drawing is viewed by the Web browser.

Include Scale and Measurement Information: This allows you to use the **Location** option in the Web browser's Whip plug-in to show scaled coordinate data.

Show Paper Boundaries: Includes a rectangular boundary at the drawing's extents.

Convert .DWG Hyperlink Extensions to .DWF: Includes hyperlinks in the DWF file.

In most cases, you would turn on all options.

7. Choose **OK** to exit the dialog boxes back to the **Plot** dialog box.
8. Accept the DWF file name listed in the **File name** text box, or type a new name. If necessary, change the location that the file will be stored in. Note the two buttons: one has an ellipsis (...), which displays the **Browse for Folder** dialog box. The second button brings up AutoCAD's internal Web browser, a simplified version of the Microsoft-branded product.

9. Choose **OK** to save the drawing in DWF format.

Viewing DWF Files

To view a DWF file, you need to use a Web browser with a special plug-in that allows the browser to correctly interpret the file. (Remember: you cannot view a DWF file with AutoCAD.) Autodesk has named their DWF plug-in "Whip!," short for "Windows HIgh Performance."

Autodesk updates the DWF plug-in approximately twice a year. Each update includes some new features. In summary, all versions of the DWF plug-in perform the following functions:

- Views DWF files created by AutoCAD within a browser.
- Right-clicking the DWF image displays a shortcut menu with commands.
- Real-time pan and zoom lets you change the view of the DWF file as quickly as a drawing file in AutoCAD.
- Embedded hyperlinks let you display other documents and files.
- File compression means that a DWF file appears in your Web browser much faster than the equivalent DWG drawing file would.
- Print the DWF file alone or along with the entire Web page.
- Works with Netscape Navigator or Microsoft Internet Explorer. A separate plug-in is required, depending upon which of the two browsers you use.
- Allows you to "drag and drop" a DWG file from a Web site into AutoCAD as a new drawing or as a block.
- Views a named view stored in the DWF file.
- Can specify a view using x,y- coordinates.
- Toggles layers off and on.

If you don't know whether the DWF plug-in is installed in your Web browser, select **Help > About Plug-ins** from the browser's menu bar. You may need to scroll through the list of plug-ins to find something like this (Figure 27-24):

If the plug-in is not installed, or is an older version, then you need to download it from Autodesk's Web site at:

http://www.autodesk.com/whip

For Netscape users, the file is quite large at 3.5MB and takes about a half-hour to download using a typical 28.8Kbaud modem. The file you download from the Autodesk Web site is either a self-installing file (has a .JAR extension) or a self-extracting installation file with a name such as Whip4.Exe. After the download is complete, follow the instructions on the screen.

For Internet Explorer users, the DWF plug-in is an ActiveX control. It is automatically installed into Explorer when you set up AutoCAD 2000.

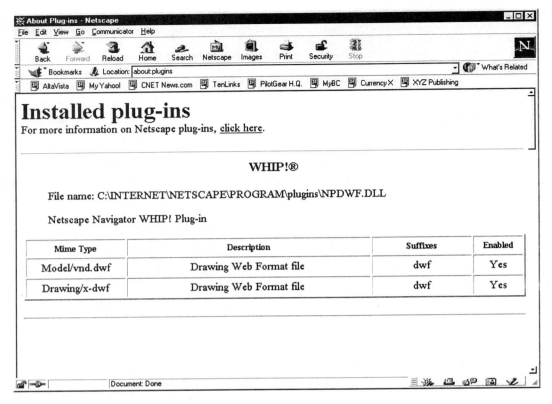

Figure 27-24 Checking the status of browser plug-ins

DWF Plug-in Commands

To display the DWF plug-in's commands, move the cursor over the DWF image and press the mouse's right button. This displays a shortcut menu with options, such as **Pan**, **Zoom**, and **Named Views** (Figure 27-25). To select an option, move the cursor over the option name and press the left mouse button.

Pan is the default option. Press the left mouse button and move the mouse. The cursor changes to an open hand, signaling that you can pan the view around the drawing. This is exactly the same as real-time panning in AutoCAD. Naturally, panning only works when you are zoomed in; it does not work in Full View mode.

Zoom is like the **ZOOM** command in AutoCAD. The cursor changes to a magnifying glass. Hold down the left mouse button and move the cursor up (to zoom in) and down (to zoom out).

Zoom Rectangle is the same as **ZOOM Window** in AutoCAD. The cursor changes to a plus sign. Click the left mouse button at one corner, then drag the rectangle to specify the size of the new view.

Fit to Window is the same as AutoCAD's **ZOOM Extents** command. You see the entire drawing.

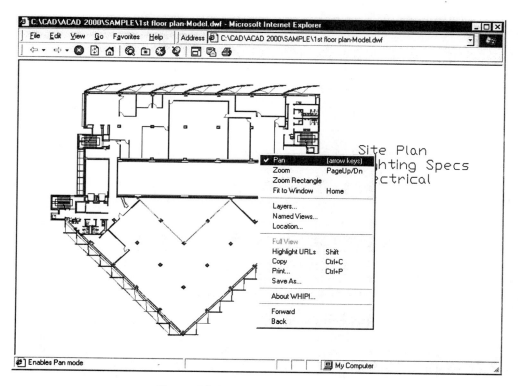

Figure 27-25 Whip's shortcut menu

Layers displays a non-modal dialog box (Figure 27-26), which lists all layers in the drawing. (A *non-modal* dialog box remains on the screen; unlike AutoCAD's modal dialog boxes, you do not need to dismiss a non-modal dialog box to continue working.) Click a layer name to toggle its visibility between on (yellow light bulb icon) and off (blue light bulb).

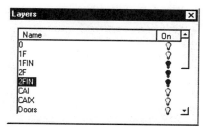

Figure 27-26 Whip's **Layer** dialog box

Named Views works only when the original DWG drawing file contained named views created with the **VIEW** command. Selecting **Named Views** displays a non- modal dialog box that allows you to select a named view (Figure 27-27). Click a named view to see it; click the small **x** in the upper-right corner to dismiss the dialog box.

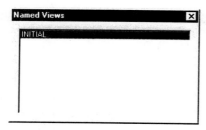

*Figure 27-27 Whip's **Named Views** dialog box*

Location displays a non-modal dialog box that shows the x,y,z-coordinates of the cursor location (Figure 27-28). Since DWF files are only 2D, the Z coordinate is always 0.

Current Location		
X: 83.6772	Y: 43.1822	Z: 0

*Figure 27-28 **Whip's Location** dialog box*

Full View causes the Web browser to display the DWF image as large as possible all by itself. This is useful for increasing the physical size of a small DWF image. When you have finished viewing the large image, right-click and choose the **Back** or choose the browser's **Back** button to return to the previous screen.

Highlight URLs displays a flashing gray effect on all objects and areas with a hyperlink (Figure 27-29). This helps you see where the hyperlinks are. To read the associated URL, pass the cursor over a highlighted area and look at the URL on the browser's status line. (A shortcut is to hold down the SHIFT key, which causes the URLs to highlight until you release the key). Choosing the **URL** opens the document with its associated application.

Copy copies the DWF image to the Windows Clipboard in EMF (enhanced Metafile or "Picture") format.

Print prints the DWF image alone. To print the entire Web page (including the DWF image), use the browser's **Print** button.

Save As saves the DWF file in three formats to your computer's hard drive:
    DWF
    BMP (Windows bitmap)
    DWG (AutoCAD drawing file) works only when a copy of the DWG file is available at the same subdirectory as the DWF file.

You cannot use the **Save As** option until the entire DWF file has been transmitted to your computer.

Figure 27-29 Highlighting hyperlinks

About WHIP displays information about the DWF file, including DWF file revision number, description, author, creator, source filename, creation time, modification time, source creation time, source modification time, current view left, current view right, current view bottom, and current view top (Figure 27-30).

Forward is almost the same as choosing the browser's **Forward** button. When the DWF image is in a frame, only that frame goes forward.

Back is almost the same as choosing the browser's **Back** button. It works differently when the DWF image is displayed in a frame.

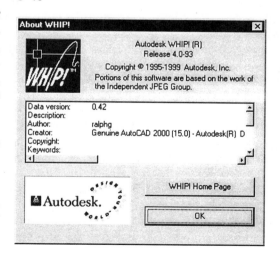

Figure 27-30 About dialog box

Drag and Drop from Browser to Drawing

The DWF plug-in allows you to perform several "drag and drop" functions. *Drag and drop* is when you use the mouse to drag an object from one application to another.

Hold down the (key to drag a DWF file from the browser into AutoCAD. Recall that AutoCAD cannot translate a DWF file into DWG drawing format. For this reason, this form of drag and drop only works when the originating DWG file exists in the same subdirectory as the DWF file. AutoCAD executes the **-INSERT** command, as follows:

> Command: _.-insert
> Enter block name or [?]: C:\CAD\ACAD 2000\SAMPLE\1st floor plan.dwg
> Specify insertion point or [Scale/X/Y/Z/Rotate/PScale/PX/PY/PZ/PRotate]: 0,0
> Enter X scale factor, specify opposite corner, or [Corner/XYZ] <1>: *Press ENTER.*
> Enter Y scale factor <use X scale factor>: *Press ENTER.*
> Specify rotation angle <0>: *Press ENTER.*

To see the inserted drawing, you may need to use the **ZOOM Extents** command.

Another drag and drop function is to drag a DWF file from the Windows Explorer (or File Manager) into the Web browser. This causes the Web browser to load the DWF plug-in, then display the DWF file. Once displayed, you can execute all of the commands listed in the previous section.

Finally, you can also drag and drop a DWF file from Windows Explorer (in Windows 95/98) or File Manager (in Windows NT) into AutoCAD. This causes AutoCAD to launch another program that is able to view the DWF file. This does not work if you do not have other software on your computer system capable of viewing DWF files.

Embedding a DWF File

To let others view your DWF file over the Internet, you need to embed the DWF file in a Web page. Here are the steps to embedding a DWF file in a Web page.

Step 1. This hype text markup language (HTML) code is the most basic method of placing a DWF file in your Web page:
> <embed src="filename.dwf">

The **<embed>** tag embeds an object in a Web page. The **src** option is short for "source." Replace **filename.dwf** with the URL of the DWF file. Remember to keep the quotation marks in place.

Step 2. HTML normally displays an image as large as possible. To control the size of the DWF file, add the **Width** and **Height** options:
> <embed width=800 height=600 src="filename.dwf">

The **Width** and **Height** values are measured in pixels. Replace 800 and 600 with any appropriate numbers, such as 100 and 75 for a "thumbnail" image, or 300 and 200 for a small image.

Step 3. To speed up a Web page's display speed, some users turn off the display of images. For this reason, it is useful to include a description, which is displayed in place of the image:
> <embed width=800 height=600 name=description src="filename.dwf">

The **Name** option displays a textual description of the image when the browser does not load images. You might replace description with the DWF filename.

Step 4. When the original drawing contains named views created by the **VIEW** command, these are transferred to the DWF file. Specify the initial view for the DWF file:

<embed width=800 height=600 name=description namedview="viewname" src="filename.dwf">

The **namedview** option specifies the name of the view to display upon loading. Replace **viewname** with the name of a valid view name. When the drawing contains named views, the user can right-click on the DWF image to get a list of all named views.

As an alternative, you can specify the 2D coordinates of the initial view:

<embed width=800 height=600 name=description view="0,0 9,12" src="filename.dwf">

The **View** option specifies the x,y-coordinates of the lower-left and upper-right corners of the initial view. Replace 0,0 9,12 with other coordinates. Since DWF is 2D only, you cannot specify a 3D viewpoint. You can use **View** or **Namedview**, but not both.

Step 5. Before a DWF image can be displayed, the Web browser must have the DWF plug-in called "Whip!". For users of Netscape Communicator, you must include a description of where to get the Whip plug-in when the Web browser is lacking it.

<embed pluginspage=http://www.autodesk.com/products/autocad/whip/whip.htm width=800 height=600 name=description view="0,0 9,12" src="filename.dwf">

The **pluginspage** option describes the page on the Autodesk Web site where the Whip-DWF plug-in can be downloaded.

The code listed above works for Netscape Navigator. To provide for users of Internet Explorer, the following HTML code must be added:

<object classid ="clsid:B2BE75F3-9197-11CF-ABF4-08000996E931" codebase = "ftp://ftp.autodesk.com/pub/autocad/plugin/whip.cab#version=2,0,0,0" width=800 height=600>
<param name="Filename" value="filename.dwf">
<param name="View" value="0,0 9,12">
<param name="Namedview" value="viewname">
<embed pluginspage=http://www.autodesk.com/products/autocad/whip/whip.htm width=800 height=600 name=description view="0,0 9,12" src="filename.dwf">
</object>

The two **<object>** and three **<param>** tags are ignored by Netscape Navigator; they are required for compatibility with Internet Explorer. The **classid** and **codebase** options tell Explorer where to find the plug-in. Remember that you can use **View** or **Namedview** but not both.

Step 6: Save the HTML file.

Chapter 27

Review Questions

1. Can you launch a Web browser from within AutoCAD? _____

2. What does DWF mean? _____

3. What is the purpose of DWF files? _____

4. URL is an acronym for? _____

5. Which of the following URLs are valid?
   www.autodesk.com
   http://www.autodesk.com
   Both of the above.
   None of the above.

6. FTP is an acronym for: _____

7. What is a "local host"? _____

8. Are hyperlinks active in an AutoCAD 2000 drawing? _____

9. The purpose of URLs is to let you create _____ between files.

10. When you attach a hyperlink to a block, the hyperlink data is _____ when you scale the block unevenly, stretch the block, or explode it.

11. Can you can attach a URL to any object? _____

12. The **-HYPERLINK** command allows you to attach a hyperlink to _____ and_____.

13. To see the location of hyperlinks in a drawing, use the _____ command.

14. Rectangular (area) hyperlinks are stored on layer:_____.

15. Compression in the DWF file causes it to take (less, more, the same) time to transmit over the Internet.

16. A DWF is created from a _____ file using the _____ command.

17. What does a "plug-in" let a Web browser do?

18. Can a Web browser view DWG drawing files over the Internet? _____

19. _____ is an HTML tag for embedding graphics in a Web page.

20. A file being transmitted over the Internet via a 28.8Kpbs modem takes about _____ minutes per megabyte.

Customizing AutoCAD

Author's Web Sites

For Faculty: Please contact the author at **stickoo@calumet.purdue.edu** to access the Web Site that contains the following:

1. **Power Point presentations, programs, and drawings used in this textbook.**
2. **Syllabus, chapter objectives and hints, and questions with answers for every chapter.**

For Students:You can download drawing-exercises, tutorials, programs, and special topics by accessing authors Web Site at **http://www.calumet.purdue.edu/public/mets/tickoo/index.html**.

Chapter 28

Template Drawings

Learning Objectives

After completing this chapter, you will be able to:

* *Create template drawings.*
* *Load template drawings using dialog boxes and the command line.*
* *Do initial drawing setup.*
* *Customize drawings with layers and dimensioning specifications.*
* *Customize drawings with viewports and paper space.*

CREATING TEMPLATE DRAWINGS

One way to customize AutoCAD is to create template drawings that contain initial drawing setup information and, if desired, visible objects and text. When the user starts a new drawing, the settings associated with the template drawing are automatically loaded. If you start a new drawing from scratch, AutoCAD loads default setup values. For example, the default limits are (0.0,0.0), (12.0,9.0) and the default layer is 0 with white color and continuous linetype. Generally, these default parameters need to be reset before generating a drawing on the computer using AutoCAD. A considerable amount of time is required to set up the layers, colors, linetypes, limits, snaps, units, text height, dimensioning variables, and other parameters. Sometimes, border lines and a title block may also be needed.

In production drawings, most of the drawing setup values remain the same. For example, the company title block, border, layers, linetypes, dimension variables, text height, LTSCALE, and other drawing setup values do not change. You will save considerable time if you save these values and reload them when starting a new drawing. You can do this by making template drawings, which can contain the initial drawing setup information, set according to company specifications. They can also contain a border, title block, tolerance table, block definitions, floating viewports in the paper space, and perhaps some notes and instructions that are common to all drawings.

THE STANDARD TEMPLATE DRAWINGS

The AutoCAD software package comes with standard template drawings like acad.dwt, acadiso.dwt, ansi_a.dwt, din_a.dwt, iso_a4.dwt, jis_a3.dwt. The ansi, din, and iso template drawings are based on the drawing standards developed by ANSI (American National Standards Institute), DIN (German), and ISO (International Organization for Standardization). When you start a new drawing, AutoCAD displays the **Create New Drawing** dialog box on the screen. To load the template drawing, select the **Use a Template** button and AutoCAD will display the list of standard template drawings. From this list you can select any template drawing according to your requirements. If you want to start a drawing with default setting, select the **Start from Scratch** button in the **Create New Drawing** dialog box. The following are some of the system variables, with the default values that are assigned to a new drawing:

System Variable Name	Default Value	
BASE	0.0000,0.0000,0.0000	
BLIPMODE	Off	
CHAMFERA	0.5000	
CHAMFERB	0.5000	
COLOR	Bylayer	
DIMALT	Off	
DIMALTD	2	
DIMALTF	25.4	
DIMPOST	None	
DIMASO	On	
DIMASZ	0.18	
DRAGMODE	Auto	
ELEVATION	0	
FILLMODE	On	
FILLETRAD	0.5000	
GRID	0.5000	
GRIDMODE	0	
ISOPLANE	Left	
LIMMIN	0.0000,0.0000	
LIMMAX	12.0000,9.0000	
LTSCALE	1.0	
MIRRTEXT	1	(Text mirrored like other objects)
ORTHOMODE	0 (Off)	
TILEMODE	1 (On)	
TRACEWID	0.0500	

Example 1

Create a template drawing with the following specifications. The name of the template drawing is **PROTO1**.

Limits	18.0,12.0
Snap	0.25
Grid	0.50

Text height	0.125
Units	Decimal
	2-digits to the right of decimal point
	Decimal degrees
	2-digits to the right of decimal point
	0 angle along positive X axis (east)
	Angle positive if measured counterclockwise

Start AutoCAD and select the **Start from Scratch** button in the **Start Up** dialog box (Figure 28-1). You can also invoke the **Create New Drawing** dialog box by selecting New in the **File** menu or entering **NEW** at AutoCAD Command prompt.

Figure 28-1 Start Up dialog box

Once you are in the Drawing Window, use the following AutoCAD commands to set up the values as given in Example 1.

Command: **LIMITS**
Specify lower left corner or [ON/OFF] <0.00,0.00>: **0,0**
Specify upper right corner <12.0,9.0>: **18.0,12.0**

Command: **SNAP**
Specify snap spacing or [ON/OFF/Aspect/Rotate/Style/Type] <0.5000>: **0.25**

Command: **GRID**
Specify grid spacing(X) or [ON/OFF/Snap/Aspect] <0.5000>: **0.50**

Command: **SETVAR**
Enter variable name or [?]: **TEXTSIZE**
Enter new value for TEXTSIZE <0.2000>: **0.125**

Using the Dialog Box. You can use the **Drawing Units** dialog box (Figure 28-2) to set the units. To invoke the **Drawing Units** dialog box, enter **DDUNITS** or **UNITS** at AutoCAD Command prompt or select **Units** in the **Format** menu.

Figure 28-2 Unit Control dialog box   *Figure 28-3* Direction Control dialog

Using UNITS Command. You can also use the **-UNITS** command to set the units.

Command: **-UNITS**
 Report formats: **Examples:**
  1. Scientific   1.55E+01
  2. Decimal   15.50
  3. Engineering   1'-3.50"
  4. Architectural   1'-3 1/2"
  5. Fractional   15 1/2

With the exception of the Engineering and Architectural formats, these formats can be used with any basic units of measurement. For example, Decimal mode is perfect for metric units as well as decimal English units.

 Enter choice, 1 to 5<2>: **2**
 Number of digits to right of decimal point (0 to 8)<4>: **2**

  Systems of angle measure: **Examples:**
  1. Decimal degrees   45.0000
  2. Degrees/minutes/seconds 45d0'0"
  3. Grads   50.0000g
  4. Radians   0.7854r
  5 Surveyor's units   N 45d0'0"

 Enter choice, 1 to 5<1>: **1**

Number of fractional places for display of angles (0 to 8)<0>: **2**
Direction for angle 0.00:

East	3 o'clock	= 0.00
North	12 o'clock	= 90.00
West	9 o'clock	= 180.00
South	6 o'clock	= 270.00

Enter direction for angle 0.00<0.00>: **0**
Do you want angles measured clockwise?<N>: **N**

Now, save the drawing as **PROTO1.DWT** using AutoCAD's **SAVE** or **SAVEAS** command. You must select template (*DWT) from the list box in the dialog box. This drawing is now saved as PROTO1.DWT on the default drive. You can also save this drawing on a floppy diskette in drives A or B.

Command: **SAVE**
Save Drawing as <Drawing.dwg>: **A:PROTO1.DWT**

LOADING A TEMPLATE DRAWING
Using the Dialog Box

You can use the template drawing any time you want to start a new drawing. To use the preset values of the template drawing, start AutoCAD or enter the **NEW** command (Command: **NEW**) to start a new drawing. AutoCAD displays the **Create New Drawing** dialog box (Figure 28-4).

You can also start a new drawing by selecting the **File** menu and then selecting the **New** option from this menu. To load the template drawing, select the **Use a Template** button; AutoCAD will display the list of template drawings. Select **PROTO1** template drawing and then select the **OK**

Figure 28-4 Create New Drawing dialog box

button to exit the dialog box. AutoCAD will start a new drawing that will have the same setup as that of template drawing, **PROTO1**.

You can have several template drawings, each with a different setup. For example, **PROTOB** for a 18" by 12" drawing, **PROTOC** for a 24" by 18" drawing, **PROTOD** for a 36" by 24" drawing, and **PROTOE** for a 48" by 36" drawing. Each template drawing can be created according to user-defined specifications. You can then load any of these template drawings as discussed previously.

Using the NEW Command

You can create a new drawing without using the dialog boxes by assigning a value of 0 to the AutoCAD system variable **FILEDIA**. To start a new drawing, enter **NEW** at the Command: prompt (Command: **NEW**) and AutoCAD will prompt you to enter the name of the drawing. The format for entering the name of the template drawing is:

Command: **NEW**
Enter template file name or [. (for none)] <current>: *Enter template drawing name.*

CUSTOMIZING DRAWINGS WITH LAYERS AND DIMENSIONING SPECIFICATIONS

Most production drawings need multiple layers for different groups of objects. In addition to layers, it is a good practice to assign different colors to different layers to control the line width at the time of plotting. You can generate a template drawing that contains the desired number of layers with linetypes and colors according to your company specifications. You can then use this template drawing to make a new drawing. The next example illustrates the procedure used for customizing a drawing with layers, linetypes, and colors.

Example 2

You want to create a template drawing (**PROTO2**) that has a border and the company's title block, as shown in Figure 28-5. In addition to this, you want the following initial drawing setup:

Limits	48.0,36.0
Snap	1.0
Grid	4.00
Text height	0.25
PLINE width	0.02
Ltscale	4.0

DIMENSIONS	
DIMSCALE	4.0
DIMTAD	1
DIMTIX	ON
DIMTOH	OFF
DIMTIH	OFF
DIMSCALE	25

(Use the **DIMSTYLE** command to save these values in the MYDIM1 dimension style file.)

LAYERS

Layer Names	Line Type	Color
0	Continuous	White
OBJ	Continuous	Red
CEN	Center	Yellow
HID	Hidden	Blue
DIM	Continuous	Green
BOR	Continuous	Magenta

Figure 28-5 Template drawing for Example 2

Start a new drawing with default parameters. You can do this by selecting the Start from Scratch button in the Create New Drawing dialog box. Once you are in the drawing editor, use the AutoCAD commands to set up the values as given for this example. Also, draw a border and a title block as shown in Figure 28-5. In this figure the hidden lines indicate the drawing limits. The border lines are 0.5 units inside the drawing limits. For the border lines, use a polyline of width 0.02 units. Use the following command sequence to produce the prototype drawing for Example 2:

Command: **LIMITS**
Specify lower left corner or [ON/OFF] <0.00,0.00>: **0,0**
Specify upper right corner <12.0,9.0>: **48.0,36.0**

Command: **SNAP**
Specify snap spacing or [ON/OFF/Aspect/Rotate/Style/Type] <0.5000>: **1.0**

Command: **GRID**
Specify grid spacing(X) or [ON/OFF/Snap/Aspect] <1.0>: **4.00**

Command: **SETVAR**
Enter variable name or [?]: **TEXTSIZE**
Enter new value for TEXTSIZE <0.2000>: **0.25**

Command: **PLINEWID**
Enter new value for PLINEWID <0.0000>: **0.02**

Command: **PLINE**
Specify start point: **1.0,1.0**
Current line-width is **0.02**
Specify next point or [Arc/Close/Halfwidth/Length/Undo/Width]:**47,1**
Specify next point or [Arc/Close/Halfwidth/Length/Undo/Width]:**47,35**
Specify next point or [Arc/Close/Halfwidth/Length/Undo/Width]:**1,35**
Specify next point or [Arc/Close/Halfwidth/Length/Undo/Width]:**C**

Command: **LTSCALE**
Enter new linetype scale factor<Current>: **1.0**

Using the Dimension Style Dialog Box. You can use the **Dimension Style Manager** dialog box (Figure 28-6) to set the dimension variables. To invoke the **Dimension Style Manager** dialog box, enter **DDIM** at AutoCAD Command prompt or select **Style** in the **Dimension** menu.

Using the DIM Command. You can also use the **DIM** command to set the dimensions. The following is the command prompt sequence for setting the dimension variables and saving the dimension style file.

Figure 28-6 Dimension Style Manager dialog box

Figure 28-7 Modify Dimension Style dialog

Command: **DIM**
Dim: **DIMSCALE**
Enter new value for dimension variable <Current>: **1.0**
Dim: **DIMTIX**
Enter new value for dimension variable <Off>: **ON**
Dim: **Dimtad**
Enter new value for dimension variable <0>: **1**
Dim: **Dimtoh**
Enter new value for dimension variable <On>: **OFF**
Dim: **Dimtih**
Enter new value for dimension variable <On>: **OFF**
Dim: **Style**
Enter new text style <STANDARD>: **MYDIM1**
Dim: **Esc**　　　　(Press the Escape key)

Using the Layer Properties Manager Dialog Box. You can use the **Layer Properties Manager** dialog box (Figure 28-8) to set the layers and linetypes. To invoke this dialog box, enter **LAYER** at AutoCAD Command prompt or select **Layer** in the **Format** menu.

Using the LAYER command. You can also use the **-LAYER** command to set the layers and linetypes. The following is the command prompt sequence for setting the layers and linetypes.

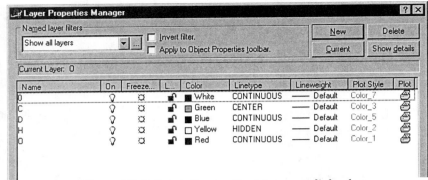

Figure 28-8 Layer Properties Manager dialog box

Command: **-LAYER**
Enter an option
[?/Make/Set/New/ON/OFF/Color/Ltype/LWeight/Plot/Freeze/Thaw/LOck/Unlock]: **N**
Enter name list for new layer(s): **OBJ,CEN,HID,DIM,BOR**

Enter an option
[?/Make/Set/New/ON/OFF/Color/Ltype/LWeight/Plot/Freeze/Thaw/LOck/Unlock]: **L**
Enter loaded linetype name or [?]<Continuous>: **HIDDEN**
Enter name list of layer(s) for linetype "HIDDEN" <0>: **HID**
Enter an option
[?/Make/Set/New/ON/OFF/Color/Ltype/LWeight/Plot/Freeze/Thaw/LOck/Unlock]: **L**
Enter loaded linetype name or [?]<Continuous>: **CENTER**
Enter name list of layer(s) for linetype "HIDDEN" <0>: **CEN**

Enter an option
[?/Make/Set/New/ON/OFF/Color/Ltype/LWeight/Plot/Freeze/Thaw/LOck/Unlock: **C**
Enter color name or number (1-255): **RED**
Enter name list of layer(s) for color 1 (red) <0>: **OBJ**
Enter an option
[?/Make/Set/New/ON/OFF/Color/Ltype/LWeight/Plot/Freeze/Thaw/LOck/Unlock: **C**
Enter color name or number (1-255): **Yellow**
Enter name list of layer(s) for color 2 (yellow) <0>: **CEN**

Enter an option
[?/Make/Set/New/ON/OFF/Color/Ltype/LWeight/Plot/Freeze/Thaw/LOck/Unlock: **C**
Enter color name or number (1-255): **Blue**
Enter name list of layer(s) for color 5 (blue) <0>: **HID**

Enter an option
[?/Make/Set/New/ON/OFF/Color/Ltype/LWeight/Plot/Freeze/Thaw/LOck/Unlock: **C**
Enter color name or number (1-255): **GREEN**
Enter name list of layer(s) for color 3 (green) <0>: **DIM**

Enter an option
[?/Make/Set/New/ON/OFF/Color/Ltype/LWeight/Plot/Freeze/Thaw/LOck/Unlock: **C**
Enter color name or number (1-255): **MAGENTA**
Enter name list of layer(s) for color 6 (magenta) <0>: **BOR**
Enter an option
[?/Make/Set/New/ON/OFF/Color/Ltype/LWeight/Plot/Freeze/Thaw/LOck/Unlock: (**RETURN**)

Next, add the title block and the text as shown in Figure 28-5. After completing the drawing, save it as PROTO2.DWT. You have created a template drawing (PROTO2) that contains all of the information given in Example 2.

CUSTOMIZING DRAWINGS ACCORDING TO PLOT SIZE AND DRAWING SCALE

You can generate a template drawing according to plot size and scale. For example, if the scale is 1/16" = 1' and the drawing is to be plotted on a 36" by 24" area, you can calculate drawing parameters like limits, **DIMSCALE**, and **LTSCALE** and save them in a template drawing. This will save considerable time in the initial drawing setup and provide uniformity in the drawings. The next example explains the procedure involved in customizing a drawing according to a certain plot size and scale. (Note, you can also use the paper space to specify the paper size and scale.)

Example 3

Generate a template drawing (**PROTO3**) with the following specifications:

Plotted sheet size	36" by 24" (Figure 28-9)
Scale	1/8" = 1.0'
Snap	3'
Grid	6'
Text height	1/4" on plotted drawing
Ltscale	Calculate
Dimscale	Calculate
Units	Architectural
	16-denominator of smallest fraction
	Angle in degrees/minutes/seconds
	4-number of fractional places for display of angles
	0 angle along positive X axis
	Angle positive if measured counterclockwise
Border	Border should be 1" inside the edges of the plotted drawing sheet, using PLINE 1/32" wide when plotted (Figure 28-9)

In this example, you need to calculate some values before you set the parameters. For example, the limits of the drawing depend on the plotted size of the drawing and the scale of the drawing. Similarly, **LTSCALE** and **DIMSCALE** depend on the limits of the drawing. The following calculations explain the procedure for finding the values of limits, ltscale, dimscale, and text height.

Chapter 28

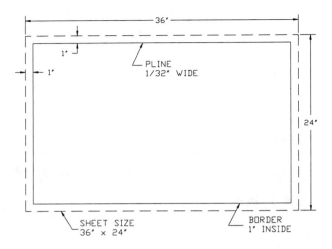

Figure 28-9 Border of prototype drawing

Limits

Given:
Sheet size   36" x 24"
Scale   1/8" = 1'
         or 1" = 8'

Calculate:
XLimit
YLimit
Since sheet size is 36" x 24" and scale is 1/8"=1'
Therefore, XLimit = 36 x 8' = 288'
         YLimit = 24 x 8' = 192'

Text height

Given:
Text height when plotted = 1/4"
Sheet size   36" x 24"
Scale   1/8" = 1'
Calculate:
Text height
Since scale is 1/8" = 1'
         or 1/8" = 12"
         or 1" = 96"
Therefore, scale factor = 96
      Text height = 1/4" x 96
                   = 24" = 2'

Ltscale and Dimscale

Known:
Since scale is 1/8" = 1'
    or 1/8" = 12"
     or 1" = 96"

Calculate:
Ltscale and Dimscale
Since scale factor = 96
Therefore, LTSCALE = Scale factor = 96
Similarly, DIMSCALE = 96
(All dimension variables, like DIMTXT and DIMASZ, will be multiplied by 96.)

Pline Width

Given:
Scale is 1/8" = 1'
Calculate:
PLINE width
Since scale is 1/8" = 1'
    or   1" = 8'
    or   1" = 96"

Therefore,
PLINE width = 1/32 x 96
      = 3"

After calculating the parameters, use the following AutoCAD commands to set up the drawing, then save the drawing as **PROTO3.DWT.**

Command: **-UNITS**

Report formats:	**Examples:**
1. Scientific	1.55E+01
2. Decimal	15.50
3. Engineering	1'-3.50"
4. Architectural	1'-3 1/2"
5. Fractional	15 1/2

With the exception of Engineering and Architectural formats, these formats can be used with any basic unit of measurement. For example, decimal mode is perfect for metric units as well as decimal English units.

Enter choice, 1 to 5<2>: **4**
Denominator of smallest fraction to display
1, 2, 4, 8, 16, 32, or 64 <16>: **16**

Systems of angle measure: **Examples:**
1. Decimal degrees   45.0000
2. Degrees/minutes/seconds 45d0'0"
3. Grads   50.0000g
4. Radians   0.7854r
5. Surveyor's units   N 45d0'0" E

Enter choice, 1 to 5<1>: **2**
Number of fractional places for display of angles (0 to 8)<0>: **4**

Direction for angle 0.00:
    East   3 o'clock   = 0d0'0"
    North   12 o'clock   = 90d0'0"
    West   9 o'clock   = 180d0'0"
    South   6 o'clock   = 270d0'0"

Enter direction for angle 0d0'0"<0d0'0">: **RETURN**
Do you want angles measured clockwise?<N>: **N**
Command: **LIMITS**
Specify lower left corner or [ON/OFF] <0'-0",0'-0">:**0,0**
Specify upper right corner <1'-0",0'-9">: **288',192'**

Command: **SNAP**
Specify snap spacing or [ON/OFF/Aspect/Rotate/Style/Type] <0'-1">: **3'**

Command: **GRID**
Specify grid spacing(X) or [ON/OFF/Snap/Aspect] <0'-0">: **6'**

Command: **SETVAR**
Enter variable name or [?] <current>: **TEXTSIZE**
Enter new value for TEXTSIZE <current>: **2'**

Command: **LTSCALE**
Enter new linetype scale factor <1.0000>: **96**

Command: **DIM**
Dim: **Dimscale**
Enter new value for dimension variable <1.0000> New value: **96**
Dim: **Style**
New text style <STANDARD>: **MYDIM2**

Command: **PLINE**
Specify start point: **8',8'**
Current line-width is **0.0000**
Specify next point or [Arc/Close/Halfwidth/Length/Undo/Width]:**W**
Specify starting width<0.00>: **3**
Specify ending width<0'-3">: **ENTER**

Specify next point or [Arc/Close/Halfwidth/Length/Undo/Width]: **280',8'**
Specify next point or [Arc/Close/Halfwidth/Length/Undo/Width]: **280',184'**
Specify next point or [Arc/Close/Halfwidth/Length/Undo/Width]: **8',184'**
Specify next point or [Arc/Close/Halfwidth/Length/Undo/Width]: **C**

Review Questions

1. The three standard template drawings that come with AutoCAD software are _____ , _____ , and _____ .

2. To use a template file, select the _____ button in the Create New Drawing dialog box.

3. To start a drawing with default setup, select the _____ button in the Create New Drawing dialog box.

4. The default value of DIMSCALE is _____ .

5. The default value for DIMTXT is _____ .

6. The default value for SNAP is _____ .

7. Architectural units can be selected by using AutoCAD's _____ or _____ commands.

8. If plot size is 36" x 24", and the scale is 1/2" = 1', then XLimit = _____ and YLimit = _____ .

9. If the plot size is 24" x 18", and the scale is 1 = 20, the XLimit = _____ and YLimit = _____ .

10. If the plot size is 200 x 150 and limits are (0.00,0.00) and (600.00,450.00), the **LTSCALE** factor = _____ . (S.Factor=600/200=3 LTSCALE=3)

Exercises

Exercise 1   *General*

Generate a template drawing **PROTOE2** with the following specifications:

Limits	48.0,36.0
Snap	0.5
Grid	2.0
Text height	0.25

PLINE width	0.03
Ltscale	Calculate
Dimscale	Calculate
Plot size	10.5 x 8

LAYERS

Layer Names	Line Type	Color
0	Continuous	White
OBJECT	Continuous	Green
CENTER	Center	Magenta
HIDDEN	Hidden	Blue
DIM	Continuous	Red
BORDER	Continuous	Cyan

Exercise 2   *General*

Generate a template drawing (**PROTOE3**) with the following specifications:

Plotted sheet size	36" x 24" (Figure 28-10)
Scale	1/2" = 1.0'
Text height	1/4" on plotted drawing
Ltscale	Calculate
Dimscale	Calculate
Units	Architectural
	32-denominator of smallest fraction to display
	Angle in degrees/minutes/seconds
	4-number of fractional places for display of angles
	0d0'0"-direction for angle
	Angle positive if measured counterclockwise
Border	Border is 1-1/2" inside the edges of the plotted drawing sheet, using PLINE 1/32" wide when plotted (Figure 28-10)

Figure 28-10 *Drawing for Exercise 3*

Chapter 29

Script Files and Slide Shows

Learning Objectives

After completing this chapter, you will be able to:
- *Write script files and use the **SCRIPT** command to run script files.*
- *Use the **RSCRIPT** and **DELAY** commands in script files.*
- *Invoke script files when loading AutoCAD.*
- *Create a slide show.*
- *Preload slides when running a slide show.*

WHAT ARE SCRIPT FILES?

AutoCAD has provided a facility called **script files** that allows you to combine different AutoCAD commands and execute them in a predetermined sequence. The commands can be written as a text file using any text editor like Notepad or AutoCAD's **EDIT** command (if the **ACAD.PGP** file is present and **EDIT** is defined in the file). These files, generally known as script files, have extension **.SCR** (example: **PLOT1.SCR**). A script file is executed with the AutoCAD **SCRIPT** command.

Script files can be used to generate a slide show, do the initial drawing setup, or plot a drawing to a predefined specification. They can also be used to automate certain command sequences that are used frequently in generating, editing, or viewing a drawing. Scripts cannot access dialog boxes or menus. When commands that open the file and plot dialog boxes are issued from a script file, AutoCAD runs the command line version of the command instead of opening the dialog box.

Example 1

Write a script file that will perform the following initial setup for a drawing (file name **SCRIPT1.SCR**). It is assumed that the drawing will be plotted on 12x9 size paper (Scale factor for plotting = 4).

Ortho	On	Zoom	All
Grid	2.0	Text height	0.125
Grid	Off	Ltscale	4.0
Snap	0.5	Dimscale	4.0
Limits	0,0 48.0,36.0		

Before writing a script file, you need to know the AutoCAD commands and the entries required in response to the command prompts. To find out the sequence of the prompt entries, you can type the command at the keyboard and then respond to different prompts. The following is a list of AutoCAD commands and prompt entries for Example 1:

Command: **ORTHO**
Enter mode [ON/OFF] <OFF>: **ON**

Command: **GRID**
Specify grid spacing(X) or [ON/OFF/Snap/Aspect] <1.0>: **2.0**

Command: **GRID**
Specify grid spacing(X) or [ON/OFF/Snap/Aspect] <1.0>: **OFF**

Command: **SNAP**
Specify snap spacing or [ON/OFF/Aspect/Rotate/Style/Type] <1.0>: **0.5**

Command: **LIMITS**
Reset Model space limits:
Specify lower left corner or [ON/OFF] <0.0,0.0>: **0,0**
Specify upper right corner <12.0,9.0>: **48.0,36.0**

Command: **ZOOM**
Specify corner of window, enter a scale factor (nX or nXP), or
[All/Center/Dynamic/Extents/Previous/Scale/Window] <real time>: **A**

Command: **SETVAR**
Enter variable name or [?]: **TEXTSIZE**
Enter new value for TEXTSIZE <0.02>: **0.125**

Command: **LTSCALE**
Enter new linetype scale factor <1.0000>: **4.0**

Command: **SETVAR**
Enter variable name or [?] <TEXTSIZE>: **DIMSCALE**
Enter new value for DIMSCALE <1.0000>: **4.0**

Once you know the AutoCAD commands and the required prompt entries, you can write the script file using the AutoCAD **EDIT** command or any text editor. The following file is a listing of the script file for Example 1:

```
ORTHO
ON
GRID
2.0
GRID
OFF
SNAP
0.5
LIMITS
0,0
48.0,36.0
ZOOM
ALL
SETVAR
TEXTSIZE
0.125
LTSCALE
4.0
SETVAR
DIMSCALE 4.0
```

Notice that the commands and the prompt entries in this file are in the same sequence as mentioned before. You can also combine several statements in one line, as shown in the following list:

```
ORTHO ON
GRID 2.0 GRID OFF
SNAP 0.5 SNAP ON
LIMITS 0,0 48.0,36.0 ZOOM ALL
SETVAR TEXTSIZE 0.125
LTSCALE 4.0
SETVAR DIMSCALE 4.0
```

Note

In the script file, a space is used to terminate a command or a prompt entry. Therefore, spaces are very important in these files. Make sure there are no extra spaces, unless they are required to press ENTER more than once.

*After you change the limits, it is a good practice to use the **ZOOM** command with the **All** option to display the new limits on the screen.*

AutoCAD ignores and does not process any lines that begin with a semicolon (;). This allows you to put comments in the file.

SCRIPT COMMAND

The AutoCAD **SCRIPT** command allows you to run a script file while you are in the drawing editor. To execute the script file, type the **SCRIPT** command and press ENTER. AutoCAD will prompt you to enter the name of the script file. You can accept the default file name or enter a new file name. The default script file name is the same as the drawing name. If you want to enter a new file name, type the name of the script file **without** the file extension (**.SCR**). (The file extension is assumed and need not be included with the file name.)

To run the script file of Example 1, type the **SCRIPT** command and press ENTER; AutoCAD will display the **Select Script File** dialog box (Figure 29-1). In the dialog box, select the file SCRIPT1 and then choose the Open button. You will see the changes taking place on the screen as the script file commands are executed. The format of the **SCRIPT** command is:

        Command: **SCRIPT**

Figure 29-1 Select Script File dialog box

You can also enter the name of the script file at the Command prompt by setting **FILEDIA**=0. The format of the **SCRIPT** command is:

        Command: **FILEDIA**
        Enter new value for FILEDIA <1>: **0**
        Command: **SCRIPT**
        Enter script file name <default>: *Script file name.*

        For example:
        Command: **SCRIPT**
        Script file <CUSTOM>: **SCRIPT1**
                    Where   **<CUSTOM>** ------------- Default drawing file name
                                      SCRIPT1 ------------------ Name of the script file

Example 2

Write a script file that will set up the following layers with the given colors and linetypes (file name **SCRIPT2.SCR**).

Layer Names	Color	Linetype	Line Weight
Object	Red	Continuous	default
Center	Yellow	Center	default
Hidden	Blue	Hidden	default
Dimension	Green	Continuous	default
Border	Magenta	Continuous	default
Hatch	Cyan	Continuous	0.05

As mentioned earlier, you need to know the AutoCAD commands and the required prompt entries before writing a script file. For Example 2, you need the following commands to create the layers with the given colors and linetypes:

Command: **LAYER**
Enter an option
[?/Make/Set/New/ON/OFF/Color/Ltype/LWeight/Plot/Freeze/Thaw/LOck/Unlock]: **N**
Enter name list for new layer(s): **OBJECT,CENTER,HIDDEN,DIM,BORDER, HATCH**

Enter an option
[?/Make/Set/New/ON/OFF/Color/Ltype/LWeight/Plot/Freeze/Thaw/LOck/Unlock]: **L**
Enter loaded linetype name or [?] <Continuous>: **CENTER**
Enter name list of layer(s) for linetype "CENTER" <0>: **CENTER**

Enter an option
[?/Make/Set/New/ON/OFF/Color/Ltype/LWeight/Plot/Freeze/Thaw/LOck/Unlock]: **L**
Enter loaded linetype name or [?] <Continuous>: **HIDDEN**
Enter name list of layer(s) for linetype "HIDDEN" <0>: **HIDDEN**

Enter an option
[?/Make/Set/New/ON/OFF/Color/Ltype/LWeight/Plot/Freeze/Thaw/LOck/Unlock]: **C**
Enter color name or number (1-255): **RED**
Enter name list of layer(s) for color 1 (red) <0>:**OBJECT**

Enter an option
[?/Make/Set/New/ON/OFF/Color/Ltype/LWeight/Plot/Freeze/Thaw/LOck/Unlock]: **C**
Enter color name or number (1-255): **YELLOW**
Enter name list of layer(s) for color 2 (yellow) <0>: **CENTER**

Enter an option
[?/Make/Set/New/ON/OFF/Color/Ltype/LWeight/Plot/Freeze/Thaw/LOck/Unlock]: **C**
Enter color name or number (1-255): **BLUE**
Enter name list of layer(s) for color 5 (blue)<0>: **HIDDEN**

Chapter 29

Enter an option
[?/Make/Set/New/ON/OFF/Color/Ltype/LWeight/Plot/Freeze/Thaw/LOck/Unlock]: **C**
Enter color name or number (1-255): **GREEN**
Enter name list of layer(s) for color 3 (green)<0>: **DIM**

Enter an option
[?/Make/Set/New/ON/OFF/Color/Ltype/LWeight/Plot/Freeze/Thaw/LOck/Unlock]: **C**
Enter color name or number (1-255): **MAGENTA**
Enter name list of layer(s) for color 6 (magenta)<0>: **BORDER**

Enter an option
[?/Make/Set/New/ON/OFF/Color/Ltype/LWeight/Plot/Freeze/Thaw/LOck/Unlock]: **C**
Enter color name or number (1-255): **CYAN**
Enter name list of layer(s) for color 4 (cyan)<0>: **HATCH**

Enter an option
[?/Make/Set/New/ON/OFF/Color/Ltype/LWeight/Plot/Freeze/Thaw/LOck/Unlock]:LW
Enter lineweight (0.0mm - 2.11mm):0.05
Enter name list of layers(s) for lineweight 0.05mm <0>:HATCH
[?/Make/Set/New/ON/OFF/Color/Ltype/LWeight/Plot/Freeze/Thaw/LOck/Unlock]: **(RETURN)**

The following file is a listing of the script file that creates different layers and assigns the given colors and linetypes to these layers:

```
;This script file will create new layers and
;assign different colors and linetypes to layers
LAYER
NEW
OBJECT,CENTER,HIDDEN,DIM,BORDER,HATCH
L
CENTER
CENTER
L
HIDDEN
HIDDEN
C
RED
OBJECT
C
YELLOW
CENTER
C
BLUE
HIDDEN
C
GREEN
DIM
C
```

MAGENTA
BORDER
C
CYAN
HATCH
(This is a blank line to terminate the **LAYER** command. End of script file.)

Example 3

Write a script file that will rotate the circle and the line, as shown in Figure 29-2, around the lower endpoint of the line through 45-degree increments. The script file should be able to produce a continuous rotation of the given objects with a delay of two seconds after every 45-degree rotation (file name **SCRIPT3.SCR**).

Figure 29-2 *Line and circle rotated through 45-degree increments*

Before writing the script file, enter the required commands and the prompt entries at the keyboard. Write down the exact sequence of the entries in which they have been entered to perform the given operations. The following is a listing of the AutoCAD command sequence needed to rotate the circle and the line around the lower endpoint of the line:

Command: **ROTATE**   *(Enter **ROTATE** command.)*
Current positive angle in UCS: ANGDIR=counterclockwise ANGBASE=0
Select objects: **W**   *(Window option to select object)*
Specify first corner: **2.25, 5.0**
Specify opposite corner: **6.25, 9.0**
Select objects: **<RETURN>**
Specify base point: **4.25,6.5**
Specify rotation angle or [Reference]: **45**

Once the AutoCAD commands, command options, and their sequences are known, you can write a script file. As mentioned earlier, you can use any text editor to write a script file. The following file is a listing of the script file that will create the required rotation of the circle and line of Example 3.

ROTATE	1
W	2
2.25,5.0	3
6.25,9.0	4
(Blank line for Return.)	5
4.25,6.5	6
45	7

Line 1
ROTATE
In this line, **ROTATE** is an AutoCAD command that rotates the objects.

Line 2
W
In this line, W is the Window option for selecting the objects that need to be edited.

Line 3
2.25,5.0
In this line, 2.25 defines the X coordinate and 5.0 defines the Y coordinate of the lower left corner of the object selection window.

Line 4
6.25,9.0
In this line, 6.25 defines the X coordinate and 9.0 defines the Y coordinate of the upper right corner of the object selection window.

Line 5
Line 5 is a blank line that terminates the object selection process.

Line 6
4.25,6.5
In this line, 4.25 defines the X coordinate and 6.5 defines the Y coordinate of the base point for rotation.

Line 7
45
In this line, 45 is the incremental angle for rotation.

Note
One of the limitations of the script files is that all the information has to be contained within the file. These files do not let you enter information. For instance, in Example 3, if you want to use the Window option to select the objects, the Window option (W) and the two points that define this window must be contained within the script file. The same is true for the base point and all other information that goes in a script file. There is no way that a script file can prompt you to enter a particular piece of information and then resume the script file, unless you embed AutoLISP commands to prompt for user input.

RSCRIPT COMMAND

The AutoCAD **RSCRIPT** command allows the user to execute the script file indefinitely until canceled. It is a very desirable feature when the user wants to run the same file continuously. For example, in the case of a slide show for a product demonstration, the **RSCRIPT** command can be used to run the script file again and again until it is terminated by pressing the ESC (Escape) key from the keyboard. Similarly, in Example 3, the rotation command needs to be repeated indefinitely to create a continuous rotation of the objects. This can be accomplished by adding **RSCRIPT** at the end of the file, as in the following file:

```
ROTATE
W
2.25,5.0
6.25,9.0
                (Blank line for Return.)
4.25,6.5
45
RSCRIPT
```

The **RSCRIPT** command on line 8 will repeat the commands from line 1 to line 7, and thus set the script file in an indefinite loop. The script file can be stopped by pressing the ESC or the BACK-SPACE key.

 Note
You cannot provide conditional statements in a script file to terminate the file when a particular condition is satisfied, unless you use the AutoLISP functions in the script file.

DELAY COMMAND

In the script files, some of the operations happen very quickly and make it difficult to see the operations taking place on the screen. It might be necessary to intentionally introduce a pause between certain operations in a script file. For example, in a slide show for a product demonstration, there must be a time delay between different slides so that the audience has enough time to see them. This is accomplished by using the AutoCAD **DELAY** command, which introduces a delay before the next command is executed. The general format of the **DELAY** command is:

> **Command: DELAY Time**
> Where   **Command** ------ AutoCAD command prompt
>   **DELAY** ---------- **DELAY** command
>   **Time** ------------ Time in milliseconds

The **DELAY** command is to be followed by the delay time in milliseconds. For example, a delay of 2,000 milliseconds means that AutoCAD will pause for approximately two seconds before executing the next command. It is approximately two seconds because computer processing speeds vary. The maximum time delay you can enter is 32,767 milliseconds (about 33 seconds). In Example 3, a two-second delay can be introduced by inserting a **DELAY** command line between line 7 and line 8, as in the following file listing:

```
ROTATE
W
2.25,5.0
6.25,9.0
            (Blank line for Return.)
4.25,6.5
45
DELAY 2000
RSCRIPT
```

The first seven lines of this file rotate the objects through a 45-degree angle. Before the **RSCRIPT** command on line 8 is executed, there is a delay of 2,000 milliseconds (about two seconds). The **RSCRIPT** command will repeat the script file that rotates the objects through another 45-degree angle. Thus, a slide show is created with a time delay of two seconds after every 45-degree increment.

RESUME COMMAND

If you cancel a script file and then want to continue it, you can do so by using the AutoCAD **RESUME** command.

Command: **RESUME**

The **RESUME** command can also be used if the script file has encountered an error that causes it to be suspended. The **RESUME** command will skip the command that caused the error and continue with the rest of the script file. If the error occurred when the command was in progress, use a leading apostrophe with the **RESUME** command (**'RESUME**) to invoke the **RESUME** command in transparent mode.

Command: **'RESUME**

COMMAND LINE SWITCHES

The command line switches can be used as arguments to the acad.exe file that launches AutoCAD. You can also use the **Options** dialog box to set the environment or by adding a set of environment variables in the autoexec.bat file. The command line switches and environment variables override the values set in the **Options** dialog box for the current session only. These switches do not alter the system registry. The following is the list of the command line switches:

Switch	Function
/c	Controls where AutoCAD stores and searches for the hardware configuration file (acad14.cfg)
/s	Specifies which directories to search for support files if they are not in the current directory
/d	Specifies which directories to search for ADI drivers
/b	Designates a script to run after AutoCAD starts
/t	Specifies a template to use when creating a new drawing
/nologo	Starts AutoCAD without first displaying the logo screen

/v	Designates a particular view of the drawing to be displayed upon start-up of AutoCAD
/r	Reconfigures AutoCAD with the default device configuration settings
/p	Specifies the profile to use on start-up

INVOKING A SCRIPT FILE WHEN LOADING AUTOCAD

The script files can also be run when loading AutoCAD, without getting into the drawing editor. The format of the command for running a script file when loading AutoCAD is:

Drive**>AutoCAD2000 [existing-drawing] [/t template] [/v view] /b script-file**

In the following example, AutoCAD will open the existing drawing (Mydwg1) and then run the script file (Setup).

Example
C:\AutoCAD2000>ACAD Mydwg1 /b Setup
> Where   **AutoCAD2000** - AutoCAD2000 subdirectory containing
> AutoCAD system files
> **ACAD** ------------ ACAD command to start AutoCAD
> **MyDwg1** -------- Existing drawing file name
> **Setup** ------------- Name of the script file

*Figure 29-3 Invoking script file when loading AutoCAD using the **Run** dialog box*

In the following example, AutoCAD will start a new drawing with the default name (Drawing), using the template file temp1, and then run the script file (Setup).

Example
C:\AutoCAD200\ACAD /t temp1 /b Setup
> Where   **temp1** ------------ Existing template file name
> **Setup** ------------- Name of the script file

or

C:\AutoCAD2000\ACAD /t c:\AutoCAD200\mytemp\temp1 /b Setup
> Where   **c:\AutoCAD2000\mytemp** ------ Path name

In the following example, AutoCAD will start a new drawing with the default name (Drawing), and then run the script file (Setup).

Example
C:\AutoCAD2000\ACAD /b Setup
      Where **Setup** ------------- Name of the script file

Here, it is assumed that the AutoCAD system files are loaded in the AutoCAD2000 directory.

Note
For invoking a script file when loading AutoCAD, the drawing file or the template file specified in the command must exist in the search path. You cannot start a new drawing with a given name.

You should avoid abbreviations to prevent any confusion. For example, a C can be used as a close option when you are drawing lines. It can also be used as a command alias for drawing a circle. If you use both of these in a script file, it might be confusing.

Example 4

Write a script file that can be invoked when loading AutoCAD and create a drawing with the following setup (filename SCRIPT4.SCR):

Grid	3.0
Snap	0.5
Limits	0,0
	36.0,24.0
Zoom	All
Text height	0.25
Ltscale	3.0
Dimscale	3.0

Layers

Name	Color	Linetype
Obj	Red	Continuous
Cen	Yellow	Center
Hid	Blue	Hidden
Dim	Green	Continuous

First, write a script file and save the file under the name SCRIPT4.SCR. The following file is a listing of this script file that does the initial setup for a drawing:

```
GRID 2.0
SNAP 0.5
LIMITS 0,0 36.0,24.0 ZOOM ALL
SETVAR TEXTSIZE 0.25
LTSCALE 3
SETVAR DIMSCALE 3.0
LAYER NEW
OBJ,CEN,HID,DIM
L CENTER CEN
```

```
L HIDDEN HID
C RED OBJ
C YELLOW CEN
C BLUE HID
C GREEN DIM
```
(Blank line for ENTER.)

After you have written and saved the file, quit the drawing editor. To run the script file, SCRIPT4, select Start, Run, and then enter the following command line:

C:\AutoCAD2000\ACAD /t C:\EX4 D:\SCRIPT4
     Where **ACAD** ------------ ACAD to load AutoCAD
                EX4 -------------- Drawing filename
                SCRIPT4 ------- Name of the script file

Here it is assumed that the template file (EX4) is on C drive and the script file (SCRIPT4) is on D drive.

Figure 29-4 *Invoking script file when loading AutoCAD using the **Run** dialog box*

When you enter this line, AutoCAD is loaded and the file EX4.DWT is opened. The script file, SCRIPT4, is then automatically loaded and the commands defined in the file are executed.

In the following example, AutoCAD will start a new drawing with the default name (Drawing), and then run the script file (SCRIPT4).

Example
C:\AutoCAD2000\ACAD /b SCRIPT4
     Where **SCRIPT4** ------- Name of the script file

Here, it is assumed that the AutoCAD system files are loaded in the AutoCAD2000 directory.

Example 5

Write a script file that will plot a 36" by 24" to maximum plot size, using your system printer/plotter. Use the Window option to select the drawing to be plotted.

Chapter 29

Before writing a script file to plot a drawing, find out the plotter specifications that must be entered in the script file to obtain the desired output. To determine the prompt entries and their sequences to set up the plotter specifications, enter the AutoCAD **-PLOT** command at the keyboard. Note the entries you make and their sequence (the entries for your printer or plotter will probably be different). The following is a listing of the plotter specification with the new entries:

Command: **-PLOT**
Detailed plot configuration? [Yes/No] <No>: **Yes**
Enter a layout name or [?] <Model>: Model
Enter an output device name or [?] <HP LaserJet 4000 Series PCL 6>: *Press ENTER.*
Enter paper size or [?] <Letter (8 1/2 x 11 in)>: *Press ENTER.*
Enter paper units [Inches/Millimeters] <Inches>: **I**
Enter drawing orientation [Portrait/Landscape] <Landscape>: *Press ENTER.*
Plot upside down? [Yes/No] <No>: **No**
Enter plot area [Display/Extents/Limits/View/Window] <Display>: **W**
Enter lower left corner of window <0.000000,0.000000>: **0,0**
Enter upper right corner of window <0.000000,0.000000>: **36,24**
Enter plot scale (Plotted Inches=Drawing Units) or [Fit] <Fit>: **F**
Enter plot offset (x,y) or [Center] <0.00,0.00>: **0,0**
Plot with plot styles? [Yes/No] <Yes>: **Yes**
Enter plot style table name or [?] (enter . for none) <>: .
Plot with lineweights? [Yes/No] <Yes>: **Yes**
Remove hidden lines? [Yes/No] <No>: **No**
Write the plot to a file [Yes/No] <N>: **No**
Save changes to model tab [Yes/No]? <N> **No**
Proceed with plot [Yes/No] <Y>: **Y**
Effective plotting area: 7.07 wide by 10.60 high
Plotting viewport 2.

Now you can write the script file by entering the responses to these prompts in the file. The following file is a listing of the script file that will plot a 36" by 24" drawing on 9" by 6" paper after making the necessary changes in the plot specifications. The comments on the right are not a part of the file.

Plot
y
                    (Blank line for ENTER, selects default layout.)
                    (Blank line for ENTER, selects default printer.)
                    (Blank line for ENTER, selects the default paper size.)
I
L
N
w
0,0
36,24
F
0,0

Y
.   *(Enter . for none)*
Y
N
N
N
Y

Note

You can use a blank line to accept the default value for a prompt. A blank line in the script file will cause a Return. However, you must not accept the default plot specifications because the file might have been altered by another user or by another script file. Therefore, always enter the actual values in the file so that when you run a script file, it does not take the default values.

Exercise 1

Write a script file that will plot a 288' by 192' drawing on a 36" x 24" sheet of paper. The drawing scale is 1/8" = 1'. (The filename is SCRIPT6.SCR. In this example assume that AutoCAD is configured for the HPGL plotter and the plotter description is HPGL-Plotter.)

WHAT IS A SLIDE SHOW?

AutoCAD provides a facility using script files to combine the slides in a text file and display them in a predetermined sequence. In this way, you can generate a slide show for a slide presentation. You can also introduce a time delay in the display so that the viewer has enough time to view a slide.

A drawing or parts of a drawing can also be displayed by using the AutoCAD display commands. For example, you can use **ZOOM**, **PAN**, or other commands to display the details you want to show. If the drawing is very complicated, it takes quite some time to display the desired information, and it may not be possible to get the desired views in the right sequence. However, with slide shows you can arrange the slides in any order and present them in a definite sequence. In addition to saving time, this will also help to minimize the distraction that might be caused by constantly changing the drawing display. Also, some drawings are confidential in nature and you may not want to display some portions or views of them. By making slides, you can restrict the information that is presented through them. You can send a slide show to a client without losing control of the drawings and the information that is contained in them.

WHAT ARE SLIDES?

A **slide** is the snapshot of a screen display; it is like taking a picture of a display with a camera. The slides do not contain any vector information like AutoCAD drawings, which means that the entities do not have any information associated with them. For example, the slides do not retain any information about the layers, colors, linetypes, start point, or endpoint of a line or viewpoint. Therefore, slides cannot be edited like drawings. If you want to make any changes in the slide, you need to edit the drawing and then make a new slide from the edited drawing.

MSLIDE COMMAND

Slides are created by using the AutoCAD **MSLIDE** command. If **FILEDIA** is set to 0, the command will prompt you to enter the slide file name.

Command: **MSLIDE**
Enter name of slide file to create <Default>: *Slide file name.*

Example
Command: **MSLIDE**
Slide File: <Drawing1> SLIDE1
       Where **Drawing1** ------- Default slide file name
              SLIDE1 --------- Slide file name

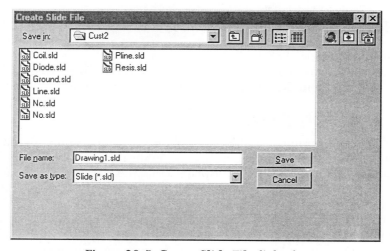

Figure 29-5 Create Slide File dialog box

In the preceding example, AutoCAD will save the slide file as **SLIDE1.SLD**. If **FILEDIA** is set to 1, the **MSLIDE** command displays the **Create Slide File** dialog (Figure 29-5) box on the screen. You can enter the slide file name in this dialog box.

Note
*In model space, you can use the **MSLIDE** command to make a slide of the existing display in the current viewport.*

If you are in the paper space viewport, you can make a slide of the display in the paper space that includes any floating viewports.

*When the viewports are not active, the **MSLIDE** command will make a slide of the current screen display.*

VSLIDE COMMAND

To view a slide, use the **VSLIDE** command. AutoCAD will then prompt you to enter the slide file name. Enter the name of the slide you want to view and press ENTER. Do not enter the extension after the slide file name. AutoCAD automatically assumes the extension **.SLD**.

> Command: **VSLIDE**
> Enter name of slide file to create<Default>: *Name.*

Example
Command: **VSLIDE**
Slide file <Drawing1>: SLIDE1
           Where   **Drawing1** ------- Default slide file name
                      SLIDE1 --------- Name of slide file

You can also use the **Select Slide File** dialog box (Figure 29-6) to view a slide.

Figure 29-6 Select Slide Files dialog box

Note

*After viewing a slide, you can use the AutoCAD **REDRAW** command to remove the slide display and return to the existing drawing on the screen.*

*Any command that is automatically followed by a redraw will also display the existing drawing. For example, AutoCAD **GRID**, **ZOOM ALL**, and **REGEN** commands will automatically return to the existing drawing on the screen.*

You can view the slides on high-resolution or low-resolution monitors. Depending on the resolution of the monitor, AutoCAD automatically adjusts the image. However, if you are using a high-resolution monitor, it is better to make the slides on the same monitor to take full advantage of that monitor.

Chapter 29

Example 7

Write a script file that will generate a slide show of the following slide files, with a time delay of 15 seconds after every slide:

    SLIDE1, SLIDE2, SLIDE3, SLIDE4

The first step in a slide show is to create the slides. Figure 29-7 shows the drawings that have been saved as slide files **SLIDE1, SLIDE2, SLIDE3,** and **SLIDE4**. The second step is to find out the sequence in which you want these slides to be displayed, with the necessary time delay, if any, between slides. Then you can use any text editor or the AutoCAD **EDIT** command (provided the **ACAD.PGP** file is present and **EDIT** is defined in the file) to write the script file with the extension **.SCR**.

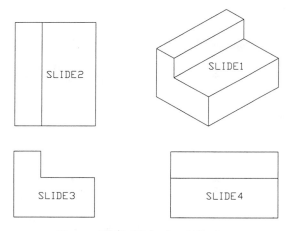

Figure 29-7 *Slides for slide show*

The following file is a listing of the script file that will create a slide show of the slides in Figure 29-7. The name of the script file is **SLDSHOW1**.

```
VSLIDE SLIDE1
DELAY 15000
VSLIDE SLIDE2
DELAY 15000
VSLIDE SLIDE3
DELAY 15000
VSLIDE SLIDE4
DELAY 15000
```

To run this slide show, type SCRIPT in response to the AutoCAD Command prompt. Now, type the name of the script file **(SLDSHOW1)** and press ENTER. The slides will be displayed on the screen, with an approximate time delay of 15 seconds between them.

PRELOADING SLIDES

In the script file of Example 7, VSLIDE SLIDE1 in line 1 loads the slide file, **SLIDE1**, and displays it on screen. After a pause of 15,000 milliseconds, it starts loading the second slide file, **SLIDE2**. Depending on the computer and the disk access time, you will notice that it takes some time to load the second slide file; the same is true for the other slides. To avoid the delay in loading the slide files, AutoCAD has provided a facility to preload a slide while viewing the previous slide. This is accomplished by placing an asterisk (*) in front of the slide file name.

VSLIDE SLIDE1	*(View slide, SLIDE1.)*
VSLIDE *SLIDE2	*(Preload slide, SLIDE2.)*
DELAY 15000	*(Delay of 15 seconds.)*
VSLIDE	*(Display slide, SLIDE2.)*
VSLIDE *SLIDE3	*(Preload slide, SLIDE3.)*
DELAY 15000	*(Delay of 15 seconds.)*
VSLIDE	*(Display slide, SLIDE3.)*
VSLIDE *SLIDE4	
DELAY 15000	
VSLIDE	
DELAY 15000	
RSCRIPT	*(Restart the script file.)*

Example 8

Write a script file to generate a continuous slide show of the following slide files, with a time delay of two seconds between slides:

SLD1, SLD2, SLD3

The slide files are located in different subdirectories, as shown in Figure 29-8. The subdirectory **SUBDIR1** is the current subdirectory.

Figure 29-8 Subdirectories of the C drive

Where **C:** -------------------- *Root directory.*
AutoCAD2000 ------------ *Subdirectory where the AutoCAD files are loaded.*
SUBDIR1 ----------------- *Drawing subdirectory.*
SUBDIR2 ----------------- *Drawing subdirectory.*
SUBDIR3 ----------------- *Drawing subdirectory.*

SLD1	--------------------	*Slide file in SUBDIR1 subdirectory.*
SLD2	--------------------	*Slide file in SUBDIR2 subdirectory.*
SLD3	--------------------	*Slide file in SUBDIR3 subdirectory.*

The following file is the listing of the script files that will generate a slide show for the slides in Example 8:

```
VSLIDE SLD1
DELAY 2000
VSLIDE C:\AutoCAD200\SUBDIR2\SLD2
DELAY 2000
VSLIDE C:\AutoCAD2000\SUBDIR3\SLD3
DELAY 2000
RSCRIPT
```

Line 1
VSLIDE SLD1
In this line, the AutoCAD command **VSLIDE** loads the slide file **SLD1**. Since, in this example, we are assuming you are in the subdirectory **SUBDIR1** and the first slide file, **SLD1**, is located in the same subdirectory, it does not require any path definition.

Line 2
DELAY 2000
This line uses the AutoCAD **DELAY** command to create a pause of approximately two seconds before the next slide is loaded.

Line 3
VSLIDE C:\AutoCAD2000\SUBDIR2\SLD2
In this line, the AutoCAD command **VSLIDE** loads the slide file **SLD2**, located in the subdirectory **SUBDIR2**. If the slide file is located in a different subdirectory, you need to define the path with the slide file.

Line 5
VSLIDE C:\AutoCAD2000\SUBDIR3\SLD3
In this line, the **VSLIDE** command loads the slide file SLD3, located in the subdirectory SUBDIR3.

Line 7
RSCRIPT
In this line, the **RSCRIPT** command executes the script file again and displays the slides on the screen. This process continues indefinitely until the script file is canceled by pressing the ESC key or the BACKSPACE key.

SLIDE SHOWS WITH RENDERED IMAGES

Slide shows can also contained rendered images. In fact, use of rendered images is highly recommended for a more dynamically pleasing, entertaining, and interesting show. AutoCAD provides the following AutoLISP function for using rendered images during a slide show presentation.

(C:REPLAY FILENAME TYPE [<XOFF> <YOFF> <XSIZE> <YSIZE>])
Where:

C:REPLAY ----------------- AutoLISP function calling AutoCAD's *Replay* command.

FILENAME --------------- Name of rendered file, without the extension. The filename is to be enclosed in quotes. Include directory path and one forward slashes (/) for directory structures.

TYPE -------------------- The rendered file type (e.g., Bmp, Tif, Tga). The file type should also be enclosed in quotes.

XOFF -------------------- The rendered file's "X" coordinate offset from 0,0.

YOFF -------------------- The rendered file's "Y" coordinate offset from 0,0.

XSIZE -------------------- The size of the rendered file to be displayed in the "X" (horizontal) direction. This information can generally be obtained when creating a rendered file with AutoCAD's **SAVEIMG** command.

YSIZE -------------------- The size of the rendered file to be displayed in the "Y" (vertical) direction. This information can generally be obtained when creating a rendered file with AutoCAD's **SAVEIMG** command.

AutoCAD ships with a file call BIGLAKE.TGA as an example of a background texture map, Figure 2-9. To display this rendered image enter following at the Command prompt. Note: The "biglake.tga" file must be in AutoCAD's support directory's search path.

(C:REPLAY "C:/PROGRAM FILES/AutoCAD2000//TEXTURES/BIGLAKE" "TGA" 150 50 944 564)
Where:

C:REPLAY: ---------------- Function for AutoCAD to perform - issue the *Replay* command.

"C:/PRO../BIGLAKE" -- Name of the rendered image file, including drive and directory.

"TGA" -------------------- The rendered image file type.

150 -------------------- The "X" offset for the image displayed.

50 -------------------- The "Y" offset for the image displayed.

944 -------------------- The "X" size (horizontal) for the image displayed.

564) -------------------- The "Y" size (vertical) for the image displayed.

Combining Slides and Rendered Images

The following is an example of a script file (replay.scr) that combines the use of AutoCAD slides and rendered images (*.bmp files) into a seamless slide show presentation. The "F_" files are the wire FRAME images, while the "R_" files are the RENDERED images. It is assumed that the BMP image files are on A drive.

```
VSLIDE A:\SLIDES\F_ROLL
DELAY 3000
(C:REPLAY "A:/RENDERS/R_ROLL" "BMP" 0 0 944 564)
DELAY 3000
VSLIDE A:\SLIDES\F_BKCASE
DELAY 3000
(C:REPLAY "A:/RENDERS/R_BKCASE" "BMP" 0 0 944 564)
DELAY 3000
VSLIDE A:\SLIDES\F_MOUSE
DELAY 3000
(C:REPLAY "A:/RENDERS/R_MOUSE" "BMP" 0 0 944 564)
DELAY 3000
VSLIDE A:\SLIDES\F_TABLE2
DELAY 3000
(C:REPLAY "A:/RENDERS/R_TABLE2" "BMP" 0 0 944 564)
DELAY 3000
VSLIDE A:\SLIDES\F_MIC_3D
DELAY 3000
(C:REPLAY "A:/RENDERS/R_MIC_3D" "BMP" 0 0 944 564)
DELAY 3000
VSLIDE A:\SLIDES\F_BOX
DELAY 3000
(C:REPLAY "A:/RENDERS/R_BOX" "BMP" 0 0 944 564)
DELAY 3000 RSCRIPT
```

Figure 29-9 *Displaying a rendered image using a script file*

Review Questions

SCRIPT FILES

1. AutoCAD has provided a facility of _____ that allows you to combine different AutoCAD commands and execute them in a predetermined sequence.

2. The _____ files can be used to generate a slide show, do the initial drawing setup, or plot a drawing to a predefined specification.

3. Before writing a script file, you need to know the AutoCAD _____ and the _____ required in response to the command prompts.

4. In a script file, you can _____ several statements in one line.

5. In a script file, the _____ are used to terminate a command or a prompt entry.

6. The AutoCAD _____ command is used to run a script file.

7. When you run a script file, the default script file name is the same as the _____ name.

8. When you run a script file, type the name of the script file without the file _____.

9. One of the limitations of script files is that all the information has to be contained _____ the file.

10. The AutoCAD _____ command allows you to re-execute a script file indefinitely until the command is canceled.

11. You cannot provide a _____ statement in a script file to terminate the file when a particular condition is satisfied.

12. The AutoCAD _____ command introduces a delay before the next command is executed.

13. The **DELAY** command is to be followed by _____ in milliseconds.

14. If the script file was canceled and you want to continue the script file, you can do so by using the AutoCAD _____ command.

SLIDE SHOWS

15. AutoCAD provides a facility through _____ files to combine the slides in a text file and display them in a predetermined sequence.

16. A _____ can also be introduced in the script file so that the viewer has enough time to view a slide.

17. Slides are the _____ of a screen display.

18. Slides do not contain any _____ information, which means that the entities do not have any information associated with them.

19. Slides _____ edited like a drawing.

20. Slides can be created using the AutoCAD _____ command.

21. Slide file names can be up to _____ characters long.

22. In model space, you can use the **MSLIDE** command to make a slide of the _____ display in the _____ viewport.

23. If you are in paper space, you can make a slide of the display in paper space that _____ any floating viewports.

24. To view a slide, use the AutoCAD _____ command.

25. If you want to make any change in the slide, you need to _____ the drawing, then make a new slide from the edited drawing.

Exercises

SCRIPT FILES

Exercise 2   *General*

Write a script file that will do the following initial setup for a new drawing:

Limits	0,0 24,18
Grid	1.0
Snap	0.25
Ortho	On
Snap	On
Zoom	All
Pline width	0.02
PLine	0,0 24,0 24,18 0,18 0,0
Units	Decimal units
	Number of decimal digits (2)
	Decimal degrees

Number of decimal digits (2)
Direction of 0 angle (3 o'clock)
Angle measured counterclockwise

Ltscale 1.5

Layers

Name	**Color**	**Linetype**
Obj	Red	Continuous
Cen	Yellow	Center
Hid	Blue	Hidden
Dim	Green	Continuous

Exercise 3 · *General*

Write a script file that will **PLOT** a given drawing according to the following specifications. (Use the plotter for which your system is configured and adjust the values accordingly.)

Plot, using the Window option
Window size (0,0 24,18)
Do not write the plot to file
Size in Inch units
Plot origin (0.0,0.0)
Maximum plot size (8.5,11 or the smallest size available on your printer/plotter)
90 degree plot rotation
No removal of hidden lines
Plotting scale (Fit)

Exercise 4 · *General*

Write a script file that will continuously rotate a line in 10-degree increments around its midpoint (Figure 29-10). The time delay between increments is one second.

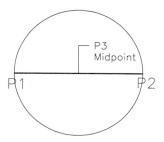

Figure 29-10 Drawing for Exercise 6

SLIDE SHOWS

Exercise 5   *General*

Make the slides shown in Figure 29-11 and write a script file for a continuous slide show. Provide a time delay of 3 seconds after every slide. (You do not have to use the slides shown in Figure 29-11; you can use any slides of your choice.)

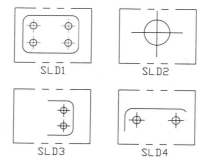

Figure 29-11 *Slides for slide show*

Chapter 30

Creating Linetypes and Hatch Patterns

Learning Objectives

After completing this chapter, you will be able to:
Create Linetypes:
- *Write linetype definitions.*
- *Create different linetypes.*
- *Create linetype files.*
- *Determine **LTSCALE** for plotting the drawing to given specifications.*
- *Define alternate linetypes and modify existing linetypes.*
- *Create string and shape complex linetypes.*

Create Hatch Patterns:
- *Understand hatch pattern definition.*
- *Create new hatch patterns.*
- *Determine the effect of angle and scale factor on hatch.*
- *Create hatch patterns with multiple descriptors.*
- *Save hatch patterns in a separate file.*
- *Define custom hatch pattern file.*
- *Add hatch pattern slides to AutoCAD slide library.*

STANDARD LINETYPES

The AutoCAD software package comes with a library of standard linetypes that has 38 different linetypes, including ISO linetypes. These linetypes are saved in the **ACAD.LIN** file. You can modify existing linetypes or create new ones.

LINETYPE DEFINITION

All linetype definitions consist of two parts: **header line and pattern line**.

Header Line

The **header line** consists of an asterisk (*) followed by the name of the linetype and the linetype description. The name and the linetype description should be separated by a comma. If there is no description, the comma that separates the linetype name and the description is not required.

The format of the header line is:

* Linetype Name, Description

Example
*HIDDENS,___ ___ ___ ___ ___ ___

            Where * ------------------- Asterisk sign
                   HIDDENS ------ Linetype name
                   , ------------------- Comma
                   __ __ __ __ ------ Linetype description

All linetype definitions require a linetype name. When you want to load a linetype or assign a linetype to an object, AutoCAD recognizes the linetype by the name you have assigned to the linetype definition. The names of the linetype definition should be selected to help the user recognize the linetype by its name. For example, a linetype name LINEFCX does not give the user any idea about the type of line. However, a linetype name like DASHDOT gives a better idea about the type of line that a user can expect.

The linetype description is a textual representation of the line. This representation can be generated by using dashes, dots, and spaces at the keyboard. The graphic is used by AutoCAD when you want to display the linetypes on the screen by using the AutoCAD **LINETYPE** command with the ? option or by using the dialog box. The linetype description cannot exceed 47 characters.

Pattern Line

The **pattern line** contains the definition of the line pattern. The definition of the line pattern consists of the alignment field specification and the linetype specification. The alignment field specification and the linetype specification are separated by a comma.

The format of the pattern line is:

Alignment Field Specification, Linetype Specification

Example
A,.75,-.25,.75
                Where **A** ------------------ Alignment field specification
                       , -------------------- Comma
                       .75,-.25,.75 ----- Linetype specification

The letter used for alignment field specification is A. This is the only alignment field supported by AutoCAD; therefore, the pattern line will always start with the letter A. The linetype specification defines the configuration of the dash-dot pattern to generate a line. The maximum number for dash length specification in the linetype is 12, provided the linetype pattern definition fits on one 80-character line.

ELEMENTS OF LINETYPE SPECIFICATION

All linetypes are created by combining the basic elements in a desired configuration. There are three basic elements that can be used to define a linetype specification.

Dash   (Pen down)
Dot   (Pen down, 0 length)
Space   (Pen up)

Example

_____ . _____ . _____ . _____

Where . -------------------- Dot (pen down with 0 length)
Blank space --------------- Space (pen up)
_____ ------------------- Dash (pen down with specified length)

The dashes are generated by defining a positive number. For example, .5 will generate a dash 0.5 units long. Similarly, spaces are generated by defining a negative number. For example, -.2 will generate a space 0.2 units long. The dot is generated by defining a 0 length.

Example
A,.5,-.2,0,-.2,.5
Where   **0** ------------------- Dot (zero length)
        -.2 ---------------- Length of space (pen up)
        .5 ------------------ Length of dash (pen down)

CREATING LINETYPES

Before creating a linetype, you need to decide the type of line you want to generate. Draw the line on a piece of paper and measure the length of each element that constitutes the line. You need to define only one segment of the line, because the pattern is repeated when you draw a line. Linetypes can be created or modified by one of the following methods:

Using the AutoCAD LINETYPE command
Using a text editor (such as Notepad).

Consider the following example, which creates a new linetype, first using the AutoCAD **LINETYPE** command and then using a text editor.

Example 1

Using the AutoCAD **LINETYPE** command, create linetype DASH3DOT (Figure 30-1) with the following specifications:

> Length of the first dash 0.5
> Blank space 0.125
> Dot
> Blank space 0.125
> Dot
> Blank space 0.125
> Dot
> Blank space 0.125

Using the AutoCAD Linetype Command

To create a linetype using the AutoCAD **LINETYPE** command, first make sure that you are in the drawing editor. Then enter the **LINETYPE** command and select the Create option to create a linetype.

Figure 30-1 Linetype specifications of DASH3DOT

> Command: -**LINETYPE**
> Enter an option [?/Create/Load/Set]: **C**

Enter the name of the linetype and the name of the library file in which you want to store the definition of the new linetype.

> Enter name of linetype to create: **DASH3DOT**

If **FILEDIA**=1, the **Create or Append Linetype File** dialog box (Figure 30-2) will appear on the screen. If **FILEDIA**=0, AutoCAD will prompt you to enter the name of the file.

> Enter linetype file name for new linetype definition <default>: **Acad**

If the linetype already exists, the following message will be displayed on the screen:

Figure 30-2 Create or Append Linetype File dialog box

Wait, checking if linetype already defined...
"Linetype" already exists in this file. Current definition is:
alighment, dash-1, dash-2, _____.
Overwrite?<N>

If you want to redefine the existing line style, enter Y; otherwise, type N or press RETURN to choose the default value of N. You can then repeat the process with a different name of the linetype.

After entering the name of the linetype and the library file name, AutoCAD will prompt you to enter the descriptive text and the pattern of the line.

Descriptive text: ***DASH3DOT,____ . . . ____ . . . ____**
Enter linetype pattern (on next line):
A,.5,-.125,0,-.125,0,-.125,0,-.125

Descriptive Text

*DASH3DOT,____ . . . ____ . . . ____

For the descriptive text, you have to type an asterisk (*) followed by the name of the linetype. For Example 1, the name of the linetype is DASH3DOT. The name *DASH3DOT can be followed by the description of the linetype; the length of this description cannot exceed 47 characters. In this example, the description is dashes and dots ____ . . . ____. It could be any text or alphanumeric string. The description is displayed on the screen when you list the linetypes.

Pattern

A,.5,-.125,0,-.125,0,-.125,0,-.125

The line pattern should start with an alignment definition. Currently, AutoCAD supports only

Chapter 30

one type of alignment—A. Therefore, it is automatically displayed on the screen when you select the **LINETYPE** command with the Create option. After entering **A** for pattern alignment, you must define the pen position. A positive number (.5 or 0.5) indicates a "pen-down" position, and a negative number (-.25 or -0.25) indicates a "pen-up" position. The length of the dash or the space is designated by the magnitude of the number. For example, 0.5 will draw a dash 0.5 units long, and -0.25 will leave a blank space of 0.25 units. A dash length of 0 will draw a dot (.). Here are the pattern definition elements for Example 1:

.5	**pen down**	**0.5 units long dash**
-.125	**pen up**	**.125 units blank space**
0	**pen down**	**dot**
-.125	**pen up**	**.125 units blank space**
0	**pen down**	**dot**
-.125	**pen up**	**.125 units blank space**
0	**pen down**	**dot**
-.125	**pen up**	**.125 units blank space**

After you enter the pattern definition, the linetype (DASH3DOT) is automatically saved in the **ACAD.LIN** file. The linetype (DASH3DOT) can be loaded using the AutoCAD **LINETYPE** command and selecting the **Load** option.

Note
The name and the description must be separated by a comma (,). The description is optional. If you decide not to give one, omit the comma after the linetype name DASH3DOT.

Using a Text Editor

You can also use a text editor (like Notepad) to create a new linetype. Using the text editor, load the file and insert the lines that define the new linetype. The following file is a partial listing of the **ACAD.LIN** file after adding a new linetype to the file:

```
*BORDER,__ __ . __ __ . __ __ . __ __ . __ __ . __ __ .
A,.5,-.25,.5,-.25,0,-.25
*BORDER2,__._.__._.__._.__._.__._.__._.__._.__._.
A,.25,-.125,.25,-.125,0,-.125
*BORDERX2,____ ____ . ____ ____ . ____ ____ .
A,1.0,-.5,1.0,-.5,0,-.5

*CENTER,____ _ ____ _ ____ _ ____ _ ____ _ ____ _ ____
A,1.25,-.25,.25,-.25
*CENTER2,___ _ ___ _ ___ _ ___ _ ___ _ ___ _ ___
A,.75,-.125,.125,-.125
*CENTERX2,_____ __ _____ __ _____ __ __
A,2.5,-.5,.5,-.5
*DASHDOT,__ . __ . __ . __ . __ . __ . __ .
A,.5,-.25,0,-.25
*DOTX2,. . . . . . . . . . . . . . . .
```

```
A,.25,-.125
*HIDDEN2,_ _ _ _ _ _ _ _ _ _ _ _ _ _ _ _ _ _ _ _ _
A,.125,-.0625
*HIDDENX2,___ ___ ___ ___ ___ ___ ___ ___ ___
A,.5,-.25
*PHANTOM,_____ __ __ _____ __ __ _____ __ __
A,1.25,-.25,.25,-.25,.25,-.25
*PHANTOM2,___ __ __ ___ __ __ ___ __ __ ___ __ _
A,.625,-.125,.125,-.125,.125,-.125
 *PHANTOMX2,_____   ___   ___   _____
```

```
*HOT_WATER_SUPPLY,Hot water supply ---- HW ---- HW ---- HW ----
A,.5,-.2,["HW",STANDARD,S=.1,R=0.0,X=-0.1,Y=-.05],-.2
*GAS_LINE,Gas line ----GAS----GAS----GAS----GAS----GAS----GAS--
A,.5,-.2,["GAS",STANDARD,S=.1,R=0.0,X=-0.1,Y=-.05],-.25
*ZIGZAG,Zig zag /\/\/\/\/\/\/\/\/\/\/\/\/\/\
A,.0001,-.2,[ZIG,ltypeshp.shx,x=-.2,s=.2],-.4,[ZIG,ltypeshp.shx,r=180,x=.2,s=.2],-.2
**DASH3DOT,___ . . . ___ . . . ___**
**A,.5,-.125,0,-.125,0,-.125,0,-.125**
```

The last two lines of this file define the new linetype, DASH3DOT. The first line contains the name DASH3DOT and the description of the line (___ . . .___). The second line contains the alignment and the pattern definition. Save the file and then load the linetype using the AutoCAD **LINETYPE** command with the Load option. The lines and polylines that this linetype will gen-

Figure 30-3 Lines created by linetype DASH3DOT

Note
If you change the LTSCALE factor, all lines in the drawing are affected by the new ratio.

CREATING LINETYPE FILES

You can start a new linetype file and then add the line definitions to this file. Use any text editor like Notepad to start a new file (NEWLT.LIN) and then add the following two lines to the file to define the DASH3DOT linetype.

> ***DASH3DOT,___ . . . ___ . . . ___**
> **A,.5,-.125,0,-.125,0,-.125,0,-.125**

You can load the DASH3DOT linetype from this file using AutoCAD's **LINETYPE** command and then selecting the LOAD option.

> Command: **-LINETYPE**
> Enter an option [?/Create/Load/Set]: **L**
> Enter linetype(s) to load: **DASHDOT**
> Enter name of linetype file to search <default>: **NEWLT**

You can also load the linetype by using **Linetype Manager** dialog box (Figure 30-4) that can be invoked by entering **LINETYPE** at the Command prompt and selecting **Linetype** from the **Format** menu.

*Figure 30-4 Loading linetypes using **Linetype Properties Manager** dialog*

ALIGNMENT SPECIFICATION

The alignment specifies the pattern alignment at the start and the end of the line, circle, or arc. In other words, the line would always start and end with the dash (___). The alignment definition "A" requires that the first element be a dash or dot (pen down), followed by a negative (pen up) segment. The minimum number of dash segments for alignment A is two. If there is not enough space for the line AutoCAD will draw a continuous line.

For example, in the linetype DASH3DOT of Example 1, the length of each line segment is 1.0 (.5 + .125 + .125 + .125 + .125 = 1.0). If the length of the line drawn is less than 1.00, the line will be drawn as a continuous line (Figure 30-5). If the length of the line is 1.00 or greater, the line will be drawn according to DASH3DOT linetype. AutoCAD automatically adjusts the length of the dashes and the line will always start and end with a dash. The length of the starting and ending dashes will be at least half the length of the dash as specified in the file. If the length of the dash as specified in the file is 0.5, the length of the starting and ending dashes will be at least 0.25. To fit a line that starts and ends with a dash, the length of these dashes can also increase as shown in Figure 30-5.

Figure 30-5 *Alignment of linetype DASH3DOT*

LTSCALE COMMAND

As we mentioned previously, the length of each line segment in the DASH3DOT linetype is 1.0 (.5 + .125 + .125 + .125 + .125 = 1.0). If you draw a line that is less than 1.0 units long, AutoCAD will draw a single dash that looks like a continuous line (Figure 30-6). This problem can be rectified by changing the linetype scale factor variable **LTSCALE** to a smaller value. This can be accomplished by using AutoCAD's **LTSCALE** command:

Command: **LTSCALE**
Enter new linetype scale factor <default>: *New value.*

The default value of the **LTSCALE** variable is 1.0. If the LTSCALE is changed to 0.75, the length of each segment is reduced by 0.75 (1.0 x 0.75 = 0.75). Then, if you draw a line 0.75 units or longer, it will be drawn according to the definition of DASH3DOT (___ . . . ___) (Figures 30-6 and 30-7).

The appearance of the lines is also affected by the limits of the drawing. Most of the AutoCAD linetypes work fine for a drawing that has the limits 12,9. Figure 30-9 shows a line of linetype DASH3DOT that is four units long and the limits of the drawing are 12,9. If you increase the limits to 48,36 the lines will appear as continuous lines. If you want the line to appear the same as before **on the screen**, the LTSCALE should be changed. Since the limits of the drawing have increased four times, the LTSCALE should also increase by the same amount. If you change the

Figure 30-6 *Alignment when Ltscale = 1*

Figure 30-7 *Alignment when Ltscale = 0.99*

scale factor to four, the line segments will also increase by a factor of four. As shown in Figure 30-9, the length of the starting and the ending dash has increased to one unit.

In general, the approximate LTSCALE factor for **screen display** can be obtained by dividing the X-limit of the drawing by the default X-limit (12.00).

LTSCALE factor for SCREEN DISPLAY = X-limits of the drawing/12.00

Example

Drawing limits are 48,36
LTSCALE factor for screen display = 48/12 = 4

Drawing sheet size is 36,24 and scale is 1/4" = 1'
LTSCALE factor for screen display = 12 x 4 x (36 / 12) = 144

Figure 30-8 *Alignment when Ltscale = 0.75*

Figure 30-9 *Linetype DASH3DOT before and after changing the LTSCALE*

LTSCALE FACTOR FOR PLOTTING

The LTSCALE factor for plotting depends on the size of the sheet you are using to plot the drawing. For example, if the limits are 48 by 36, the drawing scale is 1:1, and you want to plot the drawing on a 48" by 36" size sheet, the LTSCALE factor is 1. If you check the specification of a hidden line in the ACAD.LIN file, the length of each dash is 0.25. Therefore, when you plot a drawing with 1:1 scale, the length of each dash in a hidden line is 0.25.

However, if the drawing scale is 1/8" = 1' and you want to plot the drawing on a 48" by 36" paper, the LTSCALE factor must be 96 (8 x 12 = 96). The length of each dash in the hidden line will increase by a factor of 96 because the LTSCALE factor is 96. Therefore, the length of each dash will be 24 units (0.25 x 96 = 24). At the time of plotting, the scale factor for plotting must be 1:96 to plot the 384' by 288' drawing on a 48" by 36" size paper. Each dash of the hidden line that was 24" long on the drawing will be 0.25 (24/96 = 0.25) inch long when plotted. Similarly, if the desired text size on the paper is 1/8", the text height in the drawing must be 12" (1/8 x 96 = 12").

Ltscale Factor for PLOTTING = Drawing Scale

Sometimes your plotter may not be able to plot a 48" by 36" drawing or you might like to decrease the size of the plot so that the drawing fits within a specified area. To get the correct dash lengths for hidden, center, or other lines, you must adjust the LTSCALE factor. For example, if you want to plot the previously mentioned drawing in a 45" by 34" area, the correction factor is:

$$\text{Correction factor} = 48/45 = 1.0666$$

$$\text{New LTSCALE factor} = \text{LTSCALE factor x Correction factor} = 96 \times 1.0666 = 102.4$$

New Ltscale Factor for PLOTTING = Drawing Scale x Correction Factor

 Note

If you change the LTSCALE factor, all lines in the drawing are affected by the new ratio.

ALTERNATE LINETYPES

One of the problems with the LTSCALE factor is that it affects all the lines in the drawing. As shown in Figure 30-10(a), the length of each segment in all DASH3DOT type lines is approximately equal, no matter how long the lines. You might want to have a small segment length if the lines are small and a longer segment length if the lines are long. You can accomplish this by using CELTSCALE (discussed later in this chapter) or by defining an alternate linetype with a different segment length. For example, you can define a linetype DASH3DOT and DASH3DOTX with different line pattern specifications.

```
*DASH3DOT,____ . . . ____ . . . ____ . . . ____
A,0.5,-.125,0,-.125,0,-.125,0,-.125
*DASH3DOTX,_____ . . . _____
A,1.0,-.25,0,-.25,0,-.25,0,-.25
```

In DASH3DOT linetype the segment length is one unit, whereas in DASH3DOTX linetype the segment length is two units. You can have several alternate linetypes to produce the lines with different segment lengths. Figure 30-10(b) shows the lines generated by DASH3DOT and DASH3DOTX.

 Note

Although you might have used different linetypes with different segment lengths, the lines will be affected equally when you change the LTSCALE factor. For example, if the LTSCALE factor is 0.5, the segment length of DASH3DOT line will be 0.5 and the segment length of DASH3DOTX will be 1.0 units.

Figure 30-10 *Linetypes generated by DASH3DOT and DASH3DOTX*

MODIFYING LINETYPES

You can also modify the linetypes that are defined in the ACAD.LIN file. You need a text editor, such as Notepad, to modify the linetype. You can also use the EDIT function of DOS, or AutoCAD's **EDIT** command (provided the ACAD.PGP file is present and EDIT is defined in the file). For example, if you want to change the dash length of the border linetype from 0.5 to 0.75, load the file, then edit the pattern line of the border linetype. The following file is a partial listing of the ACAD.LIN file after changing the border and centerx2 linetypes.

```
;;  AutoCAD Linetype Definition file,  Version 2.0
;;  Copyright 1991, 1992, 1993, 1994, 1996 by Autodesk, Inc.
;;
*BORDER,__ __ . __ __ . __ __ . __ __ . __ __ . __ __ . __ __ .
A,.75,-.25,.75,-.25,0,-.25
*BORDER2,Border (.5x) __.__.__.__.__.__.__.__.__.
A,.25,-.125,.25,-.125,0,-.125
*BORDERX2,Border (2x) ___ ___ . ___ ___ . ___
A,1.0,-.5,1.0,-.5,0,-.5


*CENTER,Center ____ _ ____ _ ____ _ ____ _ ____ _ ____
A,1.25,-.25,.25,-.25
*CENTER2,Center (.5x) __ _ __ _ __ _ __ _ __ _ __
A,.75,-.125,.125,-.125
*CENTERX2,Center (2x) _____ __ _____ __ _____
A,3.5,-.5,.5,-.5


*DASHDOT,Dash dot __ . __ . __ . __ . __ . __ . __
A,.5,-.25,0,-.25
*DASHDOT2,Dash dot (.5x) _._._._._._._._._._._._.
A,.25,-.125,0,-.125
*DASHDOTX2,Dash dot (2x) ____ . ____ . ____ . __
```

A,1.0,-.5,0,-.5

*DASHED,Dashed __ __ __ __ __ __ __ __ __ __ __ __ __ __ -
A,.5,-.25
*DASHED2,Dashed (.5x) _ _ _ _ _ _ _ _ _ _ _ _ _ _ _ _ _
A,.25,-.125
*DASHEDX2,Dashed (2x) ___ ___ ___ ___ ___ __
A,1.0,-.5

*DIVIDE,Divide ____ . . ____ . . ____ . . ____ . . ____
A,.5,-.25,0,-.25,0,-.25
*DIVIDE2,Divide (.5x) __·__·__·__·__·__·__·__·__·_
A,.25,-.125,0,-.125,0,-.125
*DIVIDEX2,Divide (2x) _____ . . _____ . . _
A,1.0,-.5,0,-.5,0,-.5

*DOT,Dot . . . .
A,0,-.25
*DOT2,Dot (.5x) ....
A,0,-.125
*DOTX2,Dot (2x) . . . .
A,0,-.5

*HIDDEN,Hidden __ __ __ __ __ __ __ __ __ __ __ __ __ __
A,.25,-.125
*HIDDEN2,Hidden (.5x) _ _ _ _ _ _ _ _ _ _ _ _ _ _ _ _ __
A,.125,-.0625
*HIDDENX2,Hidden (2x) ___ ___ ___ ___ ___ ___ ___
A,.5,-.25

*PHANTOM,Phantom _____ __ __ _____ __ __ _____
A,1.25,-.25,.25,-.25,.25,-.25
*PHANTOM2,Phantom (.5x) ___ _ _ ___ _ _ ___ _ _ __
A,.625,-.125,.125,-.125,.125,-.125
*PHANTOMX2,Phantom (2x) _____ ___ ___ _
A,2.5,-.5,.5,-.5,.5,-.5
;; ISO 128 (ISO/DIS 12011) linetypes
;; The size of the line segments for each defined ISO line, is
;; defined for an usage with a pen width of 1 mm. To use them with
;; the other ISO predefined pen widths, the line has to be scaled
;; with the appropriate value (e.g. pen width 0,5 mm -> ltscale 0.5).
;;
*ACAD_ISO02W100,ISO dash __ __ __ __ __ __ __ __ __ __ __ __ __
A,12,-3
*ACAD_ISO03W100,ISO dash space __ __ __ __ __ __
A,12,-18
*ACAD_ISO04W100,ISO long-dash dot ____ . ____ . ____ . ____ . _

```
A,24,-3,.5,-3
*ACAD_ISO05W100,ISO long-dash double-dot ____ .. ____ .. ____ .
A,24,-3,.5,-3,.5,-3
*ACAD_ISO06W100,ISO long-dash triple-dot ____ ... ____ ... ____
A,24,-3,.5,-3,.5,-3,.5,-3
*ACAD_ISO07W100,ISO dot . . . . . . . . . . . . . . . . . .
A,.5,-3
*ACAD_ISO08W100,ISO long-dash short-dash ____ _ ____ _ ____ _
A,24,-3,6,-3
*ACAD_ISO09W100,ISO long-dash double-short-dash ____ _ _ ____
A,24,-3,6,-3,6,-3
*ACAD_ISO10W100,ISO dash dot __ . __ . __ . __ . __ . __ . __ .
A,12,-3,.5,-3
*ACAD_ISO11W100,ISO double-dash dot __ __ . __ __ . __ __ . __ __
A,12,-3,12,-3,.5,-3
*ACAD_ISO12W100,ISO dash double-dot __ .. __ .. __ .. __ ..
A,12,-3,.5,-3,.5,-3
*ACAD_ISO13W100,ISO double-dash double-dot __ __ .. __ __ .. _
A,12,-3,12,-3,.5,-3,.5,-3
*ACAD_ISO14W100,ISO dash triple-dot __ ... __ ... __ ... _
A,12,-3,.5,-3,.5,-3,.5,-3
*ACAD_ISO15W100,ISO double-dash triple-dot __ __ ... __ __ ..
A,12,-3,12,-3,.5,-3,.5,-3,.5,-3
;; Complex linetypes
;;
;; Complex linetypes have been added to this file.
;; These linetypes were defined in LTYPESHP.LIN in
;; Release 13, and are incorporated in ACAD.LIN in
;; Release 14.
;;
;; These linetype definitions use LTYPESHP.SHX.
;;
*FENCELINE1,Fenceline circle ——0——0——0——0——0——0—
A,.25,-.1,[CIRC1,ltypeshp.shx,x=-.1,s=.1],-.1,1
*FENCELINE2,Fenceline square ——[]——[]——[]——[]——[]——
A,.25,-.1,[BOX,ltypeshp.shx,x=-.1,s=.1],-.1,1
*TRACKS,Tracks -|-|-|-|-|-|-|-|-|-|-|-|-|-|-|-|-|-|-|-|-|-|-|-
A,.15,[TRACK1,ltypeshp.shx,s=.25],.15
*BATTING,Batting SSSSSSSSSSSSSSSSSSSSSSSSSSSSSSSSSSSSSSSSSSSSSSS
A,.0001,-.1,[BAT,ltypeshp.shx,x=-.1,s=.1],-.2,[BAT,ltypeshp.shx,r=180,x=.1,s=.1],-.1
*HOT_WATER_SUPPLY,Hot water supply —— HW —— HW —— HW ——
A,.5,-.2,["HW",STANDARD,S=.1,R=0.0,X=-0.1,Y=-.05],-.2
*GAS_LINE,Gas line ——GAS——GAS——GAS——GAS——GAS——GAS—
A,.5,-.2,["GAS",STANDARD,S=.1,R=0.0,X=-0.1,Y=-.05],-.25
*ZIGZAG,Zig zag /\/\/\/\/\/\/\/\/\/\/\/\/\/\/\
A,.0001,-.2,[ZIG,ltypeshp.shx,x=-.2,s=.2],-.4,[ZIG,ltypeshp.shx,r=180,x=.2,s=.2],-.2
```

Example 2

Create a new file, **NEWLINET.LIN**, and define a linetype, VARDASH, with the following specifications:

> Length of first dash 1.0
> Blank space 0.25
> Length of second dash 0.75
> Blank space 0.25
> Length of third dash 0.5
> Blank space 0.25
> Dot
> Blank space 0.25
> Length of next dash 0.5
> Blank space 0.25
> Length of next dash 0.75

Use a text editor and insert the following lines that define the new linetype VARDASH. Save the file as NEWLINET.LIN.

> ***VARDASH,——— —— — . — —— ———**
> **A,1,-.25,.75,-.25,.5,-.25,0,-.25,.5,-.25,.75,-.25**

The type of lines that this linetype will generate are shown in Figure 30-11.

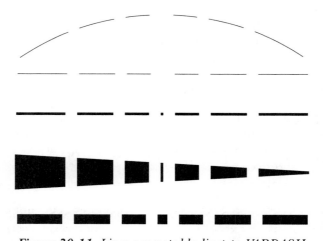

Figure 30-11 *Lines generated by linetype VARDASH*

CURRENT LINETYPE SCALING (CELTSCALE)

Like **LTSCALE**, the **CELTSCALE** system variable controls the linetype scaling. The difference is that **CELTSCALE** determines the current linetype scaling. For example, if you set the **CELTSCALE** to 0.5, all lines drawn after setting the new value for **CELTSCALE** will have the linetype scaling factor of 0.5. The value is retained in the **CELTSCALE** system variable. The first line (a) in Figure 30-12 is drawn with the **CELTSCALE** factor of 1 and the second line (b) is drawn with the **CELTSCALE** factor of 0.5. The length of the dashed is reduced by a factor of 0.5 when the **CELTSCALE** is 0.5.

The **LTSCALE** system variable controls the global scale factor. For example, if **LTSCALE** is set to 2, all lines in the drawing will be affected by a factor of 2. The net scale factor is equal to the product of **CELTSCALE** and **LTSCALE**.

*Figure 30-12 Using **CELTSCALE** to control current linetype scaling*

Figure 30-12(c) shows a line that is drawn with **LTSCALE** of 2 and **CELTSCALE** of 0.25. The net scale factor is = **LTSCALE** x **CELTSCALE** = 2 x 0.25 = 0.5.

COMPLEX LINETYPES

AutoCAD has provided a facility to create complex linetypes. The complex linetypes can be classified into two groups: string complex linetype and shape complex linetype. The difference between the two is that the string complex linetype has a text string inserted in the line, whereas the shape complex linetype has a shape inserted in the line. The facility of creating complex linetypes increases the functionality of lines. For example, if you want to draw a line around a building that indicates the fence line, you can do it by defining a complex linetype that will automatically give you the desired line with the text string (Fence). Similarly, you can define a complex linetype that will insert a shape (symbol) at predefined distances along the line.

Creating a String Complex Linetype

When writing the definition of a string complex linetype, the actual text and its attributes must be included in the linetype definition. The format of the string complex linetype is:

["String", Text Style, Text Height, Rotation, X-Offset, Y-Offset]

String. It is the actual text that you want to insert along the line. The text string must be enclosed in quotation marks (" ").

Text Style. This is the name of the text style file that you want to use for generating the text string. The text style must be predefined.

Text Height. This is the actual height of the text, if the text height defined in the text style is 0. Otherwise, it acts as a scale factor for the text height specified in the text style. In Figure 30-13, the height of the text is 0.1 units.

Rotation. This is the rotation of the text string with respect to the positive X axis. The angle is always measured with respect to the positive X axis, no matter what AutoCAD's direction setting.

The angle can be specified in radians (r), grads (g), or degrees (d). The default is degrees.

X-Offset. This is the distance of the lower left corner of the text string from the endpoint of the line segment measured along the line. If the line is horizontal, then the X-Offset distance is measured along the X axis. In Figure 30-13, the X-Offset distance is 0.05.

Y-Offset. This is the distance of the lower left corner of the text string from the endpoint of the line segment measured perpendicular to the line. If the line is horizontal, then the Y-Offset distance is measured along the Y axis.

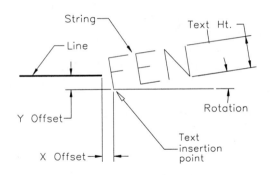

Figure 30-13   The attributes of a string complex linetype

In Figure 30-13, the Y-Offset distance is -0.05. The distance is negative because the start point of the text string is 0.05 units below the endpoint of the first line segment.

Example 3   *General*

In the following example, you will write the definition of a string complex linetype that consists of the text string "Fence" and line segments. The length of each line segment is 0.75. The height of the text string is 0.1 units, and the space between the end of the text string and the following line segment is 0.05 (Figure 30-14).

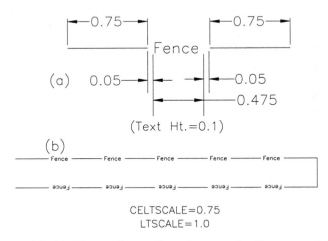

Figure 30-14   The attributes of a string complex linetype and line specifications for Example 3

Step 1

Before writing the definition of a new linetype, it is important to determine the line specification. One of the ways this can be done is to actually draw the lines and the text the way you want them to appear in the drawing. Once you have drawn the line and the text to your satisfaction, measure the distances needed to define the string complex linetype. In this example, the values are given as follows:

Text string=	Fence
Text style=	Standard
Text height=	0.1
Text rotation=	0
X-Offset=	0.05
Y-Offset=	-0.05
Length of the first line segment=	0.75
Distance between the line segments=	0.575

Step 2

Use a text editor to write the definition of the string complex linetype. You can add the definition to the AutoCAD **ACAD.LIN** file or create a separate file. The extension of the file must be **.LIN**. The following file is the listing of the **FENCE.LIN** file for Example 3. The name of the linetype is NEWFence.

```
*NEWFence1,New fence boundary line
A,0.75,["Fence",Standard,S=0.1,A=0,X=0.05,Y=-0.05],-0.575
or
A,0.75,-0.05,["Fence",Standard,S=0.1,A=0,X=0,Y=-0.05],-0.525
```

Step 3

To test the linetype, load the linetype using the **LINETYPE** command with the Load option, and assign it to a layer. Draw a line or any object to check if the line is drawn to the given specifications. Notice that the text is always drawn along X axis. Also, when you draw a line at an angle, polyline, circle, or spline, the text string does not align with the object (Figure 30-15).

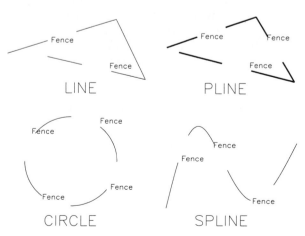

Figure 30-15 *Using string complex linetype with angle A=0*

Step 4

In the NEWFence linetype definition, the specified angle is 0 degrees (Absolute angle A = 0). Therefore, when you use the NEWFence linetype to draw a line, circle, polyline, or spline, the text string (Fence) will be at zero degrees. If you want the text string (Fence) to align with the polyline (Figure 30-16), spline, or circle, specify the angle as relative angle (R = 0) in the NEWFence linetype definition. The following is the linetype definition for NEWFence linetype with relative angle R = 0:

```
*NEWFence2,New fence boundary line
A,0.75,["Fence",Standard,S=0.1,R=0,X=0.05,Y=-0.05],-0.575
```

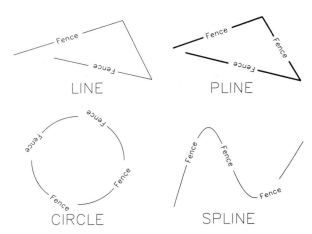

***Figure 30-16** Using a string complex linetype with angle R = 0*

Step 5

In Figure 30-16, you might notice that the text string is not properly aligned with the circumference of the circle. This is because AutoCAD draws the text string in a direction that is tangent to the circle at the text insertion point. To resolve this problem, you must define the middle point of the text string as the insertion point. Also, the line specifications should be measured accordingly. Figure 30-17 gives the measurements of the NEWFence linetype with the middle point of the text as the insertion point.

The following is the linetype definition for NEWFence linetype:

```
*NEWFence3,New fence boundary line
A,0.75,-0.287,["FENCE",Standard,S=0.1,X=-0.237,Y=-0.05],-0.287
```

 Note

If no angle is defined in the line definition, it defaults to angle R = 0.

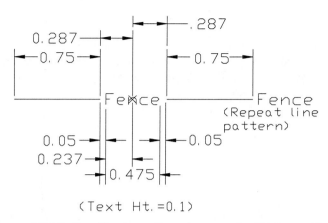

Figure 30-17 *Specifications of a string complex linetype with the middle point of the text string as the text insertion point*

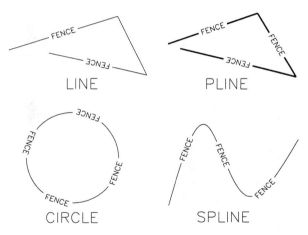

Figure 30-18 *Using a string complex linetype with the middle point of the text string as the text insertion point*

Creating a Shape Complex Linetype

As with the string complex linetype, when you write the definition of a shape complex linetype, the name of the shape, the name of the shape file, and other shape attributes, like rotation, scale, X-Offset, and Y-Offset, must be included in the linetype definition. The format of the shape complex linetype is:

[Shape Name, Shape File, Scale, Rotation, X-Offset, Y-Offset]

Shape Complex Linetype Attributes Assigned to the Shape (Figure 30-19).

Shape Name. This is the name of the shape that you want to insert along the line. The shape name must exist; otherwise, no shape will be generated along the line.

Shape File. This is the name of the compiled shape file (.SHX) that contains the definition of the shape being inserted in the line. The name of the subdirectory where the shape file is located must be in the ACAD search path. The shape files (.SHP) must be compiled before using the SHAPE command to load the shape.

Scale. This is the scale factor by which the defined shape size is to be scaled. If the scale is 1, the size of the shape will be the same as defined in the shape definition (.SHP file).

Rotation. This is the rotation of the shape with respect to the positive X axis.

X-Offset. This is the distance of the shape insertion point from the endpoint of the line segment measured along the line. If the line is horizontal, then the X-Offset distance is measured along the X axis. In Figure 30-19, the X-Offset distance is 0.2.

Y-Offset. This is the distance of the shape insertion point from the endpoint of the line segment measured perpendicular to the line. If the line is horizontal, then the Y-Offset distance is measured along the Y axis. In Figure 30-19, the Y-Offset distance is 0.

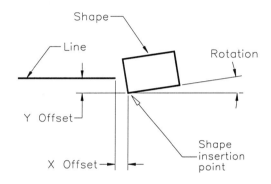

Figure 30-19 *The attributes of a shape complex linetype*

Example 4

In the following example, you will write the definition of a shape complex linetype that consists of the shape (Manhole; the name of the shape is MH) and a line. The scale of the shape is 0.1, the length of each line segment is 0.75, and the space between line segments is 0.2.

Step 1

Before writing the definition of a new linetype, it is important to determine the line specifications. One of the ways this can be done is to actually draw the lines and the shape the way you want them to appear in the drawing (Figure 30-20). Once you have drawn the line and the shape to your satisfaction, measure the distances needed to define the shape complex linetype. In this example, the values are as follows:

```
Shape name   MH
Shape file name  MHOLE.SHX   (Name of the compiled shape file.)
Scale         0.1
Rotation      0
X-Offset      0.2
Y-Offset      0
```

Length of the first line segment = 0.75
Distance between the line segments = 0.2

Figure 30-20 *The attributes of the shape complex linetype and line specifications for Example 4*

Step 2

Use a text editor to write the definition of the shape file. The extension of the file must be **.SHP**. The following file is the listing of the **MHOLE.SHP** file for Example 4. The name of the shape is MH. (For details, refer to Customizing AutoCAD by Sham Tickoo, Delmar/ITP publishers.)

```
*215,9,MH
001,10,(1,007),
001,10,(1,071),0
```

Step 3

Use the **COMPILE** command to compile the shape file (**.SHP** file). When you use this command, AutoCAD will prompt you to enter the name of the shape file (Figure 30-21). For this example, the name is **MHOLE.SHP**. The following is the command sequence for compiling the shape file:

Command: **COMPILE**
Enter shape (.SHP) or PostScript font (.PFB) file name: **MHOLE**

You can also compile the shape from the command line by setting **FILEDIA**=0 and then using the **COMPILE** command.

Step 4

Use a text editor to write the definition of the shape complex linetype. You can add the definition to the AutoCAD ACAD.LIN file or create a separate file. The extension of the file must be .LIN. The following file is the listing of the MHOLE.LIN file for Example 4. The name of the linetype is MHOLE.

*MHOLE,Line with Manholes
A,0.75,[MH,MHOLE.SHX,S=0.10,X=0.2,Y=0],-0.2

Figure 30-21 Select Shape or Font File dialog box

Step 5

To test the linetype, load the linetype using the **LINETYPE** command with the Load option and assign it to a layer. Draw a line or any object to check if the line is drawn to the given specifications. The shape is drawn upside down when you draw a line from right to left.

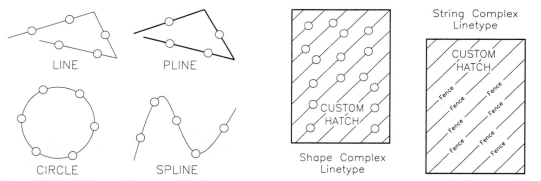

Figure 30-22 Using a shape complex linetype

Figure 30-23 Using shape and string complex linetypes to create custom hatch

HATCH PATTERN DEFINITION

The AutoCAD software comes with a hatch pattern library file, **ACAD.PAT**, that contains 67 hatch patterns. These hatch patterns are sufficient for general drafting work. However, if you need a different hatch pattern, AutoCAD lets you create your own. There is no limit to the number of hatch patterns you can define.

The hatch patterns you define can be added to the hatch pattern library file, **ACAD.PAT**. You can also create a new hatch pattern library file, provided the file contains only one hatch pattern definition, and the name of the hatch is the same as the name of the file. The hatch pattern definition consists of the following two parts: **header line and hatch descriptors**.

Header Line

The **header line** consists of an asterisk (*) followed by the name of the hatch pattern. The hatch name is the name used in the hatch command to hatch an area. After the name, you can give the hatch description, which is separated from the hatch name by a comma (,). The general format of the header line is:

*HATCH Name [, Hatch Description]
        Where   ***** ---------------------------- Asterisk
                HATCH Name ----------- Name of hatch pattern
                Hatch Description ------ Description of hatch pattern

The description can be any text that describes the hatch pattern. It can also be omitted, in which case, a comma should not follow the hatch pattern name.

Example
*DASH45, Dashed lines at 45 degrees
        Where   **DASH45** --------- Hatch name
                Dashed lines at 45 degrees -----Hatch description

Hatch Descriptors

The **hatch descriptors** consist of one or more lines that contain the definition of the hatch lines. The general format of the hatch descriptor is:

Angle, X-origin, Y-origin, D1, D2 [,Dash Length.....]
        Where   **Angle** ------------ Angle of hatch lines
                X-origin --------- X coordinate of hatch line
                Y-origin --------- Y coordinate of hatch line
                D1 ---------------- Displacement of second line (Delta-X)
                D2 ---------------- Distance between hatch lines (Delta-Y)
                Length ----------- Length of dashes and spaces (Pattern line definition)

Example
45,0,0,0,0.5,0.5,-0.125,0,-0.125
        Where   **45** ----------------- Angle of hatch line
                0 ------------------ X-Origin
                0 ------------------ Y-Origin
                0 ------------------ Delta-X
                0.5 ---------------- Delta-Y
                0.5 ---------------- Dash (pen down)
                -0.125 ------------ Space (pen up)
                0 ------------------ Dot (pen down)
                -0.125 ------------ Space (pen up)
                0.5,-0.125,0,-0.125 Pattern line definition

Hatch Angle

X-origin and Y-origin. The hatch angle is the angle that the hatch lines make with the positive X axis. The angle is positive if measured counterclockwise (Figure 30-24), and negative if the angle is measured clockwise. When you draw a hatch pattern, the first hatch line starts from the point defined by X-origin and Y-origin. The remaining lines are generated by offsetting the first hatch line by a distance specified by delta-X and delta-Y. In Figure 30-25(a), the first hatch line starts from the point with the coordinates X = 0 and Y = 0. In Figure 30-25(b) the first line of hatch starts from a point with the coordinates X = 0 and Y = 0.25.

Figure 30-24 Hatch angle

Figure 30-25 X-origin and Y-origin of hatch lines

Delta-X and Delta-Y. Delta-X is the displacement of the offset line in the direction in which the hatch lines are generated. For example, if the lines are drawn at a 0-degree angle and delta-X = 0.5, the offset line will be displaced by a distance delta-X (0.5) along the 0-angle direction. Similarly, if the hatch lines are drawn at a 45-degree angle, the offset line will be displaced by a distance delta-X (0.5) along a 45-degree direction (Figure 30-26). Delta-Y is the displacement of the offset lines measured perpendicular to the hatch lines. For example, if delta-Y = 1.0, the space between any two hatch lines will be 1.0 (Figure 30-26).

HOW HATCH WORKS

When you hatch an area, AutoCAD generates an infinite number of hatch lines of infinite length. The first hatch line always passes through the point specified by the X-origin and Y-origin. The remaining lines are generated by offsetting the first hatch line in both directions. The offset distance is determined by delta-X and delta-Y. All selected entities that form the boundary of the

Figure 30-26 Delta-X and delta-Y of hatch lines

hatch area are then checked for intersection with these lines. Any hatch lines found within the defined hatch boundaries are turned on, and the hatch lines outside the hatch boundary are turned off, as shown in Figure 30-27. Since the hatch lines are generated by offsetting, the hatch lines in different areas of the drawing are automatically aligned relative to the drawing's snap origin. Figure 30-27(a) shows the hatch lines as computed by AutoCAD. These lines are not drawn on the screen; they are shown here for illustration only. Figure 30-27(b) shows the hatch lines generated in the circle that was defined as the hatch boundary.

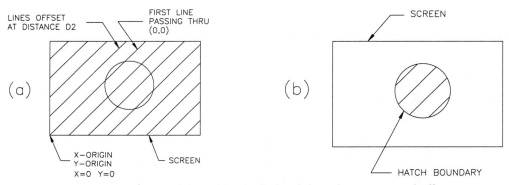

Figure 30-27 Hatch lines outside the hatch boundary are turned off

SIMPLE HATCH PATTERN

It is good practice to develop the hatch pattern specification before writing a hatch pattern definition. For simple hatch patterns it may not be that important, but for more complicated hatch patterns you should know the detailed specifications. Example 5 illustrates the procedure for developing a simple hatch pattern.

Example 5

Write a hatch pattern definition for the hatch pattern shown in Figure 30-28, with the following specifications:

Name of the hatch pattern =	HATCH1
X-Origin =	0
Y-Origin =	0
Distance between hatch lines =	0.5
Displacement of hatch lines =	0
Hatch line pattern =	Continuous

This hatch pattern definition can be added to the existing **ACAD.PAT** hatch file. You can use any text editor (like Notepad) to write the file. Load the **ACAD.PAT** file that is located in **AutoCAD2000\SUPPORT** directory and insert the following two lines at the end of the file.

*HATCH1,Hatch Pattern for Example 5
45,0,0,0,.5

Where **45** ------------------ Hatch angle
0 ------------------- X-origin
0 ------------------- Y-origin
0 ------------------- Displacement of second hatch line
.5 ------------------ Distance between hatch lines

The first field of hatch descriptors contains the angle of the hatch lines. That angle is 45 degrees with respect to the positive X axis. The second and third fields describe the X and Y coordinates of the first hatch line origin. The first line of the hatch pattern will pass through this point. If the values of the X-origin and Y-origin were 0.5 and 1.0, respectively, then the first line would pass through the point with the X coordinate of 0.5 and the Y coordinate of 1.0, with respect to the drawing origin 0,0. The remaining lines are generated by offsetting the first line, as shown in Figure 30-28.

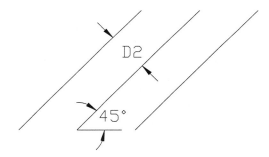

Figure 30-28 Hatch pattern angle and offset

EFFECT OF ANGLE AND SCALE FACTOR ON HATCH

When you hatch an area, you can alter the angle and displacement of hatch lines you have specified in the hatch pattern definition to get a desired hatch spacing. You can do this by entering an appropriate value for angle and scale factor in the AutoCAD **HATCH** command.

Command: **HATCH**
Enter a pattern name or [?/Solid/User defined] <default>: **Hatch1**
Specify a scale for the pattern <default>: **1**
Specify an angle for the pattern<default>: **0**

To understand how the angle and the displacement can be changed, hatch an area with the hatch pattern HATCH1 in Example 5. You will notice that the hatch lines have been generated according to the definition of hatch pattern HATCH1. Notice the effect of hatch angle and scale factor on the hatch. Figure 30-29(a) shows a hatch that is generated by the AutoCAD **HATCH** command with a 0-degree angle and a scale factor of 1.0. If the angle is 0, the hatch will be generated with the same angle as defined in the hatch pattern definition (45 degrees in Example 5). Similarly, if the scale factor is 1.0, the distance between the hatch lines will be the same as defined in the hatch pattern definition (0.5 in Example 5). Figure 30-29(b) shows a hatch that is generated when the hatch scale factor is 0.5. If you measure the distance between the successive hatch lines, it will be 0.5 x 0.5 = 0.25. Figures 30-29(c) and (d) show the hatch when the angle is 45 degrees and the scale factors are 1.0 and 0.5, respectively. You can enter any value in response to the **HATCH** command prompts to generate hatch lines at any angle and with any line spacing.

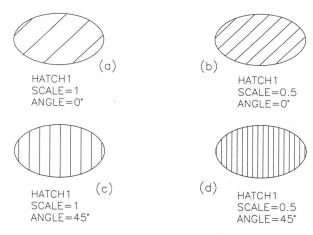

Figure 30-29 *Effect of angle and scale factor on hatch*

HATCH PATTERN WITH DASHES AND DOTS

The lines you can use in a hatch pattern definition are not restricted to continuous lines. You can define any line pattern to generate a hatch pattern. The lines can be a combination of dashes, dots, and spaces in any configuration. However, the maximum number of dashes you can specify in the line pattern definition of a hatch pattern is six. Example 6 uses a dash-dot line to create a hatch pattern.

Example 6

Write a hatch pattern definition for the hatch pattern shown in Figure 30-30, with the following specifications:

Name of the hatch pattern	HATCH2
Hatch angle =	0
X-origin =	0
Y-origin =	0
Displacement of lines (D1) =	0.25

Chapter 30

Distance between lines (D2) =   0.25
Length of each dash =   0.5
Space between dashes and dots =   0.125
Space between dots =   0.125

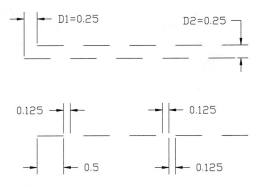

Figure 30-30 *Hatch lines made of dashes and*

You can use the AutoCAD **EDIT** command or any text editor (Notepad) to edit the **ACAD.PAT** file. The general format of the header line and the hatch descriptors is:

> ***HATCH NAME, Hatch Description**
> **Angle, X-Origin, Y-Origin, D1, D2 [,Dash Length.....]**

Substitute the values from Example 6 in the corresponding fields of header line and field descriptor:

> ***HATCH2,Hatch with dashes and dots**
> **0,0,0,0.25,0.25,0.5,-0.125,0,-0.125,0,-0.125**
> Where **0** ------------------ Angle
> **0** ------------------ X-origin
> **0** ------------------ Y-origin
> **0.25** --------------- Delta-X
> **0.25** --------------- Delta-Y
> **0.5** ---------------- Length of dash
> **-0.125** ----------- Space (pen up)
> **0** ------------------ Dot (pen down)
> **-0.125** ----------- Space (pen up)
> **0** ------------------ Dot
> **-0.125** ----------- Space

The hatch pattern this hatch definition will generate is shown in Figure 30-31. Figure 30-31(a) shows the hatch with 0-degree angle and a scale factor of 1.0. Figure 30-31(b) shows the hatch with a 45-degree angle and a scale factor of 0.5.

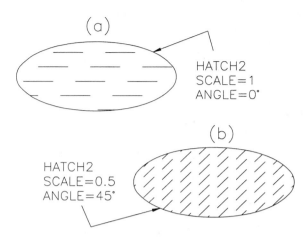

Figure 30-31 *Hatch pattern at different angles and scales*

HATCH WITH MULTIPLE DESCRIPTORS

Some hatch patterns require multiple lines to generate a shape. For example, if you want to create a hatch pattern of a brick wall, you need a hatch pattern that has four hatch descriptors to generate a rectangular shape. You can have any number of hatch descriptor lines in a hatch pattern definition. It is up to the user to combine them in any conceivable order. However, there are some shapes you cannot generate. A shape that has a nonlinear element, like an arc, cannot be generated by hatch pattern definition. However, you can simulate an arc by defining short line segments because you can use only straight lines to generate a hatch pattern. Example 7 uses three lines to define a triangular hatch pattern.

Example 7

Write a hatch pattern definition for the hatch pattern shown in Figure 30-32, with the following specifications:

Name of the hatch pattern =	HATCH3
Vertical height of the triangle =	0.5
Horizontal length of the triangle =	0.5
Vertical distance between the triangles =	0.5
Horizontal distance between the triangles =	0.5

Each triangle in this hatch pattern consists of the following three elements: a vertical line, a horizontal line, and a line inclined at 45 degrees.

Vertical Line. For the vertical line, the specifications are (Figure 30-33):
Hatch angle =   90 degrees
X-origin =   0
Y-origin =   0

Delta-X (D1) =   0
Delta-Y (D2) =   1.0
Dash length =   0.5
Space =   0.5

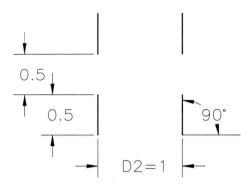

Figure 30-32 *Triangle hatch pattern*   **Figure 30-33** *Vertical line*

Substitute the values from the vertical line specification in various fields of the hatch descriptor to get the following line:

90,0,0,0,1,.5,-.5
                Where   **90** ------------------ Hatch angle
                        0 ------------------- X-origin
                        0 ------------------- Y-origin
                        0 ------------------- Delta-X
                        1 ------------------- Delta-Y
                        .5 ------------------ Dash (pen down)
                        -.5 ----------------- Space (pen up)

Horizontal Line. For the horizontal line (Figure 30-34), the specifications are:

Hatch angle =   0 degrees
X-origin =   0
Y-origin =   0.5
Delta-X (D1) =   0
Delta-Y (D2) =   1.0
Dash length =   0.5
Space =   0.5

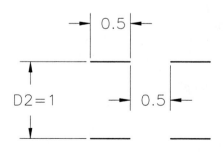

The only difference between the vertical line and the horizontal line is the angle. For the horizontal line, the angle is 0 degrees, whereas for the vertical line, the angle is 90 degrees. Substitute the values from the vertical line specification to obtain the following line:

Figure 30-34 *Horizontal line*

0,0,0.5,0,1,.5,-.5

Where **0** ------------------ Hatch angle
0 ------------------ X-origin
0.5 ---------------- Y-origin
0 ------------------ Delta-X
1 ------------------ Delta-Y
.5 ------------------ Dash (pen down)
-.5 ----------------- Space (pen up)

Line Inclined at 45 Degrees. This line is at an angle; therefore, you need to calculate the distances delta-X (D1) and delta-Y (D2), the length of the dashed line, and the length of space. Figure 30-35 shows the calculations to find these values.

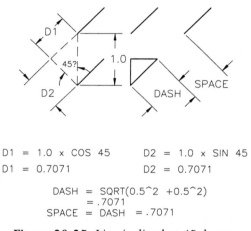

D1 = 1.0 x COS 45   D2 = 1.0 x SIN 45
D1 = 0.7071   D2 = 0.7071

DASH = SQRT(0.5^2 +0.5^2)
     = .7071
SPACE = DASH = .7071

Figure 30-35 *Line inclined at 45 degrees*

Hatch angle =   45 degrees
X-Origin =   0
Y-Origin =   0
Delta-X (D1) =   0.7071
Delta-Y (D2) =   0.7071
Dash length =   0.7071
Space =   0.7071

After substituting the values in the general format of the hatch descriptor, you will obtain the following line:

45,0,0,.7071,.7071,.7071,-.7071

Where **45** ----------------- Hatch angle
0 ------------------ X-origin
0 ------------------ Y-origin
.7071 ------------- Delta-X
.7071 ------------- Delta-Y

.7071 ------------- Dash (pen down)
-.7071 ------------ Space (pen up)

Now you can combine these three lines and insert them at the end of the **ACAD.PAT** file. You can also use the AutoCAD **EDIT** command to edit the file and insert the lines.

Figure 30-36 shows the hatch pattern that will be generated by this hatch pattern (HATCH3). In Figure 30-36(a) the hatch pattern is at a 0-degree angle and the scale factor is 0.5. In Figure 30-36(b) the hatch pattern is at a -45-degree angle and the scale factor is 0.5.

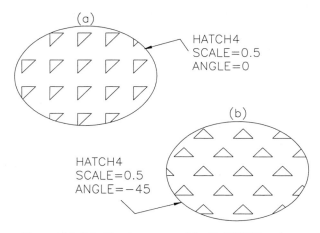

Figure 30-36 *Hatch generated by HATCH3 pattern*

The following file is a partial listing of the **ACAD.PAT** file, after adding the hatch pattern definitions from Examples 5, 6, and 7.

```
*SOLID, Solid fill
45, 0,0, 0,.125
*angle,Angle steel
0, 0,0, 0,.275, .2,-.075
90, 0,0, 0,.275, .2,-.075
*ansi31,ANSI Iron, Brick, Stone masonry
45, 0,0, 0,.125
*ansi32,ANSI Steel
45, 0,0, 0,.375
45, .176776695,0, 0,.375
*ansi33,ANSI Bronze, Brass, Copper
45, 0,0, 0,.25
45, .176776695,0, 0,.25, .125,-.0625
*ansi34,ANSI Plastic, Rubber
45, 0,0, 0,.75
45, .176776695,0, 0,.75
45, .353553391,0, 0,.75
```

```
45, .530330086,0, 0,.75
*ansi35,ANSI Fire brick, Refractory material
45, 0,0, 0,.25
45, .176776695,0, 0,.25, .3125,-.0625,0,-.0625
*ansi36,ANSI Marble, Slate, Glass
45, 0,0, .21875,.125, .3125,-.0625,0,-.0625



*swamp,Swampy area
0, 0,0, .5,.866025403, .125,-.875
90, .0625,0, .866025403,.5, .0625,-1.669550806
90, .078125,0, .866025403,.5, .05,-1.682050806
90, .046875,0, .866025403,.5, .05,-1.682050806
60, .09375,0, .5,.866025403, .04,-.96
120, .03125,0, .5,.866025403, .04,-.96
*trans,Heat transfer material
0, 0,0, 0,.25
0, 0,.125, 0,.25, .125,-.125
*triang,Equilateral triangles
60, 0,0, .1875,.324759526, .1875,-.1875
120, 0,0, .1875,.324759526, .1875,-.1875
0, -.09375,.162379763, .1875,.324759526, .1875,-.1875
*zigzag,Staircase effect
0, 0,0, .125,.125, .125,-.125
90, .125,0, .125,.125, .125,-.125
*HATCH1,Hatch at 45 Degree Angle
45,0,0,0,.5
*HATCH2,Hatch with Dashes & Dots:
0,0,0,.25,.25,0.5,-.125,0,-.125,0,-.125
*HATCH3,Triangle Hatch:
90,0,0,0,1,.5,-.5
0,0,0.5,0,1,.5,-.5
45,0,0,.7071,.7071,.7071,-.7071
```

SAVING HATCH PATTERNS IN A SEPARATE FILE

When you load a certain hatch pattern, AutoCAD looks for that definition in the ACAD.PAT file; therefore, the hatch pattern definitions must be in that file. However, you can add the new pattern definition to a different file and then copy that file to ACAD.PAT. Be sure to make a copy of the original ACAD.PAT file so that you can copy that file back when needed. Assume the name of the file that contains your custom hatch pattern definitions is CUSTOMH.PAT.

1. Copy ACAD.PAT file to ACADORG.PAT
2. Copy CUSTOMH.PAT to ACAD.PAT

If you want to use the original hatch pattern file, copy the ACADORG.PAT file to ACAD.PAT

CUSTOM HATCH PATTERN FILE

As mentioned earlier, you can add the new hatch pattern definitions to the **ACAD.PAT** file. There is no limit to the number of hatch pattern definitions you can add to this file. However, if you have only one hatch pattern definition, you can define a separate file. It has the following three requirements:

1. The name of the file has to be the same as the hatch pattern name.
2. The file can contain only one hatch pattern definition.
3. The hatch pattern name—and, therefore, the hatch file name—should be unique.
4. If you want to save the hatch pattern on the A drive, then the drive letter (A:) should precede the hatch name. For example, if the hatch name is HATCH3, the header line will be ***A:HATCH3, Triangle Hatch:** and the file name **HATCH3.PAT**.

   *HATCH3,Triangle Hatch:
   90,0,0,0,1,.5,-.5
   0,0,0.5,0,1,.5,-.5
   45,0,0,.7071,.7071,.7071,-.7071

Note
*The hatch lines can be edited after exploding the hatch with the AutoCAD **EXPLODE** command. After exploding, each hatch line becomes a separate object.*

It is good practice not to explode a hatch because it increases the size of the drawing database. For example, if a hatch consists of 100 lines, save it as a single object. However, after you explode the hatch, every line becomes a separate object and you have 99 additional objects in the drawing. Keep the hatch lines in a separate layer to facilitate editing of the hatch lines.

Assign a unique color to hatch lines so that you can control the width of the hatch lines at the time of plotting.

You can also add hatch pattern slides to the AutoCAD slide library (Refer to Customizing AutoCAD by Sham Tickoo, Delmar/ITP Publishers).

Review Questions

CREATING LINETYPES

1. The AutoCAD _____ command can be used to create a new linetype.

2. The AutoCAD _____ command can be used to load a linetype.

3. The AutoCAD _____ command can be used to change the linetype scale factor.

4. In AutoCAD, the linetypes are saved in the _____ file.

5. The linetype description should not be more than _____ characters long.

6. A positive number denotes a pen _____ segment.

7. The segment length _____ generates a dot.

8. AutoCAD supports only _____ alignment field specification.

9. A line pattern definition always starts with _____.

10. A header line definition always starts with _____.

CREATING HATCH PATTERNS

11. The **ACAD.PAT** file contains _____ number of hatch pattern definitions.

12. The header line consists of an asterisk, the pattern name, and _____.

13. The first hatch line passes through a point whose coordinates are specified by _____ and _____.

14. The perpendicular distance between the hatch lines in a hatch pattern definition is specified by _____.

15. The displacement of the second hatch line in a hatch pattern definition is specified by _____.

16. The maximum number of dash lengths that can be specified in the line pattern definition of a hatch pattern is _____.

17. The hatch lines in different areas of the drawing will automatically _____ since the hatch lines are generated by offsetting.

18. The hatch angle as defined in the hatch pattern definition can be changed further when you use the AutoCAD _____ command.

19. When you load a hatch pattern, AutoCAD looks for that hatch pattern in the _____ file.

20. The hatch lines can be edited after _____ the hatch by using the AutoCAD _____ command.

Chapter 30

Exercises

Creating Linetypes

Exercise 1   *General*

Using the AutoCAD **LINETYPE** command, create a new linetype "DASH3DASH" with the following specifications:

    Length of the first dash 0.75
    Blank space 0.125
    Dash length 0.25
    Blank space 0.125
    Dash length 0.25
    Blank space 0.125
    Dash length 0.25
    Blank space 0.125

Exercise 2   *General*

Use a text editor to create a new file, **NEWLT2.LIN**, and a new linetype, DASH2DASH, with the following specifications:

    Length of the first dash 0.5
    Blank space 0.1
    Dash length 0.2
    Blank space 0.1
    Dash length 0.2
    Blank space 0.1

Exercise 3   *General*

Using AutoCAD's **LINETYPE** command, create a linetype DASH3DOT with the following specifications:

    Length of the first dash 0.75
    Blank space 0.25
    Dot
    Blank space 0.25
    Dot
    Blank space 0.25
    Dot
    Blank space 0.25

Exercise 4
General

a. Write the definition of a string complex linetype (Hot water line) as shown in Figure 30-37(a).

b. Write the definition of a string complex linetype (Gas line) as shown in Figure 30-37(b).

Figure 30-37 *Specifications for string a complex linetype*

Creating Hatch Patterns

Exercise 5
General

Determine the hatch specifications and write a hatch pattern definition for the hatch pattern in Figure 30-38.

Figure 30-38 *Square hatch pattern*

Exercise 6 *General*

Determine the hatch pattern specifications and write a hatch pattern definition for the hatch pattern in Figure 30-39.

Figure 30-39 *Hatch pattern for Exercise 6*

Exercise 7 *General*

Determine the hatch specifications and write a hatch pattern definition for the hatch pattern as shown in Figure 30-40. Use this hatch to hatch a circle or rectangle.

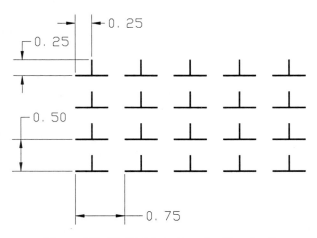

Figure 30-40 *Hatch pattern for Exercise 7*

Chapter 31

Customizing the
ACAD.PGP File

Learning Objectives

After completing this chapter, you will be able to:
- *Customize the **ACAD.PGP** file.*
- *Edit different sections of the **ACAD.PGP** file.*
- *Abbreviate commands by defining command aliases.*
- *Use the **REINIT** command to reinitialize the PGP file.*

WHAT IS THE ACAD.PGP FILE?

AutoCAD software comes with the program parameters file **ACAD.PGP**, which defines aliases for the operating system commands and some of the AutoCAD commands. When you install AutoCAD, this file is automatically copied on the **AutoCAD 2000\SUPPORT** subdirectory of the hard drive. The **ACAD.PGP** file lets you access the operating system commands from the drawing editor. For example, if you want to delete a file, all you need to do is enter DEL at the Command prompt (**Command: DEL**), and then AutoCAD will prompt you to enter the name of the file you want to delete.

The file also contains command aliases of some frequently used AutoCAD commands. For example, the command alias for the **LINE** command is L. If you enter L at the Command prompt (**Command: L**), AutoCAD will treat it as the **LINE** command. The **ACAD.PGP** file also contains comment lines that give you some information about different sections of the file.

The following file is a partial listing of the standard **ACAD.PGP** file. Some of the lines have been deleted to make the file shorter.

; AutoCAD Program Parameters File For AutoCAD 2000
; External Command and Command Alias Definitions
; Copyright (C) 1997-1999 by Autodesk, Inc.

; Each time you open a new or existing drawing, AutoCAD searches
; the support path and reads the first acad.pgp file that it finds.
; -- External Commands --
; While AutoCAD is running, you can invoke other programs or utilities
; such Windows system commands, utilities, and applications.
; You define external commands by specifying a command name to be used
; from the AutoCAD command prompt and an executable command string
; that is passed to the operating system.
; -- Command Aliases --
; You can abbreviate frequently used AutoCAD commands by defining
; aliases for them in the command alias section of acad.pgp.
; You can create a command alias for any AutoCAD command,
; device driver command, or external command.
; Recommendation: back up this file before editing it.
; External command format:
; <Command name>,[<DOS request>],<Bit flag>,[*]<Prompt>,
; The bits of the bit flag have the following meanings:
; Bit 1: if set, don't wait for the application to finish
; Bit 2: if set, run the application minimized
; Bit 4: if set, run the application "hidden"
; Bit 8: if set, put the argument string in quotes
; Fill the "bit flag" field with the sum of the desired bits.
; Bits 2 and 4 are mutually exclusive; if both are specified, only
; the 2 bit is used. The most useful values are likely to be 0
; (start the application and wait for it to finish), 1 (start the
; application and don't wait), 3 (minimize and don't wait), and 5
; (hide and don't wait). Values of 2 and 4 should normally be avoided,
; as they make AutoCAD unavailable until the application has completed.
; Bit 8 allows commands like DEL to work properly with filenames that
; have spaces such as "long filename.dwg". Note that this will interfere
; with passing space delimited lists of file names to these same commands.
; If you prefer multiplefile support to using long file names, turn off
; the "8" bit in those commands.
; Examples of external commands for command windows

```
CATALOG,   DIR /W,       8,File specification: ,        |
DEL,       DEL,        8,File to delete: ,              |
DIR,       DIR,        8,File specification: ,          |           External
EDIT,      START EDIT,    9,File to edit: ,             |  ——————— commands
SH,        ,            1,*OS Command: ,                |           area
SHELL,     ,            1,*OS Command: ,                |
START,     START,        1,*Application to start: ,     |
TYPE,      TYPE,        8,File to list: ,               |
```

; Examples of external commands for Windows
; See also the (STARTAPP) AutoLISP function for an alternative method.

```
EXPLORER,  START EXPLORER, 1,,
NOTEPAD,   START NOTEPAD,  1,*File to edit: ,
PBRUSH,    START PBRUSH,   1,,
```

; Command alias format:
;   <Alias>,*<Full command name>

; The following are guidelines for creating new command aliases.
; 1. An alias should reduce a command by at least two characters.
;   Commands with a control key equivalent, status bar button,
;   or function key do not require a command alias.
;   Examples: Control N, O, P, and S for New, Open, Print, Save.
; 2. Try the first character of the command, then try the first two,
;   then the first three.
; 3. Once an alias is defined, add suffixes for related aliases:
;   Examples: R for Redraw, RA for Redrawall, L for Line, LT for
;   Linetype.
; 4. Use a hyphen to differentiate between command line and dialog
;   box commands.
;   Example: B for Block, -B for -Block.
;
; Exceptions to the rules include AA for Area, T for Mtext, X for Explode.

; -- Sample aliases for AutoCAD commands --
; These examples include most frequently used commands.

```
3A,    *3DARRAY
3DO,   *3DORBIT
3F,    *3DFACE
3P,    *3DPOLY
A,     *ARC
ADC,    *ADCENTER
AA,    *AREA
AL,    *ALIGN
AP,    *APPLOAD
AR,    *ARRAY
ATT,    *ATTDEF
-ATT,   *-ATTDEF
ATE,    *ATTEDIT
-ATE,   *-ATTEDIT
ATTE,   *-ATTEDIT
B,     *BLOCK
-B,    *-BLOCK
BH,     *BHATCH
```

Command alias section

```
BO,      *BOUNDARY
-BO,     *-BOUNDARY
BR,      *BREAK
C,       *CIRCLE
CH,      *PROPERTIES
-CH,     *CHANGE
CHA,     *CHAMFER
COL,     *COLOR
COLOUR,  *COLOR
CO,      *COPY
D,       *DIMSTYLE
DAL,     *DIMALIGNED
DAN,     *DIMANGULAR
DBA,     *DIMBASELINE
DBC,     *DBCONNECT
DCE,     *DIMCENTER
DCO,     *DIMCONTINUE
DDI,     *DIMDIAMETER
DED,     *DIMEDIT
DI,      *DIST
DIV,     *DIVIDE



L,       *LINE
LA,      *LAYER
-LA,     *-LAYER
LE,      *QLEADER
LEN,     *LENGTHEN
LI,      *LIST
LINEWEIGHT, *LWEIGHT
LO,      *-LAYOUT
LS,      *LIST
LT,      *LINETYPE
-LT,     *-LINETYPE
LTYPE,   *LINETYPE
-LTYPE,  *-LINETYPE
LTS,     *LTSCALE
LW,      *LWEIGHT
M,       *MOVE
MA,      *MATCHPROP
ME,      *MEASURE
MI,      *MIRROR
ML,      *MLINE
MO,      *PROPERTIES
MS,      *MSPACE
MT,      *MTEXT
```

```
MV,        *MVIEW
O,         *OFFSET
OP,        *OPTIONS
ORBIT,     *3DORBIT
OS,        *OSNAP
-OS,       *-OSNAP
P,         *PAN
-P,        *-PAN
PA,        *PASTESPEC
PARTIALOPEN, *-PARTIALOPEN
PE,        *PEDIT
PL,        *PLINE
PO,        *POINT
POL,       *POLYGON
PR,        *OPTIONS
PRCLOSE,   *PROPERTIESCLOSE
PROPS,     *PROPERTIES
PRE,       *PREVIEW
PRINT,     *PLOT
PS,        *PSPACE
PU,        *PURGE
R,         *REDRAW
RA,        *REDRAWALL
RE,        *REGEN
REA,       *REGENALL
REC,       *RECTANGLE
REG,       *REGION



SP,        *SPELL
SPL,       *SPLINE
SPE,       *SPLINEDIT
ST,        *STYLE
SU,        *SUBTRACT
T,         *MTEXT
-T,        *-MTEXT
TA,        *TABLET
TH,        *THICKNESS
TI,        *TILEMODE
TO,        *TOOLBAR
TOL,       *TOLERANCE
TOR,       *TORUS
TR,        *TRIM
UC,        *DDUCS
UCP,       *DDUCSP
```

; The following are alternative aliases and aliases as supplied
; in AutoCAD Release 13.

```
AV,        *DSVIEWER
CP,        *COPY
DIMALI,    *DIMALIGNED
DIMANG,    *DIMANGULAR
DIMBASE,   *DIMBASELINE
DIMCONT,   *DIMCONTINUE
DIMDIA,    *DIMDIAMETER
DIMED,     *DIMEDIT
DIMTED,    *DIMTEDIT
DIMLIN,    *DIMLINEAR
DIMORD,    *DIMORDINATE
DIMRAD,    *DIMRADIUS
DIMSTY,    *DIMSTYLE
DIMOVER,   *DIMOVERRIDE
LEAD,      *LEADER
TM,        *TILEMODE
```

; Aliases for Hyperlink/URL Release 14 compatibility
```
SAVEURL, *SAVE
OPENURL, *OPEN
INSERTURL, *INSERT
```

; Aliases for commands discontinued in AutoCAD 2000:
```
AAD,       *DBCONNECT
AEX,       *DBCONNECT
ALI,       *DBCONNECT
ASQ,       *DBCONNECT
ARO,       *DBCONNECT
ASE,       *DBCONNECT
DDATTDEF,  *ATTDEF
DDATTEXT,  *ATTEXT
DDCHPROP,  *PROPERTIES
DDCOLOR,   *COLOR
DDLMODES,  *LAYER
DDLTYPE,   *LINETYPE
DDMODIFY,  *PROPERTIES
DDOSNAP,   *OSNAP
DDUCS,     *UCS
```

SECTIONS OF THE ACAD.PGP FILE

The contents of the AutoCAD program parameters file (**ACAD.PGP**) can be categorized into three sections. These sections merely classify the information that is defined in the **ACAD.PGP** file. They do not have to appear in any definite order in the file, and they have no section headings. For example, the comment lines can be entered anywhere in the file; the same is true with external commands and AutoCAD command aliases. The **ACAD.PGP** file can be divided into these three sections: **comments, external commands**, and **command aliases**.

Comments

The comments of ACAD.PGP file can contain any number of comment lines and can occur anywhere in the file. Every comment line must start with a semicolon (;) (This is a comment line). Any line that is preceded by a semicolon is ignored by AutoCAD. You should use the comment line to give some relevant information about the file that will help other AutoCAD users to understand, edit, or update the file.

External Command

In the external command section you can define any valid external command that is supported by your system. The information must be entered in the following format:

<Command name>, [OS Command name],<Bit flag>, [*]<Command prompt>,

Command Name. This is the name you want to use to activate the external command from the AutoCAD drawing editor. For example, you can use **goword** as a command name to load the word program (**Command: goword**). The command name must not be an AutoCAD command name or an AutoCAD system variable name. If the name is an AutoCAD command name, the command name in the **PGP** file will be ignored. Also, if the name is an AutoCAD system variable name, the system variable will be ignored. You should use the command names that reflect the expected result of the external commands. (For example, **hallo** is not a good command name for a directory file.) The command names can be uppercase or lowercase.

OS Command Name. The OS Command name is the name of a valid system command that is supported by your operating system. For example, in DOS the command to delete files is DEL; therefore, the OS Command name used in the **ACAD.PGP** file must be DEL. The following is a list of the types of commands that can be used in the PGP file:

> OS Commands (del, dir, type, copy, rename, edlin, etc.)
> Commands for starting a word processor, or text editors (word, shell, etc.)
> Name of the user-defined programs and batch files

Bit flag. This field must contain a number, preferably 8 or 1. The following are the bit flag values and their meaning:

Bit flag set to	Meaning
1	Do not wait for the application to finish
2	Runs the application minimized
4	Runs the application hidden
8	Puts the arguement string in quotes

Command Prompt. The command prompt field of the command line contains the prompt you want to display on the screen. It is an optional field that must be replaced by a comma if there is no prompt. If the operating system (OS) command that you want to use contains spaces, the prompt must be preceded by an asterisk (*). For example, the DOS command **EDIT NEW.PGP** contains a space between EDIT and NEW; therefore, the prompt used in this command line must be preceded by an asterisk. The command can be terminated by pressing ENTER. If the **OS** command consists of a single word (DIR, DEL, TYPE), the preceding asterisk must be omitted. In this case you can terminate the command by pressing the SPACEBAR or ENTER.

Command Aliases

It is time-consuming to enter AutoCAD commands at the keyboard because it requires typing the complete command name before pressing ENTER. AutoCAD provides a facility that can be used to abbreviate the commands by defining aliases for the AutoCAD commands. This is made possible by the AutoCAD program parameters file (**ACAD.PGP** file). Each command alias line consists of two fields (**L, *LINE**). The first field (**L**) defines the alias of the command; the second field (***LINE**) consists of the AutoCAD command. The AutoCAD command must be preceded by an asterisk for AutoCAD to recognize the command line as a command alias. The two fields must be separated by a comma. The blank lines and the spaces between the two fields are ignored. In addition to AutoCAD commands, you can also use aliases for AutoLISP command names, provided the programs that contain the definition of these commands are loaded.

Example 1

Add the following external commands and AutoCAD command aliases to the AutoCAD program parameters file (**ACAD.PGP**).

External Commands

Abbreviation	Command Description
GOWORD	This command loads the word processor (winword) program from the C:\Program Files\Winword.
RN	This command executes the rename command of DOS.
COP	This command executes the copy command of DOS.

Command Aliases Section

Abbreviation	Command	Abbreviation	Command
EL	Ellipse	T	Trim
CO	Copy	CH	Chamfer
O	Offset	ST	Stretch
S	Scale	MI	Mirror

The **ACAD.PGP** file is an ASCII text file. To edit this file you can use the AutoCAD EDIT command (provided the EDIT command is defined in the **ACAD.PGP** file), or any text editor (Notepad or Wordpad). The following is a partial listing of the **ACAD.PGP** file after insertion of the lines for the command aliases of Example 5. **The line numbers are not a part of the file; they are shown here for reference only.** The lines that have been added to the file are highlighted in bold.

DEL,DEL,	8,File to delete: ,	1
DIR,DIR,	8,File specification ,	2
EDIT, START EDIT,	8,File to edit: ,	3
SH,,	1,*OS Command: ,	4
SHELL,,	1,*OS Command: ,	5
START,START,	1,Application to start: ,	6
		7
GOWORD, START WINWORD,1,,		8
RN, RENAME,8,File to rename:,		9
COP,COPY,8,File to copy:,		10
DIMLIN	*DIMLINEAR	11
DIMORD,	*DIMORDINATE	12
DIMRAD,	*DIMRADIUS	13
DIMSTY,	*DIMSTYLE	14
DIMOVER,	*DIMOVERRIDE	15
LEAD,	*LEADER	16
TM,	*TILEMODE	17
EL,	***ELLIPSE**	18
CO,	***COPY**	19
O,	***OFFSET**	20
S,	***SCALE**	21
MI,	***MIRROR**	22
ST,	***STRETCH**	23

Explanation

Lines 8
GOWORD,   START WINWORD,1,,
In line 8, **goword** loads the word processor program **(winword)**. The **winword.exe** program is located in the winword directory under Program Files.

Lines 9 and 10
RN, RENAME,8,File to rename:,
COP,COPY,8,File to copy:,
Line 9 defines the alias for the DOS command **RENAME,** and the next line defines the alias for the DOS command **COPY**. The 8 is a bit flag, and the command prompt **File to rename and File to copy** is automatically displayed to let you know the format and the type of information that is expected.

Lines 18 and 19
EL, *ELLIPSE
CO, *COPY
Line 18 defines the alias **(EL)** for the AutoCAD command **ELLIPSE**, and the next line defines the alias **(CO)** for the **COPY** command. The AutoCAD commands must be preceded by an asterisk. You can put any number of spaces between the alias abbreviation and the AutoCAD command.

REINIT COMMAND

When you make any changes in the **ACAD.PGP** file, there are two ways to reinitialize the **ACAD.PGP** file. One is to quit AutoCAD and then reenter it. When you start AutoCAD, the **ACAD.PGP** file is automatically loaded.

You can also reinitialize the **ACAD.PGP** file by using the AutoCAD **REINIT** command. The **REINIT** command lets you reinitialize the I/O ports, digitizer, display, and AutoCAD program parameters file,

Figure 31-1 Re-initialization dialog

ACAD.PGP. When you enter the **REINIT** command, AutoCAD will display a dialog box (Figure 31-1). To reinitialize the **ACAD.PGP** file, select the corresponding toggle box, and then choose **OK**. AutoCAD will reinitialize the program parameters file **(ACAD.PGP)**, and then you can use the command aliases defined in the file.

Review Questions

Indicate whether the following statements are true or false.

1. The comment section can contain any number of lines. (T/F)

2. AutoCAD ignores any line that is preceded by a semicolon. (T/F)

3. The command alias must not be an AutoCAD command. (T/F)

4. The bit flag filed must contain 8. (T/F)

5. In the command alias section, the command alias must be preceded by a semicolon. (T/F)

6. You cannot use aliases for AutoLISP commands. (T/F)

7. The ACAD.PGP file does not come with AutoCAD software. (T/F)

8. The ACAD.PGP file is an ASCII file. (T/F)

Exercises

Exercise 1
General

Add the following external commands and AutoCAD command aliases to the AutoCAD program parameters file (**ACAD.PGP**).

External Command Section

Abbreviation	Command Description
MYWORDPAD	This command loads the WORDPAD program that resides in the **Program Files\Accessories** directory.
MYEXCEL	This command loads the EXCEL program that resides in the **Program Fies\Microsoft Office** directory.
CD	This command executes the CHKDSK command of DOS.
FORMAT	This command executes the FORMAT command of DOS.

Command Aliases Section

Abbreviation	Command	Abbreviation	Command
BL	**BLOCK**	LT	**LTSCALE**
INS	**INSERT**	EX	**EXPLODE**
DIS	**DISTANCE**	G	**GRID**
T	**TIME**		

Chapter 32

Pull-down, Shortcut, and Partial Menus and Customizing Toolbars

Learning Objectives

After completing this chapter, you will be able to:
- *Write pull-down menus.*
- *Load menus.*
- *Write cascading submenus in pull-down menus.*
- *Write cursor menus.*
- *Swap pull-down menus.*
- *Write partial menus.*
- *Define accelerator keys.*
- *Write toolbar definitions.*
- *Write menus to access online help.*
- *Customize toolbars.*

AUTOCAD MENU

The AutoCAD menu provides a powerful tool to customize AutoCAD. The AutoCAD software package comes with a standard menu file named **ACAD.MNU**. When you start AutoCAD, the menu file **ACAD.MNU** is automatically loaded. The AutoCAD menu file contains AutoCAD commands, separated under different headings for easy identification. For example, all draw commands are under **Draw** and all editing commands are under **Modify** menu. The headings are named and arranged to make it easier for you to locate and access the commands. However, there are some commands that you may never use. Also, some users might like to regroup and rearrange the commands so that it is easier to access those most frequently used.

AutoCAD lets the user eliminate rarely used commands from the menu file and define new ones. This is made possible by editing the existing **ACAD.MNU** file or writing a new menu file. There is no limit to the number of files you can write. You can have a separate menu file for each application. For example, you can have separate menu files for mechanical, electrical, and architectural drawings. You can load these menu files any time by using the AutoCAD **MENU** command. The menu files are text files with the extension **.MNU**. These files can be written by using any text editor like Wordpad or Notepad. The menu file can be divided into ten sections, each section identified by a.section label. AutoCAD uses the following labels to identify different sections of the AutoCAD menu file:

***SCREEN**	
***TABLET(n)**	**n** is from 1 to 4
***IMAGE**	
***POP(n)**	**n** is from 1 to 499 (For Shortcut menus n=0 and 500 to 999)
***BUTTONS(n)**	**n** is from 1 to 4
***AUX(n)**	**n** is from 1 to 4
***MENUGROUP**	
***TOOLBARS**	
***HELPSTRING**	
***ACCELERATORS**	

The tablet menu can have up to four different sections. The **POP** menu (pull-down and cursor menu) can have up to 16 sections, and auxiliary and buttons menus can have up to four sections.

Tablet Menus	Pull-Down and Cursor Menus
***TABLET1	***POP0
***TABLET2	***POP1
***TABLET3	***POP2
***TABLET4	***POP3
	***POP4
BUTTONS Menus	***POP5
***BUTTONS1	***POP6
***BUTTONS2	***POP7
***BUTTONS3	***POP8
***BUTTONS4	
Auxiliary Menus	
***AUX1	
***AUX2	***POP498
***AUX3	***POP499
***AUX4	

STANDARD MENUS

The menu is a part of the AutoCAD standard menu file, **ACAD.MNU**. The **ACAD.MNU** file is automatically loaded when you start AutoCAD, provided the standard configuration of AutoCAD has not been changed.

The menus can be selected by moving the crosshairs to the top of the screen, into the menu bar area. If you move the pointing device sideways, different menu bar titles are highlighted and you can select the desired item by pressing the pick button on your pointing device. Once the item is selected, the corresponding menu is displayed directly under the title (Figure 32-1). The menu can have 499 sections, named as POP1, POP2, POP3, . . ., POP499.

WRITING A MENU

Before you write a menu, you need to design a menu and to know the exact sequence of AutoCAD commands and the prompts associated with particular commands. To design a menu, you should select and arrange the commands in a way that provides easy access to the most frequently used commands. A careful design will save a lot of time in the long run. Therefore, consider several possible designs with different command combinations, and then

Figure 32-1 Pull-down and cascading menus

select the one best suited for the job. Suggestions from other CAD operators can prove very valuable.

The second important thing in developing a menu is to know the exact sequence of the commands and the prompts associated with each command. To better determine the prompt entries required in a command, you should enter all the commands and the prompt entries at the keyboard. The following is a description of some of the commands and the prompt entries required for Example 1.

LINE Command
Command: **LINE**

Notice the command and input sequence:

LINE
<RETURN>
CIRCLE (C,R) Command
Command: **CIRCLE**
Specify center point for circle or [3P/2P/Ttr (tan tan radius)]: *Specify center point.*
Specify radius of circle or [Diameter]: *Enter radius.*

Notice the command and input sequence:

CIRCLE
<RETURN>

Center point
<RETURN>
Radius
<RETURN>

CIRCLE (C,D) Command
Command: **CIRCLE**
Specify center point for circle or [3P/2P/Ttr (tan tan radius)]: *Specify center point.*
Specify radius of circle or [Diameter]: **D**
Specify diameter of circle: *Enter diameter.*

Notice the command and input sequence:

CIRCLE
<RETURN>
Center Point
<RETURN>
D
<RETURN>
Diameter
<RETURN>

CIRCLE (2P) Command
Command: **CIRCLE**
Specify center point for circle or [3P/2P/Ttr (tan tan radius)]: **2P**
Specify first end point of circle's diameter: *Specify first point.*
Specify second end point of circle's diameter: *Specify second point.*

Notice the command and input sequence:

CIRCLE
<RETURN>
2P
<RETURN>
Select first point on diameter
<RETURN>
Select second point on diameter
<RETURN>

ERASE Command
Command: **ERASE**

Notice the command and input sequence:

ERASE
<RETURN>

MOVE Command
Command: **MOVE**

Notice the command and prompt entry sequence:

MOVE
<RETURN>

The difference between the Center-Radius and Center-Diameter options of the **CIRCLE** command is that in the first one the RADIUS is the default, whereas in the second one you need to enter D to use the diameter option. This difference, although minor, is very important when writing a menu file. Similarly, the 2P (two-point) option of the **CIRCLE** command is different from the other two options. Therefore, it is important to know both the correct sequence of the AutoCAD commands and the entries made in response to the prompts associated with those commands.

You can use any text editor (like Notepad) to write the file. You can also use AutoCAD's **EDIT** command to write the menu file. If you use the **EDIT** command, AutoCAD will prompt you to enter the file name you want to edit. The file name can be up to eight characters long, and the file extension must be **.MNU**. If the file name exists, it will be automatically loaded; otherwise a new file will be created. To understand the process of developing a pull-down menu, consider the following example.

 Note
If AutoCAD's **EDIT** *command does not work, check the* **ACAD.PGP** *file and make sure that this command is defined in the file.*

Example 1

Write a menu for the following AutoCAD commands:

LINE	ERASE	REDRAW	SAVE
PLINE	MOVE	REGEN	QUIT
CIRCLE C,R	COPY	ZOOM ALL	PLOT
CIRCLE C,D	STRETCH	ZOOM WIN	
CIRCLE 2P	EXTEND	ZOOM PRE	
CIRCLE 3P	OFFSET		

The first step in writing any menu is to design the menu so that the commands are arranged in the desired configuration. Figure 32-2 shows one of the possible designs of this menu. This menu has four different groups of commands; therefore, it will have four sections: POP1, POP2, POP3, and POP4, and each section will have a section label. The following file is a listing of the pull-down menu file for Example 1. **The line numbers are not a part of the file; they are shown here for reference only.**

```
***POP1                                                              1
[DRAW]                                                               2
```

Figure 32-2 *Design of menu*

```
[LINE]*^C^CLINE                                                    3
[PLINE]^C^CPLINE                                                   4
[—]                                                               5
[CIR-C,R]^C^CCIRCLE                                                6
[CIR-C,D]^C^CCIRCLE \D                                             7
[CIR-2P]^C^CCIRCLE 2P                                              8
[CIR-3P]^C^CCIRCLE 3P                                              9
[—]                                                              10
[Exit]^C                                                         11
***POP2                                                          12
[EDIT]                                                           13
[ERASE]*^C^CERASE                                                14
[MOVE]^C^CMOVE                                                   15
[COPY]^C^CCOPY                                                   16
[STRETCH]^C^CSTRETCH;C                                           17
[OFFSET]^C^COFFSET                                               18
[EXTEND]^C^CEXTEND                                               19
[—]                                                             20
[Exit]^C                                                         21
***POP3                                                          22
[DISPLAY]                                                        23
[REDRAW]'REDRAW                                                  24
[REGEN]^C^CREGEN                                                 25
[—]                                                             26
[ZOOM-All]^C^C'ZOOM A                                            27
[ZOOM-Window]'ZOOM W                                             28
[ZOOM-Prev]'ZOOM PREV                                            29
[—]                                                             30
[~Exit]^C                                                       31
```

```
***POP4                                                        32
[UTILITY]                                                      33
[SAVE]^C^CSAVE;                                                34
[QUIT]^C^CQUIT                                                 35
[——]                                                           36
[PLOT]^C^CPLOT                                                 37
[—]                                                            38
[Exit]^C                                                       39
```

Explanation

Line 1
***POP1
POP1 is the section label for the first pull-down menu. All section labels in the AutoCAD menu begin with three asterisks (***), followed by the section label name, such as POP1.

Line 2
[DRAW]
In this menu item **DRAW** is the menu bar title displayed when the cursor is moved in the menu bar area. The title names should be chosen so you can identify the type of commands you expect in that particular pull-down menu. In this example, all the draw commands are under the title **DRAW** (Figure 32-3), all edit commands are under **EDIT**, and so on for other groups of items. The menu bar title can be of any length. However, it is recommended to keep them short to accommodate other menu items. Some of the display devices provide a maximum of 80 characters. To have 16 sections in a single row in the menu bar, the length of each title should not exceed five characters. If the length of the menu bar items exceeds 80 characters, AutoCAD will wrap the items that cannot be accommodated in 80 characters space, and display them in the next line. This will result in two menu item lines in the menu bar.

Figure 32-3 Draw menu

If the first line in a menu section is blank, the title of that section is not displayed in the menu bar area. Since the menu bar title is not displayed, you **cannot** access that menu. This allows you to turn off the menu section. For example, if you replace [**DRAW**] with a blank line, the **DRAW** section (POP1) of the menu will be disabled; the second section (POP2) will be displayed in its place.

Example

```
***POP1                        Section label
                               Blank line (turns off POP1)
[LINE:]^CLINE                  Menu item
[PLINE:]^CPLINE
[CIRCLE:]^CCIRCLE
```

The menu bar titles are left-justified. If the first title is not displayed, the rest of the menu titles will be shifted to the left. In Example 1, if the **DRAW** title is not displayed in the menu bar area, then the **EDIT**, **DISPLAY**, and **FILE** sections of the menu will move to the left.

Line 3
*^C^CLINE
In this menu item, the command definition starts with an asterisk (*). This feature allows the command to be repeated automatically until it is canceled by pressing ESCAPE, entering CTRL C, or by selecting another menu command. ^C^C cancels the existing command twice; **LINE** is an AutoCAD command that generates lines.

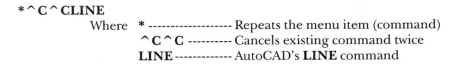

      *^C^CLINE
               Where   ***** ------------------- Repeats the menu item (command)
                            ^C^C ---------- Cancels existing command twice
                            LINE ------------- AutoCAD's **LINE** command

Line 5
[--]
To separate two groups of commands in any section, you can use a menu item that consists of two or more hyphens (--). This line automatically expands to fill the **entire width** of the menu. You can use a blank line in a menu. If any section of a menu (**POP section) has a blank line, it is ignored.

Line 11
[Exit]^C
In this menu item, **^C** command definition has been used to cancel the menu. This item provides you with one more option for canceling the menu. This is especially useful for new AutoCAD users who are not familiar with all AutoCAD features. The menu can also be canceled by any of the following actions:

1. Selecting a point.
2. Selecting an item in the screen menu area.
3. Selecting or typing another command.
4. Pressing ESC at the keyboard.
5. Selecting any menu title in the menu bar.

Line 28
[ZOOM-Window]'ZOOM W
In this menu item the single quote (') preceding the **ZOOM** command makes the **ZOOM** Window command transparent. When a command is transparent, the existing command is not canceled. After the **ZOOM** Window command (Figure 32-4), AutoCAD will automatically resume the current operation.

Figure 32-4 Display menu

      [ZOOM-Window]'ZOOM W
               Where   **W** ----------------- Window option
                          ZOOM ----------- AutoCAD **ZOOM** command
                          ' -------------------- Single quote makes **ZOOM** transparent

Line 31
[~Exit]^C
This menu item is similar to the menu item in line 11, except for the tilde (~). Since this menu item has a tilde (~), the menu item is not available (displayed grayed out), and if you select this item it will not cancel the menu. You can use this feature to disable a menu item or to indicate that the item is not a valid selection. If there is an instruction associated with the item, the instruction will not be executed when you select the item. For example, [~OSNAPS]^C^C$S=OSNAPS will not load the OSNAPS submenu on the screen.

Line 34
[SAVE]^C^CSAVE;
In this menu item, the semicolon (;) that follows the **SAVE** command enters RETURN. The semicolon is not required; the command will also work without a semicolon.

> **[SAVE]^C^CSAVE;**
>   Where **SAVE** ------------- AutoCAD **SAVE** command
>   **;** ------------------ Semicolon enters RETURN

Line 36
[----]
This menu item has four hyphens. The line will extend to fill the width of the menu. If there is only one hyphen [-], AutoCAD gives a syntex error when you load the menu.

Note

For all menus, the menu items are displayed directly beneath the menu title and are left-justified. If any menu [for example, the rightmost menu (POP16)] does not have enough space to display the entire menu item, the menu will expand to the left to accommodate the entire length of the longest menu item.

You can use // (two forward slashes) for comment lines. AutoCAD ignores the lines that start with //.

From this example it is clear that every statement in the menu is based on the AutoCAD commands and the information that is needed to complete these commands. This forms the basis for creating a menu file and should be given consideration. Following is a summary of the AutoCAD commands used in Example 1 and their equivalents in the menu file.

AutoCAD Commands	**Menu File**

Command: **LINE**   [LINE   ]^C^CLINE

Command: **CIRCLE**
Specify center point for circle or [3P/2P/Ttr (tan tan radius)]:
Specify radius of circle or [Diameter]:   [CIR-C,R]^C^CCIRCLE

Command: **CIRCLE**
Specify center point for circle or [3P/2P/Ttr (tan tan radius)]:
Specify radius of circle or [Diameter]: D

Specify diameter of circle:	[CIR-C,D] ^ C ^ CCIRCLE;\D
Command: **CIRCLE**	
Specify center point for circle or [3P/2P/Ttr (tan tan radius)]: **2P**	
Specify first end point of circle's diameter:	
Specify second end point of circle's diameter:	[CIR- 2P] ^ C ^ CCIRCLE;2P
Command: **ERASE**	[ERASE] ^ C ^ CERASE
Command: **MOVE**	[MOVE] ^ C ^ CMOVE

LOADING MENUS

AutoCAD automatically loads the **ACAD.MNU** file when you get into the AutoCAD drawing editor. However, you can also load a different menu file by using the AutoCAD **MENU** command.

Command: **MENU**

When you enter the **MENU** command, AutoCAD displays the **Select Menu File** dialog box (Figure 32-5) on the screen. Select the menu file that you want to load and then choose the **Open** button. You can also load the menu file from the command line.

Figure 32-5 Select Menu File dialog box

Command: **FILEDIA**
Enter new value for FILEDIA <1>: **0**
Command: **MENU**

Enter menu file name or [. (for none)] <ACAD>: PDM1
        Where   **PDM1** ------------ Name of menu file
               <ACAD> ------- Default menu file

After you enter the **MENU** command, AutoCAD will prompt for the file name. Enter the name of the menu file without the file extension (**.MNU**), since AutoCAD assumes the extension .MNU. AutoCAD will automatically compile the menu file into **MNC** and **MNR** files. When you load a menu file in windows, AutoCAD creates the following files:

.mnc and **.mnr** files   When you load a menu file (.mnu), AutoCAD compiles the menu file and creates **.mnc** and **.mnr** files. The .mnc file is a compiled menu file. The **.mnr** file contains the bitmaps used by the menu.

.mns file   When you load the menu file, AutoCAD also creates an **.mns** file. This is an ASCII file that is same as the **.mnu** file when you initially load the menu file. Each time you make a change in the contents of the file, AutoCAD changes the **.mns** file.

Note

*After you load the new menu, you cannot use the screen menu, buttons menu, or digitizer because the original menu, **ACAD.MNU**, is not present and the new menu does not contain these menu areas.*

*To activate the original menu again, load the menu file by using the **MENU** command:*

*Command: **MENU***
*Enter menu file name or [. (for none)] <SM1>: **ACAD***

If you need to use input from a keyboard or a pointing device, use the backslash (\). The system will pause for you to enter data.

There should be no space after the backslash (\).

The menu items, menu labels, and command definition can be uppercase, lowercase, or mixed.

You can introduce spaces between the menu items to improve the readability of the menu file. The blank lines are ignored and are not displayed on the screen.

If there are more items in the menu than the number of spaces available, the excess items are not displayed on the screen. For example, if the display device limits the number of items to 21, items in excess of 21 will not be displayed on the screen and are therefore inaccessible.

If you are using a high-resolution graphics board, you can increase the number of lines that can be displayed on the screen. On some devices this is 80 lines.

RESTRICTIONS

The menus are easy to use and provide a quick access to frequently used AutoCAD commands. However, the menu bar and the menus are disabled during the following commands:

DTEXT Command
After you assign the text height and the rotation angle to a **DTEXT** command, the menu is automatically disabled.

SKETCH Command

The menus are disabled after you set the record increment in the **SKETCH** command.

VPOINT Command

The menus are disabled while the axis tripod and compass are displayed on the screen.

ZOOM and DVIEW Commands

The menus are disabled when the dynamic zoom or dynamic view is in progress.

Exercise 1   *General*

Write a menu for the following AutoCAD commands.

DRAW	EDIT	DISP/TEXT	UTILITY
LINE	FILLET0	DTEXT,C	SAVE
PLINE	FILLET	DTEXT,L	QUIT
ELLIPSE	CHAMFER	DTEXT,R	END
POLYGON	STRETCH	ZOOM WIN	DIR
DONUT	EXTEND	ZOOM PRE	PLOT
	OFFSET		

Figure 32-6 Menu display for Exercise 1

CASCADING SUBMENUS IN MENUS

The number of items in a menu or cursor menu can be very large, and sometimes they cannot all be accommodated on one screen. For example, the maximum number of items that can be displayed on some display devices is 21. If the menu or the cursor menu has more items than can be displayed, the excess menu items are not displayed on the screen and cannot be accessed. You can overcome this problem by using cascading menus that let you define smaller groups of items within a menu section. When an item is selected, it loads the cascading menu and displays the items, defined in the cascading menu, on the screen.

The cascading feature of AutoCAD allows pull-down and cursor menus to be displayed in a hierarchical order that makes it easier to select submenus. To use the cascading feature in pull-down and cursor menus, AutoCAD has provided some special characters. For example, -> defines a cascaded submenu and <- designates the last item in the menu. The following table lists some of the characters that can be used with the pull-down or cursor menus.

Character	Character Description
--	The item label consisting of two hyphens automatically expands to fill the entire width of the menu. Example: [--]
+	Used to continue the menu item to the next line. This character has to be the last character of the menu item. Example: [Triang:]^C^CLine;1,1;+3,1;2,2;
->	This label character defines a cascaded submenu; it must precede the name of the submenu. Example: [->**Draw**]
<-	This label character designates the last item of the cascaded pull-down or cursor menu. The character must precede the label item. Example: [**<-CIRCLE 3P**]^C^C**CIRCLE;3P**
<-<-...	This label character designates the last item of the pull-down or cursor menu and also terminates the parent menu. The character must precede the label item. Example: [**<-<-Center Mark**]^C^C**_dim;_center**
$(	This label character can be used with the pull-down and cursor menus to evaluate a DIESEL expression. The character must precede the label item. Example: $(if,$(getvar,orthomode),Ortho)
~	This item indicates the label item is not available (displayed grayed out); the character must precede the item. Example: [~Application not available]
!.	When used as a prefix, it displays the item with a check mark.
&	When placed directly before a character, the character is displayed underscored. For Example, [W&Block] is displayed as W<u>B</u>lock. It also specifies the character as a menu accelerator key in the pull-down or Shortcut menu.
/c	When placed directly before an item with a character, the character is displayed underscored. For Example, [/BWBlock] is displayed as

Chapter 32

WBlock. It also specifies that the item has a menu accelarator key in the pull-down or Shortcut menu.

\t   The label text to the right of \t is displayed to the right side of the menu.

Some display devices provide space for a maximum of 80 characters. Therefore, if there are 10 menus, the length of each menu title should average eight characters. If the combined length of all menu bar titles exceeds 80 characters, AutoCAD automatically wraps the excess menu items and displays them on the next line in the menu bar. The following is a list of some additional features of the menu.

1. The section labels of the menus are ***POP1 through ***POP16. The menu bar titles are displayed in the menu bar.

2. The menus can be accessed by selecting the menu title from the menu bar at the top of the screen.

3. A maximum of 999 menu items can be defined in the menu. This includes the items that are defined in the submenus. The menu items in excess of 999 are ignored.

4. The number of menu items that can be displayed depends on the display device you are using. If the cursor or the menu contains more items than can be accommodated on the screen, the excess items are truncated. For example, if your system can display only 21 menu items, the menu items in excess of 21 are automatically truncated.

Example 2

Write a menu for the commands shown in Figure 32-7. The menu must use the AutoCAD cascading feature.

The following file is a listing of the menu for Example 2. **The line numbers are not a part of the menu; they are shown here for reference only.**

```
***POP1                                               1
[DRAW]                                                2
[LINE]^C^CLINE                                         3
[PLINE]^C^CPLINE                                       4
[->ARC]                                               5
  [ARC]^C^CARC                                         6
  [ARC,3P]^C^CARC;\\DRAG                               7
  [ARC,SCE]^C^CARC;\C;\DRAG                            8
  [ARC,SCA]^C^CARC;\C;\A;DRAG                          9
  [ARC,CSE]^C^CARC;C;\\DRAG                            10
  [ARC,CSA]^C^CARC;C;\\A;DRAG                          11
  [<-ARC,CSL]^C^CARC;C;\\L;DRAG                        12
```

Figure 32-7 Menu structure for Example 2

```
[->CIRCLE]                                              13
    [CIRCLE C,R]^C^CCIRCLE                              14
    [CIRCLE C,D]^C^CCIRCLE;\D                           15
    [CIRCLE 2P]^C^CCIRCLE;2P                            16
    [<-CIRCLE 3P]^C^CCIRCLE;3P                          17
[—]                                                     18
[Exit]^C                                                19
***POP2                                                 20
[BLOCKS]                                                21
[BLOCK]^C^CBLOCK                                        22
[INSERT]*^C^CINSERT                                     23
[WBLOCK]^C^CWBLOCK                                      24
[—]                                                     25
[Exit]^C                                                26
***POP3                                                 27
[UTILITY]                                               28
[SAVE]^C^CSAVE                                          29
[QUIT]^C^CQUIT                                          30
[PLOT]^C^CPLOT                                          31
[—]                                                     32
[Exit]^C                                                33
```

Explanation

Line 5

[->ARC]

In this menu item, **ARC** is the menu item label that is preceded by the special label character **->**. This special character indicates that the menu item has a submenu. The menu items that follow it (Lines 6-12) are the submenu items.

Figure 32-9 *Draw menu with CIRCLE submenu*

Figure 32-8 *Draw menu*

Line 12
[<-ARC,CSL] ^ C ^ CARC;C;\\L;DRAG
In this line, the menu item label **ARC,CSL** is preceded by another special label character, **<-**, which indicates the end of the submenu. The item that contains this character must be the last menu item of the submenu.

Lines 13 and 17
[->CIRCLE]
[<-CIRCLE 3P] ^ C ^ CCIRCLE;3P
The special character -> in front of **CIRCLE** indicates that the menu item has a submenu; the character <- in front of **CIRCLE 3P** indicates that this item is the last menu item in the submenu. When you select the menu item **CIRCLE** from the menu, it will automatically display the submenu on the side.

Example 3

Write a menu that has the cascading submenus for the commands shown in Figure 32-10.

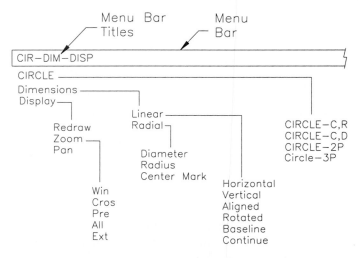

Figure 32-10 *Menu structure for Example 3*

The following file is a listing of the menu for Example 3. **The line numbers are not a part of the menu; they are shown here for reference only.**

```
***POP1                                              1
[DRAW]                                               2
[->CIRCLE]                                           3
  [CIRCLE C,R]^C^C_CIRCLE                            4
  [CIRCLE C,D]^C^C_CIRCLE;\_D                        5
  [CIRCLE 2P]^C^C_CIRCLE;_2P                         6
  [<-CIRCLE 3P]^C^C_CIRCLE;_3P                       7
[->Dimensions]                                       8
  [->Linear]                                         9
   [Horizontal]^C^C_dim;_horizontal                 10
   [Vertical]^C^C_dim;_vertical                     11
   [Aligned]^C^C_dim;_aligned                       12
   [Rotated]^C^C_dim;_rotated                       13
   [Baseline]^C^C_dim;_baseline                     14
   [<-Continue]^C^C_dim;_continue                   15
  [->Radial]                                         16
   [Diameter]^C^C_dim;_diameter                     17
   [Radius]^C^C_dim;_radius                         18
   [<-<-Center Mark]^C^C_dim;_center                19
[->DISPLAY]                                          20
  [REDRAW]^C^CREDRAW                                 21
  [->ZOOM]                                           22
   [...Win]^C^C_ZOOM;_W                             23
   [...Cros]^C^C_ZOOM;_C                            24
   [...Pre]^C^C_ZOOM;_P                             25
   [...All]^C^C_ZOOM;_A                             26
   [<-...Ext]^C^C_ZOOM;_E                           27
  [<-PAN]^C^C_Pan                                    28
```

Explanation

Lines 8 and 9
[->Dimensions]
[->Linear]

Figure 32-11 Draw menu with cascading menus

The special label character **->** in front of the menu item **Dimensions** indicates that it has a submenu, and the character -> in front of **Linear** indicates that there is another submenu. The second submenu **Linear** is within the first submenu Dimensions (Figure 32-11). The menu items on lines 10 to 15 are defined in the **Linear** submenu, and the menu items Linear and **Radial** are defined in the submenu Dimensions.

Line 16
[->Radial]
This menu item defines another submenu; the menu items on line numbers 17, 18, and 19 are part of this submenu.

Chapter 32

Line 19

[<-<-Center Mark]^C^C_dim;_center

In this menu item the special label character **<-<-** terminates the **Radial** and **Dimensions** (parent submenu) submenus.

Lines 27 and 28

[<-...Ext]^C^C_ZOOM;_E

[<-PAN]^C^C_Pan

The special character **<-** in front of the menu item **...Ext** terminates the **ZOOM** submenu (Figure 32-12); the special character in front of the menu item **PAN** terminates the **DISPLAY** submenu.

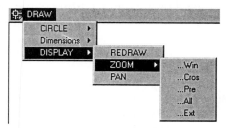

Figure 32-12 Draw pull-down menu with cascading menus

SHORTCUT AND CONTEXT MENUS

The Shortcut menus are similar to the pull-down menus, except the Shortcut menu can contain only 499 menu items compared with 999 items in the pull-down menu. The section label of the Shortcut menu can be ***POP0 and ***POP500 to ***POP 999. The Shortcut menus are displayed near or at the cursor location. Therefore, they can be used to provide convenient and quick access to some of the frequently used commands. The Shortcut menus that are in the upper range are also referred as Context menus. The following is a list of some of the features of the Shortcut menu.

1. The section label of the Shortcut menu are ***POP0 and ***POP500 to ***POP999. The menu bar title defined under this section label is not displayed in the menu bar.

2. On most systems, the menu bar title is not displayed at the top of the Shortcut menu. However, for compatibility reasons you should give a dummy menu bar title.

3. The POP0 menu can be accessed through the **$P0=*** menu command. The shortcut menus POP500 through POP999 must be referenced by their alias names. The reserved alias names for AutoCAD use are GRIPS, CMDEFAULT, CMEDIT, and CMCOMMAND. For example, to reference POP500 for grips, use **GRIPS command line under POP5000. This commands can be issued by a menu item in another menu, such as the button menu, auxiliary menu, or the screen menu. The command can also be issued from an AutoLISP or ADS program.

4. A maximum of 499 menu items can be defined in the Shortcut menu. This includes the items that are defined in the Shortcut submenus. The menu items in excess of 499 are ignored.

5. The number of menu items that can be displayed on the screen depends on the system you are using. If the Shortcut or pull-down menu contains more items than your screen can accommodate, the excess items are truncated. For example, if your system displays 21 menu items, the menu items in excess of 21 are automatically truncated.

6. The system variable **SHORTCUTMENU** controls the availability of Default, Edit, and Command mode shortcut menus. If the value is 0, it restores R14 legacy behavior and disables the Default, Edit, and Command mode shortcut menus. The default value of this variable is 11.

Example 4

Write a Shortcut menu for the following AutoCAD commands using cascading submenus. The menu should be compatible with foreign language versions of AutoCAD. Use the third button of the **BUTTONS** menu to display the cursor menu.

Osnaps	Draw	DISPLAY
Center	Line	REDRAW
Endpoint	PLINE	ZOOM
Intersection	CIR C,R	...Win
Midpoint	CIR 2P	...Cen
Nearest	ARC SCE	...Prev
Perpendicular	ARC CSE	...All
Quadrant		...Ext
Tangent		PAN
None		

The following file is a listing of the menu file for Example 4. **The line numbers are not a part of the file; they are for reference only.**

```
***AUX1                                1
;                                      2
$P0=*                                  3
***POP0                                4
[Osnaps]                               5
[Center]_Center                        6
[End point]_Endp                       7
[Intersection]_Int                     8
[Midpoint]_Mid                         9
[Nearest]_Nea                          10
[Perpendicular]_Per                    11
[Quadrant]_Qua                         12
[Tangent]_Tan                          13
[None]_Non                             14
[—]                                    15
[->Draw]                               16
  [Line]^C^C_Line                      17
  [PLINE]^C^C_Pline                    18
  [CIR C,R]^C^C_Circle                 19
  [CIR 2P]^C^C_Circle;_2P              20
  [ARC SCE]^C^C_ARC;\C                 21
  [<-ARC CSE]^C^C_Arc;C                22
[—]                                    23
[->DISPLAY]                            24
  [REDRAW]^C^_REDRAW                    25
  [->ZOOM]                             26
    [...Win]^C^C_ZOOM;_W               27
```

```
    [...Cen]^C^C_ZOOM;_C                                    28
    [...Prev]^C^C_ZOOM;_P                                   29
    [...All]^C^C_ZOOM;_A                                    30
    [<-...Ext]^C^C_ZOOM;_E                                  31
   [<-PAN]^C^C_Pan                                          32
  ***POP1                                                   33
  [SHORTCUTMENU]                                            34
  [SHORTCUTMENU=0]^C^CSHORTCUTMENU;0                        35
  [SHORTCUTMENU=11]^C^CSHORTCUTMENU;11                      36
```

Explanation

Line 1

***AUX1

AUX1 is the section label for the first auxiliary menu; *** designates the menu section. The menu items that follow it, until the second section label, are a part of this buttons menu.

Lines 2 and 3

;

$P0=*$

The semicolon (;) is assigned to the second button of the pointing device (the first button of the pointing device is the pick button); the special command **$P0=*$** is assigned to the third button of the pointing device.

Lines 4 and 5

***POP0

[Osnaps]

The menu label **POP0** is the menu section label for the Shortcut menu; Osnaps is the menu bar title. The menu bar title is not displayed, but is required. Otherwise, the first item will be interpreted as a title and will be disabled.

Line 6

[Center]_Center

In this menu item, **_Center** is the center object Snap mode. The menu files can be used with foreign language versions of AutoCAD, if AutoCAD commands and the command options are preceded by the underscore (_) character.

After loading the menu, if you press the third button of your pointing device, the Shortcut menu (Figure 32-13) will be displayed at the cursor (screen crosshairs) location. If the cursor is close to the edges of the screen, the Shortcut menu will be displayed at a location that is closest to the cursor position. When you select a submenu, the items contained in the submenu will be displayed, even if the Shortcut menu is touching the edges of the screen display area.

Figure 32-13 *Shortcut menu for Example 4*

Lines 33 and 34
***POP1
[Draw]
***POP1 defines the first pull-down menu. If no POPn sections are defined or the status line is turned off, the Shortcut menu is automatically disabled.

Exercise 2 *General*

Write a menu for the following AutoCAD commands. Use a cascading menu for the **LINE** command options in the menu. (The layout of the menu is shown in Figure 32-14.)

Figure 32-14 *Design of menu for Exercise 2*

LINE	**ZOOM All**	**TIME**
Continue	**ZOOM Win**	**LIST**
Close	**ZOOM Pre**	**DISTANCE**
Undo	**PAN**	**AREA**
.X	**DBLIST**	
.Y	**STATUS**	
.Z		
CIRCLE		
ELLIPSE		

SUBMENUS

The number of items in a pull-down menu or Shortcut menu can be very large and sometimes they cannot all be accommodated on one screen. For example, the maximum number of items that can be displayed on most of the display devices is 21. If the menu or the Shortcut menu has more than 21 items, the menu excess items are not displayed on the screen and cannot be accessed. You can overcome this problem by using submenus that let you define smaller groups of items within a menu section. When a submenu is selected, it loads the submenu items and displays them on the screen.

The menus that use AutoCAD's cascading feature are the most efficient and easy to write. The submenus follow a logical pattern that are easy to load and use without causing any confusion. It is strongly recommended to use the cascading menus whenever you need to write the pull-down or the Shortcut menus. However, AutoCAD provides the option to swap the submenus in the menus. These menus can sometimes cause distraction because the original menu is completely replaced by the submenu when swapping the menus.

Submenu Definition

A submenu definition consists of two asterisk signs (**) followed by the name of the submenu. A menu can have any number of submenus and every submenu should have a unique name. The items that follow a submenu, up to the next section label or submenu label, belong to that submenu. Following is the format of a submenu label:

Name

Where   ** ------------------ Two asterisk signs (**) designate a submenu
        Name ------------ Name of the submenu

Note

The submenu name can be up to 31 characters long.

The submenu name can consist of letters, digits, and the special characters like: $ (dollar), - (hyphen), and _ (underscore).

The submenu name cannot have any embedded blanks.

The submenu names should be unique in a menu file.

Submenu Reference

The submenu reference is used to reference or load a submenu. It consists of a "$" sign followed by a letter that specifies the menu section. The letter that specifies a menu section is Pn, where n designates the number of the menu section. The menu section is followed by "=" sign and the name of the submenu that the user wants to activate. The submenu name should be without "**". Following is the format of a submenu reference:

$Section=Submenu

Where   **$** -------------------- "$" sign
        Section ---------- Menu section specifier
        = ------------------ "=" sign
        Submenu ------- Name of submenu

Example
$P1=P1A

Where   **$P1** --------------- P1-Specifies pull-down menu section 1
        P1A --------------- Name of submenu

Displaying a Submenu

When you load a submenu in a menu, the submenu items are not automatically displayed on the screen. For example, when you load a submenu P1A that has DRAW-ARC as the first item, the current title of POP1 will be replaced by the DRAW-ARC. But the items that are defined under DRAW-ARC are not displayed on the screen. To force the display of the new items on the screen, AutoCAD uses a special command $Pn=*.

> **$Pn=***
>
>   Where   **P** ------------------ P for menu
>   **Pn** ---------------- Menu section number (1 to 10)
>   ***** ------------------ Asterisk sign (*)

LOADING MENUS

From the menu, you can load any menu that is defined in the screen or image tile menu sections by using the appropriate load commands. It may not be needed in most of the applications, but if you want to, you can load the menus that are defined in other menu sections.

Loading Screen Menus

You can load any menu that is defined in the screen menu section from the menu by using the following load command:

> **$S=X $S=LINE**
>   Where   **S** ------------------- S specifies screen menu
>   **X** ------------------ Submenu name defined in screen menu section
>   **LINE** ------------- Submenu name defined in screen menu section

The first load command ($S=X) loads the submenu X that has been defined in the screen menu section of the menu file. The X submenu can contain 21 blank lines, so that when it is loaded it clears the screen menu. The second load command ($S=LINE) loads the submenu **LINE** that has also been defined in the screen menu section of the menu file.

Loading an Image Tile Menu

You can also load an image tile menu from the menu by using the following load command:

> *$I=IMAGE1 $I=**
>   Where   **$I=Image1** ----- Load the submenu IMAGE1
>   **$I=*** ------------- To display the dialog box

This menu item consists of two load commands. The first load command $I=IMAGE1 loads the image tile submenu IMAGE1 that has been defined in the image tile menu section of the file. The second load command $I=* displays the new dialog box on the screen.

Example 5

Write a menu for the following AutoCAD commands. Use submenus for the **ARC** and **CIRCLE** commands.

LINE	**BLOCK**	**QUIT**
PLINE	**INSERT**	**SAVE**
ARC	**WBLOCK**	——
ARC 3P	**PLOT**	
ARC SCE		
ARC SCA		
ARC CSE		
ARC CSA		
ARC CSL		
CIRCLE		
CIRCLE C,R		
CIRCLE C,D		
CIRCLE 2P		

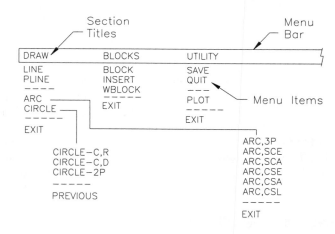

Figure 32-15 *Design of menu for Example 5*

The layout shown in Figure 32-15 is one of the possible designs for this menu. The **ARC** and **CIRCLE** commands are in separate groups that will be defined as submenus in the menu file.

The following file is a listing of the menu for Example 5. The line numbers are not a part of the menu file. They are given here for reference only.

```
***POP1                                                              1
**P1A                                                                2
[DRAW]                                                               3
[LINE]^C^CLINE                                                       4
[PLINE]^C^CPLINE                                                     5
```

```
[—]                                                              6
[ARC]^C^C$P1=P1B $P1=*                                           7
[CIRCLE]^C^C$P1=P1C $P1=*                                        8
[—]                                                              9
[Exit]^C                                                         10
                                                                 11
**P1B                                                            12
[ARC]                                                            13
[ARC,3P]^C^CARC \\DRAG                                           14
[ARC,SCE]^C^CARC \C \DRAG                                        15
[ARC,SCA]^C^CARC \C \A DRAG                                      16
[ARC,CSE]^C^CARC C \\DRAG                                        17
[ARC,CSA]^C^CARC C \\A DRAG                                      18
[ARC,CSL]^C^CARC C \\L DRAG                                      19
[—]                                                              20
[Exit]^C                                                         21
                                                                 22
**P1C                                                            23
[CIRCLE]                                                         24
[CIRCLE C,R]^C^CCIRCLE                                           25
[CIRCLE C,D]^C^CCIRCLE \D                                        26
[CIRCLE 2P]^C^CCIRCLE 2P                                         27
[—]                                                              28
[PREVIOUS]$P1=P1A $P1=*                                          29
                                                                 30
***POP2                                                          31
[BLOCKS]                                                         32
[BLOCK]^C^CBLOCK                                                 33
[INSERT]*^C^CINSERT                                              34
[WBLOCK]^C^CWBLOCK                                               35
[—]                                                              36
[Exit]$P1=P1A $P1=*                                              37
                                                                 38
***POP3                                                          39
[UTILITY]                                                        40
[SAVE]^C^CSAVE                                                   41
[QUIT]^C^CQUIT                                                   42
[~—]                                                             43
[PLOT]^C^CPLOT                                                   44
[~—]                                                             45
[Exit]^C                                                         46
                                                                 47
```

Line 2

**P1A

**P1A defines the submenu P1A. All the submenus have two asterisk signs (**) followed by the name of the submenu. The submenu can have any valid name. In this example, P1A has been chosen because it is easy to identify the location of the submenu. P indicates that it is a menu, 1 indicates that it is in the first menu (POP1), and A indicates that it is the first submenu in that section.

Line 6
[--]
The two hyphens enclosed in the brackets will automatically expand to fill the entire width of the menu. This menu item cannot be used to define a command. If it does contain a command definition, the command is ignored. For example, if the menu item is [--]^C^CLINE, the command ^C^CLINE will be ignored.

Line 7
[ARC]^C^C$P1=P1B $P1=*
In this menu item, $P1=P1B loads the submenu P1B and assigns it to the first menu section (POP1), but the new menu is not displayed on the screen. $P1=* forces the display of the new menu on the screen.

For example, if you select **CIRCLE** from the first menu (POP1), the menu bar title **DRAW** will be replaced by **CIRCLE**, but the new menu is not displayed on the screen. Now, if you select **CIRCLE** from the menu bar, the command defined under the **CIRCLE** submenu will be displayed in the menu. To force the display of the menu that is currently assigned to POP1, you can use AutoCAD's special command **$P1=***. If you select **CIRCLE** from the first menu (POP1), the **CIRCLE** submenu will be loaded and automatically displayed on the screen.

Line 21
[EXIT]^C
When you select this menu item the current menu will be canceled. It will not return to the previous submenu (**DRAW**). If you check the menu bar, it will display **ARC** as the section title, not **DRAW**. Therefore, it is not a good practice to cancel a submenu. It is better to return to the first menu before canceling it or define a command that automatically loads the previous menu and then cancels the menu.

Figure 32-16 Arc pull-down menu replaces Draw menu

        Example
        [EXIT]$P1=P1A $P1=* ^C^C

Line 29
[PREVIOUS]$P1=P1A $P1=*
In this menu item $P1=P1A loads the submenu P1A, which happens to be the previous menu in this case. You can also use $P1= to load the previous menu. $P1=* forces the display of the submenu P1A.

PARTIAL MENUS

AutoCAD has provided a facility that allows users to write their own menus and then load them in the menu bar. For example, in Windows you can write partial menus, toolbars, and definitions for accelerator keys. After you write the menu, AutoCAD lets you load the menu and use it with the standard menu. For example, you could load a partial menu and use it like a menu. You can also unload the menus that you do not want to use. These features make it convenient to use the menus that have been developed by AutoCAD users and developers.

Menu Section Labels

The following is a list of the additional menu section labels for Windows.

Section label	Description
***MENUGROUP	Menu file group name
***TOOLBARS	Toolbar definition
***HELPSTRING	Online help
***ACCELERATORS	Accelerator key definitions

Writing Partial Menus

The following example illustrates the procedure for writing a partial menu for Windows:

Example 6

In this example you will write a partial menu for Windows. The menu file has two menus, POP1 (MyDraw) and POP2 (MyEdit), as shown in Figure 32-17.

Step 1

Use a text editor to write the following menu file. The name of the file is assumed to be **MYMENU1.MNU**. The following is the listing of the menu file for this example:

Figure 32-17 *Pull-down menus for Example 6*

```
***MENUGROUP=Menu1                              1
***POP1                                         2
[/MMyDraw]                                       3
[/LLine]^C^CLine                                 4
[/CCircle]^C^CCircle                             5
[/AArc]^C^CArc                                   6
[/EEllipse]^C^CEllipse                           7
***POP2                                         8
[/EMyEdit]                                       9
[/EErase]^C^CErase                              10
[/CCopy]^C^CCopy                                11
[/MMove]^C^CMove                                12
[/OOffset]^C^COffset                            13
```

Explanation
Line 1
***MENUGROUP=Menu1
MENUGROUP is the section label and the Menu1 is the name tag for the menu group. The MENUGROUP label must precede all menu section definitions. The name of the MENUGROUP (Menu1) can be up to 32 characters long (alphanumeric), excluding spaces and punctuation marks. There is only one MENUGROUP in a menu file. All section labels must be preceded by *** (***MENUGROUP).

Line 2
***POP1
POP1 is the menu section label. The items on line numbers 3 through 7 belong to this section. Similarly, the items on line numbers 9 through 13 belong to the menu section **POP2**.

Line 3
[/MMyDraw]
/M defines the mnemonic key you can use to activate the menu item. For example, /M will display an underline under the letter M in the text string that follows it. If you enter the letter M, AutoCAD will execute the command defined in that menu item. MyDraw is the menu item label. The text string inside the brackets [ ] , except /M, has no function. It is used for displaying the function name so that the user can recognize the command that will be executed by selecting that item.

Line 4
[/LLine]^C^CLine
In this line, the /L defines the mnemonic key, and the Line that is inside the brackets is the menu item label. ^C^C cancels the command twice, and the Line is the AutoCAD **LINE** command. The part of the menu item statement that is outside the brackets is executed when you select an item from the menu. When you select Line 4, AutoCAD will execute the **LINE** command.

Step 2
Save the file and then load the partial menu file using the AutoCAD **MENULOAD** command.

Command: **MENULOAD**

When you enter the **MENULOAD** command, AutoCAD displays the **Menu Customization** dialog box (Figure 32-18). To load the menu file, enter the name of the menu file, **MYMENU1.MNU**, in the **File Name**: edit box. You can also use the **Browse...** option to invoke the **Select Menu File** dialog box. Select the name of the file, and then use the **OK** button to return to the **Menu Customization** dialog box. To load the selected menu file, choose the **LOAD** button. The name of the menu group (MENU1) will be displayed in the **Menu Groups** list box.
You can also load the menu file from the command line, as follows:

Command: **FILEDIA**
Enter new value for FILEDIA <1>: **0**   *(Disables the file dialog boxes.)*
Command: **MENULOAD**
Enter name of menu file to load: **MYMENU1.MNU**

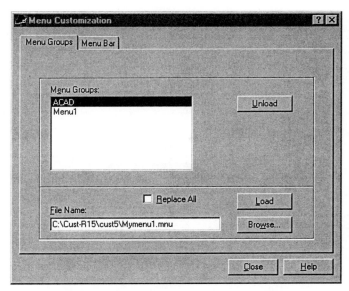

Figure 32-18 Menu Customization dialog box (Menu Groups tab)

You can also use the AutoLISP functions to set the **FILEDIA** system variable to 0 and then load the partial menu.

    Command: **(SETVAR "FILEDIA" 0)**
    Command: **(Command "MENULOAD" "MYMENU1")**

Step 3
In the **Menu Customization** dialog box, select the **Menu Bar** tab to display the menu bar options (Figure 32-19). In the **Menu Groups** list box select Menu1; the menus defined in the menu group (Menu1) will be displayed in the **Menus** list box. In the **Menus** list box select the menu (MyDraw) that you want to insert in the menu bar. In the **Menu Bar** list box select the position where you want to insert the new menu. For example, if you want to insert the new menu in front of Format, select the **Format** menu in the **Menu Bar** list box. Choose the **Insert** button to insert the selected menu (MyDraw) in the menu bar. The menu (MyDraw1) is displayed in the menu bar located at the top of your screen.

You can also load the menu from the Command line. Once the menu is loaded, use the **MENUCMD** command (AutoLISP function) to display the partial menus.

    Command: **(MENUCMD "P5=+Menu1.POP1")**
    Command: **(MENUCMD "P6=+Menu1.POP2")**

After you enter these commands, AutoCAD will display the menu titles in the menu bar, as shown in Figure 32-20. If you select MyDraw, the corresponding menu as defined in the menu file will be displayed on the screen. Similarly, selecting MyEdit will display the corresponding edit menu.

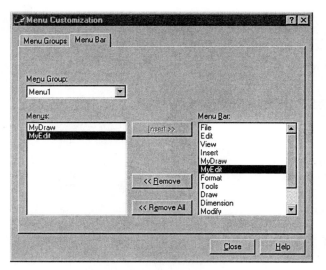

*Figure 32-19 **Menu Customization** dialog box (Menu Bar tab)*

MENUCMD is an AutoLISP function, and P5 determines where the POP1 menu will be displayed. In this example the POP1 (MyDraw) menu will be displayed as the fifth menu. Menu1 is the MENUGROUP name as defined in the menu file, and POP1 is the menu section label. The MENUGROUP name and the menu section label must be separated by a period (.).

*Figure 32-20   **MENUCMD** command places the menu titles in the menu bar*

Step 4
If you want to unload the menu (MyDraw), select the Menu Bar tab of the **Menu Customization** dialog box. In the **Menu Bar** list box select the menu item that you want to unload. Choose the **Remove** button to remove the selected item.

Step 5
You can also unload the menu groups (Menu1) using the **Menu Customization** dialog box. Enter the **MENULOAD** or **MENUUNLOAD** command to invoke the **Menu Customization** dialog box (Figure 32-18). AutoCAD will display the names of the menu files in the **Menu Groups:** list box. Select the **Menu1** menu, and then choose the **Unload** button. AutoCAD will unload the menu group. Choose the **Close** button to exit the dialog box. You can also unload the menu file from the command line, as follows:

    Command: **FILEDIA**
    Enter new value for FILEDIA <1>: **0**
    Command: **MENUUNLOAD**
    Enter the name of a MENUGROUP to unload: **MENU1.MNU**

The **MENUUNLOAD** command unloads the entire menu group. You can also unload an individual menu without unloading the entire menu group by using the following command:

Command: **(MENUCMD "P5=-)**

This command will unload the menu at position five (P5, MyDraw menu). The menu group is still loaded, but the P5 menu is not visible. The menu can also be reinitialized by using the **MENU** command to load the base menu **ACAD.MNU**. This will remove all partial menus and the tag definitions associated with the partial menus.

Accelerator Keys

AutoCAD for Windows also supports user-defined accelerator keys. For example, if you enter **C** at the Command prompt, AutoCAD draws a circle because it is a command alias for a circle as defined in the ACAD.PGP file. You cannot use the **C** key to enter the **COPY** command. To use the **C** key for entering the **COPY** command, you can define the accelerator keys. You can combine the SHIFT key with C in the menu file so that when you hold down the SHIFT key and then press the C key, AutoCAD will execute the **COPY** command. The following example illustrates the use of accelerator keys.

Example 7

In this example you will add the following accelerator keys to the partial menu of Example 6.

CONTROL+"E"	to draw an ellipse (**ELLIPSE** command)
SHIFT+"C"	to copy (**COPY** command)
[CONTROL'Q"]	to quit (**QUIT** command)

The following file is the listing of the partial menu file that uses the accelerator keys of Example 7.

```
***MENUGROUP=Menu1
***POP1
**Alias
[/MMyDraw]
[/LLine]^C^CLine
[/CCircle]^C^CCircle
[/AArc]^C^CArc
ID_Ellipse [/EEllipse]^C^CEllipse

***POP2
[/EMyEdit]
[/EErase]^C^CErase
ID_Copy [/CCopy]^C^CCopy
[/OOffset]^C^COffset
[/VMove]^C^CMov

***ACCELERATORS
ID_Ellipse [CONTROL+"E"]
ID_Copy [SHIFT+"C"]
[CONTROL'Q"]^C^CQuit
```

Chapter 32

This menu file defines three accelerator keys. The **ID_Copy [SHIFT+"C"]** accelerator key consists of two parts. The ID_Copy is the name tag, which must be the same as used earlier in the menu item definition. The SHIFT+"C" is the label that contains the modifier (SHIFT) and the keyname (C). The keyname or the string, such as "ESCAPE", must be enclosed in quotation marks. After you load the file, SHIFT+C will enter the **COPY** command and CTRL+E will draw an ellipse. Similarly, Ctrl+Q will cancel the existing command and enter the **QUIT** command.

The accelerator keys can be defined in two ways. One way is to give the name tag followed by the label containing the modifier. The modifier is followed by a single character or a special virtual key enclosed in quotation marks [CONTROL+"E"] or ["ESCAPE"]. You can also use the plus sign (+) to concatenate the modifiers [SHIFT + CONTROL + "L"]. The other way of defining an accelerator key is to give the modifier and the key string, followed by a command sequence [CONTROL "Q"]^C^CQuit.

Special Virtual Keys
The following are the special virtual keys. These keys must be enclosed in quotation marks when used in the menu file.

String	Description	String	Description
"F1"	F1 key	"NUMBERPAD0"	0 key
"F2"	F2 key	"NUMBERPAD1"	1 key
"F3"	F3 key	"NUMBERPAD2"	2 key
"F4"	F4 key	"NUMBERPAD3"	3 key
"F5"	F5 key	"NUMBERPAD4"	4 key
"F6"	F6 key	"NUMBERPAD5"	5 key
"F7"	F7 key	"NUMBERPAD6"	6 key
"F8"	F8 key	"NUMBERPAD7"	7 key
"F9"	F9 key	"NUMBERPAD8"	8 key
"F10"	F10 key	"NUMBERPAD9"	9 key
"F11"	F11 key	"UP"	UP-ARROW key
"F12"	F12 key	"DOWN"	DOWN-ARROW key
"HOME"	HOME key	"LEFT"	LEFT-ARROW key
"END"	END key	"RIGHT"	RIGHT-ARROW key
"INSERT"	INS key	"ESCAPE"	ESC key
"DELETE"	DEL key		

Valid Modifiers. The following are the valid modifiers:

String	Description
CONTROL	The CTRL key on the keyboard
SHIFT	The SHIFT key (left or right)
COMMAND	The Apple key on Macintosh keyboards
META	The meta key on UNIX keyboards

Toolbars
The contents of the toolbar and its default layout can be specified in the Toolbar section (***TOOLBARS) of the menu file. Each toolbar must be defined in a separate submenu.

Toolbar Definition. The following is the general format of the toolbar definition:

```
***TOOLBARS
**MYTOOLS1
TAG1 [Toolbar ("tbarname", orient, visible, xval, yval, rows)]
TAG2 [Button ("btnname", id_small, id_large)]macro
TAG3 [Flyout ("flyname", id_small, id_large, icon, alias)]macro
TAG4 [control (element)]
[—]
```

***TOOLBARS is the section label of the toolbar, and **MYTOOLS1** is the name of the submenu that contains the definition of a toolbar. Each toolbar can have five distinct items that control different elements of the toolbar: TAG1, TAG2, TAG3, TAG4, and separator ([—]). The first line of the toolbar (TAG1) defines the characteristics of the toolbar. In this line, **Toolbar** is the keyword, and it is followed by a series of options enclosed in parentheses. The following describes the available options.

tbarname   This is a text string that names the toolbar. The tbarname text string must consist of alphanumeric characters with no punctuation other than a dash (-) or an underscore (_).

orient   This determines the orientation of the toolbar. The acceptable values are Floating, Top, Bottom, Left, and Right. These values are not case-sensitive.

visible   This determines the visibility of the toolbar. The acceptable values are Show and Hide. These values are not case-sensitive.

xval   This is a numeric value that specifies the X ordinate in pixels. The X ordinate is measured from the left edge of the screen to the right side of the toolbar.

yval   This is a numeric value that specifies the Y ordinate in pixels. The Y ordinate is measured from the top edge of the screen to the top of the toolbar.

rows   This is a numeric value that specifies the number of rows.

The second line of the toolbar (TAG2) defines the button. In this line the **Button** is the key word and it is followed by a series of options enclosed in parentheses. The following is the description of the available options.

btnname   This is a text string that names the button. The text string must consist of alphanumeric characters with no punctuation other than a dash (-) or an underscore (_). This text string is displayed as ToolTip when you place the cursor over the button.

id_small   This is a text string that names the ID string of the small image resource (16 by 16 bitmap). The text string must consist of alphanumeric characters with no punctuation other than a dash (-) or an underscore (_). The id_small text

Chapter 32

string can also specify a user-defined bitmap (Example: ICON_16_CIRCLE).

id_big   This is a text string that names the ID string of the large image resource (32 by 32 bitmap). The text string must consist of alphanumeric characters with no punctuation other than a dash (-) or an underscore (_). The id_big text string can also specify a user-defined bitmap (Example: ICON_32_CIRCLE).

macro   The second line (TAG2), which defines a button, is followed by a command string (macro). For example, the macro can consist of $^\wedge$C$^\wedge$CLine. It follows the same syntax as that of any standard menu item definition.

The third line of the toolbar (TAG3) defines the flyout control. In this line the **Flyout** is the key word, and it is followed by a series of options enclosed in parentheses. The following describes the available options.

flyname   This is a text string that names the flyout. The text string must consist of alphanumeric characters with no punctuation other than a dash (-) or an underscore (_). This text string is displayed as ToolTip when you place the cursor over the flyout button.

id_small   This is a text string that names the ID string of the small image resource (16 by 16 bitmap). The text string must consist of alphanumeric characters with no punctuation other than a dash (-) or an underscore (_). The id_small text string can also specify a user-defined bitmap.

id_big   This is a text string that names the ID string of the large image resource (32 by 32 bitmap). The text string must consist of alphanumeric characters with no punctuation other than a dash (-) or an underscore (_). The id_big text string can also specify a user-defined bitmap.

icon   This is a Boolean key word that determines whether the button displays its own icon or the last icon selected. The acceptable values are **ownicon** and **othericon**. These values are not case-sensitive.

alias   The alias specifies the name of the toolbar submenu that is defined with the standard ****aliasname** syntax.

macro   The third line (TAG3), which defines a flyout control, is followed by a command string (macro). For example, the macro can consist of $^\wedge$C$^\wedge$CCircle. It follows the same syntax as that of any standard menu item definition.

The fourth line of the toolbar (TAG4) defines a special control element. In this line the Control is the key word, and it is followed by the type of control element enclosed in parentheses. The following describes the available control element types.

element   This parameter can have one of the following three values:
                    Layer: This specifies the layer control element.

Linetype: This specifies the linetype control element.
Color: This specifies the color control element.

The fifth line ([**--**]) defines a separator.

Example 8

In this example you will write a menu file for a toolbar for the **LINE, PLINE, CIRCLE, ELLIPSE,** and **ARC** commands. The name of the toolbar is MyDraw1 (Figure 32-21).

The following is the listing of the menu file:
MENUGROUP=M1
***TOOLBARS
**TB_MyDraw1
ID_MyDraw1[_Toolbar("MyDraw1", _Floating, _Hide, 10, 200, 1)]
ID_Line [_Button("Line", ICON_16_LINE, ICON_32_LINE)]^C^C_line
ID_Pline [_Button("Pline", ICON_16_PLine, ICON_32_PLine)]^C^C_PLine
ID_Circle[_Button("Circle", ICON_16_CirRAD, ICON_32_CirRAD)]^C^C_Circle
ID_ELLIPSE[_Button("Ellipse", ICON_16_EllCEN, ICON_32_EllCEN)]^C^C_ELLIPSE
ID_Arc[_Button("Arc 3Point", ICON_16_Arc3Pt, ICON_32_Arc3Pt)]^C^C_Arc

Figure 32-21 *MyDraw1 toolbar for Example 8 and* **Toolbars** *dialog box*

Use the **MENULOAD** command to load the MyDraw1 menu group as discussed earlier. To display the new toolbar (MyDraw1) on the screen, select Toolbars from the View menu and then select MyDraw1 in the **Menu Groups** list box. Turn the MyDraw1 toolbar on in the **Toolbars** dialog box; MyDraw1 toolbar is displayed on the screen.

You can also load the new toolbar from the command line. After using the **MENULOAD** command to load the MyDraw1 menu group, use the **-TOOLBAR** command to display the MyDraw1 toolbar.

Command: **-TOOLBAR**
Enter toolbar name or [ALL]: **MYDRAW1**
Enter an option [Show/Hide/Left/Right/Top/Bottom/Float] <Show>: **S**

Example 9

In this example you will write a menu file for a toolbar with a flyout. The name of the toolbar is MyDraw2 (Figure 32-22), and it contains two buttons, Circle and Arc. When you select the Circle button, it should display a flyout with radius, diameter, 2P, and 3P buttons (Figure 32-23). Similarly, when you select the Arc button, it should display the 3Point, SCE, and SCA buttons.

The following is the listing of the menu file:
***Menugroup=M2
***TOOLBARS
**TB_MyDraw2
ID_MyDraw2[_Toolbar("MyDraw2", _Floating, _Show, 10, 100, 1)]
ID_TbCircle[_Flyout("Circle", ICON_16_Circle, ICON_32_Circle, _OtherIcon, M2.TB_Circle)]
ID_TbArc[_Flyout("Arc", ICON_16_Arc, ICON_32_Arc, _OtherIcon, M2.TB_Arc)]
**TB_Circle
ID_TbCircle[_Toolbar("Circle", _Floating, _Hide, 10, 150, 1)]
ID_CirRAD[_Button("Circle C,R", ICON_16_CirRAD, ICON_32_CirRAD)]^C^C_Circle
ID_CirDIA[_Button("Circle C,D", ICON_16_CirDIA, ICON_32_CirDIA)]^C^C_Circle;\D
ID_Cir2Pt[_Button("Circle 2Pts", ICON_16_Cir2Pt, ICON_32_Cir2Pt)]^C^C_Circle;2P
ID_Cir3Pt[_Button("Circle 3Pts", ICON_16_Cir3Pt, ICON_32_Cir3Pt)]^C^C_Circle;3P

**TB_Arc
ID_TbArc[_Toolbar("Arc", _Floating, _Hide, 10, 150, 1)]
ID_Arc3PT[_Button("Arc,3Pts", ICON_16_Arc3PT, ICON_32_Arc3PT)]^C^C_Arc
ID_ArcSCE[_Button("Arc,SCE", ICON_16_ArcSCE, ICON_32_ArcSCE)]^C^C_Arc;\C
ID_ArcSCA[_Button("Arc,SCA", ICON_16_ArcSCA, ICON_32_ArcSCA)]^C^C_Arc;\C;\A

Explanation

ID_TbCircle[_Flyout("Circle", ICON_16_Circle, ICON_32_Circle, _OtherIcon,
M2.TB_Circle)]

In this line M2 is the MENUGROUP name (***MENUGROUP=M2) and TB_Circle is the name of the toolbar submenu. **M2.TB_Circle** will load the submenu TB_Circle that has been defined in the M2 menugroup. If M2 is missing, AutoCAD will not display the flyout when you select the Circle button.

ID_CirDIA[_Button("Circle C,D", ICON_16_**CirDIA**, ICON_32_**CirDIA**)]^C^C_Circle;\D

CirDIA is a user-defined bitmap that displays the Circle-diameter button. If you use any other name, AutoCAD will not display the desired button.

To load the toolbar, use the **MENULOAD** command to load the menu file. The **MyDraw1** toolbar will be displayed on the screen.

Figure 32-22 *Toolbar for Example 9*

Figure 32-23 *Toolbar with flyout*

Menu-Specific Help

AutoCAD for Windows allows access to online help. For example, if you want to define a helpstring for the **CIRCLE** and **ARC** commands, the syntax is as follows:

```
***HELPSTRING
ID_Copy (This command will copy the selected object.)
ID_Ellipse (This command will draw an ellipse.)
```

The *****HELPSTRING** is the section label for the helpstring menu section. The lines defined in this section start with a name tag (ID_Copy) and are followed by the label enclosed in square brackets. If you press the F1 key when the menu item is highlighted, the help engine gets activated and AutoCAD displays the helpstring defined with the name tag.

CUSTOMIZING THE TOOLBARS

AutoCAD has provided several toolbars that should be sufficient for general use. However, sometimes you may need to customize the toolbars so that the commands that you use frequently are grouped in one toolbar. This saves time in selecting commands. It also saves the drawing space because you do not need to have several toolbars on the screen. The following example explains the process involved in creating and editing the toolbars.

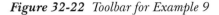

Example 10

In this example you will create a new toolbar (MyToolbar1) that has Line, Polyline, Circle (Center, Radius option), Arc (Center, Start, End option), Spline, and Paragraph Text (**MTEXT**) commands. You will also change the image and tooltip of Line button and perform other operations like deleting toolbars and buttons and copying buttons between toolbars.

1. Select the toolbars in the **View** menu. The **Toolbars** dialog box will appear on the screen. You can also invoke this dialog box by entering **TBCONFIG** at AutoCAD's Command prompt.

2. Choose **New...** button in the **Toolbars** dialog box; AutoCAD will display the **New Toolbar** dialog box at the top of the existing (Toolbars) dialog box.

3. Enter the name of the toolbar in the **Toolbar Name** edit box (Example MyToolbar1) and then chose the **OK** button to exit the dialog box. The name of the new toolbar (MyToolbar1) is displayed in the **Toolbars** dialog box (Figure 32-24).

4. Select the new toolbar, if it is not already selected, by selecting the box that is located just to the left of the toolbar name (MyToolbar1). The new toolbar (MyToolbar1) appears on the screen.

5. Choose the **Customize...** button in the **Toolbars** dialog box (Figure 32-25). The **Customize Toolbars** dialog box is displayed on the screen.

6. In the **Categories** edit box select the down arrow to display the list of toolbars and select the draw toolbar. (You can also type D to display the toolbars that start with the letter D). AutoCAD displays the draw tool buttons.

*Figure 32-24 **Toolbars** dialog box*

7. Choose and drag the Line button and position it in the MyToolbar1 toolbox. Repeat the same for Polyline, Circle (Center, Radius option), Arc (Center, Start, End option), Spline, and Text (Paragraph text) buttons.

8. Now, select the Dimensioning category and then select and drag some of the dimensioning commands to MyToolbar1.

9. Similarly, you can open any toolbar category and add commands to the new toolbar.

10. When you are done defining the commands for the new toolbar, choose the **Close** button in the **Customize Toolbars** dialog box to return to the **Toolbars** dialog box. Choose the **Close** button again to return to the AutoCAD screen.

*Figure 32-25 **MyToolbar1** toolbar and* ***Customize Toolbars*** *dialog box*

11. Test the buttons in the new toolbar (MyToolbar1).

Creating a New Image and Tooltip for a Button

1. Make sure the button with the image you want to edit is displayed on the screen. In this example we want to edit the image of the **Line** button of MyToolbar1.

2. Right-click on the **Line** button of MyToolbar1; the **Toolbars** dialog box appears on the screen. Again, right-click on the **Line** button; the **Button Properties** dialog box is displayed with the image of the existing **Line** button (Figure 32-26).

3. To edit the shape of the image, choose the **edit** button to access the **Button Editor**. Select the Grid to display the grid lines.

Figure 32-26 MyToolbar1 toolbar, Toolbars and **Button Properties** dialog box

You can edit the shape by using different tools in the **Button Editor**. You can draw a Line by choosing the **Line** button and specifying two points. You can draw a circle or an ellipse by using the **Circle** button. The **Erase** button can be used to erase the image.

4.   In this example, we want to change the color of Line image. To accomplish this, erase the existing line, and then select the color and draw a line. Also, create the shape L in the lower right corner (Figure 32-27).

5.   Choose the **SaveAs** button and save the image as **MyLine** in the Tutorial directory. Choose the **Close** button to exit the **Button Editor**.

6.   In the **Button Properties** dialog box, enter MyLine in the **Name** edit box. This changes the tooltip of this button. Now, choose the **Apply** button to apply the changes to the image. Close the dialog boxes to return to the AutoCAD screen. Notice the change in the button image and tooltip (Figure 32-28).

*Figure 32-27 **Button Editor** dialog box*

Figure 32-28 MyToollbar1 Toolbar

Deleting the Button from a Toolbar

1.   Right-click on the button that you want to remove from the toolbox. The **Toolbars** dialog box is displayed. In this example, we want to remove the **Spline** button from the MyToolbar1 toolbox.

2. Choose the **Customize...** button in the **Toolbars** dialog box. The **Customize Toolbars** dialog box is displayed.

3. Click and drag out the **Spline** button from the MyToolbar1 toolbox. The button will be deleted from the toolbox.

4. Repeat the above step to delete other buttons, if needed.

5. Close the dialog boxes to return to the screen.

Deleting a Toolbar

1. Select Toolbars from the **View** menu.

2. Select the Toolbar that you want to delete and then choose the **Delete** button. The toolbar you selected is deleted.

Copying a Tool Button

In this example we want to copy the ordinate **dimensioning** button from the **Dimensioning** toolbar to MyToolbar1.

1. Select the Toolbars from the **View** menu or right-click on any button in any toolbar.

2. In the **Toolbars** dialog box select the check box for Dimensioning and MyToolbar1. The Dimensioning and MyToolbar1 toolbars are displayed on the screen.

3. In the **Toolbars** dialog box choose the **Customizing...** button; the **Customize Toolbars** dialog box appears.

4. Hold the CTRL key down and then choose and drag the **Ordinate dimensioning** button from the **Dimensioning** toolbar to MyToolbar1. The Ordinate dimensioning toolbar is copied to MyToolbar1.

 Note
*If you do not hold down the CTRL key, the button you selected will be moved from the **Dimensioning** toolbar to MyToolbar1.*

Any changes made in the toolbars are saved in the ACAD.MNS and ACAD.MNR files. The following is the partial listing of ACAD.MNS file:

```
**MYTOOLBAR1
ID_MyToolbar1_0 [_Toolbar("MyToolbar1", _Floating, _Show, 512, 177, 1)]
ID_Line_0    [_Button("MyLine", "ICON.bmp", "ICON_24_LINE")]^C^C_line
ID_CircleCenterRadius_0 [_Button("Circle Center Radius", "ICON_16_CIRRAD",
"ICON_24_CIRRAD")]^C^C_circle
ID_Polyline_0 [_Button("Polyline", "ICON_16_PLINE", "ICON_24_PLINE")]^C^C_pline
ID_ArcCenterStartEnd_0 [_Button("Arc Center Start End", "ICON_16_ARCCSE",
"ICON_24_ARCCSE")]^C^C_arc _c
```

Creating Custom Toolbars with Flyout Icons

In this example you will create a custom toolbar with flyout buttons.

1. Right-click on any toolbar; the **Toolbars** dialog box is displayed on the screen.

2. In the **Toolbars** dialog box, choose the **New...** button to display the **New Toolbars** dialog box. Enter the name of the new toolbar (for example, MYToolbar2) and then choose the **OK** button to exit the box.

3. In the **Toolbars** dialog box, select the new toolbar name (MYToolbar2) and then choose the **Customize...** button to display the **Customize Toolbars** dialog box. From the drop-down list select custom and then drag the **flyout** button to the new toolbar.

4. Right-click twice on the **flyout** button of the new toolbar. The **Flyout Properties** dialog box (Figure 32-29) is displayed on the screen. To associate it with a predefined toolbar, select the toolbar name (for example, ACAD.Draw) from the list.

5. Choose the **Apply** button and then close the dialog boxes. If you click on the **flyout** button of the new toolbar, the corresponding **flyout** buttons are displayed.

6. Now, you can add new buttons to the toolbar or delete the ones you do not want in this toolbar.

7. If you select Show This Button's Icon, the selected icon will be displayed on the screen.

Figure 32-29 Flyout Properties dialog box and the new toolbar (MYToolbar2)

Review Questions

1. A pull-down menu can have _____ sections.

2. The length of the section title should not exceed _____ characters.

3. The section titles in a pull-down menu are _____ justified.

4. In a pull-down menu, a line consisting of two hyphens ([--]) _____ automatically to fill the _____ of the menu.

5. If the menu item begins with a tilde (~), the items will be _____ .

6. The pull-down menus are _____ when the dynamic zoom is in progress.

7. Every cascading menu in the menu file should have a _____ name.

8. The cascading menu name can be _____ characters long.

9. The cascading menu names should not have any _____ blanks.

10. In Windows you can write partial menus, toolbars, and accelerator key definitions. (T/F)

11. A menu file can contain only one MENUGROUP. (T/F)

12. You can load the partial menu file by using the AutoCAD _____ command.

13. Once the menu is loaded, you can use the _____ (AutoLISP function) to display the partial menus.

Exercises

Exercise 3   *General*

Write a menu for the following AutoCAD commands. (The layout of the menu is shown in Figure 32-30.)

LINE	DIM HORZ	DTEXT LEFT
CIRCLE C,R	DIM VERT	DTEXT RIGHT
CIRCLE C,D	DIM RADIUS	DTEXT CENTER
ARC 3P	DIM DIAMETER	DTEXT ALIGNED
ARC SCE	DIM ANGULAR	DTEXT MIDDLE
ARC CSE	DIM LEADER	DTEXT FIT

PULL-DOWN MENU

DRAW	DIM	DTEXT
LINE	DIM-HORZ	DTEXT-LEFT
CIRCLE C,R	DIM-VERT	DTEXT-RIGHT
CIRCLE C,D	DIM-RADIUS	DTEXT-CENTER
ARC 3P	DIM-DIAMETER	DTEXT-ALIGNED
ARC SCE	DIM-ANGULAR	DTEXT-MIDDLE
ARC CSE	DIM-LEADER	DTEXT-FIT

Figure 32-30 *Layout of menu*

Exercise 4   *General*

Write a menu for the following AutoCAD commands.

LINE	**BLOCK**
PLINE	**WBLOCK**
CIRCLE C,R	**INSERT**
CIRCLE C,D	**BLOCK LIST**
ELLIPSE AXIS ENDPOINT	**ATTDEF**
ELLIPSE CENTER	**ATTEDIT**

Exercise 5   *General*

Write a partial menu for Windows. The menu file should have two menus, POP1 (MyArc) and POP2 (MyDraw). The MyArc menu should contain all Arc options and must be displayed at the sixth position. Similarly, the MyDraw menu should contain **LINE**, **CIRCLE**, **PLINE**, **TRACE**, **DTEXT**, and **MTEXT** commands and should occupy the ninth position.

Exercise 6   *General*

Write a menu file for a toolbar with a flyout. The name of the toolbar is MyDrawX1, and it contains two buttons, **Polygon** and **Ellipse**. When you select the **Polygon** button, it should display a flyout with **Rectangle** and **Polygon** button. Similarly, when you choose the **Ellipse** button, it should display the **Ellipse-Center** Option and **Ellipse-Edge** Option button.

Exercise 7   *General*

Write a menu for the following AutoCAD commands. (The layouts of the menu is shown in Figure 32-31.)

LAYER NEW	**SNAP** 0.25	**UCS WORLD**
LAYER MAKE	**SNAP** 0.5	**UCS PREVIOUS**
LAYER SET	**GRID** 1.0	**VPORTS** 2
LAYER LIST	**DRID** 10.0	**VPORTS** 4
LAYER ON	**APERTURE** 5	**VPORTS SING.**
LAYER OFF	**PICKBOX** 5	

```
              PULL—DOWN  MENU

  ┌──────────────────────────────────────────┐
  │  LAYER         SETTINGS       UCS—PORT    │
  ├──────────────────────────────────────────┘
     LAYER—New      SNAP  0.25     UCS—World
     LAYER—Make     SNAP  0.5      UCS—Pre
     LAYER—Set      GRID  1.0      VPORTS—2
     LAYER—List     GRID  10.0     VPORTS—4
     LAYER—On       APERTURE  5    VPORTS—1
     LAYER—Off      PICKBOX  5
```

Figure 32-31 Design of menu for Exercise 7

Chapter 33

Tablet Menus

Learning Objectives

After completing this chapter, you will be able to:
- *Understand the advantages of tablet menus.*
- *Write and customize tablet menus.*
- *Load menus and configure tablet menus.*
- *Write tablet menus with different block sizes.*
- *Assign commands to tablet overlays.*

Figure 33-1 Sample tablet template

STANDARD TABLET MENU

The tablet menu provides a powerful alternative for entering commands. In the tablet menu, the commands are selected from the template that is secured on the surface of a digitizing tablet. To use the tablet menu you need a digitizing tablet and a pointing device. You also need a tablet template (Figure 33-1) that contains AutoCAD commands arranged in various groups for easy identification.

The standard AutoCAD menu file has four tablet menu sections: TABLET1, TABLET2, TABLET3, and TABLET4. When you start AutoCAD and get into the drawing editor, the tablet menu sections TABLET1, TABLET2, TABLET3, and TABLET4 are automatically loaded. The commands defined in these four sections are then assigned to different blocks of the template.

The first tablet menu section (TABLET1) has 225 blank blocks that can be used to assign up to 225 menu items. The remaining tablet menu sections contain AutoCAD commands, arranged in functional groups that make it easier to identify and access the commands. The commands contained in the TABLET2 section include RENDER, SOLID MODELING, DISPLAY, INQUIRY, DRAW, ZOOM, and PAPER SPACE commands. The TABLET3 section contains numbers, fractions, and angles. The commands contained in the TABLET4 section include **TEXT**, **DIMEN-SIONING**, **OBJECT SNAPS**, **EDIT**, **UTILITY**, **XREF**, and **SETTINGS**.

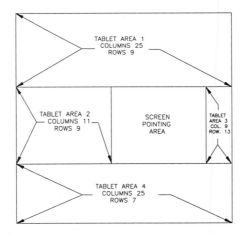

Figure 33-2 *Four tablet areas of the AutoCAD tablet template*

The AutoCAD tablet template has four tablet areas (Figure 33-2), which correspond to four tablet menu sections, TABLET1, TABLET2, TABLET3, and TABLET4.

ADVANTAGES OF A TABLET MENU

A tablet menu has the following advantages over the screen menu, pull-down menu, image menu, or keyboard.

1 In the tablet menu the commands can be arranged so that the most frequently used commands can be accessed directly. This can save considerable time in entering AutoCAD com-

mands. In the screen menu or the pull-down menu some of the commands cannot be accessed directly. For example, to generate a horizontal dimension you have to go through several steps. You first select Dimension from the root menu and then Linear. In the tablet menu you can select the Linear dimensioning command directly from the digitizer. This saves time and eliminates the distraction that takes place as you page through different screens.

2. You can have the graphical symbols of the AutoCAD commands drawn on the tablet template. This makes it much easier to recognize and select commands. For example, if you are not an expert in AutoCAD dimensioning, you may find Baseline and Continue dimensioning confusing. But if the command is supported by the graphical symbol illustrating what a command does, the chances of selecting a wrong command are minimized.

3. You can assign any number of commands to the tablet overlay. The number of commands you can assign to a tablet is limited only by the size of the digitizer and the size of the rectangular blocks.

CUSTOMIZING A TABLET MENU

As with a screen menu, you can customize the AutoCAD tablet menu. It is a powerful customizing tool to make AutoCAD more efficient.

The tablet menu can contain a maximum of four sections: TABLET1, TABLET2, TABLET3, and TABLET4. Each section represents a rectangular area on the digitizing tablet. These rectangular areas can be further divided into any number of rectangular blocks. The size of each block depends on the number of commands that are assigned to the tablet area. Also, the rectangular tablet areas can be located anywhere on the digitizer and can be arranged in any order. The AutoCAD **TABLET** command configures the tablet. The **MENU** command loads and assigns the commands to the rectangular blocks on the tablet template.

Before writing a tablet menu file, it is very important to design the layout of the design of tablet template. A well-thought-out design can save a lot of time in the long run. The following points should be considered when designing a tablet template:

1. Learn the AutoCAD commands that you use in your profession.

2. Group the commands based on their function, use, or relationship with other commands.

3. Draw a rectangle representing a template so that it is easy for you to move the pointing device around. The size of this area should be appropriate to your application. It should not be too large or too small. Also, the size of the template depends on the active area of the digitizer.

4. Divide the remaining area into four different rectangular tablet areas for TABLET1, TABLET2, TABLET3, and TABLET4. It is not necessary to use all four areas; you can have fewer tablet areas, but four is the maximum.

5. Determine the number of commands you need to assign to a particular tablet area; then determine the number of rows and columns you need to generate in each area. The size of the blocks does not need to be the same in every tablet area.

Chapter 33

6. Use the **TEXT** command to print the commands on the tablet overlay, and draw the symbols of the command, if possible.

7. Plot the tablet overlay on good-quality paper or a sheet of Mylar. If you want the plotted side of the template to face the digitizer board, you can create a mirror image of the tablet overlay and then plot the mirror image.

WRITING A TABLET MENU

When writing a tablet menu you must understand the AutoCAD commands and the prompt entries required for each command. Equally important is the design of the tablet template and the placement of various commands on it. Give considerable thought to the design and layout of the template, and, if possible, invite suggestions from AutoCAD users in your trade. To understand the process involved in developing and writing a tablet menu, consider Example 1.

Example 1

Write a tablet menu for the following AutoCAD commands. The commands are to be arranged as shown in Figure 33-3. Make a tablet menu template for configuration and command selection (filename **TM1.MNU**).

LINE	CIRCLE	PLINE
CIRCLE C,D	ERASE	CIRCLE 2P

Figure 33-3 represents one of the possible template designs, where the AutoCAD commands are in one row at the top of the template, and the screen pointing area is in the center. There is only one area in this template; therefore, you can place all these commands under the section label TABLET1. To write a menu file you can use any text editor like Notepad.

The name of the file is TM1, and the extension of the file is **.MNU. The line numbers are not part of the file. They are shown here for reference only.**

***TABLET1	1
^C^CLINE	2
^C^CPLINE	3
^C^CCIRCLE	4
^C^CCIRCLE;\D	5
^C^CCIRCLE;2P	6
^C^CERASE	7

Explanation

Line 1

***TABLET1

TABLET1 is the section label of the first tablet area. All the section labels are preceded by three asterisks (***).

   ***TABLET1

Where   *** --------------- Three asterisks designate section label.
       TABLET1 ------ Section label for TABLET1

Figure 33-3 *Design of tablet template*

Line 2
^ C ^ CLINE
^ C ^ C cancels the existing command twice; **LINE** is an AutoCAD command. There is no space between the second ^ C and **LINE**.

     ^ C ^ C LINE
            Where   **^ C ^ C** ---------- Cancels the existing command twice
                 Line ------------- AutoCAD **LINE** command

Line 3
^ C ^ CPLINE
^ C ^ C cancels the existing command twice; **PLINE** is an AutoCAD command.

Line 4
^ C ^ CCIRCLE
^ C ^ C cancels the existing command twice; **CIRCLE** is an AutoCAD command. The default input for the **CIRCLE** command is the center and the radius of the circle; therefore, no additional input is required for this line.

Line 5
^ C ^ CCIRCLE;\D
^ C ^ C cancels the existing command twice; **CIRCLE** is an AutoCAD command like the previous line. However, this command definition requires the diameter option of the circle command. This is accomplished by using \D in the command definition. There should be no space between the backslash (\) and the D, but there should always be a space **before** the backslash (\). The backslash (\) lets the user enter a point, and in this case it is the center point of the circle. After you enter the center point, the diameter option is selected by the letter D, which follows the backslash (\).

^ C ^ CCIRCLE;\D

Where   **CIRCLE** --------- **CIRCLE** command
     ; ------------------- Space for RETURN
     **** ------------------- Pause for input
     D ------------------ Diameter option

Line 6

^ C ^ CCIRCLE;2P

^ C ^ C cancels the existing command twice; **CIRCLE** is an AutoCAD command. Semicolon is for ENTER or RETURN. The 2P selects the two-point option of the **CIRCLE** command.

Line 7

^ C ^ CERASE

^ C ^ C cancels the existing command twice; **ERASE** is an AutoCAD command that erases the selected objects.

Note

In the tablet menu, the part of the menu item that is enclosed in the brackets is used for screen display only. For example, in the following menu item, T1-6 will be ignored and will have no effect on the command definition.

[T1-6] ^ C ^ CCIRCLE;2P

Where   **[T1-6]** ------------ For reference only and has no effect on the command definition
     T1 ----------------- Tablet area 1
     6 ------------------- Item number 6

The reference information can be used to designate the tablet area and the line number.

Before you can use the commands from the new tablet menu, you need to configure the tablet and load the tablet menu.

TABLET CONFIGURATION

To use the new template to select the commands, you need to configure the tablet so that AutoCAD knows the location of the tablet template and the position of the commands assigned to each block. This is accomplished by using the AutoCAD **TABLET** command. Secure the tablet template (Figure 33-3) on the digitizer with the edges of the overlay approximately parallel to the edges of the digitizer. Enter the AutoCAD **TABLET** command, select the **Configure option**, and respond to the following prompts. Figure 33-4 shows the points you need to select to configure the tablet.

Command: **TABLET**
Enter an option [ON/OFF/CAL/CFG]:**CFG**
Enter number of tablet menus desired (0–4) <current>: **1**
Do you want to realign tablet menus? [Yes/No] <N>: **Y**
Digitize upper left corner of menu area 1; **P1**
Digitize lower left corner of menu area 1; **P2**

Digitize lower right corner of menu area 1; **P3**
Enter the number of columns for menu area 1: **6**
Enter the number of rows for menu area 1: **1**
Do you want to respecify the Fixed Screen Pointing Area? [Yes/No]<N>: **Y**
Digitize lower left corner of Fixed Screen pointing area: **P4**
Digitize upper right corner of Fixed Screen pointing area: **P5**
Do you want to specify the Floating Screen Pointing Area? [Yes/No]<N>: **N**

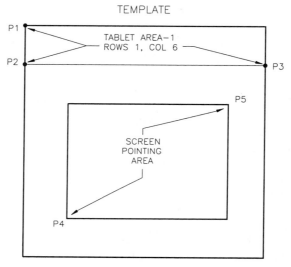

TEMPLATE

Figure 33-4 Points that need to be selected to configure the tablet

Note

The three points P1, P2, and P3 should form a 90-degree angle. If the selected points do not form a 90-degree angle, AutoCAD will prompt you to enter the points again until they do.
The tablet areas should not overlap the screen pointing area.

The screen pointing area can be any size and located anywhere on the tablet as long as it is within the active area of the digitizer. The screen pointing area should not overlap other tablet areas. The screen pointing area you select will correspond to the monitor screen area. Therefore, the length-to-width ratio of the screen pointing area should be the same as that of the monitor, unless you are using the screen pointing area to digitize a drawing.

LOADING MENUS

AutoCAD automatically loads the **ACAD.MNU** file when you get into the AutoCAD drawing editor. However, you can also load a different menu file by using the AutoCAD **MENU** command.

Command: **MENU**

When you enter the **MENU** command, AutoCAD displays the **Select Menu File** dialog box on the screen (Figure 33-5). Select the menu file that you want to load and then choose the **Open** button.

Figure 33-5 Select Menu File dialog box

You can also load the menu file from the command line.

Command: **FILEDIA**
Enter new value for FILEDIA <1>: **0**
Command: **MENU**
Menu filename <ACAD>: PDM1
            Where   **ACAD** ------------ Default menu file
                        PDM1 ----------- Name of menu file

After you enter the **MENU** command, AutoCAD will prompt for the file name. Enter the name of the menu file without the file extension (**.MNU**), since AutoCAD assumes the extension **.MNU**. AutoCAD will automatically compile the menu file into **MNC** and **MNR** files.

Exercise 1   *General*

Write a tablet menu for the following AutoCAD commands. Make a tablet menu template for configuration and command selection (filename **TME1.MNU**).

LINE	**TEXT-Center**
CIRCLE C,R	**TEXT-Left**
ARC C.S.E	**TEXT-Right**
ELLIPSE	**TEXT-Aligned**
DONUT	

Use the template in Figure 33-6 to arrange the commands. The draw and text commands should be placed in two separate tablet areas.

TABLET MENUS WITH DIFFERENT BLOCK SIZES

As mentioned earlier, the size of each tablet area can be different. The size of the blocks in these tablet areas can also be different. But the size of every block in a particular tablet area must be the

TEMPLATE

SCREEN
POINTING AREA

same. This provides you with a lot of flexibility in designing a template. For example, you may prefer to have smaller blocks for numbers, fractions, or letters, and larger blocks for draw commands. You can also arrange these tablet areas to design a template layout with different shapes, such as L-shape and T-shape.

Tablet Area-1

Tablet Area-2

Example 2

The following example illustrates the use of multiple tablet areas with different block sizes.
Write a tablet menu for the tablet overlay shown in Figure 33-7(a). Figure 33-7(b) shows the number of rows and columns in different tablet areas (filename **TM2.MNU**).
Notice that this tablet template has four different sections in addition to the screen pointing area. Therefore, this menu will have four section labels: TABLET1, TABLET2, TABLET3, and TABLET4. You can use any text editor (Notepad) to write the file. The following file is a listing of the tablet menu of Example 2.

```
***TABLET1                                                          1
 ^C^CLINE                                                           2
```

Figure 33-7(a) *Tablet overlay for Example 2*

```
^C^CPLINE                                                      3
^C^CCIRCLE                                                     4
^C^CCIRCLE;\D                                                  5
^C^CCIRCLE;2P                                                  6
***TABLET2                                                     7
^C^CERASE                                                      8
^C^CZOOM;W                                                     9
^C^CMOVE                                                      10
^C^CZOOM;P                                                    11
^C^CCOPY                                                      12
^C^CZOOM;A                                                    13
^C^COFFSET                                                    14
^C^CPAN                                                       15
***TABLET3                                                    16
;                                                            17
;                                                            18
'REDRAW                                                      19
'REDRAW                                                      20
'REDRAW                                                      21
***TABLET4                                                    22
5\                                                           23
6\                                                           24
7\                                                           25
8\                                                           26
```

9\	27
,\	28
WINDOW	29
0\	30
1\	31
2\	32
3\	33
4\	34
.\	35
CROSSING	36

Explanation

Lines 1-6
The first six lines are identical to the first six lines of the tablet menu in Example 1.

Line 9
^C^CZOOM;W
ZOOM is an AutoCAD command; W is the window option of the **ZOOM** command.

^C^CZOOM;W

Where   **ZOOM** ----------- AutoCAD **ZOOM** command
;   ------------------- Space for Return
W   ---------------- Window option of **ZOOM** command

This menu item could also be written as:

^C^CZOOM W

Space between ZOOM nad W causes a RETURN

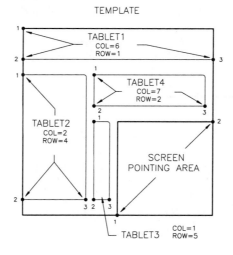

TEMPLATE

Figure 33-7(b) Number of rows and columns in different tablet

Lines 17 and 18
The semicolon (;) is for RETURN. It has the same effect as entering RETURN at the keyboard.

Lines 19-21
'REDRAW
REDRAW is an AutoCAD command that redraws the screen. Notice that there is no ^C^C in front of the **REDRAW** command. If it had ^C^C, the existing command would be canceled before redrawing the screen. This may not be desirable in most applications because you might want to redraw the screen without canceling the existing command. The single quotation (') in front of REDRAW makes the **REDRAW** command transparent.

Line 23
5
The backslash (\) is used to introduce a pause for user input. Without the backslash you cannot enter another number or a character, because after you select the digit **5** it will automatically be followed by RETURN. For example, without the backslash (\), you will not be able to enter a number like **5.6**. Therefore, you need the backslash to enable you to enter decimal numbers or any characters. To terminate the input, enter RETURN at the keyboard or select RETURN from the digitizer.

   5
                         Where \ --------- Backslash for user input
_____

ASSIGNING COMMANDS TO A TABLET

After loading the menu by means of the AutoCAD **MENU** command, you must configure the tablet. At the time of configuration AutoCAD actually generates and stores the information about the rectangular blocks on the tablet template. When you load the menu, the commands defined in the tablet menu are assigned to various blocks. For example, when you select the three points for tablet area 4, Figure 33-7(a), and enter the number of rows and columns, AutoCAD generates a grid of seven columns and two rows, as shown in the following diagram.

After Configuration

When you load the new menu, AutoCAD takes the commands under the section label TABLET4 and starts filling the blocks from left to right. That means "5", "6", "7", "8", "9", ",", and "Window" will be placed in the top row. The next seven commands will be assigned to the next row, starting from the left, as shown in the diagram on page 33-13.

After Loading Tablet Menu

5	6	7	8	9	.	Window
0	1	2	3	4	.	Cross

Similarly, tablet area 3 has been divided into five rows and one column. At first, it appears that this tablet area has only two rows and one column, as shown in Figure 33-7(a). When you configure this tablet area by specifying the three points and entering the number of rows and columns, AutoCAD divides the area into one column and five rows, as shown in the following diagrams.

After loading the menu, AutoCAD takes the commands in the TABLET3 section of the tablet menu and assigns them to the blocks. The first command (;) is placed in the first block. Since there are no more blocks in the first row, the next command (;) is placed in the second row. Similarly, the three **REDRAW** commands are placed in the next three rows. If you pick a point in the first two rows, you will select the **ENTER** command. Similarly, if you pick a point in the next three blocks, you will select the **REDRAW** command.

After Configuration

After Loading Menu

;
;
Redraw
Redraw
Redraw

This process is carried out for all the of tablet areas, and the information is stored in the AutoCAD configuration file, **ACAD.CFG**. If for any reason the configuration is not right, the tablet menu may not perform the desired function.

AUTOMATIC MENU SWAPPING

The screen menus can be automatically swapped by using the system variable **MENUCTL**. When the system variable **MENUCTL** is set to 1, AutoCAD automatically issues the **$S=CMDNAME** command, where **CMDNAME** is the name of the command that loads the submenu. For example, if you select the **LINE** command from the digitizer, menu, or enter the **LINE** command from the keyboard, the **CMDNAME** command will load the **LINE** submenu and display it in the screen menu area. To utilize this feature of AutoCAD, the command name and the submenu name must be the same. For example, if the name of the arc submenu is **ARC** and you select the **ARC** command, the arc submenu will be automatically loaded on the screen. However, if the submenu name is different (for example MYARC), then AutoCAD will not load the arc submenu on the screen. The default value of **MENUCTL** system variable is 1. If you set the **MENUCTL** variable to 0, AutoCAD will not utilize the **$S=CMDNAME** command feature to load the submenus.

Review Questions

1. The maximum number of tablet menu sections is _____.

2. A tablet menu area is _____ in shape.

3. The blocks in any tablet menu area are _____ in shape.

4. A tablet menu area can have _____ number of rectangular blocks.

5. You _____ assign the same command to more than one block on the tablet menu template.

6. The AutoCAD _____ command is used to configure the tablet menu template.

7. The AutoCAD _____ command is used to load a new menu.

Exercises

Exercise 2   *General*

Write a tablet menu for the commands shown in the tablet menu template of Figure 33-8. Make a tablet menu template for configuration and command selection.

Figure 33-8 *Tablet menu template for Exercise 4*

Chapter 34

Image Tile, Button, and Auxiliary Menus

Learning Objectives

After completing this chapter, you will be able to:
- *Write image tile menus.*
- *Reference and display submenus.*
- *Make slides for image tile menus.*
- *Write Buttons menus.*
- *Learn special handling for button menus.*
- *Define and load submenus.*

IMAGE TILE MENUS

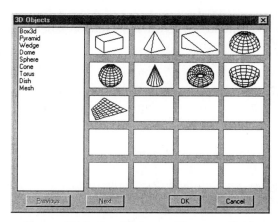

Figure 34-1 *Sample image tile menu display*

The image tile menus, also known as **icon menus**, are extremely useful for inserting a block, selecting a text font, or drawing a 3D object. You can also use the image tile menus to load an AutoLISP routine or a predefined macro. Thus, the image tile menu is a powerful tool for customizing AutoCAD.

The image tile menus can be accessed from the pull-down, tablet, button, or screen menu. However, the image tile menus **cannot** be loaded by entering the command from the keyboard. When you select an image tile, a dialog box that contains **20 image tiles** is displayed on the screen (Figure 34-1). The names of the slide files associated with image tiles appear on the left side of the dialog box with a scrolling bar that can be used to scroll the file names. The title of the image tile menu is displayed at the top of the dialog box (Figure 34-1). When you activate the image tile menu, an arrow that can be moved to select any image tile appears on the screen. You can select an image tile by selecting the slide file name from the dialog box and then choosing the **OK** button from the dialog box or double-clicking on the slide file name.

When you select the slide file, AutoCAD highlights the corresponding image tile by drawing a rectangle around the image tile (Figure 34-1). You can also select an image tile by moving the arrow to the desired image tile, and then pressing the PICK button of the pointing device. The corresponding slide file name will be automatically highlighted. And if you choose the **OK** button or double-click on the image tile, the command associated with that menu item will be executed. You can cancel an image tile menu by pressing ESCAPE on the keyboard, or selecting an image tile from the dialog box.

SUBMENUS

You can define an unlimited number of menu items in the image tile menu, but only 20 image tiles will be displayed at a time. If the number of items exceeds 20, you can use the **Next** and **Previous** buttons of the dialog box to page through different pages of image tiles. You can also define submenus that let you define smaller groups of items within an image tile menu section. When you select a submenu, the submenu items are loaded and displayed on the screen.

Submenu Definition

A submenu label consists of two asterisks (**) followed by the name of the submenu. The image tile menu can have any number of submenus, and every submenu should have a unique name. The items that follow a submenu, up to the next section label or submenu label, belong to that submenu. The format of a submenu label is:

    **Name

                Where   ****** ----------------- Two asterisks designate a submenu

                            Name ------------ Name of the submenu

Note

The submenu name can be up to 31 characters long.

The submenu name can consist of letters, digits, and special characters, like $ (dollar), - (hyphen), and _ (underscore).

The submenu name should not have any embedded blanks.

Submenu names should be unique in a menu file.

Submenu Reference

The submenu reference is used to reference or load a submenu. It consists of a $ sign followed by a letter that specifies the menu section. The letter that specifies an image tile menu section is I. The menu section is followed by an equal sign (=) and the name of the submenu you want to activate. The submenu name should be without the **. Following is the format of a submenu reference:

> **$Section=Submenu**
> Where   **$** ------------------ "$" sign
> **Section** ---------- Menu section specifier
> **=** ------------------ "=" sign
> **Submenu** ------- Name of submenu

> **$I=IMAGE1**
> Where   **I** ------------------ I specifies image tile menu section
> **IMAGE1** -------- Name of submenu

Displaying a Submenu

When you load a submenu, the new dialog box and the image tiles are not automatically displayed. For example, if you load submenu IMAGE1, the items contained in this submenu will not be displayed. To force the display of the new image tile menu on the screen, AutoCAD uses the special command $I=*:

> **$I=***
> Where   **I** ------------------ I for image tile menu
> ***** ------------------ Asterisk (*)

WRITING AN IMAGE TILE MENU

The image tile menu consists of the section label ***IMAGE followed by image tiles or image tile submenus. The menu file can contain only one image tile menu section (***IMAGE); therefore, all image tiles must be defined in this section.

> *****IMAGE**
> Where   ******* ---------------- Three asterisks designate a section label
> **IMAGE** ---------- Section label for an image tile

You can define any number of submenus in the image tile menu. All submenus have two asterisks followed by the name of the submenu (**PARTS or **IMAGE1):

> ****IMAGE1**
> Where   ****** ---------------- Two asterisks designate a submenu
> **IMAGE1** -------- Name of submenu

The first item in the image tile menu is the title of the image tile menu, which is also displayed at the top of the dialog box. The image tile dialog box title has to be enclosed in brackets ([PLC-SYMBOLS]) and should not contain any command definition. If it does contain a command definition, AutoCAD ignores the definition. The remaining items in the image tile menu file contain slide names in the brackets and the command definition outside the brackets.

***IMAGE	Image tile menu section
**BOLTS	Image tile submenu (BOLTS)
[HEX-HEAD BOLTS]	Image tile title
[BOLT1]^C^CINSERT;B1	BOLT1 is slide file name;
	B1 is block name

Example 1

Write an image tile menu that will enable you to insert the block shapes from Figure 34-2 in a drawing by selecting the corresponding image tile from the dialog box. Use the menu to load the image tile menu.

PLC SYMBOLS
NO (NORMALLY OPEN)
NC (NORMALLY CLOSED)
COIL

ELECTRIC SYMBOLS
RESIS (RESISTANCE)
DIODE
GROUND

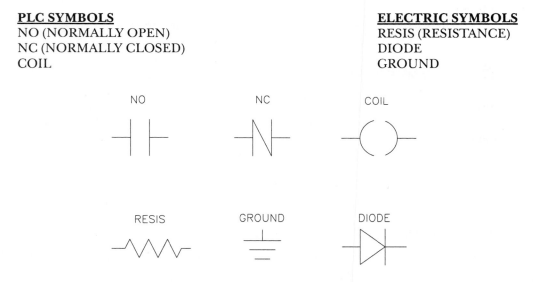

Figure 34-2 *Block shapes for the image tile menu*

As mentioned in earlier chapters, the first step in writing a menu is to design the menu so that the commands are arranged in a desired configuration. Figure 34-3 shows one possible design for the menu and the image tile menu for Example 1.

You can use the AutoCAD **EDIT** command to write the file. **The line numbers in the following file are for reference only and are not a part of the menu file.**

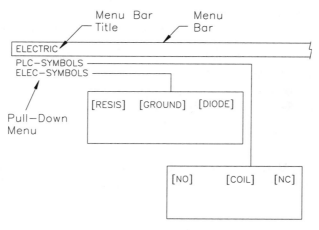

Figure 34-3 *Design of the menu and image tile menu for*

***POP1	1
[ELECTRIC]	2
[PLC-SYMBOLS]$I=IMAGE1 $I=*	3
[ELEC-SYMBOLS]$I=IMAGE2 $I=*	4
***IMAGE	5
**IMAGE1	6
[PLC-SYMBOLS]	7
[NO]^C^CINSERT;NO;\1.0;1.0;0	8
[NC]^C^CINSERT;NC;\1.0;1.0;0;	9
[COIL]^C^CINSERT;COIL	10
[No-Image]	11
[blank]	12
**IMAGE2	13
[ELECTRICAL SYMBOLS]	14
[RESIS]^C^CINSERT;RESIS;\\\\\	15
[DIODE]^C^CINSERT;DIODE;\1.0;1.0;\	16
[GROUND]^C^CINSERT;GRD;\1.5;1.5;0;;	17

Explanation

Line 1

***POP1

In this menu item, ***POP1 is the section label and defines the first section of the menu.

Line 2

[ELECTRIC]

In this menu item [ELECTRIC] is the menu bar label for the POP1 menu. It will be displayed in the menu bar.

Line 3
[PLC-SYMBOLS]$I=IMAGE1 $I=*
In this menu item, $I=IMAGE1 loads the submenu IMAGE1; $I=* displays the current image tile menu on the screen.

> **[PLC-SYMBOLS]$I=IMAGE1 $I=***
>   Where   **Image1** ---------- Loads submenu IMAGE1
> $ ------------------- Forces display of current menu

Line 5
***IMAGE
In this menu item, ***IMAGE is the section label of the image tile menu. All the image tile menus have to be defined within this section; otherwise, AutoCAD cannot locate them.

Line 6
**IMAGE1
In this menu item, **IMAGE1 is the name of the image tile submenu.

Line 7
[PLC-SYMBOLS]
When you select line 3 ([PLC-SYMBOLS]$I=IMAGE1 $I=*), AutoCAD loads the submenu IMAGE1 and displays the title of the image tile at the top of the dialog box (Figure 34-4). This title is defined in Line 7. If this line is missing, the next line will be displayed at the top of the dialog box. Image tile titles can be any length, as long as they fit the length of the dialog box.

***Figure 34-4 Image tile** box for PLC-SYMBOLS*

Line 8
[NO]^C^CINSERT;NO;\1.0;1.0;0
In this menu item, the first NO is the name of the slide and has to be enclosed within brackets. The name should not have any trailing or leading blank spaces. If the slides are not present, AutoCAD will not display any graphical symbols in the image tiles. However, the menu items will be loaded, and if you select this item, the command associated with the image tile will be executed. The second NO is the name of the block that is to be inserted. The backslash (\) pauses for user input; in this case it is the block insertion point. The first 1.0 defines the Xscale factor. The second 1.0 defines the Yscale factor, and the following 0 defines the rotation.

***Figure 34-5 Image tile** box for ELECTRICAL-SYMBOLS*

[NO]^C^CINSERT;NO;\1.0;1.0;0

Where **NO** -------------- Block name

\-------------------- Pause for block insertion point

1.0 ---------------- Xscale factor

1.0 ---------------- Yscale factor

0 ------------------ Rotation angle

When you select this item, it will automatically enter all the prompts of the **INSERT** command and insert the NO block at the given location. The only input you need to enter is the insertion point of the block.

Line 10

[COIL]^C^CINSERT;COIL

In this menu item the block name is given, but you need to define other parameters when inserting this block.

Line 11

[No-Image]

Notice the **blank space before No-Image**. If there is a space following the open bracket, AutoCAD does not look for a slide. AutoCAD instead displays the text, enclosed within the brackets, in the slide file list box of the dialog box.

Line 12

[blank]

Line 12 consists of **blank**; this displays a separator line in the list box and a blank image (no image) in the image box.

Line 15

[RESIS]^C^CINSERT;RESIS;

This menu item inserts the block RESIS. The first backslash (\) is for the block insertion point. The second and third backslashes are for the Xscale and Yscale factors. The fourth backslash is for the rotation angle. This menu item could also be written as:

[RESIS]^C^CINSERT;RESIS;

or

[RESIS]^C^CINSERT;RESIS

Line 16

[DIODE]^C^CINSERT;DIODE;\1.0;1.0;

If you select this menu item, AutoCAD will prompt you to enter the block insertion point and the rotation angle. The first backslash is for the block insertion point; the second backslash is for the rotation angle.

[DIODE]^C^CINSERT;DIODE;\1.0;1.0;

Where \-------------------- Pause for insertion point

\-------------------- Pause for rotation angle

Chapter 34

Line 17
[GROUND]^ C ^ CINSERT;GRD;\1.5;1.5;0;;
This menu item has two semicolons (;) at the end. The first semicolon after 0 is for RETURN and completes the block insertion process. The second semicolon enters a RETURN and repeats the **INSERT** command. However, when the command is repeated you will have to respond to all of the prompts. It does not accept the values defined in the menu item.

Note
The menu item repetition feature cannot be used with the image tile menus. For example, if the command definition starts with an asterisk ([GROUND]* ^ C ^ CINSERT;GRD;\1.5;1.5;0;;), the command is not automatically repeated, as is the case with a pull-down menu.

A blank line in an image tile menu terminates the menu and clears the image tiles.

The menu command $I=*, which displays the current menu, cannot be entered at the keyboard.

If you want to cancel or exit an image tile menu, press the ESC (Escape) key on the keyboard. AutoCAD ignores all other entries from the keyboard.

You can define any number of image tile menus and submenus in the image tile menu section of the menu file.

SLIDES FOR IMAGE TILE MENUS

The idea behind creating slides for the image tile menus is to display graphical symbols in the image tiles. This symbol makes it easier for you to identify the operation that the image tile will perform. Any slide can be used for the image tile. However, the following guidelines should be kept in mind when creating slides for the image tile menu:

1. When you make a slide for an image tile menu, draw the object so that it fills the entire screen. The **MSLIDE** command makes a slide of the existing screen display. If the object is small, the picture in the image tile menu will be small. Use **ZOOM** Extents or **ZOOM** Window to display the object before making a slide.

2. When you use the image tile menu, it takes some time to load the slides for display in the image tiles. The more complex the slides, the more time it will take to load them. Therefore, the slides should be kept as simple as possible and at the same time give enough information about the object.

3. Do not fill the object, because it takes a long time to load and display a solid object. If there is a solid area in the slide, AutoCAD does not display the solid area in the image tile.

4. If the objects are too long or too wide, it is better to center the image with the AutoCAD **PAN** command before making a slide.

5. The space available on the screen for image tile display is limited. Make the best use of this small area by giving only the relevant information in the form of a slide.

6. The image tiles that are displayed in the dialog box have the length-to-width ratio (aspect ratio) of 1.5:1. For example, if the length of the image tile is 1.5 units, the width is 1 unit. If the drawing area of your screen has an aspect ratio of 1.5 and the slide drawing is centered in the drawing area, the slide in the image tile will also be centered.

LOADING MENUS

AutoCAD automatically loads the **ACAD.MNU** file when you get into the AutoCAD drawing editor. However, you can also load a different menu file by using the AutoCAD **MENU** command.

Command: **MENU**

When you enter the **MENU** command, AutoCAD displays the **Select Menu File** dialog box (Figure 34-6) on the screen. Select the menu file that you want to load and then choose the **Open** button.

Figure 34-6 Select Menu File dialog box

You can also load the menu file from the command line.

Command: **FILEDIA**
Enter new value for FILEDIA <1>: **0**
Command: **MENU**
Menu filename <ACAD>: PDM1
        Where **PDM1** ------------ Name of menu file
             ACAD ------------ Default menu file

After you enter the **MENU** command, AutoCAD will prompt for the file name. Enter the name of the menu file without the file extension (**.MNU**), since AutoCAD assumes the extension **.MNU**. AutoCAD will automatically compile the menu file into **MNS** and **MNR** files.

Note
When you load the image tile menu, some of the commands will be displayed on the screen menu area. This happens because the screen menu area is empty. If the menu file contains a screen menu also, the pull-down menu items will not be displayed in the screen menu area.

When you load a new menu, the original menu you had on the screen prior to loading the new menu is disabled. You cannot select commands from the screen menu, pull-down menu, pointing device, or the digitizer, unless these sections are defined in the new menu file.

To load the original menu, use the **MENU** command again and enter the name of the menu file.

RESTRICTIONS

The pull-down and image tile menus are very easy to use and provide quick access to some of the frequently used AutoCAD commands. However, the menu bar, the pull-down menus, and the image tile menus are disabled during the following commands:

DTEXT Command
After you assign the text height and the rotation angle to a **DTEXT** command, the menu is automatically disabled.

SKETCH Command
The menus are disabled after you set the record increment in the **SKETCH** command.

VPOINT Command
The menus are disabled while the axis tripod and compass are displayed on the screen.

ZOOM Command
The menus are disabled when the dynamic zoom is in progress.

DVIEW
The menus are disabled when the dynamic view is in progress.

Exercise 1   *General*

Write an image tile menu for inserting the blocks shown in Figure 34-7. Arrange the blocks in two groups so that you have two submenus in the image tile menu.

PIPE FITTINGS	**ELECTRIC SYMBOLS**
GLOBE-P	BATTERY
GLOBE	CAPACITOR
REDUCER	COUPLER
CHECK	BREAKER

IMAGE TILE MENU ITEM LABELS

As with screen and menus, you can use menu item labels in the image menus. However, the menu item labels in the image tile menus use different formats, and each format performs a particular

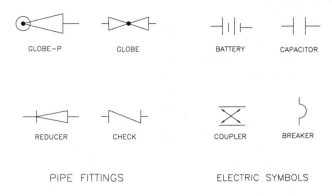

Figure 34-7 *Block shapes for Exercise 1*

function in the image tile menu. The menu item labels appear in the slide list box of the dialog box. The maximum number of characters that can be displayed in this box is 23. The characters in excess of 23 are not displayed in the list box. However, this does not affect the command that is defined with the menu item.

Menu Item Label Formats

[slidename]. In this menu item label format, **slidename** is the name of the slide displayed in the image tile. This name (slidename) is also displayed in the list box of the corresponding dialog box.

[slidename,label]. In this menu item label format, **slidename** is the name of the slide displayed in the image tile. However, unlike the previous format, the **slidename** is **not** displayed in the list box. The **label** text is displayed in the list box. For example, if the menu item label is **[BOLT1,1/2-24UNC-3LG]**, **BOLT1** is the name of the slide and **1/2-24UNC-3LG** is the label that will be displayed in the list box.

[slidelib(slidename)]. In this menu item label format, **slidename** is the name of the slide in the slide library file **slidelib**. The slide (slidename) is displayed in the image tile, and the slide file name (slidename) is also displayed in the list box of the corresponding dialog box.

[slidelib(slidename,label)]. In this menu item label format, **slidename** is the name of the slide in the slide library file **slidelib**. The slide (slidename) is displayed in the image tile, and the label text is displayed in the list box of the corresponding dialog box.

[blank]. This menu item will draw a line that extends through the width of the list box. It also displays a blank image tile in the dialog box.

[label]. If the **label** text is preceded by a space, AutoCAD does not look for a slide. The label text is displayed in the list box only. For example, if the menu item label is [EXIT]^C, the label text (EXIT) will be displayed in the list box. If you select this item, the cancel command (^C) defined with the item will be executed. The **label** text is **not** displayed in the image tile of the dialog box.

Chapter 34

BUTTON MENUS

You can use a multibutton pointing device to specify points, select objects, and execute commands. These pointing devices come with different numbers of buttons, but four-button and twelve-button pointing devices are very common. In addition to selecting points and objects, the multibutton pointing devices can be used to provide easy access to frequently used AutoCAD commands. The commands are selected by pressing the desired button; AutoCAD automatically executes the command or the macro that is assigned to that button. Figure 34-8 shows one such pointing device with 12 buttons.

Figure 34-8 *Pointing device with 12 buttons*

The AutoCAD software package comes with a standard button menu that is part of the **ACAD.MNU** file. The **standard** menu is automatically loaded when you start AutoCAD and enter the drawing editor. You can write your own button menu and assign the desired commands or macros to various buttons of the pointing device.

AUXILIARY MENUS

In a menu file, you can have up to four auxiliary menu sections (AUX1 through AUX4). The auxiliary menu sections (***AUXn) are identical to the button menu sections. The difference is in the hardware. If your computer uses a system mouse, it will automatically use the auxiliary menu.

WRITING BUTTON AND AUXILIARY MENUS

In a menu file, you can have up to four button menus (BUTTONS1 through BUTTONS4) and four auxiliary menus (AUX1 through AUX4). The buttons and the auxiliary menus are identical. However, they are OS dependent. For example, in R14 the system mouse uses auxiliary menus. If your system has a pointing device (digitizer puck), AutoCAD automatically assigns the commands defined in the BUTTONS sections of the menu file to the buttons of the pointing device. When you load the menu file, the commands defined in the BUTTONS1 section of the menu file are assigned to the pointing device (digitizer puck) and if your computer has a system mouse, the mouse will use the auxiliary menus. You can also access other button menus (BUTTONS2 through BUTTONS4) by using the following keyboard-and-button (buttons of the pointing device-digitizer puck) combinations.

Aux Menu	Buttons Menu	Keyboard + Button Sequence
AUX1	BUTTONS1	Press the button of the pointing device.
AUX2	BUTTONS2	Hold down the SHIFT key and press the button of the pointing device.
AUX3	BUTTONS3	Hold down the CTRL key and press the button of the pointing device.

AUX4	**BUTTONS4**	Hold down the SHIFT and CTRL keys and press the button of the pointing device.

One of the buttons, generally the first, is used as a pick button to specify the coordinates of the screen crosshairs and send that information to AutoCAD. This button can also be used to select commands from various other menus, such as tablet menu, screen menu, menu, and image tile menu. This button cannot be used to enter a command, but AutoCAD commands can be assigned to other buttons of the pointing device. Before writing a button menu, you should decide the commands and options you want to assign to different buttons, and know the prompts associated with those commands. The following example illustrates the working of the button menu and the procedure for assigning commands to different buttons.

Example 2

Write a buttons menu for the following AutoCAD commands. The pointing device has 12 buttons (Figure 34-9), and button number 1 is used as a pick button (filename **BM1.MNU**).

Button	Function	Button	Function
2	RETURN	3	CANCEL
4	CURSOR MENU	5	SNAP
6	ORTHO	7	AUTO
8	INT,END	9	LINE
10	CIRCLE	11	ZOOM Win
12	ZOOM Prev		

You can use the AutoCAD **EDIT** command or any other text editor to write the menu file. The following file is a listing of the button menu for Example 1. **The line numbers are for reference only and are not a part of the menu file.**

```
***BUTTONS1                              1
;                                        2
^C^C                                     3
$P0=*                                    4
^B                                       5
^O                                       6
AUTO                                     7
INT,ENDP                                 8
^C^CLINE                                 9
^C^CCIRCLE                              10
'ZOOM;Win                               11
'ZOOM;Prev                              12
```

Explanation
Line 1
***BUTTONS
***BUTTONS1 is the section label for the first button menu. When the menu is loaded, AutoCAD compiles the menu file and assigns the commands to the buttons of the pointing device.

Chapter 34

Line 2

;

This menu item assigns a semicolon (;) to button number 2. When you specify the second button on the pointing device, it enters a Return. It is like entering Return at the keyboard or the digitizer.

Line 3

^C^C

This menu item cancels the existing command twice (^C^C). This command is assigned to button number 3 of the pointing device. When you pick the third button on the pointing device, it cancels the existing command twice.

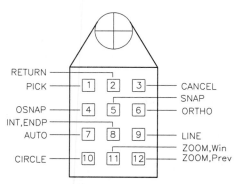

Figure 34-9 Pointing device

Line 4

$P0=*

This menu item loads and displays the cursor menu POP0, which contains various object snap modes. It is assumed that the POP0 menu has been defined in the menu file. This command is assigned to button number 4 of the pointing device. If you press this button, it will load and display the shortcut menu on the screen near the crosshairs location.

Line 5

^B

This menu item changes the Snap mode; it is assigned to button number 5 of the pointing device. When you pick the fifth button on the pointing device, it turns the Snap mode on or off. It is like holding down the CTRL key and then pressing the B key.

Line 6

^O

This menu item changes the ORTHO mode; it is assigned to button number 6. When you pick the sixth button on the pointing device, it turns the ORTHO mode on or off.

Line 7

AUTO

This menu item selects the AUTO option for creating a selection set; this command is assigned to button number 7 on the pointing device.

Line 8

INT,ENDP

In this menu item, INT is for the Intersection Osnap, and ENDP is for the Endpoint Osnap. This command is assigned to button number 8 on the pointing device. When you pick this button, AutoCAD looks for the intersection point. If it cannot find an intersection point, it then starts looking for the endpoint of the object that is within the pick box.

INT,ENDP

Where **INT** -------------- Intersection object snap

ENDP ------------ Endpoint object snap

Line 9

^C^CLINE

This menu item defines the **LINE** command; it is assigned to button number 9. When you select this button, AutoCAD cancels the existing command, and then selects the **LINE** command.

Line 10

^C^CCIRCLE

This menu item defines the **CIRCLE** command; it is assigned to button number 10. When you pick this button, AutoCAD automatically selects the **CIRCLE** command and prompts for the user input.

Line 11

'ZOOM;Win

This menu item defines a transparent **ZOOM** command with Window option; it is assigned to button number 11 of the pointing device.

'ZOOM;Win

Where **'** -------------------- Single quote makes **ZOOM** command transparent

ZOOM ----------- AutoCAD **ZOOM** command

; ------------------- Semicolon for RETURN

Win -------------- Window option of **ZOOM** command

Line 12

'ZOOM;Prev

This menu item defines a transparent **ZOOM** command with **previous** option; it is assigned to button number 12 of the pointing device.

 Note

If the button menu has more menu items than the number of buttons on the pointing device, the menu items in excess of the number of buttons are ignored. This does not include the pick button. For example, if a pointing device has three buttons in addition to the pick button, the first three menu items will be assigned to the three buttons (buttons 2, 3, and 4). The remaining lines of the button menu are ignored.

The commands are assigned to the buttons in the same order in which they appear in the file. For example, the menu item that is defined on line 3 will automatically be assigned to the fourth button of the pointing device. Similarly, the menu item that is on line 4 will be assigned to the fifth button of the pointing device. The same is true of other menu items and buttons.

Chapter 34

Review Questions

Image Tile Menus

1. The image tiles are displayed in the _____ box.

2. An **image tile** menu can be canceled by entering _____ at the keyboard.

3. The **image title** dialog box can contain a maximum of _____ image tiles.

4. A blank line in an image tile menu _____ the image tile menu.

5. The menu item repetition feature _____ be used with the image tile menu.

6. The drawing for a slide should be _____ on the entire screen before making a slide.

7. You _____ fill a solid area in a slide for image tile menu.

8. An image tile menu _____ be accessed from a tablet menu.

Button and Auxiliary Menus

9. A multibutton pointing device can be used to specify _____ , or select _____, or enter AutoCAD _____.

10. AutoCAD receives the button _____ and _____ of screen crosshairs when a button is activated on the pointing device.

11. If the number of menu items in the button menu is more than the number of buttons on the pointing device, the excess lines are _____.

12. Commands are assigned to the buttons of the pointing device in the _____ order in which they appear in the buttons menu.

13. The format of referencing or loading a submenu that has been defined in the image menu is _____.

14. The format of displaying a loaded submenu that has been defined in the image menu is _____.

15. The format of the **LOAD** command for loading a submenu that has been defined in the image menu is _____.

Exercises

Exercise 2   *General*

Write a tablet and image tile menu for inserting the following blocks. The layout of the template for the tablet menu is shown in Figure 34-10.

B1	B2	B3	C1	C2	C3
B4	B5	B6	C4	C5	C6
B7	B8	B9	C7	C8	C9

TEMPLATE

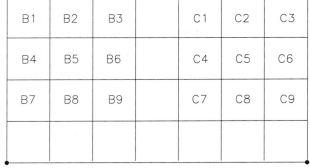

Figure 34-10 *Tablet template for Exercise 4*

Exercise 3   *General*

Write a button menu for the following AutoCAD commands. The pointing device has 10 buttons (Figure 34-11), and button number 1 is used for specifying the points. The blocks are to be inserted with a scale factor of 1.00 and a rotation of 0 degrees (file name **BME1.MNU**).

1. PICK BUTTON
2. RETURN
3. CANCEL
4. OSNAPS
5. INSERT B1
6. INSERT B2
7. INSERT B3
8. ZOOM Window
9. ZOOM All
10. ZOOM Previous

Chapter 34

Figure 34-11 *Pointing device with 10 buttons*

Chapter 35

Screen Menus

Learning Objectives

After completing this chapter, you will be able to:
- *Write screen menus.*
- *Load screen menus.*
- *Write submenus and referencing submenus.*
- *Write menu files with multiple submenus.*
- *Write menus for foreign languages.*

SCREEN MENU

When you are in the AutoCAD drawing editor the screen menu is displayed on the right of the screen. The AutoCAD screen menu displays AutoCAD at the top, followed by asterisk signs (* * * *) and a list of commands (Figure 35-1).

Depending on the scope of the menu, the size of the menu file can vary from a few lines to several hundred. A menu file consists of section labels, submenus, and menu items. A menu item consists of an item label and a command definition. The menu item label is enclosed in brackets, and the command definition (menu macro) is outside the brackets.

The menu item label that is enclosed in the brackets is displayed in the screen menu area of the monitor and is not a part of the command definition. The command definition, the part of the menu item outside the bracket, is the executable part of the menu item. To understand the process of developing and writing a screen menu, consider the following example.

[LINE   ] $S=X $S=LINE ^C^CLINE
                    Where **[LINE   ] $S=X $S=LINE ^C^CLINE** -------- Menu item
                                [LINE   ] ------- Item label or menu command name
                                $S=X $S=LINE ^C^CLINE - Command definition

Figure 35-1 *Screen display*

Example 1

Write a screen menu for the following AutoCAD commands (file name **SM1.MNU**):

LINE
CIRCLE C,R
CIRCLE C,D
CIRCLE 2P
ERASE
MOVE

The layout of these commands is shown in Figure 35-2(a). This menu is named MENU-1 and it should be displayed at the top of the screen menu. It lets you know the menu you are using. You can use any text editor to write the file. The file name can be up to eight characters long, and the file extension must be **.MNU**. For Example 1, **SM1.MNU**. **SM1** is the name of the screen menu file, and **.MNU** is the extension of this file. All menu files have the extension **.MNU**.

The following file is a listing of the screen menu for Example 1. **The line numbers on the right are not a part of the file. They are shown here for reference only.**

```
***SCREEN                                                        1
[ MENU-1          ]                                              2
[                 ]                                              3
[                 ]                                              4
[LINE             ]^C^CLINE                                      5
```

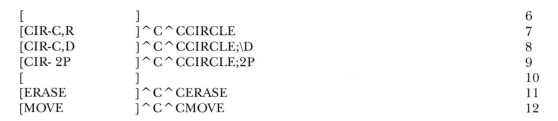

```
[                         ]                                             6
[CIR-C,R                  ] ^ C ^ CCIRCLE                               7
[CIR-C,D                  ] ^ C ^ CCIRCLE;\D                            8
[CIR- 2P                  ] ^ C ^ CCIRCLE;2P                            9
[                         ]                                             10
[ERASE                    ] ^ C ^ CERASE                                11
[MOVE                     ] ^ C ^ CMOVE                                 12
```

Figure 35-2(a) Layout of screen menu

Figure 35-2(b) Screen menu after loading the menu file

Explanation

Line 1
***SCREEN
***SCREEN is the section label for the screen menu. The lines that follow the screen menu are treated as a part of this menu. The screen menu definition will be terminated by another section label, such as ***TABLET1 or ***POP1.

Line 2
[MENU-1]
This menu item displays MENU-1 on the screen. Anything that is inside the brackets is for display only and has no effect on the command. The maximum number of characters or spaces that can be displayed inside these brackets is eight, because the width of the screen menu column on the screen is eight characters. If the number of characters is more than eight, the remaining characters are not displayed on the screen and can be used for comments. The part of the menu item that is outside the brackets is executed even if the number of characters inside the bracket is more than eight.

Lines 3 and 4
[   ]
These menu items print a blank line on the screen menu. There are eight blank spaces inside the bracket. You could also use the brackets with no spaces between the brackets ([]). When the blank spaces are printed on the screen menu, it displays a blank line. This line does not contain anything outside the bracket; therefore, no command is executed. To provide the space in the menu you can also leave a blank space in the menu file or have two brackets ([ ]). The next line, line 4, also prints a blank line.

Chapter 35

Line 5
[LINE   ]^C^CLINE
This menu item displays LINE on the screen. The first ^C (caret C) cancels the existing command, and the second ^C cancels the command again. The two **CANCEL** (^C^C) commands are required to make sure that the existing commands are canceled before a new command is executed. Most AutoCAD commands can be canceled with just one **CANCEL** command. However, some commands, like dimensioning and pedit, need to be canceled twice to get out of the command. **LINE** will prompt the user to enter the points to draw a line. Since there is nothing after the LINE, the spaces after the line automatically enters a Return.

> **[LINE   ]^C^CLINE**
> Where **[LINE   ]** --------- For screen display only
> **^C** --------------- ^C is the first **CANCEL** command
> **^C** --------------- ^C is the second **CANCEL** command
> **LINE** ------------- AutoCAD's **LINE** command

Line 7
[CIR-C,R]^C^CCIRCLE
The part of the menu item that is enclosed within the brackets is for screen display only. The part of the menu item that is outside the brackets is executed when this line is selected. ^C^C (caret C) cancels the existing command twice. **CIRCLE** is an AutoCAD command that generates a circle. **The space after CIRCLE automatically causes a RETURN. The space acts like pressing the SPACEBAR on the keyboard.**

> **[CIR-C,R]^C^CCIRCLE**
> Where **[CIR-C,R]** ----- For screen display only
> **^C** --------------- ^C for first **CANCEL** command
> **^C** --------------- ^C for second **CANCEL** command
> **CIRCLE** --------- AutoCAD's **CIRCLE** command

Line 8
[CIR-C,D]^C^CCIRCLE;\D
The part of the menu item that is enclosed in the brackets is for screen display only, and the part that is outside the brackets is the executable part. ^C^C will cancel the existing command twice.

> **[CIR-C,D]^C^CCIRCLE;\D**
> Where **^C^C** ---------- ^C^C cancels the existing command
> **CIRCLE** --------- **CIRCLE** command
> **;** ------------------- Semicolon (;) for RETURN
> **** -------------------- AutoCAD pauses for user input
> **D** ------------------ Diameter option

The **CIRCLE** command is followed by a semicolon, a backslash (\), and a D for diameter option. **The semicolon (;) after the CIRCLE command causes a RETURN, which has the same effect as entering RETURN at the keyboard. The backslash (\) pauses for user input.** In this case it is the center point of the circle. D is for the diameter option and it is automatically followed by RE-TURN. The semicolon in this example can also be replaced by a blank space, as shown in the following line. However, the semicolon is easier to spot.

> **[CIR-C,D]^C^CCIRCLE \D**
> Where   Space between CIRCLE and \ --- Blank space for RETURN

Line 9
[CIR- 2P]^C^CCIRCLE;2P
In this menu item ^C^C cancels the existing command twice. The semicolon after **CIRCLE** enters a RETURN. 2P is for the two-point option, followed by the blank space that causes a RE-TURN. You will notice that the sequence of the command and input is the same as discussed earlier. Therefore, it is essential to know the exact sequence of the command and input; otherwise, the screen menu is not going to work.

> **[CIR- 2P]^C^CCIRCLE;2P**
> Where **^C^C** ------------ **^C^C** Cancels existing command twice
> **;** -------------------- Semicolon (;) for RETURN
> **CIRCLE** --------- **CIRCLE** command
> **2P** ---------------- 2-Point option for **CIRCLE**

The semicolon after the **CIRCLE** command can be replaced by a blank space, as shown in the following line. The blank space causes a RETURN, like a semicolon (;).

> **[CIR- 2P]^C^CCIRCLE 2P**
> Where Space between CIRCLE and 2P -- Blank space or semicolon for RETURN

Line 11
[ERASE]^C^CERASE
In this menu item ^C^C cancels the existing command twice, and **ERASE** is an AutoCAD command that erases the selected objects.

> **[ERASE]^C^CERASE**
> Where **ERASE** ---------- AutoCAD **ERASE** command

Line 12
[MOVE]^C^CMOVE
In this menu item ^C^C cancels the existing command twice, and the **MOVE** command will move the selected objects.

> **[MOVE]^C^CMOVE**
> Where **Move** ------------- AutoCAD **MOVE** command

LOADING MENUS

AutoCAD automatically loads the **ACAD.MNU** file when you get into the AutoCAD drawing editor. However, you can also load a different menu file by using the AutoCAD **MENU** command.

Command: **MENU**

When you enter the **MENU** command, AutoCAD displays the **Select Menu File** dialog box (Figure 35-3) on the screen. Select the menu file that you want to load and then choose the **Open** button.

Figure 35-3 Select Menu File dialog box

You can also load the menu file from the command line.

>   Command: **FILEDIA**
>   Enter new value for FILEDIA <1>: **0**
>   Command: **MENU**
>   **Enter menu file name or [. (for none)] <current>: PDM1.MNU**
>   Where **<current>** ------ Default menu file
>   **PDM1.MNU** --- Name of menu file

Note

*1. After you load the new menu, you cannot use the screen menu, buttons menu, or digitizer because the original menu, **ACAD.MNU**, is not present and the new menu does not contain these menu areas.*

*2. To activate the original menu again, load the menu file by using the **MENU** command:*

>   *Command: **MENU***
>   *Enter menu file name or [. (for none)]<current>: **ACAD***

3. If you need to use input from a keyboard or a pointing device, use the backslash (\). The system will pause for you to enter data.

4. There should be no space after the backslash (\).

5. The menu items, menu labels, and command definition can be uppercase, lowercase, or mixed.

6. You can introduce spaces between the menu items to improve the readability of the menu file.

7. If there are more items in the menu than the number of spaces available, the excess items are not displayed on the screen. For example, if the display device limits the number of items to 21, items in excess of 21 will not be displayed on the screen and are therefore inaccessible.

8. If you are using a high-resolution graphics board, you can increase the number of lines that can be displayed on the screen. On some devices this is 80 lines.

Exercise 1   *General*

Design and write a screen menu for the following AutoCAD commands (file name **SME1.MNU**):

PLINE
ELLIPSE (Center)
ELLIPSE (Axis endpoint)
ROTATE
OFFSET
SCALE

SUBMENUS

The screen menu file can be so large that all items cannot be accommodated on one screen. For example, the maximum number of items that can be displayed on most screens is 21. If the screen menu has more than 21 items, the menu items in excess of 21 are not displayed on the screen and therefore cannot be accessed. You can overcome this problem by using submenus that enable the user to define smaller groups of items within a menu section. When a submenu is selected, it loads the submenu items and displays them on screen. However, depending on the resolution of the monitor and the graphics card, the number of items you can display can be higher and you may not need submenus.

Submenu Definition

A submenu definition consists of two asterisks (**) followed by the name of the submenu. A menu can have any number of submenus, and every submenu should have a unique name. The items that follow a submenu, up to the next section label, or submenu label belong to that submenu. The format of a submenu definition is:

**Name
        Where   ****** ----------------- Two asterisks (**) designate a submenu
                Name ------------ Name of the submenu

**DRAW1
        Where   **Edit** --------------- Name of the submenu
               ** ----------------- ** designates that DRAW1 is a submenu

Note

1. The submenu name can be up to 31 characters long.

2. The submenu name can consist of letters, digits, and such special characters as $ (dollar sign), - (hyphen), and _ (underscore).

3. The submenu name should not have any embedded blanks (spaces).

4. The submenu names should be unique in a menu file.

Submenu Reference

The submenu reference is used in a menu item to reference or load a submenu. It consists of a "$" sign followed by a letter that specifies the menu section. The letter that specifies a screen menu section is S. The section is followed by an "=" sign and the name of the submenu the user wants to activate. The submenu name should be without the **. The following is the format of a submenu reference:

> **$Section=Submenu**
> > Where **$** ------------------- "$" sign
> > **Section** ---------- Menu section specifier
> > **=** ------------------ "=" sign
> > **Submenu** ------- Name of submenu

> **$S=EDIT**
> > Where **S** ------------------- S specifies screen menu section
> > **Edit** -------------- Name of submenu

Note

$	*A special character code used to load a submenu in a menu file.*
$M=	*This is used to load a DIESEL macro from a menu item.*

The following are the section specifiers:

S	*Specifies the SCREEN menu.*
P0 - P16	*Specifies the POP menus, POP0 through POP16.*
I	*Specifies the Image Tile menu.*
B1 - B4	*Specifies the BUTTONS menu, B1 through B4.*
T1 - T4	*Specifies the TABLET menus, T1 through T4.*
A1 - A4	*Specifies the AUX menus A1 through A4.*

Nested Submenus

When a submenu is activated, the current menu is copied to a stack. If you select another submenu, the submenu that was current will be copied or pushed to the top of the stack. The maximum number of menus that can be stacked is eight. If the stack size increases to more than eight, the menu at the bottom of the stack is removed and forgotten. You can call the previous submenu by using the nested submenu call. The format of this call is:

$S=

Where $ ------------------- "$" sign
       S ------------------ Screen menu specifier
       = ----------------- "=" sign

Example 2

The maximum number of nested submenu calls is eight. Each time you call a submenu (issue $S=), this pops the last item from the stack and reactivates it.
Design a menu layout and write a screen menu for the following commands.

LINE	**ERASE**
PLINE	**MOVE**
ELLIPSE-C	**ROTATE**
ELLIPSE-E	**OFFSET**
CIR-C,R	**COPY**
CIR-C,D	**SCALE**
CIR- 2P	

As mentioned earlier, the first and the most important part of writing a menu is the design of the menu and knowing the commands and the prompts associated with those commands. You should know the way you want the menu to look and the way you want to arrange the commands for maximum efficiency. Write out the menu on a piece of paper, and check it thoroughly to make sure you have arranged the commands the way you want them. Use submenus to group the commands based on their use, function, and relationship with other submenus. Make provisions to access other frequently used commands without going through the root menu.

Figure 35-4 shows one of the possible arrangements of the commands and the design of the screen menu. It has one main menu and two submenus. One of the submenus is for draw commands, the other is for edit commands. The colon (:) at the end of the commands is not required. It is used

Figure 35-4 Screen menu design

here to distinguish the commands from those items that are not used as commands. For example, DRAW in the root menu is not a command; therefore, it has no colon at the end. On the other hand, if you select **ERASE** from the **EDIT** menu, it executes the **ERASE** command, so it has a colon (:) at the end of the command.

The following file is a listing of the menu file of Example 1. **The line numbers on the right are not a part of the file; they are given here for reference only.**

```
***SCREEN      1
[ MENU-2      ]                                                    2
[********      ]                                                    3
[             ]                                                    4
[             ]                                                    5
[             ]                                                    6
[             ]                                                    7
[DRAW         ]^C^C$S=DRAW                                          8
[EDIT         ]^C^C$S=EDIT                                          9
                                                                  10
**DRAW                                                            11
[ MENU-2      ]^C^C$S=SCREEN                                       12
[********      ]                                                   13
[             14
[*-DRAW-*     ]                                                    15
[             ]                                                    16
[LINE:        ]^C^CLINE                                            17
[PLINE:       ]^C^CPLINE;\W;0.1;0.1                                18
[ELLIP-C:     ]^C^CELLIPSE;C                                       19
[ELLIP-E:     ]^C^CELLIPSE                                         20
[CIR-C,R:     ]^C^CCIRCLE                                          21
[CIR-C,D:     ]^C^CCIRCLE;\D                                       22
[CIR-2P:      ]^C^CCIRCLE;2P                                       23
[             ]                                                    24
[             ]                                                    25
[             ]                                                    26
[             ]                                                    27
[             ]                                                    28
[             ]                                                    29
[*-PREV-*     ]^C^C$S=                                             30
[*-EDIT-*     ]^C^C$S=EDIT                                         31
                                                                  32
**EDIT                                                            33
[ MENU-2      ]^C^C$S=SCREEN                                       34
[********      ]                                                   35
[             ]                                                    36
[*-EDIT-*     ]                                                    37
[             ]                                                    38
[ERASE:       ]^C^CERASE                                           39
```

[MOVE:	]^C^CMOVE	40
[ROTATE:	]^C^CROTATE	41
[OFFSET:	]^C^COFFSET	42
[COPY:	]^C^CCOPY	43
[SCALE:	]^C^CSCALE	44
[	]	45
[	]	46
[	]	47
[	]	48
[	]	49
[	]	50
[	]	51
[*-PREV-*	]^C^C$S=	52
[*-DRAW-*	]^C^C$S=DRAW	53

Explanation

Line 1
***SCREEN
***SCREEN is the section label for the screen menu.

Line 2
[MENU-2]
This menu item displays MENU-2 at the top of the screen menu.

Line 3
[********]
This menu item prints eight asterisk signs (********) on the screen menu.

Lines 4-7
[   ]
These menu items print four blank lines on the screen menu. The brackets are not required. They could be just four blank lines without brackets.

Line 8
[DRAW   ]^C^C$S=DRAW
[DRAW   ] displays DRAW on the screen, letting you know that by selecting this function you can access the draw commands. ^C^C cancels the existing command, and $S=DRAW loads the DRAW submenu on the screen.

> **[DRAW   ]^C^C$S=DRAW**
>   Where   **^C^C** ---------- Cancels the existing command twice
>   **=** ------------------ Loads submenu DRAW
>   **DRAW** ----------- Name of submenu

Line 9
[EDIT   ]^C^C$S=EDIT

[EDIT   ] displays EDIT on the screen. ^C^C cancels the current command, and $S=EDIT loads the submenu **EDIT**.

Line 10
The blank lines between the submenus or menu items are not required. It just makes it easier to read the file.

Line 11
**DRAW
**DRAW is the name of the submenu; lines 12 through 31 are defined under this submenu.

Line 15
[*-DRAW-*]
This prints *-DRAW-* as a heading on the screen menu to let the user know that the commands listed on the menu are draw commands.

Line 18
[PLINE:]^C^CPLINE;\W;0.1;0.1
[PLINE:] displays PLINE: on the screen. ^C^C cancels the command, and **PLINE** is the AutoCAD polyline command. The semicolons are for RETURN. The semicolons can be replaced by a blank space. The backslash (\) is for user input. In this case it is the start point of the polyline. W selects the width option of the polyline. The first 0.1 is the starting width of the polyline, and the second 0.1 is the ending width. This command will draw a polyline of 0.1 width.

           [PLINE:]^C^CPLINE;\W;0.1;0.1
                   Where **PLINE** ------------ **PLINE** (Polyline) command
                         ; ------------------ RETURN
                         \-------------------- Pause for input (start pt.)
                         W ----------------- Width
                         ; ------------------ RETURN
                         0.1 --------------- Starting width
                         ; ------------------ RETURN
                         0.1 ---------------- Ending width

Line 19
[ELLIP-C:]^C^CELLIPSE;C
[ELLIP-C:] displays ELLIP-C: on the screen menu. ^C^C cancels the existing command, and **ELLIPSE** is an AutoCAD command to generate an ellipse. The semicolon is for RETURN, and C selects the center option of the **ELLIPSE** command.

           [ELLIP-C:]^C^CELLIPSE;C
                   Where **CELLIPSE** ------ **ELLIPSE** command
                         ; ------------------ RETURN
                         C ------------------ Center option for ellipse

Line 20
[ELLIP-E:]^C^CELLIPSE

[ELLIP-E:] displays ELLIP-E: on the screen menu. ^C^C cancels the existing command, and **ELLIPSE** is an AutoCAD command. Here the **ELLIPSE** command uses the default option, axis endpoint, instead of center.

Line 30
[*-PREV-*]^C^C$S=
[*-PREV-*] displays *-PREV-* on the screen menu, and ^C^C cancels the existing command. $S= restores the previous menu that was displayed on the screen before loading the current menu.

> **[*-PREV-*]^C^C$S=**
> Where **$S** ----------------- Restores the previous screen menu

Line 31
[*-EDIT-*]^C^C$S=EDIT
[*-EDIT-*] displays *-EDIT-* on the screen menu, and ^C^C cancels the existing command. $S=EDIT loads the submenu EDIT on the screen. This lets you access the **EDIT** commands without going back to the root menu and selecting **EDIT** from there.

> **[*-EDIT-*]^C^C$S=EDIT**
> Where **$S** ----------------- Loads the submenu EDIT
> **EDIT** ------------- Name of the submenu

Line 33
**EDIT
**EDIT is the name of the submenu, and lines 34 to 53 are defined under this submenu.

Line 34
[MENU-2]^C^C$S=SCREEN
[MENU-2] displays MENU-2 on the screen menu, and ^C^C cancels the existing command. $S=SCREEN loads the root menu SCREEN on the screen menu.

Line 39
[ERASE:]^C^CERASE
[ERASE:] displays ERASE: on the screen menu, and ^C^C cancels the existing command. **ERASE** is an AutoCAD command for erasing the selected objects.

Line 53
[*-DRAW-*]^C^C$S=DRAW
$S=DRAW loads the DRAW submenu on the screen. It lets you load the DRAW menu without going through the root menu. The root menu is the first menu that appears on the screen when you load a menu or start AutoCAD.

When you select DRAW from the root menu, the submenu DRAW is loaded on the screen. The menu items in the draw submenu completely replace the menu items of the root menu. If you select MENU-2 from the screen menu now, the root menu will be loaded on the screen, but some of the items are not cleared from the screen menu (Figure 35-5). This is because the root menu does not have enough menu items to completely replace the menu items of the DRAW submenu.

Chapter 35

Figure 35-5 Screen menu display after loading the root menu

One of the ways to clear the screen is to define a submenu that has 21 blank lines. When this submenu is loaded it will clear the screen. If you then load another submenu, there will be no overlap, because the screen menu has already been cleared and there are no menu items left on the screen (Figure 35-6). Example 3 illustrates the use of such a submenu.

Another way to avoid overlapping the menu items is to define every submenu so that they all have the same number of menu items. The disadvantage with this approach is that the menu file will be long, because every submenu will have 21 lines.

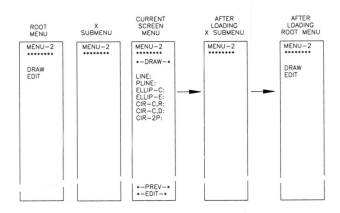

Figure 35-6 Screen menu display after loading the root menu

Exercise 2   *General*

Write a screen menu file for the following AutoCAD commands (file name **SM2.MNU**).

ARC	MIRROR
-3P	BREAK-F
-SCE	BREAK-@
-SCA	EXTEND
-SCL	STRETCH
-SEA	FILLET-0
POLYGON-C	FILLET
POLYGON-E	CHAMFER

MULTIPLE SUBMENUS

A menu file can have any number of submenus. All the submenu names have two asterisks (**) in front of them, even if there is a submenu within a submenu. Also, several submenus can be loaded in a single statement. If there is more than one submenu in a menu item, they should be separated from one another by a space. Example 3 illustrates the use of multiple submenus.

Example 3

Design the layout of the menu, and then write the screen menu for the following AutoCAD commands.

Draw	ARC	Edit	Display
LINE	3Point	EXTEND	ZOOM
Continue	SCE	STRETCH	REGEN
Close	SCA	FILLET	SCALE
Undo	CSE		PAN
.X	CSA		
.Y	CSL		
.Z			
.XY			
.XZ			
.YZ			

There are several different ways of arranging the commands, depending on your requirements. The following layout is one of the possible screen menu designs for the given AutoCAD commands (Figure 35-7).

The name of the following menu file is **SM3.MNU**. You can use a text editor to write the file. The following file is the listing of the menu file **SM3.MNU. The line numbers on the right are not a part of the file. They are shown here for reference only.**

```
***SCREEN                                                          1
**S                                                                2
[ MENU-3         ]^C^C$S=X $S=S                                    3
```

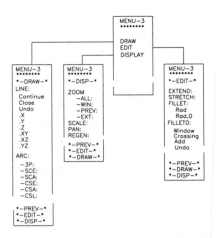

Figure 35-7 *Screen menu design with submenus*

[********	]$S=OSNAP	4
[	]	5
[DRAW	]^C^C$S=X $S=DRAW	6
[EDIT	]^C^C$S=X $S=EDIT	7
[DISPLAY	]^C^C$S=X $S=DISP	8
**DRAW 3		9
[*-DRAW-*	]	10
[	]	11
[LINE:	]^C^CLINE	12
[Continue	]^C^CLINE;;	13
[Close	]CLOSE	14
[Undo	]UNDO	15
[.X	].X	16
[.Y	].Y	17
[.Z	].Z	18
[.XY	].XY	19
[.XZ	].XZ	20
[.YZ	].YZ	21
[	]	22
[ARC:	]^C^CArc	23
[-3P:	]^C^CARC \\DRAG	24
[-SCE:	]^C^CARC \C \DRAG	25
[-SCA:	]^C^CARC \C \A DRAG	26
[-CSE:	]^C^CARC C \\DRAG	27
[-CSA:	]^C^CARC C \\A DRAG	28
[-CSL:	]^C^CARC C \\L DRAG	29
[	]	30
[*-PREV-*	]$S= $S=	31
[*-EDIT-*	]^C^C$S=X $S=EDIT	32

[*-DISP-*	]$S=X $S=DISP	33
**EDIT 3		34
[*-EDIT-*	]	35
[	]	36
[EXTEND:	]^C^CEXTEND	37
[STRETCH:	]^C^CSTRETCH;C	38
[FILLET:	]^C^CFILLET	39
[Rad	]R;\Fillet	40
[Rad 0	]R;0;Fillet	41
[FILLET0:	]^C^CFillet;R;0::	42
Win.		43
Cross.		44
Add		45
Undo		46
[	]	47
[*-PREV-*	]$S= $S=	48
[*-DRAW-*	]^C^C$S=X $S=DRAW	49
[*-DISP-*	]$S=X $S=DISP	50
**DISP 3		51
[*-DISP-*	]	52
[	]	53
[ZOOM:	]'ZOOM	54
[-ALL	]A	55
[-WIN	]W	56
[-PREV	]P	57
[-EXT	]E	58
[	]	59
[SCALE:	]'ZOOM	60
[PAN:	]'PAN	61
[REGEN:	]^C^CREGEN	62
[	]	63
[*-PREV-*	]$S= $S=	64
[*-EDIT-*	]^C^C$S=X $S=EDIT	65
[*-DRAW-*	]$S=X $S=DRAW	66
**X 3		67
[	]	68
[	]	69
[	]	70
[	]	71
[	]	72
[	]	73
[	]	74
[	]	75
[	]	76
[	]	77
[	]	78
[	]	79

Chapter 35

[	]	80
[	]	81
[	]	82
[	]	83
[	]	84
[	]	85
[	]	86
**OSNAP 2		87
[-OSNAPS-	]	88
[	]	89
[Center	]CEN $S=	90
[Endpoint	]END $S=	91
[Insert	]INS $S=	92
[Intersec	]INT $S=	93
[Midpoint	]MID $S=	94
[Nearest	]NEA $S=	95
[Node	]NOD $S=	96
[Perpend	]PER $S=	97
[Quadrant	]QUA $S=	98
[Tangent	]TAN $S=	99
[None	]NONE $S=	100
[	]	101
[	]	102
[	]	103
[	]	104
[	]	105
[*-PREV-*	]$S=	106

Explanation

Line 3

[MENU-3]^C^C$S=X $S=S

In this menu item, [MENU-3] displays MENU-3 at the top of the screen menu. ^C^C cancels the command, and $S=X loads submenu X. Similarly, $S=S loads submenu S. Submenu X, defined on line 171, consists of 18 blank lines. Therefore, when this submenu is loaded it prints blank lines on the screen and clears the screen menu area. After loading submenu X, the system loads submenu S, and the items that are defined in this submenu are displayed on the screen menu.

      [MENU-3]^C^C$S=X $S=S

           Where   **^C^C** ---------- Cancels the existing command

                     $S=X ------------ Loads submenu X (clears screen)

                     $S=S ------------- Loads submenu S

Line 4

[********]$S=OSNAP

This menu item prints eight asterisks on the screen menu, and $S=OSNAP loads submenu OSNAP. The OSNAP submenu, defined on line 191, consists of object snap modes.

Line 6
[DRAW   ]^C^C$S=X $S=DRAW
This menu item displays DRAW on the screen menu area, cancels the existing command, and then loads submenu X and submenu DRAW. Submenu X clears the screen menu area, and submenu DRAW, as defined on line 11, loads the items defined under the DRAW submenu.

Line 9
**DRAW 3
This line is the submenu label for DRAW; 3 indicates that the first line of the DRAW submenu will be printed on line 3. Nothing will be printed on line 1 or line 2. The first line of the DRAW submenu will be on line 3, followed by the rest of the menu. All the submenus except submenus S and OSNAP have a 3 at the end of the line. Therefore, the first two lines (MENU-3) and (********) will never be cleared and will be displayed on the screen all the time. If you select MENU-3 in any menu, it will load submenu S. If you select ********, it will load submenu OSNAP.

> ****DRAW 3**
> Where **DRAW** ----------- Submenu name
> **3** ------------------- Leaves two blank lines and prints from third line

Line 12
[LINE:]^C^CLINE
^C^C cancels the existing command, and **LINE** is the AutoCAD **LINE** command.

Line 13
[Continue]^C^CLINE;;
In this menu item, the **LINE** command is followed by two semicolons that continue the **LINE** command. To understand it, look at the **LINE** command to see how a continue option is used in this command:

Command: **LINE**
Specify first point: **RETURN (Continue)**
Specify next point or [Undo]:

Following is the command and prompt entry sequence for the **LINE** command, if you want to start a line from the last point:

LINE
RETURN
RETURN
SELECT A POINT

Therefore, in the screen menu file the **LINE** command has to be followed by two Returns to continue from the previous point.

Line 16
[.X   ].X

In this menu item, .X extracts the X coordinate from a point. The bracket, .X, and spaces inside the brackets ([.X   ]) are not needed. The line could consist of .X only. The same is true for lines 39 through 43.

Example

[.X	].X	can also be written (without brackets) as	.X
[.Y	].Y		.Y
[.Z	].Z		.Z

Line 31
[*-PREV-*]$S= $S=
This menu item recalls the previous menu twice. AutoCAD keeps track of the submenus that were loaded on the screen. The first **$S=** will load the previously loaded menu, and the second **$S=** will load the submenu that was loaded before that. For example, in line 16 ([ARC:]$S=X $S=ARC), two submenus have been loaded: first X, and then ARC. Submenu X is stacked before loading submenu ARC, which is current and is not stacked yet. The first $S= will recall the previous menu, in this case submenu X. The second $S= will load the menu that was on the screen before selecting the item in line 16.

> **[*-PREV-*]$S= $S=**
> Where **$S=** --------------- Loads last menu
>   **$S=** --------------- Loads next to last menu

Line 33
[*-DISP-*]$S=X $S=DISP
In this menu item, $S=X loads submenu X, and $S=DISP loads submenu DISP. Notice that there is no CANCEL (^C^C) command in the line. There are some menus you might like to load without canceling the existing command. For example, if you are drawing a line, you might want to zoom without canceling the existing command. You can select [*-DISP-*], select the appropriate zoom option, and then continue with the line command. However, if the line has a CANCEL command ([*-DISP-*]^C^C$S=X $S=DISP), you cannot continue with the **LINE** command, because the existing command will be canceled when you select *-DISP-* from the screen. In line 28 ([*-EDIT-*]^C^C$S=X $S=EDIT), ^C^C cancels the existing command, because you cannot use any editing command unless you have canceled the existing command.

Line 38
[STRETCH:]^C^CSTRETCH;C
^C^C cancels the existing command, and **STRETCH** is an AutoCAD command. The C is for the crossing option that prompts you to enter two points to select the objects.

> **[STRETCH:]^C^CSTRETCH;C**
> Where **STRETCH** ----- **STRETCH** command
>   **;** ------------------- RETURN
>   **C** ------------------- Center O'SNAP

Line 40
[RAD]R;\FILLET

This menu item selects the radius option of the **FILLET** command, and then waits for you to enter the radius. After entering the radius, execute the **FILLET** command again to generate the desired fillet between the two selected objects.

> [RAD]R;\FILLET
>
> Where **R** ----------------- Radius option of **FILLET** command
> ; ------------------ Space or semicolon for RETURN
> \-------------------- Pause for user input
> **FILLET** --------- AutoCAD **FILLET** command

Line 41
[RAD 0]R;0;FILLET
This menu item selects the radius option of the **FILLET** command and assigns it a 0 value. Then it executes the **FILLET** command to generate a 0 radius fillet between the two selected objects.

> [RAD 0]R;0;FILLET
>
> Where **R** ----------------- Radius option of **FILLET** command
> ; ------------------ Space or semicolon for RETURN
> **0** ------------------ 0 radius
> ; ------------------ Space or semicolon for RETURN
> **FILLET** --------- AutoCAD **FILLET** command

Line 42
[FILLET0:]^C^CFILLET;R 0;;
This menu item defines a **FILLET** command with 0 radius, and then generates 0 fillet between the two selected objects.

> [FILLET0:]^C^CFILLET;R 0;;
>
> Where ; ------------------ Repeats **FILLET** command
> ; ------------------ Semicolon for RETURN
> **0** ------------------ 0 radius
> Space ------------ Semicolon or space for RETURN
> **R** ----------------- R for radius option
> ; ------------------ Semicolon or space for RETURN
> **FILLET** --------- **FILLET** command

Line 54
[ZOOM:]'ZOOM
This menu item defines a transparent **ZOOM** command.

> [ZOOM:]'ZOOM
>
> Where '-------------------- Single quote (') makes **ZOOM** transparent
> **ZOOM** ----------- AutoCAD **ZOOM** command

Line 90
[Center]CEN $X=

In this menu item CEN is for center object snap, and $X= automatically recalls the previous screen menu after selecting the object.

> **[Center]CEN $S=**
>> Where   **CEN** -------------- Center object snap
>>   **$S=** --------------- Loads previous menu

Note

If any menu item on a screen menu includes more than one load command, the commands must be separated by a space.

Example

[LINE:]$S=X $S=LINE

> *Note that there is a space between X and $S.*

Similarly, if a menu item includes both a load command and an AutoCAD command, they should be separated by a space.

Example

[LINE:]$S=LINE ⌃C⌃CLINE

AUTOMATIC MENU SWAPPING

Screen menus can be automatically swapped by using the system variable **MENUCTL**. When the system variable **MENUCTL** is set to 1, AutoCAD automatically issues the **$S=CMDNAME** command, where **CMDNAME** is the command that loads the submenu. For example, if you select the **LINE** command from the digitizer or pull-down menu, or enter the **LINE** command at the keyboard, the **CMDNAME** command will load the **LINE** submenu and display it in the screen menu area. To use this feature, the command name and the submenu name must be the same. For example, if the name of the arc submenu is ARC and you select the **ARC** command, the arc submenu will be automatically loaded on the screen. However, if the submenu name is different (for example, MYARC), AutoCAD will not load the arc submenu on the screen. The default value of the **MENUCTL** system variable is 1. If you set the **MENUCTL** variable to 0, AutoCAD will not use the **$S=CMDNAME** command feature to load the submenus.

MENUECHO SYSTEM VARIABLE

If the system variable **MENUECHO** is set to 0, the commands that you select from the digitizer, screen menu, pull-down menu, or buttons menu will be displayed in the command prompt area. For example, if you select the **CIRCLE** command from the menu, AutoCAD will display **_circle Specify center point for circle or [3P/2P/Ttr (tan tan radius)]:**. If you set the value of the **MENUECHO** variable to 1, AutoCAD will suppress the echo of the menu item and display **Specify center point for circle or [3P/2P/Ttr (tan tan radius)]:** only. You will notice that the **_circle** is not displayed when **MENUECHO** is set to 1. You can use ⌃**P** in the menu item to turn the echo on or off. The **MENUECHO** system variable can also be assigned a value of 2, 4, or 8, which controls the suppression of system prompts, disabling the ⌃P toggle, and debugging aid for DIESEL macros, respectively.

MENUS FOR FOREIGN LANGUAGES

Besides English, AutoCAD has several foreign language versions. If you want to write a menu that is compatible with other foreign language versions of AutoCAD, you must precede each command and keyword in the menu file with the underscore (_) character.

Examples
[New   ]^C^C_New
[Open]^C^C_Open
[Line]^C^C_Line
[Arc-SCA]^C^C_Arc;_C;_A

Any command or keyword that starts with the underscore character will be automatically translated. If you check the ACAD.MNU file, you will find that AutoCAD has made extensive use of this feature.

Review Questions

1. The name of the menu file that comes with the AutoCAD software package is _____.

2. The AutoCAD menu file can have up to _____ main sections.

3. The tablet menu can have up to _____ main sections.

4. The section label is designated by _____.

5. A submenu is designated by _____.

6. The part of the menu item that is inside the brackets is for _____ only.

7. Only the first _____ characters can be displayed on the screen menu.

8. If the number of characters inside the bracket exceeds eight, the screen menu _____ work.

9. In a menu file you can use _____ to cancel the existing command.

10. The AutoCAD _____ command is used to load a new menu file.

11. _____ is used to pause for input in a screen menu definition.

Exercises

Exercise 3   *General*

Write a screen menu for the commands in Figure 35-8. Use the menu item ******** to load Osnaps, and use the menu item MENU-7 to load the root menu (file name SME7.MNU).

Figure 35-8 Screen menu displays

Chapter 36

AutoLISP

Learning Objectives

After completing this chapter, you will be able to:
- *Perform mathematical operations using AutoLISP.*
- *Use trigonometrical functions in AutoLISP.*
- *Understand the basic AutoLISP functions and their applications.*
- *Load and run AutoLISP programs.*
- *Use **Load/Unload Applications** dialog box.*
- *Use flowcharts to analyze problems.*
- *Test a condition using conditional functions.*

ABOUT AutoLISP

Developed by Autodesk, Inc., **AutoLISP** is an implementation of the **LISP** programming language (LISP is an acronym for **LISt Processor**.) The first reference to LISP was made by John McCarthy in the April 1960 issue of *The Communications of the ACM*.

Except for **FORTRAN** and **COBOL**, most of the languages developed in the early 1960s have become obsolete. But LISP has survived and has become a leading programming language for artificial intelligence (AI). Some of the dialects of the LISP programming language are Common LISP, BYSCO LISP, ExperLISP, GCLISP, IQLISP, LISP/80, LISP/88, MuLISP, TLCLISP, UO-LISP, Waltz LISP, and XLISP. XLISP is a public-domain LISP interpreter. The LISP dialect that resembles AutoLISP is Common LISP. The AutoLISP interpreter is embedded within the AutoCAD software package. However, AutoCAD LT and AutoCAD Versions 2.17 and lower lack the AutoLISP interpreter, therefore, you can use the AutoLISP programming language only with AutoCAD Release 2.18 and up.

The AutoCAD software package contains most of the commands used to generate a drawing. However, some commands are not provided in AutoCAD. For example, AutoCAD has no command to draw a rectangle or make global changes in the drawing text objects. With AutoLISP you can write a program in the AutoLISP programming language that will draw a rectangle or make global or selective changes in the drawing text objects. As a matter of fact, you can use AutoLISP to write any program or embed it in the menu and thus customize your system to make it more efficient.

The AutoLISP programming language has been used by hundreds of third-party software developers to write software packages for various applications. For example, the author of this text has developed a software package, **SMLayout**, that generates flat layouts of various geometrical shapes like transitions, intersection of pipes and cylinders, elbows, cones, and tank heads. There is demand for AutoLISP programmers as consultants for developing application software and custom menus.

This chapter assumes that you are familiar with AutoCAD commands and AutoCAD system variables. However, you need not be an AutoCAD or programming expert to begin learning AutoLISP. This chapter also assumes that you have no prior programming knowledge. If you are familiar with any other programming language, learning AutoLISP may be easy. A thorough discussion of various functions and a step-by-step explanation of the examples should make it fun to learn. This chapter discusses the most frequently used AutoLISP functions and their application in writing a program. For those functions not discussed in this chapter, refer to the **AutoLISP Programmers Reference Manual** from Autodesk. AutoLISP does not require any special hardware. If your system runs AutoCAD, it will also run AutoLISP. To write AutoLISP programs you can use any text editor.

MATHEMATICAL OPERATIONS

A mathematical function constitutes an important feature of any programming language. Most of the mathematical functions commonly used in programming and mathematical calculations are available in AutoLISP. You can use AutoLISP to add, subtract, multiply, and divide numbers. You can also use it to find the sine, cosine, and arctangent of angles expressed in radians. There is a host of other calculations you can do with AutoLISP. This section discusses the most frequently used mathematical functions supported by the AutoLISP programming language.

Addition

Format **(+ num1 num2 num3 - - -)**

This function (+) calculates the sum of all the numbers to the right of the plus (+) sign (num1 + num2 + num3 + . . .). The numbers can be integers or real. If the numbers are integers, then the sum is an integer. If the numbers are real, the sum is real. However, if some numbers are real and some are integers, the sum is real. In the following display, all numbers in the first two examples are integers, so the result is an integer. In the third example, one number is a real number (50.0), so the sum is a real number.

Examples
Command: (+ 2 5)   returns 7
Command: (+ 2 30 4 50)   returns 86
Command: (+ 2 30 4 50.0)   returns 86.0

Subtraction

Format **(- num1 num2 num3 - - -)**

This function **(-)** subtracts the second number from the first number (num1 - num2). If there are more than two numbers, the second and subsequent numbers are added and the sum is subtracted from the first number [num1 - (num2 + num3 + . . .)]. In the first of the following examples, 14 is subtracted from 28 and returns 14. Since both numbers are integers, the result is an integer. In the third example, 20 and 10.0 are added, and the sum of these two numbers (30.0) is subtracted from 50, returning a real number, 20.0.

Examples
Command: (- 28 14)   returns 14
Command: (- 25 7 11)   returns 7
Command: (- 50 20 10.0)   returns 20.0
Command: (- 20 30)   returns -10
Command: (- 20.0 30.0)   returns -10.0

Multiplication

Format **(* num1 num2 num3 - - -)**

This function **(*)** calculates the product of the numbers to the right of the asterisk (num1 x num2 x num3 x . . .). If the numbers are integers, the product of these numbers is an integer. If one of the numbers is a real number, the product is a real number.

Examples
Command: (* 2 5)   returns 10
Command: (* 2 5 3)   returns 30
Command: (* 2 5 3 2.0)   returns 60.0
Command: (* 2 -5.5)   returns -11.0
Command: (* 2.0 -5.5 -2)   returns 22.0

Division

Format **(/ num1 num2 num3 - - -)**

This function **(/)** divides the first number by the second number (num1/num2). If there are more than two numbers, the first number is divided by the product of the second and subsequent numbers [num1 / (num2 x num3 x . . .)]. In the fourth of the following examples, 200 is divided by the product of 5.0 and 4 [200 / (5.0 * 4)].

Examples
Command: (/ 30)   returns 30
Command: (/ 3 2)   returns 1
Command: (/ 3.0 2)   returns 1.5
Command: (/ 200.0 5.0 4)   returns 10.0
Command: (/ 200 -5)   returns -40
Command: (/ -200 -5.0)   returns 40.0

INCREMENTED, DECREMENTED, AND ABSOLUTE NUMBERS

Incremented Number

Format (**1+ number**)

This function (**1+**) adds 1 (integer) to **number** and returns a number that is incremented by 1. In the second example below, 1 is added to -10.5 and returns -9.5.

Examples
(1+ 20)	returns 21
(1+ -10.5)	returns -9.5

Decremented Number

Format (**1- number**)

This function (**1-**) subtracts 1 (integer) from the **number** and returns a number that is decremented by 1. In the second example below, 1 is subtracted from -10.5 and returns -11.5

Examples
(1- 10)	returns 9
(1- -10.5)	returns -11.5

Absolute Number

Format (**abs num**)

The **abs** function returns the absolute value of a number. The number may be an integer number or a real number. In the second example below, the function returns 20 because the absolute value of -20 is 20.

Examples
(abs 20)	returns 20
(abs -20)	returns 20
(abs -20.5)	returns 20.5

TRIGONOMETRIC FUNCTIONS

sin

Format (**sin angle**)

The **sin** function calculates the sine of an angle, where the angle is expressed in radians. In the second of the following examples, the **sin** function calculates the sine of pi (180 degrees) and returns 0.

Examples

Command: (sin 0)	returns 0.0
Command: (sin pi)	returns 0.0
Command: (sin 1.0472)	returns 0.866027

cos

Format **(cos angle)**

The **cos** function calculates the cosine of an angle, where the angle is expressed in radians. In the third of the following examples, the **cos** function calculates the cosine of pi (180 degrees) and returns -1.0.

Examples

Command: (cos 0)	returns 1.0
Command: (cos 0.0)	returns 1.0
Command: (cos pi)	returns -1.0
Command: (cos 1.0)	returns 0.540302

atan

Format **(atan num1)**

The **atan** function calculates the arctangent of **num1**, and the calculated angle is expressed in radians. In the second of the following examples, the **atan** function calculates the arctangent of 1.0 and returns 0.785398 (radians).

Examples

Command: (atan 0.5)	returns 0.463648
Command: (atan 1.0)	returns 0.785398
Command: (atan -1.0)	returns -0.785398

You can also specify a second number in the atan function:

Format **(atan num1 num2)**

If the second number is specified, the function returns the arctangent of (num1/num2) in radians. In the first of the following examples the first number (0.5) is divided by the second number (1.0), and the **atan** function calculates the arctangent of the dividend (0.5/1.0 = 0.5).

Examples

Command: (atan 0.5 1.0)	returns 0.463648 radians
Command: (atan 2.0 3.0)	returns 0.588003 radians
Command: (atan 2.0 -3.0)	returns 2.55359 radians
Command: (atan -2.0 3.00)	returns -0.588003 radians
Command: (atan -2.0 -3.0)	returns -2.55359 radians
Command: (atan 1.0 0.0)	returns 1.5708 radians
Command: (atan -0.5 0.0)	returns -1.5708 radians

angtos

Format (**angtos angle [mode [precision]]**)

The **angtos** function returns the angle expressed in radians in a string format. The format of the string is controlled by the **mode** and **precision** settings.

Examples

(angtos 0.588003 0 4)   returns "33.6901"
(angtos 2.55359 0 4)   returns "146.3099"
(angtos 1.5708 0 4)   returns "90.0000"
(angtos -1.5708 0 2)   returns "270.00"

Note

*In (**angtos angle [mode [precision]]**)*
angle   *is angle in radians*
mode   *is the angtos mode that corresponds to the AutoCAD system variable AUNITS*
The following modes are available in AutoCAD:

ANGTOS MODE	EDITING FORMAT
0	*Decimal degrees*
1	*Degrees/minutes/seconds*
2	*Grads*
3	*Radians*
4	*Surveyor's units*

*Precision is an integer number that controls the number of decimal places. Precision corresponds to the AutoCAD system variable **AUPREC**. The minimum value of **precision** is zero and the maximum is four.*

In the first example above, angle is 0.588003 radians, mode is 0 (angle in degrees), and precision is 4 (four places after decimal). The function will return 33.6901.

RELATIONAL STATEMENTS

Programs generally involve features that test a particular condition. If the condition is true, the program performs certain functions, and if the condition is not true, then the program performs other functions. For example, the relational statement (if (< x 5)) tests true if the value of the variable x is less than 5. This type of test condition is frequently used in programming. The following section discusses various relational statements used in AutoLISP programming.

Equal to

Format (**= atom1 atom2 - - - -**)

This function (=) checks whether the two atoms are equal. If they are equal, the condition is true and the function will return T. Similarly, if the specified atoms are not equal, the condition is false and the function will return nil.

Examples

(= 5 5)	returns T
(= 5 4.9)	returns nil
(= 5.5 5.5 5.5)	returns T
(= "yes" "yes")	returns T
(= "yes" "yes" "no")	returns nil

Not equal to

Format (/= atom1 atom2 - - - -)

This function (/=) checks whether the two atoms are not equal. If they are not equal, the condition is true and the function will return T. Similarly, if the specified atoms are equal, the condition is false and the function will return nil.

Examples

(/= 50 4)	returns T
(/= 50 50)	returns nil
(/= 50 -50)	returns T
(/= "yes" "no")	returns T

Less than

Format (< atom1 atom2 - - - -)

This function (<) checks whether the first atom (**atom1**) is less than the second atom (**atom2**). If it is true, then the function will return **T**. If it is not, the function will return **nil**.

Examples

(< 3 5)	returns T
(< 5 3 4 2)	returns nil
(< "x" "y")	returns T

Less than or equal to

Format (<= atom1 atom2 - - - -)

This function (<=) checks whether the first atom (**atom1**) is less than or equal to the second atom (atom2). If it is, the function will return **T**. If it is not, the function will return nil.

Examples

(<= 10 15)	returns T
(<= "c" "b")	returns nil
(<= -2.0 0)	returns T

Greater than

Format (> atom1 atom2 - - - -)

This function (>) checks whether the first atom (**atom1**) is greater than the second atom (**atom2**). If it is, the function will return **T**. If it is not, then the function will return **nil**. In the first example below, 15 is greater than 10. Therefore, this relational function is true and the function will return T. In the second example, 10 is greater than 9, but this number is not greater than the second 9 therefore, this function will return **nil**.

Examples
(> 15 10)   returns T
(> 10 9 9)   returns nil
(> "c" "b")   returns T

Greater than or equal to
Format (>= atom1 atom2 - - - -)

This function (>=) checks whether the first atom (**atom1**) is greater than or equal to the second atom (atom2). If it is, the function returns **T** otherwise, it will return nil. In the first example below, 78 is greater than 50, but 78 is not equal to 50 therefore, it will return **nil**.

Examples
(>= 78 50)   returns T
(>= "x" "y")   returns T

defun, setq, getpoint, AND Command FUNCTIONS

defun
The **defun** function is used to define a function in an AutoLISP program. The format of the **defun** function is:

(defun name [argument])
            Where **Name** ------------ Name of the function
                   Argument ------- Argument list

Examples
(defun ADNUM ( )
Defines a function ADNUM with no arguments or local symbols. This means that all variables used in the program are global variables. A global variable does not lose its value after the programs ends.

(defun ADNUM (a b c)
Defines a function ADNUM that has three arguments: **a, b,** and **c**. The variables **a, b,** and **c** receive their value from outside the program.

(defun ADNUM (/ a b)
Defines a function ADNUM that has two local variables: **a** and **b**. A local variable is one that retains its value during program execution and can be used within that program only.

(defun C:ADNUM ( )
With **C:** in front of the function name, the function can be executed by entering the name of the function at the AutoCAD Command: prompt. If **C:** is not used, the function name has to be enclosed in parentheses.

Note

AutoLISP contains some built-in functions. Do not use any of those names for function or variable names. The following is a list of some of the names reserved for AutoLISP built-in functions. (Refer to the AutoLISP Programmer's Reference manual for a complete list of AutoLISP built-in functions.)

abs	ads	alloc
and	angle	angtos
append	apply	atom
ascii	assoc	atan
atof	atoi	distance
equal	fix	float
if	length	list
load	member	nil
not	nth	null
open	or	pi
read	repeat	reverse
set	type	while

setq

The **setq** function is used to assign a value to a variable. The format of the **setq** function is:

(setq Name Value [Name Value].......)
Where **Name** ------------ Name of variable
Value ------------- Value assigned to variable

The value assigned to a variable can be any expression (numeric, string, or alphanumeric). If the value is a string, the string length cannot exceed 100 characters.

Command: **(setq X 12)**
Command: **(setq X 6.5)**
Command: **(setq X 8.5 Y 12)**

In this last expression, the number 8.5 is assigned to the variable **X**, and the number 12 is assigned to the variable **Y**.

Command: **(setq answer "YES")**

In this expression the string value "YES" is assigned to the variable **answer**.

The **setq** function can also be used in conjunction with other expressions to assign a value to a variable. In the following examples the **setq** function has been used to assign values to different variables.

(setq pt1 (getpoint "Enter start point: "))
(setq ang1 (getangle "Enter included angle: "))
(setq answer (getstring "Enter YES or NO: "))

Note
*AutoLISP uses some built-in function names and symbols. Do not assign values to any of those functions. The following functions are valid ones, but must never be used because the **pi** and **angle** functions that are reserved functions will be redefined.*

(setq pi 3.0)
(setq angle (. . .))

getpoint

The **getpoint** function pauses to enable you to enter the X, Y coordinates or X, Y, Z coordinates of a point. The coordinates of the point can be entered from the keyboard or by using the screen cursor. The format of the **getpoint** function is:

(getpoint [point] [prompt])
            Where   **Point** ------------- Enter a point, or select a point
                    Prompt ---------- Prompt to be displayed on screen

Example
(setq pt1 (getpoint))
(setq pt1 (getpoint "Enter starting point"))

Note
You cannot enter the name of another AutoLISP routine in response to the getpoint function.

A 2D or a 3D point is always defined with respect to the current user coordinate system (UCS).

Command

The **Command** function is used to execute standard AutoCAD commands from within an AutoLISP program. The AutoCAD command name and the command options have to be enclosed in double quotation marks. The format of the **Command** function is:

(Command "commandname")
            Where   **Command** ----------------- AutoLISP function
                    commandname ---------- AutoCAD command

Example
(Command "line" pt1 pt2 "")
            Where   **"Line"** ----------- AutoCAD LINE Command
                    Pt1 ---------------- First point
                    Pt2 ---------------- Second point
                    " -------------------- "" for Return

Note

Prior to AutoCAD Release 12, the **Command** *function* **could not be used** *to execute the AutoCAD PLOT command. For example: (Command "plot"...) was not a valid statement. In AutoCAD2000 Release 14 and Release 13, you can use plot with the Command function (Command "plot"...).*

The **Command** *function cannot be used to enter data with the AutoCAD DTEXT or TEXT command. (You can issue the DTEXT and TEXT command with the* **Command** *function. You can also enter text height and text rotation, but you cannot enter the text when DTEXT or TEXT prompts for text entry.)*

You cannot use the input functions of AutoLISP with the **Command** *function. The input functions are* **getpoint, getangle, getstring,** *and* **getint.** *For example, (Command "getpoint"...) or (Command "getangle"...) are not valid functions. If the program contains such a function, it will display an error message when the program is loaded.*

Example 1

Write a program that will prompt you to select three points of a triangle and then draw lines through those points to generate the triangle shown in Figure 36-1.

Most programs consist of essentially three parts: **input, output,** and **process. Process** includes what is involved in generating the desired output from the given input (Figure 36-2). Before writing a program, you must identify these three parts. In this example, the **input** to the program is the coordinates of the three points. The desired **output** is a triangle. The **process** needed to generate a triangle is to draw three lines from P1 to P2, P2 to P3, and P3 to P1. Identifying these three sections makes the programming process less confusing.

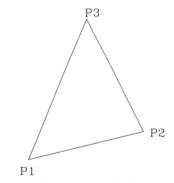

Figure 36-1 *Triangle P1, P2, P3*

The process section of the program is vital to the success of the program. Sometimes it is simple, but sometimes it involves complicated calculations. If the program involves many calculations, divide them into sections (and perhaps subsections) that are laid out in a logical and systematic order. Also, remember that programs need to be edited from time to time, perhaps by other programmers. Therefore, it is wise to document the programs as clearly and unambiguously as possible so that other programmers can understand what the program is do-

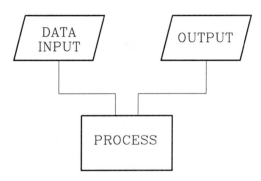

Figure 36-2 *Three elements of a Program*

ing at different stages of its execution. Give sketches, and identify points where possible.

Input

Location of point P1
Location of point P2
Location of point P3

Output

Triangle P1, P2, P3

Process

Line from P1 to P2
Line from P2 to P3
Line from P3 to P1

The following file is a listing of the AutoLISP program for Example 1. **The line numbers at the right are not a part of the program; they are shown here for reference only.**

```
;This program will prompt you to enter three points                      1
;of a triangle from the keyboard, or select three points                 2
;by using the screen cursor. P1, P2, P3 are triangle corners.            3
                                                                         4
(defun c:TRIANG1()                                                       5
   (setq P1 (getpoint "\n Enter first point of Triangle: "))             6
   (setq P2 (getpoint "\n Enter second point of Triangle: "))            7
   (setq P3 (getpoint "\n Enter third point of Triangle: "))            8
   (Command "LINE" P1 P2 P3 "C")                                         9
)                                                                        10
```

Explanation

Lines 1-3
The first three lines are comment lines describing the function of the program. These lines are important because they make it easier to edit a program. Comments should be used when needed. All comment lines must start with a semicolon (). These lines are ignored when the program is loaded.

Line 4
This is a blank line that separates the comment section from the program. Blank lines can be used to separate different modules of a program. This makes it easier to identify different sections that constitute a program. The blank lines have no effect on the program.

Line 5
(defun c:TRIANG1( )
In this line, **defun** is an AutoLISP function that defines the function **TRIANG1**. **TRIANG1** is the name of the function. The c: in front of the function name, **TRIANG1**, enables it to be executed like an AutoCAD command. If the c: is missing, the **TRIANG1** command can be executed only by enclosing it in parentheses (TRIANG1). The TRIANG1 function has three global variables (P1, P2, and P3). When you first write an AutoLISP program, it is a good practice to keep the variables global, because after you load and run the program, you can check the values of these variables by entering exclamation point (!) followed by the variable name at AutoCAD Command prompt

(Command: !P1). Once the program is tested and it works, you should make the variable local, (defun c:TRIANG1(/ P1 P2 P3)).

Line 6
(setq P1 (getpoint "\n Enter first point of Triangle: "))
In this line, the **getpoint** function pauses for you to enter the first point of the triangle. The prompt, **Enter first point of Triangle,** is displayed in the prompt area of the screen. You can enter the coordinates of this point at the keyboard or select a point by using the screen cursor. The setq function then assigns these coordinates to the variable **P1. \n** is used for the carriage return so that the statement that follows \n is printed on the next line ("n" stands for "newline").

Lines 7 and 8
(setq P2 (getpoint "\n Enter second point of Triangle: "))
(setq P3 (getpoint "\n Enter third point of Triangle: "))
These two lines prompt you to enter the second and third corners of the triangle. These coordinates are then assigned to the variables **P2** and **P3. \n** causes a carriage return so that the input prompts are displayed on the next line.

Line 9
(Command "LINE" P1 P2 P3 "C")
In this line, the **Command** function is used to enter the AutoCAD LINE command and then draw a line from P1 to P2 and from P2 to P3. "C" (for "close" option) joins the last point, P3, with the first point, P1. All AutoCAD commands and options, when used in an AutoLISP program, have to be enclosed in double quotation marks. The variables P1, P2, P3 are separated by a blank space.

Line 10
This line consists of a closing parenthesis that completes the definition of the function, TRIANG1. This parenthesis could have been combined with the previous line. It is good practice to keep it on a separate line so that any programmer can easily identify the end of a definition. In this program there is only one function defined, so it is easy to locate the end of a definition. But in some programs a number of definitions or modules within the same program might need to be clearly identified. The parentheses and blank lines help to identify the start and end of a definition or a section in the program.

LOADING AN AUTOLISP PROGRAM

There are generally two names associated with an AutoLISP program: the program file name and the function name. For example, **TRIANG.LSP** is the name of the file, not a function name. All AutoLISP file names have the extension **.LSP**. An AutoLISP file can have one or several functions defined within the same file. For example, TRIANG1 in Example 1 is the name of a function. To execute a function, the AutoLISP program file that defines that function must be loaded. Use the following command to load an AutoLISP file when you are in the drawing editor:

Command: **(load "[path]file name")**
Where **Command** ------ AutoCAD command prompt
load -------------- Loads an AutoLISP program file
file name -------- Path and name of AutoLISP program file

The AutoLISP file name and the optional path name must be enclosed in double quotes. The **load** and **file name** must be enclosed in parentheses. If the parentheses are missing, AutoCAD will try to load a shape or a text font file, not an AutoLISP file. The space between **load** and **file name** is not required. If AutoCAD is successful in loading the file, it will display the name of the function in the Command: prompt area of the screen.

To run the program, type the name of the function at the AutoCAD Command: prompt, and press ENTER (Command: **TRIANG1**). If the function name does not contain **C:** in the program, you can run the program by enclosing the function name in parentheses:

Command: **TRIANG1** or Command: **(TRIANG1)**

Note
Use a forward slash when defining the path for loading an AutoLISP program. For example, if the AutoLISP file TRIANG is in the LISP subdirectory on the C drive, use the following command to load the file. You can also use a double backslash (\\) in place of the forward slash.
Command: **(load "c:/lisp/triang")** or Command: **(load "c:\\lisp\\triang")**

You can also load an application by using the standard Windows drag and drop technique. To load a LISP program, select the file in the Windows Explorer and then drag and drop it in the graphics window of AutoCAD. The selected program will be automatically loaded. Another way to load an AutoLISP program using the **Load/Unload Application** dialog box (Figure 36-3). This dialog box can be invoked by selecting Load Applications in the **Tools** menu or by entering **APPLOAD** at the AutoCAD Command prompt.

Load/Unload Application Dialog Box

The **Load/Unload Application** dialog box (Figure 36-3) can be used to load LSP, VLX, FAS, VBA, DBX, and ObjectARX applications. VBA, DBX, and ObjectARX files are loaded immediately when you select a file. LSP, VLX, and FAS files are qued and loaded when you close the **Load/Unload Application** dialog box. The top portion of the dialog box lists the files in the selected directory. The file type can be changed by entering the file type (*.lsp) in the **Files of type:** edit box or by selecting the file type in the pop-down list. A file can be loaded by selecting the file and then choosing the Load button. The following is the description of other features of the **Load/Unload Application** dialog box:

Load

The **Load** button can be used to load and reload the selected files. The files can be selected from the file list box, Load Application tab, or History List tab. The ObjecrARX files cannot be re-loaded. You must first unload the ObjectARX file and then reload it.

Load Application Tab

When you choose the **Load Application** tab, AutoCAD displays the applications that are currently loaded. You can add files to this list by dragging the files names from the file list box and then dropping them in the Load Application list.

History List Tab

When you choose the **History List** tab, AutoCAD displays the list of files that have been previously

Figure 36-3 *Loading AutoLISP files using the **Load/***
***Unload Applications** dialog box*

loaded with Add to History selected. If the Add to History is not selected and you drag and drop the files in the History list, the files are loaded but not added to the History List.

Add to History

When Add to History is selected, it automatically adds the files to the History List when you drag and drop the files in the History List.

Unload

The **Unload** button appears when you choose the **Loaded Application** tab. To unload an application, select the file name in the Loaded Application file list and then choose the **Unload** button. LISP files and the ObjectARX files that are not registered for unloading cannot be unloaded.

Remove

The **Remove** button appears when you choose the **History List** tab. To remove a file from the History List, select the file in the History List and then choose the **Remove** button.

Startup Suit

The files in the Startup Suit are automatically loaded each time you start AutoCAD. When you choose the Startup Suit, AutoCAD displays the **Startup Suit** dialog box that contains a list of files. You can add files to the list by choosing the **Add** button. You can also drag the files from the file list box and drop them in the Startup Suit. To add files from the History List, right click on the file.

Exercise 1 *General*

Write an AutoLISP program that will draw a line between two points (Figure 36-4). The program must prompt the user to enter the X and Y coordinates of the points.

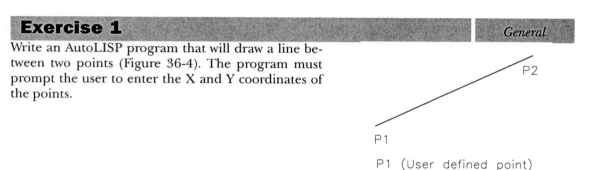

P1 (User defined point)
P2 (User defined point)

Figure 36-4 Draw line from point P1 to P2

getcorner, getdist, AND setvar FUNCTIONS

getcorner

The **getcorner** function pauses for you to enter the coordinates of a point. The coordinates of the point can be entered at the keyboard or by using the screen crosshairs. This function requires a base point, and it displays a rectangle with respect to the base point as you move the screen crosshairs around the screen. The format of the **getcorner** function is:

> (**getcorner point [prompt]**)
>   Where   **point** ----------------------- Base point
>   **prompt** -------------------- Prompt displayed on screen

Examples
(getcorner pt1)
(setq pt2 (getcorner pt1))
(setq pt2 (getcorner pt1 "Enter second point: "))

 Note
The base point and the point that you select in response to the getcorner function are located with respect to the current UCS.
If the point you select is a 3D point with X, Y, and Z coordinates, the Z coordinate is ignored. The point assumes current elevation as its Z coordinate.

getdist

The **getdist** function pauses for you to enter distance, and it then returns the distance as a real number. The format of the **getdist** function is:

> (**getdist [point] [prompt]**)
>   Where   **Point** ------------- First point for distance
>   **Prompt** ---------- Any prompt that needs to be displayed on screen

Examples
(getdist)
(setq dist (getdist))
(setq dist (getdist pt1))
(setq dist (getdist "Enter distance"))
(setq dist (getdist pt1 "Enter second point for distance"))

The distance can be entered by selecting two points on the screen. For example, if the assignment is **(setq dist (getdist))**, you can enter a number or select two points. If the assignment is **(setq dist (getdist pt1))**, where the first point (pt1) is already defined, you need to select the second point only. The getdist function will always return the distance as a real number. For example, if the current setting is architectural and the distance is entered in architectural units, the getdist function will return the distance as a real number.

setvar

The **setvar** function assigns a value to an AutoCAD system variable. The name of the system variable must be enclosed in double quotes. The format of the **setvar** function is:

(setvar "variable-name" value)
> Where **Variable-name** - AutoCAD system variable
> **Value** ------------- Value to be assigned to the system variable

Examples
(setvar "cmdecho" 0)
(setvar "dimscale" 1.5)
(setvar "ltscale" 0.5)
(setvar "dimcen" -0.25)

Example 2

Write an AutoLISP program that will generate a chamfer between two given lines by entering the chamfer angle and the chamfer distance. To generate a chamfer, AutoCAD uses the values assigned to system variables **CHAMFERA** and **CHAMFERB**. When you select the AutoCAD CHAMFER command, the first and second chamfer distances are automatically assigned to the system variables **CHAMFERA** and **CHAMFERB**. The CHAMFER command then uses these assigned values to generate a chamfer. However, in most engineering drawings, the preferred way to generate the chamfer is to enter the chamfer length and the chamfer angle, as shown in Figure 36-5.

Figure 36-5 *Chamfer with angle A and distance D*

Input	Output
First chamfer distance (D)	Chamfer between any two
Chamfer angle (A)	selected lines

<u>Process</u>
1.Calculate second chamfer distance.
2.Assign these values to the system
   variables CHAMFERA and CHAMFERB.
3.Use AutoCAD CHAMFER command.
   to generate chamfer

<u>Calculations</u>
x/d = tan a
x =   d * (tan a)
  =   d * [(sin a) / (cos a)]

The following file is a listing of the program for Example 3. **The line numbers on the right are not a part of the file; they are for reference only.**

```
;This program generates a chamfer by entering                    1
;the chamfer angle and the chamfer distance                      2
;                                                                 3
(defun c:chamf (/ d a)                                           4
(setvar "cmdecho" 0)                                             5
   (graphscr)                                                    6
   (setq d (getdist "\n Enter chamfer distance: "))             7
   (setq a (getangle "\n Enter chamfer angle: "))               8
   (setvar "chamfera" d)                                         9
   (setvar "chamferb" (* d (/ (sin a) (cos a))))               10
   (command "chamfer")                                          11
   (setvar "cmdecho" 1)                                         12
   (princ)                                                      13
)                                                               14
```

Explanation

Line 7
(setq d (getdist "\n Enter chamfer distance: "))
The **getdist** function pauses for you to enter the chamfer distance, then the **setq** function assigns that value to variable d.

Line 8
(setq a (getangle "\n Enter chamfer angle: "))
The **getangle** pauses for you to enter the chamfer angle, then the **setq** function assigns that value to variable a.

Line 9
(setvar "chamfera" d)
The **setvar** function assigns the value of variable d to AutoCAD system variable **chamfera**.

Line 10
(setvar "chamferb" (* d (/ (sin a) (cos a))))

The **setvar** function assigns the value obtained from the expression **(* d (/ (sin a) (cos a)))** to the AutoCAD system variable **chamferb**.

Line 11
(command "chamfer")
The **Command** function uses the AutoCAD **CHAMFER** command to generate a chamfer.

Exercise 2   *General*

Write an AutoLISP program that will generate the drawing shown in Figure 36-6. The program should prompt the user to enter points P1 and P2 and diameters D1 and D2.

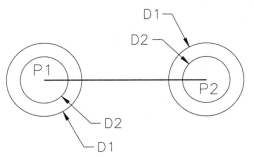

Figure 36-6 Concentric circles with connecting line

list FUNCTION

In AutoLISP the **list** function is used to define a 2D or 3D point. The list function can also be designated by using the single quote character ('), if the expression does not contain any variables or undefined items.

Examples
(Setq x (list 2.5 3 56))   returns 2.5, 3.56
(Setq x '(2.5 3.56))   returns 2.5, 3.56

car, cdr, AND cadr FUNCTIONS
car
The **car** function returns the first element of a list. If the list does not contain any elements, the function will return **nil**. The format of the **car** function is:

(car list)
            Where   **car** ---------------- Returns the first element
                    list ---------------- List of elements

Examples
(car '(2.5 3 56))   returns 2.5
(car '(x y z))   returns X

(car '((15 20) 56))   returns (15 20)
(car '( ))   returns nil

The single quotation mark signifies a list.

cdr

The **cdr** function returns a list with the first element removed from the list. The format of the **cdr** function is:

(cdr list)

> Where **cdr** ---------------- Returns a list with the first element removed
>   **list** ---------------- List of elements

Examples

(cdr '(2.5 3 56)   returns (3 56)
(cdr '(x y z))   returns (Y Z)
(cdr '((15 20) 56))   returns (56)
(cdr '( ))   returns nil

cadr

The **cadr** function performs two operations, **cdr** and **car**, to return the second element of the list. The **cdr** function removes the first element, and the **car** function returns the first element of the new list. The format of the **cadr** function is:

(cadr list)

> Where **cadr** -------------- Performs two operations (car (cdr '(x y z))
>   **list** ---------------- List of elements

Examples

(cadr '(2 3))   returns 3
(cadr '(2 3 56))   returns 3
(cadr '(x y z))   returns y
(cadr '((15 20) 56 24))   returns 56

In these examples, **cadr** performs two functions:

(cadr '(x y z))   = (car (cdr '(x y z)))
                                                       = (car (y z)) returns y

Note

In addition to the functions car, cdr, and cadr, several other functions can be used to extract different elements of a list. Following is a list of these functions, where the function f consists of a list '((x y) z w)).

(setq f '((x y) z w))
(caar f) = (car (car f))   *returns x*

(cdar f) = (cdr (car f))	*returns y*
(cadar) = (car (cdr (car f)))	*returns y*
(cddr f) = (cdr (cdr f))	*returns w*
(caddr f) = (car (cdr (cdr f)))	returns w

graphscr, textscr, princ, AND terpri FUNCTIONS

graphscr

The **graphscr** function switches from the text window to the graphics window, provided the system has only one screen. If the system has two screens, this function is ignored.

textscr

The **textscr** function switches from the graphics window to the text window, provided the system has only one screen. If the system has two screens, this function is ignored.

princ

The **princ** function prints (or displays) the value of the variable. If the variable is enclosed in double quotes, the function prints (or displays) the expression that is enclosed in the quotes. The format of the **princ** function is:

(princ [variable or expression])

Examples

(princ)	prints a blank on screen
(princ a)	prints the value of variable a on screen
(princ "Welcome")	prints Welcome on screen

terpri

The **terpri** function prints a new line on the screen, just as **\n** does. This function is used to print the line that follows the **terpri** function.

Examples

(setq p1 (getpoint "Enter first point: "))(terpri)
(setq p2 (getpoint "Enter second point: "))

The first line (Enter first point:) will be displayed in the screen's command prompt area. The **terpri** function causes a carriage return therefore, the second line (Enter second point:) will be displayed on a new line, just below the first line. If the terpri function is missing, the two lines will be displayed on the same line (Enter first point: Enter second point:).

Example 3

Write a program that will prompt you to enter two opposite corners of a rectangle and then draw the rectangle on the screen as shown in Figure 36-7.

Input
Coordinates of point P1
Coordinates of point P3

Output
Rectangle

Process
1. Calculate the coordinates of the points P2 and P4.
2. Draw the following lines.
    Line from P1 to P2
    Line from P2 to P3
    Line from P3 to P4
    Line from P4 to P1

The X and Y coordinates of points P2 and P4 can be calculated using the **car** and **cadr** functions. The **car** function **extracts** the X coordinate of a given list, and the **cadr** function extracts the Y coordinate.

X coordinate of point p2
x2 = x3
x2 = car (x3 y3)
x2 = car p3

Y coordinate of point p2
y2 = y1
y2 = CADR (x1 y1)
y2 = CADR p1

X coordinate of point p4
x4 = x1
x4 = car(x1 y1)
x4 = car p1

Y coordinate of point p4
y4 = y3
y4 = cadr (x3 y3)
y4 = cadr p3

Therefore, points p2 and p4 are:
p2 = (list (car p3) (cadr p1))
p4 = (list (car p1) (cadr p3))

Figure 36-7   *Rectangle P1 P2 P3 P4*

The following file is a listing of the program for Example 3. **The line numbers at the right are for reference only; they are not a part of the program.**

```
;This program will draw a rectangle. User will          1
;be prompted to enter the two opposite corners          2
;                                                        3
(defun c:RECT1(/ p1 p2 p3 p4)                            4
```

```
            (graphscr)                                           5
            (setvar "cmdecho" 0)                                 6
            (prompt "RECT1  command  draws  a rectangle")(terpri) 7
            (setq p1 (getpoint "Enter first corner"))(terpri)    8
            (setq p3 (getpoint "Enter opposite corner"))(terpri) 9
            (setq p2 (list (car p3) (cadr p1)))                  10
            (setq p4 (list (car p1) (cadr p3)))                  11
        (command "line" p1 p2 p3 p4 "c")                         12
        (setvar "cmdecho" 1)                                     13
        (princ)                                                  14
        )                                                        15
```

Explanation

Lines 1-3

The first three lines are comment lines that describe the function of the program. All comment lines that start with a semicolon are ignored when the program is loaded.

Line 4

(defun c:RECT1(/ p1 p2 p3 p4)

The **defun** function defines the function **RECT1**.

Line 5

(graphscr)

This function switches the text screen to the graphics screen, if the current screen happens to be a text screen. Otherwise, this function has no effect on the display screen.

Line 6

(setvar "cmdecho" 0)

The **setvar** function assigns the value 0 to the AutoCAD system variable cmdecho, which turns the echo off. When **cmdecho** is off, AutoCAD command prompts are not displayed in the command prompt area of the screen.

Line 7

(prompt "RECT1 command draws a rectangle")(terpri)

The **prompt** function will display the information in double quotes ("RECT1 command draws a rectangle"). The function **terpri** causes a carriage return so that the next text is printed on a separate line.

Line 8

(setq p1 (getpoint "Enter first corner"))(terpri)

The **getpoint** function pauses for you to enter a point (the first corner of the rectangle), and the **setq** function assigns that value to variable p1.

Line 9

(setq p3 (getpoint "Enter opposite corner"))(terpri)

The **getpoint** function pauses for you to enter a point (the opposite corner of the rectangle), and the **setq** function assigns that value to variable p3.

Line 10
(setq p2 (list (car p3) (cadr p1)))
The **cadr** function extracts the Y coordinate of point p1, and the car function extracts the X coordinate of point p3. These two values form a list, and the setq function assigns that value to variable p2.

Line 11
(setq p4 (list (car p1) (cadr p3)))
The **cadr** function extracts the Y coordinate of point p3, and the **car** function extracts the X coordinate of point p1. These two values form a list, and the **setq** function assigns that value to variable p4.

Line 12
(command "line" p1 p2 p3 p4 "c")
The command function uses the AutoCAD **LINE** command to draw lines between points p1, p2, p3, and p4. The c (close) joins the last point, p4, with the first point, p1.

Line 13
(setvar "cmdecho" 1)
The **setvar** function assigns a value of 1 to the AutoCAD system variable **cmdecho**, which turns the echo on.

Line 14
(princ)
The princ function prints a blank on the screen. If this line is missing, AutoCAD will print the value of the last expression. This value does not affect the program in any way. However, it might be confusing at times. The **princ** function is used to prevent display of the last expression in the command prompt area.

Line 15
The closing parenthesis completes the definition of the function **RECT1** and ends the program.

Note

In this program the rectangle is generated after you define the two corners of the rectangle. The rectangle is not dragged as you move the screen crosshairs to enter the second corner. However, the rectangle can be dragged by using the getcorner function, as shown in the following program listing:

```
;This program will draw a rectangle with the
;drag mode on and using getcorner function
;
(defun c:RECT2(/ p1 p2 p3 p4)
   (graphscr)
   (setvar "cmdecho" 0)
   (prompt "RECT2 command draws a rectangle")(terpri)
   (setq p1 (getpoint "enter first corner"))(terpri)
   (setq p3 (getcorner p1 "Enter opposite corner" ))(terpri)
   (setq p2 (list (car p3) (cadr p1)))
```

```
    (setq p4 (list (car p1) (cadr p3)))
(command "line" p1 p2 p3 p4 "c")
(setvar "cmdecho" 1)
(princ)
)
```

getangle AND getorient FUNCTIONS

getangle

The **getangle** function pauses for you to enter the angle then it returns the value of that angle in radians. The format of the **getangle** function is:

(getangle [point] [prompt])
               Where **point** ------------- First point of the angle
                      prompt ---------- Any prompt that needs to be displayed on screen

Examples
(getangle)
(setq ang (getangle))
(setq ang (getangle pt1))——————— pt1 is a predefined point
(setq ang (getangle "Enter taper angle"))
(setq ang (getangle pt1 "Enter second point of angle"))

The angle you enter is affected by the angle setting. The angle settings can be changed using the AutoCAD **UNITS** command or by changing the value of the AutoCAD system variables, **ANGBASE** and **ANGDIR**. Following are the default settings for measuring an angle:

The angle is measured with respect to the positive X-axis (3 o'clock position). The value of this setting is saved in the AutoCAD system variable **ANGBASE**.

The angle is positive if it is measured in the counterclockwise direction and is negative if it is measured in the clockwise direction. The value of this setting is saved in the AutoCAD system variable **ANGDIR**.

If the angle has a default setting [Figure 36-8(a)], the getangle function will return 2.35619 radians for an angle of 135.

Examples
(setq ang (getangle "Enter angle"))   returns 2.35619 for an angle of 135 degrees

Figure 36-8(b) shows the new settings of the angle, where the Y-axis is 0 degrees and the angles measured clockwise are positive. The **getangle** function will return 3.92699 for an angle of 135 degrees. The getangle function calculates the angle in the counterclockwise direction, **ignoring the direction set in the system variable ANGDIR**, with respect to the angle base as set in the system variable ANGBASE [Figure 36-9(b)].

Figure 36-8(a)   Figure 36-8(b)

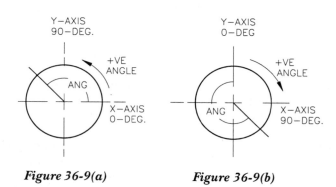

Figure 36-9(a)   Figure 36-9(b)

Examples
(setq ang (getangle "Enter angle"))   returns 3.92699

getorient

The **getorient** function pauses for you to enter the **angle,** then it returns the value of that angle in radians. The format of the **getorient** function is:

(getorient [point] [prompt])
            Where **point** ------------- First point of the angle
                    prompt ---------- Any prompt that needs to be displayed on the screen

Examples
(getorient)
(setq ang (getorient))
(setq ang (getorient pt1))
(setq ang (getorient "Enter taper angle"))
(setq ang (getorient pt1 "Enter second point of angle"))

The **getorient** function is just like the **getangle** function. Both return the value of the angle in radians. However, the **getorient** function always measures the angle with a positive X-axis (3 o'clock position) and in a counterclockwise direction. **It ignores the ANGBASE and ANGDIR settings.** If the settings have not been changed, as shown in Figure 36-10(a) (default settings for ANGDIR and ANGBASE), for an angle of 135 degrees the **getorient** function will return 2.35619 radians. If the settings are changed, as shown in Figure 36-10(b), for an angle of 135 degrees the **getorient** function will return 5.49778 radians. Although the settings have **been** changed where the angle is measured with the positive Y-axis and in a clockwise direction, the **getorient** function ignores the new settings and measures the angle from positive X-axis and in a counterclockwise direction.

Note

For the getangle and getorient functions you can enter the angle by typing the angle at the keyboard or by selecting two points on the screen. If the assignment is (setq ang (getorient pt1)), where the first point pt1 is already defined, you will be prompted to enter the second point. You can enter this point by selecting a point on the screen or by entering the coordinates of the second point.

180 degrees is equal to pi (3.14159) radians. To calculate an angle in radians, use the following relation:

Angle in radians = (pi x angle)/180

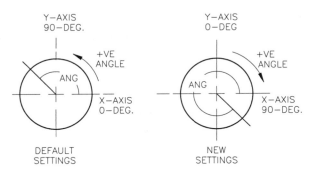

Figure 36-10(a)   *Figure 36-10(b)*

getint, getreal, getstring, AND getvar FUNCTIONS

getint

The **getint** function pauses for you to enter an integer. The function always returns an integer, even if the number you enter is a real number. The format of the **getint** function is:

(getint [prompt])
            Where   **prompt** ---------- Optional prompt that you want to display on screen

Examples
(getint)
(setq numx (getint))

(setq numx (getint "Enter number of rows: "))
(setq numx (getint "\n Enter number of rows: "))

getreal

The **getreal** function pauses for you to enter a real number and it always returns a real number, even if the number you enter is an integer. The format of the **getreal** function is:

(getreal [prompt])
               Where   **prompt** ---------- Optional prompt that is displayed on screen

Examples
(getreal)
(setq realnumx (getreal))
(setq realnumx (getreal "Enter num1: "))
(setq realnumx (getreal "\n Enter num2: "))

getstring

The **getstring** function pauses for you to enter a string value, and it always returns a string, even if the string you enter contains numbers only. The format of the **getstring** function is:

(getstring [prompt])
               Where   **prompt** ---------- Optional prompt that is displayed on screen

Examples
(getstring)
(setq answer (getstring))
(setq answer (getstring "Enter Y for yes, N for no:))
(setq answer (getstring "\n Enter Y for yes, N for no:))

Note
The maximum length of the string is 132 characters. If the string exceeds 132 characters, the excess is ignored.

getvar

The **getvar** function lets you retrieve the value of an AutoCAD system variable. The format of the **getvar** function is:

(getvar "variable")
               Where   **variable** ---------- AutoCAD system variable name

Examples
(getvar)
(getvar "dimcen")   returns 0.09
(getvar "ltscale")   returns 1.0
(getvar "limmax")   returns 12.00,9.00
(getvar "limmin")   returns 0.00,0.00

Note

The system variable name should always be enclosed in double quotes.

You can retrieve only one variable value in one assignment. To retrieve the values of several system variables, use a separate assignment for each variable.

polar AND sqrt FUNCTIONS

polar

The **polar** function defines a point at a given angle and distance from the given point (Figure 36-11). The angle is expressed in radians, measured positive in the counterclockwise direction (assuming default settings for **ANGBASE** and **ANGDIR**). The format of the **polar** function is:

(polar point angle distance)
    Where **point** ------------- Reference point
           angle ------------ Angle the point makes with the referenced point
           distance -------- Distance of the point from the referenced point

Examples
(polar pt1 ang dis)
(setq pt2 (polar pt1 ang dis))
(setq pt2 (polar '(2.0 3.25) ang dis))

sqrt

The **sqrt** function calculates the square root of a number, and the value this function returns is always a real number. The format of the **sqrt** function is:

(sqrt number)
    Where **number** ---------- Number you want to find the square root of
                                 (real or integer)

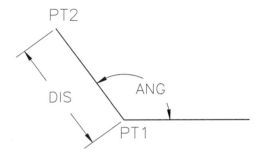

*Figure 36-11 Using the **polar** function to define a point*

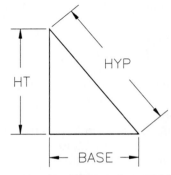

(setq hyp (sqrt (+ (* base base) (* ht ht))))
*Figure 36-12 Application of the **sqrt** function*

Examples

(sqrt 144)	returns 12.0
(sqrt 144.0)	returns 12.0
(setq x (sqrt 57.25))	returns 7.566373
(setq x (sqrt (* 25 36.5)))	returns 30.207615
(setq x (sqrt (/ 7.5 (cos 0.75))))	returns 3.2016035
(setq hyp (sqrt (+ (* base base) (* ht ht))))	

Example 4

Write an AutoLISP program that will draw an equilateral triangle outside a circle (Figure 36-13). The sides of the triangle are tangent to the circle. The program should prompt you to enter the radius and the center point of the circle.

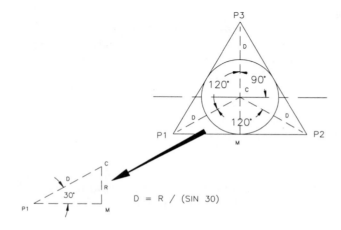

Figure 36-13 *Equilateral triangle outside a circle*

The following file is the listing of the AutoLISP program for Example 4.

```
;This program will draw a triangle outside
;the circle with the lines tangent to circle
:
(defun dtr (a)
   (* a (/ pi 180.0))
)
(defun c:trgcir(/ r c d p1 p2 p3)
(setvar "cmdecho" 0)
(graphscr)
   (setq r(getdist "\n Enter circle radius: "))
   (setq c(getpoint "\n Enter center of circle: "))
   (setq d(/ r (sin(dtr 30))))
   (setq p1(polar c (dtr 210) d))
   (setq p2(polar c (dtr 330) d))
   (setq p3(polar c (dtr 90) d))
```

```
(command "circle" c r)
(command "line" p1 p2 p3 "c")
(setvar "cmdecho" 1)
(princ)
)
```

Exercise 3   *General*

Write an AutoLISP program that will draw an isosceles triangle P1,P2,P3. The base of the triangle (P1,P2) makes an angle B with the positive X-axis (Figure 36-14). The program should prompt you to enter the starting point, P1, length L1, and angles A and B.

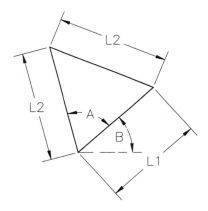

Figure 36-14 *Isosceles triangle at an angle*

Exercise 4   *General*

Write a program that will draw a slot with centerlines. The program should prompt you to enter slot length, slot width, and the layer name for the centerlines (Figure 36-15).

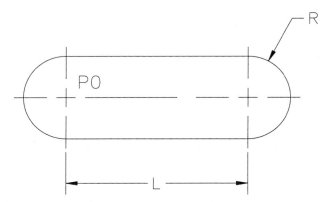

Figure 36-15 *Slot of length L and radius R*

itoa, rtos, strcase, AND prompt FUNCTIONS

itoa

The **itoa** function changes an integer into a string and returns the integer as a string. The format of the **itoa** function is:

(itoa number)

Where **Number** --------- The integer number that you want to convert into a string

Examples
(itoa 89)   returns "89"
(itoa -356)   returns "-356"

(setq intnum 7)
(itoa intnum)   returns "7"

(setq intnum 345)
(setq intstrg (itoa intnum))   returns "345"

rtos

The **rtos** function changes a real number into a string and the function returns the real number as a string. The format of the **rtos** function is:

(rtos realnum)

Where **Realnum** -------- The real number that you want to convert into a string

Examples
(rtos 50.6)   returns "50.6"
(rtos -30.0) returns "-30.0"
(setq realstrg (rtos 5.25))   returns "5.25"

(setq realnum 75.25)
(setq realstrg (rtos realnum))   returns "75.25"

The **rtos** function can also include mode and precision. The format of the **rtos** function with mode and precision is:

(rtos realnum [mode] [precision])

Where **realnum** --------- Real number
mode ------------- Unit mode, like decimal, scientific
precision -------- Number of decimal places or denominator of fractional units

strcase

The **strcase** function converts the characters of a string into uppercase or lowercase. The format of the **strcase** function is:

Chapter 36

(strcase string [true])

Where   **String** ------------ String that needs to be converted to uppercase or lowercase

True ------------- If it is not nil, all characters are converted to lowercase

The **true** is optional. If it is missing or if the value of **true** is nil, the string is converted to uppercase. If the value of true is not nil, the string is converted to lowercase.

Examples

(strcase "Welcome Home")   returns "WELCOME HOME"

(setq t 0)
(strcase "Welcome Home" t)   returns "welcome home"

(setq answer (strcase (getstring "Enter Yes or No: ")))

prompt

The **prompt** function is used to display a message on the screen in the command prompt area. The contents of the message must be enclosed in double quotes. The format of the **prompt** function is:

(prompt message)

Where   **message** --------- Message that you want to display on the screen

Examples

(prompt "Enter circle diameter: ")
(setq d (getdist (prompt "Enter circle diameter: ")))

Note

On a two-screen system, the prompt function displays the message on both screens.

Example 5

Write a program that will draw two circles of radii r1 and r2, representing two pulleys that are separated by a distance d. The line joining the centers of the two circles makes an angle a with the X-axis, as shown in Figure 36-16.

Input	Output
Radius of small circle - r1	Small circle of radius - r1
Radius of large circle - r2	Large circle of radius - r2
Distance between circles - d	Lines tangent to circles
Angle of center line - a	
Center of small circle - c1	

Process
1. Calculate distance x1, x2.
2. Calculate angle ang.

3. Locate point c2 with respect
    to point c1.
4. Locate points p1, p2, p3, p4.
5. Draw small circle with radius
    r1 and center c1.
6. Draw large circle with radius
    r2 and center c2.
7. Draw lines p1 to p2 and p3 to p4.

Calculations

$x1 = r2 - r1$

$x2 = SQRT [d^2 - (r2 - r1)^2]$

$\tan ang = x1 / x2$

$ang = atan (x1 / x2)$

$a1a = 90 + a + ang$

$a1b = 270 + a - ang$

$a2a = 90 + a + ang$

$a2b = 270 + a - ang$

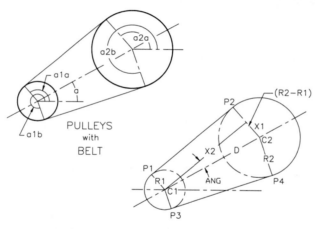

Figure 36-16 Two circles with tangent lines

The following file is a listing of the AutoLISP program for Example 5. **The line numbers on the right are not a part of the file. These numbers are for reference only.**

```
;This program draws a tangent (belt) over two              1
;pulleys that are separated by a given distance.           2
                                                           3
;This function changes degrees into radians                4
(defun dtr (a)                                              5
  (* a (/ pi 180.0))                                        6
  )                                                         7
;End of dtr function                                        8
```

```
;The belt function draws lines that are tangent to circles          9
(defun c:belt(/ r1 r2 d a c1 x1 x2 c2 p1 p2 p3 p4)                 10
    (setvar "cmdecho" 0)                                            11
    (graphscr)                                                      12
    (setq r1(getdist "\n Enter radius of small pulley: "))         13
    (setq r2(getdist "\n Enter radius of larger pulley: "))        14
    (setq d(getdist "\n Enter distance between pulleys: "))        15
    (setq a(getangle "\n Enter angle of pulleys: "))               16
    (setq c1(getpoint "\n Enter center of small pulley: "))        17
    (setq x1 (- r2 r1))                                            18
    (setq x2 (sqrt (- (* d d) (* (- r2 r1) (- r2 r1)))))          19
    (setq ang (atan (/ x1 x2)))                                    20
    (setq c2 (polar c1 a d))                                       21
    (setq p1 (polar c1 (+ ang a (dtr 90)) r1))                    22
    (setq p3 (polar c1 (- (+ a (dtr 270)) ang) r1))              23
    (setq p2 (polar c2 (+ ang a (dtr 90)) r2))                    24
    (setq p4 (polar c2 (- (+ a (dtr 270)) ang) r2))              25
                                                                    26
    ;The following line draw circles and lines                     27
    (command "circle" c1 p3)                                       28
    (command "circle" c2 p2)                                       29
    (command "line" p1 p2 "")                                      30
    (command "line" p3 p4 "")                                      31
    (setvar "cmdecho" 1)                                           32
    (princ))                                                       33
```

Explanation

Line 5
(defun dtr (a)
In this line, the **defun** function defines a function, **dtr (a)**, that converts degrees into radians.

Line 6
(* a (/ pi 180.0))
(/ pi 180) divides the value of **pi** by 180, and the product is then multiplied by angle a (180 degrees is equal to **pi** radians).

Line 10
(defun c:belt(/ r1 r2 d a c1 x1 x2 c2 p1 p2 p3 p4)
In this line, the function **defun** defines a function, c:belt, that generates two circles with tangent lines.

Line 18
(setq x1 (- r2 r1))
In this line, the function **setq** assigns a value of r2 - r1 to variable x1.

Line 19
(setq x2 (sqrt (- (* d d) (* (- r2 r1) (- r2 r1)))))

In this line, **(- r2 r1)** subtracts the value of r1 from r2 and **(* (- r2 r1) (- r2 r1))** calculates the square of (- r2 r1). **(sqrt (- (* d d) (* (- r2 r1) (- r2 r1))))** calculates the square root of the difference, and **setq x2** assigns the product of this expression to variable x2.

Line 20
(setq ang (atan (/ x1 x2)))
In this line, **(atan (/ x1 x2))** calculates the arctangent of the product of **(/ x1 x2)**. The function **setq ang** assigns the value of the angle in radians to variable **ang**.

Line 21
(setq c2 (polar c1 a d))
In this line, **(polar c1 a d)** uses the **polar** function to locate point c2 with respect to c1 at a distance d and making an angle a with the positive X-axis.

Line 22
(setq p1 (polar c1 (+ ang a (dtr 90)) r1))
In this line, **(polar c1 (+ ang a (dtr 90)) r1))** locates point p1 with respect to c1 at a distance r1 and making an angle **(+ ang a (dtr 90))** with the positive X-axis.

Line 28
(command "circle" c1 p3)
In this line, the **Command** function uses the AutoCAD **CIRCLE** command to draw a circle with center c1 and a radius defined by the point p3.

Line 30
(command "line" p1 p2 "")
In this line, the **Command** function uses the AutoCAD **LINE** command to draw a line from p1 to p2. The pair of double quotes ("") at the end introduces a Return, which terminates the LINE command.

Exercise 5   *General*

Write an AutoLISP program that will draw two lines tangent to two circles, as shown in Figure 36-17. The program should prompt you to enter the circle diameters and the center distance between the circles.

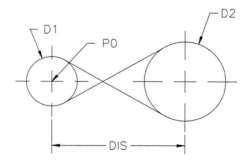

Figure 36-17 Circles with two tangent lines

FLOWCHARTS

A **flowchart** is a graphical representation of an algorithm. It can be used to analyze a problem systematically. It gives a better understanding of the problem, especially if the problem involves some conditional statements. It consists of standard symbols that represent a certain function in the program. For example, a rectangle is used to represent a process that takes place when the program is executed. The blocks are connected by lines indicating the sequence of operations. Figure 36-18 gives the standard symbols that can be used in a flowchart.

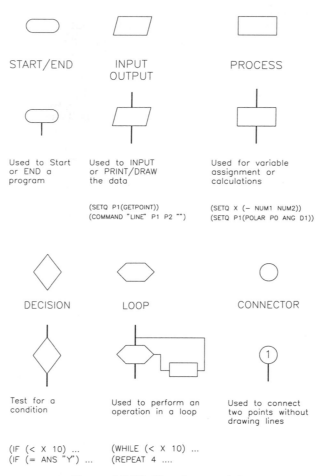

Figure 36-18 Flowchart symbols

CONDITIONAL FUNCTIONS

The relational functions discussed earlier in the chapter establish a relationship between two atoms. For example, (< x y) describes a test condition for an operation. To use such functions in a meaningful way, a conditional function is required. For example, (if (< x y) (setq z (- y x)) (setq z (-

x y))) describes the action to be taken when the condition is true (T) and when it is false (nil). If the condition is true, then z = y - x. If the condition is not true, then z = x - y. Therefore, conditional functions are very important for any programming language, including AutoLISP.

if

The **if** function (Figure 36-19) evaluates the first expression (then) if the specified condition returns "true", it evaluates the second expression (else) if the specified condition returns "nil". The format of the **if** function is:

(if condition then [else])
          Where   **condition** ------- Specified conditional statement
                   then -------------- Expression evaluated if the condition returns T
                   else -------------- Expression evaluated if the condition returns nil

Examples
(if (= 7 7) ("true"))   returns "true"
(if (= 5 7) ("true") ("false"))   returns "false"

(setq ans "yes")
(if (= ans "yes") ("Yes") ("No"))   returns "Yes"

(setq num1 8)
(setq num2 10)
(if (> num1 num2)
   (setq x (- num1 num2))
   (setq x (- num2 num1))
)   returns 2

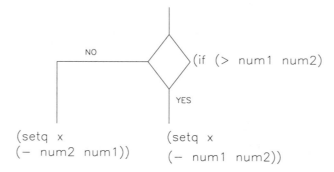

Figure 36-19 if function

Example 6

Write an AutoLISP program that will subtract a smaller number from a larger number. The program should also prompt you to enter two numbers.

Input   **Output**
Number (num1)   x = num1 - num2
Number (num2)   or
                                              x = num2 - num1

Process
If num1 > num2 then x = num1 - num2
If num1 < num2 then x = num2 - num1

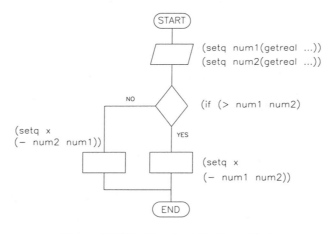

Figure 36-20 Flowchart for Example 6

The flowchart in Figure 36-20 describes the process involved in writing the program using standard flowchart symbols.

The following file is a listing of the program for Example 6. **The line numbers are not a part of the file; they are for reference only.**

```
;This program subtracts smaller number                    1
;from larger number                                        2
;                                                          3
(defun c:subnum( )                                         4
   (setvar "cmdecho" 0)                                    5
   (setq num1 (getreal "\n Enter first number: "))         6
   (setq num2 (getreal "\n Enter second number: "))        7
   (if (> num1 num2)                                       8
      (setq x (- num1 num2))                               9
      (setq x (- num2 num1))                               10
      )                                                    11
```

```
(setvar "cmdecho" 1)                                              12
(princ)                                                           13
)                                                                 14
```

Explanation

Line 8
(if (> num1 num2)
In this line, the **if** function evaluates the test expression **(> num1 num2)**. If the condition is true, it returns **T** if the condition is not true, it returns nil.

Line 9
(setq x (- num1 num2))
This expression is evaluated if the test expression **(if (> num1 num2)** returns T. The value of variable num2 is subtracted from num1, and the resulting value is assigned to variable x.

Line 10
(setq x (- num2 num1))
This expression is evaluated if the test expression **(if (> num1 num2)** returns nil. The value of variable num1 is subtracted from num2, and the resulting value is assigned to variable x.

Line 11
)
The closing parenthesis completes the definition of the if function.

Example 7

Write an AutoLISP program that will enable you to multiply or divide two numbers (Figure 36-21). The program should prompt you to enter the choice of multiplication or division. The program should also display an appropriate message if you do not enter the right choice. The following file is a listing of the AutoLISP program for Example 7:

```
;This program multiplies or divides two given numbers
(defun c:mdnum()
    (setvar "cmdecho" 0)
    (setq num1 (getreal "\n Enter first number: "))
    (setq num2 (getreal "\n Enter second number: "))
    (prompt "Do you want to multiply or divide. Enter M or D: ")
    (setq ans (strcase (getstring)))
    (if (= ans "M")
       (setq x (* num1 num2))
    )
    (if (= ans "D")
       (setq x (/ num1 num2))
    )
    (if (and (/= ans "D")(/= ans "M"))
       (prompt "Sorry! Wrong entry, Try again")
    )
```

```
(setvar "cmdecho" 1)
(princ))
```

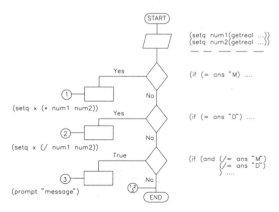

Figure 36-21 *Flow diagram for Example 7*

progn

The **progn** function can be used with the **if** function to evaluate several expressions. The format of **progn** function is:

(progn expression expression . . .)

The **if** function evaluates only one expression if the test condition returns "true". The **progn** function can be used in conjunction with the **if** function to evaluate several expressions.

Example
```
(if (= ans "yes")
  (progn
    (setq x (sin ang))
    (setq y (cos ang))
    (setq tanang (/ x y))
  ))
```

while

The **while** function (Figure 36-22) evaluates a test condition. If the condition is true (expression does not return nil), the operations that follow the while statement are repeated until the test expression returns nil. The format of the **while** function is:

(while testexpression operations)
Where **Testexpression** ----------- Expression that tests a condition
Operations --------------- Operations to be performed until the test
expression returns nil

Example

```
(while (= ans "yes")
  (setq x (+ x 1))
  (setq ans (getstring "Enter yes or no: "))
)
(while (< n 3)
     (setq x (+ x 10))
     (setq n (1+ n))
)
```

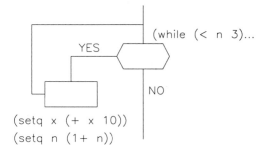

Figure 36-22 *While function*

Example 8

Write an AutoLISP program that will find the nth power of a given number. The power is an integer. The program should prompt you to enter the number and the nth power (Figure 36-23).

Input
Number x
nth power n

Output
product x^n

Process
1. Set the value of t = 1
    and c = 1.
2. Multiply t * x and assign
    that value to the variable t.
3. Repeat the process until the
    counter c is less than or
    equal to n.

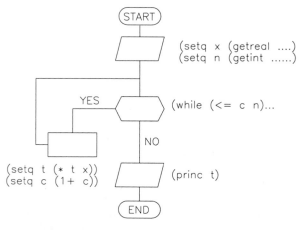

Figure 36-23 *Flowchart for Example 8*

The following file is a listing of the AutoLISP program for Example 8.

```
;This program calculates the nth
;power of a given number
(defun c:npower()
    (setvar "cmdecho" 0)
    (setq x(getreal "\n Enter a number: "))
    (setq n(getint "\n Enter Nth power-integer number: "))
    (setq t 1) (setq c 1)
    (while (<= c n)
      (setq t (* t x))
      (setq c (1+ c))
    )
    (setvar "cmdecho" 1)
    (princ t)
)
```

Example 9

Write an AutoLISP program that will generate the holes of a bolt circle (Figure 36-24). The program should prompt you to enter the center point of the bolt circle, the bolt circle diameter, the bolt circle hole diameter, the number of holes, and the start angle of the bolt circles.

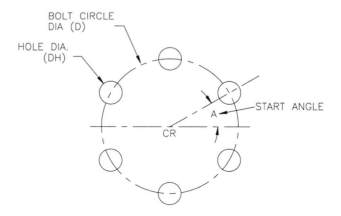

Figure 36-24 *Bolt circle with six holes*

```
;This program generates the bolt circles
;
(defun c:bc1( )
(graphscr)
(setvar "cmdecho" 0)
    (setq cr(getpoint "\n Enter center of Bolt-Circle: "))
    (setq d(getdist "\n Dia of Bolt-Circle: "))
    (setq n(getint "\n Number of holes in Bolt-Circle: "))
```

```
        (setq a(getangle "\n Enter start angle: "))
        (setq dh(getdist "\n Enter diameter of hole: "))
        (setq inc(/ (* 2 pi) n))
        (setq ang 0)
        (setq r (/ dh 2))
    (while (< ang (* 2 pi))
        (setq p1 (polar cr (+ a inc) (/ d 2)))
        (command "circle" p1 r)
        (setq a (+ a inc))
        (setq ang (+ ang inc))
        )
    (setvar "cmdecho" 1)
    (princ)
    )
```

repeat

The **repeat** function evaluates the expressions **n** number of times as specified in the **repeat** function (Figure 36-25). The variable **n** must be an integer. The format of the **repeat** function is:

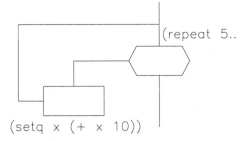

Figure 36-25 Repeat function

repeat n

           Where **n** ------------------- n is an integer that defines the number of times the expressions are to be evaluated

Example
```
(repeat 5
  (setq x (+ x 10))
  )
```

Example 10

Write an AutoLISP program that will generate a given number of concentric circles. The program should prompt you to enter the center point of the circles, the start radius, and the radius increment (Figure 36-26).

The following file is a listing of the AutoLISP program for Example 10.
```
    ;This program uses the repeat function to draw
    ;a given number of concentric circles.
    (defun c:concir( )
    (graphscr)
    (setvar "cmdecho" 0)
    (setq c (getpoint "\n Enter center point of circles: "))
    (setq n (getint "\n Enter number of circles: "))
    (setq r (getdist "\n Enter radius of first circle: "))
    (setq d (getdist "\n Enter radius increment: "))
```

```
(repeat n
  (command "circle" c r)
  (setq r (+ r d))
  )
(setvar "cmdecho" 1)
(princ)
)
```

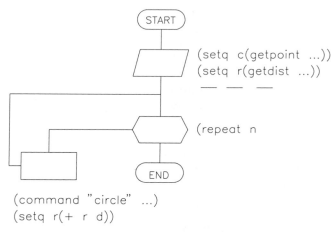

Figure 36-26 *Flowchart for Example 10*

Note

*AutoCAD allows you to load the specified AutoLISP programs automatically, each time you start AutoCAD. For example, if you are working on a project and you have loaded an AutoLISP program, the program will autoload if you start another drawing. You can enable this feature by adding the name of the file to the Startup Suite of **Load/Unload Application** dialog box. For details, see the Load/Unload Application discussed earlier in this chapter.*

Review Questions

1. Evaluate the following AutoLISP functions:

   Command: (+ 2 30 5 50)   returns _____
   Command: (+ 2 30 4 55.0)   returns _____

   (- 20 40)   returns _____
   (- 30.0 40.0)   returns _____

   (* 72 5 3 2.0)   returns _____
   (* 7 -5.5)   returns _____

(/ 299 -5)	returns _____
(/ -200 -9.0)	returns _____
(1- 99)	returns _____
(1- -18.5)	returns _____
(abs -90)	returns _____
(abs -27.5)	returns _____
(sin pi)	returns _____
(sin 1.5)	returns _____
(cos pi)	returns _____
(cos 1.2)	returns _____
(atan 1.1 0.0)	returns _____ radians
(atan -0.4 0.0)	returns _____ radians
(angtos 1.5708 0 5)	returns _____
(angtos -1.5708 0 3)	returns _____
(< "x" "y")	returns _____
(>= 80 90 79)	returns _____

2. The **setq** function is used to assign a value to _____.

3. The _____ function pauses to enable you to enter the X, Y coordinates or X, Y, Z coordinates of a point.

4. The _____ function is used to execute standard AutoCAD commands from within an AutoLISP program.

5. In an AutoLISP expression, the AutoCAD command name and the command options have to be enclosed in double quotation marks. (T/F).

6. The getdist function pauses for you to enter a _____ and it then returns the distance as a real number.

7. The _____ function assigns a value to an AutoCAD system variable. The name of the system variable must be enclosed in _____.

8. The **cadr** function performs two operations, _____ and _____, to return the second element of the list.

9. The _____ function prints a new line on the screen just as \n.

10. The _____ function pauses for you to enter the angle, then it returns the value of that angle in radians.

11. The _____ function always measures the angle with a positive X-axis and in a counter-clockwise direction.

12. The _____ function pauses for you to enter an integer. The function always returns an integer, even if the number that you enter is a real number.

13. The _____ function lets you retrieve the value of an AutoCAD system variable.

14. The _____ function defines a point at a given angle and distance from the given point (Figure 36-10).

15. The _____ function calculates the square root of a number and the value this function returns is always a real number.

16. The _____ function changes a real number into a string and the function returns the real number as a string.

17. The **if** function evaluates the test expression (**> num1 num2**). If the condition is true it returns _____, if the condition is not true, it returns_____.

18. The _____ function can be used with the **if** function to evaluate several expressions.

19. The **while** function evaluates the test condition. If the condition is true (expression does not return nil) the operations that follow the while statement are _____ until the test expression returns _____.

20. The **repeat** function evaluates the expressions n number of times as specified in the **repeat** function. The variable n must be a real number. (T/F).

Exercises

Exercise 6   *General*

Write an AutoLISP program that will draw three concentric circles with center C1 and diameters D1, D2, D3 (Figure 36-27). The program should prompt you to enter the coordinates of center point C1 and the circle diameters D1, D2, D3.

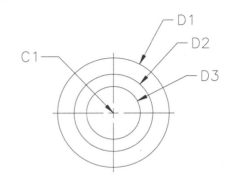

Figure 36-27 *Three concentric circles with diameters D1, D2, D3*

Exercise 7   *General*

Write an AutoLISP program that will draw a line from point P1 to point P2 (Figure 36-28). Line P1, P2 makes an angle A with the positive X-axis. Distance between the points P1 and P2 is L. The diameter of the circles is D1 (D1 = L/4).

Exercise 8   *General*

Write an AutoLISP program that will draw an isosceles triangle P1, P2, P3 (Figure 36-29). The program should prompt you to enter the starting point P1, length L1, and the included angle A.

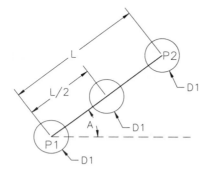

Figure 36-28 *Circles and line making an angle A with X-axis*

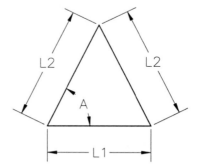

Figure 36-29 *Isosceles triangle*

Exercise 7   *General*

Write an AutoLISP program that will draw the two views of a bushing as shown in Figure 36-30. The program should prompt you to enter the starting point P0, lengths L1, L2, and the bushing diameters ID, OD, HD. The distance between the front view and the side view of bushing is DIS (DIS = 1.25 * HD). The program should also draw the hidden lines in the HID layer and center lines in the CEN layer. The center lines should extend 0.75 units beyond the object line.

Figure 36-30 *Two views of bushing*

Chapter 37

Visual LISP

Learning Objectives

After completing this chapter, you will be able to:
- *Start Visual LISP in AutoCAD.*
- *Use Visual LISP Text Editor.*
- *Load and run Visual LISP programs.*
- *Load exisiting AutoLISP files.*
- *Use Visual LISP Console.*
- *Use Visual LISP formatter and change formatting options.*
- *Debug a Visual LISP program and trace the variables.*

Visual LISP

Visual LISP is another step forward to extend the customizing power of AutoCAD. Since AutoCAD Release 2.0 in the mid 1980s, AutoCAD users have used AutoLISP to write programs for their applications, architecture, mechanical, electrical, air conditioning, civil, sheet metal, and hundreds of other applications. AutoLISP has some limitations. For example, when you use a text editor to write a program, it is difficult to locate and check parentheses, AutoLISP functions, and variables. Debugging is equally problematic, because it is hard to find out what the program is doing and what is causing an error in the program. Generally, programmers will add some statements in the program to check the values of variables at different stages of the program. Once the program is successful, the statements are removed or changed into comments. Balancing parentheses, and formatting the code are some other problems with traditional AutoLISP programming.

Visual LISP has been designed to make programming easier and efficient. It has a powerful text editor and a formatter. The text editor allows color coding of parentheses, function names, variables and other components of the program. The formatter formats the code in a easily readable format. It also has a watch facility that allows you to watch the values of variables and expressions. Visual LISP has an interactive and intelligent console that has made programming easier. It also provides context sensitive help for AutoLISP functions and apropos features for symbol name search. The debugging tools have made it easier to debug the program and check the source code. These and other features have made Visual LISP the preferred tool for writing LISP programs. Visual LISP works with AutoCAD and it contains its own set of windows. AutoCAD must be running when you are working with Visual LISP.

Overview of Visual LISP

In this overview you will learn how to start Visual LISP, use Visual LISP Text Editor to write a LISP Program, and then how to load and run the programs. As you go through the following steps, you will notice that Visual LISP has some new capabilities and features that are not available in AutoLISP.

Starting Visual LISP

Pull-down:	Tools > AutoLISP > Visual LISP Editor
Command:	VLIDE

1. Start AutoCAD.

2. In the **Tools** menu select **AutoLISP** and then select **Visual LISP Editor**. You can also start Visual LISP by entering the **VLIDE** command at the Command prompt. AutoCAD displays the Visual LISP window, Figure 37-1. If it is the first time, in the current drawing session, you are loading Visual LISP, the Trace window might appear displaying information about the current release of Visual LISP and errors that might be encountered when loading Visual LISP. The Visual LISP window has four areas; Menu, Toolbars, Console window, and Status bar, Figure 37-1. The following is a short description of these areas:

Figure 37-1 *Visual LISP window*

Menu. The menu bar is at the top of the Visual LISP window and lists different menu items. If you select a menu, AutoCAD displays the items in that menu. Also, the function of the menu item is displayed in the status bar that is located at the bottom of the Visual LISP window.

Toolbars: The toolbars provide a quick and easy way to invoke Visual LISP commands. Visual LISP has 5 toolbars; Debug, Edit, Find, Inspect, and Run. Depending on the window that is active, the display of the toolbars changes. If you move the mouse pointer over a tool and position it there for few seconds, a tool tip is displayed that indicates the function of that tool. A more detailed description of the tool appears in the status bar.

Console window. The Visual LISP Console window is contained within the Visual LISP window. It can be scrolled and positioned anywhere in the Visual LISP window. The Console window can be used to enter AutoLISP or Visual LISP commands. For example, if you want to add two numbers, enter (+ 2 9.5) next to $ sign and then press the **Enter** key. Visual LISP will return the result and display it in the same window.

Status bar. When you select a menu item or a tool in the toolbar, Visual LISP displays the related information in the status bar that is located near the bottom of the Visual LISP window.

Using Visual LISP Text Editor

1. Select **New File** from the **File** menu. The Visual LISP Text Editor window is displayed, Figure X 2. The default file name is Untitled-0 as displayed at the top of the editor window.

2. To activate the editor, click anywhere in the Visual LISP Text Editor.

3. Type the following program and notice the difference between the Visual LISP Text Editor and the text editors you have been using to write AutoLISP programs (like Notepad).

Figure 37-2 Visual LISP Text Editor

Chapter 37

```
;;;This program will draw a triangle
(defun tr1 ()
(setq p1(list 2 2))
(setq p2(list 6.0 3.0))
(setq p3(list 4.0 7.0))
(command "line" p1 p2 p3 "c")
)
```

5.   Choose the **File** menu and select the **Save** or **Save As**. In the **Save As** dialog box enter the name of the file, **Triang1.lsp**. After you save the file, the file name is displayed at the top of the editor window, Figure 37-3.

Figure 37-3 Writing program code in Visual LISP Text Editor

Loading and Running Programs

1.   Make sure the Visual Lisp Text Editor window is active. If not, click a point anywhere in the window to make it active.

2.   In the **Tools** menu select **Load Text in Editor**. You can also load the program by choosing **Load active edit window** in the **Tools** toolbar. Visual LISP displays a message in the Console window indicating that the program has been loaded. If there was a problem in loading the program, an error message will appear.

3.   To run the program, enter the function name (**tr1**) at the console prompt (-$ sign). The function name must be enclosed in parentheses. The program will draw a triangle in AutoCAD. To view the program output, switch to AutoCAD by choosing **Activate AutoCAD** in the **View** toolbar. You can also run the program from AutoCAD. Switch to AutoCAD and enter the name of the function **TR1** at the Command prompt. AutoCAD will run the program and draw a triangle on the screen, Figure 37-4.

Figure 37-4 *Program output in AutoCAD*

Exercise 1 ·   *General*

Write a LISP program that will draw an equilateral triangle. The program should prompt the user to select the starting point (bottom left corner) and the length of one of the sides of the triangle, Figure 37-5.

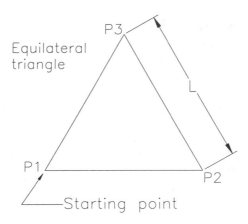

Figure 37-5 *Drawing for Exercise 1*

Loading Existing AutoLISP Files

You can also load the AutoLISP files in Visual LISP and then edit, debug, load, and run the programs from Visual LISP.

1. Start AutoCAD. In the **Tools** menu select **AutoLISP** and then select **Visual LISP Editor**. You can also start Visual AutoLISP by entering the **VLIDE** command at the Command prompt.

2. In the Visual LISP Text Editor, choose **Open File** in the **File** menu. The **Open file to edit/view** dialog box is displayed on the screen.

3. Select the AutoLISP program that you want to load and then choose **Open**. The program is loaded in the Visual LISP Text Editor.

4. To format the program in the edit window, select the **Format edit window** tool from the **Tools** toolbar. The program will automatically get formatted.

5   To load the program, choose **Load active edit window** in the **Tools** toolbar or choose **Load Text in Editor** from the **Tools** menu.

6. To run the program, enter the function name at the console prompt ($) in the Visual LISP Console window.

Visual LISP Console

Most of the programming in Visual LISP is done in the Visual LISP Text Editor. However, you can also enter the code in the Visual LISP console and see the results immediately. For example, if you enter **(sqrt 37.2)** at the console prompt (after the -$ sign) and press the **Enter** key, Visual LISP will evaluate the statement and return the value 6.09918. Similarly, enter the code **(setq x 99.3)**, **(+ 38 23.44)**, **(- 23.786 35)**, **(abs -37.5)**, **(sin 0.333)** and see the results. Each statement must be entered after the $ sign as shown in Figure 37-6.

Features of Visual LISP Console

1. In the Visual LISP console you can enter more than one statement on a line and then press the Enter key. Visual LISP will evaluate all statements and then return the value. Enter the following statement after the $ sign:
    -$(setq x 37.5) (setq y (/ x 2))
    Visual LISP will display the value of X and Y in the console, Figure 37-7

2. If you want to find the value of a variable in the code being developed, enter the variable name after the $ sign and Visual LISP will return the value and display it in the console. For example, if you want to find the value of X, enter X after the $ sign.

3. Visual LISP allows you to write an AutoLISP expression on more than one line by pressing **Ctrl+Enter** at the end of the line. For example, if you want to write the following two expressions on two lines, enter the first line and then press the **Ctrl+Enter** keys. You will notice that Visual LISP does not display the $ sign in the next line, indicating continuation of the statement on the previous line. Now enter the next line and press the **Enter** key, Figure 37-7.

$ **(setq n 38)** Press the **Ctrl+Enter** keys
(setq counter (- n 1))

Figure 37-6 *Entering LISP code in Visual LISP Console*

Figure 37-7 *Entering LISP code in Visual LISP Console*

4. To retrieve the text that has been entered in the previous statement, press the **Tab** key while at the Console prompt (-$). Each time you press the **Tab** key, the previously entered text is displayed. You can continue pressing the **Tab** key to cycle through the text that has been entered in the Visual LISP Console. If the same statement has been entered several times, pressing the Tab key will display the text only once and then jump to the statement before that. Pressing the **Shift+Tab** key displays the text in the opposite direction.

5. Pressing the **Ese** key clears the text following the Console prompt (-$). However, if you press the **Shift+Esc** keys, the text following the Console prompt is not evaluated and stays as is. The cursor jumps to the next Console prompt. For example, if you enter the expression (**setq x 15**) and then press the **Esc** key, the text is cleared. However, if you press the **Shift+Esc** keys, the expression (setq x 15) is not evaluated and the cursor jumps to the next Console prompt without clearing the text.

6. The **Tab** key also lets you do an associative search for the expression that starts with the specified text string. For example, if you want to search the expression that started with (sin, enter it at the Console prompt (-$) and then press the **Enter** key. Visual LISP will search the text in the Console window and return the statement that starts with (sin. If it cannot find the text, nothing happens, except maybe a beep.

7. If you click the **right mouse** button (right-click) anywhere in the Visual LISP Console or press the **Shift+F10** keys, Visual LISP displays the context menu, Figure 37-8. You can use the context menu to perform several tasks like Cut, Copy Paste, Clear Console Window, Find, Inspect, Add Watch, Apropros Window, Symbol Service, Undo, Redo, AutoCAD Mode, and Toggle Console Log.

8. One of the important features of Visual LISP is the facility of context-sensitive help available for the Visual LISP functions. If you need help with any Visual LISP function, enter or select the function and then choose the Help button in the **Tools** toolbar. Visual LISP will display the help for the selected function, Figure 37-9.

Figure 37-8 *Context menu displayed when you click the right mouse button*

9. Visual LISP also allows you to keep a record of the Visual LISP Console activities by saving them on the disk as a log files (.log). To create a log file, select **Toggle Console Log** in the **File** menu or select **Toggle Console Log** from the context menu. The Visual LISP Console window must be active to create a log file.

10. As you enter the text, Visual LISP automatically assigns a color to it. The colors are assigned based on the nature of the text string. For example, if the text is a built-in function or a protected symbol, the color assigned is Blue. Similarly, text strings are Magenta, integers are green, parentheses are red, real numbers are teal, and comments are magenta.

11. Although native AutoLISP and Visual LISP are separate programming environments, you can transfer any text entered in the Visual LISP Console to AutoCAD Command line. To accom-

plish this, enter the code at the Console prompt and then select **AutoCAD Mode** in the context menu or from the **Tools** menu. The Console prompt is replaced with Command prompt. Press the **Tab** key to display the text that was entered at the Console prompt. Press the ENTER key to switch to AutoCAD screen. The text is displayed at AutoCAD's Command prompt.

Figure 37-9 Context-sensitive help screen

Exercise 2   *General*

Enter the following statements in the Visual LISP Console at the console prompt (-$):

```
(+ 2 30 4 38.50)
(- 20 39 32)
(* 2.0 -7.6 31.25)
(/ -230 -7.63 2.15)
(sin 1.0472)
(atan -1.0)
(< 3 10)
(<= -2.0 0)
(setq variable_a 27.5)
(setq variable_b (getreal "Enter a value:"))
```

Using Visual LISP Text Editor

You can use the **Visual LISP Text Editor** to enter the programming code. It has several features that are not available in other text editors. For example, when you enter text, it is automatically assigned a color based on the nature of the text string. If the text is a parentheses, it is assigned red color. If the text is a Visual LIPS function, it is assigned blue color. Visual LISP Text Editor also allows you to execute an AutoLISP function without leaving the text editor, and also checks for balanced parentheses. These features make it an ideal tool for writing Visual LISP programs.

Figure 37-10 *Color coding for LISP code*

Color Coding

Visual LISP Text Editor provides color coding for files that are recognized by Visual LISP. Some of the files that it recognizes are LISP, DCL, SQL, and C language source files. When you enter text in the text editor, Visual LISP automatically determines the color and assigns it to the text, Figure 37-9. The following table shows the default color scheme:

Visual LISP Text Element	Color
Parentheses	Red
Built-in functions	Blue
Protected symbols	Blue
Comments	Magenta with gray background
Strings	Magenta
Real numbers	Teal
Integers	Green
Unrecognized items	Black (like variables)

Words in the Visual LIPS Text Editor

In most of the text editors the words are separated by space. In the Visual LISP Text Editor, the word has a different meaning. A word is a set of characters that are separated by one or more of the following special characters:

Character Description	Visual LISP Special Characters
Space	
Tab	
Single quote	

Left parentheses	(
Right parentheses	)
Double quotes	"
Semicolon	;
Newline	\n

For example, if you enter the text (Command"Line"P1 P2 P3"c), Visual LISP treats Command and Line as separate words because they are separated by double quotes. In a regular text editor (Command"Line" would have been treated as a single word. Similarly, in **(setq p1,** setq and p1 are separate words because they are separated by a space. If there was no space, Visual LISP will treat **(setqp1** as one word.

Context Sensitive Help

One of the important features of Visual LISP is the facility of context-sensitive help available for the Visual LISP functions. If you need help with any Visual LISP function, enter or select the function in the text editor and then choose the **Help** button in the **Tools** toolbar. Visual LISP will display the help for the selected function.

Context Menu

If you click the **right mouse** button (right-click) anywhere in the Visual LISP Text Editor or press the **Shift+F10** keys, Visual LISP displays the context menu, Figure 37-11. You can use the context menu to perform several tasks like Cut, Copy Paste, Clear Console Window, Find, Inspect, Add Watch, Apropos Window, Symbol Service, Undo, Redo, AutoCAD Mode, and Toggle Console Log. The following table contains a short description of these functions:

Figure 37-11 *Context menu displayed when you click the right*

Functions in the context Menu	Description of the function
Cut	Moves the text to the clipboard
Copy	Copies the text to the clipboard
Paste	Pastes the contents of the clipboard at the cursor position
Find	Finds the specified text
Go to Last Edited	Moves the cursor to the last edited position
Toggle Breakpoint	Sets or removes a breakpoint at the cursor position
Inspect	Opens the **Inspect** dialog box
Add Watch	Opens the **Add Watch** dialog box
Apropos Window	Opens **Apropos options** dialog box
Symbol Service	Opens **Symbol Service** dialog box
Undo	Reverses the last operation
Redo	Reverses the previous Undo

Visual LISP Formatter

You can use the Visual LISP Formatter to format the text entered in the text editor. When you format the text, the formatter automatically arranges the AutoLISP expressions in way that makes it easy to read and understand the code. It also makes it easier to debug the program when the program does not perform the intended function.

Figure 37-12 Using Format selection or Format window tools

Running the Formatter

With the formatter you can format all the text in the Visual LISP text editor window or the selected text. To format the text, the text editor window must be active. If it is not, click a point anywhere in the window to make it active. To format all the text, select the **Format edit window** tool in the **Tools** toolbar or select **Format code in Editor** from the **Tools** menu. To format part of the text in the text editor, select the text and then select the **Format selection** tool in the **Tools** toolbar or select **Format code in Selection** from the **Tools** menu. Figure 37-12 shows the **Tools** menu and **Tools** toolbar.

Formatting Comments

In Visual LISP you can have five types of comments and depending on the comment in the program code, Visual LISP will format and position the comment text according to its type. Following is the list of various comment types available in Visual LISP:

Comment formatting	Description
; Single semicolon	The single semicolon is indented as specified in the Single-semicolon comment indentation of AutoLISP Format option.

;; Current column comment	The comment is indented at the same position as the previous line of the program code.
;;; Heading comment	The comment appears without any indentation.
;| Inline comment|;	The Inline comments appears as any other expression.
;_ Function closing comment	The function closing comment appears just after the previous function, provided Insert form-closing comment is on in the AutoLISP Format options .

Two text editor windows are shown in Figure 37-13. The window at the top has the code without formatting. The text window at the bottom has been formatted. If you compare the two, you will see the difference formatting makes in the text display.

Figure 37-13 *Top window shows code without formatting and the bottom window shows the same code after formatting the Programming code*

Changing Formatting Options

You can change the formatting options through the **Format options** dialog box (Figure 37-14) that can be invoked by choosing **Tools** menu, **Environment Options**, and then **Visual LISP Format Options**. In this dialog box if you select **More** options button, Visual LISP will display another dialog box (Figure 37-15) listing more formatting options.

Debugging the Program

When you write a program, it is rare that the program will run the first time. Even if runs, it may not perform the desired function. The error could be a syntax error, missing parentheses, misspelled function name, improper use of a function, or simply a typographical error. It is time

Figure 37-14 *Format options dialog box*

Figure 37-15 *Format options dialog box with more options*

consuming and sometimes difficult to locate the source of the problem. Visual LISP comes with several debugging tools that makes it easier to locate the problem and debug the code. Make sure the Debug toolbar is displayed on the screen. If it is not, in the Visual LISP window click on the **View** menu and then select **Toolbars** to display the **Toolbars** dialog box. Select the **Debug** check box, choose the **Apply** button, and then choose the **Close** button to exit the dialog box. The **Debug** toolbar will appear on the screen. Figure 37-16 shows the toolbar with tool tips.

Figure 37-16 *Tools in Debug toolbar*

1. To try some of the debugging tools, enter the following program in Visual LISP Text Editor and then save the file as **triang2.lsp**:

```
;;; This  program  will  draw  a  triangle and an arc
(defun tr2 ()
  (setq p1 (getpoint "\nEnter first point p1:"))
  (setq p2 (getpoint "\nEnter second point p2:"))
  (setq p3 (getpoint "\nEnter third point p3:"))
  (command "arc" p1 p2 p3)
  (command "line" p1 p2 p3 "c")
)
```

2. To format the code, choose the **Format edit window** tool in the **Tools** toolbar. You can also format the code by selecting **Format code in Editor** in the Tools menu.

3. Load the program by choosing the **Load active edit window** tool in the **Tools** toolbar. You can also load the program from the **Tools** menu by selecting **Load Text in Editor**.

4. In the Visual LISP Text Editor, position the cursor in front of the following line and then choose the **Toggle breakpoint** tool in the **Debug** toolbar. You can also select it from the **Debug** menu. Visual LISP inserts a breakpoint at the cursor location.

   |(setq p2 (getpoint "\Enter second point p2:"))

5. In the Visual LISP Console, at the Console prompt, enter the name of the function and then press the **Enter** key to run the program.

   -$ (tr2)

   AutoCAD window will appear and the first prompt in the program (Enter first point p1:) will be displayed in the Command prompt area. Pick a point and Visual LISP window will appear. Notice, the line that follows the breakpoint is highlighted as shown in Figure 37-17.

6. Choose the **Step Into** button in the **Debug** toolbar or select **Step Into** from the **Debug** menu. You can also press the function key **F8** to invoke the **Step Into** command. The program starts

Figure 37-17 *Using Step Into command to start execution until it encounters the next expression*

execution until it encounters the next expression. The next expression that is contained within the inside parentheses is highlighted, Figure 37-18. Notice the position of the vertical bar in the Step indicator tool in the Debug toolbar. It is on the left of the Step indicator tool. Also, the cursor is just before the expression ("getpoint "\nEnter second point:).

Figure 37-18 *Using Step Into command again, the cursor jumps to the end of the expression*

7. Choose the **Step Into** button again. The AutoCAD window appears and the second prompt in the program (Enter second point p2:) is displayed in the Command prompt area. Pick a point, and the Visual LISP window returns, Figure 37-19. Notice the position of the vertical bar in the **Step indicator** tool in the **Debug** toolbar. It is just to the right of the Step Indicator. Also, the cursor is just after the expression ("getpoint "\nEnter second point:).

8. Choose the **Step Into** button again to step through the program. The entire line is highlighted and the cursor moves to the end of the expression (getpoint "Enter second point:). Notice the position of the vertical bar in the **Step indicator** tool in the **Debug** toolbar.

Figure 37-19 *Using Step Into command again, the vertical bar is displayed to the right of Step Indicator symbol*

9. Choose the **Step Into** button again, the next line of the program is highlighted and the cursor is at the start of the statement.

10 To step over the highlighted statement, choose the **Step over** tool in the **Debug** toolbar, or select **Step Over** in the Debug menu. You can also press the **Shift+F8** keys to invoke this command. The AutoCAD window is displayed and the prompt (Enter third point:) is displayed in the Command prompt area. Select a point, and the Visual LISP window appears.

11. Choose the **Step over** button again; Visual LISP highlights the next line. If you choose the Step over button again, the entire expression is executed.

12. Choose the **Step over** button until you go through all the statements and the entire program is highlighted.

Tracing Variables

Sometimes it becomes necessary to trace the values of the variables used in the program. For example, let us assume the program crashes or does not perform as desired. Now you want to locate where the problem occurred. One of the ways you can do it is by tracing the value of the variables used in the program. The following steps illustrate this procedure:

1. Open the file containing the program code in the Visual LISP Text Editor. You can open the file by selecting **Open File** from the **File** menu.

2. Load the program by selecting **Load Text in Editor** from the **Tools** menu or by selecting **Load active edit window** tool in the **Tools** toolbar.

3. Run the program by entering the name of the function (tr2) at the Console prompt (-$) in the Visual LISP Console. The program will perform the operations as defined in the program. In this program, it will draw a triangle and an arc between the user-specified points. Now, we want to find out the coordinates of the points p1, p2, and p3. To accomplish this we can use the **Watch window** tool in the **View** toolbar.

4. Highlight the variable **p1** and then choose the **Watch window** tool in the **View** toolbar. You can also select **Watch Window** in the **View** menu. Visual LISP displays the **Watch** window that lists the X, Y, and Z coordinates of point p1.

5. Position the cursor near (in front, middle, or end) the variable p2 and then choose the **Add Watch** tool in the **Watch** window. Select the **OK** button in the **Add Watch** window. The value of the selected variable is listed in the **Watch** window, Figure 37-20. Similarly you can trace the value of other variables in the program.

Figure 37-20 *Using Add Watch to trace variables in the program*

Review Questions

1. What are the different ways to start Visual LISP.
   1. _____ 2. _____

2. Name the four areas of the Visual LISP window.
   1. _____ 2. _____
   3. _____ 4. _____

3. Name the toolbars available in Visual LISP
   1. _____ 2. _____
   3. _____ 4. _____
   5. _____

4. What are the different ways of loading a Visual LISP program.
   1. _____ 2. _____

5. How can you run a Visual LISP program.
   _____

6. Can you open an AutoLISP file in the Visual LISP Text Editor. _____

7. Explain the function of the Visual LISP Console.

   _____

   _____

8. Can you enter several LISP statements in the Visual LISP Console. If yes, give an example.

   _____

9. In the Visual LISP Console, how can you enter a LISP statements in more than one line.

   _____

10. What is a context menu and how can you display it.

    _____

    _____

11. In the Visual LISP Text Editor, what are the default colors assigned to the following
    Parantheses _____ LISP functions _____
    Comments _____ Integers _____

12. What is the function of the Visual LISP Formatter and how can you format the text.

    _____

    _____

13. How can you get the heading comment and function closing comment.

    _____

14. How can you change the formatting options.

    _____

15. How can you debug a Visual LISP program.

    _____

    _____

16. How can you trace the value of variables in the Visual LISP program.

    _____

    _____

Exercises

Exercise 3   *Architectural*

Write a LISP program that will draw the staircase shown in Figure X-21. When you run the program, the user should be prompted to enter the rise and run of the staircase and the number of steps. The user should also be prompted to enter the length of the landing area.

Figure 37-21 *Drawing for Exercise 3*

Exercise 4   *Architectural*

Write a LISP program that will draw the picture frame of Figure X-22. The program should prompt the user to enter the length, width, and the thickness of the frame.

Figure 37-22 *Drawing for Exercise 4*

Chapter 38

DIESEL:
A String Expression Language

Learning Objectives

After completing this chapter, you will be able to:
- *Use DIESEL to customize a status line.*
- *Use the **MODEMACRO** system variable.*
- *Write macro expressions using DIESEL.*
- *Use AutoLISP with **MODEMACRO**.*

DIESEL

DIESEL (Direct Interpretively Evaluated String Expression Language) is a string expression language. It can be used to display a user-defined text string (macro expression) in the status line by altering the value of the AutoCAD system variable **MODEMACRO**. The value assigned to **MODEMACRO** must be a string, and the output it generates will be a string. It is fairly easy to write a macro expression in DIESEL, and it is an important tool for customizing AutoCAD. However, DIESEL is slow, and it is not intended to function like AutoLISP or DCL. You can use AutoLISP to write and assign a value to the **MODEMACRO** variable, or you can write the definition of the **MODEMACRO** expression in the menu files. A detailed explanation of the DIESEL functions and the use of DIESEL in writing a macro expression is given later in this chapter.

STATUS LINE

When you are in AutoCAD, a status line is displayed at the bottom of the graphics screen (Figure 38-1). This line contains some useful information and tools that will make it easy to change the status of some AutoCAD functions. To change the status, you must click on the buttons. For example, if you want to display grid lines on the screen, click on the **GRID** button. Similarly, if you

Figure 38-1 *Default status line display*

want to switch to paper space, click on **MODEL**. The status line contains the following information:

Coordinate Display. The coordinate information displayed in the status line can be static or dynamic. If the coordinate display is static, the coordinate values displayed in the status line change only when you specify a point. However, if the coordinate display is dynamic (default setting), AutoCAD constantly displays the absolute coordinates of the graphics cursor with respect to the UCS origin. AutoCAD can also display the polar coordinates (length<angle) if you are in an AutoCAD command.

SNAP. If SNAP is on, the cursor snaps to the snap point.

GRID. If GRID is on, grid lines are displayed on the screen.

ORTHO. If ORTHO is on, a line can be drawn in vertical or horizontal direction.

POLAR. When the POLAR snap is on, the the cursor snaps to polar angles as set in the Polar Tracking tab of the **Drafting Settings** dialog box.

OSNAP. If OSNAP is on, you can use the running object snaps. If OSNAP is off, the running object snaps are temporarily disabled. The status of OSNAP (Off or On) does not prevent you from using regular object snaps.

OTRACK. When Object Tracking is on, you can tack from a point. The object snap must be set before using Object Tracking.

MODEL and PAPER Space. AutoCAD displays MODEL in the status line when you are working in the model space. If you are working in the paper space, AutoCAD will display PAPER in place of MODEL.

LWT. When Lineweight button is on, the objects are displayed with the assigned width.

TILE. AutoCAD displays TILE, if TILEMODE is on (1). When TILEMODE is on, you are in the model space. If TILE is off, you are in the paper space (TILEMODE is 0).

MODEMACRO SYSTEM VARIABLE

The AutoCAD system variable **MODEMACRO** can be used to display a new text string in the status line. You can also display the value returned by a macro expression using the DIESEL language, which is discussed in a later section of this chapter. MODEMACRO is a system variable and you can assign a value to this variable by entering MODEMACRO at the Command prompt or by using the SETVAR command. For example, if you want to display **Customizing AutoCAD** in the status line, enter **SETVAR** at the Command: prompt and then press ENTER. AutoCAD will prompt you to enter the name of the system variable. Enter **MODEMACRO** and then press ENTER again. Now you can enter the text you want to display in the status line. After you enter **Customizing AutoCAD** and press ENTER, the status line will display the new text.

> Command: **MODEMACRO**
> or
> Command: **SETVAR**
> Variable name or ?: **MODEMACRO**
> New value for MODEMACRO, or . for none<"">: **Customizing AutoCAD**

You can also enter MODEMACRO at the Command prompt and then enter the text that you want to display in the status line.

> Command: **MODEMACRO**
> New value for MODEMACRO, or . for none<"">: **Customizing AutoCAD**

Once the value of the **MODEMACRO** variable is changed, it retains that value until you enter a new value, start a new drawing, or open an existing drawing file. If you want to display the standard text in the status line, enter a period (.) at the prompt New value for **MODEMACRO**, or . **for none <"">:**. The value assigned to the **MODEMACRO** system variable is not saved with the drawing, in any configuration file, or anywhere in the system.

> Command: **MODEMACRO**
> New value for MODEMACRO, or . for none<"">:

CUSTOMIZING THE STATUS LINE

The information contained in the status line can be divided into two parts: toggle functions and coordinate display. The toggle functions part consists of the status of Snap, Grid, Ortho, Polar Tracking, Object Snap, Object Tracking, Lineweight, Model Space, and Tile (Figure 38-1). The coordinate display displays the X, Y, and Z coordinates of the cursor. The status line can be customized to your requirements by assigning a value to the AutoCAD system variable **MODEMACRO**. The value assigned to this variable is displayed left-justified in the status bar at the bottom of the AutoCAD window. The number of characters that can be displayed in the status line depends on the system display and the size of the AutoCAD window. The coordinate display field cannot be changed or edited.

The information displayed in the status line is a valuable resource. Therefore, you must be careful when selecting the information to be displayed in the status line. For example, when working on a project, you may like to display the name of the project in the status line. If you are using several

Chapter 38

dimensioning styles, you could display the name of the current dimensioning style (DIMSTYLE) in the status line. Similarly, if you have several text files with different fonts, the name of the current text file (TEXTSTYLE) and the text height (TEXTSIZE) can be displayed in the status line. Sometimes, in 3D drawings, if you need to monitor the viewing direction (VIEWDIR), the camera coordinate information can be displayed in the status line. Therefore, the information that should be displayed in the status line depends on you and the drawing requirements. AutoCAD lets you customize this line and have any information displayed in the status line that you think is appropriate for your application.

MACRO EXPRESSIONS USING DIESEL

You can also write a macro expression using DIESEL to assign a value to the **MODEMACRO** system variable. The macro expressions are similar to AutoLISP functions, with some differences. For example, the drawing name can be obtained by using the AutoLISP statement **(getvar dwgname)**. In DIESEL, the same information can be obtained by using the macro expression **$(getvar,dwgname)**. However, unlike the case with AutoLISP, the DIESEL macro expressions return only string values. The format of a macro expression is:

$(function-name,argument1,argument2, ...)

Example
$(getvar,dwgname)

Here, **getvar** is the name of the DIESEL string function and **dwgname** is the argument of the function. There must not be any spaces between different elements of a macro expression. For example, spaces between the $ sign and the open parentheses are not permitted. Similarly, there must not be any spaces between the comma and the argument, **dwgname**. All macro expressions must start with a $ sign.

The following example illustrates the use of a macro expression using DIESEL to define and then assign a value to the **MODEMACRO** system variable.

Example 1

Using the AutoCAD MODEMACRO command, redefine the status line to display the following information in the status line:

Project name (Cust-Acad)
Name of the drawing (DEMO)
Name of the current layer (OBJ)

Note that in this example the project name is Cust-Acad, the drawing name is DEMO, and the current layer name is **OBJ**.

Before entering the **MODEMACRO** command, you need to determine how to retrieve the required information from the drawing database. For example, here the project name **(Cust-Acad)** is a user-defined name that lets you know the name of the current project. This project name is not saved in the drawing database. The name of the drawing can be obtained using the DIESEL string function **GETVAR $(getvar,dwgname)**. Similarly, the **GETVAR** function can also be used to obtain the name of the current layer, **$(getvar,clayer)**. Once you determine how to retrieve the information from the system, you can use the **MODEMACRO** system variable to obtain the new status line. For Example 1, the following DIESEL expression will define the required status line.

    Command: **MODEMACRO**
    New value for MODEMACRO, or . for none<"">: **Cust-Acad N:$(GETVAR,dwgname)**
                                     L:$(GETVAR,clayer)

Explanation
Cust-Acad
Cust-Acad is assumed to be the project name you want to display in the status line.

N:$(GETVAR,dwgname)
Here, N: is used as an abbreviation for the drawing name. The GETVAR function retrieves the name of the drawing from the system variable **dwgname** and displays it in the status line, next to N:.

L:$(GETVAR,clayer)
Here L: is used as an abbreviation for the layer name. The GETVAR function retrieves the name of the current layer from the system variable **clayer** and displays it in the status line.

The new status line is shown in Figure 38-2(a).

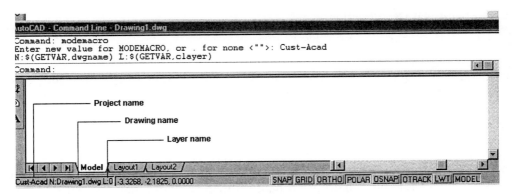

Figure 38-2(a) *Status line for Example 1*

Example 2

Using the AutoCAD **MODEMACRO** command, redefine the status line to display the following information in the status line, Figure 38-2(b):

    Name of the current textstyle
    Size of text
    User-elapsed time in minutes

In this example the abbreviations for text style, text size, and user-elapsed time in minutes are TSTYLE:, TSIZE:, and ETM:, respectively.

Command: **MODEMACRO**
New value for MODEMACRO, or . for none<"">:
      TSTYLE:$(GETVAR,TEXTSTYLE)TSIZE:$(GETVAR,TEXTSIZE)
      ETM:$(FIX,$(*,60,$(*,24,$(GETVAR,TDUSRTIMER))))

Explanation

TSTYLE:$(GETVAR,TEXTSTYLE)
The **GETVAR** function obtains the name of the current textstyle from the system variable **TEXTSTYLE** and displays it next to TSTYLE: in the status line.

TSIZE:$(GETVAR,TEXTSIZE)
The **GETVAR** function obtains the current size of the text from the system variable **TEXTSIZE** and then displays it next to TSIZE: in the status line.

Figure 38-2(b) Status line for Example 2

ETM:$(FIX,$(*,60,$(*,24,$(GETVAR,TDUSRTIMER))))
The **GETVAR** function obtains the user-elapsed time from the system variable **TDUSRTIMER** in the following format:

    <Number of days>.<Fraction>

Example
0.03206400 (time in days)
To change this time into minutes, multiply the value obtained from the system variable **TDUSRTIMER** by 24 to change it into hours, and then multiply the product by 60 to change the time into minutes. To express the minutes value without a decimal, determine the integer value using the DIESEL string function FIX.

Example
Assume that the value returned by the system variable TDUSRTIMER is 0.03206400. This time is in days. Use the following calculations to change the time into minutes, and then express the time as an integer:

    0.03206400 days x 24 = 0.769536 hr
    0.769536 hr x 60 = 46.17216 min
    integer of 46.17216 min = 46 min

USING AUTOLISP WITH MODEMACRO

Sometimes the DIESEL expressions can be as long as those shown in Example 1 and Example 2. It takes time to type the DIESEL expression, and if you make a mistake in entering the expression, you have to retype it. Also, if you need several different status line displays, you need to type them every time you want a new status line display. This can be time-consuming and sometimes confusing.

To make it convenient to change the status line display, you can use AutoLISP to write a DIESEL expression. It is easier to load an AutoLISP program, and it also eliminates any errors that might be caused by typing a DIESEL expression. The following example illustrates the use of AutoLISP to write a DIESEL expression to assign a new value to the **MODEMACRO** system variable.

Example 3

Using AutoLISP, redefine the value assigned to the **MODEMACRO** system variable to display the following information in the status line:

> Name of the current text style
> Size of text
> User-elapsed time in minutes

In this example the abbreviations for text style, text size, and user-elapsed time in minutes are TSTYLE:, TSIZE:, and ETM:, respectively.

The following file is a listing of the AutoLISP program for Example 3. The name of the file is **ETM.LSP.** The line numbers are not a part of the file; they are shown here for reference only.

```
(defun c:etm ( )                                   1
(setvar "MODEMACRO"                                2
(strcat                                            3
   "TSTYLE:$(getvar,textstyle)"                    4
   " TSIZE:$(getvar,textsize)"                     5
   " ETM:$(fix,$(*,60,$(*,24,                      6
   $(getvar,tdusrtimer))))"                        7
   )                                               8
   )                                               9
   )                                              10
```

Explanation
Line 3
(strcat
The AutoLISP function **strcat** links the string value of lines 4 through 7 and returns a single string that becomes a DIESEL expression for the **MODEMACRO** command.

Line 4
"TSTYLE:$(getvar,textstyle)"
This line is a DIESEL expression in which getvar, a DIESEL string function, retrieves the value of the system variable **textstyle** and **$(getvar,textstyle)** is replaced by the name of the textstyle. For example, if the textstyle is STANDARD, the line will return "TSTYLE:STANDARD". This is a string because it is enclosed in quotes.

Lines 6 and 7
" ETM:$(fix,$(*,60,$(*,24,
$(getvar,tdusrtimer))))"
These two lines return **ETM:** and the time in minutes as a string. The **fix** is a DIESEL string
function that changes a real number to an integer.

To load this AutoLISP file (**ETM.LSP**), use the following commands. In this example, the file
name and the function name are the same (ETM).

```
Command: (load "ETM")
ETM
Command: ETM
```

DIESEL EXPRESSIONS IN MENUS

You can also define a DIESEL expression in the screen, tablet, pull-down, or button menu. When
you select the menu item, it will automatically assign the value to the MODEMACRO system
variable and then display the new status line. The following example illustrates the use of the
DIESEL expression in the screen menu.

Example 4

Write a DIESEL macro for the screen menu that displays the following information in the status
line (Figure 38-3):

Macro-1	Macro-2	Macro-3
Project name	Pline width	Dimtad
Drawing name	Fillet radius	Dimtix
Current layer	Offset distance	Dimscale

The following file is a listing of the screen menu that contains the definition of three DIESEL
macros for Example 4. This menu can be loaded using AutoCAD's MENU command and then
entering the name of the file. If you select the first item, DIESEL1, it will automatically display the
new status line.

```
***screen
[*DIESEL*]
[DIESEL1:]^C^CMODEMACRO;$M=Cust-Acad,N:$(GETVAR,DWGNAME)+
,L:$(GETVAR,CLAYER);
[DIESEL2:]^C^CMODEMACRO;$M=PLWID:$(GETVAR,PLINEWID),+
FRAD:$(GETVAR,FILLETRAD),OFFSET:$(GETVAR,OFFSETDIST),+
LTSCALE:$(GETVAR,LTSCALE);
[DIESEL3:]^C^CMODEMACRO;$M=DTAD:$(GETVAR,DIMTAD),+
DTIX:$(GETVAR,DIMTIX),DSCALE:$(GETVAR,DIMSCALE);
```

Figure 38-3 *Status line for Example 4*

MACROTRACE SYSTEM VARIABLE

The MACROTRACE variable is an AutoCAD system variable that can be used to debug a DIESEL expression. The default value of this variable is 0 (off). It is turned on by assigning a value of 1 (on). When on, the MACROTRACE system variable will evaluate all DIESEL expressions and display the results in the command prompt area. For example, if you have defined several DIESEL expressions in a drawing session, all of them will be evaluated at the same time and the messages, if any, will be displayed in the command prompt area.

Example
Command: **MODEMACRO**
New value for MODEMACRO, or . for none<"">: **$(getvar,dwgname),$(getvar clayer)**

Note that in this DIESEL expression a comma is missing between getvar and clayer. If the MACROTRACE system variable is on, the following message will be displayed in the Command prompt area:

Eval: $(GETVAR,DWGNAME)
====>UNNAMED
Eval: $(GETVAR CLAYER)
Err: $(GETVAR CLAYER)??

This error message gives you an idea about the location of the error in a DIESEL expression. In the previous example, the first part of the expression successfully returns the name of the drawing (unnamed) and the second part of the expression results in the error message. This confirms that there is an error in the second part of the DIESEL expression. You can further determine the cause of the error by comparing it with the error messages in the following table:

Error Message	Description
$?	Syntax error
$?(func,??)	Incorrect argument to function
$(func)??	Unknown function
$(++)	Output string too long

Review Questions

1. DIESEL (direct interpretively evaluated string expression language) is a string expression language. (T/F)

2. The value assigned to the **MODEMACRO** variable is a string, and the output it generates is not a string. (T/F)

3. You cannot define a DIESEL expression in the screen menu. (T/F)

4. The coordinate information displayed in the status line can be dynamic only. (T/F)

5. Once the value of the **MODEMACRO** variable is changed, it retains that value until you enter a new value, start a new drawing, or open an existing drawing file. (T/F)

6. The number of characters that can be displayed in the layer mode field on any system is 38. (T/F)

7. The coordinate display field cannot be changed or edited. (T/F)

8. You can write a macro expression using DIESEL to assign a value to the **MODEMACRO** system variable. (T/F)

9. In DIESEL, the drawing name can be obtained by using the macro expression **$(getvar,dwgname)**. (T/F)

Exercises

Exercise 1   *General*

Using the AutoCAD **MODEMACRO** command, redefine the status line to display the following information in the status line:
   Your name
   Name of drawing

Appendix A

System Requirements and AutoCAD Installation

SYSTEM REQUIREMENTS

The following are the minimum system requirements for running AutoCAD 2000:

1. Operating systems: Windows® 95, Windows NT® 4.0, and Windows 98.
2. 32 MB of RAM
3. Pentium 133, or better/compatible processor
4. 130MB of hard disk space
5. 64MB of disk swap space (minimum)
6. 10MB of additional memory (RAM) for each concurrent session of AutoCAD
7. 2.5 MB of free disk space required at the time of installation for temporary files that are removed when installation is complete
8. 4X speed or faster CD-ROM for initial installation
9. 800 by 600 VGA video display
10. Mouse or digitizer (with Wintab driver) pointing device
11. IBM compatible parallel port and hardware lock for international single user and educational versions only
12. Serial port (for digitizers and some plotters)
13. Sound card for multimedia learning

The following hardware is optional:

1. Printer
2. Plotter
3. Digitizing tablet

INSTALLING AUTOCAD

The installation process has now been simplified that has made it easier and faster to install AutoCAD. Also, the installation procedure is more consistent with other Windows installations. The following steps describe the installation process for AutoCAD 2000:

1. The first step is to insert the AutoCAD 2000 CD in the CD-ROM drive of your computer.

2. If AutoPlay is enabled, the **Setup** dialog box is automatically displayed and the **InstallShield Wizard** is installed on your system. (AutoPlay is a Windows 95, Windows 98, and Windows NT 4.0 feature that automatically runs an executable file. The AutoPlay feature can be turned off by holding down the Shift key when you insert the CD in the CD-ROM drive, or by changing the play setting of the CD-ROM.) If your system matches the minimum hardware requirements, the **Welcome** dialog box is displayed on the screen.

3. Choose the **Next** button in the **Welcome** dialog box; the **Software License Agreement** dialog box is displayed on the screen.

4. After reading the Software License Agreement, select **Accept** to continue installation; the **Serial Number** dialog box appears on the screen.

5. Enter the Serial number and CD Key and then choose the **Next** button. (The Serial Number and the CD Key can be found at the back of the box containing the AutoCAD 2000 CD.). If the numbers you entered are correct, the **Personal Information** dialog box is displayed.

6. Enter the requested information and then choose the **Next** button. Each field must contain at least one character to display the next screen that shows the personal information you just entered. You can edit the information or choose the **Next** button to confirm the data. The **Destination Location** dialog box is displayed on the screen.

7. In the **Destination Location** dialog box, use the **Browse** button to select the directory where you want to install AutoCAD and then choose the **Next** button to display the **Setup Type** dialog box.

8. In the **Setup Type** dialog box select the type of setup you prefer (Typical, Full, Compact, or Custom). If you select Custom, the **Custom Components** dialog box is displayed. From this dialog box clear the check boxes for the components that you do not want to install and then choose the **Next** button. If your computer has enough hard disk space, the **Folder Name** dialog box is displayed.

9. In the **Folder Name** dialog box, accept the AutoCAD 2000 (default) folder or select any other folder. Choose the **Next** button; the **Setup Confirmation** dialog box is displayed.

10. If the selection you made is OK, choose the **Next** button in the **Setup Confirmation** dialog box. The installation program installs the program files on your system and when the installation is complete, the **Setup Complete** dialog box is displayed on the screen.

Appendix **B**

Express Tools

EXPRESS TOOLS

Express tools consist of programs, sample drawings, driver files, and font files that enhance the existing AutoCAD. The **Express tools** are productivity tools and are in the form of AutoLISP and ARX applications that help the user increase the speed of drafting. The **Express Tools** are Layers, Blocks, Text, Dimension, Modify, and Draw Tools.

LAYER TOOLS

Toolbar:	Express Layer Tools
Menu:	Express > Layers

Figure C-1 *Express Layer Tools* toolbar

The different **layer tools** have been added to help in the manipulation of layers.

LMAN

 When you invoke this command the **Layer Manager: Save and Restore Layer Settings** dialog box is displayed. Through this dialog box you can save, edit, and restore the layers. The layers can also be exported to or imported from a LAY file.

LAYCUR

 This command changes the layer of the selected objects to the current layer. The prompt sequence is:

Command: **LAYCUR**
Select objects to be changed to the current layer
Select objects: *Select the objects whose layer you want to change.*
Select objects: *Press ENTER.*
1 object(s) changed to layer LAYER1 (the current layer).

LAYFRZ

 This command **freezes the layer** of the selected objects. The prompt sequence is:

Command: **LAYFRZ**
Select an object on the layer to be frozen or [Options/Undo]: *Select the objects whose layer you want to freeze or enter O for Options.*
If you enter **O** then the next prompt issued is:
[No nesting/Entity level nesting/]<Block level nesting>: *Select an option.*

The **No nesting** option freezes the layer of the object selected. If a block or an xref is selected, the layer in which they are inserted are also frozen. The **Entity level nesting** freezes the layers of the objects selected even if the selected object is nested in xref or block. In the **Block level nesting**, if a block is selected then the layer in which the block is inserted is frozen. But if an xref is selected, then the layer of the object is frozen and the xref layer is not frozen.

LAYISO

 With this command the layer of the selected objects is isolated by turning all other layers off. The prompt sequence is:

Command: **LAYISO**
Select object(s) on the layer(s) to be isolated.
Select objects: *Select the objects whose layer you want to isolate.*

LAYLCK

 With this command the layer of the selected objects is locked. The prompt sequence is:

Command: **LAYLCK**
Select an object on the layer to be locked: *Select the object whose layer you want to lock.*

LAYMCH

 With this command the layer(s) of the selected object(s) is changed such that it matches the layer of the selected destination object. The prompt sequence is:

Command: **LAYMCH**
Select objects to be changed.

Select objects: *Select the object whose layer you want to change.*
Select object on destination layer or [Type-it]:

LAYOFF

The layer of the selected object is turned off. The prompt sequence is:

Command: **LAYOFF**
Select an object on the layer to be turned off or [Options/Undo]: *Select an object or specify an option.*
If you enter **O** for Options the next prompt issued is:
[No nesting/Entity level nesting/]<Block level nesting>:
If you select an object on the current layer you are prompted:
Really want layer <layer name> (the CURRENT layer) off? <N>:

TEXT TOOLS

Toolbar:	Express Text Tools
Menu:	Express > Text

The Express text commands are used to manipulate the text and attributes.

*Figure C-2 **Express Text Tools** toolbar*

ARCTEXT

This command is used to place the text along an arc. The prompt sequence is:

Command: **ARCTEXT**
Select an Arc or an Arc Aligned Text: *Select the arc or a text.*

The **Arc Aligned Text Workshop-Create** dialog box is displayed. You can enter the text in the **Text** edit box and also choose a text style and a font for the text from the respective drop-down lists in the dialog box. You can also edit an arc aligned text by selecting it and then changing the different properties through the dialog box. In the Properties area of the dialog box you can change the height, width, and offset from the arc. After making the changes, choose the **OK** button.

TEXTEXP

This command explodes text or Mtext into geometry (lines and arcs) and enables you to assign a thickness or elevation. The prompt sequence is:

Command: **TEXTEXP**
Select text to be EXPLODED: *Select the text using the object selection process.*

RTEXT

Remote Text (**RTEXT**) objects are displayed as other text or Mtext objects are, but the source for the Rtext is either an ASCII text file or the value of a DIESEL expression. Rtext objects can be edited by the **RTEDIT** command. The command sequence for **RTEXT** is:

> Command: **RTEXT**
> Current text style: STANDARD Text height: 0.2000 Text rotation: 0
> Enter an option [Style/Height/Rotation/File/Diesel] <File>: *Specify an option or source file.*

RTEDIT

This command is used to edit existing Remote Text (Rtext) objects. The prompt sequence is:

> Command: **RTEDIT**
> Select objects: Select
> Style: STANDARD Height: 0.1000, Rotation: 0
> Enter an option [Style/Height/Rotation/Edit]: *Select an option.*

The **Style** option specifies a new style for the Rtext object. The **Height** option allows you to change the height of the Rtext entity and also you can list the objects' current height. With the **Rotation** option you can specify a new rotation angle for the Rtext objects. With the **Edit** option, you can edit the Rtext objects.

TEXTFIT

 This command shrinks or stretches text objects such that they fit between the specified startpoint and endpoints. The prompt sequence is:

> Command: **TEXTFIT**
> Select text to stretch or shrink: *Select the text.*
> Specify end point or [Start point]: *Enter **S** for new start point or select an ending point.*
> If you enter **S** for a new starting point then the next prompt is:
> Pick new starting point: *Specify a new starting point.*
> Ending point: *Specify the ending point.*

TEXTMASK

 This command hides the objects behind the selected text. **TEXTMASK** works together with the **WIPEOUT** bonus routine. The prompt sequence is:

> Command: **TEXTMASK**
> Current settings: Offset factor = <default>, Mask type = <default>
> Select text objects to mask or [Masktype/Offset]: *Select the text or an option.*

If you want to remove mask from a text object that has been masked by the **TEXTMASK** command, you can use the **TEXTUNMASK** command. The command sequence is:

> Select text or MText object from which mask is to be removed.
> Select objects: *Select a masked text object.*

TXT2MTXT

This command converts one or more lines of text into Mtext. The command sequence is:

Command: **TXT2MTXT**
Select text objects or press ENTER to set Options:
Select objects: *Select the text object to be converted.*

STANDARD TOOLS

Toolbar:	Express Standard Toolbar

The Express standard commands are based on the standard AutoCAD modify commands.

Figure C-3 Express Standard Tools toolbar

MSTRETCH

 This command is used to stretch multiple objects. If the complete object is selected, this command works like the **MOVE** command. The prompt sequence is:

Command: **MSTRETCH**
Define crossing windows or crossing polygons...
Options: Crossing Polygon or Crossing first point
Specify an option [CP/C] <Crossing first point>: *Specify first point of a crossing window.*
Specify an option [CP/C/Undo] <Crossing first point>: *Specify second point of a crossing window.*
Specify an option [CP/C/Undo] <Crossing first point>: *Press ENTER.*
Specify an option [Remove objects] <Base point>: *Select a base point.*
Second base point: *Select a new base point.*

MOCORO

 This single command can be used to move, copy, rotate, and scale the selected object or objects. The prompt sequence is:

Command: **MOCORO**
Select objects: *Select objects for modifying.*
Base point: *Select a base point.*
[Move/Copy/Rotate/Scale/Base/Undo]<eXit>: *Specify an option.*

EXTRIM

 This command allows you to trim the objects by specifying a cutting edge that can be a polyline, line, circle, or arc. The prompt sequence is:

Command: **EXTRIM**
Pick a POLYLINE, LINE, CIRCLE, ARC, ELLIPSE, IMAGE or TEXT for cutting edge...
Select objects: *Select a cutting edge.*
Pick the side to trim on: *Select a point to specify the side of trimming.*

The portion of the objects in the selected side are trimmed.

MPEDIT

 This command edits multiple polylines and also converts lines and arcs to polylines. The prompt sequence is:

Command: **MPEDIT**
Select objects: *Select objects.*
Convert Lines and Arcs to polylines? [Yes/No] <Yes>: *Press ENTER.*
Enter an option [Open/Close/Join/Width/Fit/Spline/Decurve/Ltype gen/eXit] <eXit>: *Specify an option.*

WIPEOUT

 With this command the selected area is covered with the background color so as to hide it. The area you want to select must be defined by a closed polyline. The prompt sequence is:

Command: **WIPEOUT**
Select first point or [Frame/New from Polyline] <New>: *Press ENTER to create a new wipeout.*
Select a polyline: *Select the closed polyline.*
Erase polyline? Yes/No <No>: *Enter your choice.*

The area inside the polyline boundary is wiped out. You can also enter **F** at the **Select first point or [Frame/New from Polyline] <New>:** prompt to display the following prompt:

Select an option [OFF/ON] <ON>:

The **On** option displays the wipeout frame on all viewport entities. The **Off** options turns off the wipeout for all wipeout entities.

REVCLOUD

 This command is used to create a revision cloud shape from a polyline made up of sequential arcs. The prompt sequence is:

Command: **REVCLOUD**
Arc Length = <current>, Arc style = <current>l
Pick cloud starting point or [eXit/Options] <eXit>: *Specify start point or enter **O**.*

AutoCAD will display the **Revcloud Options** dialog box. As you move the crosshairs, continuous arcs are created having the set arc lengths. When the crosshairs are close to the start point, the last arc joins the start point to close the Revcloud and you come out of the command.

PACK

 With this command all the files associated with a particular drawing are copied to a specified location.

Command: **PACK**

The **Pack & Go** dialog box is displayed. All the filenames with their size, date, and drawing version (if any) are listed in the dialog box. You can choose the Tree View tab to display the files as a directory tree. If you choose the **Browse** button the **Choose Directory** dialog box is displayed where you can specify a path to copy files. The **Copy to** button copies the files to the specified path. The **Print** button allows you to print a report of information displayed in the dialog box. The **Report** button displays the **Report** dialog box specifying information about associated files.

SUPERHATCH

The Superhatch option is much like the AutoCAD **HATCH** command, but you can use images, xrefs, block, or Wipeout objects as hatch pattern. The command sequence varies with the type of hatch patterns.

For **images**:

Insertion point <0,0>: *Specify an insertion point.*
Base image size: Width: 1.00, Height: 0.24 <Unitless>
Scale factor <1>: *Specify the scale factor for insertion.*

For **blocks and xrefs**:

Insertion point: *Specify an insertion point.*
X scale factor <1> / Corner / XYZ: *Specify the X scale factor.*
Y scale factor (default=X): *Specify the Y scale factor or press ENTER.*
Rotation angle <0>: *Specify the rotation angle.*
Select a window around the block to define column and row tile distances.
Specify block [Extents] First corner <magenta rectang>: *Specify a frame for tiling and press ENTER when done.*

After the required hatch pattern is selected, the next command sequence is:

Selecting visible objects for boundary detection...Done.
Specify an option [Advanced options] <Internal point>: *Specify an internal point for hatching boundary or A for advanced options and press ENTER.*
Preparing hatch objects for display...
Done.

TFRAMES

TFRAMES command can be used for toggling the state of frames for Wipeout and image objects. For example, if frames are on, this command will turn them off, and vice versa.

Command: **TFRAMES**.

SHOWURLS

This command shows all the embedded URLs (Uniform Resource Locators) in the drawing. **SHOWURLS** also allows you to edit the associated URLs.

BLOCK TOOLS

Toolbar:	Express Block Tools

The Block Tools are used to edit the blocks
and xrefs in the drawing.

Figure C-3 Express Block Tools toolbar

NCOPY

 This command is used to copy
objects that are nested in an xref
or block. The prompt sequence is:

Command: **NCOPY**
Select nested objects to copy: *Select objects.*
Specify base point or displacement, or [Multiple]: *Select the base point or M for multiple copies.*
Second point of displacement: *Select the second point.*

BTRIM

 With this command the selected objects are trimmed to a selected cutting edge. The cutting edge can be a block or an xref object. The prompt sequence is:

Command: **BTRIM**
Select cutting edges: *Select objects for cutting edge.*
Select object to trim or [Project/Edge/Undo]: *Select the objects to trim or select an option.*

BEXTEND

 With this command the selected objects are extended to a selected boundary. The boundary can be a block or an xref object. The prompt sequence is:

Command: **BEXTEND**
Select edges for extend: Select objects for boundary edge.
Select object to extend or [Project/Edge/Undo]: *Select the objects to extend or select an option.*

XLIST

 This command lists the different properties such as object, block name, layer, color, and
linetype of a nested object in a block.

Command: **XLIST**
Select nested xref or block object to list: *Select the object.*

An **Xref/Block Nested Object List** dialog box is displayed that lists all the information about the
selected object.

CLIPIT

 This command allows you to separate some portion of block, xref drawing, or image by
removing the display of the remaining objects using a polyline, circle, or arc. The prompt

sequence is:

> Command: **CLIPIT**
> Pick a POLYLINE, CIRCLE, ARC, ELLIPSE, or TEXT object for clipping edge...
> Select objects: *Select a clipping edge.*
> Pick an IMAGE, a WIPEOUT, or an XREF/BLOCK to clip: *Select the object.*
> Enter max error distance for resolution of arcs <0.0200>: *Select a resolution value.*

The curved boundary edge is traversed with a series of short straight segments, and the resolution of arc is the distance between the midpoint of the given segment and the arc. Hence a large error value creates less segments and faster speed but the arcs become less smooth.

GATTE

 With this command the attribute values are changed globally for all insertion of specific block. The prompt sequence is:

> Command: **GATTE**
> Select block or attribute [Block name]: *Enter **B** to use a block name or select the block.*
> Known tag names for block: MDLN.
> Select attribute or type attribute name: *Select attribute or enter the tag name.*
> Number of inserts in drawing = 2   Process all of them? [Yes/No] <Yes>: *Select Yes to process all and No to process the selected attributes.*

BURST

 This command explodes a block so that the attribute values are changed to text entities. The prompt sequence is:

> Command: **BURST**
> Select objects: *Select the block containing attributes.*

DIMENSION TOOLS
DIMEX

With this command the named dimension styles and all their settings are exported to an exported file.

> Command: **DIMEX**

The **Dimension Style Export** dialog box is displayed. You can enter the desired **DIM** filename in the **Export filename:** edit box. The list of dimension styles available in the current drawing are listed in the Available **Dimension Style** list box. You can select the dimension style you wish to write to the ASCII file. In the Text Style Options area you can choose the **Full Text Style Information** radio button or **Text Style Name Only** radio button.

DIMIM

With this command the named dimension styles are imported from a DIM file into the current drawing.

Command: **DIMIM**

The **Dimension Style Import** dialog box is displayed. You can enter the desired dimension style name in the **Import filename** edit box, or from the Open dialog box that can be invoked by choosing the **Browse** button. You can retain the dimension style in the current drawing or over-write it by selecting the appropriate radio button in the Import Options area.

QLATTACH

This command is used to attach the leader line to an annotation object such as Mtext, Tolerance, or Block Reference Object. The prompt sequence is:

Command: **QLATTACH**
Select Leader: *Select the leader.*
Select Annotation: *Select the annotation object.*

QLATTACHSET

This command is used to globally attach the leader line to an annotation object such as Mtext, Tolerance, or Block Reference Object. The prompt sequence is:

Command: **QLATTACHSET**
Select objects: *Select the leader and the annotation objects.*
Select objects: *Press ENTER.*
Number of Leaders=n
Number with annotations detached=n

QLDETACHSET

This command is used to detach the leader line from an annotation object such as Mtext, Tolerance, or Block Reference Object. The prompt sequence is:

Command: **QLDETACHSET**
Select objects: *Select the leader and the annotation objects.*
Select objects: *Press ENTER.*
Number of Leaders=n
Number of annotations detached=n

SELECTION TOOLS
GETSEL

This command creates a temporary selection set.

Command: **GETSEL**
Select an object on the Source layer <*>: *Select object or press ENTER for all layers.*
Select an object of the Type you want <*>: *Select entity type or press ENTER for all.*

SSTOOLS

This command creates "anti" or exclusionary selection sets. The selection set method is preceeded by **EX**, and all the drawing objects except the ones in the selection area are selected. For example, if **W** is for window selection method, then **EXW** is for the exclusionary window selection method.

Command: **'EXW, 'EXC, 'EXP, 'EXF, 'EXWP, 'EXCP**

TOOLS COMMANDS

Menu: Express > Tools

The Express tool commands help you to manage the AutoCAD environment.

FULLSCREEN

The **FULLSCREEN** command resizes the drawing screen to a maximum area. It also hides the title bar and the menu bar in the AutoCAD window. The **FULLSCREEN** command toggles the screen size between normal and full screen.

MKLTYPE

The **MKLTYPE** command creates a new linetype based on the selected objects. This is a quick and useful method of making new ready-to-use linetype. The command line sequence is:

Command: **MKLTYPE**
Select a ".LIN" file: <acad.lin>: *Enter the name of the linetype filename.*
Enter linetype name: *Specify a new linetype name.*
Linetype description: *Specify description of the new linetype.*
Starting point for line definition: *Specify a starting point of the line.*
Ending point for line definition: *Specify an ending point.*
Select objects: *Select a drawing object to be used to define the linetype.*

MKSHAPE

The **MKSHAPE** command creates a new shape definition based on the selected drawing objects. The command sequence is:

Command: **MKSHAPE**
Select a ".SHP" file: <drawing.shp>: *Enter a shape file name to save your shape.*
Reading shape file: drawing.shp...Done.
Enter the name of the shape: *Specify a shape name.*
Enter resolution <n>: *Enter a resolution value (between 8 - 32767)*
Insertion base point: *Specify a basepoint.*
Select objects: *Select drawing objects for definition purposes, which will be treated as though they are of a continuous linetype.*
Determining geometry extents...Done.
Building coord lists...Done.
Formatting coords...Done.
Writing new shape...Done.

Compiling shape/font description file
Compilation successful. Output file C:\drawing.shx contains **n** bytes.
Use the **SHAPE** command to place shapes in your drawing.

REDIR

The **REDIR** command redefines hard-coded paths in xrefs, images, shapes, styles, and rtext. The command line sequence is:

Command: **REDIR**
Current REDIRMODE: Styles,Xrefs,Images,Rtext
Find and replace directory names
Enter old directory (use '*' for all), or ? <options>: *Enter the name of directory to be replaced or press ENTER for **options**.*
Replace "*" with: *Enter the name of the directory to be replaced with the old one.*

REDIRMODE

The **REDIRMODE** command sets the options for the **REDIR** command by specifying which objects are to be redefined. If you enter the **REDIRMODE** in the command line, the **REDIRMODE** dialog box appears where you can select object types to be redefined. The command line sequence is:

Command: **REDIRMODE**
Current REDIRMODE: Styles,Xrefs,Images,Rtext
Replace directories in Xrefs,Styles,Images,Rtext. <current>: *Enter the options (object types).*
Current REDIRMODE: *Selected object types.*

XDATA

This command allows you to attach extended entity data (xdata) to a selected entity.

Command: **XDATA**
Select object: *Select the objects.*
Application name: *Enter the name of application.*
[3Real/DIR/DISP/DIST/Hand/Int/LAyer/LOng/Pos/Real/SCale/STr/eXit]<eXit>: *Enter an option to attach the extended entity data.*

XDLIST

This command lists all the xdata associated with an object.

Command: **XDLIST**
Select object: *Select the objects.*
Application name <*>: *Enter the name of the application or press ENTER to list all.*

ADDITIONAL COMMANDS

These commands are accessed through the command line only.

BLOCK?

This command lists the different entities in a block definition.

Command: **BLOCK?**
Enter block name <Return to select>: *Press ENTER.*
Select a block: *Select the block using a selection method.*
Enter an entity type <Return for all>: *Press ENTER for all entities or enter a type of entity.*

BCOUNT

This command counts the number of insertions of each block in the drawing or in the selected objects. It then displays it in a tabular form.

Command: **BCOUNT**
Press Enter to select all or...
Select objects: *Press ENTER or select objects.*

EXPRESSMENU

This command loads the Express tools menu and displays **Express** menu on the AutoCAD menu bar. Since AutoCAD can display only 24 menus at a time, make sure that you have 23 or fewer menu items before running the **EXPRESSMENU** command.

Command: **EXPRESSMENU**

EXPRESSTOOLS

This command loads the **AutoCAD Express Tools** libraries, places the **Express** directory on the search path, and also loads and places the **Express** menu on the **AutoCAD** menu bar. **EXPESSTOOLS** adds the **Express menu group** in the **Toolbars** dialog box from where you can view **Express** toolbars.

Command: **EXPRESSTOOLS**

JULIAN

This command contains the AutoLISP functions for conversion of Julian date.

Command: **DATE**
Tue 1999/5/25 10:25:52.391

LSP

This command displays a list of all the AutoLISP commands that are available at the Command prompt. The command sequence is:

Command: **LSP**
Enter an option [?/Commands/Functions/Variables/Load]: *Specify an option.*

SSX

This command creates a selection set.

> Command: **SSX**
> Select object/<None>: *Select a template object.*
> >>Block name/Color/Entity/Flag/LAyer/LType/Pick/Style/Thickness/Vector: *Enter an option.*

It creates a selection set exactly like the selected entity or very similar to the filter list that you have adjusted.

OPERATING SYSTEM COMMANDS

TTC2TFF

The **TTC2TFF** command converts a **TTC** file (which is a TrueType font collection file that contains one or more TrueType fonts) to **TTF** files. This command is valid only in **DOS command syntax**.

> DOS command line: **TTC2TFF**.

Index